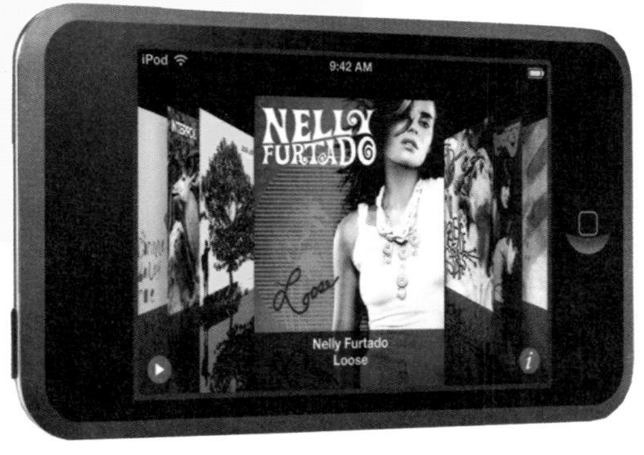

Images courtesy of Apple.

Don't have an iPod? Content can be viewed on any computer! Visit the text website for directions.

Want to see iPod in action?

Visit **www.mhhe.com/ipod** to view a demonstration of our iPod® content.

Website includes:

- Lecture presentations
  - Audio and video
  - Audio only
  - Video only
- Demonstration problems+
- Interactive self quizzes
- Accounting videos+

+Available with some textbooks

McGraw-Hill's

HOMEWORK MANAGER PLUS™ online

THE COMPLETE SOLUTION

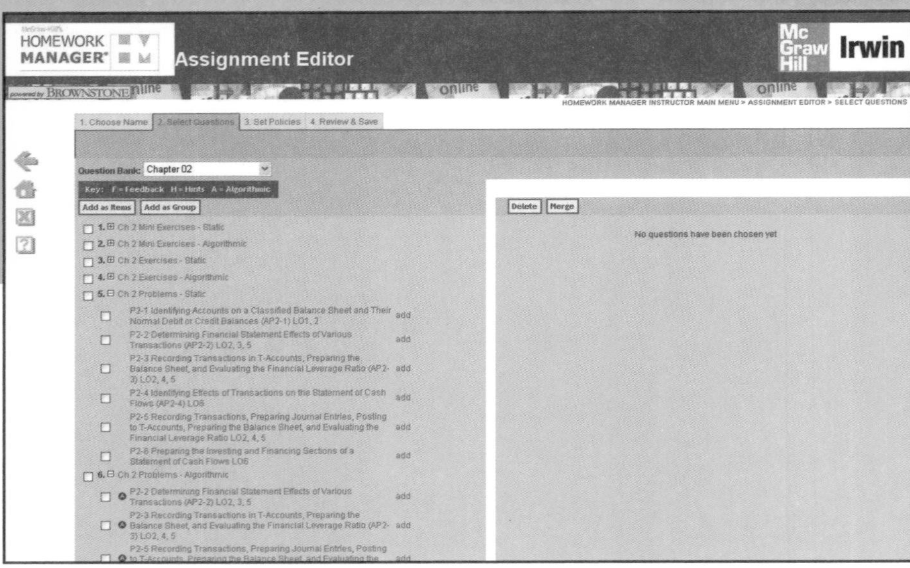

McGraw-Hill's **Homework** Manager®

™ This online homework management solution contains this textbook's end-of-chapter material. Now you have the option to build assignments from static and algorithmic versions of the text problems and exercises or to build self-graded quizzes from the additional questions provided in the online test bank.

Features:

- Assigns book-specific problems/exercises to students
- Provides integrated test bank questions for quizzes and tests
- Automatically grades assignments and quizzes, storing results in one grade book
- Dispenses immediate feedback to students regarding their work

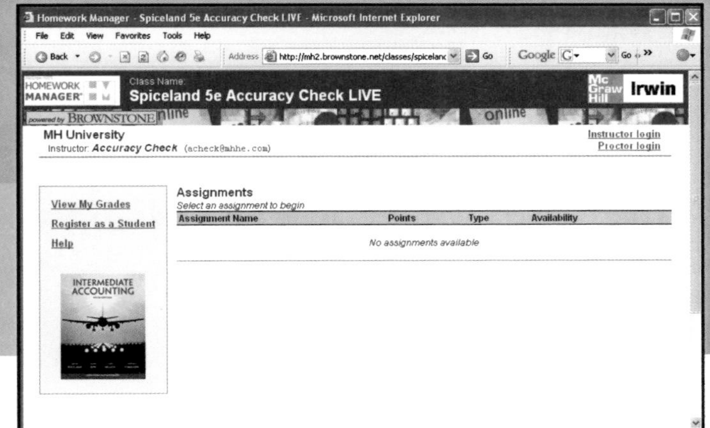

Interactive Online Version of this Textbook

In addition to the textbook, students can rely on this online version of the text for a convenient way to study. The interactive content is fully *integrated* with McGraw-Hill's Homework Manager® system to give students quick access to relevant content as they work through problems, exercises, and practice quizzes.

Features:

- Online version of the text *integrated* with McGraw-Hill's Homework Manager
- Students referred to appropriate sections of the online book as they complete an assignment or take a practice quiz
- Direct link to related material that corresponds with the learning objective within the text

Spiceland/Sepe/Nelson/Tomassini
Intermediate Accounting, 5/e
978-0-07-332445-6

2 TERM

McGraw-Hill's Homework Manager PLUS™ system combines the power of McGraw-Hill's Homework Manager® with the latest interactive learning technology to create a comprehensive, fully integrated online study package. Students working on assignments in McGraw-Hill's Homework Manager system can click a simple hotlink and instantly review the appropriate material in the Interactive Online Textbook.

By including McGraw-Hill's Homework Manager PLUS with your textbook adoption, you're giving your students a vital edge as they progress through the course and ensuring that the help they need is never more than a mouse click away. Contact your McGraw-Hill representative or visit the book's Web site to learn how to add McGraw-Hill's Homework Manager PLUS system to your adoption.

Imagine being able to create and access your test anywhere, at any time without installing the testing software. Now with **McGraw-Hill's EZ Test Online**, instructors can select questions from multiple McGraw-Hill test banks, author their own and then either print the test for paper distribution or give it online.

Use our EZ Test Online to help your students prepare to succeed with Apple® iPod® iQuiz.

Using our EZ Test Online you can make test and quiz content available for a student's Apple iPod.

Students must purchase the iQuiz game application from Apple for 99¢ in order to use the iQuiz content. It works on the iPod fifth generation iPods and better.

Instructors only need EZ Test Online to produce iQuiz ready content. Instructors take their existing tests and quizzes and export them to a file that can then be made available to the student to take as a self-quiz on their iPods. It's as simple as that.

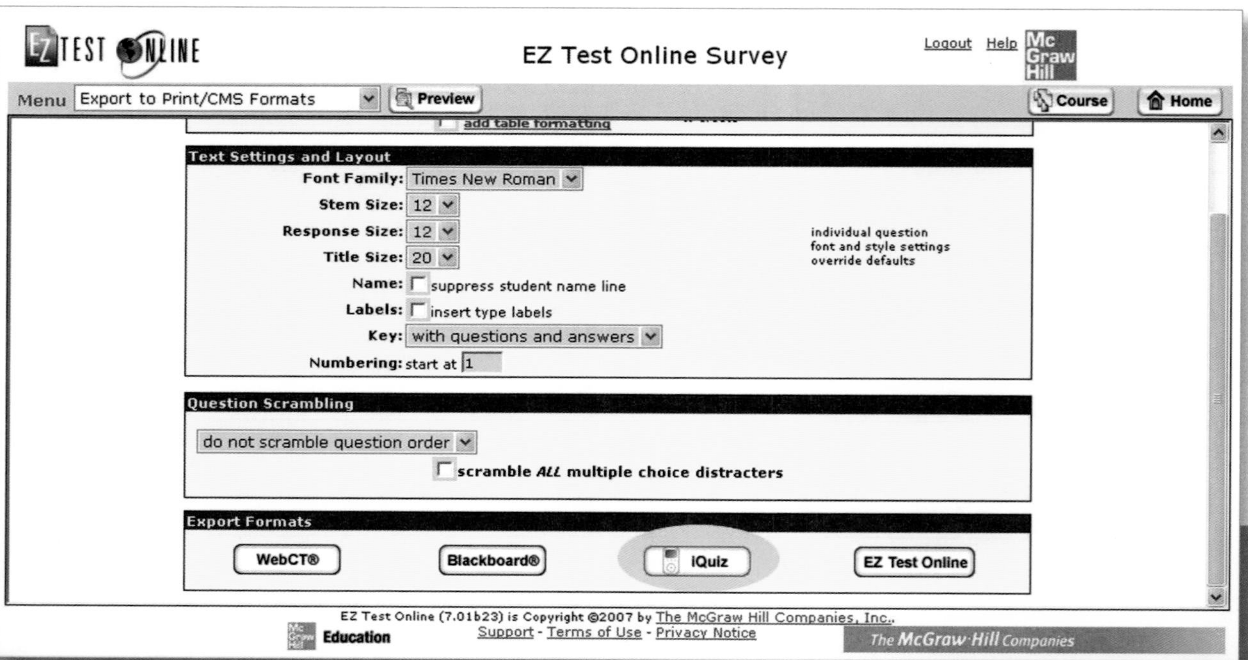

Intermediate Accounting

Volume II

Intermediate Accounting

FIFTH EDITION

J. DAVID SPICELAND
University of Memphis

JAMES F. SEPE
Santa Clara University

MARK W. NELSON
Cornell University

LAWRENCE A. TOMASSINI
The Ohio State University

Boston Burr Ridge, IL Dubuque, IA New York San Francisco St. Louis
Bangkok Bogotá Caracas Kuala Lumpur Lisbon London Madrid Mexico City
Milan Montreal New Delhi Santiago Seoul Singapore Sydney Taipei Toronto

INTERMEDIATE ACCOUNTING

Published by McGraw-Hill/Irwin, a business unit of The McGraw-Hill Companies, Inc., 1221 Avenue of the Americas, New York, NY, 10020.

This book is printed on acid-free paper.

1 2 3 4 5 6 7 8 9 0 DOW/DOW 0 9 8

ISBN-13: 978-0-07-332464-7 (volume II)
ISBN-10: 0-07-332464-7 (volume II)

Editorial director: *Stewart Mattson*
Publisher: *Tim Vertovec*
Developmental editor II: *Daryl Horrocks*
Marketing manager: *Scott S. Bishop*
Lead project manager: *Pat Frederickson*
Production supervisor: *Gina Hangos*
Interior designer: *Laurie Entringer*
Senior photo research coordinator: *Jeremy Cheshareck*
Photo researcher: *Teri Stratford*
Senior media project manager: *Kerry Bowler*
Cover design: *Laurie Entringer*
Cover credit: © *Gerolf Kalt/zefa/Corbis*
Typeface: *10.5/12 Times Lt Std-Roman*
Compositor: *Laserwords Private Limited*
Printer: *R. R. Donnelley*

The Library of Congress has cataloged the single volume edition of this work as follows.

Library of Congress Cataloging-in-Publication Data

Intermediate accounting / J. David Spiceland ... [et al.].—5th ed.
p. cm.
Rev. ed. of: Intermediate accounting / J. David Spiceland, James F. Sepe, Lawrence A. Tomassini. 4th ed.
Includes index.
ISBN-13: 978-0-07-352687-4 (combined edition : alk. paper)
ISBN-10: 0-07-352687-8 (combined edition : alk. paper)
ISBN-13: 978-0-07-332465-4 (volume I : alk. paper)
ISBN-10: 0-07-332465-5 (volume I : alk. paper)
[etc.]
1. Accounting. I. Spiceland, J. David, 1949- Intermediate accounting.
HF5635.S7838 2009
657′.044—dc22

2008019272

Dedicated to:

David's wife Charlene, daughters Denise and Jessica, and sons Michael David, Michael, and David
Jim's wife Barbara, children Kristina, Matt, and Dave, son-in-law Bob and daughter-in-law Donna, and granddaughters Kaitlyn and Meghan
Mark's wife Cathy, daughters Lizzie and Clara, and parents Mary and Richard H. Nelson
Larry's wife and children: Eve Tomassini, Nicholas, Anthony, and Katherine

About the Authors

DAVID SPICELAND

David Spiceland is professor of accounting at the University of Memphis, where he teaches intermediate accounting and other financial accounting courses at the undergraduate and master's levels. He received his BS degree in finance from the University of Tennessee, his MBA from Southern Illinois University, and his PhD in accounting from the University of Arkansas.

Professor Spiceland's primary research interests are in earnings management and educational research. He has published articles in a variety of journals including *The Accounting Review, Accounting and Business Research, Journal of Financial Research,* and *Journal of Accounting Education.* David has received university and college awards and recognition for his teaching, research, and technological innovations in the classroom.

JIM SEPE

Jim Sepe is an associate professor of accounting at Santa Clara University where he teaches primarily intermediate accounting in both the undergraduate and graduate programs. He previously taught at California Poly State University–San Luis Obispo and the University of Washington and has visited at Stanford University and the Rome campus of Loyola University of Chicago.

Professor Sepe received his BS from Santa Clara University, MBA from the University of California–Berkeley, and PhD from the University of Washington. His research interests concern financial reporting issues and the use of financial information by capital markets. He has published in *The Accounting Review,* the *Journal of Business Finance and Accounting, Financial Management,* the *Journal of Forensic Accounting,* the *Journal of Applied Business Research,* and the *Journal of Accounting Education.* He is a past recipient of the American Accounting Association's Competitive Manuscript Award and has served as a member of the editorial board of *The Accounting Review.*

Jim has received numerous awards for his teaching excellence and innovations in the classroom, including Santa Clara University's Brutocao Award for Excellence in Curriculum Innovation.

MARK NELSON

Mark Nelson is the Eleanora and George Landew Professor of Accounting at Cornell University's Johnson Graduate School of Management, where he teaches intermediate accounting at the MBA level. He received his BBA degree from Iowa State University and his MA and PhD degrees from Ohio State University. Professor Nelson has won teaching awards at Ohio State and Cornell, including three of the Johnson School's Apple Award for Teaching Excellence.

Professor Nelson's research is focused on decision making in financial accounting and auditing. His research has been published in *The Accounting Review,* the *Journal of Accounting Research, Contemporary Accounting Research, Accounting Organizations and Society, Auditing: A Journal of Practice and Theory,* and several other journals. He has won the American Accounting Association's Notable Contribution to Accounting Literature Award, and also the AAA's Wildman Medal for work judged to make the most significant contribution to the advancement of the public practice of accountancy. He has served three times as an editor or associate editor of *The Accounting Review,* and serves on the editorial boards of several journals. Professor Nelson also served for four years on the FASB's Financial Accounting Standards Advisory Council.

LARRY TOMASSINI

Larry Tomassini is professor of accounting and MIS and director of the undergraduate accounting program at The Ohio State University. He has held several endowed chair positions during his academic career, including the Ernst and Young Distinguished Professor at the University of Illinois and the Peat Marwick Mitchell Centennial Professorship in Accounting at the University of Texas.

His research has been widely published in scholarly journals, including *The Accounting Review, Accounting Horizons, Journal of Accounting Research and Contemporary Accounting Research.*

He teaches a variety of accounting courses at the undergraduate and master's levels. Recently, he was director of the Ohio State Master of Accounting Program and Vice President for Publications of the American Accounting Association.

Larry has been a pioneer in the use of Internet technology to support the teaching of accounting courses, and he has developed online versions of introductory financial and managerial accounting courses at Ohio State.

Your Vehicle to Success

"I am very impressed with this textbook and its supplements. The authors have carefully developed the book to meet the needs of a wide range of student learners. It is clearly written in understandable terms. There are many features available to provide your students with the best chance to master this material."

- Robert Gruber, University of Wisconsin—Whitewater

"SSNT have put together a comprehensive and complete intermediate accounting textbook and e-Learning system."

- Florence Atiase, University of Texas

"After reviewing this text, I would describe this text to our colleagues as an outstanding learning package and outstanding textbook."

- Habib El-Yazeed, Minnesota State University

As your students embark on their professional careers, they will be challenged to think critically and make good decisions. This new edition of *Intermediate Accounting* has been designed to ensure that your students' careers soar to the greatest heights—to be their vehicle to success!

Intermediate Accounting is the work not just of its talented authors but of the more than 130 faculty reviewers who shared their insights, experience, and opinions with us. Our reviewers helped us to build *Intermediate Accounting* into the vehicle that can propel your students to success in their accounting course, and we have the research to prove it: Spiceland was ranked #1 in improved student performance over a previous textbook, #1 in readability, and tied for #1 in overall professor satisfaction.*

Our development process began in the spring of 2006, when we received the first of what would become more than 130 in-depth reviews of *Intermediate Accounting*. A blend of Spiceland users and non-users, these reviewers explained how they use textbooks in their teaching, and many answered detailed questions about every one of Spiceland's 21 chapters. And the work of improving *Intermediate Accounting* is ongoing—even now, we're scheduling new symposia and reviewers' conferences to collect even more opinions from faculty.

Intermediate Accounting was designed from the start to be not simply a textbook, but a complete learning system, encompassing the textbook, key ancillaries, and online content, all of which are written by authors Spiceland, Sepe, Nelson, and Tomassini. The *Intermediate Accounting* learning system is built around five key attributes:

*Results from an independent market survey of intermediate accounting professors July–September 2002 by Professional Research Group, LLC.

in Intermediate Accounting

① **Clarity:** Reviewers, instructors, and students all have hailed *Intermediate Accounting's* ability to explain both simple and complex topics in language that is clear and approachable. Its highly acclaimed conversational writing style establishes a friendly dialogue between the text and each individual student. So readable is Spiceland that we've even received letters from students who bought the book themselves—despite their instructors using competing books in the course! No surprise that Spiceland was found to be the most readable intermediate accounting textbook in independent research.*

② **A Decision-Making Perspective:** Recent events have focused public attention on the key role of accounting in providing information useful to decision makers. The CPA exam, too, is redirecting its focus to emphasize the professional skills needed to critically evaluate accounting method alternatives. *Intermediate Accounting* provides a decision maker's perspective to emphasize the professional judgment and critical thinking skills required of accountants today.

③ **Flexible Technology:** Today's accounting students have come of age in a digital world, and Spiceland's Learning System reflects that trend through its comprehensive technology package. The Coach tutorial software provides a browser-based, text-integrated multimedia environment in which to review concepts and take practice quizzes, while McGraw-Hill's Homework Manager™ system offers infinite algorithmically generated practice problems in an online environment students can access whenever they want. Feedback in McGraw-Hill's Homework Manager™ system is immediate, giving students an instant snapshot of their progress in mastering the material.

④ **Consistent Quality:** The *Intermediate Accounting* author team ensures seamless compatibility throughout the Spiceland learning package by writing every major supplement themselves: Coach, Study Guide, Instructor's Resource Manual, Solutions Manual, Testbank, and website content are all created by authors Spiceland, Sepe, Nelson, and Tomassini. The end-of-chapter material, too, is written by the author team and tested in their classrooms before being included in *Intermediate Accounting*. That dedication makes Spiceland users among the most satisfied of any intermediate accounting text.*

⑤ **A Commitment to Currency:** Few disciplines see the rapid change that accounting experiences, and the Spiceland team is committed to keeping your course up to date. The fifth edition fully integrates the latest FASB standards, including *SFAS 162*, "The Hierarchy of Generally Accepted Accounting Principles"; *SFAS 161*, "Disclosures about Derivative Instruments and Hedging Activities"; *SFAS 160*, "Noncontrolling Interests in Consolidated Financial Statements—An Amendment of ARB No. 51"; *SFAS 141(R), "Business Combination"*; *SFAS 159* "The Fair Value Option for Financial Assets and Financial Liabilities"; *FIN 48*, "Accounting for Uncertainty in Income Taxes"; and *SFAS 158*, "Employers' Accounting for Defined Benefit Pension and Other Postretirement Plans".

*Results from an independent market survey of intermediate accounting professors July–September 2002 by Professional Research Group, LLC.

"The best available text for the intermediate accounting courses at both the graduate and undergraduate level."

- Gerard M. Engeholm, Pace University

"It is an excellent intermediate text with real-world examples and practical current commentary."

- Simon Pearlman, California State University—Long Beach

"When someone other than the authors prepares the [end-of-chapter material] they generally do not mirror the material that is presented in the chapters and they contain quite a few errors."

- Gloria Worthy, Southwest Tennessee Community College

"Overall, I find the Spiceland end-of-chapter material far superior to that in Kieso in terms of quantity, especially as it relates to the diversity of the problem material."

- Chula King, University of West Florida

What Stands Out in the Fifth Edition?

New Coauthor Mark Nelson

A new coauthor, Mark Nelson of Cornell University, has joined the Spiceland author team for the fifth edition. Mark is an award-winning full professor at Cornell University, where he has been teaching out of Spiceland for several years. Mark is an active and well-known instructor of financial accounting, while also serving as an editor of *The Accounting Review* and member of the Financial Accounting Standards Advisory Council.

"The Star Problems are challenging—a good way to illustrate the more difficult concepts and calculations."

- Kenneth R. Henry, Florida International University

Star Problems

Star problems are a new feature in the fifth edition. These are problems (more than one-third new) in each chapter that are designated by a ★ to indicate that they are particularly challenging, requiring students to combine multiple concepts or requiring judgment beyond explicit explanation in chapter discussions.

Fair Value Option

New coverage of *SFAS No. 159* ("The Fair Value Option for Financial Assets and Financial Liabilities") and *SFAS No. 157* ("Fair Value Measurements") has been added to chapters 1, 12 and 14. Extensive assignment materials related to the fair value option have also been added.

Option to Report Liabilities at Fair Value

● LO3

***SFAS No. 159* gives a company the option to value financial assets and liabilities at fair value.**

Companies are not required to, but have the option to, value some or all of their financial assets and liabilities at fair value. This choice is permitted by *SFAS No. 159*, "The Fair Value Option for Financial Assets and Financial Liabilities." In Chapter 12, we saw examples of the option being applied to financial assets—specifically, companies reporting their investments in securities at fair value. Now, we see how liabilities, too, can be reported at fair value.

How does a liability's fair value change? Remember that there are two sides to every investment. For example, if a company has an investment in **General Motors'** bonds, that investment is an asset to the investor, and the same bonds are a liability to General Motors. So, the same market forces that influence the fair value of an investment in debt securities (interest rates, economic conditions, risk, etc.) influence the fair value of liabilities. For bank loans or other de[illegible]at aren't t[illegible] on a market exchange, the mix of factors will diff[illegible]

"A significant improvement over KWW in terms of thoroughness for schools wanting a rigorous textbook."

- Mark Dawkins, University of Georgia

P 2–11
Accrual accounting; financial statements

● LO4 LO6 LO8

McGuire Corporation began operations in 2009. The company purchases computer equipment from manufacturers and then sells to retail stores. During 2009, the bookkeeper used a check register to record all receipts and cash disbursements. No other journals were used. The following is a recap of the cash receipts a[illegible] disbursements made during the year.

Cash receipts:	
Sale of common stock	$ 50,000
Collections from customers	320,000
Borrowed from local bank on April 1, note signed requiring principal and interest at 12% to be paid on March 31, 2010	40,000

Revising a book as successful as Intermediate Accounting takes judiciousness and a strong vision of what a textbook should be. New features aren't piled on for their own sake; only when our users consistently point out an opportunity for improvement does the Spiceland team take action. The result is a book that never loses its original strengths as it gains in usefulness and flexibility with each revision.

New Coverage of International Financial Reporting Standards

The United States is moving rapidly toward converging U.S. GAAP with the **International Financial Reporting Standards (IFRS)** that are followed by most of the rest of the world. An extensive discussion has been added to Chapter 1 that provides an overview of the background and current status of the convergence process. Separate IFRS boxes within chapters highlight emerging issues and key differences between U.S. and international GAAP in the context of the chapter topics. End-of-chapter assignment material has been added to reinforce students' understanding of these differences.

INTERNATIONAL FINANCIAL REPORTING STANDARDS

Lease Classification. We discussed four classification criteria used under U.S. GAAP to determine whether a lease is a capital lease. Under IFRS, a lease is a capital lease (called a finance lease under *IAS No. 17*, "Leases"), if substantially all risks and rewards of ownership are transferred. Judgment is made based on a number of "indicators" including some similar to the specific criteria of U.S. GAAP. More judgment, less specificity, is applied.

CPA and CMA Review Questions

A new **CPA and CMA Review Questions** section has been added to the end-of-chapter material between the Exercises and Problems. The CPA questions are multiple choice questions used in the Kaplan CPA Review Course and focus on the key topics within each chapter, permitting quick and efficient reinforcement of those topics as well as conveying a sense of the way the topics are covered in the CPA exam. The CMA questions are adapted from questions that previously appeared on Certified Management Accountant (CMA) exams.

CPA AND CMA REVIEW QUESTIONS

CPA Exam Questions

KAPLAN SCHWESER

● LO3

The following questions are used in the Kaplan CPA Review Course examination. Determine the response that best completes the stateme

1. A company leases the following asset:
   - Fair value of $200,000.
   - Useful life of 5 years with no salvage value.
   - Lease term is 4 years.
   - Annual lease payment is $30,000 and the lease rate is 11%.
   - The company's overall borrowing rate is 9.5%.
   - The firm can p equipment

"*Intermediate Accounting* is current, complete, well written, and highly detailed. It belongs in the library of anyone who is preparing for the CPA exam."

- Barbara K. Parks, American Intercontinental University – Online

Market-Leading Technology

iPod Content

Harness the power of one of the most popular technology tools students use today—the Apple iPod®. Our innovative approach allows students to download audio and video presentations right into their iPod and take learning materials with them wherever they go.

Students just need to visit the Online Learning Center at **www.mhhe.com/spiceland5e** to download our iPod content. For each chapter of the book, they will be able to download audio narrated lecture presentations, slideshows and even self-quizzes designed for use on various versions of iPods.

It makes review and study time as easy as putting on headphones.

"SSNT's *Intermediate Accounting* is a very comprehensive, well-written text, that includes extensive EOC assignment material and student supplements. It achieves an effective balance of both preparer and user perspectives throughout the text."

- Michael G. Welker,
Drexel University

"We encourage our students to sit for the exam, and it would prepare them for the testing mode and environment they will encounter when taking the exam."

- Ronald Kilgore,
University of Tennessee

CPA Simulations

Students sitting for the new computerized CPA exam will confront an interface unlike any they've encountered before; from finding information in a research database to entering data into a spreadsheet, the CPA exam doesn't look or act like any other software program. Kaplan CPA Exam Simulations allow students to practice intermediate accounting concepts in a web-based environment identical to that used in the actual CPA exam. There'll be no hesitation or confusion when your students sit for the real exam: they'll know exactly what they need to do.

There's more to making a book better than adding new features. Organizing and updating the content is one of the foremost challenges a textbook faces, and Intermediate Accounting undergoes continual refinement to ensure that the content is as fresh and as easy to present and teach as possible.

Major Content Changes

A great many events have impacted accounting over the past few years, and *Intermediate Accounting* integrates every important development just where it belongs. A few examples of key updates for 5e:

- The **Testbank** is a key component of our Learning System and has been an area of major emphasis in the authors' development of the fifth edition. An extensive review process was undertaken to ensure the most complete, accurate, and flexible Testbank available. It been revised for all the changes and additions to the text. Greater variety has been added at each level of rigor. The fifth edition Testbank has over 800 new test items and more extensive explanations of solutions.
- The **financial statements** and **disclosure notes** of Google now are packaged with the textbook as well as available through a link at the text website. These replace the FedEx statements previously in a text appendix. The statements and notes are the basis for text references and cases in most chapters.
- For Chapter 5, the sections dealing with long-term contracts and profitability analysis have been rewritten for clarity. More end-of-chapter material has been added for these areas as well.
- Chapter 1, 12, and 14 have been revised to incorporate the latest fair value standards.
- Chapter 17 was extensively revised to incorporate *SFAS No. 158,* "Employers' Accounting for Defined Benefit Pension and Other Postretirement Plans." Since the publication of the Revised Fourth Edition, additional edits have been made for clarity.
- Chapter 12 has been rewritten to more clearly cover accounting for investments when the investor lacks significant influence. This section has been reordered to cover held-to-maturity investments, then trading securities, and then available-for-sale securities.
- For selected chapters, instructions are now included in the margin for using financial calculators.

"SSNT5e is a strong competitor to Kieso, and meets or exceeds Kieso in most areas. I prefer its organization to Kieso."

- Derek Oler, Indiana University

"An excellent intermediate text that presents the material in a well-organized manner. Read-ability, crisp graphics and layout make it the number once choice of students."

- Denise de la Rosa, Grand Valley State University

What Keeps Spiceland Users Coming Back?

Financial Reporting Cases

Each chapter opens with a Financial Reporting Case that places the student in the role of the decision maker, engaging the student in an interesting situation related to the accounting issues to come. Then, the cases pose questions of the student in the role of decision maker. Marginal notations throughout the chapter point out locations where each question is addressed. Finally, the questions are answered at the end of the chapter.

FINANCIAL REPORTING CASE **SOLUTION**

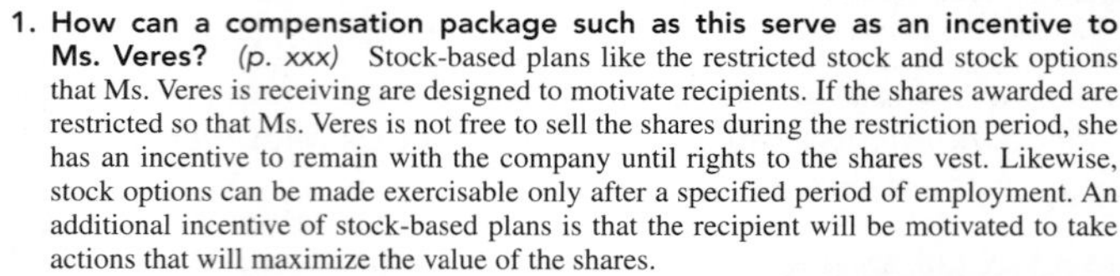

1. **How can a compensation package such as this serve as an incentive to Ms. Veres?** *(p. xxx)* Stock-based plans like the restricted stock and stock options that Ms. Veres is receiving are designed to motivate recipients. If the shares awarded are restricted so that Ms. Veres is not free to sell the shares during the restriction period, she has an incentive to remain with the company until rights to the shares vest. Likewise, stock options can be made exercisable only after a specified period of employment. An additional incentive of stock-based plans is that the recipient will be motivated to take actions that will maximize the value of the shares.
2. **Ms. Veres received a "grant of restricted stock." How should NEV account for the grant?** *(p. xxx)* The compensation as...

"The case at the beginning of each chapter is very captivating. After I read the case, I wanted to get paper and pencil and answer the questions."

- Carol Shaver, Louisiana Tech University

Decision Makers' Perspective

These sections appear throughout the text to illustrate how accounting information is put to work in today's firms. With the CPA exam placing greater focus on application of skills in realistic work settings, these discussions help your students gain an edge that will remain with them as they enter the workplace.

INTERMEDIATE

DECISION MAKERS' PERSPECTIVE

Cash often is referred to as a *nonearning* asset because it earn... managers invest idle cash in either cash equivalents or short-te... provide a return. Management's goal is to hold the minimum... conduct normal business operations, meet its obligations, and... ties. Too much cash reduces profits through lost returns, while... This tradeoff between risk and return is an ongoing choice m... ers. Whether the choice made is appropriate is an ongoing asse... creditors.

A company must have cash available for the compensating... previous section as well as for planned disbursements relate... ing, and financing cash flows. However, because cash inflow... planned amounts, a company needs an additional cash cushion as a precaution against that contingency...

"This is an excellent feature of the book. It is so important to know why and how information is used and not just memorizing the "right" answers."

- Jeff Mankin, Lipscomb University

Earnings Management

With 86 percent of intermediate accounting faculty teaching earnings management in their courses,* Spiceland's integrated coverage of this key topic throughout the book is especially helpful.

Real World Case 5–1
Chainsaw Al; revenue recognition and earnings management

● LO1

In May 2001, the Securities and Excha... the group with financial reporting frau... is a recognized designer, manufacture... Eastpak, First Alert, Grillmaster, Mixm... Sunbeam needed help: its profits had d... 50% from its high. To the rescue: Alb... ruthless executive known for his ability... ing jobs.

The strategy appeared to work. In 19... the brokerage firm of **Paine Webber** do... Webber had noticed unusually high acc...

"I think that this discussion, and others like it in the text, is excellent. Being a former CFO, I spend a fair amount of time talking with students about how earnings can be managed, in the hands of a biased (unethical?) CFO."

- Ron Tilden, University of Washington, Bothell

In talking to so many intermediate accounting faculty, we heard more than how to improve the book—there was much, much more that both users and nonusers insisted we keep exactly as it was. Here are some of the features that have made Spiceland such a phenomenal success in its previous editions.

Additional Consideration Boxes

These are "on the spot" considerations of important, but incidental or infrequent aspects of the primary topics to which they relate. Their parenthetical nature, highlighted by enclosure in Additional Consideration boxes, helps maintain an appropriate level of rigor of topic coverage without sacrificing clarity of explanation.

ADDITIONAL CONSIDERATION

Some lessors use what's called the "gross metho lease. By this method, the lessor debits lease payments and credits *unearned interest revenue* payments and the present value of the payment be recorded as interest revenue over the term entry by the gross method at the inception of th

Lease receivable ($100,000 × 6) ....
Unearned interest revenue (difference) .....
Inventory of equipment (lessor's cost) ....

The same ultimate result is achieved either wa to more easily demonstrate the lessee's entries and the lessor's entries being "two sides of the same coin." Whichever method is used, both the lessee and the lessor must report in the disclosure notes both the net and gross amounts of the lease.

"This is a good technique that I actually use in my class and its good to see it in a book!"

- Ramesh Narasimhan, Montclair State University

Ethical Dilemmas

Because ethical ramifications of business decisions impact so many individuals as well as the core of our economy, Ethical Dilemmas are incorporated within the context of accounting issues as they are discussed. These features lend themselves very well to impromptu class discussions and debates.

ETHICAL DILEMMA

"I know we had discussed that they'r option becomes exercisable," Ferris in Jenkins, you know how fast computers be worth only $10,000 in three years."

The computers to which Ferris ref of the criteria for classification as a ca purchase option. Under the lease opti three years.

"We could avoid running up our de

How could debt be avoided?

Do you perceive an ethical problem

"Having ethical dilemma boxes in every chapter is much more significant than having a separate chapter devoted to ethics. Students can relate to the importance of being ethical in every aspect of business dealings."

- Gloria Worthy, Southwest Tennessee Community College

Broaden Your Perspective Cases

Finish each chapter with these powerful and effective cases, a great way to reinforce and expand concepts learned in the chapter.

BROADEN YOUR PERSPECTIVE

Apply your critical-thinking ability to the knowledge you've gained. These cases will provide you an opportunity to develop your research, analysis, judgment, and communication skills. You will also work with other students, integrate what you've learned, apply it in real-world situations, and consider its global and ethical ramifications. This practice will broaden your knowledge and further develop your decision-making abilities.

Judgment Case 1–1 The development of accounting standards

● LO3

In 1934, Congress created the Securiti power and responsibility for setting acc

Required:

1. Explain the relationship between the over time, been delegated the respon
2. Can you think of any reasons why th

Research Case 1–2 Accessing SEC information

Internet access to the World Wide Web ers. Many chapters in this text contain R ing issue. The purpose of this case is to Commission (SEC)

"I think students would benefit tremendously from the cases."

- Joyce Njoroge, Drake University

*Results from an independent market survey of intermediate accounting professors July–September 2002 by Professional Research Group, LLC.

What's New in the Fifth Edition?

Chapter 1
ENVIRONMENT AND THEORETICAL STRUCTURE OF FINANCIAL ACCOUNTING

- Revised the section on our global marketplace to reflect the most recent developments in the move toward global accounting standards.
- Enhanced the coverage of the Sarbanes-Oxley Act to include information about the cost of compliance.
- Revised the section on the elements of financial statements to provide a more concise presentation of the material.
- Added a section on the evolution of accounting principles that includes discussions of the move to the asset/liability approach and the move toward fair value in standard setting. The fair value discussion includes information on two new, important FASB standards, *SFAS No. 157* and *SFAS No. 159.*
- Moved the section on ethics in accounting to earlier in the chapter to provide a better flow of material.

Chapter 2
REVIEW OF THE ACCOUNTING PROCESS

- Enhanced the section on the conversion of cash basis to accrual basis to provide a more thorough analysis of the process and added additional end-of-chapter material on this topic.

Chapter 3
THE BALANCE SHEET AND FINANCIAL DISCLOSURES

- The introductory material on financial disclosures and disclosure notes has been enhanced to provide more thorough coverage of the topic.

Chapter 4
THE INCOME STATEMENT AND STATEMENT OF CASH FLOWS

- The section on comprehensive income has been moved from the beginning of Part A to the end. It will be easier for students to grasp this difficult topic after first covering the content and structure of the income statement.
- In the discussion of changes in accounting principles, a section has been added that addresses the accounting treatment of mandated changes in principles.
- The statement of cash flows illustration in Part B of the chapter has been expanded to include additional transactions. Presentation of cash flows from investing and financing activities also has been added to the illustration.

Chapter 5
INCOME MEASUREMENT AND PROFITABILITY ANALYSIS

- The section dealing with long-term contracts has been rewritten to clarify the similarities and differences between the percentage-of-completion and completed contract methods. Discussion has been added that clarifies the intuition underlying those approaches.
- Added discussion of multiple-deliverable revenue-recognition arrangements to cover the accounting approach indicated by EITF 00-21.
- Rewrote Part B of the chapter (Profitability Analysis) to organize it around the DuPont framework, adding discussion of leverage and using a peer analysis to illustrate the framework, and added end-of-chapter assignment material on this topic.

Chapter 6
TIME VALUE OF MONEY CONCEPTS

- Added discussion and illustration of how to use Excel and a calculator to determine present value and future value.

Chapter 7
CASH AND RECEIVABLES

- Enhanced the discussion of the valuation of noninterest-bearing notes including a computation aid for determining present value with Excel and with a calculator.

Chapter 8
INVENTORIES: MEASUREMENT

- Added information in the updated chapter-opening financial reporting case on LIFO liquidations.
- Added end-of-chapter material on physical quantities included in inventory, LIFO liquidations, and dollar-value LIFO.

Chapter 9
INVENTORIES: ADDITIONAL ISSUES

- Added a graphic to help students in their understanding of the lower-of-cost-or-market approach to valuing inventory.

Chapter 10
OPERATIONAL ASSETS: ACQUISITION AND DISPOSITION

- Updated material where necessary to reflect the issuance of *SFAS No. 141(R),* primarily the additional consideration that discusses negative goodwill and the section on purchased research and development.
- Revised the section on nonmonetary exchanges to provide more thorough coverage of the topic.

Chapter 11
OPERATIONAL ASSETS: UTILIZATION AND IMPAIRMENT

- The journal entry to record impairment losses has been added to impairment illustrations.

Chapter 12
INVESTMENTS

- Rewrote Part A (which covers accounting for investments when the investor lacks significant influence). This section has been reordered to cover held-to-maturity investments, then trading securities, and then available-for-sale securities. The same set of investments illustrate each approach, and a summary table compares and contrasts accounting under the three approaches to highlight similarities and differences among alternative approaches.
- Added coverage of *SFAS No. 157* and determining fair value. Tied investor accounting for held-to-maturity investments to the debt issuer's accounting discussed under long-term liabilities in Chapter 14.
- Simplified the explanation of fair-value adjustments at period end for both trading securities and available-for-sale securities by using the same basic journal-entry structure for both, while highlighting the effects on net income and other comprehensive income.
- Enhanced Part B (which covers the equity method) by illustrating equity-method accounting for one of the investments discussed in Part A.
- Added a summary table that compares and contrasts accounting under the fair-value and equity-method approaches to help students understand similarities and differences between these approaches.
- Added a new learning objective for the fair value option to correspond with new discussion of *SFAS No. 159* and the fair value option in both Parts A and Parts B. Also added end-of-chapter assignment material on this topic.

We received an incredible amount of feedback prior to writing the fifth edition of Intermediate Accounting. The following list of changes and improvements is a testament to our users and their commitment to making Intermediate Accounting the best book of its kind.

- Rewrote the decision-maker perspective to highlight the effects of alternative accounting approaches on income recognition and gains and losses and to emphasize the potential for earnings management.

Chapter 13 CURRENT LIABILITIES AND CONTINGENCIES

- Added discussion of accounting for contingent liabilities that a company acquires when it purchases another company under *SFAS No. 141(R)*, "Business Combinations."
- Revised coverage of contingencies for tax uncertainties that according to *FIN 48*, "Accounting for Uncertainty in Income Taxes" are no longer considered loss contingencies and added end-of-chapter assignment material on this topic

Chapter 14 BONDS AND LONG-TERM NOTES

- Since it's rare to have a delay in issuing bonds that causes them to be issued between interest dates, discussion of this infrequent event is moved to an appendix to the chapter.
- *SFAS No. 159*, "The Fair Value Option for Financial Assets and Financial Liabilities," gives companies the option to value some or all of their financial assets and liabilities at fair value. Discussion of how the fair value option is applied to liabilities has been added to the chapter, and extensive assignment materials related to the fair value option have been added.
- Added computation aids for determining present values with Excel and with a calculator.

Chapter 15 LEASES

- In an important pedagogical improvement, lessor accounting for nonoperating leases has been changed from the "gross method" of recording the lease receivable to the net method. Instruction is greatly simplified as students now immediately see that the lessee's entries and the lessor's entries are "two sides of the same coin." End-of-chapter assignment materials have been revised accordingly.
- Added computation aids for determining present values with Excel and with a calculator.

Chapter 16 ACCOUNTING FOR INCOME TAXES

- Added a new section, "Coping with Uncertainty in Income Taxes," and related end-of-chapter assignment materials in response to *FIN 48*, "Accounting for Uncertainty in Income Taxes."
- Enhanced the deferred tax accounting illustrations.

Chapter 17 PENSIONS AND OTHER POSTRETIREMENT BENEFIT PLANS

- Enhanced and simplified the illustrations of recording the expense, gains and losses, and prior service cost for both pensions and other postretirement benefit plans prescribed by *SFAS No. 158*.
- Improved the format of the pension spreadsheet.

Chapter 18 SHAREHOLDERS' EQUITY

- Simplified and modernized the discussion of stock issuance by eliminating coverage of share purchase contracts.

Chapter 19 SHARE-BASED COMPENSATION AND EARNINGS PER SHARE

- Enhanced the discussion of incentive and nonqualified plans and their tax treatment.
- Restricted stock awards are quickly replacing stock options as the share-based compensation plan of choice. In response, the discussion of EPS calculation is expanded to include the effect of these stock award plans as well as stock option plans that are not fully vested. Coverage is presented in a way that allows flexibility in the extent to which it is included in lesson plans and assignments.
- Coverage of SARs is moved to an appendix to the chapter. SARs along with options are becoming less popular. Their decline in popularity and their relatively complexity cause many to choose not to cover this topic.

Chapter 20 ACCOUNTING CHANGES AND ERROR CORRECTIONS

- Some changes in reporting entity are a result of changes in accounting rules, but the more frequent change in entity occurs when one company acquires another one. Discussion has been added to describe the disclosure required in these situations as prescribed by *SFAS No. 141(R)*.

Chapter 21 STATEMENT OF CASH FLOWS REVISITED

- This chapter continues to be devoted entirely to in-depth coverage of the statement of cash flows to complement and extend the more fundamental presentation of the statement in Chapter 4.

How Does Spiceland Help My Students Improve Their Performance?

Online Learning Center (OLC)

www.mhhe.com/spiceland5e

Today's students are every bit as comfortable using a web browser as they are reading a printed book. That's why we offer an Online Learning Center (OLC) that follows **Intermediate Accounting** chapter by chapter. It doesn't require any building or maintenance on your part, and is ready to go the moment you and your students type in the URL.

As your students study, they can refer to the OLC website for such benefits as:

- iPod content
- Self-grading quizzes
- Electronic flash cards
- Audio narrated PowerPoints
- Alternate exercises and problems
- Check figures
- Practice exams
- FASB pronouncements, summaries and updates
- Text updates

A secured Instructor Resource Center stores your essential course materials to save you prep time before class. The Instructor's Resource Manual, Solutions Manual, PowerPoint, and sample syllabi are now just a couple of clicks away. You will also find useful packaging information and transition notes.

The OLC website also serves as a doorway to other technology solutions such as PageOut, which is free to *Intermediate Accounting* adopters.

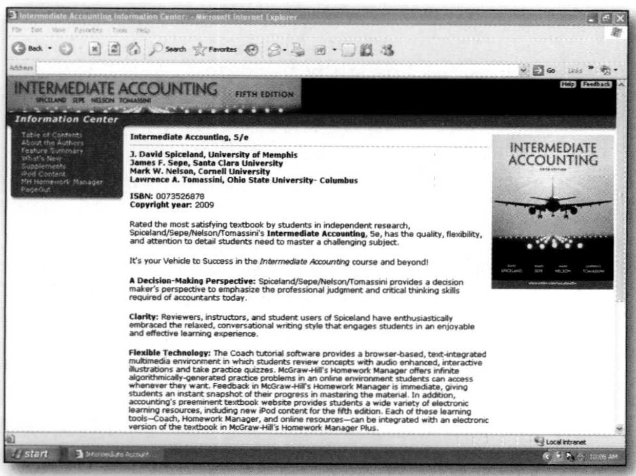

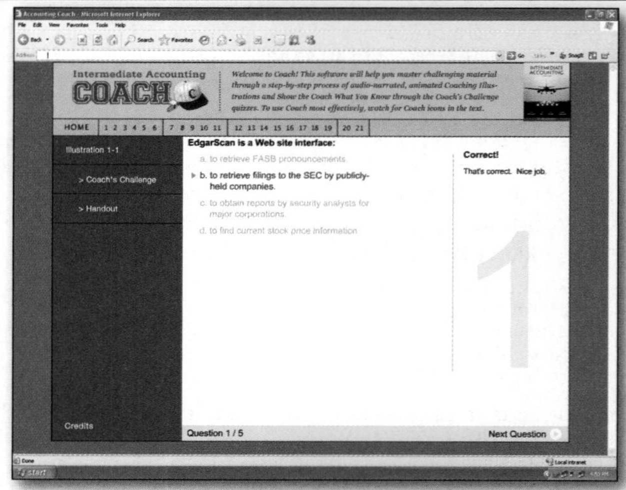

Coach

Coach is our award-winning tutorial software designed to help students understand critical accounting concepts. First, Coach actually provides spoken, narrated feedback as it helps students work through problems, rather than acting as just a reservoir of content that couldn't fit in the text. Second, the concept, content, and execution of Coach have been driven by and are part of the philosophy of the text authors.

Coach helps students master challenging material through a clear, step-by-step model. **Coaching Illustrations** are animated illustrations and examples similar to those found in the text that walk students through difficult concepts in a step-by-step manner. Look for the Coach icon in the text to identify these illustrations. **Show the Coach What You Know** provides students with a fun and interactive way to quiz themselves on key terminology and concepts.

> **"It is wonderful. I have my students evaluate each course I teach and rate the resources used. Time after time, students rate Coach as their number one choice. They love the interaction."**
>
> *- Janice Stoudemire, Midlands Technical College*

Intermediate Accounting's digital learning tools provide a comprehensive and cutting-edge environment for your students to practice in—and all digital content is prepared by the authors themselves.

McGraw-Hill's Homework Manager system is a Web-based supplement that duplicates problems directly from the textbook end-of-chapter material, using algorithms to provide a limitless supply of online self-graded practice for students, or assignments and tests with unique versions of every problem. Say goodbye to cheating in your classroom; say hello to the power and flexibility you've been waiting for in creating assignments.

The enhanced version of McGraw-Hill's Homework Manager system integrates all of Spiceland's online and multimedia assets to allow your students to brush up on a topic before doing their homework. You now have the option to give your students pre-populated hints and feedback. The Testbank has been added to McGraw-Hill's Homework Manager system so you can create online quizzes and exams and have them autograded and recorded in the same gradebook as your homework assignments. The enhanced version provides you with the option of incorporating the complete online version of the textbook, so your students can easily reference the chapter material as they do their homework assignment, even when their textbook is far away.

HOMEWORK MANAGER PLUS

McGraw-Hill's Homework Manager system is also a useful grading tool. All assignments can be delivered over the Web and are graded automatically, with the results stored in your private gradebook. Detailed results let you see at a glance how each student does on an assignment or an individual problem—you can even see how many tries it took them to solve it.

Students receive full access to McGraw-Hill's Homework Manager system when they purchase Homework Manager Plus® software, or you can have McGraw-Hill's Homework Manager system pass codes shrinkwrapped with the textbook. Students can also purchase access to McGraw-Hill's Homework Manager software directly from your class home page.

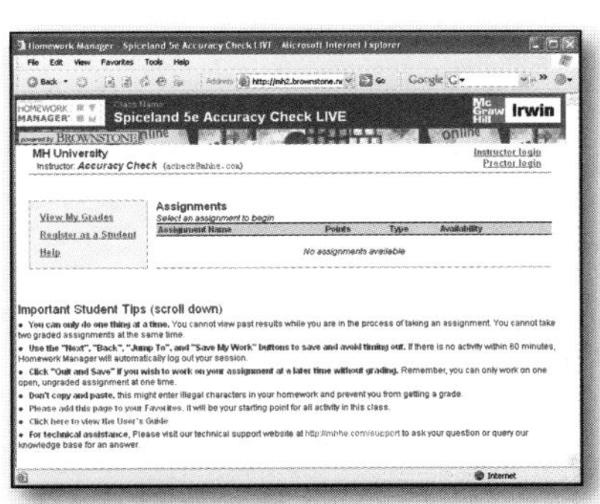

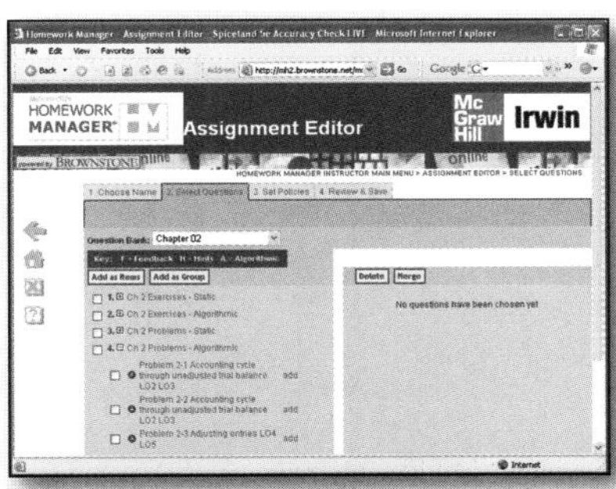

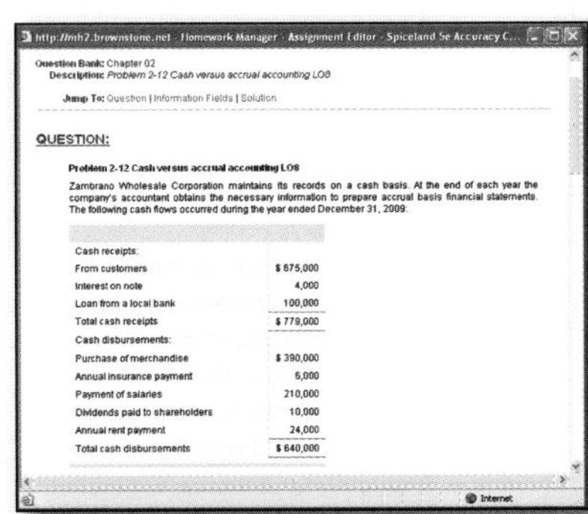
Question Bank: Chapter 02
Description: Problem 2-12 Cash versus accrual accounting LO8

Jump To: Question | Information Fields | Solution

QUESTION:

Problem 2-12 Cash versus accrual accounting LO8

Zambrano Wholesale Corporation maintains its records on a cash basis. At the end of each year the company's accountant obtains the necessary information to prepare accrual basis financial statements. The following cash flows occurred during the year ended December 31, 2009:

Cash receipts:	
From customers	$ 675,000
Interest on note	4,000
Loan from a local bank	100,000
Total cash receipts	$ 779,000
Cash disbursements:	
Purchase of merchandise	$ 390,000
Annual insurance payment	6,000
Payment of salaries	210,000
Dividends paid to shareholders	10,000
Annual rent payment	24,000
Total cash disbursements	$ 640,000

McGraw-Hill's Homework Manager Plus™ combines the power of McGraw-Hill's Homework Manager system with the latest interactive learning technology to create a comprehensive, fully integrated online study package.

Students using McGraw-Hill's Homework Manager Plus system can access not only McGraw-Hill's Homework Manager® software itself, but the interactive online textbook as well. For more than a textbook on a screen, this resource is completely integrated into McGraw-Hill's Homework Manager software, allowing students working on assignments to click a hotlink and instantly review the appropriate material in the textbook.

By including McGraw-Hill's Homework Manager Plus system with your textbook adoption, you're giving your students a vital edge as they progress through the course and ensuring that the help they need is never more than a mouse click away.

How Does Spiceland Help Me Build a Better Course?

> **"The two [technology assets] that I find most exciting are Homework Manager and ALEKS. These alone are powerful reasons to choose this textbook."**
>
> *- Chula King, University of West Florida*

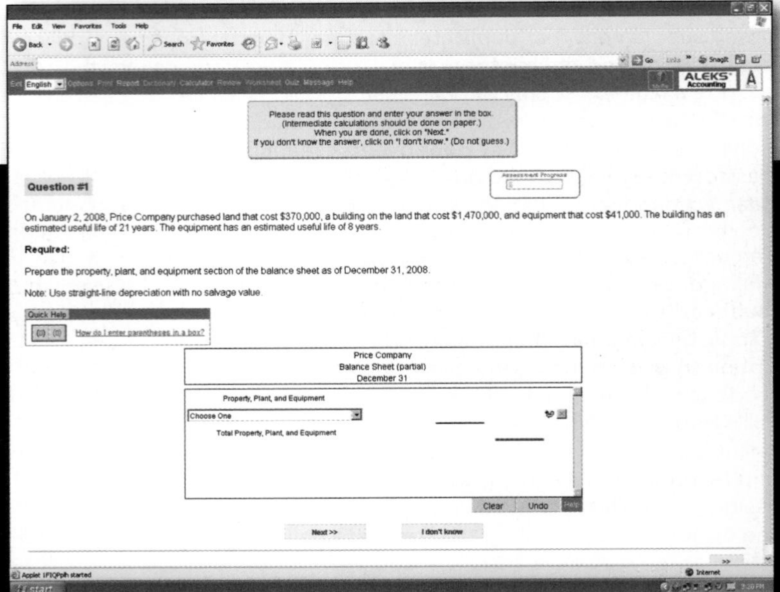

ALEKS for the Accounting Cycle uses innovative adaptive learning technology to provide individualized guided learning to each and every student. ALEKS defines the key concepts, offers explanations and opportunities to practice, analyzes and corrects errors, and moves on to new topics when the student is ready.

When a student completes an initial assessment with ALEKS, the system analyzes the student's responses and determines an individual knowledge state for that student with great efficiency. From then on, ALEKS sets an appropriate learning path for the student by carefully analyzing his or her responses and determining what material is ready to be learned next.

You'll see increased motivation and confidence in your students after they use ALEKS. You'll see improved performance in courses where ALEKS is deployed, as well as fewer drops. And you'll see it all with minimal effort on your part—that's how easy it is to integrate ALEKS into your course.

What are the benefits of ALEKS for the Accounting Cycle?

- Intermediate accounting students can use ALEKS for a review of the accounting cycle. Since ALEKS is self-guided, you can reduce the time spent in your intermediate course reviewing material from financial accounting.
- ALEKS can be used as the curriculum for a bridge course between financial accounting and intermediate accounting.
- MBA students can use ALEKS for a self-guided review of accounting to prepare for their MBA program. Since it is online, students can do their work from anywhere in the world.

Contact your McGraw-Hill representative today and learn more about ALEKS, or email **aleks@mcgraw-hill.com.**

From innovative self-guided assessment and guidance to complete online course solutions, McGraw-Hill/Irwin lets you take full advantage of everything the digital age has to offer.

Flexible Online Course Content

No matter what platform you use, McGraw-Hill is committed to making your online course a success. We provide free, WebCT- and Blackboard-compatible course cartridges containing all the content you need.

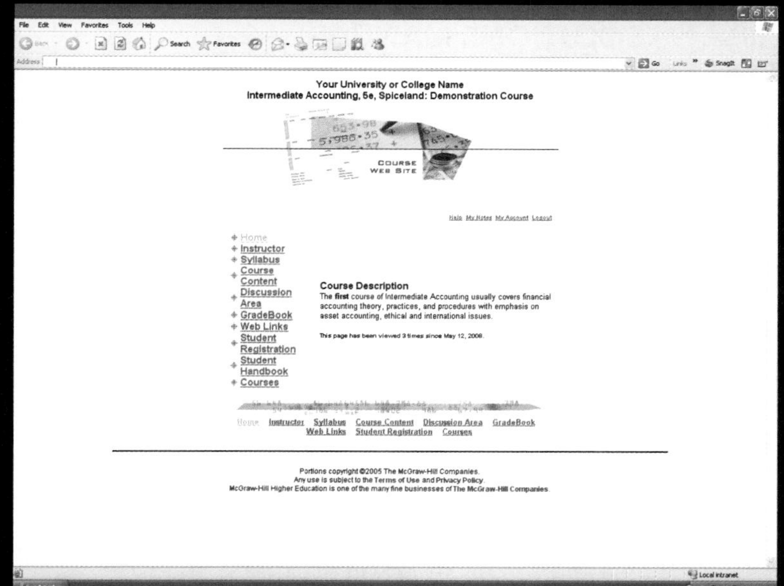

> **"The course I will use this text for is a 'blended' course . . . partially online and partially on campus. This will be very useful."**
>
> *- Kathy Simons, Bryant College*

PageOut—McGraw-Hill's Course Management System

PageOut is the easiest way to create a Website for your accounting course.

There's no need for HTML coding, graphic design, or a thick how-to book. Just fill in a series of boxes with simple English and click on one of our professional designs. In no time, your course is online with a Website that contains your syllabus!

Should you need assistance in preparing your Website, we can help. Our team of product specialists is ready to take your course materials and build a custom Website to your specifications. You simply need to call a McGraw-Hill/Irwin PageOut specialist to start the process. Best of all, PageOut is free when you adopt *Intermediate Accounting*! To learn more, please visit **www.pageout.net.**

To see how these platforms can assist your online course, visit **www.mhhe.com**

A GREAT LEARNING SYSTEM DOESN'T STOP WITH THE BOOK.

INSTRUCTOR SUPPLEMENTS

ASSURANCE OF LEARNING READY

Many educational institutions today are focused on the notion of assurance of learning, an important element of some accreditation standards. *Intermediate Accounting* is designed specifically to support your assurance of learning initiatives with a simple, yet powerful, solution.

Each Testbank question for *Intermediate Accounting* maps to a specific chapter learning outcome/objective listed in the text. You can use our Testbank software, *EZ Test*, to easily query for learning outcomes/objectives that directly relate to the learning objectives for your course. You can then use the reporting features of *EZ Test* to aggregate student results in similar fashion, making the collection and presentation of assurance of learning data simple and easy. You can also use our Algorithmic-Diploma Testbank to do this.

AACSB STATEMENT

McGraw-Hill Companies is a proud corporate member of AACSB International. Recognizing the importance and value of AACSB accreditation, we have sought to recognize the curricula guidelines detailed in AACSB standards for business accreditation by connecting selected Testbank questions in *Intermediate Accounting* to the general knowledge and skill guidelines found in the AACSB standards.

The statements contained in *Intermediate Accounting* are provided only as a guide for the users of this text. The AACSB leaves content coverage and assessment clearly within the realm and control of individual schools, the mission of the school, and the faculty. The AACSB also charges schools with the obligation of doing assessment against their own content and learning goals. While *Intermediate Accounting* and its teaching package make no claim of any specific AACSB qualification or evaluation, we have labeled questions according to the six general knowledge and skills areas.

INSTRUCTOR'S RESOURCE MANUAL

This manual provides for each chapter: (a) a chapter overview; (b) a comprehensive lecture outline; (c) extensive teaching transparency masters that can be modified to suit an instructor's particular needs or preferences; (d) a variety of suggested class activities (real world, ethics, Google, professional development activities including research, analysis, communication and judgment, and others); and (e) an assignment chart indicating topic, learning objective, and estimated completion time for every question, exercise, problem, and case.

> **"Very readable, impressive web-based supplements, excellent topic coverage."**
>
> *- Karen Foust, Tulane University*

SOLUTIONS MANUAL

The Solutions Manual includes detailed solutions for every question, exercise, problem, and case in the text.

INSTRUCTOR'S CD-ROM

ISBN-13: 9780073324494 (ISBN-10: 0073324493)

This all-in-one resource contains the Instructor's Resource Manual, Solutions Manual, Testbank Word files, Computerized, Testbank, and PowerPoint® slides.

TESTBANK

Written by the authors, this comprehensive Testbank contains over 3,700 problems and true/false, multiple-choice, matching, and essay questions.

COMPUTERIZED TESTBANK WITH ALGORITHMIC PROBLEM GENERATOR

ISBN-13: 9780073324333 (ISBN-10: 0073324337)

The Computerized Testbank is an algorithmic problem generator enabling instructors to create similarly structured problems with different values, allowing every student to be assigned a unique quiz or test. The user-friendly interface allows faculty to easily create different versions of the same test, change the answer order, edit or add questions, and even conduct online testing.

AUDIO POWERPOINT SLIDES

The Audio PowerPoint slides are created by Jon Booker and Charles Caldwell of Tennessee Technological University and Susan Galbreath of David Lipscomb University. The slides include an accompanying audio lecture with notes and are available on the Online Learning Center (OLC).

Intermediate Accounting authors Spiceland, Sepe, Nelson and Tomassini know from their years of teaching experience what separates a great textbook from a merely adequate one. Every component of the learning package must be imbued with the same style and approach, and that's why the Intermediate Accounting authors write every major ancillary themselves, whether printed or online. It's one more thing that sets Intermediate Accounting far above the competition.

STUDENT SUPPLEMENTS

STUDY GUIDE

Volume 1: ISBN-13: 9780073324593 (ISBN-10: 0073324590)
Volume 2: ISBN-13: 9780073324609 (ISBN-10: 0073324604)

The Study Guide, written by the text authors, provides chapter summaries, detailed illustrations, and a wide variety of self-study questions, exercises, and multiple-choice problems (with solutions).

WORKING PAPERS

ISBN-13: 9780073324630 (ISBN-10: 0073324639)

Working Papers provide students with formatted templates to aid them in doing homework assignments.

EXCEL TEMPLATES

Selected end-of-chapter exercises and problems, marked in the text with an icon, can be solved using these Microsoft Excel templates, located on the OLC.

UNDERSTANDING CORPORATE ANNUAL REPORTS

Seventh Edition, by William R. Pasewark

ISBN-13: 9780073526935 (ISBN-10: 0073526932)

This project provides students with instruction for obtaining an annual report from a publicly traded corporation and for making an industry or competitor comparison.

> **"This is a well-written text, with good integration. It has a full range of computerized and other support materials; and the authors personally write and check the practice questions, examples, and text items."**
>
> *- Elaine Henry, University of Miami*

ALTERNATE EXERCISES AND PROBLEMS

This online manual includes additional exercises and problems for each chapter in the text. Available on the OLC.

COACH

This step-by-step, tutorial software is available on the OLC and integrated throughout the text to help students better understand intermediate accounting topics.

PRACTICE SETS

Student ISBN-13: 9780073324449 (ISBN-10: 0073324442)

Grady Wholesale Practice Set: Review of the Accounting Cycle

> **"The text is a well written, easy to read intermediate accounting text with lots of graphics and color."**
>
> *- Patty Lobingier, Virginia Polytechnic Institute*

Acknowledgments

Fifth Edition Reviewers

Habib Abo-El-Yazeed, *Minnesota State University—Mankato*
Noel Addy, *Mississippi State University*
Pervaiz Alam, *Kent State University*
Joseph W. Antenucci, *Youngstown State University*
Marie Archambault, *Marshall University*
Jack Aschkenazi, *American Intercontinental University*
Florence Atiase, *University of Texas*
Joyce Barden, *DeVry University—Phoenix*
John Bildersee, *New York University*
Robert Bloom, *John Carroll University*
William J. Bradberry, *Bluefield State College*
Russell Briner, *University of Texas*
Nat R. Briscoe, *Northwestern State University*
R. Eugene Bryson, *University of Alabama—Huntsville*
Gary Burkette, *East Tennessee State University*
Al Case, *Southern Oregon University*
Jack M. Cathey, *University North Carolina—Charlotte*
Teresa Conover, *University of North Texas*
Cheryl Corke, *Genesee Community College*
Charles D'Alessandro, *SUNY—Suffolk*
Mark Dawkins, *University of Georgia*
Denise De La Rosa, *Grand Valley State University*
Susan A. Dehner, *Delaware Tech Community College—Dover*
Larry A. Deppe, *Weber State University*
Wendy Duffy, *Illinois State University*
Gerard M. Engeholm, *Pace University*
Kathryn K. Epps, *Kennesaw State University*
Patricia A. Fedje, *Minot State University*
Anita Feller, *University of Illinois—Champaign*
Karen Foust, *Tulane University*
Jeanne Gerard, *Franklin Pierce College*
Aloke Ghosh, *Bernard M. Baruch College*
Lori Grady, *Bucks County Community College*
Julia Grant, *Case Western Reserve University*
Mary Halford, *Prince Georges Community College*
John M. Hassell, *Indiana University–Purdue University Indianapolis*
Kenneth Henry, *Florida International University—Miami*
Paula Irwin, *Muhlenberg College*
Marianne James, *California State University—Los Angeles*
Cynthia Jeffrey, *Iowa State University*
Ronald Kilgore, *University of Tennessee—Martin*
Gordon Klein, *University of California—Los Angeles*
Philip Lee, *Nashville State Tech Community College*
Tim M. Lindquist, *University of Northern Iowa*
Danny S. Litt, *University of California—Los Angeles*
Patty Lobingier, *Virginia Polytechnic Institute*
Susan Logorda, *Lehigh Carbon Community College*
Jeff Mankin, *Lipscomb University*
Josephine Mathias, *Mercer County Community College*
Robert W. McGee, *Barry University*
Anita Morgan, *CTU Online*
Barbara Muller, *Arizona State University*
Ramesh Narasimhan, *Montclair University*
Siva Nathan, *Georgia State University*
Joyce Njoroge, *Drake University*
George Nogler, *University of Massachusetts—Lowell*
Derek Oler, *Indiana University*
Mitchell Oler, *Virginia Tech*
William A. Padley, *Madison Area Technical College—Truax*
Hong Pak, *California State Poly University—Pomona*
Barbara K. Parks, *American Intercontinental University*
Keith Patterson, *Brigham Young University*
Simon Pearlman, *California State University—Long Beach*
Anthony R. Piltz, *Rocky Mountain College*
Terence Pitre, *University of South Carolina*
David Plumlee, *University of Utah*
Grace Pownall, *Emory University*
Angela Sandberg, *Jacksonville State University*
Alex Sannella, *Rutgers University*
Paul Schloemer, *Ashland University*
Kathy Sevigny, *Bridgewater State College*
Carol Shaver, *Louisiana Tech University*
Ronald Singleton, *Western Washington University*
Kenneth Smith, *Salisbury University*
Katherene P. Terrell, *University of Central Oklahoma*

As you know if you've read this far, Intermediate Accounting would not be what it is without the passionate feedback of our colleagues. Through your time and effort, we were able to create a learning system that truly responds to the needs of the market, and for that, we sincerely thank each of you.

Michael Tyler, *Barry University*

Michael G. Welker, *Drexel University*

Gloria Worthy, *Southwest Tennessee University*

Jing-Wen Yang, *California State University—East Bay*

Fifth Edition Reviewers' Conference Attendees

Reviewers' conferences give our authors a valuable opportunity to interact with textbook users face to face, hearing firsthand their successes and difficulties in the classroom. That feedback was particularly valuable in crafting the fifth edition of *Intermediate Accounting,* and the Spiceland team extends special thanks to all those who participated:

Matilda Abavana, *Essex County College*

Noel D. Addy, Jr., *Mississippi State University*

Matthew Anderson, *Michigan State University*

Florence Atiase, *University of Texas*

Yoel Beniluz, *Rutgers University*

Lila Bergman, *Hunter College*

Russell Briner, *University of Texas*

Al Case, *Southern Oregon University*

Lanny Chasteen, *Oklahoma State University*

C. S. Agnes Cheng, *University of Houston*

Stanley Chu, *Bernard M. Baruch College*

Kwang Chung, *Pace University*

Edwin Cohen, *DePaul University*

Teresa Conover, *University of North Texas*

John Corless, *California State University—Sacramento*

Bobbie W. Daniels, *Jackson State University*

Mark Dawkins, *University of Georgia*

Gerard M. Engeholm, *Pace University*

Kathryn K. Epps, *Kennesaw State University*

Ehsan H. Feroz, *University of Washington—Tacoma*

Gail E. Fraser, *Kean University*

Frank Heflin, *Florida State University—Tallahassee*

Kenneth Henry, *Florida International University—Miami*

Agatha Jeffers, *Montclair State University*

Keith Jones, *George Mason University*

Khondkar Karim, *Rochester Institute of Technology*

Lisa Koonce, *University of Texas—Austin*

Cynthia L. Krom, *Marist College*

Joan Lacher, *Nassau Community College*

Janice Lawrence, *University of Nebraska—Lincoln*

Kevin Lightner, *San Diego State University*

Heidemarie Lundblad, *California State University—Northridge*

Robert W. McGee, *Barry University*

Mike Metzcar, *Indiana Wesleyan University*

Charles Miller, *California Polytechnic State University*

Sia Nassiripour, *William Paterson University*

Emeka Ofobike, *University of Akron*

Hong S. Pak, *California State Poly University—Pomona*

Rachel Pernia, *Essex County College*

Joann Pinto, *Montclair State University*

Frederick M. Richardson, *Virginia Polytech Institute*

Michael Riordan, *James Madison University*

Byung Ro, *Purdue University—West Lafayette*

Pamela Roush, *University of Central Florida*

Huldah A. Ryan, *Iona College*

Anwar Salimi, *California State Poly University—Pomona*

Gerald Savage, *Essex County College*

Gary Schader, *Kean University*

Nancy Snow, *University of Toledo*

Paulette Tandy, *University of Nevada—Las Vegas*

Katherene P. Terrell, *University of Central Oklahoma*

Robert Terrell, *University of Central Oklahoma*

Karen Turner, *University of Northern Colorado*

Michael L. Werner, *University of Miami—Coral Gables*

Previous Edition Reviewers and Focus Group Attendees

The Spiceland team also extends sincere thanks to the reviewers of our previous editions, without whose input we could not have made *Intermediate Accounting* the extraordinary success it has been.

Charlene Abendroth, *California State University—Hayward*

Marie Archambault, *Marshall University*

Peter Aghimien, *Indiana University—South Bend*

Tony Amoruso, *West Virginia University*

James Anderson, *St. Cloud Tech College*

Matt Anderson, *Michigan State University*

Florence Atiase, *University of Texas at Austin*

Craig Bain, *Northern Arizona University*

James Bannister, *University of Hartford*

Katherine Barker, *Lander University*

Acknowledgments

Homer Bates, *University of North Florida*
Daniel Bayak, *Lehigh University*
Jan Bell, *California State University—Northridge*
Whit Broome, *University of Virginia—Charlottesville*
Kevin Brown, *Drexel University*
John Brozovsky, *Virginia Tech*
Eddy Burks, *Athens State University*
Ronald Campbell, *North Carolina A&T University*
Al Case, *Southern Oregon University*
John Cezair, *Fayetteville State University*
Nandini Chandar, *Rutgers University*
Gyan Chandra, *Miami University, Oxford, Ohio**
Otto Chang, *California State University—Santa Barbara*
Kim Charland, *Kansas State University*
Betty Chavis, *California State University—Fullerton*
Alan Cherry, *Loyola Marymount University*
Steve Christian, *Jackson Community College*
Bryan Church, *Georgia Institute of Technology*
Marilyn G. Ciolino, *Delgado Community College*
Lynn Clements, *Florida Southern College*
Bob Cluskey, *State University of West Georgia*
Christie L. Comunale, *Long Island University—C.W. Post Campus*
Betty Conner, *University of Colorado at Denver*
Ellen Cook, *University of Louisiana at Lafayette*
Araya Debessay, *University of Delaware*
Marinus Debruine, *Grand Valley State University*
Larry Deppe, *Weber State University*
Judi Doing, *University of Arizona*
Orapin Duangploy, *University of Houston Downtown*
Wendy Duffy, *Illinois State University*
Tim Eaton, *Marquette University*
Jerry Engeholm, *Pace University*
Kathleen Fitzpatrick, *University of Toledo Community Tech College*
Sandra Fleak, *Truman State University*
Dick Fleischman, *John Carroll University*
Karen Foust, *Tulane University*
Clyde Galbraith, *West Chester University of Pennsylvania*
Susan Galbreath, *David Lipscomb University*
John Garlick, *Fayetteville State University*
Jennifer Gaver, *University of Georgia*
Nashwa George, *Montclair State University*
John Gillett, *Bradley University*
Sid Glandon, *University of Texas at El Paso*
Geoffrey Goldsmith, *Belhaven College*
Janet Greenlee, *University of Dayton*
Robert Gruber, *University of Wisconsin—Whitewater*
Amy Haas, *Kingsborough Community College*
Seth Hammer, *Towson University*
Coby Harmon, *University of California—Santa Barbara*
Charles Harter, *North Dakota State University—Fargo*
Robert Hatanaka, *University of Hawaii at Manoa*
Roger Hehman, *University of Cincinnati—Blue Ash*
Lyle Hicks, *Danville Area Community College*
Steve Hunt, *Western Illinois University*
Eliot Kamlet, *Binghamton University*
Ronald Kilgore, *University of Tennessee—Martin*
Chula King, *University of West Florida*
Gordon Klein, *University of California Los Angeles*
Larry Klein, *Bentley College*
David Knight, *Boro of Manhattan Community College*
Mary-Jo Kranacher, *York College, CUNY*
Jerry Krueze, *Western Michigan University**
Linda Kuechler, *Daemen College*
Tara Laken, *Joliet Junior College*
Jerry Lehman, *Madison Area Technical College—Truax*
Barbara Lippincott, *University of Tampa*
Susan Lynn, *University of Baltimore*
Mostafa Maksy, *Northeastern Illinois University*
Danny Matthews, *Midwestern State University*
Kevin McNelis, *New Mexico State University*
Wilda Meixner, *Texas State University—San Marcos*
Cathy Miller, *University of Michigan—Flint*
Bonnie Moe, *University of Illinois—Springfield*
Kathy Moffeit, *State University of West Georgia*
Jackie Moffitt, *Louisiana State University*
Louella Moore, *Arkansas State University*
Joe Moran, *College of DuPage*
Joe Morris, *Southeastern Louisiana University*
Barbara Muller, *Arizona State University—West*
Emeka Ofobike, *University of Akron*
Steven Onaitis, *University of Pittsburgh—Pittsburgh*
Janet C. Papiernik, *Indiana University—Purdue University—Fort Wayne*
Patricia Parker, *Columbus State Community College*
Sy Pearlman, *California State University—Long Beach*
Gary Pieroni, *University of California Berkeley*
Joanne Pinto, *Montclair State University*
Marion Posey, *Pace University*
Mike Prockton, *Finger Lakes Community College*
Judy Ramage, *Christian Bros University*
Donald Raux, *Siena College*
Sara Reiter, *SUNY—Bingham*
Randall Rentfro, *Florida Atlantic University—Fort Lauderdale*
David Roberts, *Texas A & M University International*
Luther Ross, *Central Piedmont Community College*
Eric Rothenburg, *Kingsborough Community College*
Marc Rubin, *Miami University, Oxford, Ohio*
John Rude, *Bloomsburg University of Pennsylvania*
Robert W. Rutledge, *Texas State University*
Maria Sanchez, *Rider University*
Angela Sandberg, *Jacksonville State University*
Alex Sannella, *Rutgers University—Newark*
Stanley Sauber, *Brooklyn College*
Gary Schader, *Kean University*
Carol G. Schaver, *Louisiana Tech University*
Paul Schloemer, *Ashland University*
Barbara Scofield, *University of Texas—Permian Basin*
Jerry Scott, *Ivy Tech State College*
Michael Serif, *Dowling College*
Rebecca Shortridge, *Ball State University*
Kathy Simons, *Bryant College*
Lorraine Stern, *York College, CUNY*
Doug Stevens, *Syracuse University*
Janice Stoudemire, *Midlands Technical College*

Lynn Suberly, *Valdosta State University**

John Surdick, *Xavier University*

Debbie Tanju, *University of Alabama at Birmingham*

Peter Theuri, *Northern Kentucky University*

Ron Tilden, *University of Washington, Bothell*

Michael Toerner, *Southern University—Baton Rouge*

Michael Trebesh, *Alma College*

Richard A. Turpen, *University of Alabama at Birmingham*

Michael Tyler, *Barry University*

Irwin Uhr, *Hunter College*

Frank Urbancic, *University of Southern Alabama*

Herbert Vessel, *Southern University—Baton Rouge*

James Voss, *Pennsylvania State Behrend-Erie*

Larry Walther, *University of Texas—Arlington**

Weiman Wang, *Tulane University*

Scott White, *Lindenwood University*

Gloria Worthy, *Southwest Tennessee Community College—Macon Campus*

Suzanne Wright, *Pennsylvania State University-University Park*

Robert Wyatt, *Drury University*

Thomas Yandow, *Norwich University*

George Young, *Florida Atlantic University—Fort Lauderdale*

Kay Zekany, *Ohio Northern University*

Mary Zenner, *College of Lake County*

* Completed in-depth review of Testbank

We Are Grateful

We would like to acknowledge Barbara Muller, Arizona State University, for her detailed accuracy check of the Testbank; also, Patty Lobingier (Virginia Polytechnic Iusricure), Marianne James (California State, Los Angeles), and Jing-Wen Yang (California State University—East Bay) completed helpful reviews of the Testbank before we started revisions. Bill Padley of Madison Area Technical College contributed greatly to the production of the Working Papers. In addition, we thank Jon A. Booker and Charles W. Caldwell of Tennessee Technological University and Susan C. Galbreath of David Lipscomb University for crafting the PowerPoint Slides; and Jack E. Terry, ComSource Associates, for developing the Excel Templates.

Ilene Persoff, CW Post Campus/Long Island University and Beth Woods, Accuracy Counts, made significant contributions to the accuracy of the text, end-of-chapter material, and solutions manual. In addition, we appreciate the help and guidance received from Teresa Conover from North Texas University, for her insights regarding the International Financial Reporting Standards. A big thank you to Jerry Kreuze of Western Michigan University for his detailed analysis of the end-of-chapter material. We appreciate the assistance of James Lynch at KPMG, who provided us with valuable feedback on various difficult issues.

We appreciate the excellent Homework Manager accuracy checking work completed by Mark McCarthy, East Carolina University; Angela Sandberg, Jacksonville State University; Ilene Persoff, CW Post Campus/Long Island University; Lisa N. Bostick, The University of Tampa; Patty Lobingier, Virginia Polytechnic Institute; Marc A. Giullian, Montana State University; Barbara Muller, Arizona State University; Lori Grady, Bucks County Community College; and William Padley, Madison Area Technical College.

We are most grateful for the talented assistance and support from the many people at McGraw-Hill/Irwin. We would particularly like to thank Brent Gordon, editor in chief; Stewart Mattson, editorial director; Tim Vertovec, publisher; Daryl Horrocks, developmental editor; Scott Bishop, marketing manager; Greg Patterson, regional sales manager; Pat Frederickson, lead project manager; Gina Hangos, production supervisor; Laurie Entringer, designer; Jeremy Cheshareck, photo research coordinator; and Kerry Bowler, media project manager.

Finally, we extend our thanks to Kaplan CPA Review for their assistance developing simulations for our inclusion in the end-of-chapter material, as well as Google for allowing us to use its Annual Report throughout the text. We also acknowledge permission from the AICPA to adapt material from the Uniform CPA Examination, the IMA for permission to adapt material from the CMA Examination, and Dow Jones & Co., Inc., for permission to excerpt material from *The Wall Street Journal.*

David Spiceland Jim Sepe
Mark Nelson Larry Tomassini

Contents in Brief

Financial Instruments and Liabilities

3 SECTION

Additional Financial Reporting Issues

4 SECTION

Contents

3 SECTION Financial Instruments and Liabilities

13 CHAPTER Current Liabilities and Contingencies, 650

14 CHAPTER Bonds and Long-Term Notes, 702

15 CHAPTER Leases, 758

16 CHAPTER Accounting for Income Taxes, 820

SECTION 4 Additional Financial Reporting Issues

19 CHAPTER Share-Based Compensation and Earnings Per Share, 1000

20 CHAPTER Accounting Changes and Error Corrections, 1060

This page is intentionally blank

13

CHAPTER

Current Liabilities and Contingencies

/// OVERVIEW

With the discussion of investments in Chapter 12, we concluded our six-chapter coverage of assets that began in Chapter 7. This is the first of six chapters devoted to liabilities. Here we focus on short-term liabilities. Bonds and long-term notes are discussed in Chapter 14. Obligations relating to leases, income taxes, pensions, and other postretirement benefits are the subjects of the following four chapters. In Part A of this chapter, we discuss liabilities that are classified appropriately as current. In Part B we turn our attention to situations in which there is uncertainty as to whether an obligation really exists. These are designated as loss contingencies.

LEARNING OBJECTIVES

After studying this chapter, you should be able to:

- **LO1** Define liabilities and distinguish between current and long-term liabilities.
- **LO2** Account for the issuance and payment of various forms of notes and record the interest on the notes.
- **LO3** Characterize accrued liabilities and liabilities from advance collection and describe when and how they should be recorded.
- **LO4** Determine when a liability can be classified as a noncurrent obligation.
- **LO5** Identify situations that constitute contingencies and the circumstances under which they should be accrued.
- **LO6** Demonstrate the appropriate accounting treatment for contingencies, including unasserted claims and assessments.

FINANCIAL REPORTING CASE

Dinstuhl's Dad

"My dad is confused," your friend Buzz Dinstuhl proclaimed at the office one morning. "You see, we're competing against each other in that investment game I told you about, and one of his hot investments is Syntel Microsystems. When he got their annual report yesterday afternoon, he started analyzing it, you know, really studying it closely. Then he asked me about this part here." Buzz pointed to the current liability section of the balance sheet and related disclosure note:

SYNTEL MICROSYSTEMS, INC.
Balance Sheet
December 31, 2009 and 2008
($ in millions)

Current Liabilities	**2009**	**2008**
Accounts payable	$233.5	$241.6
Short-term borrowings (Note 3)	187.0	176.8
Accrued liabilities	65.3	117.2
Accrued loss contingency	76.9	—
Other current liabilities	34.6	45.2
Current portion of long-term debt	44.1	40.3
Total current liabilities	$641.4	$621.1

Note 3: Short-Term Borrowings (in part)

The components of short-term borrowings and their respective weighted average interest rates at the end of the period are as follows:

$ in millions

	2009		**2008**	
	Amount	**Average Interest Rate**	**Amount**	**Average Interest Rate**
Commercial paper	$ 34.0	5.2%	$ 27.1	5.3%
Bank loans	218.0	5.5	227.7	5.6
Amount reclassified to long-term liabilities	(65.0)	—	(78.0)	—
Total short-term borrowings	$187.0		$176.8	

The Company maintains bank credit lines sufficient to cover outstanding short-term borrowings. As of December 31, 2009, the Company had $200.0 million fee-paid lines available.

At December 31, 2009 and 2008, the Company classified $65.0 million and $78.0 million, respectively, of commercial paper and bank notes as long-term debt. The Company has the intent and ability, through formal renewal agreements, to renew these obligations into future periods.

Note 6: Contingencies (in part)

Between 2007 and 2008, the Company manufactured cable leads that, the Company has learned, contribute to corrosion of linked components with which they are installed. At December 31, 2009, the Company accrued $132.0 million in anticipation of remediation and claims settlement deemed probable, of which $76.9 million is considered a current liability.

"So, what's the problem?" you asked.

"Well, he thinks I'm some sort of financial wizard because I'm in the business."

"And because you tell him so all the time," you interrupted.

"Maybe so, but he's been told that current liabilities are riskier than long-term liabilities, and now he's focusing on that. He can't see why some long-term debt is reported here in the current section. And it also looks like some is reported the other way around; some current liabilities reported as long term. Plus, the contingency amount seems like it's not even a contractual liability. Then he wants to know what some of those terms mean. Lucky for me, I had to leave before I had to admit I didn't know the answers. You're the accounting graduate; help me out."

By the time you finish this chapter, you should be able to respond appropriately to the questions posed in this case. Compare your response to the solution provided at the end of the chapter.

QUESTIONS ///

1. What are accrued liabilities? What is commercial paper? (page 657)
2. Why did Syntel Microsystems include some long-term debt in the current liability section? (page 662)
3. Did they also report some current amounts as long-term debt? Explain. (page 662)
4. Must obligations be known contractual debts in order to be reported as liabilities? (page 666)
5. Is it true that current liabilities are riskier than long-term liabilities? (page 676)

PART A CURRENT LIABILITIES

Before a business can invest in an asset it first must acquire the money to pay for it. This can happen in either of two ways—funds can be provided by owners or the funds must be borrowed. You may recognize this as a description of the basic accounting equation: liabilities and owners' equity on the right-hand side of the equation represent the two basic sources of the assets on the left-hand side. You studied assets in the chapters leading to this one and you will study owners' equity later. This chapter and the next four describe the various liabilities that constitute creditors' claims on a company's assets.

Liabilities and owners' equity accounts represent specific sources of a company's assets.

Characteristics of Liabilities

Most liabilities obligate the debtor to pay cash at specified times and result from legally enforceable agreements.

You already know what liabilities are. You encounter them every day. The multibillion dollar national debt we hear discussed almost daily is a liability of all of us. Our creditors are the individuals and institutions that have bought debt securities from (loaned money to) our government. Similarly, when businesses issue notes and bonds, their creditors are the banks, individuals, and organizations that exchange cash for those securities. If you are paying for a car or a home with monthly payments, you have a personal liability. Each of these obligations represents the most common type of liability—one to be paid in cash and for which the amount and timing are specified by a legally enforceable contract.

Entities routinely incur most liabilities to acquire the funds, goods, and services they need to operate and just as routinely settle the liabilities they incur.[1]

Some liabilities are not contractual obligations and may not be payable in cash.

However, to be reported as a **liability**, an obligation need not be payable in cash. Instead, it may require the company to transfer other assets or to provide services. It also need not be represented by a written agreement nor be legally enforceable. Even the amount and timing

[1]"Elements of Financial Statements," *Statement of Financial Accounting Concepts No. 6* (Stamford, Conn.: FASB, 1985), par. 38.

of repayment need not be precisely known. From a financial reporting perspective, a liability has three essential characteristics. Liabilities:

LO1

1. Are *probable, future* sacrifices of economic benefits.
2. Arise from *present* obligations (to transfer goods or provide services) to other entities.
3. Result from *past* transactions or events.[2]

Notice that the definition of a liability involves the present, the future, and the past. It is a present responsibility to sacrifice assets in the future because of a transaction or other event that already has happened.

Later in the chapter we'll discuss several liabilities that possess these characteristics but have elements of uncertainty regarding the amount and timing of payments and sometimes even their existence.

What Is a Current Liability?

In a classified balance sheet, we categorize liabilities as either **current liabilities** or long-term liabilities. Listing financial statement elements by classification provides additional clarification concerning the nature of those elements. In the case of liabilities, the additional information provided by the classification relates to their relative riskiness. Will payment require the use of current assets and reduce the amount of liquid funds available for other uses? If so, are sufficient liquid funds available to pay currently maturing obligations in addition to meeting current operating needs? Or is the due date comfortably in the future, permitting resources to be used for other purposes without risking default or without compromising operating efficiency? Classifying liabilities as either current or long term helps investors and creditors assess the riskiness of a business's obligations in this regard. In this chapter, we focus on current liabilities. The next three chapters address liabilities classified as long term.

Classifying liabilities as either current or long term helps investors and creditors assess the relative risk of a business's liabilities.

We often characterize current liabilities as obligations payable within one year or within the firm's operating cycle, whichever is longer. This general definition usually applies. However, a more discriminating definition identifies current liabilities as those expected to be satisfied with *current assets* or by the creation of other *current liabilities.*[3]

***Current liabilities* are expected to require current assets and usually are payable within one year.**

As you study the liabilities discussed in this chapter, you should be aware that a practical expediency usually affects the way current liabilities are reported on the balance sheet. Conceptually, liabilities should be recorded at their present values. In other words, the amount recorded is the present value of all anticipated future cash payments resulting from the debt (specifically, principal and interest payments). This is due to the time value of money.[4] However, in practice, liabilities payable within one year ordinarily are recorded instead at their maturity amounts.[5] The inconsistency usually is inconsequential because the relatively short-term maturity of current liabilities makes the interest or time value component immaterial.

Current liabilities ordinarily are reported at their maturity amounts.

The most common obligations reported as current liabilities are accounts payable, notes payable, commercial paper, income tax liability, accrued liabilities, and contingencies. Liabilities related to income taxes are the subject of Chapter 16. We discuss the others here.

Before we examine specific current liabilities, let's use the current liability section of the balance sheet of **General Mills, Inc.**, and related disclosure notes to overview the chapter and to provide perspective on the liabilities we discuss (Graphic 13–1).

Incurred but not yet paid

[2]Ibid.

[3]Committee on Accounting Procedure, American Institute of CPAs, *Accounting Research and Terminology Bulletin, Final Edition* (New York: AICPA, August 1961), p. 21.

[4]You learned the concept of the time value of money and the mechanics of present value calculations in Chapter 6.

[5]In fact, those arising in connection with suppliers in the normal course of business and due within a year are specifically exempted from present value reporting by "Interest on Receivables and Payables," *Accounting Principles Board Opinion No. 21* (New York: AICPA, August 1971), par. 3.

GRAPHIC 13–1
Current Liabilities—General Mills

GENERAL MILLS, INC.
Excerpt from Balance Sheet ($ in millions)
May 27, 2007 and May 28, 2006

Liabilities

Current Liabilities:	**2007**	**2006**
Accounts payable	$ 778	$ 673
Current portion of long-term debt	1,734	2,131
Notes payable	1,254	1,503
Other current liabilities	2,079	1,831
Total current liabilities	$5,845	$6,138

In practice, there is little uniformity regarding precise captions used to describe current liabilities or in the extent to which accounts are combined into summary captions. The presentation here is representative and fairly typical.

8. Notes Payable
The components of notes payable and their respective weighted average interest rates at the end of the period are as follows:

	2007		**2006**	
Dollars in millions:	**Note Payable**	**Weighted Average Interest Rate**	**Note Payable**	**Weighted Average Interest Rate**
U.S. commercial paper	$ 477	5.4%	$ 713	5.1%
Euro commercial paper	639	5.4	462	5.1
Financial institutions	138	9.8	328	5.7
Total notes payable	$1,254	5.8%	$1,503	5.2%

To ensure availability of funds, we maintain bank credit lines sufficient to cover our outstanding short-term borrowings. Our commercial paper borrowings are supported by $2.95 billion of fee-paid committed credit lines and $351 million in uncommitted lines. As of May 27, 2007, there were no amounts outstanding on the fee-paid committed credit lines and $133 million was drawn on the uncommitted lines, all by our international operations. Our committed lines consist of a $1.1 billion credit facility expiring in October 2007, a $750 million credit facility expiring in January 2009, and a $1.1 billion credit facility expiring in October 2010.

Real World Financials

Amounts reported on the face of the balance sheet seldom are sufficient to adequately describe current liabilities. Additional descriptions are provided in disclosure notes.

You may want to refer back to portions of Graphic 13–1 as corresponding liabilities are described later in the chapter. We discuss accounts payable and notes payable first.

Open Accounts and Notes

Many businesses buy merchandise or supplies on credit. Most also find it desirable to borrow cash from time to time to finance their activities. In this section we discuss the liabilities these borrowing activities create: namely, trade accounts and trade notes, bank loans, and commercial paper.

Accounts Payable and Trade Notes Payable

Buying merchandise on account in the ordinary course of business creates *accounts payable*.

Accounts payable are obligations to suppliers of merchandise or of services purchased on *open account.* Most trade credit is offered on open account. This means that the only formal credit instrument is the invoice. Because the time until payment usually is short (often 30, 45, or 60 days), these liabilities typically are noninterest-bearing and are reported at their face amounts. As shown in Graphic 13–1, General Mills's accounts payable in 2007 was $778 million. The key accounting considerations relating to accounts payable are determining their existence and ensuring that they are recorded in the appropriate accounting period. You studied these issues and learned how cash discounts are handled during your study of inventories in Chapter 8.

Trade notes payable differ from accounts payable in that they are formally recognized by a written promissory note. Often these are of a somewhat longer term than open accounts and sometimes they bear interest.

Short-Term Notes Payable

The most common way for a corporation to obtain temporary financing is to arrange a short-term bank loan. When a company borrows cash from a bank and signs a promissory note (essentially an IOU), the firm's liability is reported as *notes payable* (sometimes *bank loans* or *short-term borrowings*). About two-thirds of bank loans are short term, but because many are routinely renewed, some tend to resemble long-term debt. In fact, in some cases we report them as long-term financing (as you'll see later in the chapter).

Very often, smaller firms are unable to tap into the major sources of long-term financing to the extent necessary to provide for their capital needs. So they must rely heavily on short-term financing. Even large companies typically utilize short-term debt as a significant and indispensable component of their capital structure. One reason is that short-term funds usually offer lower interest rates than long-term debt. Perhaps most importantly, corporations desire flexibility. As a rule, managers want as many financing alternatives as possible.

A *line of credit* allows a company to borrow cash without having to follow formal loan procedures and paperwork.

CREDIT LINES. Usually short-term bank loans are arranged under an existing line of credit with a bank or group of banks. These can be noncommitted or committed lines of credit. A *noncommitted* line of credit is an informal agreement that permits a company to borrow up to a prearranged limit without having to follow formal loan procedures and paperwork. Banks sometimes require the company to maintain a compensating balance on deposit with the bank, say, 5% of the line of credit.[6] The 2006 annual report of IBM Corporation illustrates a noncommitted line of credit (Graphic 13–2).

GRAPHIC 13–2
Disclosure of Credit Lines—IBM Corporation

Real World Financials

K. Borrowings (in part)

On June 28, 2006, the company entered into a new 5-year $10 billion Credit Agreement with JPMorgan Chase Bank, N.A., as Administrative Agent, and Citibank, N.A., as Syndication Agent . . . . The new Credit Agreement permits the company and its Subsidiary Borrowers to borrow up to $10 billion on a revolving basis.

A *committed* line of credit is a formal arrangement usually requiring a commitment fee and sometimes a compensating balance.

A *committed* line of credit is a more formal agreement that usually requires the firm to pay a commitment fee to the bank. A typical annual commitment fee is ¼% of the total committed funds. Banks often require smaller firms to keep compensating balances in the bank. A disclosure note in the 2006 annual report of the Walgreen Co. describes a committed line of credit as shown in Graphic 13–3.

GRAPHIC 13–3
Disclosure of Committed Line of Credit—Walgreen Company

Real World Financials

Short-Term Borrowings (in part)

At August 31, 2006, the company had a syndicated bank line of credit facility of $200 million to support the company's short-term commercial paper program. The company pays a nominal facility fee to the financing bank to keep this line of credit facility active.

General Mills's disclosure notes that we looked at in Graphic 13–1 indicate that the company has both noncommitted and committed lines of credit.

INTEREST. When a company borrows money, it pays the lender interest in return for using the lender's money during the term of the loan. You might think of the interest as the "rent" paid for using money. Interest is stated in terms of a percentage rate to be applied to the face amount of the loan. Because the stated rate typically is an annual rate, when calculating interest for a short-term note we must adjust for the fraction of the annual period the loan spans. Interest on notes is calculated as:

$$\text{Face amount} \times \text{Annual rate} \times \text{Time to maturity}$$

[6]A compensating balance is a deposit kept by a company in a low-interest or noninterest-bearing account at the bank. The required deposit usually is some percentage of the committed amount or the amount used (say, 2% to 5%). The effect of the compensating balance is to increase the borrower's effective interest rate and the bank's effective rate of return.

This is demonstrated in Illustration 13–1.

ILLUSTRATION 13–1
Note Issued for Cash

● LO2

Interest on notes is calculated as:
Face amount × Annual rate × Time to maturity

On May 1, Affiliated Technologies, Inc., a consumer electronics firm borrowed $700,000 cash from First BancCorp under a noncommitted short-term line of credit arrangement and issued a six-month, 12% promissory note. Interest was payable at maturity.

May 1		
Cash	700,000	
Notes payable		700,000
November 1		
Interest expense ($700,000 × 12% × 6/12)	42,000	
Notes payable	700,000	
Cash ($700,000 + 42,000)		742,000

Sometimes a bank loan assumes the form of a so-called **noninterest-bearing note.** Obviously, though, no bank will lend money without interest. Noninterest-bearing loans actually do bear interest, but the interest is deducted (or discounted) from the face amount to determine the cash proceeds made available to the borrower at the outset. For example, the preceding note could be packaged as a $700,000 noninterest-bearing note, with a 12% discount rate. In that case, the $42,000 interest would be discounted at the outset, rather than explicitly stated:[7]

The proceeds of the note are reduced by the interest in a noninterest-bearing note.

May 1		
Cash (difference)	658,000	
Discount on notes payable ($700,000 × 12% × 6/12)	42,000	
Notes payable (face amount)		700,000
November 1		
Interest expense	42,000	
Discount on notes payable		42,000
Notes payable (face amount)	700,000	
Cash		700,000

Notice that the amount borrowed under this arrangement is only $658,000, but the interest is calculated as the discount rate times the $700,000 face amount. This causes the *effective* interest rate to be higher than the 12% stated rate:

When interest is discounted from the face amount of a note, the effective interest rate is higher than the stated discount rate.

$$\frac{\$42{,}000 \text{ Interest for 6 months}}{\$658{,}000 \text{ Amount borrowed}} = 6.38\% \text{ Rate for 6 months}$$

To annualize:

$$6.38\% \times 12/6 = 12.76\% \text{ Effective interest rate}$$

We studied short-term notes from the perspective of the lender (note receivable) in Chapter 7.

[7]Be sure to understand that we are actually recording the note at $658,000, not $700,000, but are recording the interest portion separately in a contra-liability account, discount on notes payable. The entries shown reflect the gross method. By the net method, the interest component is netted against the face amount of the note as follows:

May 1		
Cash	658,000	
Notes payable		658,000
November 1		
Interest expense ($700,000 × 12% × 6/12)	42,000	
Notes payable	658,000	
Cash		700,000

SECURED LOANS. Sometimes short-term loans are *secured,* meaning a specified asset of the borrower is pledged as collateral or security for the loan. Although many kinds of assets can be pledged, the secured loans most frequently encountered in practice are secured by inventory or accounts receivable. For example, **Collins Industries, Inc.,** which sells vehicle chassis to major vehicle manufacturers, disclosed the secured notes described in Graphic 13–4.

Inventory or accounts receivable often are pledged as security for short-term loans.

GRAPHIC 13–4
Disclosure of Notes Secured by Inventory—Collins Industries, Inc.

Note 4: Chassis Floorplan Notes Payable (in part)

Chassis floorplan notes are payable to a financing subsidiary of a chassis manufacturer. These notes are secured by the related chassis and are payable upon the earlier of the date the Company sells the chassis or 180 days from the date of the note.

When accounts receivable serve as collateral, we refer to the arrangement as *pledging* accounts receivable. Sometimes, the receivables actually are sold outright to a finance company as a means of short-term financing. This is called *factoring* receivables.[8]

Commercial Paper

Some large corporations obtain temporary financing by issuing **commercial paper,** often purchased by other companies as a short-term investment. Commercial paper refers to unsecured notes sold in minimum denominations of $25,000 with maturities ranging from 30 to 270 days (beyond 270 days the firm would be required to file a registration statement with the SEC). Interest often is discounted at the issuance of the note. Usually commercial paper is issued directly to the buyer (lender) and is backed by a line of credit with a bank (see the **Walgreens** disclosure note in Graphic 13–3). This allows the interest rate to be lower than in a bank loan. Commercial paper has become an increasingly popular way for large companies to raise funds, the total amount having expanded over fivefold in the last decade.

Large, highly rated firms sometimes sell *commercial paper* to borrow funds at a lower rate than through a bank loan.

The name *commercial paper* refers to the fact that a paper certificate traditionally is issued to the lender to signify the obligation, although there is a trend toward total computerization of paper sold directly to the lender so that no paper is created. Since commercial paper is a form of notes payable, recording its issuance and payment is exactly the same as our earlier illustration.

FINANCIAL Reporting Case

Q1, p. 652

In a statement of cash flows, the cash a company receives from using notes to borrow funds as well as the cash it uses to repay the notes are reported among cash flows from financing activities. Most of the other liabilities we study in this chapter are integrally related to a company's primary operations and thus are part of operating activities. We discuss long-term notes in the next chapter.

Accrued Liabilities

● LO3

Accrued liabilities represent expenses already incurred but not yet paid (accrued expenses). These liabilities are recorded by adjusting entries at the end of the reporting period, prior to preparing financial statements. You learned how to record accrued liabilities in your study of introductory accounting and you reinforced your understanding in Chapter 2. Common examples are salaries and wages payable, income taxes payable, and interest payable.

Accrued Interest Payable

Accrued interest payable arises in connection with notes like those discussed earlier in this chapter (as well as other forms of debt). For example, to continue Illustration 13–1, let's assume the fiscal period for Affiliated Technologies ends on June 30, two months after the six-month note is issued. The issuance of the note, intervening adjusting entry, and note payment would be recorded as shown in Illustration 13–1A.

Liabilities accrue for expenses that are incurred but not yet paid.

[8]Both methods of accounts receivable financing were discussed in Chapter 7, "Cash and Receivables."

[9]Elsewhere in your accounting curriculum, often in advanced accounting, you will learn how foreign-currency-denominated loans are translated into dollars in U.S. financial statements.

ILLUSTRATION 13–1A

Note with Accrued Interest

At June 30, two months' interest has accrued and is recorded to avoid misstating expenses and liabilities on the June 30 financial statements.

Issuance of Note on May 1		
Cash	700,000	
Note payable		700,000
Accrual of Interest on June 30		
Interest expense ($700,000 × 12% × 2/12)	14,000	
Interest payable		14,000
Note Payment on November 1		
Interest expense ($700,000 × 12% × 4/12)	28,000	
Interest payable (from adjusting entry)	14,000	
Note payable	700,000	
Cash ($700,000 + 42,000)		742,000

Salaries, Commissions, and Bonuses

Compensation for employee services can be in the form of hourly wages, salary, commissions, bonuses, stock compensation plans, or pensions.[10] Accrued liabilities arise in connection with compensation expense when employee services have been performed as of a financial statement date, but employees have yet to be paid. These accrued expenses/accrued liabilities are recorded by adjusting entries at the end of the reporting period, prior to preparing financial statements.

VACATIONS, SICK DAYS, AND OTHER PAID FUTURE ABSENCES. Suppose a firm grants two weeks of paid vacation each year to nonsalaried employees. Some take their vacations during the year earned and are compensated then. Some wait. Is the compensation an expense during the year for only those who actually are paid that year for their absence? When you recall what you've learned about accrual accounting, you probably conclude otherwise.

An employer should accrue an expense and the related liability for employees' compensation for future absences (such as vacation pay) if the obligation meets four conditions. These conditions, all of which must be met for accrual, are listed in Graphic 13–5.

GRAPHIC 13–5

Conditions for Accrual of Paid Future Absences

1. The obligation is attributable to employees' services already performed.
2. The paid absence can be taken in a later year—the benefit vests (will be compensated even if employment is terminated) or the benefit can be accumulated over time.
3. Payment is probable.
4. The amount can be reasonably estimated.

If these conditions look familiar, it's because they are simply the characteristics of a liability we discussed earlier, adapted to relate to a potential obligation for future absences of employees. Also, be sure to recognize the consistency of these conditions with accruing loss contingencies only when the obligation is both (a) probable and (b) can be reasonably estimated. The situation is demonstrated in Illustration 13–2.

The liability for paid absences usually is accrued at the existing wage rate rather than at a rate estimated to be in effect when absences occur.[11] So, if wage rates have risen, the difference between the accrual and the amount paid increases compensation expense that year. For example, let's assume all the carryover vacation time is taken in 2010 and the actual amount paid to employees is $5,700,000:

[10]We discuss pensions in Chapter 17 and share-based compensation plans in Chapter 19.

[11]Actually, *SFAS 43* is silent on how the liability should be measured. In practice, most companies accrue at the current rate because it avoids estimates and usually produces a lower expense and liability. Then, later, they remeasure periodically at updated rates.

ILLUSTRATION 13–2
Paid Future Absences

Davidson-Getty Chemicals has 8,000 employees. Each employee earns two weeks of paid vacation per year. Vacation time not taken in the year earned can be carried over to subsequent years. During 2009, 2,500 employees took both weeks' vacation, but at the end of the year, 5,500 employees had vacation time carryovers as follows:

Employees	Vacation Weeks Earned but Not Taken	Total Carryover Weeks
2,500	0	0
2,000	1	2,000
3,500	2	7,000
8,000		9,000

During 2009, compensation averaged $600 a week per employee.

When Vacations Were Taken in 2009

Salaries and wages expense (2,500 × 2 wks. × $600) + (2,000 × 1 wk. × $600)	4,200,000	
Cash (or wages payable)		4,200,000

December 31, 2009 (adjusting entry)

Salaries and wages expense (9,000 carryover weeks × $600)	5,400,000	
Liability—compensated future absences		5,400,000

When the necessary conditions are met, compensated future absences are accrued in the year the compensation is earned.

When Year 2009 Vacations Are Taken in 2010

Liability—compensated future absences (account balance)	5,400,000	
Salaries and wages expense (difference)	300,000	
Cash (or salaries and wages payable) (given)		5,700,000

Company policy and actual practice should be considered when deciding whether the rights to payment for absences have been earned by services already rendered. Consider an illustrative situation. Suppose scientists in a private laboratory are eligible for paid sabbaticals every seven years. Should a liability be accrued at the end of a scientist's sixth year? No—if sabbatical leave is granted only to perform research beneficial to the employer. Yes—if past practice indicates that sabbatical leave is intended to provide unrestricted compensated absence for past service and other conditions are met.

Customary practice should be considered when deciding whether an obligation exists.

Custom and practice also influence whether unused rights to paid absences expire or can be carried forward. Obviously, if rights vest (payable even if employment is terminated) they haven't expired. But holiday time, military leave, maternity leave, and jury time typically do not accumulate if unused, so a liability for those benefits usually is not accrued. On the other hand, if it's customary that a particular paid absence, say holiday time, can be carried forward—if employees work on holidays, in this case—a liability is accrued if it's probable that employees will be compensated in a future year.

Interestingly, sick pay quite often meets the conditions for accrual but is specifically excluded by *SFAS 43*, "Accounting for Compensated Absences," from mandatory accrual. Its exclusion is because future absence depends on future illness, which usually is not a certainty. However, similar to other forms of paid absences, the decision of whether to accrue nonvesting sick pay should be based on actual policy and practice. If company policy or custom is that employees are paid sick pay even when their absences are not due to illness, it's appropriate to record a liability for unused sick pay. For example, some companies routinely allow unused sick pay benefits to be accumulated and paid at retirement (or to beneficiaries if death comes before retirement). If each condition is met except that the company finds it impractical to reasonably estimate the amount of compensation for future absences, a disclosure note should describe the situation.

Accrual of sick pay is not required, but is permitted.

A wide variety of bonus plans provide compensation tied to performance other than stock prices.

Bonuses sometimes take the place of permanent annual raises.

ANNUAL BONUSES. Sometimes compensation packages include annual bonuses tied to performance objectives designed to provide incentive to executives. The most common performance measures are earnings per share, net income, and operating income, each being used by about a quarter of firms having bonus plans. Nonfinancial performance measures, such as customer satisfaction and product or service quality, also are used.[12] In recent years, **annual bonuses** have been gaining in popularity, not just for executives, but for nonmanagerial personnel as well. Unfortunately for employees, bonuses often take the place of annual raises. This allows a company to increase employee pay without permanently locking in the increases in salaries. Bonuses are compensation expense of the period in which they are earned.

Liabilities from Advance Collections

Liabilities are created when amounts are received that will be returned or remitted to others. Deposits and advances from customers and collections for third parties are cases in point.

Deposits and Advances from Customers

Collecting cash from a customer as a refundable deposit or as an advance payment for products or services creates a liability to return the deposit or to supply the products or services.[13]

REFUNDABLE DEPOSITS. In some businesses it's typical to require customers to pay cash as a deposit that will be refunded when a specified event occurs. You probably have encountered such situations. When apartments are rented, security or damage deposits often are collected. Utility companies frequently collect deposits when service is begun. Similarly, deposits sometimes are required on returnable containers, to be refunded when the containers are returned. The situation is demonstrated in Illustration 13–3.

ILLUSTRATION 13–3
Refundable Deposits

Rancor Chemical Company sells combustible chemicals in expensive, reusable containers. Customers are charged a deposit for each container delivered and receive a refund when the container is returned. Deposits collected on containers delivered during the year were $300,000. Deposits are forfeited if containers are not returned within one year. Ninety percent of the containers were returned within the allotted time. Deposits charged are twice the actual cost of containers. The inventory of containers remains on the company's books until deposits are forfeited.

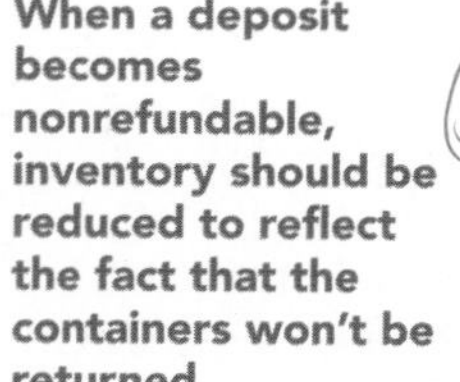

When a deposit becomes nonrefundable, inventory should be reduced to reflect the fact that the containers won't be returned.

When Deposits Are Collected		
Cash	300,000	
Liability—refundable deposits		300,000
When Containers Are Returned*		
Liability—refundable deposits	270,000	
Cash		270,000
When Deposits Are Forfeited*		
Liability—refundable deposits	30,000	
Revenue—sale of containers		30,000
Cost of goods sold	15,000	
Inventory of containers		15,000

*Of course, not all containers are returned at the same time, nor does the allotted return period expire at the same time for all containers not returned. These entries summarize the several individual returns and forfeitures.

[12] C. D. Ittner, D. F. Larker, and M. V. Rajan, "The Choice of Performance Measures in Annual Bonus Contracts," Working Paper, The Wharton School, University of Pennsylvania (August 1995).

[13] *SFAC 6* specifically identifies customer advances and deposits as liabilities under the definition provided in that statement. "Elements of Financial Statements," *Statement of Financial Accounting Concepts No. 6* (Stamford, CT: FASB, 1985), par. 197.

ADVANCES FROM CUSTOMERS. At times, businesses require advance payments from customers that will be applied to the purchase price when goods are delivered or services provided. Gift certificates, magazine subscriptions, layaway deposits, special order deposits, and airline tickets are examples. These customer advances represent liabilities until the related product or service is provided. For instance, one of the largest liabilities reported by **Readers Digest Association, Inc.,** is deferred revenue from the sale of magazine subscriptions ($394 million in 2006). Advances are demonstrated in Illustration 13–4.

ILLUSTRATION 13–4
Customer Advance

Tomorrow Publications collects magazine subscriptions from customers at the time subscriptions are sold. Subscription revenue is recognized over the term of the subscription. Tomorrow collected $20 million in subscription sales during its first year of operations. At December 31, the average subscription was one-fourth expired.

	($ in millions)	
When Advance Is Collected		
Cash	20	
Unearned subscriptions revenue		20
When Product Is Delivered		
Unearned subscriptions revenue	5	
Subscriptions revenue		5

A customer advance produces an obligation that is satisfied when the product or service is provided.

The **New York Times Company** described its recognition of revenue from newspaper subscriptions in the disclosure note shown in Graphic 13–6.

GRAPHIC 13–6
Advances from Customers—The New York Times Company

Real World Financials

Note 1: Summary of Significant Accounting Policies (in part)
Proceeds from subscriptions are deferred at the times of sale as unexpired subscriptions and are included in revenues on a pro rata basis over the terms of the subscriptions.

Like refundable deposits, customer advances forfeited (for instance, gift certificates not redeemed) create revenue when they are deemed forfeited. Liability accounts produced by customer deposits and advances are classified as current or long-term liabilities depending on when the obligation is expected to be satisfied.

Collections for Third Parties

Companies often make collections for third parties from customers or from employees and periodically remit these amounts to the appropriate governmental (or other) units. Amounts collected this way represent liabilities until remitted.

An example is sales taxes. For illustration, assume a state sales tax rate of 4% and local sales tax rate of 3%. Adding the tax to a $100 sale creates a $7 liability until the tax is paid:

Cash (or accounts receivable)	107	
Sales revenue		100
Sales taxes payable ([4% + 3%] × $100)		7

Sales taxes collected from customers represent liabilities until remitted.

Payroll-related deductions such as withholding taxes, Social Security taxes, employee insurance, employee contributions to retirement plans, and union dues also create current liabilities until the amounts collected are paid to appropriate parties. These payroll-related liabilities are explored further in the appendix to this chapter.

Amounts collected from employees in connection with payroll also represent liabilities until remitted.

Although recorded in separate liability accounts, accrued liabilities usually are combined and reported under a single caption or perhaps two accrued liability captions in the balance sheet.

A Closer Look at the Current and Noncurrent Classification

● LO4

Given a choice, do you suppose management would prefer to report an obligation as a current liability or as a noncurrent liability? Other things being equal, most would choose the noncurrent classification. The reason is that in most settings outsiders (like banks, bondholders, and shareholders) consider debt that is payable currently to be riskier than debt that need not be paid for some time. Relatedly, the long-term classification enables the company to report higher working capital (current assets minus current liabilities) and a higher current ratio (current assets/current liabilities). Working capital and the current ratio often are explicitly restricted in loan contracts. As you study this section, you should view the classification choice from this perspective. That is, the question is not so much "What amount should be reported as a current liability?" but rather "What amount can be excluded from classification as a current liability?"

Current Maturities of Long-Term Debt

FINANCIAL Reporting Case

Q2, p. 652

The currently maturing portion of a long-term debt must be reported as a current liability.

Long-term obligations (bonds, notes, lease liabilities, deferred tax liabilities) usually are reclassified and reported as current liabilities when they become payable within the upcoming year (or operating cycle, if longer than a year). For example, a 20-year bond issue is reported as a long-term liability for 19 years but normally is reported as a current liability on the balance sheet prepared during the 20th year of its term to maturity.[14] General Mills reported $1,734 million of its long-term debt as a current liability in 2007 (see Graphic 13–1, page 654).

Obligations Callable by the Creditor

Long-term liabilities that are due on demand—by terms of the contract or violation of contract covenants—must be reported as current liabilities.

The requirement to classify currently maturing debt as a current liability includes debt that is *callable* (in other words, due on demand) *by the creditor* in the upcoming year (or operating cycle, if longer), even if the debt is not expected to be called. The current liability classification also is intended to include situations in which the creditor has the right to demand payment because an *existing violation* of a provision of the debt agreement makes it callable (say, working capital has fallen below a contractual minimum). This also includes situations in which debt is not yet callable but will be callable within the year if an existing violation is not corrected within a specified grace period (unless it's probable the violation will be corrected within the grace period or waived by the creditor).[15]

When Short-Term Obligations Are Expected to Be Refinanced

FINANCIAL Reporting Case

Q3, p. 652

Reconsider the 20-year bond issue we discussed earlier. Normally we would reclassify it as a current liability on the balance sheet prepared during its 20th year. But suppose a second 20-year bond issue is sold specifically to refund the first issue when it matures. Do we have a long-term liability for 19 years, a current liability for a year, and then another long-term liability? Or, do we have a single 40-year, long-term liability? If we look beyond the outward form of the transactions, the substance of the events obviously supports a single, continuing, noncurrent obligation. The concept of substance over form influences the classification of obligations expected to be refinanced.

---

[14] Debt to be refinanced is an exception we discuss later.

[15] "Classification of Obligations That Are Callable by the Creditor," *Statement of Financial Accounting Standards No. 78* (Stamford, Conn.: FASB, 1983).

Short-term obligations (including the callable obligations we discussed in the previous section) that are expected to be refinanced on a long-term basis can be reported as noncurrent, rather than current, liabilities only if two conditions are met. The firm (1) must intend to refinance on a long-term basis and (2) must actually have demonstrated the ability to do so. Ability to refinance on a long-term basis can be demonstrated by either an existing refinancing agreement or by actual financing prior to the issuance of the financial statements.[16] An example will provide perspective (Illustration 13–5).

Short-term obligations can be reported as noncurrent liabilities if the company (a) *intends* to refinance on a long-term basis and (b) demonstrates the *ability* to do so by a refinancing agreement or by actual financing.

ILLUSTRATION 13–5
Short-Term Obligations that Are Expected to Be Refinanced on a Long-Term Basis

Brahm Bros. Ice Cream had $12 million of notes that mature in May 2010 and also had $4 million of bonds issued in 1984 that mature in February 2010. On December 31, 2009, the company's fiscal year-end, management intended to refinance both on a long-term basis.

On February 7, 2010, the company issued $4 million of 20-year bonds, applying the proceeds to repay the bond issue that matured that month. In early March, prior to the actual issuance of the 2009 financial statements, Brahm Bros. negotiated a line of credit with a commercial bank for up to $7 million any time during 2010. Any borrowings will mature two years from the date of borrowing. Interest is at the prime London interbank borrowing rate.*

	December 31, 2009
Classification	($ in 000s)
Current Liabilities	
Notes payable	$5,000
Long-Term Liabilities	
Notes payable	$7,000
Bonds payable	4,000

Management's ability to refinance the bonds on a long-term basis was demonstrated by actual financing prior to the issuance of the financial statements. Ability to refinance $7 million of the notes is demonstrated by a refinancing agreement. The remaining $5 million must be reported as a current liability.

*This is a widely available rate often used as a basis for establishing interest rates on lines of credit and often abbreviated as LIBOR.

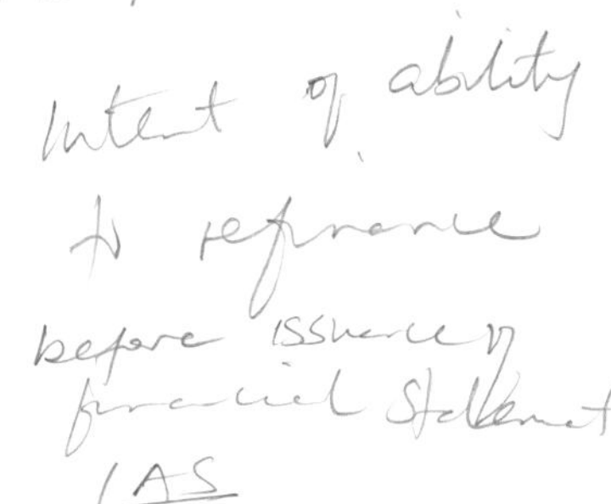

If shares of stock had been issued to refinance the bonds in the illustration, the bonds still would be excluded from classification as a current liability. The specific form of the long-term refinancing (bonds, bank loans, equity securities) is irrelevant when determining the appropriate classification. Requiring companies to actually demonstrate the ability to refinance on a long-term basis in addition to merely intending to do so avoids intentional or unintentional understatements of current liabilities.

It's important to remember that several weeks usually pass between the end of a company's fiscal year and the date the financial statements for that year actually are issued.

Events occurring during that period can be used to clarify the nature of financial statement elements at the reporting date. Here we consider refinancing agreements and actual securities transactions to support a company's ability to refinance on a long-term basis. Later in the chapter we use information that becomes available during this period to decide how loss contingencies are reported.

INTERNATIONAL FINANCIAL REPORTING STANDARDS

Classification of Liabilities to be Refinanced. Under U.S. GAAP, liabilities payable within the coming year are classified as long-term liabilities if refinancing is completed before date of issuance of the financial statements. Under IFRS, refinancing must be completed before the balance sheet date. The FASB is considering an exposure draft proposing the IFRS method.

[16] "Classification of Obligations Expected to Be Refinanced," *Statement of Financial Accounting Standards No. 6* (Stamford, Conn.: FASB, 1975).

CONCEPT REVIEW EXERCISE

CURRENT LIABILITIES

The following selected transactions relate to liabilities of Southern Communications, Inc., for portions of 2009 and 2010. Southern's fiscal year ends on December 31.

Required:
Prepare the appropriate journal entries for these transactions.

2009

July 1	Arranged an uncommitted short-term line of credit with First City Bank amounting to $25,000,000 at the bank's prime rate (11.5% in July). The company will pay no commitment fees for this arrangement.
Aug. 9	Received a $30,000 refundable deposit from a major customer for copper-lined mailing containers used to transport communications equipment.
Oct. 7	Received most of the mailing containers covered by the refundable deposit and a letter stating that the customer will retain containers represented by $2,000 of the deposit and forfeits that amount. The cost of the forfeited containers was $1,500.
Nov. 1	Borrowed $7 million cash from First City Bank under the line of credit arranged in July and issued a nine-month promissory note. Interest at the prime rate of 12% was payable at maturity.
Dec. 31	Recorded appropriate adjusting entries for the liabilities described above.

2010

Feb. 12	Using the unused portion of the credit line as support, issued $9 million of commercial paper and issued a six-month promissory note. Interest was discounted at issuance at a 10% discount rate.
Aug. 1	Paid the 12% note at maturity.
12	Paid the commercial paper at maturity.

SOLUTION 2009

July 1
No entry is made for a line of credit until a loan actually is made. The existence and terms of the line would be described in a disclosure note.

August 9

	Debit	Credit
Cash	30,000	
Liability—refundable deposits		30,000

October 7

	Debit	Credit
Liability—refundable deposits	30,000	
Cash		28,000
Revenue—sale of containers		2,000
Cost of goods sold	1,500	
Inventory of containers		1,500

November 1

	Debit	Credit
Cash	7,000,000	
Notes payable		7,000,000

December 31

	Debit	Credit
Interest expense ($7,000,000 × 12% × $^2/_{12}$)	140,000	
Interest payable		140,000

2010

February 12

	Debit	Credit
Cash ($9,000,000 − [$9,000,000 × 10% × $^6/_{12}$])	8,550,000	
Discount on notes payable (difference)	450,000	
Note payable		9,000,000

Note that the effective interest rate is [($9,000,000 × 10% × $^6/_{12}$) ÷ $8,550,000] × $^{12}/_6$ = $450,000 ÷ $8,550,000 × 2 = 10.53%

(continued)

(concluded)

August 1		
Interest expense ($7,000,000 × 12% × 7/12)	490,000	
Interest payable (from adjusting entry)	140,000	
Note payable (face amount)	7,000,000	
Cash ($7,000,000 + $630,000)		7,630,000
August 12		
Interest expense ($9,000,000 × 10% × 6/12)	450,000	
Discount on notes payable		450,000
Note payable (face amount)	9,000,000	
Cash ($8,550,000 + $450,000)		9,000,000

CONTINGENCIES

PART **B**

The feature that distinguishes the contingencies we discuss in this part of the chapter from the liabilities we discussed previously is uncertainty as to whether an obligation really exists. The existing uncertainty will be resolved only when some future event occurs (or doesn't occur). We will discuss gain contingencies, too, because of their similarity to loss contingencies.

Loss Contingencies

● LO5

Ford Motor Company's financial statements recently indicated potential obligations from pending lawsuits (shown in Graphic 13–7).

GRAPHIC 13–7
Disclosure of Pending Litigation—Ford Motor Company

Note 12: Litigation and Claims (in part)

Various legal actions, governmental investigations and proceedings and claims are pending or may be instituted or asserted in the future against the company and its subsidiaries, including those arising out of alleged defects in the company's products, governmental regulations relating to safety, emissions and fuel economy, financial services, intellectual property rights, product warranties and environmental matters. Certain of the pending legal actions are, or purport to be, class actions. Some of the foregoing matters involve or may involve compensatory, punitive, or antitrust or other treble damage claims in very large amounts, or demands for recall campaigns, environmental remediation programs, sanctions, or other relief which, if granted, would require very large expenditures.

The disclosure indicates that if certain events occur, "very large expenditures" would result. Do these contingencies represent liabilities of Ford? Certainly the liabilities *may* exist on the date of the financial statements. But how likely is an unfavorable outcome? Also, precise amounts of any obligations Ford may have are unknown. But can the amounts be estimated? These are the key questions addressed by accounting standards for loss contingencies.

A **loss contingency** is an existing, uncertain situation involving potential loss depending on whether some future event occurs. Whether a contingency is accrued and reported as a liability depends on (a) the likelihood that the confirming event will occur and (b) what can be determined about the amount of loss. Consider an EPA investigation of possible violation of clean air laws, pending at year end, and for which the outcome will not be known until after the financial statements are issued. The likelihood must be assessed that the company will pay penalties, and if so, what the payment amount will be.

A *loss contingency* involves an existing uncertainty as to whether a loss really exists, where the uncertainty will be resolved only when some future event occurs.

Note that the cause of the uncertainty must occur before the statement date. Otherwise, regardless of the likelihood of the eventual outcome, no liability could have existed at the statement date. Recall that one of the essential characteristics of a liability is that it results "from past transactions or events."

FINANCIAL Reporting Case

Q4, p. 652

Likelihood That a Liability Exists

Accounting standards require that the likelihood that the future event(s) will confirm the incurrence of the liability be (somewhat arbitrarily) categorized as probable, reasonably possible, or remote:[17]

Probable	Confirming event is likely to occur.
Reasonably possible	The chance the confirming event will occur is more than remote but less than likely.
Remote	The chance the confirming event will occur is slight.

● LO6

Also key to reporting a contingent liability is its dollar amount. The amount of the potential loss is classified as either known, reasonably estimable, or not reasonably estimable. A liability is accrued if it is both probable that the confirming event will occur and the amount can be at least reasonably estimated. A general depiction of the accrual of a loss contingency is:

Accrual of a Loss Contingency—Liability

Loss (or expense)	x,xxx	
Liability		x,xxx

ADDITIONAL CONSIDERATION

If one amount within a range of possible loss appears better than other amounts within the range, that amount is accrued. When no amount within the range appears more likely than others, the *minimum* amount should be *recorded* and the possible *additional loss* should be *disclosed.*[18]

In a recent annual report (Graphic 13–8), **Union Pacific** reported a loss contingency it had accrued for a claim against it by government agencies for which the company deemed payment was both probable and reasonably estimable.

GRAPHIC 13–8
Accrual of Loss Contingency—Union Pacific

Real World Financials

10. Commitments and Contingencies (in part)

We accrue the cost of remediation where our obligation is probable and such costs can be reasonably estimated. . . . Our environmental liability activity was as follows:

Millions of Dollars	**2006**	2005	2004
Beginning balance	**$213**	$201	$187
Accruals	**39**	45	46
Payments	**(42)**	(33)	(32)
Ending balance at December 31	**$210**	$213	$201

It is important to note that some loss contingencies don't involve liabilities at all. Some contingencies when resolved cause a noncash asset to be impaired, so accruing it means reducing the related asset rather than recording a liability:

Accrual of a Loss Contingency—Asset Impairment

Loss (or expense)	x,xxx	
Asset (or valuation account)		x,xxx

The most common loss contingency of this type is an uncollectible receivable. You have recorded these before without knowing you were accruing a loss contingency (*Debit:* bad debt expense; *Credit:* allowance for uncollectible accounts).

[17]Because "Accounting for Uncertainty in Income Taxes," *FASB Interpretation No. 48* (Norwalk, Conn.: FASB, 2006) provides guidance on accounting for uncertainty in income taxes, *SFAS No. 5* no longer applies to income taxes. *FIN 48* changes the threshold for recognition of tax positions from the most probable amount to the amount that has a "more likely than not" chance of being sustained upon examination. We discuss *FIN 48* in Chapter 16.

[18]"Reasonable Estimation of the Amount of the Loss," *FASB Interpretation No. 14* (Stamford, Conn.: FASB, 1976).

If one or both of these criteria is not met, but there is at least a reasonable possibility that the loss will occur, a disclosure note should describe the contingency. It also should provide an estimate of the possible loss or range of loss, if possible. If an estimate cannot be made, a statement to that effect is needed.

A loss contingency is disclosed in notes to the financial statements if there is at least a reasonable possibility that the loss will occur.

Varian Medical Systems, Inc. designs and manufactures cancer therapy systems. VMS felt that the loss contingency from an investment was reasonably possible and accordingly did not accrue a liability but provided the information noted in Graphic 13–9.

GRAPHIC 13–9
Disclosure of Loss Contingency—VMS, Inc.

Note 9 (in part)

. . . we agreed to invest $5 million in a consortium to participate in the acquisition of a minority interest in dpiX LLC ("dpiX"), which supplies us with amorphous silicon based thin-film transistor arrays. Based on information provided by dpiX, management currently believes it is reasonably possible that we will recognize a loss of up to $5 million on this investment.

Graphic 13–10 highlights appropriate accounting treatment for each possible combination of (a) the likelihood of an obligation's being confirmed and (b) the determinability of its dollar amount.

GRAPHIC 13–10
Accounting Treatment of Loss Contingencies

	Dollar Amount of Potential Loss		
Likelihood	**Known**	**Reasonably Estimable**	**Not Reasonably Estimable**
Probable	Liability accrued and disclosure note	Liability accrued and disclosure note	Disclosure note only
Reasonably possible	Disclosure note only	Disclosure note only	Disclosure note only
Remote	No disclosure required*	No disclosure required*	No disclosure required*

*Except for certain guarantees and other specified off-balance-sheet risk situations discussed in the next chapter.

A loss contingency is accrued only if a loss is probable and the amount can reasonably be estimated.

Product Warranties and Guarantees

MANUFACTURER'S ORIGINAL WARRANTY. Satisfaction guaranteed! Your money back if not satisfied! If anything goes wrong in the first five years or 50,000 miles . . . ! Three-year guarantee! These and similar promises accompany most consumer goods. The reason—to boost sales. It follows, then, that any costs of making good on such guarantees should be recorded as expenses in the same accounting period the products are sold (matching principle). The obstacle is that much of the cost usually occurs later, sometimes years later. This is a loss contingency. There may be a future sacrifice of economic benefits (cost of satisfying the guarantee) due to an existing circumstance (the guaranteed products have been sold) that depends on an uncertain future event (customer claim).

Most consumer products are accompanied by a guarantee.

As you might expect, meeting the accrual criteria is more likely for some types of loss contingencies than for others. For instance, the outcome of pending litigation is particularly difficult to predict. On the other hand, the criteria for accrual almost always are met for some types of loss contingencies. Product warranties (or product guarantees) inevitably entail costs. And while we usually can't predict the liability associated with an individual sale, reasonably accurate estimates of the *total* liability for a period usually are possible, based on prior experience. So the contingent liability for warranties and guarantees usually is accrued. The estimated warranty (guarantee) liability is credited and warranty (guarantee) expense is debited in the reporting period in which the product under warranty is sold. This is demonstrated in Illustration 13–6.

The contingent liability for product warranties almost always is accrued.

ILLUSTRATION 13–6
Product Warranty

Caldor Health, a supplier of in-home health care products, introduced a new therapeutic chair carrying a two-year warranty against defects. Estimates based on industry experience indicate warranty costs of 3% of sales during the first 12 months following the sale and 4% the next 12 months. During December 2009, its first month of availability, Caldor sold $2 million of the chairs.

The costs of satisfying guarantees should be recorded as expenses in the same accounting period the products are sold.

During December		
Cash (and accounts receivable)	2,000,000	
Sales revenue		2,000,000
December 31, 2009 (adjusting entry)		
Warranty expense ([3% + 4%] × $2,000,000)	140,000	
Estimated warranty liability		140,000

When customer claims are made and costs are incurred to satisfy those claims, the liability is reduced (let's say $61,000 in 2010):

Estimated warranty liability	61,000	
Cash, wages payable, parts and supplies, etc		61,000

Estimates of warranty costs cannot be expected to be precise. However, if the estimating method is monitored and revised when necessary, overestimates and underestimates should cancel each other over time. The estimated liability may be classified as current or as part current and part long-term, depending on when costs are expected to be incurred.

SFAC No. 7 provides a framework for using future cash flows in accounting measurements.

EXPECTED CASH FLOW APPROACH. In Chapter 6, you learned of a framework for using future cash flows as the basis for measuring assets and liabilities, introduced by the FASB in 2000 with *Statement of Financial Accounting Concepts No. 7,* "Using Cash Flow Information and Present Value in Accounting Measurements."[19] The approach described in the Concept Statement offers a way to take into account *any uncertainty concerning the amounts and timing of the cash flows.* Although future cash flows in many instances are contractual and certain, the amounts and timing of cash flows are less certain in other situations, such as warranty obligations.

As demonstrated in Illustration 13–6, the traditional way of measuring a warranty obligation is to report the "best estimate" of future cash flows, ignoring the time value of money on the basis of immateriality. However, when the warranty obligation spans more than one year and we can associate probabilities with possible cash flow outcomes, the approach described by *SFAC No. 7* offers a more plausible estimate of the warranty obligation. This new "expected cash flow approach" incorporates specific probabilities of cash flows into the analysis. In Chapter 6, we discussed the expected cash flow approach to determining present value. Illustration 13–7 provides an example.

EXTENDED WARRANTY CONTRACTS. It's difficult these days to buy a CD player, a digital camera, a car, or almost any durable consumer product without being asked to buy an extended warranty agreement. An extended warranty provides warranty protection beyond the manufacturer's original warranty. Because an extended warranty is priced and sold separately from the warranted product, it essentially constitutes a separate sales transaction. The accounting question is "when should the revenue from the sale be recognized?"

By the accrual concept, revenue is recognized when earned, not necessarily when cash is received. Because the earning process for an extended warranty continues during the contract period, revenue should be recognized over the same period. So, revenue from separately priced extended warranty contracts is deferred as a liability at the time of sale and recognized on a straight-line basis over the contract period. Notice that this is similar to an advance payment for products or services that, as we discussed earlier, creates a liability to supply the products or services. We demonstrate accounting for extended warranties in Illustration 13–8.

[19]"Using Cash Flow Information and Present Value in Accounting Measurements," *Statement of Financial Accounting Concepts No. 7* (Norwalk, Conn.: FASB, 2000). Recall that Concept Statements do not directly prescribe GAAP, but instead provide structure and direction to financial accounting.

ILLUSTRATION 13–7
Product Warranty

Caldor Health, a supplier of in-home health care products, introduced a new therapeutic chair carrying a two-year warranty against defects. During December of 2009, its first month of availability, Caldor sold $2 million of the chairs. Industry experience indicates the following probability distribution for the potential warranty costs:

Warranty Costs	Probability
2010	
$50,000	20%
$60,000	50%
$70,000	30%
2011	
$70,000	20%
$80,000	50%
$90,000	30%

Probabilities are associated with possible cash outcomes.

An arrangement with a service firm requires that costs for the two-year warranty period be settled at the end of 2010 and 2011. The risk-free rate of interest is 5%. Applying the expected cash flow approach, at the end of the 2009 fiscal year, Caldor would record a warranty liability (and expense) of $131,564, calculated as follows:

$50,000 × 20% =	$10,000	
60,000 × 50% =	30,000	
70,000 × 30% =	21,000	
	$61,000	
	× .95238*	$ 58,095
$70,000 × 20% =	$14,000	
80,000 × 50% =	40,000	
90,000 × 30% =	27,000	
	$81,000	
	× .90703†	73,469
		$131,564

*Present value of $1, $n = 1$, $i = 5\%$ (from Table 2)
†Present value of $1, $n = 2$, $i = 5\%$ (from Table 2)

The probability-weighted cash outcomes provide the expected cash flows.

The present value of the expected cash flows is the estimated liability.

December 31, 2009 (adjusting entry)

Warranty expense	131,564	
Estimated warranty liability (calculated above)		131,564

ILLUSTRATION 13–8
Extended Warranty

Brand Name Appliances sells major appliances that carry a one-year manufacturer's warranty. Customers are offered the opportunity at the time of purchase to also buy a three-year extended warranty for an additional charge. On January 3, 2009, Brand Name sold a $60 extended warranty.

January 3, 2009

Cash (or accounts receivable)	60	
Unearned revenue—extended warranties		60

December 31, 2010, 2011, 2012 (adjusting entries)

Unearned revenue—extended warranties	20	
Revenue—extended warranties ($60 ÷ 3)		20

The manufacturer's warranty covers 2009. Revenue from the extended warranty is recognized during the three years of the contract period.

Remember that the costs incurred to satisfy customer claims under the extended warranties also will be recorded during the same three-year period, achieving a proper matching of revenues and expenses. If sufficient historical evidence indicates that the costs of satisfying customer claims will be incurred on other than a straight-line basis, revenue should be recognized by the same pattern (proportional to the costs).[20]

[20]"Accounting for Separately Priced Extended Warranty and Product Maintenance Contracts," *FASB Technical Bulletin 90-1,* 1990.

Premiums

Cash rebates have become commonplace. Cash register receipts, bar codes, rebate coupons, or other proofs of purchase often can be mailed to the manufacturer for cash rebates. Sometimes promotional offers promise premiums other than cash (like toys, dishes, and utensils) to buyers of certain products. Of course the purpose of these premium offers is to stimulate sales. So it follows that the estimated amount of the cash rebates or the cost of noncash premiums estimated to be given out represents both an expense and an estimated liability in the reporting period the product is sold. Like a manufacturer's warranty, this loss contingency almost always meets accrual criteria. Premiums are illustrated in Illustration 13–9.

ILLUSTRATION 13–9
Premiums

The costs of promotional offers should be recorded as expenses in the same accounting period the products are sold.

CMX Corporation offered $2 cash rebates on a particular model of hand-held hair dryers. To receive the rebate, customers must mail in a rebate certificate enclosed in the package plus the cash register receipt. Previous experience indicates that 30% of coupons will be redeemed. One million hair dryers were sold in 2009 and total payments to customers were $225,000.

Promotional expense (30% × $2 × 1,000,000)	600,000	
Estimated premium liability		600,000
To record the estimated liability for premiums.		
Estimated premium liability	225,000	
Cash		225,000
To record payments to customers for coupons.		

The remaining liability of $375,000 is reported in the 2009 balance sheet and is reduced as future rebates are paid. The liability should be classified as current or long term depending on when future rebates are expected to be paid.

Of course, if premiums actually are included in packages of products sold, no contingent liability is created. For example, the costs of toys in Cracker Jack boxes and cereal boxes, and phone cards and compact discs in drink cartons are simply expenses of the period the product is sold, for which the amount is readily determinable.

ADDITIONAL CONSIDERATION

Cents-off coupons are a popular marketing tool. Coupons clipped from newspapers, from mail offers, or included in packages are redeemable for cash discounts at the time promoted items are purchased. Issuing the coupons creates a contingent liability to be recorded in the period the coupons are issued. However, because the hoped-for sales don't materialize until later, a question arises as to when the related expense should be recognized. Logically, since the purpose of coupon offers is to stimulate sales, the expense properly should be deferred until the coupons are redeemed (when the sales occur).

Illustration

On December 18, 2009, Craft Foods distributed coupons in newspaper inserts offering 50 cents off the purchase price of one of its cereal brands when coupons are presented to retailers. Retailers are reimbursed by Craft for the face amount of coupons plus 10% for handling. Previous experience indicates that 20% of coupons will be redeemed. Coupons issued had a total face amount of $1,000,000 and total payments to retailers in 2009 were $50,000. Retailers were paid $170,000 in 2010.

Promotional expense (redeemed in 2009)	50,000	
Cash		50,000
To record payments to retailers for coupons in 2009.		
Deferred promotional expense (an asset)	170,000	
Estimated coupon liability ([20% × $1,000,000 × 1.10] – $50,000)		170,000
To record the estimated liability for coupons in 2009.		

(continued)

(concluded)

Estimated coupon liability	170,000	
Cash		170,000
Promotional expense (redeemed in 2010)	170,000	
Deferred promotional expense		170,000

To record payments to retailers for coupons in 2010.

This situation, though prevalent, is not addressed by promulgated accounting standards. In practice, most firms either (a) recognize the entire expense with the liability in the period the coupons are issued, like we record premiums, or (b) recognize no liability in the period the coupons are issued, recording the expense when reimbursements are made. One reason is that the same coupons are reissued periodically, making it difficult to associate specific reimbursements with specific offers. Another reason is that the time lag between the time a merchant receives a coupon from customers and the time it's presented to the manufacturer for reimbursement prevents appropriate apportionment of the expense.

Litigation Claims

Pending litigation similar to that disclosed by **Ford** in Graphic 13–7 on page xxx is not unusual. In fact, the majority of medium and large corporations annually report loss contingencies due to litigation. By far the most common disclosure is nonspecific regarding the actual litigation but uses wording similar to this contingency disclosure from an annual report of **Sun Microsystems** (Graphic 13–11).

GRAPHIC 13–11
Disclosure of Litigation Contingencies—Sun Microsystems, Inc.

Real World Financials

Note 10: Commitments and Contingencies (in part)

From time to time and in the ordinary course of business, the Company may be subject to various claims, charges, and litigation. In the opinion of management, final judgments from such pending claims, charges, and litigation, if any, against the Company would not have a material adverse effect on its consolidated financial position, results of operations, or cash flows.

In practice, accrual of a loss from pending or ongoing litigation is rare. Imagine why. Suppose you are chief financial officer of Feinz Foods. Feinz is the defendant in a $44 million class action suit. The company's legal counsel informally advises you that chances that the company will emerge victorious in the lawsuit are quite doubtful. Counsel feels the company might lose $30 million. Now suppose you decide to accrue a $30 million loss in your financial statements. Later, in the courtroom, your disclosure that Feinz management feels it is probable that the company will lose $30 million would be welcome ammunition for the opposing legal counsel. Understanding this, most companies rely on the knowledge that in today's legal environment the outcome of litigation is highly uncertain, making likelihood predictions difficult. Companies usually do not record a loss until after the ultimate settlement has been reached or negotiations for settlement are substantially completed. Instead, disclosure notes typically describe the specifics of the litigation along with whether management feels an adverse outcome would materially affect the financial position of the company. As you can see in Graphic 13–12, **ExxonMobil Corporation,** in a recent quarterly report, disclosed but did not accrue damages from a lawsuit it lost, even after the award was affirmed by trial court, because the company was appealing the verdict.

GRAPHIC 13–12
Disclosure of a Lawsuit—ExxonMobil

Real World Financials

17. Litigation and Other Contingencies (in part)

. . . . , a state court jury in New Orleans, Louisiana, returned a verdict against the corporation and three other entities in a case brought by a landowner claiming damage to his property. The jury awarded the plaintiff $56 million in compensatory damages and $1 billion in punitive damages. The award has been affirmed by the trial court, and the corporation is in the process of taking an appeal to the Louisiana Fourth Circuit Court of Appeals. The ultimate outcome is not expected to have a materially adverse effect upon the corporation's operations or financial condition.

Subsequent Events

It's important to remember several weeks usually pass between the end of a company's fiscal year and the date the financial statements for that year actually are issued. Events occurring during this period can be used to clarify the nature of financial statement elements at the report date. This situation can be represented by the following time line:

When the cause of a loss contingency occurs before the year-end, a clarifying event before financial statements are issued can be used to determine how the contingency is reported.

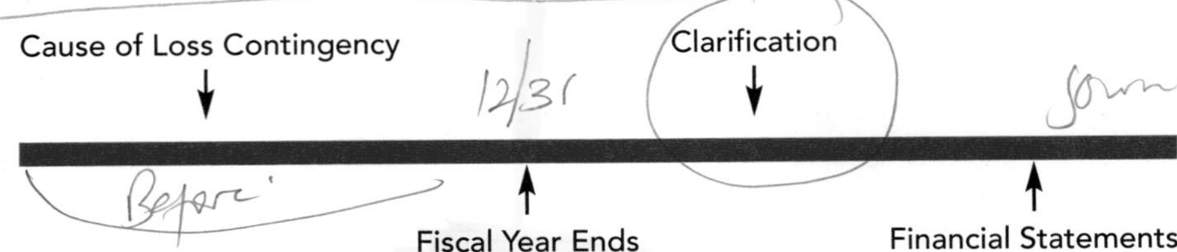

For instance, if information becomes available that sheds light on a claim that existed when the fiscal year ended, that information should be used in determining the probability of a loss contingency materializing and in estimating the amount of the loss. The settlement of a lawsuit after the December 31 report date of **ADESA Inc.** apparently influenced its accrual of a loss contingency (Graphic 13–13).

GRAPHIC 13–13
Accrual of Litigation Contingency—ADESA, Inc.

Real World Financials

Note 21 Commitments and Contingencies (in part)

In January 2007, the settlement agreement was finalized and the federal district court formally dismissed the litigation. The Company recorded provisions totaling approximately $0.6 million in the third quarter of 2006 . . . .

For a loss contingency to be accrued, the cause of the lawsuit must have occurred before the accounting period ended. It's not necessary that the lawsuit actually was filed during that reporting period.

Sometimes, the cause of a loss contingency occurs after the end of the year but before the financial statements are issued:

If an event giving rise to a contingency occurs after the year-end, a liability should not be accrued.

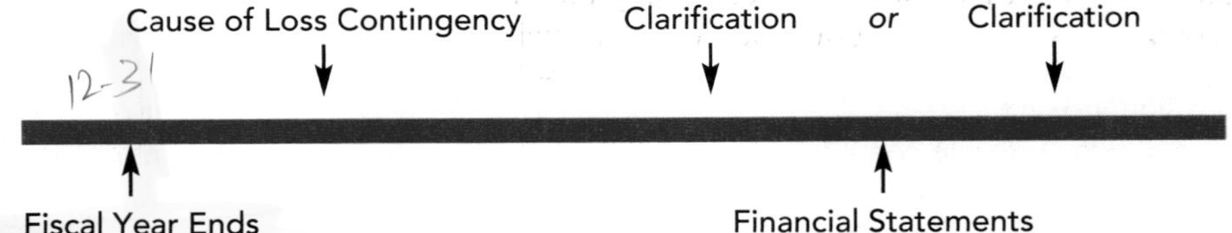

When a contingency comes into existence after the year-end, a liability cannot be accrued because it didn't exist at the end of the year. However, if the failure to disclose the possible loss would cause the financial statements to be misleading, the situation should be described in a disclosure note, including the effect of the possible loss on key accounting numbers affected.[21]

In fact, *any* event occurring after the fiscal year-end but before the financial statements are issued that has a material effect on the company's financial position must be disclosed in a subsequent events disclosure note. Examples are an issuance of debt or equity securities, a business combination, and discontinued operations.

A disclosure note of **IBM** from its 2006 annual report is shown in Graphic 13–14 and describes an event that occurred in the first quarter of 2007.

GRAPHIC 13–14
Subsequent Events—IBM

Real World Financials

X. Subsequent events (in part)

On January 25, 2007, the company and Ricoh Company announced an agreement to form a joint venture, the InfoPrint Solutions Company (joint venture), which will be based on the company's Printing Systems Division (a division of the Systems and Technology Group segment). The company will transfer its printer business to the joint venture and initially receive 49 percent ownership of the joint venture.

[21]"Accounting for Contingencies," *Statement of Financial Accounting Standards No. 5* (Stamford, Conn.: FASB, 1975), par. 11.

ADDITIONAL CONSIDERATION

Contingent liabilities that a company acquires when it purchases another company are treated differently from those that arise during the normal course of business. *SFAS No. 141(R),* "Business Combinations," requires that accounting for an *acquired* contingency depends on whether the contingency arose from a contract (such as a warranty agreement) or in some other way (such as litigation). Non-contractual contingencies are ignored if they are not viewed as "more likely than not." All other contingencies are recognized at fair value as of the acquisition date. In the future, the contingent liability is shown in the balance sheet at the higher of acquisition-date fair value or the amount that would be recognized under *SFAS No. 5* if the contingent liability arose in the normal course of business. Any quarter-by-quarter changes are reported as gains or losses in the income statement.

Unasserted Claims and Assessments

It must be probable that an unasserted claim or assessment or an unfiled lawsuit will occur before considering whether and how to report the possible loss.

Even if a claim has yet to be made when the financial statements are issued, a contingency may warrant accrual or disclosure. However, an unfiled lawsuit or an unasserted claim or assessment need not be disclosed unless it is *probable that the suit, claim, or assessment will occur.* If it is probable, then the likelihood of an unfavorable outcome and the feasibility of estimating a dollar amount should be considered in deciding whether and how to report the possible loss.

For example, suppose a trucking company frequently transports hazardous waste materials and is subject to environmental laws and regulations. Management has identified several sites at which it is or may be liable for remediation. For those sites for which no penalties have been asserted, management must assess the likelihood that a claim will be made, and if so, whether the company actually will be held liable. If management feels an assessment is probable, the possible remediation penalty *might* need to be reported. An estimated loss and contingent liability would be accrued if an unfavorable outcome is probable and the amount can be reasonably estimated. However, note disclosure alone would be appropriate if an unfavorable settlement is only reasonably possible, and no action is needed if chances of that outcome are remote. Notice that when the claim or assessment is unasserted as yet, a two-step process is involved in deciding how it should be reported:

1. Is a claim or assessment probable? (If the answer to this question is no, no disclosure is needed; skip step 2.)
2. Only if a claim or assessment is probable should we evaluate (a) the likelihood of an unfavorable outcome and (b) whether the dollar amount can be estimated.

If the conclusion of step 1 is that the claim or assessment *is not* probable, no further action is required. If the conclusion of step 1 is that the claim or assessment *is* probable, the decision as to whether or not a liability is accrued or disclosed is precisely the same as when the claim or assessment already has been asserted.

As described in a recent disclosure note (see Graphic 13–15), **Union Pacific** felt that some unasserted claims meet the criteria for accrual under this two-step decision process.

GRAPHIC 13–15
Unasserted Claims—Union Pacific Corporation

Real World Financials

12. Commitments and Contingencies (in part)

The Corporation and its subsidiaries periodically enter into financial and other commitments in connection with their businesses. It is not possible at this time for the Corporation to determine fully the effect of all unasserted claims on its consolidated financial condition, results of operations or liquidity; however, to the extent possible, where unasserted claims can be estimated and where such claims are considered probable, the Corporation has recorded a liability.

Notice that the treatment of contingent liabilities is consistent with the accepted definition of liabilities as (a) probable, future sacrifices of economic benefits (b) that arise from

Accrued loss contingencies meet the *SFAC 6* definition of liabilities.

present obligations to other entities and (c) that result from past transactions or events.[22] The inherent uncertainty involved with contingent liabilities means additional care is required to determine whether future sacrifices of economic benefits are probable and whether the amount of the sacrifices can be quantified.

INTERNATIONAL FINANCIAL REPORTING STANDARDS

Contingencies. Accounting for contingencies is part of a broader international standard, *IAS No. 37*, "Provisions, Contingent Liabilities and Contingent Assets." U.S. GAAP has no equivalent general standards on "provisions," but provides specific guidance on contingencies in *SFAS No. 5*, "Accounting for Contingencies." A difference in accounting relates to determining the existence of a loss contingency. We accrue a loss contingency under U.S. GAAP if it's both probable and can be reasonably estimated. IFRS is similar, but the threshold is "more likely than not." This is a lower threshold than "probable."

Another difference in accounting relates to whether to report a long-term contingency at its face amount or its present value. Under IFRS, present value of the estimated cash flows is reported when the effect of *time value of money is material.* According to U.S. GAAP, though, discounting of cash flows is allowed when the *timing of cash flows is certain.* Here's a portion of a footnote from the financial statements of Electrolux, which reports under IFRS:

Real World Financials

Note 29: U.S. GAAP information (in part)

Discounted provisions

Under IFRS and U.S. GAAP, provisions are recognized when the Group has a present obligation as a result of a past event, and it is probable that an outflow of resources will be required to settle the obligation, and a reliable estimate can be made of the amount of the obligation. Under IFRS, where the effect of time value of money is material, the amount recognized is the present value of the estimated expenditures. *IAS 37* states that long-term provisions shall be discounted if the time value is material. According to U.S. GAAP discounting of provisions is allowed when the timing of cash flow is certain.

Gain Contingencies

Never accrue! Don't make Journal entry

Important

A gain contingency is an uncertain situation that might result in a gain. For example, in a pending lawsuit, one side—the defendant—faces a loss contingency; the other side—the plaintiff—has a gain contingency. As we discussed earlier, loss contingencies are accrued when the event confirming the obligation is probable and the amount can reasonably be estimated. However, gain contingencies are not accrued. The nonparallel treatment of gain contingencies follows the same conservative reasoning that motivates reporting some assets at lower of cost or market. Specifically, it's desirable to anticipate losses, but recognizing gains should await their realization.

Gain contingencies are not accrued.

If you feel compelled put note very conservative to mislead

Though gain contingencies are not recorded in the accounts, material ones are disclosed in notes to the financial statements. Care should be taken that the disclosure note not give "misleading implications as to the likelihood of realization."[23]

CONCEPT REVIEW EXERCISE

CONTINGENCIES

Hanover Industries manufactures and sells food products and food processing machinery. While preparing the December 31, 2009, financial statements for Hanover, the following information was discovered relating to contingencies and possible adjustments to liabilities. Hanover's 2009 financial statements were issued on April 1, 2010.

a. On November 12, 2009, a former employee filed a lawsuit against Hanover alleging age discrimination and asking for damages of $750,000. At December 31, 2009, Hanover's

[22] "Elements of Financial Statements," *Statement of Financial Accounting Concepts No. 6* (Stamford, Conn.: FASB, 1985).

[23] "Accounting For Contingencies," *Statement of Financial Accounting Standards No. 5* (Stamford, Conn.: FASB, 1975), par. 17.

attorney indicated that the likelihood of losing the lawsuit was possible but not probable. On March 5, 2010, Hanover agreed to pay the former employee $125,000 in return for withdrawing the lawsuit.

b. Hanover believes there is a possibility a service provider may claim that it has been undercharged for outsourcing a processing service based on verbal indications of the company's interpretation of a negotiated rate. The service provider has not yet made a claim for additional fees as of April 2010, but Hanover feels it will. Hanover 's accountants and legal counsel believe the charges were appropriate but that if an assessment is made, there is a reasonable possibility that subsequent court action would result in an additional tax liability of $55,000.
c. Hanover grants a one-year warranty for each processing machine sold. Past experience indicates that the costs of satisfying warranties are approximately 2% of sales. During 2009, sales of processing machines totaled $21,300,000. 2009 expenditures for warranty repair costs were $178,000 related to 2009 sales and $220,000 related to 2008 sales. The January 1, 2009, balance of the warranty liability account was $250,000.
d. Hanover is the plaintiff in a $600,000 lawsuit filed in 2008 against Ansdale Farms for failing to deliver on contracts for produce. The suit is in final appeal. Legal counsel advises that it is probable that Hanover will prevail and will be awarded $300,000 (considered a material amount).
e. Included with certain food items sold in 2009 were coupons redeemable for a kitchen appliance at the rate of five coupons per appliance. During 2009, 30,000 coupons were issued and 5,000 coupons were redeemed. Although this is the first such promotion in years, past experience indicates that 60% of coupons are never redeemed. An inventory of kitchen appliances is maintained, and a count shows that 1,000 are on hand at December 31, 2009, with a normal retail value of $20,000 and a cost to Hanover of $8,000.

Required:

1. Determine the appropriate means of reporting each situation. Briefly explain your reasoning.
2. Prepare any necessary journal entries and state whether a disclosure note is needed.

SOLUTION

a. This is a loss contingency. Hanover can use the information occurring after the end of the year in determining appropriate disclosure. The cause for the suit existed at the end of the year. Hanover should accrue the $125,000 loss because an agreement has been reached confirming the loss and the amount is known.

Loss—litigation	125,000	
Liability—litigation		125,000

A disclosure note also is appropriate.

b. At the time financial statements are issued, a claim is as yet unasserted. However, an assessment is probable. Thus, (a) the likelihood of an unfavorable outcome and (b) whether the dollar amount can be estimated are considered. No accrual is necessary because an unfavorable outcome is not probable. But because an unfavorable outcome is reasonably possible, a disclosure note is appropriate.

Note: If the likelihood of a claim being asserted is not probable, disclosure is not required even if an unfavorable outcome is thought to be probable in the event of an assessment and the amount is estimable.

c. The contingency for warranties should be accrued because it is probable that expenditures will be made and the amount can be estimated from past experience. When customer claims are made and costs are incurred to satisfy those claims the liability is reduced.

Warranty expense (2% × $21,300,000)	426,000	
Estimated warranty liability		426,000
Estimated warranty liability ($178,000 + 220,000)	398,000	
Cash, wages payable, parts and supplies, etc.		398,000

The liability at December 31, 2009, would be reported as $278,000:

Warranty Liability
(in 000s)

		250	Balance, Jan. 1
		426	2009 expense
2009 expenditures	398		
		278	Balance, Dec. 31

A disclosure note also is appropriate.

d. This is a gain contingency. Gain contingencies cannot be accrued even if the gain is probable and reasonably estimable. The gain should be recognized only when realized. It can be disclosed, but care should be taken to avoid misleading language regarding the realizability of the gain.

e. The contingency for premiums should be accrued because it is probable that coupons will be redeemed and the amount can be estimated from past experience. When coupons are redeemed and appliances are issued, the liability is reduced.

Promotional expense (40% × [30,000 ÷ 5] × $8*)	19,200	
Estimated premium liability		19,200
Estimated premium liability ([5,000 ÷ 5] × $8*)	8,000	
Inventory of premiums		8,000

*$8,000 ÷ 1,000 = $8

The liability at December 31, 2009, would be reported as $11,200:

Premium Liability

		19,200	2009 expense
2009 expenditures	8,000		
		11,200	Balance, Dec. 31

A disclosure note also is appropriate.

DECISION MAKERS' PERSPECTIVE

An analyst of risk should be concerned with a company's ability to meet its short-term obligations.

Current liabilities impact a company's liquidity. Liquidity refers to a company's cash position and overall ability to obtain cash in the normal course of business. A company is said to be liquid if it has sufficient cash (or other assets convertible to cash in a relatively short time) to pay currently maturing debts. Because the lack of liquidity can cause the demise of an otherwise healthy company, it is critical that managers as well as outside investors and creditors maintain close scrutiny of this aspect of a company's well-being.

Keeping track of the current ratio is one of the most common ways of doing this. The current ratio is intended as a measure of short-term solvency and is determined by dividing current assets by current liabilities.

FINANCIAL Reporting Case

Q5, p. 652

When we compare liabilities that must be satisfied in the near term with assets that either are cash or will be converted to cash in the near term, we get a useful measure of a company's liquidity. A ratio of 1 to 1 or higher often is considered a rule-of-thumb standard, but like other ratios, acceptability should be evaluated in the context of the industry in which the company operates and other specific circumstances. Keep in mind, though, that industry averages are only one indication of adequacy and that the current ratio is but one indication of liquidity.

A manager should actively monitor a company's liquidity.

We can adjust for the implicit assumption of the current ratio that all current assets are equally liquid. The acid-test, or quick, ratio is similar to the current ratio but is based on a more conservative measure of assets available to pay current liabilities. Specifically, the numerator, quick assets, includes only cash and cash equivalents, short-term investments, and accounts receivable. By eliminating current assets such as inventories and prepaid expenses that are less readily convertible into cash, the acid-test ratio provides a more rigorous indication of a company's short-term solvency than does the current ratio.

If either of these liquidity ratios is less than that of the industry as a whole, does that mean that liquidity is a problem? Perhaps; perhaps not. It does, though, raise a red flag that suggests caution when assessing other areas. It's important to remember that each ratio is but one piece of the puzzle. For example, profitability is probably the best long-run indication of liquidity. Also, management may be very efficient in managing current assets so that some current assets—receivables or inventory—are more liquid than they otherwise would be and more readily available to satisfy liabilities. The turnover ratios discussed in earlier chapters help measure the efficiency of asset management in this regard.

A liquidity ratio is but one indication of a company's liquidity.

Given the actual and perceived importance of a company's liquidity in the minds of analysts, it's not difficult to adopt a management perspective and imagine efforts to manipulate the ratios that measure liquidity. For instance, a company might use its economic muscle or persuasive powers to influence the timing of accounts payable recognition by asking suppliers to change their delivery schedules. Because accounts payable is included in the denominator in most measures of liquidity, such as the current ratio, the timing of their recognition could mean the difference between an unacceptable ratio and an acceptable one, or between violating a debt covenant and compliance. For example, suppose a company with a current ratio of 1.25 (current assets of \$5 million and current liabilities of \$4 million) is in violation of a debt covenant requiring a minimum current ratio of 1.3. By delaying the delivery of \$1 million of inventory, the ratio would increase to 1.33 (current assets of \$4 million and current liability of \$3 million).

Analysts should be alert for efforts to manipulate measures of liquidity.

It is important for creditors and analysts to be attentive for evidence of activities that would indicate timing strategies, such as unusual variations in accounts payable levels. You might notice that such timing strategies are similar to earnings management techniques we discussed previously—specifically, manipulating the timing of revenue and expense recognition in order to "smooth" income over time.

In the next chapter, we continue our discussion of liabilities. Our focus will shift from current liabilities to long-term liabilities in the form of bonds and long-term notes.

FINANCIAL REPORTING CASE SOLUTION

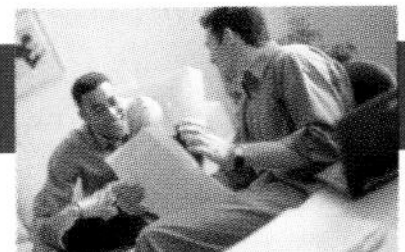

1. **What are accrued liabilities? What is commercial paper?** *(p. 657)* Accrued liabilities are reported for expenses already incurred but not yet paid (accrued expenses). These include salaries and wages payable, income taxes payable, and interest payable. Commercial paper is a form of notes payable sometimes used by large corporations to obtain temporary financing. It is sold to other companies as a short-term investment. It represents unsecured notes sold in minimum denominations of \$25,000 with maturities ranging from 30 to 270 days. Typically, commercial paper is issued directly to the buyer (lender) and is backed by a line of credit with a bank.
2. **Why did Syntel Microsystems include some long-term debt in the current liability section?** *(p. 662)* Syntel Microsystems did include some long-term debt in the current liability section. The currently maturing portion of a long-term debt must be reported as a current liability. Amounts are reclassified and reported as current liabilities when they become payable within the upcoming year.
3. **Did they also report some current amounts as long-term debt? Explain.** *(p. 662)* Yes they did. It is permissible to report short-term obligations as noncurrent liabilities if the company (a) intends to refinance on a long-term basis and (b) demonstrates the ability to do so by a refinancing agreement or by actual financing. As the disclosure note explains, this is the case for a portion of Syntel's currently payable debt.
4. **Must obligations be known contractual debts in order to be reported as liabilities?** *(p. 666)* No. From an accounting perspective, it is not necessary that obligations be known, legally enforceable debts to be reported as liabilities. They must only be probable and the dollar amount reasonably estimable.

5. Is it true that current liabilities are riskier than long-term liabilities? *(p. 676)*
Other things being equal, current liabilities generally are considered riskier than long-term liabilities. For that reason, management usually would rather report a debt as long term. Current debt, though, is not necessarily risky. The liquidity ratios we discussed in the chapter attempt to measure liquidity. Remember, any such measure must be assessed in the context of other factors: industry standards, profitability, turnover ratios, and risk management activities, to name a few. ●

THE BOTTOM LINE

- **LO1** Liabilities are present obligations to sacrifice assets in the future because of something that already has occurred. Current liabilities are expected to require current assets (or the creation of other current liabilities) and usually are payable within one year. (p. 653)
- **LO2** Short-term bank loans usually are arranged under an existing line of credit with a bank or group of banks. When interest is discounted from the face amount of a note (a so-called noninterest-bearing note), the effective interest rate is higher than the stated discount rate. Large, highly rated firms sometimes sell commercial paper directly to the buyer (lender) to borrow funds at a lower rate than through a bank loan. (p. 656)
- **LO3** Accrued liabilities are recorded by adjusting entries for expenses already incurred, but for which cash has yet to be paid (accrued expenses). Familiar examples are salaries and wages payable, income taxes payable, and interest payable. (p. 657)
- **LO4** Short-term obligations can be reported as noncurrent liabilities if the company (a) intends to refinance on a long-term basis and (b) demonstrates the ability to do so by actual financing or a formal agreement to do so. (p. 662)
- **LO5** A loss contingency is an existing, uncertain situation involving potential loss depending on whether some future event occurs. Whether a contingency is accrued and reported as a liability depends on (a) the likelihood that the confirming event will occur and (b) what can be determined about the amount of loss. It is accrued if it is both probable that the confirming event will occur and the amount can be at least reasonably estimated. (p. 665)
- **LO6** A clarifying event before financial statements are issued, but after the year-end, can be used to determine how the contingency is reported. An unasserted suit, claim, or assessment warrants accrual or disclosure if it is probable it will be asserted. A gain contingency is a contingency that might result in a gain. A gain contingency is not recognized until it actually is realized. (p. 666) ●

APPENDIX 13 PAYROLL-RELATED LIABILITIES

All firms incur liabilities in connection with their payrolls. These arise primarily from legal requirements to withhold taxes from employees' paychecks and from payroll taxes on the firms themselves. Some payroll-related liabilities result from voluntary payroll deductions of amounts payable to third parties.

EMPLOYEES' WITHHOLDING TAXES Employers are required by law to withhold federal (sometimes state) income taxes and Social Security taxes from employees' paychecks and remit these to the Internal Revenue Service. The amount withheld for federal income taxes is determined by a tax table furnished by the IRS and varies according to the amount earned and the number of exemptions claimed by the employee. Also, the Federal Insurance Contributions Act (FICA) requires employers to withhold a percentage of each employee's earnings up to a specified maximum. Both the percentage and the maximum are changed intermittently. As this text went to print, the deduction for Social Security was 6.2% of the first $108,000 an employee earns. Additionally, a deduction for Medicare tax was 1.45% with no limit on the base amount. The employer also must pay an equal (matching) amount on behalf of the employee.

VOLUNTARY DEDUCTIONS Besides the required deductions for income taxes and Social Security taxes, employees often authorize their employers to deduct other amounts from their paychecks. These deductions might include union dues, contributions to savings or retirement plans, and insurance premiums. Amounts deducted this way represent liabilities until paid to the appropriate organizations.

EMPLOYERS' PAYROLL TAXES One payroll tax mentioned previously is the employer's matching amount of FICA taxes. The employer also must pay federal and state unemployment taxes on behalf of its employees. The Federal Unemployment Tax Act (FUTA) requires a tax of 6.2% of the first $7,000 earned by each employee. This amount is reduced by a 5.4% (maximum) credit for contributions to state unemployment programs, so the net federal rate often is .8%.[24] In many states the state rate is 5.4% but may be reduced by merit ratings affected by the employer's employment experience.

FRINGE BENEFITS In addition to salaries and wages, withholding taxes, and payroll taxes, many companies provide employees a variety of fringe benefits. Most commonly, employers pay all or part of employees' insurance premiums and/or contributions to retirement income plans.

Representative payroll-related liabilities are presented in Illustration 13A–1.

ILLUSTRATION 13A–1
Payroll-Related Liabilities

Crescent Lighting and Fixtures' payroll for the second week in January was $100,000. The following deductions, fringe benefits, and taxes apply:

Federal income taxes to be withheld	$20,000
State income taxes to be withheld	3,000
Medical insurance premiums (Blue Cross)—70% paid by employer	1,000
Employee contribution to voluntary retirement plan (Fidelity Investments)—contributions matched by employer	4,000
Union dues (Local No. 222)—paid by employees	100
Life insurance premiums (Prudential Life)—100% paid by employer	200
Social Security tax rate	6.2%
Medicare tax rate	1.45%
Federal unemployment tax rate (after state deduction)	0.80%
State unemployment tax rate	5.40%

Salaries and wages expense (total amount earned)	100,000	
Withholding taxes payable (federal income tax)		20,000
Withholding taxes payable (state income tax)		3,000
Social Security taxes payable (6.2%)		6,200
Medicare taxes payable (1.45%)		1,450
Payable to Blue Cross (insurance premiums—30%)		300
Payable to Fidelity Investments (employees' investment)		4,000
Payable to Local No. 222 (union dues)		100
Salaries and wages payable (net pay)		64,950
Payroll tax expense (total)	13,850	
Social Security taxes payable (employer's matching amount)		6,200
Medicare taxes payable (employer's matching amount)		1,450
FUTA payable (federal unemployment tax: .8%)		800
State unemployment tax payable (5.4%)		5,400
Salaries and wages expense (fringe benefits)	4,900	
Payable to Blue Cross (insurance premiums—70%)		700
Payable to Fidelity Investments (matching amount)		4,000
Payable to Prudential life (insurance premiums)		200

Amounts withheld from paychecks represent liabilities until remitted to third parties.

The employer's share of FICA and unemployment taxes constitute the employer's payroll tax expense.

Fringe benefits are part of salaries and wages expense and represent liabilities until remitted to third parties.

As you study the illustration, you should note the similarity among all payroll-related liabilities. Amounts withheld—voluntarily or involuntarily—from paychecks are liabilities until turned over to appropriate third parties. Payroll taxes and expenses for fringe benefits are incurred as a result of services performed by employees and also are liabilities until paid to appropriate third parties. ●

[24]All states presently have unemployment tax programs.

QUESTIONS FOR REVIEW OF KEY TOPICS

Q 13–1 What are the essential characteristics of liabilities for purposes of financial reporting?

Q 13–2 What distinguishes current liabilities from long-term liabilities?

Q 13–3 Bronson Distributors owes a supplier $100,000 on open account. The amount is payable in three months. What is the theoretically correct way to measure the reportable amount for this liability? In practice, how will it likely be reported? Why?

Q 13–4 Bank loans often are arranged under existing lines of credit. What is a line of credit? How does a noncommitted line of credit differ from a committed line?

Q 13–5 Banks sometimes loan cash under noninterest-bearing notes. Is it true that banks lend money without interest?

Q 13–6 How does commercial paper differ from a bank loan? Why is the interest rate often less for commercial paper?

Q 13–7 Salaries of $5,000 have been earned by employees by the end of the period but will not be paid to employees until the following period. How should the expense and related liability be recorded? Why?

Q 13–8 Under what conditions should an employer accrue an expense and the related liability for employees' compensation for future absences? How do company custom and practice affect the accrual decision?

Q 13–9 How are refundable deposits and customer advances similar? How do they differ?

Q 13–10 Amounts collected for third parties represent liabilities until remitted. Provide several examples of this kind of collection.

Q 13–11 Consider the following liabilities of Future Brands, Inc., at December 31, 2009, the company's fiscal year-end. Should they be reported as current liabilities or long-term liabilities?

1. $77 million of 8% notes are due on May 31, 2013. The notes are callable by the Company's bank, beginning March 1, 2010.
2. $102 million of 8% notes are due on May 31, 2014. A debt covenant requires Future to maintain a current ratio (ratio of current assets to current liabilities) of at least 2 to 1. Future is in violation of this requirement but has obtained a waiver from the bank until May 2010, since both companies feel Future will correct the situation during the first half of 2010.

Q 13–12 Long-term obligations usually are reclassified and reported as current liabilities when they become payable within the upcoming year (or operating cycle, if longer than a year). So, a 25-year bond issue is reported as a long-term liability for 24 years but normally is reported as a current liability on the balance sheet prepared during the 25th year of its term to maturity. Name a situation in which this would not be the case.

Q 13–13 Define a loss contingency. Provide three examples.

Q 13–14 List and briefly describe the three categories of likelihood that a future event(s) will confirm the incurrence of the liability for a loss contingency.

Q 13–15 Under what circumstances should a loss contingency be accrued?

Q 13–16 Suppose the analysis of a loss contingency indicates that an obligation is not probable. What accounting treatment if any is warranted?

Q 13–17 Name two loss contingencies that almost always are accrued.

Q 13–18 Distinguish between the accounting treatment of a manufacturer's warranty and an extended warranty. Why the difference?

Q 13–19 At December 31, the end of the reporting period, the analysis of a loss contingency indicates that an obligation is only reasonably possible, though its dollar amount is readily estimable. During February, before the financial statements are issued, new information indicates the loss is probable. What accounting treatment is warranted?

Q 13–20 After the end of the reporting period, a contingency comes into existence. Under what circumstances, if any, should the contingency be reported in the financial statements for the period ended?

Q 13–21 Suppose the Environmental Protection Agency is in the process of investigating Ozone Ruination Limited for possible environmental damage but has not proposed a penalty as of December 31, 2009, the company's fiscal year-end. Describe the two-step process involved in deciding how this unasserted assessment should be reported.

Q 13–22 You are the plaintiff in a lawsuit. Your legal counsel advises that your eventual victory is inevitable. "You will be awarded $12 million," your attorney confidently asserts. Describe the appropriate accounting treatment.

BRIEF EXERCISES

BE 13–1
Bank loan; accrued interest
● LO2 LO3

On October 1, Eder Fabrication borrowed $60 million and issued a nine-month, 12% promissory note. Interest was payable at maturity. Prepare the journal entry for the issuance of the note and the appropriate adjusting entry for the note at December 31, the end of the reporting period.

BE 13–2
Non-interest-bearing note; accrued interest
● LO2 LO3

On October 1, Eder Fabrication borrowed $60 million and issued a nine-month promissory note. Interest was discounted at issuance at a 12% discount rate. Prepare the journal entry for the issuance of the note and the appropriate adjusting entry for the note at December 31, the end of the reporting period.

BE 13–3
Determining accrued interest
● LO2 LO3

On July 1, Orcas Lab issued a $100,000, 12%, 8-month note. Interest is payable at maturity. What is the amount of interest expense that should be recorded in a year-end adjusting entry if the fiscal year-end is (a) December 31? (b) September 30?

BE 13–4
Commercial paper
● LO2

Branch Corporation issued $12 million of commercial paper on March 1 on a nine-month note. Interest was discounted at issuance at a 9% discount rate. Prepare the journal entry for the issuance of the commercial paper and its repayment at maturity.

BE 13–5
Non-interest-bearing note; effective interest rate
● LO2

Life.com issued $10 million of commercial paper on April 1 on a nine-month note. Interest was discounted at issuance at a 6% discount rate. What is the effective interest rate on the commercial paper?

BE 13–6
Advance collection
● LO3

On December 12, 2009, Pace Electronics received $24,000 from a customer toward a cash sale of $240,000 of diodes to be completed on January 16, 2010. What journal entries should Pace record on December 12 and January 16?

BE 13–7
Sales tax
● LO3

During December, Rainey Equipment made a $600,000 credit sale. The state sales tax rate is 6% and the local sales tax rate is 1.5%. Prepare the appropriate journal entry.

BE 13–8
Warranties
● LO5 LO6

Right Medical introduced a new implant that carries a five-year warranty against manufacturer's defects. Based on industry experience with similar product introductions, warranty costs are expected to approximate 1% of sales. Sales were $15 million and actual warranty expenditures were $20,000 for the first year of selling the product. What amount (if any) should Right report as a liability at the end of the year?

BE 13–9
Product recall
● LO5 LO6

Consultants notified management of Goo Goo Baby Products that a crib toy poses a potential health hazard. Counsel indicated that a product recall is probable and is estimated to cost the company $5.5 million. How will this affect the company's income statement and balance sheet this period?

BE 13–10
Contingency
● LO5 LO6

Skill Hardware is the plaintiff in a $16 million lawsuit filed against a supplier. The litigation is in final appeal and legal counsel advises that it is virtually certain that Skill will win the lawsuit and be awarded $12 million. How should Skill account for this event?

BE 13–11
Contingency
● LO5 LO6

Bell International can estimate the amount of loss that will occur if a foreign government expropriates some company property. Expropriation is considered reasonably possible. How should Bell report the loss contingency?

BE 13–12
Contingencies
● LO5 LO6

Household Solutions manufactures kitchen storage products. During the year, the company became aware of potential costs due to (1) a possible product defect that is reasonably possible and can be reasonably estimated, (2) a safety hazard that is probable and cannot be reasonably estimated, and (3) a new product warranty that is probable and can be reasonably estimated. Which, if any, of these costs should be accrued?

BE 13–13
Unasserted assessment
● LO5 LO6

At March 13, 2010, the Environmental Protection Agency is in the process of investigating a possible emissions leak last summer at a facility of Now Chemical. The EPA has not yet proposed a penalty assessment. Now's fiscal year ends on December 31, 2009, and its financial statements are published in March, 2010. Management feels an assessment is *reasonably possible,* and if an assessment is made an unfavorable settlement of $13 million is *probable.* What, if any, action should Now take for its financial statements?

EXERCISES

available with McGraw-Hill's Homework Manager www.mhhe.com/spiceland5e 

An alternate exercise and problem set is available on the text website: www.mhhe.com/spiceland5e

E 13–1
Bank loan; accrued interest
● LO2 LO3

On November 1, 2009, Quantum Technology, a geothermal energy supplier, borrowed $16 million cash to fund a geological survey. The loan was made by Nevada BancCorp under a noncommitted short-term line of credit arrangement. Quantum issued a nine-month, 12% promissory note. Interest was payable at maturity. Quantum's fiscal period is the calendar year.

Required:

1. Prepare the journal entry for the issuance of the note by Quantum Technology.
2. Prepare the appropriate adjusting entry for the note by Quantum on December 31, 2009.
3. Prepare the journal entry for the payment of the note at maturity.

E 13–2
Determining accrued interest in various situations
● LO2 LO3

On July 1, 2009, Ross-Livermore Industries issued nine-month notes in the amount of $400 million. Interest is payable at maturity.

Required:

Determine the amount of interest expense that should be recorded in a year-end adjusting entry under each of the following independent assumptions:

	Interest Rate	Fiscal Year-End
1.	12%	December 31
2.	10%	September 30
3.	9%	October 31
4.	6%	January 31

E 13–3
Short-term notes
● LO2

The following selected transactions relate to liabilities of United Insulation Corporation. United's fiscal year ends on December 31.

Required:

Prepare the appropriate journal entries through the maturity of each liability.

2009	
Jan. 13	Negotiated a revolving credit agreement with Parish Bank that can be renewed annually upon bank approval. The amount available under the line of credit is $20 million at the bank's prime rate.
Feb. 1	Arranged a three-month bank loan of $5 million with Parish Bank under the line of credit agreement. Interest at the prime rate of 10% was payable at maturity.
May 1	Paid the 10% note at maturity.
Dec. 1	Supported by the credit line, issued $10 million of commercial paper on a nine-month note. Interest was discounted at issuance at a 9% discount rate.
31	Recorded any necessary adjusting entry(s).
2010	
Sept. 1	Paid the commercial paper at maturity.

E 13–4
Paid future absences
● LO3

JWS Transport Company's employees earn vacation time at the rate of 1 hour per 40-hour work period. The vacation pay vests immediately (that is, an employee is entitled to the pay even if employment terminates). During 2009, total wages paid to employees equaled $404,000, including $4,000 for vacations actually taken in 2009 but not including vacations related to 2009 that will be taken in 2010. All vacations earned before 2009 were taken before January 1, 2009. No accrual entries have been made for the vacations. No over-time premium and no bonuses were paid during the period.

Required:

Prepare the appropriate adjusting entry for vacations earned but not taken in 2009.

E 13–5
Paid future absences
● LO3

On January 1, 2009, Poplar Fabricators Corporation agreed to grant its employees two weeks' vacation each year, with the stipulation that vacations earned each year can be taken the following year. For the year ended December 31, 2009, Poplar Fabricators' employees each earned an average of $900 per week. Seven hundred vacation weeks earned in 2009 were not taken during 2009.

Required:

1. Prepare the appropriate adjusting entry for vacations earned but not taken in 2009.
2. Suppose wage rates for employees have risen by an average of 5 percent by the time vacations actually are taken in 2010. Also, assume wages earned in 2010 (including vacations earned and taken in 2010) were $31 million. Prepare a journal entry that summarizes 2010 wages and the payment for 2009 vacations taken in 2010.

E 13–6
Customer advances; sales taxes

● LO1

Bavarian Bar and Grill opened for business in November 2009. During its first two months of operation, the restaurant sold gift certificates in various amounts totaling $5,200, mostly as Christmas presents. They are redeemable for meals within two years of the purchase date, although experience within the industry indicates that 80% of gift certificates are redeemed within one year. Certificates totaling $1,300 were presented for redemption during 2009 for meals having a total price of $2,100. The sales tax rate on restaurant sales is 4%, assessed at the time meals (not gift certificates) are purchased. Sales taxes will be remitted in January.

Required:

1. Prepare the appropriate journal entries (in summary form) for the gift certificates sold during 2009 (keeping in mind that, in actuality, each sale of a gift certificate or a meal would be recorded individually).
2. Determine the liability for gift certificates to be reported on the December 31, 2009, balance sheet.
3. What is the appropriate classification (current or noncurrent) of the liabilities at December 31, 2009? Why?

E 13–7
Customer deposits

● LO3

Diversified Semiconductors sells perishable electronic components. Some must be shipped and stored in reusable protective containers. Customers pay a deposit for each container received. The deposit is equal to the container's cost. They receive a refund when the container is returned. During 2009, deposits collected on containers shipped were $850,000.

Deposits are forfeited if containers are not returned within 18 months. Containers held by customers at January 1, 2009, represented deposits of $530,000. In 2009, $790,000 was refunded and deposits forfeited were $35,000.

Required:

1. Prepare the appropriate journal entries for the deposits received and returned during 2009.
2. Determine the liability for refundable deposits to be reported on the December 31, 2009, balance sheet.

E 13–8
Various transactions involving advance collections

● LO3

The following selected transactions relate to liabilities of Interstate Farm Implements for December of 2009. Interstate's fiscal year ends on December 31.

Required:

Prepare the appropriate journal entries for these transactions.

1. On December 15, received $7,500 from Bradley Farms toward the purchase of a $98,000 tractor to be delivered on January 6, 2010.
2. During December, received $25,500 of refundable deposits relating to containers used to transport equipment parts.
3. During December, credit sales totaled $800,000. The state sales tax rate is 5% and the local sales tax rate is 2%. (This is a summary journal entry for the many individual sales transactions for the period.)

E 13–9
Current—noncurrent classification of debt

● LO1 LO4

An annual report of Sprint Corporation contained a rather lengthy narrative entitled "Review of Segmental Results of Operation." The narrative noted that short-term notes payable and commercial paper outstanding at the end of the year aggregated $756 million and that during the following year "This entire balance will be replaced by the issuance of long-term debt or will continue to be refinanced under existing long-term credit facilities."

Required:

How did Sprint report the debt in its balance sheet? Why?

E 13–10
Current—noncurrent classification of debt

● LO1 LO4

At December 31, 2009, Newman Engineering's liabilities include the following:

1. $10 million of 9% bonds were issued for $10 million on May 31, 1988. The bonds mature on May 31, 2020, but bondholders have the option of calling (demanding payment on) the bonds on May 31, 2010. However, the option to call is not expected to be exercised, given prevailing market conditions.
2. $14 million of 8% notes are due on May 31, 2013. A debt covenant requires Newman to maintain current assets at least equal to 175% of its current liabilities. On December 31, 2009, Newman is in violation of this covenant. Newman obtained a waiver from National City Bank until June 2010, having convinced the bank that the company's normal 2 to 1 ratio of current assets to current liabilities will be reestablished during the first half of 2010.
3. $7 million of 11% bonds were issued for $7 million on August 31, 1978. The bonds mature on July 31, 2010. Sufficient cash is expected to be available to retire the bonds at maturity.

Required:

What portion of the debt can be excluded from classification as a current liability (that is, reported as a noncurrent liability)? Explain.

E 13–11
Warranties

● LO5 LO6

Cupola Awning Corporation introduced a new line of commercial awnings in 2009 that carry a two-year warranty against manufacturer's defects. Based on their experience with previous product introductions, warranty costs are expected to approximate 3% of sales. Sales and actual warranty expenditures for the first year of selling the product were:

Sales	Actual Warranty Expenditures
$5,000,000	$37,500

Required:

1. Does this situation represent a loss contingency? Why or why not? How should Cupola account for it?
2. Prepare journal entries that summarize sales of the awnings (assume all credit sales) and any aspects of the warranty that should be recorded during 2009.
3. What amount should Cupola report as a liability at December 31, 2009?

E 13–12
Extended warranties
● LO5 LO6

Carnes Electronics sells consumer electronics that carry a 90-day manufacturer's warranty. At the time of purchase, customers are offered the opportunity to also buy a two-year extended warranty for an additional charge. During the year, Carnes received $412,000 for these extended warranties (approximately evenly throughout the year).

Required:

1. Does this situation represent a loss contingency? Why or why not? How should it be accounted for?
2. Prepare journal entries that summarize sales of the extended warranties (assume all credit sales) and any aspects of the warranty that should be recorded during the year.

E 13–13
Contingency; product recall
● LO5 LO6

Sound Audio manufactures and sells audio equipment for automobiles. Engineers notified management in December 2009 of a circuit flaw in an amplifier that poses a potential fire hazard. An intense investigation indicated that a product recall is virtually certain, estimated to cost the company $2 million. The fiscal year ends on December 31.

Required:

1. Should this loss contingency be accrued, disclosed only, or neither? Explain.
2. What loss, if any, should Sound Audio report in its 2009 income statement?
3. What liability, if any, should Sound Audio report in its 2009 balance sheet?
4. Prepare any journal entry needed.

E 13–14
Impairment of accounts receivable
● LO5 LO6

The Manda Panda Company uses the allowance method to account for bad debts. At the beginning of 2009, the allowance account had a credit balance of $75,000. Credit sales for 2009 totaled $2,400,000 and the year-end accounts receivable balance was $490,000. During this year, $73,000 in receivables were determined to be uncollectible. Manda Panda anticipates that 3% of all credit sales will ultimately become uncollectible. The fiscal year ends on December 31.

Required:

1. Does this situation describe a loss contingency? Explain.
2. What is the bad debt expense that Manda Panda should report in its 2009 income statement?
3. Prepare the appropriate journal entry to record the contingency.
4. What is the net realizable value (book value) Manda Panda should report in its 2009 balance sheet?

E 13–15
Premiums
● LO5 LO6

Drew-Richards iMusic is a regional music media reseller. As a promotion, it offered $5 cash rebates on specific CDs. Customers must mail in a proof-of-purchase seal from the package plus the cash register receipt to receive the rebate. Experience suggests that 70% of the rebates will be claimed. Twenty thousand of the CDs were sold in 2009. Total rebates to customers in 2009 were $22,000 and were recorded as promotional expense when paid. The fiscal year ends on December 31.

Required:

1. What is the promotional expense that Drew-Richards should report in its 2009 income statement?
2. What is the premium liability that Drew-Richards should report in its 2009 balance sheet?
3. Prepare the appropriate journal entry to record the contingency.

E 13–16
Unasserted assessment
● LO6

At April 1, 2010, the Environmental Protection Agency is in the process of investigating a possible chemical leak last June at a facility of Shu Lamination, Inc. The EPA has not yet proposed a penalty assessment. Shu's fiscal year ends on December 31, 2009. The company's financial statements are published in April 2010.

Required:

For each of the following scenarios, determine the appropriate way to report the situation. Explain your reasoning and prepare any necessary journal entry.

1. Management feels an assessment is *reasonably possible,* and if an assessment is made an unfavorable settlement of $13 million is *reasonably possible.*
2. Management feels an assessment is *reasonably possible,* and if an assessment is made an unfavorable settlement of $13 million is *probable.*
3. Management feels an assessment is *probable,* and if an assessment is made an unfavorable settlement of $13 million is *reasonably possible.*
4. Management feels an assessment is *probable,* and if an assessment is made an unfavorable settlement of $13 million is *probable.*

E 13–17
Various transactions involving contingencies

● LO5 LO6

The following selected transactions relate to contingencies of Classical Tool Makers, Inc., which began operations in July 2009. Classical's fiscal year ends on December 31. Financial statements are published in April 2010.

Required:

Prepare the appropriate journal entries to record any amounts that should be recorded as a result of each of these contingencies and indicate whether a disclosure note is indicated.

1. Classical's products carry a one-year warranty against manufacturer's defects. Based on previous experience, warranty costs are expected to approximate 4% of sales. Sales were $2 million (all credit) for 2009. Actual warranty expenditures were $30,800 and were recorded as warranty expense when incurred.
2. Although no customer accounts have been shown to be uncollectible, Classical estimates that 2% of credit sales will eventually prove uncollectible.
3. In December 2009, the state of Tennessee filed suit against Classical, seeking penalties for violations of clean air laws. On January 23, 2010, Classical reached a settlement with state authorities to pay $1.5 million in penalties.
4. Classical is the plaintiff in a $4 million lawsuit filed against a supplier. The suit is in final appeal and attorneys advise that it is virtually certain that Classical will win the case and be awarded $2.5 million.
5. In November 2009, Classical became aware of a design flaw in an industrial saw that poses a potential electrical hazard. A product recall appears unavoidable. Such an action would likely cost the company $500,000.
6. Classical offered $25 cash rebates on a new model of jigsaw. Customers must mail in a proof-of-purchase seal from the package plus the cash register receipt to receive the rebate. Experience suggests that 60% of the rebates will be claimed. Ten thousand of the jigsaws were sold in 2009. Total rebates to customers in 2009 were $105,000 and were recorded as promotional expense when paid.

E 13–18
Disclosures of liabilities

● LO1 through LO6

Indicate (by letter) the way each of the items listed below should be reported in a balance sheet at December 31, 2009.

	Item	Reporting Method
____	1. Commercial paper.	N. Not reported
____	2. Noncommitted line of credit.	C. Current liability
____	3. Customer advances.	L. Long-term liability
____	4. Estimated warranty cost.	D. Disclosure note only
____	5. Accounts payable.	A. Asset
____	6. Long-term bonds that will be callable by the creditor in the upcoming year unless an existing violation is not corrected (there is a reasonable possibility the violation will be corrected within the grace period).	
____	7. Note due March 3, 2010.	
____	8. Interest accrued on note, Dec. 31, 2009.	
____	9. Short-term bank loan to be paid with proceeds of sale of common stock.	
____	10. A determinable gain that is contingent on a future event that appears extremely likely to occur in three months.	
____	11. Unasserted assessment of back taxes that probably will be asserted, in which case there would probably be a loss in six months.	
____	12. Unasserted assessment of back taxes with a reasonable possibility of being asserted, in which case there would probably be a loss in 13 months.	
____	13. A determinable loss from a past event that is contingent on a future event that appears extremely likely to occur in three months.	
____	14. Bond sinking fund.	
____	15. Long-term bonds callable by the creditor in the upcoming year that are not expected to be called.	

E 13–19
Warranty expense; change in estimate

● LO5 LO6

Woodmier Lawn Products introduced a new line of commercial sprinklers in 2008 that carry a one-year warranty against manufacturer's defects. Because this was the first product for which the company offered a warranty, trade publications were consulted to determine the experience of others in the industry. Based on that experience, warranty costs were expected to approximate 2% of sales. Sales of the sprinklers in 2008 were $2.5 million.

Accordingly, the following entries relating to the contingency for warranty costs were recorded during the first year of selling the product:

Accrued liability and expense		
Warranty expense (2% × $2,500,000)	50,000	
Estimated warranty liability		50,000
Actual expenditures (summary entry)		
Estimated warranty liability	23,000	
Cash, wages payable, parts and supplies, etc.		23,000

In late 2009, the company's claims experience was evaluated and it was determined that claims were far more than expected—3% of sales rather than 2%.

Required:

1. Assuming sales of the sprinklers in 2009 were $3.6 million and warranty expenditures in 2009 totaled $88,000, prepare any journal entries related to the warranty.
2. Assuming sales of the sprinklers were discontinued after 2008, prepare any journal entry(s) in 2009 related to the warranty.

E 13–20
Change in accounting estimate

● LO3

The Commonwealth of Virginia filed suit in October 2007 against Northern Timber Corporation, seeking civil penalties and injunctive relief for violations of environmental laws regulating forest conservation. When the 2008 financial statements were issued in 2009, Northern had not reached a settlement with state authorities, but legal counsel advised Northern Timber that it was probable the ultimate settlement would be $1,000,000 in penalties. The following entry was recorded:

Loss—litigation	1,000,000	
Liability—litigation		1,000,000

Late in 2009, a settlement was reached with state authorities to pay a total of $600,000 to cover the cost of violations.

Required:

1. Prepare any journal entries related to the change.
2. Briefly describe other steps Northern should take to report the change.

E 13–21
Contingency; Dow Chemical Company disclosure

● LO5 LO6

Real World Financials

The Dow Chemical Company provides chemical, plastic, and agricultural products and services to various consumer markets. The following excerpt is taken from the disclosure notes of Dow's 2006 annual report:

> At December 31, 2006, the Company had accrued obligations of $347 million for environmental remediation and restoration costs, including $31 million for the remediation of Superfund sites. This is management's best estimate of the costs for remediation and restoration with respect to environmental matters for which the Company has accrued liabilities, although the ultimate cost with respect to these particular matters could range up to twice that amount. Inherent uncertainties exist in these estimates primarily due to unknown conditions, changing governmental regulations and legal standards regarding liability, and evolving technologies for handling site remediation and restoration.

Required:

Does the excerpt describe a loss contingency? Under what conditions would Dow accrue such a contingency? What journal entry did Dow use to record the provision (loss)?

E 13–22
Payroll-related liabilities

● Appendix

Lee Financial Services pays employees monthly. Payroll information is listed below for January 2009, the first month of Lee's fiscal year. Assume that none of the employees exceeded any relevant wage base.

Salaries	$500,000
Federal income taxes to be withheld	100,000
Federal unemployment tax rate	0.80%
State unemployment tax rate (after FUTA deduction)	5.40%
Social Security (FICA) tax rate	7.65%

Required:

Prepare the appropriate journal entries to record salaries and wages expense and payroll tax expense for the January 2009 pay period.

CPA AND CMA REVIEW QUESTIONS

CPA Exam Questions

KAPLAN SCHWESER

The following questions are used in the Kaplan CPA Review Course to study current liabilities and contingencies while preparing for the CPA examination. Determine the response that best completes the statements or questions.

● LO6

1. In December 2009, Mill Co. began including one coupon in each package of candy that it sells and offering a toy in exchange for 50 cents and five coupons. The toys cost Mill 80 cents each. Eventually 60% of the coupons will be redeemed. During December, Mill sold 110,000 packages of candy and no coupons were redeemed. In its December 31, 2009, balance sheet, what amount should Mill report as estimated liability for coupons?
   a. $ 3,960
   b. $10,560
   c. $19,800
   d. $52,800

● LO6

2. During 2009, Gum Co. introduced a new product carrying a two-year warranty against defects. The estimated warranty costs related to dollar sales are 2% within 12 months following the sale and 4% in the second 12 months following the sale. Sales and actual warranty expenditures for the years ended December 31, 2009, and 2010, are as follows:

	Sales	Actual Warranty Expenditures
2009	$150,000	$2,250
2010	250,000	7,500
	$400,000	$9,750

   What amount should Gum report as estimated warranty liability in its December 31, 2010, balance sheet?
   a. $ 2,500
   b. $ 4,250
   c. $11,250
   d. $14,250

● LO3

3. On March 1, 2008, Fine Co. borrowed $10,000 and signed a two-year note bearing interest at 12% per annum compounded annually. Interest is payable in full at maturity on February 28, 2010. What amount should Fine report as a liability for accrued interest at December 31, 2009?
   a. $ 0
   b. $1,000
   c. $1,200
   d. $2,320

● LO3

4. North Corp. has an employee benefit plan for compensated absences that gives employees 10 paid vacation days and 10 paid sick days. Both vacation and sick days can be carried over indefinitely. Employees can elect to receive payment in lieu of vacation days; however, no payment is given for sick days not taken. At December 31, 2009, North's unadjusted balance of liability for compensated absences was $21,000. North estimated that there were 150 vacation days and 75 sick days available at December 31, 2009. North's employees earn an average of $100 per day. In its December 31, 2009, balance sheet, what amount of liability for compensated absences is North required to report?
   a. $15,000
   b. $21,000
   c. $22,500
   d. $36,000

● LO5

5. In May 2006, Caso Co. filed suit against Wayne, Inc., seeking $1,900,000 in damages for patent infringement. A court verdict in November 2009 awarded Caso $1,500,000 in damages, but Wayne's appeal is not expected to be decided before 2011. Caso's counsel believes it is probable that Caso will be successful against Wayne for an estimated amount in the range between $800,000 and $1,100,000, with $1,000,000 considered the most likely amount. What amount should Caso record as income from the lawsuit in the year ended December 31, 2009?
   a. $ 0
   b. $ 800,000
   c. $1,000,000
   d. $1,500,000

● LO4

6. On December 31, 2009, Largo, Inc., had a $750,000 note payable outstanding, due July 31, 2010. Largo borrowed the money to finance construction of a new plant. Largo planned to refinance the note by issuing long-term bonds. Because Largo temporarily had excess cash, it prepaid $250,000 of the note on January 12, 2010. In February 2010, Largo completed a $1,500,000 bond offering. Largo will use the bond offering proceeds to repay the note payable at its maturity and to pay construction costs during 2010. On March 3, 2010, Largo issued its 2009 financial statements. What amount of the note payable should Largo include in the current liabilities section of its December 31, 2009, balance sheet?

a. $250,000
b. $750,000
c. $500,000
d. $ 0

CMA Exam Questions

The following questions dealing with current liabilities and contingencies are adapted from questions that previously appeared on Certified Management Accountant (CMA) examinations. The CMA designation sponsored by the Institute of Management Accountants (**www.imanet.org**) provides members with an objective measure of knowledge and competence in the field of management accounting. Determine the response that best completes the statements or questions.

● LO5

1. An employee has the right to receive compensation for future paid leave, and the payment of compensation is probable. If the obligation relates to rights that vest but the amount cannot be reasonably estimated, the employer should

a. Accrue a liability with proper disclosure.
b. Not accrue a liability nor disclose the situation.
c. Accrue a liability; however, the additional disclosure is not required.
d. Not accrue a liability; however, disclosure is required.

● LO5

2. The accrual of a contingent liability and the related loss should be recorded when the

a. Loss resulting from a future event may be material in relation to income.
b. Future event that gives rise to the liability is unusual in nature and nonrecurring.
c. Amount of the loss resulting from the event is reasonably estimated and the occurrence of the loss is probable.
d. Event that gives rise to the liability is unusual and its occurrence is probable.

● LO6

3. For the past 3 months, Kenton Inc. has been negotiating a labor contract with potentially significant wage increases. Before completing the year-end financial statements on November 30, Kenton determined that the contract was likely to be signed in the near future. Kenton has estimated that the effect of the new contract will cost the company either $100,000, $200,000, or $300,000. Also Kenton believes that each estimate has an equal chance of occurring and that the likelihood of the new contract being retroactive to the fiscal year ended November 30 is probable. According to SFAS 5, Kenton should

a. Do nothing because no loss will occur if the contract is never signed.
b. Disclose each loss contingency amount in the notes to the November 30 financial statements.
c. Accrue $100,000 in the income statement, and disclose the nature of the contingency and the additional loss exposure.
d. Follow conservatism and accrue $300,000 in the income statement, and disclose the nature of the contingency.

● LO4

4. Lister Company intends to refinance a portion of its short-term debt next year and is negotiating a long-term financing agreement with a local bank. This agreement will be noncancelable and will extend for 2 years. The amount of short-term debt that Lister Company can exclude from its statement of financial position at December 31

a. May exceed the amount available for refinancing under the agreement.
b. Depends on the demonstrated ability to consummate the refinancing.
c. Must be adjusted by the difference between the present value and the market value of the short-term debt.
d. Is reduced by the proportionate change in the working capital ratio.

PROBLEMS

available with McGraw-Hill's Homework Manager www.mhhe.com/spiceland5e

An alternate exercise and problem set is available on the text website: www.mhhe.com/spiceland5e

P 13–1
Bank loan; accrued interest
● LO2 LO3

Blanton Plastics, a household plastic product manufacturer, borrowed $14 million cash on October 1, 2009, to provide working capital for year-end production. Blanton issued a four-month, 12% promissory note to N,C&I Bank under a prearranged short-term line of credit. Interest on the note was payable at maturity. Each firm's fiscal period is the calendar year.

Required:

1. Prepare the journal entries to record (a) the issuance of the note by Blanton Plastics and (b) N,C&I Bank's receivable on October 1, 2009.
2. Prepare the journal entries by both firms to record all subsequent events related to the note through January 31, 2010.
3. Suppose the face amount of the note was adjusted to include interest (a noninterest-bearing note) and 12% is the bank's stated discount rate. (a) Prepare the journal entries to record the issuance of the noninterest-bearing note by Blanton Plastics on October 1, 2009, the adjusting entry at December 31, and payment of the note at maturity. (b) What would be the effective interest rate?

P 13–2
Various transactions involving liabilities
● LO1 through LO4

Camden Biotechnology began operations in September 2009. The following selected transactions relate to liabilities of the company for September 2009 through March 2010. Camden's fiscal year ends on December 31. Its financial statements are issued in April.

2009

a. On September 5, opened checking accounts at Second Commercial Bank and negotiated a short-term line of credit of up to $15,000,000 at the bank's prime rate (10.5% at the time). The company will pay no commitment fees.
b. On October 1, borrowed $12 million cash from Second Commercial Bank under the line of credit and issued a five-month promissory note. Interest at the prime rate of 10% was payable at maturity. Management planned to issue 10-year bonds in February to repay the note.
c. Received $2,600 of refundable deposits in December for reusable containers used to transport and store chemical-based products.
d. For the September–December period, sales on account totaled $4,100,000. The state sales tax rate is 3% and the local sales tax rate is 3%. (This is a summary journal entry for the many individual sales transactions for the period.)
e. Recorded the adjusting entry for accrued interest.

2010

f. In February, issued $10 million of 10-year bonds at face value and paid the bank loan on the March 1 due date.
g. Half of the storage containers covered by refundable deposits were returned in March. The remaining containers are expected to be returned during the next six months.

Required:

1. Prepare the appropriate journal entries for these transactions.
2. Prepare the current and long-term liability sections of the December 31, 2009, balance sheet. Trade accounts payable on that date were $252,000.

P 13–3
Current—noncurrent classification of debt
● LO1 LO4

The balance sheet at December 31, 2009, for Nevada Harvester Corporation includes the liabilities listed below:

a. 11% bonds with a face amount of $40 million were issued for $40 million on October 31, 2000. The bonds mature on October 31, 2020. Bondholders have the option of calling (demanding payment on) the bonds on October 31, 2010, at a redemption price of $40 million. Market conditions are such that the call is not expected to be exercised.
b. Management intended to refinance $6 million of its 10% notes that mature in May 2010. In early March, prior to the actual issuance of the 2009 financial statements, Nevada Harvester negotiated a line of credit with a commercial bank for up to $5 million any time during 2010. Any borrowings will mature two years from the date of borrowing.
c. Noncallable 12% bonds with a face amount of $20 million were issued for $20 million on September 30, 1988. The bonds mature on September 30, 2010. Sufficient cash is expected to be available to retire the bonds at maturity.
d. A $12 million 9% bank loan is payable on October 31, 2015. The bank has the right to demand payment after any fiscal year-end in which Nevada Harvester's ratio of current assets to current liabilities falls below a contractual minimum of 1.7 to 1 and remains so for six months. That ratio was 1.45 on December 31, 2009,

due primarily to an intentional temporary decline in inventory levels. Normal inventory levels will be reestablished during the first quarter of 2010.

Required:

1. Determine the amount that can be excluded from classification as a current liability (that is, reported as a noncurrent liability) for each. Explain the reasoning behind your classifications.
2. Prepare the liability section of a classified balance sheet and any necessary footnote disclosure for Nevada Harvester at December 31, 2009. Accounts payable and accruals are $22 million.

P 13–4
Various liabilities

● LO1 through LO4

The unadjusted trial balance of the Manufacturing Equitable at December 31, 2009, the end of its fiscal year, included the following account balances. Manufacturing's 2009 financial statements were issued on April 1, 2010.

Accounts receivable	$ 92,500
Accounts payable	35,000
Bank notes payable	600,000
Mortgage note payable	1,200,000

Other information:

a. The bank notes, issued August 1, 2009, are due on July 31, 2010, and pay interest at a rate of 10%, payable at maturity.

b. The mortgage note is due on March 1, 2010. Interest at 9% has been paid up to December 31 (assume 9% is a realistic rate). Manufacturing intended at December 31, 2009, to refinance the note on its due date with a new 10-year mortgage note. In fact, on March 1, Manufacturing paid $250,000 in cash on the principal balance and refinanced the remaining $950,000.

c. Included in the accounts receivable balance at December 31, 2009, were two subsidiary accounts that had been overpaid and had credit balances totaling $18,000. The accounts were of two major customers who were expected to order more merchandise from Manufacturing and apply the overpayments to those future purchases.

d. On November 1, 2009, Manufacturing rented a portion of its factory to a tenant for $30,000 per year, payable in advance. The payment for the 12 months ended October 31, 2010, was received as required and was credited to rent revenue.

Required:

1. Prepare any necessary adjusting journal entries at December 31, 2009, pertaining to each item of other information (a–d).
2. Prepare the current and long-term liability sections of the December 31, 2009, balance sheet.

P 13–5
Bonus compensation; algebra

● LO3

Sometimes compensation packages include bonuses designed to provide performance incentives to employees. The difficulty a bonus can cause accountants is not an accounting problem, but a math problem. The complication is that the bonus formula sometimes specifies that the calculation of the bonus is based in part on the bonus itself. This occurs anytime the bonus is a percentage of income because expenses are components of income, and the bonus is an expense.

Regalia Fashions has an incentive compensation plan through which a division manager receives a bonus equal to 10% of the division's net income. Division income in 2009 before the bonus and income tax was $150,000. The tax rate is 30%.

Required:

1. Express the bonus formula as one or more algebraic equation(s).*
2. Using these formulas calculate the amount of the bonus.
3. Prepare the adjusting entry to record the bonus compensation.
4. Bonus arrangements take many forms. Suppose the bonus specifies that the bonus is 10% of the division's income before tax, but after the bonus itself. Calculate the amount of the bonus.

P 13–6
Various contingencies

● LO5 LO6

Eastern Manufacturing is involved with several situations that possibly involve contingencies. Each is described below. Eastern's fiscal year ends December 31, and the 2009 financial statements are issued on March 15, 2010.

a. Eastern is involved in a lawsuit resulting from a dispute with a supplier. On February 3, 2010, judgment was rendered against Eastern in the amount of $107 million plus interest, a total of $122 million. Eastern plans to appeal the judgment and is unable to predict its outcome though it is not expected to have a material adverse effect on the company.

b. In November, 2008, the State of Nevada filed suit against Eastern, seeking civil penalties and injunctive relief for violations of environmental laws regulating hazardous waste. On January 12, 2010, Eastern reached a settlement with state authorities. Based upon discussions with legal counsel, the Company feels it is probable that $140 million will be required to cover the cost of violations. Eastern believes that the ultimate settlement of this claim will not have a material adverse effect on the company.

*Remember when you were studying algebra, and you wondered if you would ever use it?

c. Eastern is the plaintiff in a $200 million lawsuit filed against United Steel for damages due to lost profits from rejected contracts and for unpaid receivables. The case is in final appeal and legal counsel advises that it is probable that Eastern will prevail and be awarded $100 million.

d. At March 15, 2010, the Environmental Protection Agency is in the process of investigating possible soil contamination at various locations of several companies including Eastern. The EPA has not yet proposed a penalty assessment. Management feels an assessment is reasonably possible, and if an assessment is made an unfavorable settlement of up to $33 million is reasonably possible.

Required:

1. Determine the appropriate means of reporting each situation. Explain your reasoning.
2. Prepare any necessary journal entries and disclosure notes.

P 13–7
Frequent flyer program

● LO5 LO6

Northeast Airlines operates a frequent flyer marketing program under which mileage credits are earned by flying on Northeast. The program was designed to retain and increase the business of frequent travelers by offering incentives for their continued patronage. Awards are issued to members at the 20,000 miles level. All awards have an expiration date three years from the date earned. Experience indicates that 25% of free travel earned will actually be redeemed. Northeast accounts for its frequent flyer obligation on the accrual basis using the incremental cost method. The incremental costs include food, beverage, and an additional cost per passenger that is based on engineering formulas to determine the average fuel cost per pound per hour. Northeast's liability for free travel at the beginning of 2009 was $25 million. The incremental cost of free travel taken (redeemed) in 2009 was $8 million. The costs of free travel earned for miles traveled in 2009 are estimated to be $40 million. The fiscal year ends on December 31.

Required:

1. Is it appropriate for Northeast to account for its frequent flyer program on the accrual basis? Why?
2. What is the expense that Northeast should report in its 2009 income statement?
3. What is the liability that Northeast should report in its 2009 balance sheet?
4. Prepare the appropriate journal entry to record the year-end accrual of the 2009 expense.

P 13–8
Expected cash flow approach; product recall

● LO6

The Heinrich Tire Company recalled a tire in its subcompact line in December 2009. Costs associated with the recall were originally thought to approximate $50 million. Now, though, while management feels it is probable the company will incur substantial costs, all discussions indicate that $50 million is an excessive amount. Based on prior recalls in the industry, management has provided the following probability distribution for the potential loss:

Loss Amount	Probability
$40 million	20%
$30 million	50%
$20 million	30%

An arrangement with a consortium of distributors requires that all recall costs be settled at the end of 2010. The risk-free rate of interest is 5%.

Required:

1. Applying the expected cash flow approach of *SFAC No. 7,* estimate Heinrich's liability at the end of the 2009 fiscal year.
2. Prepare the journal entry to record the contingent liability (and loss).
3. Prepare the journal entry to accrue interest on the liability at the end of 2010.
4. Prepare the journal entry to pay the liability at the end of 2010, assuming the actual cost is $30 million. Heinrich records an additional loss if the actual costs are higher or a gain if the costs are lower.
5. By the traditional approach to measuring loss contingencies, what amount would Heinrich record at the end of 2009 for the loss and contingent liability?

P 13–9
Subsequent events

● LO6

Lincoln Chemicals became involved in investigations by the U.S. Environmental Protection Agency in regard to damages connected to waste disposal sites. Below are four possibilities regarding the timing of (A) the alleged damage caused by Lincoln, (B) an investigation by the EPA, (C) the EPA assessment of penalties, and (D) ultimate settlement. In each case, assume that Lincoln is unaware of any problem until an investigation is begun. Also assume that once the EPA investigation begins, it is probable that a damage assessment will ensue and that once an assessment is made by the EPA, it is reasonably possible that a determinable amount will be paid by Lincoln.

Required:

For each case, decide whether (a) a loss should be accrued in the financial statements with an explanatory note, (b) a disclosure note only should be provided, or (c) no disclosure is necessary.

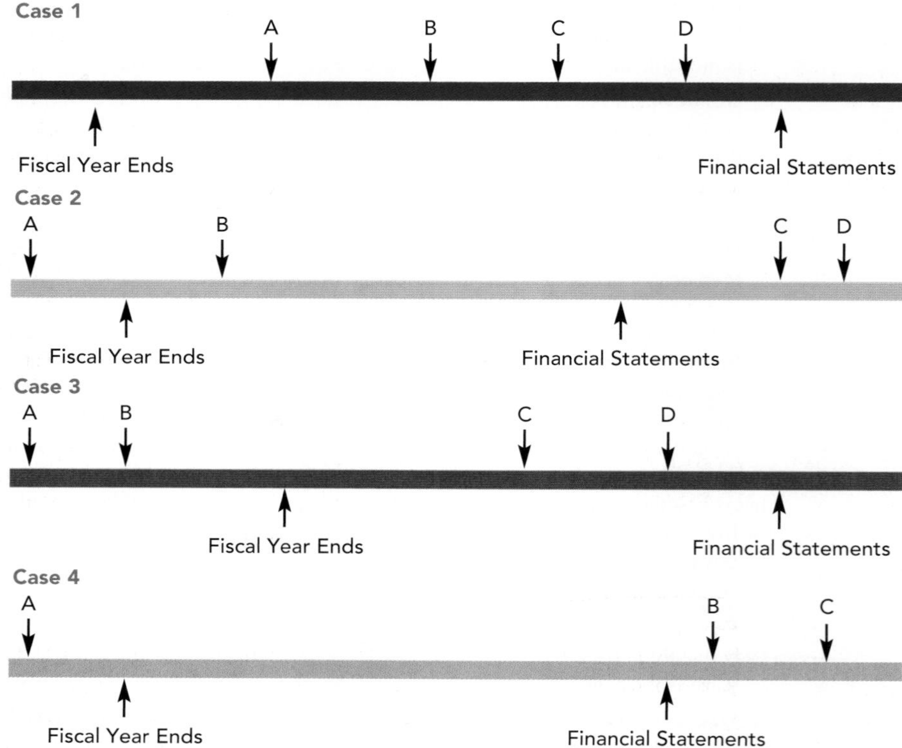

P 13–10
Subsequent events; classification of debt; loss contingency; financial statement effects

● LO4 LO5

Van Rushing Hunting Goods' fiscal year ends on December 31. At the end of the 2009 fiscal year, the company had notes payable of $12 million due on February 8, 2010. Rushing sold 2 million shares of its $0.25 par, common stock on February 3, 2010, for $9 million. The proceeds from that sale along with $3 million from the maturation of some 3-month CDs were used to pay the notes payable on February 8.

Through his attorney, one of Rushing's construction workers notified management on January 5, 2010, that he planned to sue the company for $1 million related to a work-site injury on December 20, 2009. As of December 31, 2009, management had been unaware of the injury, but reached an agreement on February 23, 2010, to settle the matter by paying the employee's medical bills of $75,000.

Rushing's financial statements were finalized on March 3, 2010.

Required:

1. What amount(s) if any, related to the situations described should Rushing report among current liabilities in its balance sheet at December 31, 2009? Why?
2. What amount(s) if any, related to the situations described should Rushing report among long-term liabilities in its balance sheet at December 31, 2009? Why?
3. How would your answers to requirements 1 and 2 differ if the settlement agreement had occurred on March 15, 2010, instead? Why?
4. How would your answers to requirements 1 and 2 differ if the work-site injury had occurred on January 3, 2010, instead? Why?

P 13–11
Concepts; terminology

● LO1 through LO4

Listed below are several terms and phrases associated with current liabilities. Pair each item from List A (by letter) with the item from List B that is most appropriately associated with it.

List A	List B
____ 1. Face amount × Interest rate × Time.	a. Informal agreement
____ 2. Payable with current assets.	b. Secured loan
____ 3. Short-term debt to be refinanced with common stock.	c. Refinancing prior to the issuance of the financial statements
____ 4. Present value of interest plus present value of principal.	d. Accounts payable
____ 5. Noninterest-bearing.	e. Accrued liabilities
____ 6. Noncommitted line of credit.	f. Commercial paper
____ 7. Pledged accounts receivable.	g. Current liabilities
____ 8. Reclassification of debt.	h. Long-term liability
____ 9. Purchased by other corporations.	i. Usual valuation of liabilities
____ 10. Expenses not yet paid.	j. Interest on debt
____ 11. Liability until refunded.	k. Customer advances
____ 12. Applied against purchase price.	l. Customer deposits

P 13–12
Various liabilities; frequent flyer program; balance sheet classification; prepare liability section of balance sheet; write footnotes

● LO4 LO5

Transit Airlines provides regional jet service in the Mid-South. The following is information on liabilities of Transit at December 31, 2009. Transit's fiscal year ends on December 31. Its annual financial statements are issued in April.

1. Transit operates a frequent flyer program under which customers earn mileage credits by flying on Transit. Awards are issued to members at the 30,000 miles level. All awards have an expiration date five years from the date earned. Transit's experience suggests that 30% of free travel earned actually will be redeemed. Transit accounts for its frequent flyer obligation on the accrual basis using the incremental cost method. The incremental costs include food, beverage, and an additional cost per passenger that is based on formulas to determine the average fuel cost per pound per hour. Transit's liability for free travel at the beginning of 2009 was $60 million. The incremental cost of free travel taken (redeemed) in 2009 was $12 million. The costs of free travel for miles traveled in 2009 are estimated to be $90 million. Twenty percent of the frequent flyer liability is deemed current.
2. Transit has outstanding 6.5% bonds with a face amount of $90 million. The bonds mature on July 31, 2018. Bondholders have the option of calling (demanding payment on) the bonds on July 31, 2010, at a redemption price of $90 million. Market conditions are such that the call option is not expected to be exercised.
3. A $30 million 8% bank loan is payable on October 31, 2015. The bank has the right to demand payment after any fiscal year-end in which Transit's ratio of current assets to current liabilities falls below a contractual minimum of 1.9 to 1 and remains so for 6 months. That ratio was 1.75 on December 31, 2009, due primarily to an intentional temporary decline in parts inventories. Normal inventory levels will be reestablished during the sixth week of 2010.
4. Transit management intended to refinance $45 million of 7% notes that mature in May of 2010. In late February 2010, prior to the issuance of the 2009 financial statements, Transit negotiated a line of credit with a commercial bank for up to $40 million any time during 2010. Any borrowings will mature two years from the date of borrowing.
5. Transit is involved in a lawsuit resulting from a dispute with a food caterer. On February 13, 2010, judgment was rendered against Transit in the amount of $53 million plus interest, a total of $54 million. Transit plans to appeal the judgment and is unable to predict its outcome though it is not expected to have a material adverse effect on the company.

Required:

1. Determine the liability associated with Transit's frequent flyer program at December 31, 2009. What is the current portion of the debt?
2. How should the 6.5% bonds be classified by Transit among liabilities in its balance sheet? Explain.
3. How should the 8% bank loan be classified by Transit among liabilities in its balance sheet? Explain.
4. How should the 7% notes be classified by Transit among liabilities in its balance sheet? Explain.
5. How should the lawsuit be reported by Transit? Explain.
6. Prepare the liability section of a classified balance sheet for Transit Airlines at December 31, 2009. Transit's accounts payable and accruals were $43 million.
7. Draft appropriate footnote disclosures for Transit's financial statements at December 31, 2009, for each of the five items described.

P 13–13
Payroll-related liabilities

● Appendix

Alamar Petroleum Company offers its employees the option of contributing retirement funds up to 5% of their wages or salaries, with the contribution being matched by Alamar. The company also pays 80% of medical and life insurance premiums. Deductions relating to these plans and other payroll information for the first biweekly payroll period of February are listed as follows:

Wages and salaries	$2,000,000
Employee contribution to voluntary retirement plan	84,000
Medical insurance premiums	42,000
Life insurance premiums	9,000
Federal income taxes to be withheld	400,000
Local income taxes to be withheld	53,000
Payroll taxes:	
Federal unemployment tax rate	0.80%
State unemployment tax rate (after FUTA deduction)	5.40%
Social Security tax rate	6.2%
Medicare tax rate	1.45%

Required:

Prepare the appropriate journal entries to record salaries and wages expense and payroll tax expense for the biweekly pay period. Assume that no employee's cumulative wages exceed the relevant wage bases.

BROADEN YOUR PERSPECTIVE

Apply your critical-thinking ability to the knowledge you've gained. These cases will provide you an opportunity to develop your research, analysis, judgment, and communication skills. You also will work with other students, integrate what you've learned, apply it in real world situations, and consider its global and ethical ramifications. This practice will broaden your knowledge and further develop your decision-making abilities.

Research Case 13–1
Bank loan; accrued interest

● LO1 LO2

A fellow accountant has solicited your opinion regarding the classification of short-term obligations repaid prior to being replaced by a long-term security. Cheshire Foods, Inc., issued $5,000,000 of short-term commercial paper during 2008 to finance construction of a plant. At September 30, 2009, Cheshire's fiscal year-end, the company intends to refinance the commercial paper by issuing long-term bonds. However, because Cheshire temporarily has excess cash, in November 2009 it liquidates $2,000,000 of the commercial paper as the paper matures. In December 2009, the company completes a $10,000,000 long-term bond issue. Later during December, it issues its September 30, 2009 financial statements. The proceeds of the long-term bond issue are to be used to replenish $2,000,000 in working capital, to pay $3,000,000 of commercial paper as it matures in January 2010, and to pay $5,000,000 of construction costs expected to be incurred later that year to complete the plant.

You initially are hesitant because you don't recall encountering a situation in which short-term obligations were repaid prior to being replaced by a long-term security. However, you are encouraged by remembering that this general topic is covered by an FASB pronouncement to which you have access: "Classification of Obligations Expected to Be Refinanced," *Statement of Financial Accounting Standards No. 6* (Stamford, Conn.: FASB, 1975). Also, "Classification of Obligation Repaid Prior to Being Replaced by a Long-Term Security," *FASB Interpretation No. 8,* addresses this situation specifically.

Required:

Determine how the $5,000,000 of commercial paper should be classified by consulting the FASB pronouncement. Before doing so, formulate your own opinion on the proper treatment.

Real World Case 13–2
Returnable containers

● LO1 LO3

Real World Financials

The **Zoo Doo Compost Company** processes a premium organic fertilizer made with the help of the animals at the Memphis Zoo. Zoo Doo is sold in a specially designed plastic pail that may be kept and used for household chores or returned to the seller. The fertilizer is sold for $12.50 per two-gallon pail (including the $1.76 cost of the pail). For each pail returned, Zoo Doo donates $1 to the Memphis Zoo and the pail is used again.[25]

Required:

The founder and president of this start-up firm has asked your opinion on how to account for the donations to be made when fertilizer pails are returned. (Ignore any tax implications.)

Research Case 13–3
Relationship of liabilities to assets and owners' equity

● LO1

SFAC No. 6 states that "an entity's assets, liabilities, and equity (net assets) all pertain to the same set of probable future economic benefits." Explain this statement.

Judgment Case 13–4
Paid future absences

● LO3

Cates Computing Systems develops and markets commercial software for personal computers and workstations. Three situations involving compensation for possible future absences of Cates's employees are described below.

a. Cates compensates employees at their regular pay rate for time absent for military leave, maternity leave, and jury time. Employees are allowed predetermined absence periods for each type of absence.
b. Members of the new product development team are eligible for three months' paid sabbatical leave every four years. Five members of the team have just completed their fourth year of participation.
c. Company policy permits employees four paid sick days each year. Unused sick days can accumulate and can be carried forward to future years.

Required:

1. What are the conditions that require accrual of an expense and related liability for employees' compensation for future absences?
2. For each of the three situations, indicate the circumstances under which accrual of an expense and related liability is warranted.

Ethics Case 13–5
Outdoors R Us

● LO1

Outdoors R Us owns several membership-based campground resorts throughout the Southwest. The company sells campground sites to new members, usually during a get-acquainted visit and tour. The campgrounds offer a wider array of on-site facilities than most. New members sign a multiyear contract, pay a down payment, and make monthly installment payments. Because no credit check is made and many memberships originate on a spur-of-the-moment basis, cancellations are not uncommon.

[25]Case based on Kay McCullen, "Take The Zoo Home With You!" *Head Lions,* July 1991 and a conversation with the Zoo Doo Compost Company president, Pierce Ledbetter.

Business has been brisk during its first three years of operations, and since going public in 1998, the market value of its stock has tripled. The first sign of trouble came in 2009 when the new sales dipped sharply.

One afternoon, two weeks before the end of the fiscal year, Diane Rice, CEO, and Gene Sun, controller, were having an active discussion in Sun's office.

Sun: I've thought more about our discussion yesterday. Maybe something can be done about profits.
Rice: I hope so. Our bonuses and stock value are riding on this period's performance.
Sun: We've been recording unearned revenues when new members sign up. Rather than recording liabilities at the time memberships are sold, I think we can justify reporting sales revenue for all memberships sold.
Rice: What will be the effect on profits?
Sun: I haven't run the numbers yet, but let's just say very favorable.

Required:

1. Why do you think liabilities had been recorded previously?
2. Is the proposal ethical?
3. Who would be affected if the proposal is implemented?

Trueblood Case 13–6
Contingencies; research *FIN 45*

● LO5

The following Trueblood case is recommended for use with this chapter. The case provides an excellent opportunity for class discussion, group projects, and writing assignments. The case, along with Professor's Discussion Material, can be obtained from the Deloitte Foundation at its website: www.deloitte.com/us/truebloodcases.

Case 05–5: *Guarantees-R-Us*

This case gives students the opportunity to extend their knowledge beyond chapter coverage by researching *FASB Interpretation No. 45,* "Guarantor's Accounting and Disclosure Requirements for Guarantees, Including Indirect Guarantees of Indebtedness of Others" and applying that pronouncement to decide whether specific guarantees are loss contingencies.

Communication Case 13–7
Exceptions to the general classification guideline; group interaction

● LO4

Domestic Transfer and Storage is a large trucking company headquartered in the Midwest. Rapid expansion in recent years has been financed in large part by debt in a variety of forms. In preparing the financial statements for 2010, questions have arisen regarding the way certain of the liabilities are to be classified in the company's classified balance sheet.

A meeting of several members of the accounting area is scheduled for tomorrow, April 8, 2010. You are confident that that meeting will include the topic of debt classification. You want to appear knowledgeable at the meeting, but realizing it's been a few years since you have dealt with classification issues, you have sought out information you think relevant. Questionable liabilities at the company's fiscal year-end (January 31, 2010) include the following:

a. $15 million of 9% commercial paper is due on July 31, 2010. Management intends to refinance the paper on a long-term basis. In early April, 2010, Domestic negotiated a credit agreement with a commercial bank for up to $12 million any time during the next three years, any borrowings from which will mature two years from the date of borrowing.
b. $17 million of 11% notes were issued on June 30, 2007. The notes are due on November 30, 2010. The company has investments of $20 million classified as "available for sale."
c. $25 million of 10% notes were due on February 28, 2010. On February 21, 2010, the company issued 30-year, 9.4% bonds in a private placement to institutional investors.
d. Recently, company management has considered reducing debt in favor of a greater proportion of equity financing. $20 million of 12% bonds mature on July 31, 2010. Discussions with underwriters, which began on January 4, 2010, resulted in a contractual arrangement on March 15 under which new common shares will be sold in July for approximately $20 million.

In order to make notes to yourself in preparation for the meeting concerning the classification of these items, you decide to discuss them with a colleague. Specifically, you want to know what portion of the debt can be excluded from classification as a current liability (that is, reported as a noncurrent liability) and why.

Required:

1. What is the appropriate classification of each liability? Develop a list of arguments in support of your view prior to the class session for which the case is assigned.
2. In class, your instructor will pair you (and everyone else) with a classmate (who also has independently developed a position). You will be given three minutes to argue your view to your partner. Your partner likewise will be given three minutes to argue his or her view to you. During these three-minute presentations, the listening partner is not permitted to speak.
3. Then after each person has had a turn attempting to convince his or her partner, the two partners will have a three-minute discussion to decide which classifications are more convincing. Arguments will be merged into a single view for each pair.

4. After the allotted time, a spokesperson for each of the four liabilities will be selected by the instructor. Each spokesperson will field arguments from the class as to the appropriate classification. The class then will discuss the merits of the classification and attempt to reach a consensus view, though a consensus is not necessary.

Communication Case 13–8
Various contingencies

● LO5 LO6

"I see an all-nighter coming on," Gayle grumbled. "Why did Mitch just now give us this assignment?" Your client, Western Manufacturing is involved with several situations that possibly involve contingencies. The assignment Gayle refers to is to draft appropriate accounting treatment for each situation described below in time for tomorrow's meeting of the audit group. Western's fiscal year is the calendar year 2009, and the 2009 financial statements are issued on March 15, 2010.

1. During 2009, Western experienced labor disputes at three of its plants. Management hopes an agreement will soon be reached. However negotiations between the Company and the unions have not produced an acceptable settlement and, as a result, strikes are ongoing at these facilities since March 1, 2010. It is virtually certain that material costs will be incurred but the amount of possible costs cannot be reasonably ascertained.
2. In accordance with a 2007 contractual agreement with A. J. Conner Company, Western is entitled to $37 million for certain fees and expense reimbursements. These were written off as bad debts in 2008. A. J. Conner has filed for bankruptcy. The bankruptcy court on February 4, 2010, ordered A. J. Conner to pay $23 million immediately upon consummation of a proposed merger with Garner Holding Group.
3. Western warrants most products it sells against defects in materials and workmanship for a period of a year. Based on their experience with previous product introductions, warranty costs are expected to approximate 2% of sales. A warranty liability of $39 million was reported at December 31, 2008. Sales of warranted products during 2009 were $2,100 million and actual warranty expenditures were $40 million. Expenditures in excess of the existing liability were debited to warranty expense.
4. Western is involved in a suit filed in January 2010 by Crump Holdings seeking $88 million, as an adjustment to the purchase price in connection with the Company's sale of its textile business in 2009. The suit alleges that Western misstated the assets and liabilities used to calculate the purchase price for the textile division. Legal counsel advises that it is reasonably possible that Western could end up losing an indeterminable amount not expected to have a material adverse effect on the Company's financial position.

Required:

1. Determine the appropriate means of reporting each situation.
2. In a memo to the audit manager, Mitch Riley, explain your reasoning. Include any necessary journal entries and drafts of appropriate disclosure notes.

Judgment Case 13–9
Loss contingency and full disclosure

● LO5 LO6

In the March 2010 meeting of Valleck Corporation's board of directors, a question arose as to the way a possible obligation should be disclosed in the forthcoming financial statements for the year ended December 31. A veteran board member brought to the meeting a draft of a disclosure note that had been prepared by the controller's office for inclusion in the annual report. Here is the note:

> On May 9, 2009, the United States Environmental Protection Agency (EPA) issued a Notice of Violation (NOV) to Valleck alleging violations of the Clean Air Act. Subsequently, in June 2009, the EPA commenced a civil action with respect to the foregoing violation seeking civil penalties of approximately $853,000. The EPA alleges that Valleck exceeded applicable volatile organic substance emission limits. The Company estimates that the cost to achieve compliance will be $190,000; in addition the Company expects to settle the EPA lawsuit for a civil penalty of $205,000 which will be paid in 2012.

"Where did we get the $205,000 figure?" he asked. On being informed that this is the amount negotiated last month by company attorneys with the EPA, the director inquires, "Aren't we supposed to report a liability for that in addition to the note?"

Required:

Explain whether Valleck should report a liability in addition to the note. Why or why not? For full disclosure, should anything be added to the disclosure note itself?

Communication Case 13–10
Change in loss contingency; write a memo

● LO5 LO6

Late in 2009, you and two other officers of Curbo Fabrications Corporation just returned from a meeting with officials of The City of Jackson. The meeting was unexpectedly favorable even though it culminated in a settlement with city authorities that required your company pay a total of $475,000 to cover the cost of violations of city construction codes. Jackson had filed suit in November 2007, against Curbo Fabrications Corporation, seeking civil penalties and injunctive relief for violations of city construction codes regulating earthquake damage standards. Alleged violations involved several construction projects completed during the previous three years. When the financial statements were issued in 2008, Curbo had not reached a settlement with state authorities, but legal counsel had advised the Company that it was probable the ultimate settlement would be $750,000 in penalties. The following entry had been recorded:

Loss—litigation	750,000	
Liability—litigation		750,000

The final settlement, therefore, was a pleasant surprise. While returning from the meeting, your conversation turned to reporting the settlement in the 2009 financial statements. You drew the short straw and were selected to write a memo to Janet Zeno, the financial vice president, advising the proper course of action.

Required:

Write the memo. Include descriptions of any journal entries related to the change in amounts. Briefly describe other steps Curbo should take to report the settlement.

Research Case 13–11
Researching the way contingencies are reported; retrieving information from the Internet

● LO5 LO6

EDGAR (Electronic Data Gathering, Analysis, and Retrieval system) performs automated collection, validation, indexing, acceptance, and forwarding of submissions by companies and others who are required by law to file forms with the U.S. Securities and Exchange Commission (SEC). All publicly traded domestic companies use EDGAR to make the majority of their filings. Form 10-K, which includes the annual report, is required to be filed on EDGAR. The SEC makes this information available on the Internet.

Required:

1. Access EDGAR on the Internet at: www.sec.gov.
2. Search for a public company with which you are familiar. Access its most recent 10-K filing. Search or scroll to find the financial statements and related notes.
3. Specifically, look for any contingency(s) reported in the disclosure notes. Identify the nature of the contingency(s) described and explain the reason(s) the loss or losses was or was not accrued.
4. Repeat requirements 2 and 3 for two additional companies.

Communication Case 13–12
Accounting changes

● LO5 LO6

Kevin Brantly is a new hire in the controller's office of Fleming Home Products. Two events occurred in late 2009 that the company had not previously encountered. The events appear to affect two of the company's liabilities, but there is some disagreement concerning whether they also affect financial statements of prior years. Each change occurred during 2009 before any adjusting entries or closing entries were prepared. The tax rate for Fleming is 40% in all years.

- Fleming Home Products introduced a new line of commercial awnings in 2008 that carry a one-year warranty against manufacturer's defects. Based on industry experience, warranty costs were expected to approximate 3% of sales. Sales of the awnings in 2008 were $3,500,000. Accordingly, warranty expense and a warranty liability of $105,000 were recorded in 2008. In late 2009, the company's claims experience was evaluated and it was determined that claims were far fewer than expected—2% of sales rather than 3%. Sales of the awnings in 2009 were $4,000,000 and warranty expenditures in 2009 totaled $91,000.
- In November 2007, the State of Minnesota filed suit against the company, seeking penalties for violations of clean air laws. When the financial statements were issued in 2008, Fleming had not reached a settlement with state authorities, but legal counsel advised Fleming that it was probable the company would have to pay $200,000 in penalties. Accordingly, the following entry was recorded:

Loss—litigation	200,000	
Liability—litigation		200,000

Late in 2009, a settlement was reached with state authorities to pay a total of $350,000 in penalties.

Required:

Kevin's supervisor, perhaps unsure of the answer, perhaps wanting to test Kevin's knowledge, e-mails the message, "Kevin, send me a memo on how we should handle our awning warranty and that clean air suit." Wanting to be accurate, Kevin consults his reference materials. What will he find? Prepare the memo requested.

Real World Case 13–13
Frequent flyer miles

● LO1 LO3

Real World Financials

Most airlines offer a frequent flyer program under which passengers can earn free travel. Northwest Airlines Corporation described its program in a recent annual report:

> **Frequent Flyer Program (in part):** The Company utilizes a number of estimates in accounting for its WorldPerks frequent flyer program. The Company accounts for the frequent flyer program obligations by recording a liability for the estimated incremental cost of flight awards expected to be redeemed on Northwest and other airline partners. Customers are expected to redeem their mileage, and a liability is recorded, when their accounts accumulate the minimum number of miles needed to obtain one flight award.
>
> The number of estimated travel awards outstanding and expected to be redeemed at December 31, 2006, 2005, and 2004 was approximately 3.6, 3.6, and 3.8 million, respectively. Northwest recorded a liability for these estimated awards of $269 million, $248 million and $215 million at December 31, 2006, 2005 and 2004, respectively.

	($ in millions)	
Current Liabilities	**2006**	**2005**
Air traffic liability	$1,557	$1,586
Accrued compensation and benefits	301	303
Accounts payable	624	342
Collections as agent	138	116
Accrued aircraft rent	49	74
Other accrued liabilities	329	295
Current maturities of long-term debt	213	74
	3,211	2,790

Required:

1. Why does Northwest's frequent flyer program produce a liability?
2. Is incremental cost the appropriate measure of the liability? Why?
3. Is the liability current, long-term, or both?
4. Prepare journal entry appropriate to recognize Northwest's expense and liability assuming the liability for the frequent flyer program is included in the Air Traffic liability.

Real World Case 13–14
Lawsuit settlement; SkillSoft

● LO5 LO6

Real World Financials

SkillSoft is a leading provider of content resources and complementary technologies for integrated enterprise learning. The company's fiscal year ends January 31, 2006, and it plans to file its financial statements with the SEC on April, 17, 2006. On April 13, the company issued the following press release (in part):

> NASHUA, N.H., April 13 /PRNewswire-FirstCall/—SkillSoft PLC (Nasdaq: SKIL), . . . has agreed . . . to settle a lawsuit filed against it and certain of its former and current officers and directors in late 2004 related to the 2002 securities class action lawsuit. This lawsuit included substantially the same claims as those set forth in the previously settled 2002 securities class action lawsuit. Under the terms of the settlement, SkillSoft will pay a total of $1.79 million to the plaintiffs prior to April 17, 2006.

Required:

1. From an accounting perspective, how should SkillSoft have treated the settlement?
2. Relying on the information provided by the press release, re-create the journal entry SkillSoft recorded for the settlement.
3. Suppose the settlement had occurred after April 17. How should SkillSoft have treated the settlement?

Ethics Case 13–15
Profits guaranteed

● LO5

This was Joel Craig's first visit to the controller's corner office since being recruited for the senior accountant position in May. Because he'd been directed to bring with him his preliminary report on year-end adjustments, Craig presumed he'd done something wrong in preparing the report. That he had not was Craig's first surprise. His second surprise was his boss's request to reconsider one of the estimated expenses.

S & G Fasteners was a new company, specializing in plastic industrial fasteners. All products carry a generous long-term warranty against manufacturer's defects. "Don't you think 4% of sales is a little high for our warranty expense estimate?" his boss wondered. "After all, we're new at this. We have little experience with product introductions. I just got off the phone with Blanchard (the company president). He thinks we'll have trouble renewing our credit line with the profits we're projecting. The pressure's on."

Required:

1. Should Craig follow his boss's suggestion?
2. Does revising the warranty estimate pose an ethical dilemma?
3. Who would be affected if the suggestion is followed?

IFRS Case 13–16
Current liabilities and contingencies; differences between U.S. GAAP and IFRS

● LO4 LO5

As a second-year financial analyst for A.J. Straub Investments, you are performing an initial analysis on Fizer Pharmaceuticals. A difficulty you've encountered in making comparisons with its chief rival is that Fizer uses U.S. GAAP and the competing company uses International Financial Reporting Standards. Some areas of concern are the following:

1. Fizer has been designated as a potentially responsible party by the United States Environmental Protection Agency with respect to certain waste sites. These claims are in various stages of administrative or judicial proceedings and include demands for recovery of past governmental costs and for future investigations or remedial actions. Fizer accrues costs associated with environmental matters when they become probable and reasonably estimable. Counsel has advised that the likelihood of payments of about $70 million is slightly more than 50%. Accordingly, payment is judged reasonably possible and the contingency was disclosed in a footnote.

2. Fizer had $10 million of bonds issued in 1985 that mature in February 2010. On December 31, 2009, the company's fiscal year-end, management intended to refinance the bonds on a long-term basis. On February 7, 2010, Fizer issued $10 million of 20-year bonds, applying the proceeds to repay the bond issue that matured that month. The bonds were reported in Fizer's balance sheet as long-term debt.
3. Fizer reported in its 2009 financial statements a long-term contingency at its face amount rather than its present value even though the difference was considered material. The reason the cash flows were not discounted is that their timing is uncertain.

Required:

If Fizer used IFRS as does its competitor, how would the items described be reported differently?

Analysis Case 13–17
Analyzing financial statements; liquidity ratios

● LO1

IGF Foods Company is a large, primarily domestic, consumer foods company involved in the manufacture, distribution and sale of a variety of food products. Industry averages are derived from Troy's *The Almanac of Business and Industrial Financial Ratios.* Following are the 2009 and 2008 comparative balance sheets for IGF. (The financial data we use are from actual financial statements of a well-known corporation, but the company name used is fictitious and the numbers and dates have been modified slightly.)

IGF FOODS COMPANY
Comparative Balance Sheets
Years Ended December 31, 2009 and 2008
($ in millions)

	2009	2008
Assets		
Current assets:		
Cash	$ 48	$ 142
Accounts receivable	347	320
Marketable securities	358	—
Inventories	914	874
Prepaid expenses	212	154
Total current assets	$1,879	$1,490
Property, plant, and equipment (net)	2,592	2,291
Intangibles (net)	800	843
Other assets	74	60
Total assets	$5,345	$4,684
Liabilities and Shareholders' Equity		
Current liabilities:		
Accounts payables	$ 254	$ 276
Accrued liabilities	493	496
Notes payable	518	115
Current portion of long-term debt	208	54
Total current liabilities	$1,473	$ 941
Long-term debt	534	728
Deferred income taxes	407	344
Total liabilities	$2,414	$2,013
Shareholders' equity:		
Common stock	180	180
Additional paid-in capital	21	63
Retained earnings	2,730	2,428
Total shareholders' equity	$2,931	$2,671
Total liabilities and shareholders' equity	$5,345	$4,684

Liquidity refers to a company's cash position and overall ability to obtain cash in the normal course of business. A company is said to be liquid if it has sufficient cash or is capable of converting its other assets to cash in a relatively short period of time so that currently maturing debts can be paid.

Required:

1. Calculate the current ratio for IGF for 2009. The average ratio for the stocks listed on the New York Stock Exchange in a comparable time period was 1.5. What information does your calculation provide an investor?
2. Calculate IGF's acid-test or quick ratio for 2009. The ratio for the stocks listed on the New York Stock Exchange in a comparable time period was .80. What does your calculation indicate about IGF's liquidity?

Analysis Case 13–18
Reporting current liabilities; liquidity

● LO1

Google

Refer to the financial statements and related disclosure notes of **Google** located in the company's 2007 annual report included with all new copies of the text. They also can be found at **www.Google.com**. At the end of its 2007 fiscal year, Google reported current liabilities of $2 billion in its balance sheet.

Required:

1. What are the five components of current liabilities?
2. Are current assets sufficient to cover current liabilities? What is the current ratio for 2007? How does the ratio compare with 2006?
3. Google reported accrued expenses among its current liabilities. What were the two largest accrued expenses in 2007 aside from "other"? What are accrued expenses and when does Google record them?
4. Google reports "accrued revenue share" among its liabilities. This represents amounts owed to Google's "Adsense" partners which Google pays individual affiliates when they are owed at least $100. How does this policy of not paying Adsense earnings until that minimum amount is owned benefit Google?

Real World Case 13–19
Contingencies

● LO5

Real World Financials

The following is an excerpt from *USAToday.com* in July 2007:

> **Microsoft** (MSFT) on Thursday extended the warranty on its Xbox 360 video game console and said it will take a charge of more than $1 billion to pay for "anticipated costs." Under the new warranty, Microsoft will pay for shipping and repairs for three years, worldwide, for consoles afflicted with what gamers call "the red ring of death." Previously, the warranty expired after a year for U.S. customers and two years for Europeans. The charge will be $1.05 billion to $1.15 billion for the quarter ended June 30. Microsoft reports its fourth-quarter results July 19.

Required:

1. Why must Microsoft report this charge of over $1 billion entirely in one quarter, the last quarter of the company's fiscal year ended June 30, 2007?
2. When the announcement was made, analyst Richard Doherty stated that either a high number of Xbox 360s will fail or the company is being overly conservative in its warranty estimate. From an accounting standpoint, what will Microsoft do in the future if the estimate of future repairs is overly conservative (too high)?

14

CHAPTER

Bonds and Long-Term Notes

/// OVERVIEW

This chapter continues the presentation of liabilities. Specifically, the discussion focuses on the accounting treatment of long-term liabilities. Long-term notes and bonds are discussed, as well as the extinguishment of debt and debt convertible into stock.

LEARNING OBJECTIVES

After studying this chapter, you should be able to:

- **LO1** Identify the underlying characteristics of debt instruments and describe the basic approach to accounting for debt.
- **LO2** Account for bonds issued at par, at a discount, or at a premium, recording interest at the effective rate or by the straight-line method.
- **LO3** Understand the option to report liabilities at their fair values.
- **LO4** Characterize the accounting treatment of notes, including installment notes, issued for cash or for noncash consideration.
- **LO5** Describe the disclosures appropriate to long-term debt in its various forms.
- **LO6** Record the early extinguishment of debt and its conversion into equity securities.

FINANCIAL REPORTING CASE

Service Leader, Inc.

The mood is both upbeat and focused on this cool October morning. Executives and board members of Service Leader, Inc., are meeting with underwriters and attorneys to discuss the company's first bond offering in its 20-year history. You are attending in the capacity of company controller and two-year member of the board of directors. The closely held corporation has been financed entirely by equity, internally generated funds, and short-term bank borrowings.

Bank rates of interest, though, have risen recently and the company's unexpectedly rapid, but welcome, growth has prompted the need to look elsewhere for new financing. Under consideration are 15-year, 6.25% first mortgage bonds with a principal amount of $70 million. The bonds would be callable at 103 any time after June 30, 2011, and convertible into Service Leader common stock at the rate of 45 shares per $1,000 bond.

Other financing vehicles have been discussed over the last two months, including the sale of additional stock, nonconvertible bonds, and unsecured notes. This morning *The Wall Street Journal* indicated that market rates of interest for debt similar to the bonds under consideration are about 6.5%.

By the time you finish this chapter, you should be able to respond appropriately to the questions posed in this case. Compare your response to the solution provided at the end of the chapter.

QUESTIONS ///

1. What does it mean that the bonds are "first mortgage" bonds? What effect does that have on financing? (page 705)
2. From Service Leader's perspective, why are the bonds callable? What does that mean? (page 705)
3. How will it be possible to sell bonds paying investors 6.25% when other, similar investments will provide the investors a return of 6.5%? (page 706)
4. Would accounting differ if the debt were designated as notes rather than bonds? (page 719)
5. Why might the company choose to make the bonds convertible into common stock? (page 728)

The Nature of Long-Term Debt

● LO1

A company must raise funds to finance its operations and often the expansion of those operations. Presumably, at least some of the necessary funding can be provided by the company's own operations, though some funds must be provided by external sources. Ordinarily, external financing includes some combination of equity and debt funding. We explore debt financing first.

Liabilities signify *creditors'* interest in a company's assets.

In the present chapter, we focus on debt in the form of bonds and notes. The following three chapters deal with liabilities also, namely those arising in connection with leases (Chapter 15), deferred income taxes (Chapter 16), and pensions and employee benefits (Chapter 17). Some employee benefits create equity rather than debt, which are discussed in Chapter 19. In Chapter 18, we examine shareholders' interest arising from external *equity* financing. In Chapter 21, we see that cash flows from both debt and equity financing are reported together in a statement of cash flows as "cash flows from financing activities."

As you read this chapter, you will find the focus to be on the liability side of the transactions we examine. Realize, though, that the mirror image of a liability is an asset (bonds payable/investment in bonds, note payable/note receivable, etc.). So as we discuss accounting for debts from the viewpoint of the issuers of the debt instruments, we also will take the opportunity to see how the lender deals with the corresponding asset. Studying the two sides of the same transaction in tandem will emphasize their inherent similarities.

A note payable and a note receivable are two sides of the same coin.

Accounting for a liability is a relatively straightforward concept. This is not to say that all debt instruments are unchallenging, "plain vanilla" loan agreements. Quite the contrary, the financial community continually devises increasingly exotic ways to flavor financial instruments in the attempt to satisfy the diverse and evolving tastes of both debtors and creditors.

Packaging aside, a liability requires the future payment of cash in specified (or estimated) amounts, at specified (or projected) dates. As time passes, interest accrues on debt. As a general rule, the periodic interest is the effective interest rate times the amount of the debt outstanding during the period. This same principle applies regardless of the specific form of the liability—note payable, bonds payable, lease liability, pension obligation, or other debt instruments. Also, as a general rule, long-term liabilities are reported at their present values. The present value of a liability is the present value of its related cash flows (principal and/or interest payments), discounted at the effective rate of interest at issuance.

Periodic interest is the effective interest rate times the amount of the debt outstanding during the interest period.

We begin our study of long-term liabilities by examining accounting for bonds. We follow that section with a discussion of debt in the form of notes in Part B. It's important to note that, although particulars of the two forms of debt differ, the basic approach to accounting for each type is precisely the same. In Part C, we look at various ways bonds and notes are retired or converted into other securities.

PART A

BONDS

A bond issue divides a large liability into many smaller liabilities.

A company can borrow cash from a bank or other financial institution by signing a promissory note. We discuss notes payable later in the chapter. Medium-and large-sized corporations often choose to borrow cash by issuing bonds. In fact, the most common form of corporate debt is bonds. A bond issue, in effect, breaks down a large debt (large corporations often borrow hundreds of millions of dollars at a time) into manageable parts—usually $1,000 or $5,000 units. This avoids the necessity of finding a single lender who is both willing and able to loan a large amount of money at a reasonable interest rate. So rather than signing a $400 million note to borrow cash from a financial institution, a company may find it more economical to sell 400,000 $1,000 bonds to many lenders—theoretically up to 400,000 lenders.

Corporations issuing bonds are obligated to repay a stated amount at a specified *maturity date* and periodic *interest* between the issue date and maturity.

Bonds obligate the issuing corporation to repay a stated amount (variously referred to as the *principal, par value, face amount,* or *maturity value*) at a specified *maturity date.* Maturities for bonds typically range from 10 to 40 years. In return for the use of the money borrowed, the company also agrees to pay *interest* to bondholders between the issue date and maturity. The periodic interest is a stated percentage of face amount (variously referred to as the *stated rate, coupon rate,* or *nominal rate*). Ordinarily, interest is paid semiannually on designated interest dates beginning six months after the day the bonds are "dated."

The Bond Indenture

A *bond indenture* describes the specific promises made to bondholders.

The specific promises made to bondholders are described in a document called a **bond indenture.** Because it would be impractical for the corporation to enter into a direct agreement with each of the many bondholders, the bond indenture is held by a trustee, usually a commercial bank or other financial institution, appointed by the issuing firm to represent the rights of the bondholders. If the company fails to live up to the terms of the bond indenture, the trustee may bring legal action against the company on behalf of the bondholders.

Most corporate bonds are debenture bonds. A **debenture bond** is secured only by the "full faith and credit" of the issuing corporation. No specific assets are pledged as security. Investors in debentures usually have the same standing as the firm's other general creditors. So in case of bankruptcy, debenture holders and other general creditors would be treated equally. An exception is the **subordinated debenture,** which is not entitled to receive any liquidation payments until the claims of other specified debt issues are satisfied.

A **mortgage bond**, on the other hand, is backed by a lien on specified real estate owned by the issuer. Because a mortgage bond is considered less risky than debentures, it typically will command a lower interest rate.

FINANCIAL Reporting Case

Q1, p. 703

Today most corporate bonds are registered bonds. Interest checks are mailed directly to the owner of the bond, whose name is registered with the issuing company. Years ago, it was typical for bonds to be structured as **coupon bonds** (sometimes called *bearer bonds*). The name of the owner of a coupon bond was not registered. Instead, to collect interest on a coupon bond the holder actually clipped an attached coupon and redeemed it in accordance with instructions in the indenture. A carryover effect of this practice is that we still often see the term *coupon rate* in reference to the stated interest rate on bonds.

FINANCIAL Reporting Case

Q2, p. 703

Most corporate bonds are **callable** (or redeemable). The call feature allows the issuing company to buy back, or call, outstanding bonds from bondholders before their scheduled maturity date. This feature affords the company some protection against being stuck with relatively high-cost debt in the event interest rates fall during the period before maturity. The call price must be prespecified and often exceeds the bond's face amount (a call premium), sometimes declining as maturity is approached.

For example, financial statements of **Emhart Corporation** included this footnote disclosure:

Real World Financials

The Company's 9¼% (9.65% effective interest rate, after discount) sinking fund debentures are callable at prices decreasing from 105% of face amount currently to 100% in 2006.

Mandatory sinking fund redemptions retire a bond issue gradually over its term to maturity.

"No call" provisions usually prohibit calls during the first few years of a bond's life. Very often, calls are mandatory. That is, the corporation may be required to redeem the bonds on a prespecified, year-by-year basis. Bonds requiring such **sinking fund** redemptions often are labeled *sinking fund debentures.*

Serial bonds provide a more structured (and less popular) way to retire bonds on a piecemeal basis. Serial bonds are retired in installments during all or part of the life of the issue. Each bond has its own specified maturity date. So for a typical 30-year serial issue, 25 to 30 separate maturity dates might be assigned to specific portions of the bond issue.

Convertible bonds are retired as a consequence of bondholders choosing to convert them into shares of stock. We look closer at convertible bonds a little later in the chapter.

Recording Bonds at Issuance

● LO2

Bonds represent a liability to the corporation that issues the bonds and an asset to a company that buys the bonds as an investment. Each side of the transaction is the mirror image of the other.[1] This is demonstrated in Illustration 14–1.

ILLUSTRATION 14–1
Bonds Sold at Face Amount

On January 1, 2009, Masterwear Industries issued $700,000 of 12% bonds. Interest of $42,000 is payable semiannually on June 30 and December 31. The bonds mature in three years (an unrealistically short maturity to shorten the illustration). The entire bond issue was sold in a private placement to United Intergroup, Inc., at the face amount.

At Issuance (January 1)

Masterwear (Issuer)		
Cash	700,000	
Bonds payable (face amount)		700,000
United (Investor)		
Investment in bonds (face amount)	700,000	
Cash		700,000

[1]You should recall from Chapter 12 that investments in bonds that are to be held to maturity by the investor are reported at amortized cost, which is the method described here. However, also remember that investments in debt securities *not* to be held to maturity are reported at the fair value of the securities held, as described in Chapter 12.

Most bonds these days are issued on the day they are dated (date printed in the indenture contract). On rare occasions, there may be a delay in issuing bonds that causes them to be issued between interest dates, in which case the interest that has accrued since the day they are dated is added to the bonds' price. We discuss this infrequent event in an appendix to this chapter.

Determining the Selling Price

FINANCIAL Reporting Case

Q3, p. 703

The price of a bond issue at any particular time is not necessarily equal to its face amount. The $700,000, 12% bond issue in the previous illustration, for example, may sell for more than face amount (at a **premium**) or less than face amount (at a **discount**), depending on how the 12% *stated* interest rate compares with the prevailing *market* or *effective rate* of interest (for securities of similar risk and maturity). For instance, if the 12% bonds are competing in a market in which similar bonds are providing a 14% return, the bonds could be sold only at a price less than $700,000. On the other hand, if the market rate is only 10%, the 12% stated rate would seem relatively attractive and the bonds would sell at a premium over face amount. The reason the stated rate often differs from the market rate, resulting in a discount or premium, is the inevitable delay between the date the terms of the issue are established and the date the issue comes to market.

Other things being equal, the lower the perceived riskiness of the corporation issuing bonds, the higher the price those bonds will command.

In addition to the characteristic terms of a bond agreement as specified in the indenture, the market rate for a specific bond issue is influenced by the creditworthiness of the company issuing the bonds. To evaluate the risk and quality of an individual bond issue, investors rely heavily on bond ratings provided by **Standard & Poor's Corporation** and by **Moody's Investors Service, Inc.** See the bond ratings in Graphic 14–1.

GRAPHIC 14–1
Bond Ratings*

	S&P	Moody's
Investment Grades:		
Highest	AAA	Aaa
High	AA	Aa
Medium	A	A
Minimum investment grade	BBB	Baa
"Junk" Ratings:		
Speculative	BB	Ba
Very speculative	B	B
Default or near default	CCC	Caa
	CC	Ca
	C	C
	D	

*Adapted from *Bond Record* (New York: Moody's Investors Service, monthly) and *Bond Guide* (New York: Standard & Poor's Corporation, monthly).

A bond issue will be priced by the marketplace to yield the market rate of interest for securities of similar risk and maturity.

Forces of supply and demand cause a bond issue to be *priced to yield the market rate.* In other words, an investor paying that price will earn an effective rate of return on the investment equal to the market rate. The price is calculated as the present value of all the cash flows required of the bonds, where the discount rate used in the present value calculation is the market rate. Specifically, the price will be the present value of the periodic cash interest payments (face amount × stated rate) plus the present value of the principal payable at maturity, both discounted at the market rate.

Bonds priced at a discount are described in Illustration 14–2.

ILLUST
Bonds
Discou

On January 1, 2009, Masterwear Industries issued $700,000 of 12% bonds, dated January 1. Interest of $42,000 is payable semiannually on June 30 and December 31. The bonds mature in three years. The market yield for bonds of similar risk and maturity is 14%. The entire bond issue was purchased by United Intergroup, Inc.

Calculation of the Price of the Bonds

		Present Values
Interest	$ 42,000 × 4.76654* =	$200,195
Principal	$700,000 × 0.66634† =	466,438
Present value (price) of the bonds		$666,633

*Present value of an ordinary annuity of $1: $n = 6$, $i = 7\%$ (Table 4).
†Present value of $1: $n = 6$, $i = 7\%$ (Table 2).
Because interest is paid semiannually, the present value calculations use: (a) one-half the stated rate (6%) to determine cash payments, (b) one-half the market rate (7%) as the discount rate, and (c) six (3 × 2) semiannual periods.

Note: Present value tables are provided at the end of this textbook. If you need to review the concept of the time value of money, refer to the discussions in Chapter 6.

Rounding: Because present value tables truncate decimal places, the solution may be slightly different if you use a calculator or Excel.

Using Excel, enter:
=PV(.07,6,42000,700000)
Output: 666,634

Using a calculator:
Enter: N 6 I 7
PMT −42000 FV −700000
Output: PV 666,634

The calculation is illustrated in Graphic 14–2.

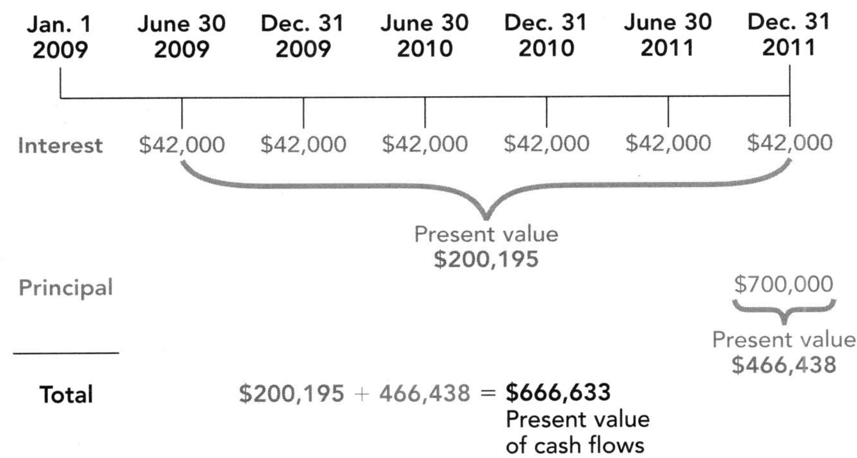

GRAPHIC 14–2
Cash Flows from a Bond Issue

Because of the time value of money, the present value of the future cash flows is less than the total payments of $952,000.

Although the cash flows total $952,000, the present value of those future cash flows as of January 1, 2009, is only $666,633. This is due to the time value of money.

Journal Entries at Issuance—Bonds Sold at a Discount

Masterwear (Issuer)		
Cash (price calculated above)	666,633	
Discount on bonds payable (difference)	33,367	
Bonds payable (face amount)		700,000
United (Investor)		
Investment in bonds (face amount)	700,000	
Discount on bond investment (difference)		33,367
Cash (price calculated above)		666,633

Note: In practice, investors often record their investments using the "net method." Issuers, too, are not required to use the "gross method" demonstrated here. By the net method, the entries above would be:

Masterwear		
Cash	666,633	
Bonds payable		666,633
United		
Investment in bonds	666,633	
Cash		666,633

When bond prices are quoted in financial media, they typically are stated in terms of a percentage of face amount. Thus, a price quote of 98 means a $1,000 bond will sell for $980; a bond priced at 101 will sell for $1,010.

Determining Interest—Effective Interest Method

The *effective interest* on debt is the market rate of interest multiplied by the outstanding balance of the debt.

Interest accrues on an outstanding debt at a constant percentage of the debt each period. Of course, under the concept of accrual accounting, the periodic effective interest is not affected by the time at which the cash interest actually is paid. Recording interest each period as the *effective market rate of interest multiplied by the outstanding balance of the debt* (during the interest period) is referred to as the **effective interest method.** Although giving this a label—the effective interest method—implies some specialized procedure, this simply is an application of the accrual concept, consistent with accruing all expenses as they are incurred.

Continuing our example, we determined that the amount of debt when the bonds are issued is $666,633. Since the effective interest rate is 14%, interest recorded (as expense to the issuer and revenue to the investor) for the first six-month interest period is $46,664:

$666,633	×	[14% ÷ 2]	=	$46,664
Outstanding balance		Effective rate		Effective interest

However, the bond indenture calls for semiannual interest payments of only $42,000—the *stated* rate (6%) times the *face amount* ($700,000). As always, when only a portion of an expense is paid, the remainder becomes a liability—in this case an addition to the already outstanding liability. So the difference, $4,664, increases the liability and is reflected as a reduction in the discount (a valuation account). This is illustrated in Graphic 14–3.

GRAPHIC 14–3
Change in Debt When Effective Interest Exceeds Cash Paid

The unpaid portion of the effective interest increases the existing liability.

			Account Balances		
	Outstanding Balance		Bonds Payable (face amount)		Discount on Bonds Payable
January 1	$666,633	=	$700,000	less	$33,367
Interest accrued at 7%	46,664				
Portion of interest paid	(42,000)				(4,664)
June 30	$671,297	=	$700,000	less	$28,703

Interest accrues on the outstanding debt at the effective rate. Interest paid is the amount specified in the bond indenture—the stated rate times the face amount. These amounts and the change in the outstanding debt are recorded as follows:

Journal Entries—The Interest Method

The effective interest is calculated each period as the market rate times the amount of the debt outstanding during the interest period.

At the first Interest Date (June 30)

Masterwear (Issuer)		
Interest expense (market rate × outstanding balance)	46,664	
Discount on bonds payable (difference)		4,664
Cash (stated rate × face amount)		42,000
United (Investor)		
Cash (stated rate × face amount)	42,000	
Discount on bond investment (difference)	4,664	
Interest revenue (market rate × outstanding balance)		46,664

Because the balance of the debt changes each period, the dollar amount of interest (balance × rate) also will change each period. To keep up with the changing amounts, it usually is convenient to prepare a schedule that reflects the changes in the debt over its term to maturity. An amortization schedule for the situation under discussion is shown in Graphic 14–4.

Amounts for the journal entries each interest date are found in the first three columns of the schedule. Traditionally, this schedule has been referred to as an **amortization schedule**—a

GRAPHIC 14–4
Amortization Schedule—Discount

Date	Cash Interest	Effective Interest	Increase in Balance	Outstanding Balance
	(6% × Face amount)	(7% × Outstanding balance)	(Discount reduction)	
1/1/09				666,633
6/30/09	42,000	.07 (666,633) = 46,664	4,664	671,297
12/31/09	42,000	.07 (671,297) = 46,991	4,991	676,288
6/30/10	42,000	.07 (676,288) = 47,340	5,340	681,628
12/31/10	42,000	.07 (681,628) = 47,714	5,714	687,342
6/30/11	42,000	.07 (687,342) = 48,114	6,114	693,456
12/31/11	42,000	.07 (693,456) = 48,544*	6,544	700,000
	252,000	285,367	33,367	

*Rounded.

Since less cash is paid each period than the effective interest, the unpaid difference increases the outstanding balance of the debt.

reference to alleged amortization of the discount.[2] This is an apparent carryover from earlier days when the discount was considered to be an asset to be amortized. To the contrary, the discount is a valuation account, having no existence apart from the related debt. As you learned in the previous paragraphs, changes in its balance are the derived result of changes in the outstanding debt, when portions of periodic accrued interest go unpaid.[3]

Terms such as *unamortized or deferred discount or premium* and *to amortize discount or premium* are carryovers from the days when debt discount was considered to be an amortizable asset and do not describe accurately either the assets or liabilities and events involved or the interest method of accounting for them.[4]

However, because this terminology is so prevalent in practice, we too will use the label *amortization schedule.* Be sure to realize, though, that this label is a misnomer—nothing is being amortized. The essential point to remember is that the effective interest method is a straightforward application of the accrual concept, whereby interest expense (or revenue) is accrued periodically at the effective rate. It involves neither deferring expenses (or revenues) nor amortizing deferrals.

A liability should be reported at its present value.

Determining interest in this manner has a convenient side effect. It results in reporting the liability at the present value of future cash payments—the appropriate valuation method for any liability.[5] This is obvious at issuance; we actually calculated the present value to be $666,633. What perhaps is not quite as obvious is that the outstanding amount of debt each subsequent period (shown in the right-hand column of the amortization schedule) is still the present value of the remaining cash flows, discounted at the original rate.

ADDITIONAL CONSIDERATION

Although the reported amount each period is the **present value** of the bonds, at any date after issuance this amount is not necessarily equal to the **market value** of the bonds. This is because the **market** rate of interest will not necessarily remain the same as the rate implicit in the original issue price (the effective rate). Of course, for negotiable financial instruments, the issue price is the market price at any given time. Differences between market values and present values based on the original rate are holding gains and losses. If we were to use the market rate to revalue bonds on each reporting date—that is, recalculate the present value using the market rate—the reported amount always would be the market value.

[2]You learned in earlier chapters that amortization is the accounting process of reducing an asset or liability by periodic write-downs or payments [*SFAC 6,* par. 142].

[3]Or as we see later, the debt changes when periodic interest is overpaid. This occurs when debt is sold at a premium, rather than at a discount.

[4]"Elements of Financial Statements," *Statement of Financial Accounting Concepts No. 6,* par. 36 (Stamford, Conn.: FASB, 1985), par. 239.

[5]"Interest on Receivables and Payables," *APB Opinion No. 21* (New York: AICPA, 1971).

Zero-Coupon Bonds

A zero-coupon bond pays no interest. Instead, it offers a return in the form of a "deep discount" from the face amount. For illustration, let's look at the zero-coupon bonds issued by **General Mills, Inc.**. Two billion, two hundred thirty million dollars face amount of the 20-year securities sold for $1.501 million. As the amortization schedule in Graphic 14–5 demonstrates, they were priced to yield 2%.

GRAPHIC 14–5
Zero-Coupon Securities—General Mills, Inc.

Real World Financials

($ in millions)	Cash Interest	Effective Interest	Increase in Balance	Outstanding Balance*
	(0% × Face amount)	(2% × Outstanding debt)	(Discount reduction)	
				1,501
2002	0	.02 (1,501) = 30	30	1,531
2003	0	.02 (1,531) = 31	31	1,561
2004	0	.02 (1,561) = 31	31	1,593
◆	◆	◆	◆	◆
◆	◆	◆	◆	◆
◆	◆	◆	◆	◆
2021	0	.02 (2,143) = 43	43	2,186
2022	0	.02 (2,186) = 44	44	2,230
		729	729	

*Some numbers appear not to total because the underlying calculations are not rounded.

Zero-coupon bonds provide us a convenient opportunity to reinforce a key concept we just learned: that we accrue the interest expense (or revenue) each period at the effective rate regardless of how much cash interest actually is paid (zero in this case). An advantage of issuing zero-coupon bonds or notes is that the corporation can deduct for tax purposes the annual interest expense (see schedule) but has no related cash outflow until the bonds mature. However, the reverse is true for investors in "zeros." Investors receive no periodic cash interest, even though annual interest revenue is reportable for tax purposes. So those who invest in zero-coupon bonds usually have tax-deferred or tax-exempt status, such as pension funds, individual retirement accounts (IRAs), and charitable organizations. Zero-coupon bonds and notes have popularity but still constitute a relatively small proportion of corporate debt.

Bonds Sold at a Premium

In Illustration 14–2, Masterwear Industries sold the bonds at a price that would yield an effective rate higher than the stated rate. The result was a discount. On the other hand, if the 12% bonds had been issued when the market yield for bonds of similar risk and maturity was *lower* than the stated rate, say 10%, the issue would have been priced at a *premium.* Because the 12% rate would seem relatively attractive in a 10% market, the bonds would command an issue price of more than $700,000, calculated in Illustration 14–3 on the next page.

Interest on bonds sold at a premium is determined in precisely the same manner as on bonds sold at a discount. Again, interest is the effective interest rate applied to the debt outstanding during each period (balance at the end of the previous interest period), and the cash paid is the stated rate times the face amount, as shown in Graphic 14–6 on the next page.

Notice that the debt declines each period. This is because the effective interest each period is less than the cash interest paid. The overpayments each period reduce the amount owed. Remember, this is precisely the opposite of when debt is sold at a discount, when the effective

On January 1, 2009, Masterwear Industries issued $700,000 of 12% bonds, dated January 1. Interest of $42,000 is payable semiannually on June 30 and December 31. The bonds mature in three years. The market yield for bonds of similar risk and maturity is 10%. The entire bond issue was purchased by United Intergroup, Inc.

Calculation of the Price of the Bonds

		Present Values
Interest	$ 42,000 × 5.07569* =	$213,179
Principal	$700,000 × 0.74622† =	522,354
Present value (price) of the bonds		$735,533

*Present value of an ordinary annuity of $1: $n = 6$, $i = 5\%$.
†Present value of $1: $n = 6$, $i = 5\%$.

ILLUSTRATION 14–3
Bonds Sold at a Premium

Because interest is paid *semiannually*, the present value calculations use:
a. one-half the stated rate (6%),
b. one-half the market rate (5%), and
c. 6 (3 × 2) semiannual periods.

Masterwear (Issuer)		
Cash (price calculated above)	735,533	
Bonds payable (face amount)		700,000
Premium on bonds payable (difference)		35,533
United (Investor)		
Investment in bonds (face amount)	700,000	
Premium on bond investment (difference)	35,533	
Cash (price calculated above)		735,533

Journal Entries at Issuance—Bonds Sold at Premium

Date	Cash Interest	Effective Interest	Decrease in Balance	Outstanding Balance
	(6% × Face amount)	(5% × Outstanding balance)	(Premium reduction)	
1/1/09				735,533
6/30/09	42,000	.05 (735,533) = 36,777	5,223	730,310
12/31/09	42,000	.05 (730,310) = 36,516	5,484	724,826
6/30/10	42,000	.05 (724,826) = 36,241	5,759	719,067
12/31/10	42,000	.05 (719,067) = 35,953	6,047	713,020
6/30/11	42,000	.05 (713,020) = 35,651	6,349	706,671
12/31/11	42,000	.05 (706,671) = 35,329*	6,671	700,000
	252,000	216,467	35,533	

*Rounded.

GRAPHIC 14–6
Amortization Schedule—Premium

Since *more* cash is paid each period than the effective interest, the debt outstanding is reduced by the overpayment.

interest each period is more than the cash paid, and the underpayment of interest adds to the amount owed. This is illustrated in Graphic 14-7 on the next page.

In practice, bonds rarely are issued at a premium. Because of the delay between the date the terms of the bonds are established and when the bonds are issued, it's difficult to set the stated rate equal to the ever-changing market rate. Knowing that, for marketing reasons, companies deliberately set the terms to more likely create a small discount rather than a premium at the issue date. Some investors are psychologically prone to prefer buying at a discount rather than a premium even if the yield is the same (the market rate).

GRAPHIC 14–7
Premium and Discount Amortization Compared

Whether bonds are issued at a premium or a discount, the outstanding balance becomes zero at maturity.

ADDITIONAL CONSIDERATION

The preceding illustrations describe bonds sold at a discount and at a premium. The same concepts apply to bonds sold at face amount. But some of the procedures would be unnecessary. For instance, calculating the present value of the interest and the principal always will give us the face amount when the effective rate and the stated rate are the same:

Calculation of the Price of the Bonds

			Present Values
Interest	$ 42,000 × 4.91732*	=	$206,528
Principal	$700,000 × 0.70496†	=	493,472
Present value (price) of the bonds			$700,000

*Present value of an ordinary annuity of $1: $n = 6, i = 6\%$.
†Present value of $1: $n = 6, i = 6\%$.

When Financial Statements are Prepared Between Interest Dates

Any interest that has accrued since the last interest date must be recorded by an adjusting entry prior to preparing financial statements.

When an accounting period ends between interest dates, it is necessary to record interest that has accrued since the last interest date. As an example, refer again to Illustration 14–2 on page 707. If the fiscal years of Masterwear and United end on October 31 and interest was last paid and recorded on June 30, four months' interest must be accrued in a year-end adjusting entry. Because interest is recorded for only a portion of a semiannual period, amounts recorded are simply the amounts shown in the amortization schedule (Graphic 14–4, p. 709) times the appropriate fraction of the semiannual period (in this case 4/6).

Adjusting Entries—To Accrue Interest

To avoid understating interest in the financial statements, four months' interest is recorded at the end of the reporting period.

At October 31

Masterwear (Issuer)		
Interest expense (4/6 × 46,991)	31,327	
Discount on bonds payable (4/6 × 4,991)		3,327
Interest payable (4/6 × 42,000)		28,000
United (Investor)		
Interest receivable (4/6 × 42,000)	28,000	
Discount on bond investment (4/6 × 4,991)	3,327	
Interest revenue (4/6 × 46,991)		31,327

Two months later, when semiannual interest is paid next, the remainder of the interest is allocated to the first two months of the next accounting year—November and December:

At the December 31 Interest Date		
Masterwear (Issuer)		
Interest expense (2/6 × 46,991)	15,664	
Interest payable (from adjusting entry)	28,000	
Discount on bonds payable (2/6 × 4,991)		1,664
Cash (stated rate × face amount)		42,000
United (Investor)		
Cash (stated rate × face amount)	42,000	
Discount on bond investment (2/6 × 4,991)	1,664	
Interest receivable (from adjusting entry)		28,000
Interest revenue (2/6 × 46,991)		15,664

Of the six-months' interest paid December 31, only the November and December interest is expensed in the new fiscal year.

The Straight-Line Method—A Practical Expediency

In some circumstances the profession permits an exception to the conceptually appropriate method of determining interest for bond issues. A company is allowed to determine interest indirectly by allocating a discount or a premium equally to each period over the term to maturity—if doing so produces results that are not materially different from the usual (and preferable) interest method.[6] The decision should be guided by whether the **straight-line method** would tend to mislead investors and creditors in the particular circumstance.

By the straight-line method, the discount in Illustration 14–2 and Graphic 14–4 would be allocated equally to the six semiannual periods (three years):

$33,367 ÷ 6 periods = $5,561 per period

At Each of the Six Interest Dates		
Masterwear (Issuer)		
Interest expense (to balance)	47,561	
Discount on bonds payable (discount ÷ 6 periods)		5,561
Cash (stated rate × face amount)		42,000
United (Investor)		
Cash (stated rate × face amount)	42,000	
Discount on bond investment (discount ÷ 6 periods)	5,561	
Interest revenue (to balance)		47,561

Journal Entries—Straight-Line Method

By the straight-line method, interest (expense and revenue) is a plug figure, resulting from calculating the amount of discount reduction.

Allocating the discount or premium equally over the life of the bonds by the straight-line method results in a constant dollar amount of interest each period. An amortization schedule, then, would serve little purpose. For example, if we prepared one for the straight-line method in this situation, it would provide the same amounts each period as shown in Graphic 14–8.

GRAPHIC 14–8

Amortization Schedule—Straight-Line Method

	Cash Interest	Recorded Interest	Increase in Balance	Outstanding Balance
	(6% × Face amount)	(Cash + Discount reduction)	($33,367 ÷ 6)	
1/1/09				666,633
6/30/09	42,000	(42,000 + 5,561) = 47,561	5,561	672,194
12/31/09	42,000	(42,000 + 5,561) = 47,561	5,561	677,755
6/30/10	42,000	(42,000 + 5,561) = 47,561	5,561	683,316
12/31/10	42,000	(42,000 + 5,561) = 47,561	5,561	688,877
6/30/11	42,000	(42,000 + 5,561) = 47,561	5,561	694,438
12/31/11	42,000	(42,000 + 5,561) = 47,561	5,561	700,000*
	252,000	285,366	33,366	

*Rounded.

By the straight-line method, the amount of the discount to be reduced periodically is calculated, and the recorded interest is the plug figure.

[6] Ibid.

Determining interest by allocating the discount (or premium) on a straight-line basis is a practical expediency permitted in some situations by the materiality concept.

Remember, constant dollar amounts are not produced when the effective interest method is used. By that method, the dollar amounts of interest vary over the term to maturity because the percentage rate of interest remains constant but is applied to a changing debt balance.

Also, be sure to realize that the straight-line method is not an alternative method of determining interest in a conceptual sense. Instead, it is an application of the materiality concept, by which an appropriate application of GAAP (e.g., the effective interest method) can be by-passed for reasons of practical expediency in situations when doing so has no material effect on the results. Based on the frequency with which the straight-line method is used in practice, we can infer that managers very frequently conclude that its use has no material impact on investors' decisions.

CONCEPT REVIEW EXERCISE

ISSUING BONDS AND RECORDING INTEREST

On January 1, 2009, the Meade Group issued $8,000,000 of 11% bonds, dated January 1. Interest is payable semiannually on June 30 and December 31. The bonds mature in four years. The market yield for bonds of similar risk and maturity is 10%.

Required:

1. Determine the price these bonds sold for to yield the 10% market rate and record their issuance by the Meade Group.
2. Prepare an amortization schedule that determines interest at the effective rate and record interest on the first interest date, June 30, 2009.

SOLUTION

1. Determine the price these bonds sold for to yield the 10% market rate and record their issuance by the Meade Group.

Calculation of the Price of the Bonds

There are eight semiannual periods and one-half the market rate is 5%.

Interest	$ 440,000 × 6.46321*	=	$2,843,812
Principal	$8,000,000 × 0.67684†	=	5,414,720
Present value (price) of the bonds			$8,258,532

*Present value of an ordinary annuity of $1: $n = 8$, $i = 5\%$.
†Present value of $1: $n = 8$, $i = 5\%$.

Journal Entries at Issuance

Cash (price calculated above)	8,258,532	
Bonds payable (face amount)		8,000,000
Premium on bonds payable (difference)		258,532

2. Prepare an amortization schedule that determines interest at the effective rate and record interest on the first interest date, June 30, 2009.

More cash is paid each period than the effective interest, so the debt outstanding is *reduced by the "overpayment."*

Amortization Schedule

Date	Cash Interest	Effective Interest	Decrease in Balance	Outstanding Balance
	(5.5% × Face amount)	(5% × Outstanding balance)	(Premium reduction)	
1/1/09				8,258,532
6/30/09	440,000	.05 (8,258,532) = 412,927	27,073	8,231,459
12/31/09	440,000	.05 (8,231,459) = 411,573	28,427	8,203,032
6/30/10	440,000	.05 (8,203,032) = 410,152	29,848	8,173,184
12/31/10	440,000	.05 (8,173,184) = 408,659	31,341	8,141,843
6/30/11	440,000	.05 (8,141,843) = 407,092	32,908	8,108,935
12 /31/11	440,000	.05 (8,108,935) = 405,447	34,553	8,074,382
6/30/12	440.000	.05 (8,074,382) = 403,719	36,281	8,038,101
12/31/12	440,000	.05 (8,038,101) = 401,899*	38,101	8,000,000
	3,520,000	3,261,468	258,532	

*Rounded.

Interest expense (5% × $8,258,532)	412,927	
Premium on bonds payable (difference)	27,073	
Cash (5.5% × $8,000,000)		440,000
To record interest for six months.		

Debt Issue Costs

Rather than sell bonds directly to the public, corporations usually sell an entire issue to an underwriter who then resells them to other security dealers and the public. By committing to purchase bonds at a set price, an investment house such as **Smith Barney, Goldman Sachs,** and **Merrill Lynch** is said to underwrite any risks associated with a new issue. The underwriting fee is the spread between the price the underwriter pays and the resale price.

Alternatively, the issuing company may choose to sell the debt securities directly to a single investor (as we assumed in previous illustrations)—often a pension fund or an insurance company. This is referred to as *private placement.* Issue costs are less because privately placed securities are not subject to the costly and lengthy process of registering with the SEC that is required of public offerings. Underwriting fees also are avoided.[7]

With either publicly or privately sold debt, the issuing company will incur costs in connection with issuing bonds or notes, such as legal and accounting fees and printing costs, in addition to registration and underwriting fees. These **debt issue costs** are recorded *separately* and are amortized over the term of the related debt. GAAP requires a debit to an asset account—debt issue costs. The asset is allocated to expense, usually on a straight-line basis.

Costs of issuing debt securities are recorded as a debit to an asset account, "debt issue costs," and amortized to expense over the term to maturity.

For example, let's assume issue costs in Illustration 14–3 had been $12,000. The entries for the issuance of the bonds would include a separate asset account for the issue costs:

Cash (price minus issue costs)	723,533	
Debt issue costs	12,000	
Bonds payable (face amount)		700,000
Premium on bonds payable (price minus face amount)		35,533

The premium (or discount) is unaffected by debt issue costs because they are recorded in a separate account.

Semiannual amortization of the asset would be:

Debt issue expense ($12,000 ÷ 6)	2,000	
Debt issue costs		2,000

ADDITIONAL CONSIDERATION

The treatment of issue costs just described is required by APB Opinion No. 21. A conceptually more appealing treatment would be to reduce the recorded amount of the debt by the debt issue costs instead of recording the costs separately as an asset. The cost of these services reduces the net cash the issuing company receives from the sale of the financial instrument. A lower [net] amount is borrowed at the same cost, increasing the effective interest rate. However, unless the recorded amount of the debt is reduced by the issue costs, the higher rate is not reflected in a higher recorded interest expense.[8] The actual increase in the effective interest rate would be reflected in the interest expense if the issue cost is allowed to reduce the premium (or increase the discount) on the debt:

Cash (price calculated above)	723,533	
Bonds payable (face amount)		700,000
Premium on bonds payable (difference)		23,533

(continued)

[7]Rule 144A of the Securities Act of 1933, as amended, allows for the private resale of unregistered securities to "qualified institutional buyers," which are generally large institutional investors with assets exceeding $100 million.

[8]When the same amortization method is used for both, net income is unaffected by whether the cost is amortized as a separate debt issue expense or is reflected in a higher interest expense.

ADDITIONAL CONSIDERATION—concluded

Also, this approach is consistent with the treatment of issue costs when equity securities are sold. You will see in Chapter 18 that the effect of share issue costs is to reduce the amount credited to stock accounts.

This treatment also is suggested by the FASB in *SFAC 6.* Remember, though, that concept statements do not constitute GAAP, so until a new FASB standard is issued to supersede *APB Opinion 21,* the generally accepted practice is to record debt issue costs as assets.

INTERNATIONAL FINANCIAL REPORTING STANDARDS

Distinction between Debt and Equity for Preferred Stock. The primary standard for distinguishing between debt and equity in the United States is *SFAS No. 150,* "Accounting for Certain Financial Instruments: Characteristics of both Liabilities and Equity"; and under IFRS, it's *IAS No. 32,* "Financial Instruments: Disclosure and Presentation." Differences in the definitions and requirements under these standards can result in the same instrument being classified differently between debt and equity under IFRS and U.S. GAAP. Most preferred stock (preference shares) is reported under IFRS as debt with the dividends reported in the income statement as interest expense. Under U.S. GAAP, that's the case only for "manditorily redeemable" preferred stock. Unilever describes such a difference in a disclosure note:

> **Additional Information for U.S. Investors [in part]**
> **Preference Shares**
> Under *IAS 32,* Unilever recognises preference shares that provide a fixed preference dividend as borrowings with preference dividends recognised in the income statement. Under U.S. GAAP such preference shares are classified in shareholders' equity with dividends treated as a deduction to shareholder's equity.

Option to Report Liabilities at Fair Value

● LO3

***SFAS No. 159* gives a company the option to value financial assets and liabilities at fair value.**

Companies are not required to, but have the option to, value some or all of their financial assets and liabilities at fair value. This choice is permitted by *SFAS No. 159,* "The Fair Value Option for Financial Assets and Financial Liabilities." In Chapter 12, we saw examples of the option being applied to financial assets—specifically, companies reporting their investments in securities at fair value. Now, we see how liabilities, too, can be reported at fair value.

How does a liability's fair value change? Remember that there are two sides to every investment. For example, if a company has an investment in **General Motors'** bonds, that investment is an asset to the investor, and the same bonds are a liability to General Motors. So, the same market forces that influence the fair value of an investment in debt securities (interest rates, economic conditions, risk, etc.) influence the fair value of liabilities. For bank loans or other debts that aren't traded on a market exchange, the mix of factors will differ, but in any case, changes in the current market rate of interest will be a major contributor to changes in fair value.

Determining Fair Value

Changes in interest rates cause changes in the fair value of liabilities.

For demonstration, we revisit the Masterwear Industries bonds that sold at a discount in Illustration 14–2 on page 707. Now, suppose it's six months later, the market rate of interest has fallen to 11%, and June 30 is the end of Masterwear's fiscal year. A decline in market interest rates means bond prices rise. Let's say that checking market prices in *The Wall Street Journal* indicates that the fair value of the Masterwear bonds on June 30, 2009, is $714,943. Referring to the amortization schedule on page 707, we see that on the same date, with 5 periods remaining to maturity, the present value of the bonds—their price—would have been $671,297 if the market rate still had been 14% (7% semiannually).

ADDITIONAL CONSIDERATION

If the bonds are not traded on a market exchange, their fair value would not be readily observable. In that case, the next most preferable way to determine fair value according to *SFAS No. 157* would be to calculate the fair value as the present value of the remaining cash flows discounted at the current interest rate. If the rate is 11% (5.5% semiannually), as we're assuming now, that present value would be $714,943:

			Present Values
Interest	$ 42,000 × 4.27028*	=	$179,352
Principal	$700,000 × 0.76513†	=	535,591
Present value of the bonds			$714,943

*Present value of an ordinary annuity of $1: $n = 5$, $i = 5.5\%$.
†Present value of $1: $n = 5$, $i = 5.5\%$.

When the bonds were issued, Masterwear had a choice—report this liability (a) at its amortized initial measurement throughout the term to maturity or (b) at its current fair value on each reporting date. Had the company *not* elected the fair value option, on June 30 it would report the $671,297 we calculated earlier for the amortization schedule. On the other hand, if Masterwear had elected the fair value option, it would report the bonds at their current fair value, $714,943.

Reporting Changes in Fair Value

If a company chooses the option to report at fair value, then it must report *changes* in fair value in the income statement. In our example, Masterwear would report the increase in fair value from $666,633 to $714,943, or $48,310. Note, though, that part of the change is due to the unpaid interest we discussed earlier. Here's a recap.

At June 30, 2009, the interest that accrued during the first six months was $46,664, but only $42,000 of that was paid in cash; so the debt balance increased by the $4,664 unpaid interest. We recorded the following entry:

Interest expense	46,664	
Discount on bonds payable		4,664
Cash		42,000

Bonds payable less: discount carrying value

Amortizing the discount in this entry increased the book value of the liability by $4,664 to $671,297:

January 1 book value and fair value	$666,633
Increase from discount amortization	4,664
June 30 book value (amortized initial amount)	$671,297

FAIR VALUE RISES. Comparing that amount with the fair value of the bonds on that date provides the amount needed to adjust the bonds to their fair value.

June 30 fair value	$714,943
June 30 book value (amortized initial amount)	671,297
Fair value adjustment needed	$ 43,646

When the fair value option is elected, we report changes in fair value in the income statement.

Rather than increasing the bonds payable account itself, though, we instead adjust it *indirectly* with a credit to a valuation allowance (or contra) account:

Unrealized holding loss	43,646	
Fair value adjustment ($714,943 – 671,297)		43,646

Masterwear must recognize the unrealized holding loss in the June 30, 2009, income statement. Notice that the effect on earnings is:

Electing the FVO means reporting unrealized holding gains and losses in earnings.

Interest expense	$46,664
Unrealized holding loss	43,646
Net decrease in earnings	$90,310

The new carrying value of the bonds is now the fair value:

The *credit* balance in the fair value adjustment *increases* the carrying value; the discount reduces it.

Bonds payable	$700,000
Less: Discount ($33,367 – 4,664)	(28,703)
Amortization table value	$671,297
Plus: Fair value adjustment	43,646
Carrying value, June 30	$714,943

FAIR VALUE FALLS. Suppose the fair value at June 30, 2009, had been $650,000 instead of $714,943. In that case, Masterwear would record a *reduction* in the liability from $671,297 to $650,000, or $21,297. The entry would be:

Fair value adjustment ($671,297 – 650,000)	21,297	
Unrealized holding gain		21,297

The effect on earnings in the second scenario is:

Interest expense	$46,664
Unrealized holding gain	(21,297)
Net decrease in earnings	$25,367

The new carrying value of the bonds is the fair value:

The *debit* balance in the fair value adjustment *reduces* the carrying value, as does the discount.

Bonds payable	$700,000
Less: Discount ($33,367 – 4,664)	(28,703)
Amortization table value	$671,297
Less: Fair value adjustment	(21,297)
Carrying value, June 30	$650,000

The outstanding balance in the last column of the amortization schedule at any date up to and including the balance at maturity will be the bonds payable less the discount (for instance $671,297 at June 30, 2009, on page xxx). But the amount we report in the balance sheet at any reporting date, the fair value, will be that amortized initial amount from the amortization schedule plus or minus the fair value adjustment. That's the $714,943 or the $650,000 in the two scenarios above.

Mix and Match

Companies choose which financial instruments to report at fair value.

Remember from our discussions in prior chapters that if a company elects the fair value option, it's not necessary that the company elect the option to report all of its financial instruments at fair value or even all instruments of a particular type at fair value. They can "mix and match" on an instrument-by-instrument basis. So Masterwear, for instance, might choose to report these bonds at fair value but all its other liabilities at their amortized initial measurement. However, the company must make the election when the item originates, in this case when the bonds are issued, and is not allowed to switch methods once a method is chosen.

National Penn Bank Shares elected the option to report one of its liabilities (bonds) at fair value and accordingly reported the change in its fair value as a gain in its 2007 income statement. Graphic 14–9 presents an excerpt from a disclosure note describing that election.

The corporate bond is the basic long-term debt instrument for most large companies. But for many firms, the debt instrument often used is a *note*. We discuss notes next.

GRAPHIC 14–9

Electing the Option to Report a Liability at Fair Value—National Penn Bank Shares

Real World Financials

11. FAIR VALUE MEASUREMENTS (in part)

The Company early adopted *SFAS No. 159* as of January 1, 2007, and elected the fair value option for one discreet financial instrument. . . . Specifically, the fair value option was applied to the Company's only fixed rate subordinated debt liabilities with a cost basis of $65.2 million. This subordinated debt has a fixed rate of 7.85% and a maturity date of September 30, 2032, with a call provision after September 30, 2007. The Company believes that by electing the fair value option for this financial instrument, it will . . . provide more comparable accounting treatment for this long-term fixed rate debt with the Company's long-term fair valued assets for which the debt is a funding instrument, such as the long-term municipal bonds held in the Company's investment portfolio. . . . The Company recorded a gain of $151,000 in noninterest income for the change in fair value of the subordinated debt for the three months ended March 31, 2007.

PART B

● LO4

LONG-TERM NOTES

When a company borrows cash from a bank and signs a promissory note (essentially an IOU), the firm's liability is reported as a *note payable.* Or a note might be issued in exchange for a noncash asset—perhaps to purchase equipment on credit. In concept, notes are accounted for in precisely the same way as bonds. In fact, we could properly substitute notes payable for bonds payable in each of our previous illustrations.

FINANCIAL Reporting Case

Q4, p. 703

Note Issued for Cash

The interest rate stated in a note is likely to be equal to the market rate because the rate usually is negotiated at the time of the loan. So discounts and premiums are less likely for notes than on bonds. Accounting for a note issued for cash is demonstrated in Illustration 14–4.

ILLUSTRATION 14–4

Note Issued for Cash

On January 1, 2009, Skill Graphics, Inc., a product-labeling and graphics firm, borrowed $700,000 cash from First BancCorp and issued a three-year, $700,000 promissory note. Interest of $42,000 was payable semiannually on June 30 and December 31.

At Issuance		
Skill Graphics (Borrower)		
Cash	700,000	
Notes payable (face amount)		700,000
First BancCorp (Lender)		
Notes receivable (face amount)	700,000	
Cash		700,000
At Each of the Six Interest Dates		
Skill Graphics (Borrower)		
Interest expense	42,000	
Cash (stated rate × face amount)		42,000
First BancCorp (Lender)		
Cash (stated rate × face amount)	42,000	
Interest revenue		42,000
At Maturity		
Skill Graphics (Borrower)		
Notes payable	700,000	
Cash (face amount)		700,000
First BancCorp (Lender)		
Cash (face amount)	700,000	
Notes receivable		700,000

Note Exchanged for Assets or Services

Occasionally the *stated* interest rate is not indicative of the *market* rate at the time a note is negotiated. The value of the asset (cash or noncash) or service exchanged for the note establishes the market rate.[9] For example, let's assume Skill Graphics purchased a package-labeling machine from Hughes–Barker Corporation by issuing a 12%, $700,000, three-year note that requires interest to be paid semiannually. Let's also assume that the machine could have been purchased at a cash price of $666,633. You probably recognize this numerical situation as the one used earlier to illustrate bonds sold at a discount (Illustration 14–2). Reference to the earlier example will confirm that exchanging this $700,000 note for a machine with a cash price of $666,633 implies an annual market rate of interest of 14%. That is, 7% is one-half the discount rate that yields a present value of $666,633 for the note's cash flows (interest plus principal):

			Present Values
Interest	$ 42,000 × 4.76654*	=	$200,195
Principal	$700,000 × 0.66634†	=	466,438
Present value of the note			$666,633

*Present value of an ordinary annuity of $1: $n = 6$, $i = 7\%$.
†Present value of $1: $n = 6$, $i = 7\%$.

This is referred to as the **implicit rate of interest**—the rate implicit in the agreement. It may be that the implicit rate is not apparent. Sometimes the value of the asset (or service) is not readily determinable, but the interest rate stated in the transaction is unrealistic relative to the rate that would be expected in a similar transaction under similar circumstances. Deciding what the appropriate rate should be is called *imputing* an interest rate.

A basic concept of accounting is *substance over form.*

For example, suppose the machine exchanged for the 12% note is custom-made for Skill Graphics so that no customary cash price is available with which to work backwards to find the implicit rate. In that case, the appropriate rate would have to be found externally. It might be determined, for instance, that a more realistic interest rate for a transaction of this type, at this time, would be 14%. Then it would be apparent that Skill Graphics actually paid less than $700,000 for the machine and that part of the face amount of the note in effect makes up for the lower than normal interest rate. You learned early in your study of accounting that the economic essence of a transaction should prevail over its outward appearance. In keeping with this basic precept, the accountant should look beyond the *form* of this transaction and record its *substance.* The amount actually paid for the machine is the present value of the cash flows called for by the loan agreement, discounted at the market rate—imputed in

ADDITIONAL CONSIDERATION

For another example, let's assume the more realistic interest rate for a transaction of this type is, say, 16%. In that case we would calculate the real cost of the machine by finding the present value of both the interest and the principal, discounted at half the 16% rate:

			Present Values
Interest	$ 42,000 × 4.62288*	=	$194,161
Principal	$700,000 × 0.63017†	=	441,119
Present value of the note			$635,280

*Present value of an ordinary annuity of $1: $n = 6$, $i = 8\%$.
†Present value of $1: $n = 6$, $i = 8\%$.

Both the asset acquired and the liability used to purchase it would be recorded at $635,280.

[9]If the debt instrument is negotiable and a dependable exchange price is readily available, the market value of the debt may be better evidence of the value of the transaction than the value of a noncash asset, particularly if it has no established cash selling price. The value of the asset or the debt, whichever is considered more reliable, should be used to record the transaction (*APB 21*).

this case to be 14%. So both the asset acquired and the liability used to purchase it should be recorded at the real cost, $666,633.

The accounting treatment is the same whether the amount is determined directly from the market value of the machine (and thus the note) or indirectly as the present value of the note (and thus the value of the asset):[10]

Ref 707.

Journal Entries at Issuance—Note with Unrealistic Interest Rate

Skill Graphics (Buyer/Issuer)		
Machinery (cash price)	666,633	
Discount on note payable (difference)	33,367	
Notes payable (face amount)		700,000
Hughes–Barker (Seller/Lender)		
Notes receivable (face amount)	700,000	
Discount on note payable (difference)		33,367
Sales revenue (cash price)		666,633

Likewise, whether the effective interest rate is determined as the rate implicit in the agreement, given the asset's market value, or whether the effective rate is imputed as the appropriate interest rate if the asset's value is unknown, both parties to the transaction should record periodic interest (interest expense to the borrower, interest revenue to the lender) at the effective rate, rather than the stated rate.

Ref Page 708

Journal Entries—The Interest Method

The effective interest (expense to the issuer; revenue to the investor) is calculated each period as the effective rate times the amount of the debt outstanding during the interest period.

At the first Interest Date (June 30)		
Skill Graphics (Borrower)		
Interest expense (effective rate × outstanding balance)	46,664	
Discount on notes payable (difference)		4,664
Cash (stated rate × face amount)		42,000
Hughes–Barker (Seller/Lender)		
Cash (stated rate × face amount)	42,000	
Discount on notes receivable (difference)	4,664	
Interest revenue (effective rate × outstanding balance)		46,664

The interest expense (interest revenue for the lender) varies as the balance of the note changes over time. See the amortization schedule in Graphic 14–10 on the next page.[11]

Installment Notes

You may have recently purchased a car, or maybe a house. If so, unless you paid cash, you signed a note promising to pay the purchase price over, say, four years for the car, or 30 years for the house. Car and house notes usually call for payment in monthly installments rather than by a single amount at maturity. Corporations, too, often borrow using installment notes. Typically, installment payments are equal amounts each period. Each payment includes both an amount that represents interest and an amount that represents a reduction of the outstanding balance (principal reduction). The periodic reduction of the balance is sufficient that at maturity the note is completely paid. This amount is easily calculated by

[10]The method shown is the *gross method*. Alternatively, the *net method* can be used as follows:

Skill Graphics (Buyer/Issuer)		
Machinery (cash price)	666,633	
Notes payable (face amount)		666,633
Hughes–Barker (Seller/Lender)		
Notes receivable (face amount)	666,633	
Sales revenue (cash price)		666,633

Under the gross method the note is recorded at the face amount and a contra account, called *discount on note payable,* is recorded for the difference between face value and present value. This discount represents the interest to be recognized over the term of the loan. As payments are made, the note is reduced by the full amount of the payment. Interest revenue (and interest expense) are recognized by a reduction in the discount on note and a credit to interest revenue (debit to interest expense). After the last payment, the discount and note accounts both will be zero. Over the term of the note, the note is shown net of the discount in the balance sheet.

[11]The creation of amortization schedules is simplified by an electronic spreadsheet such as Microsoft Excel.

GRAPHIC 14–10
Amortization Schedule—Note

Since less cash is paid each period than the effective interest, the unpaid difference (the discount reduction) increases the outstanding balance of the debt.

Date	Cash Interest	Effective Interest	Increase in Balance	Outstanding Balance
	(6% × Face amount)	(7% × Outstanding balance)	(Discount reduction)	
1/1/09				666,633
6/30/09	42,000	.07 (666,633) = 46,664	4,664	671,297
12/31/09	42,000	.07 (671,297) = 46,991	4,991	676,288
6/30/10	42,000	.07 (676,288) = 47,340	5,340	681,628
12/31/10	42,000	.07 (681,628) = 47,714	5,714	687,342
6/30/11	42,000	.07 (687,342) = 48,114	6,114	693,456
12/31/11	42,000	.07 (693,456) = 48,544*	6,544	700,000
	252,000	285,367	33,367	

*Rounded.

dividing the amount of the loan by the appropriate discount factor for the present value of an annuity. The installment payment amount that would pay the note above is:

$666,633	÷	4.76654	=	$139,857
Amount of loan		(from Table 4 $n = 6, i = 7.0\%$)		Installment payment

Consider Graphic 14–11.

GRAPHIC 14–11
Amortization Schedule—Installment Note

Each installment payment includes interest on the outstanding debt at the effective rate. The remainder of each payment reduces the outstanding balance.

Date	Cash Payment	Effective Interest	Decrease in Debt	Outstanding Balance
		(7% × Outstanding balance)		
1/1/09				666,633
6/30/09	139,857	.07 (666,633) = 46,664	93,193	573,440
12/31/09	139,857	.07 (573,440) = 40,141	99,716	473,724
6/30/10	139,857	.07 (473,724) = 33,161	106,696	367,028
12/31/10	139,857	.07 (367,028) = 25,692	114,165	252,863
6/30/11	139,857	.07 (252,863) = 17,700	122,157	130,706
12/31/11	139,857	.07 (130,706) = 9,151*	130,706	0
	839,142	172,509	666,633	

*Rounded.

The procedure is the same as for a note whose principal is paid at maturity, but the periodic cash payments are larger and there is no lump-sum payment at maturity. We calculated the amount of the payments so that after covering the interest on the existing debt each period, the excess would exactly amortize the debt to zero at maturity (rather than to a designated maturity amount).

For installment notes, the outstanding balance of the note does not eventually become its face amount as it does for notes with designated maturity amounts. Instead, at the maturity date the balance is zero. Consequently, the significance is lost of maintaining separate balances for the face amount (in a note account) and the discount (or premium). So an installment note typically is recorded at its net carrying amount in a single note payable (or receivable) account:

Journal Entries at Issuance—Installment Note

Skill Graphics (Buyer/Issuer)		
Machinery	666,633	
Note payable		666,633
Hughes–Barker (Seller/Lender)		
Note receivable	666,633	
Sale revenue		666,633

Each payment includes both an amount that represents interest and an amount that represents a reduction of principal.

At the first Interest Date (June 30)		
Skill Graphics (Borrower)		
Interest expense (effective rate × outstanding balance)	46,664	
Note payable (difference)	93,193	
Cash (installment payment calculated above)		139,857
Hughes–Barker (Seller/Lender)		
Cash (installment payment calculated above)	139,857	
Note receivable (difference)		93,193
Interest revenue (effective rate × outstanding balance)		46,664

ADDITIONAL CONSIDERATION

You will learn in the next chapter that the liability associated with a capital lease is accounted for the same way as this installment note. In fact, if the asset described above had been leased rather than purchased, the cash payments would be designated lease payments rather than installment loan payments, and a virtually identical amortization schedule would apply.

The reason for the similarity is that we view a capital lease as being, in substance, equivalent to an installment purchase/sale. Naturally, then, accounting treatment of the two essentially identical transactions should be consistent. Be sure to notice the parallel treatment as you study leases in the next chapter.

Financial Statement Disclosures

● LO5

In the balance sheet, long-term debt (liability for the debtor; asset for the creditor) typically is reported as a single amount, net of any discount or increased by any premium, rather than at its face amount accompanied by a separate valuation account for the discount or premium. Any portion of the debt to be paid (received) during the upcoming year, or operating cycle if longer, should be reported as a current amount.

Supplemental disclosure is required of the fair value of bonds, notes, and other financial instruments.

The fair value of financial instruments must be disclosed either in the body of the financial statements or in disclosure notes.[12] These fair values are available for bonds and other securities traded on market exchanges in the form of quoted market prices. On the other hand, financial instruments not traded on market exchanges require other evidence of market value. For example, the market value of a note payable might be approximated by the present value of principal and interest payments using a current discount rate commensurate with the risks involved.

For all long-term borrowings, disclosures also should include the aggregate amounts maturing and sinking fund requirements (if any) for each of the next five years.[13] To comply, **Procter & Gamble**'s 2007 annual report stated:

Real World Financials

The fair value and scheduled amounts should be disclosed for the next five years.

($ in millions)

The fair value of the long-term debt was $23,122 and $36,027 June 30, 2007 and 2006, respectively. Long-term debt maturities during the next five years are as follows:

2008—$2,544; 2009—$5,751; 2010—$1,982; 2011—$1,877 and 2012—$67.

[12] "Disclosures About Fair Values of Financial Instruments," *Statement of Financial Accounting Standards No. 107* (Norwalk, Conn.: FASB, 1991).

[13] "Disclosure of Long-Term Obligations," *Statement of Financial Accounting Standards No. 47* (Stamford, Conn.: FASB, 1981), par. 10b.

Borrowing is a financing activity; lending is an investing activity.

Paying or receiving interest is an operating activity.

In a statement of cash flows, issuing bonds or notes are reported as cash flows from financing activities by the issuer (borrower) and cash flows from investing activities by the investor (lender). Similarly, when the debt is repaid, the issuer (borrower) reports the cash outflow as a financing activity while the investor (lender) reports it as a cash inflow from investing activities. However, because both interest expense and interest revenue are components of the income statement, both parties to the transaction report cash payments for interest among operating activities.

DECISION MAKERS' PERSPECTIVE

Business decisions involve risk. Failure to properly consider risk in those decisions is one of the most costly, yet one of the most common mistakes investors and creditors can make. Long-term debt is one of the first places decision makers should look when trying to get a handle on risk.

Generally speaking, debt increases risk.

To evaluate a firm's risk, you might start by calculating its debt to equity ratio.

In general, debt increases risk. As an owner, debt would place you in a subordinate position relative to creditors because the claims of creditors must be satisfied first in case of liquidation. In addition, debt requires payment, usually on specific dates. Failure to pay debt interest and principal on a timely basis may result in default and perhaps even bankruptcy. The debt to equity ratio, total liabilities/shareholders' equity, often is calculated to measure the degree of risk. Other things being equal, the higher the debt to equity ratio, the higher the risk. The type of risk this ratio measures is called *default risk* because it presumably indicates the likelihood a company will default on its obligations.

As a manager, you would try to create favorable financial leverage to earn a return on borrowed funds in excess of the cost of borrowing the funds.

Debt also can be an advantage. It can be used to enhance the return to shareholders. This concept, known as leverage, was described and illustrated in Chapter 3. If a company earns a return on borrowed funds in excess of the cost of borrowing the funds, shareholders are provided with a total return greater than what could have been earned with equity funds alone. This desirable situation is called *favorable financial leverage.* Unfortunately, leverage is not always favorable. Sometimes the cost of borrowing the funds exceeds the returns they generate. This illustrates the typical risk-return trade-off faced by shareholders.

As an external analyst or a manager, you are concerned with a company's ability to repay debt.

Creditors demand interest payments as compensation for the use of their capital. Failure to pay interest as scheduled may cause several adverse consequences, including bankruptcy. Therefore, another way to measure a company's ability to pay its obligations is by comparing interest payments with income available to pay those charges. The times interest earned ratio does this by dividing income before subtracting interest expense or income tax expense by interest expense.

Two points about this ratio are important. First, because interest is deductible for income tax purposes, income before interest and taxes is a better indication of a company's ability to pay interest than is income after interest and taxes (i.e., net income). Second, income before interest and taxes is a rough approximation for cash flow generated from operations. The primary concern of decision makers is, of course, the cash available to make interest payments. In fact, this ratio often is computed by dividing cash flow generated from operations by interest payments.

For illustration, let's compare the ratios for **Coca-Cola** and **PepsiCo**. Graphic 14–12 on the next page provides condensed financial statements adapted from 2006 annual reports of those companies.

The debt to equity ratio indicates the extent of trading on the equity, or financial leverage.

The debt to equity ratio is higher for PepsiCo:

$$\text{Debt to equity ratio} = \frac{\text{Total liabilities}}{\text{Shareholders' equity}}$$

$$\text{Coca-cola} = \frac{\$13,043}{\$16,920} = .77$$

$$\text{PepsiCo} = \frac{\$14,562}{\$15,368} = .95$$

Remember, that's not necessarily a positive or a negative. Let's look closer. When the return on shareholders' equity is greater than the return on assets, management is using debt

GRAPHIC 14–12
Condensed Financial Statements—Coca-Cola, PepsiCo

Real World Financials

Balance Sheets	($ in millions)	
	Coca-Cola	**PepsiCo**
Assets		
Current assets	$ 8,441	$ 9,130
Property, plant, and equipment (net)	6,903	9,687
Intangibles and other assets	14,619	11,113
Total assets	$29,963	$29,930
Liabilities and Shareholders' Equity		
Current liabilities	$ 8,890	$ 6,860
Long-term liabilities	4,153	7,702
Total liabilities	$13,043	$14,562
Shareholders' equity	16,920	15,368
Total liabilities and shareholders' equity	$29,963	$29,930
Income Statements		
Net sales	$24,088	$35,137
Cost of goods sold	(8,164)	(15,762)
Gross profit	$15,924	$19,375
Operating and other expenses	(9,126)	(12,147)
Interest expense	(220)	(239)
Income before taxes	$ 6,578	$ 6,989
Tax expense	(1,498)	(1,347)
Net income	$ 5,080	$ 5,642

funds to enhance the earnings for shareholders. Both firms do this. We calculate return on assets as follows:

The rate of return on assets indicates profitability without regard to how resources are financed.

$$\text{Rate of return on assets} = \frac{\text{Net income}}{\text{Total assets}}$$

$$\text{Coca-Cola} = \frac{\$5,080}{\$29,963} = 17.0\%$$

$$\text{PepsiCo} = \frac{\$5,642}{\$29,930} = 18.9\%$$

The return on assets indicates a company's overall profitability, ignoring specific sources of financing. In this regard, PepsiCo's profitability exceeds that of Coca-Cola by about 11% ([18.9 − 17.0]/17.0). That advantage is even greater when we compare the return to shareholders:

The rate of return on shareholders' equity indicates the effectiveness of employing resources provided by owners.

$$\text{Rate of return on shareholders' equity} = \frac{\text{Net income}}{\text{Shareholders' equity}}$$

$$\text{Coca-Cola} = \frac{\$5,080}{\$16,920} = 30.0\%$$

$$\text{PepsiCo} = \frac{\$5,642}{\$15,368} = 36.7\%$$

PepsiCo's higher leverage has been used to provide a return to shareholders roughly 22% higher than Coca-Cola's. PepsiCo increased its return to shareholders 1.94 times (36.7%/18.9%) the return on assets. Coca-Cola increased its return to shareholders 1.76 times (30%/17%) the return on assets. Interpret this with caution, though. First, the difference is small. Second, PepsiCo's higher leverage means higher risk as well. In down times, PepsiCo's return to shareholders will suffer proportionally more than will Coca-Cola's.

From the perspective of a creditor, we might look at which company offers the most comfortable margin of safety in terms of its ability to pay fixed interest charges:

The times interest earned ratio indicates the margin of safety provided to creditors.

$$\text{Times interest earned ratio} = \frac{\text{Net income plus interest plus taxes}}{\text{Interest}}$$

$$\text{Coca-Cola} = \frac{\$5{,}080 + 220 + 1{,}498}{\$220} = 30.9 \text{ times}$$

$$\text{PepsiCo} = \frac{\$5{,}642 + 239 + 1{,}347}{\$239} = 30.2 \text{ times}$$

In this regard, both firms provide an adequate margin of safety. The interest coverage ratios seem to indicate an ample safety cushion for creditors, particularly when considered in conjunction with their debt-equity ratios.

Decision makers should be alert to gains and losses that have nothing to do with a company's normal operating activities.

Liabilities also can have misleading effects on the income statement. Decision makers should look carefully at gains and losses produced by early extinguishment of debt. These have nothing to do with a company's normal operating activities. Unchecked, corporate management can be tempted to schedule debt buybacks to provide discretionary income in down years or even losses in up years to smooth income over time.

Outside analysts as well as managers should actively monitor risk management activities.

Alert investors and lenders also look outside the financial statements for risks associated with "off-balance-sheet" financing and other commitments that don't show up on the face of financial statements but nevertheless expose a company to risk. Relatedly, most companies attempt to actively manage the risk associated with these and other obligations. It is important for top management to understand and closely monitor risk management strategies. Some of the financial losses that have grabbed headlines in recent years, were permitted by a lack of oversight and scrutiny by senior management of companies involved. It is similarly important for investors and creditors to become informed about risks companies face and how well-equipped those companies are in managing that risk. The supplemental disclosures designed to communicate the degree of risk associated with the financial instruments we discuss in this chapter contribute to that understanding. We examine the significance of lease commitments in the next chapter.

INTERNATIONAL FINANCIAL REPORTING STANDARDS

Capital markets are operating more and more as a global marketplace. Firms competing for international resources, such as debt funding, include domestic corporations, multinational corporations, as well as foreign corporations and joint ventures. This poses several problems for lenders and other resource providers attempting to evaluate alternatives across international boundaries.

One persistent problem is the lack of uniformity in accounting standards used to produce the financial statements being compared. The gap has narrowed in recent years, but analysts must be aware of differences in accounting methods from country to country. Other considerations are being familiar with the accounting consequences of translating results from abroad into dollars, institutional, political, cultural, and tax differences, and identifying appropriate international industry standards for comparison.

CONCEPT REVIEW EXERCISE

NOTE WITH AN UNREALISTIC INTEREST RATE

Cameron-Brown, Inc., constructed for Harmon Distributors a warehouse that was completed and ready for occupancy on January 2, 2009. Harmon paid for the warehouse by issuing a $900,000, four-year note that required 7% interest to be paid on December 31 of each year. The warehouse was custom-built for Harmon, so its cash price was not known. By comparison with similar transactions, it was determined that an appropriate interest rate was 10%.

Required:

1. Prepare the journal entry for Harmon's purchase of the warehouse on January 2, 2009.
2. Prepare (a) an amortization schedule for the four-year term of the note and (b) the journal entry for Harmon's first interest payment on December 31, 2009.
3. Suppose Harmon's note had been an installment note to be paid in four equal payments. What would be the amount of each installment if payable (a) at the end of each year, beginning December 31, 2009? or (b) at the beginning of each year, beginning on January 2, 2009?

SOLUTION

1. Prepare the journal entry for Harmon's purchase of the warehouse on January 2, 2009.

	Present Values
Interest	$ 63,000 × 3.16987* = $199,702
Principal	$900,000 × 0.68301† = 614,709
Present value of the note	$814,411

*Present value of an ordinary annuity of $1: $n = 4$, $i = 10\%$.
†Present value of $1: $n = 4$, $i = 10\%$.

Warehouse (price determined above)	814,411	
Discount on notes payable (difference)	85,589	
Notes payable (face amount)		900,000

2. Prepare (a) an amortization schedule for the four-year term of the note and (b) the journal entry for Harmon's first interest payment on December 31, 2009.

a.

Dec. 31	Cash Interest	Effective Interest	Increase in Balance	Outstanding Balance
	(7% × Face amount)	(10% × Outstanding balance)	(Discount reduction)	
				814,411
2009	63,000	.10 (814,411) = 81,441	18,441	832,852
2010	63,000	.10 (832,852) = 83,285	20,285	853,137
2011	63,000	.10 (853,137) = 85,314	22,314	875,451
2012	63,000	.10 (875,451) = 87,549*	24,549	900,000
	252,000	337,589	85,589	

*Rounded.

Each period the unpaid interest increases the outstanding balance of the debt.

b.

Interest expense (effective rate × outstanding balance)	81,441	
Discount on notes payable (difference)		18,441
Cash (stated rate × face amount)		63,000

The effective interest is the market rate times the amount of the debt outstanding during the year.

3. Suppose Harmon's note had been an installment note to be paid in four equal payments. What would be the amount of each installment if payable (a) at the end of each year, beginning December 31, 2009? or (b) at the beginning of each year, beginning on January 2, 2009?

a. $814,411 Amount of loan ÷ 3.16987 (from Table 4 $n = 4$, $i = 10\%$) = $256,923 Installment payment

b. $814,411 Amount of loan ÷ 3.48685 (from Table 6 $n = 4$, $i = 10\%$) = $233,566 Installment payment

Because money has a time value, installment payments delayed until the end of each period must be higher than if the payments are made at the beginning of each period.

PART C DEBT RETIRED EARLY, CONVERTIBLE INTO STOCK, OR PROVIDING AN OPTION TO BUY STOCK

Early Extinguishment of Debt

● LO6

As the previous illustration demonstrated, debt paid in installments is systematically retired over the term to maturity so that at the designated maturity date the outstanding balance is zero. When a maturity amount is specified as in our earlier illustrations, any discount or premium has been systematically reduced to zero as of the maturity date and the debt is retired simply by paying the maturity amount. However, a gain or a loss may result when debt is retired before its scheduled maturity.

Earlier we noted that a call feature accompanies most bonds to protect the issuer against declining interest rates. Even when bonds are not callable, the issuing company can retire bonds early by purchasing them on the open market. Regardless of the method, when debt of any type is retired prior to its scheduled maturity date, the transaction is referred to as **early extinguishment of debt.**

Any difference between the outstanding debt and the amount paid to retire that debt represents either a gain or a loss.

To record the extinguishment, the account balances pertinent to the debt obviously must be removed from the books. Of course cash is credited for the amount paid—the call price or market price. The difference between the carrying amount of the debt and the reacquisition price represents either a gain or a loss on the early extinguishment of debt. Let's continue an earlier example to illustrate the retirement of debt prior to its scheduled maturity (Illustration 14–5):

ILLUSTRATION 14–5
Early Extinguishment of Debt

On January 1, 2010, Masterwear Industries called its $700,000, 12% bonds when their carrying amount was $676,288. The indenture specified a call price of $685,000. The bonds were issued previously at a price to yield 14%.

Bonds payable (face amount)	700,000	
Loss on early extinguishment[14] ($685,000 – 676,288)	8,712	
Discount on bonds payable ($700,000 – 676,288)		23,712
Cash (call price)		685,000

Convertible Bonds

FINANCIAL Reporting Case

Q5, p. 703

Convertible bonds can be exchanged for shares of stock at the option of the investor.

Convertible bonds have features of both debt and equity.

Sometimes corporations include a convertible feature as part of a bond offering. **Convertible bonds** can be converted into (that is, exchanged for) shares of stock at the option of the bondholder. Among the reasons for issuing convertible bonds rather than straight debt are (a) to sell the bonds at a higher price (which means a lower effective interest cost),[15] (b) to use as a medium of exchange in mergers and acquisitions, and (c) to enable smaller firms or debt-heavy companies to obtain access to the bond market. Sometimes convertible bonds serve as an indirect way to issue stock when there is shareholder resistance to direct issuance of additional equity.

Central to each of these reasons for issuing convertible debt is that the conversion feature is attractive to investors. This hybrid security has features of both debt and equity. The owner has a fixed-income security that can become common stock if and when the firm's prosperity makes that feasible. This increases the investor's upside potential while limiting the downside risk. The conversion feature has monetary value. Just how valuable it is depends on both the conversion terms and market conditions. But from an accounting perspective the question raised is how to account for its value. To evaluate the question, consider Illustration 14–6.

It would appear that the conversion feature is valued by the market at $5 million—the difference between the market value of the convertible bonds, $103 million, and the market value

[14]For several years the FASB required companies to report gains and losses from early extinguishment of debt as extraordinary items, but no longer. Now, these gains and losses are subject to the same criteria as other gains and losses for such treatment; namely, that they be both (a) unusual and (b) infrequent. *Statement of Financial Accounting Standards No. 145,* "Rescission of FASB Statements No. 4, 44, and 64, Amendment of FASB Statement No. 13, and Technical Corrections" (Norwalk, Conn.: FASB, 2002).

[15]Remember, there is an inverse relationship between bond prices and interest rates. When the price is higher, the rate (yield) is lower, and vice versa.

ILLUSTRATION 14–6
Convertible Bonds

On January 1, 2009, HTL Manufacturers issued $100 million of 8% convertible debentures due 2019 at 103 (103% of face value). The bonds are convertible at the option of the holder into $1 par common stock at a conversion ratio of 40 shares per $1,000 bond. HTL recently issued nonconvertible, 20-year, 8% debentures at 98.

of the nonconvertible bonds, $98 million. Some accountants argue that we should record the value of the conversion option in a shareholders' equity account ($5 million in this case) and the debt value in the bond accounts ($100 million bonds payable less $2 million discount). In fact, *SFAS 150* indicates that convertible securities and similar securities will be dealt with in phase 2 of the FASB's project on hybrid securities.[16] In the meantime, the currently accepted practice is to record the entire issue price as debt in precisely the same way as for nonconvertible bonds.[17] Treating the features as two inseparable parts of a single security avoids the practical difficulty of trying to measure the separate values of the debt and the conversion option. We sidestepped this difficulty in our illustration by assuming that HTL had recently issued nonconvertible bonds that were otherwise similar to the convertible bonds.

Because of the inseparability of their debt and equity features, the entire issue price of convertible bonds is recorded as debt, as if they are nonconvertible bonds.

Journal Entry at Issuance—Convertible Bonds

	($ in millions)	
Cash (103% × $100 million)	103	
Convertible bonds payable (face amount)		100
Premium on bonds payable (difference)		3

The value of the conversion feature is not separately recorded.

Since we make no provision for the separate value of the conversion option, all subsequent entries, including the periodic reduction of the premium, are exactly the same as if these were nonconvertible bonds. So the illustrations and examples of bond accounting we discussed earlier would pertain equally to nonconvertible or convertible bonds.

SFAS 150 did address accounting for "freestanding" hybrid securities. It requires that stock or other financial instruments that a company is obligated to buy back (manditorily redeemable) must be reported in the balance sheet as a liability, not as shareholders' equity.

INTERNATIONAL FINANCIAL REPORTING STANDARDS

Convertible bonds. Under IFRS, convertible debt is divided into its liability and equity elements. Under U.S. GAAP, the entire issue price is recorded as a liability.

When the Conversion Option is Exercised

If and when the bondholder exercises his or her option to convert the bonds into shares of stock, the bonds are removed from the accounting records and the new shares issued are recorded at the same amount (in other words, at the book value of the bonds). To illustrate, assume that half the convertible bonds issued by HTL Manufacturers are converted at a time when the remaining unamortized premium is $2 million:

Journal Entry at Conversion

	($ in millions)	
Convertible bonds payable (½ the account balance)	50	
Premium on bonds payable (½ the account balance)	1	
Common stock [(50,000 bonds × 40 shares) × $1 par]		2
Paid-in capital—excess of par (to balance)		49

The 2 million shares issued are recorded at the $51 million book value of the bonds retired.

[16]"Accounting for Certain Financial Instruments with Characteristics of Both Liabilities and Equity," *Statement of Financial Accounting Standards No. 150* (Norwalk, Conn.: FASB, 2003).

[17]"Accounting for Convertible Debt and Debt Issued with Stock Purchase Warrants," *Accounting Principles Board Opinion No. 14* (New York: APB, 1969).

ADDITIONAL CONSIDERATION

The method just described is referred to as the *book value method,* since the new shares are recorded at the book value of the bonds being redeemed. It is by far the most popular method in practice. Another acceptable approach, the *market value method,* records the new shares at the market value of the shares themselves or of the bonds, whichever is more determinable. Because the market value most likely will differ from the book value of the bonds, a gain or loss on conversion will result. Assume for illustration that the market value of HTL's stock is $30 per share at the time of the conversion:

	($ in millions)	
Convertible bonds payable (1/2 the account balance)	50	
Premium on bonds payable (1/2 the account balance)	1	
Loss on conversion of bonds (to balance)	9	
Common stock [(50,000 bonds × 40 shares) × $1 par]		2
Paid-in capital in excess of par [(50,000 × 40 shares) × $29]		58

If a single investor had purchased the 50,000 bonds being converted, that company would record the conversion as follows:

	($ in millions)	
Investment in common stock	51	
Investment in convertible bonds (account balance)		50
Premium on bond investment (account balance)		1

Induced Conversion

Investors often are reluctant to convert bonds to stock, even when share prices have risen significantly since the convertible bonds were purchased. This is because the market price of the convertible bonds will rise along with market prices of the stock. So companies sometimes try to induce conversion. The motivation might be to reduce debt and become a better risk to potential lenders or achieve a lower debt-to-equity ratio.

One way is through the call provision. As we noted earlier, most corporate bonds are callable by the issuing corporation. When the specified call price is less than the conversion value of the bonds (the market value of the shares), calling the convertible bonds provides bondholders with incentive to convert. Bondholders will choose the shares rather than the lower call price.

Any additional consideration provided to induce conversion of convertible debt is recorded as an expense of the period.

Occasionally, corporations may try to encourage voluntary conversion by offering an added inducement in the form of cash, stock warrants, or a more attractive conversion ratio. When additional consideration is provided to induce conversion, the fair value of that consideration is considered an expense incurred to bring about the conversion.[18]

Bonds with Detachable Warrants

Another (less common) way to sweeten a bond issue is to include **detachable stock purchase warrants** as part of the security issue. A stock warrant gives the investor an option to purchase a stated number of shares of common stock at a specified *option price,* often within a given period of time. Like a conversion feature, warrants usually mean a lower interest rate and often enable a company to issue debt when borrowing would not be feasible otherwise.

The issue price of bonds with detachable warrants is allocated between the two different securities on the basis of their market values.

However, unlike the conversion feature for convertible bonds, warrants can be separated from the bonds. This means they can be exercised independently or traded in the market separately from bonds, having their own market price. In essence, two different securities—the bonds and the warrants—are sold as a package for a single issue price. Accordingly, the issue price is allocated between the two different securities on the basis of their market values. If the independent market value of only one of the two securities is reliably determinable, that value establishes the allocation. This is demonstrated in Illustration 14–7.

[18]"Induced Conversions of Convertible Debt," *Statement of Financial Accounting Standards No. 84* (Stamford, Conn.: FASB, 1985).

ILLUSTRATION 14–7
Bonds with Detachable Warrants

On January 1, 2009, HTL Manufacturers issued $100 million of 8% debentures due 2016 at 103 (103% of face value). Accompanying each $1,000 bond were 20 warrants. Each warrant permitted the holder to buy one share of $1 par common stock at $25 per share. Shortly after issuance, the warrants were listed on the stock exchange at $3 per warrant.

	($ in millions)	
Cash (103% × $100 million)	103	
Discount on bonds payable (difference)	3	
Bonds payable (face amount)		100
Paid-in capital—stock warrants outstanding* (100,000 bonds × 20 warrants × $3)		6

*Reported as part of shareholders' equity rather than as a liability.

ADDITIONAL CONSIDERATION

Market imperfections may cause the separate market values not to sum to the issue price of the package. In this event, allocation is achieved on the basis of the relative market values of the two securities. Let's say the bonds have a separate market price of $940 per bond (priced at 94):

Market Values	Dollars	Percent
Bonds (100,000 bonds × $940)	$ 94	94%
Warrants (100,000 bonds × 20 warrants × $3)	6	6
Total	$100	100%

Proportion of Issue Price Allocated to Bonds:

$103 million × 94% = $96,820,000

Proportion of Issue Price Allocated to Warrants:

$103 million × 6% = $6,180,000

	($ in millions)	
Cash (103% × $100 million)	103.00	
Discount on bonds payable ($100 million – $96.82 million)	3.18	
Bonds payable (face amount)		100.00
Paid-in capital—stock warrants outstanding		6.18

Notice that this is the same approach we used in Chapter 10 to allocate a single purchase price to two or more assets bought for that single price. We also will allocate the total selling price of two equity securities sold for a single issue in proportion to their relative market values in Chapter 18.

If one-half of the warrants (1 million) in Illustration 14–7 are exercised when the market value of HTL's common stock is $30 per share, 1 million shares would be issued for one warrant each plus the exercise price of $25 per share.

Journal Entry at Exercise of Detachable Warrants

	($ in millions)	
Cash (1,000,000 warrants × $25)	25	
Paid-in capital—stock warrants outstanding (1,000,000 warrants × $3)	3	
Common stock (1,000,000 shares × $1 par per share)		1
Paid-in capital—excess of par (to balance)		27

The $30 market value at the date of exercise is not used in valuing the additional shares issued. The new shares are recorded at the total of the previously measured values of both the warrants and the shares.

CONCEPT REVIEW EXERCISE

ISSUANCE AND EARLY EXTINGUISHMENT OF DEBT

The disclosure notes to the 2009 financial statements of Olswanger Industries included the following:

Note 12: Bonds

On October 3, 2008, the Corporation sold bonds with an aggregate principal amount of $500,000,000 bearing a 14% interest rate. The bonds will mature on September 15, 2018 and are unsecured subordinated obligations of the Corporation. Interest is payable semiannually on March 15 and September 15. The Corporation may redeem the bonds at any time beginning September 15, 2008, as a whole or from time to time in part, through maturity, at specified redemption prices ranging from 112% of principal in declining percentages of principal amount through 2015 when the percentage is set at 100% of principal amount. The cost of issuing the bonds, totaling $11,000,000, and the discount of $5,000,000 are being amortized over the life of the bonds, using the straight-line method and the interest method, respectively. Amortization of these items for the year ended December 31, 2009, was $960,000 and $252,000, respectively.

During the year ended December 31, 2009, the Corporation repurchased, in open market transactions, $200,000,000 in face amount of the bonds for $224,000,000, including accrued interest. The unamortized cost of issuing these bonds and the unamortized discount, $3,972,000 and $1,892,000, respectively, have been deducted in the current period.

From the information provided by Olswanger in Note 12, you should be able to recreate some of the journal entries the company recorded in connection with this bond issue.

Required:

1. Prepare the journal entry for the issuance of these bonds on October 3, 2008. (Be sure to include accrued interest for the half-month period between September 15 and October 3.)
2. Prepare the journal entry for the repurchase of these bonds, assuming the date of repurchase was November 15, 2009. The accrued interest for the two-month period between September 15 and November 15 would be $200,000,000 × 14% × 2/12 = $4,667,000 (rounded). Assume the entry to accrue interest was recorded separately, so the cash paid to repurchase the bonds was $219,333,000 [$224,000,000 (amount given) − $4,667,000].

SOLUTION

1. Prepare the journal entry for the issuance of these bonds on October 3, 2008.

	($ in 000s)	
Cash (to balance)	486,916	
Bond issue costs (given in note)	11,000	
Discount on bonds payable (given in note)	5,000	
Bonds payable (face amount—given in note)		500,000
Interest payable (accrued interest—see below*)		2,916

*Accrued interest: $500,000 × 14% × 0.5/12 = $2,916

2. Prepare the journal entry for the repurchase of these bonds, assuming the date of repurchase was November 15, 2009.

	($ in 000s)	
Bonds payable (face amount repurchased)	200,000	
Loss on early extinguishment (to balance)	25,197	
Discount on bonds payable (given in note)		1,892
Bond issue costs (given in note)		3,972
Cash (given in requirement 2)		219,333

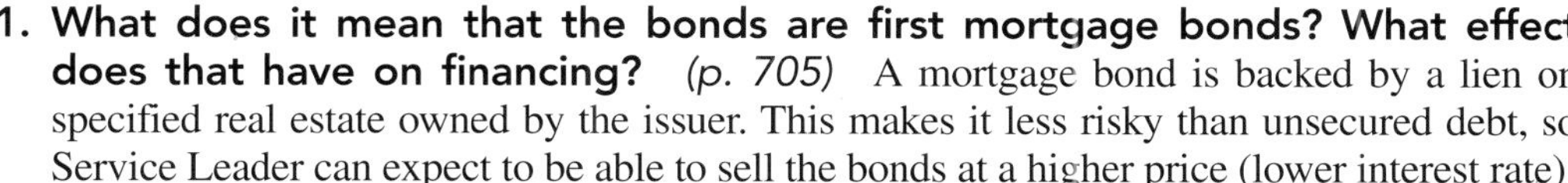

FINANCIAL REPORTING CASE SOLUTION

1. **What does it mean that the bonds are first mortgage bonds? What effect does that have on financing?** *(p. 705)* A mortgage bond is backed by a lien on specified real estate owned by the issuer. This makes it less risky than unsecured debt, so Service Leader can expect to be able to sell the bonds at a higher price (lower interest rate).
2. **From Service Leader's perspective, why are the bonds callable? What does that mean?** *(p. 705)* The call feature gives Service Leader some protection against being stuck with relatively high-cost debt in case interest rates fall during the 15 years to maturity. Service Leader can buy back, or call, the bonds from bondholders before the 15-year maturity date, after June 30, 2008. The call price is prespecified at 103 percent of the face value—$1,030 per $1,000 bond.
3. **How will it be possible to sell bonds paying investors 6.25% when other, similar investments will provide the investors a return of 6.5%?** *(p. 706)* Service Leader will be able to sell its 6.25% bonds in a 6.5% market only by selling them at a discounted price, below face amount. Bonds are priced by the marketplace to yield the market rate of interest for securities of similar risk and maturity. The price will be the present value of all the periodic cash interest payments (face amount × stated rate) plus the present value of the principal payable at maturity, both discounted at the market rate.
4. **Would accounting differ if the debt were designated as notes rather than bonds?** *(p. 719)* No. Other things being equal, whether they're called bonds, notes, or some other form of debt, the same accounting principles apply. They will be recorded at present value and interest will be recorded at the market rate over the term to maturity.
5. **Why might the company choose to make the bonds convertible into common stock?** *(p. 728)* Convertible bonds can be converted at the option of the bondholders into shares of stock. Sometimes the motivation for issuing convertible bonds rather than straight debt is to use the bonds as a medium of exchange in mergers and acquisitions, as a way for smaller firms or debt-heavy companies to obtain access to the bond market, or as an indirect way to issue stock when there is shareholder resistance to direct issuance of additional equity. None of these seems pertinent to Service Leader. The most likely reason is to sell at a higher price. The conversion feature is attractive to investors. Investors have a fixed-income security that can become common stock if circumstances make that attractive. The investor has additional possibilities for higher returns, with downside risk limited by the underlying debt. ●

THE BOTTOM LINE

- **LO1** A liability requires the future payment of cash in specified amounts at specified dates. As time passes, interest accrues on debt at the effective interest rate times the amount of the debt outstanding during the period. This same principle applies regardless of the specific form of the liability. (p. 703)
- **LO2** Forces of supply and demand cause a bond to be priced to yield the market rate, calculated as the present value of all the cash flows required, where the discount rate is the market rate. Interest accrues at the effective market rate of interest multiplied by the outstanding balance (during the interest period). A company is permitted to allocate a discount or a premium equally to each period over the term to maturity if doing so produces results that are not materially different from the interest method. (p. 705)
- **LO3** Companies are not required to, but have the option to, value some or all of their liabilities at fair value. If the option is elected, an increase (or decrease) in fair value from one balance sheet to the next is reported as a loss (or gain) in the income statement. It's a one-time election for each liability when the liability is created. (p. 716)
- **LO4** In concept, notes are accounted for in precisely the same way as bonds. When a note is issued with an unrealistic interest rate, the effective market rate is used both to determine the amount recorded in the transaction and to record periodic interest thereafter. (p. 719)

- **LO5** In the balance sheet, disclosure should include, for all long-term borrowings, the aggregate amounts maturing and sinking fund requirements (if any) for each of the next five years. Supplemental disclosures are needed for (a) off-balance-sheet credit or market risk, (b) concentrations of credit risk, and (c) the fair value of financial instruments. (p. 723)
- **LO6** A gain or loss on early extinguishment of debt should be recorded for the difference between the reacquisition price and the carrying amount of the debt. Convertible bonds are accounted for as straight debt, but the value of the equity feature is recorded separately for bonds issued with detachable warrants. (p. 728)

APPENDIX 14A BONDS ISSUED BETWEEN INTEREST DATES

All bonds sell at their price plus any interest that has accrued since the last interest date.

We assumed that the bonds in the previous example were sold on the day they were dated (date printed in the indenture contract). But suppose a weak market caused a delay in selling the bonds until two months after that date (four months before semiannual interest was to be paid). In that case, the buyer would be asked to pay the seller **accrued interest** for two months in addition to the price of the bonds. For illustration, assume Masterwear was unable to sell the bonds in the previous example until March 1—two months after they are dated. This variation is shown in Illustration 14A–1. United would pay the price of the bonds ($700,000) plus $14,000 accrued interest:

$700,000	×	12%	×	2/12	=	$14,000
Face amount		Annual rate		Fraction of the annual period		Accrued interest

ILLUSTRATION 14A–1
Bonds Sold at Face Amount between Interest Dates

At Issuance (March 1)

	Debit	Credit
Masterwear (Issuer)		
Cash (price plus accrued interest)	714,000	
Bonds payable (face amount)		700,000
Interest payable (accrued interest determined above)		14,000
United (Investor)		
Investment in bonds (face amount)	700,000	
Interest receivable (accrued interest determined above)	14,000	
Cash (price plus accrued interest)		714,000

Since the investor will hold the bonds for only four months before receiving six months' interest, two months' accrued interest must be added to the price paid.

The issuer incurs interest expense, and the investor earns interest revenue, for only the four months the bonds are outstanding.

When Masterwear pays semiannual interest on June 30, a full six months' interest is paid. But having received two months' accrued interest in advance, Masterwear's *net* interest expense will be four months' interest, for the four months the bonds have been outstanding at that time. Likewise, when United receives six months' interest—after holding the bonds for only four months—United will net only the four months' interest to which it is entitled:

At the first Interest Date (June 30)

	Debit	Credit
Masterwear (Issuer)		
Interest expense (6 mo. – 2 mo. = 4 mo.)	28,000	
Interest payable[19] (accrued interest determined above)	14,000	
Cash (stated rate × face amount)		42,000
United (Investor)		
Cash (stated rate × face amount)	42,000	
Interest receivable (accrued interest determined above)		14,000
Interest revenue (6 mo. – 2 mo. = 4 mo.)		28,000

[19]Some accountants prefer to credit interest expense, rather than interest payable, when the bonds are sold. When that is done, this entry would require simply a debit to interest expense and a credit to cash for $42,000. The interest expense account would then reflect the same *net* debit of four months' interest ($42,000 – $14,000).

Interest Expense

Debit	Credit
	2 months
6 months	
4 months	

Similarly, the investor could debit interest revenue, rather than interest receivable when buying the bonds.

TROUBLED DEBT RESTRUCTURING

APPENDIX 14B

A respected real estate developer, Brillard Properties, was very successful developing and managing a number of properties in the southeastern United States. To finance these investments, the developer had borrowed hundreds of millions of dollars from several regional banks. For years, events occurred as planned. The investments prospered. Cash flow was high. Interest payments on the debt were timely and individual loans were repaid as they matured.

Almost suddenly, however, the real estate climate in the region soured. Investments that had provided handsome profits now did not provide the cash flow necessary to service the debt. Bankers who had loaned substantial funds to Brillard now faced a dilemma. Because contractual interest payments were unpaid, the bankers had the legal right to demand payment, which would force the developer to liquidate all or a major part of the properties to raise the cash. Sound business practice? Not necessarily.

If creditors force liquidation, they then must share among themselves the cash raised from selling the properties—at forced sale prices. Believing the developer's financial difficulties were caused by temporary market forces, not by bad management, the bankers felt they could minimize their losses by *restructuring* the debt agreements, rather than by forcing liquidation.

When changing the original terms of a debt agreement is motivated by financial difficulties experienced by the debtor (borrower), the new arrangement is referred to as a **troubled debt restructuring.** By definition, a troubled debt restructuring involves some concessions on the part of the creditor (lender). A troubled debt restructuring may be achieved in either of two ways:

1. The debt may be *settled* at the time of the restructuring.
2. The debt may be *continued,* but with *modified terms.*

Debt Is Settled

In the situation described above, one choice the bankers had was to try to actually settle the debt outright at the time of the troubled debt restructuring. For instance, a bank holding a $30 million note from the developer might agree to accept a property valued at, let's say, $20 million as final settlement of the debt. In that case, the developer has a $10 million gain equal to the difference between the carrying amount of the debt and the fair value of the property transferred. The debtor may need to adjust the carrying amount of an asset to its fair value prior to recording its exchange for a debt. The developer in our example, for instance, would need to change the recorded amount for the property specified in the exchange agreement if it is carried at an amount other than its $20 million fair market value. In such an instance, an ordinary gain or loss on disposition of assets should be recorded as shown in Illustration 14B–1.

In all areas of accounting, a noncash transaction is recorded at fair value.

The payment to settle a debt in a troubled debt restructuring might be cash, or a noncash asset (as in the example here), or even shares of the debtor's stock. An example of shares of stock being given in exchange for debt forgiveness is the celebrated reorganization of TWA in 1992 (since acquired by American Airlines), when creditors received a 55% stake in the company's common shares in return for forgiving about $1 billion of the airline's $1.5 billion debt. In any case, the debtor's gain is the difference between the carrying amount of the debt and the fair value of the asset(s) or equity securities transferred.

ILLUSTRATION 14B–1
Debt Settled

First Prudent Bank agrees to settle Brillard's $30 million debt in exchange for property having a fair value of $20 million. The carrying amount of the property on Brillard's books is $17 million:

	($ in millions)	
Land ($20 million minus $17 million)	3	
Gain on disposition of assets		3
Note payable (carrying amount)	30	
Gain on troubled debt restructuring		10
Land (fair value)		20

An asset is adjusted to fair value prior to recording its exchange for a debt.

Debt Is Continued, but with Modified Terms

We assumed in the previous example that First Prudent Bank agreed to accept property in full settlement of the debt. A more likely occurrence would be that the bank allows the debt to continue, but modifies the terms of the debt agreement to make it easier for the debtor to comply. The bank might agree to reduce or delay the scheduled *interest payments*. Or, it may agree to reduce or delay the *maturity amount*. Often a troubled debt restructuring will call for some combination of these concessions.

The carrying amount of a debt is the current balance of the primary debt plus any accrued (unpaid) interest.

Let's say the stated interest rate on the note in question is 10% and annual interest payments of \$3 million (10% × \$30 million) are payable in December of each of two remaining years to maturity. Also assume that the developer was unable to pay the \$3 million interest payment for the year just ended. This means that the amount owed—the carrying amount (or book value) of the debt—is \$33 million (\$30 million plus one year's accrued interest).

Two quite different situations are created when the terms of a debt are modified, depending on whether the cash payments are reduced to the extent that interest is eliminated.

According to generally accepted accounting principles, the way the debtor accounts for the restructuring depends on the extent of the reduction in cash payments called for by the restructured arrangement. More specifically, the accounting procedure depends on whether, under the new agreement, total cash payments (a) are *less than* the carrying amount of the debt or (b) still *exceed* the carrying amount of the debt.

WHEN TOTAL CASH PAYMENTS ARE LESS THAN THE CARRYING AMOUNT OF THE DEBT By the original agreement, the debtor was to pay at maturity the \$30 million loaned, plus enough periodic interest to provide a 10% effective rate of return. If the new agreement calls for less cash than the \$33 million now owed, interest is presumed to have been eliminated.

As one of many possibilities, suppose the bank agrees to (1) forgive the interest accrued from last year, (2) reduce the two remaining interest payments from \$3 million each to \$2 million each, and (3) reduce the face amount from \$30 million to \$25 million. Clearly, the debtor will pay less by the new agreement than by the original one. In fact, if we add up the total payments called for by the new agreement, the total [(\$2 million × 2) plus \$25 million] is less than the \$33 million carrying amount. Because the \$29 million does not exceed the amount owed, the restructured debt agreement no longer provides interest on the debt. Actually, the new payments are \$4 million short of covering the debt itself. So, after the debt restructuring, no interest expense is recorded. All subsequent cash payments are considered to be payment of the debt itself. Consider Illustration 14B–2.

ILLUSTRATION 14B–2

Cash Payments Less than the Debt

Brillard Properties owes First Prudent Bank \$30 million under a 10% note with two years remaining to maturity. Due to financial difficulties of the developer, the previous year's interest (\$3 million) was not paid. First Prudent Bank agrees to:

1. Forgive the interest accrued from last year.
2. Reduce the remaining two interest payments to \$2 million each.
3. Reduce the principal to \$25 million.

Analysis:			
	Carrying amount	\$30 million + \$3 million =	\$33 million
	Future payments	(\$2 million × 2) + \$25 million =	29 million
	Gain		\$ 4 million

	(\$ in millions)	
Accrued interest payable (10% × \$30 million)	3	
Note payable (\$30 million – \$29 million)	1	
Gain on debt restructuring		4

Carrying Amount		
Before Restr.	**Adj.**	**After Restr.**
\$30	(1)	\$29
3	(3)	0
\$33	(4)	\$29

After restructuring, no interest expense is recorded. All cash payments are considered to be payment of the note itself.

When the total future cash payments are less than the carrying amount of the debt, the difference is recorded as a gain at the date of restructure. No interest should be recorded thereafter. That is, all subsequent cash payments result in reductions of principal.

	($ in millions)	
At Each of the Two Interest Dates		
Note payable	2	
Cash (revised "interest" amount)		2
At Maturity		
Note payable	25	
Cash (revised principal amount)		25

The $25 million payment at maturity reduces the note to zero.

WHEN TOTAL CASH PAYMENTS EXCEED THE CARRYING AMOUNT OF THE DEBT Let's modify the example in the previous section. Now suppose the bank agrees to delay the due date for all cash payments until maturity and accept $34,333,200 at that time in full settlement of the debt. Rather than just reducing the cash payments as in the previous illustration, the payments are delayed. It is not the nature of the change that creates the need to account differently for this situation, but the amount of the total cash payments under the agreement relative to the carrying amount of the debt. This situation is demonstrated in Illustration 14B–3.

ILLUSTRATION 14B–3

Cash Payments More than the Debt

Brillard Properties owes First Prudent Bank $30 million under a 10% note with two years remaining to maturity. Due to Brillard's financial difficulties, the previous year's interest ($3 million) was not paid. First Prudent Bank agrees to:

1. Delay the due date for all cash payments until maturity.
2. Accept $34,333,200 at that time in full settlement of the debt.

Analysis:	Future payments		$34,333,200
	Carrying amount	$30 million + $3 million =	33,000,000
	Interest		$ 1,333,200

Calculation of the New Effective Interest Rate

- $33,000,000 ÷ $34,333,200 = .9612, the Table 2 value for $n = 2$, $i = ?$
- In row 2 of Table 2, the number .9612 is in the 2% column. So, this is the new effective interest rate.

The discount rate that equates the present value on the debt ($33 million) and its future value ($34,333,200) is the effective rate of interest.

Now the total payments called for by the new agreement, $34,333,200, exceed the $33 million carrying amount. Because the payments exceed the amount owed, the restructured debt agreement still provides interest on the debt—but less than before the agreement was revised. No longer is the effective rate 10%. The accounting objective now is to determine what the new effective rate is and *record interest for the remaining term of the loan at that new, lower rate,* as shown in Illustration 14B–3.

As long as cash payments exceed the amount owed there will be interest—although at a lower effective rate.

Because the total future cash payments are not less than the carrying amount of the debt, no reduction of the existing debt is necessary and no entry is required at the time of the debt restructuring. Even though no cash is paid until maturity under the restructured debt agreement, interest expense still is recorded annually—but at the new rate.

Unpaid interest is accrued at the effective rate times the carrying amount of the note.

At the End of the First Year		
Interest expense [2% × ($30,000,000 + 3,000,000)]	660,000	
Accrued interest payable		660,000
At the End of the Second Year		
Interest expense [2% × ($30,000,000 + 3,660,000)]	673,200	
Accrued interest payable		673,200
At Maturity (End of the Second Year)		
Note payable	30,000,000	
Accrued interest payable ($3,000,000 + 660,000 + 673,200)	4,333,200	
Cash (required by new agreement)		34,333,200

The carrying amount of the debt is increased by the unpaid interest from the previous year.

The total of the accrued interest account plus the note account is equal to the amount scheduled to be paid at maturity.

ADDITIONAL CONSIDERATION

To keep up with the changing amounts, it may be convenient to prepare an amortization schedule for the debt.

Year	Cash Interest	Effective Interest	Increase in Balance	Outstanding Balance
		(2% × Outstanding balance)		
				33,000,000
1	0	.02 (33,000,000) = 660,000	660,000	33,660,000
2	0	.02 (33,660,000) = 673,200	673,200	34,333,200
	0	1,333,200	1,333,200	

An amortization schedule is particularly helpful if there are several years remaining to maturity.

In our example, the restructured debt agreement called for a single cash payment at maturity ($34,333,200). If more than one cash payment is required (as in the agreement in our earlier example), calculating the new effective rate is more difficult. The concept would remain straightforward: (1) determine the interest rate that provides a present value of all future cash payments that is equal to the current carrying amount and (2) record the interest at that rate thereafter. Mechanically, though, the computation by hand would be cumbersome, requiring a time-consuming trial-and-error calculation. Since our primary interest is understanding the concepts involved, we will avoid the mathematical complexities of such a situation.

You also should be aware that when a restructuring involves modification of terms, accounting for a liability by the debtor, as described in this section, and accounting for a receivable by the creditor, which was described in Chapter 12, are inconsistent. You may recall that when a creditor's investment in a receivable becomes impaired, due to a troubled debt restructuring or for any other reason, the receivable is remeasured based on the discounted present value of currently expected cash flows at the loan's original effective rate (regardless of the extent to which expected cash receipts have been reduced). For ease of comparison, the example in this chapter (Illustration 14B–3) describes the same situation as the example in Chapter 12 (Illustration 12B–2). There is no conceptual justification for the asymmetry between debtors' and creditors' accounting for troubled debt restructurings. The FASB will likely reconsider debtors' accounting in the future.[20] ●

[20]"Accounting by Creditors for Impairment of a Loan," *Statement of Financial Accounting Standards No. 114* (Norwalk, Conn.: FASB, 1993), par. 63.

QUESTIONS FOR REVIEW OF KEY TOPICS

Q 14–1 How is periodic interest determined for outstanding liabilities? For outstanding receivables? How does the approach compare from one form of debt instrument (say bonds payable) to another (say notes payable)?

Q 14–2 As a general rule, how should long-term liabilities be reported on the debtor's balance sheet?

Q 14–3 How are bonds and notes the same? How do they differ?

Q 14–4 What information is contained in a bond indenture? What purpose does it serve?

Q 14–5 On January 1, 2009, Brandon Electronics issued $85 million of 11.5% bonds, dated January 1. The market yield for bonds of maturity issued by similar firms in terms of riskiness is 12.25%. How can Brandon sell debt paying only 11.5% in a 12.25% market?

Q 14–6 How is the price determined for a bond (or bond issue)?

Q 14–7 A zero-coupon bond pays no interest. Explain.

Q 14–8 When bonds are issued at a premium the debt declines each period. Explain.

Q 14–9 Compare the two commonly used methods of determining interest on bonds.

Q 14–10 *APB Opinion No. 21* requires that debt issue costs be recorded separately and amortized over the term of the related debt. Describe a logical alternative to this accounting treatment.

Q 14–11 Cordova Tools has bonds outstanding during a year in which the market rate of interest has risen. If Cordova has elected the fair value option for the bonds, will it report a gain or a loss on the bonds for the year? Explain.

Q 14–12 When a note's stated rate of interest is unrealistic relative to the market rate, the concept of substance over form should be employed. Explain.

Q 14–13 Mandatorily redeemable shares obligate the issuing company to buy back the shares in exchange for cash or other assets. Where in the balance sheet are these securities reported?

Q 14–14 How does an installment note differ from a note for which the principal is paid as a single amount at maturity?

Q 14–15 Long-term debt can be reported either (a) as a single amount, net of any discount or increased by any premium or (b) at its face amount accompanied by a separate valuation account for the discount or premium. Any portion of the debt to be paid during the upcoming year, or operating cycle if longer, should be reported as a current amount. Regarding amounts to be paid in the future, what additional disclosures should be made in connection with long-term debt?

Q 14–16 Early extinguishment of debt often produces a gain or a loss. How is the gain or loss determined?

Q 14–17 What criteria are used to classify a gain or loss on early extinguishment of debt as an extraordinary item in the income statement?

Q 14–18 Both convertible bonds and bonds issued with detachable warrants have features of both debt and equity. How does the accounting treatment differ for the two hybrid securities? Why is the accounting treatment different?

Q 14–19 At times, companies try to induce voluntary conversion by offering an added incentive—maybe cash, stock warrants, or a more favorable conversion ratio. How is such an inducement accounted for? How is it measured?

Q 14–20 (Based on Appendix A) Why will bonds always sell at their price plus any interest that has accrued since the last interest date?

Q 14–21 (Based on Appendix B) When the original terms of a debt agreement are changed because of financial difficulties experienced by the debtor (borrower), the new arrangement is referred to as a *troubled debt restructuring*. Such a restructuring can take a variety of forms. For accounting purposes, these possibilities are categorized. What are the accounting classifications of troubled debt restructurings?

Q 14–22 (Based on Appendix B) Pratt Industries owes First National Bank $5 million but, due to financial difficulties, is unable to comply with the original terms of the loan. The bank agrees to settle the debt in exchange for land having a fair value of $3 million. The carrying amount of the property on Pratt's books is $2 million. For the reporting period in which the debt is settled, what amount(s) will Pratt report on its income statement in connection with the troubled debt restructuring?

Q 14–23 (Based on Appendix B) The way a debtor accounts for the restructuring depends on the extent of the reduction in cash payments called for by the restructured arrangement. Describe, in general, the accounting procedure for the two basic cases: when, under the new agreement, total cash payments (a) are less than the carrying amount of the debt or (b) still exceed the carrying amount of the debt.

BRIEF EXERCISES

BE 14–1
Bond interest

● LO1

Holiday Brands issued $30 million of 6%, 30-year bonds for $27.5 million. What is the amount of interest that Holiday will pay semiannually to bondholders?

BE 14–2
Determining the price of bonds

● LO2

A company issued 5%, 20-year bonds with a face amount of $80 million. The market yield for bonds of similar risk and maturity is 6%. Interest is paid semiannually. At what price did the bonds sell?

BE 14–3
Determining the price of bonds

● LO2

A company issued 6%, 15-year bonds with a face amount of $75 million. The market yield for bonds of similar risk and maturity is 6%. Interest is paid semiannually. At what price did the bonds sell?

BE 14–4
Determining the price of bonds

● LO2

A company issued 5%, 20-year bonds with a face amount of $100 million. The market yield for bonds of similar risk and maturity is 4%. Interest is paid semiannually. At what price did the bonds sell?

BE 14–5
Effective interest on bonds
● LO2

On January 1, a company issued 7%, 15-year bonds with a face amount of $90 million for $82,218,585 to yield 8%. Interest is paid semiannually. What was interest expense at the effective interest rate on June 30, the first interest date?

BE 14–6
Effective interest on bonds
● LO2

On January 1, a company issued 3%, 20-year bonds with a face amount of $80 million for $69,033,776 to yield 4%. Interest is paid semiannually. What was the interest expense at the effective interest rate on the December 31 annual income statement?

BE 14–7
Straight-line interest on bonds
● LO2

On January 1, a company issued 3%, 20-year bonds with a face amount of $80 million for $69,033,776 to yield 4%. Interest is paid semiannually. What was the straight-line interest expense on the December 31 annual income statement?

BE 14–8
Investment in bonds
● LO2

On January 1, a company purchased 3%, 20-year corporate bonds for $69,033,776 as an investment. The bonds have a face amount of $80 million and are priced to yield 4%. Interest is paid semiannually. Prepare the journal entry to record revenue at the effective interest rate on December 31, the second interest payment date.

BE 14–9
Reporting bonds at fair value
● LO3

AI Tool and Dye issued 8% bonds with a face amount of $160 million on January 1, 2009. The bonds sold for $150 million. For bonds of similar risk and maturity the market yield was 9%. Upon issuance, AI elected the option to report these bonds at their fair value. On June 30, 2009, the fair value of the bonds was $145 million as determined by their market value on the NASDAQ. Will AI report a gain or will it report a loss when adjusting the bonds to fair value? If the change in fair value is attributable to a change in the interest rate, did the rate increase or decrease?

BE 14–10
Note with unrealistic interest rate
● LO4

Snipes Construction paid for earth-moving equipment by issuing a $300,000, 3-year note that specified 2% interest to be paid on December 31 of each year. The equipment's retail cash price was unknown, but it was determined that a reasonable interest rate was 5%. At what amount should Snipes record the equipment and the note? What journal entry should it record for the transaction?

BE 14–11
Installment note
● LO4

On January 1, a company borrowed cash by issuing a $300,000, 5%, installment note to be paid in three equal payments at the end of each year beginning December 31. What would be the amount of each installment? Prepare the journal entry for the second installment payment.

BE 14–12
Early extinguishment; effective interest
● LO6

A company retired $60 million of its 6% bonds at 102 ($61.2 million) before their scheduled maturity. At the time, the bonds had a remaining discount of $2 million. Prepare the journal entry to record the redemption of the bonds.

BE 14–13
Bonds with detachable warrants
● LO6

Hoffman Corporation issued $60 million of 5%, 20-year bonds at 102. Each of the 60,000 bonds was issued with 10 detachable stock warrants, each of which entitled the bondholder to purchase, for $20, one share of $1 par common stock. At the time of sale, the market value of the common stock was $25 per share and the market value of each warrant was $5. Prepare the journal entry to record the issuance of the bonds.

BE 14–14
Convertible bonds
● LO6

Hoffman Corporation issued $60 million of 5%, 20-year bonds at 102. Each of the 60,000 bonds was convertible into one share of $1 par common stock. Prepare the journal entry to record the issuance of the bonds.

EXERCISES

available with McGraw-Hill's Homework Manager www.mhhe.com/spiceland5e 

An alternative exercise and problem set is available on the text website: www.mhhe.com/spiceland5e

E 14–1
Bond valuation
● LO2

Your investment department has researched possible investments in corporate debt securities. Among the available investments are the following $100 million bond issues, each dated January 1, 2009. Prices were determined by underwriters at different times during the last few weeks.

	Company	Bond Price	Stated Rate
1.	BB Corp.	$109 million	11%
2.	DD Corp.	$100 million	10%
3.	GG Corp.	$ 91 million	9%

Each of the bond issues matures on December 31, 2028, and pays interest semiannually on June 30 and December 31. For bonds of similar risk and maturity, the market yield at January 1, 2009, is 10%.

Required:

Other things being equal, which of the bond issues offers the most attractive investment opportunity at the prices stated? the least attractive? Why?

E 14–2
Determine the price of bonds in various situations

● LO2

Determine the price of a $1 million bond issue under each of the following independent assumptions:

	Maturity	Interest Paid	Stated Rate	Effective (market) Rate
1.	10 years	annually	10%	12%
2.	10 years	semiannually	10%	12%
3.	10 years	semiannually	12%	10%
4.	20 years	semiannually	12%	10%
5.	20 years	semiannually	12%	12%

E 14–3
Determine the price of bonds; issuance; effective interest

● LO2

The Bradford Company issued 10% bonds, dated January 1, with a face amount of $80 million on January 1, 2009. The bonds mature in 2018 (10 years). For bonds of similar risk and maturity, the market yield is 12%. Interest is paid semiannually on June 30 and December 31.

Required:

1. Determine the price of the bonds at January 1, 2009.
2. Prepare the journal entry to record their issuance by The Bradford Company on January 1, 2009.
3. Prepare the journal entry to record interest on June 30, 2009 (at the effective rate).
4. Prepare the journal entry to record interest on December 31, 2009 (at the effective rate).

E 14–4
Investor; effective interest

● LO2

(Note: This is a variation of the previous exercise modified to consider the investor's perspective.) The Bradford Company sold the entire bond issue described in the previous exercise to Saxton-Bose Corporation.

Required:

1. Prepare the journal entry to record the purchase of the bonds by Saxton-Bose on January 1, 2009.
2. Prepare the journal entry to record interest revenue on June 30, 2009 (at the effective rate).
3. Prepare the journal entry to record interest revenue on December 31, 2009 (at the effective rate).

E 14–5
Bonds; issuance; effective interest; financial statement effects

● LO2

Myriad Solutions, Inc., issued 10% bonds, dated January 1, with a face amount of $320 million on January 1, 2009 for $283,294,720. The bonds mature in 2019 (10 years). For bonds of similar risk and maturity the market yield is 12%. Interest is paid semiannually on June 30 and December 31.

Required:

1. What would be the net amount of the liability Myriad would report in its balance sheet at December 31, 2009?
2. What would be the amount related to the bonds that Myriad would report in its income statement for the year ended December 31, 2009?
3. What would be the amount(s) related to the bonds that Myriad would report in its statement of cash flows for the year ended December 31, 2009?

E 14–6
Bonds; issuance; effective interest

● LO2

The Gorman Group issued $900,000 of 13% bonds on June 30, 2009 for $967,707. The bonds were dated on June 30 and mature on June 30, 2029 (20 years). The market yield for bonds of similar risk and maturity is 12%. Interest is paid semiannually on December 31 and June 30.

Required:

1. Prepare the journal entry to record their issuance by The Gorman Group on June 30, 2009.
2. Prepare the journal entry to record interest on December 31, 2009 (at the effective rate).
3. Prepare the journal entry to record interest on June 30, 2010 (at the effective rate).

E 14–7
Determine the price of bonds; issuance; straight-line method

● LO2

Universal Foods issued 10% bonds, dated January 1, with a face amount of $150 million on January 1, 2009. The bonds mature on December 31, 2023 (15 years). The market rate of interest for similar issues was 12%. Interest is paid semiannually on June 30 and December 31. Universal uses the straight-line method.

Required:

1. Determine the price of the bonds at January 1, 2009.
2. Prepare the journal entry to record their issuance by Universal Foods on January 1, 2009.

3. Prepare the journal entry to record interest on June 30, 2009.
4. Prepare the journal entry to record interest on December 31, 2016.

E 14–8
Investor; straight-line method
● LO2

(Note: This is a variation of the previous exercise modified to consider the investor's perspective.) Universal Foods sold the entire bond issue described in the previous exercise to Wang Communications.

Required:

1. Prepare the journal entry to record the purchase of the bonds by Wang Communications on January 1, 2009.
2. Prepare the journal entry to record interest revenue on June 30, 2009.
3. Prepare the journal entry to record interest revenue on December 31, 2016.

E 14–9
Issuance of bonds; effective interest; amortization schedule; financial statement effects
● LO2

When Patey Pontoons issued 6% bonds on January 1, 2009, with a face amount of $600,000, the market yield for bonds of similar risk and maturity was 7%. The bonds mature December 31, 2012 (4 years). Interest is paid semiannually on June 30 and December 31.

Required:

1. Determine the price of the bonds at January 1, 2009.
2. Prepare the journal entry to record their issuance by Patey on January 1, 2009.
3. Prepare an amortization schedule that determines interest at the effective rate each period.
4. Prepare the journal entry to record interest on June 30, 2009.
5. What is the amount(s) related to the bonds that Patey will report in its balance sheet at December 31, 2009?
6. What is the amount(s) related to the bonds that Patey will report in its income statement for the year ended December 31, 2009? (Ignore income taxes.)
7. Prepare the appropriate journal entries at maturity on December 31, 2012.

E 14–10
Issuance of bonds; effective interest; amortization schedule
● LO2

National Orthopedics Co. issued 9% bonds, dated January 1, with a face amount of $500,000 on January 1, 2009. The bonds mature in 2012 (4 years). For bonds of similar risk and maturity the market yield was 10%. Interest is paid semiannually on June 30 and December 31.

Required:

1. Determine the price of the bonds at January 1, 2009.
2. Prepare the journal entry to record their issuance by National on January 1, 2009.
3. Prepare an amortization schedule that determines interest at the effective rate each period.
4. Prepare the journal entry to record interest on June 30, 2009.
5. Prepare the appropriate journal entries at maturity on December 31, 2012.

E 14–11
Bonds; effective interest; adjusting entry
● LO2

On February 1, 2009, Strauss-Lombardi issued 9% bonds, dated February 1, with a face amount of $800,000. The bonds sold for $731,364 and mature on January 31, 2029 (20 years). The market yield for bonds of similar risk and maturity was 10%. Interest is paid semiannually on July 31 and January 31. Strauss-Lombardi's fiscal year ends December 31.

Required:

1. Prepare the journal entry to record their issuance by Strauss-Lombardi on February 1, 2009.
2. Prepare the journal entry to record interest on July 31, 2009 (at the effective rate).
3. Prepare the adjusting entry to accrue interest on December 31, 2009.
4. Prepare the journal entry to record interest on January 31, 2010.

E 14–12
Bonds; straight-line method; adjusting entry
● LO2

On March 1, 2009, Stratford Lighting issued 14% bonds, dated March 1, with a face amount of $300,000. The bonds sold for $294,000 and mature on February 28, 2029 (20 years). Interest is paid semiannually on August 31 and February 28. Stratford uses the straight-line method and its fiscal year ends December 31.

Required:

1. Prepare the journal entry to record the issuance of the bonds by Stratford Lighting on March 1, 2009.
2. Prepare the journal entry to record interest on August 31, 2009.
3. Prepare the journal entry to accrue interest on December 31, 2009.
4. Prepare the journal entry to record interest on February 28, 2010.

E 14–13
Issuance of bonds; effective interest
● LO2

Federal Semiconductors issued 11% bonds, dated January 1, with a face amount of $800 million on January 1, 2009. The bonds sold for $739,814,813 and mature in 2028 (20 years). For bonds of similar risk and maturity the market yield was 12%. Interest is paid semiannually on June 30 and December 31.

Required:

1. Prepare the journal entry to record their issuance by Federal on January 1, 2009.
2. Prepare the journal entry to record interest on June 30, 2009 (at the effective rate).
3. Prepare the journal entry to record interest on December 31, 2009 (at the effective rate).

4. At what amount will Federal report the bonds among its liabilities in the December 31, 2009, balance sheet?

E 14–14
Reporting bonds at fair value
● LO3

(Note: This is a variation of the previous exercise modified to consider the fair value option for reporting liabilities.)

Federal Semiconductors issued 11% bonds, dated January 1, with a face amount of $800 million on January 1, 2009. The bonds sold for $739,814,813 and mature in 2028 (20 years). For bonds of similar risk and maturity the market yield was 12%. Interest is paid semiannually on June 30 and December 31. Federal determines interest at the effective rate. Federal elected the option to report these bonds at their fair value. On December 31, 2009, the fair value of the bonds was $730 million as determined by their market value in the over-the-counter market.

Required:

1. Prepare the journal entry to adjust the bonds to their fair value for presentation in the December 31, 2009, balance sheet.
2. Assume the fair value of the bonds on December 31, 2010, had risen to $736 million. Prepare the journal entry to adjust the bonds to their fair value for presentation in the December 31, 2010, balance sheet.

E 14–15
Reporting bonds at fair value
● LO3

On January 1, 2009, Rapid Airlines issued $200 million of its 8% bonds for $184 million. The bonds were priced to yield 10%. Interest is payable semiannually on June 30 and December 31. Rapid Airlines records interest at the effective rate and elected the option to report these bonds at their fair value. On December 31, 2009, the fair value of the bonds was $188 million as determined by their market value in the over-the-counter market.

Required:

1. Prepare the journal entry to record interest on June 30, 2009 (the first interest payment).
2. Prepare the journal entry to record interest on December 31, 2009 (the second interest payment).
3. Prepare the journal entry to adjust the bonds to their fair value for presentation in the December 31, 2009, balance sheet.

E 14–16
Reporting bonds at fair value; calculate fair value
● LO3

On January 1, 2009, Essence Communications issued $800,000 of its 10-year, 8% bonds for $700,302. The bonds were priced to yield 10%. Interest is payable semiannually on June 30 and December 31. Essence Communications records interest at the effective rate and elected the option to report these bonds at their fair value. On December 31, 2009, the market interest rate for bonds of similar risk and maturity was 9%. The bonds are not traded on an active exchange.

Required:

1. Using the information provided, estimate the fair value of the bonds at December 31, 2009.
2. Prepare the journal entry to record interest on June 30, 2009 (the first interest payment).
3. Prepare the journal entry to record interest on December 31, 2009 (the second interest payment).
4. Prepare the journal entry to adjust the bonds to their fair value for presentation in the December 31, 2009, balance sheet.

E 14–17
Note with unrealistic interest rate; amortization schedule
● LO4

Amber Mining and Milling, Inc., contracted with Truax Corporation to have constructed a custom-made lathe. The machine was completed and ready for use on January 1, 2009. Amber paid for the lathe by issuing a $600,000, three-year note that specified 4% interest, payable annually on December 31 of each year. The cash market price of the lathe was unknown. It was determined by comparison with similar transactions that 12% was a reasonable rate of interest.

Required:

1. Prepare the journal entry on January 1, 2009, for Amber Mining and Milling's purchase of the lathe.
2. Prepare an amortization schedule for the three-year term of the note.
3. Prepare the journal entries to record (a) interest for each of the three years and (b) payment of the note at maturity.

E 14–18
Installment note; amortization schedule
● LO4

American Food Services, Inc., acquired a packaging machine from Barton and Barton Corporation. Barton and Barton completed construction of the machine on January 1, 2009. In payment for the $4 million machine, American Food Services issued a four-year installment note to be paid in four equal payments at the end of each year. The payments include interest at the rate of 10%.

Required:

1. Prepare the journal entry for American Food Services' purchase of the machine on January 1, 2009.
2. Prepare an amortization schedule for the four-year term of the installment note.
3. Prepare the journal entry for the first installment payment on December 31, 2009.
4. Prepare the journal entry for the third installment payment on December 31, 2011.

E 14–19
Installment note
● LO4

LCD Industries purchased a supply of electronic components from Entel Corporation on November 1, 2009. In payment for the $24 million purchase, LCD issued a 1-year installment note to be paid in equal monthly payments at the end of each month. The payments include interest at the rate of 12%.

Required:

1. Prepare the journal entry for LCD's purchase of the components on November 1, 2009.
2. Prepare the journal entry for the first installment payment on November 30, 2009.
3. What is the amount of interest expense that LCD will report in its income statement for the year ended December 31, 2009?

E 14–20
Early extinguishment
● LO6

The balance sheet of Indian River Electronics Corporation as of December 31, 2008, included 12.25% bonds having a face amount of $90 million. The bonds had been issued in 2001 and had a remaining discount of $3 million at December 31, 2008. On January 1, 2009, Indian River Electronics called the bonds before their scheduled maturity at the call price of 102.

Required:

Prepare the journal entry by Indian River Electronics to record the redemption of the bonds at January 1, 2009.

E 14–21
Convertible bonds
● LO6

On January 1, 2009, Gless Textiles issued $12 million of 9%, 10-year convertible bonds at 101. The bonds pay interest on June 30 and December 31. Each $1,000 bond is convertible into 40 shares of Gless's $1 par common stock. Century Services purchased 10% of the issue as an investment.

Required:

1. Prepare the journal entries for the issuance of the bonds by Gless and the purchase of the bond investment by Century.
2. Prepare the journal entries for the June 30, 2013, interest payment by both Gless and Century assuming both use the straight-line method.
3. On July 1, 2014, when Gless's common stock had a market price of $33 per share, Century converted the bonds it held. Prepare the journal entries by both Gless and Century for the conversion of the bonds (book value method).

E 14–22
IFRS; convertible bonds
● LO5

Refer to the situation described in the previous exercise.

Required:

How might your solution to requirement 1 for the issuer of the bonds differ if Gless Textiles prepares its financial statements according to International Accounting Standards? Include any appropriate journal entry in your response.

E 14–23
Bonds with detachable warrants
● LO6

On August 1, 2009, Limbaugh Communications issued $30 million of 10% nonconvertible bonds at 104. The bonds are due on July 31, 2029. Each $1,000 bond was issued with 20 detachable stock warrants, each of which entitled the bondholder to purchase, for $60, one share of Limbaugh Communications' $10 par common stock. Interstate Containers purchased 20% of the bond issue. On August 1, 2009, the market value of the common stock was $58 per share and the market value of each warrant was $8.

In February, 2020, when Limbaugh's common stock had a market price of $72 per share and the unamortized discount balance was $1 million, Interstate Containers exercised the warrants it held.

Required:

1. Prepare the journal entries on August 1, 2009, to record (a) the issuance of the bonds by Limbaugh and (b) the investment by Interstate.
2. Prepare the journal entries for both Limbaugh and Interstate in February, 2020, to record the exercise of the warrants.

E 14–24
New debt issues; offerings announcements
● LO2

When companies offer new debt security issues, they publicize the offerings in the financial press and on internet sites. Assume the following were among the debt offerings reported in December 2009:

New Securities Issues

Corporate

National Equipment Transfer Corporation—$200 million bonds via lead managers Second Tennessee Bank N.A. and Morgan, Dunavant & Co., according to a syndicate official. Terms: maturity, Dec. 15, 2015; coupon 7.46%; issue price, par; yield, 7.46%; noncallable, debt ratings: Ba-1 (Moody's Investors Service, Inc.), BBB+ (Standard & Poor's).
IgWig Inc.—$350 million of notes via lead manager Stanley Brothers, Inc., according to a syndicate official. Terms: maturity, Dec. 1, 2017; coupon, 6.46%; Issue price, 99; yield, 6.56%; call date, NC; debt ratings: Baa-1 (Moody's Investors Service, Inc.), A (Standard & Poor's).

Required:

1. Prepare the appropriate journal entries to record the sale of both issues to underwriters. Ignore share issue costs and assume no accrued interest.
2. Prepare the appropriate journal entries to record the first semiannual interest payment for both issues.

E 14–25
Error in amortization schedule
● LO4

Wilkins Food Products, Inc. acquired a packaging machine from Lawrence Specialists Corporation. Lawrence completed construction of the machine on January 1, 2007. In payment for the machine Wilkins issued a three-year installment note to be paid in three equal payments at the end of each year. The payments include interest at the rate of 10%.

Lawrence made a conceptual error in preparing the amortization schedule which Wilkins failed to discover until 2009. The error had caused Wilkins to understate interest expense by $45,000 in 2007 and $40,000 in 2008.

Required:

1. Determine which accounts are incorrect as a result of these errors at January 1, 2009, before any adjustments. Explain your answer. (Ignore income taxes.)
2. Prepare a journal entry to correct the error.
3. What other step(s) would be taken in connection with the error?

E 14–26
Error correction; accrued interest on bonds
● LO2

At the end of 2008, Majors Furniture Company failed to accrue $61,000 of interest expense that accrued during the last five months of 2008 on bonds payable. The bonds mature in 2022. The discount on the bonds is amortized by the straight-line method. The following entry was recorded on February 1, 2009, when the semiannual interest was paid:

Interest expense	73,200	
Discount on bonds payable		1,200
Cash		72,000

Required:
Prepare any journal entry necessary to correct the error as well as any adjusting entry for 2009 related to the situation described. (Ignore income taxes.)

E 14–27
Accrued interest
● Appendix A

On March 1, 2009, Brown-Ferring Corporation issued $100 million of 12% bonds, dated January 1, 2009, for $99 million (plus accrued interest). The bonds mature on December 31, 2028, and pay interest semiannually on June 30 and December 31. Brown-Ferring's fiscal period is the calendar year.

Required:

1. Determine the amount of accrued interest that was included in the proceeds received from the bond sale.
2. Prepare the journal entry for the issuance of the bonds by Brown-Ferring.

E 14–28
Troubled debt restructuring; debt settled
● Appendix B

At January 1, 2009, Transit Developments owed First City Bank Group $600,000, under an 11% note with three years remaining to maturity. Due to financial difficulties, Transit was unable to pay the previous year's interest.

First City Bank Group agreed to settle Transit's debt in exchange for land having a fair value of $450,000. Transit purchased the land in 2005 for $325,000.

Required:
Prepare the journal entry(s) to record the restructuring of the debt by Transit Developments.

E 14–29
Troubled debt restructuring; modification of terms
● Appendix B

At January 1, 2009, Brainard Industries, Inc., owed Second BancCorp $12 million under a 10% note due December 31, 2011. Interest was paid last on December 31, 2007. Brainard was experiencing severe financial difficulties and asked Second BancCorp to modify the terms of the debt agreement. After negotiation Second BancCorp agreed to:

a. Forgive the interest accrued for the year just ended.
b. Reduce the remaining two years' interest payments to $1 million each and delay the first payment until December 31, 2010.
c. Reduce the unpaid principal amount to $11 million.

Required:
Prepare the journal entries by Brainard Industries, Inc., necessitated by the restructuring of the debt at (1) January 1, 2009, (2) December 31, 2010, and (3) December 31, 2011.

E 14–30
Troubled debt restructuring; modification of terms
● Appendix B

At January 1, 2009, NCI Industries, Inc., was indebted to First Federal Bank under a $240,000, 10% unsecured note. The note was signed January 1, 2005, and was due December 31, 2010. Annual interest was last paid on December 31, 2007. NCI was experiencing severe financial difficulties and negotiated a restructuring of the terms of the debt agreement. First Federal agreed to reduce last year's interest and the remaining two years' interest payments to $11,555 each and delay all payments until December 31, 2010, the maturity date.

Required:
Prepare the journal entries by NCI Industries, Inc., necessitated by the restructuring of the debt at: (1) January 1, 2009; (2) December 31, 2009; and (3) December 31, 2010.

CPA AND CMA REVIEW QUESTIONS

CPA Exam Questions

SCHWESER

The following questions are used in the Kaplan CPA Review Course to study long-term liabilities while preparing for the CPA examination. Determine the response that best completes the statements or questions.

● LO1

1. The market price of a bond issued at a discount is the present value of its principal amount at the market (effective) rate of interest
   a. Less the present value of all future interest payments at the rate of interest stated on the bond.
   b. Plus the present value of all future interest payments at the rate of interest stated on the bond.
   c. Plus the present value of all future interest payments at the market (effective) rate of interest.
   d. Less the present value of all future interest payments at the market (effective) rate of interest.

● LO6

2. On June 30, 2009, King Co. had outstanding 9%, $5,000,000 face value bonds maturing on June 30, 2014. Interest was payable semiannually every June 30 and December 31. On June 30, 2009, after amortization was recorded for the period, the unamortized bond premium and bond issue costs were $30,000 and $50,000, respectively. On that date, King acquired all its outstanding bonds on the open market at 98 and retired them. At June 30, 2009, what amount should King recognize as gain before income taxes on redemption of bonds?
   a. $ 20,000
   b. $ 80,000
   c. $120,000
   d. $180,000

● LO2

3. On July 1, 2009, Pell Co. purchased Green Corp. 10-year, 8% bonds with a face amount of $500,000 for $420,000. The bonds mature on June 30, 2017, and pay interest semiannually on June 30 and December 31. Using the interest method, Pell recorded bond discount amortization of $1,800 for the six months ended December 31, 2009. From this long-term investment, Pell should report 2009 revenue of
   a. $16,800
   b. $18,200
   c. $20,000
   d. $21,800

● LO2

4. The following information pertains to Camp Corp.'s issuance of bonds on July 1, 2009:

Face amount	$800,000
Terms	10 years
Stated interest rate	6%
Interest payment dates	Annually on July 1
Yield	9%

	At 6%	At 9%
Present value of $1 for 10 periods	0.558	0.422
Future value of $1 for 10 periods	1.791	2.367
Present value of ordinary annuity of $1 for 10 periods	7.360	6.418

   What should be the issue price for each $1,000 bond?
   a. $ 700
   b. $ 807
   c. $ 864
   d. $1,000

● LO2

5. For a bond issue that sells for less than its par value, the market rate of interest is
   a. Higher than the rate stated on the bond.
   b. Dependent on the rate stated on the bond.
   c. Equal to the rate stated on the bond.
   d. Less than the rate stated on the bond.

● LO2

6. On January 31, 2009, Beau Corp. issued $300,000 maturity value, 12% bonds for $300,000 cash. The bonds are dated December 31, 2008, and mature on December 31, 2018. Interest will be paid semiannually on June 30

and December 31. What amount of accrued interest payable should Beau report in its September 30, 2009, balance sheet?

a. $ 9,000
b. $18,000
c. $27,000
d. $24,000

● LO6

7. On January 1, 2004, Fox Corp. issued 1,000 of its 10%, $1,000 bonds for $1,040,000. These bonds were to mature on January 1, 2014, but were callable at 101 any time after December 31, 2007. Interest was payable semiannually on July 1 and January 1. On July 1, 2009, Fox called all of the bonds and retired them. Bond premium was amortized on a straight-line basis. Before income taxes, Fox's gain or loss in 2009 on this early extinguishment of debt was

a. $ 8,000 gain
b. $10,000 loss
c. $12,000 gain
d. $30,000 gain

● LO2

8. A bond issue on June 1, 2009, has interest payment dates of April 1 and October 1. Bond interest expense for the year ended December 31, 2009, is for a period of

a. Three months
b. Four months
c. Six months
d. Seven months

CMA Exam Questions

IMA

The following questions dealing with long-term liabilities are adapted from questions that previously appeared on Certified Management Accountant (CMA) examinations. The CMA designation sponsored by the Institute of Management Accountants (www.imanet.org) provides members with an objective measure of knowledge and competence in the field of management accounting. Determine the response that best completes the statements or questions.

Questions 1 and 2 are based on the following information. On January 1, Matthew Company issued 7% term bonds with a face amount of $1,000,000 due in 8 years. Interest is payable semiannually on January 1 and July 1. On the date of issue, investors were willing to accept an effective interest rate of 6%.

● LO1

1. The bonds were issued on January 1 at

a. a premium.
b. an amortized value.
c. book value.
d. a discount.

● LO2

2. Assume the bonds were issued on January 1 for $1,062,809. Using the effective interest amortization method, Matthew Company recorded interest expense for the 6 months ended June 30 in the amount of

a. $35,000
b. $70,000
c. $63,769
d. $31,884

● LO5

3. A bond issue sold at a premium is valued on the statement of financial position at the

a. maturity value.
b. maturity value plus the unamortized portion of the premium.
c. cost at the date of investment.
d. maturity value less the unamortized portion of the premium.

PROBLEMS

available with McGraw-Hill's Homework Manager www.mhhe.com/spiceland5e 

An alternate exercise and problem set is available on the text website: www.mhhe.com/spiceland5e

P 14–1
Determining the price of bonds; discount and premium; issuer and investor

● LO2

On January 1, 2009, Instaform, Inc., issued 10% bonds with a face amount of $50 million, dated January 1. The bonds mature in 2028 (20 years). The market yield for bonds of similar risk and maturity is 12%. Interest is paid semiannually.

Required:

1. Determine the price of the bonds at January 1, 2009, and prepare the journal entry to record their issuance by Instaform.

2. Assume the market rate was 9%. Determine the price of the bonds at January 1, 2009, and prepare the journal entry to record their issuance by Instaform.
3. Assume Broadcourt Electronics purchased the entire issue in a private placement of the bonds. Using the data in requirement 2, prepare the journal entry to record their purchase by Broadcourt.

P 14–2
Effective interest; financial statement effects
● LO2

On January 1, 2009, Baddour, Inc. issued 10% bonds with a face amount of $160 million. The bonds were priced at $140 million to yield 12%. Interest is paid semiannually on June 30 and December 31. Baddour's fiscal year ends September 30.

Required:
1. What amount(s) related to the bonds would Baddour report in its balance sheet at September 30, 2009?
2. What amount(s) related to the bonds would Baddour report in its income statement for the year ended September 30, 2009?
3. What amount(s) related to the bonds would Baddour report in its statement of cash flows for the year ended September 30, 2009? In which section(s) should the amount(s) appear?

P 14–3
Straight-line and effective interest compared
● LO2
eXcel

On January 1, 2009, Bradley Recreational Products issued $100,000, 9%, four-year bonds. Interest is paid semiannually on June 30 and December 31. The bonds were issued at $96,768 to yield an annual return of 10%.

Required:
1. Prepare an amortization schedule that determines interest at the effective interest rate.
2. Prepare an amortization schedule by the straight-line method.
3. Prepare the journal entries to record interest expense on June 30, 2011, by each of the two approaches.
4. Explain why the pattern of interest differs between the two methods.
5. Assuming the market rate is still 10%, what price would a second investor pay the first investor on June 30, 2011, for $10,000 of the bonds?

P 14–4
Bond amortization schedule
● LO2

On January 1, 2009, Tennessee Harvester Corporation issued debenture bonds that pay interest semiannually on June 30 and December 31. Portions of the bond amortization schedule appear below:

Payment	Cash Interest	Effective Interest	Increase in Balance	Outstanding Balance
				6,627,273
1	320,000	331,364	11,364	6,638,637
2	320,000	331,932	11,932	6,650,569
3	320,000	332,528	12,528	6,663,097
4	320,000	333,155	13,155	6,676,252
5	320,000	333,813	13,813	6,690,065
6	320,000	334,503	14,503	6,704,568
~	~	~	~	~
~	~	~	~	~
~	~	~	~	~
38	320,000	389,107	69,107	7,851,247
39	320,000	392,562	72,562	7,923,809
40	320,000	396,191	76,191	8,000,000

Required:
1. What is the face amount of the bonds?
2. What is the initial selling price of the bonds?
3. What is the term to maturity in years?
4. Interest is determined by what approach?
5. What is the stated annual interest rate?
6. What is the effective annual interest rate?
7. What is the total cash interest paid over the term to maturity?
8. What is the total effective interest expense recorded over the term to maturity?

P 14–5
Issuer and investor; effective interest; amortization schedule; adjusting entries
● LO2

On February 1, 2009, Cromley Motor Products issued 9% bonds, dated February 1, with a face amount of $80 million. The bonds mature on January 31, 2013 (4 years). The market yield for bonds of similar risk and maturity was 10%. Interest is paid semiannually on July 31 and January 31. Barnwell Industries acquired $80,000 of the bonds as a long-term investment. The fiscal years of both firms end December 31.

Required:
1. Determine the price of the bonds issued on February 1, 2009.

2. Prepare amortization schedules that indicate (a) Cromley's effective interest expense and (b) Barnwell's effective interest revenue for each interest period during the term to maturity.
3. Prepare the journal entries to record (a) the issuance of the bonds by Cromley and (b) Barnwell's investment on February 1, 2009.
4. Prepare the journal entries by both firms to record all subsequent events related to the bonds through January 31, 2011.

P 14–6
Issuer and investor; straight-line method; adjusting entries

● LO2

On April 1, 2009, Western Communications, Inc., issued 12% bonds, dated March 1, 2009, with face amount of \$30 million. The bonds sold for \$29.3 million and mature on February 28, 2012. Interest is paid semiannually on August 31 and February 28. Stillworth Corporation acquired \$30,000 of the bonds as a long-term investment. The fiscal years of both firms end December 31, and both firms use the straight-line method.

Required:

1. Prepare the journal entries to record (a) issuance of the bonds by Western and (b) Stillworth's investment on April 1, 2009.
2. Prepare the journal entries by both firms to record all subsequent events related to the bonds through maturity.

P 14–7
Issuer and investor; effective interest

● LO2

McWherter Instruments sold \$400 million of 8% bonds, dated January 1, on January 1, 2009. The bonds mature on December 31, 2028 (20 years). For bonds of similar risk and maturity, the market yield was 10%. Interest is paid semiannually on June 30 and December 31. Blanton Technologies, Inc., purchased \$400,000 of the bonds as a long-term investment.

Required:

1. Determine the price of the bonds issued on January 1, 2009.
2. Prepare the journal entries to record (a) their issuance by McWherter and (b) Blanton's investment on January 1, 2009.
3. Prepare the journal entries by (a) McWherter and (b) Blanton to record interest on June 30, 2009 (at the effective rate).
4. Prepare the journal entries by (a) McWherter and (b) Blanton to record interest on December 31, 2009 (at the effective rate).

P 14–8
Bonds; effective interest; partial period interest; financial statement effects

● LO2

The fiscal year ends December 31 for Lake Hamilton Development. To provide funding for its Moonlight Bay project, LHD issued 5% bonds with a face amount of \$500,000 on November 1, 2009. The bonds sold for \$442,215, a price to yield the market rate of 6%. The bonds mature October 31, 2028 (20 years). Interest is paid semiannually on April 30 and October 31.

Required:

1. What amount of interest expense related to the bonds will LHD report in its income statement for the year ending December 31, 2009?
2. What amount(s) related to the bonds will LHD report in its balance sheet at December 31, 2009?
3. What amount of interest expense related to the bonds will LHD report in its income statement for the year ending December 31, 2010?
4. What amount(s) related to the bonds will LHD report in its balance sheet at December 31, 2010?

P 14–9
Zero-coupon bonds

● LO2

On January 1, 2009, Darnell Window and Pane issued \$18 million of 10-year, zero-coupon bonds for \$5,795,518.

Required:

1. Prepare the journal entry to record the bond issue.
2. Determine the effective rate of interest.
3. Prepare the journal entry to record annual interest expense at December 31, 2009.
4. Prepare the journal entry to record annual interest expense at December 31, 2010.
5. Prepare the journal entry to record the extinguishment at maturity.

P 14–10
Determine bond price; record interest; report bonds at fair value

● LO3

On January 1, 2009, NFB Visual Aids issued \$800,000 of its 20-year, 8% bonds. The bonds were priced to yield 10%. Interest is payable semiannually on June 30 and December 31. NFB Visual Aids records interest at the effective rate and elected the option to report these bonds at their fair value. On December 31, 2009, the fair value of the bonds was \$668,000 as determined by their market value in the over-the-counter market.

Required:

1. Determine the price of the bonds at January 1, 2009, and prepare the journal entry to record their issuance.
2. Prepare the journal entry to record interest on June 30, 2009 (the first interest payment).
3. Prepare the journal entry to record interest on December 31, 2009 (the second interest payment).
4. Prepare the journal entry to adjust the bonds to their fair value for presentation in the December 31, 2009, balance sheet.

P 14–11
Report bonds at fair value; quarterly reporting

● LO3

Appling Enterprises issued 8% bonds with a face amount of $400,000 on January 1, 2009. The bonds sold for $331,364 and mature in 2028 (20 years). For bonds of similar risk and maturity the market yield was 10%. Interest is paid semiannually on June 30 and December 31. Appling determines interest at the effective rate. Appling elected the option to report these bonds at their fair value. The fair values of the bonds at the end of each quarter during 2009 as determined by their market values in the over-the-counter market were the following:

March 31	$350,000
June 30	340,000
September 30	335,000
December 31	342,000

Required:
1. By how much will Appling's earnings be increased or decreased by the bonds (ignoring taxes) in the March 31 *quarterly* financial statements?
2. By how much will Appling's earnings be increased or decreased by the bonds (ignoring taxes) in the June 30 *quarterly* financial statements?
3. By how much will Appling's earnings be increased or decreased by the bonds (ignoring taxes) in the September 30 *quarterly* financial statements?
4. By how much will Appling's earnings be increased or decreased by the bonds (ignoring taxes) in the December 31 *annual* financial statements?

P 14–12
Notes exchanged for assets

● LO4

At the beginning of the year, Lambert Motors issued the three notes described below. Interest is paid at year-end.
1. The company issued a two-year, 12%, $600,000 note in exchange for a tract of land. The current market rate of interest is 12%.
2. Lambert acquired some office equipment with a fair value of $94,643 by issuing a one-year, $100,000 note. The stated interest on the note is 6%.
3. The company purchased a building by issuing a three-year installment note. The note is to be repaid in equal installments of $1 million per year beginning one year hence. The current market rate of interest is 12%.

Required:
Prepare the journal entries to record each of the three transactions and the interest expense at the end of the first year for each.

P 14–13
Note with unrealistic interest rate

● LO4

At January 1, 2009, Brant Cargo acquired equipment by issuing a five-year, $150,000 (payable at maturity), 4% note. The market rate of interest for notes of similar risk is 10%.

Required:
1. Prepare the journal entry for Brant Cargo to record the purchase of the equipment.
2. Prepare the journal entry for Brant Cargo to record the interest at December 31, 2009.
3. Prepare the journal entry for Brant Cargo to record the interest at December 31, 2010.

P 14–14
Noninterest-bearing installment note

● LO4

At the beginning of 2009, VHF Industries acquired a machine with a fair market value of $6,074,700 by issuing a four-year, noninterest-bearing note in the face amount of $8 million. The note is payable in four annual installments of $2 million at the end of each year.

Required:
1. What is the effective rate of interest implicit in the agreement?
2. Prepare the journal entry to record the purchase of the machine.
3. Prepare the journal entry to record the first installment payment at December 31, 2009.
4. Prepare the journal entry to record the second installment payment at December 31, 2010.
5. Suppose the market value of the machine was unknown at the time of purchase, but the market rate of interest for notes of similar risk was 11%. Prepare the journal entry to record the purchase of the machine.

P 14–15
Note and installment note with unrealistic interest rate

● LO4

Braxton Technologies, Inc., constructed a conveyor for A&G Warehousers that was completed and ready for use on January 1, 2009. A&G paid for the conveyor by issuing a $100,000, four-year note that specified 5% interest to be paid on December 31 of each year. The conveyor was custom-built for A&G, so its cash price was unknown. By comparison with similar transactions it was determined that a reasonable interest rate was 10%.

Required:
1. Prepare the journal entry for A&G's purchase of the conveyor on January 1, 2009.
2. Prepare an amortization schedule for the four-year term of the note.
3. Prepare the journal entry for A&G's third interest payment on December 31, 2011.
4. If A&G's note had been an installment note to be paid in four equal payments at the end of each year beginning December 31, 2009, what would be the amount of each installment?

5. Prepare an amortization schedule for the four-year term of the installment note.
6. Prepare the journal entry for A&G's third installment payment on December 31, 2011.

P 14–16
Early extinguishment of debt

● LO6

Three years ago American Insulation Corporation issued 10 percent, $800,000, 10-year bonds for $770,000. Debt issue costs were $3,000. American Insulation exercised its call privilege and retired the bonds for $790,000. The corporation uses the straight-line method both to determine interest and to amortize debt issue costs.

Required:
Prepare the journal entry to record the call of the bonds.

P 14–17
Early extinguishment; effective interest

● LO6

The long-term liability section of Twin Digital Corporation's balance sheet as of December 31, 2008, included 12% bonds having a face amount of $20 million and a remaining discount of $1 million. Disclosure notes indicate the bonds were issued to yield 14%.

Interest is recorded at the effective interest rate and paid on January 1 and July 1 of each year. On July 1, 2009, Twin Digital retired the bonds at 102 ($20.4 million) before their scheduled maturity.

Required:
1. Prepare the journal entry by Twin Digital to record the semiannual interest on July 1, 2009.
2. Prepare the journal entry by Twin Digital to record the redemption of the bonds on July 1, 2009.

P 14–18
Investments in bonds; accrued interest; sale

● Appendix A

The following transactions relate to bond investments of Livermore Laboratories. The company's fiscal year ends on December 31. Livermore uses the straight-line method to determine interest.

2009	
July 1	Purchased $16 million of Bracecourt Corporation 10% debentures, due in 20 years (June 30, 2029), for $15.7 million. Interest is payable on January 1 and July 1 of each year.
Oct. 1	Purchased $30 million of 12% Framm Pharmaceuticals debentures, due May 31, 2019, for $31,160,000 plus accrued interest. Interest is payable on June 1 and December 1 of each year.
Dec. 1	Received interest on the Framm bonds.
31	Accrued interest.
2010	
Jan. 1	Received interest on the Bracecourt bonds.
June 1	Received interest on the Framm bonds.
July 1	Received interest on the Bracecourt bonds.
Sept. 1	Sold $15 million of the Framm bonds at 101 plus accrued interest.
Dec. 1	Received interest on the remaining Framm bonds.
31	Accrued interest.
2011	
Jan. 1	Received interest on the Bracecourt bonds.
Feb. 28	Sold the remainder of the Framm bonds at 102 plus accrued interest.
Dec. 31	Accrued interest.

Required:
1. Prepare the appropriate journal entries for these long-term bond investments.
2. By how much will Livermore Labs' earnings increase in each of the three years as a result of these investments? (Ignore income taxes.)

P 14–19
Debt issue costs; issuance; expensing; early extinguishment

● LO2 LO6

Cupola Fan Corporation issued 10%, $400,000, 10-year bonds for $385,000 on June 30, 2009. Debt issue costs were $1,500. Interest is paid semiannually on December 31 and June 30. One year from the issue date (July 1, 2010), the corporation exercised its call privilege and retired the bonds for $395,000. The corporation uses the straight-line method both to determine interest and to amortize debt issue costs.

Required:
1. Prepare the journal entry to record the issuance of the bonds.
2. Prepare the journal entries to record the payment of interest and amortization of debt issue costs on December 31, 2009.
3. Prepare the journal entries to record the payment of interest and amortization of debt issue costs on June 30, 2010.
4. Prepare the journal entries to record the call of the bonds.

P 14–20
Concepts; terminology

● LO1 through LO6

Listed below are several terms and phrases associated with long-term debt. Pair each item from List A (by letter) with the item from List B that is most appropriately associated with it.

	List A	List B
______	1. Effective rate times balance	a. Straight-line method
______	2. Promises made to bondholders	b. Discount
______	3. Present value of interest plus present value of principal	c. Liquidation payments after other claims satisfied d. Name of owner not registered
______	4. Call feature	e. Premium
______	5. Debt issue costs	f. Checks are mailed directly
______	6. Market rate higher than stated rate	g. No specific assets pledged
______	7. Coupon bonds	h. Bond indenture
______	8. Convertible bonds	i. Backed by a lien
______	9. Market rate less than stated rate	j. Interest expense
______	10. Stated rate times face amount	k. May become stock
______	11. Registered bonds	l. Legal, accounting, printing
______	12. Debenture bond	m. Protection against falling rates
______	13. Mortgage bond	n. Periodic cash payments
______	14. Materiality concept	o. Bond price
______	15. Subordinated debenture	

P 14–21
Early extinguishment
● LO6

The long-term liability section of Eastern Post Corporation's balance sheet as of December 31, 2008, included 10% bonds having a face amount of $40 million and a remaining premium of $6 million. On January 1, 2009, Eastern Post retired some of the bonds before their scheduled maturity.

Required:

Prepare the journal entry by Eastern Post to record the redemption of the bonds under each of the independent circumstances below:

1. Eastern Post called half the bonds at the call price of 102 (102% of face amount).
2. Eastern Post repurchased $10 million of the bonds on the open market at their market price of $10.5 million.

P 14–22
Convertible bonds; induced conversion; bonds with detachable warrants
● LO6

Bradley-Link's December 31, 2009, balance sheet included the following items:

Long-Term Liabilities	($ in millions)
9.6% convertible bonds, callable at 101 beginning in 2010, due 2013 (net of unamortized discount of $2) [note 8]	$198
10.4% registered bonds callable at 104 beginning in 2019, due 2023 (net of unamortized discount of $1) [note 8]	49
Shareholders' Equity	
Paid-in capital—stock warrants outstanding	4

Note 8: Bonds (in part)

The 9.6% bonds were issued in 1996 at 97.5 to yield 10%. Interest is paid semiannually on June 30 and December 31. Each $1,000 bond is convertible into 40 shares of the Company's $1 par common stock.

The 10.4% bonds were issued in 2000 at 102 to yield 10%. Interest is paid semiannually on June 30 and December 31. Each $1,000 bond was issued with 40 detachable stock warrants, each of which entitles the holder to purchase one share of the Company's $1 par common stock for $25, beginning 2010.

On January 3, 2010, when Bradley-Link's common stock had a market price of $32 per share, Bradley-Link called the convertible bonds to force conversion. 90% were converted; the remainder were acquired at the call price. When the common stock price reached an all-time high of $37 in December of 2010, 40% of the warrants were exercised.

Required:

1. Show the journal entries that were recorded when each of the two bond issues was originally sold in 1996 and 2000.
2. Prepare the journal entry to record (book value method) the conversion of 90% of the convertible bonds in January 2010 and the retirement of the remainder.
3. Assume Bradley-Link induced conversion by offering $150 cash for each bond converted. Prepare the journal entry to record (book value method) the conversion of 90% of the convertible bonds in January 2010.
4. Assume Bradley-Link induced conversion by modifying the conversion ratio to exchange 45 shares for each bond rather than the 40 shares provided in the contract. Prepare the journal entry to record (book value method) the conversion of 90% of the convertible bonds in January 2010.

5. Prepare the journal entry to record the exercise of the warrants in December 2010.
6. By how much will Bradley-Link's paid-in capital change as a result of the conversion of 90% of the bonds under each of the three scenarios described in requirements 3, 4, and 5?

P 14–23
Troubled debt restructuring

● Appendix B

At January 1, 2009, Rothschild Chair Company, Inc., was indebted to First Lincoln Bank under a $20 million, 10% unsecured note. The note was signed January 1, 2006, and was due December 31, 2012. Annual interest was last paid on December 31, 2007. Rothschild Chair Company was experiencing severe financial difficulties and negotiated a restructuring of the terms of the debt agreement.

Required:

Prepare all journal entries by Rothschild Chair Company, Inc., to record the restructuring and any remaining transactions relating to the debt under each of the independent circumstances below:

1. First Lincoln Bank agreed to settle the debt in exchange for land having a fair value of $16 million but carried on Rothschild Chair Company's books at $13 million.
2. First Lincoln Bank agreed to (a) forgive the interest accrued from last year, (b) reduce the remaining four interest payments to $1 million each, and (c) reduce the principal to $15 million.
3. First Lincoln Bank agreed to defer all payments (including accrued interest) until the maturity date and accept $27,775,000 at that time in settlement of the debt.

BROADEN YOUR PERSPECTIVE

Apply your critical-thinking ability to the knowledge you've gained. These cases will provide you an opportunity to develop your research, analysis, judgment, and communication skills. You also will work with other students, integrate what you've learned, apply it in real world situations, and consider its global and ethical ramifications. This practice will broaden your knowledge and further develop your decision-making abilities.

Communication Case 14–1
Convertible securities and warrants; concepts

● LO6

It is not unusual to issue long-term debt in conjunction with an arrangement under which lenders receive an option to buy common stock during all or a portion of the time the debt is outstanding. Sometimes the vehicle is convertible bonds; sometimes warrants to buy stock accompany the bonds and are separable. Interstate Chemical is considering these options in conjunction with a planned debt issue.

"You mean we have to report $7 million more in liabilities if we go with convertible bonds? Makes no sense to me," your CFO said. "Both ways seem pretty much the same transaction. Explain it to me, will you?"

Required:

Write a memo. Include in your explanation each of the following:

1. The differences in accounting for proceeds from the issuance of convertible bonds and of debt instruments with separate warrants to purchase common stock.
2. The underlying rationale for the differences.
3. Arguments that could be presented for the alternative accounting treatment.

Real World Case 14–2
Zero-coupon debt; Hewlett-Packard Company

● LO2

Real World Financials

The 2007 first quarter report of **Hewlett-Packard Company** reports zero-coupon notes issued at the end of its 1997 fiscal year. One billion, eight hundred million dollars face amount of 20-year debt sold for $968 million, a price to yield 3.149%. In fiscal 2002, HP repurchased $257 million in face value of the notes for a purchase price of $127 million, resulting in a gain on the early extinguishment of debt.

Required:

1. What journal entry did Hewlett-Packard use to record the sale in 1997?
2. Using an electronic spreadsheet, prepare an amortization schedule for the notes. Assume interest is calculated annually and use numbers expressed in millions of dollars; that is, the face amount is $1,800.
3. What was the effect on HP's earnings in 1998? Explain.
4. From the amortization schedule, determine the book value of the debt at the end of 2002.
5. What journal entry did Hewlett-Packard use to record the early extinguishment of debt in 2002, assuming the purchase was made at the end of the year?

Communication Case 14–3
Is convertible debt a liability or is it shareholders' equity? Group Interaction

● LO6

Some financial instruments can be considered compound instruments in that they have features of both debt and shareholders' equity. The most common example encountered in practice is convertible debt—bonds or notes convertible by the investor into common stock. A topic of debate for several years has been whether:

View 1: Issuers should account for an instrument with both liability and equity characteristics entirely as a liability or entirely as an equity instrument depending on which characteristic governs.

View 2: Issuers should account for an instrument as consisting of a liability component and an equity component that should be accounted for separately.

In considering this question, you should disregard what you know about the current position of the FASB on the issue. Instead, focus on conceptual issues regarding the practicable and theoretically appropriate treatment, unconstrained by GAAP. Also, focus your deliberations on convertible bonds as the instrument with both liability and equity characteristics.

Required:

1. Which view do you favor? Develop a list of arguments in support of your view prior to the class session for which the case is assigned.
2. In class, your instructor will pair you (and everyone else) with a classmate (who also has independently developed an argument).
   a. You will be given three minutes to argue your view to your partner. Your partner likewise will be given three minutes to argue his or her view to you. During these three-minute presentations, the listening partner is not permitted to speak.
   b. After each person has had a turn attempting to convince his or her partner, the two partners will have a three-minute discussion in which they will decide which view is more convincing. Arguments will be merged into a single view for each pair.
3. After the allotted time, a spokesperson for each of the two views will be selected by the instructor. Each spokesperson will field arguments from the class in support of that view's position and list the arguments on the board. The class then will discuss the merits of the two lists of arguments and attempt to reach a consensus view, though a consensus is not necessary.

Analysis Case 14–4
Issuance of bonds
● LO2

The following appeared in the October 15, 2009, issue of the *Financial World Journal:*

This announcement is not an offer of securities for sale or an offer to buy securities.
New Issue October 15, 2009

$750,000,000
CRAFT FOODS, INC.
7.75% Debentures Due October 1, 2019
Price 99.57%
plus accrued interest if any from date of issuance

Copies of the prospectus and the related prospectus supplement may be obtained from such of the undersigned as may legally offer these securities under applicable securities laws.

Keegan Morgan & Co. Inc.
Coldwell Bros. & Co.
Robert Stacks & Co.
Sherwin-William & Co.

Required:

1. Explain what is being described by the announcement.
2. Can you think of a psychological reason for the securities to be priced as they are?
3. What are the accounting considerations for Craft Foods, Inc.? Describe how Craft recorded the sale.

Judgment Case 14–5
Noninterest-bearing debt
● LO4

While reading a recent issue of *Health & Fitness,* a trade journal, Brandon Wilde noticed an ad for equipment he had been seeking for use in his business. The ad offered oxygen therapy equipment under the following terms:

Model BL 44582
$204,000 zero interest loan
Quarterly payments of $17,000 for only 3 years

The ad captured Wilde's attention, in part because he recently had been concerned that the interest charges incurred by his business were getting out of line. The price, though, was somewhat higher than prices for this model he had seen elsewhere.

Required:

Advise Mr. Wilde on the purchase he is considering.

Judgment Case 14–6
Noninterest-bearing note exchanged for cash and other privileges

The Jaecke Group, Inc., manufactures various kinds of hydraulic pumps. In June 2009, the company signed a four-year purchase agreement with one of its main parts suppliers, Hydraulics, Inc. Over the four-year period, Jaecke has agreed to purchase 100,000 units of a key component used in the manufacture of its pumps. The agreement allows Jaecke to purchase the component at a price lower than the prevailing market price at the time of purchase. As part of the agreement, Jaecke will lend Hydraulics $200,000 to be

● LO4

repaid after four years with no stated interest (the prevailing market rate of interest for a loan of this type is 10%).

Jaecke's chief accountant has proposed recording the note receivable at $200,000. The parts inventory purchase from Hydraulics over the next four years will then be recorded at the actual prices paid.

Required:

Do you agree with the accountant's valuation of the note and his intention to value the parts inventory acquired over the four-year period of the agreement at actual prices paid? If not, how would you account for the initial transaction and the subsequent inventory purchases?

Communication Case 14–7
Note receivable exchanged for cash and other services

● LO4

The Pastel Paint Company recently loaned $300,000 to KIX 96, a local radio station. The radio station signed a noninterest-bearing note requiring the $300,000 to be repaid in three years. As part of the agreement, the radio station will provide Pastel with a specified amount of free radio advertising over the three-year term of the note.

The focus of this case is the valuation of the note receivable by Pastel Paint Company and the treatment of the "free" advertising provided by the radio station. Your instructor will divide the class into two to six groups depending on the size of the class. The mission of your group is to reach consensus on the appropriate note valuation and accounting treatment of the free advertising.

Required:

1. Each group member should deliberate the situation independently and draft a tentative argument prior to the class session for which the case is assigned.
2. In class, each group will meet for 10 to 15 minutes in different areas of the classroom. During that meeting, group members will take turns sharing their suggestions for the purpose of arriving at a single group treatment.
3. After the allotted time, a spokesperson for each group (selected during the group meetings) will share the group's solution with the class. The goal of the class is to incorporate the views of each group into a consensus approach to the situation.

Ethics Case 14–8
Debt for equity swaps; have your cake and eat it too

● LO6

The cloudy afternoon mirrored the mood of the conference of division managers. Claude Meyer, assistant to the controller for Hunt Manufacturing, wore one of the gloomy faces that was just emerging from the conference room. "Wow, I knew it was bad, but not that bad," Claude thought to himself. "I don't look forward to sharing those numbers with shareholders."

The numbers he discussed with himself were fourth quarter losses which more than offset the profits of the first three quarters. Everyone had known for some time that poor sales forecasts and production delays had wreaked havoc on the bottom line, but most were caught off guard by the severity of damage.

Later that night he sat alone in his office, scanning and rescanning the preliminary financial statements on his computer monitor. Suddenly his mood brightened. "This may work," he said aloud, though no one could hear. Fifteen minutes later he congratulated himself, "Yes!"

The next day he eagerly explained his plan to Susan Barr, controller of Hunt for the last six years. The plan involved $300 million in convertible bonds issued three years earlier.

Meyer: By swapping stock for the bonds, we can eliminate a substantial liability from the balance sheet, wipe out most of our interest expense, and reduce our loss. In fact, the book value of the bonds is significantly more than the market value of the stock we'd issue. I think we can produce a profit.

Barr: But Claude, our bondholders are not inclined to convert the bonds.

Meyer: Right. But, the bonds are callable. As of this year, we can call the bonds at a call premium of 1%. Given the choice of accepting that redemption price or converting to stock, they'll all convert. We won't have to pay a cent. And, since no cash will be paid, we won't pay taxes either.

Required:

Do you perceive an ethical dilemma? What would be the impact of following up on Claude's plan? Who would benefit? Who would be injured?

Judgment Case 14–9
Analyzing financial statements; financial leverage; interest coverage

● LO1

IGF Foods Company is a large, primarily domestic, consumer foods company involved in the manufacture, distribution, and sale of a variety of food products. Industry averages are derived from Troy's *The Almanac of Business and Industrial Financial Ratios.* Following are the 2009 and 2008 comparative income statements and balance sheets for IGF. (The financial data we use are from actual financial statements of a well-known corporation, but the company name is fictitious and the numbers and dates have been modified slightly to disguise the company's identity.)

IGF FOODS COMPANY
Years Ended December 31, 2009 and 2008
($ in millions)

Comparative Income Statements	**2009**	**2008**
Net sales	$6,440	$5,800
Cost of goods sold	(3,667)	(3,389)
Gross profit	2,773	2,411
Operating expenses	(1,916)	(1,629)
Operating income	857	782
Interest expense	(54)	(53)
Income from operations before tax	803	729
Income taxes	(316)	(287)
Net income	$ 487	$ 442
Comparative Balance Sheets		
Assets		
Total current assets	$1,879	$1,490
Property, plant, and equipment (net)	2,592	2,291
Intangibles (net)	800	843
Other assets	74	60
Total assets	$5,345	$4,684
Liabilities and Shareholders' Equity		
Total current liabilities	$1,473	$ 941
Long-term debt	534	728
Deferred income taxes	407	344
Total liabilities	2,414	2,013
Shareholders' equity:		
Common stock	180	180
Additional paid-in capital	21	63
Retained earnings	2,730	2,428
Total shareholders' equity	2,931	2,671
Total liabilities and shareholders' equity	$5,345	$4,684

Long-term solvency refers to a company's ability to pay its long-term obligations. Financing ratios provide investors and creditors with an indication of this element of risk.

Required:

1. Calculate the debt to equity ratio for IGF for 2009. The average ratio for the stocks listed on the New York Stock Exchange in a comparable time period was 1.0. What information does your calculation provide an investor?
2. Is IGF experiencing favorable or unfavorable financial leverage?
3. Calculate IGF's times interest earned ratio for 2009. The coverage for the stocks listed on the New York Stock Exchange in a comparable time period was 5.1. What does your calculation indicate about IGF's risk?

Real World Case 14–10
Researching the way long-term debt is reported; retrieving information from the Internet

● LO1 through LO4

Real World Financials

EDGAR, the Electronic Data Gathering. Analysis, and Retrieval system, performs automated collection, validation, indexing, acceptance and forwarding of submissions by companies and others who are required by law to file forms with the U.S. Securities and Exchange Commission (SEC). All publicly traded domestic companies use EDGAR to make the majority of their filings. (Some foreign companies do so voluntarily.) Form 10-K, including the annual report, is required to be filed on EDGAR. The SEC makes this information available on the Internet.

Required:

1. Access EDGAR on the Internet at **www.sec.gov** or the **Procter & Gamble** website: **www.pg.com**.
2. Search for Procter & Gamble. Access its 2007 10-K filing. Search or scroll to find the financial statements and related notes.
3. What is the total debt (including current liabilities and deferred taxes) reported on the balance sheet? How has that amount changed over the most recent two years?
4. Compare the total liabilities (including current liabilities and deferred taxes) with the shareholders' equity and calculate the debt to equity ratio for the most recent two years. Has the proportion of debt financing and equity financing changed recently?
5. Does P&G obtain more financing through notes, bonds, or commercial paper? Are required debt payments increasing or decreasing over time? Is any long-term debt classified as short-term or vice versa? Why?

Analysis Case 14–11
Bonds; conversion; extinguishment

● LO6

On August 31, 2006, Chickasaw Industries issued $25 million of its 30-year, 6% convertible bonds dated August 31, priced to yield 5%. The bonds are convertible at the option of the investors into 1,500,000 shares of Chickasaw's common stock. Chickasaw records interest at the effective rate. On August 31, 2009, investors in Chickasaw's convertible bonds tendered 20% of the bonds for conversion into common stock that had a market value of $20 per share on the date of the conversion. On January 1, 2008, Chickasaw Industries issued $40 million of its 20-year, 7% bonds dated January 1 at a price to yield 8%. On December 31, 2009, the bonds were extinguished early through acquisition in the open market by Chickasaw for $40.5 million.

Required:

1. Using the book value method, would recording the conversion of the 6% convertible bonds into common stock affect earnings? If so, by how much? Would earnings be affected if the market value method is used? If so, by how much?
2. Were the 7% bonds issued at face value, at a discount, or at a premium? Explain.
3. Would the amount of interest expense for the 7% bonds be higher in the first year or second year of the term to maturity? Explain.
4. How should gain or loss on early extinguishment of debt be determined? Does the early extinguishment of the 7% bonds result in a gain or loss? Explain.

CPA SIMULATION 14–1

Ace Company
Long-Term Debt

CPA Review

Test your knowledge of the concepts discussed in this chapter, practice critical professional skills necessary for career success, and prepare for the computer-based CPA exam by accessing our CPA simulations at the text website: www.mhhe.com/spiceland5e.

The Ace Company simulation tests your knowledge of a) the way we account for and report bonds from the perspective of both the issuer and investor, b) reporting the cash flows related to bonds, and c) capitalization of interest on funds provided by bonds and used to construct a building, as we studied in Chapter 10.

As on the CPA exam itself, you will be asked to use tools including a spreadsheet, a calculator, and professional accounting standards, to conduct research, derive solutions, and communicate conclusions related to these issues in a simulated environment headed by the following interactive tabs:

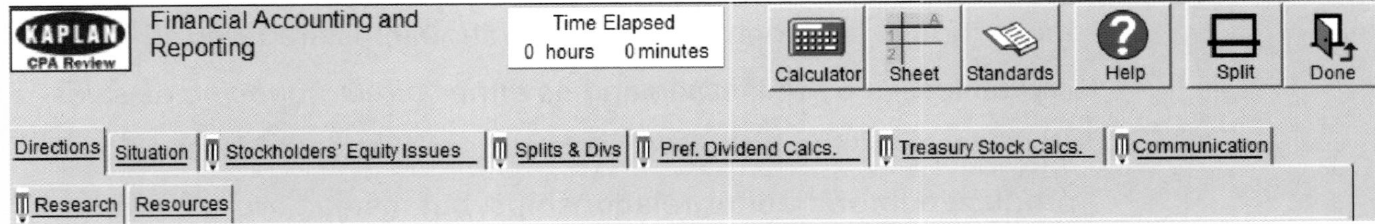

Specific tasks in the simulation include:

- Determining the selling price of bonds and analyzing the way an investor should report an investment in bonds.
- Applying judgment in the classification of cash flows from bond transactions on a statement of cash flows.
- Determining the amount of interest to be capitalized as part of the cost of an asset constructed with funding provided by bonds.
- Demonstrating an understanding of the way interest is calculated on debt.
- Communicating the way we account for convertible debt and debt with detachable warrants.
- Researching the way early extinguishments of debt is reported.

15

CHAPTER

Leases

/// OVERVIEW

In the previous chapter, we saw how companies account for their long-term debt. The focus of that discussion was *bonds* and *notes.* In this chapter we continue our discussion of debt, but we now turn our attention to liabilities arising in connection with *leases.* Leases that produce such debtor/creditor relationships are referred to as *capital* leases by the lessee and as either *direct financing* or *sales-type* leases by the lessor. We also will see that some leases do not produce debtor/creditor relationships, but instead are accounted for as rental agreements. These are designated as *operating* leases.

LEARNING OBJECTIVES

After studying this chapter, you should be able to:

- LO1 Identify and describe the operational, financial, and tax objectives that motivate leasing.
- LO2 Explain why some leases constitute rental agreements and some represent purchases/sales accompanied by debt financing.
- LO3 Explain the basis for each of the criteria and conditions used to classify leases.
- LO4 Record all transactions associated with operating leases by both the lessor and lessee.
- LO5 Describe and demonstrate how both the lessee and lessor account for a nonoperating lease.
- LO6 Describe and demonstrate how the lessor accounts for a sales-type lease.
- LO7 Explain how lease accounting is affected by the residual value of a leased asset.
- LO8 Describe the way a bargain purchase option affects lease accounting.
- LO9 Explain the impact on lease accounting of executory costs, the discount rate, initial direct costs, and contingent rentals.
- LO10 Explain sale-leaseback agreements and other special leasing arrangements and their accounting treatment.

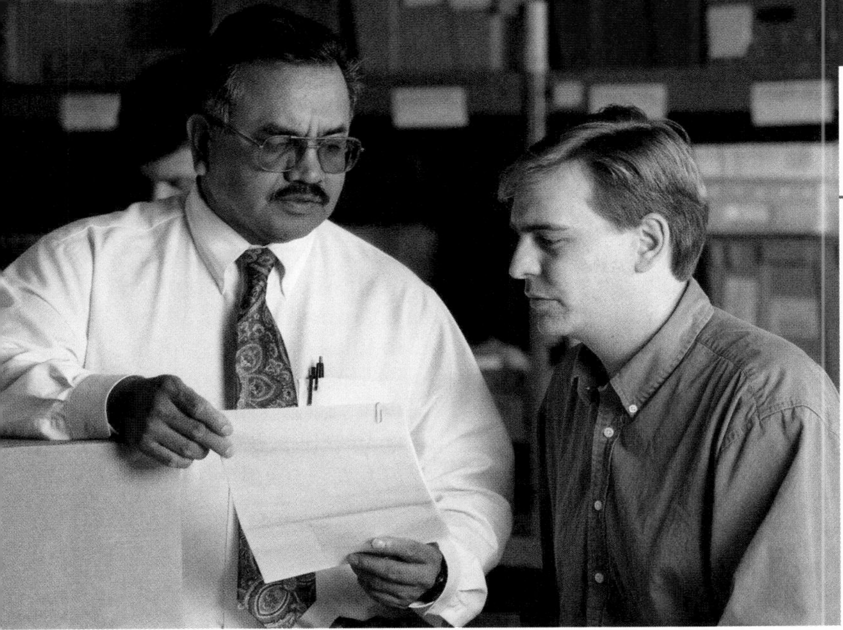

FINANCIAL REPORTING CASE

It's a Hit!

"Don't get too comfortable with those big numbers," said Aaron Sanchez, controller for your new employer. "It's likely our revenues will take a hit over the next couple of years as more of our customers lease our machines rather than buy them."

You've just finished your first look at Higher Graphics' third quarter earnings report. Like most companies in your industry, HG leases its labeling machines to some customers and sells them to others. Eager to understand the implications of your new supervisor's concerns, you pull out your old intermediate accounting book and turn to the leases chapter.

By the time you finish this chapter, you should be able to respond appropriately to the questions posed in this case. Compare your response to the solution provided at the end of the chapter.

QUESTIONS ///

1. How would HG's revenues "take a hit" as a result of more customers leasing rather than buying labeling machines? (page 645)
2. Under what kind of leasing arrangements would the "hit" not occur? (page 773)

PART A ACCOUNTING BY THE LESSOR AND LESSEE

We all are familiar with leases. If you ever have leased an apartment, you know that a lease is a contractual arrangement by which a **lessor** (owner) provides a **lessee** (user) the right to use an asset for a specified period of time. In return for this right, the lessee agrees to make stipulated, periodic cash payments during the term of the lease. An apartment lease is a typical rental agreement in which the fundamental rights and responsibilities of ownership are retained by the lessor; the lessee merely uses the asset temporarily. Businesses, too, lease assets under similar arrangements. These are referred to as **operating leases.** Many contracts, though, are formulated outwardly as leases, but in reality are installment purchases/sales. These are called **capital leases** (**direct financing** or **sales-type leases** to the lessor). Graphic 15–1 compares the classification possibilities.

An apartment lease is a typical rental agreement referred to as an *operating lease.*

GRAPHIC 15–1
Basic Lease Classifications

Lessee	Lessor
Operating lease	Operating lease
Capital lease	Direct financing lease
	Sales-type lease

After looking at some of the possible advantages of leasing assets rather than buying them in certain circumstances, we will explore differences in leases further.

DECISION MAKERS' PERSPECTIVE—Advantages of Leasing

● LO1

When a young entrepreneur started a computer training center a few years ago, she had no idea how fast her business would grow. Now, while she knows she needs computers, she doesn't know how many. Just starting out, she also has little cash with which to buy them.

The mutual funds department of a large investment firm often needs new computers and peripherals—fast. The department manager knows he can't afford to wait up to a year, the time it sometimes takes, to go through company channels to obtain purchase approval.

The U.S. Navy once leased a fleet of tankers to avoid asking Congress for appropriations.

An established computer software publisher recently began developing a new line of business software. The senior programmer has to be certain he's testing the company's products on the latest versions of computer hardware. And yet he views large expenditures on equipment subject to rapid technological change and obsolescence as risky business.

Leasing can facilitate asset acquisition.

Each of these individuals is faced with different predicaments and concerns. The entrepreneur is faced with uncertainty and cash flow problems, the department manager with time constraints and bureaucratic control systems, the programmer with fear of obsolescence. Though their specific concerns differ, these individuals have all met their firms' information technology needs with the same solution: each has decided to lease the computers rather than buy them.

The number one method of external financing by U.S. businesses is leasing.

Computers are by no means the only assets obtained through leasing arrangements. To the contrary, leasing has grown to be the most popular method of external financing of corporate assets in America. The airplane in which you last flew probably was leased, as was the gate from which it departed. Your favorite retail outlet at the local shopping mall likely leases the space it operates. Many companies actually exist for the sole purpose of acquiring assets and leasing them to others. And, leasing often is a primary method of "selling" a firm's products. **IBM** and **Boeing** are familiar examples.

In light of its popularity, you may be surprised that leasing usually is more expensive than buying. Of course, the higher apparent cost of leasing is because the lessor usually shoulders at least some of the financial and risk burdens that a purchaser normally would assume. So, why the popularity?

Tax incentives often motivate leasing.

The lease decisions described above are motivated by operational incentives. Tax and market considerations also motivate firms to lease. Sometimes leasing offers tax saving advantages over outright purchases. For instance, a company with little or no taxable income—maybe a business just getting started, or one experiencing an economic downturn—will get little benefit from depreciation deductions. But the company can benefit *indirectly* by leasing assets rather than buying. By allowing the *lessor* to retain ownership and thus benefit from depreciation deductions, the lessee often can negotiate lower lease payments. Lessees with sufficient taxable income to take advantage of the depreciation deductions, but still in lower tax brackets than lessors, also can achieve similar indirect tax benefits.

The desire to obtain "off-balance-sheet financing" also is sometimes a leasing stimulus. When funds are borrowed to purchase an asset, the liability has a detrimental effect on the company's debt-equity ratio and other quantifiable indicators of riskiness. Similarly, the purchased asset increases total assets and correspondingly lowers calculations of the rate of return on assets. Despite research that indicates otherwise, management actions continue to reflect a belief that the financial market is naive and is fooled by off-balance-sheet financing. Managers continue to avoid reporting assets and liabilities by leasing rather than buying and by constructing lease agreements in such a way that capitalizing the assets and liabilities is not required.[1]

Leasing sometimes is used as a means of off-balance-sheet financing.

Whether or not there is any real effect on security prices, sometimes off-balance-sheet financing helps a firm avoid exceeding contractual limits on designated financial ratios (like the debt to equity ratio, for instance).[2] When the operational, tax, and financial market advantages are considered, the *net* cost of leasing often is less than the cost of purchasing.

Operational, tax, and financial market incentives often make leasing an attractive alternative to purchasing.

Capital Leases and Installment Notes Compared

● LO2

You learned in the previous chapter how to account for an installment note. To a great extent, then, you already have learned how to account for a capital lease. To illustrate, let's recall the situation described in the previous chapter. We assumed that Skill Graphics purchased a package-labeling machine from Hughes–Barker Corporation by issuing a three-year installment note that required six semiannual installment payments of $139,857 each. That arrangement provided for the purchase of the $666,633 machine as well as interest at an annual rate of 14% (7% twice each year). Remember, too, that each installment payment consisted of part interest (7% times the outstanding balance) and part payment for the machine (the remainder of each payment).

Now let's suppose that Skill Graphics instead acquired the package-labeling machine from Hughes–Barker Corporation under a three-year *lease* that required six semiannual rental payments of $139,857 each. Obviously, the fundamental nature of the transaction remains the same regardless of whether it is negotiated as an installment purchase or as a lease. So, it would be inconsistent to account for this lease in a fundamentally different way than for an installment purchase:

Comparison of a Note and Capital Lease

In keeping with the basic accounting concept of substance over form, accounting for a capital lease parallels that for an installment purchase.

At Inception (January 1)		
Installment Note		
Machinery	666,633	
Note payable		666,633
Capital Lease		
Leased machinery	666,633	
Lease payable		666,633

[1]You will learn later in the chapter that accounting standards are designed to identify lease arrangements that, despite their outward appearance, are in reality purchases of assets. Assets acquired by these arrangements, *capital leases,* are required to be recorded as well as the related lease liability. Managers often structure lease terms so that capitalization requirements are avoided.

[2]It is common for debt agreements, particularly long-term ones, to include restrictions on the debtor as a way to provide some degree of protection to the creditor. Sometimes a minimum level is specified for current assets relative to current liabilities, net assets, debt as a ratio of equity, or many other financial ratios. Often a restriction is placed on dividend payments, share repurchases, or other activities that might impede the debtor's ability to repay the debt. Typically, the debt becomes due on demand when the debtor becomes in violation of such a debt covenant, often after a specified grace period.

Consistent with the nature of the transaction, interest expense accrues each period at the effective rate times the outstanding balance:

Interest Compared for a Note and Capital Lease

Each payment includes both an amount that represents interest and an amount that represents a reduction of principal.

At the First Semiannual Payment Date (June 30)

Installment Note		
Interest expense (7% × $666,633)	46,664	
Note payable (difference)	93,193	
Cash (installment payment)		139,857
Capital Lease		
Interest expense (7% × $666,633)	46,664	
Lease payable (difference)	93,193	
Cash (rental payment)		139,857

Because the lease payable balance declines with each payment, the interest becomes less each period. An amortization schedule is convenient to track the changing amounts as shown in Graphic 15–2.

GRAPHIC 15–2
Lease Amortization Schedule

Each rental payment includes interest on the outstanding balance at the effective rate. The remainder of each payment reduces the outstanding balance.

Date	Payments	Effective Interest	Decrease in Balance	Outstanding Balance
		(7% × Outstanding balance)		
				666,633
1	139,857	.07(666,633) = 46,664	93,193	573,440
2	139,857	.07(573,440) = 40,141	99,716	473,724
3	139,857	.07(473,724) = 33,161	106,696	367,028
4	139,857	.07(367,028) = 25,692	114,165	252,863
5	139,857	.07(252,863) = 17,700	122,157	130,706
6	139,857	.07(130,706) = 9,151*	130,706	0
	839,142	172,509	666,633	

*Rounded

You should recognize this as essentially the same amortization schedule we used in the previous chapter in connection with our installment note example. The reason for the similarity is that we view a capital lease as being, in substance, equivalent to an installment purchase. So naturally the accounting treatment of the two essentially identical transactions should be consistent.

Lease Classification

A lease is accounted for as either a rental agreement or a purchase/sale accompanied by debt financing. The choice of accounting method hinges on the nature of the leasing arrangement.

A basic concept of accounting is substance over form.

Capital leases are agreements that we identify as being formulated outwardly as leases, but which are in reality installment purchases. Sometimes the true nature of an arrangement is obvious. For example, a 10-year noncancelable lease of a computer with a 10-year useful life, by which title passes to the lessee at the end of the lease term, obviously more nearly represents a purchase than a rental agreement. But what if the terms of the contract do not transfer title, and the lease term is for only seven years of the asset's 10-year life? Suppose contractual terms permit the lessee to obtain title under certain prearranged conditions? What if compensation provided by the lease contract is nearly equal to the value of the asset under lease? These situations are less clear-cut.

Accounting for leases attempts to see through the legal form of the agreements to determine their economic substance.

Professional judgment is needed to differentiate between leases that represent rental agreements and those that in reality are installment purchases/sales. The essential question is whether the usual risks and rewards of ownership have been transferred to the lessee.

But judgment alone is likely to lead to inconsistencies in practice. The desire to encourage consistency in practice motivated the FASB to provide guidance for distinguishing between the two fundamental types of leases.[3] As you study the classification criteria in the following paragraphs, keep in mind that some leases clearly fit the classifications we give them, but others fall in a gray area somewhere between the two extremes. For those, we end up forcing them into one category or the other by somewhat arbitrary criteria.

Classification Criteria

A lessee should classify a lease transaction as a capital lease if it includes a noncancelable lease term and one or more of the four criteria listed in Graphic 15–3 are met.[4] Otherwise, it is an operating lease.

● LO3

GRAPHIC 15–3
Criteria for Classification as a Capital Lease

1. The agreement specifies that ownership of the asset transfers to the lessee.
2. The agreement contains a bargain purchase option.
3. The noncancelable lease term is equal to 75% or more of the expected economic life of the asset.
4. The present value of the minimum lease payments is equal to or greater than 90% of the fair value of the asset.

Let's look closer at these criteria.

Criterion 1: Transfer of ownership.

Since our objective is to determine when the risks and rewards of ownership have been transferred to the lessee, the first criterion is self-evident. If legal title passes to the lessee during, or at the end of, the lease term, obviously ownership attributes are transferred.

Criterion 2: Bargain purchase option.

A **bargain purchase option (BPO)** is a provision in the lease contract that gives the lessee the option of purchasing the leased property at a bargain price. This is defined as a price sufficiently lower than the expected fair value of the property (when the option becomes exercisable) that the exercise of the option appears reasonably assured at the inception of the lease. Because exercise of the option appears reasonably assured, transfer of ownership is expected. So the logic of the second criterion is similar to that of the first. Applying criterion 2 in practice, though, often is more difficult because it is necessary to make a judgment now about whether a future option price will be a bargain.

Criterion 3: Lease term is 75% of economic life.

If an asset is leased for most of its useful life, then most of the benefits and responsibilities of ownership are transferred to the lessee. We presume, quite arbitrarily, that 75% or more of the **expected economic life** of the asset is an appropriate threshold point for this purpose.

Although the intent of this criterion is fairly straightforward, implementation sometimes is troublesome. First, the lease term may be uncertain. It may be renewable beyond its initial term. Or the lease may be cancelable after a designated noncancelable period. When either is an issue, we ordinarily consider the lease term to be the noncancelable[5] term of the lease plus any periods covered by **bargain renewal options.**[6] A bargain renewal option gives the lessee the option to renew the lease at a bargain rate. That is, the rental payment is sufficiently lower than the expected fair rental of the property at the date the option becomes exercisable that exercise of the option appears reasonably assured.

[3]"Accounting for Leases," *Statement of Financial Accounting Standards No. 13* (Stamford, Conn.: FASB, 1980), par. 7.

[4]Noncancelable in this context does not preclude the agreement from specifying that the lease is cancelable after a designated noncancelable lease term. If no portion of the lease term is noncancelable, it is an operating lease. Later in this section, we discuss treatment of any cancelable portion of the lease term.

[5]Noncancelable in this context is a lease that is cancelable only by (a) the occurrence of some remote contingency, (b) permission of the lessor, (c) a new lease with the same lessor, or (d) payment by the lessee of a penalty in an amount such that continuation of the lease appears, at inception, reasonably assured. "Accounting for Leases: Sale and Leaseback Transactions Involving Real Estate, Sales-Type Leases of Real Estate, Definition of the Lease Term, Initial Direct Costs of Direct Financing Leases," *Statement of Financial Accounting Standards No. 98* (Stamford, Conn.: FASB, 1988), par. 22.

[6]If applicable, the lease term also should include (a) periods for which failure to renew the lease imposes a penalty on the lessee in an amount such that renewal appears reasonably assured, (b) periods covered by ordinary renewal options during which a guarantee by the lessee of the lessor's debt directly or indirectly related to the leased property is expected to be in effect or a loan from the lessee to the lessor directly or indirectly related to the leased property is expected to be outstanding, (c) periods covered by ordinary renewal options preceding the date that a bargain purchase option is exercisable, or (d) periods representing renewals or extensions of the lease at the lessor's option. "Accounting for Leases: Sale and Leaseback Transactions Involving Real Estate, Sales-Type Leases of Real Estate, Definition of the Lease Term, Initial Direct Costs of Direct Financing Leases," *Statement of Financial Accounting Standards No. 98* (Stamford, Conn.: FASB, 1988), par. 22.

ADDITIONAL CONSIDERATION

Periods covered by bargain renewal options are not included in the lease term if a **bargain purchase option** is present. This is because the lease term should not extend beyond the date a bargain purchase option becomes exercisable. For example, assume a BPO allows a lessee to buy a leased delivery truck at the end of the noncancelable five-year lease term. Even if an option to renew the lease beyond that date is considered to be a bargain renewal option, that extra period would not be included as part of the lease term. Remember, we presume the BPO will be exercised after the initial five-year term, making the renewal option irrelevant.

Another implementation issue is estimating the economic life of the leased property. This is the estimated remaining time the property is expected to be economically usable for its intended purpose, with normal maintenance and repairs, at the inception of the lease. Estimates of the economic life of leased property are subject to the same uncertainty limitations of most estimates. This uncertainty presents the opportunity to arrive at estimates that cause this third criterion not to be met.

Finally, if the inception of the lease occurs during the last 25% of an asset's economic life, this third criterion does not apply. This is consistent with the basic premise of this criterion that most of the risks and rewards of ownership occur during the first 75% of an asset's life.

Criterion 4: Present value of payments is 90% of fair value.

If the lease payments required by a lease contract substantially pay for a leased asset, it is logical to identify the arrangement as a lease equivalent to an installment purchase. This situation is considered to exist when the present value of the **minimum lease payments** is equal to or greater than 90% of the fair value of the asset at the inception of the lease. In general, minimum lease payments are payments the lessee is required to make in connection with the lease. We look closer at the make-up of minimum lease payments later in the chapter.

The 90% recovery criterion often is the decisive one. As mentioned earlier, lessees often try to avoid writing a lease agreement that will require recording an asset and liability. When this is an objective, it usually is relatively easy to avoid meeting the first three criteria. However, when the underlying motive for the lease agreement is that the lessee substantively acquire the asset, it is more difficult to avoid meeting the 90% recovery criterion without defeating that motive. New ways, though, continually are being devised to structure leases to avoid meeting this criterion. Later we will look at some popular devices that are used.

Again consistent with the basic premise that most of the risks and rewards of ownership occur during the first 75% of an asset's life, this fourth criterion does not apply if the inception of the lease occurs during the last 25% of an asset's economic life.

Additional Lessor Conditions

As we saw in the previous section, the lessee accounts for a capital lease as if an asset were purchased—records both an asset and a liability at the inception of the lease. Consistency would suggest that the lessor in the same lease transaction should record the sale of an asset. Indeed, consistency is a goal of the FASB's lease accounting standards. The four classification criteria discussed in the previous section apply to both parties to the transaction, lessees and lessors. However, a fundamental difference is that for a lessor to record the sale side of the transaction, it is necessary also to satisfy the conditions of the realization principle we discussed in Chapter 5. In particular, the FASB specifies that for the lessor to record a lease as a direct financing lease or a sales-type lease, two conditions must be met in addition to one of the four classification criteria. These are listed in Graphic 15–4.

GRAPHIC 15–4
Additional Conditions for Classification as a Nonoperating Lease by the Lessor

1. The collectibility of the lease payments must be reasonably predictable.
2. If any costs to the lessor have yet to be incurred, they are reasonably predictable. (Performance by the lessor is substantially complete.)

In the case of a sales-type lease (discussed later in Part A of this chapter) in which the lessor recognizes sales revenue, the reason for these additional conditions is apparent; collectibility of payments and substantial completion of the earnings process are conditions of the revenue realization principle. This logic is extended to agreements classified as direct financing leases. Although sales revenue is not recorded in a direct financing lease, the leased asset is removed from the lessor's books and is replaced by a receivable.

Although uniformity of classification is a goal of lease accounting standards, it is obvious that the additional conditions allow inconsistencies.[7] Indeed, in lease negotiations an objective of the parties involved often is to devise terms that will result in a sale by the lessor but an operating lease by the lessee.[8]

Additional lessor conditions for classification as a nonoperating lease are consistent with criteria of the revenue realization principle.

In the remaining sections of Part A of this chapter we consider, in order, operating leases, direct financing leases (capital leases to the lessee), and sales-type leases (capital leases to the lessee).

INTERNATIONAL FINANCIAL REPORTING STANDARDS

Lease Classification. We discussed four classification criteria used under U.S. GAAP to determine whether a lease is a capital lease. Under IFRS, a lease is a capital lease (called a finance lease under *IAS No. 17*, "Leases"), if substantially all risks and rewards of ownership are transferred. Judgment is made based on a number of "indicators" including some similar to the specific criteria of U.S. GAAP. More judgment, less specificity, is applied.

Operating Leases

If a lease does not meet any of the criteria for a capital lease it is considered to be more in the nature of a rental agreement and is referred to as an **operating lease**.[9] We assume that the fundamental rights and responsibilities of ownership are retained by the lessor and that the lessee merely is using the asset temporarily. In keeping with that presumption, a sale is not recorded by the lessor; a purchase is not recorded by the lessee. Instead, the periodic rental payments are accounted for merely as rent by both parties to the transaction—rent revenue by the lessor, rent expense by the lessee.

FINANCIAL Reporting Case

Q1, p. 759

● LO4

Let's look at an example that illustrates the relatively straightforward accounting for operating leases. The earlier example comparing a capital lease to an installment purchase assumed rental payments at the *end* of each period. A more typical leasing arrangement requires rental payments at the *beginning* of each period. This more realistic payment schedule is assumed in Illustration 15–1.

Journal entries for Illustration 15–1 are shown in Illustration 15–1A.

In an operating lease, rent is recognized on a straight-line basis unless another systematic method more clearly reflects the benefits of the asset's use. So, if rental payments are uneven—for instance, if rent increases are scheduled—the total scheduled payments ordinarily would be expensed equally (straight-line basis) over the lease term.[10]

Advance Payments

Often lease agreements call for advance payments to be made at the inception of the lease that represent prepaid rent. For instance, it is common for a lessee to pay a bonus in return for negotiating more favorable lease terms. Such payments are recorded as prepaid rent and allocated (normally on a straight-line basis) to rent expense/rent revenue over the lease term. So the rent that is periodically reported in those cases consists of the periodic rent

[7]"Accounting for Leases," *Statement of Financial Accounting Standards No. 13* (Stamford, Conn.: FASB, 1980).

[8]Later in the chapter we discuss ways this is done.

[9]The term *operating lease* got its name long ago when a lessee routinely received from the lessor an operator along with leased equipment.

[10]"Accounting for Operating Leases With Scheduled Rent Increases," *FASB Technical Bulletin 85-3* (Stamford, Conn.: FASB, 1985), par. 1.

ILLUSTRATION 15–1

Application of Classification Criteria

Using Excel, enter:
=PV(.10,4,100000,, 1)
Output: 348685.2

Using a calculator:
enter: BEG mode N 4 I 10
PMT −100000 FV
Output: PV 348685

On January 1, 2009, Sans Serif Publishers, Inc., a computer services and printing firm, leased a color copier from CompuDec Corporation.

The lease agreement specifies four annual payments of $100,000 beginning January 1, 2009, the inception of the lease, and at each January 1 thereafter through 2012. The useful life of the copier is estimated to be six years.

Before deciding to lease, Sans Serif considered purchasing the copier for its cash price of $479,079. If funds were borrowed to buy the copier, the interest rate would have been 10%.

How should this lease be classified? We apply the four classification criteria:

1. Does the agreement specify that ownership of the asset transfers to the lessee? — No
2. Does this agreement contain a bargain purchase option? — No
3. Is the lease term equal to 75% or more of the expected economic life of the asset? — No (4 yrs < 75% of 6 yrs)
4. Is the present value of the minimum lease payments equal to or greater than 90% of the fair value of the asset? — No ($348,685 < 90% of $479,079)

$100,000 × 3.48685* = $348,685
(Lease payments) (Present value)

Since none of the four classification criteria is met, this is an operating lease.

*Present value of an annuity due of $1: $n = 4$, $i = 10\%$. Recall from Chapter 6 that we refer to periodic payments at the beginning of each period as an *annuity due*.

ILLUSTRATION 15–1A

Journal Entries for an Operating Lease

At the beginning of the year, the rent payments are prepaid rent to the lessee and unearned rent to the lessor.

The lessor retains the asset on its books, and accordingly records depreciation on the asset.

The operating lease described in Illustration 15–1 is recorded as follows:

At Each of the Four Payment Dates

Sans Serif Publishers, Inc. (Lessee)		
Prepaid rent	100,000	
Cash		100,000
CompuDec Corporation (Lessor)		
Cash	100,000	
Unearned rent revenue		100,000

At the End of Each Year

Sans Serif Publishers, Inc. (Lessee)		
Rent expense	100,000	
Prepaid rent		100,000
CompuDec Corporation (Lessor)		
Unearned rent revenue	100,000	
Rent revenue		100,000
Depreciation expense	x,xxx	
Accumulated depreciation		x,xxx

payments themselves plus an allocated portion of prepaid rent. This is demonstrated in Illustration 15–1B.

Sometimes advance payments include security deposits that are refundable at the expiration of the lease or prepayments of the last period's rent. A refundable security deposit is recorded as a long-term receivable (by the lessee) and liability (by the lessor) unless it is not expected to be returned. A prepayment of the last period's rent is recorded as prepaid rent and allocated to rent expense/rent revenue during the last period of the lease term.

At times, lease agreements call for uneven rent payments during the term of the lease. One way this can occur is when the initial payment (or maybe several payments) is waived. This is called a **rent abatement.**

Alternatively, rent payments may be scheduled to increase periodically over the lease term. In any event, the total rent over the term of the lease is allocated to individual periods on a straight-line basis. This means the (temporarily) unpaid portion of rent expense must be credited to deferred rent expense payable until later in the lease term when rent payments exceed rent expense.

ILLUSTRATION 15–1B

Journal Entries—Operating Lease with Advance Payment

Assume Sans Serif paid a $40,000 bonus (advance payment) at the inception of the lease described in Illustration 15–1 in return for lower periodic payments—$90,000 each.

At the Inception of the Lease		
Sans Serif Publishers, Inc. (Lessee)		
Prepaid rent (bonus payment)	40,000	
Cash		40,000
CompuDec Corporation (Lessor)		
Cash	40,000	
Unearned rent revenue (bonus payment)		40,000
At Each of the Four Payment Dates		
Sans Serif Publishers, Inc. (Lessee)		
Prepaid rent (annual rent payment)	90,000	
Cash		90,000
CompuDec Corporation (Lessor)		
Cash	90,000	
Unearned rent revenue (annual rent payment)		90,000
At the End of Each Year		
Sans Serif Publishers, Inc. (Lessee)		
Rent expense (annual rent)	90,000	
Prepaid rent		90,000
Rent expense (bonus allocation)	10,000	
Prepaid rent ($40,000 ÷ 4)		10,000
CompuDec Corporation (Lessor)		
Unearned rent revenue	90,000	
Rent revenue (annual rent)		90,000
Unearned rent revenue ($40,000 ÷ 4)	10,000	
Rent revenue (bonus allocation)		10,000
Depreciation expense	x,xxx	
Accumulated depreciation		x,xxx

Advance payments in operating leases are deferred and allocated to rent over the lease term.

Rent comprises the periodic rent payments plus an allocated portion of the advance payment.

Leasehold Improvements

The cost of a *leasehold improvement* is depreciated over its useful life to the lessee.

Sometimes a lessee will make improvements to leased property that reverts back to the lessor at the end of the lease. If a lessee constructs a new building or makes modifications to existing structures, that cost represents an asset just like any other capital expenditure. Like other assets, its cost is allocated as depreciation expense over its useful life to the lessee, which will be the shorter of the physical life of the asset or the lease term.[11] Theoretically, such assets can be recorded in accounts descriptive of their nature, such as buildings or plant. In practice, the traditional account title used is **leasehold improvements**.[12] In any case, the undepreciated cost usually is reported in the balance sheet under the caption *property, plant, and equipment.* Movable assets like office furniture and equipment that are not attached to the leased property are not considered leasehold improvements.

Hundreds of firms in 2005 corrected the way they accounted for leases.

During 2005 hundreds of companies, particularly in the retail and restaurant industries, underwent one of the most widespread accounting correction events ever. Corrections were in the way these companies, including **Pep Boys**, **Ann Taylor**, **Target**, and **Domino's Pizza**, had allocated the cost of leasehold improvements. Rather than expensing leasehold improvements properly over the lease terms, these firms for years had inappropriately expensed the cost over the longer estimated useful lives of the properties. Prompting the

[11]If the agreement contains an option to renew, and the likelihood of renewal is uncertain, the renewal period is ignored.

[12]Also, traditionally, depreciation sometimes is labeled amortization when in connection with leased assets and leasehold improvements. This is of little consequence. Remember, both depreciation and amortization refer to the process of allocating an asset's cost over its useful life.

sweeping revisions was a Securities and Exchange Commission letter on February 7, 2005, urging companies to follow long-standing accounting standards in this area. A result of the improper practices was to defer expense, thereby accelerating earnings. For instance, **McDonald's Corp.** recorded a charge of $139 million in its 2004 fourth quarter to adjust for the difference.

Let's turn our attention now to accounting for leases that meet the criteria and conditions for classification as nonoperating leases by both the lessee and the lessor.

Nonoperating Leases—Lessee and Lessor

LO5

In the operating lease illustration, we assumed Sans Serif leased a copier directly from its manufacturer. Now, in Illustration 15–2 on page 769, let's assume a financial intermediary provided financing by acquiring the copier and leasing it to the user.

A leased asset is recorded by the lessee at the *present value of the minimum lease payments* or the asset's fair value, whichever is lower.

A lease that transfers substantially all of the benefits and risks incident to ownership of property should be accounted for as the acquisition of an asset and the incurrence of an obligation by the lessee and as a sale or financing by the lessor.[13]

The amount recorded (capitalized) by the lessee is the present value of the minimum lease payments. However, if the fair value of the asset is lower than this amount, the recorded value of the asset should be limited to fair value. Unless the lessor is a manufacturer or dealer, the fair value typically will be the lessor's cost ($479,079 in this case). However, if considerable time has elapsed between the purchase of the property by the lessor and the inception of the lease, the fair value might be different. When the lessor is a manufacturer or dealer, the fair value of the property at the inception of the lease ordinarily will be its normal selling price (reduced by any volume or trade discounts). We study this situation (a sales-type lease) later. In unusual cases, market conditions may cause fair value to be less than the normal selling price.

Interest is a function of time. It accrues at the effective rate on the balance outstanding during the period.

Be sure to note that the entire $100,000 first rental payment is applied to principal reduction.[14] Because it occurred at the inception of the lease, no interest had yet accrued. Subsequent rental payments include interest on the outstanding balance as well as a residual portion that reduces that outstanding balance. As of the second rental payment date, one year's interest has accrued on the $379,079 balance outstanding during 2010, recorded as in Illustration 15–2A on page 770. Notice that the outstanding balance is reduced by $62,092—the portion of the $100,000 payment remaining after interest is covered.

ADDITIONAL CONSIDERATION

Some lessors use what's called the "gross method" to record the receivable in a nonoperating lease. By this method, the lessor debits lease receivable for the gross sum of the lease payments and credits *unearned interest revenue* for the difference between the total of the payments and the present value of the payments since that's the amount that eventually will be recorded as interest revenue over the term of the lease. In Illustration 15–2, the lessor's entry by the gross method at the inception of the lease would be:

Lease receivable ($100,000 × 6)	600,000	
Unearned interest revenue (difference)		120,921
Inventory of equipment (lessor's cost)		479,079

The same ultimate result is achieved either way. We use the net method in our illustrations to more easily demonstrate the lessee's entries and the lessor's entries being "two sides of the same coin." Whichever method is used, both the lessee and the lessor must report in the disclosure notes both the net and gross amounts of the lease.

[13] "Accounting for Leases," *Statement of Financial Accounting Standards No. 13* (Stamford, Conn.: FASB, 1980).

[14] Another way to view this is to think of the first $100,000 as a down payment with the remaining $379,079 financed by 5 (i.e., 6 – 1) *year-end* lease payments.

ILLUSTRATION 15–2
Nonoperating Leases

On January 1, 2009, Sans Serif Publishers, Inc., leased a copier from First LeaseCorp. First LeaseCorp purchased the equipment from CompuDec Corporation at a cost of $479,079.

The lease agreement specifies annual payments beginning January 1, 2009, the inception of the lease, and at each December 31 thereafter through 2013. The six-year lease term ending December 31, 2014, is equal to the estimated useful life of the copier.

First LeaseCorp routinely acquires electronic equipment for lease to other firms. The interest rate in these financing arrangements is 10%.

Since the lease term is equal to the expected useful life of the copier (>75%), the transaction must be recorded by the lessee as a **capital lease.**[15] If we assume also that collectibility of the lease payments and any costs to the lessor that are yet to be incurred are reasonably predictable, this qualifies also as a **direct financing lease** to First LeaseCorp. To achieve its objectives, First LeaseCorp must (a) recover its $479,079 investment as well as (b) earn interest revenue at a rate of 10%. So, the lessor determined that annual rental payments would be $100,000:

$479,079	÷	4.79079*	=	$100,000
Lessor's cost				Rental payments

*Present value of an annuity due of $1: $n = 6$, $i = 10\%$.

Using Excel, enter:
=PMT(.10,6,479079,, 1)
Output: 100000

Of course, Sans Serif Publishers, Inc., views the transaction from the other side. The price the lessee pays for the copier is the present value of the rental payments:

$100,000	×	4.79079*	=	$479,079
Rental payments				Lessee's cost

*Present value of an annuity due of $1: $n = 6$, $i = 10\%$.

Using a calculator:
enter: BEG mode N 6 I 10
PV −479079 FV
Output: PMT 100000

Direct Financing Lease (January 1, 2009)

Sans Serif Publishers, Inc. (Lessee)		
Leased equipment (present value of lease payments)	479,079	
Lease payable (present value of lease payments)		479,079
First LeaseCorp (Lessor)		
Lease receivable (present value of lease payments)	479,079	
Inventory of equipment (lessor's cost)		479,079

First Lease Payment (January 1, 2009)*

Sans Serif Publishers, Inc. (Lessee)		
Lease payable	100,000	
Cash		100,000
First LeaseCorp (Lessor)		
Cash	100,000	
Lease receivable		100,000

The first lease payment reduces the balances in the lease payable and the lease receivable by $100,000 to $379,079.

*Of course, the entries to record the lease and the first payment could be combined into a single entry since they occur at the same time.

The amortization schedule in Graphic 15–5 on page 770 shows how the lease balance and the effective interest change over the six-year lease term. Each rental payment after the first includes both an amount that represents interest and an amount that represents a reduction of principal. The periodic reduction of principal is sufficient that, at the end of the lease term, the outstanding balance is zero.

An interesting aspect of the amortization schedule that you may want to note at this point relates to a disclosure requirement that we discuss at the end of the chapter. Among other things, the lessee and lessor must report separately the current and noncurrent portions of the outstanding lease balance. Both amounts are provided by the amortization schedule. For example, if we want the amounts to report on the 2009 balance sheet, refer to the next row of the schedule. The portion of the 2010 payment that represents principal ($68,301) is the *current* (as of December 31, 2009) balance. The *noncurrent* amount is the balance outstanding

[15]The fourth criterion also is met. The present value of lease payments ($479,079) is 100% (>90%) of the fair value of the copier ($479,079). Meeting any one of the four criteria is sufficient.

ILLUSTRATION 15–2A
Journal Entries for the Second Lease Payment

LESSEE Net Payable
$479,079
(100,000)
$379,079
(62,092)
$316,987

LESSOR Net Receivable
$479,079
(100,000)
$379,079
(62,092)
$316,987

Second Lease Payment (December 31, 2009)

Sans Serif Publishers, Inc. (Lessee)		
Interest expense [10% × ($479,079 – 100,000)]	37,908	
Lease payable (difference)	62,092	
Cash (lease payment)		100,000
First LeaseCorp (Lessor)		
Cash (lease payment)	100,000	
Lease receivable		62,092
Interest revenue [10% × ($479,079 – 100,000)]		37,908

GRAPHIC 15–5
Lease Amortization Schedule

The first rental payment includes no interest.

The total of the cash payments ($600,000) provides for:
1. Payment for the copier ($479,079).
2. Interest ($120,921) at an effective rate of 10%.

	Payments	Effective Interest	Decrease in Balance	Outstanding Balance
		(10% × Outstanding balance)		
1/1/09				479,079
1/1/09	100,000		100,000	379,079
12/31/09	100,000	.10 (379,079) = 37,908	62,092	316,987
12/31/10	100,000	.10 (316,987) = 31,699	68,301	248,686
12/31/11	100,000	.10 (248,686) = 24,869	75,131	173,555
12/31/12	100,000	.10 (173,555) = 17,355	82,645	90,910
12/31/13	100,000	.10 (90,910) = 9,090*	90,910	0
	600,000	120,921*	479,079	

*Adjusted for rounding of other numbers in the schedule.

after the 2010 reduction ($248,686). These amounts are the current and noncurrent lease liability for the lessee and the current and noncurrent net investment for the lessor.

Depreciation

Depreciation is recorded for leased assets in a manner consistent with the lessee's usual policy for depreciating its operational assets.

Because a capital lease assumes the lessee purchased the asset, the lessee depreciates its cost.

End of Each Year

Sans Serif Publishers, Inc. (Lessee)		
Depreciation expense ($479,079 ÷ 6 years*)	79,847	
Accumulated depreciation		79,847

*If the lessee depreciates assets by the straight-line method.

The depreciation period is restricted to the lease term unless the lease provides for transfer of title or a BPO.

DEPRECIATION PERIOD. The lessee normally should depreciate a leased asset over the term of the lease. However, if ownership transfers or a bargain purchase option is present (i.e., either of the first two classification criteria is met), the asset should be depreciated over its useful life. This means depreciation is recorded over the useful life of the asset to the lessee.

A description of leased assets and related depreciation provided in a recent disclosure note (Graphic 15–6) of **Kroger Company** is representative of leased asset disclosures.

3. PROPERTY, PLANT AND EQUIPMENT, NET

Property, plant and equipment, net consists of:

$ in millions	2006	2005
Land	$ 1,690	$ 1,675
Buildings and land improvements	5,402	5,142
Equipment	8,255	7,980
Leasehold improvements	4,221	3,917
Construction-in-progress	822	511
Leased property under capital leases	592	561
	20,982	19,786
Accumulated depreciation and amortization	(9,203)	(8,421)
Total	$11,779	$11,365

Accumulated depreciation for leased property under capital leases was $288 at February 3, 2007 and $263 at January 28, 2006.

GRAPHIC 15–6

Disclosure of Leased Assets—Kroger Company

Real World Financials

Accrued Interest

If a company's reporting period ends at any time between payment dates, it's necessary to record (as an adjusting entry) any interest that has accrued since interest was last recorded. We purposely avoided this step in the previous illustration by assuming that the lease agreement specified rental payments on December 31—the end of the reporting period. But if payments were made on another date, or if the company's fiscal year ended on a date other than December 31, accrued interest would be recorded prior to preparing financial statements. For example, if lease payments were made on January 1 of each year, the effective interest amounts shown in the lease amortization schedule still would be appropriate but would be recorded one day prior to the actual rental payment. For instance, the second cash payment of $100,000 would occur on January 1, 2010, but the interest component of that payment ($37,908) would be accrued a day earlier as shown in Illustration 15–2B.

At each financial statement date, any interest that has accrued since interest was last recorded must be accrued for all liabilities and receivables, including those relating to leases.

December 31, 2009 (to accrue interest)		
Sans Serif Publishers, Inc. (Lessee)		
Interest expense [10% × ($479,079 – 100,000)]	37,908	
Interest payable		37,908
First LeaseCorp (Lessor)		
Interest receivable	37,908	
Interest revenue [10% × ($479,079 – 100,000)]		37,908
Second Lease Payment (January 1, 2010)		
Sans Serif Publishers, Inc. (Lessee)		
Interest payable (from adjusting entry above)	37,908	
Lease payable (difference)	62,092	
Cash (lease payment)		100,000
First LeaseCorp (Lessor)		
Cash (lease payment)	100,000	
Lease receivable (difference)		62,092
Interest receivable (from adjusting entry above)		37,908

ILLUSTRATION 15–2B

Journal Entries When Interest Is Accrued Prior to the Lease Payment

Notice that this is consistent with recording accrued interest on any debt, whether in the form of a note, a bond, or a lease.

We assumed in this illustration that First LeaseCorp bought the copier for $479,079 and then leased it for the same price. There was no profit on the "sale" itself. The only income derived by the lessor was interest revenue earned over the lease term. In effect, First LeaseCorp financed the purchase of the copier by Sans Serif Publishers. This type of lease is a direct financing lease. This kind of leasing is a thriving industry. It is a profitable part of operations for banks and other financial institutions (Citicorp is one of the largest). Some leasing companies do nothing else. Often leasing companies, like **IBM Credit Corporation**, are subsidiaries of larger corporations, formed for the sole purpose of conducting financing activities for their parent corporations.

CONCEPT REVIEW EXERCISE

DIRECT FINANCING LEASE

United Cellular Systems leased a satellite transmission device from Pinnacle Leasing Services on January 1, 2010. Pinnacle paid $625,483 for the transmission device. Its fair value is $625,483.

Terms of the Lease Agreement and Related Information:

Lease term	3 years (6 semiannual periods)
Semiannual rental payments	$120,000 – beginning of each period
Economic life of asset	3 years
Interest rate	12%

Required:

1. Prepare the appropriate entries for both United Cellular Systems and Pinnacle Leasing Services on January 1, the inception of the lease.
2. Prepare an amortization schedule that shows the pattern of interest expense for United Cellular Systems and interest revenue for Pinnacle Leasing Services over the lease term.
3. Prepare the appropriate entries to record the second lease payment on July 1, 2010, and adjusting entries on December 31, 2010 (the end of both companies' fiscal years).

SOLUTION

1. Prepare the appropriate entries for both United Cellular Systems and Pinnacle Leasing Services on January 1, the inception of the lease.

Calculation of the present value of minimum lease payments.

Present value of periodic rental payments:

($120,000 × 5.21236*) = $625,483

*Present value of an annuity due of $1: n = 6, i = 6%.

January 1, 2010

United Cellular Systems (Lessee)		
Leased equipment (calculated above)	625,483	
Lease payable (calculated above)		625,483
Lease payable	120,000	
Cash (lease payment)		120,000
Pinnacle Leasing Services (Lessor)		
Lease receivable (calculated above)	625,483	
Inventory of equipment (lessor's cost)		625,483
Cash (lease payment)	120,000	
Lease receivable		120,000

2. Prepare an amortization schedule that shows the pattern of interest expense for United Cellular Systems and interest revenue for Pinnacle Leasing Services over the lease term.

Date	Payments	Effective Interest	Decrease in Balance	Outstanding Balance
		(6% × Outstanding balance)		
1/1/10				625,483
1/1/10	120,000		120,000	505,483
7/1/10	120,000	.06 (505,483) = 30,329	89,671	415,812
1/1/11	120,000	.06 (415,812) = 24,949	95,051	320,761
7/1/11	120,000	.06 (320,761) = 19,246	100,754	220,007
1/1/12	120,000	.06 (220,007) = 13,200	106,800	113,207
7/1/12	120,000	.06 (113,207) = 6,793*	113,207	0
	720,000	94,517	625,483	

*Adjusted for rounding of other numbers in the schedule.

3. Prepare the appropriate entries to record the second lease payment on July 1, 2010, and adjusting entries on December 31, 2010 (the end of both companies' fiscal years).

July 1, 2010

United Cellular Systems (Lessee)		
Interest expense [6% × ($625,483 − 120,000)]	30,329	
Lease payable (difference)	89,671	
Cash (lease payment)		120,000
Pinnacle Leasing Services (Lessor)		
Cash (lease payment)	120,000	
Lease receivable (difference)		89,671
Interest revenue [6% × ($625,483 − 120,000)]		30,329

December 31, 2010

United Cellular Systems (Lessee)		
Interest expense (6% × $415,812: from schedule)	24,949	
Interest payable		24,949
Depreciation expense ($625,483 ÷ 3 years)	208,494	
Accumulated depreciation		208,494
Pinnacle Leasing Services (Lessor)		
Interest receivable	24,949	
Interest revenue (6% × $415,812: from schedule)		24,949

Let's turn our attention now to situations in which the lessors are manufacturers or retailers and use lease arrangements as a means of selling their products.

Sales-Type Leases

LO6

FINANCIAL Reporting Case

Q2, p. 759

A **sales-type lease** differs from a direct financing lease in only one respect. In addition to interest revenue earned over the lease term, the lessor receives a manufacturer's or dealer's profit on the "sale" of the asset.[16] This additional profit exists when the fair value of the asset (usually the present value of the minimum lease payments, or "selling price") exceeds the cost or carrying value of the asset sold. Accounting for a sales-type lease is the same as for a direct financing lease except for recognizing the profit at the inception of the lease.[17]

To illustrate, let's modify our previous illustration. Assume all facts are the same except Sans Serif Publishers leased the copier directly from CompuDec Corporation, rather than through the financing intermediary. Also assume CompuDec's cost of the copier was $300,000. If you recall that the lease payments (their present value) provide a selling price

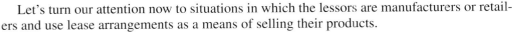

INTERNATIONAL FINANCIAL REPORTING STANDARDS

Joint Lease Project. The IASB and FASB are collaborating on a joint project for a revision of leasing standards. The Boards have agreed that a "right of use" model (where the lessee recognizes an asset representing the right to use the leased asset for the lease term and also recognizes a corresponding liability for the lease rentals, whatever the term of the lease) is the only approach which recognizes assets and liabilities that corresponded to the conceptual framework definitions. Many people expect the new standard to result in most, if not all, leases being recorded as an intangible asset for the right of use and a liability for the present value of the lease payments.

The impact of any changes will be significant; U.S. companies alone have over $1.25 *trillion* in operating lease obligations.

[16]A lessor need not be a manufacturer or a dealer for the arrangement to qualify as a sales-type lease. The existence of a profit (or loss) on the sale is the distinguishing factor.

[17]It is possible that the asset's carrying value will exceed its fair value, in which case a dealer's loss should be recorded.

ILLUSTRATION 15–3
Sales-Type Lease

On January 1, 2009, Sans Serif Publishers, Inc., leased a copier from CompuDec Corporation at a price of $479,079.

The lease agreement specifies annual payments of $100,000 beginning January 1, 2009, the inception of the lease, and at each December 31 thereafter through 2013. The six-year lease term ending December 31, 2014, is equal to the estimated useful life of the copier.

CompuDec manufactured the copier at a cost of $300,000.

CompuDec's interest rate for financing the transaction is 10%.

Sales-Type Lease*

CompuDec Corporation (Lessor)		
Lease receivable (present value of lease payments)	479,079	
Cost of goods sold (lessor's cost)	300,000	
Sales revenue (present value of lease payments)		479,079
Inventory of equipment (lessor's cost)		300,000

Sales revenue	$479,079
– COGS	300,000
Dealer's profit	$179,079

Remember, no interest has accrued when the first payment is made at the inception of the lease.

First Lease Payment*

CompuDec Corporation (Lessor)		
Cash	100,000	
Lease receivable		100,000

*Of course, the entries to record the lease and the first payment could be combined into a single entry:

Lease receivable ($479,079 – $100,000)	379,079	
Cost of goods sold	300,000	
Cash	100,000	
Sales revenue		479,079
Inventory of equipment		300,000

Recording a sales-type lease is similar to recording a sale of merchandise on account:

A/R	{price}	
Sales rev		{price}
COGS	{cost}	
Inventory		{cost}

of $479,079, you see that CompuDec receives a gross profit on the sale of $479,079 – 300,000 = $179,079. This sales-type lease is demonstrated in Illustration 15–3.

You should recognize the similarity between recording both the revenue and cost components of this sale by lease and recording the same components of other sales transactions. As in the sale of any product, gross profit is the difference between sales revenue and cost of goods sold.

All entries other than the entry at the inception of the lease, which includes the gross profit on the sale, are the same for a sales-type lease and a direct financing lease.

Accounting by the lessee is not affected by how the lessor classifies the lease. All lessee entries are precisely the same as in the previous illustration of a direct financing lease.

Graphic 15–7 shows the relationships among various lease components, using dollar amounts from the previous illustration.

GRAPHIC 15–7
Lease Payment Relationships

The difference between the total payments and their present value (selling price of the asset) represents interest.

If the price is higher than the cost to the lessor, the lessor realizes a profit on the sale.

Lessor:		**Lessee:**
SALES-TYPE LEASE **Gross Investment in Lease***	**$600,000**	**CAPITAL LEASE** **Minimum Lease Payments**
	Less: Interest during lease term ($120,921)	
Selling Price (present value of payments)	Equals: **$479,079**	**Purchase Price** (present value of payments)
	Less: Profit on sale† ($179,079)	
Cost to Lessor	Equals: **$300,000**	**(irrelevant to lessee)**

*The lessor's gross investment in the lease also would include any *unguaranteed* residual value in addition to the minimum lease payments. Also, any residual value guaranteed by the lessee is included in the minimum lease payments (both companies). We address these issues later in the chapter.

†If profit is zero, this would be a direct financing lease.

PART B

RESIDUAL VALUE AND BARGAIN PURCHASE OPTIONS

Residual Value

The **residual value** of leased property is an estimate of what its commercial value will be at the end of the lease term. In our previous examples of nonoperating leases, we assumed that the residual value was negligible. But now let's consider the economic effect of a leased asset that does have a residual value and how that will affect the way both the lessee and the lessor account for the lease agreement.

● LO7

Suppose the copier leased in Illustration 15–3 was expected to be worth $60,000 at the end of the six-year lease term. Should this influence the lessor's (CompuDec) calculation of periodic rental payments? Other than the possible influence on rental payments, should the lessee (Sans Serif Publishers) be concerned with the residual value of the leased assets? The answer to both questions is maybe. We'll use Illustration 15–4 to see why.

ILLUSTRATION 15–4
Residual Value

On January 1, 2009, Sans Serif Publishers, Inc., leased a color copier from CompuDec Corporation at a price of $479,079. The lease agreement specifies annual payments beginning January 1, 2009, the inception of the lease, and at each December 31 thereafter through 2013. The estimated useful life of the copier is seven years. At the end of the six-year lease term, ending December 31, 2014, the copier is expected to be worth $60,000.

CompuDec manufactured the copier at a cost of $300,000.*

CompuDec's interest rate for financing the transaction is 10%.

*This provision is to be consistent with Illustration 15–3 which described a sales-type lease. However, our discussion of the effect of a residual value would be precisely the same if our illustration were of a direct financing lease (for instance, if the lessor's cost were $479,079) except that, neither sales revenue nor cost of goods sold would be recorded in a direct financing lease.

In deciding whether the residual value affects how the lease is recorded, the first question that influences the answer is "Who gets the residual value?"

Who Gets the Residual Value?

If the lessee obtains title, the lessor's computation of rental payments is unaffected by any residual value.

LESSEE OBTAINS TITLE. Consider CompuDec (the lessor) first. Suppose Sans Serif will own the copier at the end of the lease term—by transfer of title or by the expected exercise of a bargain purchase option. In that case, it is Sans Serif, not CompuDec, who will benefit by the residual value. So the lessor can't count on the $60,000 residual value to help recover its $479,079 investment. The lessor's computation of rental payments of $100,000 therefore is unaffected by the residual value.

On the other side of the transaction, the residual value influences the lessee only by the fact that depreciation calculations reflect a reduced depreciable amount. However, in determining the amount to capitalize as a leased asset and to record as a lease liability, the residual value is ignored. The capitalized amount is simply the present value of the minimum lease payments.

If the lessor retains title, the amount to be recovered through periodic lease payments is reduced by the present value of the residual amount.

LESSOR RETAINS TITLE. On the other hand, if CompuDec retains title to the asset, then it would anticipate receiving the $60,000 residual value at the conclusion of the lease term. That amount would contribute to the total amount to be recovered by the lessor and would reduce the amount needed to be recovered from the lessee through periodic rental payments. The amount of each payment would be reduced from $100,000 to $92,931, calculated in Illustration 15–4A.

ILLUSTRATION 15–4A
Lessor's Calculation of Rental Payments When Lessor Retains Residual Value

Amount to be recovered (fair value)	$479,079
Less: Present value of the residual value ($60,000 × .56447*)	(33,868)
Amount to be recovered through periodic rental payments	$445,211
Rental payments at the beginning of each of the next six years: ($445,211 ÷ 4.79079†)	$ 92,931

*Present value of $1: $n = 6$, $i = 10\%$.
†Present value of an annuity due of $1: $n = 6$, $i = 10\%$.

On the other side of the transaction, the lessee (Sans Serif Publishers) considers the purchase price of the copier to include, at a minimum, the present value of the periodic rental payments ($445,211):

$$\underset{\text{Rental payments}}{\$92{,}931} \times 4.79079^{*} = \underset{\text{Present value}}{\$445{,}211^{\dagger}}$$

*Present value of an annuity due of $1: $n = 6$, $i = 10\%$.
†The multiplication actually produces $445,212.9. We use $445,211 to be consistent with the lessor's calculation ($445,211 ÷ 4.79079 = $92,931). The difference is due to rounding.

Whether or not the lessee's cost also includes an amount for the residual value depends on whether the residual value is viewed as an additional "payment" by the lessee. It is viewed as an additional payment when the lessee *guarantees* the residual value to be a particular amount at the end of the lease term.

When the Residual Value is Guaranteed By the Lessee

Sometimes the lease agreement includes a guarantee by the lessee that the lessor will recover a specified residual value when custody of the asset reverts back to the lessor at the end of the lease term. This not only reduces the lessor's risk but also provides incentive for the lessee to exercise a higher degree of care in maintaining the leased asset to preserve the residual value. The lessee promises to return not only the property but also sufficient cash to provide the lessor with a minimum combined value. In effect, the guaranteed residual value is an additional lease payment that is to be paid in property, or cash, or both. As such, it is included in the minimum lease payments and affects the amount the lessee records as both a leased asset and a lease liability, as shown in Illustration 15–4B.

ILLUSTRATION 15–4B
Lessee's Calculation of the Present Value of Minimum Lease Payments Including a Guaranteed Residual Value

Present value of periodic rental payments ($92,931 × 4.79079*)	$445,211
Plus: Present value of the residual value ($60,000 × .56447)†	33,868
Present value of minimum lease payments (Recorded as a leased asset and a lease liability)	$479,079

*Present value of an annuity due of $1: $n = 6$, $i = 10\%$.
†Present value of $1: $n = 6$, $i = 10\%$.

You should notice that the lessee's calculation of the amount to capitalize is precisely the reverse of the lessor's calculation of periodic rental payments. This is because when the residual value is guaranteed, both view it as an additional lease payment. In accordance with

SFAS 13, the guaranteed residual value is a component of the minimum lease payı both the lessor and lessee.[18] We see in Graphic 15–8 how this affects the accountin; lease as reflected in the lease amortization schedule for CompuDec and Sans Serif.

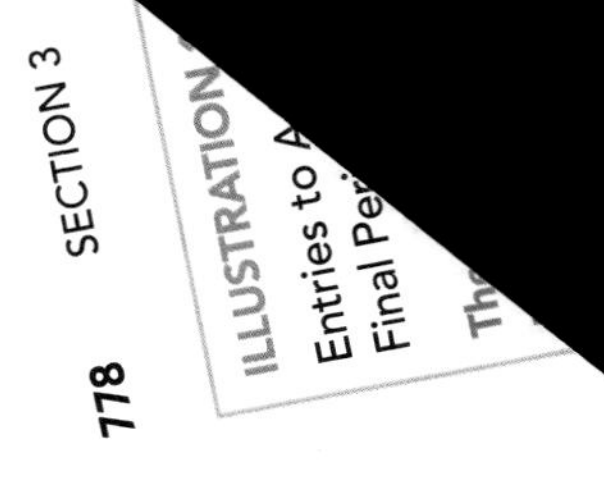

	Payments	Effective Interest	Decrease in Balance	Outstan Balanc
		(10% × Outstanding balance)		
1/1/09				479,079
1/1/09	92,931		92,931	386,148
12/31/09	92,931	.10 (386,148) = 38,615	54,316	331,832
12/31/10	92,931	.10 (331,832) = 33,183	59,748	272,084
12/31/11	92,931	.10 (272,084) = 27,208	65,723	206,361
12/31/12	92,931	.10 (206,361) = 20,636	72,295	134,066
12/31/13	92,931	.10 (134,066) = 13,407	79,524	54,542
12/31/14	60,000	.10 (54,542) = 5,458*	54,542	0
	617,586	138,507	479,079	

*Adjusted for rounding of other numbers in the schedule.

…ual value as an additional component of its investment in the lease.

The lessee views it as an additional payment only if the residual value is guaranteed by the lessee.

Be aware of several points the amortization schedule reveals. First, the six periodic cash payments are now $92,931 as we calculated previously. Notice also that we now include the $60,000 residual value as an additional lease payment. Despite the different composition of the minimum lease payments, their present value ($479,079) is the same as when we assumed $100,000 periodic payments and no residual value. However, the effective interest that will be recorded over the lease term (as interest expense by the lessee and interest revenue by the lessor) now is more: $138,507. (It was $120,921 before.) The higher interest reflects the fact that payments are farther in the future, causing the outstanding lease balances (and interest on those balances) to be higher during the lease term. Also, note that the total of the lease payments now is more: $617,586. (It was $600,000 before.) This total is referred to as the lessor's **gross investment in the lease** and is shown in Illustration 15–4C.

The lessor's *gross investment in the lease* is the total of periodic rental payments and any residual value.

ILLUSTRATION 15–4C

Sales-Type Lease with Guaranteed Residual Value

Sales-Type Lease, January 1, 2009

Sans Serif Publishers, Inc. (Lessee)		
Leased equipment (present value of lease payments)	479,079	
Lease payable (present value of lease payments)		479,079
CompuDec Corporation (Lessor)		
Lease receivable (present value of minimum lease payments*)	479,079	
Cost of goods sold (lessor's cost)	300,000	
Sales revenue (present value of minimum lease payments*)		479,079
Inventory of equipment (lessor's cost)		300,000

Sales revenue	$479,079
– COGS	300,000
Dealer's profit	$179,079

First Lease Payment, January 1, 2009

Sans Serif Publishers, Inc. (Lessee)		
Lease payable	92,931	
Cash		92,931
CompuDec Corporation (Lessor)		
Cash	92,931	
Lease receivable		92,931

*Minimum lease payments include the $60,000 residual value because it's guaranteed.

[18]Later you will see that when the residual value is *not* guaranteed, it is *not* considered a component of minimum lease payments for either the lessor or the lessee; but it still is considered a part of the lessor's gross investment in the lease and affects the amount of periodic lease payments.

15–4D

ccompany
odic Payment

residual value reduces the asset's depreciable cost to $419,079.

As the outstanding balance becomes less toward the end of the lease term, the portion of each payment that represents interest also becomes less.

December 31, 2013		
Sans Serif Publishers, Inc. (Lessee)		
Depreciation expense [($479,079 – 60,000)* ÷ 6 years]	69,847	
Accumulated depreciation		69,847
Interest expense (10% × outstanding balance)	13,407	
Lease payable (difference)	79,524	
Cash (lease payment)		92,931
CompuDec Corporation (Lessor)		
Cash (lease payment)	92,931	
Lease receivable		79,524
Interest revenue (10% × outstanding balance)		13,407

*The depreciable cost is reduced by the lessee-guaranteed residual value.

Notice, too, that the timing of the $60,000 payment is December 31, 2014, the end of the lease term. Remember, the final periodic cash payment on December 31, 2013, is at the beginning of the final year. The journal entries that accompany this final cash payment are shown in Illustration 15–4D.

At December 31, 2014, the lessee's book value of the fully depreciated copier is its $60,000 estimated residual value. If we assume that the actual residual value also is at least $60,000, then the lessee is not obligated to pay cash in addition to returning the copier to the lessor (demonstrated in Illustration 15–4E).[19]

ILLUSTRATION 15–4E

End of Lease Term—Actual Residual Value Equals the Guaranteed Amount

The sixth and final depreciation charge increases the balance in accumulated depreciation to $419,079.

The copier is reinstated on the books of the lessor at its fair value at the end of the lease term.

December 31, 2014		
Sans Serif Publishers, Inc. (Lessee)		
Depreciation expense [($479,079 – 60,000)* ÷ 6 years]	69,847	
Accumulated depreciation		69,847
Interest expense (10% × outstanding balance)	5,458	
Lease payable (difference)	54,542	
Accumulated depreciation (account balance)	419,079	
Leased equipment (account balance)		479,079
CompuDec Corporation (Lessor)		
Inventory of equipment (residual value)	60,000	
Lease receivable (account balance)		54,542
Interest revenue (10% × outstanding balance)		5,458

*The depreciable cost is reduced by the lessee-guaranteed residual value.

However, if we assume that the actual residual value at December 31, 2014, is only $25,000, then the lessee is required to pay $35,000 cash to the lessor in addition to returning the copier. The lessee records this payment as a loss.[20]

When the Residual Value is Not Guaranteed

If the lessee doesn't guarantee the residual value, the asset and liability are recorded as the PV of periodic rental payments only.

The previous example demonstrates that when the residual value is guaranteed, both the lessor and lessee view it as a component of minimum lease payments. But what if the lessee does *not* guarantee the residual value? In that case, the lessee is not obligated to make any payments other than the periodic rental payments. As a result, the present value of the minimum lease payments—recorded as a leased asset and a lease liability—is simply the present value of periodic rental payments ($445,211). The same is true when the residual value is guaranteed by a third-party guarantor. (Insurance companies sometimes assume this role.)

[19]If the actual value is *more* than the estimated residual value, the lessor may realize a gain if and when the asset subsequently is sold, but the potential gain does not affect the entries at the end of the lease term.

[20]Sometimes by mutual agreement the lessee will sell the leased asset at the end of the lease term and remit the proceeds (plus any deficiency under the guarantee) to the lessor.

From the lessor's perspective, the residual value is a component of minimum lease payments only if it is guaranteed (by either the lessee or a third-party guarantor). Yet, even if it is not guaranteed, the lessor still expects to receive it. So, if we modify the previous illustration to assume the residual value is not guaranteed, the lessor's receivable still is $479,079, the present value of the lease payments, including the residual value, but the sales revenue is only $445,211—the present value of the minimum lease payments *not* including the residual value. In other words, sales revenue includes the present value only of the periodic rental payments, not the unguaranteed residual value. Cost of goods sold is similarly reduced by the present value of the unguaranteed residual value, as shown in Illustration 15–4F.

The lessor's minimum lease payments include a residual value only if it is guaranteed (by either the lessee or a third party guarantor).

ILLUSTRATION 15–4F

Sales-Type Lease with Unguaranteed Residual Value

Sales-Type Lease

Sans Serif Publishers, Inc. (Lessee)		
Leased equipment (present value of lease payments)	445,211	
Lease payable (present value of lease payments)		445,211
CompuDec Corporation (Lessor)		
Lease receivable (PV of lease payments plus PV of $60,000 residual value)	479,079	
Cost of goods sold ($300,000 – 33,868)	266,132	
Sales revenue ($479,079 – 33,868)*		445,211
Inventory of equipment (lessor's cost)		300,000

First Lease Payment

Sans Serif Publishers, Inc. (Lessee)		
Lease payable	92,931	
Cash		92,931
CompuDec Corporation (Lessor)		
Cash	92,931	
Lease receivable		92,931

*Also can be calculated as the present value of the lessor's minimum lease payments, which do not include the unguaranteed residual value.

Dealer's profit is the same as when the residual value is guaranteed because both sales revenue and COGS are reduced by the same amounts.

Sales revenue does not include the unguaranteed residual value because the revenue to be recovered from the lessee is lease payments only. The remainder of the lessor's gross investment is to be recovered—not from payment by the lessee (as is presumed when the residual value is guaranteed), but by selling, re-leasing, or otherwise obtaining value from the asset when it reverts back to the lessor. You might want to view the situation this way: The portion of the asset sold is the portion not represented by the unguaranteed residual value. So, both the asset's cost and its selling price are reduced by the present value of the portion not sold.

The lessor's lease receivable is $479,079 even when the residual value is not guaranteed. However, the lessee's lease liability would be only $445,211 at the inception of the lease and would become zero with the final payment at the beginning of the final year, with reductions occurring in accordance with the pattern described by the schedule in Graphic 15–9.

When the lessee doesn't guarantee the residual value, the lessee's net liability and the lessor's net receivable will differ because the former does not include the unguaranteed residual amount.

GRAPHIC 15–9

Lessee's Amortization Schedule—Residual Value Not Guaranteed

	Payments	Effective Interest	Decrease in Balance	Outstanding Balance
		(10% × Outstanding balance)		
1/1/09				445,211
11/1/09	92,931		92,931	352,280
12/31/09	92,931	.10 (352,280) = 35,228	57,703	294,577
12/31/10	92,931	.10 (294,577) = 29,458	63,473	231,104
12/31/11	92,931	.10 (231,104) = 23,110	69,821	161,283
12/31/12	92,931	.10 (161,283) = 16,128	76,803	84,480
12/31/13	92,931	.10 (84,480) = 8,451*	84,480	0
	557,586	112,375*	445,211*	

*Adjusted for rounding of other numbers in the schedule.

Because the lessee does not guarantee the residual value, the lessee does not consider it to be an additional lease payment.

When the residual value is not guaranteed, the lessor bears any loss that results from the actual residual value of the leased asset being less than the original estimate.

Graphic 15–10 summarizes the effect of the residual value of a leased asset for each of the various possibilities regarding the nature of the residual value.

GRAPHIC 15–10
Effect of a Residual Value: A Summary

Is the residual value of a leased asset included in:

	the Lessor's		the Lessee's
	(a) Gross Investment in Lease *Computation of Payments*	(b) Minimum Lease Payments *Sales Revenue*	**(c) Minimum Lease Payments *Asset & Liability***
Lessee gets the residual value (by transfer of title or the expected exercise of a bargain purchase option)	No	No	No
Lessor gets the residual value (title does not transfer; no bargain purchase option)			
• Residual value is not guaranteed	Yes	No	No
• Residual value is guaranteed by the lessee.	Yes	Yes	Yes
• Residual value is guaranteed by a third party guarantor.	Yes	Yes	No

(a) if included in the lessor's gross investment in the lease, the residual value is part of the computation by the **lessor** of the amount of the periodic rental payments
(b) the present value of the lessor's minimum lease payments is sales revenue in a sales-type lease
(c) the present value of the lessee's minimum lease payments is the amount to be capitalized as an asset and a liability

Bargain Purchase Options

LO8

We mentioned earlier that a **bargain purchase option (BPO)** is a provision of some lease contracts that gives the lessee the option of purchasing the leased property at a bargain price. We discussed BPOs in the context of how they affect the classification of leases, but none of our earlier illustrations included a situation in which a BPO was present. You should have noted that a bargain price is defined in such a way that an additional cash payment is expected when a BPO is included in the agreement. Remember, a bargain price is one that is sufficiently below the property's expected fair value that the exercise of the option appears reasonably assured. Because exercise of the option appears at the inception of the lease to be reasonably assured, payment of the option price is expected to occur when the option becomes exercisable.

When a BPO is present, both the lessor and the lessee view the option price as an additional lease payment.

The logic applied to lessee-guaranteed residual values in the previous section applies here too. The expectation that the option price will be paid effectively adds an additional cash flow to the lease for both the lessee and the lessor. That additional payment is included as a component of minimum lease payments for both the lessor and the lessee. It therefore (a) reduces the amount of the periodic rent payments the *lessor* will receive from the lessee and (b) is included in the computation of the amount to be capitalized (as an asset and liability) by the *lessee.* In fact, the way a BPO is included in these calculations is precisely the same way that a lessee-guaranteed residual value is included. This is demonstrated in Graphic 15–11.

GRAPHIC 15–11
Effect of a Bargain Purchase Option

- ✔ The **lessor,** when computing periodic rental payments, subtracts the present value of the BPO from the amount to be recovered (fair market value) to determine the amount that must be recovered from the lessee through the periodic rent payments.
- ✔ The **lessee** *adds* the present value of the BPO price to the present value of periodic payments when computing the amount to be recorded as a leased asset and a lease liability.

To emphasize the similarity in the way a lessee-guaranteed[21] residual value and a BPO affect the calculations, let's assume the $60,000 in our last illustration is an option price that could be paid by Sans Serif at the conclusion of the lease to purchase the copier. To make this a "bargain" purchase option let's say the residual value at the same time is expected now to be $75,000. This situation is assumed in Illustration 15–5.

ILLUSTRATION 15–5
Bargain Purchase Option

On January 1, 2009, Sans Serif Publishers, Inc., leased a color copier from CompuDec Corporation at a price of $479,079. The lease agreement specifies annual payments beginning December 31, 2009, the inception of the lease, and at each December 31 thereafter through 2013. The estimated useful life of the copier is seven years. At the end of the six-year lease term the copier is expected to be worth $75,000 on December 31, 2014, and Sans Serif has the option to purchase it for $60,000 on that date. The residual value after seven years is zero.[22]

CompuDec manufactured the copier at a cost of $300,000.
CompuDec's interest rate for financing the transaction is 10%.

Amount to be recovered (fair market value)	$479,079
Less: Present value of the BPO price ($60,000 × .56447*)	(33,868)
Amount to be recovered through periodic rental payments	$445,211
Rental payments at the beginning of each of the next six years: ($445,211 ÷ 4.79079†)	$ 92,931

*Present value of $1: $n = 6$, $i = 10\%$.
†Present value of an annuity due of $1: $n = 6$, $i = 10\%$.

The lessor's selling price is reduced by the present value of the BPO price to determine the amount that must be recovered from the periodic rental payments.

When we compare the way the *BPO* affected the lessor's (CompuDec's) calculation with the way the lessee-guaranteed residual value affected the calculation earlier, we see that they are exactly the same. That's the case also for the lessee (Sans Serif Publishers) as shown in Illustration 15–5A.

ILLUSTRATION 15–5A
Lessee's Calculation of the Present Value of Minimum Lease Payments When a BPO Is Present

Present value of periodic rental payments ($92,931 × 4.79079*)	$445,211
Plus: Present value of the BPO price ($60,000 × .56447†)	33,868
Present value of minimum lease payments (recorded as a leased asset and a lease liability)	$479,079

*Present value of an annuity due of $1: $n = 6$, $i = 10\%$.
†Present value of $1: $n = 6$, $i = 10\%$.

You should recognize this as the same calculation we used when there was no BPO but the residual value was guaranteed and so was considered an additional lease payment. A question you might have at this point is: Why are we now ignoring the residual value? Earlier it was considered an additional lease payment. Yet, now we view the BPO price as an additional lease payment but ignore the residual value. The reason is obvious when you recall an essential characteristic of a BPO—it's expected to be exercised. So, when it is exercised, title to the leased asset passes to the lessee and with title, any residual value. And remember, when the lessee gets the residual value it is ignored by both parties to the lease.

Because a BPO is expected to be exercised, its exercise price is viewed as one more cash payment.

When a BPO is present, the residual value becomes irrelevant.

The lease amortization schedule for CompuDec and Sans Serif when a BPO is included in the lease agreement (Graphic 15–12) should look familiar to you also.

[21]The lessee-guaranteed qualification here refers to what you learned in the previous section: a residual value is part of the lessee's minimum lease payments only when guaranteed by the lessee; the lessor includes in its computation of rent payments any residual values that revert to the lessor—guaranteed or not.

[22]Our discussion of the effect of a bargain purchase option would be precisely the same if our illustration were of a direct financing lease (for instance, if the lessor's cost were $479,079) except that, of course, neither sales revenue nor cost of goods sold would be recorded in a direct financing lease.

GRAPHIC 15–12
Amortization Schedule—with BPO

	Payments	Effective Interest	Decrease in Balance	Outstanding Balance
		(10% × Outstanding balance)		
1/1/09				479,079
1/1/09	92,931		92,931	386,148
12/31/09	92,931	.10 (386,148) = 38,615	54,316	331,832
12/31/10	92,931	.10 (331,832) = 33,183	59,748	272,084
12/31/11	92,931	.10 (272,084) = 27,208	65,723	206,361
12/31/12	92,931	.10 (206,361) = 20,636	72,295	134,066
12/31/13	92,931	.10 (134,066) = 13,407	79,524	54,542
12/31/14	60,000	.10 (54,542) = 5,458*	54,542	0
	617,586	138,507	479,079	

*Adjusted for rounding of other numbers in the schedule.

Both the lessor and lessee view the BPO price ($60,000) as an additional cash payment.

Recording the exercise of the option is similar to recording the periodic rent payments. That is, a portion of the payment covers interest for the year, and the remaining portion reduces the outstanding balance (to zero with this last payment), as shown in Illustration 15–5B.

ILLUSTRATION 15–5B
Journal Entries—with BPO

December 31, 2014

Sans Serif Publishers, Inc. (Lessee)		
Depreciation expense ($479,079* ÷ 7 years)	68,440	
Accumulated depreciation		68,440
Interest expense (10% × $54,542)	5,458	
Lease payable (difference)	54,542	
Cash (BPO price)		60,000
CompuDec Corporation (Lessor)		
Cash (BPO price)	60,000	
Lease receivable (account balance)		60,000
Unearned interest revenue (account balance)	5,458	
Interest revenue (10% × outstanding balance)		5,458

*The residual value is zero after the full seven-year useful life.

The depreciation entries reflect the fact that the lessee anticipates using the copier for its full seven-year life.

The cash payment expected when the BPO is exercised represents part interest, part principal just like the other cash payments.

Note that depreciation also is affected by the BPO. As pointed out earlier, the lessee normally depreciates a leased asset over the term of the lease. But if ownership transfers by contract or by the expected exercise of a bargain purchase option, the asset should be depreciated over the asset's useful life. This reflects the fact that the lessee anticipates using the leased asset for its full useful life. In this illustration, the copier is expected to be useful for seven years, so depreciation is $68,440 ($479,079 ÷ 7 years).

When a BPO Is Exercisable before the End of the Lease Term

The length of the lease term is limited to the time up to when a bargain purchase option becomes exercisable.

We assumed in this example that the BPO was exercisable on December 31, 2014—the end of the lease term. This assumption was convenient to illustrate the similarity between how a residual value and a BPO are dealt with when accounting for leases. It also is a very realistic assumption. Sometimes, though, the lease contract specifies that a BPO becomes exercisable before the designated lease term ends. Since a BPO is expected to be exercised, the lease term ends for accounting purposes when the option becomes exercisable. For example, let's say the BPO in the previous example could be exercised a year earlier—at the end of the fifth year. The effect this would have on accounting for the lease is to change the lease term from six years to five. All calculations would be modified accordingly. Stated differently, minimum lease payments include only the periodic cash payments specified in the agreement that occur prior to the date a BPO becomes exercisable. (We assume the option is exercised at that time and the lease ends.)

We have seen how minimum lease payments are affected by a residual value and by a bargain purchase option. Let's now consider how maintenance, insurance, taxes, and other costs usually associated with ownership (called *executory costs*) affect minimum lease payments.

ETHICAL DILEMMA

"I know we had discussed that they're supposed to be worth $24,000 when our purchase option becomes exercisable," Ferris insisted. "That's why we agreed to the lease terms. But, Jenkins, you know how fast computers become dated. We can make a good case that they'll be worth only $10,000 in three years."

The computers to which Ferris referred were acquired by lease. The lease meets none of the criteria for classification as a capital lease except that it contains an apparent bargain purchase option. Under the lease option, the computers can be purchased for $10,000 after three years.

"We could avoid running up our debt that way," Jenkins agreed.

How could debt be avoided?

Do you perceive an ethical problem?

PART C

OTHER LEASE ACCOUNTING ISSUES

Executory Costs

● LO9

One of the responsibilities of ownership that is transferred to the lessee in a capital lease is the responsibility to pay for maintenance, insurance, taxes, and any other costs usually associated with ownership. These are referred to as **executory costs.** Lease agreements usually are written in such a way that these costs are borne by the lessee. These expenditures simply are expensed by the lessee as incurred: repair expense, insurance expense, property tax expense, and so on. Let's return, for example, to Illustration 15–2. Now, suppose that a $2,000 per year maintenance agreement was arranged with an outside service for the leased copier. Sans Serif (the lessee) would expense this fee each year as incurred:

Maintenance expense	2,000	
Cash (annual fee)		2,000

The lessee simply expenses executory costs as incurred.

The lessor is unaffected by executory costs paid by the lessee.

Sometimes, as an expediency, a lease contract will specify that the lessor is to pay executory costs, but that the lessee will reimburse the lessor through higher rental payments. When rental payments are inflated for this reason, these executory costs are excluded in determining the minimum lease payments. They still are expensed by the lessee, even though paid through the lessor. For demonstration, let's modify Illustration 15–2 to assume the periodic rental payments were increased to $102,000 with the provision the lessor (First LeaseCorp) pays the maintenance fee. We do this in Illustration 15–6 on the next page.

Any portion of rental payments that represents maintenance, insurance, taxes, or other executory costs is not considered part of minimum lease payments.

Discount Rate

An important factor in the overall lease equation that we've glossed over until now is the discount rate used in present value calculations. Because lease payments occur in future periods, we must consider the time value of money when evaluating their present value. The rate is important because it influences virtually every amount reported in connection with the lease by both the lessor and the lessee.

One rate is implicit in the lease agreement. This is the effective interest rate the lease payments provide the lessor over and above the price at which the asset is sold under the lease. It is the desired rate of return the lessor has in mind when deciding the size of the

ILLUSTRATION 15–6

Rental Payments Including Executory Costs Paid by the Lessor

On January 1, 2009, Sans Serif Publishers, Inc., leased a copier from First LeaseCorp. First LeaseCorp purchased the equipment from CompuDec Corporation at a cost of $479,079.

- Six annual payments of $102,000 beginning January 1, 2009.
- Payments include $2,000 which First LeaseCorp will use to pay an annual maintenance fee.
- The interest rate in these financing arrangements is 10%.
- Capital lease to Sans Serif.
- Direct financing lease to First LeaseCorp.

Executory costs that are included in periodic rental payments to be paid by the lessor are, in effect, indirectly paid by the lessee—and expensed by the lessee.

First Payment (January 1, 2009)

Sans Serif Publishers, Inc. (Lessee)		
Maintenance expense (2009 fee)	2,000	
Lease payable	100,000	
Cash (lease payment)		102,000
First LeaseCorp (Lessor)		
Cash (rental payment)	102,000	
Lease receivable		100,000
Maintenance fee payable*		2,000

*This assumes the $2,000 maintenance fee has not yet been paid to the outside maintenance service.

The lessee uses the lower of the interest rate implicit in the lease or the lessee's own incremental borrowing rate.

lease payments. (Refer to our earlier calculations of the periodic rental payments.) Usually the lessee is aware of the lessor's implicit rate or can infer it from the asset's fair value.[23] When the lessor's implicit rate is unknown, the lessee should use its own incremental borrowing rate. This is the rate the lessee would expect to pay a bank if funds were borrowed to buy the asset. When the lessor's implicit rate *is* known, the lessee should use the lower of the two rates.[24]

When the Lessee's Incremental Borrowing Rate is Less Than the Lessor's Implicit Rate

Instances are few in which the lessee actually would use its incremental borrowing rate. Here's why. We noted earlier that, like any other asset, a leased asset should not be recorded at more than its fair value. Look what happens to the present value payments if Sans Serif uses a discount rate less than the 10% rate implicit in Illustration 15–6 (let's say 9%):

$100,000 × 4.88965*	=	$488,965
Rental payments		Lessee's cost

*Present value of an annuity due of $1: $n = 6$, $i = 9\%$.

But remember, the fair value of the copier was $479,079. The $100,000 amount for the rental payments was derived by the lessor, contemplating a fair value of $479,079 and a desired interest rate of return (implicit rate) of 10%. So, using a discount rate lower than the lessor's implicit rate usually would result in the present value of minimum lease payments being more than the fair value.

This conclusion does not hold when the leased asset has an unguaranteed residual value. You will recall that the lessor's determinations always include any residual value that accrues to the lessor; but when the lessee doesn't guarantee the residual value, it is *not* included in the lessee's present value calculations. Combining two previous examples, let's modify our demonstration of an unguaranteed residual value (Illustration 15–6) to assume the lessee's incremental borrowing rate was 9%. Because the residual value was expected to contribute to the lessor's recovery of the $479,079 fair value, the rental payments were only $92,931. But, the lessee would ignore the unguaranteed residual value and calculate its cost of the leased asset to be $454,400.

$92,931 × 4.88965*	=	$454,400
Rental payments		Lessee's cost

*Present value of an annuity due of $1: $n = 6$, $i = 9\%$.

[23]The corporation laws of some states, Florida for instance, actually require the interest rate to be expressly stated in the lease agreement.

[24]*Incremental borrowing rate* refers to the fact that lending institutions tend to view debt as being increasingly risky as the level of debt increases. Thus, additional (i.e., incremental) debt is likely to be loaned at a higher interest rate than existing debt, other things being equal.

In this case, the present value of minimum lease payments would be *less than* the fair value even though a lower discount rate is used. But again, if there is no residual value, or if the lessee guarantees the residual value, or if the unguaranteed residual value is relatively small, a discount rate lower than the lessor's implicit rate will result in the present value of minimum lease payments being more than the fair value.

When the Lessor's Implicit Rate is Unknown

What if the lessee is unaware of the lessor's implicit rate? This is a logical question in light of the rule that says the lessee should use its own incremental borrowing rate when the lessor's implicit rate is unknown to the lessee. But in practice the lessor's implicit rate usually is known. Even if the lessor chooses not to explicitly disclose the rate, the lessee usually can deduce the rate using information he knows about the value of the leased asset and the lease payments. After all, in making the decision to lease rather than buy, the lessee typically becomes quite knowledgeable about the asset.

Even so, it is possible that a lessee might be unable to derive the lessor's implicit rate. This might happen, for example, if the leased asset has a relatively high residual value. Remember, a residual value (guaranteed or not) is an ingredient in the lessor's calculation of the rental payments. Sometimes it may be hard for the lessee to identify the residual value estimated by the lessor if the lessor chooses not to make it known.[25] The longer the lease term or the more risk of obsolescence the leased asset is subject to, the less of a factor the residual value typically is.

ADDITIONAL CONSIDERATION

As pointed out earlier, the management of a lessee company sometimes will try to structure a lease to avoid the criteria that would cause the lease to be classified as a capital lease in order to gain the questionable advantages of off-balance-sheet financing. On the other hand, a lessor normally would prefer recording a **nonoperating** lease, other things being equal. Two ways sometimes used to structure a lease to qualify as an operating lease by the lessee, but as a nonoperating lease by the lessor are: (1) cause the two parties to use different interest rates and (2) avoid including the residual value in the lessee's minimum lease payments. Let's see how they work:

1. Cause the Two Parties to Use Different Interest Rates.

It was pointed out earlier that a lessee sometimes can claim to be unable to determine the lessor's implicit rate. Not knowing the lessor's implicit rate would permit the lessee to use its own incremental borrowing rate. If higher than the lessor's implicit rate, the present value it produces may cause the 90% of fair value criterion **not** to be met for the lessee (thus an operating lease) even though the criterion is met for the lessor (thus a nonoperating lease).

2. Avoid Including the Residual Value in the Lessee's Minimum Lease Payments.

The residual value, if guaranteed by the lessee or by a third party guarantor, is included in the minimum lease payments by the lessor when applying the 90% of fair value criterion and thus increases the likelihood that it is met. However, when the residual value is guaranteed by a third-party guarantor and not by the lessee, it is **not** included in the lessee's minimum lease payments. So, if a residual value is sufficiently large and guaranteed by a third-party guarantor, it may cause the 90% of fair value criterion to be met by the lessor, but not by the lessee.

Both schemes are unintentionally encouraged by lease accounting rules. As long as arbitrary cutoff points are used (90% of fair value in this case), maneuvers will be devised to circumvent them.

Lessor's Initial Direct Costs

The costs incurred by the lessor that are associated directly with originating a lease and are essential to acquire that lease are referred to as **initial direct costs.** They include legal fees,

[25]Disclosure requirements provide that the lessor company must disclose the components of its investments in nonoperating leases, which would include any estimated residual values. But the disclosures are aggregate amounts, not amounts of individual leased assets.

INTERNATIONAL FINANCIAL REPORTING STANDARDS

Present Value of Minimum Lease Payments. Under *IAS No. 17,* both parties to a lease generally use the rate implicit in the lease to discount minimum lease payments. Under U.S. GAAP, lessors use the implicit rate and lessees use the incremental borrowing rate unless the implicit rate is known and is the lower rate.

Lessor

commissions, evaluating the prospective lessee's financial condition, and preparing and processing lease documents. The method of accounting for initial direct costs depends on the nature of the lease. Remember, a lessor can classify a lease as (1) an operating lease, (2) a direct financing lease, or (3) a sales-type lease. The accounting treatment for initial direct costs by each of the three possible lease types is summarized below.

1. For *operating leases,* initial direct costs are recorded as assets and amortized over the term of the lease. Since the only revenue an operating lease produces is rental revenue, and that revenue is recognized over the lease term, initial direct costs also are automatically recognized over the lease term to match these costs with the rent revenues they help generate.
2. In *direct financing leases,* interest revenue is earned over the lease term, so initial direct costs are matched with the interest revenues they help generate. Therefore, initial direct costs are not expensed at the outset but are deferred and recognized over the lease term. This can be accomplished by increasing the lessor's *lease receivable* by the total of initial direct costs. Then, as unearned interest revenue is recognized over the lease term at a constant effective rate, the initial direct costs are recognized at the same rate (that is, proportionally).
3. For *sales-type leases,* initial direct costs are expensed at the inception of the lease. Since the usual reason for a sales-type lease is for a manufacturer or a dealer to sell its product, it's reasonable to recognize the costs of creating the transaction as a selling expense in the period of the sale.

Contingent Rentals

Sometimes rental payments may be increased (or decreased) at some future time during the lease term, depending on whether or not some specified event occurs. Usually the contingency is related to revenues, profitability, or usage above some designated level. For example, a recent annual report of **Wal-Mart Stores** included the note re-created in Graphic 15–13.

GRAPHIC 15–13
Disclosure of Contingent Rentals—Wal-Mart Stores

9 Commitments (in part)

Certain of the leases provide for contingent additional rentals based on percentage of sales. The additional rentals amounted to $41 million, $27 million and $32 million in 2007, 2006 and 2005, respectively.

Contingent rentals are *not* included in the minimum lease payments because they are not determinable at the inception of the lease. Instead, they are included as components of income when (and if) they occur. Increases or decreases in rental payments that are dependent only on the passage of time are not contingent rentals; these are part of minimum lease payments.

Although contingent rentals are not included in minimum lease payments, they are reported in disclosure notes by both the lessor and lessee.

A Brief Summary

Leasing arrangements often are complex. In studying this chapter you've encountered several features of lease agreements that alter the way we make several of the calculations needed to account for leases. Graphic 15–14 provides a concise review of the essential lease accounting components, using calculations from a hypothetical lease situation to provide a numerical perspective.

GRAPHIC 15–14 Lease Terms and Concepts: A Summary

Lease Situation for Calculations

($ in 000s)			
Lease term (years)	4	Lessor's cost	$300
Asset's useful life (years)	5	Residual value:	
Lessor's implicit rate (known by lessee)	12%	Guaranteed by lessee	$8
Lessee's incremental borrowing rate	13%	Guaranteed by third party[a]	$6
Rental payments (including executory costs) at the beginning of each year	$102	Unguaranteed	$5
		Executory costs paid annually by lessor	$2
		Bargain purchase option	none
		Initial direct costs	3

Amount	Description	Calculation
Lessor's:		
Gross investment in the lease[b]	Total of periodic rental payments[c] plus any residual value that reverts to the lessor (guaranteed or not) or plus BPO price[d]	($100 × 4) + ($8 + 6 + 5) = $419
Net investment in the lease	Present value of the gross investment (discounted at lessor's rate) plus any initial direct costs in a direct financing lease	($100 × 3.40183[e]) + ($19 × .63552[f]) = $352[g]
Minimum lease payments	Total of periodic rental payments[c] plus residual value guaranteed to the lessor (by lessee and/or by third party) or plus BPO price[d]	($100 × 4) + ($8 + 6) = $414
Sales revenue	Present value of lessor's minimum lease payments; also, net investment − present value of unguaranteed residual value	($100 × 3.40183[e]) + ($14 × .63552[f]) = $349; also: $352 − ($5 × .63552) = $349
Cost of goods sold	Lessor's cost − Present value of unguaranteed residual value	$300 − ($5 × .63552[f]) = $297
Dealer's profit	Sales revenue − Cost of goods sold; also, Net investment − Lessor's cost	$349 − 297 = $52; also, $352 − 300 = $52
Lessee's:		
Minimum lease payments	Total of periodic rental payments[c] plus residual value guaranteed by lessee or plus BPO price[d]	($100 × 4) + $8 = $408
Leased asset	Present value of minimum lease payments (using lower of lessor's rate and lessee's incremental borrowing rate); cannot exceed fair value	($100 × 3.40183[e]) + ($8 × .63552[f]) = $345
Lease liability at inception	Same as leased asset	($100 × 3.40183[e]) + ($8 × .63552[f]) = $345

[a]Beyond any amount guaranteed by the lessee (amount guaranteed is $8 + 6 minus any amount paid by the lessee).
[b]This is the amount to be recovered by the lessor and therefore is used in the calculation of periodic lease payments.
[c]Any portion of rental payments that represents maintenance, insurance, taxes, or other executory costs is not considered part of minimum lease payments. In this case, rentals are reduced as follows: $102 − 2 = $100.
[d]In this context, a residual value and a BPO price are mutually exclusive: if a BPO exists, any residual value is expected to remain with the lessee and is not considered an additional payment.
[e]Present value of annuity due of $1: $n = 4$, $i = 12\%$.
[f]Present value of $1: $n = 4$, $i = 12\%$.
[g]Since this is a sales-type lease ($352 − 300 = $52 dealer's profit), initial direct costs are expensed at the lease's inception and do not increase the net investment in the lease.

Lease Disclosures

Lease disclosure requirements are quite extensive for both the lessor and lessee. Virtually all aspects of the lease agreement must be disclosed. For *all* leases (a) a general description of the leasing arrangement is required as well as (b) minimum future payments, in the aggregate and for each of the five succeeding fiscal years. Other required disclosures are specific to the type of lease and include: residual values, contingent rentals, unearned interest, sublease rentals, and executory costs. Some representative examples are shown in Graphics 15–15 (lessor) and 15–16 (lessee).

IBM is a manufacturer that relies heavily on leasing as a means of selling its products. Its disclosure of sales-type leases is shown in Graphic 15–15.

GRAPHIC 15–15

Lessor Disclosure of Sales-Type Leases—IBM Corporation

Real World Financials

F Financing Receivables (in part)
(dollars in millions)

At December 31:	2006	2005
Short term:		
Net investment in sales-type leases	$ 4,590	$ 4,435
Commercial financing receivables	5,814	5,053
Customer loans receivable	4,196	3,752
Installment payment receivables	496	510
Total	$15,095	$13,750
Long term:		
Net investment in sales-type leases	$ 5,471	$ 5,393
Commercial financing receivables	32	17
Customer loans receivable	4,214	3,901
Installment payment receivables	351	317
Total	$10,068	$ 9,628

Net investment in sales-type leases is for leases that relate principally to IBM equipment and are generally for terms ranging from two to seven years. Net investment in sales-type leases includes unguaranteed residual values of $854 million and $792 million at December 31, 2006 and 2005, respectively, and is reflected net of unearned income of $1,005 million and $939 million and of allowance for uncollectible accounts of $135 million and $176 million at those dates, respectively.

Wal-Mart Stores leases facilities under both operating and capital leases. Its long-term obligations under these lease agreements are disclosed in a note to its financial statements (see Graphic 15–16) on the next page.

INTERMEDIATE ACCOUNTING

Leasing sometimes is used as a means of off-balance-sheet financing.

DECISION MAKERS' PERSPECTIVE—Financial Statement Impact

As indicated in the Decision Makers' Perspective at the beginning of the chapter, leasing can allow a firm to conserve assets, to avoid some risks of owning assets, and to obtain favorable tax benefits. These advantages are desirable. It also was pointed out earlier that some firms try to obscure the realities of their financial position through off-balance-sheet financing or by avoiding violating terms of contracts that limit the amount of debt a company can have. Accounting guidelines are designed to limit the ability of firms to hide financial realities. Nevertheless, investors and creditors should be alert to the impact leases can have on a company's financial position and on its risk.

Note 9 Commitments (in part)

The Company and certain of its subsidiaries have long-term leases for stores and equipment. Rentals (including, for certain leases, amounts applicable to taxes, insurance, maintenance, other operating expenses and contingent rentals) under all operating leases were $1.4 billion, $1.0 billion, and $1.1 billion in 2007, 2006, and 2005, respectively. Aggregate minimum annual rentals at January 31, 2007, under non-cancelable leases are as follows (in millions):

Fiscal Year	Operating Leases	Capital Leases
2008	$ 842	$ 538
2009	826	540
2010	768	520
2011	698	505
2012	634	480
Thereafter	6,678	3,132
Total minimum rentals	$10,446	5,715
Less estimated executory costs		29
Net minimum lease payments		5,686
Less imputed interest at rates ranging from 3.0% to 15.6%		1,888
Present value of minimum lease payments		$3,798

GRAPHIC 15–16

Lessee Disclosure of Leases—Wal-Mart Stores

Real World Financials

Balance Sheet and Income Statement

Lease liabilities affect the debt to equity ratio and the rate of return on assets.

Lease transactions identified as nonoperating impact several of a firm's financial ratios. Because we record liabilities for capital leases, the debt-equity ratio (liabilities divided by shareholders' equity) is immediately impacted. Because we also record leased assets, the immediate impact on the rate of return on assets (net income divided by assets) is negative, but the lasting effect depends on how leased assets are utilized to enhance future net income. As illustrated in this chapter, the financial statement impact of a capital lease is no different from that of an installment purchase.

Do operating leases create long-term commitments equivalent to liabilities?

Even operating leases, though, can significantly affect risk. Operating leases represent long-term commitments that can become a problem if business declines and cash inflows drop off. For example, long-term lease commitments became a big problem for **Businessland** in the early 1990s. The company's revenues declined but it was saddled with lease commitments for numerous facilities the company no longer occupied. Its stock's market price declined from $11.88 to $.88 in one year.

The net income difference between treating a lease as a capital lease versus an operating lease generally is not significant.

Whether leases are capitalized or treated as operating leases affects the income statement as well as the balance sheet. However, the impact generally is not significant. Over the life of a lease, total expenses are equal regardless of the accounting treatment of a lease. If the lease is capitalized, total expenses comprise interest and depreciation. The total of these equals the total amount of rental payments, which would constitute rent expense if not capitalized. There is, however, a timing difference between lease capitalization and operating lease treatment, but the timing difference usually isn't great.

The difference in impact on the balance sheet between capital leases and operating leases is significant.

The more significant difference between capital leases and operating leases is the impact on the balance sheet. As mentioned above, a capital lease adds to both the asset and liability side of the balance sheet; operating leases do not affect the balance sheet at all. How can external financial statement users adjust their analysis to incorporate the balance sheet differences between capital and operating leases? A frequently offered suggestion is to capitalize all noncancelable lease commitments, including those related to operating leases. Some financial analysts, in fact, do this on their own to get a better feel for a company's actual debt position.

To illustrate, refer to Graphic 15–16, which reveals the operating lease commitments disclosed by **Wal-Mart Stores.** If these lease arrangements were considered nonoperating, these payments would be capitalized (reported at the present value of all future payments). By making some reasonable assumptions, we can estimate the present value of all future payments to be made on existing operating leases. For example, the interest rates used by Wal-Mart to discount rental payments on capital leases range from 3.0% to 15.6%. If we use the approximate average rate of 10%, and make certain other assumptions, we can determine the debt equivalent of the operating lease commitments as shown in Graphic 15–17.

GRAPHIC 15–17
Estimating the Debt Equivalent of Operating Lease Commitments

Capitalized Value or Debt Equivalent of Wal-Mart's Operating Leases

Fiscal Years	Operating Leases	PV Factor 10%	Present Value
2008	$ 842	.909	$ 765
2009	826	.826	682
2010	768	.751	577
2011	698	.683	477
2012	634	.621	394
Thereafter	6,678	.386*	2,578
Total minimum rentals	$10,446		$5,473

*This is the PV factor for $i = 10\%$, $n = 10$, which treats payments after 2012 as occurring in 2017, an assumption due to not knowing precise dates of specific payments after 2012.

If capitalized, these operating lease commitments would add $5,473 million to Wal-Mart's liabilities and approximately $5,473 to the company's assets.[26] Let's look at the impact this would have on the company's debt to equity ratio and its return on assets ratio using selected financial statement information taken from Wal-Mart's annual report for the fiscal year ending January 31, 2007, shown below:

	($ in millions)
Total assets	$151,193
Total liabilities	89,620
Total shareholders' equity	61,573
Net income	11,284

The debt to equity and return on assets ratios are calculated in Graphic 15–18 without considering the capitalization of operating leases and then again after adding $5,473 million to both total assets and total liabilities. In the calculation of return on assets, we use only the year-end total assets rather than the average total assets for the year. Also, we assume no impact on income.

GRAPHIC 15–18
Ratios with and without Capitalization of Operating Leases

	Without Capitalization ($ in millions)	With Capitalization
Debt to equity ratio	$\frac{\$89,620}{\$61,573} = 1.46$	$\frac{\$95,093}{\$61,573} = 1.54$
Return on assets	$\frac{\$11,284}{\$151,193} = 7.5\%$	$\frac{\$11,284}{\$156,666} = 7.2\%$

[26]If these operating leases were capitalized, both assets and liabilities would increase by the same amount at inception of the lease. However, in later years, the leased asset account balance and the lease liability account will, generally, not be equal. The leased asset account is reduced by depreciation and the lease liability account is reduced (amortized) down to zero using the effective interest method.

The debt to equity ratio rises from 1.46 to 1.54, and the return on assets ratio declines from 7.5% to 7.2%.

Statement of Cash Flow Impact

OPERATING LEASES. Remember, lease payments for operating leases represent rent—expense to the lessee, revenue for the lessor. These amounts are included in net income, so both the lessee and lessor report cash payments for operating leases in a statement of cash flows as cash flows from operating activities.

Operating leases are not reported on a statement of cash flows at the lease's inception.

CAPITAL LEASES AND DIRECT FINANCING LEASES. You've learned in this chapter that capital leases are agreements that we identify as being formulated outwardly as leases, but which are in reality installment purchases, so we account for them as such. Each rental payment (except the first if paid at inception) includes both an amount that represents interest and an amount that represents a reduction of principal. In a statement of cash flows, then, the lessee reports the interest portion as a cash outflow from operating activities and the principal portion as a cash outflow from financing activities. On the other side of the transaction, the lessor in a direct financing lease reports the interest portion as a cash inflow from operating activities and the principal portion as a cash inflow from investing activities. Both the lessee and lessor report the lease at its inception as a noncash investing/financing activity.

The interest portion of a capital lease payment is a cash flow from operating activities and the principal portion is a cash flow from financing activities.

SALES-TYPE LEASES. A sales-type lease differs from a direct-financing lease for the lessor in that we assume the lessor is actually selling its product. Consistent with reporting sales of products under installment sales agreements rather than lease agreements, the lessor reports cash receipts from a sales-type lease as cash inflows from operating activities.

Cash receipts from a sales-type lease are cash flows from operating activities.

CONCEPT REVIEW EXERCISE

VARIOUS LEASE ACCOUNTING ISSUES

(This is an extension of the previous Concept Review Exercise.)
United Cellular Systems leased a satellite transmission device from Satellite Technology Corporation on January 1, 2010. Satellite Technology paid $500,000 for the transmission device. Its retail value is $653,681.

Terms of the Lease Agreement and Related Information:	
Lease term	3 years (6 semiannual periods)
Semiannual rental payments	$123,000—beginning of each period
Economic life of asset	4 years
Implicit interest rate (Also lessee's incremental borrowing rate)	12%
Unguaranteed residual value	$40,000
Regulatory fees paid by lessor	$3,000/twice each year (included in rentals)
Lessor's initial direct costs	$4,500
Contingent rental payments	Additional $4,000 if revenues exceed a specified base

Required:

1. Prepare an amortization schedule that describes the pattern of interest expense over the lease term for United Cellular Systems.
2. Prepare an amortization schedule that describes the pattern of interest revenue over the lease term for Satellite Technology.
3. Prepare the appropriate entries for both United Cellular Systems and Satellite Technology on January 1 and June 30, 2010.
4. Prepare the appropriate entries for both United Cellular Systems and Satellite Technology on December 31, 2012 (the end of the lease term), assuming the device is returned to the lessor and its actual residual value is $14,000 on that date.

SOLUTION

1. Prepare an amortization schedule that describes the pattern of interest expense over the lease term for United Cellular Systems.

Calculation of the Present Value of Minimum Lease Payments:

Present value of periodic rental payments excluding executory costs of $3,000:

($120,000 × 5.21236*) = $625,483

*Present value of an annuity due of $1: $n = 6$, $i = 6\%$.

Note: The *unguaranteed* residual value is excluded from minimum lease payments for both the lessee and lessor.

Date	Payments	Effective Interest	Decrease in Balance	Outstanding Balance
		(6% × Outstanding balance)		
1/1/10				625,483
1/1/10	120,000		120,000	505,483
6/30/10	120,000	.06 (505,483) = 30,329	89,671	415,812
1/1/11	120,000	.06 (415,812) = 24,949	95,051	320,761
6/30/11	120,000	.06 (320,761) = 19,246	100,754	220,007
1/1/12	120,000	.06 (220,007) = 13,200	106,800	113,207
6/30/12	120,000	.06 (113,207) = 6,793*	113,207	0
	720,000	94,517	625,483	

*Adjusted for rounding of other numbers in the schedule.

2. Prepare an amortization schedule that describes the pattern of interest revenue over the lease term for Satellite Technology.

Calculation of the Lessor's Net Investment:

Present value of periodic rental payments excluding executory costs of $3,000 ($120,000 × 5.21236*)	$625,483
Plus: Present value of the unguaranteed residual value ($40,000 × .70496†)	28,198
Lessor's net investment in lease	$653,681

*Present value of an annuity due of $1: $n = 6$, $i = 6\%$.
†Present value of $1: $n = 6$, $i = 6\%$.
Note: The *unguaranteed* residual value is excluded from minimum lease payments, but is part of the lessor's gross and net investment in the lease.

Date	Payments	Effective Interest	Decrease in Balance	Outstanding Balance
		(6% × Outstanding balance)		
1/1/10				653,681
1/1/10	120,000		120,000	533,681
6/30/10	120,000	.06 (533,681) = 32,021	87,979	445,702
1/1/11	120,000	.06 (445,702) = 26,742	93,258	352,444
6/30/11	120,000	.06 (352,444) = 21,147	98,853	253,591
1/1/12	120,000	.06 (253,591) = 15,215	104,785	148,806
6/30/12	120,000	.06 (148,806) = 8,928	111,072	37,734
12/31/12	40,000	.06 (37,734) = 2,266*	37,734	0
	760,000	106,319	653,681	

*Adjusted for rounding of other numbers in the schedule.

3. Prepare the appropriate entries for both United Cellular Systems and Satellite Technology on January 1 and June 30, 2010.

January 1, 2010

United Cellular Systems (Lessee)

Leased equipment (calculated above)	625,483	
Lease payable (calculated above)		625,483
Lease payable (payment less executory costs)	120,000	
Regulatory fees expense (executory costs)	3,000	
Cash (lease payment)		123,000

Satellite Technology (Lessor)		
Lease receivable (PV of lease payments + PV $40,000 residual value)[a]	653,681	
Cost of goods sold [$500,000 – ($40,000[a] × .70496)]	471,802	
Sales revenue (present value of minimum lease payments[b])		625,483
Inventory of equipment (lessor's cost)		500,000
Selling expense	4,500	
Cash (initial direct costs)		4,500
Cash (lease payment)	123,000	
Regulatory fees payable (or cash)		3,000
Lease receivable (payment less executory costs)		120,000

[a]This is the unguaranteed residual value.
[b]Also, $653,681 – ($40,000[a] × .70496).

June 30, 2010		
United Cellular Systems (Lessee)		
Interest expense [6% × ($625,483 – 120,000)]	30,329	
Lease payable (difference)	89,671	
Regulatory fees expense (annual fee)	3,000	
Cash (lease payment)		123,000
Satellite Technology (Lessor)		
Cash (lease payment)	123,000	
Regulatory fees payable (or cash)		3,000
Lease receivable (to balance)		87,979
Interest revenue [6% × ($653,681 – 120,000)]		32,021

4. Prepare the appropriate entries for both United Cellular Systems and Satellite Technology on December 31, 2012 (the end of the lease term), assuming the device is returned to the lessor and its actual residual value is $14,000 on that date.

December 31, 2012		
United Cellular Systems (Lessee)		
Depreciation expense ($625,483 ÷ 3 years)	208,494	
Accumulated depreciation		208,494
Accumulated depreciation (account balance)	625,483	
Leased equipment (account balance)		625,483
Satellite Technology (Lessor)		
Inventory of equipment (actual residual value)	14,000	
Loss on leased assets ($40,000 – 14,000)	26,000	
Lease receivable (account balance)		37,734
Interest revenue (6% × $37,734: from schedule)		2,266

PART D

SPECIAL LEASING ARRANGEMENTS

Sale-Leaseback Arrangements

LO10

In a **sale-leaseback transaction,** the owner of an asset sells it and immediately leases it back from the new owner. Sound strange? Maybe, but this arrangement is common. In a sale-leaseback transaction two things happen:

1. The seller-lessee receives cash from the sale of the asset.
2. The seller-lessee pays periodic rent payments to the buyer-lessor to retain the use of the asset.

What motivates this kind of arrangement? The two most common reasons are: (1) If the asset had been financed originally with debt and interest rates have fallen, the sale-leaseback transaction can be used to effectively refinance at a lower rate. (2) The most likely motivation for a sale-leaseback transaction is to generate cash.

Capital Leases

Recording a sale-leaseback transaction follows the basic accounting concept of substance over form.

Illustration 15–7 demonstrates a sale-leaseback involving a capital lease. The sale and simultaneous leaseback of the warehouses should be viewed as a single borrowing transaction. Although there appear to be two separate transactions, look closer at the substance of the agreement. Teledyne still retains the use of the warehouses that it had prior to the sale leaseback. What is different? Teledyne has $900,000 cash and a noncancelable obligation to make annual payments of $133,155. In substance, Teledyne simply has borrowed $900,000 to be repaid over 10 years along with 10% interest. From the perspective of substance over form, we do not immediately recognize the $300,000 gain on the sale of the warehouses but defer the gain to be recognized over the term of the lease (or the useful life of the asset if title is expected to transfer outright or by the exercise of a BPO).

ILLUSTRATION 15–7
Sale-Leaseback

Teledyne Distribution Center was in need of cash. Its solution: sell its four warehouses for $900,000, then lease back the warehouses to obtain their continued use. The warehouses had a carrying value on Teledyne's books of $600,000 (original cost $950,000). Other information:

1. The sale date is December 31, 2009.
2. The noncancelable lease term is 10 years and requires annual payments of $133,155 beginning December 31, 2009. The estimated remaining useful life of the warehouses is 10 years.
3. The annual rental payments (present value $900,000) provides the lessor with a 10% rate of return on the financing arrangement.* Teledyne's incremental borrowing rate is 10%.
4. Teledyne depreciates its warehouses on a straight-line basis.

The gain on sale-leaseback is deferred and recognized over the lease term as a reduction of depreciation expense.

December 31, 2009		
Cash	900,000	
Accumulated depreciation ($950,000 – 600,000)	350,000	
Warehouses (cost)		950,000
Deferred gain on sale-leaseback (difference)		300,000
Leased warehouses (present value of lease payments)	900,000	
Lease payable (present value of lease payments)		900,000
Lease payable	133,155	
Cash		133,155
December 31, 2010		
Interest expense [10% × ($900,000 – 133,155)]	76,685	
Lease payable (difference)	56,470	
Cash (rental payment)		133,155
Depreciation expense ($900,000 ÷ 10 years)	90,000	
Accumulated depreciation		90,000
Deferred gain on sale-leaseback ($300,000 ÷ 10 years)	30,000	
Depreciation expense		30,000

*$133,155 × 6.75902 = $900,000 ($899,997.30 rounded)
Rent payments; (from Table 6) $n = 10$, $i = 10\%$; Present value

Since the lease term is equal to the expected useful life of the warehouses (>75%), the leaseback must be recorded by the lessee as a capital lease.[27] There typically is an interdependency between the lease terms and the price at which the asset is sold. The earnings process is not complete at the time of sale but is completed over the term of the lease. So, viewing the sale and the leaseback as a single transaction is consistent with the realization principle. Look closely at the 2010 entries to see the net effect of recording the sale leaseback this way. Amortizing the deferred gain over the lease term as a reduction of depreciation expense decreases depreciation each year to $60,000.[28] Interest expense is $76,685. If Teledyne had *not* sold the warehouses ($600,000 carrying value) and had borrowed $900,000 cash by issuing an installment note, the 2010 effect would have been virtually identical:

December 31, 2010		
Interest expense [10% × ($900,000 – 133,155)]	76,685	
Note payable (difference)	56,470	
Cash (installment payment)		133,155
Depreciation expense ($600,000 ÷ 10 years)	60,000	
Accumulated depreciation		60,000

Depreciating the carrying value of the warehouses over their remaining useful life produces depreciation equal to the net depreciation recorded in a sale-leaseback.

The deferred gain is reported in the balance sheet as a valuation (contra) account, offsetting the leased asset. The 2010 balance sheet effect of the sale-leaseback transaction and a $900,000 installment note are compared in Graphic 15–19. Once again, the effect is virtually identical.

GRAPHIC 15–19
Comparison of a Sale-Leaseback and a Purchase

	Sale-Leaseback	**Retain Asset; Borrow Cash**
Assets		
Leased asset	$900,000	$950,000
Less: Accumulated depreciation	(90,000)	(410,000)
Less: Deferred gain ($300,000 – 30,000)	(270,000)	
	$540,000	$540,000
Liabilities		
Lease payable ($900,000 – 133,155 – 56,470)	$710,375	
Note payable ($900,000 – 133,155 – 56,470)		$710,375

Accounting by the buyer/lessor is no different in a sale-leaseback transaction than another lease transaction. That is, it records a lease in accordance with the usual lease guidelines.

Operating Leases

If the leaseback portion of the previous sale-leaseback transaction were classified as an operating lease, the gain still would be deferred but would be recognized as a reduction of rent expense rather than depreciation. There is no leased asset to depreciate.[29]

December 31, 2010		
Deferred gain on sale-leaseback ($300,000 ÷ 10 years)	30,000	
Rent expense		30,000

Those of you with a healthy sense of skepticism will question whether the leaseback portion of our sale-leaseback situation could qualify as an operating lease. After all, the

[27]The fourth criterion also is met. The present value of lease payments ($900,000) is 100% (>90%) of the fair value of the warehouses ($900,000). Meeting any one of the four criteria is sufficient.

[28]If depreciation is over the useful life of the leased asset rather than the lease term because ownership is expected to transfer to the lessee, amortization of the deferred gain also would be over the useful life. If a leaseback of land is a capital lease, the amortization of the deferred gain is recorded as revenue.

[29]The deferred gain would be reported as a deferred liability since it could not be offset against a leased asset.

10-year lease term is equal to the 10-year remaining useful life. But when you remember that neither the third (75% of economic life) nor the fourth (90% recovery) classification criterion applies if the inception of the lease occurs during the last 25% of an asset's economic life, you see the possibility of an operating lease. Suppose, for instance, that the original useful life of the warehouses was 40 years. In that case, the current lease term would occur during the last 25% of an asset's economic life and we would have an operating lease.

Losses on Sale-Leasebacks

In a sale-leaseback, any gain on the sale of the asset is deferred and amortized. However, a real loss on the sale of the property is recognized immediately—not deferred. A real loss means the fair value is less than the carrying amount of the asset. On the other hand, if the fair value exceeds the carrying amount, but the asset is sold to the buyer/lessor for less than the carrying amount, an artificial loss is produced that is probably in substance a prepayment of rent and should be deferred and amortized.

INTERNATIONAL FINANCIAL REPORTING STANDARDS

Recognizing a Gain on a Sale and Leaseback Transaction. When the leaseback is an operating lease, under *IAS No. 17,* the gain is recognized immediately but is amortized over the lease term under U.S. GAAP. When the leaseback is a finance (capital) lease, under *IAS No. 17,* the gain is recognized over the lease term, but is recognized over the useful life of the asset under U.S. GAAP.

Real Estate Leases

Some leases involve land—exclusively or in part. The concepts we discussed in the chapter also relate to **real estate leases.** But the fact that land has an unlimited life causes us to modify how we account for some leases involving real estate.

Leases of Land Only

Only the first (title transfers) and second (BPO) classification criteria apply in a land lease.

Because the useful life of land is indefinite, the risks and rewards of ownership cannot be presumed transferred from the lessor to the lessee unless title to the land is expected to transfer—outright or by the expected exercise of a bargain purchase option (criterion 1 or criterion 2). Since the useful life is undefined, the third and fourth criteria are not applicable. Relatedly, because the leased asset is land, depreciation is inappropriate.

Leases of Land and Building

When the leased property includes both land and a building and the lease transfers ownership or is expected to by exercise of a BPO, the lessee should record each leased asset separately. The present value of the minimum lease payments is allocated between the leased land and leased building accounts on the basis of their relative market values.

When (a) the leased property includes both land and a building, (b) neither of the first two criteria is met, and (c) the fair value of the land is 25% or more of the combined fair value, both the lessee and the lessor treat the land as an operating lease and the building as any other lease.

When neither of the first two criteria is met, the question arises as to whether the third and fourth criteria apply. Because they logically should apply to the building (because its life is limited) but not to the land (because its life is unlimited), the profession employs an arbitrary guideline. If the fair value of the land is less than 25% of the combined fair value, it is in effect ignored and both the lessee and the lessor treat the land and building as a single unit. The single leased asset is depreciated as if land were not involved. If the fair value of the land is 25% or more of the combined fair value, both the lessee and the lessor treat the land and building as two separate leases. Thus, the land lease is an operating lease, and the building lease is classified and accounted for in the manner described in the chapter.

Leases of Only Part of a Building

Some of the most common of leases involve leasing only part of a building. For instance, businesses frequently lease space in an office building or individual stores in a shopping mall. Practical difficulties arise when applying lease accounting procedures in these situations. What is the cost of the third shop from the entrance in a $14 million mall? What is the fair value of a sixth floor office suite in a 40-floor office complex? Despite practical difficulties, usual lease accounting treatment applies. It may, however, be necessary to employ real estate appraisals or replacement cost information to arrive at reasonable estimates of cost or fair value.

Usual lease accounting procedures apply to leases that involve only part of a building, although extra effort may be needed to arrive at reasonable estimates of cost and fair value.

INTERNATIONAL FINANCIAL REPORTING STANDARDS

Leases of Land and Buildings. Under *IAS No. 17,* land and buildings elements are considered separately unless the land element is not material. Under U.S. GAAP, land and building elements generally are accounted for as a single unit, unless land represents more than 25% of the total fair value of the leased property.

Leveraged Leases

In a **leveraged lease,** a third-party, long-term creditor provides nonrecourse financing for a lease agreement between a lessor and lessee. The term *leveraged* refers to the fact that the lessor acquires title to the asset after borrowing a large part of the investment.

A *leveraged lease* involves significant long-term, nonrecourse financing by a third-party creditor.

From the lessee's perspective, accounting for a leveraged lease is not distinguishable from accounting for a nonleveraged lease. Accounting for leveraged leases by the lessor is similar to that for nonleveraged leases. A lessor records its investment (receivable) net of the nonrecourse debt. The lessor's liability to the lender should be offset against its lease receivable from the lessee because its role is in substance that of a mortgage broker. That is, the lessor earns income by serving as an agent for a firm wishing to acquire property and a lender seeking an investment. The lessor borrows enough cash from the lender to acquire the property, which is in turn leased to the lessee under a capital lease. Payments from the lessee are applied to the note held by the lender. The note may be assumed by the lessee *without recourse* such that the lessor is absolved of responsibility for its payment. In order to qualify for favorable treatment under the tax code, the lessor must maintain at least a minimum percentage of equity position in the asset. Also, the lessor should report income from the lease only in those years when the receivable exceeds the liability.

A lessor records its investment (receivable) net of the nonrecourse debt and reports income from the lease only in those years when the receivable exceeds the liability.

FINANCIAL REPORTING CASE SOLUTION

1. **How would HG's revenues "take a hit" as a result of more customers leasing than buying labeling machines?** *(p. 645)* When HG leases machines under operating leases, it reports revenue as it collects "rent" over the lease term. When HG sells machines, on the other hand, it recognizes revenue "up front" in the year of sales. Actually, total revenues are not necessarily less with a lease, but are spread out over the several years of the lease term. This delays the recognition of revenues, creating the "hit" in the reporting periods in which a shift to leasing occurs.
2. **Under what kind of leasing arrangements would the "hit" not occur?** *(p. 773)* The hit will not occur when HG leases its machines under sales-type leases. In those cases, despite the fact that the contract specifies a lease, in effect, HG actually sells its machines under the arrangement. Consequently, HG will recognize sales revenue (and cost of goods sold) at the inception of the lease. The amount recognized is roughly th same as if customers actually buy the machines. As a result, the income statement wi not receive the hit created by the substitution of operating leases for outright sales. ●

THE BOTTOM LINE

- **LO1** Leasing is used as a means of financing assets as well as achieving operational and tax objectives. (p. 760)
- **LO2** In keeping with the concept of substance over form, a lease is accounted for as either a rental agreement or a purchase/sale accompanied by debt financing. (p. 761)
- **LO3** A lessee should classify a lease transaction as a capital lease if it is noncancelable and if one or more of four classification criteria are met. Otherwise, it is an operating lease. A lessor records a lease as a direct financing lease or a sales-type lease only if two conditions relating to revenue realization are met in addition to one of the four classification criteria. (p. 763)
- **LO4** In an operating lease a sale is not recorded by the lessor; a purchase is not recorded by the lessee. Instead, the periodic rental payments are accounted for merely as rent revenue by the lessor and rent expense by the lessee. (p. 765)
- **LO5** In a capital lease the lessee records a leased asset at the present value of the minimum lease payments. A nonoperating lease is recorded by the lessor as a sales-type lease or direct financing lease, depending on whether the lease provides the lessor a dealer's profit. (p. 768)
- **LO6** A sales-type lease requires recording sales revenue and cost of goods sold by the lessor at the inception of the lease. All other entries are the same as in a direct financing lease. (p. 773)
- **LO7** A lessee-guaranteed residual value is included as a component of minimum lease payments for both the lessor and the lessee. An unguaranteed residual value is not (but is part of the lessor's gross investment in the lease). (p. 775)
- **LO8** A bargain purchase option is included as a component of minimum lease payments for both the lessor and the lessee. The lease term effectively ends when the BPO is exercisable. (p. 780)
- **LO9** Executory costs (maintenance, insurance, taxes, and any other costs usually associated with ownership) are expenses of the lessee. Any costs incurred by the lessor that are associated directly with originating a lease and are essential to acquire that lease are called *initial direct costs* and are expensed in accordance with the matching principle. To find the present value of minimum lease payments to capitalize as an asset and liability, the lessee usually uses a discount rate equal to the lower of the rate implicit in the lease agreement and its own incremental borrowing rate. Contingent rentals are *not* included in the minimum lease payments because they are not determinable at the inception of the lease. (p. 783)
- **LO10** A gain on the sale of an asset in a sale leaseback arrangement is deferred and amortized over the lease term (or asset life if title is expected to transfer to the lessee). The lease portion of the transaction is evaluated and accounted for like any lease. (p. 793)

QUESTIONS FOR REVIEW OF KEY TOPICS

Q 15–1 The basic concept of "substance over form" influences lease accounting. Explain.

Q 15–2 How is interest determined in a nonoperating lease transaction? How does the approach compare to other forms of debt (say bonds payable or notes payable)?

Q 15–3 How are leases and installment notes the same? How do they differ?

Q 15–4 A lessee should classify a lease transaction as a capital lease if it is noncancelable and one or more of four classification criteria are met. Otherwise, it is an operating lease. What are these criteria?

Q 15–5 What is a bargain purchase option? How does it differ from other purchase options?

Q 15–6 Lukawitz Industries leased equipment to Seminole Corporation for a four-year period, at which time possession of the leased asset will revert back to Lukawitz. The equipment cost Lukawitz $4 million and has an expected useful life of six years. Its normal sales price is $5.6 million. The present value of the minimum lease payments for both the lessor and lessee is $5.2 million. The first payment was made at the inception of the lease. Collectibility of the remaining lease payments is reasonably assured, and Lukawitz has no material cost uncertainties. How should this lease be classified (a) by Lukawitz Industries (the lessor) and (b) by Seminole Corporation (the lessee)? Why?

Q 15–7 Can the present value of minimum lease payments differ between the lessor and lessee? If so, how?

Q 15–8 Compare the way a bargain purchase option and a residual value are treated by the lessee when determining minimum lease payments.

Q 15–9 What are executory costs? How are they accounted for by the lessee in a capital lease when paid by the lessee? When paid by the lessor? Explain.

Q 15–10 The discount rate influences virtually every amount reported in connection with a lease by both the lessor and the lessee. What is the lessor's discount rate when determining the present value of minimum lease payments? What is the lessee's discount rate?

Q 15–11 A lease might specify that rental payments may be increased (or decreased) at some future time during the lease term depending on whether or not some specified event occurs such as revenues or profits exceeding some designated level. Under what circumstances are contingent rentals included or excluded from minimum lease payments? If excluded, how are they recognized in income determination?

Q 15–12 The lessor's initial direct costs often are substantial. What are initial direct costs?

Q 15–13 When are initial direct costs recognized in an operating lease? In a direct financing lease? In a sales-type lease? Why?

Q 15–14 In a sale-leaseback transaction the owner of an asset sells it and immediately leases it back from the new owner. This dual transaction should be viewed as a single borrowing transaction. Why?

Q 15–15 Explain how the general classification criteria are applied to leases that involve land.

Q 15–16 What are the guidelines for determining when a material amount of land is involved in a lease?

Q 15–17 How does a leveraged lease differ from a nonleveraged lease?

BRIEF EXERCISES

BE 15–1
Operating lease
● LO4

At the beginning of its fiscal year, Lakeside, Inc. leased office space to LTT Corporation under a seven-year operating lease agreement. The contract calls for quarterly rent payments of $25,000 each. The office building was acquired by Lakeside at a cost of $2 million and was expected to have a useful life of 25 years with no residual value. What will be the effect of the lease on LTT's earnings for the first year (ignore taxes)?

BE 15–2
Operating lease
● LO4

In the situation described in the previous brief exercise, what will be the effect of the lease on Lakeside's earnings for the first year (ignore taxes)?

BE 15–3
Operating lease; advance payment
● LO4

Ward Products leased office space under a 10-year operating lease agreement. The lease specified 120 monthly rent payments of $5,000 each, beginning at the inception of the lease. In addition to the first rent payment, Ward also paid a $100,000 advance payment at the lease's inception. What will be the effect of the lease on Ward's earnings for the first year (ignore taxes)?

BE 15–4
Lease classification
● LO3 LO5

Corinth Co. leased equipment to Athens Corporation for an eight-year period, at which time possession of the leased asset will revert back to Corinth. The equipment cost Corinth $16 million and has an expected useful life of 12 years. Its normal sales price is $22.4 million. The present value of the minimum lease payments for both the lessor and lessee is $20.4 million. The first payment was made at the inception of the lease. Collectibility of the remaining lease payments is reasonably assured, and Corinth has no material cost uncertainties. How should Athens classify this lease? Why?

BE 15–5
Lease classification
● LO3 LO5

In the situation described in BE 15-4, how should Corinth classify this lease? Why?

BE 15–6
Net investment in leases
● LO5

The 2006 annual report of the Sonic Corporation reported minimum lease payments receivable of $6,827,000 and a net investment in direct financing leases of $3,815,000. What accounts for the difference between these two amounts? Explain.

BE 15–7
Nonoperating lease; calculate interest
● LO5

A lease agreement calls for quarterly lease payments of $5,376 over a 10-year lease term, with the first payment at July 1, the lease's inception. The interest rate is 8%. Both the fair value and the cost of the asset to the lessor are $150,000. What would be the amount of interest expense the lessee would record in conjunction with the second quarterly payment at October 1? What would be the amount of interest revenue the lessor would record in conjunction with the second quarterly payment at October 1?

BE 15–8
Capital lease; lessee; balance sheet effects
● LO5

A lease agreement that qualifies as a capital lease calls for annual lease payments of $26,269 over a six-year lease term, with the first payment at January 1, the lease's inception. The interest rate is 5%. If lessee's fiscal year is the calendar year, what would be the amount of the lease liability that the lessee would report in its balance sheet at the end of the first year? What would be the interest payable?

BE 15–9
Capital lease; lessee; income statement effects
● LO5

In the situation described in BE 15–8, what would be the pretax amounts related to the lease that the lessee would report in its income statement for the year ended December 31?

BE 15–10
Sales-type lease; lessor; income statement effects
● LO6

In the situation described in BE 15–8, assume the asset being leased cost the lessor $125,000 to produce. Determine the price at which the lessor is "selling" the asset (present value of the lease payments). What would be the pretax amounts related to the lease that the lessor would report in its income statement for the year ended December 31?

BE 15–11
Sales-type lease; lessor; calculate lease payments
● LO6

Manning Imports is contemplating an agreement to lease equipment to a customer for five years. Manning normally sells the asset for a cash price of $100,000. Assuming that 8% is a reasonable rate of interest, what must be the amount of quarterly lease payments (beginning at the inception of the lease) in order for Manning to recover its normal selling price as well as be compensated for financing the asset over the lease term?

BE 15–12
Guaranteed residual value; direct financing lease
● LO5 through LO7

On January 1, James Industries leased equipment to a customer for a four-year period, at which time possession of the leased asset will revert back to James. The equipment cost James $700,000 and has an expected useful life of six years. Its normal sales price is $700,000. The residual value after four years, guaranteed by the lessee, is $100,000. Lease payments are due on December 31 of each year, beginning with the first payment at the end of the first year. Collectibility of the remaining lease payments is reasonably assured, and there are no material cost uncertainties. The interest rate is 5%. Calculate the amount of the annual lease payments.

BE 15–13
Bargain purchase option; lessor; direct financing lease
● LO5 LO6 LO8

Ace Leasing acquires equipment and leases it to customers under long-term direct financing leases. Universal earns interest under these arrangements at a 6% annual rate. Ace leased a machine it purchased for $600,000 under an arrangement that specified annual payments beginning at the inception of the lease for five years. The lessee had the option to purchase the machine at the end of the lease term for $100,000 when it was expected to have a residual value of $160,000. Calculate the amount of the annual lease payments.

EXERCISES

available with McGraw-Hill's Homework Manager www.mhhe.com/spiceland5e 

An alternative exercise and problem set is available on the text website: www.mhhe.com/spiceland5e

E 15–1
Operating lease
● LO4

On January 1, 2009, Nath-Langstrom Services, Inc., a computer software training firm, leased several computers from ComputerWorld Corporation under a two-year operating lease agreement. The contract calls for four rent payments of $10,000 each, payable semiannually on June 30 and December 31 each year. The computers were acquired by ComputerWorld at a cost of $90,000 and were expected to have a useful life of six years with no residual value.

Required:

Prepare the appropriate entries for both (a) the lessee and (b) the lessor from the inception of the lease through the end of 2009. (Use straight-line depreciation.)

E 15–2
Operating lease; advance payment; leasehold improvement
● LO4

On January 1, 2009, Winn Heat Transfer leased office space under a three-year operating lease agreement. The arrangement specified three annual rent payments of $80,000 each, beginning January 1, 2009, the inception of the lease, and at each January 1 through 2011. Winn also paid a $96,000 advance payment at the inception of the lease in addition to the first $80,000 rent payment. With permission of the owner, Winn made structural modifications to the building before occupying the space at a cost of $180,000. The useful life of the building and the structural modifications were estimated to be 30 years with no residual value.

Required:

Prepare the appropriate entries for Winn Heat Transfer from the inception of the lease through the end of 2009. Winn's fiscal year is the calendar year. Winn uses straight-line depreciation.

E 15–3
Capital lease; lessee
● LO5

(Note: Exercises 3, 4, and 5 are three variations of the same basic situation.)
Manufacturers Southern leased high-tech electronic equipment from Edison Leasing on January 1, 2009. Edison purchased the equipment from International Machines at a cost of $112,080.

Related Information:

Lease term	2 years (8 quarterly periods)
Quarterly rental payments	$15,000—beginning of each period
Economic life of asset	2 years
Fair value of asset	$112,080
Implicit interest rate	8%
(Also lessee's incremental borrowing rate)	

Required:
Prepare a lease amortization schedule and appropriate entries for Manufacturers Southern from the inception of the lease through January 1, 2010. Depreciation is recorded at the end of each fiscal year (December 31) on a straight-line basis.

E 15–4
Direct financing lease; lessor

● LO5

Edison Leasing leased high-tech electronic equipment to Manufacturers Southern on January 1, 2009. Edison purchased the equipment from International Machines at a cost of $112,080.

Related Information:

Lease term	2 years (8 quarterly periods)
Quarterly rental payments	$15,000—beginning of each period
Economic life of asset	2 years
Fair value of asset	$112,080
Implicit interest rate	8%
(Also lessee's incremental borrowing rate)	

Required:
Prepare a lease amortization schedule and appropriate entries for Edison Leasing from the inception of the lease through January 1, 2010. Edison's fiscal year ends December 31.

E 15–5
Sales-type lease; lessor

● LO6

Manufacturers Southern leased high-tech electronic equipment from International Machines on January 1, 2009. International Machines manufactured the equipment at a cost of $85,000.

Related Information:

Lease term	2 years (8 quarterly periods)
Quarterly rental payments	$15,000—beginning of each period
Economic life of asset	2 years
Fair value of asset	$112,080
Implicit interest rate	8%
(Also lessee's incremental borrowing rate)	

Required:
1. Show how International Machines determined the $15,000 quarterly rental payments.
2. Prepare appropriate entries for International Machines to record the lease at its inception, January 1, 2009, and the second rental payment on April 1, 2009.

E 15–6
Capital lease

● LO5

American Food Services, Inc., leased a packaging machine from Barton and Barton Corporation. Barton and Barton completed construction of the machine on January 1, 2009. The lease agreement for the $4 million (fair market value) machine specified four equal payments at the end of each year. The useful life of the machine was expected to be four years with no residual value. Barton and Barton's implicit interest rate was 10% (also American Food Services' incremental borrowing rate).

Required:
1. Prepare the journal entry for American Food Services at the inception of the lease on January 1, 2009.
2. Prepare an amortization schedule for the four-year term of the lease.
3. Prepare the journal entry for the first lease payment on December 31, 2009.
4. Prepare the journal entry for the third lease payment on December 31, 2011.

(Note: You may wish to compare your solution to this exercise with that of Exercise 14–18 which deals with a parallel situation in which the packaging machine was acquired with an installment note.)

(Note: Exercises 7, 8, and 9 are three variations of the same situation.)

E 15–7
Capital lease; lessee; balance sheet and income statement effects

● LO5

On June 30, 2009, Georgia-Atlantic, Inc. leased a warehouse facility from IC Leasing Corporation. The lease agreement calls for Georgia-Atlantic to make semiannual lease payments of $562,907 over a three-year lease term, payable each June 30 and December 31, with the first payment at June 30, 2009. Georgia-Atlantic's incremental borrowing rate is 10%, the same rate IC uses to calculate lease payment amounts. Depreciation is recorded on a straight-line basis at the end of each fiscal year. The fair value of the warehouse is $3 million.

Required:

1. Determine the present value of the lease payments at June 30, 2009 (to the nearest $000) that Georgia-Atlantic uses to record the leased asset and lease liability.
2. What pretax amounts related to the lease would Georgia-Atlantic report in its balance sheet at December 31, 2009?
3. What pretax amounts related to the lease would Georgia-Atlantic report in its income statement for the year ended December 31, 2009?

E 15–8
Direct financing lease; lessor; balance sheet and income statement effects

● LO5

On June 30, 2009, Georgia-Atlantic, Inc., leased a warehouse facility from IC Leasing Corporation. The lease agreement calls for Georgia-Atlantic to make semiannual lease payments of $562,907 over a three-year lease term, payable each June 30 and December 31, with the first payment at June 30, 2009. Georgia-Atlantic's incremental borrowing rate is 10%, the same rate IC used to calculate lease payment amounts. IC purchased the warehouse from Builders, Inc. at a cost of $3 million.

Required:

1. What pretax amounts related to the lease would IC report in its balance sheet at December 31, 2009?
2. What pretax amounts related to the lease would IC report in its income statement for the year ended December 31, 2009?

E 15–9
Sales-type lease; lessor; balance sheet and income statement effects

● LO6

On June 30, 2009, Georgia-Atlantic, Inc., leased a warehouse facility from Builders, Inc. The lease agreement calls for Georgia-Atlantic to make semiannual lease payments of $562,907 over a three-year lease term, payable each June 30 and December 31, with the first payment at June 30, 2009. Georgia-Atlantic's incremental borrowing rate is 10%, the same rate Builders used to calculate lease payment amounts. Builders constructed the warehouse at a cost of $2.5 million.

Required:

1. Determine the price at which Builders is "selling" the warehouse (present value of the lease payments) at June 30, 2009 (to the nearest $000).
2. What pretax amounts related to the lease would Builders report in its balance sheet at December 31, 2009?
3. What pretax amounts related to the lease would Builders report in its income statement for the year ended December 31, 2009?

E 15–10
Lessor calculation of annual lease payments; lessee calculation of asset and liability

● LO5

Each of the three independent situations below describes a nonoperating lease in which annual lease payments are payable at the beginning of each year. The lessee is aware of the lessor's implicit rate of return.

	Situation		
	1	2	3
Lease term (years)	10	20	4
Lessor's rate of return	11%	9%	12%
Lessee's incremental borrowing rate	12%	10%	11%
Fair value of leased asset	$600,000	$980,000	$185,000

Required:

For each situation, determine:

a. The amount of the annual lease payments as calculated by the lessor.
b. The amount the lessee would record as a leased asset and a lease liability.

E 15–11
Lessor calculation of annual lease payments; lessee calculation of asset and liability

● LO5

(Note: This is a variation of the previous exercise modified to assume lease payments are at the end of each period.)

Each of the three independent situations below describes a nonoperating lease in which annual lease payments are payable at the *end* of each year. The lessee is aware of the lessor's implicit rate of return.

	Situation		
	1	2	3
Lease term (years)	10	20	4
Lessor's rate of return	11%	9%	12%
Lessee's incremental borrowing rate	12%	10%	11%
Fair value of leased asset	$600,000	$980,000	$185,000

Required:

For each situation, determine:

a. The amount of the annual lease payments as calculated by the lessor.
b. The amount the lessee would record as a leased asset and a lease liability.

E 15–12
Calculation of annual lease payments; residual value

● LO5 through LO7

Each of the four independent situations below describes a nonoperating lease in which annual lease payments are payable at the beginning of each year. Determine the annual lease payments for each:

	Situation			
	1	**2**	**3**	**4**
Lease term (years)	4	7	5	8
Lessor's rate of return	10%	11%	9%	12%
Fair value of leased asset	$50,000	$350,000	$75,000	$465,000
Lessor's cost of leased asset	$50,000	$350,000	$45,000	$465,000
Residual value:				
Guaranteed by lessee	0	$ 50,000	0	$ 30,000
Unguaranteed	0	0	$ 7,000	$ 15,000

E 15–13
Lease concepts; direct financing leases; guaranteed and unguaranteed residual value

● LO5 through LO7

Each of the four independent situations below describes a direct financing lease in which annual lease payments of $100,000 are payable at the beginning of each year. Each is a capital lease for the lessee. Determine the following amounts at the inception of the lease:

A. The lessor's:
   1. Minimum lease payments
   2. Gross investment in the lease
   3. Net investment in the lease

B. The lessee's:
   4. Minimum lease payments
   5. Leased asset
   6. Lease liability

	Situation			
	1	**2**	**3**	**4**
Lease term (years)	7	7	8	8
Lessor's and lessee's discount rate	9%	11%	10%	12%
Residual value:				
Guaranteed by lessee	0	$50,000	0	$40,000
Unguaranteed	0	0	$50,000	$60,000

E 15–14
Calculation of annual lease payments; BPO

● LO5 through LO8

For each of the three independent situations below determine the amount of the annual lease payments. Each describes a nonoperating lease in which annual lease payments are payable at the beginning of each year. Each lease agreement contains an option that permits the lessee to acquire the leased asset at an option price sufficiently lower than the expected market value that the exercise of the option appears reasonably certain.

	Situation		
	1	**2**	**3**
Lease term (years)	5	12	4
Lessor's rate of return	12%	11%	9%
Fair value of leased asset	$60,000	$420,000	$185,000
Lessor's cost of leased asset	$50,000	$420,000	$145,000
Bargain purchase option:			
Option price	$10,000	$ 50,000	$ 22,000
Exercisable at end of year:	5	5	3

E 15–15
Capital lease; bargain purchase option; lessee

● LO5 through LO8

Federated Fabrications leased a tooling machine on January 1, 2009, for a three-year period ending December 31, 2011. The lease agreement specified annual payments of $36,000 beginning with the first payment at the inception of the lease, and each December 31 through 2010. The company had the option to purchase the machine on December 30, 2011, for $45,000 when its fair value was expected to be $60,000. The machine's estimated useful life was six years with no salvage value. Federated depreciates assets by the straight-line method. The company was aware that the lessor's implicit rate of return was 12%, which was less than Federated's incremental borrowing rate.

Required:

1. Calculate the amount Federated should record as a leased asset and lease liability for this capital lease.
2. Prepare an amortization schedule that describes the pattern of interest expense for Federated over the lease term.
3. Prepare the appropriate entries for Federated from the inception of the lease through the end of the lease term.

E 15–16
Bargain purchase option; lessor; direct financing lease

● LO5 through LO8

Universal Leasing leases electronic equipment to a variety of businesses. The company's primary service is providing alternate financing by acquiring equipment and leasing it to customers under long-term direct financing leases. Universal earns interest under these arrangements at a 10% annual rate.

The company leased an electronic typesetting machine it purchased for $30,900 to a local publisher, Desktop Inc., on December 31, 2008. The lease contract specified annual payments of $8,000 beginning January 1, 2009, the inception of the lease, and each December 31 through 2010 (three-year lease term). The publisher had the option to purchase the machine on December 30, 2011, the end of the lease term, for $12,000 when it was expected to have a residual value of $16,000.

Required:

1. Show how Universal calculated the $8,000 annual lease payments for this direct financing lease.
2. Prepare an amortization schedule that describes the pattern of interest revenue for Universal Leasing over the lease term.
3. Prepare the appropriate entries for Universal Leasing from the inception of the lease through the end of the lease term.

E 15–17
Executory costs; lessor and lessee

● LO5 through LO7 LO9

On January 1, 2009, NRC Credit Corporation leased equipment to Brand Services under a direct financing lease designed to earn NRC a 12% rate of return for providing long-term financing. The lease agreement specified:

a. 10 annual payments of $55,000 (including executory costs) beginning January 1, 2009, the inception of the lease and each December 31 thereafter through 2017.

b. The estimated useful life of the leased equipment is 10 years with no residual value. Its cost to NRC was $316,412.

c. The lease qualifies as a capital lease to Brand.

d. A 10-year service agreement with Quality Maintenance Company was negotiated to provide maintenance of the equipment as required. Payments of $5,000 per year are specified, beginning January 1, 2009. NRC was to pay this executory cost as incurred, but lease payments reflect this expenditure.

e. A partial amortization schedule, appropriate for both the lessee and lessor, follows:

	Payments	Effective Interest	Decrease in Balance	Outstanding Balance
		(12% × Outstanding balance)		
				316,412
1/1/09	50,000		50,000	266,412
12/31/09	50,000	.12 (266,412) = 31,969	18,031	248,381
12/31/10	50,000	.12 (248,381) = 29,806	20,194	228,187

Required:

Prepare the appropriate entries for both the lessee and lessor to record:

1. The lease at its inception.
2. The second lease payment and depreciation (straight line) on December 31, 2009.

E 15–18
Executory costs plus management fee; lessor and lessee

● LO5 through LO7 LO9

Refer to the lease agreement described in the previous exercise. Assume the contract specified that NRC (the lessor) was to pay, not only the $5,000 maintenance fees, but also insurance of $700 per year, and was to receive a $250 management fee for facilitating service and paying executory costs. The lessee's lease payments were increased to include an amount sufficient to reimburse executory costs plus NRC's fee.

Required:

Prepare the appropriate entries for both the lessee and lessor to record the **second** lease payment, executory costs, and depreciation (straight line) on December 31, 2009.

E 15–19
Lessor's initial direct costs; operating, direct financing and sales-type leases

● LO4 through LO6 LO9

Terms of a lease agreement and related facts were:

a. Leased asset had a retail cash selling price of $100,000. Its useful life was six years with no residual value (straight-line depreciation).

b. Annual lease payments at the beginning of each year were $20,873, beginning January 1.

c. Lessor's implicit rate when calculating annual rental payments was 10%.

d. Costs of negotiating and consummating the completed lease transaction incurred by the lessor were $2,062.

e. Collectibility of the lease payments by the lessor was reasonably predictable and there were no costs to the lessor that were yet to be incurred.

Required:

Prepare the appropriate entries for the lessor to record the lease, the initial payment at its inception, and at the December 31 fiscal year-end under each of the following three independent assumptions:

1. The lease term is three years and the lessor paid $100,000 to acquire the asset (operating lease).

2. The lease term is six years and the lessor paid $100,000 to acquire the asset (direct financing lease). Also assume that adjusting the net investment by initial direct costs reduces the effective rate of interest to 9%.
3. The lease term is six years and the lessor paid $85,000 to acquire the asset (sales-type lease).

E 15–20
Lessor's initial direct costs; operating lease
● LO9

The following relate to an operating lease agreement:

a. The lease term is 3 years, beginning January 1, 2009.
b. The leased asset cost the lessor $800,000 and had a useful life of eight years with no residual value. The lessor uses straight-line depreciation for its depreciable assets.
c. Annual lease payments at the beginning of each year were $137,000.
d. Costs of negotiating and consummating the completed lease transaction incurred by the lessor were $2,400.

Required:
Prepare the appropriate entries for the lessor from the inception of the lease through the end of the lease term.

E 15–21
Lessor's initial direct costs; direct financing lease
● LO9

Terms of a lease agreement and related facts were:

a. Costs of negotiating and consummating the completed lease transaction incurred by the lessor were $4,242.
b. The retail cash selling price of the leased asset was $500,000. Its useful life was three years with no residual value.
c. Collectibility of the lease payments by the lessor was reasonably predictable and there were no costs to the lessor that were yet to be incurred.
d. The lease term is three years and the lessor paid $500,000 to acquire the asset (direct financing lease).
e. Annual lease payments at the beginning of each year were $184,330.
f. Lessor's implicit rate when calculating annual rental payments was 11%.

Required:
1. Prepare the appropriate entries for the lessor to record the lease and related payments at its inception, January 1, 2009.
2. Calculate the effective rate of interest revenue after adjusting the net investment by initial direct costs.
3. Record any entry(s) necessary at December 31, 2009, the fiscal year-end.

E 15–22
Lessor's initial direct costs; sales-type lease
● LO9

The lease agreement and related facts indicate the following:

a. Leased equipment had a retail cash selling price of $300,000. Its useful life was five years with no residual value.
b. Collectibility of the lease payments by the lessor was reasonably predictable and there were no costs to the lessor that were yet to be incurred.
c. The lease term is five years and the lessor paid $265,000 to acquire the equipment (sales-type lease).
d. Lessor's implicit rate when calculating annual lease payments was 8%.
e. Annual lease payments beginning January 1, 2009, the inception of the lease, were $69,571.
f. Costs of negotiating and consummating the completed lease transaction incurred by the lessor were $7,500.

Required:
Prepare the appropriate entries for the lessor to record:
1. The lease and the initial payment at its inception.
2. Any entry(s) necessary at December 31, 2009, the fiscal year-end.

E 15–23
Sale-leaseback; capital lease
● LO10

To raise operating funds, Signal Aviation sold an airplane on January 1, 2009, to a finance company for $770,000. Signal immediately leased the plane back for a 13-year period, at which time ownership of the airplane will transfer to Signal. The airplane has a fair value of $800,000. Its cost and its book value were $620,000. Its useful life is estimated to be 15 years. The lease requires Signal to make payments of $102,771 to the finance company each January 1. Signal depreciates assets on a straight-line basis. The lease has an implicit rate of 11%.

Required:
Prepare the appropriate entries for Signal on:
1. January 1, 2009, to record the sale-leaseback.
2. December 31, 2009, to record necessary adjustments.

E 15–24
IFRS; sale leaseback; capital lease
● LO10

Refer to the situation described in the previous exercise.

Required:
How might your solution differ if Signal Aviation prepares its financial statements according to International Accounting Standards? Include any appropriate journal entries in your response.

E 15–25
Sale-leaseback; operating lease

● LO10

To raise operating funds, National Distribution Center sold its office building to an insurance company on January 1, 2009, for $800,000 and immediately leased the building back. The operating lease is for the final 12 years of the building's estimated 50-year useful life. The building has a fair value of $800,000 and a book value of $650,000 (its original cost was $1 million). The rental payments of $100,000 are payable to the insurance company each December 31. The lease has an implicit rate of 9%.

Required:
Prepare the appropriate entries for National Distribution Center on:

1. January 1, 2009, to record the sale-leaseback.
2. December 31, 2009, to record necessary adjustments.

E 15–26
IFRS; sale leaseback; operating lease

● LO10

Refer to the situation described in the previous exercise.

Required:
How might your solution differ if National Distribution Center prepares its financial statements according to International Accounting Standards? Include any appropriate journal entries in your response.

E 15–27
Concepts; terminology

● LO3 through LO9

Listed below are several terms and phrases associated with leases. Pair each item from List A (by letter) with the item from List B that is most appropriately associated with it.

List A	List B
____ 1. Effective rate times balance.	a. PV of BPO price.
____ 2. Realization principle.	b. Lessor's net investment.
____ 3. Minimum lease payments plus unguaranteed residual value.	c. Lessor's gross investment.
____ 4. Periodic lease payments plus lessee-guaranteed residual value.	d. Operating lease.
____ 5. PV of minimum lease payments plus PV of unguaranteed residual value.	e. Depreciable assets.
____ 6. Initial direct costs.	f. Loss to lessee.
____ 7. Rent revenue.	g. Executory costs.
____ 8. Bargain purchase option.	h. Depreciation longer than lease term.
____ 9. Leasehold improvements.	i. Disclosure only.
____ 10. Cash to satisfy residual value guarantee.	j. Interest expense.
____ 11. Capital lease expense.	k. Additional lessor conditions.
____ 12. Deducted in lessor's computation of lease payments.	l. Lessee's minimum lease payments.
____ 13. Title transfers to lessee.	m. Purchase price less than fair value.
____ 14. Contingent leases.	n. Sales-type lease selling expense.
____ 15. Lease payments plus lessee-guaranteed and third-party-guaranteed residual value.	o. Lessor's minimum lease payments.

E 15–28
Real estate lease; land and building

● LO10

On January 1, 2009, Cook Textiles leased a building with two acres of land from Peck Development. The lease is for 10 years at which time Cook has an option to purchase the property for $100,000. The building has an estimated life of 20 years with a residual value of $150,000. The lease calls for Cook to assume all costs of ownership and to make annual payments of $200,000 due at the beginning of each year. On January 1, 2009, the estimated value of the land was $400,000. Cook uses the straight-line method of depreciation and pays 10% interest on borrowed money. Peck's implicit rate is unknown.

Required:
Prepare Cook Company's journal entries related to the lease in 2009.

CPA AND CMA REVIEW QUESTIONS

CPA Exam Questions

KAPLAN SCHWESER

● LO3

The following questions are used in the Kaplan CPA Review Course to study leases while preparing for the CPA examination. Determine the response that best completes the statements or questions.

1. A company leases the following asset:
   - Fair value of $200,000.
   - Useful life of 5 years with no salvage value.
   - Lease term is 4 years.
   - Annual lease payment is $30,000 and the lease rate is 11%.
   - The company's overall borrowing rate is 9.5%.
   - The firm can purchase the equipment at the end of the lease period for $45,000.

What type of lease is this?

a. Operating.
b. Capital.
c. Financing.
d. Long term.

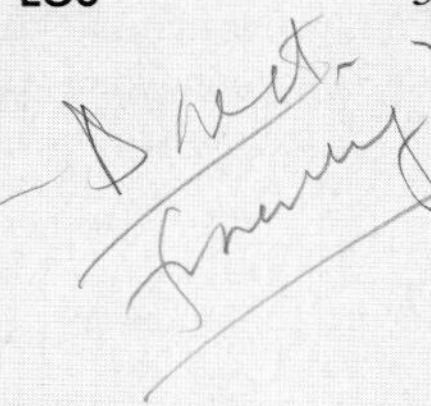

● LO5 2. On January 1, 2009, Blaugh Co. signed a long-term lease for an office building. The terms of the lease required Blaugh to pay $10,000 annually, beginning December 30, 2009, and continuing each year for 30 years. The lease qualifies as a capital lease. On January 1, 2009, the present value of the lease payments is $112,500 at the 8% interest rate implicit in the lease. In Blaugh's December 31, 2009, balance sheet, the capital lease liability should be

a. $102,500
b. $111,500
c. $112,500
d. $290,000

● LO5 3. Glade Co. leases computer equipment to customers under direct-financing leases. The equipment has no residual value at the end of the lease and the leases do not contain bargain purchase options. Glade wishes to earn 8% interest on a five-year lease of equipment with a fair value of $323,400. The present value of an annuity due of $1 at 8% for five years is 4.312. What is the total amount of interest revenue that Glade will earn over the life of the lease?

a. $ 51,600
b. $ 75,000
c. $129,360
d. $139,450

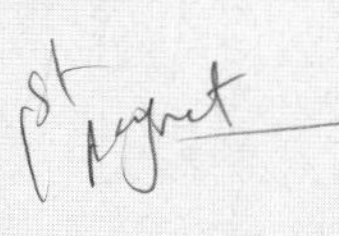

● LO6 4. Peg Co. leased equipment from Howe Corp. on July 1, 2009, for an eight-year period expiring June 30, 2017. Equal payments under the lease are $600,000 and are due on July 1 of each year. The first payment was made on July 1, 2009. The rate of interest contemplated by Peg and Howe is 10%. The cash selling price of the equipment is $3,520,000, and the cost of the equipment on Howe's accounting records is $2,800,000. The lease is appropriately recorded as a sales-type lease. What is the amount of profit on the sale and interest revenue that Howe should record for the year ended December 31, 2009?

	Profit on Sale	Interest Revenue
a.	$ 45,000	$146,000
b.	$ 45,000	$176,000
c.	$720,000	$146,000
d.	$720,000	$176,000

● LO7 5. At the inception of a capital lease, the guaranteed residual value should be

a. Included as part of minimum lease payments at present value.
b. Included as part of minimum lease payments at future value.
c. Included as part of minimum lease payments only to the extent that guaranteed residual value is expected to exceed estimated residual value.
d. Excluded from minimum lease payments.

● LO8 6. On January 2, 2009, Nori Mining Co. (lessee) entered into a 5-year lease for drilling equipment. Nori accounted for the acquisition as a capital lease for $240,000, which includes a $10,000 bargain purchase option. At the end of the lease, Nori expects to exercise the bargain purchase option. Nori estimates that the equipment's fair value will be $20,000 at the end of its 8-year life. Nori regularly uses straight-line depreciation on similar equipment. For the year ended December 31, 2009, what amount should Nori recognize as depreciation expense on the leased asset?

a. $27,500
b. $30,000
c. $48,000
d. $46,000

● LO9 7. Neal Corp. entered into a nine-year capital lease on a warehouse on December 31, 2009. Lease payments of $52,000, which includes real estate taxes of $2,000, are due annually, beginning on December 31, 2010, and every December 31 thereafter. Neal does not know the interest rate implicit in the lease; Neal's incremental borrowing rate is 9%. The rounded present value of an ordinary annuity for nine years at 9% is 6.0. What amount should Neal report as capitalized lease liability at December 31, 2009?

a. $300,000
b. $312,000
c. $450,000
d. $468,000

● LO10

8. On December 31, 2009, Bain Corp. sold a machine to Ryan and simultaneously leased it back for one year. Pertinent information at this date follows:

Sales price	$360,000
Carrying amount	330,000
Present value of lease payments ($3,000 for 12 months at 12%)	34,100
Estimated remaining useful life	12 years

In Bain's December 31, 2009, balance sheet, the deferred revenue from the sale of this machine should be

a. $ 0
b. $ 4,100
c. $34,100
d. $30,000

CMA Exam Questions

The following questions dealing with leases are adapted from questions that previously appeared on Certified Management Accountant (CMA) examinations. The CMA designation sponsored by the Institute of Management Accountants (**www.imanet.org**) provides members with an objective measure of knowledge and competence in the field of management accounting. Determine the response that best completes the statements or questions.

● LO5

1. For a direct-financing lease, the gross investment of the lessor is equal to the
   a. Present value of the minimum lease payments minus the unguaranteed residual value accruing to the lessor at the end of the lease term.
   b. Lower of 90% of the present value of the minimum lease payments or the fair value of the leased asset.
   c. Difference between the fair value of the leased asset and the unearned interest revenue.
   d. Minimum lease payments plus the unguaranteed residual value accruing to the lessor at the end of the lease term.

● LO9

2. Initial direct costs incurred by the lessor under a sales-type lease should be
   a. Deferred and allocated over the economic life of the leased property.
   b. Expensed in the period incurred.
   c. Deferred and allocated over the term of the lease in proportion to the recognition of rental income.
   d. Added to the gross investment in the lease and amortized over the term of the lease as a yield adjustment.

● LO8

3. Howell Corporation, a publicly traded corporation, is the lessee in a leasing agreement with Brandon Inc. to lease land and a building. If the lease contains a bargain purchase option, Howell should record the land and the building as a(n)
   a. Operating lease and capital lease, respectively.
   b. Capital lease and operating lease, respectively.
   c. Capital lease but recorded as a single unit.
   d. Capital lease but separately classified.

PROBLEMS

available with McGraw-Hill's Homework Manager www.mhhe.com/spiceland5e 

An alternate exercise and problem set is available on the text website: www.mhhe.com/spiceland5e

P 15–1
Operating lease; scheduled rent increases

● LO4

On January 1, 2009, Sweetwater Furniture Company leased office space under a 21-year operating lease agreement. The contract calls for annual rent payments on December 31 of each year. The payments are $10,000 the first year and increase by $500 per year. Benefits expected from using the office space are expected to remain constant over the lease term.

Required:

Record Sweetwater's rent payment at December 31, 2013 (the fifth rent payment) and December 31, 2023 (the 15th rent payment).

P 15–2
Lease amortization schedule

● LO5 LO7

On January 1, 2009, National Insulation Corporation (NIC) leased office space under a capital lease. Lease payments are made annually. Title does not transfer to the lessee and there is no bargain purchase option. Portions of the lessee's lease amortization schedule appear below:

Jan. 1	Payments	Effective Interest	Decrease in Balance	Outstanding Balance
2009				192,501
2009	20,000		20,000	172,501
2010	20,000	17,250	2,750	169,751
2011	20,000	16,975	3,025	166,726
2012	20,000	16,673	3,327	163,399
2013	20,000	16,340	3,660	159,739
2014	20,000	15,974	4,026	155,713
—	—	—	—	—
—	—	—	—	—
—	—	—	—	—
2026	20,000	7,364	12,636	61,006
2027	20,000	6,101	13,899	47,107
2028	20,000	4,711	15,289	31,818
2029	35,000	3,182	31,818	0

Required:
1. What is NIC's lease liability at the inception of the lease (after the first payment)?
2. What amount would NIC record as a leased asset?
3. What is the lease term in years?
4. What is the asset's residual value expected at the end of the lease term?
5. How much of the residual value is guaranteed by the lessee?
6. What is the effective annual interest rate?
7. What is the total amount of minimum lease payments?
8. What is the total effective interest expense recorded over the term of the lease?

P 15–3
Direct financing and sales-type lease; lessee and lessor

● LO3 LO5 LO6

Rand Medical manufactures lithotripters. Lithotripsy uses shock waves instead of surgery to eliminate kidney stones. Physicians' Leasing purchased a lithotripter from Rand for $2,000,000 and leased it to Mid-South Urologists Group, Inc., on January 1, 2009.

Lease Description:	
Quarterly lease payments	$130,516—beginning of each period
Lease term	5 years (20 quarters)
No residual value; no BPO	
Economic life of lithotripter	5 years
Implicit interest rate and lessee's incremental borrowing rate	12%
Fair value of asset	$2,000,000

Collectibility of the lease payments is reasonably assured, and there are no lessor costs yet to be incurred.

Required:
1. How should this lease be classified by Mid-South Urologists Group and by Physicians' Leasing?
2. Prepare appropriate entries for both Mid-South Urologists Group and Physicians' Leasing from the inception of the lease through the second rental payment on April 1, 2009. Depreciation is recorded at the end of each fiscal year (December 31).
3. Assume Mid-South Urologists Group leased the lithotripter directly from the manufacturer, Rand Medical, which produced the machine at a cost of $1.7 million. Prepare appropriate entries for Rand Medical from the inception of the lease through the second lease payment on April 1, 2009.

P 15–4
Capital lease

● LO5

At the beginning of 2009, VHF Industries acquired a machine with a fair value of $6,074,700 by signing a four-year lease. The lease is payable in four annual payments of $2 million at the end of each year.

Required:
1. What is the effective rate of interest implicit in the agreement?
2. Prepare the lessee's journal entry at the inception of the lease.
3. Prepare the journal entry to record the first lease payment at December 31, 2009.
4. Prepare the journal entry to record the second lease payment at December 31, 2010.
5. Suppose the fair value of the machine and the lessor's implicit rate were unknown at the time of the lease, but that the lessee's incremental borrowing rate of interest for notes of similar risk was 11%. Prepare the lessee's entry at the inception of the lease.

(Note: You may wish to compare your solution to Problem 15–4 with that of Problem 14–14, which deals with a parallel situation in which the machine was acquired with an installment note.)

(Note: Problems 5, 6, and 7 are three variations of the same basic situation.)

P 15–5
Capital lease; lessee; financial statement effects

● LO5

Werner Chemical, Inc., leased a protein analyzer on September 30, 2009. The five-year lease agreement calls for Werner to make quarterly lease payments of $391,548, payable each September 30, December 31, March 31, June 30, with the first payment at September 30, 2009. Werner's incremental borrowing rate is 12%. Depreciation is recorded on a straight-line basis at the end of each fiscal year. The useful life of the equipment is five years.

Required:

1. Determine the present value of the lease payments at September 30, 2009 (to the nearest $000).
2. What pretax amounts related to the lease would Werner report in its balance sheet at December 31, 2009?
3. What pretax amounts related to the lease would Werner report in its income statement for the year ended December 31, 2009?
4. What pretax amounts related to the lease would Werner report in its statement of cash flows for the year ended December 31, 2009?

P 15–6
Direct financing lease; lessor; financial statement effects

● LO5

Abbott Equipment leased a protein analyzer to Werner Chemical, Inc., on September 30, 2009. Abbott purchased the machine from NutraLabs, Inc., at a cost of $6 million. The five-year lease agreement calls for Werner to make quarterly lease payments of $391,548, payable each September 30, December 31, March 31, June 30, with the first payment at September 30, 2009. Abbot's implicit interest rate is 12%.

Required:

1. What pretax amounts related to the lease would Abbott report in its balance sheet at December 31, 2009?
2. What pretax amounts related to the lease would Abbott report in its income statement for the year ended December 31, 2009?
3. What pretax amounts related to the lease would Abbott report in its statement of cash flows for the year ended December 31, 2009?

P 15–7
Sales-type lease; lessor; financial statement effects

● LO6

NutraLabs, Inc., leased a protein analyzer to Werner Chemical, Inc., on September 30, 2009. NutraLabs manufactured the machine at a cost of $5 million. The five-year lease agreement calls for Werner to make quarterly lease payments of $391,548, payable each September 30, December 31, March 31, June 30, with the first payment at September 30, 2009. NutraLabs' implicit interest rate is 12%.

Required:

1. Determine the price at which NutraLabs is "selling" the equipment (present value of the lease payments) at September 30, 2009 (to the nearest $000).
2. What pretax amounts related to the lease would NutraLabs report in its balance sheet at December 31, 2009?
3. What pretax amounts related to the lease would NutraLabs report in its income statement for the year ended December 31, 2009?
4. What pretax amounts related to the lease would NutraLabs report in its statement of cash flows for the year ended December 31, 2009?

(Note: Problems 8, 9, and 10 are three variations of the same basic situation.)

P 15–8
Guaranteed residual value; direct financing lease

● LO3 LO5 LO7

eXcel

On December 31, 2009, Rhone-Metro Industries leased equipment to Western Soya Co. for a four-year period ending December 31, 2013, at which time possession of the leased asset will revert back to Rhone-Metro. The equipment cost Rhone-Metro $365,760 and has an expected useful life of six years. Its normal sales price is $365,760. The lessee-guaranteed residual value at December 31, 2013, is $25,000. Equal payments under the lease are $100,000 and are due on December 31 of each year. The first payment was made on December 31, 2009. Collectibility of the remaining lease payments is reasonably assured, and Rhone-Metro has no material cost uncertainties. Western Soya's incremental borrowing rate is 12%. Western Soya knows the interest rate implicit in the lease payments is 10%. Both companies use straight-line depreciation.

Required:

1. Show how Rhone-Metro calculated the $100,000 annual lease payments.
2. How should this lease be classified (a) by Western Soya Co. (the lessee) and (b) by Rhone-Metro Industries (the lessor)? Why?
3. Prepare the appropriate entries for both Western Soya Co. and Rhone-Metro on December 31, 2009.
4. Prepare an amortization schedule(s) describing the pattern of interest over the lease term for the lessee and the lessor.
5. Prepare all appropriate entries for both Western Soya and Rhone-Metro on December 31, 2010 (the second lease payment and depreciation).
6. Prepare the appropriate entries for both Western Soya and Rhone-Metro on December 31, 2013 assuming the equipment is returned to Rhone-Metro and the actual residual value on that date is $1,500.

P 15–9
Unguaranteed residual value; executory costs; sales-type lease

● LO6 LO7 LO9

Rhone-Metro Industries manufactures equipment that is sold or leased. On December 31, 2009, Rhone-Metro leased equipment to Western Soya Co. for a four-year period ending December 31, 2013, at which time possession of the leased asset will revert back to Rhone-Metro. The equipment cost $300,000 to manufacture and has an expected useful life of six years. Its normal sales price is $365,760. The expected residual value of $25,000 at December 31, 2013, is not guaranteed. Equal payments under the lease are $104,000 (including $4,000 executory costs) and are due on December 31 of each year. The first payment was made on December 31, 2009. Collectibility of the remaining lease payments is reasonably assured, and Rhone-Metro has no material cost uncertainties. Western Soya's incremental borrowing rate is 12%. Western Soya knows the interest rate implicit in the lease payments is 10%. Both companies use straight-line depreciation.

Required:

1. Show how Rhone-Metro calculated the $104,000 annual lease payments.
2. How should this lease be classified (a) by Western Soya Co. (the lessee) and (b) by Rhone-Metro Industries (the lessor)? Why?
3. Prepare the appropriate entries for both Western Soya Co. and Rhone-Metro on December 31, 2009.
4. Prepare an amortization schedule(s) describing the pattern of interest over the lease term for the lessee and the lessor.
5. Prepare the appropriate entries for both Western Soya and Rhone-Metro on December 31, 2010 (the second lease payment and depreciation).
6. Prepare the appropriate entries for both Western Soya and Rhone-Metro on December 31, 2013, assuming the equipment is returned to Rhone-Metro and the actual residual value on that date is $1,500.

P 15–10
Bargain purchase option exercisable before lease term ends; executory costs; sales-type lease

● LO3 LO6 LO8 LO9

Rhone-Metro Industries manufactures equipment that is sold or leased. On December 31, 2009, Rhone-Metro leased equipment to Western Soya Co. for a noncancelable stated lease term of four years ending December 31, 2013, at which time possession of the leased asset will revert back to Rhone-Metro. The equipment cost $300,000 to manufacture and has an expected useful life of six years. Its normal sales price is $365,760. The expected residual value of $25,000 at December 31, 2013, is not guaranteed. Western Soya Co. can exercise a bargain purchase option on December 30, 2012, at an option price of $10,000. Equal payments under the lease are $134,960 (including $4,000 annual executory costs) and are due on December 31 of each year. The first payment was made on December 31, 2009. Collectibility of the remaining lease payments is reasonably assured, and Rhone-Metro has no material cost uncertainties. Western Soya's incremental borrowing rate is 12%. Western Soya knows the interest rate implicit in the lease payments is 10%. Both companies use straight-line depreciation.

Hint: A lease term ends for accounting purposes when an option becomes exercisable if it's expected to be exercised (i.e., a BPO).

Required:

1. Show how Rhone-Metro calculated the $134,960 annual lease payments.
2. How should this lease be classified (a) by Western Soya Co. (the lessee) and (b) by Rhone-Metro Industries (the lessor)? Why?
3. Prepare the appropriate entries for both Western Soya Co. and Rhone-Metro on December 31, 2009.
4. Prepare an amortization schedule(s) describing the pattern of interest over the lease term for the lessee and the lessor.
5. Prepare the appropriate entries for both Western Soya and Rhone-Metro on December 31, 2010 (the second rent payment and depreciation).
6. Prepare the appropriate entries for both Western Soya and Rhone-Metro on December 30, 2012, assuming the BPO is exercised on that date.

P 15–11
Operating lease to lessee—nonoperating lease to lessor

● LO3 LO4 LO5 LO7

Allied Industries manufactures high-performance conveyers that often are leased to industrial customers. On December 31, 2009, Allied leased a conveyer to Poole Carrier Corporation for a three-year period ending December 31, 2012, at which time possession of the leased asset will revert back to Allied. Equal payments under the lease are $200,000 and are due on December 31 of each year. The first payment was made on December 31, 2009. Collectibility of the remaining lease payments is reasonably assured, and Allied has no material cost uncertainties. The conveyer cost $450,000 to manufacture and has an expected useful life of six years. Its normal sales price is $659,805. The expected residual value of $150,000 at December 31, 2012, is guaranteed by United Assurance Group. Poole Carrier's incremental borrowing rate and the interest rate implicit in the lease payments are 10%.

Required:

1. Show how Allied Industries calculated the $200,000 annual lease payments.
2. How should this lease be classified (a) by Allied (the lessor) and (b) by Poole (the lessee)? Why?
3. Prepare the appropriate entries for both Poole and Allied on December 31, 2009.
4. Prepare an amortization schedule(s) describing the pattern of interest over the lease term.
5. Prepare the appropriate entries for both Poole and Allied on December 31, 2010, 2011, and 2012, assuming the conveyer is returned to Allied at the end of the lease and the actual residual value on that date is $105,000.

P 15–12
Lease concepts; direct financing leases; guaranteed and unguaranteed residual value

● LO3 LO5 LO7

Each of the four independent situations below describes a direct financing lease in which annual lease payments of $10,000 are payable at the beginning of each year. Each is a capital lease for the lessee. Determine the following amounts at the inception of the lease:

A. The lessor's:
   1. Minimum lease payments
   2. Gross investment in the lease
   3. Net investment in the lease
B. The lessee's:
   4. Minimum lease payments
   5. Leased asset
   6. Lease liability

	Situation			
	1	2	3	4
Lease term (years)	4	4	4	4
Asset's useful life (years)	4	5	5	5
Lessor's implicit rate (known by lessee)	11%	11%	11%	11%
Lessee's incremental borrowing rate	11%	12%	11%	12%
Residual value:				
Guaranteed by lessee	0	$4,000	0	0
Guaranteed by third party	0	0	$4,000	0
Unguaranteed	0	0	0	$4,000

P 15–13
Lease concepts

● LO3 LO5 LO7

Four independent situations are described below. For each, annual lease payments of $100,000 (not including any executory costs paid by lessor) are payable at the beginning of each year. Each is a nonoperating lease for both the lessor and lessee. Determine the following amounts at the inception of the lease:

A. The lessor's:
   1. Minimum lease payments
   2. Gross investment in the lease
   3. Net investment in the lease
   4. Sales revenue
   5. Cost of goods sold
   6. Dealer's profit
B. The lessee's:
   7. Minimum lease payments
   8. Leased asset
   9. Lease liability

	Situation			
	1	2	3	4
Lease term (years)	4	5	6	4
Lessor's cost	$369,175	$449,896	$500,000	$400,000
Asset's useful life (years)	6	7	7	5
Lessor's implicit rate (known by lessee)	10%	12%	9%	10%
Lessee's incremental borrowing rate	9%	10%	11%	12%
Residual value:				
Guaranteed by lessee	0	$ 53,000	$ 40,000	$ 60,000
Guaranteed by third party*	0	0	0	$ 50,000
Unguaranteed	$ 30,000	0	$ 35,000	$ 40,000
Executory costs paid annually by lessor	$ 1,000	$ 8,000	$ 5,000	$ 10,000

*Over and above any amount guaranteed by the lessee (after a deductible equal to any amount guaranteed by the lessee).

P 15–14
Executory costs; lessor and lessee

● LO3 LO5 LO9

Branif Leasing leases mechanical equipment to industrial consumers under direct financing leases that earn Branif a 10% rate of return for providing long-term financing. A lease agreement with Branson Construction specified 20 annual payments of $100,000 beginning December 31, 2009, the inception of the lease. The estimated useful life of the leased equipment is 20 years with no residual value. Its cost to Branif was $936,500. The lease qualifies as a capital lease to Branson. Maintenance of the equipment was contracted for through a 20-year service agreement with Midway Service Company requiring 20 annual payments of $3,000 beginning December 31, 2009. Both companies use straight-line depreciation.

Required:

Prepare the appropriate entries for both the lessee and lessor to record the second lease payment and depreciation on December 31, 2010, under each of three independent assumptions:

1. The lessee pays executory costs as incurred.
2. The contract specifies that the lessor pays executory costs as incurred. The lessee's lease payments were increased to $103,000 to include an amount sufficient to reimburse these costs.
3. The contract specifies that the lessor pays executory costs as incurred. The lessee's lease payments were increased to $103,300 to include an amount sufficient to reimburse these costs plus a 10% management fee for Branif.

P 15–15
Sales-type lease; bargain purchase option exercisable before lease term ends; lessor and lessee

● LO3 LO5 LO6 LO7 LO8

Mid-South Auto Leasing leases vehicles to consumers. The attraction to customers is that the company can offer competitive prices due to volume buying and requires an interest rate implicit in the lease that is one percent below alternate methods of financing. On September 30, 2009, the company leased a delivery truck to a local florist, Anything Grows.

The lease agreement specified quarterly payments of $3,000 beginning September 30, 2009, the inception of the lease, and each quarter (December 31, March 31, and June 30) through June 30, 2012 (three-year lease term). The florist had the option to purchase the truck on September 29, 2011, for $6,000 when it was expected to have a residual value of $10,000. The estimated useful life of the truck is four years. Mid-South Auto Leasing's quarterly interest rate for determining payments was 3% (approximately 12% annually). Mid-South paid $25,000 for the truck. Both companies use straight-line depreciation. Anything Grows' incremental interest rate is 12%.

Hint: A lease term ends for accounting purposes when an option becomes exercisable if it's expected to be exercised (i.e., a BPO).

Required:

1. Calculate the amount of dealer's profit that Mid-South would recognize in this sales-type lease. (Be careful to note that, although payments occur on the last calendar day of each quarter, since the first payment was at the inception of the lease, payments represent an annuity due.)
2. Prepare the appropriate entries for Anything Grows and Mid-South on September 30, 2009.
3. Prepare an amortization schedule(s) describing the pattern of interest expense for Anything Grows and interest revenue for Mid-South Auto Leasing over the lease term.
4. Prepare the appropriate entries for Anything Grows and Mid-South Auto Leasing on December 31, 2009.
5. Prepare the appropriate entries for Anything Grows and Mid-South on September 29, 2011, assuming the bargain purchase option was exercised on that date.

P 15–16
Lessee-guaranteed residual value; third-party-guaranteed residual value; unguaranteed residual value; executory costs; different interest rates for lessor and lessee

● LO3 LO5 LO7 LO9

On December 31, 2009, Yard Art Landscaping leased a delivery truck from Branch Motors. Branch paid $40,000 for the truck. Its retail value is $45,114.

The lease agreement specified annual payments of $11,000 beginning December 31, 2009, the inception of the lease, and at each December 31 through 2012. Branch Motors' interest rate for determining payments was 10%. At the end of the four-year lease term (December 31, 2013) the truck was expected to be worth $15,000. The estimated useful life of the truck is five years with no salvage value. Both companies use straight-line depreciation.

Yard Art guaranteed a residual value of $6,000. Guarantor Assurance Corporation was engaged to guarantee a residual value of $11,000, but with a deductible equal to any amount paid by the lessee ($11,000 reduced by any amount paid by the lessee). Yard Art's incremental borrowing rate is 9%.

A $1,000 per year maintenance agreement was arranged for the truck with an outside service firm. As an expediency, Branch Motors agreed to pay this fee. It is, however, reflected in the $11,000 lease payments.

Collectibility of the lease payments by Yard Art is reasonably predictable and there are no costs to the lessor that are yet to be incurred.

Required:

1. How should this lease be classified by Yard Art Landscaping (the lessee)? Why?
2. Calculate the amount Yard Art Landscaping would record as a leased asset and a lease liability.
3. How should this lease be classified by Branch Motors (the lessor)? Why?
4. Show how Branch Motors calculated the $11,000 annual lease payments.
5. Calculate the amount Branch Motors would record as sales revenue.
6. Prepare the appropriate entries for both Yard Art and Branch Motors on December 31, 2009.
7. Prepare an amortization schedule that describes the pattern of interest expense over the lease term for Yard Art.
8. Prepare an amortization schedule that describes the pattern of interest revenue over the lease term for Branch Motors.
9. Prepare the appropriate entries for both Yard Art and Branch Motors on December 31, 2010.

10. Prepare the appropriate entries for both Yard Art and Branch Motors on December 31, 2012 (the final lease payment).
11. Prepare the appropriate entries for both Yard Art and Branch Motors on December 31, 2013 (the end of the lease term), assuming the truck is returned to the lessor and the actual residual value of the truck was $4,000 on that date.

P 15–17
Integrating problem; bonds; note; lease

● LO5

You are the new controller for Moonlight Bay Resorts. The company CFO has asked you to determine the company's interest expense for the year ended December 31, 2009. Your accounting group provided you the following information on the company's debt:

1. On July 1, 2009, Moonlight Bay issued bonds with a face amount of $2,000,000. The bonds mature in 20 years and interest of 9% is payable semiannually on June 30 and December 31. The bonds were issued at a price to yield investors 10%. Moonlight Bay records interest at the effective rate.
2. At December 31, 2008, Moonlight Bay had a 10% installment note payable to Third Merchantile Bank with a balance of $500,000. The annual payment is $60,000, payable each June 30.
3. On January 1, 2009, Moonlight Bay leased a building under a capital lease calling for four annual lease payments of $40,000 beginning January 1, 2009. Moonlight Bay's incremental borrowing rate on the date of the lease was 11% and the lessor's implicit rate, which was known by Moonlight Bay, was 10%.

Required:
Calculate interest expense for the year ended December 31, 2009.

P 15–18
Initial direct costs; direct financing lease

● LO3 LO5 LO9

Bidwell Leasing purchased a single-engine plane for its fair value of $645,526 and leased it to Red Baron Flying Club on January 1, 2009.

Terms of the lease agreement and related facts were:

a. Eight annual payments of $110,000 beginning January 1, 2009, the inception of the lease, and at each December 31 through 2015. Bidwell Leasing's implicit interest rate was 10%. The estimated useful life of the plane is eight years. Payments were calculated as follows:

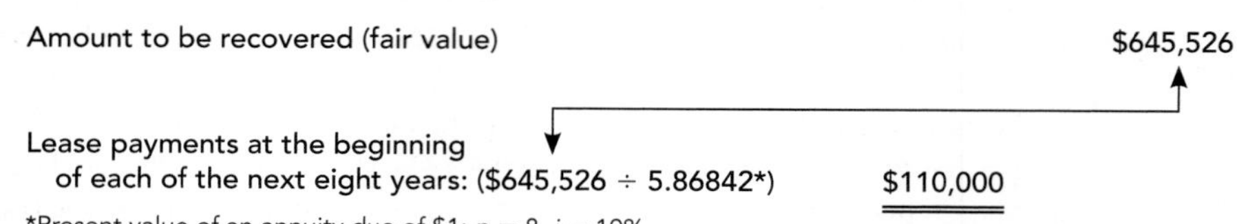

Amount to be recovered (fair value)	$645,526
Lease payments at the beginning of each of the next eight years: ($645,526 ÷ 5.86842*)	$110,000

*Present value of an annuity due of $1: $n = 8$, $i = 10\%$.

b. Red Baron's incremental borrowing rate is 11%.
c. Costs of negotiating and consummating the completed lease transaction incurred by Bidwell Leasing were $18,099.
d. Collectibility of the lease payments by Bidwell Leasing is reasonably predictable and there are no costs to the lessor that are yet to be incurred.

Required:

1. How should this lease be classified (a) by Bidwell Leasing (the lessor) and (b) by Red Baron (the lessee)?
2. Prepare the appropriate entries for both Red Baron Flying Club and Bidwell Leasing on January 1, 2009.
3. Prepare an amortization schedule that describes the pattern of interest expense over the lease term for Red Baron Flying Club.
4. Determine the effective rate of interest for Bidwell Leasing for the purpose of recognizing interest revenue over the lease term.
5. Prepare an amortization schedule that describes the pattern of interest revenue over the lease term for Bidwell Leasing.
6. Prepare the appropriate entries for both Red Baron and Bidwell Leasing on December 31, 2009 (the second lease payment). Both companies use straight-line depreciation.
7. Prepare the appropriate entries for both Red Baron and Bidwell Leasing on December 31, 2015 (the final lease payment).

P 15–19
Initial direct costs; sales-type lease

● LO3 LO6 LO9

(Note: This problem is a variation of the preceding problem, modified to cause the lease to be a sales-type lease.)

Bidwell Leasing purchased a single-engine plane for $400,000 and leased it to Red Baron Flying Club for its fair value of $645,526 on January 1, 2009.

Terms of the lease agreement and related facts were:

a. Eight annual payments of $110,000 beginning January 1, 2009, the inception of the lease, and at each December 31 through 2015. Bidwell Leasing's implicit interest rate was 10%. The estimated useful life of the plane is eight years. Payments were calculated as follows:

Amount to be recovered (fair value)		$645,526
Lease payments at the beginning of each of the next eight years: ($645,526 ÷ 5.86842*)	$110,000	

*Present value of an annuity due of $1: n = 8, i = 10%.

b. Red Baron's incremental borrowing rate is 11%.

c. Costs of negotiating and consummating the completed lease transaction incurred by Bidwell Leasing were $18,099.

d. Collectibility of the lease payments by Bidwell Leasing is reasonably predictable and there are no costs to the lessor that are yet to be incurred.

Required:

1. How should this lease be classified (a) by Bidwell Leasing (the lessor) and (b) by Red Baron (the lessee)?
2. Prepare the appropriate entries for both Red Baron Flying Club and Bidwell Leasing on January 1, 2009.
3. Prepare an amortization schedule that describes the pattern of interest expense over the lease term for Red Baron Flying Club.
4. Prepare the appropriate entries for both Red Baron and Bidwell Leasing on December 31, 2009 (the second lease payment). Both companies use straight-line depreciation.
5. Prepare the appropriate entries for both Red Baron and Bidwell Leasing on December 31, 2015 (the final lease payment).

P 15–20
Sale-leaseback

● LO5 LO10

To raise operating funds, North American Courier Corporation sold its building on January 1, 2009, to an insurance company for $500,000 and immediately leased the building back. The lease is for a 10-year period ending December 31, 2018, at which time ownership of the building will revert to North American Courier. The building has a carrying amount of $400,000 (original cost $1,000,000). The lease requires North American to make payments of $88,492 to the insurance company each December 31. The building had a total original useful life of 30 years with no residual value and is being depreciated on a straight-line basis. The lease has an implicit rate of 12%.

Required:

1. Prepare the appropriate entries for North American on (a) January 1, 2009, to record the sale-leaseback and (b) December 31, 2009, to record necessary adjustments.
2. Show how North American's December 31, 2009, balance sheet and income statement would reflect the sale-leaseback.

P 15–21
Real estate lease; land and building

● LO10

On January 1, 2009, Cook Textiles leased a building with two acres of land from Peck Development. The lease is for 10 years. No purchase option exists and the property will revert to Peck at the end of the lease. The building and land combined have a fair market value on January 1, 2009, of $1,450,000 and the building has an estimated life of 20 years with a residual value of $150,000. The lease calls for Cook to assume all costs of ownership and to make annual payments of $200,000 due at the beginning of each year. On January 1, 2009, the estimated value of the land was $400,000. Cook uses the straight-line method of depreciation and pays 10% interest on borrowed money. Peck's implicit rate is unknown.

Required:

1. Prepare journal entries for Cook Textiles for 2009. Assume the land could be leased without the building for $59,000 each year.
2. Assuming the land had a fair value on January 1, 2009, of $200,000 and could be leased alone for $30,000, prepare journal entries for Cook Textiles for 2009.

P15–22
IFRS; real estate lease; land and building

● LO10

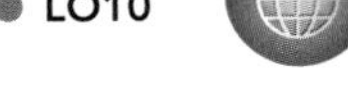

Refer to the situation described in Problem 15–21.

Required:

How might your solution differ if Cook Textiles prepares its financial statements according to International Accounting Standards?

BROADEN YOUR PERSPECTIVE

Apply your critical-thinking ability to the knowledge you've gained. These cases will provide you an opportunity to develop your research, analysis, judgment, and communication skills. You also will work with other students, integrate what you've learned, apply it in real world situations, and consider its global and ethical ramifications. This practice will broaden your knowledge and further develop your decision-making abilities.

Analysis Case 15–1
Reporting leases; off-balance-sheet financing;

● LO1 through LO5

Real World Financials

Refer to the most recent financial statements and related disclosure notes of **FedEx Corporation.** You can find these at the FedEx website, **www.fedex.com**, or by using Edgar at **www.sec.gov**. Management's Discussion and Analysis states that "Generally, management's practice in recent years with respect to funding new aircraft acquisitions has been to finance such aircraft through long-term lease transactions that qualify as off-balance-sheet operating leases under applicable accounting rules."

Required:

1. What does FedEx's management mean when it says some leases "qualify as off-balance-sheet" financing?
2. See the note on Lease Commitments in the disclosure notes. What is FedEx's capital lease liability?
3. If the operating leases were capitalized, approximately how much would that increase the capital lease liability?
4. What effect would that have on the company's debt-equity ratio? (Refer to the balance sheet.)

Research Case 15–2
Locate and extract relevant information and authoritative support for a financial reporting issue; capital lease; sublease of a leased asset

● LO1 through LO5

"I don't see that in my intermediate accounting text I saved from college," you explain to another member of the accounting division of Dowell Chemical Corporation. "This will take some research." Your comments pertain to the appropriate accounting treatment of a proposed sublease of warehouses Dowell has used for product storage.

Dowell leased the warehouses one year ago on December 31. The five-year lease agreement called for Dowell to make quarterly lease payments of $2,398,303, payable each December 31, March 31, June 30, and September 30, with the first payment at the lease's inception. As a capital lease, Dowell had recorded the leased asset and liability at $40 million, the present value of the lease payments at 8%. Dowell records depreciation on a straight-line basis at the end of each fiscal year.

Today, Jason True, Dowell's controller, explained a proposal to sublease the underused warehouses to American Tankers, Inc. for the remaining four years of the lease term. American Tankers would be substituted as lessee under the original lease agreement. As the new lessee, it would become the primary obligor under the agreement, but Dowell would be secondarily liable for fulfilling the obligations under the lease agreement. Indications are that it would be reasonably possible, though not likely, that American Tankers would default and Dowell would be required to fulfill those obligations. "Check on how we would need to account for this and get back to me," he had said.

Required:

1. After the first full year under the warehouse lease, what is the balance in Dowell's lease liability? An amortization schedule will be helpful in determining this amount.
2. After the first full year under the warehouse lease, what is the carrying amount (after accumulated depreciation) of Dowell's leased warehouses?
3. Obtain the original FASB Standard on accounting for leases. You might gain access from the FASB website at **www.fasb.org/st/**, through FARS, (the FASB Financial Accounting Research System,) from your school library, or some other source. Determine the appropriate accounting treatment for the proposed sublease. What is the specific citation that Dowell would rely on in applying that accounting treatment?
4. What, if any, journal entry would Dowell record in connection with the sublease?
5. What, if any, disclosure would Dowell provide in its financial statements in connection with the sublease? Why?

Communication Case 15–3
Classification issues; lessee accounting; group interaction

● LO3 LO7 LO8

Interstate Automobiles Corporation leased 40 vans to VIP Transport under a four-year noncancelable lease on January 1, 2009. Information concerning the lease and the vans follows:

a. Equal annual lease payments of $300,000 are due on January 1, 2009, and thereafter on December 31 each year. The first payment was made January 1, 2009. Interstate's implicit interest rate is 10% and known by VIP.
b. VIP has the option to purchase all of the vans at the end of the lease for a total of $290,000. The vans' estimated residual value is $300,000 at the end of the lease term and $50,000 at the end of 7 years, the estimated life of each van.
c. VIP estimates the fair value of the vans to be $1,240,000. Interstate's cost was $1,050,000.
d. VIP's incremental borrowing rate is 11%.
e. VIP will pay the executory costs (maintenance, insurance, and other fees not included in the annual lease payments) of $1,000 per year. The depreciation method is straight-line.
f. The collectibility of the lease payments is reasonably predictable, and there are no important cost uncertainties.

Your instructor will divide the class into two to six groups depending on the size of the class. The mission of your group is to assess the proper recording and reporting of the lease described.

Required:

1. Each group member should deliberate the situation independently and draft a tentative argument prior to the class session for which the case is assigned.
2. In class, each group will meet for 10 to 15 minutes in different areas of the classroom. During that meeting, group members will take turns sharing their suggestions for the purpose of arriving at a single group treatment.

3. After the allotted time, a spokesperson for each group (selected during the group meetings) will share the group's solution with the class. The goal of the class is to incorporate the views of each group into a consensus approach to the situation.

   Specifically, you should address:

   a. Identify potential advantages to VIP of leasing the vans rather than purchasing them.
   b. How should the lease be classified by VIP? by Interstate?
   c. Regardless of your response to previous requirements, suppose VIP recorded the lease on January 1, 2009, as a capital lease in the amount of $1,100,000. What would be the appropriate journal entries related to the capital lease for the second lease payment on December 31, 2009?

Ethics Case 15–4
Leasehold improvements

● LO3

American Movieplex, a large movie theater chain, leases most of its theater facilities. In conjunction with recent operating leases, the company spent $28 million for seats and carpeting. The question being discussed over breakfast on Wednesday morning was the length of the depreciation period for these leasehold improvements. The company controller, Sarah Keene, was surprised by the suggestion of Larry Person, her new assistant.

Keene: Why 25 years? We've never depreciated leasehold improvements for such a long period.

Person: I noticed that in my review of back records. But during our expansion to the Midwest, we don't need expenses to be any higher than necessary.

Keene: But isn't that a pretty rosy estimate of these assets' actual life? Trade publications show an average depreciation period of 12 years.

Required:

1. How would increasing the depreciation period affect American Movieplex's income?
2. Does revising the estimate pose an ethical dilemma?
3. Who would be affected if Person's suggestion is followed?

IFRS Case 15–5
Capitalizing operating leases; financial statement effects

● LO5

Google

In concert with the International Accounting Standards Board, the FASB is rethinking accounting for leases. Because obligations to make operating lease payments contribute to a company's riskiness, some accountants speculate that new lease standards might require leases now considered to be operating leases to be capitalized the way we now record capital leases.

Refer to the financial statements and related disclosure notes of Google located in the company's 2007 annual report included with all new copies of the text. You also can locate the **2007** report online at www.google.com. Find the section entitled, "Contractual Obligations as of December 31, 2007," within the MANAGEMENT'S DISCUSSION AND ANALYSIS OF FINANCIAL CONDITION AND RESULTS OF OPERATIONS. Note the discussion of Google's various noncancelable operating lease agreements for certain of its offices, land, and data centers throughout the world.

Required:

1. What is the total of Google's operating lease commitments?
2. If the operating leases were capitalized, approximately how much would that increase Google's debt? [Assume a 6% interest rate and state clearly any other assumptions you make in your calculations.]
3. Referring also to Google's balance sheet, determine the effect that capitalizing the leases would have on the company's debt-equity ratio.

Real World Case 15–6
Lease concepts

● LO1 through LO6

Real World Financials

Safeway, Inc., is one of the world's largest food retailers, operating 1,761 stores in the United States and Canada. Approximately two-thirds of the premises that the company occupies are leased. Its financial statements and disclosure notes revealed the following information:

Balance Sheet
($ in millions)

	2006	2005
Assets		
Property:		
Property under capital lease	$777.4	$779.1
Less: Accumulated amortization	(291.4)	(256.7)
Liabilities		
Current liabilities:		
Current obligations under capital leases	40.8	39.1
Long-term debt:		
Obligation under capital leases	607.9	644.1

Required:

1. Discuss some possible reasons why Safeway leases rather than purchases most of its premises.
2. The net asset "property under capital lease" has a 2006 balance of $486 million ($777.4 − 291.4). Liabilities for capital leases total $648.7 ($40.8 + 607.9). Why do the asset and liability amounts differ?

3. Prepare a 2007 summary entry to record Safeway's lease payments, which were $104 million.
4. Assuming that all property under capital lease is depreciated over the life of the lease, and that all 2006 amortization (depreciation) applied to leased assets held at the beginning of the year, what is the average life of Safeway's capital leases?
5. What is the approximate average interest rate on Safeway's capital leases? (Hint: See Req. 3)

Research Case 15–7
Researching lease disclosures; retrieving information from the Internet

● LO3 LO4 LO5

EDGAR, the Electronic Data Gathering, Analysis, and Retrieval system, performs automated collection, validation, indexing, acceptance, and forwarding of submissions by companies and others who are required by law to file forms with the U.S. Securities and Exchange Commission (SEC). All publicly traded domestic companies use EDGAR to make the majority of their filings. (Some foreign companies do so voluntarily.) Form 10-K which includes the annual report, is required to be filed on EDGAR. The SEC makes this information available on the Internet.

Required:

1. Access EDGAR on the Internet at www.sec.gov.
2. Search for a company with which you are familiar and which you believe leases some of its facilities. (Retail firms and airlines are good candidates.) Access the company's most recent 10-K filing. Search or scroll to find the financial statements and related notes.

Real World Financials

3. From the disclosure notes, determine the total capital lease obligation of the firm. What percentage does this represent of total liabilities (including current liabilities and deferred taxes) reported on the balance sheet?
4. Compare the company's rental commitments over the next five years and beyond five years for capital leases and operating leases. If operating leases were capitalized, would the company's reported debt change significantly?
5. Repeat steps 2–4 for another firm in the same industry. Are leasing practices similar between the two firms?

Real World Case 15–8
Sale-leaseback; FedEx

● LO10

FedEx Corporation, the world's largest express transportation company, leases much of its aircraft, land, facilities, and equipment. A portion of those leases are part of sale and leaseback arrangements. An excerpt from FedEx's 2008 disclosure notes describes the company's handling of gains from those arrangements:

> **Deferred Gains**
>
> Gains on the sale and leaseback of aircraft and other property and equipment are deferred and amortized ratably over the life of the lease as a reduction of rent expense.

Required:

Real World Financials

1. Why should companies defer gains from sale-leaseback arrangements?
2. Based on the information provided in the disclosure note, determine whether the leases in the leaseback portion of the arrangements are considered by FedEx to be capital leases or operating leases. Explain.

Communication Case 15–9
Where's the gain?

● LO1 LO2 LO3 LO10

General Tools is seeking ways to maintain and improve cash balances. As company controller, you have proposed the sale and leaseback of much of the company's equipment. As seller-lessee, General Tools would retain the right to essentially all of the remaining use of the equipment. The term of the lease would be six years. A gain would result on the sale portion of the transaction. The lease portion would be classified appropriately as a capital lease.

You previously convinced your CFO of the cash flow benefits of the arrangement, but now he doesn't understand the way you will account for the transaction. "I really had counted on that gain to bolster this period's earnings. What gives?" he wondered. "Put it in a memo, will you? I'm having trouble following what you're saying to me."

Required:

Write a memo to your CFO. Include discussion of each of these points:

1. How the sale portion of the sale-leaseback transaction should be accounted for at the lease's inception.
2. How the gain on the sale portion of the sale-leaseback transaction should be accounted for during the lease.
3. How the leaseback portion of the sale-leaseback transaction should be accounted for at the lease's inception.
4. The conceptual basis for capitalizing certain long-term leases.

Trueblood Case 15–10
Lease inception date issues

● LO3

The following Trueblood case is recommended for use with this chapter. The case provides an excellent opportunity for class discussion, group projects, and writing assignments. The case, along with Professor's Discussion Material, can be obtained by searching for "Trueblood Cases" on the Deloitte Foundation website: www.deloitte.com.

Case 07-7: *Porky's Revenge*

This case gives students the opportunity to extend their knowledge beyond chapter coverage by determining the lease commencement date. It focuses on a major issue in accounting for leases, but one which had often not been appropriately applied, resulting in incorrect accounting for many leases. It pertains to the situation described in the chapter in which over 200 companies in early 2005 accounted incorrectly for leases.

CPA SIMULATION 15–1

GA Company
Leases

KAPLAN SCHWESER

CPA Review

Test your knowledge of the concepts discussed in this chapter, practice critical professional skills necessary for career success, and prepare for the computer-based CPA exam by accessing our CPA simulations at the text website: www.mhhe.com/spiceland5e.

The GA Company simulation tests your knowledge of a) the way we account for and report leases from the perspective of both the lessor and lessee, b) how lease accounting is influenced by bargain purchase options and guaranteed residual value, and c) accounting for sale-leaseback arrangements.

As on the CPA exam itself, you will be asked to use tools including a spreadsheet, a calculator, and professional accounting standards, to conduct research, derive solutions, and communicate conclusions related to these issues in a simulated environment headed by the following interactive tabs:

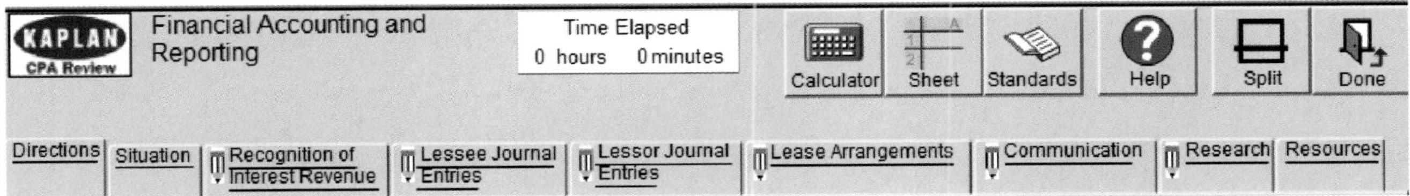

Specific tasks in the simulation include:

- Complete a worksheet pertaining to interest revenue recognition on a sales-type lease.
- Demonstrating an understanding of the way a lessee accounts for a capital lease.
- Demonstrating an understanding of the way a lessor accounts for a sales-type lease.
- Applying judgment in deciding how bargain purchase options, residual value, and sale-leaseback arrangements affect lease accounting.
- Communicating the criteria applied when classifying leases.
- Researching whether sale leaseback treatment is appropriate in a specific situation described.

16 CHAPTER

Accounting for Income Taxes

/// OVERVIEW

In this chapter we explore the financial accounting and reporting standards for the effects of income taxes. The discussion defines and illustrates temporary differences, which are the basis for recognizing deferred tax assets and deferred tax liabilities, as well as nontemporary differences, which have no deferred tax consequences. You will learn how to adjust deferred tax assets and deferred tax liabilities when tax laws or rates change. We also discuss accounting for operating loss carrybacks and carryforwards and intraperiod tax allocation.

LEARNING OBJECTIVES

After studying this chapter, you should be able to:

- **LO1** Describe the types of temporary differences that cause deferred tax liabilities and determine the amounts needed to record periodic income taxes.
- **LO2** Identify and describe the types of temporary differences that cause deferred tax assets.
- **LO3** Describe when and how a valuation allowance is recorded for deferred tax assets.
- **LO4** Explain why nontemporary differences have no deferred tax consequences.
- **LO5** Explain how a change in tax rates affects the measurement of deferred tax amounts.
- **LO6** Determine income tax amounts when multiple temporary differences exist.
- **LO7** Describe when and how an operating loss carryforward and an operating loss carryback are recognized in the financial statements.
- **LO8** Explain how deferred tax assets and deferred tax liabilities are classified and reported in a classified balance sheet and describe related disclosures.
- **LO9** Demonstrate how to account for uncertainty in income tax decisions.
- **LO10** Explain intraperiod tax allocation.

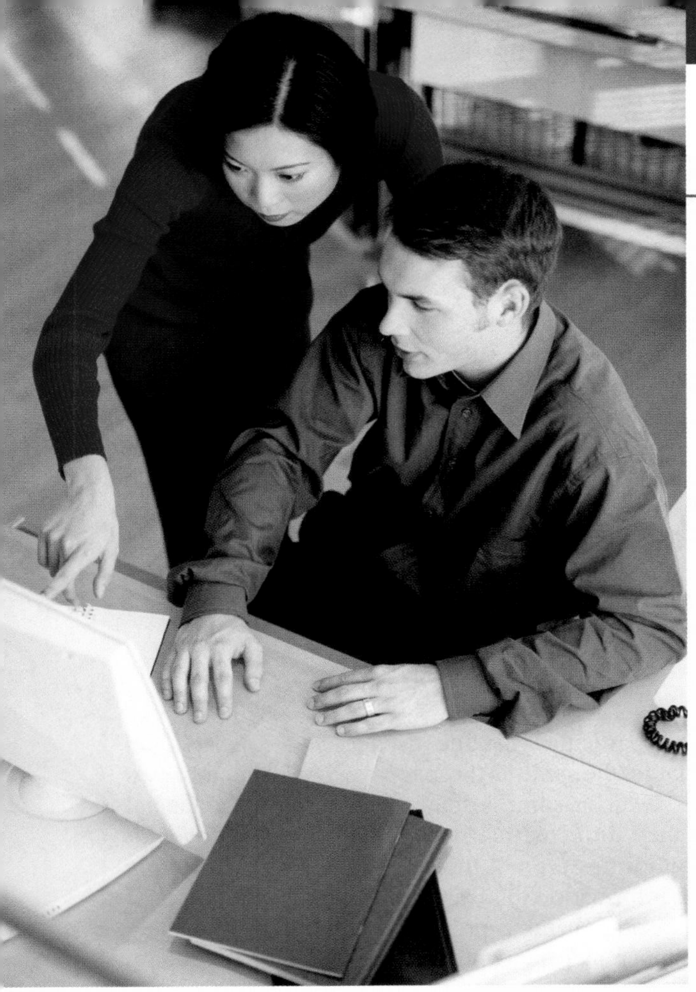

FINANCIAL REPORTING CASE

What's the Difference?

The board of directors for Times-Lehrer Industries is meeting for the first time since Laura Lynn was asked to join the board. Laura was the director of the regional office of United Charities. Although she has broad experience with the tax advantages of charitable giving and the vast array of investment vehicles available to donors, her 30 years of experience with not-for-profit organizations has not exposed her to the issues involved with corporate taxation. This gap in her considerable business knowledge causes her to turn to you, Times-Lehrer's CFO and long-time friend, who recommended Laura for appointment to the board.

"I must say," Laura confided, "I've looked long and hard at these statements, and I can't quite grasp why the amount reported for income tax expense is not the same as the amount of income taxes we paid. What's the difference?"

By the time you finish this chapter, you should be able to respond appropriately to the questions posed in this case. Compare your response to the solution provided at the end of the chapter.

QUESTIONS ///

1. What's the difference? Explain to Laura how differences between financial reporting standards and income tax rules might cause the two tax amounts to differ. (page 822)
2. What is the conceptual advantage of determining income tax expense as we do? (page 822)
3. Are there differences between financial reporting standards and income tax rules that will not contribute to the difference between income tax expense and the amount of income taxes paid? (page 834)

PART A

DEFERRED TAX ASSETS AND DEFERRED TAX LIABILITIES

FINANCIAL Reporting Case

Q1, p. 821

A manufacturer of leather accessories in the Midwest is obligated to pay the Internal Revenue Service $24 million in income taxes as determined by its 2009 income tax return. Another $9 million in income taxes also is attributable to 2009 activities. Conveniently, though, tax laws permit the company to defer paying the additional $9 million until subsequent tax years by reporting certain revenues and expenses on the tax return in years other than when reported on the income statement. Does the company have only a current income tax liability of $24 million? Or does it also have a deferred income tax liability for the other $9 million? To phrase the question differently: Should the company report a 2009 income tax expense of the $24 million tax payable for the current year, or $33 million to include the future tax effects of events already recognized? For perspective on this question, we should look closer at the circumstances that might create the situation. Such circumstances are called *temporary differences.*

Conceptual Underpinning

FINANCIAL Reporting Case

Q2, p. 821

The goals of financial accounting and tax accounting are not the same.

When a company prepares its tax return for a particular year, the revenues and expenses (and losses) included on the return are, by and large, the same as those reported on the company's income statement for the same year. However, in some instances tax laws and financial accounting standards differ. The reason they differ is that the fundamental objectives of financial reporting and those of taxing authorities are not the same. Financial accounting standards are established to provide useful information to investors and creditors. Congress, through the Internal Revenue Service, on the other hand, is primarily concerned with raising public revenues in a socially acceptable manner and, frequently, with influencing the behavior of taxpayers. In pursuing the latter objective, Congress uses tax laws to encourage activities it deems desirable, such as investment in productive assets, and to discourage activities it deems undesirable, such as violations of law.

Accounting for income taxes is consistent with the accrual concept of accounting.

A consequence of differences between GAAP and tax rules is that tax payments frequently occur in years different from when the revenues and expenses that cause the taxes are generated. The financial reporting issue is *when* the tax expense should be recognized. The issue has generated considerable controversy for decades. In 1967 the profession, through *APB 11,* embraced the concept of reporting income tax expense in the same period as events that give rise to the expense, regardless of when the tax actually is paid.[1] You may recognize this approach as being consistent with the accrual concept of accounting. The primary focus of that pronouncement was the matching principle. Income tax expense was calculated on the basis of pretax income reported on the income statement. Differences between the expense and the tax currently paid were reported on the balance sheet not as deferred tax liabilities (or assets) but as nebulous deferred credits (or debits).[2]

***APB 11* focused on the income statement and the matching principle.**

APB 11 was replaced in 1987 by *SFAS 96,* which reiterated the objective of reporting deferred taxes but redirected the focus to an asset-liability approach.[3] This balance sheet focus emphasizes reporting the future tax sacrifice or benefit attributable to temporary differences between the reported amount of an asset or liability in the financial statements and its tax basis.[4] Plagued by implementation complexities, *SFAS 96* was delayed three times and then replaced in 1992 with *SFAS 109* before ever becoming mandatory.[5] The current standard modified some of the more troublesome measurement and recognition requirements but retained the essential flavor of *SFAS 96.* That is, the objective of accounting for income taxes is to recognize a deferred tax liability or deferred tax asset for the tax consequences of amounts that will become taxable or deductible in future years as a result of transactions

***SFAS 109* focuses on the balance sheet and the recognition of liabilities and assets.**

[1]"Accounting for Income Taxes," *Accounting Principles Board Opinion No. 11* (New York: AICPA, 1967).
[2]Some critics at the time referred to these amounts as "UGOs: Unidentified Growing Objects."
[3]"Accounting for Income Taxes," *Statement of Financial Accounting Standards No. 96* (Stamford, Conn.: FASB, 1987).
[4]Research supports the notion that deferred tax liabilities are, in fact, viewed by investors as real liabilities.
[5]"Accounting for Income Taxes," *Statement of Financial Accounting Standards No. 109* (Norwalk, Conn.: FASB, 1992).

or events that already have occurred. Future taxable amounts and future deductible amounts arise as a result of temporary differences. We discuss those now.

Temporary Differences

● LO1

The differences in the rules for computing taxable income and those for financial reporting often cause amounts to be included in taxable income in a year later—or earlier—than the year in which they are recognized for financial reporting purposes, or not to be included in taxable income at all. For example, you learned in Chapter 4 that income from selling properties on an installment basis is reported for financial reporting purposes in the year of the sale. But tax laws permit installment income to be reported on the tax return as it actually is received (by the installment method). This means taxable income might be less than accounting income in the year of an installment sale but higher than accounting income in later years when installment income is collected.

The situation just described creates what's referred to as a **temporary difference** between pretax *accounting* income and *taxable* income and, consequently, between the reported amount of an asset or liability in the financial statements and its tax basis. In our example, the asset for which the temporary difference exists is the installment receivable that's recognized for financial reporting purposes, but not for tax purposes.

Deferred Tax Liabilities

It's important to understand that a temporary difference *originates* in one period and *reverses*, or turns around, in one or more subsequent periods. The temporary difference described above originates in the year the installment sales are made and are reported on the *income statement* and then reverses when the installments are collected and income is reported on the *tax return*. An example is provided in Illustration 16–1.

Kent Land Management reported pretax accounting income in 2009, 2010, and 2011 of $100 million, plus additional 2009 income of $40 million from installment sales of property. However, the installment sales income is reported on the tax return when collected, in 2010 ($10 million) and 2011 ($30 million).* The enacted tax rate is 40% each year.†

($ in millions)	Temporary Difference			
	Originates	Reverses		
	2009	2010	2011	Total
Pretax accounting income	$140	$100	$100	$340
Installment sale income on the income statement	(40)	0	0	(40)
Installment sale income on the tax return	0	10	30	40
Taxable income (tax return)	$100	$110	$130	$340

ILLUSTRATION 16–1

Revenue Reported on the Tax Return after the Income Statement

In 2009, taxable income is less than accounting income because income from installment sales is not reported on the tax return until 2010–2011.

*The installment method is not available to accrual method taxpayers. H.R. 1180, sec. 536, 1999.

†The enacted rate refers to the tax rate indicated by currently enacted tax legislation (as distinguished from anticipated legislation). This is discussed later in the chapter.

Notice that pretax accounting income and taxable income total the same amount over the three-year period but are different in each individual year. In 2009, taxable income is $40 million *less* than accounting income because it does not include income from installment sales. The difference is temporary, though. That situation reverses over the next two years. In 2010 and 2011 taxable income is *more* than accounting income because income on the installment sales, reported on the income statement in 2009, becomes taxable during the next two years as installments are collected.

Because tax laws permit the company to delay reporting this income as part of taxable income, the company is able to defer paying the tax on that income. The tax is not avoided,

The 2009 tax liability is paid in the next two years.

just deferred. In the meantime, the company has a liability for the income tax deferred. The liability originates in 2009 and is paid over the next two years as follows:

Deferred Tax Liability

($ in millions)			
		16	2009 ($40 × 40%)
2010 ($10 × 40%)	4		
2011 ($30 × 40%)	12		
		0	Balance after 3 years

At the end of 2009, financial and taxable income for 2010 and 2011 are, of course, not yet known. We assumed knowledge of that information above so we could compare the three-year effect of the temporary difference, but seeing the future is unnecessary to determine amounts needed to record income taxes in 2009. This is demonstrated in Illustration 16–1A.

ILLUSTRATION 16–1A
Determining and Recording Income Taxes—2009

($ in millions)	Current Year 2009	Future Taxable Amounts 2010	2011	Future Taxable Amounts (total)
Pretax accounting income	$140			
Temporary difference:				
Installment income	(40)	$10	$30	$40
Taxable income (tax return)	100			
Enacted tax rate	40%			40%
Tax payable currently	40			
Deferred tax liability				$16

Reported in the income statement, not on the tax return

Deferred Tax Liability

Desired ending balance	$16
Less: Beginning balance	0
Change in balance	$16

Deferred tax liability

	0 beg. bal.
	16 change
	16 ending bal.

Journal Entry at the End of 2009

Income tax expense (to balance)	56	
Income tax payable (determined above)		40
Deferred tax liability (determined above)		16

With **future taxable amounts** of $40 million, taxable at 40%, a $16 million **deferred tax liability** is indicated. Since no previous balance exists, we add this amount to the liability.

Each year, income tax expense comprises both the current and the deferred tax consequences of events and transactions already recognized. This means we:

1. Calculate the income tax that is payable currently.
2. Separately calculate the change in the deferred tax liability (or asset).
3. Combine the two to get the income tax expense.

Deferred tax liability

	16 beg. bal.
change 4	
	12 ending bal.

Using the 2010 and 2011 income numbers, the journal entries to record income taxes those years would be:

At the end of 2010, the deferred tax liability should have a balance of $12 million. Because the balance from 2009 is $16 million, we reduce it by $4 million.

2010	($ in millions)	
Income tax expense (to balance)	40	
Deferred tax liability [($30 million × 40%) − 16 million]	4	
Income tax payable ($110 million × 40%)		44

2011		
Income tax expense (to balance)	40	
Deferred tax liability ($0 million – 12 million)	12	
Income tax payable ($130 million × 40%)		52

At the end of 2011, the deferred tax liability should have a balance of zero. So, we eliminate the $12 million balance.

The FASB's Balance Sheet Approach

Our perspective in this example so far has centered around the income effects of the installment sales and thus on the changes in the deferred tax liability as the temporary difference reverses. Another perspective is to consider the balance sheet effect. From this viewpoint, we regard a deferred tax liability (or asset) to be the tax effect of the temporary difference between the *financial statement carrying amount* of an asset or liability and its *tax basis*. The tax basis of an asset or liability is its original value for tax purposes reduced by any amounts included to date on tax returns. In our example, a temporary book-tax difference exists for a receivable from installment sales that's recognized for financial reporting purposes but not for tax purposes. When a company sells something on an installment basis, it reports a receivable. From a tax perspective, though, there is no receivable because a "taxable sale" doesn't occur until installments are collected. This is shown in Illustration 16–1B.

An installment receivable has no tax basis.

ILLUSTRATION 16–1B
Balance Sheet Perspective

December 31 ($ in millions)	2009		2010		2011	
Receivable from installment sales:						
Accounting basis	$40	$40	$(10)	$30	$(30)	$0
Tax basis	(0)	(0)	(0)	(0)	(0)	(0)
Temporary difference	$40	$40	$(10)	$30	$(30)	$0
Tax rate	↑	× 40%	↑	× 40%	↑	× 40%
Deferred tax liability		$16		$12		$0
	Originating Difference		Reversing Differences			

The deferred tax liability each year is the tax rate times the temporary difference between the financial statement carrying amount of the receivable and its tax basis.

Of course, the income statement view and the balance sheet view are two different perspectives on the very same event. In this example, we derive the same deferred tax liability whether we view it as a result of a temporary difference (a) between accounting and taxable income or (b) between the financial statement carrying amount of an installment receivable and its tax basis. Conceptually, though, the balance sheet approach strives to establish deferred tax assets and liabilities that meet the definitions of assets and liabilities provided by the FASB's conceptual framework. As specified by *SFAC 6,* assets represent "probable future economic benefits obtained or controlled by a particular entity as a result of past transactions or events," and liabilities are "probable future sacrifices of economic benefits as a result of past transactions or events."[6] In our example, the probable future sacrifices of economic benefits are the payments of $4 million in 2010 and $12 million in 2011. The past transactions or events resulting in the future tax payments are the installment sales in 2009.

SFAS 109 takes a balance sheet approach to establishing deferred tax assets and liabilities that meet the definitions of assets and liabilities provided by the FASB's conceptual framework.

This balance sheet approach, sometimes called the "asset/liability approach," is a perspective that extends beyond accounting for deferred taxes. In fact, the FASB and IASB increasingly appear to be moving to that perspective in their approach to accounting standards. The movement toward fair values we discussed in Chapters 12 (Investments) and 14 (Bonds and Long-term Notes) is consistent with that perspective. Measuring assets and liabilities at their fair values and then reporting changes in those fair values as holding gains and losses in the income statement is a fundamental departure from the "transactions approach," by which we report in the income statement the effects of external transactions such as gains and losses from the sale of assets and liabilities.

Recent accounting standards provide evidence that the FASB is embracing a "balance sheet approach" to accounting.

[6] "Elements of Financial Statements," *Statement of Financial Accounting Concepts No. 6* (Stamford, Conn.: FASB, 1985), par. 25, 35.

Types of Temporary Differences

Examples of temporary differences are provided in Graphic 16–1.

GRAPHIC 16–1
Types of Temporary Differences

	Revenues (or gains)	**Expenses (or losses)**
Items reported on the tax return *after* the income statement	• Installment sales of property (installment method for taxes). • Unrealized gain from recording investments at fair value (taxable when asset is sold).	• Estimated expenses and losses (tax deductible when paid). • Unrealized loss from recording investments at fair value or inventory at LCM (tax deductible when asset is sold).
Items reported on the tax return *before* the income statement	• Rent collected in advance. • Subscriptions collected in advance. • Other revenue collected in advance.	• Accelerated depreciation on tax return (straight-line depreciation in the income statement). • Prepaid expenses (tax deductible when paid).

- The temporary differences shown in the diagonal purple areas create *deferred tax liabilities* because they result in *taxable* amounts in some future year(s) when the related assets are recovered or the related liabilities are settled (when the temporary differences reverse).
- The temporary differences in the opposite diagonal blue areas create *deferred tax assets* because they result in *deductible* amounts in some future year(s) when the related assets are recovered or the related liabilities are settled (when the temporary differences reverse).

ADDITIONAL CONSIDERATION

Temporary differences between the reported amount of an asset or liability in the financial statements and its tax basis are primarily caused by revenues, expenses, gains, and losses being included in taxable income in a year earlier or later than the year in which they are recognized for financial reporting purposes as illustrated in Graphic 16–1. Other events also can cause temporary differences between the reported amount of an asset or liability in the financial statements and its tax basis. Three other such events that are beyond the scope of this textbook are briefly described in "Accounting for Income Taxes," *Statement of Financial Accounting Standards No. 109* (Norwalk, Conn.: FASB, 1992), par. 11 e–h. Our discussions in this chapter focus on temporary differences caused by the timing of revenue and expense recognition, but it's important to realize that the concept of temporary differences embraces all differences that will result in taxable or deductible amounts in future years.

Be sure to notice that deferred tax liabilities can arise from either (a) a revenue being reported on the tax return after the income statement or (b) an expense being reported on the tax return before the income statement. Our previous illustration was of the first type. We look at the second in Illustration 16–2.

Notice, too, that this temporary difference originates during more than a single year before it begins to reverse. This usually is true when depreciation is the cause of the temporary difference. Tax laws typically permit the cost of a depreciable asset to be deducted on the tax return sooner than it is reported as depreciation on the income statement.[7] This

[7]Presently, the accelerated depreciation method prescribed by the tax code is the modified accelerated cost recovery system (MACRS). The method is described in Chapter 11.

ILLUSTRATION 16–2
Expense Reported on the Tax Return before the Income Statement

Courts Temporary Services reported pretax accounting income in 2009, 2010, 2011, and 2012 of $100 million. In 2009, an asset was acquired for $100 million. The asset is depreciated for financial reporting purposes over four years on a straight-line basis (no residual value). For tax purposes the asset's cost is deducted (by MACRS) over 2009–2012 as follows: $33 million, $44 million, $15 million, and $8 million. No other depreciable assets were acquired. The enacted tax rate is 40% each year.

($ in millions)	Temporary Difference: Originates		Reverses		
	2009	**2010**	**2011**	**2012**	**Total**
Pretax accounting income	$100	$100	$100	$100	$400
Depreciation on the income statement	25	25	25	25	100
Depreciation on the tax return	(33)	(44)	(15)	(8)	(100)
Taxable income (tax return)	$ 92	$ 81	$110	$117	$400

To determine taxable income, we add back to accounting income the actual depreciation taken in the income statement and then subtract the depreciation deduction allowed on the tax return.

means taxable income will be less than pretax accounting income in the income statement during the years the tax deduction is higher than income statement depreciation, but higher than pretax accounting income in later years when the situation reverses.

2009 income taxes would be recorded as follows in Illustration 16–2A:

ILLUSTRATION 16–2A
Determining and Recording Income Taxes—2009

($ in millions)	Current Year 2009	Future Taxable Amounts 2010	2011	2012	Future Taxable Amounts (total)
Pretax accounting income	$ 100				
Temporary difference:					
Depreciation	(8)	$(19)	$10	$17	$8
Taxable income	$ 92				
Enacted tax rate	40%				40%
Tax payable currently	$36.8				
Deferred tax liability					$3.2

Tax depreciation is $8 million more than in the income statement.

Deferred Tax Liability

Ending balance	$3.2
Less: Beginning balance	0.0
Change in balance	$3.2

Journal Entry at the End of 2009

Income tax expense (to balance)	40	
Income tax payable (determined above)		36.8
Deferred tax liability (determined above)		3.2

Taxable income is $8 million less than accounting income because that much more depreciation is deducted on the 2009 tax return ($33 million) than is reported on the income statement ($25 million).

Income tax expense is comprised of two components: the amount payable now and the amount deferred until later.

Let's follow the determination of income taxes for this illustration all the way through the complete reversal of the temporary difference. We assume accounting income is $100 million each year and that the only difference between pretax accounting income and taxable income is caused by depreciation. 2010 income taxes would be determined as shown in Illustration 16–2B on the next page.

Notice that each year the appropriate balance is determined for the deferred tax liability. That amount is compared with any existing balance to determine whether the account must be either increased or decreased.

ILLUSTRATION 16–2B
Determining and Recording Income Taxes—2010

The cumulative temporary difference ($27 million) is both (a) the sum of the amounts originating in 2009 ($8 million) and in 2010 ($19 million) and (b) the sum of the amounts reversing in 2011 ($10 million) and in 2012 ($17 million).

Since a balance of $3.2 million already exists, $7.6 million must be added.

($ in millions)

	2009	Current Year 2010	Future Taxable Amounts 2011	Future Taxable Amounts 2012	Future Taxable Amounts (total)
Pretax accounting income		$ 100			
Temporary difference:					
Depreciation	$(8)	(19)	$10	$17	$ 27
Taxable income (tax return)		81			
Enacted tax rate		40%			40%
Tax payable currently		$32.4			
Deferred tax liability					$10.8

Deferred Tax Liability

Ending balance	$10.8
Less: Beginning balance	(3.2)
Change in balance	$ 7.6

Journal Entry at the End of 2010

Income tax expense (to balance)	40	
Income tax payable (determined above)		32.4
Deferred tax liability (determined above)		7.6

Income taxes for 2011 would be recorded as shown in Illustration 16–2C.

ILLUSTRATION 16–2C
Determining and Recording Income Taxes—2011

A credit balance of $6.8 million is needed in the deferred tax liability account.

Since a credit balance of $10.8 million already exists, $4 million must be deducted (debited).

A portion of the tax deferred from 2009 and 2010 is now being paid in 2011.

($ in millions)

	2009	2010	Current Year 2011	Future Taxable Amounts 2012	Future Taxable Amounts (total)
Pretax accounting income			$100		
Temporary difference:					
Depreciation	$(8)	$(19)	10	$17	$ 17
Taxable income (tax return)			$110		
Enacted tax rate			40%		40%
Tax payable currently			$ 44		
Deferred tax liability					$ 6.8

Deferred Tax Liability

Ending balance	$ 6.8
Less: Beginning balance	(10.8)
Change in balance	$(4.0)

Journal Entry at the End of 2011

Income tax expense (to balance)	40	
Deferred tax liability (determined above)	4	
Income tax payable (determined above)		44

ILLUSTRATION 16–2D
Determining and Recording Income Taxes—2012

($ in millions)	2009	2010	2011	Current Year 2012	Future Taxable Amounts (total)
Pretax accounting income				$100	
Temporary difference:					
Depreciation	$(8)	$(19)	$10	17	$ 0
Taxable income (tax return)				$117	
Enacted tax rate				40%	40%
Tax payable currently				$ 46.8	
Deferred tax liability					$ 0.0

Deferred Tax Liability

Ending balance	$ 0.0
Less: Beginning balance	(6.8)
Change in balance	$(6.8)

Journal Entry at the End of 2012

Income tax expense (to balance)	40.0	
Deferred tax liability (determined above)	6.8	
Income tax payable (determined above)		46.8

Because the entire temporary difference has now reversed, there is a zero cumulative temporary difference, and the balance in the deferred tax liability should be zero.

Since a credit balance of $6.8 million exists, that amount must be deducted (debited).

The final portion of the tax deferred from 2009 and 2010 is paid in 2012.

Income taxes for 2012 would be recorded as shown in Illustration 16–2D. Notice there that the deferred tax liability is increased in 2009–2010 and decreased in 2011–2012.

Deferred Tax Liability

($ in millions)	Debit	Credit	
		3.2	2009 ($ 8 × 40%)
2011 ($10 × 40%)	4.0	7.6	2010 ($19 × 40%)
2012 ($17 × 40%)	6.8		
		0	Balance after 4 years

The deferred tax liability increases the first two years and is paid over the next two years.

We can see this result from the alternate perspective of looking at the temporary book–tax difference that exists for the depreciable asset. Its carrying amount is its cost minus accumulated straight-line depreciation. Its tax basis is cost minus the accumulated cost recovery for tax purposes:

($ in millions)		December 31	2009		2010		2011		2012
Depreciable asset:									
Accounting basis	$100	$(25)	$ 75	$(25)	$ 50	$(25)	$ 25	$(25)	$ 0
Tax basis	100	(33)	67	(44)	23	(15)	8	(8)	0
Temporary difference		$ 8	$ 8	$ 19	$ 27	$(10)	$ 17	$(17)	$ 0
Enacted tax rate			40%		40%		40%		40%
Deferred tax liability			$3.2		$10.8		$6.8		$ 0
		Originating Differences				Reversing Differences			

A balance sheet perspective focuses on the difference between the carrying amount and the tax basis.

Deferred Tax Assets

● LO2

The temporary differences illustrated to this point produce future taxable amounts when the temporary differences reverse. Future taxable amounts mean taxable income will be increased relative to pretax accounting income in one or more future years. Sometimes, though, the future tax consequence of a temporary difference will be to decrease taxable income relative to accounting income. Such situations produce what's referred to as **future deductible amounts.** These have favorable tax consequences that are recognized as **deferred tax assets.**

Deferred tax assets are recognized for the future tax benefits of temporary differences that create future deductible amounts.

Two examples indicated in Graphic 16–1 are (1) estimated expenses that are recognized on income statements when incurred but deducted on tax returns in later years when actually paid and (2) revenues that are taxed when collected but recognized on income statements in later years when actually earned. An example of the first type is provided in Illustration 16–3.

ILLUSTRATION 16–3
Expense Reported on the Tax Return after the Income Statement

RDP Networking reported pretax accounting income in 2009, 2010, and 2011 of $70 million, $100 million, and $100 million, respectively. The 2009 income statement includes a $30 million warranty expense that is deducted for tax purposes when paid in 2010 ($15 million) and 2011 ($15 million).* The income tax rate is 40% each year.

($ in millions)	Temporary Difference			
	Originates	Reverses		
	2009	2010	2011	Total
Pretax accounting income	$ 70	$100	$100	$270
Warranty expense on the income statement	30			30
Warranty expense on the tax return		(15)	(15)	(30)
Taxable income (tax return)	$100	$ 85	$ 85	$270

In 2009, taxable income is more than pretax accounting income because the warranty expense is not deducted on the tax return until paid.

*Remember from Chapter 13 that warranty expense is estimated for the period the products are sold even though the actual cost isn't incurred until later periods.

At the end of 2009, the amounts needed to record income tax for 2009 would be determined as shown in Illustration 16–3A.

ILLUSTRATION 16–3A
Determining and Recording Income Taxes—2009

($ in millions)

	Current Year 2009	Future Deductible Amounts 2010	Future Deductible Amounts 2011	Future Deductible Amounts (total)
Pretax accounting income	$ 70			
Temporary difference:				
Warranty expense	30	$(15)	$(15)	$(30)
Taxable income (tax return)	$100			
Enacted tax rate	40%			40%
Tax payable currently	$ 40			
Deferred tax asset				$(12)

Deferred Tax Asset

Ending balance	$ 12
Less: Beginning balance	0
Change in balance	$ 12

Journal Entry at the End of 2009

Income tax expense (to balance)	28	
Deferred tax asset (determined above)	12	
Income tax payable (determined above)		40

Because the warranty expense was subtracted on the 2009 income statement but isn't deductible on the 2009 tax return, it is added back to pretax accounting income to find taxable income.

The amounts deductible in 2010 and 2011 will produce tax benefits that are recognized now as a deferred tax asset.

At the end of 2009 and 2010, the company reports a deferred tax asset for future income tax benefits.

Deferred Tax Asset

			($ in millions)
2009 ($30 × 40%)	12		
		6	2010 ($15 × 40%)
		6	2011 ($15 × 40%)
Balance after 3 years	0		

Income taxes payable in 2010 and 2011 are less than otherwise payable because of the taxes prepaid in 2009.

If we continue the assumption of $85 million taxable income in each of 2010 and 2011, income tax those years would be recorded this way:

2010		
Income tax expense (to balance)	40	
Deferred tax asset ($15 million × 40%)		6
Income tax payable ($85 million × 40%)		34
2011		
Income tax expense (to balance)	40	
Deferred tax asset ($15 million × 40%)		6
Income tax payable ($85 million × 40%)		34

The deferred tax asset represents the future tax benefit from the reversal of a temporary difference between the financial statement carrying amount of the warranty liability and its tax basis.

($ in millions)	December 31					
	2009		2010		2011	
Warranty liability:						
Accounting basis	$30	$30	$(15)	$15	$(15)	$0
Tax basis	(0)	(0)	(0)	(0)	(0)	(0)
Temporary difference	$30	$30	$(15)	$15	$(15)	$0
Tax rate		× 40%		× 40%		× 40%
Deferred tax asset	↑ Originating Difference	$12	↑ Reversing Differences	$ 6	↑	$0

A liability is recognized for financial reporting purposes when the guaranteed product is sold:

2009 Warr. exp 30
Liability 30

and reduced when the expense is paid:

2010 Liability 15
Cash 15

2011 Liability 15
Cash 15

From a tax perspective, there is no liability.

The preceding was an illustration of an estimated expense that is reported on the income statement when incurred but deducted on tax returns in later years when actually paid. A second type of temporary difference that gives rise to a deferred tax asset is a *revenue* that is taxed when collected but recognized on income statements in later years when actually earned. Illustration 16–4 on the next page demonstrates this second type.

A deferred tax asset is recognized when an existing temporary difference will produce future deductible amounts.

Notice that this temporary difference produces future *deductible* amounts. In 2009, taxable income is $20 million *more* than pretax accounting income because it includes the unearned subscriptions revenue not yet reported on the income statement. However, in 2010 and 2011 taxable income is *less* than accounting income because the subscription revenue is earned and reported on the income statements but not on the tax returns of those two years.

In effect, tax laws require the company to prepay the income tax on this revenue, which is a sacrifice now but will benefit the company later when it avoids paying the taxes when the revenue is earned. In the meantime, the company has an asset representing this future income tax benefit.

ILLUSTRATION 16–4
Revenue Reported on the Tax Return *before* the Income Statement

In 2009, taxable income is more than accounting income because subscription revenue is not reported on the income statement until 2010–2011.

Tomorrow Publications reported pretax accounting income in 2009, 2010, and 2011 of $80 million, $115 million, and $105 million, respectively. The 2009 income statement does *not* include $20 million of magazine subscriptions received that year for one- and two-year subscriptions. The subscription revenue is reported for tax purposes in 2009. The revenue will be earned in 2010 ($15 million) and 2011 ($5 million). The income tax rate is 40% each year.

($ in millions)	Temporary Difference			
	Originates	Reverses		
	2009	2010	2011	Total
Pretax accounting income	$ 80	$115	$105	$300
Subscription revenue on the income statement		(15)	(5)	(20)
Subscription revenue on the tax return	20	0	0	20
Taxable income (tax return)	$100	$100	$100	$300

At the end of 2009, the amounts needed to record income tax for 2009 would be determined as shown in Illustration 16–4A.

ILLUSTRATION 16–4A
Determining and Recording Income Taxes—2009

($ in millions)

	2009	Future Deductible Amounts 2010	2011	Future Deductible Amounts (total)
Pretax accounting income	$ 80			
Temporary difference:				
Subscription revenue	20	$(15)	$(5)	$(20)
Taxable income	$100			
Enacted tax rate	40%			40%
Tax payable currently	$ 40			
Deferred tax asset				$ (8)

$20 million is taxable now, but not yet in the income statement.

Deferred Tax Asset

Ending balance	$ 8
Less: Beginning balance	0
Change in balance	$ 8

Deferred tax asset

beg. bal. 0	
change 8	
end. bal. 8	

Journal Entry at the End of 2009

Income tax expense (to balance)	32	
Deferred tax asset (determined above)	8	
Income tax payable (determined above)		40

At the end of 2009 and 2010, the company reports a deferred tax asset for future tax benefits.

Income taxes payable in 2010 and 2011 are less than otherwise payable because of the taxes prepaid in 2009.

Deferred Tax Asset

			($ in millions)
2009 ($20 × 40%)	8		
		6	2010 ($15 × 40%)
		2	2011 ($ 5 × 40%)
Balance after 3 years	0		

Again, we could also determine the deferred tax asset as the future tax benefit from the reversal of a temporary difference between the financial statement carrying amount of the subscription liability and its tax basis.[8]

($ in millions)	December 31					
	2009		2010		2011	
Liability—subscriptions:						
Accounting basis	$20	$20	$(15)	$ 5	$(5)	$ 0
Tax basis	(0)	(0)	(0)	(0)	(0)	(0)
Temporary difference	$20	$20	$(15)	$ 5	$(5)	$ 0
Tax rate	↑	× 40%	↑	× 40%	↑	× 40%
Deferred tax asset		$ 8		$ 2		$ 0
	Originating Difference		Reversing Differences			

A liability is recognized for financial reporting purposes when the cash is received:

2009 Cash	**20**	
Liability		**20**

and reduced when the revenue is earned:

2010 Liability	**15**	
Revenue		**15**
2011 Liability	**5**	
Revenue		**5**

From a tax perspective, there is no liability.

Valuation Allowance

● LO3

Deferred tax assets are recognized for all deductible temporary differences.[9] However, a deferred tax asset is then reduced by a valuation allowance if it is "more likely than not" that some portion or all of the deferred tax asset will not be realized.[10] Remember, a future deductible amount reduces taxable income and saves taxes only if there is taxable income to be reduced when the future deduction is available. So, a valuation allowance is needed if taxable income is anticipated to be insufficient to realize the tax benefit.

For example, let's say that in the previous illustration management determines that it's more likely than not that $3 million of the deferred tax asset will not ultimately be realized. The deferred tax asset would be reduced by the creation of a valuation allowance as follows:

A valuation allowance is needed if it is more likely than not that some portion or all of a deferred tax asset will not be realized.

	($ in millions)	
Income tax expense	3	
Valuation allowance—deferred tax asset		3

The effect is to increase the income tax expense as a result of reduced expectations of future tax savings. In the 2009 balance sheet, the deferred tax asset would be reported at its estimated net realizable value:

Deferred tax asset	$8
Less: Valuation allowance—deferred tax asset	(3)
	$5

A deferred tax asset is reported at its estimated net realizable value.

ADDITIONAL CONSIDERATION

The decision as to whether a valuation allowance is needed should be based on the weight of all available evidence. The real question is whether or not there will be sufficient taxable income in future years for the anticipated tax benefit to be realized. The benefit of future deductible amounts can be realized only if future income is at least equal to the deferred deductions. After all, a deduction reduces taxes only if it reduces taxable income.

[8]It is less intuitive to view an unearned revenue (Illustration 16–4) as producing future deductible amounts when the unearned revenue liability is settled than it is to view the future deductibility of an estimated expense (Illustration 16–3) as a future deductible amount. Nevertheless, the recognition of deferred tax assets for the future tax benefits of unearned revenue liability temporary differences is consistent with the asset/liability approach of *SFAS 109* because these unearned revenue liabilities are reported as if they represent future refundable amounts and therefore future deductible amounts. This point is argued persuasively by Hugo Nurnberg, "Deferred Tax Assets under FASB *Statement No. 96*," *Accounting Horizons,* December 1989.

[9]Unless the deductibility itself is uncertain. In that case, whether we recognize a deferred tax asset (and if so, its amount) is determined in accordance with *FIN 48* discussed later in the chapter.

[10]"More likely than not" means a likelihood of more than 50%, "Accounting for Income Taxes," *Statement of Financial Accounting Standards No. 109* (Norwalk, Conn.: FASB, 1992), par. 17.

All evidence—both positive and negative—should be considered. For instance, operating losses in recent years or anticipated circumstances that would adversely affect future operations would constitute negative evidence. On the other hand, a strong history of profitable operations or sizable, existing contracts would constitute positive evidence of sufficient taxable income to be able to realize the deferred tax asset.

Managerial actions that could be taken to reduce or eliminate a valuation allowance when deferred tax assets are not otherwise expected to be realized must be considered. These tax-planning strategies include any prudent and feasible actions management might take to realize a tax benefit while it is available.

This having been said, it should be clear that the decision as to whether or not a valuation allowance is used, as well as how large the allowance should be, rests squarely on managerial judgment. Because that decision directly impacts the amount of income tax expense and therefore reported income, it has obvious implications for earnings quality assessment from an analyst's perspective.

At the end of each reporting period, the valuation allowance is reevaluated. The appropriate balance is decided on and the balance is adjusted—up or down—to create that balance. For instance, let's say that at the end of the following year, 2010, available evidence indicates that $500,000 of the deferred tax asset at the end of 2010 will not be realized. We would adjust the valuation allowance to reflect the indicated amount:

	($ in millions)	
Valuation allowance—deferred tax asset ($3 million – 0.5 million)	2.5	
Income tax expense		2.5

The disclosure note shown in Graphic 16–2 accompanied the 2006 annual report of **Lucent Technologies** indicating that some of its deferred tax assets were not expected to be realized:

GRAPHIC 16–2
Valuation Allowance—Lucent Technologies

Real World Financials

Although profits were generated in recent periods and we are no longer in a cumulative loss position in the U.S., a substantial amount of the profits were generated from a pension credit that is not currently taxable. As a result, we concluded that there was not sufficient positive evidence to enable us to conclude that it was more likely than not that the net U.S. deferred tax assets would be realized. Therefore, we have maintained a valuation allowance on our net U.S. deferred tax assets as of September 30, 2006 and 2005.

INTERNATIONAL FINANCIAL REPORTING STANDARDS

Recognition of Deferred Tax Assets. Under *IAS 12*, "Income Taxes," deferred tax assets are recorded only if realization of the tax benefit is "probable." As we discussed earlier, we recognize all deferred tax assets under U.S. GAAP assets (unless the future deductible amounts are uncertain), but record a valuation allowance unless realization is "more likely than not."

● LO4

Nontemporary Differences

FINANCIAL Reporting Case

Q3, p. 821

So far, we've dealt with temporary differences between the reported amount of an asset or liability in the financial statements and its tax basis. You learned that temporary differences result in future taxable or deductible amounts when the related asset or liability is recovered or settled. However, some differences are caused by transactions and events that under existing tax law will never affect taxable income or taxes payable. Interest received from

INTERNATIONAL FINANCIAL REPORTING STANDARDS

Nontax Differences Affect Taxes. Despite the similar approaches for accounting for taxation under *IAS 12*, "Income Taxes," and *SFAS No.109*, "Accounting for Income Taxes," differences in reported amounts for deferred taxes are among the most frequent between IFRS and U.S. GAAP. Although differences in the specific IFRS and U.S. GAAP guidance in several areas account for many of the disparities, the principal reason is that a great many of the nontax differences between IFRS and U.S. GAAP affect net income and shareholders' equity and therefore have consequential effects on deferred taxes.

investments in bonds issued by state and municipal governments, for instance, is exempt from taxation. Interest revenue of this type is, of course, reported as revenue on the recipient's income statement but not on its tax return—not now, not later. Pretax accounting income exceeds taxable income. This situation will not reverse in a later year. Taxable income in a later year will not exceed pretax accounting income because the tax-free income will never be reported on the tax return.

These permanent differences are disregarded when determining the tax payable currently, the deferred tax effect, and therefore the income tax expense.[11] This is why we adjust accounting income in the illustrations that follow to eliminate any permanent differences from taxable income. Graphic 16–3 provides examples of differences with no deferred tax consequences.

Permanent differences are disregarded when determining both the tax payable currently and the deferred tax asset or liability.

GRAPHIC 16–3
Differences without Deferred Tax Consequences

- Interest received from investments in bonds issued by state and municipal governments (not taxable).
- Investment expenses incurred to obtain tax-exempt income (not tax deductible).
- Life insurance proceeds on the death of an insured executive (not taxable).
- Premiums paid for life insurance policies when the payer is the beneficiary (not tax deductible).
- Compensation expense pertaining to some employee stock option plans (not tax deductible).
- Expenses due to violations of the law (not tax deductible).
- Portion of dividends received from U.S. corporations that is not taxable due to the dividends received deduction.[12]
- Tax deduction for depletion of natural resources (percentage depletion) that permanently exceeds the income statement depletion expense (cost depletion).[13]
- Tax deduction for goodwill amortization over 15 years (goodwill is not amortized for financial reporting purposes).[14]

Provisions of the tax laws, in some instances, dictate that the amount of a revenue that is taxable or expense that is deductible permanently differs from the amount reported on the income statement.

To compare temporary and **nontemporary differences,** we can modify Illustration 16–1 to include nontaxable income in Kent Land Management's 2010 pretax accounting income. We do this in Illustration 16–5. Note that the existence of an amount that causes a permanent difference has no effect on income taxes payable, deferred taxes, or income tax expense.

To this point, we've seen that our objective in accounting for income taxes is to recognize the tax consequences of amounts that will become taxable or deductible in future years as a result of transactions or events that already have occurred. To achieve the objective, we

[11]The term permanent difference was used in *APB 11* to describe differences with no deferred tax consequences. Although the term itself is not used in more recent pronouncements (*SFAS 96* and *SFAS 109*), it still is useful to describe nontemporary differences.

[12]When a corporation owns shares of another U.S. corporation, a percentage of the dividends from those shares is exempt from taxation due to the dividends received deduction. The percentage is 70% if the investor owns less than 20% of the investee's shares, 80% for 20% to 80% ownership, and 100% for more than 80% ownership.

[13]The cost of natural resources is reported as depletion expense over their extraction period for financial reporting purposes; but tax rules prescribe sometimes different percentages of cost to be deducted for tax purposes. There usually is a difference between the cost depletion and percentage depletion that doesn't eventually reverse.

[14]Recall, though, that goodwill might become "impaired," at which time all or a portion of it will be subtracted from earnings. Because this amount would impact the income statement in a period different from the one in which it is deducted on the tax return, it would represent a temporary difference.

ILLUSTRATION 16–5
Temporary and Permanent Differences

Kent Land Management reported pretax accounting income in 2009 of $100 million except for additional income of $40 million from installment sales of property and $5 million interest from investments in municipal bonds in 2009. The installment sales income is reported for tax purposes in 2010 ($10 million) and 2011 ($30 million). The enacted tax rate is 40% each year.

($ in millions)	Current Year 2009	Future Taxable Amounts 2010	Future Taxable Amounts 2011	Future Taxable Amounts (total)
Pretax accounting income	$145			
Permanent difference:				
Municipal bond interest	(5)			
Temporary difference:				
Installment income	(40)	$10	$30	$40
Taxable income (tax return)	$100			
Enacted tax rate	40%			40%
Tax payable currently	$ 40			
Deferred tax liability				$16

Deferred Tax Liability

Ending balance	$16
Less: Beginning balance	0
Change in balance	$16

Journal Entry at the End of 2009

Income tax expense (to balance)	56	
Income tax payable (determined above)		40
Deferred tax liability (determined above)		16

Because interest on municipal bonds is tax exempt, it is reported only in the income statement. This difference between pretax accounting income and taxable income does not reverse later.

record a deferred tax liability or deferred tax asset for future taxable amounts or future deductible amounts that arise as a result of temporary differences. Permanent differences, on the other hand, do not create future taxable amounts and future deductible amounts and therefore have no tax consequences.

Permanent differences affect a company's effective tax rate.

You might notice here that because of the permanent difference, Kent's "effective" tax rate is less than its 40% statutory rate. The effective rate is the total tax to be paid (eventually), $56 million, divided by accounting income, $145 million, or 38.6%. Without the $5 million municipal bond interest, the effective rate would have been $56 million divided by $140 million, or 40%. Nontaxable revenues and gains, as we have for Kent, cause the effective rate to be *lower* than the statutory rate; whereas, nondeductible expenses and losses would cause the effective rate to be *higher* than the statutory rate. Companies report a comparison of their effective and statutory tax rates in disclosure notes, as in Graphic 16–4's example from **FedEx**'s 2007 financial statements.

GRAPHIC 16–4
Effective Tax Rate—FedEx Corporation.

Real World Financials

Note 11: Income Taxes (in part)

A reconciliation of the statutory federal income tax rate to FedEx's effective income tax rate for the years ended May 31 was as follows:

	2007	2006	2005
Statutory U.S. income tax rate	35.0%	35.0%	35.0%
Increase resulting from:			
State income taxes, net of federal benefit	2.0	2.1	1.7
Other, net	0.3	0.6	0.7
Effective tax rate	37.3%	37.7%	37.4%

CONCEPT REVIEW EXERCISE

TEMPORARY AND PERMANENT DIFFERENCES

Mid-South Cellular Systems began operations in 2009. That year the company reported pre-tax accounting income of $70 million, which included the following amounts:

1. Compensation expense of $3 million related to employee stock option plans granted to organizers was reported on the 2009 income statement. This expense is not deductible for tax purposes.
2. An asset with a four-year useful life was acquired last year. It is depreciated by the straight-line method on the income statement. MACRS is used on the tax return, causing deductions for depreciation to be more than straight-line depreciation the first two years but less than straight-line depreciation the next two years ($ in millions):

	Depreciation		
	Income Statement	**Tax Return**	**Difference**
2009	$150	$198	$ (48)
2010	150	264	(114)
2011	150	90	60
2012	150	48	102
	$600	$600	$ 0

The enacted tax rate is 40%.

Required:
Prepare the journal entry to record Mid-South Cellular's income taxes for 2009.

SOLUTION

($ in millions)	Current Year 2009	Future Taxable Amounts 2010	2011	2012	Future Taxable Amounts (total)
Pretax accounting income	$70				
Permanent difference:					
Compensation expense	3				
Temporary difference:					
Depreciation	(48)	$(114)	$60	$102	$ 48
Taxable income (tax return)	$25				
Enacted tax rate	40%				40%
Tax payable currently	$10				
Deferred tax liability					$19.2

Because the compensation expense is not tax deductible, taxable income does not include that $3 million deduction and is higher by that amount than accounting income.

Deferred Tax Liability

Ending balance	$19.2
Less: Beginning balance	0.0
Change in balance	$19.2

Journal Entry at the End of 2009

Income tax expense (to balance)	29.2	
Income tax payable (determined above)		10.0
Deferred tax liability (determined above)		19.2

Income tax expense is composed of: (1) the tax payable now and (2) the tax deferred until later.

PART B

OTHER TAX ACCOUNTING ISSUES

Tax Rate Considerations

● LO5

To measure the deferred tax liability or asset, we multiply the temporary difference by the currently *enacted* tax rate that will be effective in the year(s) the temporary difference reverses.[15] We do not base calculations on *anticipated* legislation that would alter the

[15]The current U.S. corporate tax rate is 34%, or 35% for corporations with taxable income over $75,000. Most states tax corporate income at rates less than 10%. We use 40% in most of our illustrations to simplify calculations.

INTERNATIONAL FINANCIAL REPORTING STANDARDS

Tax Rate for Measuring Deferred Tax Assets and Liabilities. Deferred taxes are based on currently enacted tax rates under U.S. GAAP. Under IFRS, deferred taxes are based on "substantially enacted" rates, meaning whatever rate is "virtually certain" to apply.

company's tax rate. A conceptual case can be made that expected rate changes should be anticipated when measuring the deferred tax liability or asset. However, this is one of many examples of the frequent trade-off between relevance and reliability. In this case, the FASB chose to favor reliability by waiting until an anticipated change actually is enacted into law before recognizing its tax consequences.

When Enacted Tax Rates Differ

A deferred tax liability (or asset) is based on enacted tax rates and laws.

Existing tax laws may call for enacted tax rates to be different in two or more future years in which a temporary difference is expected to reverse. When a phased-in change in rates is scheduled to occur, the specific tax rates of each future year are multiplied by the amounts reversing in each of those years. The total is the deferred tax liability or asset.

To illustrate, let's again modify our Kent Land Management illustration, this time to assume a scheduled change in tax rates. See Illustration 16–6.

ILLUSTRATION 16–6
Scheduled Change in Tax Rates

Kent Land Management reported pretax accounting income in 2009 of $100 million except for additional income of $40 million from installment sales of property and $5 million interest from investments in municipal bonds in 2009. The installment sales income is reported for tax purposes in 2010 ($10 million) and 2011 ($30 million). The enacted tax rates are 40% for 2009 and 2010, and 35% for 2011.

The tax effects of the future taxable amounts depend on the tax rates at which those amounts will be taxed.

($ in millions)	Current Year 2009	Future Taxable Amounts 2010	2011	(total)
Pretax accounting income	$145			
Permanent difference:				
Municipal bond interest	(5)			
Temporary difference:				
Installment income	(40)	$10	$ 30	
Taxable income (tax return)	$100			
Enacted tax rate	40%	40%	35%	
Tax payable currently	$ 40			
Deferred tax liability		$ 4	$10.5	$14.5

Deferred Tax Liability

Ending balance	$14.5
Less: Beginning balance	0.0
Change in balance	$14.5

Journal Entry at the End of 2009

Income tax expense (to balance)	54.5	
Income tax payable (determined above)		40.0
Deferred tax liability (determined above)		14.5

Be sure to note that the 2010 rate (40%) as well as the 2011 rate (35%) already is enacted into law as of 2009 when the deferred tax liability is established. In the next section we discuss how to handle a change resulting from new legislation.

Changes in Tax Laws or Rates

Tax laws sometimes change. If a change in a tax law or rate occurs, the deferred tax liability or asset must be adjusted. Remember, the deferred tax liability or asset is meant to reflect the amount to be paid or recovered in the future. When legislation changes that amount, the deferred tax liability or asset also should change. The effect is reflected in operating income in the year of the enactment of the change in the tax law or rate.

As a result of a change [in tax law or rate] deferred tax consequences become larger or smaller.[16]

For clarification, reconsider the previous illustration. Without a change in tax rates and assuming that pretax accounting income reported in the income statement in 2010 is $100 million (with no additional temporary or permanent differences), the 2010 income tax amounts would be determined as shown in Illustration 16–6A.

($ in millions)

	2009	Current Year 2010	Future Taxable Amount 2011	
Pretax accounting income		$100		
Temporary difference:				
Installment income	(40)	10	$ 30	
Taxable income (tax return)		$110		
Enacted tax rate		40%	35%	
Tax payable currently		$ 44		
Deferred tax liability			$10.5	$10.5

Deferred Tax Liability

Ending balance	$10.5
Less: Beginning balance	(14.5)
Change in balance	$ (4.0)

Journal Entry at the End of 2010

Income tax expense (to balance)	40	
Deferred tax liability (determined above)	4	
Income tax payable (determined above)		44

ILLUSTRATION 16–6A
Reversal of Temporary Difference *without* a Tax Rate Change

The 40% 2010 rate and the 35% 2011 rate are established by previously enacted legislation.

Now assume Congress passed a new tax law in 2010 that will cause the 2011 tax rate to be 30% instead of the previously scheduled 35% rate. Because a deferred tax liability was established in 2009 with the expectation that the 2011 taxable amount would be taxed at 35%, it would now be adjusted to reflect taxation at 30%, instead. This is demonstrated in Illustration 16–6B on the next page.

Notice that the methods used to determine the deferred tax liability and the change in that balance are the same as without the rate change—the calculation merely uses the new rate (30%) rather than the old rate (35%). So recalculating the desired balance in the deferred tax liability each period and comparing that amount with any previously existing balance automatically takes into account tax rate changes.

When a tax rate changes, the deferred tax liability or asset should be adjusted with the effect reflected in operating income in the year of the change.

Also notice that the income tax expense ($38.5 million) is $1.5 million less than it would have been without the tax rate change ($40 million). The effect of the change is included in income tax expense. In fact, this is highlighted if we separate the previous entry into

[16]"Accounting for Income Taxes," *Statement of Financial Accounting Standards No. 109* (Norwalk, Conn.: FASB, 1992), par. 112.

ILLUSTRATION 16–6B
Reversal of Temporary Difference with a Tax Rate Change

The deferred tax liability would have been $10.5 million (30 million × 35%) if the tax rate had not changed.

($ in millions)

	2009	Current Year 2010	Future Taxable Amount 2011	
Pretax accounting income		$100		
Temporary difference:				
Installment income	(40)	10	$ 30	
Taxable income (tax return)		$110		
Enacted tax rate		40%	30%*	
Tax payable currently		$ 44		
Deferred tax liability			$ 9	$ 9.0

*2011 rate enacted into law in 2010.

Deferred Tax Liability

Ending balance	$ 9.0
Less: Beginning balance	(14.5)
Change in balance	$ (5.5)

Journal Entry at the End of 2010

Income tax expense (to balance)	38.5	
Deferred tax liability (determined above)	5.5	
Income tax payable (determined above)		44.0

its component parts: (1) record the income tax expense without the tax rate change and (2) separately record the adjustment of the deferred tax liability for the change:

Journal Entries at the End of 2010	($ in millions)	
Income tax expense	40	
Deferred tax liability	4	
Income tax payable		44
Deferred tax liability [$30 million × (35% – 30%)]	1.5	
Income tax expense		1.5

The tax consequence of a change in a tax law or rate is recognized in the period the change is enacted. In this case, the consequence of a lower tax rate is a reduced deferred tax liability, recognized as a reduction in income tax expense in 2010 when the change occurs.

Multiple Temporary Differences

● LO6

It would be unusual for any but a very small company to have only a single temporary difference in any given year. Having multiple temporary differences, though, doesn't change any of the principles you've learned so far in connection with single differences. All that's necessary is to categorize all temporary differences according to whether they create (a) future taxable amounts or (b) future deductible amounts. The total of the future taxable amounts is multiplied by the future tax rate to determine the appropriate balance for the deferred tax liability, and the total of the future deductible amounts is multiplied by the future tax rate to determine the appropriate balance for the deferred tax asset. This is demonstrated in Illustration 16–7 on the next page.

ILLUSTRATION 16–7
Multiple Temporary Differences

2009

During 2009, its first year of operations, Eli-Wallace Distributors reported pretax accounting income of $200 million which included the following amounts:

1. Income from installment sales of warehouses in 2009 of $9 million to be reported for tax purposes in 2010 ($5 million) and 2011 ($4 million).
2. Depreciation is reported by the straight-line method on an asset with a four-year useful life. On the tax return, deductions for depreciation will be more than straight-line depreciation the first two years but less than straight-line depreciation the next two years ($ in millions):

	Income Statement	Tax Return	Difference
2009	$ 50	$ 66	$(16)
2010	50	88	(38)
2011	50	30	20
2012	50	16	34
	$200	$200	$ 0

3. Estimated warranty expense that will be deductible on the tax return when actually paid during the next two years. Estimated deductions are as follows ($ in millions):

	Income Statement	Tax Return	Difference
2009	$7		$7
2010		$4	(4)
2011		3	(3)
	$7	$7	$0

2010

During 2010, pretax accounting income of $200 million included an estimated loss of $1 million from having accrued a loss contingency. The loss is expected to be paid in 2012 at which time it will be tax deductible.

The enacted tax rate is 40% each year.

Look at Illustration 16–7A on page 842 to see how Eli-Wallace determines the income tax amounts for 2009. Then turn to Illustration 16–7B on page 843 to see how those amounts are determined for 2010.

After the journal entry at the end of 2010, the balances of both the deferred tax asset and the deferred tax liability reflect the desired amounts as follows ($ in millions):

Deferred Tax Asset			Deferred Tax Liability	
2.8		2009 balance		10.0
	1.2	Adjustment		13.2
1.6		2010 balance		23.2

The deferred tax asset declines and the deferred tax liability increases during 2010.

Of course, if a phased-in change in rates is scheduled to occur, it would be necessary to determine the total of the future taxable amounts and the total of the future deductible amounts for each future year as outlined previously. Then the specific tax rates of each future year would be multiplied by the two totals in each of those years. Those annual tax effects would then be summed to get the deferred tax liability and the deferred tax asset.

Net Operating Losses

● LO7

A **net operating loss** is negative taxable income: tax-deductible expenses exceed taxable revenues. Of course, there is no tax payable for the year an operating loss occurs because there's no taxable income. In addition, tax laws permit the operating loss to be used to reduce taxable income in other, profitable years. Offsetting operating profits with operating losses is achieved by either a carryback of the loss to prior years or a carryforward of the

ILLUSTRATION 16–7A

Multiple Temporary Differences—2009

Temporary differences are grouped according to whether they create future taxable amounts or future *deductible* amounts.

The desired balances in the deferred tax liability and the deferred tax asset are separately determined.

Income tax expense is composed of three components: (1) the tax payable now plus (2) the tax deferred until later, reduced by (3) the deferred tax benefit.

($ in millions)

	Current Year 2009	Future Taxable (Deductible) Amounts 2010	2011	2012	Future Taxable Amounts (total)	Future Deductible Amounts (total)
Pretax accounting income	$ 200					
Temporary differences:						
Installment sales	(9)	$ 5	$ 4		$ 9	
Depreciation	(16)	(38)	20	$34	16	
Warranty expense	7	(4)	(3)			$ (7)
Taxable income (tax return)	$ 182				$25	(7)
Enacted tax rate	40%				40%	40%
Tax payable currently	$72.8					
Deferred tax liability					$10	
Deferred tax asset						$(2.8)
					↓ Deferred Tax Liability	↓ Deferred Tax Asset
Ending balances:					$10	$ 2.8
Less: Beginning balances:					0	(0.0)
Change in balances					$10	$ 2.8

Journal Entry at the End of 2009

Income tax expense (to balance)	80.0	
Deferred tax asset (determined above)	2.8	
Deferred tax liability (determined above)		10.0
Income tax payable (determined above)		72.8

Can elect to carry back or forward. Make before due date

loss to later years, or both. In essence, the tax deductible expenses that can't be deducted this year because they exceed taxable revenues can be deducted in other years. Specifically, the operating loss can be carried back 2 years and forward for up to 20 years:

Carryforward ⟶ Up to 20 Years

2007	2008	LOSS	2010	2011	2012	⟶	2028	2029

2 years ⟵ Carryback

Tax laws permit a choice. A company can elect an **operating loss carryback** if taxable income was reported in either of the two previous years. By reducing taxable income of a previous year, the company can receive an immediate refund of taxes paid that year.

If taxable income was not reported in either of the two previous years or higher tax rates are anticipated in the future, a company might elect to forgo the operating loss carryback and carry the loss forward for up to 20 years to offset taxable income of those years. Even if a loss carryback is elected, any loss that remains after the two-year carryback can be carried forward. The carryback election is a choice that must be made in the year of the operating loss and the choice is irrevocable. It usually is advantageous to carry back losses because by filing an amended tax return to get a refund, a company can realize the benefit much sooner than if the loss is carried forward.

The accounting question is: *When* should the tax benefit created by an operating loss be recognized on the income statement? The answer is: In the year the loss occurs.

Operating Loss Carryforward

First consider a loss carryforward. You have learned in this chapter that a deferred tax asset is recognized for the future tax benefit of temporary differences that create future deductible amounts. An operating loss carryforward also creates future deductible amounts. Logically,

($ millions)	2009	Current Year 2010	Future Taxable (Deductible) Amounts 2011	2012	Future Taxable Amounts (total)*	Future Deductible Amounts (total)*
Pretax accounting income		$200				
Temporary differences:						
Installment sales	$ (9)	$ 5	$ 4		$ 4	
Depreciation	(16)	(38)	20	$34	54	
Warranty expense	7	(4)	(3)			$ (3)
Estimated loss		1		(1)		(1)
Taxable income (tax return)		$164			$58	$ (4)
Enacted tax rate		40%			40%	40%
Tax payable currently		$ 65.6				
Deferred tax liability					$23.2	
Deferred tax asset						$(1.6)
					Deferred Tax Liability	**Deferred Tax Asset**
Ending balances:					$23.2	$ 1.6
Less: Beginning balances:					(10.0)	(2.8)
Change in balances					$13.2	$ (1.2)

Journal Entry at the End of 2010

Income tax expense (to balance)	80.0	
Deferred tax asset (determined above)		1.2
Deferred tax liability (determined above)		13.2
Deferred tax payable (determined above)		65.6

ILLUSTRATION 16–7B
Multiple Temporary Differences—2010

The future taxable amount of installment sales ($4 million) is equal to the cumulative temporary difference ($9 million − 5 million).

Similarly, the total of other future taxable and deductible amounts are equal to the cumulative temporary differences in the related assets and liabilities.

Analysis indicates that the deferred tax liability should be increased further and the deferred tax asset should be reduced.

*Total future taxable and deductible amounts also are equal to the cumulative temporary differences in the related assets and liabilities.

then, a deferred tax asset is recognized for an operating loss carryforward also. This is demonstrated on the next page in Illustration 16–8.

The income tax benefit of an operating loss carryforward is recognized for accounting purposes in the year the operating loss occurs. The net after-tax operating loss reflects the future tax savings that the operating loss is expected to create:

Income Statement (partial)

	($ in millions)
Operating loss before income taxes	$125
Less: Income tax benefit—operating loss	(50)
Net operating loss	$ 75

The income tax benefit of an operating loss carryforward is recognized in the year the operating loss occurs.

VALUATION ALLOWANCE. Just as for all deductible temporary differences, deferred tax assets are recognized for any operating loss without regard to the likelihood of having taxable income in future years sufficient to absorb future deductible amounts. However, the deferred tax asset is then reduced by a valuation allowance if it is more likely than not that some portion or all of the deferred tax asset will not be realized. Remember, a valuation allowance both reduces the net deferred tax asset and increases the income tax expense just as if that portion of the deferred tax asset had not been recognized.

Operating Loss Carryback

To compare the treatment of an operating loss carryback, let's modify the illustration to assume that there was taxable income in the two years prior to the operating loss and that

ILLUSTRATION 16–8
Operating Loss Carryforward

An operating loss carryforward can be deducted from taxable income in future years.

The tax benefit of being able to deduct amounts in the future represents a deferred tax asset.

During 2009, its first year of operations, American Laminating Corporation reported an operating loss of $125 million for financial reporting and tax purposes. The enacted tax rate is 40%.

($ in millions)

	Current Year 2009	Future Deductible Amounts (total)
Operating loss	$(125)	
Loss carryforward	125	$(125)
	$ 0	
Enacted tax rate	40%	40%
Tax payable	$ 0	
Deferred tax asset		$ (50)

Deferred Tax Asset

Ending balance	$50
Less: Beginning balance	0
Change in balance	$50

Journal Entry at the End of 2009

Deferred tax asset (determined above)	50	
Income tax benefit—operating loss (to balance)		50

An operating loss must be applied to the earlier year first and then brought forward to the next year.

American Laminating elected a loss carryback (see Illustration 16–9 on the next page). Note that the operating loss must be applied to the earlier year first and then brought forward to the next year. If any of the loss remains after reducing taxable income to zero in the two previous years, the remainder is carried forward to future years as an operating loss carryforward.

The income tax benefit of both an operating loss carryback and an operating loss carry forward is recognized for accounting purposes in the year the operating loss occurs. The net after-tax operating loss reflects the reduction of past taxes from the loss carryback and future tax savings that the loss carryforward is expected to create:

		($ in millions)
Operating loss before income taxes		$125
Less: Income tax benefit:		
Tax refund from loss carryback	$29	
Future tax savings from loss carryforward	20	49
Net operating loss		$ 76

Notice that the income tax benefit ($49 million) is less than it was when we assumed a carryforward only ($50 million). This is because the tax rate in one of the carryback years (2007) was lower than the carryforward rate (40%).

Financial Statement Presentation

Balance Sheet Classification

● LO8

In a classified balance sheet, deferred tax assets and deferred tax liabilities are classified as either current or noncurrent according to how the related assets or liabilities are classified for financial reporting. For instance, a deferred tax liability arising from different depreciation methods being used for tax and book purposes would be classified as noncurrent because depreciable assets are reported as noncurrent. A deferred tax asset or deferred tax liability is considered to be related to an asset or liability if reduction (including amortization) of that asset or liability will cause the temporary difference to reverse.

ILLUSTRATION 16–9

Operating Loss Carryback and Carryforward

During 2009, American Laminating Corporation reported an operating loss of $125 million for financial reporting and tax purposes. The enacted tax rate is 40% for 2009. Taxable income, tax rates, and income taxes paid in the two previous years were as follows:

	Taxable Income	Taxable Rates	Income Taxes Paid
2007	$20 million	35%	$ 7 million
2008	55 million	40%	22 million

Here's how the income tax benefit of the operating loss carryback and the operating loss carryforward is determined:

($ in millions)

	Prior Years		Current Year	Future Deductible Amounts
	2007	2008	2009	(total)
Operating loss			$(125)	
Loss carryback	$(20)	$(55)	75	
Loss carryforward			50	$(50)
			$ 0	
Enacted tax rate	35%	40%	40%	40%
Tax payable (refundable)	$ (7)	$(22)	$ 0	
Deferred tax asset				$(20)
Deferred Tax Asset				↓
Ending balance				$ 20
Less: Beginning balance				0
Change in balance				$ 20

Journal Entry at the End of 2009

Receivable—income tax refund ($7 + 22)	29	
Deferred tax asset (determined above)	20	
Income tax benefit—operating loss (to balance)		49

An *operating loss carryback* can be deducted from taxable income in the two prior years, creating a refund of taxes paid those years.

The portion of an operating loss that remains after a carryback is carried forward.

The income tax benefit of an operating loss carryback, like a carryforward, is recognized in the year the operating loss occurs.

Let's carry the illustration forward one year (see Illustration 16–9A) and assume a performance turnaround in 2010 resulted in pretax accounting income of $15 million.

ILLUSTRATION 16–9A

Determining and Recording Income Taxes—2010

($ in millions)

	2009	Current Year 2010	Future Deductible Amounts (total)
Pretax accounting income		$15	
Temporary difference:			
Loss carryforward	$50	(15)	$(35)
Taxable income (tax return)		$ 0	
Enacted tax rate		40%	40%
Tax payable currently		$ 0	
Deferred tax asset			$(14)
Deferred Tax Asset			↓
Ending balance			$ 14.0
Less: Beginning balance			(20.0)
Change in balance			$ (6.0)

Journal Entry at the End of 2010

Income tax expense (to balance)	6	
Deferred tax asset (determined above)		6

$15 million of the carryforward can be used to offset 2010 income. The remaining $35 million is carried forward up to 19 more years.

The $20 million deferred tax asset is reduced to $14 million.

A net current amount and a net noncurrent amount are reported as either an asset or a liability.

Most companies will have several different types of temporary differences that give rise to deferred tax amounts. The several deferred tax assets and liabilities should not be reported individually but combined instead into two summary amounts. Current deferred tax assets and liabilities should be offset (netted together). The resulting *net current* amount is then reported as either a current asset (if deferred tax assets exceed deferred tax liabilities) or current liability (if deferred tax liabilities exceed deferred tax assets). Similarly, a single *net noncurrent* amount should be reported as a net noncurrent asset or a net noncurrent liability. This is demonstrated in Illustration 16–10.

ILLUSTRATION 16–10
Balance Sheet Classification and Presentation

The current or noncurrent classification of deferred tax assets and deferred tax liabilities is the same as that of the related assets or liabilities.

Warren Properties, Inc. had future taxable amounts and future deductible amounts relating to temporary differences between the tax bases of the assets and liabilities indicated below and their financial reporting amounts:

($ in millions)

Related Balance Sheet Account	Classification Current—C Noncurrent—N	Future Taxable (Deductible) Amounts	Tax Rate	Deferred Tax (Asset) Liability C	N
Receivable—installment sales of land	C	$ 10	× 40%	$ 4	
Receivable—installment sales of land	N	5	× 40%		$ 2
Depreciable assets	N	105	× 40%		42
Allowance—uncollectible accounts	C	(15)	× 40%	(6)	
Liability—subscriptions received	C	(20)	× 40%	(8)	
Estimated warranty liability	C	(30)	× 40%	(12)	
Net current liability (asset)				$(22)	
Net noncurrent liability (asset)					$ 44
Balance Sheet Presentation					
Current Assets:					
Deferred tax asset	$22				
Long-Term Liabilities:					
Deferred tax liability	$44				

Note: Before offsetting assets and liabilities within the current and noncurrent categories, the **total** of deferred tax assets is $26 ($6 + 8 + 12) and the **total** of deferred tax liabilities is $48 ($4 + 2 + 42).

DEFERRED TAX AMOUNT NOT RELATED TO A SPECIFIC ASSET OR LIABILITY. Sometimes, a deferred tax asset or a deferred tax liability cannot be identified with a specific asset or liability. When that's the case, it should be classified according to when the underlying temporary difference is expected to reverse. For instance, some organization costs are recognized as expenses for financial reporting purposes when incurred, but are deducted for tax purposes in later years. When such expenditures are made, an expense is recorded, but no asset or liability is recognized on the balance sheet. The deferred tax asset recognized for the future deductible amounts is classified as a current asset for the tax effect of the deduction expected next year, and as a noncurrent asset for the tax effect of the deductions expected in later years.

A deferred tax asset or liability that is not related to a specific asset or liability should be classified according to when the underlying temporary difference is expected to reverse.

Operating loss carryforwards also are unrelated to a specific asset or liability and so are classified as current or noncurrent according to when future income is expected to be sufficient to realize the benefit of the carryforward.

A valuation allowance is allocated between current and noncurrent on a pro rata basis.

VALUATION ALLOWANCE. Any valuation allowance for deferred tax assets should be allocated between the current and noncurrent amount in proportion to the amounts of deferred tax assets that are classified as current and noncurrent. In our illustration, all three

INTERNATIONAL FINANCIAL REPORTING STANDARDS

Classification of Deferred Taxes. Under U.S. GAAP, deferred tax liabilities and deferred tax assets are classified in the balance sheet as current and noncurrent based on the classification of the underlying asset or liability. Under IFRS, though, they always are classified as noncurrent.

deferred tax assets were classified as current, so any valuation allowance would be reported with the net current deferred tax asset.

Disclosure Notes

DEFERRED TAX ASSETS AND DEFERRED TAX LIABILITIES. Additional disclosures are required pertaining to amounts reported on the balance sheet. Disclosure notes should reveal the:

- Total of all deferred tax liabilities ($48 million in our Illustration 16–10 Note).
- Total of all deferred tax assets ($26 million in our Illustration 16–10 Note).
- Total valuation allowance recognized for deferred tax assets.
- Net change in the valuation allowance.
- Approximate tax effect of each type of temporary difference (and carryforward).

In its 2007 balance sheet, the Harris Corporation, manufacturer of wireless communications products, reported net current deferred tax assets of $94.3 million and net noncurrent deferred tax liabilities of $61.8 million. The composition of this amount was provided in the disclosure note shown in Graphic 16–5.

GRAPHIC 16–5
Disclosure of Deferred Taxes—Harris Corporation

Real World Financials

Note 22: Income Taxes (in part)
The components of deferred tax assets (liabilities) are as follows:

	2007		2006	
	Current	**Noncurrent**	**Current**	**Noncurrent**
	(In millions)			
Inventory valuations	$ 35.7	$ —	$ 30.3	$ —
Accruals	96.8	4.4	74.6	1.6
Depreciation	—	(28.7)	—	(18.4)
Domestic tax loss and credit carryforwards	—	93.4	—	34.6
International tax loss and credit carryforwards	—	68.3	—	69.9
International research and development expense deferrals	—	27.9	—	22.6
Acquired intangibles	—	(108.9)	—	(62.1)
FAS 158 unfunded pension liability	—	10.8	—	—
All other—net	(5.1)	5.8	1.7	(8.0)
	127.4	73.0	106.6	40.2
Valuation allowance	(33.1)	(134.8)	(1.6)	(68.8)
	$ 94.3	$ (61.8)	$105.0	$ (28.6)

OPERATING LOSS CARRYFORWARDS. In addition, the amounts and expiration dates should be revealed for any operating loss carryforwards. Remember, operating losses can be carried forward for reduction of future taxable income for 20 years. This potential tax benefit can foreshadow desirable cash savings for the company if earnings sufficient to absorb the loss carryforwards are anticipated before their expiration date. The presence of large operating loss carryforwards also can make an unprofitable company an attractive target for acquisition by a company that could use those loss carryforwards to shelter its own earnings from taxes with that loss deduction. If the IRS determines that an acquisition is made solely to obtain the tax benefits of operating loss carryforwards, the deductions will not be allowed. However, motivation is difficult to determine, so it is not uncommon for companies to purchase operating loss carryforwards.

INCOME TAX EXPENSE. Disclosures also are required pertaining to the income tax expense reported on the income statement. Disclosure notes should reveal the:

- Current portion of the tax expense (or tax benefit).
- Deferred portion of the tax expense (or tax benefit), with separate disclosure of amounts attributable to:
  - Portion that does not include the effect of the following separately disclosed amounts.
  - Operating loss carryforwards.
  - Adjustments due to changes in tax laws or rates.
  - Adjustments to the beginning-of-the-year valuation allowance due to revised estimates.
  - Tax credits.

Coping with Uncertainty in Income Taxes

● LO9

Few expense items in the income statement rival the size of the income tax expense line, and few are subject to the complexities of implementation and interpretation inherent in reporting income tax expense. As you might imagine, most companies strive to legitimately reduce their overall tax burden and reduce or delay cash outflows for taxes.

The IRS frequently disagrees with the stance a company takes on its tax return.

Toward that end, they might enter into tax-advantaged transactions or structure tax-optimized methods of transacting with affiliates and others. Even without additional tax-motivated activities, most companies' tax returns will include many tax positions inherent to normal business activities that are subject to multiple interpretations. Despite good faith positions taken in preparing tax returns, those judgments may not ultimately prevail if challenged by the IRS. Judgments frequently are subjected to legal scrutiny before the uncertainty ultimately is resolved.

Consider the decision by Derrick Company to claim a deduction on its tax return that will save the company $8 million in 2009 income taxes. Derrick knows that, historically, the IRS has challenged many deductions of this type. Since tax returns usually aren't examined for one, two, or more years, uncertainty exists.

TWO-STEP DECISION PROCESS. *FASB Interpretation No. 48 (FIN 48)* indicates how companies should deal with that uncertainty.[17] This guidance allows companies to recognize in the financial statements the tax benefit of a position it takes, such as Derrick's decision to take the 2009 deduction, only if it is "more likely than not" (greater than 50% chance) to be sustained if challenged. Guidance also prescribes how to *measure* the amount to be recognized. The decision, then, is a "two-step" process.

The identified tax position must have a "more-likely-than-not" probability—a more than 50 percent chance—of being sustained on examination.

Step 1. A tax benefit may be reflected in the financial statements only if it is "more likely than not" that the company will be able to sustain the tax return position, based on its technical merits.

Step 2. A tax benefit should be measured as the largest amount of benefit that is cumulatively greater than 50 percent likely to be realized (demonstrated later).

For the step-one decision as to whether the position can be sustained, *FIN 48* requires companies to assume that the position is reviewed by the IRS or other taxing authority (state and local governments) and litigated to the "highest court possible," and that the IRS has knowledge of all relevant facts.

[17]"Accounting for Uncertainty in Income Taxes, an Interpretation of FASB Statement No. 109," *FASB Interpretation No. 48* (Norwalk, Conn.: FASB, June 2006).

NOT "MORE LIKELY THAN NOT." Let's say that in the step-one decision, Derrick believes the more-likely-than-not criterion is *not* met. This means that none of the tax benefit is allowed to be recorded in 2009. The effect is that the income tax expense must be recorded at the same amount as if the tax deduction is not available.

Suppose, for instance, that Derricks's current income tax payable is $24 million after being reduced by the full $8 million tax benefit.[18] However, if it's more likely than not that the tax benefit isn't allowable, the benefit can't be recognized as a reduction of tax expense. So, Derrick would record (a) tax expense as if there is no deduction, (b) income tax payable that reflects the benefit of the deduction, and (c) a liability that represents the potential obligation to pay the additional taxes if the deduction is not ultimately upheld:

If there's a less than 50-50 chance of the company's position being sustained on examination, the tax expense can't reflect the tax benefit.

	($ in millions)	
Income tax expense (without $8 tax benefit)	32	
Income tax payable (with $8 tax benefit)		24
Liability—unrecognized tax benefit		8

The $8 million liability can be viewed as a "reserve" to cover the possibility that tax officials might disallow the tax treatment the income tax payable presumes.

The $8 million difference is the tax not paid, but potentially due if the deduction is not upheld. Because the ultimate outcome probably won't be determined within the upcoming year, the Liability—unrecognized tax benefit likely will be reported as a long-term liability.

MEASURING THE TAX BENEFIT. Now, let's say that even though Derrick is aware of the IRS's tendency to challenge deductions of this sort, management believes the more-likely-than-not criterion *is* met. Since we determine in step one that a tax benefit can be recognized, we now need to decide how much. That's step two.

Suppose the following table represents management's estimates of the likelihood of various amounts of tax benefit that would be upheld:

Likelihood Table ($ in millions)					
Amount of the tax benefit that management expects to be sustained	$8	$7	$6	$5	$4
Percentage likelihood that the tax position will be sustained at this level	10%	20%	25%	25%	20%
Cumulative probability that the tax position will be sustained	10%	30%	55%	80%	100%

The largest amount that has a greater-than-50%-chance of being realized is $6 million (10% + 20% + 25% = 55%).

The amount of tax benefit that Derrick can recognize in the financial statements (reduce tax expense) is $6 million because it represents the largest amount of benefit that is more than 50 percent likely to be the end result. So, Derrick would record (a) tax expense as if there is a $6 million benefit, (b) income tax payable that reflects the entire $8 million benefit of the deduction, and (c) a liability that represents the potential obligation to pay the additional taxes if the deduction is not ultimately upheld:

	($ in millions)	
Income tax expense (without $6 tax benefit)	26	
Income tax payable (with $8 tax benefit)		24
Liability—unrecognized tax benefit ($8 – 6)		2

Only $6 million of the tax benefit is recognized in income tax expense.

RESOLUTION OF THE UNCERTAINTY. Now let's consider alternative possibilities for resolution of the uncertainty associated with the tax position. Note that, in each case, the "Liability—unrecognized tax benefit" gets reduced to zero and the balancing entry is to tax expense in the period in which the uncertainty is resolved.

1. **Worst case scenario.** The entire position disallowed, such that Derrick owes $8 million tax (plus interest and penalties, which we are ignoring)

[18]For illustration, if pretax accounting income is $80 million, the tax rate is 40%, and the questionable deduction is $20 million, income tax payable would be [$80 million – 20 million] × 40% = $24 million.

	($ in millions)	
Tax expense	6	
Liability—unrecognized tax benefit	2	
Income tax payable (or cash)		8

2. **Best case scenario.** The entire position is upheld, so Derrick owes no additional tax

	($ in millions)	
Liability—unrecognized tax benefit	2	
Income tax expense		2

3. **Intermediate scenario.** The $6 million position is allowed as expected, so Derrick owes the expected $2 million tax (plus interest and penalties, which we are ignoring)

	($ in millions)	
Liability—unrecognized tax benefit	2	
Income tax payable (or cash)		2

Intraperiod Tax Allocation

● LO10

You should recall that an income statement reports certain items separately from income (or loss) from continuing operations when such items are present. Specifically, (a) discontinued operations and (b) extraordinary items are given a place of their own on the income statement to better allow the user of the statement to isolate irregular components of net income from those that represent ordinary, recurring business operations. Presumably, this permits the user to more accurately project future operations without neglecting events that affect current performance.[19] Following this logic, each component of net income should reflect the income tax effect directly associated with that component.

Consequently, the total income tax expense for a reporting period should be allocated among the income statement items that gave rise to it. Each of the following items should be reported net of its respective income tax effects:

- Income (or loss) from continuing operations.
- Discontinued operations.
- Extraordinary items.

The related tax effect can be either a tax expense or a tax benefit. For example, an extraordinary gain adds to a company's tax expense, while an extraordinary loss produces a tax reduction because it reduces taxable income and therefore reduces income taxes. So a company with a tax rate of 40% would report $100 million pretax income that includes a $10 million extraordinary gain this way:

	($ in millions)
Income before tax and extraordinary item ($100 – 10)	$ 90
Less: Income tax expense ($90 × 40%)	(36)
Income before extraordinary item	54
Extraordinary gain (net of $4 income tax)	6
Net income	$ 60

A gain causes an increase in taxes.

If the $100 million pretax income included a $10 million extraordinary loss rather than an extraordinary gain, the loss would be reported net of associated tax savings:

	($ in millions)
Income before tax and extraordinary item ($100 + 10)	$110
Less: Income tax expense ($110 × 40%)	(44)
Income before extraordinary item	66
Extraordinary loss (net of $4 income tax benefit)	(6)
Net income	$ 60

A loss causes a reduction in taxes.

[19]This was discussed in Chapter 3.

ADDITIONAL CONSIDERATION

If the extraordinary gain in the earlier example had been of a type taxable at a capital gains tax rate of 30%, it would have been reported net of the specific tax associated with that gain:

Extraordinary gain (net of $3 income tax)	$7

Allocating income taxes within a particular reporting period is intraperiod tax allocation.

Allocating income taxes among financial statement components in this way within a particular reporting period is referred to as *intraperiod tax allocation*. You should recognize the contrast with *inter*period tax allocation—terminology sometimes used to describe allocating income taxes between two or more reporting periods by recognizing deferred tax assets and liabilities. While interperiod tax allocation is challenging and controversial, intraperiod tax allocation is relatively straightforward and substantially free from controversy.

Conceptual Concerns

Some accountants disagree with the FASB's approach to accounting for income taxes. Some of the most persistent objections are outlined below.

SHOULD DEFERRED TAXES NOT BE RECOGNIZED? Some feel the income tax expense for a reporting period should be the income tax actually payable currently. Reasons often cited include the contentions that the legal liability for taxes is determined only by the tax return and that taxes are based on aggregate taxable income, not individual components of the aggregate amount. The FASB counters that it is not only possible, but desirable, to separate the tax consequences of individual components of income from the financial reporting of those events. If tax laws permit a company to defer paying tax on a particular event, it is only when, not whether, the tax will be paid that is impacted. Recognizing the tax effect when the event occurs, regardless of when the tax will be paid is consistent with accounting on an accrual rather than a cash basis.

SHOULD DEFERRED TAXES BE RECOGNIZED FOR ONLY SOME ITEMS? Critics sometimes argue that the tax liability for certain recurring events will never be paid and therefore do not represent a liability.[20] An example often cited is the temporary difference due to depreciation. Because the temporary difference recurs frequently (as new assets are acquired), new originating differences more than offset reversing differences causing the balance in the deferred tax liability account to continually get larger. The contention is that no future tax payment will be required, so no liability should be recorded. The FASB's counter argument is that, although the aggregate amount of depreciation differences may get larger, the deferred tax liability for a particular depreciable asset usually does require payment. This is analogous to specific accounts payable requiring payment even though the total balance of accounts payable may grow larger year by year.

SHOULD DEFERRED TAXES BE DISCOUNTED? Some accountants contend that deferred tax assets and liabilities should reflect the time value of money by determining those amounts on a discounted (present value) basis.[21] For some deferred tax amounts such as operating loss carryforwards that might be realized after perhaps 20 years in some cases, the time value might be significant. Practical considerations weighed heavily in the FASB's decision not to permit discounting. Discounting usually would require detailed scheduling of the reversals of all differences reversing in the future, and the selection of appropriate discount rates would pose practical difficulties.

[20]For example, see Paul Chaney and Debra Jeter, "Accounting for Deferred Taxes: Simplicity? Usefulness?" *Accounting Horizons*, June 1989, pp. 7–8.

[21]For example, see Harry Wolk, Dale Martin, and Virginia Nichols, "*Statement of Financial Standards No. 96:* Some Theoretical Problems," *Accounting Horizons*, June 1989, p. 4.

SHOULD CLASSIFICATION BE BASED ON THE TIMING OF TEMPORARY DIFFERENCE REVERSALS? Some feel that deferred tax assets and liabilities should be classified in a balance sheet as current or noncurrent according to the timing of the reversal of the temporary differences that gave rise to them. By this view, those deferred tax assets and liabilities related to temporary differences that will reverse within the coming year should be classified as current, others as noncurrent. Advocates of this view consider it to be consistent with the asset-liability perspective on deferred tax amounts. Again, practical considerations are reflected in the FASB's requirement that a deferred tax asset or deferred tax liability should be classified in a balance sheet as current or noncurrent according to the classification of the asset or liability to which it is related. Classifying a deferred tax liability related to depreciation as noncurrent because the depreciable asset is classified as noncurrent, for example, does not require detailed scheduling of the year-by-year originations and reversals of temporary differences related to depreciation.

DECISION MAKERS' PERSPECTIVE

Income taxes represent one of the largest expenditures that many firms incur. When state, local, and foreign taxes are considered along with federal taxes, the total bite can easily consume 40% of income. A key factor, then, in any decision that managers make should be the impact on taxes. Decision makers must constantly be alert to options that minimize or delay taxes. During the course of this chapter, we encountered situations that avoid taxes (for example, interest on municipal bonds) and those that delay taxes (for example, using accelerated depreciation on the tax return). Astute managers make investment decisions that consider the tax effect of available alternatives. Similarly, outside analysts should consider how effectively management has managed its tax exposure and monitor the current and prospective impact of taxes on their interests in the company.

Investment patterns and other disclosures can indicate potential tax expenditures.

Consider an example. Large, capital-intensive companies with significant investments in buildings and equipment often have sizable deferred tax liabilities from temporary differences in depreciation. If new investments cause the level of depreciable assets to at least remain the same over time, the deferred tax liability can be effectively delayed indefinitely. Investors and creditors should be watchful for situations that might cause material paydowns of that deferred tax liability, such as impending plant closings or investment patterns that suggest declining levels of depreciable assets. Unexpected additional tax expenditures can severely diminish an otherwise attractive prospective rate of return.

Operating loss carryforwards can indicate significant future tax savings.

You also learned in the chapter that deferred tax assets represent future tax benefits. One such deferred tax asset that often reflects sizable future tax deductions is an operating loss carryforward. When a company has a large operating loss carryforward, a large amount of future income can be earned tax free. This tax shelter can be a huge advantage, not to be overlooked by careful analysts.

Deferred tax liabilities increase risk as measured by the debt to equity ratio.

Managers and outsiders are aware that increasing debt increases risk. Deferred tax liabilities increase reported debt. As discussed and demonstrated in the previous chapter, financial risk often is measured by the debt to equity ratio, total liabilities divided by shareholders' equity. Other things being equal, the higher the debt to equity ratio, the higher the risk. Should the deferred tax liability be included in the computation of this ratio? Some analysts will argue that it should be excluded, observing that in many cases the deferred tax liability account remains the same or continually grows larger. Their contention is that no future tax payment will be required. Others, though, contend that is no different from the common situation in which long-term borrowings tend to remain the same or continually grow larger. Research supports the notion that deferred tax liabilities are, in fact, viewed by investors as real liabilities and they appear to discount them according to the timing and likelihood of the liabilities' settlement.[22]

[22]See Dan Givoly and Carla Hayn, "The Valuation of the Deferred Tax Liability: Evidence from the Stock Market," *The Accounting Review*, April 1992, pp. 394–410.

Anytime managerial discretion can materially impact reported earnings, analysts should be wary of the implications for earnings quality assessment. We indicated earlier that the decision as to whether or not a valuation allowance is used, as well as the size of the allowance, is largely discretionary. Alert investors should not overlook the potential for "earnings management" here. In fact, recent empirical evidence indicates that some companies do use the deferred tax asset valuation allowance account to manage earnings upward to meet analyst forecasts.[23]

In short, managers who make decisions based on estimated pretax cash flows and outside investors and creditors who make decisions based on pretax income numbers are perilously ignoring one of the most important aspects of those decisions. Taxes should be a primary consideration in any business decision.

CONCEPT REVIEW EXERCISE

MULTIPLE DIFFERENCES AND OPERATING LOSS

Mid-South Cellular Systems began operations in 2009. That year the company reported taxable income of $25 million. In 2010, its second year of operations, pretax accounting income was $88 million, which included the following amounts:

1. Insurance expense of $14 million, representing one-third of a $42 million, three-year casualty and liability insurance policy that is deducted for tax purposes entirely in 2010.
2. Insurance expense for a $1 million premium on a life insurance policy for the company president. This is not deductible for tax purposes.
3. An asset with a four-year useful life was acquired last year. It is depreciated by the straight-line method on the income statement. MACRS is used on the tax return, causing deductions for depreciation to be more than straight-line depreciation the first two years but less than straight-line depreciation the next two years ($ in millions):

	Income Statement	Tax Return	Difference
2009	$150	$198	$ (48)
2010	150	264	(114)
2011	150	90	60
2012	150	48	102
	$600	$600	0

4. Equipment rental revenue of $80 million, which does not include an additional $20 million of advance payment for 2011 rent. $100 million of rental revenue is reported on the 2010 income tax return.

The enacted tax rate is 40%.

Required:

1. Prepare the journal entry to record Mid-South Cellular's income taxes for 2010.
2. What is Mid-South Cellular's 2010 net income?
3. Show how any deferred tax amount(s) should be reported on the 2010 balance sheet. Assume taxable income is expected in 2011 sufficient to absorb any deductible amounts carried forward from 2010.

[23]Rego, Sonja O., and Mary Margaret Frank, "Do Managers Use the Valuation Allowance Account to Manage Earnings Around Certain Earnings Targets?" (April 16, 2004). Darden Business School Working Paper No. 03-09.

SOLUTION

1. Prepare the journal entry to record Mid-South Cellular's income taxes for 2010.

($ in millions)

Differences in tax reporting and financial reporting of both the prepaid insurance and the depreciation create future taxable amounts.

Both the advance rent and the operating loss carryforward create future deductible amounts.

	2009	Current Year 2010	Future Taxable (Deductible) Amounts 2011	2012	Future Taxable Amounts (total)	Future Deductible Amounts (total)
Pretax accounting income		$ 88				
Permanent difference:						
Life insurance premium		1				
Temporary differences:						
Prepaid insurance		(28)	$ 14	$ 14	$ 28	
Depreciation	$(48)	(114)	60	102	162	
Advance rent received		20	(20)			$(20)
Operating loss		$ (33)				
Loss carryback	(25)	25				
Loss carryforward		8				(8)
		$ 0			$190	$(28)
Enacted tax rate	40%	40%			40%	40%
Tax payable (refundable)	$(10)	$ 0				
Deferred tax liability					$ 76.0	
Deferred tax asset						$(11.2)

	Deferred Tax Liability	Deferred Tax Asset
Ending balances:	$76.0	$11.2
Less: Beginning balance ($48* × 40%)	(19.2)	(0.0)
Change in balances	$56.8	$11.2

*2009's only temporary difference.

Income tax expense is composed of three components: (1) the tax deferred until later, reduced by (2) the deferred tax benefit and (3) the refund of 2009 taxes paid.

Journal Entry at the End of 2010

Income tax expense (to balance)	35.6	
Receivable—income tax refund (determined above)	10.0	
Deferred tax asset (determined above)	11.2	
Deferred tax liability (determined above)		56.8

Note: Adjusting pretax accounting income by the nontemporary difference and the three temporary differences creates a negative taxable income, which is a net operating loss.

2. What is Mid-South Cellular's 2010 net income?

Pretax accounting income	$88.0
Income tax expense	(35.6)
Net income	$52.4

3. Show how any deferred tax amount(s) should be reported in the 2010 balance sheet. Assume taxable income is expected in 2011 sufficient to absorb any deductible amounts carried forward from 2010.

(continued)

(concluded)

	($ in millions)				
	Classification Current—C Noncurrent—N	Future Taxable (Deductible) Amounts	Tax Rate	Deferred Tax (Asset) Liability C	N
Related balance sheet account					
Prepaid insurance	C	28	× 40%	11.2	
Depreciable assets	N	162	× 40%		64.8
Liability—rent received in advance	C	(20)	× 40%	(8.0)	
Unrelated to any balance sheet account					
Operating loss carryforward	C*	(8)	× 40%	(3.2)	
Net current liability (asset)				0.0	
Net noncurrent liability (asset)					64.8

*Deferred tax asset classified entirely as current because 2011 income is expected to be sufficient to realize the benefit of the carryforward.

No net current amount
Long-term liabilities:
Deferred tax liability $64.8

Note: These net amounts ($0.0 + 64.8 = $64.8) sum to the net **total** deferred tax liabilities and deferred tax assets from requirement 1 ($76.0 − 11.2 = $64.8).

FINANCIAL REPORTING CASE SOLUTION

1. **What's the difference? Explain to Laura how differences between financial reporting standards and income tax rules might cause the two tax amounts to differ.** *(p. 822)* The differences in the rules for computing taxable income and those for financial reporting often cause amounts to be included in taxable income in a different year(s) from the year in which they are recognized for financial reporting purposes. Temporary differences result in future taxable or deductible amounts when the temporary differences reverse. As a result, tax payments frequently occur in years different from the years in which the revenues and expenses that cause the taxes are generated.
2. **What is the conceptual advantage of determining income tax expense as we do?** *(p. 822)* Income tax expense is the combination of the current tax effect and the deferred tax consequences of the period's activities. Under the asset-liability approach, the objective of accounting for income taxes is to recognize a deferred tax liability or deferred tax asset for the tax consequences of amounts that will become taxable or deductible in future years as a result of transactions or events that already have occurred. A result is to recognize both the current and the deferred tax consequences of the operations of a reporting period.
3. **Are there differences between financial reporting standards and income tax rules that will not contribute to the difference between income tax expense and the amount of income taxes paid?** *(p. 834)* Yes. Some differences between accounting income and taxable income are caused by transactions and events that will never affect taxable income or taxes payable. These differences between accounting income and taxable income do not reverse later. These are permanent differences which are disregarded when determining (a) the tax payable currently, (b) the deferred tax effect, and therefore (c) the income tax expense. ●

THE BOTTOM LINE

● **LO1** Temporary differences produce future taxable amounts when the taxable income will be increased relative to pretax accounting income in one or more future years. These produce deferred tax liabilities for the taxes to be paid on the future taxable amounts. Income tax expense for the year includes an amount for which payment (or receipt) is deferred in addition to the amount for which payment is due currently. The deferred amount is the change in the tax liability (or asset). (p. 823)

● **LO2** When the future tax consequence of a temporary difference will be to decrease taxable income relative to pretax accounting income, future deductible amounts are created. These have favorable tax consequences that are recognized as deferred tax assets. (p. 830)

● **LO3** Deferred tax assets are recognized for all deductible temporary differences. However, a deferred tax asset is then reduced by a valuation allowance if it is more likely than not that some portion or all of the deferred tax asset will not be realized. (p. 833)

● **LO4** Nontemporary differences between the reported amount of an asset or liability in the financial statements and its tax basis are those caused by transactions and events that under existing tax law will never affect taxable income or taxes payable. These are disregarded when determining both the tax payable currently and the deferred tax effect. (p. 834)

● **LO5** The deferred tax liability (or asset) for which payment (or receipt) is deferred is based on enacted tax rates applied to the taxable or deductible amounts. If a change in a tax law or rate occurs, the deferred tax liability or asset is adjusted to reflect the change in the amount to be paid or recovered. That effect is reflected in operating income in the year of the enactment of the change in the tax law or rate. (p. 837)

● **LO6** When multiple temporary differences exist, the total of the future **taxable** amounts is multiplied by the future tax rate to determine the appropriate balance for the deferred tax liability, and the total of the future **deductible** amounts is multiplied by the future tax rate to determine the appropriate balance for the deferred tax asset. (p. 840)

● **LO7** Tax laws permit an operating loss to be used to reduce taxable income in other, profitable years by either a carryback of the loss to prior years (2) or a carryforward of the loss to later years (up to 20). The tax benefit of an operating loss carryback or an operating loss carryforward is recognized in the year of the loss. (p. 841)

● **LO8** Deferred tax assets and deferred tax liabilities are classified as either current or noncurrent according to how the related assets or liabilities are classified for financial reporting. Disclosure notes should reveal additional relevant information needed for full disclosure pertaining to deferred tax amounts reported on the balance sheet, the components of income tax expense, and available operating loss carryforwards. (p. 844)

● **LO9** A tax benefit may be reflected in the financial statements only if it is "more likely than not" that the company will be able to sustain the tax return position, based on its technical merits. It should be measured as the largest amount of benefit that is cumulatively greater than 50 percent likely to be realized. (p. 848)

● **LO10** Through intraperiod tax allocation, the total income tax expense for a reporting period is allocated among the financial statement items that gave rise to it; specifically, income (or loss) from continuing operations, discontinued operations, extraordinary items, and prior period adjustments (to the beginning retained earnings balance) (p. 850). ●

QUESTIONS FOR REVIEW OF KEY TOPICS

Q 16–1 A member of the board of directors is concerned that the company's income statement reports income tax expense of $12.3 million, but the income tax obligation to the government for the year is only $7.9 million. How might the corporate controller explain this apparent discrepancy?

Q 16–2 A deferred tax liability (or asset) is described as the tax effect of the temporary difference between the financial statement carrying amount of an asset or liability and its tax basis. Explain this tax effect of the temporary difference. How might it produce a deferred tax liability? A deferred tax asset?

Q 16–3 Sometimes a temporary difference will produce future deductible amounts. Explain what is meant by future deductible amounts. Describe two general situations that have this effect. How are such situations recognized in the financial statements?

Q 16–4 The benefit of future deductible amounts can be achieved only if future income is sufficient to take advantage of the deferred deductions. For that reason, not all deferred tax assets will ultimately be realized. How is this possibility reflected in the way we recognize deferred tax assets?

Q 16–5 Temporary differences result in future taxable or deductible amounts when the related asset or liability is recovered or settled. Some differences, though, are not temporary. What events create nontemporary or permanent differences? What effect do these have on the determination of income taxes payable? Of deferred income taxes?

Q 16–6 Identify three examples of differences with no deferred tax consequences.

Q 16–7 The income tax rate for Hudson Refinery has been 35% for each of its 12 years of operation. Company forecasters expect a much-debated tax reform bill to be passed by Congress early next year. The new tax measure would increase Hudson's tax rate to 42%. When measuring this year's deferred tax liability, which rate should Hudson use?

Q 16–8 Suppose a tax reform bill is enacted that causes the corporate tax rate to change from 34% to 36%. How would this affect an existing deferred tax liability? How would the change be reflected in income?

Q 16–9 An operating loss occurs when tax-deductible expenses exceed taxable revenues. Tax laws permit the operating loss to be used to reduce taxable income in other, profitable years by either a carryback of the loss to prior years or a carryforward of the loss to later years. How are loss carrybacks and loss carryforwards recognized for financial reporting purposes?

Q 16–10 How are deferred tax assets and deferred tax liabilities reported in a classified balance sheet?

Q 16–11 Additional disclosures are required pertaining to deferred tax amounts reported on the balance sheet. What are the needed disclosures?

Q 16–12 Additional disclosures are required pertaining to the income tax expense reported on the income statement. What are the needed disclosures?

Q 16–13 The means of dealing with uncertainty in tax positions is prescribed by *FASB Interpretation No. 48 (FIN 48)*. Describe the two-step process provided by *FIN 48*.

Q 16–14 What is intraperiod tax allocation?

Q 16–15 Some accountants believe that deferred taxes should be recognized only for some temporary differences. What is the conceptual basis for this argument? What is the counter argument that serves as the basis for the FASB's requirement that deferred taxes should be recognized for all temporary differences?

BRIEF EXERCISES

BE 16–1
Temporary difference; deferred tax liability
● LO1

A company reports *pretax accounting income* of $10 million, but because of a single temporary difference, *taxable income* is only $7 million. No temporary differences existed at the beginning of the year, and the tax rate is 40%. Prepare the appropriate journal entry to record income taxes.

BE 16–2
Temporary difference; deferred tax asset
● LO2

A company reports *pretax accounting income* of $10 million, but because of a single temporary difference, *taxable income* is $12 million. No temporary differences existed at the beginning of the year, and the tax rate is 40%. Prepare the appropriate journal entry to record income taxes.

BE 16–3
Single temporary difference; income tax payable given
● LO2

In 2009, Ryan Management collected rent revenue for 2010 tenant occupancy. For financial reporting, the rent is recognized as income in the period earned, but for income tax reporting it is taxed when collected. The unearned portion of the rent collected in 2009 was $50 million. Taxable income is $180 million. No temporary differences existed at the beginning of the year, and the tax rate is 40%. Prepare the appropriate journal entry to record income taxes.

BE 16–4
Single temporary difference; income tax payable given
● LO2

Refer to the situation described in BE 16–3. Suppose the unearned portion of the rent collected was $40 million at the end of 2010. Taxable income is $200 million. Prepare the appropriate journal entry to record income taxes.

BE 16–5
Valuation allowance
● LO2 LO3

At the end of the year, the deferred tax asset account had a balance of $12 million attributable to a cumulative temporary difference of $30 million in a liability for estimated expenses. Taxable income is $35 million. No temporary differences existed at the beginning of the year, and the tax rate is 40%. Prepare the journal entry(s) to record income taxes assuming it is more likely than not that one-fourth of the deferred tax asset will not ultimately be realized.

BE 16–6
Valuation allowance
● LO2 LO3

Hypercom Corporation is a provider of electronic card payment terminals, peripherals, network products, and software. In its 2006 annual report, it reported current and long-term deferred tax assets totaling about $61 million. The company also reported valuation allowances totaling about $61 million. What would motivate Hypercom to have a valuation allowance almost equal to its deferred tax assets?

BE 16–7
Single temporary difference; determine taxable income; determine prior year deferred tax amount

● LO1

Kara Fashions uses straight-line depreciation for financial statement reporting and MACRS for income tax reporting. Three years after its purchase, one of Kara's buildings has a carrying value of $400,000 and a tax basis of $300,000. There were no other temporary differences and no nontemporary differences. Taxable income was $4 million and Kara's tax rate is 40%. What is deferred tax liability to be reported in the balance sheet? Assuming that balance was $32,000 the previous year, prepare the appropriate journal entry to record income taxes this year.

BE 16–8
Temporary and nontemporary differences; determine deferred tax consequences

● LO1 LO4

Differences between financial statement and taxable income were as follows:

	($ in millions)
Pretax accounting income	$300
Permanent difference	(24)
	276
Temporary difference	(18)
Taxable income	$258

The cumulative temporary difference to date is $40 million (also the future taxable amount). The enacted tax rate is 40%. What is deferred tax asset or liability to be reported in the balance sheet?

BE 16–9
Single temporary difference; nontemporary difference; calculate taxable income

● LO1 LO4

Shannon Polymers uses straight-line depreciation for financial reporting purposes for equipment costing $800,000 and with an expected useful life of four years and no residual value. For tax purposes, the deduction is 40%, 30%, 20%, and 10% in those years. Pretax accounting income the first year the equipment was used was $900,000, which includes interest revenue of $20,000 from municipal bonds. Other than the two described, there are no differences between accounting income and taxable income. The enacted tax rate is 40%. Prepare the journal entry to record income taxes.

BE 16–10
Single temporary difference; multiple tax rates

● LO5

J-Matt, Inc., had pretax accounting income of $291,000 and taxable income of $300,000 in 2009. The only difference between accounting and taxable income is estimated product warranty costs for sales this year. Warranty payments are expected to be in equal amounts over the next three years. Recent tax legislation will change the tax rate from the current 40% to 30% in 2011. Determine the amounts necessary to record J-Matt's income taxes for 2009 and prepare the appropriate journal entry.

BE 16–11
Change in tax rate; single temporary difference

● LO5

Superior Developers sells lots for residential development. When lots are sold, Superior recognizes income for financial reporting purposes in the year of the sale. For some lots, Superior recognizes income for tax purposes when collected. In the *prior* year, income recognized for financial reporting purposes for lots sold this way was $20 million, which would be collected equally over the next two years. The enacted tax rate was 40%. This year, a new tax law was enacted, revising the tax rate from 40% to 35% beginning next year. Calculate the amount by which Superior should reduce its deferred tax liability this year.

BE 16–12
Operating loss carryforward

● LO7

During its first year of operations, Nile.com reported an operating loss of $15 million for financial reporting and tax purposes. The enacted tax rate is 40%. Prepare the journal entry to recognize the income tax benefit of the operating loss.

BE 16–13
Operating loss carryback

● LO7

AirParts Corporation reported an operating loss of $25 million for financial reporting and tax purposes. Taxable income last year and the previous year, respectively, was $20 million and $15 million. The enacted tax rate each year is 40%. Prepare the journal entry to recognize the income tax benefit of the operating loss. AirParts elects the carryback option.

BE 16–14
Tax uncertainty

● LO9

First Bank has some question as to the tax-free nature of $5 million of its municipal bond portfolio. This amount is excluded from First Bank's taxable income of $55 million. Management has determined that there is a 65% chance that the tax-free status of this interest can't withstand scrutiny of taxing authorities. Assuming a 40% tax rate, what amount of income tax expense should the bank report?

BE 16–15
Intraperiod tax allocation

● LO10

Southeast Airlines had pretax earnings of $65 million, including an extraordinary gain of $10 million. The company's tax rate is 40%. What is the amount of income tax expense that Southeast should report in its income statement? How should the extraordinary gain be reported?

EXERCISES

available with McGraw-Hill's Homework Manager www.mhhe.com/spiceland5e 

An alternate exercise and problem set is available on the text website: www.mhhe.com/spiceland5e

E 16–1
Single temporary difference; taxable income given
● LO1

Alvis Corporation reports *pretax accounting income* of $400,000, but due to a single temporary difference, *taxable income* is only $250,000. At the beginning of the year, no temporary differences existed.

Required:

1. Assuming a tax rate of 35%, what will be Alvis's net income?
2. What will Alvis report in the balance sheet pertaining to income taxes?

E 16–2
Single temporary difference; income tax payable given
● LO2

In 2009, DFS Medical Supply collected rent revenue for 2010 tenant occupancy. For income tax reporting, the rent is taxed when collected. For financial statement reporting, the rent is recognized as income in the period earned. The unearned portion of the rent collected in 2009 amounted to $300,000 at December 31, 2009. DFS had no temporary differences at the beginning of the year.

Required:

Assuming an income tax rate of 40% and 2009 income tax payable of $950,000, prepare the journal entry to record income taxes for 2009.

E 16–3
Single temporary difference; future deductible amounts; taxable income given
● LO2

Lance Lawn Services reports bad debt expense using the allowance method. For tax purposes, the expense is deducted when accounts prove uncollectible (the direct write-off method). At December 31, 2009, Lance has accounts receivable and an allowance for uncollectible accounts of $20 million and $1 million, respectively, and taxable income of $75 million. At December 31, 2008, Lance reported a deferred tax asset of $435,000 related to this difference in reporting bad debts, its only temporary difference. The enacted tax rate is 40% each year.

Required:

Prepare the appropriate journal entry to record Lance's income tax provision for 2009.

E 16–4
Deferred tax asset; taxable income given; valuation allowance
● LO3

At the end of 2008, Payne Industries had a deferred tax asset account with a balance of $30 million attributable to a temporary book–tax difference of $75 million in a liability for estimated expenses. At the end of 2009, the temporary difference is $70 million. Payne has no other temporary differences and no valuation allowance for the deferred tax asset. Taxable income for 2009 is $180 million and the tax rate is 40%.

Required:

1. Prepare the journal entry(s) to record Payne's income taxes for 2009, assuming it is more likely than not that the deferred tax asset will be realized.
2. Prepare the journal entry(s) to record Payne's income taxes for 2009, assuming it is more likely than not that one-half of the deferred tax asset will ultimately be realized.

E 16–5
IFRS; valuation allowance
● LO3

Refer to the situation described in the previous exercise.

Required:

Assume that Payne Industries believes that, while there is a greater than 50% likelihood that half the tax benefit will be realized, due to a downturn this year in product demand, it's "probable" that only one-fourth will be realized. ("Probable" typically is viewed as indicating a higher probability than "more likely than not.") How might your solution to requirement 2 differ if Payne prepares its financial statements according to International Accounting Standards? Include any appropriate journal entry(s) in your response.

E 16–6
Deferred tax asset; income tax payable given; previous balance in valuation allowance
● LO3

(This is a variation of Exercise 16–4, modified to assume a previous balance in the valuation allowance.)

At the end of 2008, Payne Industries had a deferred tax asset account with a balance of $30 million attributable to a temporary book-tax difference of $75 million in a liability for estimated expenses. At the end of 2009, the temporary difference is $70 million. Payne has no other temporary differences. Taxable income for 2009 is $180 million and the tax rate is 40%.

Payne has a valuation allowance of $10 million for the deferred tax asset at the beginning of 2009.

Required:

1. Prepare the journal entry(s) to record Payne's income taxes for 2009, assuming it is more likely than not that the deferred tax asset will be realized.
2. Prepare the journal entry(s) to record Payne's income taxes for 2009, assuming it is more likely than not that one-half of the deferred tax asset will ultimately be realized.

E 16–7
Single temporary difference; determine taxable income; determine prior year deferred tax amount

On January 1, 2006, Ameen Company purchased a building for $36 million. Ameen uses straight-line depreciation for financial statement reporting and MACRS for income tax reporting. At December 31, 2008, the carrying value of the building was $30 million and its tax basis was $20 million. At December 31, 2009, the carrying value of the building was $28 million and its tax basis was $13 million. There were no other temporary differences and no nontemporary differences. Pretax accounting income for 2009 was $20 million.

Required:

● LO1

1. Prepare the appropriate journal entry to record Ameen's 2009 income taxes. Assume an income tax rate of 40%.
2. What is Ameen's 2009 net income?

E 16–8
Single temporary difference; taxable income given; calculate deferred tax liability

● LO1

Ayres Services acquired an asset for $80 million in 2009. The asset is depreciated for financial reporting purposes over four years on a straight-line basis (no residual value). For tax purposes the asset's cost is depreciated by MACRS. The enacted tax rate is 40%. Amounts for pretax accounting income, depreciation, and taxable income in 2009, 2010, 2011, and 2012 are as follows:

	($ in millions)			
	2009	**2010**	**2011**	**2012**
Pretax accounting income	$330	$350	$365	$400
Depreciation on the income statement	20	20	20	20
Depreciation on the tax return	(25)	(33)	(15)	(7)
Taxable income	$325	$337	$370	$413

Required:

For December 31 of each year, determine (a) the temporary book–tax difference for the depreciable asset and (b) the balance to be reported in the deferred tax liability account.

E 16–9
Identifying future taxable amounts and future deductible amounts

● LO1 LO2

Listed below are 10 causes of temporary differences. For each temporary difference, indicate (by letter) whether it will create future deductible amounts (D) or future taxable amounts (T).

Temporary Difference

____ 1. Accrual of loss contingency, tax-deductible when paid.
____ 2. Newspaper subscriptions; taxable when received, recognized for financial reporting when earned.
____ 3. Prepaid rent, tax-deductible when paid.
____ 4. Accrued bond interest expense, tax-deductible when paid.
____ 5. Prepaid insurance, tax-deductible when paid.
____ 6. Unrealized loss from recording investments available for sale at fair value (tax-deductible when investments are sold).
____ 7. Bad debt expense; allowance method for financial reporting; direct write-off for tax purposes.
____ 8. Advance rent receipts on an operating lease (as the lessor), taxable when received.
____ 9. Straight-line depreciation for financial reporting; accelerated depreciation for tax purposes.
____ 10. Accrued expense for employee postretirement benefits, tax-deductible when subsequent payments are made.

E 16–10
Identifying future taxable amounts and future deductible amounts

● LO1 LO2

(This is a variation of the previous exercise, modified to focus on the balance sheet accounts related to the deferred tax amounts.)

Listed below are 10 causes of temporary differences. For each temporary difference indicate the balance sheet account for which the situation creates a temporary difference.

Temporary Difference

1. Accrual of loss contingency, tax-deductible when paid.
2. Newspaper subscriptions; taxable when received, recognized for financial reporting when earned.
3. Prepaid rent, tax-deductible when paid.
4. Accrued bond interest expense, tax-deductible when paid.
5. Prepaid insurance, tax-deductible when paid.
6. Unrealized loss from recording investments available for sale at fair value (tax-deductible when investments are sold).
7. Bad debt expense; allowance method for financial reporting; direct write-off for tax purposes.
8. Advance rent receipts on an operating lease (as the lessor), taxable when received.
9. Straight-line depreciation for financial reporting; accelerated depreciation for tax purposes.
10. Accrued expense for employee postretirement benefits, tax-deductible when subsequent payments are made.

E 16–11
Single temporary difference; nontemporary difference; calculate taxable income
● LO1 LO4

Southern Atlantic Distributors began operations in January 2009 and purchased a delivery truck for $40,000. Southern Atlantic plans to use straight-line depreciation over a four-year expected useful life for financial reporting purposes. For tax purposes, the deduction is 50% of cost in 2009, 30% in 2010, and 20% in 2011. Pretax accounting income for 2009 was $300,000, which includes interest revenue of $40,000 from municipal bonds. The enacted tax rate is 40%.

Required:

Assuming no differences between accounting income and taxable income other than those described above:

1. Prepare the journal entry to record income taxes in 2009.
2. What is Southern Atlantic's 2009 net income?

E 16–12
Single temporary difference; nontemporary difference (goodwill); calculate taxable income
● LO1 LO4

Peridot Developers, Inc., began operations in December 2009. Peridot sells plots of land for industrial development. Peridot recognizes income for financial reporting purposes in the year it sells the plots. For some of the plots sold, Peridot recognizes the income for tax purposes when collected. Income Peridot recognized for financial reporting purposes in 2009 for plots sold this way was $40 million. The company expected to collect this amount over the next two years as follows:

2010	$24 million
2011	16 million
	$40 million

Peridot's pretax *accounting* income for 2009 was $63 million. On its tax return, Peridot is amortizing $45 million of goodwill over the 15-year period permitted by tax laws. Goodwill is not amortizable for financial reporting purposes and thus is not reflected in pretax accounting income. The enacted tax rate is 40 percent.

Required:

1. Assuming no differences between accounting income and taxable income other than those described above, prepare the journal entry to record income taxes in 2009.
2. What is Peridot's 2009 net income?

E 16–13
Single temporary difference; multiple tax rates
● LO2 LO5

Allmond Corporation, organized on January 3, 2009, had pretax accounting income of $14 million and taxable income of $20 million for the year ended December 31, 2009. The 2009 tax rate is 35%. The only difference between accounting income and taxable income is estimated product warranty costs. Expected payments and scheduled tax rates (based on recent tax legislation) are as follows:

2010	$2 million	30%
2011	1 million	30%
2012	1 million	30%
2013	2 million	25%

Required:

1. Determine the amounts necessary to record Allmond's income taxes for 2009 and prepare the appropriate journal entry.
2. What is Allmond's 2009 net income?

E 16–14
Change in tax rates; calculate taxable income
● LO1 LO5

Arnold Industries has pretax accounting income of $33 million for the year ended December 31, 2009. The tax rate is 40%. The only difference between accounting income and taxable income relates to an operating lease in which Arnold is the lessee. The inception of the lease was December 28, 2009. An $8 million advance rent payment at the inception of the lease is tax-deductible in 2009 but, for financial reporting purposes, represents prepaid rent expense to be recognized equally over the four-year lease term.

Required:

1. Determine the amounts necessary to record Arnold's income taxes for 2009 and prepare the appropriate journal entry.
2. Determine the amounts necessary to record Arnold's income taxes for 2010 and prepare the appropriate journal entry. Pretax accounting income was $50 million for the year ended December 31, 2010.
3. Assume a new tax law is enacted in 2010 that causes the tax rate to change from 40% to 30% beginning in 2011. Determine the amounts necessary to record Arnold's income taxes for 2010 and prepare the appropriate journal entry.
4. Why is Arnold's 2010 income tax expense different when the tax rate change occurs from what it would be without the change?

E 16–15
Deferred taxes; change in tax rates
● LO1 LO5

Bronson Industries reported a deferred tax liability of $8 million for the year ended December 31, 2008, related to a temporary difference of $20 million. The tax rate was 40%. The temporary difference is expected to reverse in 2010 at which time the deferred tax liability will become payable. There are no other temporary differences in 2008–2010. Assume a new tax law is enacted in 2009 that causes the tax rate to change from 40% to 30% beginning in 2010. (The rate remains 40% for 2009 taxes.) Taxable income in 2009 is $30 million.

Required:
Determine the effect of the change and prepare the appropriate journal entry to record Bronson's income tax expense in 2009. What adjustment, if any, is needed to revise retained earnings as a result of the change?

E 16–16
Multiple temporary differences; record income taxes
● LO6

The information that follows pertains to Esther Food Products:

a. At December 31, 2009, temporary differences were associated with the following future taxable (deductible) amounts:

Depreciation	$60,000
Prepaid expenses	17,000
Warranty expenses	(12,000)

b. No temporary differences existed at the beginning of 2009.

c. Pretax accounting income was $80,000 and taxable income was $15,000 for the year ended December 31, 2009.

d. The tax rate is 40%.

Required:
Determine the amounts necessary to record income taxes for 2009 and prepare the appropriate journal entry.

E 16–17
Multiple temporary differences; record income taxes
● LO6

The information that follows pertains to Richards Refrigeration, Inc.:

a. At December 31, 2009, temporary differences existed between the financial statement carrying amounts and the tax bases of the following:

	($ in millions)		
	Carrying Amount	**Tax Basis**	**Future Taxable (Deductible) Amount**
Buildings and equipment (net of accumulated depreciation)	$120	$90	$30
Prepaid insurance	50	0	50
Liability—loss contingency	25	0	(25)

b. No temporary differences existed at the beginning of 2009.

c. Pretax accounting income was $200 million and taxable income was $145 million for the year ended December 31, 2009. The tax rate is 40%.

Required:
1. Determine the amounts necessary to record income taxes for 2009 and prepare the appropriate journal entry.
2. What is the 2009 net income?

E 16–18
Calculate income tax amounts under various circumstances
● LO1 LO2

Four independent situations are described below. Each involves future deductible amounts and/or future taxable amounts produced by temporary differences:

	($ in thousands) Situation			
	1	**2**	**3**	**4**
Taxable income	$85	$215	$195	$260
Future deductible amounts	15		20	20
Future taxable amounts		15	15	30
Balance(s) at beginning of the year:				
Deferred tax asset	2		9	4
Deferred tax liability		2	2	

The enacted tax rate is 40%.

Required:
For each situation, determine the:
a. Income tax payable currently.
b. Deferred tax asset—balance.

c. Deferred tax asset—change (dr) cr.
d. Deferred tax liability—balance.
e. Deferred tax liability—change (dr) cr.
f. Income tax expense.

E 16–19
Determine taxable income

● LO1 LO2

Eight independent situations are described below. Each involves future deductible amounts and/or future taxable amounts produced by:

($ in millions)
Temporary Differences Reported First on:

	The Income Statement		The Tax Return	
	Revenue	**Expense**	**Revenue**	**Expense**
1.		$20		
2.	$20			
3.			$20	
4.				$20
5.	15	20		
6.		20	15	
7.	15	20		10
8.	15	20	5	10

Required:
For each situation, determine taxable income assuming pretax accounting income is $100 million.

E 16–20
Two temporary differences; nontemporary difference

● LO1 LO2 LO4

For the year ended December 31, 2009, Fidelity Engineering reported pretax accounting income of $977,000. Selected information for 2009 from Fidelity's records follows:

Interest income on municipal bonds	$32,000
Depreciation claimed on the 2009 tax return in excess of depreciation on the income statement	55,000
Carrying amount of depreciable assets in excess of their tax basis at year-end	85,000
Warranty expense reported on the income statement	26,000
Actual warranty expenditures in 2009	16,000

Fidelity's income tax rate is 40%. At January 1, 2009, Fidelity's records indicated balances of zero and $12,000 in its deferred tax asset and deferred tax liability accounts, respectively.

Required:
1. Determine the amounts necessary to record income taxes for 2009 and prepare the appropriate journal entry.
2. What is Fidelity's 2009 net income?

E 16–21
Operating loss carryforward

● LO7

During 2009, its first year of operations, Baginski Steel Corporation reported an operating loss of $375,000 for financial reporting and tax purposes. The enacted tax rate is 40%.

Required:
1. Prepare the journal entry to recognize the income tax benefit of the operating loss. Assume the weight of available evidence suggests future taxable income sufficient to benefit from future deductible amounts from the operating loss carryforward.
2. Show the lower portion of the 2009 income statement that reports the income tax benefit of the operating loss.

E 16–22
Operating loss carryback

● LO7

Wynn Sheet Metal reported an operating loss of $100,000 for financial reporting and tax purposes in 2009. The enacted tax rate is 40%. Taxable income, tax rates, and income taxes paid in Wynn's first four years of operation were as follows:

	Taxable Income	Tax Rates	Income Taxes Paid
2005	$60,000	30%	$18,000
2006	70,000	30	21,000
2007	80,000	40	32,000
2008	60,000	45	27,000

Required:
1. Prepare the journal entry to recognize the income tax benefit of the operating loss. Wynn elects the carryback option.
2. Show the lower portion of the 2009 income statement that reports the income tax benefit of the operating loss.

E 16–23
Operating loss carryback and carryforward
● LO7

(This exercise is based on the situation described in the previous exercise, modified to include a carryforward in addition to a carryback.)

Wynn Sheet Metal reported an operating loss of $160,000 for financial reporting and tax purposes in 2009. The enacted tax rate is 40%. Taxable income, tax rates, and income taxes paid in Wynn's first four years of operation were as follows:

	Taxable Income	Tax Rates	Income Taxes Paid
2005	$60,000	30%	$18,000
2006	70,000	30	21,000
2007	80,000	40	32,000
2008	60,000	45	27,000

Required:

1. Prepare the journal entry to recognize the income tax benefit of the operating loss. Wynn elects the carryback option.
2. Show the lower portion of the 2009 income statement that reports the income tax benefit of the operating loss.

E 16–24
Balance sheet classification
● LO8

At December 31, DePaul Corporation had a $16 million balance in its deferred tax asset account and a $68 million balance in its deferred tax liability account. The balances were due to the following cumulative temporary differences:

1. Estimated warranty expense, $15 million: expense recorded in the year of the sale; tax-deductible when paid (one-year warranty).
2. Depreciation expense, $120 million: straight-line on the income statement; MACRS on the tax return.
3. Income from installment sales of properties, $50 million: income recorded in the year of the sale; taxable when received equally over the next five years.
4. Bad debt expense, $25 million: allowance method for accounting; direct write-off for tax purposes.

Required:

Show how any deferred tax amounts should be classified and reported in the December 31 balance sheet. The tax rate is 40%.

E 16–25
IFRS; balance sheet classification
● LO8

Refer to the situation described in the previous exercise.

Required:

How might your solution differ if DePaul Corporation prepares its financial statements according to International Accounting Standards? Include any appropriate journal entry in your response.

E 16–26
Single temporary difference; nontemporary difference; multiple tax rates; balance sheet classification
● LO1 LO4 LO5 LO8

Case Development began operations in December 2009. When property is sold on an installment basis, Case recognizes installment income for financial reporting purposes in the year of the sale. For tax purposes, installment income is reported by the installment method. 2009 installment income was $600,000 and will be collected over the next three years. Scheduled collections and enacted tax rates for 2010–2012 are as follows:

2010	$150,000	30%
2011	250,000	40
2012	200,000	40

Pretax accounting income for 2009 was $810,000, which includes interest revenue of $10,000 from municipal bonds. The enacted tax rate for 2009 is 30%.

Required:

1. Assuming no differences between accounting income and taxable income other than those described above, prepare the appropriate journal entry to record Case's 2009 income taxes.
2. What is Case's 2009 net income?
3. How should the deferred tax amount be classified in a classified balance sheet?

E 16–27
Two temporary differences; nontemporary difference; multiple tax rates; balance sheet classification
● LO1 LO2 LO4 LO5 LO6 LO8

(This exercise is a variation of the previous exercise, modified to include a second temporary difference.)

Case Development began operations in December 2009. When property is sold on an installment basis, Case recognizes installment income for financial reporting purposes in the year of the sale. For tax purposes, installment income is reported by the installment method. 2009 installment income was $600,000 and will be collected over the next three years. Scheduled collections and enacted tax rates for 2010–2012 are as follows:

2010	$150,000	30%
2011	250,000	40
2012	200,000	40

Case also had product warranty costs of $80,000 expensed for financial reporting purposes in 2009. For tax purposes, only the $20,000 of warranty costs actually paid in 2009 was deducted. The remaining $60,000 will be deducted for tax purposes when paid over the next three years as follows:

2010	$20,000
2011	25,000
2012	15,000

Pretax *accounting* income for 2009 was $810,000, which includes interest revenue of $10,000 from municipal bonds. The enacted tax rate for 2009 is 30%.

Required:

1. Assuming no differences between accounting income and taxable income other than those described above, prepare the appropriate journal entry to record Case's 2009 income taxes.
2. What is Case's 2009 net income?
3. How should the deferred tax amounts be classified in a classified balance sheet?

E 16–28
Identifying income tax deferrals

● LO1 LO2 LO4 LO7

Listed below are ten independent situations. For each situation indicate (by letter) whether it will create a deferred tax asset (A), a deferred tax liability (L), or neither (N).

Situation

____ 1. Advance payments on an operating lease deductible when paid.
____ 2. Estimated warranty costs, tax deductible when paid.
____ 3. Rent revenue collected in advance; cash basis for tax purposes.
____ 4. Interest received from investments in municipal bonds.
____ 5. Prepaid expenses tax deductible when paid.
____ 6. Operating loss carryforward.
____ 7. Operating loss carryback.
____ 8. Bad debt expense; allowance method for accounting; direct write-off for tax.
____ 9. Organization costs expensed when incurred, tax deductible over 15 years.
____ 10. Life insurance proceeds received upon the death of the company president.

E 16–29
Concepts; terminology

● LO1 through LO8

Listed below are several terms and phrases associated with accounting for income taxes. Pair each item from List A (by letter) with the item from List B that is most appropriately associated with it.

List A	List B
____ 1. No tax consequences.	a. Deferred tax liability.
____ 2. Originates, then reverses.	b. Deferred tax asset.
____ 3. Revise deferred tax amounts.	c. 2 years.
____ 4. Operating loss.	d. Current and deferred tax consequence combined.
____ 5. Future tax effect of prepaid expenses tax deductible when paid.	e. Temporary difference.
____ 6. Loss carryback.	f. Specific tax rates times amounts reversing each year.
____ 7. Future tax effect of estimated warranty expense.	g. Nontemporary differences.
____ 8. Valuation allowance.	h. When enacted tax rate changes.
____ 9. Phased-in change in rates.	i. Same as related asset or liability.
____ 10. Balance sheet classifications.	j. "More likely than not" test.
____ 11. Individual tax consequences of financial statement components.	k. Intraperiod tax allocation.
____ 12. Income tax expense.	l. Negative taxable income.

E 16–30
Tax credit; uncertainty regarding sustainability; *FIN 48*

● LO9

Delta Catfish Company has taken a position in its tax return to claim a tax credit of $10 million (direct reduction in taxes payable) and has determined that its sustainability is "more likely than not," based on its technical merits. Delta has developed the probability table shown below of all possible material outcomes:

Probability Table ($ in millions)

Amount of the tax benefit that management expects to receive	$10	$ 8	$ 6	$ 4	$ 2
Percentage likelihood that the tax benefit will be sustained at this level	10%	20%	25%	20%	25%

Delta's taxable income is $85 million for the year. Its effective tax rate is 40%. The tax credit would be a direct reduction in current taxes payable.

Required:

1. At what amount would Delta measure the tax benefit in its income statement?
2. Prepare the appropriate journal entry for Delta to record its income taxes for the year.

E 16–31
Intraperiod tax allocation

● LO10

The following income statement does not reflect intraperiod tax allocation.

Required:

Recast the income statement to reflect intraperiod tax allocation.

INCOME STATEMENT
For the Fiscal Year Ended March 31, 2009
($ in millions)

Revenues	$830
Cost of goods sold	(350)
Gross profit	480
Operating expenses	(180)
Income tax expense	(86)
Income before discontinued operations and extraordinary item	214
Loss from discontinued operations	(10)
Extraordinary casualty loss	(75)
Net income	$129

The company's tax rate is 40%.

CPA AND CMA REVIEW QUESTIONS

CPA Exam Questions

KAPLAN SCHWESER

The following questions are used in the Kaplan CPA Review Course to study accounting for income taxes while preparing for the CPA examination. Determine the response that best completes the statements or questions.

● LO1

1. Scott Corp. received cash of $20,000 that was included in revenues in its 2009 financial statements, of which $12,000 will not be taxable until 2010. Scott's enacted tax rate is 30% for 2009, and 25% for 2010. What amount should Scott report in its 2009 balance sheet for deferred income tax liability?
   a. $2,000
   b. $2,400
   c. $3,000
   d. $3,600

● LO2

2. West Corp. leased a building and received the $36,000 annual rental payment on June 15, 2009. The beginning of the lease was July 1, 2009. Rental income is taxable when received. West's tax rates are 30% for 2009 and 40% thereafter. West had no other permanent or temporary differences. West determined that no valuation allowance was needed. What amount of deferred tax asset should West report in its December 31, 2009, balance sheet?
   a. $ 5,400
   b. $ 7,200
   c. $10,800
   d. $14,400

● LO3

3. In its December 31, 2009, balance sheet, Shin Co. had income taxes payable of $13,000 and a current deferred tax asset of $20,000 before determining the need for a valuation account. Shin had reported a current deferred tax asset of $15,000 at December 31, 2008. No estimated tax payments were made during 2009. At December 31, 2009, Shin determined that it was more likely than not that 10% of the deferred tax asset would not be realized. In its 2009 income statement, what amount should Shin report as total income tax expense?
   a. $ 8,000
   b. $ 8,500
   c. $10,000
   d. $13,000

● LO5

4. Stone Co. began operations in 2009 and reported $225,000 in income before income taxes for the year. Stone's 2009 tax depreciation exceeded its book depreciation by $25,000. Stone also had nondeductible book expenses of $10,000 related to permanent differences. Stone's tax rate for 2009 was 40%, and the enacted rate for years after 2009 is 35%. In its December 31, 2009, balance sheet, what amount of deferred income tax liability should Stone report?

a. $ 8,750
b. $10,000
c. $12,250
d. $14,000

LO5

5. Black Co. organized on January 2, 2009, had pretax financial statement income of $500,000 and taxable income of $800,000 for the year ended December 31, 2009. The only temporary differences are accrued product warranty costs, which Black expects to pay as follows:

2010	$100,000
2011	$ 50,000
2012	$ 50,000
2013	$100,000

The enacted income tax rates are 25% for 2009, 30% for 2010 through 2012, and 35% for 2013. Black believes that future years' operations will produce profits. In its December 31, 2009, balance sheet, what amount should Black report as deferred tax asset?

a. $50,000
b. $75,000
c. $90,000
d. $95,000

LO7

6. Dix, Inc., a calendar-year corporation, reported the following operating income (loss) before income tax for its first three years of operations:

2007	$100,000
2008	(200,000)
2009	400,000

There are no permanent or temporary differences between operating income (loss) for financial and income tax reporting purposes. When filing its 2008 tax return, Dix did not elect to forego the carryback of its loss for 2008. Assume a 40% tax rate for all years. What amount should Dix report as its income tax liability at December 31, 2009?

a. $ 60,000
b. $ 80,000
c. $120,000
d. $160,000

LO10

7. An example of intraperiod income tax allocation is
   a. Reporting an extraordinary item in the income statement, net of direct tax effects.
   b. Interest income on municipal obligations.
   c. Estimated expenses for major repairs accrued for financial statement purposes in one year, but deducted for income tax purposes when paid in a subsequent year.
   d. Rental income included in income for income tax purposes when collected, but deferred for financial statement purposes until earned in a subsequent year.

CMA Exam Questions

The following questions dealing with accounting for income taxes are adapted from questions that previously appeared on Certified Management Accountant (CMA) examinations. The CMA designation sponsored by the Institute of Management Accountants (www.imanet.org) provides members with an objective measure of knowledge and competence in the field of management accounting. Determine the response that best completes the statements or questions.

LO2

1. Which one of the following temporary differences will result in a deferred tax asset?
   a. Use of the straight-line depreciation method for financial statement purposes and the modified Accelerated Cost Recovery System (MACRS) for income tax purposes.
   b. Installment sale profits accounted for on the accrual basis for financial statement purposes and on a cash basis for income tax purposes.
   c. Advance rental receipts accounted for on the accrual basis for financial statement purposes and on a cash basis for tax purposes.
   d. Investment gains accounted for under the equity method for financial statement purposes and under the cost method for income tax purposes.

Questions 2 and 3 are based on the following information. Bearings Manufacturing Company Inc. purchased a new machine on January 1, 2010 for $100,000. The company uses the straight-line depreciation method with an estimated equipment life of 5 years and a zero salvage value for financial statement purposes, and uses the 3-year Modified Accelerated Cost Recovery System (MACRS) with an estimated equipment life of 3 years for income tax reporting purposes. Bearings is subject to a 35% marginal income tax rate. Assume that the deferred tax liability at the beginning of the year is zero and that Bearings has a positive earnings tax position. The MACRS depreciation rates for 3-year equipment are shown below.

Year	Rate
1	33.33%
2	44.45
3	14.81
4	7.41

● LO1

2. What is the deferred tax liability at December 31, 2010 (rounded to the nearest whole dollar)?
   a. $7,000
   b. $33,330
   c. $11,666
   d. $4,666

● LO5

3. For Bearings Manufacturing Company Inc., assume that the following new corporate income tax rates will go into effect:

2011–2013	40%
2014	45%

   What is the amount of the deferred tax asset/liability at December 31, 2010 (rounded to the nearest whole dollar)?
   a. $0
   b. $9,000
   c. $2,668
   d. $6,332

PROBLEMS

available with McGraw-Hill's Homework Manager www.mhhe.com/spiceland5e 

An alternate exercise and problem set is available on the text website: www.mhhe.com/spiceland5e

P 16–1
Determine deferred tax assets and liabilities

● LO1 LO2

Corning-Howell reported taxable income in 2009 of $120 million. At December 31, 2009, the reported amount of some assets and liabilities in the financial statements differed from their tax bases as indicated below:

	Carrying Amount	Tax Basis
Assets		
Current		
Accounts receivable (net of allowance)	$ 10 million	$ 12 million
Prepaid insurance	20 million	0
Prepaid rent expense (operating lease)	6 million	0
Noncurrent		
Buildings and equipment (net)	360 million	280 million
Liabilities		
Current		
Liability—subscriptions received	14 million	0
Long-term		
Liability—postretirement benefits	594 million	0
Shareholders' Equity		
Unrealized gain from recording investments available for sale at fair market value*	4 million	0

*Taxable when investments are sold.

The total deferred tax asset and deferred tax liability amounts at January 1, 2009, were $250 million and $40 million, respectively. The enacted tax rate is 40% each year.

Required:

1. Determine the total deferred tax asset and deferred tax liability amounts at December 31, 2009.
2. Determine the increase (decrease) in the deferred tax asset and deferred tax liability accounts at December 31, 2009.

3. Determine the income tax payable currently for the year ended December 31, 2009.
4. Prepare the journal entry to record income taxes for 2009.
5. Show how the deferred tax amounts should be classified and reported in the 2009 balance sheet.

P 16–2
Temporary difference; determine deferred tax amount for three years; balance sheet classification

● LO2 LO8

Times-Roman Publishing Company reports the following amounts in its first three years of operation:

($ in 000s)	2009	2010	2011
Pretax accounting income	$250	$240	$230
Taxable income	290	220	260

The difference between pretax accounting income and taxable income is due to subscription revenue for one-year magazine subscriptions being reported for tax purposes in the year received, but reported on the income statement in later years when earned. The income tax rate is 40% each year. Times-Roman anticipates profitable operations in the future.

Required:

1. What is the balance sheet account for which a temporary difference is created by this situation?
2. For each year, indicate the cumulative amount of the temporary difference at year-end.
3. Determine the balance in the related deferred tax account at the end of each year. Is it a deferred tax asset or a deferred tax liability?
4. How should the deferred tax amount be classified and reported in the balance sheet?

P 16–3
Change in tax rate; single temporary difference

● LO5

Dixon Development began operations in December 2009. When lots for industrial development are sold, Dixon recognizes income for financial reporting purposes in the year of the sale. For some lots, Dixon recognizes income for tax purposes when collected. Income recognized for financial reporting purposes in 2009 for lots sold this way was $12 million, which will be collected over the next three years. Scheduled collections for 2010–2012 are as follows:

2010	$ 4 million
2011	5 million
2012	3 million
	$12 million

Pretax accounting income for 2009 was $16 million. The enacted tax rate is 40%.

Required:

1. Assuming no differences between accounting income and taxable income other than those described above, prepare the journal entry to record income taxes in 2009.
2. Suppose a new tax law, revising the tax rate from 40% to 35%, beginning in 2011, is enacted in 2010, when pretax accounting income was $15 million. Prepare the appropriate journal entry to record income taxes in 2010.
3. If the new tax rate had not been enacted, what would have been the appropriate balance in the deferred tax liability account at the end of 2010? Why?

P 16–4
Change in tax rate; record taxes for four years

● LO5

Zekany Corporation would have had identical income before taxes on both its income tax returns and income statements for the years 2009 through 2012 except for differences in depreciation on an operational asset. The asset cost $120,000 and is depreciated for income tax purposes in the following amounts:

2009	$39,600
2010	52,800
2011	18,000
2012	9,600

The operational asset has a four-year life and no residual value. The straight-line method is used for financial reporting purposes.

Income amounts before depreciation expense and income taxes for each of the four years were as follows.

	2009	2010	2011	2012
Accounting income before taxes and depreciation	$60,000	$80,000	$70,000	$70,000

Assume the average and marginal income tax rate for 2009 and 2010 was 30%; however, during 2010 tax legislation was passed to raise the tax rate to 40% beginning in 2011. The 40% rate remained in effect through the years 2011 and 2012. Both the accounting and income tax periods end December 31.

Required:

Prepare the journal entries to record income taxes for the years 2009 through 2012.

P 16–5
Change in tax rate; permanent and temporary differences; record taxes for four years

● LO1 LO4 LO5

The DeVille Company reported pretax accounting income on its income statement as follows:

2009	$350,000
2010	270,000
2011	340,000
2012	380,000

Included in the income of 2009 was an installment sale of property in the amount of $50,000. However, for tax purposes, DeVille reported the income in the year cash was collected. Cash collected on the installment sale was $20,000 in 2010, $25,000 in 2011, and $5,000 in 2012.

Included in the 2011 income was $15,000 interest from investments in municipal bonds.

The enacted tax rate for 2009 and 2010 was 30%, but during 2010 new tax legislation was passed reducing the tax rate to 25% for the years 2011 and beyond.

Required:

Prepare the year-end journal entries to record income taxes for the years 2009–2012.

P 16–6
Multiple temporary differences; temporary difference yet to originate; multiple tax rates; classification

● LO5 LO6 LO8

You are the new accounting manager at the Barry Transport Company. Your CFO has asked you to provide input on the company's income tax position based on the following:

1. Pretax accounting income was $41 million and taxable income was $8 million for the year ended December 31, 2009.
2. The difference was due to three items:
   a. Tax depreciation exceeds book depreciation by $30 million in 2009 for the business complex acquired that year. This amount is scheduled to be $60 million, ($50 million), and ($40 million) in 2010, 2011, and 2012, respectively.
   b. Insurance of $9 million was paid in 2009 for 2010 coverage.
   c. A $6 million loss contingency was accrued in 2009, to be paid in 2011.
3. No temporary differences existed at the beginning of 2009.
4. The tax rate is 40%.

Required:

1. Determine the amounts necessary to record income taxes for 2009 and prepare the appropriate journal entry.
2. How should the deferred tax amounts be classified in a classified balance sheet?
3. Assume the enacted federal income tax law specifies that the tax rate will change from 40% to 35% in 2011. When scheduling the reversal of the depreciation difference, you were uncertain as to how to deal with the fact that the difference will continue to originate in 2010 before reversing the next two years. Upon consulting **PricewaterhouseCoopers'** *Comperio* database, you found:

   .441 Depreciable and amortizable assets
   Only the reversals of the temporary difference at the balance sheet date would be scheduled. Future originations are not considered in determining the reversal pattern of temporary differences for depreciable assets. *FAS 109* is silent as to how the balance sheet date temporary differences are deemed to reverse, but the FIFO pattern is intended.

   You interpret that to mean that, when future taxable amounts are being scheduled, and a portion of a temporary difference has yet to originate, only the reversals of the *temporary difference at the balance sheet date* can be scheduled and multiplied by the tax rate that will be in effect when the difference reverses. Future originations (like the depreciation difference the second year) are not considered when determining the timing of the reversal. For the existing temporary difference, it is assumed that the difference will reverse the first year the difference begins reversing.

   Determine the amounts necessary to record income taxes for 2009 and prepare the appropriate journal entry.

P 16–7
Multiple temporary differences; nontemporary difference; calculate taxable income; balance sheet classification

● LO1 LO2 LO4 LO6 LO8

Sherrod, Inc., reported pretax accounting income of $76 million for 2009. The following information relates to differences between pretax accounting income and taxable income:

a. Income from installment sales of properties included in pretax accounting income in 2009 exceeded that reported for tax purposes by $3 million. The installment receivable account at year-end had a balance of $4 million (representing portions of 2008 and 2009 installment sales), expected to be collected equally in 2010 and 2011.
b. Sherrod was assessed a penalty of $2 million by the Environmental Protection Agency for violation of a federal law in 2009. The fine is to be paid in equal amounts in 2009 and 2010.
c. Sherrod rents its operating facilities but owns one asset acquired in 2008 at a cost of $80 million. Depreciation is reported by the straight-line method assuming a four-year useful life. On the tax return, deductions for depreciation will be more than straight-line depreciation the first two years but less than straight-line depreciation the next two years ($ in millions):

	Income Statement	Tax Return	Difference
2008	$20	$26	$ (6)
2009	20	35	(15)
2010	20	12	8
2011	20	7	13
	$80	$80	$ 0

d. Bad debt expense is reported using the allowance method, $3 million in 2009. For tax purposes, the expense is deducted when accounts prove uncollectible (the direct write-off method), $2 million in 2009. At December 31, 2009, the allowance for uncollectible accounts was $2 million (after adjusting entries). The balance was $1 million at the end of 2008.

e. In 2009, Sherrod accrued an expense and related liability for estimated paid future absences of $7 million relating to the company's new paid vacation program. Future compensation will be deductible on the tax return when actually paid during the next two years ($4 million in 2010; $3 million in 2011).

f. During 2008, accounting income included an estimated loss of $2 million from having accrued a loss contingency. The loss is paid in 2009 at which time it is tax deductible.

Balances in the deferred tax asset and deferred tax liability accounts at January 1, 2009, were $1.2 million and $2.8 million, respectively. The enacted tax rate is 40% each year.

Required:

1. Determine the amounts necessary to record income taxes for 2009 and prepare the appropriate journal entry.
2. What is the 2009 net income?
3. Show how any deferred tax amounts should be classified and reported in the 2009 balance sheet.

P 16–8
Multiple temporary differences; nontemporary difference; taxable income given; two years; balance sheet classification; change in tax rate

● LO1 LO2 LO4 LO4 LO6 LO8

Arndt, Inc., reported the following for 2009 and 2010 ($ in millions):

	2009	2010
Revenues	$888	$983
Expenses	760	800
Pretax accounting income (income statement)	$128	$183
Taxable income (tax return)	$120	$200
Tax rate: 40%		

a. Expenses each year include $30 million from a two-year casualty insurance policy purchased in 2009 for $60 million. The cost is tax-deductible in 2009.

b. Expenses include $2 million insurance premiums each year for life insurance on key executives.

c. Arndt sells one-year subscriptions to a weekly journal. Subscription sales collected and taxable in 2009 and 2010 were $33 million and $35 million, respectively. Subscriptions included in 2009 and 2010 financial reporting revenues were $25 million ($10 million collected in 2008 but not earned until 2009) and $33 million, respectively. Hint: View this as two temporary differences—one reversing in 2009; one originating in 2009.

d. 2009 expenses included a $17 million unrealized loss from reducing investments (classified as trading securities) to fair value. The investments were sold in 2010.

e. During 2008, accounting income included an estimated loss of $5 million from having accrued a loss contingency. The loss was paid in 2009 at which time it is tax deductible.

f. At January 1, 2009, Arndt had a deferred tax asset of $6 million and no deferred tax liability.

Required:

1. Which of the five differences described are temporary and which are nontemporary differences? Why?
2. Prepare a schedule that (a) reconciles the difference between pretax accounting income and taxable income and (b) determines the amounts necessary to record income taxes for 2009. Prepare the appropriate journal entry.
3. Show how any 2009 deferred tax amounts should be classified and reported on the 2009 balance sheet.
4. Prepare a schedule that (a) reconciles the difference between pretax accounting income and taxable income and (b) determines the amounts necessary to record income taxes for 2010. Prepare the appropriate journal entry.
5. Explain how any 2010 deferred tax amounts should be classified and reported on the 2010 balance sheet.
6. Suppose that during 2010, tax legislation was passed that will lower Arndt's effective tax rate to 35% beginning in 2011. Repeat requirement 4.

P 16–9
Single temporary difference originates each year for four years

● LO2

Alsup Consulting sometimes performs services for which it receives payment at the conclusion of the engagement, up to six months after services commence. Alsup recognizes service revenue for financial reporting purposes when the services are performed. For tax purposes, revenue is reported when fees are collected. Service revenue, collections, and pretax accounting income for 2008–2011 are as follows:

	Service Revenue	Collections	Pretax Accounting Income
2008	$650,000	$620,000	$186,000
2009	750,000	770,000	250,000
2010	715,000	700,000	220,000
2011	700,000	720,000	200,000

There are no differences between accounting income and taxable income other than the temporary difference described above. The enacted tax rate for each year is 40%.

Required:

1. Prepare the appropriate journal entry to record Alsup's 2009 income taxes.
2. Prepare the appropriate journal entry to record Alsup's 2010 income taxes.
3. Prepare the appropriate journal entry to record Alsup's 2011 income taxes.

(Hint: You may find it helpful to prepare a schedule that shows the balances in service revenue receivable at December 31, 2008–2011.)

P 16–10
Operating loss carryback and carryforward; temporary difference; nontemporary difference

● LO2 LO4 LO7

Fores Construction Company reported a pretax operating loss of $135 million for financial reporting purposes in 2009. Contributing to the loss were (a) a penalty of $5 million assessed by the Environmental Protection Agency for violation of a federal law and paid in 2009 and (b) an estimated loss of $10 million from accruing a loss contingency. The loss will be tax deductible when paid in 2010.

The enacted tax rate is 40%. There were no temporary differences at the beginning of the year and none originating in 2009 other than those described above. Taxable income in Fores's two previous years of operation was as follows:

2007	$75 million
2008	30 million

Required:

1. Prepare the journal entry to recognize the income tax benefit of the operating loss in 2009. Fores elects the carryback option.
2. Show the lower portion of the 2009 income statement that reports the income tax benefit of the operating loss.
3. Prepare the journal entry to record income taxes in 2010 assuming pretax accounting income is $60 million. No additional temporary differences originate in 2010.

P 16–11
Valuation allowance; General Motors Corporation

● LO3 LO8

Real World Financials

Here's an excerpt from a press release by **General Motors Corporation** in November 2007 announcing the largest deferred tax asset write-down ever:

> **DETROIT**—General Motors Corp. (NYSE: GM) today announced it will record a net non-cash charge of $39 billion for the third quarter of 2007 related to establishing a valuation allowance against its deferred tax assets (DTAs) in the U.S., Canada and Germany.
>
> *SFAS No. 109* guidelines require that a valuation allowance should now be established due to more recent events and developments during the 2007 third quarter. A significant negative factor was the company's three-year historical cumulative loss in the third quarter of 2007 in the U.S., Canada and Germany on an adjusted basis. Another significant factor was the ongoing weakness at GMAC Financial Services related to its Residential Capital, LLC (ResCap) mortgage business, including substantial U.S. losses incurred in 2007. Finally, the company faces more challenging near-term automotive market conditions in the U.S. and Germany.

The following is an excerpt from a disclosure note in GM's 2006 balance sheet:

Temporary differences and carryforwards that gave rise to deferred tax assets and liabilities included the following:

	December 31,			
	2006 Deferred Tax		2005 Deferred Tax	
	Assets	Liabilities	Assets	Liabilities
	($ in millions)			
Postretirement benefits other than pensions	18,609	—	12,757	—
Pension and other employee benefit plans	5,044	6,137	3,807	12,985
Warranties, dealer and customer allowances, claims, and discounts	4,070	47	6,739	52
Depreciation and amortization	6,098	2,008	5,713	2,584
Tax carryforwards	13,293	—	12,139	—
Lease transactions	—	199	—	4,351
Miscellaneous foreign	2,992	40	4,580	371
Other	8,240	2,194	10,922	3,677
Subtotal	58,346	10,625	56,657	24,020
Valuation allowances	(6,523)	—	(6,284)	—
Total deferred taxes	51,823	10,625	50,373	24,020
Net deferred tax assets	41,198		26,353	

Required:

1. As indicated in the note, GM had both deferred tax assets and deferred tax liabilities at the end of 2006. The balance sheet that year, though, reported only deferred tax assets. In fact, it reported both current and noncurrent deferred tax assets but no deferred tax liabilities. Explain why GM's deferred tax liabilities were not explicitly reported. Explain what the current and noncurrent deferred tax assets represent.
2. What is a valuation allowance against deferred tax assets? When must such an allowance be recorded? Use GM's situation to help illustrate your response. Assume an effective tax rate of 35%.
3. The press release mentions three items that influenced GM's decision to record a valuation allowance. Explain how each might bear upon the decision.
4. Is the write-down of deferred tax assets permanent? Under what circumstances might some or all of the $39 billion be reclaimed?

P 16–12
Integrating problem—bonds, leases, taxes

● LO2 LO5

The long-term liabilities section of CPS Transportation's December 31, 2008, balance sheet included the following:

a. A capital lease liability with 15 remaining lease payments of $10,000 each, due annually on January 1:

Lease liability	$76,061
Less current portion	2,394
	$73,667

The incremental borrowing rate at the inception of the lease was 11% and the lessor's implicit rate, which was known by CPS Transportation, was 10%.

b. A deferred income tax liability due to a single temporary difference. The only difference between CPS Transportation's taxable income and pretax accounting income is depreciation on a machine acquired on January 1, 2008, for $500,000. The machine's estimated useful life is five years, with no salvage value. Depreciation is computed using the straight-line method for financial reporting purposes and the MACRS method for tax purposes. Depreciation expense for tax and financial reporting purposes for 2009 through 2012 is as follows:

Year	MACRS Depreciation	Straight-line Depreciation	Difference
2009	$160,000	$100,000	$60,000
2010	80,000	100,000	(20,000)
2011	70,000	100,000	(30,000)
2012	60,000	100,000	(40,000)

The enacted federal income tax rates are 35% for 2008 and 40% for 2009 through 2012. For the year ended December 31, 2009, CPS's income before income taxes was $900,000.

On July 1, 2009, CPS Transportation issued $800,000 of 9% bonds. The bonds mature in 20 years and interest is payable each January 1 and July 1. The bonds were issued at a price to yield the investors 10%. CPS records interest at the effective interest rate.

Required:

1. Determine CPS Transportation's income tax expense and net income for the year ended December 31, 2009.
2. Determine CPS Transportation's interest expense for the year ended December 31, 2009.
3. Prepare the long-term liabilities section of CPS Transportation's December 31, 2009, balance sheet.

P 16–13
Temporary difference; nontemporary difference; application of FIN 48

● LO2 LO3 LO4 LO9

Tru Developers, Inc., sells plots of land for industrial development. Tru recognizes income for financial reporting purposes in the year it sells the plots. For some of the plots sold this year, Tru took the position that it could recognize the income for tax purposes when the installments are collected. Income that Tru recognized for financial reporting purposes in 2009 for plots in this category was $60 million. The company expected to collect 60% of each sale in 2010 and 40% in 2011. This amount over the next two years as follows:

2010	$36 million
2011	24 million
	$60 million

Tru's pretax accounting income for 2009 was $90 million. In its income statement, Tru reported interest income of $15 million, unrelated to the land sales, for which the company's position is that the interest is not taxable. Accordingly, the interest was not reported in the tax return. There are no differences between accounting income and taxable income other than those described above. The enacted tax rate is 40 percent.

Management believes the tax position taken on the land sales has a greater than 50% chance of being upheld based on its technical merits, but the position taken on the interest has a less than 50% chance of being upheld. It is further believed that the following likelihood percentages apply to the tax treatment of the land sales ($ in millions):

Amount Qualifying for Installment Sales Treatment	Percentage Likelihood of Tax Treatment Being Sustained
$60	20%
50	20%
40	20%
30	20%
20	20%

Required:

1. What portion of the tax benefit of tax-free interest will Tru recognize in its 2009 tax return?
2. What portion of the tax benefit of tax-free interest will Tru recognize in its 2009 financial statements?
3. What portion of the tax on the $60 million income from the plots sold on an installment basis will Tru defer in its 2009 tax return? What portion of the tax on the $60 million income from the plots sold on an installment basis will Tru defer in its 2009 financial statements? How is the difference between these two amounts reported?
4. Prepare the journal entry to record income taxes in 2009 assuming full recognition of the tax benefits in the financial statements of both differences between pretax accounting income and taxable income.
5. Prepare the journal entry to record income taxes in 2009 assuming the recognition of the tax benefits in the financial statements you indicated in requirements 1–3.

BROADEN YOUR PERSPECTIVE

Apply your critical-thinking ability to the knowledge you've gained. These cases will provide you an opportunity to develop your research, analysis, judgment, and communication skills. You also will work with other students, integrate what you've learned, apply it in real world situations, and consider its global and ethical ramifications. This practice will broaden your knowledge and further develop your decision-making abilities.

Analysis Case 16–1
Basic concepts

● LO1 through LO8

One of the longest debates in accounting history is the issue of deferred taxes. The controversy began in the 1940s and has continued, even after the FASB issued *Statement of Financial Accounting Standards No. 109* in 1992. At issue is the appropriate treatment of tax consequences of economic events that occur in years other than that of the events themselves.

Required:

1. Distinguish between temporary differences and permanent differences. Provide an example of each.
2. Distinguish between intraperiod tax allocation and interperiod tax allocation (deferred tax accounting). Provide an example of each.
3. How are deferred tax assets and deferred tax liabilities classified and reported in the financial statements?

Integrating Case 16–2
Postretirement benefits
● LO2

Statement of Financial Accounting Standards No. 106 establishes accounting standards for postretirement benefits other than pensions, most notably postretirement health care benefits. Essentially, the standard requires companies to accrue compensation expense each year employees perform services, for the expected cost of providing future postretirement benefits that can be attributed to that service. Typically, companies do not prefund these costs for two reasons: (a) unlike pension liabilities, no federal law requires companies to fund nonpension postretirement benefits and (b) funding contributions, again unlike for pension liabilities, are not tax deductible. (The costs aren't tax deductible until paid to, or on behalf of, employees.)

Required:

1. As a result of being required to record the periodic postretirement expense and related liability, most companies now report lower earnings and higher liabilities. How might many companies also report higher assets as a result of *SFAS 106?*
2. One objection to *SFAS 109,* "Accounting for Income Taxes," as cited in the chapter is the omission of requirements to discount deferred tax amounts to their present values. This objection is inappropriate in the context of deferred tax amounts necessitated by accounting for postretirement benefits. Why?

Judgment Case 16–3
Intraperiod tax allocation
● LO10

Russell-James Corporation is a diversified consumer products company. During 2009, Russell-James discontinued its line of cosmetics, which constituted discontinued operations for financial reporting purposes. As vice president of the food products division, you are interested in the effect of the discontinuance on the company's profitability. One item of information you requested was an income statement. The income statement you received was labeled *preliminary* and *unaudited:*

RUSSELL-JAMES CORPORATION
Income Statement
For the Year Ended December 31, 2009
($ in millions, except per share amounts)

Revenues		$300
Cost of goods sold		90
Gross profit		210
Selling and administrative expenses		(60)
Income from continuing operations before income taxes		150
Income taxes		(22)
Income from continuing operations		128
Discontinued operations:		
Loss from operations of cosmetics division	$(100)	
Gain from disposal of cosmetics division	15	(85)
Income before extraordinary item		43
Extraordinary loss from earthquake		(10)
Net income		$ 33
Per Share of Common Stock (100 million shares):		
Income from continuing operations		$1.28
Loss from operations of cosmetics division		(1.00)
Gain from disposal of cosmetics division		.15
Income before extraordinary item		.43
Extraordinary loss from earthquake		(.10)
Net income		$ .33

You are somewhat surprised at the magnitude of the loss incurred by the cosmetics division prior to its disposal. Another item that draws your attention is the apparently low tax rate indicated by the statement ($22 ÷ 150 = 15%). Upon further investigation you are told the company's tax rate is 40%.

Required:

1. Recast the income statement to reflect intraperiod tax allocation.
2. How would you reconcile the income tax expense shown on the statement above with the amount your recast statement reports?

Trueblood Accounting Case 16–4
Valuation allowance

● LO3

The following Trueblood case is recommended for use with this chapter. The case provides an excellent opportunity for class discussion, group projects, and writing assignments. The case, along with Professor's Discussion Material, can be obtained from the Deloitte Foundation at its website: **www.deloitte.com/us/truebloodcases.**

Case 07-6: *Graphic Inc.*

This case gives the students an opportunity to understand that judgment is involved in determining whether a valuation allowance should be recorded on deferred income tax assets. Students will identify and weigh positive and negative evidence to assess whether or how much of a valuation allowance should be recorded against an entity's deferred income tax assets.

Judgment Case 16–5
Analyzing the effect of deferred tax liabilities on firm risk; Fed Ex Corporation

● LO8

Real World Financials

The following is a portion of the 2007 balance sheet of **FedEx Corporation**:

	2007	2006
Liabilities and Stockholders' Investment		
Current Liabilities		
Current portion of long-term debt	$ 639	$ 850
Accrued salaries and employee benefits	1,354	1,325
Accounts payable	2,016	1,908
Accrued expenses	1,419	1,390
Total current liabilities	5,428	5,473
Long-Term Debt, Less Current Portion	2,007	1,592
Other Long-Term Liabilities		
Deferred income taxes	897	1,367
Pension, postretirement healthcare and other benefit obligations	1,164	944
Self-insurance accruals	759	692
Deferred lease obligations	655	658
Deferred gains, principally related to aircraft transactions	343	373
Other liabilities	91	80
Total other long-term liabilities	3,909	4,114
Commitments and Contingencies		
Common Stockholders' Investment		
Common stock, $0.10 par value; 800 million shares authorized; 308 million shares issued for 2007 and 306 million shares issued for 2006	31	31
Additional paid-in capital	1,689	1,438
Retained earnings	11,970	10,068
Accumulated other comprehensive loss	(1,030)	(24)
Treasury stock	(4)	(2)
Total common stockholders' investment	12,656	11,511
	$24,000	$22,690

FedEx's debt to equity ratio in 2007 was .90, calculated as $11,344 ÷ $12,656. Some analysts argue that long-term deferred tax liabilities should be excluded from liabilities when computing the debt to equity ratio.

Required:

1. What is the rationale for the argument that long-term deferred tax liabilities should be excluded from liabilities when computing the debt to equity ratio?
2. What would be the effect on FedEx's debt to equity ratio of excluding deferred tax liabilities from its calculation? What would be the percentage change?
3. What might be the rationale for not excluding long-term deferred tax liabilities from liabilities when computing the debt to equity ratio?

Integrating Case 16–6
Income taxes and investment securities; Dominion Resources

● LO1 LO2 LO8

Real World Financials

Dominion Resources, Inc., is one of the nation's largest producers of energy. Corporate headquarters are in Richmond, Va. The following is an excerpt from the company's 2006 annual report.

INVESTMENT SECURITIES (IN PART)

Available-for-sale securities are reported at fair value with realized gains and losses and any other-than-temporary declines in fair value included in other income and unrealized gains and losses reported as a component of AOCI, net of tax.

Dominion's statement of comprehensive income for 2006 reported an "Unrealized gain on investment securities, net of $83 million tax expense of $126 million."

Required:

1. Explain how investment securities classified as available for sale are accounted for.
2. What would have been Dominion's journal entry to reflect the 2006 fair value of the investments?

Communication Case 16–7
Deferred taxes, changing rates; write a memo

● LO1 LO4 LO5

You are the new controller for Engineered Solutions. The company treasurer, Randy Patey, believes that as a result of pending legislation, the current 40% income tax rate will be decreased for 2010 to 35% and is uncertain which tax rate to apply in determining deferred taxes for 2009. Patey also is uncertain which differences should be included in that determination and has solicited your help. Your accounting group provided you the following information.

Two items are relevant to the decisions. One is the $50,000 insurance premium the company pays annually for the CEO's life insurance policy for which the company is the beneficiary. The second is that Engineered Solutions purchased a building on January 1, 2008, for $6,000,000. The machine's estimated useful life is 30 years from the date of purchase, with no salvage value. Depreciation is computed using the straight-line method for financial reporting purposes and the MACRS method for tax purposes. As a result, the building's tax basis is $5,200,000 at December 31, 2009.

Required:

Write a memo to Patey that:

a. Identifies the objectives of accounting for income taxes.
b. Differentiates temporary differences and nontemporary differences.
c. Explains which tax rate to use.
d. Calculates the deferred tax liability at December 31, 2009.

Integrating Case 16–8
Tax effects of accounting changes and error correction; six situations

● LO1 LO2 LO8

Williams-Santana, Inc., is a manufacturer of high-tech industrial parts that was started in 1997 by two talented engineers with little business training. In 2009, the company was acquired by one of its major customers. As part of an internal audit, the following facts were discovered. The audit occurred during 2009 before any adjusting entries or closing entries were prepared. The income tax rate is 40% for all years.

a. A five-year casualty insurance policy was purchased at the beginning of 2007 for $35,000. The full amount was debited to insurance expense at the time.
b. On December 31, 2008, merchandise inventory was overstated by $25,000 due to a mistake in the physical inventory count using the periodic inventory system.
c. The company changed inventory cost methods to FIFO from LIFO at the end of 2009 for both financial statement and income tax purposes. The change will cause a $960,000 increase in the beginning inventory at January 1, 2008.
d. At the end of 2008, the company failed to accrue $15,500 of sales commissions earned by employees during 2008. The expense was recorded when the commissions were paid in early 2009.
e. At the beginning of 2007, the company purchased a machine at a cost of $720,000. Its useful life was estimated to be 10 years with no salvage value. The machine has been depreciated by the doubledeclining-balance method. Its carrying amount on December 31, 2008, was $460,800. On January 1, 2009, the company changed to the straight-line method.
f. Additional industrial robots were acquired at the beginning of 2006 and added to the company's assembly process. The $1,000,000 cost of the equipment was inadvertently recorded as repair expense. Robots have 10-year useful lives and no material salvage value. This class of equipment is depreciated by the straight-line method for both financial reporting and income tax reporting.

Required:

For each situation:

1. Identify whether it represents an accounting change or an error. If an accounting change, identify the type of change.
2. Prepare any journal entry necessary as a direct result of the change or error correction as well as any adjusting entry for 2009 related to the situation described. Any tax effects should be adjusted for through the deferred tax liability account.
3. Briefly describe any other steps that should be taken to appropriately report the situation.

Real World Case 16–9
Disclosure issues; balance sheet classifications

● LO1 LO2 LO8

Real World Financials

The income tax disclosure note accompanying the 2007 financial statements of the **Walgreen Company** is reproduced below:

(6) Income Taxes

The provision for income taxes consists of the following (In Millions):

	2007	2006	2005
Current provision			
Federal	$1,027.9	$ 970.1	$841.4
State	96.7	137.4	125.5
	1,124.6	1,107.5	966.9
Deferred provision			
Federal	18.3	(88.8)	(57.8)
State	4.9	(15.2)	(13.0)
	23.2	(104.0)	(70.8)
	$1,147.8	$1,003.5	$896.1

The deferred tax assets and liabilities included in the Consolidated Balance Sheets consist of the following (In Millions):

	2007	2006
Deferred tax assets		
Compensation and benefits	$ 203.7	$ 177.8
Insurance	191.5	178.4
Postretirement benefits	179.4	126.1
Accrued rent	135.3	130.5
Inventory	44.7	41.0
Legal	44.1	18.8
Other	159.7	103.0
	958.4	775.6
Deferred tax liabilities		
Accelerated depreciation	702.6	643.7
Inventory	199.0	142.1
Intangible assets	85.5	—
Other	72.2	30.9
	1,059.3	816.7
Net deferred tax liabilities	$ 100.9	$ 41.1

Income taxes paid were $1.204 billion, $1.111 billion and $928.2 million during the fiscal years ended August 31, 2007, 2006 and 2005, respectively.

Required:

1. In its 2007 balance sheet, Walgreen reported as a noncurrent liability, "Deferred income taxes" of $158.2 million. Why is this different from the $100.9 million "net deferred tax liability" reported in the disclosure note?
2. Re-create the journal entry that summarizes the entries Walgreen used to record its 2007 income taxes.

Research Case 16–10

Researching the way tax deductions are reported on a corporation tax return; retrieving a tax form from the Internet

● LO1 LO2 LO3 LO8

The U.S. Treasury maintains an information site on the Internet. As part of this site the Internal Revenue Service provides tax information and services. Among those services is a server for publications and forms which allows a visitor to download a variety of IRS forms and publications.

Required:

1. Access the Treasury site on the Internet. The web address is www.ustreas.gov. After exploring the information available there, navigate to the IRS server for forms and publications via the IRS home page.
2. Download the corporation tax return, Form 1120.
3. Note the specific deductions listed that are deductible from total income to arrive at taxable income. Are any deductions listed that might not also be included among expenses on the income statement?
4. One of the deductions indicated is "net operating loss deduction." Under what circumstances might a company report an amount for this item?
5. Based on how taxable income is determined, how might temporary differences be created between taxable income and pretax income on the income statement?

Analysis Case 16–11
Reporting deferred taxes

● LO1 LO2 LO3 LO7 LO8

Real World Financials

Google

Refer to the financial statements and related disclosure notes of Google Inc. included with all new copies of the book. In Google's balance sheet, deferred income taxes in 2006 are reported as both an asset ($29.7 million) and a liability ($40.4 million).

Required:

1. Explain why deferred income taxes can be reported as both an asset and a liability. Why is the deferred tax asset reported as current and the deferred tax liability as long term in 2006? Is that also the situation in 2007?
2. Note 13 in the disclosure notes indicates that deferred tax assets are $100.7 million in 2006 and deferred tax liabilities are $111.4 million. How can that be explained in light of the two amounts reported in the balance sheet?
3. Does Google feel the need to record a valuation allowance for its deferred tax assets?

Analysis Case 16–12
Consult financial statements; analyze tax disclosures; recreate journal entry

● LO1 LO2 LO3 LO7 LO8

Real World Financials

Kroger Co. is one of the largest retail food companies in the United States as measured by total annual sales. The Kroger Co. operates supermarkets, convenience stores, and manufactures and processes food that its supermarkets sell. Kroger's stores operate under names such as Dillon Food Stores, City Market, Sav-Mor, Kwik Shop, and Ralph's.

Like most corporations, Kroger has significant deferred tax assets and liabilities resulting from accounting for income taxes in accordance with *SFAS 109.* Using Edgar, (www.sec.gov.com/) or the company's website check the company's annual report for the year ended February 1, 2007.

Required:

1. From the income statement, determine the income tax expense for the year. What is the current portion and the deferred portion of the expense? (See the "Taxes Based on Income" note in the Notes to Consolidated Financial Statements.) Why is the income tax expense from the income statement different from the "provision for income taxes in the disclosure note"?
2. How are the deferred taxes classified in Kroger's balance sheet? (See the "Taxes Based on Income" note in the Notes to Consolidated Financial Statements.) What amounts are reported among current assets or liabilities and among noncurrent assets or liabilities? Why?

CPA SIMULATION 16–1

Kerry Oil
Deferred Taxes

CPA Review

Test your knowledge of the concepts discussed in this chapter, practice critical professional skills necessary for career success, and prepare for the computer-based CPA exam by accessing our CPA simulations at the text website: www.mhhe.com/spiceland5e.

The Kerry Oil simulation tests your knowledge of the financial reporting implications of income taxes.

As on the CPA exam itself, you will be asked to use tools including a spreadsheet, a calculator, and professional accounting standards, to conduct research, derive solutions, and communicate conclusions related to these issues in a simulated environment headed by the following interactive tabs:

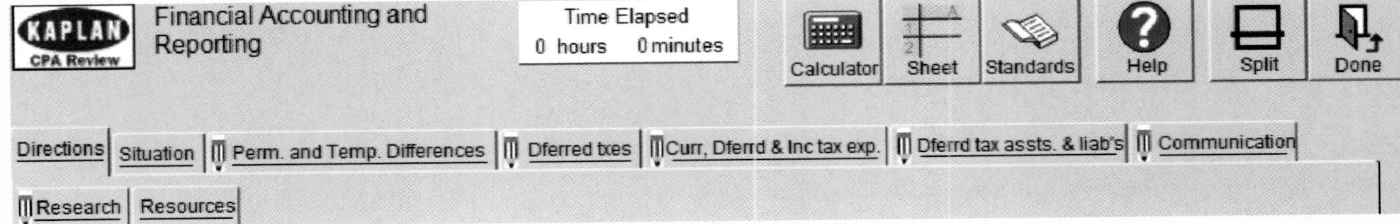

Specific tasks in the simulation include:

- Demonstrating an understanding of temporary and nontemporary differences.
- Analyze transactions for their deferred tax reporting implications.
- Calculating the current and deferred tax components of income tax expense for multiple temporary differences.
- Applying judgment in deciding the deferred tax effects of a variety of transactions.
- Communicating the deferred tax effects of the two deferred tax reporting issues.
- Researching factors that might influence whether a valuation allowance might not be required in spite of evidence to the contrary.

17 CHAPTER

Pensions and Other Postretirement Benefits

/// OVERVIEW

Employee compensation comes in many forms. Salaries and wages, of course, provide direct and current payment for services provided. However, it's commonplace for compensation also to include benefits payable after retirement. We discuss pension benefits and other postretirement benefits in this chapter. Accounting for pension benefits recognizes that they represent deferred compensation for current service. Accordingly, the cost of these benefits is recognized on an accrual basis during the years that employees earn the benefits.

LEARNING OBJECTIVES

After studying this chapter, you should be able to:

- **LO1** Explain the fundamental differences between a defined contribution pension plan and a defined benefit pension plan.
- **LO2** Distinguish among the vested benefit obligation, the accumulated benefit obligation, and the projected benefit obligation.
- **LO3** Describe the five events that might change the balance of the PBO.
- **LO4** Explain how plan assets accumulate to provide retiree benefits and understand the role of the trustee in administering the fund.
- **LO5** Describe the funded status of pension plans and how that amount is reported.
- **LO6** Describe how pension expense is a composite of periodic changes that occur in both the pension obligation and the plan assets.
- **LO7** Record for pension plans the periodic expense and funding as well as new gains and losses and new prior service cost as they occur.
- **LO8** Understand the interrelationships among the elements that constitute a defined benefit pension plan.
- **LO9** Describe the nature of postretirement benefit plans other than pensions and identify the similarities and differences in accounting for those plans and pensions.
- **LO10** Explain how the obligation for postretirement benefits is measured and how the obligation changes.
- **LO11** Determine the components of postretirement benefit expense.

FINANCIAL REPORTING CASE

United Dynamics

You read yesterday that many companies in the United States have pension plans that are severely underfunded. This caught your attention in part because you have your office interview tomorrow with United Dynamics. You hadn't really thought that much about the pension plan of your potential future employer, in part because your current employer has a defined contribution 401K plan, for which funding is not a concern. However, United Dynamics is an older firm with a defined benefit plan, for which funding is the employer's responsibility.

To prepare for your interview, you obtained a copy of United Dynamics' financial statements. Unfortunately, the financial statements themselves are of little help. You are unable to find any pension liability on the balance sheet, but the statement does report a relatively small "pension asset." The income statement reports pension expense for each of the years reported. For help, you search the disclosure notes. In part, the pension disclosure note reads as follows:

Note 7: Pension Plan

United Dynamics has a defined benefit pension plan covering substantially all of its employees. Plan benefits are based on years of service and the employee's compensation during the last three years of employment. The company's funding policy is consistent with the funding requirements of federal law and regulations. The net periodic pension expense for the company included the following components. The company's pension expense was as follows ($ in millions):

	2009	2008	2007
Current service costs	$ 43	$ 47	$ 42
Interest cost on projected benefit obligation	178	164	152
Return on assets	(213)	(194)	(187)
Amortization of prior service cost	43	43	43
Amortization of net gain	(2)	(1)	—
Net pension costs	$ 49	$ 59	$ 50

(continued)

By the time you finish this chapter, you should be able to respond appropriately to the questions posed in this case. Compare your response to the solution provided at the end of the chapter.

QUESTIONS ///

1. Why is underfunding not a concern in your present employment? (page 885)
2. Were you correct that the pension liability is not reported on the balance sheet? What is the liability? (page 887)
3. What is the amount of the plan assets available to pay benefits? What are the factors that can cause that amount to change? (page 893)
4. What does the "pension asset" represent? Are you interviewing with a company whose pension plan is severely underfunded? (page 894)
5. How is the pension expense influenced by changes in the pension liability and plan assets? (page 895)

(concluded)

The following table describes the change in projected benefit obligation for the plan years ended December 31, 2009, and December 31, 2008 ($ in millions):

	2009	2008
Projected benefit obligation at beginning of year	$2,194	$2,121
Service cost	43	47
Interest cost	178	164
Actuarial (gain) loss	319	(40)
Benefits paid	(106)	(98)
Projected benefit obligation at end of year	$2,628	$2,194

The weighted-average discount rate and rate of increase in future compensation levels used in determining the actuarial present value of the projected benefit obligations in the above table were 8.1% and 4.3%, respectively, at December 31, 2009, and 7.73% and 4.7%, respectively, at December 31, 2008. The expected long-term rate of return on assets was 9.1% at December 31, 2009 and 2008.

The following table describes the change in the fair value of plan assets for the plan years ended December 31, 2009 and 2008 ($ in millions):

	2009	2008
Fair value of plan assets at beginning of year	$2,340	$2,133
Actual return on plan assets	215	178
Employer contributions	358	127
Benefits paid	(106)	(98)
Fair value of plan assets at end of year	$2,807	$2,340

"Ouch! I can't believe how much of my accounting I forgot," you complain to yourself. "I'd better get out my old intermediate accounting book."

PART A THE NATURE OF PENSION PLANS

Over 60 million American workers are covered by pension plans. The United States' pension funds tripled in size during the previous two decades and now are roughly the size of Japan's gross national product. This powerful investment base now controls about one-fourth of the stock market. At the company level, the enormous size of pension funds is reflected in a periodic pension cost that constitutes one of the largest expenses many companies report. The corporate liability for providing pension benefits, though largely off-balance-sheet, is huge. Obviously, then, the financial reporting responsibility for pensions has important social and economic implications.

Pension plans are designed to provide income to individuals during their retirement years. This is accomplished by setting aside funds during an employee's working years so that at retirement the accumulated funds plus earnings from investing those funds are available to replace wages. Actually, an individual who periodically invests in stocks, bonds, certificates of deposit (CDs), or other investments for the purpose of saving for retirement is establishing a personal pension fund. Often, such individual plans take the form of individual retirement accounts (IRAs) to take advantage of tax breaks offered by that arrangement. In employer plans, some or all of the periodic contributions to the retirement fund often are provided by the employer.

Pension plans often enhance productivity, reduce turnover, satisfy union demands, and allow employers to compete in the labor market.

Corporations establish pension plans for a variety of reasons. Sponsorship of pension plans provides employees with a degree of retirement security and fulfills a moral obligation felt by many employers. This security also can induce a degree of job satisfaction and perhaps loyalty that might enhance productivity and reduce turnover. Motivation to sponsor a plan sometimes comes from union demands and often relates to being competitive in the labor market.

ADDITIONAL CONSIDERATION

When established according to tight guidelines, a pension plan gains important tax advantages. Such arrangements are called *qualified plans* because they qualify for favorable tax treatment. In a qualified plan, the employer is permitted an immediate tax deduction for amounts paid into the pension fund (within specified limits). The employees, on the other hand, are not taxed at the time employer contributions are made—only when retirement benefits are received. Moreover, earnings on the funds set aside by the employer are not taxed while in the pension fund, so the earnings accumulate tax free. If you are familiar with the tax advantages of IRAs, you probably recognize the similarity between those individual plans and corporate pension arrangements.

For a pension plan to be qualified for special tax treatment it must meet these general requirements.

1. It must cover at least 70% of employees.
2. It cannot discriminate in favor of highly compensated employees.
3. It must be funded in advance of retirement through contributions to an irrevocable trust fund.
4. Benefits must vest after a specified period of service, commonly five years. (We discuss this in more detail later.)
5. It complies with specific restrictions on the timing and amount of contributions and benefits.

Qualified pension plans offer important tax benefits.

LO1

Sometimes, employers agree to annually contribute a specific (defined) amount to a pension fund on behalf of employees but make no commitment regarding benefit amounts at retirement. In other arrangements, employers don't specify the amount of annual contributions but promise to provide determinable (defined) amounts at retirement. These two arrangements describe defined contribution pension plans and defined benefit pension plans, respectively:

- **Defined contribution pension plans** promise fixed annual contributions to a pension fund (say, 5% of the employees' pay). Employees choose (from designated options) where funds are invested—usually stocks or fixed-income securities. Retirement pay depends on the size of the fund at retirement.
- **Defined benefit pension plans** promise fixed retirement benefits defined by a designated formula. Typically, the pension formula bases retirement pay on the employees' (a) years of service, (b) annual compensation (often final pay or an average for the last few years), and sometimes (c) age. Employers are responsible for ensuring that sufficient funds are available to provide promised benefits.

Today, more than two-thirds of workers covered by pension plans are covered by defined contribution plans, fewer than one-third by defined benefit plans. This represents a radical shift from previous years when the traditional defined benefit plan was far more common. However, very few new pension plans are of the defined benefit variety. In fact, many companies are terminating long-standing defined benefit plans and substituting defined contribution plans. Why the shift? There are three main reasons:

Virtually all new pension plans are defined contribution plans.

1. Government regulations make defined benefit plans cumbersome and costly to administer.
2. Employers are increasingly unwilling to bear the risk of defined benefit plans; with defined contribution plans, the company's obligation ends when contributions are made.
3. There has been a shift among many employers from trying to "buy long-term loyalty" (with defined benefit plans) to trying to attract new talent (with more mobile defined contribution plans).

The two categories of pension plans are depicted in Graphic 17–1.

GRAPHIC 17–1
Defined Contribution and Defined Benefit Pension Plans

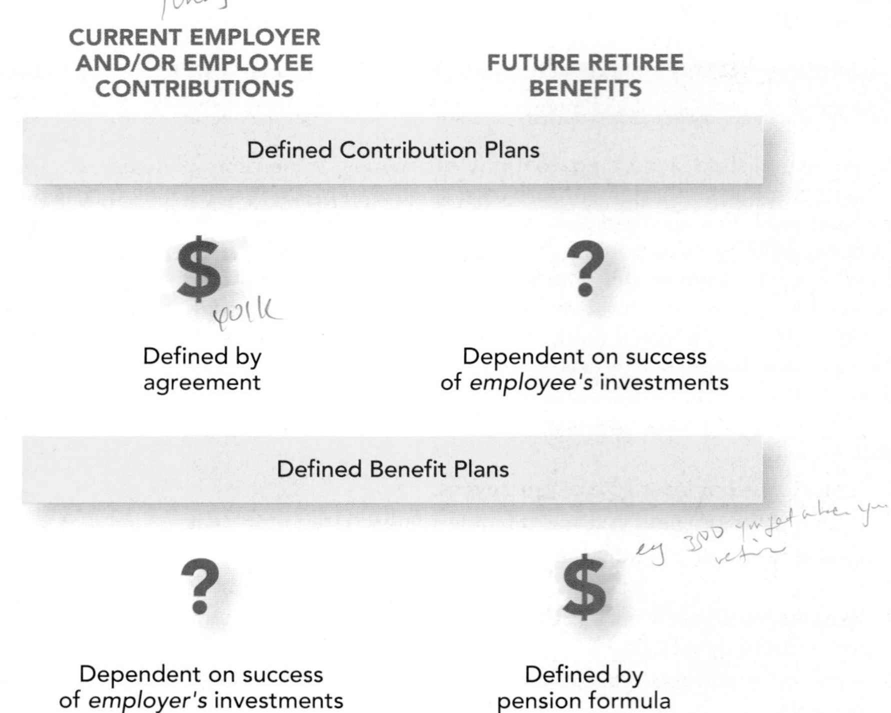

Both types of plans have a common goal: to provide income to employees during their retirement years. Still, the two types of plans differ regarding who bears the risk—the employer or the employees—for whether the retirement objectives are achieved. The two types of plans also have entirely different implications for accounting and financial reporting. Our discussion of defined contribution plans will be brief. Although these are now the most popular type of corporate pension plan, their relative simplicity permits a rather straightforward accounting treatment that requires little explanation. On the other hand, defined benefit plans require considerably more complex accounting treatment and constitute the primary focus of this chapter.

Defined Contribution Pension Plans

Defined contribution plans promise defined periodic contributions to a pension fund, without further commitment regarding benefit amounts at retirement.

Defined contribution pension plans are becoming increasingly popular vehicles for employers to provide retirement income without the paperwork, cost, and risk generated by the more traditional defined benefit plans. Defined contribution plans promise fixed periodic contributions to a pension fund. Retirement income depends on the size of the fund at retirement. No further commitment is made by the employer regarding benefit amounts at retirement.

These plans have several variations. In money purchase plans, employers contribute a fixed percentage of employees' salaries. Thrift plans, savings plans, and 401(k) plans (named after the Tax Code section that specifies the conditions for the favorable tax treatment of these plans) permit voluntary contributions by employees. These contributions typically are matched to a specified extent by employers. Over 70% of American workers participate in 401(k) plans. More than two trillion dollars are invested in these plans.

When plans link the amount of contributions to company performance, labels include profit-sharing plans, incentive savings plans, 401(k) profit-sharing plans, and similar titles. When employees make contributions to the plan in addition to employer contributions, it's called a *contributory* plan. Sometimes the amount the employer contributes is tied to the amount of the employee contribution.[1] Variations are seemingly endless. An example from a recent annual report of **Cisco Systems** is re-created in Graphic 17–2.

[1] One popular way for employer companies to provide contributions is with shares of its own common stock. If so, the arrangements usually are designed to comply with government requirements to be designated an employee stock ownership plan (ESOP).

Note 10: Employee Benefit Plans (in part)
Employee 401(k) Plans. The Company sponsors the Cisco Systems, Inc. 401(k) Plan (the "Plan") to provide retirement benefits for its employees. As allowed under Section 401(k) of the Internal Revenue Code, the Plan provides for tax-deferred salary contributions for eligible employees. The Plan allows employees to contribute from 1% to 25% of their annual compensation to the Plan on a pretax and after-tax basis. Employee contributions are limited to a maximum annual amount as set periodically by the Internal Revenue Code. The Company matches pretax employee contributions up to 100% of the first 4% of eligible earnings that are contributed by employees. All matching contributions vest immediately. The Company's matching contributions to the Plan totaled $131 million, $96 million, and $84 million in fiscal 2007, 2006, and 2005, respectively.

GRAPHIC 17–2
Defined Contribution Plan—Cisco Systems

Real World Financials

Accounting for these plans is quite easy. Each year, the employer simply records pension expense equal to the amount of the annual contribution. Suppose a plan promises an annual contribution equal to 3% of an employee's salary. If an employee's salary is $110,000 in a particular year, the employer would simply recognize pension expense in the amount of the contribution:

FINANCIAL Reporting Case

Q1, p. 881

Pension expense	3,300	
Cash ($110,000 × 3%)		3,300

For defined contribution plans, the employer simply records pension expense equal to the cash contribution.

The employee's retirement benefits are totally dependent upon how well investments perform. Who bears the risk (or reward) of that uncertainty? The employee would bear the risk of uncertain investment returns and, potentially, settle for far less at retirement than at first expected.[2] On the other hand, the employer would be free of any further obligation. Because the actual investments are held by an independent investment firm, the employer is free of that recordkeeping responsibility as well.

Risk is reversed in a defined benefit plan. Because specific benefits are promised at retirement, the employer would be responsible for making up the difference when investment performance is less than expected. We look at defined benefit plans next.

Defined Benefit Pension Plans

Defined benefit plans promise fixed retirement benefits defined by a designated formula.

When setting aside cash to fund a pension plan, the uncertainty surrounding the rate of return on plan assets is but one of several uncertainties inherent in a defined benefit plan. Employee turnover affects the number of employees who ultimately will become eligible for retirement benefits. The age at which employees will choose to retire as well as life expectancies will impact both the length of the retirement period and the amount of the benefits. Inflation, future compensation levels, and interest rates also have obvious influence on eventual benefits.

Uncertainties complicate determining how much to set aside each year to ensure that sufficient funds are available to provide promised benefits.

This is particularly true when pension benefits are defined by a pension formula, as usually is the case. A typical formula might specify that a retiree will receive annual retirement benefits based on the employee's years of service and annual pay at retirement (say, pay level in the final year, highest pay achieved, or average pay in the last two or more years). For example, a pension formula might define annual retirement benefits as:

1½% × Years of service × Final year's salary

By this formula, the annual benefits to an employee who retires after 30 years of service, with a final salary of $100,000, would be:

1½% × 30 years × $100,000 = $45,000

[2]Of course, this is not entirely unappealing to the employee. Defined contribution plans allow an employee to select investments in line with his or her own risk preferences and often provide greater retirement benefits and flexibility than defined benefit plans.

A pension formula typically defines retirement pay based on the employees' (a) years of service, (b) annual compensation, and sometimes (c) age.

Typically, a firm will hire an actuary, a professional trained in a particular branch of statistics and mathematics, to assess the various uncertainties (employee turnover, salary levels, mortality, etc.) and to estimate the company's obligation to employees in connection with its pension plan. Such estimates are inherently subjective, so regardless of the skill of the actuary, estimates invariably deviate from the actual outcome to one degree or another.[3] For instance, the return on assets can turn out to be more or less than expected. These deviations are referred to as *gains* and *losses* on pension assets. When it's necessary to revise estimates related to the pension obligation because it's determined to be more or less than previously thought, these revisions are referred to as *losses* and *gains,* respectively, on the pension liability. Later, we will discuss the accounting treatment of gains and losses from either source. The point here is that the risk of the pension obligation changing unexpectedly or the pension funds being inadequate to meet the obligation is borne by the employer with a defined benefit pension plan.

Pension gains and losses occur when the *pension obligation* is lower or higher than expected.

Pension gains and losses occur when the *return on plan assets* is higher or lower than expected.

The key elements of a defined benefit pension plan are:

1. The *employer's obligation* to pay retirement benefits in the future.
2. The *plan assets* set aside by the employer from which to pay the retirement benefits in the future.
3. The *periodic expense* of having a pension plan.

Neither the pension obligation nor the plan assets are reported individually in the balance sheet.

As you will learn in this chapter, the first two of these elements are not reported individually in the financial statements. This may seem confusing at first because it is inconsistent with the way you're accustomed to treating assets and liabilities. Even though they are not separately reported, it's critical that you understand the composition of both the pension obligation and the plan assets because (a) they are reported as a net amount in the balance sheet, and (b) their balances are reported in disclosure notes. And, importantly, the pension expense reported in the income statement is a direct composite of periodic changes that occur in both the pension obligation and the plan assets.

The pension expense is a direct composite of periodic changes that occur in both the pension obligation and the plan assets.

For this reason, we will devote a considerable portion of our early discussion to understanding the composition of the pension obligation and the plan assets before focusing on the derivation of pension expense and required financial statement disclosures. We will begin with a quick overview of how periodic changes that occur in both the pension obligation and the plan assets affect pension expense. Next we will explore how those changes occur, beginning with changes in the pension obligation followed by changes in plan assets. We'll then return to pension expense for a closer look at how those changes influence its calculation. After that, we will bring together the separate but related parts by using a simple spreadsheet to demonstrate how each element of the pension plan articulates with the other elements.

> In applying accrual accounting to pensions, this *Statement (87)* retains three fundamental aspects of past pension accounting: *delayed recognition* of certain events, reporting *net cost,* and *offsetting* liabilities and assets. Those three features of practice have shaped financial reporting for many years . . . and they conflict in some respects with accounting principles applied elsewhere.[4]

Pension Expense—An Overview

The annual pension expense reflects changes in both the pension obligation and the plan assets. Graphic 17–3 provides a brief overview of how these changes are included in pension expense. After the overview, we'll look closer at each of the components.

Next we explore each of these pension expense components in the context of its being a part of either (a) the pension obligation or (b) the plan assets. After you learn how the expense components relate to these elements of the pension plan, we'll return to explore further how they are included in the pension expense.

---

[3]We discuss changes in more detail in Chapter 20.

[4]"Employers' Accounting for Pensions," *Statement of Financial Accounting Standards No. 87* (Stamford, Conn.: FASB, 1985).

GRAPHIC 17–3
Components of Pension Expense

Components of Pension Expense

+	**Service cost** ascribed to employee service during the period
+	**Interest** accrued on the pension liability
−	**Return** on the plan assets*
	Amortized portion of:
+	**Prior service cost** attributed to employee service before an amendment to the pension plan
+ or (−)	**Losses or (gains)** from revisions in the pension liability or from investing plan assets
=	**Pension expense**

*The actual return is adjusted for any difference between actual and expected return, resulting in the *expected* return being reflected in pension expense. This loss or gain from investing plan assets is combined with losses and gains from revisions in the pension liability for deferred inclusion in pension expense. (See the last component of pension expense.)

Interest and investment return are financing aspects of the pension cost.

The recognition of some elements of the pension expense is delayed.

PART B

THE PENSION OBLIGATION AND PLAN ASSETS

The Pension Obligation

FINANCIAL Reporting Case

Q2, p. 881

Now we consider more precisely what is meant by the pension obligation. Unfortunately, there's not just one definition, nor is there uniformity concerning which definition is most appropriate for pension accounting. Actually, three different ways to measure the pension obligation have meaning in pension accounting, as shown in Graphic 17–4.

GRAPHIC 17–4
Ways to Measure the Pension Obligation

1. **Accumulated benefit obligation (ABO)** The actuary's estimate of the total retirement benefits (at their discounted present value) earned so far by employees, applying the pension formula using existing compensation levels.
2. **Vested benefit obligation (VBO)** The portion of the accumulated benefit obligation that plan participants are entitled to receive regardless of their continued employment.
3. **Projected benefit obligation (PBO)** The actuary's estimate of the total retirement benefits (at their discounted present value) earned so far by employees, applying the pension formula using estimated future compensation levels. (If the pension formula does not include future compensation levels, the PBO and the ABO are the same.)

Later you will learn that the projected benefit obligation is the basis for some elements of the periodic pension expense. Remember, there is but one obligation; these are three ways to measure it. The relationship among the three is depicted in Graphic 17–5 on the next page.

Now let's look closer at how the obligation is measured in each of these three ways. Keep in mind, though, that it's not the accountant's responsibility to actually derive the measurement; a professional actuary provides these numbers. However, for the accountant to effectively use the numbers provided, she or he must understand their derivation.

● LO2

Vested Benefit Obligation

Suppose an employee leaves the company to take another job. Will she still get earned benefits at retirement? The answer depends on whether the benefits are vested under the terms of this particular pension plan. If benefits are fully vested—yes. **Vested benefits** are those that employees have the right to receive even if their employment were to cease today.

Pension plans typically require some minimum period of employment before benefits vest. Before the Employee Retirement Income Security Act (ERISA) was passed in 1974, horror stories relating to lost benefits were commonplace. It was possible, for example, for an employee to be dismissed a week before retirement and be left with no pension benefits. Vesting requirements were tightened drastically to protect employees. These requirements have been changed periodically since then. Beginning in 1989, benefits must vest (a) fully within five years or (b) 20% within three years with another 20% vesting each subsequent

The benefits of most pension plans vest after five years.

GRAPHIC 17–5
Alternative Measures of the Pension Obligation

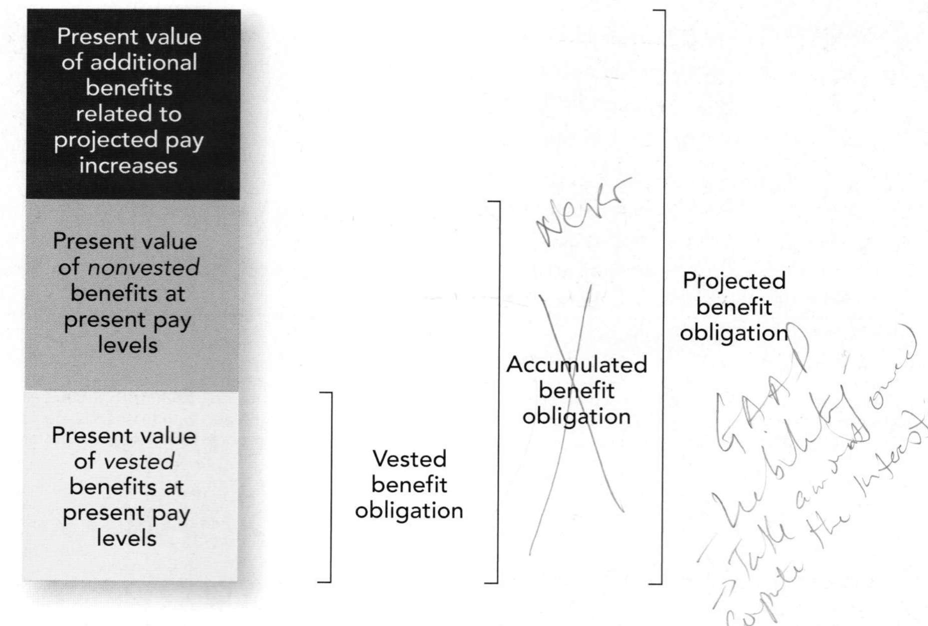

year until fully vested after seven years. Five-year vesting is most common. ERISA also established the Pension Benefit Guaranty Corporation (PBGC) to impose liens on corporate assets for unfunded pension liabilities in certain instances and to administer terminated pension plans. The PBGC is financed by premiums from employers equal to specified amounts for each covered employee. It makes retirement payments for terminated plans and guarantees basic vested benefits when pension liabilities exceed assets.

Accumulated Benefit Obligation

The *accumulated benefit obligation* ignores possible pay increases in the future.

The **accumulated benefit obligation (ABO)** is an estimate of the discounted present value of the retirement benefits earned so far by employees, applying the plan's pension formula using existing compensation levels. When we look at a detailed calculation of the projected benefit obligation below, keep in mind that simply substituting the employee's existing compensation in the pension formula for her projected salary at retirement would give us the accumulated benefit obligation.

Projected Benefit Obligation

● LO3

As described earlier, when the ABO is estimated, the most recent salary is included in the pension formula to estimate future benefits, even if the pension formula specifies the final year's salary. No attempt is made to forecast what that salary would be the year before retirement. Of course, the most recent salary certainly offers an objective number to measure the obligation, but is it realistic? Since it's unlikely that there will be no salary increases between now and retirement, a more meaningful measurement should include a projection of what the salary might be at retirement.[5] Measured this way, the liability is referred to as the **projected benefit obligation (PBO)**. The PBO measurement may be less reliable than the ABO but is more relevant and representationally faithful.

The *PBO* estimates retirement benefits by applying the pension formula using projected future compensation levels.

To understand the concepts involved, it's helpful to look at a numerical example. We'll simplify the example (Illustration 17–1) by looking at how pension amounts would be determined for a single employee. Keep in mind though, that in actuality, calculations would be made (by the actuary) for the entire employee pool rather than on an individual-by-individual basis.

[5]To project future salaries for a group of employees, actuaries usually assume some percentage rate of increase in compensation levels in upcoming years. Recent estimates of the rate of compensation increase have ranged from 4.5% to 7.5% with 4.5% being the most commonly reported expectation (AICPA, *Accounting Trends and Techniques*, 2007).

Jessica Farrow was hired by Global Communications in 1998. The company has a defined benefit pension plan that specifies annual retirement benefits equal to:

1.5% × Service years × Final year's salary

Farrow is expected to retire in 2037 after 40 years service. Her retirement period is expected to be 20 years. At the end of 2007, 10 years after being hired, her salary is $100,000. The interest rate is 6%. The company's actuary projects Farrow's salary to be $400,000 at retirement.*

What is the company's projected benefit obligation with respect to Jessica Farrow?

Steps to calculate the projected benefit obligation:

1. Use the pension formula (including a projection of future salary levels) to determine the retirement benefits earned to date.
2. Find the present value of the retirement benefits as of the retirement date.
3. Find the present value of retirement benefits as of the current date.

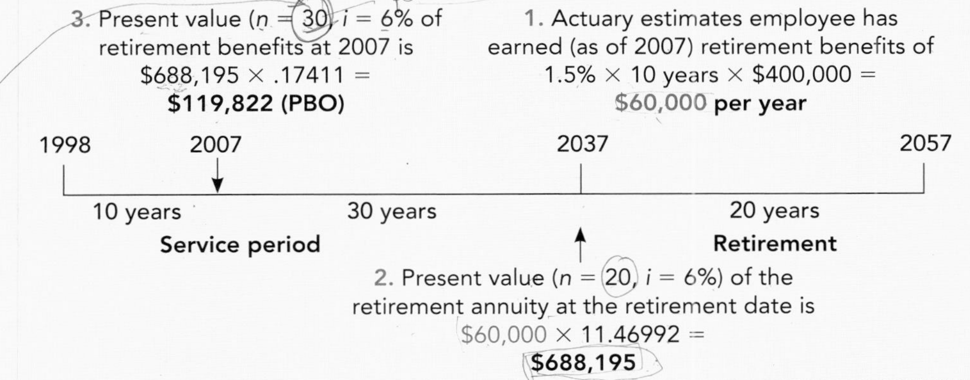
3. Present value (n = 30, i = 6% of retirement benefits at 2007 is
$688,195 × .17411 =
$119,822 (PBO)
1. Actuary estimates employee has earned (as of 2007) retirement benefits of
1.5% × 10 years × $400,000 =
$60,000 per year
1998
2007
2037
2057
10 years
30 years
20 years
Service period
Retirement
2. Present value (n = 20, i = 6%) of the retirement annuity at the retirement date is
$60,000 × 11.46992 =
$688,195

ILLUSTRATION 17–1

Projected Benefit Obligation

The actuary includes projected salaries in the pension formula. The projected benefit obligation is the present value of those benefits.

Using Excel, enter:
=PV(.06,20,60000)
Output: 688195

Using a calculator:
enter: N 20 I 6
PMT −60000 FV
Output: PV 688195

*This salary reflects an estimated compound rate of increase of about 5% and should take into account expectations concerning inflation, promotions, productivity gains, and other factors that might influence salary levels.

If the actuary's estimate of the final salary hasn't changed, the PBO a year later at the end of 2008 would be $139,715 as demonstrated in Illustration 17–1A.

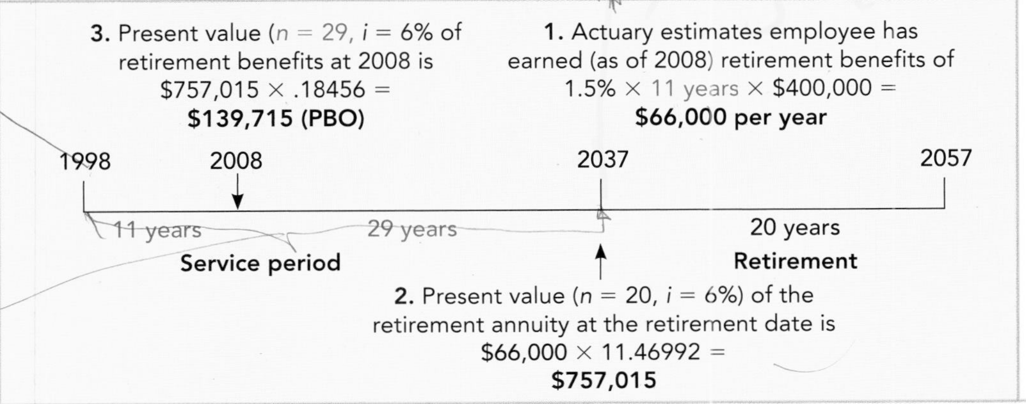
3. Present value (n = 29, i = 6% of retirement benefits at 2008 is
$757,015 × .18456 =
$139,715 (PBO)
1. Actuary estimates employee has earned (as of 2008) retirement benefits of
1.5% × 11 years × $400,000 =
$66,000 per year
1998
2008
2037
2057
11 years
29 years
20 years
Service period
Retirement
2. Present value (n = 20, i = 6%) of the retirement annuity at the retirement date is
$66,000 × 11.46992 =
$757,015

ILLUSTRATION 17–1A

PBO in 2008

In 2008 the pension formula includes one more service year.

Also, 2008 is one year closer to the retirement date for the purpose of calculating the present value.

CHANGES IN THE PBO. Notice that the PBO increased during 2008 (Illustration 17–1A) from $119,822 to $139,715 for two reasons:

1. One more service year is included in the pension formula calculation (service cost).
2. The employee is one year closer to retirement, causing the present value of benefits to increase due to the time value of future benefits (interest cost).

These represent two of the events that might possibly cause the balance of the PBO to change. Let's elaborate on these and the three other events that might change the balance of the PBO. The five events are (1) service cost, (2) interest cost, (3) prior service cost, (4) gains and losses, and (5) payments to retired employees.

Each year's service adds to the obligation to pay benefits.

1. Service cost. As we just witnessed in the illustration, the PBO increases each year by the amount of that year's **service cost.** This represents the increase in the projected benefit obligation attributable to employee service performed during the period. As we explain later, it also is the primary component of the annual pension expense.

Interest accrues on the PBO each year.

2. Interest cost. The second reason the PBO increases is called the **interest cost.** Even though the projected benefit obligation is not formally recognized as a liability in the company's balance sheet, it is a liability nevertheless. And, as with other liabilities, interest accrues on its balance as time passes. The amount can be calculated directly as the assumed discount rate multiplied by the projected benefit obligation at the beginning of the year.[6]

ADDITIONAL CONSIDERATION

We can verify the increase in the PBO as being caused by the service cost and interest cost as follows:

PBO at the beginning of 2008 (end of 2007)					\$119,822
Service cost: (1.5% × 1 yr. × \$400,000)	×	11.46992*	×	.18456†	12,701
Annual retirement benefits from 2008 service		To discount to 2037		To discount to 2008	
Interest cost: \$119,822 × 6%					7,189
PBO at the end of 2008					\$139,712‡

*Present value of an ordinary annuity of \$1: $n = 20$, $i = 6\%$.
†Present value of \$1: $n = 29$, $i = 6\%$.
‡Differs from \$139,715 due to rounding.

3. Prior service cost. Another reason the PBO might change is when the pension plan itself is *amended* to revise the way benefits are determined. For example, Global Communications in our illustration might choose to revise the pension formula by which benefits are calculated. Let's back up and assume the formula's salary percentage is increased in 2008 from 1.5% to 1.7%:

1.7% × Service years × Final year's salary
(revised pension formula)

Obviously, the annual service cost from this date forward will be higher than it would have been without the amendment. This will cause a more rapid future expansion of the PBO. But it also might cause an immediate increase in the PBO as well. Here's why.

When a pension plan is amended, credit often is given for employee service rendered in prior years. The cost of doing so is called *prior service cost.*

Suppose the amendment becomes effective for future years' service only, without consideration of employee service to date. As you might imagine, the morale and dedication of long-time employees of the company could be expected to suffer. So, for economic as well as ethical reasons, most companies choose to make amendments retroactive to prior years. In other words, the more beneficial terms of the revised pension formula are not applied just to future service years, but benefits attributable to all prior service years also are recomputed under the more favorable terms. Obviously, this decision is not without cost to the company. Making the amendment retroactive to prior years adds an extra layer of retirement benefits, increasing the company's benefit obligation. The increase in the PBO attributable to making a plan amendment retroactive is referred to as **prior service cost.**[7] For instance, Graphic 17–6 presents an excerpt from an annual report of **Ecolab, Inc.** describing the increase in its PBO as a result of making an amendment retroactive:

[6]Assumed discount rates should reflect rates used currently in annuity contracts. Discount rates recently reported have ranged from 4.5% to 9%, with 5.5% being the most commonly assumed rate (AICPA, *Accounting Trends and Techniques,* 2007).

[7]Prior service cost also is created if a defined benefit pension plan is initially adopted by a company that previously did not have one, and the plan itself is made retroactive to give credit for prior years' service. Prior service cost is created by plan amendments far more often than by plan adoptions because most companies already have pension plans, and new pension plans in recent years have predominantly been defined contribution plans.

Note 1: Retirement Plans (in part)
. . . The Company amended its U.S. pension plan to change the formula for pension benefits and to provide a more rapid vesting schedule. The plan amendments resulted in a $6 million increase in the projected benefits obligation.

GRAPHIC 17–6
Prior Service Cost—Ecolab, Inc.

Real World Financials

Let's put prior service cost in the context of our illustration.

At the end of 2007, and therefore the beginning of 2008, the PBO is $119,822. If the plan is amended on January 3, 2008, the PBO could be recomputed as:

Retroactive benefits from an amendment add additional costs, increasing the company's PBO. This increase is the prior service cost.

	PBO without Amendment		PBO with Amendment	
1.	1.5% × 10 yrs. × $400,000	= $ 60,000	1.7% × 10 yrs. × $400,000	= $ 68,000
2.	$60,000 × 11.46992	= 688,195	$68,000 × 11.46992	= 779,955
3.	$688,195 × .17411	= 119,822	$779,955 × .17411	= 135,798

$15,976
Prior service cost

The $15,976 increase in the PBO attributable to applying the more generous terms of the amendment to prior service years is the prior service cost. And, because we assumed the amendment occurred at the beginning of 2008, both the 2008 service cost and the 2008 interest cost would change as a result of the prior service cost. This is how:

Prior service cost increased the PBO at the beginning of the year.

PBO at the beginning of 2008 (end of 2007)			$119,822
Prior service cost (determined above)			15,976
PBO including prior service cost at the beginning of 2008			135,798
Service cost: (1.7% × 1 yr. × $400,000)	× 11.46992*	× .18456†	14,395
Annual retirement benefits from 2008 service	To discount to 2037	To discount to 2008	
Interest cost: $135,798‡ × 6%			8,148
PBO at the end of 2008			$158,341

*Present value of an ordinary annuity of $1: $n = 20$, $i = 6\%$.
†Present value of $1: $n = 29$, $i = 6\%$.
‡Includes the beginning balance plus the prior service cost because the amendment occurred at the beginning of the year.

ADDITIONAL CONSIDERATION

We can verify the PBO balance by calculating it directly:

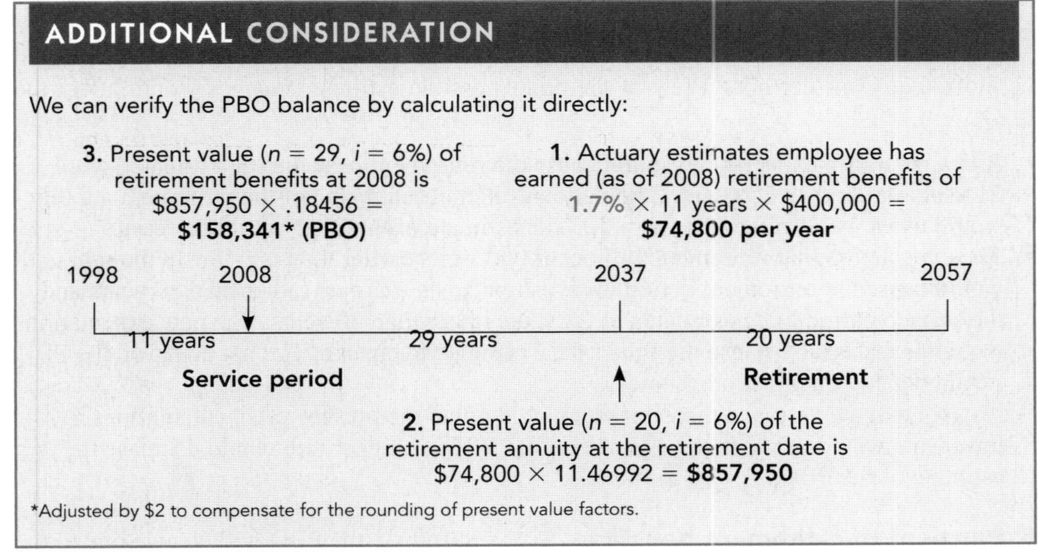
3. Present value (n = 29, i = 6%) of retirement benefits at 2008 is $857,950 × .18456 = $158,341* (PBO)
1. Actuary estimates employee has earned (as of 2008) retirement benefits of 1.7% × 11 years × $400,000 = $74,800 per year
1998
2008
2037
2057
11 years
29 years
20 years
Service period
Retirement
2. Present value (n = 20, i = 6%) of the retirement annuity at the retirement date is $74,800 × 11.46992 = $857,950

*Adjusted by $2 to compensate for the rounding of present value factors.

The pension formula reflects the plan amendment.

The plan amendment would affect not only the year in which it occurs, but also each subsequent year because the revised pension formula determines each year's service cost. Continuing our illustration to 2009 demonstrates this:

During 2009, the PBO increased as a result of service cost and interest cost.

PBO at the beginning of 2009 (end of 2008)				$158,341
Service cost: (1.7% × 1 yr. × $400,000)	×	11.46992*	× .19563†	15,258
Annual retirement benefits from 2009 service		To discount to 2037	To discount to 2009	
Interest cost: $158,341 × 6%				9,500
PBO at the end of 2009				$183,099

*Present value of an ordinary annuity of $1: $n = 20$, $i = 6\%$.
†Present value of $1: $n = 28$, $i = 6\%$.

Decreases and increases in estimates of the PBO because of periodic reevaluation of uncertainties are called gains and losses.

4. Gain or loss on the PBO. We mentioned earlier that a number of estimates are necessary to derive the PBO. When one or more of these estimates requires revision, the estimate of the PBO also will require revision. The resulting decrease or increase in the PBO is referred to as a *gain* or *loss,* respectively. Let's modify our illustration to imitate the effect of revising one of the several possible estimates involved. Suppose, for instance, that new information at the end of 2009 about inflation and compensation trends suggests that the estimate of Farrow's final salary should be increased by 5% to $420,000. This would affect the estimate of the PBO as follows:

Changing the final salary estimate changes the PBO.

	PBO *without* Revised Estimate		PBO *with* Revised Estimate	
1.	1.7% × 12 yrs. × $400,000	= $ 81,600	1.7% × 12 yrs. × $420,000	= $ 85,680
2.	$81,600 × 11.46992	= 935,945	$85,680 × 11.46992	= 982,743
3.	$935,945 × .19563	= 183,099	$982,743 × .19563	= 192,254

$9,155
Loss on PBO

The difference of $9,155 represents a loss on the PBO because the obligation turned out to be higher than previously expected. Now there would be three elements of the increase in the PBO during 2009.[8]

The revised estimate caused the PBO to increase.

PBO at the beginning of 2009	$158,341
Service cost (calculated above)	15,258
Interest cost (calculated above)	9,500
Loss on PBO (calculated above)	9,155
PBO at the end of 2009	$192,254

If a revised estimate causes the PBO to be lower than previously expected, a gain would be indicated. Consider how a few of the other possible estimate changes would affect the PBO:

- A change in life expectancies might cause the retirement period to be estimated as 21 years rather than 20 years. Calculation of the present value of the retirement annuity would use $n = 21$, rather than $n = 20$. The estimate of the PBO would increase.
- The expectation that retirement will occur two years earlier than previously thought would cause the retirement period to be estimated as 22 years rather than 20 years and the service period to be estimated as 28 years rather than 30 years. The new expectation would probably also cause the final salary estimate to change. The net effect on the PBO would depend on the circumstances.
- A change in the assumed discount rate would affect the present value calculations. A lower rate would increase the estimate of the PBO. A higher rate would decrease the estimate of the PBO.

Payment of retirement benefits reduces the PBO.

5. Payment of retirement benefits. We've seen how the PBO will change due to the accumulation of service cost from year to year, the accrual of interest as time passes, making plan amendments retroactive to prior years, and periodic adjustments when estimates

[8]The increase in the PBO due to amending the pension formula (prior service cost) occurred in 2008.

change. Another change in the PBO occurs when the obligation is reduced as benefits actually are paid to retired employees.

The payment of such benefits is not applicable in our present illustration because we've limited the situation to calculations concerning an individual employee who is several years from retirement. Remember, though, in reality the actuary would make these calculations for the entire pool of employees covered by the pension plan. But the concepts involved would be the same. Graphic 17–7 summarizes the five ways the PBO can change.

GRAPHIC 17–7
Components of Change in the PBO

The Projected Benefits Obligation Changes as a Result of:

Cause	Effect	Frequency
Service cost	+	Each period
Interest cost	+	Each period (except the first period of the plan, when no obligation exists to accrue interest)
Prior service cost	+	Only if the plan is amended (or initiated) that period
Loss or gain on PBO	+ or –	Whenever revisions are made in the pension liability estimate
Retiree benefits paid	–	Each period (unless no employees have yet retired under the plan)

Illustration Expanded to Consider the Entire Employee Pool

The PBO is not formally recognized in the balance sheet.

For our single employee, the PBO at the end of 2009 is $192,254. Let's say now that Global Communications has 2,000 active employees covered by the pension plan and 100 retired employees receiving retirement benefits. Illustration 17–2 expands the numbers to represent all covered employees.

ILLUSTRATION 17–2
The PBO Expanded to Include All Employees

The changes in the PBO for Global Communications during 2009 were as follows:

	($ in millions)*
PBO at the beginning of 2009† (amount assumed)	$400
Service cost, 2009 (amount assumed)	41
Interest cost: $400 × 6%	24
Loss (gain) on PBO (amount assumed)	23
Less: Retiree benefits paid (amount assumed)	(38)
PBO at the end of 2009	$450

*Of course, these expanded amounts are not simply the amounts for Jessica Farrow multiplied by 2,000 employees because her years of service, expected retirement date, and salary are not necessarily representative of other employees. Also, the expanded amounts take into account expected employee turnover and current retirees.
†Includes the prior service cost that increased the PBO when the plan was amended in 2008.

Pension Plan Assets

● LO4

So far our focus has been on the employer's obligation to provide retirement benefits in the future. We turn our attention now to the resources with which the company will satisfy that obligation—the **pension plan assets.** Like the PBO, the pension plan assets are not formally recognized on the balance sheet but are actively monitored in the employer's informal records. Its balance, too, must be reported in disclosure notes to the financial statements, and as explained below, the return on these assets is included in the calculation of the periodic pension expense.

We assumed in the previous section that Global Communications' obligation is $450 million for service performed to date. When employees retire, will there be sufficient funds to provide the anticipated benefits? To ensure sufficient funding, Global will contribute cash each year to a pension fund.

FINANCIAL Reporting Case

Q3, p. 881

A *trustee* manages pension plan assets.

The assets of a pension fund must be held by a **trustee.** A trustee accepts employer contributions, invests the contributions, accumulates the earnings on the investments, and pays benefits from the plan assets to retired employees or their beneficiaries. The trustee can be an individual, a bank, or a trust company. Plan assets are invested in stocks, bonds, and other income-producing assets. The accumulated balance of the annual employer contributions plus the return on the investments (dividends, interest, market price appreciation) must be sufficient to pay benefits as they come due.

When an employer estimates how much it must set aside each year to accumulate sufficient funds to pay retirement benefits as they come due, it's necessary to estimate the return those investments will produce. This is the **expected return on plan assets.** The higher the return, the less the employer must actually contribute. On the other hand, a relatively low return means the difference must be made up by higher contributions. In practice, recent estimates of the rate of return have ranged from 4.5% to 9.5%, with 8.5% being the most commonly reported expectation.[9] In Illustration 17–3, we shift the focus of our numerical illustration to emphasize Global's pension plan assets.

ILLUSTRATION 17–3

How Plan Assets Change

Global Communications funds its defined benefit pension plan by contributing each year the year's service cost plus a portion of the prior service cost. Cash of $48 million was contributed to the pension fund at the end of 2009.

Plan assets at the beginning of 2009 were valued at $300 million. The expected rate of return on the investment of those assets was 9%, but the actual return in 2009 was 10%. Retirement benefits of $38 million were paid at the end of 2009 to retired employees.

What is the value of the company's pension plan assets at the end of 2009?

A trustee accepts employer contributions, invests the contributions, accumulates the earnings on the investments, and pays benefits from the plan assets.

	($ in millions)
Plan assets at the beginning of 2009	$300
Return on plan assets (10% × $300)	30
Cash contributions	48
Less: Retiree benefits paid	(38)
Plan assets at the end of 2009	$340

An *underfunded* pension plan means the PBO exceeds plan assets.

Recall that Global's PBO at the end of 2009 is $450 million. Because the plan assets are only $340 million, the pension plan is said to be *underfunded.* One reason is that we assumed Global incurred a $60 million prior service cost from amending the pension plan at the beginning of 2008, and that cost is being funded over several years. Another factor is the loss from increasing the PBO due to the estimate revision, since funding has been based on the previous estimate. Later, we'll assume earlier revisions also have increased the PBO. Of course, actual performance of the investments also impacts a plan's funded status.

An *overfunded* pension plan means plan assets exceed the PBO.

It is not unusual for pension plans today to be underfunded. Historically the funded status of pension plans has varied considerably. Prior to the Employee Retirement Income Security Act (ERISA) in 1974, many plans were grossly underfunded. The new law established minimum funding standards among other matters designed to protect plan participants. The new standards brought most plans closer to full funding. Then the stock market boom of the 1980s caused the value of plan assets for many pension funds to swell to well over their projected benefit obligations. More than 80% of pension plans were overfunded. As a result, managers explored ways to divert funds to other areas of operations. Today a majority of plans again are underfunded. Many of the underfunded plans are with troubled companies, placing employees at risk. The PBGC guarantees are limited to about $3,400 per month, often less than promised pension benefits.

● LO5

Reporting the Funded Status of the Pension Plan

FINANCIAL Reporting Case

Q4, p. 881

A company's PBO is not reported among liabilities in the balance sheet. Similarly, the plan assets a company sets aside to pay those benefits are not reported among assets in the balance sheet. However, firms do report the net difference between those two amounts, referred

[9]AICPA, *Accounting Trends and Techniques,* 2007.

to as the "funded status" of the plan.[10] From our previous discussion, we see the funded status for Global to be the following at Dec. 31, 2009, and Dec. 31, 2008:

	($ in millions)	
	2009	**2008**
Projected benefit obligation (PBO)	$450	$400
Fair value of plan assets	340	300
Underfunded status	$110	$100

A company must report in its balance sheet a liability for the underfunded (or asset for the overfunded) status of its postretirement plans.

Because the plan is underfunded, Global reports a net pension liability of $110 million in its 2009 balance sheet and $100 million in 2008. If the plan becomes overfunded in the future, Global will report a net pension asset instead.

Now, let's look at all the ways that changes in the PBO and the pension plan assets affect pension expense.

DETERMINING PENSION EXPENSE

PART C

The Relationship between Pension Expense and Changes in the PBO and Plan Assets

● LO6

Like wages, salaries, commissions, and other forms of pay, pension expense is part of a company's compensation for employee services each year. Accordingly, the accounting objective is to achieve a matching of the costs of providing this form of compensation with the benefits of the services performed. However, the fact that this form of compensation actually is paid to employees many years after the service is performed means that other elements in addition to the annual service cost will affect the ultimate pension cost. These other elements are related to changes that occur over time in both the pension liability and the pension plan assets. Graphic 17–8 provides a summary of how some of these changes influence pension expense.

The matching principle and the time period assumption dictate that the costs be allocated to the periods the services are performed.

GRAPHIC 17–8
Components of the Periodic Pension Expense

Changes in the PBO	Pension Expense	Changes in Plan Assets
Service cost—increase in the employer's obligation attributed to employee service during the current period	*Included currently:* → **Service cost**	**Expected return on the plan assets**—estimated long-term return from changes in the value of plan assets, due to dividends, interest, and market price changes, plus (minus):
Interest cost—interest accrued on the obligation during the current period (balance at the beginning of the period multiplied by the interest rate)	→ **Interest cost**	→ **(Expected return on the plan assets)**
Prior service cost—increase in the employer's obligation due to giving credit to employees for years of service provided before the pension plan is amended (or initiated)	*Delayed recognition:* Amortized portion of: → **Prior service cost**	**Gains or (losses) on the plan assets**—return on plan assets lower or (higher) than expected
Losses or (gains) on the PBO—increases or (decreases) in the estimate of the PBO from revisions in underlying assumptions	→ **Net loss or (gain)**	**Cash contributions**—payments into the fund by the employer
Less: Payments to retirees		**Less: Payments to retirees**

Report net Amt (over + you have).

FINANCIAL Reporting Case

Q5, p. 881

The pension expense reported in the income statement is a composite of periodic changes that occur in both the pension obligation and the plan assets.

[10]"Employers' Accounting for Defined Benefit Pension and Other Postretirement Plans—an amendment of FASB Statements No. 87, 88, 106, and 132(R)," *Statement of Financial Accounting Standards No. 158* (Stamford, Conn.: FASB, 2006).

We've examined each of the components of pension expense from the viewpoint of its effect on the PBO or on plan assets, using the Global Communications illustration to demonstrate that effect. Now, let's expand the same illustration to see how these changes affect *pension expense*. Illustration 17– 4 provides this expanded example.

ILLUSTRATION 17–4
Pension Expense

Reports from the actuary and the trustee of plan assets indicate the following changes during 2009 in the PBO and plan assets of Global Communications.

These are the changes in the PBO and in the plan assets we previously discussed (Illustration 17–2 and Illustration 17–3).

($ in millions)	PBO		Plan Assets
Beginning of 2009	$400	*Beginning* of 2009	$300
Service cost	41	Return on plan assets,*	
Interest cost, 6%	24	10% (9% expected)	30
Loss (gain) on PBO	23	Cash contributions	48
Less: Retiree benefits	(38)	Less: Retiree benefits	(38)
End of 2009	$450	*End* of 2009	$340

A *prior service cost* of $60 million was incurred at the beginning of the previous year (2008) due to a plan amendment increasing the PBO. At the beginning of 2009 Global had a *net loss* of $55 million (previous losses exceeded previous gains). The average remaining service life of employees is estimated at 15 years.

2009 Pension Expense

Global's 2009 Pension Expense Is Determined as Follows:	($ in millions)
Service cost	$41
Interest cost	24
Expected return on the plan assets ($30 actual, less $3 gain)	(27)
Amortization of prior service cost (calculated later)	4
Amortization of net loss (calculated later)	1
Pension expense	$43

*Expected rates of return anticipate the performance of various investments of plan assets. This is not necessarily the same as the discount rate used by the actuary to estimate the pension obligation. Assumed rates of return recently reported have ranged from 4.5% to 9.5%, with 8.5% being the most commonly assumed rate (AICPA, *Accounting Trends and Techniques*, 2007).

Components of Pension Expense

Illustration 17–4 demonstrates the relationship between some of the changes in the PBO and in plan assets and the components of pension expense: service cost, interest cost, the return on plan assets, prior service cost amortization, and net gain or loss amortization. Let's look at these five components of pension expense one at a time.

1. SERVICE COST. The $41 million service cost represents the increase in the projected benefit obligation attributable to employee service performed during 2009 (benefits earned by employees during the year). Each year this is the first component of the pension expense.

Interest cost is the discount rate times the PBO balance at the beginning of the year.

2. INTEREST COST. The interest cost is calculated as the interest rate (actuary's discount rate) multiplied by the projected benefit obligation at the beginning of the year. In 2009, this is 6% times $400 million, or $24 million.

The PBO is not formally recognized as a liability in the company's balance sheet, but it is a liability nevertheless. The interest expense that accrues on its balance is not separately reported on the income statement but is instead combined with the service cost (and other amounts) as the second component of the annual pension expense.

The return earned on investment securities increases the plan asset balance.

3. RETURN ON PLAN ASSETS. Remember, plan assets comprise funds invested in stocks, bonds, and other securities that presumably will generate dividends, interest, and capital gains. Each year these earnings represent the return on plan assets during that year. When accounting for the return, we need to differentiate between its two modes: the *expected* return and the *actual* return.

Actual versus expected return. We've assumed Global's expected rate of return is 9%, so its expected return on plan assets in 2009 was 9% times $300 million, or $27 million. But, as previously indicated, the actual rate of return in 2009 was 10%, producing an actual return on plan assets of 10% times $300 million, or $30 million.

Obviously, investing plan assets in income-producing assets lessens the amounts employers must contribute to the fund. So, the return on plan assets reduces the net cost of having a pension plan. Accordingly, the return on plan assets each year *reduces* the amount recorded as pension expense. Just as the interest expense that accrues on the PBO is included as a component of pension expense rather than being separately reported, the investment revenue on plan assets is not separately reported either. In actuality, both the interest and return-on-assets components of pension expense do not directly represent employee compensation. Instead, they are financial items created only because the pension payment is delayed while the obligation is funded currently.

The interest and return-on-assets components are financial items created only because the compensation is delayed and the obligation is funded currently.

Adjustment for loss or gain. A controversial question is *when* differences between the actual and expected return should be recognized in pension expense. It seems logical that since the net cost of having a pension plan is reduced by the actual return on plan assets, the charge to pension expense should be the actual return on plan assets. However, the FASB concluded that the actual return should first be adjusted by any difference between that return and what the return had been expected to be. So, it's actually the *expected* return that is included in the calculation of pension expense. In our illustration, Global's pension expense is reduced by the expected return of $27 million.

The return on plan assets reduces the net *cost of having a* pension plan.

The difference between the actual and expected return is considered a loss or gain on plan assets. Although we don't include these losses and gains as part of pension expense when they occur, it's possible they will affect pension expense at a later time. On the next page, we will discuss how that might happen.

Any loss or gain is not included in pension expense right away.

4. AMORTIZATION OF PRIOR SERVICE COST. Recall that the $60 million increase in Global's PBO due to recalculating benefits employees earned in prior years as a result of a plan amendment is referred to as the prior service cost. Obviously, prior service cost adds to the cost of having a pension plan. But when should this cost be recognized as pension expense? An argument can be made that the cost should be recognized as expense in the year of the amendment when the cost increases the company's pension obligation. In fact, some members of the FASB have advocated this approach. At present, though, we amortize the cost gradually to pension expense. Here's the rationalization.

Prior service cost is recognized as pension expense over the future service period of the employees whose benefits are recalculated.

Amending a pension plan, and especially choosing to make that amendment retroactive, typically is done with the idea that future operations will benefit from those choices. For that reason, the cost is not recognized as pension expense in the year the plan is amended. Instead, it is recognized as pension expense over the time that the employees who benefited from the retroactive amendment will work for the company in the future. Presumably, this future service period is when the company will receive the benefits of its actions.

In our illustration, the amendment occurred in 2008, increasing the PBO at that time. For the individual employee, Jessica Farrow, the prior service cost was calculated to be $15,976. Our illustration assumes that, for *all* plan participants, the prior service cost was $60 million at the beginning of 2008. The prior service cost at the beginning of 2009 is $56 million. The following section explains how this amount was computed.

One assumption in our illustration is that the average remaining service life of the active employee group is 15 years. To recognize the $60 million prior service cost in equal annual amounts over this period, the amount amortized as an increase in pension expense each year is $4 million:[11]

[11]An alternative to this straight-line approach, called the *service method,* attempts to allocate the prior service cost to each year in proportion to the fraction of the total remaining service years worked in each of those years. This method is described in the chapter appendix.

By the straight-line method, prior service cost is recognized over the average remaining service life of the active employee group.

Amortization of Prior Service Cost:	($ in millions)
Service cost	$41
Interest cost	24
Expected return on the plan assets	(27)
Amortization of prior service cost–AOCI	4
Amortization of net loss–AOCI	1
Pension expense	**$43**

Prior service cost is not expensed as it is incurred. Instead, it is reported as a component of AOCI to be amortized over time.

Be sure to note that, even though we're amortizing it, the prior service cost is not an asset, but instead a part of *accumulated other comprehensive income* (AOCI), a shareholders' equity account. This is a result of the FASB's current disinclination to treat the cost as an expense as it is incurred. The Board, instead, prefers to ascribe it the off-the-income-statement designation as *other comprehensive income* (OCI) in the same manner as the handful of losses and gains also categorized the same way and not reported among the gains and losses in the traditional income statement. You first learned about comprehensive income in Chapter 4 and again in Chapter 12. We'll revisit it again later in this chapter.

The prior service cost declines by $4 million each year:

Prior Service Cost – AOCI	($ in millions)
Prior service cost at the beginning of 2009	$56
Less: 2009 amortization	(4)
Prior service cost at the end of 2009	$52

5. AMORTIZATION OF A NET LOSS OR NET GAIN. You learned previously that gains and losses can occur when expectations are revised concerning either the PBO or the return on plan assets. Graphic 17–9 summarizes the possibilities.

GRAPHIC 17–9
Gains and Losses

Gains and losses occur when either the PBO or the return on plan assets turns out to be different than expected.

	Projected Benefit Obligation	Return on Plan Assets
Higher than expected	Loss	Gain
Lower than expected	Gain	Loss

Like the prior service cost we just discussed, we don't include these gains and losses as part of pension expense in the income statement, but instead report them as OCI in the statement of comprehensive income as they occur. We then report the gains and losses on a cumulative basis as a net loss–AOCI or a net gain–AOCI, depending on whether we have greater losses or gains over time. We report this amount in the balance sheet as a part of *accumulated other comprehensive income* (AOCI), a shareholders' equity account.

There is no conceptual justification for not including losses and gains in earnings. After all, these increases and decreases in either the PBO or plan assets immediately impact the net cost of providing a pension plan and, conceptually, should be included in pension expense as they occur.

Nevertheless, The FASB requires that income statement recognition of gains and losses from either source be delayed. Why?—for practical reasons.

Income Smoothing

The FASB acknowledged the conceptual shortcoming of delaying the recognition of a gain or a loss while opting for this more politically acceptable approach. Delayed recognition was favored by a dominant segment of corporate America that was concerned with the effect of allowing gains and losses to immediately impact reported earnings. In 2006, the FASB decided to formally reconsider all aspects of accounting for postretirement benefit plans, including this treatment of gains and losses.[14] The project will consider overhauling the entire system for accounting for and reporting on postretirement benefits. This result might include immediately including gains and losses in pension expense, thereby eliminating income smoothing.

The Board believes that it would be conceptually appropriate and preferable to [have] . . . no delay in recognition of gains and losses, or perhaps [to have] . . . gains and losses reported currently in comprehensive income but not in earnings. However, it concluded that those approaches would be too great a change from past practice to be adopted at the present time.[12]

Delayed recognition of gains and losses achieves income smoothing at the expense of conceptual integrity.

The practical justification for delayed recognition is that, over time, gains and losses might cancel one another out. Given this possibility, why create unnecessary fluctuations in reported income by letting temporary gains and losses decrease and increase (respectively) pension expense? Of course, as years pass there may be more gains than losses, or vice versa, preventing their offsetting one another completely. So, if a net gain or a net loss gets "too large," pension expense must be adjusted.

The Board acknowledges that the delayed recognition included in this Statement results in excluding the most current and most relevant information.[13]

SFAS No. 87 defines too large rather arbitrarily as being when a net gain or a net loss at the beginning of a year exceeds an amount equal to 10% of the PBO, or 10% of plan assets, whichever is higher.[15] *SFAS No. 87* refers to this threshold amount as the "corridor." When the corridor is exceeded, the excess is not charged to pension expense all at once. Instead, as a further concession to income smoothing, only a portion of the excess is included in pension expense. The minimum amount that should be included is the excess divided by the average remaining service period of active employees expected to receive benefits under the plan.[16]

A net gain or a net loss affects pension expense only if it exceeds an amount equal to 10% of the PBO, or 10% of plan assets, whichever is higher.

In our illustration, we're assuming a net loss–AOCI of $55 million at the beginning of 2009. Also recall that the PBO and plan assets are $400 million and $300 million, respectively, at that time. The amount amortized to 2009 pension expense is $1 million, calculated as follows:

Determining Net Loss Amortization—2009	($ in millions)
Net loss (previous losses exceeded previous gains)	$55
10% of $400 ($400 is greater than $300); the "corridor"	(40)
Excess at the beginning of the year	$15
Average remaining service period	÷ 15 years
Amount amortized to 2009 pension expense	$ 1

Because the net loss exceeds an amount equal to the greater of 10% of the PBO or 10% of plan assets, part of the excess is amortized to pension expense.

The pension expense is increased because a net loss is being amortized. If a net *gain* were being amortized, the amount would be *deducted* from pension expense because a gain would indicate that the net cost of providing the pension plan had decreased.

Amortization of the Net Loss–AOCI:	($ in millions)
Service cost	$41
Interest cost	24
Expected return on the plan assets	(27)
Amortization of prior service cost–AOCI	4
Amortization of net loss–AOCI	1
Pension expense	$43

Amortization of a net gain would decrease pension expense.

Amortization of a net loss increases pension expense.

[12] FASB, "Employers' Accounting for Pension and Other Postretirement Benefits," *Preliminary Views*, November 1982, par. 107.

[13] Ibid., par. 88.

[14] "Employers' Accounting for Defined Benefit Pension and Other Postretirement Plans—an amendment of FASB Statements No. 87, 88, 106, and 132(R)," *Statement of Financial Accounting Standards No. 158* (Stamford, Conn.: FASB, 2006), par. B16.

[15] For this purpose the FASB specifies the market-related value of plan assets. This can be either the fair value or a weighted-average fair value over a period not to exceed five years. We will uniformly assume fair value in this chapter.

[16] Companies are permitted to amortize the entire net loss (or gain) rather than just the excess, but few choose that option. (*SFAS 87*, par. 33.)

This amortization reduces the net loss–AOCI in 2009 by $1 million. Also recall that Global incurred (a) a $23 million loss in 2009 from revising estimates relating to the PBO and (b) a $3 million gain when the 2009 return on plan assets was higher than expected. These three changes affected the net loss–AOCI in 2009 as follows:

New losses add to a net loss; new gains reduce a net loss.

Net Loss–AOCI	($ in millions)
Net loss–AOCI at the beginning of 2009	$55
Less: 2009 amortization	(1)
Plus: 2009 loss on PBO	23
Less: 2009 gain on plan assets	(3)
Net loss–AOCI at the end of 2009	$74

ADDITIONAL CONSIDERATION

The $74 million balance at the end of 2009 would be the beginning balance in 2010. It would be compared with the 2010 beginning balances in the PBO and plan assets to determine whether amortization would be necessary in 2010. If you were to look back to our analyses of the changes in those two balances, you would see the 2010 beginning balances in the PBO and plan assets to be $450 million and $340 million, respectively. The amount amortized to 2010 pension expense will be $1.93 million, calculated as follows:

	($ in millions)
Net loss (previous losses exceeded previous gains)	$ 74
10% of $450 ($450 is greater than $340)	(45)
Excess at the beginning of the year	$29
Average remaining service period	÷ 15 years*
Amount amortized to 2010 pension expense	**$1.93**

*Assumes the average remaining service period of active employees is still 15 years in 2010 due to new employees joining the firm.

PART D

REPORTING ISSUES

Recording Gains and Losses

● LO7

As we discussed earlier, gains and losses (either from changing assumptions regarding the PBO or from the return on assets being higher or lower than expected) are deferred and not immediately included in pension expense and net income. Instead, we report them as *other comprehensive income (OCI)* in the statement of comprehensive income. So Global records a *loss–OCI* for the $23 million loss that occurs in 2009 when it revises its estimate of future salary levels causing its PBO estimate to increase. Global also records a $3 million *gain–OCI* that occurred when the $30 million actual return on plan assets exceeded the $27 million expected return. Here's the entry:

Losses and gains (as well as any new prior service cost should it occur) are reported as OCI.

To Record Gains and Losses	($ in millions)	
Loss–OCI (from change in assumption)	23	
PBO		23
Plan assets	3	
Gain–OCI ($30 actual return on assets – $27 expected return)		3

The loss is an increase in the PBO due to a change in an assumption. In this entry, we are recording that increase in the PBO account balance. If the change in assumption had caused the PBO to be reduced instead, we would debit the PBO here and credit a gain–OCI.

Similarly, the gain due to the actual return on plan assets exceeding the expected return is an increase in plan assets. In the next section, we increase plan assets for the expected return (as a component of pension expense) so the two adjustments together cause the plan assets account balance to reflect the actual return (expected increase plus the additional increase represented by the gain). Of course, if the actual return had been less than expected, we would debit a loss–OCI and credit plan assets here.

ADDITIONAL CONSIDERATION

Just as we record new losses and gains as they occur, we also will record a change in the prior service cost account for any new prior service cost should it occur. For instance, if Global revised its pension formula again and recalculated its PBO using the more generous formula, causing a $40 million increase in the PBO, the company would record the new prior service cost this way:

To Record New Prior Service Cost	($ in millions)	
Prior service cost–OCI (increase in PBO due to plan amendment)	40	
PBO		40

If an amendment *reduces* rather than increases the PBO, the *negative prior service cost* would reduce both the prior service cost and pension liability.

INTERNATIONAL FINANCIAL REPORTING STANDARDS

Actuarial Gains and Losses. We've seen that *SFAS No. 158* requires that actuarial gains and losses be included among OCI items in the statement of comprehensive income, thus subsequently become part of AOCI. This is permitted under *IAS No. 19*, but not required.

Then, if gains and losses *are* included in comprehensive income, under *IAS No. 19* they cannot subsequently be amortized to expense and recycled or reclassified from other comprehensive income as is required under *SFAS No. 158* if the net gain or net loss exceeds the 10% threshold.

Recording the Pension Expense

Recall from Illustration 17–4 that Global's 2009 pension expense is $43 million. The expense includes the $41 million service cost and the $24 million interest cost, both of which, as we learned earlier, add to Global's PBO. Similarly, the expense includes a $27 million expected return on plan assets, which adds to the plan assets.[17] These changes are reflected in the following entry:

Each component of the pension expense is recorded in the journal entry to record pension expense.

Service cost	$41
Interest cost	24
Expected return on assets	(27)
Amortization of prior service cost	4
Amortization of net loss	1
Pension expense	$43

To Record Pension Expense	($ in millions)	
Pension expense (total)	43	
Plan assets ($27 expected return on assets).	27	
PBO ($41 Service Cost + $24 Interest Cost). . . .		65
Amortization of prior service cost—OCI (2009 amortization)		4
Amortization of net loss—OCI (2009 amortization)		1

Service cost and interest cost increase the PBO. The return on assets increases plan assets.

[17]The increase in plan assets is the $30 million *actual* return, but the $27 million *expected* return is the component of pension expense because the $3 million gain isn't included in expense. We saw in the previous section that the $3 million gain also increases plan assets.

INTERNATIONAL FINANCIAL REPORTING STANDARDS

Prior Service Cost. Under *IAS No. 19,* prior service cost (called past service cost under IFRS) is expensed immediately to the extent it relates to benefits that have vested. The amount not yet expensed (nonvested portion) is reported as an offset or increase to the defined benefit obligation.

Under U.S. GAAP, prior service cost is not expensed immediately, but is included among OCI items in the statement of comprehensive income and thus subsequently becomes part of AOCI where it is amortized over the average remaining service period.

New gains and losses and prior service cost are reported as OCI. So is the amortization of their accumulated balances.

The pension expense also includes the $4 million amortization of the prior service cost and the $1 million amortization of the net loss. As we discussed earlier, we report prior service cost when it arises as well as gains and losses as they occur as *other comprehensive income (OCI)* in the statement of comprehensive income. These OCI items accumulate as Prior service cost–AOCI and Net loss (or gain)–AOCI. So, when we amortize these AOCI accounts, we report the amortization amounts in the statement of comprehensive income as well.

Amortization reduces the Prior service cost–AOCI and the Net loss–AOCI. Since these accounts have debit balances, we credit the amortization accounts. If we were amortizing a net gain, we would *debit* the account because a net gain has a credit balance.

65 ↑ PBO
27 ↑ *Less: plan assets*
38 ↑ Net pension liability

Remember, we report the funded status of the plan in the balance sheet. That's the difference between the PBO and plan assets. In this case, it's a net pension liability since the plan is underfunded; that is, the PBO exceeds plan assets.

Recording the Funding of Plan Assets

When Global adds its annual cash investment to its plan assets, the value of those plan assets increases by $48 million:

PBO
48 ↑ *Less: plan assets*
48 ↑ Net pension liability

To Record Funding	($ in millions)	
Plan assets	48	
Cash (contribution to plan assets)		48

It's not unusual for the cash contribution to differ from that year's pension expense. After all, determining the periodic pension expense and the funding of the pension plan are two separate processes. Pension expense is an accounting decision. How much to contribute each year is a financing decision affected by cash flow and tax considerations, as well as minimum funding requirements of ERISA. Subject to these considerations, cash contributions are actuarially determined with the objective of accumulating (along with investment returns) sufficient funds to provide promised retirement benefits.

The pension expense is, of course, reported in the income statement. In addition, the composition of that amount must be reported in disclosure notes. For instance, Samsonite Corporation described the composition of its pension expense in the disclosure note in its 2007 annual report, shown in Graphic 17–10.

GRAPHIC 17–10
Disclosure of Pension Expense—Samsonite

The components of pension expense are itemized in the disclosure note.

Real World Financials

(15) Pension and Other Employee Benefits (in part)

(in thousands)	2007	2006	2005
Components of net periodic benefit costs			
Service cost	**$ 1,664**	1,769	1,572
Interest cost	**12,210**	12,482	12,389
Expected return on plan assets	**(13,476)**	(13,395)	(14,081)
Amortization of prior service cost	**261**	267	270
Recognized net actual (gain) loss	**4,795**	4,866	2,567
Total net periodic benefit cost	**$ 5,454**	5,989	2,717

Comprehensive Income

Comprehensive income, as you may recall from Chapter 4, is a more expansive view of income than traditional net income. In fact, it encompasses all changes in equity other than from transactions with owners.[18] So, in addition to net income, comprehensive income includes up to four other changes in equity. A statement of comprehensive income is demonstrated in Illustration 17–5, highlighting the presentation of the components of OCI pertaining to Global's pension plan.

ILLUSTRATION 17–5
Statement of Comprehensive Income

	($ in millions)	
Net income		$xxx
Other comprehensive income:		
Unrealized holding gains (losses) on investments	$ x	
Pension plan:		
Loss—due to revising a PBO estimate*	(23)	
Gain—return on plan assets exceeds expected*	3	
Amortization of net loss	1	
Amortization of prior service cost	4	
Deferred gains (losses) from derivatives	x	
Gains (losses) from foreign currency translation	x	xx
Comprehensive income		$xxx

Gains and losses, as well as any new prior service cost should it arise, are among the OCI items reported in the period they occur.

*From Illustration 17–4 on p. xxx
Note: These amounts are shown without considering taxes. Actually each of the elements of comprehensive income *should be reported net of tax*. For instance, if the tax rate is 40%, the gain would be reported as $13.8 million: $23 million less a $9.2 million tax benefit.

Other comprehensive income (OCI) items are reported both (a) as they occur and (b) as an accumulated balance as shown in Illustrations 17–6 and 17–7.[19]

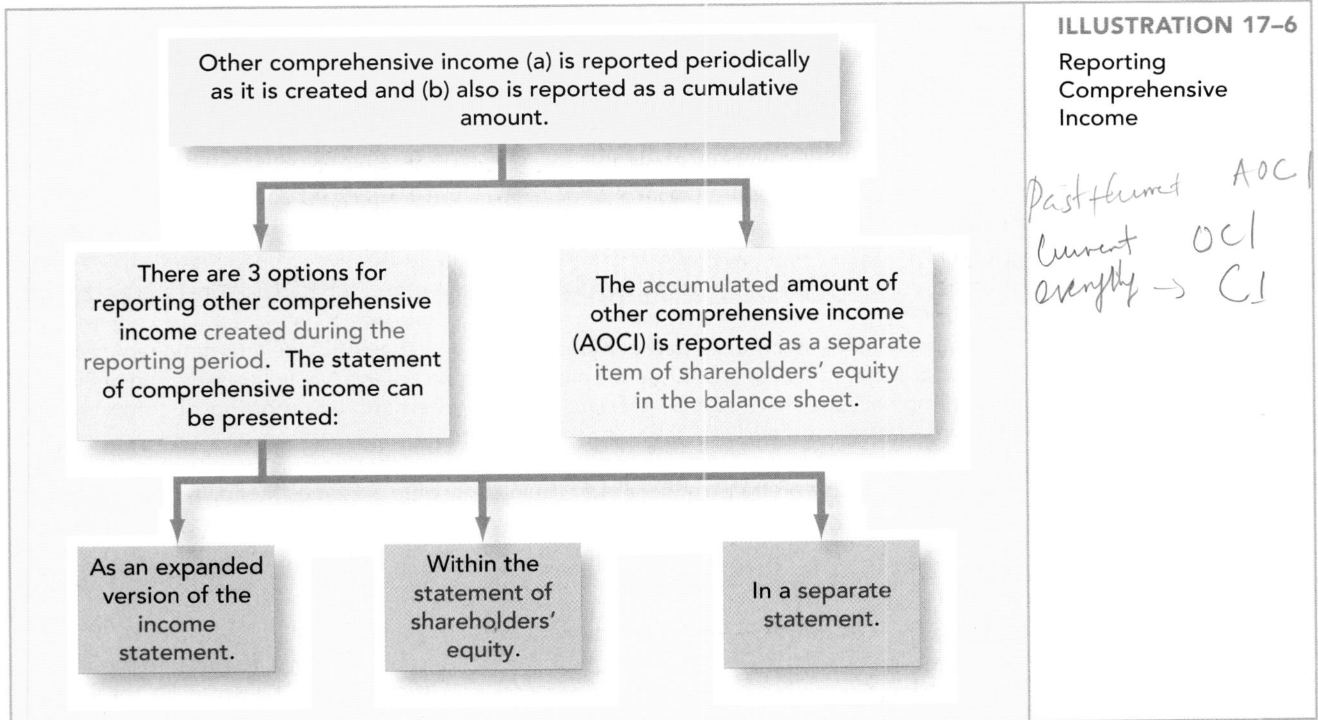

Other comprehensive income (a) is reported periodically as it is created and (b) also is reported as a cumulative amount.
There are 3 options for reporting other comprehensive income created during the reporting period. The statement of comprehensive income can be presented:
The accumulated amount of other comprehensive income (AOCI) is reported as a separate item of shareholders' equity in the balance sheet.
As an expanded version of the income statement.
Within the statement of shareholders' equity.
In a separate statement.

ILLUSTRATION 17–6
Reporting Comprehensive Income

[18] Transactions with owners primarily include dividends and the sale or purchase of shares of the company's stock.
[19] The statement of comprehensive income can be reported either (a) as an extension of the income statement, (b) in a disclosure note, or (c) as part of the statement of shareholders' equity.

ILLUSTRATION 17–7
Balance Sheet Presentation of Pension Amounts

If the plan had been overfunded, Global would have reported a pension asset among its assets rather than this pension liability.

The net loss and prior service cost *reduce* shareholders' equity.

Global Communication
Balance Sheets
For Years Ended December 31

	2009	**2008**
Assets		
Current assets	$xxx	$xxx
Property, plant, and equipment	xxx	xxx
Liabilities		
Current Liabilities	$xxx	$xxx
Net pension liability	110	100
Other long-term liabilities	xxx	xxx
Shareholders' Equity		
Common stock	$xxx	$xxx
Retained earnings	xxx	xxx
Accumulated other comprehensive income:		
Net unrealized holding gains and losses on investments—AOCI	xxx	xxx
Net loss–AOCI*	(74)	(55)
Prior service cost—AOCI*	(52)	(56)

*These are debit balances and therefore negative components of accumulated other comprehensive income; a net gain–AOCI would have a credit balance and be a positive component of accumulated other comprehensive income.

Reporting OCI as it occurs and also as an accumulated balance is consistent with the way we report net income and its accumulated counterpart, retained earnings.

In addition to reporting the gains or losses (and other elements of comprehensive income) that occur in the current reporting period, we also report these amounts on a *cumulative* basis in the balance sheet. Comprehensive income includes (a) net income and (b) OCI. Notice that we report net income that occurs in the current reporting period in the income statement and also report accumulated net income (that hasn't been distributed as dividends) in the balance sheet as retained earnings. Similarly, we report OCI as it occurs in the current reporting period (see Illustration 17–5) and also report *accumulated other comprehensive income* in the balance sheet. In its 2009 balance sheet, Global will report the amounts as shown in Illustration 17–7.

Look back to the schedule on page 900 to see how the net loss–AOCI increased from $55 million to $74 million during 2009 and the schedule on page 898 to see how the prior service cost—AOCI decreased from $56 million to $52 million. The pension liability represents the underfunded status of Global's pension plan on the two dates.

INTERNATIONAL FINANCIAL REPORTING STANDARDS

Comprehensive Income. As part of a joint project with the FASB, the International Accounting Standards Board (IASB) in 2007 issued a revised version of *IAS No. 1*, "Presentation of Financial Statements," that revised the standard to bring international reporting of comprehensive income largely in line with U.S. standards. It provides the option of presenting revenue and expense items and components of other comprehensive income either in (a) a single statement of comprehensive income or (b) in an income statement followed by a statement of comprehensive income. U.S. GAAP also allows reporting other comprehensive income in the statement of shareholders' equity, which is the way most U.S. companies report it.

Income Tax Considerations

OCI items are reported net of tax, in both the (a) statement of comprehensive income and (b) AOCI.

We have ignored the income tax effects of the amounts in order to focus on the core issues. Note, though, that as gains and losses occur, they are reported net of tax (tax expense for a gain, tax savings for a loss) in the statement of comprehensive income.[20] Likewise, AOCI in the balance sheet also is reported net of tax.

[20]Similarly, if any new prior service cost should arise due to a plan amendment, it too would be reported net of tax.

Putting the Pieces Together

● LO8

In preceding sections, we've discussed (1) the projected benefit obligation (including changes due to periodic service cost, accrued interest, revised estimates, plan amendments, and the payment of benefits); (2) the plan assets (including changes due to investment returns, employer contributions, and the payment of benefits); (3) prior service cost; (4) gains and losses; (5) the periodic pension expense (comprising components of each of these); and (6) the funded status of the plan. These elements of a pension plan are interrelated. It's helpful to see how each element relates to the others. One way is to bring each part together in a *pension spreadsheet.* We do this for our 2009 Global Communications Illustration in Graphic 17–11.

GRAPHIC 17–11
Pension Spreadsheet

			AOCI		Income Statement	Asset	Asset or Liability
($ in millions) Note: ( )s indicate credits; debits otherwise	PBO	Plan Assets	Prior Service Cost	Net Loss	Pension Expense	Cash	Net Pension (Liability) / Asset
Balance, Jan. 1, 2009	(400)	300	56	55			(100)
Service cost	(41)				41		(41)
Interest cost	(24)				24		(24)
Expected return on assets		27			(27)		27
Adjust for: Gain on assets		3		(3)			3
Amortization of:							
Prior service cost–AOCI			(4)		4		
Net loss–AOCI				(1)	1		
Loss on PBO	(23)			23			(23)
Prior service cost (new)*	0		0				0
Contributions to fund		48				(48)	48
Retiree benefits paid	38	(38)					
Balance, Dec. 31, 2009	(450)	340	52	74	43		(110)

*This amount was $60 million in the 2007 pension spreadsheet.

When the PBO exceeds plan assets, we have a net pension liability. If plan assets exceed the PBO we have a net pension asset.

Each change in one of the accounts in the formal records (the blue-shaded area) affects exactly two such accounts.

You should spend several minutes studying this spreadsheet, focusing on the relationships among the elements that constitute a postretirement benefit pension plan. Notice that the first numerical column simply repeats the actuary's report of how the PBO changed during the year, as explained previously (Illustration 17–2). Likewise, the second column reproduces the changes in plan assets we discussed earlier (Illustration 17–3). We've also previously noted the changes in the prior service cost–AOCI (page 898) and the net loss–AOCI (page 900) that are duplicated in the third and fourth columns. The fifth column repeats the calculation of the 2009 pension expense we determined earlier (page 896), and the cash contribution to the pension fund is the sole item in the next column.

The last column shows the changes in the funded status of the plan. Be sure to notice that the funded status is the difference between the PBO (column 1) and the plan assets (column 2). That means that each of the changes we see in either of the first two columns also is reflected as a change in the funded status in the last column. For example, we noted earlier that when Global added $48 million to its plan assets, the pension liability decreased since it's the excess of the PBO over plan assets. We see that result in our spreadsheet.

Notice that each change in a formal account (blue-shaded columns) is reflected in exactly two of those columns. Any of the changes that affect the net pension liability (or asset) also is reported in one of the first two (pink) columns due to the relationship described in the previous paragraph.

INTERNATIONAL FINANCIAL REPORTING STANDARDS

Limitation on Recognition of Pension Assets. Under *IAS No. 19*, pension assets can't be recognized in excess of the net total of unrecognized past (prior) service cost and actuarial losses plus the present value of benefits available from refunds or reduction of future contributions to the plan. There is no such limitation under U.S. GAAP.

DECISION MAKERS' PERSPECTIVE

Although financial statement items are casualties of the political compromises of *SFAS No. 87*, information provided in the disclosure notes fortunately makes up for some of the deficiencies. *SFAS No. 132* revised the pension disclosure requirements.[21] Foremost among the useful disclosures are changes in the projected benefit obligation, changes in the fair value of plan assets, and a breakdown of the components of the annual pension expense. Other information also is made available to make it possible for interested analysts to reconstruct the financial statements with pension assets and liabilities included. We'll look at specific disclosures after we discuss postretirement benefits other than pensions because the two types of plans are reported together.

Pension amounts reported in the disclosure notes fill a reporting gap left by the minimal disclosures in the primary financial statements.

Investors and creditors must be cautious of the nontraditional treatment of pension information when developing financial ratios as part of an analysis of financial statements. The various elements of pensions that are not reported separately on the balance sheet and income statement (PBO, plan assets, gains and losses) can be included in ratios such as the debt to equity ratio or return on assets, but only by deliberately obtaining those numbers from the disclosure notes and adjusting the computation of the ratios. Similarly, without adjustment, profitability ratios and the times interest earned ratio will be distorted because pension expense includes the financial components of interest and return on assets.

Earnings quality (as defined in Chapter 4 and discussed in other chapters) also can be influenced by amounts reported in pension disclosures. Companies with relatively sizeable unrecognized pension costs (prior service cost, net gain or loss) can be expected to exhibit a relatively high "transitory" earnings component. Recall that transitory earnings are expected to be less predictive of future earnings than the "permanent" earnings component.

Settlement or Curtailment of Pension Plans

Companies sometimes terminate defined benefit plans to reduce costs and lessen risk.

Companies sometimes terminate defined benefit plans to siphon off excess pension fund assets for other purposes.

To cut down on cumbersome paperwork and lessen their exposure to the risk posed by defined benefit plans, many companies are providing defined contribution plans instead. Sometimes the motivation to terminate a plan is to take advantage of the excess funding position of many plans that was created by the stock market boom of the 1980s and 1990s and to divert these assets to another purpose. This trend was given impetus in 1982 when **Tengelmann Group** took over ailing **A&P** and used the acquired company's excess pension plan assets to finance its turnaround. Since then, so-called reversion assets have been used, not only in takeovers, but by existing management as well. **Exxon** (now **ExxonMobil**), for instance, used $1.6 billion from its $5.6 billion pension fund to bolster operations during a period of depressed oil prices in 1986. Asset reversions are not as common now as in the 1980s, largely because of excise taxes on amounts recovered when plans are terminated and other restrictive legislation taken by Congress to limit terminations.

[21]"Employers' Disclosures about Pensions and Other Postretirement Benefits," *Statement of Financial Accounting Standards No. 132* (revised 2003), (Stamford, Conn.: FASB, 2003).

When a plan is terminated, *SFAS No. 88* requires a gain or loss to be reported at that time.[22] For instance, **Melville Corporation** described the termination of its pension plan in the following disclosure note:

GRAPHIC 17–12
Gain on the Termination of a Defined Benefit Plan—Melville Corporation

Retirement Plans (in part)
. . . As a result of the termination of the defined benefit plans, and after the settlement of the liability to plan participants through the purchase of nonparticipating annuity contracts or lump-sum rollovers into the new 401(k) Profit Sharing Plan, the Company recorded a nonrecurring gain of approximately $4,000,000 which was the amount of plan assets that reverted to the Company. This was accounted for in accordance with *Statement of Financial Accounting Standards No. 88,* "Employers' Accounting for Settlements and Curtailments of Defined Benefit Pension Plans and for Termination Benefits."

CONCEPT REVIEW EXERCISE

PENSION PLANS

Allied Services, Inc. has a noncontributory, defined benefit pension plan. Pension plan assets had a fair market value of $900 million at December 31, 2008.

On January 3, 2009, Allied amended the pension formula to increase benefits for each service year. By making the amendment retroactive to prior years, Allied incurred a prior service cost of $75 million, adding to the previous projected benefit obligation of $875 million. The prior service cost is to be amortized (expensed) over 15 years. The service cost is $31 million for 2009. Both the actuary's discount rate and the expected rate of return on plan assets were 8%. The actual rate of return on plan assets was 10%.

At December 31, 2009, $16 million was contributed to the pension fund and $22 million was paid to retired employees. Also, at that time, the actuary revised a previous assumption, increasing the PBO estimate by $10 million. The net loss AOCI at the beginning of the year was $13 million.

Required:

Determine each of the following amounts as of December 31, 2009, the fiscal year-end for Allied: (1) projected benefit obligation; (2) plan assets; and (3) pension expense.

SOLUTION

($ in millions)	Projected Benefit Obligation	Plan Assets	Pension Expense
Balances at Jan. 1	$ 875	$900	$ 0
Prior service cost	75		
Service cost	31		31
Interest cost [($875 + 75)* × 8%]	76		76
Return on plan assets:			
Actual ($900 × 10%)		90	
Expected ($900 × 8%)			(72)
Amortization of prior service cost ($75 ÷ 15)			5
Amortization of net loss			0†
Loss on PBO	10		
Cash contribution		16	
Retirement payments	(22)	(22)	
Balance at Dec. 31	$1,045	$984	$40

Note: The $18 million gain on plan assets ($90 – 72 million) is not recognized yet; it is carried forward to be combined with previous and future gains and losses, which will be recognized only if the net gain or net loss exceeds 10% of the higher of the PBO or plan assets.
*Since the plan was amended at the beginning of the year, the prior service cost increased the PBO at that time.
†Since the net loss ($13) does not exceed 10% of $900 (higher than $875), no amortization is required for 2009.

[22] "Employers' Accounting for Settlements and Curtailments of Defined Benefit Pension Plans and for Termination Benefits," *Statement of Financial Accounting Standards No. 88* (Stamford, Conn.: FASB, 1985).

PART **E**

POSTRETIREMENT BENEFITS OTHER THAN PENSIONS

As we just discussed, most companies have pension plans that provide for the future payments of retirement benefits to compensate employees for their current services. Many companies also furnish *other postretirement benefits* to their retired employees. These may include medical coverage, dental coverage, life insurance, group legal services, and other benefits. By far the most common is health care benefits. One of every three U.S. workers in medium- and large-size companies participates in health care plans that provide for coverage that continues into retirement. The aggregate impact is considerable; the total obligation for all U.S. corporations is about $500 billion.

Prior to 1993, employers accounted for postretirement benefit costs on a pay-as-you-go basis, meaning the expense each year was simply the amount of insurance premiums or medical claims paid, depending on the way the company provided health care benefits. *SFAS No. 106* requires a completely different approach. The expected future health care costs for retirees now must be recognized as an expense over the years necessary for employees to become entitled to the benefits.[23] This is the accrual basis that also is the basis for pension accounting.

● LO9

In fact, accounting for postretirement benefits is similar in most respects to accounting for pension benefits. This is because the two forms of benefits are fundamentally similar. Each is a form of deferred compensation earned during the employee's service life and each can be estimated as the present value of the cost of providing the expected future benefits. **General Motors** described its plan as shown in Graphic 17–13.

GRAPHIC 17–13
Disclosures—General Motors

Real World Financials

Note 5: Other Postretirement Benefits (in part)
The Corporation and certain of its domestic subsidiaries maintain hourly and salaried benefit plans that provide postretirement medical, dental, vision, and life insurance to retirees and eligible dependents. These benefits are funded as incurred from the general assets of the Corporation. Effective January 1, 1992, the Corporation adopted *SFAS No. 106,* Employers Accounting for Postretirement Benefits Other Than Pensions. This Statement requires that the cost of such benefits be recognized in the financial statements during the period employees provide service to the Corporation.

Despite the similarities, though, there are a few differences in the characteristics of the benefits that necessitate differences in accounting treatment. Because accounting for the two types of retiree benefits is so nearly the same, our discussion in this portion of the chapter will emphasize the differences. This will allow you to use what you learned earlier in the chapter regarding pension accounting as a foundation for learning how to account for other postretirement benefits, supplementing that common base only when necessary. Focusing on the differences also will reinforce your understanding of pension accounting.

What Is a Postretirement Benefit Plan?

Before addressing the accounting ramifications, let's look at a typical retiree health care plan.[24] First, it's important to distinguish retiree health care benefits from health care benefits provided during an employee's working years. The annual cost of providing *preretirement* benefits is simply part of the annual compensation expense. However, many companies offer coverage that continues into retirement. It is the deferred aspect of these *postretirement* benefits that creates an accounting issue.

Eligibility usually is based on age and/or years of service.

Usually a plan promises benefits in exchange for services performed over a designated number of years, or reaching a particular age, or both. For instance, a plan might specify that employees are eligible for postretirement benefits after both working 20 years and reaching

[23] "Employers' Accounting for Postretirement Benefits Other Than Pensions," *Statement of Financial Accounting Standards No. 106* (Norwalk, Conn.: FASB, 1990). The Standard became effective (with some exceptions) in 1993.

[24] For convenience, our discussion focuses on health care benefits because these are by far the most common type of postretirement benefits other than pensions. But the concepts we discuss apply equally to other forms of postretirement benefits.

age 62 while in service. Eligibility requirements and the nature of benefits usually are specified by a written plan, or sometimes only by company practice.

Postretirement Health Benefits and Pension Benefits Compared

Keep in mind that retiree health benefits differ fundamentally from pension benefits in some important respects:

1. The amount of *pension* benefits generally is based on the number of years an employee works for the company so that the longer the employee works, the higher are the benefits. On the other hand, the amount of *postretirement health care* benefits typically is unrelated to service. It's usually an all-or-nothing plan in which a certain level of coverage is promised upon retirement, independent of the length of service beyond that necessary for eligibility.
2. Although coverage might be identical, the cost of providing the coverage might vary significantly from retiree to retiree and from year to year because of differing medical needs.
3. Postretirement health care plans often require the retiree to share in the cost of coverage through monthly contribution payments. For instance, a company might pay 80% of insurance premiums, with the retiree paying 20%. The net cost of providing coverage is reduced by these contributions as well as by any portion of the cost paid by Medicare or other insurance.
4. Coverage often is provided to spouses and eligible dependents.

Determining the Net Cost of Benefits

To determine the postretirement benefit obligation and the postretirement benefit expense, the company's actuary first must make estimates of what the postretirement benefit costs will be for current employees. Then, as illustrated in Graphic 17–14, contributions to those costs by employees are deducted, as well as Medicare's share of the costs (for retirement years when the retiree will be 65 or older), to determine the estimated net cost of benefits to the employer:

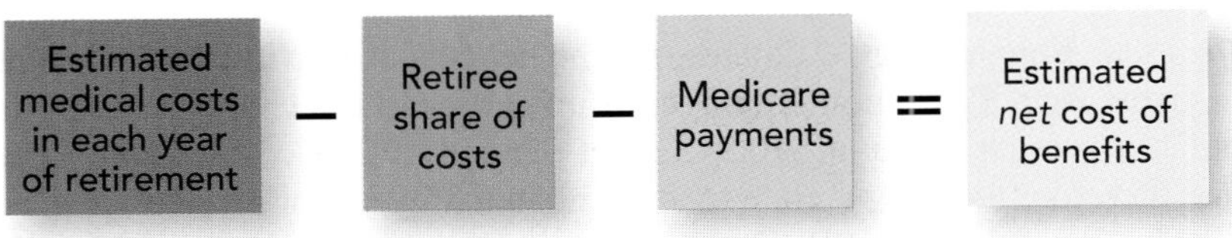

GRAPHIC 17–14
Estimating the Net Cost of Benefits

Remember, postretirement health care benefits are anticipated actual costs of providing the promised health care, rather than an amount estimated by a defined benefit formula. This makes these estimates inherently more intricate, particularly because health care costs in general are notoriously difficult to forecast. And, since postretirement health care benefits are partially paid by the retiree and by Medicare, these cost-sharing amounts must be estimated as well.

On the other hand, estimating postretirement benefits costs is similar in many ways to estimating pension costs. Both estimates entail a variety of assumptions to be made by the company's actuary. Many of these assumptions are the same; for instance, both require estimates of:

Many of the assumptions needed to estimate postretirement health care benefits are the same as those needed to estimate pension benefits.

1. A discount rate.
2. Expected return on plan assets (if the plan is funded).
3. Employee turnover.
4. Expected retirement age.
5. Expected compensation increases (if the plan is pay-related).
6. Expected age of death.
7. Number and ages of beneficiaries and dependents.

Of course, the relative importance of some estimates is different from that for pension plans. Dependency status, turnover, and retirement age, for example, take on much greater significance. Also, additional assumptions become necessary as a result of differences between pension plans and other postretirement benefit plans. Specifically, it's necessary to estimate:

Some additional assumptions are needed to estimate postretirement health care benefits besides those needed to estimate pension benefits.

1. The current cost of providing health care benefits at each age that participants might receive benefits.
2. Demographic characteristics of plan participants that might affect the amount and timing of benefits.
3. Benefit coverage provided by Medicare, other insurance, or other sources that will reduce the net cost of employer-provided benefits.
4. The expected health care cost trend rate.[25]

The postretirement benefit obligation is the discounted present value of the benefits during retirement.

Taking these assumptions into account, the company's actuary estimates what the net cost of postretirement benefits will be for current employees in each year of their expected retirement. The discounted present value of those costs is the expected postretirement benefit obligation.

Postretirement Benefit Obligation

● LO10

There are two related obligation amounts. As indicated in Graphic 17–15, one measures the total obligation and the other refers to a specific portion of the total:

GRAPHIC 17–15
Two Views of the Obligation for Postretirement Benefits Other Than Pensions

1. **Expected postretirement benefit obligation (EPBO):** The actuary's estimate of the *total* postretirement benefits (at their discounted present value) expected to be received by plan participants.
2. **Accumulated postretirement benefit obligation (APBO):** The portion of the EPBO attributed to employee service to date.

The accumulated postretirement benefit obligation (APBO) is analogous to the projected benefit obligation (PBO) for pensions. Like the PBO, the APBO is reported in the balance sheet only to the extent that it exceeds plan assets.

Measuring the Obligation

To illustrate, assume the actuary estimates that the net cost of providing health care benefits to Jessica Farrow (our illustration employee from earlier in the chapter) during her retirement years has a present value of $10,842 as of the end of 2007. This is the EPBO. If the benefits (and therefore the costs) relate to an estimated 35 years of service[26] and 10 of those years have been completed, the APBO would be:

$3,098 represents the portion of the EPBO related to the first 10 years of the 35-year service period.

$10,842	×	10/35	=	$3,098
EPBO		Fraction attributed to service to date		APBO

If the assumed discount rate is 6%, a year later the EPBO will have grown to $11,493 simply because of a year's interest accruing at that rate ($10,842 × 1.06 = $11,493). Notice that there is no increase in the EPBO for service because, unlike the obligation in most pension plans, the total obligation is not increased by an additional year's service.

The APBO, however, is the portion of the EPBO related to service up to a particular date. Consequently, the APBO will have increased both because of interest and because the service fraction will be higher (service cost):

$3,612 represents the portion of the EPBO related to the first 11 years of the 35-year service period.

$11,493	×	11/35	=	$3,612
EPBO		Fraction attributed to service to date		APBO

[25]Health care cost trend rates recently reported have ranged from 5.5% to 13.5%, with 9% being the most commonly assumed rate. AICPA, *Accounting Trends and Techniques,* 2007.

[26]Assigning the costs to particular service years is referred to as the *attribution* of the costs to the years the benefits are assumed earned. We discuss attribution in the next section.

The two elements of the increase in 2008 can be separated as follows:

APBO at the beginning of the year	$3,098
Interest cost: $3,098 × 6%	186
Service cost:($11,493 × 1/35) portion of EPBO attributed to the year	328
APBO at the end of the year	$3,612

The APBO increases each year due to (a) interest accrued on the APBO and (b) the portion of the EPBO attributed to that year.

Attribution

Attribution is the process of assigning the cost of benefits to the years during which those benefits are assumed to be earned by employees. The approach required by *SFAS No. 106* is to assign an equal fraction of the EPBO to each year of service from the employee's date of hire to the employee's full eligibility date.[27] This is the date the employee has performed all the service necessary to have earned all the retiree benefits estimated to be received by the employee.[28] In our earlier example, we assumed the attribution period was 35 years and accordingly accrued 1/35 of the EPBO each year. The amount accrued each year increases both the APBO and the postretirement benefit expense. In Illustration 17–8 we see how the 35-year attribution (accrual) period was determined.

The cost of benefits is attributed to the years during which those benefits are assumed to be earned by employees.

ILLUSTRATION 17–8
Determining the Attribution Period

Jessica Farrow was hired by Global Communications at age 22 at the beginning of 1998 and is expected to retire at the end of 2037 at age 61. The retirement period is estimated to be 20 years.*

Global's employees are eligible for postretirement health care benefits after both reaching age 56 while in service and having worked 20 years.

Since Farrow becomes fully eligible at age 56 (the end of 2032), retiree benefits are attributed to the 35-year period from her date of hire through that date. Graphically, the situation can be described as follows:

Attribution Period
35 years

Retirement Period
20 years

Age 22	Age 56	Age 61	Age 81
1998	**2032**	**2037**	**2057**
Date hired	Full-eligibility date	Retirement	

*You probably recognize this as the situation used earlier in the chapter to illustrate pension accounting.

The attribution period spans each year of service from the employee's date of hire to the employee's full eligibility date.

Some critics of *SFAS No. 106* feel there is a fundamental inconsistency between the way we measure the benefits and the way we assign the benefits to specific service periods. The benefits (EPBO) are measured with the concession that the employee may work beyond the full eligibility date; however, the attribution period does not include years of service after that date. The counterargument is the fact that at the full eligibility date the employee will have earned the right to receive the full benefits expected under the plan and the amount of the benefits will not increase with service beyond that date.[29]

The attribution period does not include years of service beyond the full eligibility date even if the employee is expected to work after that date.

[27]If the plan specifically grants credit only for service from a date after employee's date of hire, the beginning of the attribution period is considered to be the beginning of that credited service period, rather than the employee's date of hire.

[28]Or any beneficiaries and covered dependents.

[29]"Employers' Accounting for Postretirement Benefits Other Than Pensions," *Statement of Financial Accounting Standards No. 106* (Norwalk, Conn.: FASB, 1990), par. 219–239.

● LO11

Accounting for Postretirement Benefit Plans Other Than Pensions

We account for pensions and for other postretirement benefits essentially the same way.

As we just discussed, it's necessary to attribute a portion of the accumulated postretirement benefit obligation to each year as the service cost for that year as opposed to measuring the actual benefits employees earn during the year as we did for pension plans. That's due to the fundamental nature of these other postretirement plans under which employees are ineligible for benefits until specific eligibility criteria are met, at which time they become 100% eligible. This contrasts with pension plans under which employees earn additional benefits each year until they retire.

GRAPHIC 17–16
Measuring Service Cost

Measuring the service cost differs, though, due to a fundamental difference in the way employees acquire benefits under the two types of plans.

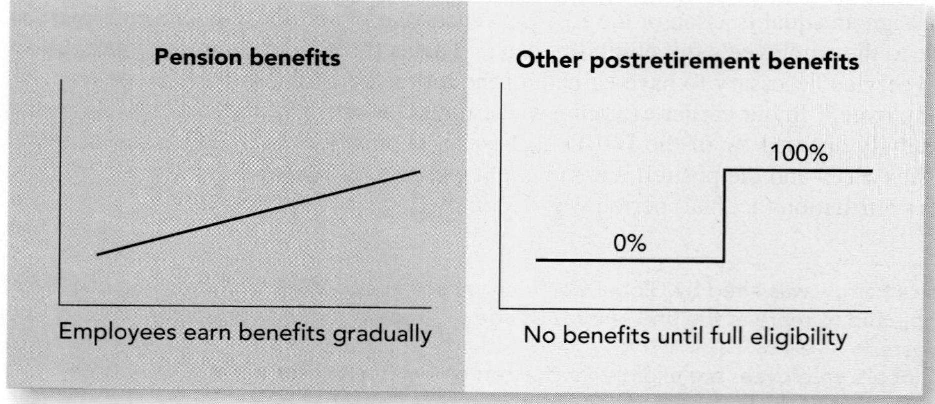

The way we measure service cost is the primary difference between accounting for pensions and for other postretirement benefits. Otherwise, though, accounting for the two is virtually identical. For example, a company with an underfunded postretirement benefit plan with existing prior service cost and net loss–AOCI would record the following journal entries annually:

We record the annual expense and funding for other postretirement benefit plans the same way we do for pensions.

We record losses and gains (as well as any new prior service cost should it occur) the same way we do for pensions.

To Record Postretirement Benefit Expense		
Postretirement benefit expense (total)	xx	
Plan assets (expected return on assets)	xx	
Amortization of net gain–OCI (current amortization)	xx	
APBO (service cost + interest cost)		xx
Amortization of net loss–OCI (current amortization)		xx
Amortization of prior service cost–OCI[30] (current amortization)		xx
To Record Cash Funding of Plan Assets		
Plan assets	xx	
Cash (contribution to plan assets)		xx
To Record Gains and Losses		
Loss–OCI (from change in assumption)	xx	
APBO		xx
or		
APBO	xx	
Gain–OCI (from change in assumption)		xx
Plan assets	xx	
Gain–OCI (actual return on assets − expected return)		xx
or		
Gain–OCI (expected return on assets − actual return)	xx	
Plan assets		xx

[30]The prior service cost for other postretirement benefits is amortized over the average remaining time until "full eligibility" for employees rather than until retirement as is the case for pension plans. This is consistent with recording "regular" service cost over the time to full eligibility.

Earlier this year, you were elected to the board of directors of Champion International, Inc. Champion has offered its employees postretirement health care benefits for 35 years. The practice of extending health care benefits to retirees began modestly. Most employees retired after age 65, when most benefits were covered by Medicare. Costs also were lower because life expectancies were shorter and medical care was less expensive. Because costs were so low, little attention was paid to accounting for these benefits. The company simply recorded an expense when benefits were provided to retirees. *SFAS No. 106* changed all that. Now, the obligation for these benefits must be anticipated and reported in the annual report. Worse yet, the magnitude of the obligation has grown enormously, almost unnoticed. Health care costs have soared in recent years. Medical technology and other factors have extended life expectancies. Of course, the value to employees of this benefit has grown parallel to the growth of the burden to the company.

Without being required to anticipate future costs, many within Champion's management were caught by surprise at the enormity of the company's obligation. Equally disconcerting was the fact that such a huge liability now must be exposed to public view. Now you find that several board members are urging the dismantling of the postretirement plan altogether.

What do you think?

A Comprehensive Illustration

We assumed earlier that the EPBO at the end of 2007 was determined by the actuary to be $10,842. This was the present value on that date of all anticipated future benefits. Then we noted that the EPBO at the end of the next year would have grown by 6% to $11,493. This amount, too, would represent the present value of the same anticipated future benefits, but as of a year later. The APBO, remember, is the portion of the EPBO attributed to service performed to a particular date. So, we determined the APBO at the end of 2008 to be $11,493 × $^{11}/_{35}$, or $3,612. We determined the $328 service cost noted earlier for 2008 as the portion of the EPBO attributed to that year: $11,493 × $^{1}/_{35}$.

Now, let's review our previous discussion of how the EPBO, the APBO, and the postretirement benefit expense are determined by calculating those amounts a year later, at the end of 2009. Before doing so, however, we can anticipate (a) the EPBO to be $11,493 × 1.06, or $12,182, (b) the APBO to be $^{12}/_{35}$ of that amount, or $4,177, and (c) the 2007 service cost to be $^{1}/_{35}$ of that amount, or $348. In Illustration 17–9 we see if our expectations are borne out by direct calculation.

Assume the actuary has estimated the net cost of retiree benefits in each year of Jessica Farrow's 20-year expected retirement period to be the amounts shown in the calculation below. She is fully eligible for benefits at the end of 2032 and is expected to retire at the end of 2037.

Calculating the APBO and the postretirement benefit expense at the end of 2009, 12 years after being hired, begins with estimating the EPBO.

Steps to calculate (a) the EPBO, (b) the APBO, and (c) the annual service cost at the end of 2009, 12 years after being hired, are:

(a). 1. Estimate the cost of retiree benefits in each year of the expected retirement period and deduct anticipated Medicare reimbursements and retiree cost-sharing to derive the net cost to the employer in each year of the expected retirement period.
2. Find the present value of each year's net benefit cost as of the *retirement date.*
3. Find the present value of the total net benefit cost as of the *current date.* This is the EPBO.

(b). Multiply the EPBO by the attribution factor, (service to date/total attribution period). This is the APBO. The service cost in any year is simply one year's worth of the EPBO.

(c). Multiply the EPBO by $^{1}/_{\text{total attribution period}}$.

ILLUSTRATION 17–9
Determining the Postretirement Benefit Obligation

The EPBO is the discounted present value of the total benefits expected to be earned.

The fraction of the EPBO considered to be earned this year is the service cost.

The fraction of the EPBO considered to be earned so far is the APBO.

The steps are demonstrated in Illustration 17–9A.

ILLUSTRATION 17–9A

EPBO, APBO, and Service Cost in 2009

The actuary estimates the net cost to the employer in each year the retiree is expected to receive benefits.

As of the retirement date, the lump-sum equivalent of the expected yearly costs is $62,269.

The EPBO in 2009 is the present value of those benefits.

The APBO is the portion of the EPBO attributed to service to date.

The service cost is the portion of the EPBO attributed to a particular year's service.

(a.1). Actuary estimates the net cost of benefits paid during retirement years:

(a.2). Present value [n = 1, 2, 3, 4, . . . 19, 20: i = 6%] of the net benefits as of the retirement date:

Year	Age	Net Benefit	Present Value at 2037
2038	62	5,000	4,717
2039	63	5,600	4,984
2040	64	6,300	5,290
2041	65	3,000	2,376
~	~	~	~
2056	80	9,550	3,156
2057	81	10,300	3,212
			$62,269

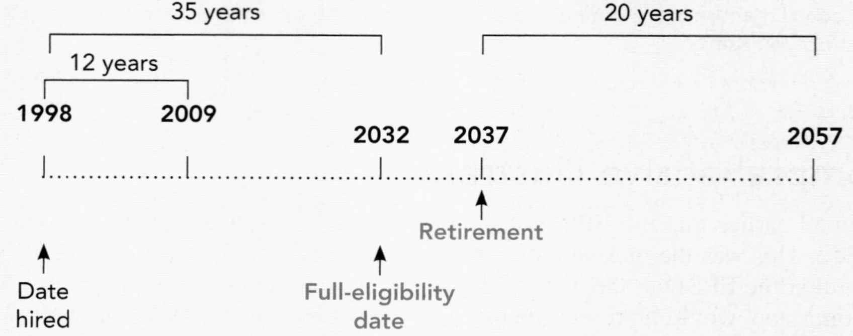

(a.3). Present value (n = 28, i = 6%) of postretirement benefits at 2009 is $62,269 × .19563 = $12,182 (EPBO)

(b). $12,182 × 12⁄35 = $4,177 (APBO)

(c). $12,182 × 1⁄35 = $348 (Service Cost)

DECISION MAKERS' PERSPECTIVE

Postretirement benefit amounts reported in the disclosure notes fill a reporting gap left by the minimal disclosures in the primary financial statements.

When they analyze financial statements, investors and creditors should be wary of the non-standard way companies report pension and other postretirement information. Recall that in the balance sheet, firms do not separately report the benefit obligation and the plan assets. Also, companies have considerable latitude in making the several assumptions needed to estimate the components of postretirement benefit plans. Fortunately, information provided in the disclosure notes makes up for some of the deficiency in balance sheet information and makes it possible for interested analysts to modify their analysis. As for pensions, the choices companies make for the discount rate, expected return on plan assets, and the compensation growth rate can greatly impact postretirement benefit expense and earnings quality. The disclosures required are very similar to pension disclosures. In fact, disclosures for the two types of retiree benefits typically are combined.[31] Disclosures include:

- Descriptions of the plans.
- Estimates of the obligations (PBO, ABO, vested benefit obligation, EPBO, and APBO).
- The percentage of total plan assets for each major category of assets (equity securities, debt securities, real estate, other) as well as a description of investment strategies, including any target asset allocations and risk management practices.

[31] "Employers' Disclosures about Pensions and Other Postretirement Benefits," *Statement of Financial Accounting Standards No. 132* (Stamford, Conn.: FASB, 1998).

- A breakdown of the components of the annual pension and postretirement benefit expenses for the years reported.
- The discount rates, the assumed rate of compensation increases used to measure the PBO, the expected long-term rate of return on plan assets, and the expected rate of increase in future medical and dental benefit costs.
- Estimated benefit payments presented separately for the next five years and in the aggregate for years 6–10.
- Estimate of expected contributions to fund the plan for the next year.
- Disclosures related to the modifications *SFAS No. 158* introduced, including (a) any changes to the net gain or net loss and prior service cost arising during the period, (b) the accumulated amounts of these components of accumulated other comprehensive income, and (c) the amounts of those balances expected to be amortized in the next year.
- Other information to make it possible for interested analysts to reconstruct the financial statements with plan assets and liabilities included.

CONCEPT REVIEW EXERCISE

OTHER POSTRETIREMENT BENEFITS

Technology Group, Inc., has an unfunded retiree health care plan. The actuary estimates the net cost of providing health care benefits to a particular employee during his retirement years to have a present value of $24,000 as of the end of 2009 (the EPBO). The benefits and therefore the expected postretirement benefit obligation relate to an estimated 36 years of service and 12 of those years have been completed. The interest rate is 6%.

Required:

Pertaining to the one employee only:

1. What is the accumulated postretirement benefit obligation at the end of 2009?
2. What is the expected postretirement benefit obligation at the end of 2010?
3. What is the service cost to be included in 2010 postretirement benefit expense?
4. What is the interest cost to be included in 2010 postretirement benefit expense?
5. What is the accumulated postretirement benefit obligation at the end of 2010?
6. Show how the APBO changed during 2010 by reconciling the beginning and ending balances.
7. What is the 2010 postretirement benefit expense, assuming no net gains or losses and no prior service cost?

SOLUTION

1. What is the accumulated postretirement benefit obligation at the end of 2009?

$24,000	×	12⁄36	=	$8,000
EPBO 2009		Fraction earned		APBO 2009

2. What is the expected postretirement benefit obligation at the end of 2010?

$24,000	×	1.06	=	$25,440
EPBO 2009		To accrue interest		EPBO 2010

3. What is the service cost to be included in 2010 postretirement benefit expense?

$25,440	×	1⁄36	=	$707
EPBO 2010		Earned in 2010		Service cost

4. What is the interest cost to be included in 2010 postretirement benefit expense?

$8,000 (beginning APBO) × 6% = $480

5. What is the accumulated postretirement benefit obligation at the end of 2010?

$25,440	×	13⁄36	=	$9,187
EPBO 2010		Fraction earned		APBO 2010

6. Show how the APBO changed during 2010 by reconciling the beginning and ending balances.

APBO at the beginning of 2010 (from req. 1)	$8,000
Service cost: (from req. 3)	707
Interest cost: (from req. 4)	480
APBO at the end of 2010 (from req. 5)	$9,187

7. What is the 2010 postretirement benefit expense, assuming no net gains or losses and no prior service cost?

Service cost	$ 707
Interest cost	480
Actual return on the plan assets	(not funded)
Adjusted for: gain or loss on the plan assets	(not funded)
Amortization of prior service cost	none
Amortization of net gain or loss	none
Postretirement benefit expense	$1,187

FINANCIAL REPORTING CASE SOLUTION

1. **Why is underfunding not a concern in your present employment?** *(p. 885)* In a defined contribution plan, the employer is not obliged to provide benefits beyond the annual contribution to the employees' plan. No liability is created. Unlike retirement benefits paid in a defined benefit plan, the employee's retirement benefits in a defined contribution plan are totally dependent on how well invested assets perform in the marketplace.
2. **Were you correct that the pension liability is not reported on the balance sheet? What is the liability?** *(p. 887)* Yes. The pension liability is measured (in three ways) and tracked informally, but not reported on the balance sheet. It is disclosed, however, in the notes. For United Dynamics, the PBO in 2009 is $2,628 million.
3. **What is the amount of the plan assets available to pay benefits? What are the factors that can cause that amount to change?** *(p. 893)* The plan assets at the end of 2009 total $2,807 million. A trustee accepts employer contributions, invests the contributions, accumulates the earnings on the investments, and pays benefits from the plan assets. So the amount is increased each year by employer cash contributions and (hopefully) a return on assets invested. It is decreased by amounts paid out to retired employees.
4. **What does the "pension asset" represent? Are you interviewing with a company whose pension plan is severely underfunded?** *(p. 894)* The pension asset is not the plan assets available to pay pension benefits. Instead, it's the net difference between those assets and the pension obligation. United Dynamics' plan assets exceed the pension obligation in each year presented.
5. **How is the pension expense influenced by changes in the pension liability and plan assets?** *(p. 895)* The pension expense reported on the income statement is a composite of periodic changes that occur in both the pension obligation and the plan assets. For United Dynamics in 2009, the pension expense included the service cost and interest cost, which are changes in the PBO, and the return on plan assets. It also included an amortized portion of prior service costs (a previous change in the PBO) and of net gains (gains and losses result from changes in both the PBO and plan assets).

THE BOTTOM LINE

- LO1 Pension plans are arrangements designed to provide income to individuals during their retirement years. *Defined contribution* plans promise fixed annual contributions to a pension fund, without further commitment regarding benefit amounts at retirement. *Defined benefit* plans promise fixed retirement benefits defined by a designated formula. The employer sets aside cash each year to provide sufficient funds to pay promised benefits. (p. 883)

- **LO2** The *accumulated benefit obligation* is an estimate of the discounted present value of the retirement benefits earned so far by employees, applying the plan's pension formula to *existing* compensation levels. The vested benefit obligation is the portion of the accumulated benefit obligation that plan participants are entitled to receive regardless of their continued employment. The *projected benefit obligation* estimates retirement benefits by applying the pension formula to *projected future* compensation levels. (p. 887)
- **LO3** The PBO can change due to the accumulation of *service cost* from year to year, the accrual of *interest* as time passes, making plan amendments retroactive to prior years (prior service cost), and periodic adjustments when estimates change (gains and losses). The obligation is reduced as benefits actually are paid to retired employees. (p. 888)
- **LO4** The plan assets consist of the accumulated balance of the annual employer contributions plus the return on the investments less benefits paid to retirees. (p. 893)
- **LO5** The difference between an employer's obligation (PBO for pensions, APBO for other postretirement benefit plans) and the resources available to satisfy that obligation (plan assets) is the funded status of the pension plan. The employer must report the "funded status" of the plan in the balance sheet as a net pension liability if the obligation exceeds the plan assets or as a net pension asset if the plan assets exceed the obligation. (p. 894)
- **LO6** The pension expense is a composite of periodic changes in both the pension obligation and the plan assets. Service cost is the increase in the PBO attributable to employee service and is the primary component of pension expense. The interest and return-on-assets components are financial items created only because the pension payment is delayed and the obligation is funded currently. Prior service cost is recognized over employees' future service period. Also, neither a loss (gain) on the PBO nor a loss (gain) on plan assets is immediately recognized in pension expense; they are recognized on a delayed basis to achieve income smoothing. (p. 895)
- **LO7** Recording pension expense causes the net pension liability/asset to change by the service cost, the interest cost, and the expected return on plan assets. Any amortization amounts included in the expense will reduce the *accumulated other comprehensive income* balances being amortized, e.g., net loss—AOCI and prior service cost–AOCI. Similarly, the plan assets are increased by the annual cash investment. New losses and gains (as well as any new prior service cost should it occur) are recognized as other comprehensive income. (p. 900)
- **LO8** The various elements of a pension plan—projected benefit obligation, plan assets, prior service cost, gains and losses, pension expense, and the funded status of the plan—are interrelated. One way to see how each element relates to the other is to bring each part together in a *pension spreadsheet.* (p. 905)
- **LO9** Accounting for postretirement benefits is similar in most respects to accounting for pension benefits. Like pensions, other postretirement benefits are a form of deferred compensation. Unlike pensions, their cost is attributed to the years from the employee's date of hire to the full eligibility date. (p. 908)
- **LO10** The expected postretirement benefit obligation (EPBO) is the actuary's estimate of the total postretirement benefits (at their discounted present value) expected to be received by plan participants. The accumulated postretirement benefit obligation (APBO) is the portion of the EPBO attributed to employee service to date. (p. 910)
- **LO11** The components of postretirement benefit expense are essentially the same as those for pension expense. (p. 912)

SERVICE METHOD OF ALLOCATING PRIOR SERVICE COST

APPENDIX 17

When amortizing prior service cost, our objective is to match the cost with employee service. The straight-line method described in this chapter allocates an equal amount of the prior service cost to each year of the 15-year average service period of affected employees. But consider this: fewer of the affected employees will be working for the company toward the end of that period than at the beginning. Some probably will retire or quit in each year following the amendment.

An allocation approach that reflects the declining service pattern is called the **service method.** This method allocates the prior service cost to each year in proportion to the fraction of the total remaining service years worked in each of those years. To do this, it's necessary to estimate how many of the 2,000 employees working at the beginning of 2008 when the amendment is made will still be employed in each year after the amendment.

Let's suppose, for example, that the actuary estimates that a declining number of these employees still will be employed in each of the next 28 years as indicated in the abbreviated schedule below. The portion of the prior service cost amortized to pension expense each year is \$60 million times a declining fraction. Each year's fraction is that year's service divided by the 28-year total (30,000). This is demonstrated in Graphic 17A–1.

GRAPHIC 17A–1
Service Method of Amortizing Prior Service Cost

By the service method, prior service cost is recognized each year in proportion to the fraction of the total remaining service years worked that year.

Year	Number of Employees Still Employed (assumed for the illustration)	Fraction of Total Service Years		Prior Service Cost ($ in millions)		Amount Amortized ($ in millions)
2008	2,000	2,000/30,000	×	$60	=	$ 4.0
2009	2,000	2,000/30,000	×	60	=	4.0
2010	1,850	1,850/30,000	×	60	=	3.7
2011	1,700	1,700/30,000	×	60	=	3.4
2012	1,550	1,550/30,000	×	60	=	3.1
—	—	—	×	—	=	—
2033	400	400/30,000	×	60	=	.8
2034	250	250/30,000	×	60	=	.5
2035	100	100/30,000	×	60	=	.2
Totals	30,000 Total number of service years	30,000/30,000				$60.0 Total amount amortized

The service method amortized an equal amount *per employee* each year.

Conceptually, the service method achieves a better matching of the cost and benefits. In fact, this is the FASB's recommended approach. However, *SFAS No. 87* permits the consistent use of any method that amortizes the prior service cost at least as quickly.[32] The straight-line method meets this condition and is the approach most often used in practice. In our illustration, the cost is completely amortized over 15 years rather than the 28 years required by the service method. The 15-year average service life is simply the total estimated service years divided by the total number of employees in the group:

30,000 years	÷	2,000	=	15 years
Total number of service years		Total number of employees		Average service years

[32]"Employers' Accounting for Pensions," *Statement of Financial Accounting Standards No. 87* (Stamford, Conn.: FASB, 1985), par. 26.

QUESTIONS FOR REVIEW OF KEY TOPICS

Q 17–1 What is a pension plan? What motivates a corporation to offer a pension plan for its employees?

Q 17–2 Qualified pension plans offer important tax benefits. What is the special tax treatment and what qualifies a pension plan for these benefits?

Q 17–3 Lamont Corporation has a pension plan in which the corporation makes all contributions and employees receive benefits at retirement based on the balance in their accumulated pension fund. What type of pension plan does Lamont have?

Q 17–4 What is the vested benefit obligation?

Q 17–5 Differentiate between the accumulated benefit obligation and the projected benefit obligation.

Q 17–6 Name five events that might change the balance of the PBO.

Q 17–7 Name three events that might change the balance of the plan assets.

Q 17–8 What are the components that might be included in the calculation of net pension cost recognized for a period by an employer sponsoring a defined benefit pension plan?

Q 17–9 Define the service cost component of the periodic pension expense.

Q 17–10 Define the interest cost component of the periodic pension expense.

Q 17–11 The return on plan assets is the increase in plan assets (at fair value), adjusted for contributions to the plan and benefits paid during the period. How is the return included in the calculation of the periodic pension expense?

Q 17–12 Define prior service cost. How is it reported in the financial statements? How is it included in pension expense?

Q 17–13 How should gains or losses related to pension plan assets be recognized? How does this treatment compare to that for gains or losses related to the pension obligation?

Q 17–14 Is a company's PBO reported in the balance sheet? Its plan assets? Explain.

Q 17–15 What two components of pension expense may be negative (i.e., reduce pension expense)?

Q 17–16 Which are the components of pension expense that involve delayed recognition?

Q 17–17 Evaluate this statement: The excess of the actual return on plan assets over the expected return decreases the employer's pension cost.

Q 17–18 When accounting for pension costs, how should the payment into the pension fund be recorded? How does it affect the funded status of the plan?

Q 17–19 TFC, Inc. revises its estimate of future salary levels, causing its PBO estimate to increase by $3 million. How is the $3 reflected in TFC's financial statements?

Q 17–20 A pension plan is underfunded when the employer's obligation (PBO) exceeds the resources available to satisfy that obligation (plan assets) and overfunded when the opposite is the case. How is this funded status reported on the balance sheet if plan assets exceed the PBO? If the PBO exceeds plan assets?

Q 17–21 What are two ways to measure the obligation for postretirement benefits other than pensions? Define these measurement approaches.

Q 17–22 How are the costs of providing postretirement benefits other than pensions expensed?

Q 17–23 The components of postretirement benefit expense are similar to the components of pension expense. In what fundamental way does the service cost component differ between these two expenses?

Q 17–24 The EPBO for Branch Industries at the end of 2009 was determined by the actuary to be $20,000 as it relates to employee Will Lawson. Lawson was hired at the beginning of 1995. He will be fully eligible to retire with health care benefits in 15 years but is expected to retire in 25 years. What is the APBO as it relates to Will Lawson?

BRIEF EXERCISES

BE 17–1
Changes in the projected benefit obligation
● LO3

The projected benefit obligation was $80 million at the beginning of the year. Service cost for the year was $10 million. At the end of the year, pension benefits paid by the trustee were $6 million and there were no pension-related other comprehensive income accounts requiring amortization. The actuary's discount rate was 5%. What was the amount of the projected benefit obligation at year-end?

BE 17–2
Changes in the projected benefit obligation
● LO3

The projected benefit obligation was $80 million at the beginning of the year and $85 million at the end of the year. At the end of the year, pension benefits paid by the trustee were $6 million and there were no pension-related other comprehensive income accounts requiring amortization. The actuary's discount rate was 5%. What was the amount of the service cost for the year?

BE 17–3
Changes in the projected benefit obligation
● LO3

The projected benefit obligation was $80 million at the beginning of the year and $85 million at the end of the year. Service cost for the year was $10 million. At the end of the year, there was no prior service cost and a negligible net loss–pensions. The actuary's discount rate was 5%. What was the amount of the retiree benefits paid by the trustee?

BE 17–4
Changes in the projected benefit obligation
● LO3

The projected benefit obligation was $80 million at the beginning of the year and $85 million at the end of the year. Service cost for the year was $10 million. At the end of the year, pension benefits paid by the trustee were $6 million. The actuary's discount rate was 5%. At the end of the year, the actuary revised the estimate of the percentage rate of increase in compensation levels in upcoming years. What was the amount of the gain or loss the estimate change caused?

BE 17–5
Changes in pension plan assets
● LO4

Pension plan assets were $80 million at the beginning of the year. The return on plan assets was 5%. At the end of the year, retiree benefits paid by the trustee were $6 million and cash invested in the pension fund was $7 million. What was the amount of the pension plan assets at year-end?

BE 17–6
Changes in pension plan assets
● LO4

Pension plan assets were $80 million at the beginning of the year and $83 million at the end of the year. The return on plan assets was 5%. At the end of the year, cash invested in the pension fund was $7 million. What was the amount of the retiree benefits paid by the trustee?

BE 17–7
Changes in pension plan assets
● LO4

Pension plan assets were $100 million at the beginning of the year and $104 million at the end of the year. At the end of the year, retiree benefits paid by the trustee were $6 million and cash invested in the pension fund was $7 million. What was the percentage rate of return on plan assets?

BE 17–8
Pension expense
● LO6

The projected benefit obligation was $80 million at the beginning of the year. Service cost for the year was $10 million. At the end of the year, pension benefits paid by the trustee were $6 million and there were no pension-related other comprehensive income accounts requiring amortization. The actuary's discount rate was 5%. The actual return on plan assets was $5 million although it was expected to be only $4 million. What was the pension expense for the year?

BE 17–9
Pension expense; prior service cost
● LO6

The pension plan was amended last year, creating a prior service cost of $20 million. Service cost and interest cost for the year were $10 million and $4 million, respectively. At the end of the year, there was a negligible balance in the net gain–pensions account. The actual return on plan assets was $4 million although it was expected to be $6 million. On average, employees' remaining service life with the company is 10 years. What was the pension expense for the year?

BE 17–10
Net gain
● LO6

The projected benefit obligation and plan assets were $80 million and $100 million, respectively, at the beginning of the year. Due primarily to favorable stock market performance in recent years, there also was a net gain of $30 million. On average, employees' remaining service life with the company is 10 years. As a result of the net gain, what was the increase or decrease in pension expense for the year?

BE 17–11
Reporting the funded status of pension plans
● LO5

JDS Foods' projected benefit obligation, accumulated benefit obligation, and plan assets were $40 million, $30 million, and $25 million, respectively, at the end of the year. What, if any, pension liability must be reported in the balance sheet? What would JDS report if the plan assets were $45 million instead?

BE 17–12
Recording pension expense
● LO7

The Warren Group's pension expense is $67 million. This amount includes a $70 million service cost, a $50 million interest cost, a $55 million reduction for the expected return on plan assets, and a $2 million amortization of a prior service cost. How is the net pension liability affected when the pension expense is recorded?

BE 17–13
Recording pension expense
● LO7

Andrews Medical reported a net loss–AOCI in last year's balance sheet. This year, the company revised its estimate of future salary levels causing its PBO estimate to decline by $4 million. Also, the $8 million actual return on plan assets fell short of the $9 million expected return. How does this gain and loss affect Andrews' income statement, statement of comprehensive income, and balance sheet?

BE 17–14
Postretirement benefits; determine the APBO and service cost
● LO9, LO10

Prince Distribution, Inc., has an unfunded postretirement benefit plan. Medical care and life insurance benefits are provided to employees who render 10 years service and attain age 55 while in service. At the end of 2009, Jim Lukawitz is 31. He was hired by Prince at age 25 (6 years ago) and is expected to retire at age 62. The expected postretirement benefit obligation for Lukawitz at the end of 2009 is $50,000 and $54,000 at the end of 2010. Calculate the accumulated postretirement benefit obligation at the end of 2009 and 2010 and the service cost for 2009 and 2010 as pertaining to Lukawitz.

BE 17–15
Postretirement benefits; changes in the APBO
● LO11

On January 1, 2009, Medical Transport Company's accumulated postretirement benefit obligation was $25 million. At the end of 2009, retiree benefits paid were $3 million. Service cost for 2009 is $7 million. Assumptions regarding the trend of future health care costs were revised at the end of 2009, causing the actuary to revise downward the estimate of the APBO by $1 million. The actuary's discount rate is 8%. Determine the amount of the accumulated postretirement benefit obligation at December 31, 2009.

EXERCISES

available with McGraw-Hill's Homework Manager www.mhhe.com/spiceland5e

An alternate exercise and problem set is available on the text website: www.mhhe.com/spiceland5e

Indicate by letter whether each of the events listed below increases **(I)**, decreases **(D)**, or has no effect **(N)** on an employer's projected benefit obligation.

E 17–1
Changes in the PBO

● LO3

Events

____ 1. Interest cost.
____ 2. Amortization of prior service cost.
____ 3. A decrease in the average life expectancy of employees.
____ 4. An increase in the average life expectancy of employees.
____ 5. A plan amendment that increases benefits is made retroactive to prior years.
____ 6. An increase in the actuary's assumed discount rate.
____ 7. Cash contributions to the pension fund by the employer.
____ 8. Benefits are paid to retired employees.
____ 9. Service cost.
____ 10. Return on plan assets during the year are lower than expected.
____ 11. Return on plan assets during the year are higher than expected.

E 17–2
Determine the projected benefit obligation

● LO3

On January 1, 2009, Burleson Corporation's projected benefit obligation was $30 million. During 2009 pension benefits paid by the trustee were $4 million. Service cost for 2009 is $12 million. Pension plan assets (at fair value) increased during 2009 by $6 million as expected. At the end of 2009, there was no prior service cost and a negligible balance in net loss–pensions. The actuary's discount rate was 10%.

Required:
Determine the amount of the projected benefit obligation at December 31, 2009.

E 17–3
Components of pension expense

● LO6

Indicate by letter whether each of the events listed below increases (**I**), decreases (**D**), or has no effect (**N**) on an employer's periodic pension expense in the year the event occurs.

Events

____ 1. Interest cost.
____ 2. Amortization of prior service cost–AOCI.
____ 3. Excess of the expected return on plan assets over the actual return.
____ 4. Expected return on plan assets.
____ 5. A plan amendment that increases benefits is made retroactive to prior years.
____ 6. Actuary's estimate of the PBO is increased.
____ 7. Cash contributions to the pension fund by the employer.
____ 8. Benefits are paid to retired employees.
____ 9. Service cost.
____ 10. Excess of the actual return on plan assets over the expected return.
____ 11. Amortization of net loss–AOCI.
____ 12. Amortization of net gain–AOCI.

E 17–4
Recording pension expense

● LO6 LO7

Harrison Forklift's pension expense includes a service cost of $10 million. Harrison began the year with a pension liability of $28 million (underfunded pension plan).

Required:
Prepare the appropriate general journal entries to record Harrison's pension expense in each of the following independent situations regarding the other components of pension expense ($ in millions):

1. Interest cost, $6; expected return on assets, $4; amortization of net loss, $2.
2. Interest cost, $6; expected return on assets, $4; amortization of net gain, $2.
3. Interest cost, $6; expected return on assets, $4; amortization of net loss, $2; amortization of prior service cost, $3 million.

E 17–5
Determine pension plan assets

● LO4

The following data relate to Voltaire Company's defined benefit pension plan:

	($ in millions)
Plan assets at fair value, January 1	$600
Expected return on plan assets	60
Actual return on plan assets	48
Contributions to the pension fund (end of year)	100
Amortization of net loss	10
Pension benefits paid (end of year)	11
Pension expense	72

Required:
Determine the amount of pension plan assets at fair value on December 31.

E 17–6
Changes in the pension obligation; determine service cost

● LO3 LO6

Pension data for Millington Enterprises include the following:

	($ in millions)
Discount rate, 10%	
Projected benefit obligation, January 1	$360
Projected benefit obligation, December 31	465
Accumulated benefit obligation, January 1	300
Accumulated benefit obligation, December 31	415
Cash contributions to pension fund, December 31	150
Benefit payments to retirees, December 31	54

Required:
Assuming no change in actuarial assumptions and estimates, determine the service cost component of pension expense for the year ended December 31.

E 17–7
Changes in plan assets; determine cash contributions

● LO4

Pension data for Fahy Transportation, Inc., include the following:

	($ in millions)
Discount rate, 7%	
Expected return on plan assets, 10%	
Actual return on plan assets, 11%	
Projected benefit obligation, January 1	$730
Plan assets (fair value), January 1	700
Plan assets (fair value), December 31	750
Benefit payments to retirees, December 31	66

Required:
Assuming cash contributions were made at the end of the year, what was the amount of those contributions?

E 17–8
Components of pension expense

● LO6

Pension data for Sterling Properties include the following:

	($ in 000s)
Service cost, 2009	$112
Projected benefit obligation, January 1, 2009	850
Plan assets (fair value), January 1, 2009	900
Prior service cost–AOCI (2009 amortization, $8)	80
Net loss–AOCI (2009 amortization, $1)	101
Discount rate, 6%	
Expected return on plan assets, 10%	
Actual return on plan assets, 11%	

Required:
Determine pension expense for 2009.

E 17–9
Determine pension expense

● LO6 LO7

Abbott and Abbott has a noncontributory, defined benefit pension plan. At December 31, 2009, Abbott and Abbott received the following information:

Projected Benefit Obligation	($ in millions)
Balance, January 1	$120
Service cost	20
Interest cost	12
Benefits paid	(9)
Balance, December 31	$143
Plan Assets	
Balance, January 1	$ 80
Actual return on plan assets	9
Contributions 2009	20
Benefits paid	(9)
Balance, December 31	$100

The expected long-term rate of return on plan assets was 10%. There was no prior service cost and a negligible net loss–AOCI on January 1, 2009.

Required:
1. Determine Abbott and Abbott's pension expense for 2009.
2. Prepare the journal entries to record Abbott and Abbott's pension expense and funding for 2009.

E 17–10
Components of pension expense; journal entry

● LO6 LO7

Pension data for Barry Financial Services, Inc., include the following:

	($ in 000s)
Discount rate, 7%	
Expected return on plan assets, 10%	
Actual return on plan assets, 9%	
Service cost, 2009	$ 310
January 1, 2009:	
Projected benefit obligation	2,300
Accumulated benefit obligation	2,000
Plan assets (fair value)	2,400
Prior service cost–AOCI (2009 amortization, $25)	325
Net gain–AOCI (2009 amortization, $6)	330
December 31, 2009:	
Cash contributions to pension fund, December 31, 2009	245
Benefit payments to retirees, December 31, 2009	270

Required:

1. Determine pension expense for 2009.
2. Prepare the journal entries to record pension expense and funding for 2009.

E 17–11
PBO calculations; ABO calculations; present value concepts

● LO1 LO2 LO3

Clark Industries has a defined benefit pension plan that specifies annual retirement benefits equal to:

1.2% × Service years × Final year's salary

Stanley Mills was hired by Clark at the beginning of 1990. Mills is expected to retire at the end of 2034 after 45 years of service. His retirement is expected to span 15 years. At the end of 2009, 20 years after being hired, his salary is $80,000. The company's actuary projects Mills's salary to be $270,000 at retirement. The actuary's discount rate is 7%.

Required:

1. Estimate the amount of Stanley Mills's annual retirement payments for the 15 retirement years earned as of the end of 2009.
2. Suppose Clark's pension plan permits a lump-sum payment at retirement in lieu of annuity payments. Determine the lump-sum equivalent as the present value as of the retirement date of annuity payments during the retirement period.
3. What is the company's projected benefit obligation at the end of 2009 with respect to Stanley Mills?
4. What is the company's accumulated benefit obligation at the end of 2009 with respect to Stanley Mills?
5. If we assume no estimates change in the meantime, what is the company's projected benefit obligation at the end of 2010 with respect to Stanley Mills?
6. What portion of the 2010 increase in the PBO is attributable to 2010 service (the service cost component of pension expense) and to accrued interest (the interest cost component of pension expense)?

E 17–12
Determining the amortization of net loss or net gain

● LO6

Hicks Cable Company has a defined benefit pension plan. Three alternative possibilities for pension-related data at January 1, 2009, are shown below:

	($ in 000s)		
	Case 1	**Case 2**	**Case 3**
Net loss (gain)–AOCI, Jan. 1	$ 320	$ (330)	$ 260
2009 loss (gain) on plan assets	(11)	(8)	2
2009 loss (gain) on PBO	(23)	16	(265)
Accumulated benefit obligation, Jan. 1	(2,950)	(2,550)	(1,450)
Projected benefit obligation, Jan. 1	(3,310)	(2,670)	(1,700)
Fair value of plan assets, Jan. 1	2,800	2,700	1,550
Average remaining service period of active employees (years)	12	15	10

Required:

1. For each independent case, calculate any amortization of the net loss or gain that should be included as a component of pension expense for 2009.
2. For each independent case, determine the net loss–AOCI or net gain–AOCI as of January 1, 2010.

E 17–13
Pension spreadsheet

A partially completed pension spreadsheet showing the relationships among the elements that comprise the defined benefit pension plan of Universal Products is given below. The actuary's discount rate is 5%. At the end

● LO8

of 2007, the pension formula was amended, creating a prior service cost of $120,000. The expected rate of return on assets was 8%, and the average remaining service life of the active employee group is 20 years in the current year as well as the previous two years.

Required:

Copy the incomplete spreadsheet and fill in the missing amounts.

			AOCI		Income Statement	Asset	Asset or Liability
( )s indicate credits; debits otherwise ($ in 000s)	**PBO**	**Plan Assets**	**Prior Service Cost**	**Net Loss**	**Pension Expense**	**Cash**	**Net Pension (Liability)/ Asset**
Balance, Jan. 1, 2009	(800)	600	114	80			(200)
Service cost					84		
Interest cost, 5%	(40)						
Expected return on assets					(48)		
Adjust for:							
Loss on assets				6			
Amortization:							
Prior service cost							
Amortization:							
Net loss							
Gain on PBO							12
Prior service cost	0						
Cash funding						(68)	
Retiree benefits							
Balance, Dec. 31, 2009	(862)		108				

E 17–14
Effect of pension expense components on balance sheet accounts

● LO7 LO8

Warrick Boards calculated pension expense for its underfunded pension plan as follows:

	($ in 000s)
Service cost	$224
Interest cost	150
Expected return on the plan assets ($100 actual, less $10 gain)	(90)
Amortization of prior service cost	8
Amortization of net loss	2
Pension expense	$294

Required:

Which elements of Warrick's balance sheet are affected by the components of pension expense? What are the specific changes in these accounts?

E 17–15
Determine and record pension expense, funding, and gains and losses

● LO6 LO7

Actuary and trustee reports indicate the following changes in the PBO and plan assets of Douglas-Roberts Industries during 2009:

Prior service cost at Jan. 1, 2009, from plan amendment at the beginning of 2006 (amortization: $4 million per year)	$28 million
Net loss–AOCI at Jan.1, 2009 (previous losses exceeded previous gains)	$80 million
Average remaining service life of the active employee group	10 years
Actuary's discount rate	7%

($ in millions) PBO			Plan Assets
Beginning of 2009	$600	*Beginning* of 2009	$400
Service cost	80	Return on plan assets,	
Interest cost, 7%	42	8% (10% expected)	32
Loss (gain) on PBO	(14)	Cash contributions	90
Less: Retiree benefits	(38)	Less: Retiree benefits	(38)
End of 2009	$670	*End* of 2009	$484

Required:

1. Determine Douglas-Roberts' pension expense for 2009 and prepare the appropriate journal entries to record the expense as well as the cash contribution to plan assets.
2. Prepare the appropriate journal entry(s) to record any 2009 gains and losses.

E 17–16
Concepts; terminology

● LO2 through LO8

Listed below are several terms and phrases associated with pensions. Pair each item from List A (by letter) with the item from List B that is most appropriately associated with it.

List A	List B
____ 1. Future compensation levels estimated.	a. Actual return exceeds expected
____ 2. All funding provided by the employer.	b. Net gain–AOCI
____ 3. Credit to OCI and debit to plan assets.	c. Vested benefit obligation
____ 4. Retirement benefits specified by formula.	d. Projected benefit obligation
____ 5. Trade-off between relevance and reliability.	e. Choice between PBO and ABO
____ 6. Cumulative gains in excess of losses.	f. Noncontributory pension plan
____ 7. Current pay levels implicitly assumed.	g. Accumulated benefit obligation
____ 8. Created by the passage of time.	h. Plan assets
____ 9. Not contingent on future employment.	i. Interest cost
____ 10. Risk borne by employee.	j. Delayed recognition in earnings
____ 11. Increased by employer contributions.	k. Defined contribution plan
____ 12. Caused by plan amendment.	l. Defined benefit plan
____ 13. Loss on plan assets.	m. Prior service cost
____ 14. Excess over 10% of plan assets or PBO.	n. Amortize net loss–AOCI

E 17–17
Record pension expense, funding, and gains and losses; determine account balances

● LO6 LO7 LO8

Beale Management has a noncontributory, defined benefit pension plan. On December 31, 2009 (the end of Beale's fiscal year), the following pension-related data were available:

Projected Benefit Obligation	($ in millions)
Balance, January 1, 2009	$480
Service cost	82
Interest cost, discount rate, 5%	24
Gain due to changes in actuarial assumptions in 2009	(10)
Pension benefits paid	(40)
Balance, December 31, 2009	$536
Plan Assets	
Balance, January 1, 2009	$500
Actual return on plan assets	40
(Expected return on plan assets, $45)	
Cash contributions	70
Pension benefits paid	(40)
Balance, December 31, 2009	$570
January 1, 2009, balances:	
Pension asset	$ 20
Prior service cost–AOCI (amortization $8 per year)	48
Net gain–AOCI (any amortization over 15 years)	80

Required:

1. Prepare the 2009 journal entry to record pension expense.
2. Prepare the 2009 journal entry to record the contribution to plan assets.
3. Prepare the journal entry(s) to record any 2009 gains and losses.
4. Determine the balances at December 31, 2009, in the pension asset, the net gain–AOCI, and prior service cost–AOCI and show how the balances changed during 2009. [Hint: You might find T-accounts useful.]

E 17–18
Pension spreadsheet

● LO8

Refer to the data provided in Exercise 17–17.

Required:

Prepare a pension spreadsheet to show the relationship among the PBO, plan assets, prior service cost, the net gain, pension expense, and the net pension asset.

E 17–19
Determine pension expense; prior service cost

● LO6

Lacy Construction has a noncontributory, defined benefit pension plan. At December 31, 2009, Lacy received the following information:

Projected Benefit Obligation	($ in millions)
Balance, January 1	$360
Service cost	60
Interest cost	36
Benefits paid	(27)
Balance, December 31	$429

Plan Assets	
Balance, January 1	$240
Actual return on plan assets	27
Contributions 2009	60
Benefits paid	(27)
Balance, December 31	$300

The expected long-term rate of return on plan assets was 10%. There were no AOCI balances related to pensions on January 1, 2009. At the end of 2009, Lacy amended the pension formula creating a prior service cost of $12 million, one-third of which is related to employees whose pension benefits have vested.

Required:

1. Determine Lacy's pension expense for 2009.
2. Prepare the journal entry(s) to record Lacy's pension expense, funding, gains or losses, and prior service cost for 2009.

E 17–20
IFRS; prior service cost

● LO7

Refer to the situation described in Exercise 17–19.

Required:

How might your solution differ if Lacy Construction prepares its financial statements according to International Accounting Standards? Include any appropriate journal entries in your response.

E 17–21
Classifying accounting changes and errors

● LO8

Indicate with the appropriate letter the nature of each adjustment described below:

Type of Adjustment

A. Change in principle
B. Change in estimate
C. Correction of an error
D. Neither an accounting change nor an error

____ 1. Change in actuarial assumptions for a defined benefit pension plan.

____ 2. Determination that the projected benefit obligation under a pension plan exceeded the fair value of plan assets at the end of the previous year by $17,000. The only pension-related amount on the balance sheet was a net pension liability of $30,000.

____ 3. Pension plan assets for a defined benefit pension plan achieving a rate of return in excess of the amount anticipated.

____ 4. Instituting a pension plan for the first time and adopting *Statement of Financial Accounting Standards No. 158,* "Employers' Accounting for Defined Benefit Pension and Other Postretirement Plans."

E 17–22
Postretirement benefits; determine APBO, EPBO

● LO10

Classified Electronics has an unfunded retiree health care plan. Each of the company's three employees has been with the firm since its inception at the beginning of 2008. As of the end of 2009, the actuary estimates the total net cost of providing health care benefits to employees during their retirement years to have a present value of $72,000. Each of the employees will become fully eligible for benefits after 28 more years of service but aren't expected to retire for 35 more years. The interest rate is 6%.

Required:

1. What is the expected postretirement benefit obligation at the end of 2009?
2. What is the accumulated postretirement benefit obligation at the end of 2009?
3. What is the expected postretirement benefit obligation at the end of 2010?
4. What is the accumulated postretirement benefit obligation at the end of 2010?

E 17–23
Postretirement benefits; determine APBO, service cost, interest cost; prepare journal entry

● LO10 LO11

The following data are available pertaining to Household Appliance Company's retiree health care plan for 2009:

Number of employees covered	2
Years employed as of January 1, 2009	3 [each]
Attribution period	25 years
Expected postretirement benefit obligation, Jan. 1	$50,000
Expected postretirement benefit obligation, Dec. 31	$53,000
Interest rate	6%
Funding	none

Required:

1. What is the accumulated postretirement benefit obligation at the beginning of 2009?
2. What is interest cost to be included in 2009 postretirement benefit expense?

3. What is service cost to be included in 2009 postretirement benefit expense?
4. Prepare the journal entry to record the postretirement benefit expense for 2009.

E 17–24
Postretirement benefits; determine EPBO; attribution period

● LO10 LO11

Lorin Management Services has an unfunded postretirement benefit plan. On December 31, 2009, the following data were available concerning changes in the plan's accumulated postretirement benefit obligation with respect to one of Lorin's employees:

APBO at the beginning of 2009	$16,364
Interest cost: ($16,364 × 10%)	1,636
Service cost: ($44,000 × 1⁄22) Portion of EPBO attributed to 2009	2,000
APBO at the end of 2009	$20,000

Required:
1. Over how many years is the expected postretirement benefit obligation being expensed (attribution period)?
2. What is the expected postretirement benefit obligation at the *end* of 2009?
3. When was the employee hired by Lorin?
4. What is the expected postretirement benefit obligation at the *beginning* of 2009?

E 17–25
Postretirement benefits; components of postretirement benefit expense

● LO11

Data pertaining to the postretirement health care benefit plan of Sterling Properties include the following for 2009:

	($ in 000s)
Service cost	$124
Accumulated postretirement benefit obligation, January 1	700
Plan assets (fair market value), January 1	50
Prior service cost–AOCI	none
Net gain–AOCI (2009 amortization, $1)	91
Retiree benefits paid (end of year)	87
Contribution to health care benefit fund (end of year)	185
Discount rate, 7%	
Return on plan assets (actual and expected), 10%	

Required:
1. Determine the postretirement benefit expense for 2009.
2. Prepare the appropriate journal entries to record the postretirement benefit expense and funding for 2009.

E 17–26
Postretirement benefits; amortization of net loss

● LO11

Cahal-Michael Company has a postretirement health care benefit plan. On January 1, 2009, the following plan-related data were available:

	($ in 000s)
Net loss–AOCI	$ 336
Accumulated postretirement benefit obligation	2,800
Fair value of plan assets	500
Average remaining service period to retirement	14 years (same in previous 10 yrs.)

The rate of return on plan assets during 2009 was 10%, although it was expected to be 9%. The actuary revised assumptions regarding the APBO at the end of the year, resulting in a $39,000 increase in the estimate of that obligation.

Required:
1. Calculate any amortization of the net loss that should be included as a component of postretirement benefit expense for 2009.
2. Assume the postretirement benefit expense for 2009, not including the amortization of the net loss component, is $212,000. What is the expense for the year?
3. Determine the net loss or gain as of December 31, 2009.

E 17–27
Postretirement benefits; determine and record expense

● LO11

Gorky-Park Corporation provides postretirement health care benefits to employees who provide at least 12 years of service and reach age 62 while in service. On January 1, 2009, the following plan-related data were available:

	($ in millions)
Accumulated postretirement benefit obligation	$130
Fair value of plan assets	none
Average remaining service period to retirement	25 years (same in previous 10 yrs.)
Average remaining service period to full eligibility	20 years (same in previous 10 yrs.)

On January 1, 2009, Gorky-Park amends the plan to provide certain dental benefits in addition to previously provided medical benefits. The actuary determines that the cost of making the amendment retroactive increases the APBO by $20 million. Management chooses to amortize the prior service cost on a straight-line basis. The service cost for 2009 is $34 million. The interest rate is 8%.

Required:

1. Calculate the postretirement benefit expense for 2009.
2. Prepare the journal entry to record the expense.

E 17–28
Postretirement benefits; negative plan amendment
● LO11

Southeast Technology provides postretirement health care benefits to employees. On January 1, 2009, the following plan-related data were available:

	($ in 000s)
Prior service cost—originated in 2004	$ 50
Accumulated postretirement benefit obligation	530
Fair value of plan assets	none
Average remaining service period to retirement	20 years (same in previous 10 yrs.)
Average remaining service period to full eligibility	15 years (same in previous 10 yrs.)

On January 1, 2009, Southeast amends the plan in response to spiraling health care costs. The amendment establishes an annual maximum of $3,000 for medical benefits that the plan will provide. The actuary determines that the effect of this amendment is to decrease the APBO by $80,000. Management amortizes prior service cost on a straight-line basis. The interest rate is 8%. The service cost for 2009 is $114,000.

Required:

1. Calculate the prior service cost amortization for 2009.
2. Calculate the postretirement benefit expense for 2009.

E 17–29
Prior service cost; service method; straight-line method (Based on Appendix)

Frazier Refrigeration amended its defined benefit pension plan on December 31, 2009, to increase retirement benefits earned with each service year. The consulting actuary estimated the prior service cost incurred by making the amendment retroactive to prior years to be $110,000. Frazier's 100 present employees are expected to retire at the rate of approximately 10 each year at the end of each of the next 10 years.

Required:

1. Using the service method, calculate the amount of prior service cost to be amortized to pension expense in each of the next 10 years.
2. Using the straight-line method, calculate the amount of prior service cost to be amortized to pension expense in each of the next 10 years.

CPA AND CMA REVIEW QUESTIONS

CPA Exam Questions

SCHWESER

The following questions are used in the Kaplan CPA Review Course to study pensions and other postretirement benefits while preparing for the CPA examination. Determine the response that best completes the statements or questions.

● LO11

1. At December 31, 2008, Johnston and Johnston reported in its balance sheet as part of accumulated other comprehensive income a net loss of $37 million related to its postretirement benefit plan. The actuary for J&J increased her estimate of J&J's future health care costs at the end of 2009. J&J's entry to record the effect of this change will include
   a. a debit to other comprehensive income and a credit to postretirement benefit liability.
   b. a debit to postretirement benefit liability and a credit to other comprehensive income.
   c. a debit to pension expense and a credit to postretirement benefit liability.
   d. a debit to pension expense and a credit to other comprehensive income.

● LO5

2. Wolf, Inc., began a defined benefit pension plan for its employees on January 1, 2009. The following data are provided for 2009 as of December 31, 2009:

Projected benefit obligation	$385,000
Accumulated benefit obligation	340,000
Plan assets at fair value	255,000
Pension expense	95,000
Employer's cash contribution (end of year)	255,000

What amount should Wolf report as a net pension liability at December 31, 2009?

a. $ 0
b. $ 45,000
c. $ 85,000
d. $130,000

● LO7

3. A statement of comprehensive income for a company with a defined benefit pension plan does *not* include

a. net income.
b. the return on plan assets.
c. gains from the return on assets exceeding expectations.
d. losses from changes in estimates regarding the pension obligation.

● LO8

4. JWS Corporation has a defined benefit pension plan. JWS reported a net pension liability in last year's balance sheet. This year, the company revised its estimate of future salary levels causing its projected benefit obligation estimate to decline by $8. Also, the $16 million actual return on plan assets was less than the $18 million expected return. As a result

a. the net pension liability will decrease by $8 million.
b. the statement of comprehensive income will report a $2 million gain and an $8 million loss.
c. the net pension liability will increase by $6 million.
d. accumulated other comprehensive income will increase by $6 million.

● LO8

5. Amortizing a net gain for pensions and other postretirement benefit plans will

a. decrease retained earnings and decrease accumulated other comprehensive income.
b. increase retained earnings and increase accumulated other comprehensive income.
c. decrease retained earnings and increase accumulated other comprehensive income.
d. increase retained earnings and decrease accumulated other comprehensive income.

CMA Exam Questions

The following questions dealing with pensions and other postretirement benefits are adapted from questions that previously appeared on Certified Management Accountant (CMA) examinations. The CMA designation sponsored by the Institute of Management Accountants (**www.imanet.org**) provides members with an objective measure of knowledge and competence in the field of management accounting. Determine the response that best completes the statements or questions.

● LO3

1. According to *SFAS No. 87*, "Employer's Accounting for Pension Plans," the projected benefit obligation (PBO) is best described as the

a. Present value of benefits accrued to date based on future salary levels.
b. Present value of benefits accrued to date based on current salary levels.
c. Increase in retroactive benefits at the date of the amendment of the plan.
d. Amount of the adjustment necessary to reflect the difference between actual and estimated actuarial returns.

● LO6

2. On November 30, the Board of Directors of Baldwin Corporation amended its pension plan giving retroactive benefits to its employees. The information below is provided at November 30.

Accumulated benefit obligation (ABO)	$825,000
Projected benefit obligation (PBO)	900,000
Plan assets (fair value)	307,500
Market-related asset value	301,150
Prior service cost	190,000
Average remaining service life of employees	10 years
Useful life of pension goodwill	20 years

Using the straight-line method of amortization, the amount of prior service cost charged to expense during the year ended November 30 is

a. $9,500.
b. $19,000.
c. $30,250.
d. $190,000.

PROBLEMS

available with McGraw-Hill's Homework Manager www.mhhe.com/spiceland5e 

An alternate exercise and problem set is available on the text website: www.mhhe.com/spiceland5e

(Note: Problems 1–5 are variations of the same situation, designed to focus on different elements of the pension plan.)

P 17–1
ABO calculations; present value concepts

● LO2 LO3

Sachs Brands' defined benefit pension plan specifies annual retirement benefits equal to: 1.6% × service years × final year's salary, payable at the end of each year. Angela Davenport was hired by Sachs at the beginning of 1995 and is expected to retire at the end of 2029 after 35 years' service. Her retirement is expected to span 18 years. Davenport's salary is $90,000 at the end of 2009 and the company's actuary projects her salary to be $240,000 at retirement. The actuary's discount rate is 7%.

Required:

1. Draw a time line that depicts Davenport's expected service period, retirement period, and a 2009 measurement date for the pension obligation.
2. Estimate by the accumulated benefits approach the amount of Davenport's annual retirement payments earned as of the end of 2009.
3. What is the company's accumulated benefit obligation at the end of 2009 with respect to Davenport?
4. If no estimates are changed in the meantime, what will be the accumulated benefit obligation at the end of 2012 (three years later) when Davenport's salary is $100,000?

P 17–2
PBO calculations; present value concepts

● LO3

Sachs Brands' defined benefit pension plan specifies annual retirement benefits equal to: 1.6% × service years × final year's salary, payable at the end of each year. Angela Davenport was hired by Sachs at the beginning of 1995 and is expected to retire at the end of 2029 after 35 years' service. Her retirement is expected to span 18 years. Davenport's salary is $90,000 at the end of 2009 and the company's actuary projects her salary to be $240,000 at retirement. The actuary's discount rate is 7%.

Required:

1. Draw a time line that depicts Davenport's expected service period, retirement period, and a 2009 measurement date for the pension obligation.
2. Estimate by the projected benefits approach the amount of Davenport's annual retirement payments earned as of the end of 2009.
3. What is the company's projected benefit obligation at the end of 2009 with respect to Davenport?
4. If no estimates are changed in the meantime, what will be the company's projected benefit obligation at the end of 2012 (three years later) with respect to Davenport?

P 17–3
Service cost, interest, and PBO calculations; present value concepts

● LO3

Sachs Brands' defined benefit pension plan specifies annual retirement benefits equal to: 1.6% × service years × final year's salary, payable at the end of each year. Angela Davenport was hired by Sachs at the beginning of 1995 and is expected to retire at the end of 2029 after 35 years' service. Her retirement is expected to span 18 years. Davenport's salary is $90,000 at the end of 2009 and the company's actuary projects her salary to be $240,000 at retirement. The actuary's discount rate is 7%.

Required:

1. What is the company's projected benefit obligation at the beginning of 2009 (after 14 years' service) with respect to Davenport?
2. Estimate by the projected benefits approach the portion of Davenport's annual retirement payments attributable to 2009 service.
3. What is the company's service cost for 2009 with respect to Davenport?
4. What is the company's interest cost for 2009 with respect to Davenport?
5. Combine your answers to requirements 1, 3, and 4 to determine the company's projected benefit obligation at the end of 2009 (after 15 years' service) with respect to Davenport.

P 17–4
Prior service cost; components of pension expense; present value concepts

● LO3 LO6

Sachs Brands' defined benefit pension plan specifies annual retirement benefits equal to: 1.6% × service years × final year's salary, payable at the end of each year. Angela Davenport was hired by Sachs at the beginning of 1995 and is expected to retire at the end of 2029 after 35 years' service. Her retirement is expected to span 18 years. Davenport's salary is $90,000 at the end of 2009 and the company's actuary projects her salary to be $240,000 at retirement. The actuary's discount rate is 7%.

At the beginning of 2010, the pension formula was amended to:

1.75% × Service years × Final year's salary

The amendment was made retroactive to apply the increased benefits to prior service years.

Required:

1. What is the company's prior service cost at the beginning of 2010 with respect to Davenport after the amendment described above?
2. Since the amendment occurred at the *beginning* of 2010, amortization of the prior service cost begins in 2010. What is the prior service cost amortization that would be included in pension expense?
3. What is the service cost for 2010 with respect to Davenport?
4. What is the interest cost for 2010 with respect to Davenport?
5. Calculate pension expense for 2010 with respect to Davenport, assuming plan assets attributable to her of $150,000 and a rate of return (actual and expected) of 10%.

P 17–5
Gain on PBO; present value concepts
● LO3 LO6

Sachs Brands' defined benefit pension plan specifies annual retirement benefits equal to: 1.6% × service years × final year's salary, payable at the end of each year. Angela Davenport was hired by Sachs at the beginning of 1995 and is expected to retire at the end of 2029 after 35 years' service. Her retirement is expected to span 18 years. Davenport's salary is $90,000 at the end of 2009 and the company's actuary projects her salary to be $240,000 at retirement. The actuary's discount rate is 7%.

At the beginning of 2010, changing economic conditions caused the actuary to reassess the applicable discount rate. It was decided that 8% is the appropriate rate.

Required:

Calculate the effect of the change in the assumed discount rate on the PBO at the beginning of 2010 with respect to Davenport.

P 17–6
Determine the PBO; plan assets; pension expense; two years
● LO3 LO4 LO6

Stanley-Morgan Industries adopted a defined benefit pension plan on April 12, 2009. The provisions of the plan were not made retroactive to prior years. A local bank, engaged as trustee for the plan assets, expects plan assets to earn a 10% rate of return. A consulting firm, engaged as actuary, recommends 6% as the appropriate discount rate. The service cost is $150,000 for 2009 and $200,000 for 2010. Year-end funding is $160,000 for 2009 and $170,000 for 2010. No assumptions or estimates were revised during 2009.

Required:

Calculate each of the following amounts as of both December 31, 2009, and December 31, 2010:

1. Projected benefit obligation
2. Plan assets
3. Pension expense
4. Net pension asset/liability

P 17–7
Determining the amortization of net gain
● LO6

Herring Wholesale Company has a defined benefit pension plan. On January 1, 2009, the following pension-related data were available:

	($ in 000s)
Net gain–AOCI	$ 170
Accumulated benefit obligation	1,170
Projected benefit obligation	1,400
Fair value of plan assets	1,100
Average remaining service period of active employees (expected to remain constant for the next several years)	15 years

The rate of return on plan assets during 2009 was 9%, although it was expected to be 10%. The actuary revised assumptions regarding the PBO at the end of the year, resulting in a $23,000 decrease in the estimate of that obligation.

Required:

1. Calculate any amortization of the net gain that should be included as a component of net pension expense for 2009.
2. Assume the net pension expense for 2009, not including the amortization of the net gain component, is $325,000. What is pension expense for the year?
3. Determine the net loss–AOCI or net gain–AOCI as of January 1, 2010.

P 17–8
Pension spreadsheet; record pension expense and funding; new gains and losses

A partially completed pension spreadsheet showing the relationships among the elements that constitute Car Inc.'s defined benefit pension plan follows. Six years earlier, Carney revised its pension formula and recalc benefits earned by employees in prior years using the more generous formula. The prior service cost cre the recalculation is being amortized at the rate of $5 million per year. At the end of 2009, the pension f amended again, creating an additional prior service cost of $40 million. The expected rate of return actuary's discount rate were 10%, and the average remaining service life of the active employee g

● LO7 LO8

( )s indicate credits; debits otherwise ($ in millions)	PBO	Plan Assets	AOCI Prior Service Cost	AOCI Net Loss	Income Statement Pension Expense	Asset Cash	Asset or Liability Net Pension (Liability) / Asset
Balance, Jan. 1, 2009	(830)	680	20	93			(150)
Service cost	?				74		?
Interest cost	?				?		?
Expected return on asset		?			?		?
Adjust for:							
Loss on assets		(7)		?			?
Amortization of:							
Prior service cost			?		?		
Net loss				?	?		
Loss on PBO	?			?			(13)
Prior service cost	?		?				?
Cash funding		?				?	84
Retiree benefits	?	?					
Balance, Dec. 31, 2009	?	775	?	?	?		?

Required:

1. Copy the incomplete spreadsheet and fill in the missing amounts.
2. Prepare the 2009 journal entry to record pension expense.
3. Prepare the 2009 journal entry to record the cash contribution to plan assets.
4. Prepare the journal entry(s) to record any 2009 gains and losses and new prior service cost in 2009.

P 17–9
Determine pension expense; PBO; plan assets; pension asset/liability; journal entries

● LO3 through LO8

U.S. Metallurgical, Inc. reported the following balances in its financial statements and disclosure notes at December 31, 2008.

Plan assets	$ 400,000
Projected benefit obligation	320,000

U.S.M.'s actuary determined that 2009 service cost is $60,000. Both the expected and actual rate of return on plan assets are 9%. The interest (discount) rate is 5%. U.S.M. contributed $120,000 to the pension fund at the end of 2009, and retirees were paid $44,000 from plan assets.

Required:

Determine the following amounts at the end of 2009.

1. Pension expense
2. Projected benefit obligation
3. Plan assets
4. Net pension asset/liability
5. Prepare journal entries to record the pension expense and funding of plan assets to verify the change in the net pension asset/liability.

17–10
pension

The Kollar Company has a defined benefit pension plan. Pension information concerning the fiscal years 2009 and 2010 are presented below ($ in millions):

Information Provided by Pension Plan Actuary:

...ojected benefit obligation as of December 31, 2008 = $1,800.

... cost from plan amendment on January 2, 2009 = $400 (straight-line amortization for 10-year ...ervice period).

...9 = $520.

...10 = $570.

...d by actuary on projected benefit obligation for 2009 and 2010 = 10%.

...rees in 2009 = $400.

...tirees in 2010 = $450.

...n actuarial assumptions or estimates.

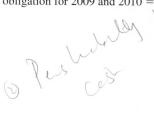

Information Provided by Pension Fund Trustee:

a. Plan asset balance at fair value on January 1, 2009 = $1,600.
b. 2009 contributions = $540.
c. 2010 contributions = $590.
d. Expected long-term rate of return on plan assets = 12%.
e. 2009 actual return on plan assets = $180.
f. 2010 actual return on plan assets = $210.
g. Net gain–AOCI on January 1, 2009 = $230.
h. Net gains and losses are amortized for 10 years for 2009 and 2010.

Required:

1. Calculate pension expense for 2009 and 2010.
2. Prepare the journal entries for 2009 and 2010 to record pension expense.
3. Prepare the journal entries for 2009 and 2010 to record the cash contribution to plan assets.
4. Prepare the journal entries for 2009 and 2010 to record any gains and losses and new prior service cost.

P 17–11
Determine the PBO, plan assets, pension expense; prior service cost

● LO3 LO4 LO6

Lewis Industries adopted a defined benefit pension plan on January 1, 2009. By making the provisions of the plan retroactive to prior years, Lewis incurred a prior service cost of $2 million. The prior service cost was funded immediately by a $2 million cash payment to the fund trustee on January 2, 2009. However, the cost is to be amortized (expensed) over 10 years. The service cost—$250,000 for 2009—is fully funded at the end of each year. Both the actuary's discount rate and the expected rate of return on plan assets were 9%. The actual rate of return on plan assets was 11%. At December 31, the trustee paid $16,000 to an employee who retired during 2009.

Required:

Determine each of the following amounts as of December 31, 2009, the fiscal year-end for Lewis:

1. Projected benefit obligation
2. Plan assets
3. Pension expense

P 17–12
Relationship among pension elements

● LO3 through LO8

The funded status of Hilton Paneling, Inc.'s defined benefit pension plan and the balances in prior service cost and the net gain–pensions, are given below.

	($ in 000s)	
	2009 Beginning Balances	**2009 Ending Balances**
Projected benefit obligation	$2,300	$2,501
Plan assets	2,400	2,591
Funded status	100	90
Prior service cost–AOCI	325	300
Net gain–AOCI	330	300

Retirees were paid $270,000 and the employer contribution to the pension fund was $245,000 at the end of 2009. The expected rate of return on plan assets was 10%, and the actuary's discount rate is 7%. There were no changes in actuarial estimates and assumptions regarding the PBO.

Required:

Determine the following amounts for 2009:

1. Actual return on plan assets
2. Loss or gain on plan assets
3. Service cost
4. Pension expense
5. Average remaining service life of active employees (used to determine amortization of the net gain)

P 17–13
Comprehensive—pension elements; spreadsheet

● LO8

The following pension-related data pertain to Metro Recreation's noncontributory, defined benefit pension plan for 2009:

	($ in 000s)	
	Jan. 1	**Dec. 31**
Projected benefit obligation	$4,100	$4,380
Accumulated benefit obligation	3,715	3,950
Plan assets (fair value)	4,530	4,975
Interest (discount) rate, 7%		
Expected return on plan assets, 10%		
Prior service cost–AOCI (from Dec. 31, 2008, amendment)	840	
Net loss–AOCI	477	
Average remaining service life: 12 years		
Gain due to changes in actuarial assumptions		44
Contributions to pension fund (end of year)		340
Pension benefits paid (end of year)		295

Required:
Prepare a pension spreadsheet that shows the relationships among the various pension balances, shows the changes in those balances, and computes pension expense for 2009.

P 17–14
Comprehensive—reporting a pension plan; pension spreadsheet; determine changes in balances; two years

● **LO3 through LO8**

Actuary and trustee reports indicate the following changes in the PBO and plan assets of Lakeside Cable during 2009:

Prior service cost at Jan. 1, 2009, from plan amendment at the beginning of 2007 (amortization: $4 million per year)	$32 million
Net loss–pensions at Jan.1, 2009 (previous losses exceeded previous gains)	$40 million
Average remaining service life of the active employee group	10 years
Actuary's discount rate	8%

($ in millions)	**PBO**		**Plan Assets**
Beginning of 2009	$300	*Beginning* of 2009	$200
Service cost	48	Return on plan assets,	
Interest cost, 8%	24	7.5% (10% expected)	15
Loss (gain) on PBO	(2)	Cash contributions	45
Less: Retiree benefits	(20)	Less: Retiree benefits	(20)
End of 2009	$350	*End* of 2009	$240

Required:
1. Determine Lakeside's pension expense for 2009 and prepare the appropriate journal entries to record the expense as well as the cash contribution to plan assets.
2. Determine the new gains and/or losses in 2009 and prepare the appropriate journal entry(s) to record them.
3. Prepare a pension spreadsheet to assist you in determining end of 2009 balances in the PBO, plan assets, prior service cost–AOCI, the net loss–AOCI, and the pension liability.
4. Assume the following actuary and trustee reports indicating changes in the PBO and plan assets of Lakeside Cable during 2010:

($ in millions)	**PBO**		**Plan Assets**
Beginning of 2010	$350	*Beginning* of 2010	$240
Service cost	38	Return on plan assets,	
Interest cost at 8%	28	15% (10% expected)	36
Loss (gain) on PBO	5	Cash contributions	30
Less: Retiree benefits	(16)	Less: Retiree benefits	(16)
End of 2010	$405	*End* of 2010	$290

Determine Lakeside's pension expense for 2010 and prepare the appropriate journal entries to record the expense and the cash funding of plan assets.

5. Determine the new gains and/or losses in 2010 and prepare the appropriate journal entry(s) to record them.

6. Using T-accounts, determine the balances at December 31, 2010, in the net loss–AOCI and prior service cost–AOCI.
7. Confirm the balances determined in Requirement 6 by preparing a pension spreadsheet.

P 17–15
Integrating Problem—Deferred tax effects of pension entries; integrate concepts learned in Chapter 16

● LO7

To focus on the core issues, we ignored the income tax effects of the pension amounts we recorded in the chapter. Reproduced below are the journal entries from the chapter that Global Communications used to record its pension expense and funding in 2009 and the new gain and loss that occurred that year.

	($ in millions)	
To Record Pension Expense		
Pension expense (total)	43	
Plan assets (expected return on plan assets)	27	
PBO ($41 service cost + $24 interest cost)		65
Amortization of prior service cost–OCI (2009 amortization)		4
Amortization of net loss–OCI (2009 amortization)		1

To Record Funding		
Plan assets	48	
Cash (contribution to plan assets)		48

To Record Gains and Losses		
Loss–OCI (from change in assumption)	23	
PBO		23
Plan assets	3	
Gain–OCI (from actual return exceeding expec ted return)		3

Required:
1. Recast these journal entries to include the income tax effects of the events being recorded. Assume that Global's tax rate is 40%. [Hint: Costs are incurred and recognized for financial reporting purposes now, but the tax impact comes much later—when these amounts are deducted for tax purposes as actual payments for retiree benefits occur in the future. As a result, the tax effects are deferred, creating the need to record deferred tax assets and deferred tax liabilities. So, you may want to refer back to Chapter 16 to refresh your memory on these concepts.]
2. Prepare a statement of comprehensive income for 2009 assuming Global's only other sources of comprehensive income were net income of $300 million and a $20 million net unrealized holding gain on investments in securities available for sale.

P 17–16
Postretirement benefits; EPBO calculations; APBO calculations; components of postretirement benefit expense; present value concepts

● LO9 LO10

Century-Fox Corporation's employees are eligible for postretirement health care benefits after both being employed at the end of the year in which age 60 is attained and having worked 20 years. Jason Snyder was hired at the end of 1986 by Century-Fox at age 34 and is expected to retire at the end of 2014 (age 62). His retirement is expected to span five years (unrealistically short to simplify calculations). The company's actuary has estimated the net cost of retiree benefits in each retirement year as shown below. The discount rate is 6%. The plan is not prefunded.

Year	Expected Age	Net Cost
2015	63	$4,000
2016	64	4,400
2017	65	2,300
2018	66	2,500
2019	67	2,800

Assume costs are incurred at the end of each year.

Required:
1. Draw a time line that depicts Snyder's attribution period for retiree benefits and expected retirement period.
2. Calculate the present value of the net benefits as of the expected retirement date.
3. With respect to Snyder, what is the company's expected postretirement benefit obligation at the end of 2009?
4. With respect to Snyder, what is the company's accumulated postretirement benefit obligation at the end of 2009?
5. With respect to Snyder, what is the company's accumulated postretirement benefit obligation at the end of 2010?
6. What is the service cost to be included in 2010 postretirement benefit expense?
7. What is the interest cost to be included in 2010 postretirement benefit expense?
8. Show how the APBO changed during 2010 by reconciling the beginning and ending balances.

P 17–17
Postretirement benefits; schedule of postretirement benefit costs

● LO9 through LO11

Stockton Labeling Company has a retiree health care plan. Employees become fully eligible for benefits after working for the company eight years. Stockton hired Misty Newburn on January 1, 2009. As of the end of 2009, the actuary estimates the total net cost of providing health care benefits to Newburn during her retirement years to have a present value of $18,000. The actuary's discount rate is 10%.

Required:

Prepare a schedule that shows the EPBO, the APBO, the service cost, the interest cost, and the postretirement benefit expense for each of the years 2009–2016.

P 17–18
Postretirement benefits; relationship among elements of postretirement benefit plan

● LO9 through LO11

The information below pertains to the retiree health care plan of Thompson Technologies:

	($ in 000s)	
	2009 Beginning Balances	**2009 Ending Balances**
Accumulated postretirement benefit obligation	$460	$485
Plan assets	0	75
Funded status	(460)	(410)
Prior service cost–AOCI	120	110
Net gain–AOCI	(50)	(49)

Thompson began funding the plan in 2009 with a contribution of $127,000 to the benefit fund at the end of the year. Retirees were paid $52,000. The actuary's discount rate is 5%. There were no changes in actuarial estimates and assumptions.

Required:

Determine the following amounts for 2009:

1. Service cost.
2. Postretirement benefit expense.
3. Net postretirement benefit liability

P 17–19
Pension disclosure; amortization of actuarial gain or loss; Samsonite

● LO3 through LO7

Real World Financials

The **Samsonite Group** is a leader in the luggage and travel product industry. The following is an excerpt from a disclosure note in a recent annual report of Samsonite.

(15) Pension and Other Employee Benefits (in part)
Pension Benefits ($ in 000s):

	Year Ended January 31,		
	2007	2006	2005
Change in Benefit Obligation			
Benefit obligation at beginning of year	**$ 229,484**	224,522	206,024
Service cost	**1,664**	1,769	1,572
Interest cost	**12,210**	12,482	12,389
Actuarial (gain)/loss	**2,424**	7,590	21,349
Benefits paid	**(16,893)**	(16,946)	(16,814)
Translation adjustment	**(34)**	67	2
Benefit obligations at end of year	**$ 228,855**	229,484	224,522
Change in Plan Assets			
Fair value of plan assets at beginning of year	**$ 167,091**	177,061	178,875
Actual return on plan assets	**18,412**	6,680	14,986
Employer contributions	**2,737**	237	228
Mexican plan termination	**—**	—	(215)
Translation adjustment	**(31)**	59	1
Benefits paid	**(16,893)**	(16,946)	(16,814)
Fair value of plan assets at end of year	**$ 171,316**	167,091	177,061

Required:

1. What amount did Samsonite report in its balance sheet related to the pension plan at January 31, 2007?
2. When calculating pension expense at January 31, 2007, what amount did Samsonite include as the amortization of Unrecognized net actuarial loss, which was $56,481,000 at the beginning of the year? The average remaining service life of employees was 7 years.
3. The expected return on plan assets was $13,476,000 for the year ending January 31, 2007, and $261,000 of prior service cost was amortized in 2007. What was the pension expense?
4. What were the appropriate journal entries to record Samsonite's pension expense and to record gains and/or losses related to the pension plan?

BROADEN YOUR PERSPECTIVE

Apply your critical-thinking ability to the knowledge you've gained. These cases will provide you an opportunity to develop your research, analysis, judgment, and communication skills. You also will work with other students, integrate what you've learned, apply it in real world situations, and consider its global and ethical ramifications. This practice will broaden your knowledge and further develop your decision-making abilities.

Judgment Case 17–1
Choose your retirement option

● LO1 LO3 LO4 LO5

"I only get one shot at this?" you wonder aloud. Mrs. Montgomery, human resources manager at Covington State University, has just explained that newly hired assistant professors must choose between two retirement plan options. "Yes, I'm afraid so," she concedes. "But you do have a week to decide."

Mrs. Montgomery's explanation was that your two alternatives are: (1) the state's defined benefit plan and (2) a defined contribution plan under which the university will contribute each year an amount equal to 8% of your salary. The defined benefit plan will provide annual retirement benefits determined by the following formula: 1.5% × years of service × salary at retirement.

"It's a good thing I studied pensions in my accounting program," you tell her. "Now let's see. You say the state is currently assuming our salaries will rise about 3% a year, and the interest rate they use in their calculations is 6%? And, for someone my age, you say they assume I'll retire after 40 years and draw retirement pay for 20 years. I'll do some research and get back to you."

Required:

1. You were hired at the beginning of 2009 at a salary of $100,000. If you choose the state's defined benefit plan and projections hold true, what will be your annual retirement pay? What is the present value of your retirement annuity as of the anticipated retirement date (end of 2048)?
2. Suppose instead that you choose the defined contribution plan. Assuming that the rate of increase in salary is the same as the state assumes and that the rate of return on your retirement plan assets will be 6% compounded annually, what will be the future value of your plan assets as of the anticipated retirement date (end of 2048)? What will be your annual retirement pay (assuming continuing investment of remaining assets at 6%)?
3. Based on this numerical comparison, which plan would you choose? What other factors must you also consider in making the choice?

Hint: The calculations are greatly simplified using an electronic spreadsheet such as Excel. There are many ways to set up the spreadsheet. One relatively easy way is to set up the first few rows with the formulas as shown below, then use the "fill down" function to fill in the remaining 38 rows, and use the Insert: Name: Define: function to name column A "n". Note that multiplying each contribution by (1.06)n, where *n* equals the remaining number of years to retirement, calculates the future value of each contribution invested at 6% until retirement.

	A	B	C	D
1	Years to			Future Value
2	Retirement	Salary	Contribution	at Retirement
3	40	100000	=B3*0.08	=C3*1.06^n
4	=A3-1	=B3*1.03	=B4*0.08	=C4*1.06^n

Communication Case 17–2
Pension concepts

● LO2 through LO8

Noel Zoeller is the newly hired assistant controller of Kemp Industries, a regional supplier of hardwood derivative products. The company sponsors a defined benefit pension plan that covers its 420 employees. On reviewing last year's financial statements, Zoeller was concerned about some items reported in the disclosure notes relating to the pension plan. Portions of the relevant note follow:

Note 8: Pensions
The company has a defined benefit pension plan covering substantially all of its employees. Pension benefits are based on employee service years and the employee's compensation during the last two years of employment. The company contributes annually the maximum amount permitted by the federal tax code. Plan contributions provide for benefits expected to be earned in the future as well as those earned to date. The following reconciles the plan's funded status and amount recognized in the balance sheet at December 31, 2009 ($ in 000s).

Actuarial Present Value Benefit Obligations:	
Accumulated benefit obligation (including vested benefits of $318)	$(1,305)
Projected benefit obligation	(1,800)
Plan assets at fair value	1,575
Projected benefit obligation in excess of plan assets	$ (225)

Kemp's comparative income statements reported net periodic pension expense of $108,000 in 2009 and $86,520 in 2008. Since employment has remained fairly constant in recent years, Zoeller expressed concern over the increase in the pension expense. He expressed his concern to you, a three-year senior accountant at Kemp. "I'm also interested in the differences in these liability measurements," he mentioned.

Required:

Write a memo to Zoeller. In the memo:

1. Explain to Zoeller how the composition of the net periodic pension expense can create the situation he sees. Briefly describe the components of pension expense.
2. Briefly explain how pension gains and losses are recognized in earnings.
3. Describe for him the differences and similarities between the accumulated benefit obligation and the projected benefit obligation.
4. Explain how the "Projected benefit obligation in excess of plan assets" is reported in the financial statements.

Judgment Case 17–3
Barlow's wife; relationship among pension elements

● LO8

LGD Consulting is a medium-sized provider of environmental engineering services. The corporation sponsors a noncontributory, defined benefit pension plan. Alan Barlow, a new employee and participant in the pension plan, obtained a copy of the 2009 financial statements, partly to obtain additional information about his new employer's obligation under the plan. In part, the pension footnote reads as follows:

Note 8: Retirement Benefits
The Company has a defined benefit pension plan covering substantially all of its employees. The benefits are based on years of service and the employee's compensation during the last two years of employment. The company's funding policy is consistent with the funding requirements of federal law and regulations. Generally, pension costs accrued are funded. Plan assets consist primarily of stocks, bonds, commingled trust funds, and cash.

The change in projected benefit obligation for the plan years ended December 31, 2009, and December 31, 2008:

($ in 000s)	**2009**	**2008**
Projected benefit obligation at beginning of year	$3,786	$3,715
Service cost	103	94
Interest cost	287	284
Actuarial (gain) loss	302	(23)
Benefits paid	(324)	(284)
Projected benefit obligation at end of year	$4,154	$3,786

The weighted average discount rate and rate of increase in future compensation levels used in determining the actuarial present value of the projected benefit obligations in the above table were 7.0% and 4.3%, respectively, at December 31, 2009, and 7.75% and 4.7%, respectively, at December 31, 2008. The expected long-term rate of return on assets was 10.0% at December 31, 2009 and 2008.

The change in the fair value of plan assets for the plan years ended December 31, 2009 and 2008:

($ in 000s)	2009	2008
Fair value of plan assets at beginning of year	$3,756	$3,616
Actual return on plan assets	1,100	372
Employer contributions	27	52
Benefits paid	(324)	(284)
Fair value of plan assets at end of year	$4,559	$3,756

Included in the Consolidated Balance Sheets are the following components of accumulated other comprehensive income:

($ in 000s)	2009	2008
Net actuarial gain	$(620)	$(165)
Prior service cost	44	46

Net periodic defined benefit pension cost for fiscal 2009, 2008, and 2007 included the following components:

($ in 000s)	2009	2008	2007
Service cost	$ 103	$ 94	$ 112
Interest cost	287	284	263
Expected return on plan assets	(342)	(326)	(296)
Amortization of prior service cost	2	2	1
Recognized net actuarial (gain) loss	(2)	2	4
Net periodic pension cost	$ 48	$ 56	$ 84

In attempting to reconcile amounts reported in the footnote with amounts reported in the income statement and balance sheet, Barlow became confused. He was able to find the pension expense on the income statement but was unable to make sense of the balance sheet amounts. Expressing his frustration to his wife, Barlow said, "It appears to me that the company has calculated pension expense as if they have the pension liability and pension assets they include in the footnote, but I can't seem to find those amounts in the balance sheet. In fact, there are several amounts here I can't seem to account for. They also say they've made some assumptions about interest rates, pay increases, and profits on invested assets. I wonder what difference it would make if they assumed other numbers,"

Barlow's wife took accounting courses in college and remembers most of what she learned about pension accounting. She attempts to clear up her husband's confusion.

Required:

Assume the role of Barlow's wife. Answer the following questions for your husband.

1. Is Barlow's observation correct that the company has calculated pension expense on the basis of amounts not reported in the balance sheet?
2. What amount would the company report as a pension liability in the balance sheet?
3. What amount would the company report as a pension asset in the balance sheet?
4. Which of the other amounts reported in the disclosure note would the company report in the balance sheet?
5. The disclosure note reports a net actuarial gain as well as an actuarial loss. How are these related? What do the amounts mean?
6. Which components of the pension expense represent deferred recognition? Where are these deferred amounts reported prior to amortization?

Communication Case 17–4
Barlow's wife; relationship among pension elements

● LO8

The focus of this case is question 1 in the previous case. Your instructor will divide the class into two to six groups, depending on the size of the class. The mission of your group is to assess the correctness of Barlow's observation and to suggest the appropriate treatment of the pension obligation. The suggested treatment need not be that required by GAAP.

Required:

1. Each group member should deliberate the situation independently and draft a tentative argument prior to the class session for which the case is assigned.
2. In class, each group will meet for 10 to 15 minutes in different areas of the classroom. During that meeting, group members will take turns sharing their suggestions for the purpose of arriving at a single group treatment.
3. After the allotted time, a spokesperson for each group (selected during the group meetings) will share the group's solution with the class. The goal of the class is to incorporate the views of each group into a consensus approach to the situation.

Real World Case 17–5
Types of pension plans; disclosures

● LO1

Real World Financials

Google

Refer to the financial statements and related disclosure notes of **Google, Inc.** located in the company's annual report included with all new copies of the text. The financial statements also can be found at the company's website: **www.google.com** or via EDGAR at **www.sec.gov**.

Required:

1. What type of pension plan does Google sponsor for its employees? Explain.
2. Who bears the "risk" of factors that might reduce retirement benefits in this type of plan? Explain.
3. Suppose a Google employee contributes $10,000 to the pension plan during her first year of employment and directs investments to a municipal bond mutual fund. If she leaves Google early in her second year, after the mutual fund's value has increased by 2%, how much will she be entitled to roll over into an Individual Retirement Account (IRA)?
4. How did Google account for its participation in the pension plan in 2007?

Ethics Case 17–6
401(k) plan contributions

● LO1

You are in your third year as internal auditor with VXI International, manufacturer of parts and supplies for jet aircraft. VXI began a defined contribution pension plan three years ago. The plan is a so-called 401(k) plan (named after the Tax Code section that specifies the conditions for the favorable tax treatment of these plans) that permits voluntary contributions by employees. Employees' contributions are matched with one dollar of employer contribution for every two dollars of employee contribution. Approximately $500,000 of contributions are deducted from employee paychecks each month for investment in one of three employer-sponsored mutual funds.

While performing some preliminary audit tests, you happen to notice that employee contributions to these plans usually do not show up on mutual fund statements for up to two months following the end of pay periods from which the deductions are drawn. On further investigation, you discover that when the plan was first begun, contributions were invested within one week of receipt of the funds. When you question the firm's investment manager about the apparent change in the timing of investments, you are told, "Last year Mr. Maxwell (the CFO) directed me to initially deposit the contributions in the corporate investment account. At the close of each quarter, we add the employer matching contribution and deposit the combined amount in specific employee mutual funds."

Required:

1. What is Mr. Maxwell's apparent motivation for the change in the way contributions are handled?
2. Do you perceive an ethical dilemma?

Research Case 17–7
Researching pension disclosures; retrieving information from the Internet

● LO1 LO3 LO4

All publicly traded domestic companies use EDGAR, the Electronic Data Gathering, Analysis, and Retrieval system, to make the majority of their filings with the SEC. You can access EDGAR on the Internet at **www.sec.gov**.

Required:

1. Search for a company with which you are familiar and which you believe is likely to have a pension plan. (Older, established firms are good candidates.) Access the company's most recent 10-K filing. Search or scroll to find the financial statements and related notes.
2. From the disclosure notes, determine the type of pension plan(s) the company has.
3. For any defined contribution plans, determine the contributions the company made to the plans on behalf of employees during the most recent three years.
4. For any defined benefit plans, determine the projected benefit obligation for the most recent year. Compare this obligation with the company's total long-term debt. What interest rate was used in estimating the PBO?
5. Repeat steps 2 through 4 for a second firm. Compare and contrast the types of pension plans offered. Are actuarial assumptions the same for defined benefit plans?

Real World Case 17–8
Types of pension plans; reporting postretirement plans; disclosures

● LO5 LO8

Real World Financials

Refer to the most recent financial statements and related disclosure notes of **FedEx Corporation**. The financial statements can be found at the company's website: **www.fedex.com** or via EDGAR at **www.sec.gov**.

Required:

1. What pension and other postretirement benefit plans does FedEx sponsor for its employees? Explain.
2. What amount does FedEx report in its balance sheet for its pension and other postretirement benefit plans? Explain.
3. FedEx reports three actuarial assumptions used in its pension calculations. Did reported changes in those assumptions from the previous year increase or decrease the projected benefit obligation? Why?

Real World Case 17–9
Pension amendment

● LO5 LO8

Charles Rubin is a 30-year employee of **General Motors**. Charles was pleased with recent negotiations between his employer and the United Auto Workers. Among other favorable provisions of the new agreement, the pact also includes a 13% increase in pension payments for workers under 62 with 30 years of service who retire during the agreement. Although the elimination of a cap on outside income earned by retirees has been generally viewed as an incentive for older workers to retire, Charles sees promise for his dream of becoming a part-time engineering consultant after retirement. What has caught Charles's attention is the following excerpt from an article in *the financial press:*

Real World Financials

> **General Motors Corp.** will record a $170 million charge due to increases in retirement benefits for hourly United Auto Workers employees.
>
> The charge stems from GM's new tentative labor contract with the UAW. According to a filing with the Securities and Exchange Commission, the charge amounts to 22 cents a share and is tied to the earnings of GM's Hughes Electronics unit.
>
> The company warned that its "unfunded pension obligation and pension expense are expected to be unfavorably impacted as a result of the recently completed labor negotiations."

Taking advantage of an employee stock purchase plan, Charles has become an active GM stockholder as well as employee. His stockholder side is moderately concerned by the article's reference to the unfavorable impact of the recently completed labor negotiations.

Required:

1. When a company modifies its pension benefits the way General Motors did, what name do we give the added cost? How is it accounted for?
2. What does GM mean when it says its "unfunded pension obligation and pension expense are expected to be unfavorably impacted as a result of the recently completed labor negotiations"?

Analysis Case 17–10
Effect of pensions on earnings

● LO7

While doing some online research concerning a possible investment you come across an article that mentions in passing that a representative of **Morgan Stanley** had indicated that a company's pension plan had benefited its reported earnings. Curiosity piqued, you seek your old Intermediate Accounting text.

Required:

1. Can the net periodic pension "cost" cause a company's reported earnings to increase? Explain.
2. Companies must report the actuarial assumptions used to make estimates concerning pension plans. Which estimate influences the earnings effect in requirement 1? Can any of the other estimates influence earnings? Explain.

Research Case 17–11
Researching the way employee benefits are tested on the CPA Exam; retrieving information from the Internet

● LO9 LO10 LO11

The board of examiners of the American Institute of Certified Public Accountants (AICPA) is responsible for preparing the CPA examination. The boards of accountancy of all 50 states, the District of Columbia, Guam, Puerto Rico, the U.S. Virgin Islands, and the Mariana Islands use the examination as the primary way to measure the technical competence of CPA candidates. The content for each examination section is specified by the AICPA and described in outline form.

Required:

1. Access the AICPA web site on the Internet. The web address is **www.aicpa.org**.
2. Access the CPA exam section within the site. Locate the exam content portion of the section.
3. In which of the four separately graded sections of the exam are postretirement benefits tested?
4. From the AICPA site, access the Board of Accountancy for your state. What are the education requirements in your state to sit for the CPA exam?

CPA SIMULATION 17–1

Schachter Company
Liabilities and Postretirement Benefitis

CPA Review

Test your knowledge of the concepts discussed in this chapter, practice critical professional skills necessary for career success, and prepare for the computer-based CPA exam by accessing our CPA simulations at the text website: www.mhhe.com/spiceland5e.

The Schachter Company simulation tests your knowledge of contingencies, bonds, leases, deferred income taxes, transferring accounts receivables in a secured borrowing, and postretirement benefits.

As on the CPA exam itself, you will be asked to use tools including a spreadsheet, a calculator, and professional accounting standards to conduct research, derive solutions, and communicate conclusions related to these issues in a simulated environment headed by the following interactive tabs:

KAPLAN CPA Review | Financial Accounting and Reporting | Time Elapsed 0 hours 0 minutes | Calculator | Sheet | Standards | Help | Split | Done

Directions | Situation | Contingencies | Dferrd Taxes | Bonds | Bonds and Leases | Communication | Research | Resources

Specific tasks in the simulation include:

- Demonstrating an understanding of financial reporting effects of various contingencies.
- Applying judgment in deciding the deferred tax effects of a variety of transactions.
- Calculating interest and liabilities relating to bonds and leases.
- Communicating the way to calculate financial ratios related to liabilities and what they attempt to measure.
- Researching appropriate accounting for the transfer of accounts receivable to a third party.

CHAPTER 18

Shareholders' Equity

/// OVERVIEW

We turn our attention from liabilities, which represent the creditors' interests in the assets of a corporation, to the shareholders' residual interest in those assets. The discussions distinguish between the two basic sources of shareholders' equity: (1) *invested capital* and (2) *earned* capital. We explore the expansion of corporate capital through the issuance of shares and the contraction caused by the retirement of shares or the purchase of treasury shares. In our discussions of retained earnings, we examine cash dividends, property dividends, stock dividends, and stock splits.

LEARNING OBJECTIVES

After studying this chapter, you should be able to:

- **LO1** Describe the components of shareholders' equity and explain how they are reported in a statement of shareholders' equity.
- **LO2** Describe comprehensive income and its components.
- **LO3** Record the issuance of shares when sold for cash and for noncash consideration.
- **LO4** Describe what occurs when shares are retired and how the retirement is recorded.
- **LO5** Distinguish between accounting for retired shares and for treasury shares.
- **LO6** Describe retained earnings and distinguish it from paid-in capital.
- **LO7** Explain the basis of corporate dividends, including the similarities and differences between cash and property dividends.
- **LO8** Explain stock dividends and stock splits and how we account for them.

FINANCIAL REPORTING CASE

Textron Inc.

Finally, you have some uninterrupted time to get back on the net. Earlier today you noticed on the Internet that the market price of Textron Inc.'s common stock was up almost 10%. You've been eager to look into why this happened, but have had one meeting after another all day.

al World
ancials

Textron Inc. is an $11 billion multi-industry company operating in 32 countries known for its Bell Helicopter, Cessna Aircraft, and other brands. You've been a stockholder of Textron since the beginning of the year when your uncle bragged to you about his company's Cessna. The dividends of 19 cents a share that you receive quarterly are nice, but that's not why you bought the stock; you were convinced at the time that the stock price was poised to rise rapidly. A few well-placed clicks of the mouse and you come across the following news article:

> PROVIDENCE, RI–July 19, 2007–Textron Inc. (Business Wire) today reported a 26% increase in earnings per share from continuing operations on a 15% revenue increase. The company also raised earnings and cash flow guidance for 2007. "We experienced another strong quarter of solid revenue growth and improved profitability," said Textron Chairman, President and CEO Lewis B. Campbell.
>
> The Board approved a two-for-one split of its Common Stock shares. The stock split will be effected through a 100% stock dividend, payable on August 24, 2007 to shareholders of record as of the close of business on August 3, 2007. Textron's Common Stock will begin trading at the split-adjusted price on August 27, 2007.
>
> In addition, Textron's Board of Directors has approved a 19% increase in the company's annualized Common Stock dividend rate from $0.775 per share to $0.92 per share, stated on a post-split basis. Related to this action, Textron's Board of Directors declared a quarterly dividend of $0.23 per common share to holders of record as of the close of business on September 14, 2007.
>
> Furthermore, the Board of Directors has authorized the repurchase of up to 24 million shares of Textron's Common Stock, stated on a post-split basis.

Source: "Textron Reports Strong Second Quarter Results," *Business Wire,* July 19, 2007.

By the time you finish this chapter, you should be able to respond appropriately to the questions posed in this case. Compare your response to the solution provided at the end of the chapter.

QUESTIONS ///

1. Do you think the stock price increase is related to Textron's share repurchase plan? (page 960)
2. What are Textron's choices in accounting for the share repurchases? (page 961)
3. What effect does the quarterly cash dividend of 23 cents a share have on Textron's assets? Its liabilities? Its shareholders' equity? (page 967)
4. What effect did the stock split have on Textron's assets? Its liabilities? Its shareholders' equity? (page 970)

PART A

THE NATURE OF SHAREHOLDERS' EQUITY

A corporation raises money to fund its business operations by some mix of debt and equity financing. In earlier chapters, we examined debt financing in the form of notes, bonds, leases, and other liabilities. Amounts representing those liabilities denote *creditors' interest* in the company's assets. Now we focus on various forms of equity financing. Specifically, in this chapter we consider transactions that affect shareholders' equity—those accounts that represent the *ownership interests* of shareholders.

● LO1

In principle, shareholders' equity is a relatively straightforward concept. Shareholders' equity is a residual amount—what's left over after creditor claims have been subtracted from assets (in other words, net assets). You probably recall the residual nature of shareholders' equity from the basic accounting equation:

Net assets equal shareholders' equity.

$$\underbrace{\text{Assets} - \text{Liabilities}}_{\text{Net Assets}} = \text{Shareholder's equity}$$

Shareholders' equity accounts denote the ownership interests of shareholders.

Ownership interests of shareholders arise primarily from two sources: (1) amounts *invested* by shareholders in the corporation and (2) amounts *earned* by the corporation on behalf of its shareholders. These two sources are reported as (1) paid-in capital and (2) retained earnings.

Despite being a seemingly clear-cut concept, shareholders' equity and its component accounts often are misunderstood and misinterpreted. As we explore the transactions that affect shareholders' equity and its component accounts, try not to allow yourself to be overwhelmed by unfamiliar terminology or to be overly concerned with precise account titles. Terminology pertaining to shareholders' equity accounts is notoriously diverse. To give you one example—retained earnings is reported variously as *retained income* (**Smucker**), *reinvested earnings* (**Verizon**), *earnings reinvested* (**ExxonMobil**), *earnings retained in the business* (**Campbell Soup**), *retained earnings reinvested and employed in the business* (**L.S. Starret Company**), *accumulated* equity (**Federated Department Stores**), and *accumulated earnings* (**Intel**). Every shareholders' equity account has several aliases. Indeed, shareholders' equity itself is often referred to as *stockholders' equity, shareowners' equity, shareholders' investment,* and many other similar titles.

GAAP permits many choices in accounting for transactions affecting shareholders' equity.

Complicating matters, transactions that affect shareholders' equity are influenced by corporation laws of individual states in which companies are located. And, as we see later, generally accepted accounting principles provide companies with considerable latitude when choosing accounting methods in this area.

Keeping this perspective in mind while you study the chapter should aid you in understanding the essential concepts. At a very basic level, each transaction we examine can be viewed simply as an increase or decrease in shareholders' equity, per se, without regard to specific shareholders' equity accounts. In fact, for a business organized as a single proprietorship, all capital changes are recorded in a single owner's equity account. The same concepts apply to a corporation. But for corporations, additional considerations make it desirable to separate owners' equity into several separate shareholders' equity accounts. These additional considerations—legal requirements and disclosure objectives—are discussed in later sections of this chapter. So, as you study the separate effects of transactions on retained earnings and specific paid-in capital accounts, you may find it helpful to ask yourself frequently "What is the net effect of this transaction on shareholders' equity?" or, equivalently, "By how much are net assets (assets minus liabilities) affected by this transaction?"

Legal requirements and disclosure objectives make it preferable to separate a corporation's capital into several separate shareholders' equity accounts.

Financial Reporting Overview

Before we examine the events that underlie specific shareholders' equity accounts, let's overview how individual accounts relate to each other. The condensed balance sheet of Exposition Corporation, a hypothetical company, in Graphic 18–1 provides that perspective.

Graphic 18–1 depicts a rather comprehensive situation. It's unlikely that any one company would have shareholders' equity from all of these sources at any one time. Remember

GRAPHIC 18–1
Detailed Shareholders' Equity Presentation

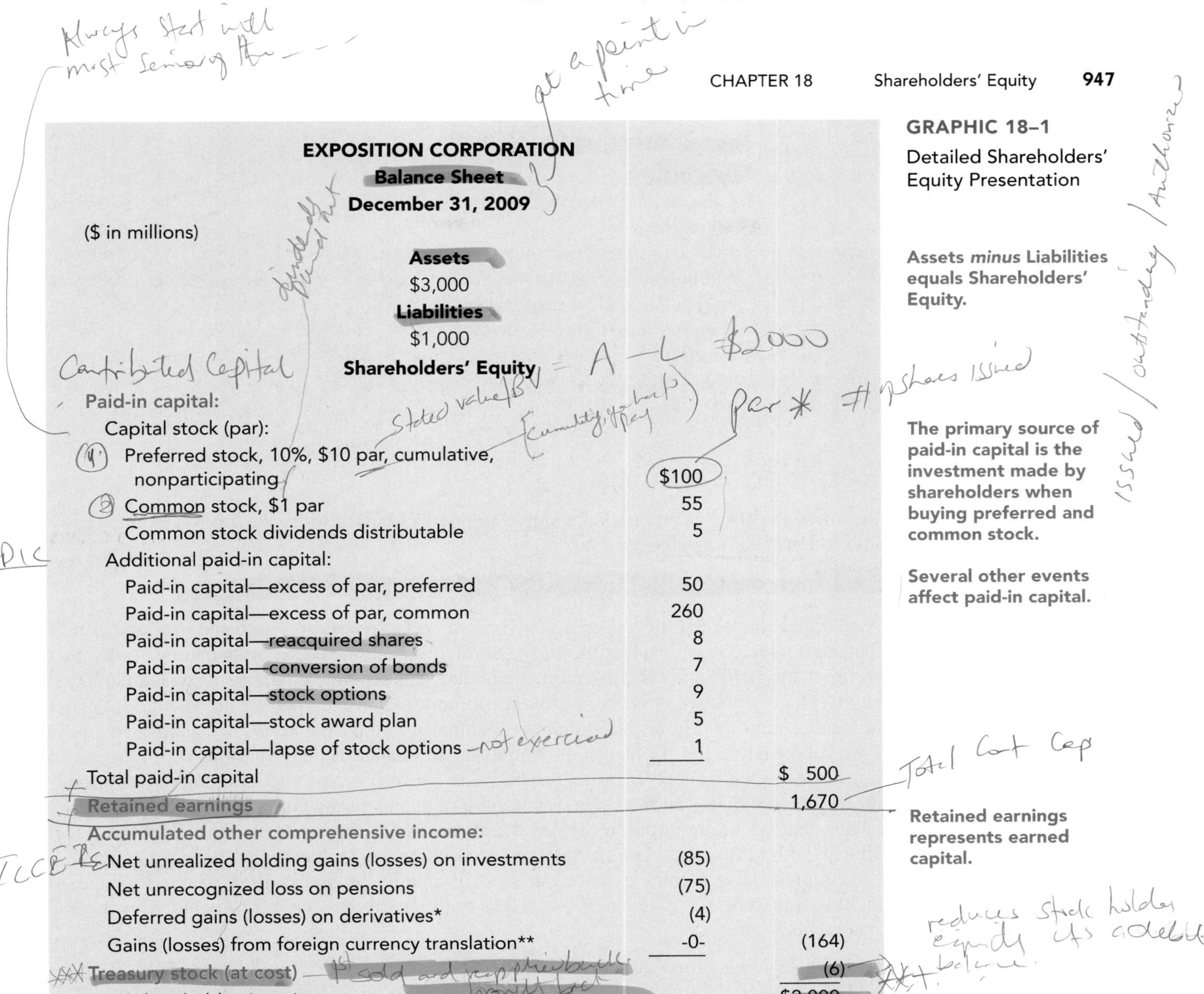

EXPOSITION CORPORATION
Balance Sheet
December 31, 2009

($ in millions)

Assets
$3,000
Liabilities
$1,000
Shareholders' Equity

Paid-in capital:		
Capital stock (par):		
Preferred stock, 10%, $10 par, cumulative, nonparticipating	$100	
Common stock, $1 par	55	
Common stock dividends distributable	5	
Additional paid-in capital:		
Paid-in capital—excess of par, preferred	50	
Paid-in capital—excess of par, common	260	
Paid-in capital—reacquired shares	8	
Paid-in capital—conversion of bonds	7	
Paid-in capital—stock options	9	
Paid-in capital—stock award plan	5	
Paid-in capital—lapse of stock options	1	
Total paid-in capital		$ 500
Retained earnings		1,670
Accumulated other comprehensive income:		
Net unrealized holding gains (losses) on investments	(85)	
Net unrecognized loss on pensions	(75)	
Deferred gains (losses) on derivatives*	(4)	
Gains (losses) from foreign currency translation**	-0-	(164)
Treasury stock (at cost)		(6)
Total shareholders' equity		$2,000

Assets *minus* Liabilities equals Shareholders' Equity.

The primary source of paid-in capital is the investment made by shareholders when buying preferred and common stock.

Several other events affect paid-in capital.

Retained earnings represents earned capital.

*When a derivative designated as a cash flow hedge is adjusted to fair value, the gain or loss is deferred as a component of other comprehensive income and included in earnings later, at the same time as earnings are affected by the hedged transaction (described in Appendix A at the end of the book).
**Gains or losses from changes in foreign currency exchange rates. This item is discussed elsewhere in your accounting curriculum. The amount could be an addition to or reduction in shareholders' equity.

that, at this point, our objective is only to get a general perspective of the items constituting shareholders' equity. You should, however, note a few aspects of the statement shown in Graphic 18–1. First, although company records would include separate accounts for each of these components of shareholders' equity, in the balance sheet, Exposition would report a more condensed version similar to that in Graphic 18–1A on the next page.

The four classifications within shareholders' equity are paid-in capital, retained earnings, accumulated other comprehensive income, and treasury stock. We discuss these now in the context of Exposition Corporation.

Paid-in capital

The two primary components of shareholders' equity are paid-in capital and retained earnings.

Paid-in capital consists primarily of amounts invested by shareholders when they purchase shares of stock from the corporation. In addition, amounts sometimes are invested (or disinvested) by others on behalf of the shareholders. For Exposition Corporation, shareholders invested $470 million ($100 + 55 + 5 + 260 + 50). An additional $30 million ($8 + 7 + 9 + 5 + 1) of paid-in capital arose from financing activities, bringing the total to $500 million. Later in this chapter, we consider in more detail the events and transactions that affect paid-in capital.

GRAPHIC 18–1A
Typical Shareholders' Equity Presentation

Preferred stock, 10%	$ 100
Common stock	60
Additional paid-in capital	340
Retained earnings	1,670
Accumulated other comprehensive income:	
Net unrealized holding losses on investments	(85)
Net unrealized loss on pensions	(75)
Deferred losses on derivatives	(4)
Treasury stock	(6)
Total shareholders' equity	$2,000

Retained Earnings

Retained earnings is reported as a single amount, $1,670 million. We discuss retained earnings in Part C of this chapter.

LO2

Accumulated Other Comprehensive Income

Some accounts can be viewed as contra-shareholders' equity accounts.

Comprehensive income includes net income as well as other gains and losses that change shareholders' equity but are not included in traditional net income.

Also notice that shareholders' equity of Exposition Corporation is adjusted for three events that are not included in net income and so don't affect retained earnings but are part of "other comprehensive income" and therefore are included as separate components of shareholders' equity.[1] **Comprehensive income** provides a more expansive view of the change in shareholders' equity than does traditional net income. It is the total *nonowner* change in equity for a reporting period. In fact, it encompasses all changes in equity other than those from transactions with owners. Transactions between the corporation and its shareholders primarily include dividends and the sale or purchase of shares of the company's stock. Most nonowner changes are reported in the income statement. So, the changes other than those that are part of traditional net income are the ones reported as "other comprehensive income."

Comprehensive income extends our view of income beyond conventional net income to include four types of gains and losses that traditionally haven't been included in income statements:

1. Net holding gains (losses) on investments.
2. Gains (losses) from and amendments to postretirement benefit plans.
3. Deferred gains (losses) on derivatives.
4. Gains (losses) from foreign currency translation.

The first of these are the gains and losses on securities "available-for-sale" that occur when the fair values of these investments increase or decrease. As you learned in Chapter 12, these gains and losses aren't included in earnings until they are realized through the sale of the securities but are considered a component of *other comprehensive income* in the meantime. Similarly, as we discussed in Chapter 17, net gains and losses as well as "prior service cost" on pensions sometimes affect other comprehensive income but not net income. You have not yet studied the third and fourth potential components of other comprehensive income. As described in Appendix A, "Derivatives" at the back of this textbook, when a derivative designated as a "*cash flow hedge*" is adjusted to fair value, the gain or loss is deferred as a component of other comprehensive income and included in earnings later, at the same time as earnings are affected by the hedged transaction. Gains and losses from changes in foreign currency exchange rates are discussed elsewhere in your accounting curriculum, but also are included in other comprehensive income (OCI) but not net income.

OCI shares another trait with net income. Just as net income is reported periodically in the income statement and also on a cumulative basis as part of retained earnings, OCI too, is reported periodically in the statement of comprehensive income and also as **accumulated other comprehensive income** in the balance sheet along with retained earnings. In other

[1]Comprehensive income was introduced in Chapter 4 and revisited in Chapters 12 and 17.

words, we report two attributes of OCI: (1) components of comprehensive income *created during the reporting period* and (2) the comprehensive income *accumulated* over the current and prior periods.

The first attribute—components of comprehensive income *created during the reporting period*—can be reported either as (a) an expanded version of the income statement, (b) part of the statement of shareholders' equity, or (c) a separate statement. Regardless of the placement a company chooses, the presentation is similar. It will report net income, other components of comprehensive income, and total comprehensive income, similar to the presentation in Graphic 18–2. Note that each component is reported net of its related income tax expense or income tax benefit.

GRAPHIC 18–2
Comprehensive Income

		($ in millions)
Net income		$xxx
Other comprehensive income:		
Net unrealized holding gains (losses) on investments (net of tax)*	$ x	
Gains (losses) from and amendments to postretirement benefit plans (net of tax)†	(x)	
Deferred gains (losses) on derivatives (net of tax)‡	(x)	
Gains (losses) from foreign currency translation (net of tax)§	x	xx
Comprehensive income		$xxx

*Changes in the market value of securities available-for-sale (described in Chapter 12).
†Gains and losses due to revising assumptions or market returns differing from expectations and prior service cost from amending the plan (described in Chapter 17).
‡When a derivative designated as a cash flow hedge is adjusted to fair value, the gain or loss is deferred as a component of comprehensive income and included in earnings later, at the same time as earnings are affected by the hedged transaction (described in the Derivatives Appendix to the text).
§Gains or losses from changes in foreign currency exchange rates. The amount could be an addition to or reduction in shareholders' equity. (This item is discussed elsewhere in your accounting curriculum.)

Comprehensive income includes net income as well as other gains and losses that change shareholders' equity but are not included in traditional net income.

The second measure—the comprehensive income *accumulated* over the current and prior periods—is reported as a separate component of shareholders' equity following retained earnings, similar to the presentation by Exposition Corporation in Graphic 18–1. Note that amounts reported here—accumulated other comprehensive income (AOCI)—represent the *cumulative* sum of the changes in each component created during each reporting period (Graphic 18–2) throughout all prior years.

Treasury Stock

We discuss the final component of shareholders' equity—treasury stock—later in the chapter. It indicates that some of the shares previously sold were bought back by the corporation from shareholders.

You seldom if ever will see this degree of detail reported in the presentation of paid-in capital. Instead, companies keep track of individual additional paid-in capital accounts in company records but ordinarily report these amounts as a single subtotal—additional paid-in capital. Pertinent rights and privileges of various securities outstanding such as dividend

Ordinarily, less detail is reported than is kept in company records.

INTERNATIONAL FINANCIAL REPORTING STANDARDS

Comprehensive Income. As part of a joint project with the FASB, the International Accounting Standards Board (IASB) in 2007 issued a revised version of *IAS No. 1*, "Presentation of Financial Statements," that revised the standard to bring international reporting of comprehensive income largely in line with U.S. standards. It provides the option of presenting revenue and expense items and components of other comprehensive income either in (a) a single statement of comprehensive income or (b) in an income statement followed by a statement of comprehensive income. U.S. GAAP also allows reporting other comprehensive income in the statement of shareholders' equity, which is the way most U.S. companies report it.

and liquidation preferences, call and conversion information, and voting rights are summarized in disclosure notes.[2] The shareholders' equity portion of the balance sheet of **Southwest Airlines,** shown in Graphic 18–3, is a typical presentation format.

GRAPHIC 18–3
Typical Presentation Format—Southwest Airlines

Real World Financials

Details of each class of stock are reported on the face of the balance sheet or in disclosure notes.

SOUTHWEST AIRLINES, INC.
Balance Sheet
[Shareholders' Equity Section]
($ in millions)

	2006	2005
Stockholders' equity:		
Common stock, $1.00 par value: 2,000,000,000 shares authorized; 807,611,634 and 801,641,645 shares issued in 2006 and 2005, respectively	808	802
Capital in excess of par value	1,142	963
Retained earnings	4,307	4,018
Accumulated other comprehensive income	582	892
Treasury stock, at cost: 24,302,215 shares in 2006	(390)	—
Total stockholders' equity	6,449	6,675

A *statement of shareholders' equity* reports the transactions that cause changes in its shareholders' equity account balances.

The balance sheet reports annual balances of shareholders' equity accounts. However, companies also should disclose the sources of the changes in those accounts.[3] This is the purpose of the **statement of shareholders' equity.** To illustrate, Graphic 18–4 on the next page shows how Southwest Airlines reported the changes in its shareholders' equity balances (shown in Graphic 18–3).

The changes that Southwest Airlines's statements of shareholders' equity reveal are net income and two other items of comprehensive income, the purchase of treasury stock, the issuance of common stock, and dividends declared.

The Corporate Organization

A company may be organized in any of three ways: (1) a sole proprietorship, (2) a partnership, or (3) a corporation. In your introductory accounting course, you studied each form. In this course we focus exclusively on the corporate form of organization.

Corporations are the dominant form of business organization.

Most well-known companies, such as **Microsoft, IBM,** and **General Motors,** are corporations. Also, many smaller companies—even one-owner businesses—are corporations. Although fewer in number than proprietorships and partnerships, in terms of business volume, corporations are the predominant form of business organization.

Accounting for most transactions is the same regardless of the form of business organization.

In most respects, transactions are accounted for in the same way regardless of the form of business organization. Assets and liabilities are unaffected by the way a company is organized. The exception is the method of accounting for capital, the ownership interest in the company. Rather than recording all changes in ownership interests in a single capital account for each owner, as we do for sole proprietorships and partnerships, we use the several capital accounts overviewed in the previous section to record those changes for a corporation. Before discussing how we account for specific ownership changes, let's look at the characteristics of a corporation that make this form of organization distinctive and require special accounting treatment.

Limited Liability

A corporation is a separate legal entity—separate and distinct from its owners.

The owners are not personally liable for debts of a corporation. Unlike a proprietorship or a partnership, a corporation is a separate legal entity, responsible for its own debts. Shareholders' liability is limited to the amounts they invest in the company when they purchase shares (unless the shareholder also is an officer of the corporation). The limited liability of shareholders is perhaps the single most important advantage of corporate organization. In

[2]"Disclosure of Information about Capital Structure," *Statement of Financial Accounting Standards No. 129* (Norwalk, Conn.: FASB, 1997).
[3]"Omnibus Opinion," *APB Opinion No. 12* (New York: AICPA, 1967).

other forms of business, creditors may look to the personal assets of owners for satisfaction of business debt.

GRAPHIC 18–4 Changes in Stockholders' Equity—Southwest Airlines

SOUTHWEST AIRLINES
Consolidated Statements of Stockholders' Equity

(In millions, except per share amounts)	Common Stock	Capital in Excess of Par Value	Retained Earnings	Accumulated Other Comprehensive Income (Loss)	Treasury Stock	Total
Balance at December 31, 2003	**$789**	**$ 612**	**$3,506**	**$ 122**	**$ —**	**$5,029**
Purchase of shares of treasury stock	—	—	—	—	(246)	(246)
Issuance of common and treasury stock pursuant to employee stock plans	1	7	(93)	—	175	90
Tax benefit of options exercised	—	23	—	—	—	23
Share-based compensation	—	135	—	—	—	135
Cash dividends, $.018 per share	—	—	(14)	—	—	(14)
Comprehensive income (loss)						
Net income	—	—	215	—	—	215
Unrealized gain on derivative instruments	—	—	—	293	—	293
Other	—	—	—	2	—	2
Total comprehensive income						510
Balance at December 31, 2004	**$790**	**$ 777**	**$3,614**	**$ 417**	**$ (71)**	**$5,527**
Purchase of shares of treasury stock	—	—	—	—	(55)	(55)
Issuance of common and treasury stock pursuant to employee stock plans	12	59	(66)	—	126	131
Tax benefit of options exercised	—	47	—	—	—	47
Share-based compensation	—	80	—	—	—	80
Cash dividends, $.018 per share	—	—	(14)	—	—	(14)
Comprehensive income (loss)						
Net income	—	—	484	—	—	484
Unrealized gain on derivative instruments	—	—	—	474	—	474
Other	—	—	—	1	—	1
Total comprehensive income						959
Balance at December 31, 2005	**$802**	**$ 963**	**$4,018**	**$ 892**	**$ —**	**$6,675**
Purchase of shares of treasury stock	—	—	—	—	(800)	(800)
Issuance of common and treasury stock pursuant to employee stock plans	6	39	(196)	—	410	259
Tax benefit of options exercised	—	60	—	—	—	60
Share-based compensation	—	80	—	—	—	80
Cash dividends, $.018 per share	—	—	(14)	—	—	(14)
Comprehensive income (loss)						
Net income	—	—	499	—	—	499
Unrealized loss on derivative instruments	—	—	—	(306)	—	(306)
Other	—	—	—	(4)	—	(4)
Total comprehensive income						189
Balance at December 31, 2006	**$808**	**$1,142**	**$4,307**	**$ 582**	**$(390)**	**$6,449**

Ease of Raising Capital

Ownership interest in a corporation is easily transferred.

A corporation is better suited to raising capital than is a proprietorship or a partnership. All companies can raise funds by operating at a profit or by borrowing. However, attracting equity capital is easier for a corporation. Because corporations sell ownership interest in the form of shares of stock, ownership rights are easily transferred. An investor can sell his/her ownership interest at any time and without affecting the corporation or its operations.

Shareholders do not have a mutual agency relationship.

From the viewpoint of a potential investor, another favorable aspect of investing in a corporation is the lack of mutual agency. Individual partners in a partnership have the power to bind the business to a contract. Therefore, an investor in a partnership must be careful regarding the character and business savvy of fellow co-owners. On the other hand, shareholders' participation in the affairs of a corporation is limited to voting at shareholders' meetings (unless the shareholder also is a manager). Consequently, a shareholder needn't exercise the same degree of care that partners must in selecting co-owners.

Obviously, then, a corporation offers advantages over the other forms of organization, particularly in its ability to raise investment capital. As you might guess, though, these benefits do not come without a price.

Disadvantages

Corporations are subject to expensive government regulation.

Paperwork! To protect the rights of those who buy a corporation's stock or who loan money to a corporation, the state in which the company is incorporated and the federal government impose expensive reporting requirements. Primarily the required paperwork is intended to ensure adequate disclosure of information needed by investors and creditors.

Corporations create double taxation.

You read earlier that corporations are separate legal entities. As such, they also are separate taxable entities. Often this causes what is referred to as *double taxation.* Corporations first pay income taxes on their earnings. Then, when those earnings are distributed as cash dividends, shareholders pay personal income taxes on the previously taxed earnings. Proprietorships and partnerships are not taxed at the business level; each owner's share of profits is taxed only as personal income.

Types of Corporations

When referring to corporations in this text, we are referring to corporations formed by private individuals for the purpose of generating profits. These corporations raise capital by selling stock. There are, however, other types of corporations.

Not-for-profit corporations may be owned:
1. **By the public sector.**
2. **By a governmental unit.**

Some corporations such as churches, hospitals, universities, and charities do not sell stock and are not organized for profit. Also, some not-for-profit corporations are government-owned—the **Federal Deposit Insurance Corporation (FDIC),** for instance. Accounting for not-for-profit corporations is discussed elsewhere in the accounting curriculum.

Corporations organized for profit may be:
1. **Publicly held and traded:**
   a. **On an exchange.**
   b. **Over-the-counter.**
2. **Privately held.**

Corporations organized for profit may be publicly held or privately (or closely) held. The stock of publicly held corporations is available for purchase by the general public. You can buy shares of **General Electric, Ford Motor Company,** or **ExxonMobil** through a stockbroker. These shares are traded on the New York Stock Exchange. Other publicly held stock, like **Intel** and **Microsoft,** are available through Nasdaq (National Association of Securities Dealers Automated Quotations).

Privately held companies' shares are held by only a few individuals and are not available to the general public.

On the other hand, shares of privately held companies are owned by only a few individuals (perhaps a family) and are not available to the general public. Corporations whose stock is privately held do not need to register those shares with the Securities and Exchange Commission and are spared the voluminous, annual reporting requirements of the SEC. Of course, new sources of equity financing are limited when shares are privately held, as is the market for selling existing shares.

Frequently, companies begin as smaller, privately held corporations. Then as success broadens opportunities for expansion, the corporation goes public. For example, in 2008 **Visa** decided to take public the privately held company. The result was the largest technology initial public offering ever.

Hybrid Organizations

A corporation can elect to comply with a special set of tax rules and be designated an **S corporation.** S corporations have characteristics of both regular corporations and partnerships. Owners have the limited liability protection of a corporation, but income and expenses are passed through to the owners as in a partnership, avoiding double taxation.

Two relatively recent business structures have evolved in response to liability issues and tax treatment—limited liability companies and limited liability partnerships.

A **limited liability company** offers several advantages. Owners are not liable for the debts of the business, except to the extent of their investment. Unlike a limited partnership, all members of a limited liability company can be involved with managing the business without losing liability protection. Like an S corporation, income and expenses are passed through to the owners as in a partnership, avoiding double taxation, but there are no limitations on the number of owners as in an S corporation.

A **limited liability partnership** is similar to a limited liability company, except it doesn't offer all the liability protection available in the limited liability company structure. Partners are liable for their own actions but not entirely liable for the actions of other partners.

The Model Business Corporation Act

Corporations are formed in accordance with the corporation laws of individual states. State laws are not uniform, but share many similarities, thanks to the widespread adoption of the **Model Business Corporation Act.**[4] This act is designed to serve as a guide to states in the development of their corporation statutes. It presently serves as the model for the majority of states.

The *Model Business Corporation Act* serves as the model for the corporation statutes of most states.

State laws regarding the nature of shares that can be authorized, the issuance and repurchase of those shares, and conditions for distributions to shareholders obviously influence actions of corporations. Naturally, differences among state laws affect how we account for many of the shareholders' equity transactions discussed in this chapter. For that reason, we will focus on the normal case, as described by the Model Business Corporation Act, and note situations where variations in state law might require different accounting. Your goal is not to learn diverse procedures caused by peculiarities of state laws, but to understand the broad concepts of accounting for shareholders' equity that can be applied to any specific circumstance.

Variations among state laws influence GAAP pertaining to shareholders' equity transactions.

The process of incorporating a business is similar in all states. The **articles of incorporation** (sometimes called the *corporate charter*) describe (a) the nature of the firm's business activities, (b) the shares to be issued, and (c) the composition of the initial **board of directors.** The board of directors establishes corporate policies and appoints officers who manage the corporation.

At least some of the shares authorized by the articles of incorporation are sold at the inception of the corporation. Frequently, the initial shareholders include members of the board of directors or officers (who may be one and the same). Ultimately, it is the corporation's shareholders that control the company. Shareholders are the owners of the corporation. By voting their shares, it is they who determine the makeup of the board of directors—who in turn appoint officers, who in turn manage the company.

Shareholders' investment in a corporation ordinarily is referred to as paid-in capital. In the next section, we examine the methods normally used to maintain records of shareholders' investment and to report such paid-in capital in financial statements.

PAID-IN CAPITAL

PART B

Fundamental Share Rights

In reading the previous paragraphs, you noted that corporations raise equity funds by selling shares of the corporation. Shareholders are the owners of a corporation. If a corporation has only one class of shares, no designation of the shares is necessary, but they typically are labeled *common shares.* Ownership rights held by common shareholders, unless specifically withheld by agreement with the shareholders, are:

a. The right to vote on matters that come before the shareholders, including the election of corporate directors. Each share represents one vote.
b. The right to share in profits when dividends are declared. The percentage of shares owned by a shareholder determines his/her share of dividends distributed.
c. The right to share in the distribution of assets if the company is liquidated. The percentage of shares owned by a shareholder determines his/her share of assets after creditors and preferred shareholders are paid.

[4] *Revised Model Business Corporation Act,* the American Bar Association, 1994.

Another right sometimes given to common shareholders is the right to maintain one's percentage share of ownership when new shares are issued. This is referred to as a *preemptive right.* Each shareholder is offered the opportunity to buy a percentage of any new shares issued equal to the percentage of shares he/she owns at the time. In most states this right must be specifically granted; in others, it is presumed unless contractually excluded.

For reasons of practicality, the preemptive right usually is excluded.

This right usually is withheld because of the inconvenience it causes corporations when they issue new shares. The exclusion of the preemptive right ordinarily is inconsequential because few shareholders own enough stock to be concerned about their ownership percentage.

Distinguishing Classes of Shares

It is not uncommon for a firm to have more than one, and perhaps several, classes of shares, each with different rights and limitations. To attract investors, companies have devised quite a variety of ownership securities.

If more than one class of shares is authorized by the articles of incorporation, the specific rights of each (for instance, the right to vote, residual interest in assets, and dividend rights) must be stated. Also, some designation must be given to distinguish each class.

Some of the distinguishing designations often used are:

Terminology varies in the way companies differentiate among share types.

1. Class A, class B, and so on (**Tyson Foods**).
2. Preferred stock, common stock, and class B stock (**Hershey Foods**).
3. Common and preferred (**Hewlett Packard**).
4. Capital stock (**Reader's Digest**).
5. Common and serial preferred (**Smucker**).

It often is difficult to predict the rights and privileges of shares on the basis of whether they are labeled *common* or *preferred.*

In your introductory study of accounting, you probably became most familiar with the common stock–preferred stock distinction. That terminology has deep roots in tradition. Early English corporate charters provided for shares that were preferred over others as to dividends and liquidation rights. These provisions were reflected in early American corporation laws. But as our economy developed, corporations increasingly felt the need for innovative ways of attracting investment capital. The result has been a gradual development of a wide range of share classifications that cannot easily be identified by these historical designations.

To reflect the flexibility that now exists in the creation of equity shares, the Model Business Corporation Act, and thus many state statutes, no longer mention the words common and preferred. But the influence of tradition lingers. Most corporations still designate shares as common or preferred. For consistency with practice, the illustrations you study in this chapter use those designations. As you consider the examples, keep in mind that the same concepts apply regardless of the language used to distinguish shares.

Typical Rights of Preferred Shares

An issue of shares with certain preferences or features that distinguish it from the class of shares customarily called common shares may be assigned any of the several labels mentioned earlier. Very often the distinguishing designation is **preferred shares.** The special rights of preferred shareholders usually include one or both of the following:

a. Preferred shareholders typically have a preference to a specified amount of dividends (stated dollar amount per share or % of par value per share). That is, if the board of directors declares dividends, preferred shareholders will receive the designated dividend before any dividends are paid to common shareholders.
b. Preferred shareholders customarily have a preference (over common shareholders) as to the distribution of assets in the event the corporation is dissolved.

Preferred shareholders sometimes have the **right of conversion** which allows them to exchange shares of preferred stock for common stock at a specified conversion ratio. Alternatively, a **redemption privilege** might allow preferred shareholders the option, under specified conditions, to return their shares for a predetermined redemption price. For instance, in 2007, **Samsonite Corporation** had outstanding 11 million shares of convertible preferred stock. Preferred shareholders have preference over common stockholders in dividends and liquidation rights. Each preferred share is convertible into common shares or an equivalent amount of cash. Similarly, shares may be redeemable at the option of the issuing corporation (sometimes referred to as *callable*).

Shares may be:
1. ***Convertible*** into a specified number of another class of shares.
2. ***Redeemable*** at the option of:
   a. Shareholders.
   b. The corporation.

Preferred shares may be **cumulative** or **noncumulative.** Typically, preferred shares are cumulative, which means that if the specified dividend is not paid in a given year, the unpaid dividends (called *dividends in arrears*) accumulate and must be made up in a later dividend year before any dividends are paid on common shares.

Preferred shares may be **participating** or **nonparticipating.** A participating feature allows preferred shareholders to receive additional dividends beyond the stated amount. If the preferred shares are fully participating, the distribution of dividends to common and preferred shareholders is a pro rata allocation based on the relative par value amounts of common and preferred stock outstanding. Participating preferred stock, previously quite common, is rare today.

If preferred shares are not cumulative, dividends not declared in any given year need never be paid.

Remember that the designations of common and preferred imply no necessary rights, privileges, or limitations of the shares so designated. Such relative rights must be specified by the contract with shareholders. A corporation can create classes of preferred shares that are indistinguishable from common shares in voting rights and/or the right to participate in assets (distributed as dividends or distributed upon liquidation). Likewise, it is possible to devise classes of common shares that possess preferential rights, superior to those of preferred shares.

Is It Equity or Is It Debt

You probably also can imagine an issue of preferred shares that is almost indistinguishable from a bond issue. Let's say, for instance, that preferred shares call for annual cash dividends of 10% of the par value, dividends are cumulative, and the shares must be redeemed for cash in 10 years. Although the declaration of dividends rests in the discretion of the board of directors, the contract with preferred shareholders can be worded in such a way that directors are compelled to declare dividends each year the company is profitable. For a profitable company, it would be difficult to draw the line between this issue of preferred shares and a 10%, 10-year bond issue. Even in a more typical situation, preferred shares are somewhat hybrid securities—a cross between equity and debt.

The line between debt and equity is hard to draw.

Sometimes the similarity to debt is even more obvious. Suppose shares are mandatorily redeemable—the company is obligated to buy back the shares at a specified future date.

INTERNATIONAL FINANCIAL REPORTING STANDARDS

Distinction between Debt and Equity for Preferred Stock. The primary standard for distinguishing between debt and equity in the United States is *SFAS No.150*, "Accounting for Certain Financial Instruments: Characteristics of both Liabilities and Equity"; under IFRS it's *IAS No. 32*, "Financial Instruments: Disclosure and Presentation." Differences [illegible] definitions and requirements under these standards can result in the same instrum[illegible] classified differently between debt and equity under IFRS and U.S. GAAP. M[illegible] stock (preference shares) is reported under IFRS as debt with the dividend[illegible] income statement as interest expense. Under U.S. GAAP, that's the case onl[illegible] redeemable" preferred stock. **Unilever** describes such a difference in a disc[illegible]

Additional Information for U.S. Investors [in part]
Preference Shares
Under *IAS 32*, Unilever recognises preference shares that provide a fixed preferen[illegible] as borrowings with preference dividends recognised in the income statement. Under [illegible] such preference shares are classified in shareholders' equity with dividends treated as a [illegible] to shareholder's equity.

● LO3

Mandatorily redeemable shares are classified as liabilities.

The fact that the company is obligated to pay cash (or other assets) at a fixed or determinable date in the future makes this financial instrument tantamount to debt. A mandatorily redeemable financial instrument must be reported in the balance sheet as a liability, not as shareholders' equity.[5] **Nike,** for instance, reported its mandatorily redeemable preferred shares as a liability in its 2007 balance sheet.

The Concept of Par Value

We have inherited the archaic concept of par value from early corporate law.

Another prevalent practice (besides labeling shares as common and preferred) that has little significance other than historical is assigning a par value to shares. The concept of par value dates back as far as the concept of owning shares of a business. Par value originally indicated the real value of shares. All shares were issued at that price.

During the late 19th and early 20th centuries, many cases of selling shares for less than par value—known as *watered shares*—received a great deal of attention and were the subject of a number of lawsuits. Investors and creditors contended that they relied on the par value as the permanent investment in the corporation and therefore net assets must always be at least that amount. Not only was par value assumed to be the amount invested by shareholders, but it also was defined by early corporation laws as the amount of net assets not available for distribution to shareholders (as dividends or otherwise).

Shares with nominal par value became common to dodge elaborate statutory rules pertaining to par value shares.

Many companies began turning to par value shares with very low par values—often pennies—to escape the watered shares liability of issuing shares below an arbitrary par value and to limit the restrictions on distributions. This practice is common today.

Accountants and attorneys have been aware for decades that laws pertaining to par value and legal capital not only are bewildering but fail in their intent to safeguard creditors from payments to shareholders. Actually, to the extent that creditors are led to believe that they are afforded protection, they are misled. Like the designations of common and preferred shares, the concepts of par value and legal capital have been eliminated entirely from the Model Business Corporation Act.[6]

Most shares continue to bear arbitrarily designated par values.

Many states already have adopted these provisions of the Model Act. But most established corporations issued shares prior to changes in the state statutes. Consequently, most companies have par value shares outstanding and continue to issue previously authorized par value shares. The evolution will be gradual to the simpler, more meaningful provisions of the Model Act.

In the meantime, accountants must be familiar with the outdated concepts of par value and legal capital in order to properly record and report transactions related to par value shares. For that reason, most of the discussion in this chapter centers around par value shares. Largely, this means only that proceeds from shareholders' investment is allocated between stated capital and additional paid-in capital. Be aware, though, that in the absence of archaic laws that prompted the creation of par value shares, there is no theoretical reason to do so.

Accounting for the Issuance of Shares

Shares Issued For Cash

When shares are sold for cash (see Illustration 18–1), the capital stock account (usually common or preferred) is credited for the amount representing stated capital. When shares have a designated par value, that amount denotes stated capital and is credited to the stock account. Proceeds in excess of this amount are credited to paid-in capital—excess of par.

[5] "Accounting for Certain Financial Instruments with Characteristics of Both Liabilities and Equity," *Statement of Financial Accounting Standards No. 150* (Norwalk, Conn.: FASB, 2003).

[6] *Revised Model Business Corporation Act,* the American Bar Association, 1994, official comment to Section 6.21.

ILLUSTRATION 18–1
Shares Sold for Cash

Dow Industrial sells 100,000 of its common shares, $1 par per share, for $10 per share:

	($ in 000s)	
Cash (100,000 shares at $10 price per share)	1,000	
Common stock (100,000 shares at $1 par per share)		100
Paid-in capital—excess of par (remainder)		900

The entire proceeds from the sale of no-par stock are deemed stated capital and recorded in the stock account. If the shares are no-par, the entry is as follows:

Cash (100,000 shares at $10 price per share)	1,000	
Common stock		1,000

The total amount received from the sale of no-par shares is credited to the stock account.

Shares Issued for Noncash Consideration

Occasionally, a company might issue its shares for consideration other than cash. It is not uncommon for a new company, yet to establish a reliable cash flow, to pay for promotional and legal services with shares rather than with cash. Similarly, shares might be given in payment for land, or for equipment, or for some other noncash asset.

Shares should be issued at fair value.

Even without a receipt of cash to establish the fair value of the shares at the time of the exchange, the transaction still should be recorded at fair value. Best evidence of fair value might be:

- A quoted market price for the shares.
- A selling price established in a recent issue of shares for cash.
- The amount of cash that would have been paid in a cash purchase of the asset or service.
- An independent appraisal of the value of the asset received.
- Other available evidence.

Whichever evidence of fair value seems more clearly evident should be used.[7]

Illustration 18–2 demonstrates a situation where the quoted market price is the best evidence of fair value.

ILLUSTRATION 18–2
Shares Sold for Noncash Consideration

DuMont Chemicals issues 1 million of its common shares, $1 par per share, in exchange for a custom-built factory for which no cash price is available. Today's issue of *The Wall Street Journal* lists DuMont's stock at $10 per share:

	($ in millions)	
Property, plant, and equipment (1 million shares at $10 per share)	10	
Common stock (1 million shares at $1 par per share)		1
Paid-in capital—excess of par (remainder)		9

The quoted market price for the shares issued might be the best evidence of fair value.

More than One Security Issued for a Single Price

Although uncommon, a company might sell more than one security—perhaps common shares and preferred shares—for a single price. As you might expect, the cash received usually is the sum of the separate market values of the two securities. Of course, each is then recorded at its market value. However, if only one security's value is known, the second security's market value is inferred from the total selling price as demonstrated in Illustration 18–3 on the next page.

Because the shares sell for a total of $100 million, and the market value of the common shares is known to be $40 million (4 million × $10), the preferred shares are inferred to have a market value of $60 million.

[7]Although stock issuances are not specifically mentioned in *APB Opinion No. 29*, this treatment is consistent with the general rule for accounting for noncash transactions as described in that pronouncement, pars. 18 and 25.

ILLUSTRATION 18–3

More than One Security Sold for a Single Price

When only one security's value is known ($40 million), the second security's market value ($60 million) is assumed from the total selling price ($100 million).

AP&P issues 4 million of its common shares, $1 par per share, and 4 million of its preferred shares, $10 par, for $100 million. Today's issue of *The Wall Street Journal* lists AP&P's common at $10 per share. There is no established market for the preferred shares:

	($ in millions)	
Cash	100	
Common stock (4 million shares × $1 par)		4
Paid-in capital—excess of par common		36
Preferred stock (4 million shares × $10 par)		40
Paid-in capital—excess of par, preferred		20

ADDITIONAL CONSIDERATION

In the unlikely event that the total selling price is not equal to the sum of the two market prices (when both market values are known), the total selling price is allocated between the two securities, in proportion to their relative market values. You should note that this is the same approach we use (a) when more than one asset is purchased for a single purchase price to allocate the single price to the various assets acquired, (b) when detachable warrants and bonds are issued for a single price, and (c) in any other situation when more than one item is associated with a single purchase price or selling price.

Share Issue Costs

Share issue costs reduce the net cash proceeds from selling the shares and thus paid-in capital—excess of par.

Real World Financials

When a company sells shares, it obtains the legal, promotional, and accounting services necessary to effect the sale. The cost of these services reduces the net proceeds from selling the shares. Since paid-in capital—excess of par is credited for the excess of the proceeds over the par value of the shares sold, the effect of share issue costs is to reduce the amount credited to that account. For example, on completing a public offering of 825,000 shares at a price of $17.75 per share, the **Duriron Company, Inc.**, noted in its financial statements: "The proceeds of the offering, after deducting all associated costs, were $13,491,000 or $16.35 per newly issued share." Duriron's entry to record the sale was:

The cash proceeds is the net amount received after paying share issue costs.

	($ in millions)	
Cash (825,000 shares at $16.35 net price per share)	13.49	
Common stock (825,000 shares at $1.25 par per share)		1.03
Paid-in capital—excess of par (remainder)		12.46

Like interest, debt issue costs are an expense of borrowing funds.

You should notice that not separately reporting issue costs differs from how *debt* issue costs are recorded. In Chapter 14 you learned that the costs associated with a debt issue are recorded in a separate debt issue costs account and amortized to expense over the life of the debt.

It can be argued that share issue costs and debt issue costs are fundamentally different. That view would argue that a debt issue has a fixed maturity and, like interest expense, debt issue costs are part of the expense of borrowing funds for that period of time (even though it's recorded in a separate expense account—debt issue expense). Selling shares, on the other hand, represents a perpetual equity interest. Dividends paid on that capital investment are not an expense; neither are the costs of obtaining that capital investment (share issue costs).

Like dividends, share issue costs are not an expense.

Although expensing debt issue costs presently is required by GAAP, the FASB has suggested in *Concept Statement 6* that those costs should be treated the same way as share issue costs. That is, the recorded amount of the debt would be reduced by the debt issue costs instead of recording the costs separately as an asset. Remember, though, that concept statements do not constitute GAAP, so until a new FASB standard is issued to supersede *APB Opinion 21,* the prescribed practice is to record debt issue costs as assets and expense the asset over the maturity of the debt.

CONCEPT REVIEW EXERCISE

EXPANSION OF CORPORATE CAPITAL

Situation: The shareholders' equity section of the balance sheet of National Foods, Inc. included the following accounts at December 31, 2007:

Shareholders' Equity	($ in millions)
Paid-in capital:	
Common stock, 120 million shares at $1 par	$ 120
Paid-in capital—excess of par	836
Retained earnings	2,449
Total shareholders' equity	$3,405

Required:

1. During 2008, several transactions affected the stock of National Foods. Prepare the appropriate entries for these events.
   a. On March 11, National Foods issued 10 million of its 9.2% preferred shares, $1 par per share, for $44 per share.
   b. On November 22, 1 million common shares, $1 par per share, were issued in exchange for eight labeling machines. Each machine was built to custom specifications so no cash price was available. National Food's stock was listed at $10 per share.
   c. On November 23, 1 million of the common shares and 1 million preferred shares were sold for $60 million. The preferred shares had not traded since March and their market value was uncertain.
2. Prepare the shareholders' equity section of the comparative balance sheets for National Foods at December 31, 2008 and 2007. Assume that net income for 2008 was $400 million and the only other transaction affecting shareholders' equity was the payment of the 9.2% dividend on the 11 million preferred shares ($1 million).

SOLUTION

1. During 2008 several transactions affected the stock of National Foods. Prepare the appropriate entries for these events.
   a. On March 11, National Foods issued 10 million of its preferred shares, $1 par per share, for $44 per share.

	($ in millions)	
Cash	440	
Preferred stock (10 million shares × $1 par per share)		10
Paid-in capital—excess of par, preferred		430

   b. On November 22, 1 million common shares, $1 par per share, were issued in exchange for 8 labeling machines:

Machinery (fair value of shares)	10	
Common stock (1 million shares × $1 par per share)		1
Paid-in capital—excess of par, common (1 million shares × $9)		9

The transaction was recorded at the fair market value of the shares exchanged for the machinery.

   c. On November 23, 1 million of the common shares and 1 million preferred shares were sold for $60 million:

Cash	60	
Common stock (1 million shares × $1 par per share)		1
Paid-in capital—excess of par, common		9
Preferred stock (1 million shares × $1 par per share)		1
Paid-in capital—excess of par, preferred (to balance)		49

Since the value of only the common stock was known, the preferred stock's market value ($50/share) was inferred from the total selling price.

2. Prepare the shareholders' equity section of the comparative balance sheets for National Foods at December 31, 2008 and 2007.

NATIONAL FOODS, INC.
Balance Sheet
[Shareholders' Equity Section]

	($ in millions)	
	2008	**2007**
Shareholders' Equity		
Preferred stock, 9.2%, $1 par (2008: $10 million + 1 million)	$ 11	$ —
Common stock, $1 par (2008: $120 million + 1 million + 1 million)	122	120
Paid-in capital—excess of par, preferred (2008: $430 million + 49 million)	479	—
Paid-in capital—excess of par, common (2008: $836 million + 9 million + 9 million)	854	836
Retained earnings (2007: $2,449 million + 400 million − 1 million)	2,848	2,449
Total shareholders' equity	$4,314	$3,405

Note: This situation is continued in the next Concept Review Exercise on page 964.

Share Buybacks

● LO4

In the previous section we examined various ways stock might be issued. In this section, we look at situations in which companies reacquire shares previously sold. Most medium- and large-size companies buy back their own shares. Many have formal share repurchase plans to buy back stock over a series of years.

DECISION MAKER'S PERSPECTIVE

Decreasing the supply of shares in the marketplace supports the price of remaining shares.

When a company's management feels the market price of its stock is undervalued, it may attempt to support the price by decreasing the supply of stock in the marketplace. A **Johnson & Johnson** announcement that it planned to buy back up to $5 billion of its outstanding shares triggered a buying spree that pushed the stock price up by more than 3 percent.

FINANCIAL Reporting Case

Q1, p. 945

When announcing plans to repurchase up to $1 billion of its shares, **Compaq** chairman and chief executive officer Michael Capellas explained, "At current price levels, we believe Compaq's stock offers a tremendous investment opportunity for the company."[8] Although clearly a company may attempt to increase net assets by buying its shares at a low price and selling them back later at a higher price, that investment is not viewed as an asset. Similarly, increases and decreases in net assets from that activity are not reported as gains and losses in the company's income statement. Instead, buying and selling its shares are transactions between the corporation and its owners, analogous to retiring shares and then selling previously unissued shares. You should note the contrast between a company's purchasing of its own shares and its purchasing of shares in another corporation as an investment.

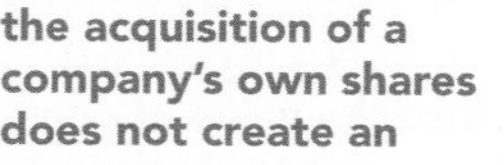

Unlike an investment in another firm's shares, the acquisition of a company's own shares does not create an asset.

Though not considered an investment, the repurchase of shares often is a judicious use of a company's cash. By increasing per share earnings and supporting share price, shareholders benefit. When **IBM** announced its second $3.5 billion buyback of common stock the same year, **Merrill Lynch & Co.** commented, "I think it's a reasonable use of cash. How many investment opportunities do they have that can return cost of capital? They should be investing up to that point, and beyond that they should return cash to the shareholders."[9]

To the extent this strategy is effective, a share buyback can be viewed as a way to "distribute" company profits without paying dividends. Capital gains from any stock price increase are taxed at lower capital gains tax rates than ordinary income tax rates on dividends.

[8] "HP, Compaq Resume Stock Buyback," *CNET News.com*, September 17, 2001.
[9] "IBM Sets Another Big Buyback of Its Shares," *The New York Times*, October 28, 1998.

Perhaps the primary motivation for most stock repurchases is to offset the increase in shares that routinely are issued to employees under stock award and stock option compensation programs. **Microsoft** reported its stock buyback program designed to offset the effect of its stock option and stock purchase plans as shown in Graphic 18–5.

Companies buy back shares to offset the increase in shares issued to employees.

> **Note 11: Stockholders' Equity (in part)**
> Our board of directors has approved a program to repurchase shares of our common stock to reduce the dilutive effect of our stock option and stock purchase plans.

GRAPHIC 18–5
Disclosure of Share Repurchase Program—Microsoft

Real World Financials

Similarly, shares might be reacquired to distribute in a stock dividend, a proposed merger, or as a defense against a hostile takeover.[10]

Whatever the reason shares are repurchased, a company has a choice of how to account for the buyback:

1. The shares can be formally retired.
2. The shares can be called treasury stock.

Unfortunately, the choice is not dictated by the nature of the buyback, but by practical motivations of the company.

Shares Formally Retired or Viewed as Treasury Stock

When a corporation retires its own shares, those shares assume the same status as authorized but unissued shares, just the same as if they never had been issued. We saw earlier in the chapter that when shares are sold, both cash (usually) and shareholders' equity are increased; the company becomes larger. Conversely, when cash is paid to **retire stock**, the effect is to decrease both cash and shareholders' equity; the size of the company literally is reduced.

FINANCIAL Reporting Case

Q2, p. 945

Out of tradition and for practical reasons, companies usually reacquire shares of previously issued stock without formally retiring them.[11] Shares repurchased and not retired are referred to as **treasury stock.** Because reacquired shares are essentially the same as shares that never were issued at all, treasury shares have no voting rights nor do they receive cash dividends. Like the concepts of par value and legal capital, the concept of treasury shares no longer is recognized in most state statutes.[12] Some companies, in fact, are eliminating treasury shares from their financial statements as corporate statutes are modernized. **Microsoft** retires the shares it buys back rather than labeling them treasury stock.

Reacquired shares are equivalent to authorized but unissued shares.

Accounting for Retired Shares

When shares are formally retired, we should reduce precisely the same accounts that previously were increased when the shares were sold, namely, common (or preferred) stock and paid-in capital—excess of par. The first column of Illustration 18–4 on the next page demonstrates this. The paid-in capital—excess of par account shows a balance of $900 million while the common stock account shows a balance of $100 million. Thus the 100 million outstanding shares were originally sold for an average of $9 per share above par, or $10 per share. Consequently, when 1 million shares are retired (regardless of the retirement price), American Semiconductor should reduce its common stock account by $1 per share and its paid-in capital—excess of par by $9 per share. Another way to view the reduction is that because 1% of the shares are retired, both share account balances (common stock and paid-in capital—excess of par) are reduced by 1%.

[10]A corporate takeover occurs when an individual or group of individuals acquires a majority of a company's outstanding common stock from present shareholders. Corporations that are the object of a hostile takeover attempt—a public bid for control of a company's stock against the company's wishes—often take evasive action involving the reacquisition of shares.

[11]The concept of treasury shares originated long ago when new companies found they could sell shares at an unrealistically low price equal to par value to incorporators, who then donated those shares back to the company. Since these shares already had been issued (though not outstanding), they could be sold at whatever the real market price was without adjusting stated capital.

Because treasury shares are already issued, different rules apply to their purchase and resale than to unissued shares. Companies can:

a. Issue shares without regard to preemptive rights of shareholders.
b. Distribute shares as a dividend to shareholders even without a balance in retained earnings.

[12]*The Revised Model Business Corporation Act* eliminated the concept of treasury shares in 1984 after 1980 revisions had eliminated the concepts of par value and legal capital. Most state laws have since followed suit.

ILLUSTRATION 18–4
Comparison of Share Retirement and Treasury Stock Accounting—Share Buybacks

American Semiconductor's balance sheet included the following:

Shareholders' Equity	($ in millions)
Common stock, 100 million shares at $1 par	$ 100
Paid-in capital—excess of par	900
Paid-in capital—share repurchase	2
Retained earnings	2,000

Formally retiring shares restores the balances in both the Common stock account and Paid-in capital—excess of par to what those balances would have been if the shares never had been issued.

When we view a buyback as treasury stock the cost of acquiring the shares is "temporarily" debited to the treasury stock account.

Retirement			**Treasury Stock**	
Reacquired 1 million of its common shares				
Case 1: Shares repurchased at $7 per share				
Common stock ($1 par × 1 million shares)	1		Treasury stock (cost)	7
Paid-in capital—excess of par ($9 per shares)	9			
Paid-in capital—share repurchase (difference)		3		
Cash		7	Cash	7
OR				
Case 2: Shares repurchased at $13 per share				
Common stock ($1 par × 1 million shares)	1		Treasury stock (cost)	13
Paid-in capital—excess of par ($9 per shares)	9			
Paid-in capital—share repurchase	2*			
Retained earnings (difference)	1			
Cash		13	Cash	13

*Because there is a $2 million credit balance.

How we treat the difference between the cash paid to buy the shares and the amount the shares originally sold for (amounts debited to common stock and paid-in capital—excess of par) depends on whether the cash paid is *less* than the original issue price (credit difference) or the cash paid is *more* than the original issue price (debit difference):

1. If a *credit* difference is created (as in Case 1 of Illustration 18–4), we credit paid-in capital—share repurchase.
2. If a *debit* difference is created (as in Case 2 of Illustration 18–4), we debit paid-in capital—share repurchase, but only if that account already has a credit balance. Otherwise, we debit retained earnings. (Reducing the account beyond its previous balance would create a negative balance.)

***Paid-in capital—share repurchase* is debited to the extent of its credit balance before debiting retained earnings.**

Why is paid-in capital credited in Case 1 and retained earnings debited in Case 2? The answer lies in the fact that the payments made by a corporation to repurchase its own shares are a distribution of corporate assets to shareholders.

Payments made by a corporation to retire its own shares are viewed as a distribution of corporate assets to shareholders.

In Case 1, only $7 million is distributed to shareholders to retire shares that originally provided $10 million of paid-in capital. Thus, some of the original investment ($3 million in this case) remains and is labeled *paid-in capital—share repurchase.*

In Case 2, more cash ($13 million) is distributed to shareholders to retire shares than originally was paid in. The amount paid in comprises the original investment of $10 million for the shares being retired plus $2 million of paid-in capital created by previous repurchase transactions—$12 million total. Thirteen million is returned to shareholders. The additional $1 million paid is viewed as a dividend on the shareholders' investment, and thus a reduction of retained earnings.[13]

[13]In the next section of this chapter, you will be reminded that dividends reduce retained earnings. (You first learned this in your introductory accounting course.)

INTERNATIONAL FINANCIAL REPORTING STANDARDS

Reacquired Shares. IFRS does not permit the "retirement" of shares. All buybacks are treated as treasury stock.

Accounting for Treasury Stock

● LO5

We view the purchase of treasury stock as a temporary reduction of shareholders' equity, to be reversed later when the treasury stock is resold. The cost of acquiring the shares is "temporarily" debited to the treasury stock account (second column of Illustration 18–4). At this point, the shares are considered to be issued, but not outstanding.

Recording the effects on specific shareholders' equity accounts is delayed until later when the shares are reissued. In the meantime, the shares assume the fictional status we discussed earlier of being neither unissued nor outstanding. Effectively, we consider the purchase of treasury stock and its subsequent resale to be a "single transaction."

When a share repurchase is viewed as treasury stock, recording the effects on specific shareholders' equity accounts is delayed until the shares are reissued.

ADDITIONAL CONSIDERATION

The approach to accounting for treasury stock we discuss in this chapter is referred to as the "cost method." Another permissible approach is the "par value method." It is essentially identical to formally retiring shares, which is why it sometimes is referred to as the *retirement method of accounting for treasury stock.* In fact, if we substitute Treasury stock for Common stock in each of the journal entries we used to account for retirement of shares in Illustrations 18–4 and 18–5, we have the par value method. Because the method has virtually disappeared from practice, we do not discuss it further in this chapter.

BALANCE SHEET EFFECT. Formally retiring shares restores the balances in both the Common stock account and Paid-in capital—excess of par to what those balances would have been if the shares never had been issued at all. As discussed above, any net increase in assets resulting from the sale and subsequent repurchase is reflected as Paid-in capital—share repurchase. On the other hand, any net decrease in assets resulting from the sale and subsequent repurchase is reflected as a reduction in retained earnings.

In contrast, when a share repurchase is viewed as treasury stock, the cost of the treasury stock is simply reported as a reduction in total shareholders' equity. Reporting under the two approaches is compared in Graphic 18–6 using the situation described above for American Semiconductor after the purchase of treasury stock in Illustration 18–4 (Case 2) on page 962. Notice that either way total shareholders' equity is the same.

GRAPHIC 18–6
Reporting Share Buyback in the Balance Sheet

	($ in millions)	
	Shares Retired	**Treasury Stock**
Shareholders' Equity		
Paid-in capital:		
Common stock, 100 million shares at $1 par	$ 99	$ 100
Paid-in capital—excess of par	891	900
Paid-in capital—reacquired shares		2
Retained earnings	1,999	2,000
Less: Treasury stock, 1 million shares (at cost)		(13)
Total shareholders' equity	$2,989	$2,989

Retirement reduces common stock and associated shareholders' equity accounts.

Treasury stock reduces total shareholders' equity.

Resale of Shares

...es are ...or the par value ...od is used, we ...ew any subsequent sale as the sale of new shares.

After shares are formally retired, any subsequent sale of shares is simply the sale of new, unissued shares and is accounted for accordingly. This is demonstrated in the first column of Illustration 18–5.

ILLUSTRATION 18–5

Comparison of Share Retirement and Treasury Stock Accounting—Subsequent Sale of Shares

After formally retiring shares, we record a subsequent sale of shares exactly like any sale of shares.

The resale of treasury shares is viewed as the consummation of the "single transaction" begun when the treasury shares were purchased.

American Semiconductor sold 1 million shares after reacquiring shares at $13 per share (Case 2 in Illustration 18–4).

Retirement			Treasury Stock		
Sold 1 million shares					
Case A: Shares sold at $14 per share					
Cash	14		Cash	14	
Common stock (par)		1	Treasury stock (cost)		13
Paid-in capital—excess of par		13	Paid-in capital—share repurchase		1
OR					
Case B: Shares sold at $10 per share					
Cash	10		Cash	10	
Common stock (par)		1	Retained earnings (to balance)	1	
Paid-in capital—excess of par		9	Paid-in capital—share repurchase	2*	
			Treasury stock (cost)		13

*Because there is a $2 million credit balance.

The resale of treasury shares is viewed as the consummation of the single transaction begun when the treasury shares were repurchased. The effect of the single transaction of purchasing treasury stock and reselling it for more than cost (Case 2 of Illustration 18–4 and Case A of Illustration 18–5) is to *increase* both cash and shareholders' equity (by $1 million). The effect of the single transaction of purchasing treasury stock and reselling it for less than cost (Case 2 of Illustration 18–4 and Case B of Illustration 18–5) is to *decrease* both cash and shareholders' equity (by $3 million).

Allocating the cost of treasury shares occurs when the shares are resold.

Note that retained earnings may be debited in a treasury stock transaction, but not credited. Also notice that transactions involving treasury stock have no impact on the income statement. This follows the reasoning discussed earlier that a corporation's buying and selling of its own shares are transactions between the corporation and its owners and not part of the earnings process.

ADDITIONAL CONSIDERATION

Treasury Shares Acquired at Different Costs

Notice that the treasury stock account always is credited for the cost of the reissued shares ($13 million in Illustration 18–5). When shares are reissued, if treasury stock on hand has been purchased at different per share prices, the cost of the shares sold must be determined using a cost flow assumption—FIFO, LIFO, or weighted average—similar to determining the cost of goods sold when inventory items are acquired at different unit costs.

Determining the cost of treasury stock sold is similar to determining the cost of goods sold.

CONCEPT REVIEW EXERCISE

TREASURY STOCK

Situation: The shareholders' equity section of the balance sheet of National Foods, Inc. included the following accounts at December 31, 2008.

Shareholders' Equity	($ in millions)
Paid-in capital:	
Preferred stock, 11 million shares at $1 par	$ 11
Common stock, 122 million shares at $1 par	122
Paid-in capital—excess of par, preferred	479
Paid-in capital—excess of par, Common	854
Retained earnings	2,848
Total shareholders' equity	$4,314

Required:

1. National Foods reacquired common shares during 2009 and sold shares in two separate transactions later that year. Prepare the entries for both the purchase and subsequent sale of shares during 2009 assuming that the shares were (a) retired and (b) considered to be treasury stock.
   a. National Foods purchased 6 million shares at $10 per share.
   b. National Foods sold 2 million shares at $12 per share.
   c. National Foods sold 2 million shares at $7 per share.
2. Prepare the shareholders' equity section of National Foods' balance sheet at December 31, 2009, assuming the shares were both (a) retired and (b) viewed as treasury stock. Net income for 2009 was $400 million, and preferred shareholders were paid $1 million cash dividends.

SOLUTION

1. National Foods reacquired common shares during 2009 and sold shares in two separate transactions later that year. Prepare the entries for both the purchase and subsequent sale of shares during 2009 assuming that the shares were (a) retired and (b) considered to be treasury stock.

a. National Foods purchased 6 million shares at $10 per share:

Retirement ($ in millions)			**Treasury Stock** ($ in millions)		
Common stock (6 million shares × $1) ...	6		Treasury stock (6 million shares × $10)	60	
Paid-in capital—excess of par (6 million shares × $7*)	42		Cash		60
Retained earnings (to balance)	12				
Cash		60			

*$854 million ÷ 122 million shares

b. National Foods sold 2 million shares at $12 per share: ($ in millions)

Cash	24		Cash	24	
Common stock (2 million shares × $1)..................		2	Treasury stock (2 million shares × $10)		20
Paid-in capital—excess of par.........		22	Paid-in capital—reacquired shares		4

c. National Foods sold 2 million shares at $7 per share: ($ in millions)

Cash	14		Cash	14	
Common stock (2 million shares × $1 par)		2	Paid-in capital—reacquired shares	4	
Paid-in capital—excess of par		12	Retained earnings (to balance)	2	
			Treasury stock (2 million shares × $10)		20

2. Prepare the shareholders' equity section of National Foods' balance sheet at December 31, 2009, assuming the shares were both (a) retired and (b) viewed as treasury stock.

NATIONAL FOODS, INC.
Balance Sheet
[Shareholders' Equity Section]
At December 31, 2009

	($ in millions)	
	Shares Retired	**Treasury Stock**
Shareholders' Equity		
Preferred stock, 11 million shares at $1 par	$ 11	$ 11
Common stock, 122 million shares at $1 par	120	122
Paid-in capital—excess of par, preferred	479	479
Paid-in capital—excess of par, common	846*	854
Retained earnings	3,235†	3,245‡
Treasury stock, at cost; 2 million common shares	—	(20)
Total shareholders' equity	$4,691	$4,691

*$854 – 42 + 22 + 12
†$2,848 – 12 + 400 – 1
‡$2,848 – 2 + 400 – 1

Note: This situation is continued in the next Concept Review Exercise on page 973.

PART C

RETAINED EARNINGS

Characteristics of Retained Earnings

● LO6

In the previous section we examined *invested* capital. Now we consider *earned* capital, that is, retained earnings. In general, retained earnings represents a corporation's accumulated, undistributed net income (or net loss). A more descriptive title used by some companies is reinvested earnings. A credit balance in this account indicates a dollar amount of assets previously earned by the firm but not distributed as dividends to shareholders. We refer to a debit balance in retained earnings as a **deficit. Microsoft** reported a deficit of $29.5 billion as of June 30, 2007.

Real World Financials

You saw in the previous section that the buyback of shares (as well as the resale of treasury shares in some cases) can decrease retained earnings. We examine in this section the effect on retained earnings of dividends and stock splits.

Dividends

 LO7

Shareholders' initial investments in a corporation are represented by amounts reported as paid-in capital. One way a corporation provides a return to its shareholders on their investments is to pay them a **dividend,** typically cash.[14]

Dividends are distributions of assets the company has earned on behalf of its shareholders. If dividends are paid that exceed the amount of assets earned by the company, then management is, in effect, returning to shareholders a portion of their investments, rather than providing them a return on that investment. So most companies view retained earnings as the amount available for dividends.[15]

Liquidating Dividend

Any dividend not representing a distribution of earnings should be debited to paid-in capital.

In unusual instances in which a dividend exceeds the balance in retained earnings, the excess is referred to as a **liquidating dividend** because some of the invested capital is being

[14]Dividends are not the only return shareholders earn; when market prices of their shares rise, shareholders benefit also. Indeed, many companies have adopted policies of never paying dividends but reinvesting all assets they earn. The motivation is to accommodate more rapid expansion and thus, presumably, increases in the market price of the stock.

[15]Ordinarily, this is not the legal limitation. Most states permit a company to pay dividends so long as, after the dividend, its assets would not be "less than the sum of its total liabilities plus the amount that would be needed, if the corporation were to be dissolved at the time of the distribution, to satisfy the preferential rights upon dissolution of shareholders whose preferential rights are superior to those receiving the distribution." (Revised Model Business Corporation Act, American Bar Association, 1994.) Thus, legally, a corporation can distribute amounts equal to total shareholders' equity less dissolution preferences of senior equity securities (usually preferred stock). Note that Microsoft has recently paid cash dividends despite a deficit (negative retained earnings).

liquidated. This might occur when a corporation is being dissolved and assets (not subject to a superior claim by creditors) are distributed to shareholders. Any portion of a dividend not representing a distribution of earnings should be debited to additional paid-in capital rather than retained earnings.

Retained Earnings Restrictions

Sometimes the amount available for dividends purposely is reduced by management. A restriction of retained earnings designates a portion of the balance in retained earnings as being *unavailable for dividends.* A company might restrict retained earnings to indicate management's intention to withhold for some specific purpose the assets represented by that portion of the retained earnings balance. For example, management might anticipate the need for a specific amount of assets in upcoming years to repay a maturing debt, to cover a contingent loss, or to finance expansion of the facilities. Be sure to understand that the restriction itself does not set aside cash for the designated event but merely communicates management's intention not to distribute the stated amount as a dividend.

A restriction of retained earnings communicates management's intention to withhold assets represented by a specified portion of the retained earnings balance.

A restriction of retained earnings normally is indicated by a disclosure note to the financial statements. Although instances are rare, a formal journal entry may be used to reclassify a portion of retained earnings to an "appropriated" retained earnings account.

Normally a restriction of retained earnings is indicated by a disclosure note.

Cash Dividends

Microsoft Corp. today announced that its Board of Directors declared a quarterly dividend of $0.10 per share. The dividend is payable March 8, 2007, to shareholders of record on Feb. 13, 2007.[16]

You learned in Chapter 14 that paying interest to creditors is a contractual obligation. No such legal obligation exists for paying dividends to shareholders. A liability is not recorded until a company's board of directors votes to declare a dividend. In practice, though, corporations ordinarily try to maintain a stable dividend pattern over time.

FINANCIAL Reporting Case

Q3, p. 945

When directors declare a cash dividend, we reduce retained earnings and record a liability. Before the payment actually can be made, a listing must be assembled of shareholders entitled to receive the dividend. A specific date is stated as to when the determination will be made of the recipients of the dividend. This date is called the **date of record.** Registered owners of shares of stock on this date are entitled to receive the dividend—even if they sell those shares prior to the actual cash payment. To be a registered owner of shares on the date of record, an investor must purchase the shares before the **ex-dividend date.** This date usually is two business days before the date of record. Shares purchased on or after that date are purchased ex dividend—without the right to receive the declared dividend. As a result, the market price of a share typically will decline by the amount of the dividend, other things being equal, on the ex-dividend date. Consider Illustration 18–6.

The name of an investor who buys shares on the *ex-dividend date* or later will not appear on the company's list of registered owners until after the *date of record.*

On June 1, the board of directors of Craft Industries declares a cash dividend of $2 per share on its 100 million shares, payable to shareholders of record June 15, to be paid July 1:

	($ in millions)	
June 1—Declaration Date		
Retained earnings	200	
Cash dividends payable (100 million shares at $2/share)		200
June 13—Ex-Dividend Date		
No entry		
June 15—Date of Record		
No entry		
July 1—Payment Date		
Cash dividends payable	200	
Cash		200

ILLUSTRATION 18–6
Cash Dividends

At the declaration date, retained earnings is reduced and a liability is recorded.

Registered owners of shares on the date of record are entitled to receive the dividend.

[16]Microsoft press release, December 8, 2004.

A sufficient balance in retained earnings permits a dividend to be declared. Remember, though, that retained earnings is a shareholders' equity account representing a dollar claim on assets in general, but not on any specific asset in particular. Sufficient retained earnings does not ensure sufficient cash to make payment. These are two separate accounts having no necessary connection with one another. When a dividend is "paid from retained earnings," this simply means that sufficient assets previously have been earned to pay the dividend without returning invested assets to shareholders.

Property Dividends

The *fair value* of the assets to be distributed is the amount recorded for a property dividend.

Because cash is the asset most easily divided and distributed to shareholders, most corporate dividends are cash dividends. In concept, though, any asset can be distributed to shareholders as a dividend. When a noncash asset is distributed, it is referred to as a **property dividend** (often called *a dividend in kind*).

MobilePro Corp. recently declared to its shareholders a property dividend in shares of **STI** stock that MobilePro was holding as an investment. Securities held as investments are the assets most often distributed in a property dividend due to the relative ease of dividing these assets among shareholders and determining their fair market values.

A property dividend should be recorded at the fair value of the assets to be distributed. This may require revaluing the asset to fair value prior to recording the dividend. If so, a gain or loss is recognized for the difference between book value and fair value. This is demonstrated in Illustration 18–7.

ILLUSTRATION 18–7
Property Dividends

On October 1 the board of directors of Craft Industries declares a property dividend of 2 million shares of Beaman Corporation's preferred stock that Craft had purchased in March as an investment (book value: $9 million). The investment shares have a fair value of $5 per share, $10 million, and are payable to shareholders of record October 15, to be distributed November 1:

Before recording the property dividend, the asset first must be written up to fair value.

	($ in millions)	
October 1—Declaration Date		
Investment in Beaman Corporation preferred stock	1	
Gain on appreciation of investment ($10 − 9)		1
Retained earnings (2 million shares at $5 per share)	10	
Property dividends payable		10
October 15—Date of Record		
No entry		
November 1—Payment Date		
Property dividends payable	10	
Investment in Beaman Corporation preferred stock		10

Stock Dividends and Splits

Stock Dividends

● LO8

A **stock dividend** is the distribution of additional shares of stock to current shareholders of the corporation. Be sure to note the contrast between a stock dividend and either a cash or property dividend. A stock dividend affects neither the assets nor the liabilities of the firm. Also, because each shareholder receives the same percentage increase in shares, shareholders' proportional interest in (percentage ownership of) the firm remains unchanged.

The prescribed accounting treatment of a stock dividend requires that shareholders' equity items be reclassified by reducing one or more shareholders' equity accounts and simultaneously increasing one or more paid-in capital accounts. The amount reclassified depends on the size of the stock dividend. For a small stock dividend, typically less than 25%, the fair market value of the additional shares distributed is transferred from retained earnings to paid-in capital as demonstrated in Illustration 18–8.[17]

[17]The Committee on Accounting Procedure prescribes this accounting treatment in "Restatement and Revision of Accounting Research Bulletins," *Accounting Research Bulletin No. 43* (New York: AICPA, 1961), Chap. 7, sec. B, pars. 10–14. In this pronouncement, a small stock dividend is defined as one 20 to 25% or less. For filings with that agency, the SEC has refined the definition to comprise stock distributions of less than 25%.

ILLUSTRATION 18–8
Stock Dividend

A small stock dividend requires reclassification to paid-in capital of retained earnings equal to the fair value of the additional shares distributed.

Craft declares and distributes a 10% common stock dividend (10 million shares) when the market value of the $1 par common stock is $12 per share.

	($ in millions)	
Retained earnings (10 million shares at $12 per share)	120	
Common stock (10 million shares at $1 par per share)		10
Paid-in capital—excess of par (remainder)		110

ADDITIONAL CONSIDERATION

The entry above is recorded on the declaration date. Since the additional shares are not yet issued, some accountants would prefer to credit "common stock dividends issuable" at this point, instead of common stock. In that case, when the shares are issued, common stock dividends issuable is debited and common stock credited. The choice really is inconsequential; either way the $10 million amount would be reported as part of paid-in capital on a balance sheet prepared between the declaration and distribution of the shares.

STOCK MARKET REACTION TO STOCK DISTRIBUTIONS. As a Craft shareholder owning 10 shares at the time of the 10% stock dividend, you would receive an 11th share. Since each is worth $12, would you benefit by $12 when you receive the additional share from Craft? Of course not. If the value of each share were to remain $12 when the 10 million new shares are distributed, the total market value of the company would grow by $120 million (10 million shares × $12 per share).

A corporation cannot increase its market value simply by distributing additional stock certificates. Because all shareholders receive the same percentage increase in their respective holdings, you, and all other shareholders, still would own the same percentage of the company as before the distribution. Accordingly, the per share value of your shares should decline from $12 to $10.91 so that your 11 shares would be worth $120—precisely what your 10 shares were worth prior to the stock dividend. Any failure of the stock price to actually adjust in proportion to the additional shares issued probably would be due to information other than the distribution reaching shareholders at the same time.

The market price per share will decline in proportion to the increase in the number of shares distributed in a stock dividend.

Then, what justification is there for recording the additional shares at market value? In 1941 (and reaffirmed in 1953), accounting rulemakers felt that many shareholders are deceived by small stock dividends, believing they benefit by the market value of their additional shares.[18] Furthermore they erroneously felt that these individual beliefs are collectively reflected in the stock market by per share prices that remain unchanged by stock dividends. Consequently, their prescribed accounting treatment is to reduce retained earnings by the same amount as if cash dividends were paid equal to the market value of the shares issued.

Early rulemakers felt that per share market prices do not adjust in response to an increase in the number of shares.

This obsolete reasoning is inconsistent with our earlier conclusion that the market price per share will decline in approximate proportion to the increase in the number of shares distributed. Our intuitive conclusion is supported also by formal research.[19]

Besides being based on fallacious reasoning, accounting for stock dividends by artificially reclassifying "earned" capital as "invested" capital conflicts with the reporting objective of reporting shareholders' equity by source. Despite these limitations, this outdated accounting standard still applies.

Capitalizing retained earnings for a stock dividend artificially reclassifies earned capital as invested capital.

[18]"Restatement and Revision of Accounting Research Bulletins," *Accounting Research Bulletin No. 43* (New York: AICPA, 1961), chap. 7.

[19]Foster and Vickrey, "The Information Content of Stock Dividend Announcements," *Accounting Review* (April 1978), and Spiceland and Winters, "The Market Reaction to Stock Distributions: The Effect of Market Anticipation and Cash Returns," *Accounting and Business Research* (Summer 1986).

Companies sometimes declare a stock dividend in lieu of a real dividend.

REASONS FOR STOCK DIVIDENDS. Since neither the corporation nor its shareholders apparently benefits from stock dividends, why do companies declare them?[20] Occasionally, a company tries to give shareholders the illusion that they are receiving a real dividend.

Companies sometimes declare a stock dividend so they can capitalize retained earnings.

Another reason is merely to enable the corporation to take advantage of the accepted accounting practice of capitalizing retained earnings. Specifically, a company might wish to lower an existing balance in retained earnings—otherwise available for *cash* dividends—so it can reinvest the earned assets represented by that balance without carrying a large balance in retained earnings.

Stock Splits

FINANCIAL Reporting Case

Q4, p. 945

A frequent reason for issuing a stock dividend is actually to induce the per share market price decline that follows. For instance, after a company declares a 100% stock dividend on 100 million shares of common stock, with a per share market price of $12, it then has 200 million shares, each with an approximate market value of $6. The motivation for reducing the per share market price is to increase the stock's *marketability* by making it attractive to a larger number of potential investors.

> **ADDITIONAL CONSIDERATION**
>
> No cash dividends are paid on treasury shares. Usually stock dividends aren't paid on treasury shares either. Treasury shares are essentially equivalent to shares that never have been issued. In some circumstances, though, the intended use of the repurchased shares will give reason for the treasury shares to participate in a stock dividend. For instance, if the treasury shares have been specifically designated for issuance to executives in a stock option plan or stock award plan it would be appropriate to adjust the number of shares by the stock distribution.

A large stock dividend is known as a stock split.

A stock distribution of 25% or higher, although often called a "large" stock dividend, is more often referred to as a stock split.[21] Thus, a 100% stock dividend could be labeled a 2-for-1 stock split. Conceptually, the proper accounting treatment of a stock dividend or a stock split is to make no journal entry, avoiding the reclassification of earned capital as invested capital. This, in fact, is the prescribed accounting treatment for a stock split.

Since the same common stock account balance (total par) represents twice as many shares, the par value per share should be reduced by one-half. In the previous example, if the par were $1 per share before the stock distribution, then after the 2-for-1 stock split, the par would be $.50 per share.

> Following on the heels of an enormous run up in price in shares, Apple Computer announced Friday a two-for-one stock split. Each share held on Feb. 18 gets an additional share. The company plans to start trading on a split-adjusted basis at the end of February. "It potentially makes it more attractive to individual investors," said Steve Lidberg, an analyst at Pacific Crest Securities, who doesn't own shares of Apple. "Outside of that, it doesn't impact at all the way I think of the company."[22]

Stock Splits Effected in the Form of Stock Dividends (Large Stock Dividends)

If the per share par value of the shares is not changed, the stock distribution is referred to as a *stock split effected in the form of a stock dividend,* or simply a *stock dividend.* In that case, a journal entry increases the common stock account by the par value of the additional shares. To avoid reducing retained earnings in these instances, most companies reduce (debit) paid-in capital—excess of par to offset the credit to common stock (Illustration 18–9).

[20]After hitting a high in the 1940s, the number of stock dividends has declined significantly. Currently, about 3% of companies declare stock dividends in any given year.

[21]"Restatement and Revision of Accounting Research Bulletins," *Accounting Research Bulletin No. 43* (New York: AICPA, 1961), Chap. 7, sec. B, par. 11.

[22]"Apple's Share Price Surge Results in Stock Split," *CNN Money,* February 11, 2005.

ILLUSTRATION 18–9

Stock Split Effected in the Form of a Stock Dividend

If the *per share* par value of the shares is not changed, a stock distribution is referred to as a *stock split effected in the form of a stock dividend.*

Craft declares and distributes a 2-for-1 stock split effected in the form of a 100% stock dividend (100 million shares) when the market value of the $1 par common stock is $12 per share:

	($ in millions)	
Paid-in capital—excess of par	100	
Common stock (100 million shares at $1 par per share)		100

Notice that this entry does not reclassify earned capital as invested capital. Some companies, though, choose to debit retained earnings instead.[23]

Some companies capitalize retained earnings when recording a stock split effected in the form of a stock dividend.

	($ in millions)	
Retained earnings	100	
Common stock (10 million shares × $1 par per share)		100

Nike, Inc., described its recent stock split in its disclosure notes as shown in Graphic 18–7.

GRAPHIC 18–7

Stock Split Disclosure—Nike, Inc.

Real World Financials

Note 1—Summary of Significant Accounting Policies
Stock Split
On February 15, 2007 the Board of Directors declared a two-for-one stock split of the Company's Class A and Class B common shares, which was effected in the form of a 100% common stock dividend distributed on April 2, 2007. All references to share and per share amounts in the consolidated financial statements and accompanying notes to the consolidated financial statements have been retroactively restated to reflect the two-for-one stock split.

ADDITIONAL CONSIDERATION

A company choosing to capitalize retained earnings when recording a stock split effected in the form of a stock dividend may elect to capitalize an amount other than par value. Accounting guidelines are vague in this regard, stating only that legal amounts are minimum requirements and do not prevent the capitalization of a larger amount per share.

Source: "Restatement and Revision of Accounting Research Bulletins," *Accounting Research Bulletin No. 43* (New York: AICPA, 1961), Chap. 7, sec. B, par. 14.

REVERSE STOCK SPLIT. A **reverse stock split** occurs when a company decreases, rather than increases, its outstanding shares. After a 1-for-4 reverse stock split, for example, 100 million shares, $1 par per share, would become 25 million shares, $4 par per share. No journal entry is necessary. Of course the market price per share theoretically would quadruple, which usually is the motivation for declaring a reverse stock split. Companies that reverse split their shares frequently are struggling companies trying to accomplish with the split what the market has been unwilling to do—increase the stock price.

FRACTIONAL SHARES. Typically, a stock dividend or stock split results in some shareholders being entitled to fractions of whole shares. For example, if a company declares a 25% stock dividend, or equivalently a 5-for-4 stock split, a shareholder owning 10 shares would be entitled to 2½ shares. Another shareholder with 15 shares would be entitled to 3¾ shares.

Cash payments usually are made when shareholders are entitled to fractions of whole shares.

[23]The 2004 *Accounting Trends & Techniques* reports that 19 of its 600 sample companies reported a stock split. Of those, 7 debited additional paid-in capital, 5 debited retained earnings, and 7 made no entry. Thus all but 7 were handled as stock splits effected in the form of stock dividends.

Cash payments usually are made to shareholders for **fractional shares.** In the situation described above, for instance, if the market price at declaration is $12 per share, the shareholder with 15 shares would receive 3 additional shares and $9 in cash ($12 × ¾).

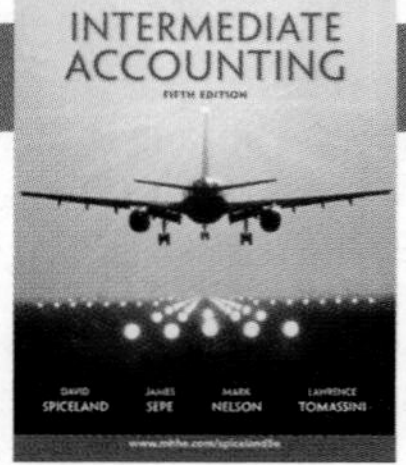

DECISION MAKER'S PERSPECTIVE

The return on shareholders' equity is a popular measure of profitability.

Profitability is the key to a company's long-run survival. A summary measure of profitability often used by investors and potential investors, particularly common shareholders, is the return on shareholders' equity. This ratio measures the ability of company management to generate net income from the resources that owners provide. The ratio is computed by dividing net income by average shareholders' equity. A variation of this ratio often is used when a company has both preferred and common stock outstanding. The return to common shareholders' equity is calculated by subtracting dividends to preferred shareholders from the numerator and using average common shareholders' equity as the denominator. The modified ratio focuses on the profits generated on the assets provided by common shareholders.

Book value measures have limited use in financial analysis.

Although the ratio is useful when evaluating the effectiveness of management in employing resources provided by owners, analysts must be careful not to view it in isolation or without considering how the ratio is derived. Keep in mind that shareholders' equity is a measure of the book value of equity, equivalent to the book value of net assets. Book value measures quickly become out of line with market values. An asset's book value usually equals its market value on the date it's purchased; the two aren't necessarily the same after that. Equivalently, the market value of a share of stock (or of total shareholders' equity) usually is different from its book value. As a result, to supplement the return on shareholders' equity ratio, analysts often relate earnings to the market value of equity, calculating the earnings-price ratio. This ratio is simply the earnings per share divided by the market price per share.

To better understand the differences between the book value ratio and the market value ratio, let's consider the following condensed information reported by Sharp-Novell Industries for 2009 and 2008:

($ in 000s except per share amounts)	2009	2008
Sales	$3,500	$3,100
Net income	125	114
Current assets	$ 750	$ 720
Property, plant, and equipment (net)	900	850
Total assets	$1,650	$1,570
Current liabilities	$ 550	$ 530
Long-term liabilities	540	520
Paid-in capital	210	210
Retained earnings	350	310
Liabilities and shareholders' equity	$1,650	$1,570
Shares outstanding	50,000	50,000
Stock price (average)	$42.50	$42.50

The 2009 return on shareholders' equity is computed by dividing net income by average shareholders' equity:

$$\$125 \div [(\$560 + 520)/2] = 23.1\%$$

The earnings-price ratio is the earnings per share divided by the market price per share:

$$\text{Earnings per share (2009)} = \$125 \div 50 = \$2.50$$
$$\text{Earnings-price ratio} = \$2.50 \div 42.50 = 5.9\%$$

Share retirement and treasury stock transactions can affect the return to owners.

Obviously, the return on the market value of equity is much lower than on the book value of equity. This points out the importance of looking at more than a single ratio when making decisions. While 23.1% may seem like a desirable return, 5.9% is not nearly so attractive.

Companies often emphasize the return on shareholders' equity in their annual reports. Alert investors should not accept this measure of achievement at face value. For some companies this is a meaningful measure of performance; but for others, the market-based ratio means more, particularly for a mature firm whose book value and market value are more divergent.

Decisions managers make with regard to shareholders' equity transactions can significantly impact the return to shareholders. For example, when a company buys back shares of its own stock, the return on shareholders' equity goes up. Net income is divided by a smaller amount of shareholders' equity. On the other hand, the share buyback uses assets, reducing the resources available to earn net income in the future. So, managers as well as outside analysts must carefully consider the decision to reacquire shares in light of the current economic environment, the firm's investment opportunities, and cost of capital to decide whether such a transaction is in the long-term best interests of owners. Investors should be wary of buybacks during down times because the resulting decrease in shares and increase in earnings per share can be used to mask a slowdown in earnings growth.

The decision to pay dividends requires similar considerations. When earnings are high, are shareholders better off receiving substantial cash dividends or having management reinvest those funds to finance future growth (and future dividends)? The answer, of course, depends on the particular circumstances involved. Dividend decisions should reflect managerial strategy concerning the mix of internal versus external financing, alternative investment opportunities, and industry conditions. High dividends often are found in mature industries and low dividends in growth industries.

Dividend decisions should be evaluated in light of prevailing circumstances.

ETHICAL DILEMMA

Interworld Distributors has paid quarterly cash dividends since 1980. The dividends have steadily increased from $.25 per share to the latest dividend declaration of $2.00 per share. The board of directors is eager to continue this trend despite the fact that revenues fell significantly during recent months as a result of worsening economic conditions and increased competition. The company founder and member of the board proposes a solution. He suggests a 5% stock dividend in lieu of a cash dividend to be accompanied by the following press announcement:

"In lieu of our regular $2.00 per share cash dividend, Interworld will distribute a 5% stock dividend on its common shares, currently trading at $40 per share. Changing the form of the dividend will permit the Company to direct available cash resources to the modernization of physical facilities in preparation for competing in the 21st century."

What do you think?

CONCEPT REVIEW **EXERCISE**

CHANGES IN RETAINED EARNINGS

Situation: The shareholders' equity section of the balance sheet of National Foods, Inc., included the following accounts at December 31, 2009:

Shareholders' Equity	($ in millions)
Paid-in capital	
Preferred stock, 9.09%, 11 million shares at $1 par	$ 11
Common stock, 122 million shares at $1 par	122
Paid-in capital—excess of par, preferred	479
Paid-in capital—excess of par, common	854
Retained earnings	3,245
Treasury stock, at cost, 2 million common shares	(20)
Total shareholders' equity	$4,691

Required:

1. During 2010, several events and transactions affected the retained earnings of National Foods. Prepare the appropriate entries for these events.

a. On March 1, the board of directors declared a cash dividend of $1 per share on its 120 million outstanding shares (122 million − 2 million treasury shares), payable on April 3 to shareholders of record March 11.
b. On March 5, the board of directors declared a property dividend of 120 million shares of **Kroger** common stock that National Foods had purchased in February as an investment (book value: $900 million). The investment shares had a fair value of $8 per share and were distributed March 30 to shareholders of record March 15.
c. On April 13, a 3-for-2 stock split was declared and distributed. The stock split was effected in the form of a 50% stock dividend. The market value of the $1 par common stock was $20 per share.
d. On October 13, a 10% common stock dividend was declared and distributed when the market value of the $1 par common stock was $12 per share. Fractional share rights for 1 million equivalent whole shares were paid in cash.
e. On December 1, the board of directors declared the 9.09% cash dividend on the 11 million preferred shares, payable on December 23 to shareholders of record December 11.

2. Prepare a statement of shareholders' equity for National Foods reporting the changes in shareholders' equity accounts for 2008, 2009, and 2010. Refer to the previous two Concept Reviews in this chapter for the 2008 and 2009 changes. For 2009, assume that shares were reacquired as treasury stock. Also, look back to the statement of shareholders' equity in Graphic 18–4 on page 951 for the format of the statement. Assume that net income for 2010 is $225 million.

SOLUTION

1. During 2010, several events and transactions affected the retained earnings of National Foods. Prepare the appropriate entries for these events.

a. Cash dividend of $1 per share on its 120 million *outstanding* common shares (122 million − 2 million treasury shares), payable on April 3 to shareholders of record March 11 (Note: Dividends aren't paid on treasury shares.):

The declaration of a dividend reduces retained earnings and creates a liability.

March 1—Declaration Date	($ in millions)	
Retained earnings	120	
Cash dividends payable (120 million shares at $1/share)		120
March 11—Date of Record		
No entry		
April 3—Payment Date		
Cash dividends payable	120	
Cash		120

b. Property dividend of 120 million shares of Kroger common stock:

The investment first must be written up to the $960 million fair value ($ 8 × 120 million shares).

The liability is satisfied when the Kroger shares are distributed to shareholders.

March 5—Declaration Date	($ in millions)	
Investment in Kroger common stock	60	
Gain on appreciation of investment ($960 − 900)		60
Retained earnings (fair value of asset to be distributed)	960	
Property dividends payable		960
March 15—Date of Record		
No entry		
March 30—Payment Date		
Property dividends payable	960	
Investment in Kroger common stock		960

c. 3-for-2 stock split effected in the form of a 50% stock dividend:

120 million shares times 50% equals 60 million new shares—recorded at par.

	($ in millions)	
April 13		
Paid-in capital—excess of par*	60	
Common stock (60 million shares at $1 par per share)		60

*Alternatively, retained earnings may be debited.

d. 10% common stock dividend—fractional share rights for 1 million equivalent whole shares:

	($ in millions)	
October 13		
Retained earnings (18 million shares* at $12 per share)	216	
Common stock (17 million shares at $1 par per share)		17
Paid-in capital—excess of par (17 million shares at $11 per share above par)		187
Cash (1 million shares at $12 market price per share)		12

*(120 million + 60 million) × 10% = 18 million shares

The stock dividend occurs after the 3-for-2 stock split; thus 18 million shares are distributed.

The $12 fair value of the additional shares is capitalized in this small stock dividend.

e. 9.09% cash dividend on the 11 million preferred shares, payable on December 23 to shareholders of record December 11:

	($ in millions)	
December 1—Declaration Date		
Retained earnings	1	
Cash dividends payable ($11 million par × 9.09%)		1
December 11—Date of Record		
NO ENTRY		
December 23—Payment Date		
Cash dividends payable	1	
Cash		1

Preferred shareholders annually receive the designated percentage (9.09%) of the preferred's par value ($1 million), if dividends are declared.

2. Prepare a statement of shareholders' equity for National Foods reporting the changes in shareholders' equity accounts for 2008, 2009, and 2010.

NATIONAL FOODS
Statement of Shareholders' Equity
For the Years Ended December 31, 2010, 2009, and 2008

($ in millions)

	Preferred Stock	Common Stock	Additional Paid-In Capital	Retained Earnings	Treasury Stock (at cost)	Total Share holder's Equity
Balance at January 1, 2008		120	836	2,449		3,405
Sale of preferred shares	10		430			440
Issuance of common shares		1	9			10
Issuance of common and preferred shares	1	1	58			60
Net income				400		400
Cash dividends, preferred	—	—	—	(1)	—	(1)
Balance at December 31, 2008	11	122	1,333	2,848		4,314
Purchase of treasury shares					(60)	(60)
Sale of treasury shares			4		20	24
Sale of treasury shares			(4)	(2)	20	14
Net income				400		400
Cash dividends, preferred	—	—	—	(1)	—	(1)
Balance at December 31, 2009	11	122	1,333	3,245	(20)	4,691
Cash dividends, common				(120)		(120)
Property dividends, common				(960)		(960)
3-for-2 split effected in the form of a stock dividend		60	(60)			
10% stock dividend		17	187	(216)		(12)
Preferred dividends				(1)		(1)
Net income	—	—	—	225	—	225
Balance at December 31, 2010	11	199	1,460	2,173	(20)	3,823

These are the transactions from Concept Review Exercise—Expansion of Corporate Capital.

These are the transactions from Concept Review Exercise—Treasury Stock.

These are the transactions from Concept Review Exercise—Changes in Retained Earnings.

FINANCIAL REPORTING CASE SOLUTION

1. **Do you think the stock price increase is related to Textron's share repurchase plan?** *(p. 960)* The stock price increase probably is related to Textron's buyback plan. The marketplace realizes that decreasing the supply of shares supports the price of remaining shares. However, the repurchase of shares is not necessarily the best use of a company's cash. Whether it is in the shareholders' best interests depends on what other opportunities the company has for the cash available.
2. **What are Textron's choices in accounting for the share repurchases?** *(p. 961)* When a corporation reacquires its own shares, those shares assume the same status as authorized but unissued shares, just as if they never had been issued. However, for exactly the same transaction, companies can choose between two accounting alternatives: (a) formally retiring them or (b) accounting for the shares repurchased as treasury stock. In actuality, Textron's uses alternative (b).
3. **What effect does the quarterly cash dividend of 45 cents a share have on Textron's assets? Its liabilities? Its shareholders' equity?** *(p. 967)* Each quarter, when directors declare a cash dividend, retained earnings are reduced and a liability is recorded. The liability is paid with cash on the payment date. So, the net effect is a decrease in Textron's assets and its shareholders' equity. The effect on liabilities is temporary.
4. **What effect did the stock split have on Textron's assets? Its liabilities? Its shareholders' equity?** *(p. 970)* Conceptually, the proper accounting treatment of a stock split is to make no journal entry. However, since Textron refers to the stock distribution as a "stock split effected through a 100% stock dividend," a journal entry would increase the common stock account by the par value of the additional shares and would reduce paid-in capital—excess of par. This merely moves an amount from one part of shareholders' equity to another. Regardless of the accounting method, there is no change in Textron's assets, liabilities, or total shareholders' equity. ●

THE BOTTOM LINE

● **LO1** Shareholders' equity is the owners' residual interest in a corporation's assets. It arises primarily from (1) amounts invested by shareholders and (2) amounts earned by the corporation on behalf of its shareholders. These are reported as (1) paid-in capital and (2) retained earnings. A statement of shareholders' equity reports the sources of the changes in individual shareholders' equity accounts. (p. 946)

● **LO2** Comprehensive income encompasses all changes in equity except those caused by transactions with owners (like dividends and the sale or purchase of shares). It includes traditional net income as well as "other comprehensive income." (p. 948)

● **LO3** Shares sold for consideration other than cash (maybe services or a noncash asset) should be recorded at the fair value of the shares or the noncash consideration, whichever seems more clearly evident. (p. 956)

● **LO4** When a corporation retires previously issued shares, those shares assume the same status as authorized but unissued shares—just the same as if they had never been issued. Payments made to retire shares are viewed as a distribution of corporate assets to shareholders. (p. 960)

● **LO5** When reaquired shares are viewed as treasury stock, the cost of acquiring the shares is temporarily debited to the treasury stock account. Recording the effects on specific shareholders' equity accounts is delayed until later when the shares are reissued. (p. 963)

● **LO6** Retained earnings represents, in general, a corporation's accumulated, undistributed or reinvested net income (or net loss). Distributions of earned assets are dividends. (p. 966)

● **LO7** Most corporate dividends are paid in cash. When a noncash asset is distributed, it is referred to as a property dividend. The fair value of the assets to be distributed is the amount recorded for a property dividend. (p. 966)

● **LO8** A stock dividend is the distribution of additional shares of stock to current shareholders. For a small stock dividend (25% or less), the fair value of the additional shares distributed is transferred from retained earnings to paid-in capital. For a stock distribution of 25% or higher, the par value of the additional shares is reclassified within shareholders' equity if referred to as a stock split effected in the form of a stock dividend, but if referred to merely as a stock split, no journal entry is recorded. (p. 968) ●

APPENDIX 18

QUASI REORGANIZATIONS

A firm undergoing financial difficulties, but with favorable future prospects, may use a **quasi reorganization** to write down inflated asset values and eliminate an accumulated deficit (debit balance in retained earnings). To effect the reorganization the following procedures are followed:

1. The firm's assets (and perhaps liabilities) are revalued (up or down) to reflect fair values, with corresponding credits or debits to retained earnings. This process typically increases the deficit.
2. The debit balance in retained earnings (deficit) is eliminated against additional paid-in capital. If additional paid-in capital is not sufficient to absorb the entire deficit, a reduction in capital stock may be necessary (with an appropriate restating of the par amount per share).
3. Retained earnings is dated. That is, disclosure is provided to indicate the date the deficit was eliminated and when the new accumulation of earnings began.

The procedure is demonstrated in Illustration 18A–1. The shareholders approved the quasi reorganization effective January 1, 2009. The plan was to be accomplished by a reduction of inventory by $75 million, a reduction in property, plant, and equipment (net) of $175 million, and appropriate adjustments to shareholders' equity.

ILLUSTRATION 18A–1
Quasi Reorganization

The Emerson-Walsch Corporation has incurred operating losses for several years. A newly elected board of directors voted to implement a quasi reorganization, subject to shareholder approval. The balance sheet, on December 31, 2008, immediately prior to the restatement, includes the data shown below.

	($ in millions)
Cash	$ 75
Receivables	200
Inventory	375
Property, plant, and equipment (net)	400
	$1,050
Liabilities	$ 400
Common stock (800 million shares at $1 par)	800
Additional paid-in capital	150
Retained earnings (deficit)	(300)
	$1,050

	($ in millions)	
To Revalue Assets:		
Retained earnings	75	
Inventory		75
Retained earnings	175	
Property, plant, and equipment		175
To Eliminate a Portion of the Deficit against Available Additional Paid-In Capital:		
Additional paid-in capital	150	
Retained earnings		150
To Eliminate the Remainder of the Deficit against Common Stock:		
Common stock	400	
Retained earnings		400

When assets are revalued to reflect fair values, the process often increases the deficit.

The deficit, $550 ($300 + 75 + 175), can be only partially absorbed by the balance of additional paid-in capital.

The remaining deficit, $400 ($300 + 75 + 175 – 150), must be absorbed by reducing the balance in common stock.

The balance sheet immediately after the restatement would include the following:

Assets and liabilities reflect current values.

Because a reduced balance represents the same 800 million shares, the par amount per share must be reduced.

The deficit is eliminated.

	($ in millions)
Cash	$ 75
Receivables	200
Inventory	300
Property, plant, and equipment (net)	225
	$800
Liabilities	$400
Common stock (800 million shares at $.50 par)	400
Additional paid-in capital	0
Retained earnings (deficit)	0
	$800

Note A: Upon the recommendation of the board of directors and approval by shareholders a quasi reorganization was implemented January 1, 2009. The plan was accomplished by a reduction of inventory by $75 million, a reduction in property, plant, and equipment (net) of $175 million, and appropriate adjustments to shareholders' equity. The balance in retained earnings reflects the elimination of a $300 million deficit on that date.

QUESTIONS FOR REVIEW OF KEY TOPICS

Q 18–1 Identify and briefly describe the two primary sources of shareholders' equity.

Q 18–2 The balance sheet reports the balances of shareholders' equity accounts. What additional information is provided by the statement of shareholders' equity?

Q 18–3 What is comprehensive income? How does comprehensive income differ from net income? Where do companies report it in a balance sheet?

Q 18–4 Identify the three common forms of business organization and the primary difference between the way they are accounted for.

Q 18–5 Corporations offer the advantage of limited liability. Explain what is meant by that statement.

Q 18–6 Distinguish between not-for-profit and for-profit corporations.

Q 18–7 Distinguish between publicly held and privately (or closely) held corporations.

Q 18–8 How does the Model Business Corporation Act affect the way corporations operate?

Q 18–9 The owners of a corporation are its shareholders. If a corporation has only one class of shares, they typically are labeled common shares. Indicate the ownership rights held by common shareholders, unless specifically withheld by agreement.

Q 18–10 What is meant by a shareholder's preemptive right?

Q 18–11 Terminology varies in the way companies differentiate among share types. But many corporations designate shares as common or preferred. What are the two special rights usually given to preferred shareholders?

Q 18–12 Most preferred shares are cumulative. Explain what this means.

Q 18–13 The par value of shares historically indicated the real value of shares and all shares were issued at that price. The concept has changed with time. Describe the meaning of par value as it has evolved to today.

Q 18–14 At times, companies issue their shares for consideration other than cash. What is the measurement objective in those cases?

Q 18–15 Companies occasionally sell more than one security for a single price. How is the issue price allocated among the separate securities?

Q 18–16 The costs of legal, promotional, and accounting services necessary to effect the sale of shares are referred to as share issue costs. How are these costs recorded? Compare this approach to the way debt issue costs are recorded.

Q 18–17 When a corporation acquires its own shares, those shares assume the same status as authorized but unissued shares, as if they never had been issued. Explain how this is reflected in the accounting records if the shares are formally retired.

Q 18–18 Discuss the conceptual basis for accounting for a share buyback as treasury stock.

Q 18–19 The prescribed accounting treatment for stock dividends implicitly assumes that shareholders are fooled by small stock dividends and benefit by the market value of their additional shares. Explain this statement. Is it logical?

Q 18–20 Brandon Components declares a 2-for-1 stock split. What will be the effects of the split, and how should it be recorded?

Q 18–21 What is a reverse stock split? What would be the effect of a reverse stock split on one million $1 par shares? On the accounting records?

Q 18–22 Suppose you own 80 shares of IBM common stock when the company declares a 4% stock dividend. What will you receive as a result?

Q 18–23 (Based on Appendix 18) A quasi reorganization is sometimes employed by a firm undergoing financial difficulties, but with favorable future prospects. What are two objectives of this procedure? Briefly describe the procedural steps.

BRIEF EXERCISES

BE 18–1
Comprehensive income
● LO1

Schaeffer Corporation reports $50 million accumulated other comprehensive income in its balance sheet as a component of shareholders' equity. In a related disclosure note reporting comprehensive income for the year, the company reveals net income of $400 million and other comprehensive income of $15 million. What was the balance in accumulated other comprehensive income in last year's balance sheet?

BE 18–2
Stock issued
● LO3

Penne Pharmaceuticals sold 8 million shares of its $1 par common stock to provide funds for research and development. If the issue price is $12 per share, what is the journal entry to record the sale of the shares?

BE 18–3
Stock issued
● LO3

Lewelling Company issued 100,000 shares of its $1 par common stock to the Michael Morgan law firm as compensation for 4,000 hours of legal services performed. Morgan's usual rate is $240 per hour. By what amount should Lewelling's paid-in capital—excess of par increase as a result of this transaction?

BE 18–4
Retirement of shares
● LO4

Horton Industries' shareholders' equity included 100 million shares of $1 par common stock and a balance in paid-in capital—excess of par of $900 million. Assuming that Horton retires shares it reacquires (restores their status to that of authorized but unissued shares), by what amount will Horton's total paid-in capital decline if it reacquires 2 million shares at $8.50 per share?

BE 18–5
Retirement of shares
● LO4

Agee Storage issued 35 million shares of its $1 par common stock at $16 per share several years ago. Last year, for the first time, Agee reacquired 1 million shares at $14 per share. Assuming that Agee retires shares it reacquires (restores their status to that of authorized but unissued shares), by what amount will Agee's total paid-in capital decline if it now reacquires 1 million shares at $19 per share?

BE 18–6
Treasury stock
● LO5

The Jennings Group reacquired 2 million of its shares at $70 per share as treasury stock. Last year, for the first time, Jennings sold 1 million treasury shares at $71 per share. By what amount will Jennings' retained earnings decline if it now sells the remaining 1 million treasury shares at $67 per share?

BE 18–7
Treasury stock
● LO5

In previous years, Cox Transport reacquired 2 million treasury shares at $20 per share and, later, 1 million treasury shares at $26 per share. By what amount will Cox's paid-in capital—share repurchase increase if it now sells 1 million treasury shares at $29 per share and determines cost as the weighted-average cost of treasury shares?

BE 18–8
Treasury stock
● LO5

Refer to the situation described in BE 18–7. By what amount will Cox's paid-in capital—share repurchase increase if it determines the cost of treasury shares by the FIFO method?

BE 18–9
Cash dividend
● LO7
Real World Financials

Following is a Microsoft press release:

In March 2007 Microsoft Corp. today announced that its Board of Directors declared a quarterly dividend of $0.10 per share. The dividend is payable March 18, 2007, to shareholders of record on Feb. 13, 2007.

Prepare the journal entries Microsoft used to record the declaration and payment of the cash dividend for its 9,355 million shares.

BE 18–10
Property dividend
● LO7

LaRoe Moving and Storage, a family-owned corporation, declared a property dividend of 1,000 shares of GE common stock that LaRoe had purchased in February for $37,000 as an investment. GE's shares had a market value of $35 per share on the declaration date. Prepare the journal entries to record the property dividend on the declaration and payment dates.

BE 18–11
Stock dividend
● LO8

On June 13, the board of directors of Siewert, Inc. declared a 5% stock dividend on its 60 million, $1 par, common shares, to be distributed on July 1. The market price of Siewert common stock was $25 on June 13. Prepare the journal entry to record the stock dividend.

BE 18–12
Stock split
● LO8

Refer to the situation described in BE 18–11, but assume a 2-for-1 stock split instead of the 5% stock dividend. Prepare the journal entry to record the stock split if it is *not* to be effected in the form of a stock dividend. What is the par per share after the split?

BE 18–13
Stock split
● LO8

Refer to the situation described in BE 18–11, but assume a 2-for-1 stock split instead of the 5% stock dividend. Prepare the journal entry to record the stock split if it is to be effected in the form of a 100% stock dividend. What is the par per share after the split?

EXERCISES

available with McGraw–Hill's Homework Manager www.mhhe.com/spiceland5e 

An alternate exercise and problem set is available on the text website: www.mhhe.com/spiceland5e

E 18–1
Comprehensive income
● LO2

The following is an excerpt from a disclosure note from the 2009 annual report of Kaufman Chemicals, Inc:

COMPREHENSIVE INCOME (LOSS)

The components of comprehensive income, net of tax, are as follows (in millions):

Years Ended December 31	2009	2008	2007
Net income	$856	$766	$594
Other comprehensive income:			
Change in net unrealized gains on available-for-sale investments, net of tax of $22, ($14), and $15 in 2009, 2008, and 2007, respectively	34	(21)	23
Other	(2)	(1)	1
Total	$888	$744	$618

Kaufman reports Accumulated other comprehensive income in its balance sheet as a component of shareholders' equity as follows:

	($ in millions)	
	2009	2008
Shareholders' equity:		
Common stock	355	355
Additional paid-in capital	8,567	8,567
Retained earnings	6,544	5,988
Accumulated other comprehensive income	107	75
Total shareholders' equity	$15,573	$14,985

Required:

1. What is comprehensive income and how does it differ from net income?
2. How is comprehensive income reported in a balance sheet?
3. Why is Kaufman's 2009 balance sheet amount different from the 2009 amount reported in the disclosure note? Explain.
4. From the information provided, determine how Kaufman calculated the $107 million Accumulated other comprehensive income in 2009.

E 18–2
Stock issued for cash; Wright Medical Group
● LO3
Real World Financials

The following is a news item reported by Reuters:

WASHINGTON, Jan 29 (Reuters)—**Wright Medical Group,** a maker of reconstructive implants for knees and hips, on Tuesday filed to sell 3 million shares of common stock.

In a filing with the U.S. Securities and Exchange Commission, it said it plans to use the proceeds from the offering for general corporate purposes, working capital, research and development, and acquisitions.

After the sale there will be about 31.5 million shares outstanding in the Arlington, Tennessee-based company, according to the SEC filing.

Wright shares closed at $17.15 on Nasdaq.

The common stock of Wright Medical Group has a par of $.01 per share.

Required:

Prepare the journal entry to record the sale of the shares assuming the price existing when the announcement was made and ignoring share issue costs.

E 18–3
Issuance of shares; noncash consideration

● LO3

During its first year of operations, Eastern Data Links Corporation entered into the following transactions relating to shareholders' equity. The articles of incorporation authorized the issue of 8 million common shares, $1 par per share, and 1 million preferred shares, $50 par per share.

Required:

Prepare the appropriate journal entries to record each transaction.

Feb. 12	Sold 2 million common shares, for $9 per share.
13	Issued 40,000 common shares to attorneys in exchange for legal services.
13	Sold 80,000 of its common shares and 4,000 preferred shares for a total of $945,000.
Nov. 15	Issued 380,000 of its common shares in exchange for equipment for which the cash price was known to be $3,688,000.

E 18–4
Redeemable shares

● LO3

Williams Industries has outstanding 30 million common shares, 20 million Class A shares, and 20 million Class B shares. Williams has the right but not the obligation to repurchase the Class A shares if a change in ownership of the voting common shares causes J. P. Williams, founder and CEO, to have less than 50% ownership. Williams has the unconditional obligation to repurchase the Class B shares upon the death of J. P. Williams.

Required:

Which, if any, of the shares should be reported in Williams's balance sheet as liabilities? Explain.

E 18–5
Share issue costs; issuance

● LO3

ICOT Industries issued 15 million of its $1 par common shares for $424 million on April 11. Legal, promotional, and accounting services necessary to effect the sale cost $2 million.

Required:

1. Prepare the journal entry to record the issuance of the shares.
2. Explain how recording the share issue costs differ from the way debt issue costs are recorded (discussed in Chapter 14).

E 18–6
Retirement of shares

● LO4

Borner Communications' articles of incorporation authorized the issuance of 130 million common shares. The transactions described below effected changes in Borner's outstanding shares. Prior to the transactions, Borner's shareholders' equity included the following:

Shareholders' Equity	($ in millions)
Common stock, 100 million shares at $1 par	$100
Paid-in capital—excess of par	300
Retained earnings	210

Required:

Assuming that Borner Communications retires shares it reacquires (restores their status to that of authorized but unissued shares), record the appropriate journal entry for each of the following transactions:

1. On January 7, 2009, Borner reacquired 2 million shares at $5.00 per share.
2. On August 23, 2009, Borner reacquired 4 million shares at $3.50 per share.
3. On July 25, 2010, Borner sold 3 million common shares at $6 per share.

E 18–7
Retirement of shares

● LO4

In 2009, Borland Semiconductors entered into the transactions described below. In 2006, Borland had issued 170 million shares of its $1 par common stock at $34 per share.

Required:

Assuming that Borland retires shares it reacquires, record the appropriate journal entry for each of the following transactions:

1. On January 2, 2009, Borland reacquired 10 million shares at $32.50 per share.
2. On March 3, 2009, Borland reacquired 10 million shares at $36 per share.
3. On August 13, 2009, Borland sold 1 million shares at $42 per share.
4. On December 15, 2009, Borland sold 2 million shares at $36 per share.

E 18–8
Treasury stock

● LO5

In 2009, Western Transport Company entered into the treasury stock transactions described below. In 2007, Western Transport had issued 140 million shares of its $1 par common stock at $17 per share.

Required:

Prepare the appropriate journal entry for each of the following transactions:

1. On January 23, 2009, Western Transport reacquired 10 million shares at $20 per share.
2. On September 3, 2009, Western Transport sold 1 million treasury shares at $21 per share.
3. On November 4, 2009, Western Transport sold 1 million treasury shares at $18 per share.

E 18–9
Treasury stock; weighted-average and FIFO cost

● LO5

At December 31, 2008, the balance sheet of Meca International included the following shareholders' equity accounts:

Shareholders' Equity	($ in millions)
Common stock, 60 million shares at $1 par	$ 60
Paid-in capital—excess of par	300
Retained earnings	410

Required:

Assuming that Meca International views its share buybacks as treasury stock, record the appropriate journal entry for each of the following transactions:

1. On February 12, 2009, Meca reacquired 1 million common shares at $13 per share.
2. On June 9, 2010, Meca reacquired 2 million common shares at $10 per share.
3. On May 25, 2011, Meca sold 2 million treasury shares at $15 per share—determine cost as the weighted-average cost of treasury shares.
4. For the previous transaction, assume Meca determines the cost of treasury shares by the FIFO method.

E 18–10
Reporting shareholders' equity after share repurchase

● LO4 LO5

On two previous occasions, the management of Dennison and Company, Inc. repurchased some of its common shares. Between buyback transactions, the corporation issued common shares under its management incentive plan. Shown below is shareholders' equity following these share transactions, as reported by two different methods of accounting for reacquired shares.

	($ in millions)	
	Method A	Method B
Shareholders' equity		
Paid-in capital:		
Preferred stock, $10 par	$ 150	$ 150
Common stock, $1 par	200	197
Additional paid-in capital	1,204	1,201
Retained earnings	2,994	2,979
Less: Treasury stock	(21)	
Total shareholders' equity	$4,527	$4,527

Required:

1. Infer from the presentation which method of accounting for reacquired shares is represented by each of the two columns.
2. Explain why presentation formats are different and why some account balances are different for the two methods.

E 18–11
Change from treasury stock to retired stock

● LO4 LO5

In keeping with a modernization of corporate statutes in its home state, UMC Corporation decided in 2009 to discontinue accounting for reacquired shares as treasury stock. Instead, shares repurchased will be viewed as having been retired, reassuming the status of unissued shares. As part of the change, treasury shares held were reclassified as retired stock. At December 31, 2008 UMC's balance sheet reported the following shareholders' equity:

	($ in millions)
Common stock, $1 par	$ 200
Paid-in capital—excess of par	800
Retained earnings	956
Treasury stock (4 million shares at cost)	(25)
Total shareholders' equity	$1,931

Required:

Identify the type of accounting change this decision represents, and prepare the journal entry to effect the reclassification of treasury shares as retired shares.

E 18–12
Transactions affecting retained earnings

● LO6 LO7

Shown below in T-account format are the changes affecting the retained earnings of Brenner-Jude Corporation during 2009. At January 1, 2009, the corporation had outstanding 105 million common shares, $1 par per share.

Retained Earnings ($ in millions)

		90	Beginning balance
Retirement of 5 million common shares for $22 million	2		
		88	Net income for the year
Declaration and payment of a $.33 per share cash dividend	33		
Declaration and distribution of a 4% stock dividend	20		
		123	Ending balance

Required:

1. From the information provided by the account changes you should be able to recreate the transactions that affected Brenner-Jude's retained earnings during 2009. Prepare the journal entries that Brenner-Jude must have recorded during the year for these transactions.
2. Prepare a statement of retained earnings for Brenner-Jude for the year ended 2009.

E 18–13
Effect of cumulative, nonparticipating preferred stock on dividends—3 years

● LO7

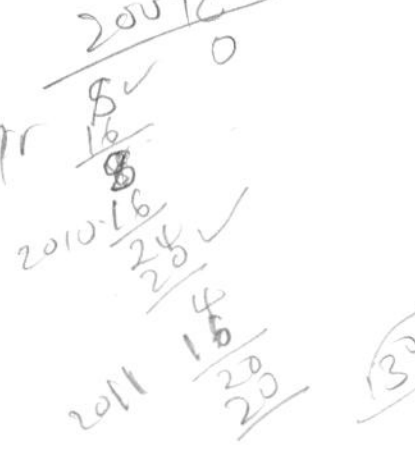

The shareholders' equity of WBL Industries includes the items shown below. The board of directors of WBL declared cash dividends of $8 million, $20 million, and $150 million in its first three years of operation—2009, 2010, and 2011, respectively.

	($ in millions)
Common stock	$100
Paid-in capital—excess of par, common	980
Preferred stock, 8%	200
Paid-in capital—excess of par, preferred	555

Required:

Determine the amount of dividends to be paid to preferred and common shareholders in each of the three years, assuming that the preferred stock is cumulative and nonparticipating.

	Preferred	Common
2009		
2010		
2011		

E 18–14
Stock dividend

● LO8

The shareholders' equity of Core Technologies Company on June 30, 2008, included the following:

Common stock, $1 par; authorized, 8 million shares; issued and outstanding, 3 million shares	$ 3,000,000
Paid-in capital—excess of par	12,000,000
Retained earnings	14,000,000

On April 1, 2009, the board of directors of Core Technologies declared a 10% stock dividend on common shares, to be distributed on June 1. The market price of Core Technologies' common stock was $30 on April 1, 2009, and $40 on June 1, 2009.

Required:

Prepare the journal entry to record the distribution of the stock dividend on the declaration date.

E 18–15
Stock split; Hanmi Financial Corporation

● LO8

Real World Financials

Hanmi Financial Corporation is the parent company of Hanmi Bank. The company's stock split was announced in the following Business Wire:

LOS ANGELES (BUSINESS WIRE) Jan. 20—Hanmi Financial Corporation (Nasdaq), announced that the Board of Directors has approved a two-for-one stock split to be effected in the form of a 100 percent common stock dividend. Hanmi Financial Corporation stockholders of record at the close of business on January 31 will receive one additional share of common stock for every share of common stock then held. Distribution of additional shares issued as a result of the split is expected to occur on or about February 15.

At the time of the stock split, 24.5 million shares of common stock, $.001 par per share, were outstanding.

Required:

1. Prepare the journal entry, if any, that Hanmi recorded at the time of the stock split.
2. What is the probable motivation for declaring the 2-for-1 stock split to be effected by a dividend payable in shares of common stock?
3. If Hanmi's stock price had been $36 at the time of the split, what would be its approximate value after the split (other things equal)?

E 18–16
Cash for fractional share rights

● LO8

Douglas McDonald Company's balance sheet included the following shareholders' equity accounts at December 31, 2008:

	($ in millions)
Paid-in capital:	
Common stock, 900 million shares at $1 par	$ 900
Paid-in capital—excess of par	15,800
Retained earnings	14,888
Total shareholders' equity	$31,588

On March 16, 2009, a 4% common stock dividend was declared and distributed. The market value of the common stock was $21 per share. Fractional share rights represented 2 million equivalent whole shares. Cash was paid in place of the fractional share rights.

Required:

1. What is a fractional share right?
2. Prepare the appropriate entries for the declaration and distribution of the stock dividend.

E 18–17
Transactions affecting retained earnings

● LO6 through LO8

The balance sheet of Consolidated Paper, Inc. included the following shareholders' equity accounts at December 31, 2008:

	($ in millions)
Paid-in capital:	
Preferred stock, 8.8%, 90,000 shares at $1 par	$ 90,000
Common stock, 364,000 shares at $1 par	364,000
Paid-in capital—excess par, preferred	1,437,000
Paid-in capital—excess of par, common	2,574,000
Retained earnings	9,735,000
Treasury stock, at cost; 4,000 common shares	(44,000)
Total shareholders' equity	$14,156,000

During 2009, several events and transactions affected the retained earnings of Consolidated Paper.

Required:

1. Prepare the appropriate entries for these events:
   a. On March 3 the board of directors declared a property dividend of 240,000 shares of Leasco International common stock that Consolidated Paper had purchased in January as an investment (book value: $700,000). The investment shares had a fair value of $3 per share and were distributed March 31 to shareholders of record March 15.
   b. On May 3 a 5-for-4 stock split was declared and distributed. The stock split was effected in the form of a 25% stock dividend. The market value of the $1 par common stock was $11 per share.
   c. On July 5 a 2% common stock dividend was declared and distributed. The market value of the common stock was $11 per share.
   d. On December 1 the board of directors declared the 8.8% cash dividend on the 90,000 preferred shares, payable on December 28 to shareholders of record December 20.
   e. On December 1 the board of directors declared a cash dividend of $.50 per share on its common shares, payable on December 28 to shareholders of record December 20.
2. Prepare the shareholders' equity section of the balance sheet for Consolidated Paper, Inc. for the year ended at December 31, 2009. Net income for the year was $810,000.

E 18–18
Profitability ratio

● LO1

Comparative balance sheets for Softech Canvas Goods for 2009 and 2008 are shown below. Softech pays no dividends, instead reinvesting all earnings for future growth.

Comparative Balance Sheets
($ in 000s)

	December 31	
	2009	**2008**
Assets:		
Cash	$ 50	$ 40
Accounts receivable	100	120
Short-term investments	50	40
Inventory	200	140
Property, plant, and equipment (net)	600	550
	$1,000	$890
Liabilities and Shareholders' Equity:		
Current liabilities	$ 240	$210
Bonds payable	160	160
Paid-in capital	400	400
Retained earnings	200	120
	$1,000	$890

Required:
1. Determine the return on shareholders' equity for 2009.
2. What does the ratio measure?

E 18–19
New equity issues; offerings announcements
● LO3

When companies offer new equity security issues, they publicize the offerings in the financial press and on Internet sites. Assume the following were among the equity offerings reported in December 2009:

NEW SECURITIES ISSUES

Equity

American Materials Transfer Corporation (AMTC)—7.5 million common shares, $.001 par, priced at $13.546 each through underwriters led by Second Tennessee Bank N.A. and Morgan, Dunavant & Co., according to a syndicate official.

Proactive Solutions Inc. (PSI)—Offering of nine million common shares, $.01 par, was priced at $15.20 a share via lead manager Stanley Brothers, Inc., according to a syndicate official.

Required:
Prepare the appropriate journal entries to record the sale of both issues to underwriters. Ignore share issue costs.

E 18–20
Stock buyback; Adobe Systems; press announcement
● LO4 LO5
Real World Financials

The following excerpt is from an article reported in the April 9, 2007, online issue of *Reuters*.

Adobe Systems Incorporated (Nasdaq:ADBE)—April 9, 2007 announces its Board of Directors has approved a new stock repurchase program that authorizes the company to repurchase in aggregate up to 20 million shares of the company's common stock. The Board also authorized an additional $500 million in funds to repurchase shares under its existing stock repurchase program designed to offset dilution from stock issuances.

The par amount per share for Adobe's common stock is $.0001. Paid-in capital—excess of par is $40.48 per share on average. The market price was $43 on April 9, 2007.

Required:
1. Suppose Adobe reacquires the 20 million shares through repurchase on the open market at $43 per share. Prepare the appropriate journal entry to record the purchase. Adobe considers the shares it buys back to be treasury stock.
2. Suppose Adobe considers the shares it buys back to be retired rather than treated as treasury stock. Prepare the appropriate journal entry to record the purchase.
3. What does the company mean by saying that the buyback will serve "to offset dilution from stock issuances"?

CPA AND CMA REVIEW QUESTIONS

CPA Exam Questions

The following questions are used in the Kaplan CPA Review Course to study shareholders' equity while preparing for the CPA examination. Determine the response that best completes the statements or questions.

● LO4

1. In 2007, Fogg, Inc., issued $10 par value common stock for $25 per share. No other common stock transactions occurred until March 31, 2009, when Fogg acquired some of the issued shares for $20 per share and retired them. Which of the following statements correctly states an effect of this acquisition and retirement?
   a. 2009 net income is decreased.
   b. Additional paid-in capital is decreased.
   c. 2009 net income is increased.
   d. Retained earnings is increased.

● LO5

2. Copper, Inc., initially issued 100,000 shares of $1 par value stock for $500,000 in 2006. In 2008, the company repurchased 10,000 shares for $100,000. In 2009, 5,000 of the repurchased shares were resold for $80,000. In its balance sheet dated December 31, 2009, Copper, Inc.'s Treasury Stock account shows a balance of:
   a. $ 0
   b. $ 20,000
   c. $ 50,000
   d. $100,000

● LO7

3. On June 27, 2009, Brite Co. distributed to its common stockholders 100,000 outstanding common shares of its investment in Quik, Inc., an unrelated party. The carrying amount on Brite's books of Quik's $1 par common stock was $2 per share. Immediately after the distribution, the market price of Quik's stock was $2.50 per share. In its income statement for the year ended June 30, 2009, what amount should Brite report as gain before income taxes on disposal of the stock?
   a. $ 0
   b. $ 50,000
   c. $200,000
   d. $250,000

● LO8

4. Whipple Company has 1,000,000 shares of common stock authorized with a par value of $3 per share, of which 600,000 shares are outstanding. When the market value was $8 per share, Whipple issued a stock dividend whereby for each six shares held one share was issued as a stock dividend. The par value of the stock was not changed. What entry should Whipple make to record this transaction?

a. Retained earnings	$300,000	
Common stock		$300,000
b. Additional paid-in capital	300,000	
Common stock		300,000
c. Retained earnings	800,000	
Common stock		300,000
Additional paid-in capital		500,000
d. Additional paid-in capital	800,000	
Common stock		300,000
Retained earnings		500,000

● LO8

5. When a company issues a stock dividend which of the following would be affected?
   a. Earnings per share.
   b. Total assets.
   c. Total liabilities.
   d. Total stockholder's equity.

6. Long Co. had 100,000 shares of common stock issued and outstanding at January 1, 2009. During 2009, Long took the following actions:

March 15	Declared a 2-for-1 stock split, when the fair value of the stock was $80 per share.
December 15	Declared a $0.50 per share cash dividend.

In Long's statement of shareholders' equity for 2009, what amount should Long report as dividends?

a. $ 50,000
b. $100,000
c. $850,000
d. $950,000

CMA Exam Questions

The following questions dealing with shareholders' equity are adapted from questions that previously appeared on Certified Management Accountant (CMA) examinations. The CMA designation sponsored by the Institute of Management Accountants (www.imanet.org) provides members with an objective measure of knowledge and competence in the field of management accounting. Determine the response that best completes the statements or questions.

● LO1

1. The par value of common stock represents
   a. the estimated fair value of the stock when it was issued.
   b. the liability ceiling of a shareholder when a company undergoes bankruptcy proceedings.
   c. the total value of the stock that must be entered in the issuing corporation's records.
   d. the amount that must be recorded on the issuing corporation's record as paid-in capital.

● LO1

2. The equity section of Smith Corporation's statement of financial position is presented below.

Preferred stock, $100 par	$12,000,000
Common stock, $5 par	10,000,000
Paid-in capital in excess of par	18,000,000
Retained earnings	9,000,000
Shareholders' equity	$49,000,000

The common shareholders of Smith Corporation have preemptive rights. If Smith Corporation issues 400,000 additional share of common stock at $6 per share, a current holder of 20,000 shares of Smith Corporation's common stock must be given the option to buy

   a. 1,000 additional shares.
   b. 3,774 additional shares.
   c. 4,000 additional shares.
   d. 3,333 additional shares.

● LO8

3. A stock dividend
   a. increases the debt to equity ratio of a firm.
   b. decreases future earnings per share.
   c. decreases the size of the firm.
   d. increases shareholders' wealth.

PROBLEMS

available with McGraw-Hill's Homework Manager www.mhhe.com/spiceland5e 

An alternate exercise and problem set is available on the text website: www.mhhe.com/spiceland5e

P 18–1
Various stock transactions; correction of journal entries

● LO3

Part A

During its first year of operations, the McCollum Corporation entered into the following transactions relating to shareholders' equity. The corporation was authorized to issue 100 million common shares, $1 par per share.

Required:

Prepare the appropriate journal entries to record each transaction.

Jan. 9	Issued 40 million common shares for $20 per share.
Mar. 11	Issued 5,000 shares in exchange for custom-made equipment. McCollum's shares have traded recently on the stock exchange at $20 per share.

Part B

A new staff accountant for the McCollum Corporation recorded the following journal entries during the second year of operations. McCollum retires shares that it reacquires (restores their status to that of authorized but unissued shares).

		($ in millions)	
Jan. 12	Land	2	
	Paid-in capital—donation of land		2
Sept. 1	Common stock	2	
	Retained earnings	48	
	Cash		50
Dec. 1	Cash	26	
	Common stock		1
	Gain on sale of previously issued shares		25

Required:
Prepare the journal entries that should have been recorded for each of the transactions.

P 18–2
Share buyback—comparison of retirement and treasury stock treatment

● LO4 LO5

The shareholders' equity section of the balance sheet of TNL Systems, Inc. included the following accounts at December 31, 2008:

Shareholders' Equity	($ in millions)
Common stock, 240 million shares at $1 par	$ 240
Paid-in capital—excess of par	1,680
Paid-in capital—share repurchase	1
Retained earnings	1,100

Required:

1. During 2009, TNL Systems reacquired shares of its common stock and later sold shares in two separate transactions. Prepare the entries for both the purchase and subsequent resale of the shares assuming the shares are (a) retired and (b) viewed as treasury stock.
   a. On February 5, 2009, TNL Systems purchased 6 million shares at $10 per share.
   b. On July 9, 2009, the corporation sold 2 million shares at $12 per share.
   c. On November 14, 2011, the corporation sold 2 million shares at $7 per share.
2. Prepare the shareholders' equity section of TNL Systems' balance sheet at December 31, 2011, comparing the two approaches. Assume all net income earned in 2009–2011 was distributed to shareholders as cash dividends.

P 18–3
Reacquired shares—comparison of retired shares and treasury shares

● LO4 LO5

eXcel

National Supply's shareholders' equity included the following accounts at December 31, 2008:

Shareholders' Equity	($ in millions)
Common stock, 6 million shares at $1 par	$ 6,000,000
Paid-in capital—excess of par	30,000,000
Retained earnings	86,500,000

Required:

1. National Supply reacquired shares of its common stock in two separate transactions and later sold shares. Prepare the entries for each of the transactions under each of two separate assumptions: the shares are (a) retired and (b) accounted for as treasury stock.

February 15, 2009	Reacquired 300,000 shares at $8 per share.
February 17, 2010	Reacquired 300,000 shares at $5.50 per share.
November 9, 2011	Sold 200,000 shares at $7 per share (assume FIFO cost).

2. Prepare the shareholders' equity section of National Supply's balance sheet at December 31, 2011, assuming the shares are (a) retired and (b) accounted for as treasury stock. Net income was $14 million in 2009, $15 million in 2010, and $16 million in 2011. No dividends were paid during the three-year period.

P 18–4
Statement of retained earnings

● LO4 through LO7

Comparative statements of retained earnings for Renn-Dever Corporation were reported in its 2009 annual report as follows.

RENN-DEVER CORPORATION
Statements of Retained Earnings

For the Years Ended December 31,	2009	2008	2007
Balance at beginning of year	**$6,794,292**	**$5,464,052**	**$5,624,552**
Net income (loss)	3,308,700	2,240,900	(160,500)
Deductions:			
Stock dividend (34,900 shares)	242,000		
Common shares retired (110,000 shares)		212,660	
Common stock cash dividends	889,950	698,000	0
Balance at end of year	**$8,971,042**	**$6,794,292**	**$5,464,052**

At December 31, 2006, common shares consisted of the following:

Common stock, 1,855,000 shares at $1 par	$1,855,000
Paid-in capital—excess of par	7,420,000

Required:

Infer from the reports the events and transactions that affected Renn-Dever Corporation's retained earnings during 2007, 2008, and 2009. Prepare the journal entries that reflect those events and transactions.

P 18–5
Shareholders' equity transactions; statement of shareholders' equity

● LO1 LO6 through LO8

Listed below are the transactions that affected the shareholders' equity of Branch-Rickie Corporation during the period 2009–2011. At December 31, 2008, the corporation's accounts included:

	($ in 000s)
Common stock, 105 million shares at $1 par	$105,000
Paid-in capital—excess of par	630,000
Retained earnings	970,000

a. November 1, 2009, the board of directors declared a cash dividend of $.80 per share on its common shares, payable to shareholders of record November 15, to be paid December 1.

b. On March 1, 2009, the board of directors declared a property dividend consisting of corporate bonds of Warner Corporation that Branch-Rickie was holding as an investment. The bonds had a fair value of $1.6 million, but were purchased two years previously for $1.3 million. Because they were intended to be held to maturity, the bonds had not been previously written up. The property dividend was payable to shareholders of record March 13, to be distributed April 5.

c. On July 12, 2010, the corporation declared and distributed a 5% common stock dividend (when the market value of the common stock was $21 per share). Cash was paid for fractional share rights representing 250,000 equivalent whole shares.

d. On November 1, 2010, the board of directors declared a cash dividend of $.80 per share on its common shares, payable to shareholders of record November 15, to be paid December 1.

e. On January 15, 2011, the board of directors declared and distributed a 3-for-2 stock split effected in the form of a 50% stock dividend when the market value of the common stock was $22 per share.

f. On November 1, 2011, the board of directors declared a cash dividend of $.65 per share on its common shares, payable to shareholders of record November 15, to be paid December 1.

Required:

1. Prepare the journal entries that Branch-Rickie recorded during the three-year period for these transactions.
2. Prepare comparative statements of shareholders' equity for Branch-Rickie for the three-year period ($ in 000s). Net income was $330 million, $395 million, and $455 million for 2009, 2010, and 2011, respectively.

P 18–6
Statement of shareholders' equity

● LO1 LO3 through LO8

Comparative statements of shareholders' equity for Anaconda International Corporation were reported as follows for the fiscal years ending December 31, 2009, 2010, and 2011.

ANACONDA INTERNATIONAL CORPORATION
Statements of Shareholders' Equity
For the Years Ended Dec. 31, 2009, 2010, and 2011
($ in millions)

	Preferred Stock $10 par	Common Stock $1 par	Additional Paid-In Capital	Retained Earnings	Total Shareholders' Equity
Balance at January 1, 2009		55	495	1,878	2,428
Sale of preferred shares	10		470		480
Sale of common shares		7	63		70
Cash dividend, preferred				(1)	(1)
Cash dividend, common				(16)	(16)
Net income	—	—	—	290	290
Balance at December 31, 2009	10	62	1,028	2,151	3,251
Retirement of shares		(3)	(27)	(20)	(50)
Cash dividend, preferred				(1)	(1)
Cash dividend, common				(20)	(20)
3-for-2 split effected in the form of a dividend	5		(5)		
Net income	—	—	—	380	380

(continued)

(concluded)

Balance at December 31, 2010	**15**	**59**	**996**	**2,490**	**3,560**
Common stock dividend		6	59	(65)	
Cash dividend, preferred				(1)	(1)
Cash dividend, common				(22)	(22)
Net income				412	412
Balance at December 31, 2011	**15**	**65**	**1,055**	**2,814**	**3,949**

Required:

1. Infer from the statements the events and transactions that affected Anaconda International Corporation's shareholders' equity during 2009, 2010, and 2011. Prepare the journal entries that reflect those events and transactions.
2. Prepare the shareholders' equity section of Anaconda's comparative balance sheets at December 31, 2011 and 2010.

P 18–7
Reporting shareholders' equity; comprehensive income; Cisco Systems

● LO1 through LO4

Real World Financials

The following is the 2007 Statement of Shareholders' Equity from Cisco Systems' 2007 annual report. Remember that for comparative purposes, three years are reported in these statements. The 2006 and 2005 portions of the statement are not shown here for brevity of presentation.

CISCO SYSTEMS, INC.
Consolidated Statements of Shareholders' Equity (in part)

($ in millions)	Shares of Common Stock	Common Stock and Additional Paid-In Capital	Retained Earnings (Accumulated Deficit)	Accumulated Other Comprehensive Income	Total Shareholders' Equity
Balance at July 29, 2006	**6,059**	**$24,257**	**$ (617)**	**$272**	**$ 23,912**
Net income	—	—	7,333	—	7,333
Change in unrealized gains and losses on investments, net of tax	—	—	—	124	124
Other	—	—	—	166	166
Comprehensive income					7,623
Issuance of common stock	325	5,306	—	—	5,306
Repurchase of common stock	(297)	(1,296)	(6,485)	—	(7,781)
Tax benefits from employee stock incentive plans	—	995	—	—	995
Purchase acquisitions	13	462	—	—	462
Employee share-based compensation expense	—	929	—	—	929
Share-based compensation expense related to acquisitions and investments	—	34	—	—	34
Balance at July 28, 2007	**6,100**	**$30,687**	**$ 231**	**$562**	**$ 31,480**

Required:

1. What is the purpose of the statement of shareholders' equity?
2. How does Cisco account for its share buybacks?
3. For its share buybacks in fiscal year 2007, was the price Cisco paid for the shares repurchased more or less than the average price at which Cisco had sold the shares previously? Reconstruct the journal entry Cisco used to record the buyback.
4. What is comprehensive income? What is other comprehensive income?
5. What caused the change in Cisco's comprehensive income in fiscal year 2007? What was the amount of Accumulated other comprehensive income (loss) that Cisco reported in its July 28, 2007 balance sheet? Be specific.

P 18–8
Share issue costs; issuance; dividends; early retirement

● LO3 LO4 LO7

During its first year of operations, Cupola Fan Corporation issued 30,000 of $1 par Class B shares for $385,000 on June 30, 2009. Share issue costs were $1,500. One year from the issue date (July 1, 2010), the corporation retired 10% of the shares for $39,500.

Required:

1. Prepare the journal entry to record the issuance of the shares.
2. Prepare the journal entry to record the declaration of a $2 per share dividend on December 1, 2009.
3. Prepare the journal entry to record the payment of the dividend on December 31, 2009.
4. Prepare the journal entry to record the retirement of the shares.

(Note: You may wish to compare your solution to this problem with that of Problem 14–19, which deals with parallel issues of debt issue costs and the retirement of debt.)

P 18–9
Effect of preferred stock characteristics on dividends

● LO7

The shareholders' equity of Kramer Industries includes the data shown below. During 2009, cash dividends of $150 million were declared. Dividends were not declared in 2007 or 2008.

	($ in millions)
Common stock	$200
Paid-in capital—excess of par, common	800
Preferred stock, 10%, nonparticipating	100
Paid-in capital—excess of par, preferred	270

Required:
Determine the amount of dividends payable to preferred shareholders and to common shareholders under each of the following two assumptions regarding the characteristics of the preferred stock.

Assumption A—The preferred stock is noncumulative.
Assumption B—The preferred stock is cumulative.

P 18–10
Transactions affecting retained earnings

● LO3 through LO8

Indicate by letter whether each of the transactions listed below increases **(I)**, decreases **(D)**, or has no effect **(N)** on retained earnings. Assume the shareholders' equity of the transacting company includes only common stock, paid-in capital—excess of par, and retained earnings at the time of each transaction.

Transactions

Example: __N__ 1. Sale of common stock
______ 2. Purchase of treasury stock at a cost *less* than the original issue price
______ 3. Purchase of treasury stock at a cost *greater* than the original issue price
______ 4. Declaration of a property dividend
______ 5. Sale of treasury stock for *more* than cost
______ 6. Sale of treasury stock for *less* than cost
______ 7. Net income for the year
______ 8. Declaration of a cash dividend
______ 9. Payment of a previously declared cash dividend
______ 10. Issuance of convertible bonds for cash
______ 11. Declaration and distribution of a 5% stock dividend
______ 12. Retirement of common stock at a cost *less* than the original issue price
______ 13. Retirement of common stock at a cost *greater* than the original issue price
______ 14. A stock split effected in the form of a stock dividend
______ 15. A stock split in which the par value per share is reduced (not effected in the form of a stock dividend)
______ 16. A net loss for the year

P 18–11
Stock dividends received on investments; integrative problem

● LO8

Ellis Transport Company acquired 1.2 million shares of stock in L&K Corporation at $44 per share. They are classified by Ellis as "available for sale." Ellis sold 200,000 shares at $46, received a 10% stock dividend, and then later in the year sold another 100,000 shares at $43.
Hint: There is no entry for the stock dividend, but a new investment per share must be calculated for use later when the shares are sold.

Required:
Prepare journal entries to record these transactions.

P 18–12
Various shareholders' equity topics; comprehensive

● LO1 LO3 through LO8

Part A

In late 2008, the Nicklaus Corporation was formed. The corporate charter authorizes the issuance of 5,000,000 shares of common stock carrying a $1 par value, and 1,000,000 shares of $5 par value, noncumulative, nonparticipating preferred stock. On January 2, 2009, 3,000,000 shares of the common stock are issued in exchange for cash at an average price of $10 per share. Also on January 2, all 1,000,000 shares of preferred stock are issued at $20 per share.

Required:

1. Prepare journal entries to record these transactions.
2. Prepare the shareholders' equity section of the Nicklaus balance sheet as of March 31, 2009. (Assume net income for the first quarter 2009 was $1,000,000.)

Part B

During 2009, the Nicklaus Corporation participated in three treasury stock transactions:

a. On June 30, 2009, the corporation reacquires 200,000 shares for the treasury at a price of $12 per share.
b. On July 31, 2009, 50,000 treasury shares are reissued at $15 per share.
c. On September 30, 2009, 50,000 treasury shares are reissued at $10 per share.

Required:

1. Prepare journal entries to record these transactions.
2. Prepare the Nicklaus Corporation shareholders' equity section as it would appear in a balance sheet prepared at September 30, 2009. (Assume net income for the second and third quarter was $3,000,000.)

Part C

On October 1, 2009, Nicklaus Corporation receives permission to replace its $1 par value common stock (5,000,000 shares authorized, 3,000,000 shares issued, and 2,900,000 shares outstanding) with a new common stock issue having a $.50 par value. Since the new par value is one-half the amount of the old, this represents a 2-for-1 stock split. That is, the shareholders will receive two shares of the $.50 par stock in exchange for each share of the $1 par stock they own. The $1 par stock will be collected and destroyed by the issuing corporation.

On November 1, 2009, the Nicklaus Corporation declares a $.05 per share cash dividend on common stock and a $.25 per share cash dividend on preferred stock. Payment is scheduled for December 1, 2009, to shareholders of record on November 15, 2009.

On December 2, 2009, the Nicklaus Corporation declares a 1% stock dividend payable on December 28, 2009, to shareholders of record on December 14. At the date of declaration, the common stock was selling in the open market at $10 per share. The dividend will result in 58,000 (.01 × 5,800,000) additional shares being issued to shareholders.

Required:

1. Prepare journal entries to record the declaration and payment of these stock and cash dividends.
2. Prepare the December 31, 2009, shareholders' equity section of the balance sheet for the Nicklaus Corporation. (Assume net income for the fourth quarter was $2,500,000.)
3. Prepare a statement of shareholders' equity for Nicklaus Corporation for 2009.

P 18–13
Quasi reorganization (based on Appendix 18)

● LO1

A new CEO was hired to revive the floundering Champion Chemical Corporation. The company had endured operating losses for several years, but confidence was emerging that better times were ahead. The board of directors and shareholders approved a quasi reorganization for the corporation. The reorganization included devaluing inventory for obsolescence by $105 million and increasing land by $5 million. Immediately prior to the restatement, at December 31, 2009, Champion Chemical Corporation's balance sheet appeared as follows (in condensed form):

CHAMPION CHEMICAL CORPORATION
Balance Sheet
At December 31, 2009
($ in millions)

Cash	$ 20
Receivables	40
Inventory	230
Land	40
Buildings and equipment (net)	90
	$420
Liabilities	$240
Common stock (320 million shares at $1 par)	320
Additional paid-in capital	60
Retained earnings (deficit)	(200)
	$420

Required:

1. Prepare the journal entries appropriate to record the quasi reorganization on January 1, 2010.
2. Prepare a balance sheet as it would appear immediately after the restatement.

BROADEN YOUR PERSPECTIVE

Apply your critical-thinking ability to the knowledge you've gained. These cases will provide you an opportunity to develop your research, analysis, judgment, and communication skills. You also will work with other students, integrate what you've learned, apply it in real world situations, and consider its global and ethical ramifications. This practice will broaden your knowledge and further develop your decision-making abilities.

Real World Case 18–1
Initial public offering of common stock; Dolby Laboratories

● LO3

Real World Financials

Ray Dolby started **Dolby Laboratories** nearly 40 years ago and since then has been a leader in the entertainment industry and consumer electronics. Closely held since its founding in 1965, Dolby decided to go public in 2005. Here's an AP news report:

FEB. 14, 2005

DOLBY'S IPO EXPECTED TO PLAY SWEET MUSIC

The initial public offering market is hoping for a big bang this week from Dolby Laboratories Inc. The San Francisco company, whose sound systems and double-D logo are ubiquitous in the movie industry as well as in consumer electronics, plans to sell 27.5 million shares for $13.50 to $15.50 each. Founded by Cambridge-trained scientist Ray Dolby 39 years ago, the company started out manufacturing noise-reduction equipment for the music industry that eliminated the background "hiss" on recordings, and has since expanded to encompass everything from digital audio systems to Dolby Surround sound. The company's IPO, which is lead-managed by underwriters Morgan Stanley and Goldman Sachs Group Inc., is expected to do well not only because of its brand recognition, but also because of its strong financials. *(AP)*

Required:

1. Assuming the shares are issued at the midpoint of the price range indicated, how much capital did the IPO raise for Dolby Laboratories before any underwriting discount and offering expenses?
2. If the par amount is $.01 per share, what journal entry did Dolby use to record the sale?

Analysis Case 18–2
Statement of shareholders' equity

● LO1 LO3 LO6 LO7

The shareholders' equity portion of the balance sheet of Sessel's Department Stores, Inc., a large regional specialty retailer, is as follows:

SESSEL'S DEPARTMENT STORES, INC.
Comparative Balance Sheets
Shareholders' Equity Section

($ in 000s, except per share amounts)	Dec. 31, 2009	Dec. 31, 2008
Shareholders' Equity		
Preferred stock—$1 par value; 20,000 total shares authorized,		
Series A—600 shares authorized, issued, and outstanding, $50 per share liquidation preference	$ 57,700	$ —
Series B—33 shares authorized, no shares outstanding		
Common stock—$.10 par; 200,000 shares authorized, 19,940 and 18,580 shares issued and outstanding at Dec. 31, 2009, and Dec. 31, 2008, respectively	1,994	1,858
Additional paid-in capital	227,992	201,430
Retained income	73,666	44,798
Total shareholders' equity	$361,352	$248,086

Disclosures elsewhere in Sessel's annual report revealed the following changes in shareholders' equity accounts for 2009, 2008, 2007:

2009:

1. The only changes in retained earnings during 2009, were preferred dividends on preferred stock of $3,388,000 and net income.
2. The preferred stock is convertible. During the year, 6,592 shares were issued. All shares were converted into 320,000 shares of common stock. No gain or loss was recorded on the conversion.
3. Common shares were issued in a public offering and upon the exercise of stock options. On the statement of shareholders' equity, Sessel's reports these two items on a single line entitled: "Issuance of shares."

2008:

1. Net income: $12,126,000.
2. Issuance of common stock: 5,580,000 shares at $112,706,000.

2007:

1. Net income: $13,494,000.
2. Issuance of common stock: 120,000 shares at $826,000.

Required:

From these disclosures, prepare comparative statements of shareholders' equity for 2009, 2008, and 2007.

Communication Case 18–3
Is preferred stock debt or equity? Group interaction

● LO1

An unsettled question in accounting for stock is: Should preferred stock be recognized as a liability, or should it be considered equity? Under International Financial Reporting Standards, preferred stock (preference shares) often is reported as debt with the dividends reported in the income statement as interest expense. Under U.S. GAAP, that is the case only for "manditorily redeemable" preferred stock.

Two opposing viewpoints are:

View 1: Preferred stock should be considered equity.

View 2: Preferred stock should be reported as a liability.

In considering this question, focus on conceptual issues regarding the practicable and theoretically appropriate treatment, unconstrained by GAAP.

Required:

1. Which view do you favor? Develop a list of arguments in support of your view prior to the class session for which the case is assigned.
2. In class, your instructor will pair you (and everyone else) with a classmate (who also has independently developed an argument).
   a. You will be given three minutes to argue your view to your partner. Your partner likewise will be given three minutes to argue his or her view to you. During these three-minute presentations, the listening partner is not permitted to speak.
   b. Then after each person has had a turn attempting to convince his or her partner, the two partners will have a three-minute discussion in which they will decide which view is more convincing and arguments will be merged into a single view for each pair.
3. After the allotted time, a spokesperson for each of the two views will be selected by the instructor. Each spokesperson will field arguments from the class in support of that view's position and list the arguments on the board. The class then will discuss the merits of the two lists of arguments and attempt to reach a consensus view, though a consensus is not necessary.

Research Case 18–4
Comprehensive income; locate and extract relevant information and authoritative support for a financial reporting issue; integrative; Cisco Systems

● LO2

Real World Financials

Titan Networking became a public company through an IPO (initial public offering) two weeks ago. You are looking forward to the challenges of being assistant controller for a publicly owned corporation. One such challenge came in the form of a memo in this morning's in-box. "We need to start reporting comprehensive income in our financials," the message from your boss said. "Do some research on that, will you? That concept didn't exist when I went to school." In response, you sought out the financial statements of Cisco Systems, the networking industry leader. The following is an excerpt from a disclosure note from Cisco's 2007 annual report:

Comprehensive Income (Loss) (in part)

The components of comprehensive income (loss), net of tax, are as follows (in millions):

	Years Ended		
	July 28, 2007	July 29, 2006	July 30, 2005
Net income (loss)	$7,333	$5,580	$5,741
Other comprehensive income (loss):			
Change in unrealized gains and losses on investments net of tax benefit (expense) of $43, $(57), and $(61) in fiscal 2007, 2006, and 2005, respectively	128	(64)	(25)
Other	166	61	10
Comprehensive income before minority interest	$7,627	$5,577	$5,726
Change in minority interest	(4)	1	77
Total	$7,623	$5,578	$5,803

Required:

1. Locate the financial statements of Cisco at www.sec.gov or Cisco's website. Search the 2007 annual report for information about how Cisco accounts for comprehensive income. What does Cisco report in its balance sheet regarding comprehensive income?
2. Consult the FASB pronouncements at www.fasb.org/st/ or from some other source. What authoritative literature does Cisco rely on when reporting comprehensive income? When did the requirement become effective?
3. What is comprehensive income? How does it differ from net income? Where is it reported in a balance sheet? Why does Cisco's 2007 balance sheet amount differ from the 2007 amount reported in the disclosure note? Explain.
4. The primary component of Other comprehensive income for Cisco is "Change in net unrealized gains on investments." What does this mean? From the information Cisco's financial statements provide, determine how the company calculated the $562 million accumulated other comprehensive income in fiscal 2007.
5. What might be possible causes for the "Other" component of Cisco's Other comprehensive income?

Judgment Case 18–5
Treasury stock; stock split; cash dividends; Alcoa

● LO5 through LO8

Real World Financials

Alcoa is the world's leading producer of primary aluminum, fabricated aluminum, and alumina. The following is a press release from the company:

ALCOA ANNOUNCES 33% INCREASE IN BASE DIVIDEND, 2-FOR-1 STOCK SPLIT

PITTSBURGH—Alcoa today announced that its Board of Directors approved a base quarterly dividend increase of 33.3%, to 25 cents per common share from 18.75 cents per share. For a full year, base dividends will now total $1.00 compared with 75 cents before the increase.

2-FOR-1 STOCK SPLIT

The Board declared a two-for-one split of Alcoa's common stock. The stock split is subject to approval of Alcoa shareholders who must approve an amendment to the company's articles to increase the authorized shares of common stock at Alcoa's annual meeting. Shareholders of record on May 26 will receive an additional common share for each share held, which will be distributed on June 9.

COMMITMENT TO STOCK REPURCHASE PROGRAM

Alcoa restated its commitment to its previously authorized share repurchase program which it announced last year.

Required:

1. What are the two primary reporting alternatives Alcoa has in accounting for the repurchase of its shares? What would be the effect of the optional courses of action on total shareholders' equity? Explain. What would be the effect of the optional courses of action on how stock would be presented in Alcoa's balance sheet? If the shares are later resold for an amount greater than cost, how should Alcoa account for the sale?
2. What are the two primary courses of action Alcoa has in accounting for the stock split, and how would the choice affect Alcoa's shareholders' equity? Why?
3. How should Alcoa account for the cash dividend, and how would it affect Alcoa's balance sheet? Why?

Communication Case 18–6
Issuance of shares; share issue costs; prepare a report

● LO3

You are the newest member of the staff of Brinks & Company, a medium-size investment management firm. You are supervised by Les Kramer, an employee of two years. Les has a reputation as being technically sound but has a noticeable gap in his accounting education. Knowing you are knowledgeable about accounting issues, he requested you provide him with a synopsis of accounting for share issue costs.

"I thought the cost of issuing securities is recorded separately and expensed over time," he stated in a handwritten memo. "But I don't see that for IBR's underwriting expenses. What gives?"

He apparently was referring to a disclosure note on a page of IBR's annual report, photocopied and attached to his memo. To raise funds for expansion, the company sold additional shares of its $.10 par common stock. The following disclosure note appeared in the company's most recent annual report:

NOTES TO CONSOLIDATED FINANCIAL STATEMENTS

Note 10—Stock Transactions (in part)

In February and March, the Company sold 2,395,000 shares of Common Stock at $22.25 per share in a public offering. Net proceeds to the Company were approximately $50.2 million after the underwriting discount and offering expenses.

Required:

Write a formal memo to your supervisor. Briefly explain how share issue costs are accounted for and how that accounting differs from that of debt issue costs. To make sure your explanation is understood in context of the footnote, include in your memo the following:

a. At what total amount did the shares sell to the public? How is the difference between this amount and the $50.2 million net proceeds accounted for?
b. The appropriate journal entry to record the sale of the shares.

Analysis Case 18–7

Analyzing financial statements; price-earnings ratio; dividend payout ratio

● LO1

IGF Foods Company is a large, primarily domestic, consumer foods company involved in the manufacture, distribution, and sale of a variety of food products. Industry averages are derived from Troy's *The Almanac of Business and Industrial Financial Ratios* and Dun and Bradstreet's *Industry Norms and Key Business Ratios.* Following are the 2009 and 2008 comparative income statements and balance sheets for IGF. The market price of IGF's common stock is $47 during 2009. (The financial data we use are from actual financial statements of a well-known corporation, but the company name used in our illustration is fictitious and the numbers and dates have been modified slightly to disguise the company's identity.)

IGF FOODS COMPANY
Years Ended December 31, 2009 and 2008

($ in millions)	2009	2008
Comparative Income Statements		
Net sales	$6,440	$5,800
Cost of goods sold	(3,667)	(3,389)
Gross profit	2,773	2,411
Operating expenses	(1,916)	(1,629)
Operating income	857	782
Interest expense	(54)	(53)
Income from operations before tax	803	729
Income taxes	(316)	(287)
Net income	$ 487	$ 442
Net income per share	$ 2.69	$2.44
Average shares outstanding	181 million	181 million
Comparative Balance Sheets		
Assets		
Current assets:		
Cash	$ 48	$ 142
Accounts receivable	347	320
Marketable securities	358	—
Inventories	914	874
Prepaid expenses	212	154
Total current assets	$1,879	$1,490
Property, plant, and equipment (net)	2,592	2,291
Intangibles (net)	800	843
Other assets	74	60
Total assets	$5,345	$4,684
Liabilities and Shareholders' Equity		
Current liabilities:		
Accounts payable	$ 254	$ 276
Accrued liabilities	493	496
Notes payable	518	115
Current portion of long-term debt	208	54
Total current liabilities	1,473	941
Long-term debt	534	728
Deferred income taxes	407	344
Total liabilities	2,414	2,013
Shareholders' equity:		
Common stock, $1 par	180	180
Additional paid-in capital	21	63
Retained earnings	2,730	2,428
Total shareholders' equity	2,931	2,671
Total liabilities and shareholders' equity	$5,345	$4,684

Profitability is the key to a company's long-run survival. Profitability measures focus on a company's ability to provide an adequate return relative to resources devoted to company operations.

Required:

1. Calculate the return on shareholders' equity for IGF. The average return for the stocks listed on the New York Stock Exchange in a comparable period was 18.8%. What information does your calculation provide an investor?
2. Calculate IGF's earnings per share and earnings-price ratio. The average return for the stocks listed on the New York Stock Exchange in a comparable time period was 5.4%. What does your calculation indicate about IGF's earnings?

Ethics Case 18–8
The Swiss label maker; value of shares issued for equipment

● LO3

Bricker Graphics is a privately held company specializing in package labels. Representatives of the firm have just returned from Switzerland, where a Swiss firm is manufacturing a custom-made high speed, color labeling machine. Confidence is high that the new machine will help rescue Bricker from sharply declining profitability. Bricker's chief operating officer, Don Benson, has been under fire for not achieving the company's performance goals of achieving a rate of return on assets of at least 12%.

The afternoon of his return from Switzerland, Benson called Susan Sharp into his office. Susan is Bricker's Controller.

Benson: I wish you had been able to go. We have some accounting issues to consider.
Sharp: I wish I'd been there, too. I understand the food was marvelous. What are the accounting issues?
Benson: They discussed accepting our notes at the going rate for a face amount of $12.5 million. We also discussed financing with stock.
Sharp: I thought we agreed, debt is the way to go for us now.
Benson: Yes, but I've been thinking. We can issue shares for a total of $10 million. The labeler is custom-made and doesn't have a quoted selling price, but the domestic labelers we considered went for around $10 million. It sure would help our rate of return if we keep the asset base as low as possible.

Required:

1. How will Benson's plan affect the return measure? What accounting issue is involved?
2. Is the proposal ethical?
3. Who would be affected if the proposal is implemented?

Research Case 18–9
Researching the way shareholders' equity transactions are reported; retrieving financial statements from the Internet

● LO1 LO6

EDGAR, the Electronic Data Gathering, Analysis, and Retrieval system, performs automated collection, validation, indexing, and forwarding of submissions by companies and others who are required by law to file forms with the U.S. Securities and Exchange Commission (SEC). All publicly traded domestic companies use EDGAR to make the majority of their filings. (Filings by foreign companies are not required to be filed on EDGAR, but some of these companies do so voluntarily.) Form 10-K or 10-KSB, which includes the annual report, is required to be filed on EDGAR. The SEC makes this information available on the Internet.

Required:

1. Access EDGAR on the Internet at www.sec.gov.
2. Search for a public company with which you are familiar. Access its most recent 10-K filing. Search or scroll to find the statement of shareholders' equity and related note(s). If a statement of shareholders' equity is not provided, try another company.
3. Determine from the statement the transactions that occurred during the most recent three years that affected retained earnings.
4. Determine from the statement the transactions that occurred during the most recent three years that affected common stock. Were any of these transactions identified in requirement 3 also?
5. Cross-reference your findings with amounts reported on the balance sheet. How do these two statements articulate with one another?

Real World Case 18–10
Reporting preferred shares; AMCON Distributing Co.

● LO1 LO3

Real World Financials

AMCON Distributing Company is primarily engaged in the wholesale distribution of consumer products in the Great Plains and Rocky Mountain regions. The following disclosure note appeared in the company's 2007 annual report:

3. CONVERTIBLE PREFERRED STOCK (in part):
The Company has the following Convertible Preferred Stock outstanding as of September 2007:

	Series A	Series B	Series C
Date of issuance:	June 17, 2004	Oct. 8, 2004	Mar 6, 2006
Optionally redeemable beginning	June 18, 2006	Oct. 9, 2006	Mar 4, 2008
Par value (gross proceeds):	$2,500,000	$2,000,000	$2,000,000

(continued)

(concluded)

Number of shares:	100,000	80,000	80,000
Liquidation preference per share:	$25.00	$25.00	$25.00
Conversion price per share:	$30.31	$24.65	$13.62
Number of common shares in which to be converted:	82,481	81,136	146,842
Dividend rate:	6.785%	6.37%	6.00%

The Preferred Stock is convertible at any time by the holders into a number of shares of AMCON common stock equal to the number of preferred shares being converted times a fraction equal to $25.00 divided by the conversion price. The conversion prices for the Preferred Stock are subject to customary adjustments in the event of stock splits, stock dividends and certain other distributions on the Common Stock. Cumulative dividends for the Preferred Stock are payable in arrears, when, as and if declared by the Board of Directors, on March 31, June 30, September 30 and December 31 of each year.

The Preferred Stock are optionally redeemable by the Company beginning on various dates, as listed above, at redemption prices equal to 112% of the liquidation preference. The redemption prices decrease 1% annually thereafter until the redemption price equals the liquidation preference after which date it remains the liquidation preference.

Required:

1. What amount of dividends is paid annually to a preferred shareholder owning 100 shares of the Series A preferred stock?
2. If dividends are not paid in 2008 and 2009, but are paid in 2010, what amount of dividends will the shareholder receive?
3. If the investor chooses to convert the shares in 2008, how many shares of common stock will the investor receive for his/her 100 shares?
4. If AMCON chooses to redeem the shares on June 18, 2008, what amount will the investor be paid for his/her 100 shares?

Communication Case 18–11

Should the present two-category distinction between liabilities and equity be retained? group interaction.

● LO1

The current conceptual distinction between liabilities and equity defines liabilities independently of assets and equity, with equity defined as a residual amount. The present proliferation of financial instruments that combine features of both debt and equity and the difficulty of drawing a distinction have led many to conclude that the present two-category distinction between liabilities and equity be eliminated. Two opposing viewpoints are:

View 1: The distinction should be maintained.

View 2: The distinction should be eliminated and financial instruments should instead be reported in accordance with the priority of their claims to enterprise assets.

One type of security that often is mentioned in the debate is convertible bonds. Although stock in many ways, such a security also obligates the issuer to transfer assets at a specified price and redemption date. Thus it also has features of debt. In considering this question, focus on conceptual issues regarding the practicable and theoretically appropriate treatment, unconstrained by GAAP.

Required:

1. Which view do you favor? Develop a list of arguments in support of your view prior to the class session for which the case is assigned.
2. In class, your instructor will pair you (and everyone else) with a classmate (who also has independently developed an argument).
   a. You will be given three minutes to argue your view to your partner. Your partner likewise will be given three minutes to argue his or her view to you. During these three-minute presentations, the listening partner is not permitted to speak.
   b. Then after each person has had a turn attempting to convince his or her partner, the two partners will have a three-minute discussion in which they will decide which view is more convincing and arguments will be merged into a single view for each pair.
3. After the allotted time, a spokesperson for each of the two views will be selected by the instructor. Each spokesperson will field arguments from the class in support of that view's position and list the arguments on the board. The class then will discuss the merits of the two lists of arguments and attempt to reach a consensus view, though a consensus is not necessary.

CPA SIMULATION 18–1

Hanson Corporation
Shareholders' Equity

CPA Review

Test your knowledge of the concepts discussed in this chapter, practice critical professional skills necessary for career success, and prepare for the computer-based CPA exam by accessing our CPA simulations at the text website: **www.mhhe.com/spiceland5e.**

The Hansen Corporation simulation tests your knowledge of a variety of shareholders' equity reporting issues.

As on the CPA exam itself, you will be asked to use tools including a spreadsheet, a calculator, and professional accounting standards, to conduct research, derive solutions, and communicate conclusions related to these issues in a simulated environment headed by the following interactive tabs:

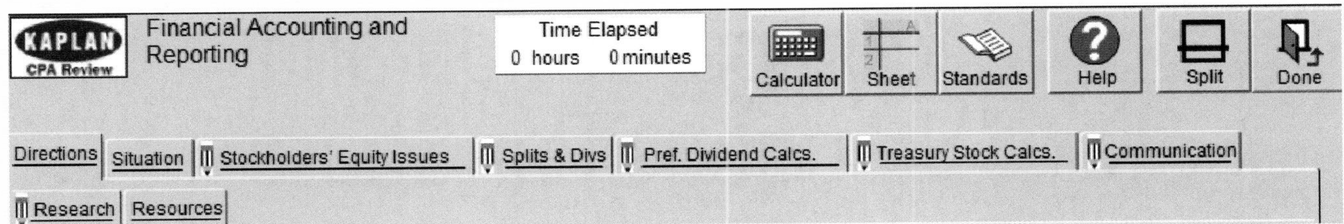

Specific tasks in the simulation include:

- Applying judgment in deciding the financial reporting implications of a variety of shareholders' equity transactions.
- Determining the financial statement effects of stock dividends and stock splits.
- Calculating dividends on preferred stock.
- Demonstrating an understanding of financial reporting effects of treasury stock transactions.
- Communicating the benefits of a stock buyback.
- Researching appropriate accounting for manditorily redeemable preferred stock.

19 CHAPTER

Share-Based Compensation and Earnings Per Share

/// OVERVIEW

We've discussed a variety of employee compensation plans in prior chapters, including pension and other postretirement benefits in Chapter 17. In this chapter we look at some common forms of compensation in which the amount of the compensation employees receive is tied to the market price of company stock. We will see that these *share-based* compensation plans—stock awards, stock options, and stock appreciation rights—create shareholders' equity, the topic of the previous chapter and also often affect the way we calculate earnings per share, the topic of the second part of the current chapter. Specifically, we view these as *potential common shares* along with convertible securities and calculate earnings per share as if they already had been exercised or converted into additional common shares.

LEARNING OBJECTIVES

After studying this chapter, you should be able to:

- **LO1** Explain and implement the accounting for stock award plans.
- **LO2** Explain and implement the accounting for stock options.
- **LO3** Explain and implement the accounting for employee share purchase plans.
- **LO4** Distinguish between a simple and a complex capital structure.
- **LO5** Describe what is meant by the weighted-average number of common shares.
- **LO6** Differentiate the effect on EPS of the sale of new shares, a stock dividend or stock split, and the reacquisition of shares.
- **LO7** Describe how preferred dividends affect the calculation of EPS.
- **LO8** Describe how options, rights, and warrants are incorporated in the calculation of EPS.
- **LO9** Describe how convertible securities are incorporated in the calculation of EPS.
- **LO10** Explain the way contingently issuable shares are incorporated in the calculation of EPS.
- **LO11** Describe the way EPS information should be reported in an income statement.

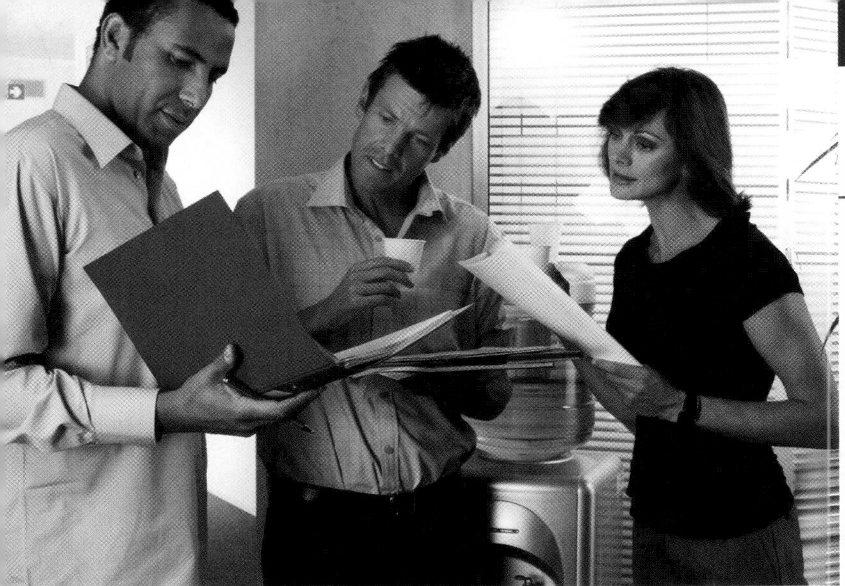

FINANCIAL REPORTING CASE

Proper Motivation?

The coffee room discussion Thursday morning was particularly lively. Yesterday's press release describing National Electronic Ventures' choice of Sandra Veres as its president and chief operating officer was today's hot topic in all the company's departments. The press release noted that Ms. Veres's compensation package includes elements beyond salary that are intended to not only motivate her to accept the offer, but also to remain with the company and work to increase shareholder value. Excerpts from the release follow:

> National Electronic Ventures, Inc. today announced it had attracted G. Sandra Veres, respected executive from the wireless communications industry to succeed chairman Walter Kovac. Veres will assume the new role as CEO on Jan. 1, 2009. Ms. Veres will receive a compensation package at NEV of more than $1 million in salary, stock options to buy more than 800,000 shares and a grant of restricted stock.

By the time you finish this chapter, you should be able to respond appropriately to the questions posed in this case. Compare your response to the solution provided at the end of the chapter.

QUESTIONS ///

1. How can a compensation package such as this serve as an incentive to Ms. Veres? (page 1002)
2. Ms. Veres received a "grant of restricted stock." How should NEV account for the grant? (page 1002)
3. Included were stock options to buy more than 800,000 shares. How will the options affect NEV's compensation expense? (page 1004)
4. How will the presence of these and other similar stock options affect NEV's earnings per share? (page 1017)

PART A SHARE-BASED COMPENSATION

Employee compensation plans frequently include share-based awards. These may be outright awards of shares, stock options, or cash payments tied to the market price of shares. Sometimes only key executives participate in a stock benefit plan. Typically, an executive compensation plan is tied to performance in a strategy that uses compensation to motivate its recipients. Some firms pay their directors entirely in shares. Actual compensation depends on the market value of the shares. Obviously, that's quite an incentive to act in the best interests of shareholders.

FINANCIAL Reporting Case

Q1, p. 1001

Although the variations of share-based compensation plans are seemingly endless, each shares common goals. Whether the plan is a stock award plan, a stock option plan, a stock appreciation rights (SARs) plan, or one of the several similar plans, the goals are to provide compensation to designated employees, while sometimes providing those employees with some sort of performance incentive. Likewise, our goals in accounting for each of these plans are the same for each: (1) to determine the fair value of the compensation and (2) to expense that compensation over the periods in which participants perform services. The issue is not trivial. In 2007 the median chief executive was holding stock and stock options 32 times the amount of his/her cash salary (80 times salary among the largest 10 percent).

The accounting objective is to record compensation expense over the periods in which related services are performed.

Stock Award Plans

Usually, restricted shares are subject to forfeiture if the employee doesn't remain with the company.

● LO1

Executive compensation sometimes includes a grant of shares of stock. Usually, such shares are restricted in such a way as to provide some incentive to the recipient. Typically, restricted stock award plans are tied to continued employment. In a **restricted stock** plan, shares actually are awarded in the name of the employee, although the company might retain physical possession of the shares. The employee has all rights of a shareholder, subject to certain restrictions or forfeiture. Ordinarily, the shares are subject to forfeiture by the employee if employment is terminated within some specified number of years from the date of grant. The employee usually is not free to sell the shares during the restriction period and a statement to that effect often is inscribed on the stock certificates. These restrictions give the employee incentive to remain with the company until rights to the shares vest. Graphic 19–1 describes the restricted award plan for the **Sears Holdings Corporation.**

GRAPHIC 19–1
Restricted Stock Award Plan—Sears Holdings
Real World Financials

Stock-based Compensation (in part)

The Company has granted restricted stock awards to certain associates. These restricted stock awards typically vest in full three years from the date of grant, provided the grantee remains employed by the Company as of the vesting date. The fair value of these awards is equal to the market price of the Company's common stock on the date of grant.

FINANCIAL Reporting Case

Q2, p. 1001

The compensation associated with a share of restricted stock (or nonvested stock) is the market price at the grant date of an unrestricted share of the same stock. This amount is accrued as compensation expense over the service period for which participants receive the shares, usually from the date of grant to when restrictions are lifted (the vesting date).[1] This is demonstrated in Illustration 19–1.

Once the shares vest and the restrictions are lifted, paid-in capital—restricted stock is replaced by common stock and paid-in capital—excess of par.

The amount of the compensation is measured at the date of grant—at the market price on that date. Any market price changes that might occur after that don't affect the total compensation.

[1]Restricted stock plans usually are designed to comply with Tax Code Section 83 to allow employee compensation to be nontaxable to the employee until the year the shares become substantially vested, which is when the restrictions are lifted. Likewise, the employer gets no tax deduction until the compensation becomes taxable to the employee.

ILLUSTRATION 19–1
Restricted Stock Award Plan

Under its restricted stock award plan, Universal Communications grants five million of its $1 par common shares to certain key executives at January 1, 2009. The shares are subject to forfeiture if employment is terminated within four years. Shares have a current market price of $12 per share.

January 1, 2009
No entry

Calculate total compensation expense:

$12	Fair value per share
× 5 million	Shares awarded
= $60 million	Total compensation

The total compensation is the market value of the shares ($12) times five million shares.

The total compensation is to be allocated to expense over the four-year service (vesting) period: 2009–2012

$60 million ÷ 4 years = $15 million per year

The $60 million is accrued to compensation expense over the four-year service period.

December 31, 2009, 2010, 2011, 2012	($ in millions)	
Compensation expense ($60 million ÷ 4 years)	15	
Paid-in capital—restricted stock		15
December 31, 2012		
Paid-in capital—restricted stock (5 million shares at $12)	60	
Common stock (5 million shares at $1 par)		5
Paid-in capital—excess of par (difference)		55

When restrictions are lifted, paid-in capital—restricted stock, is replaced by common stock and paid-in capital—excess of par.

ADDITIONAL CONSIDERATION

An alternative way of accomplishing the same result is to debit deferred compensation for the full value of the restricted shares ($60 million in the illustration) on the date they are granted:

Deferred compensation (5 million shares at $12)	60	
Common stock (5 million shares at $1 par)		5
Paid-in capital—excess of par (difference)		55

If so, deferred compensation is reported as a reduction in shareholders' equity, resulting in a zero net effect on shareholders' equity. Then, deferred compensation is credited when compensation expense is debited over the service period. Just as in Illustration 19–1, the result is an increase in both compensation expense and shareholders' equity each year over the vesting period.

If restricted stock is forfeited because, say, the employee leaves the company, entries previously made related to that specific employee would simply be reversed. This would result in a decrease in compensation expense in the year of forfeiture. The total compensation, adjusted for the forfeited amount, is then allocated over the remaining service period.

Stock Option Plans

● LO2

More commonly, employees aren't actually awarded shares, but rather are given the option to buy shares in the future. In fact, **stock options** have become an integral part of the total compensation package for key officers of most medium and large companies.[2] As with any compensation plan, the accounting objective is to report compensation expense during the period of service for which the compensation is given.

[2]In a recent survey of 600 corporations, 590 companies disclosed the existence of stock option plans (AICPA, *Accounting Trends and Techniques,* 2007).

Expense—The Great Debate

Stock option plans give employees the option to purchase (a) a specified number of shares of the firm's stock, (b) at a specified price, (c) during a specified period of time. One of the most heated controversies in standard-setting history has been the debate over the amount of compensation to be recognized as expense for stock options. At issue is how the value of stock options is measured, which for most options determines whether any expense at all is recognized.

Historically, options have been measured at their **intrinsic values**—the simple difference between the market price of the shares and the option price at which they can be acquired. For instance, an option that permits an employee to buy $25 stock for $10 has an intrinsic value of $15. However, plans in which the exercise price equals the market value of the underlying stock at the date of grant (which describes most executive stock option plans) have no intrinsic value and therefore result in zero compensation when measured this way, even though the fair value of the options can be quite significant. Chief executives of U.S. companies cashed in stock options in 2006 for a median gain of over $3.3 million. In 2006, **Occidental Petroleum**'s CEO, Ray Irani, exercised enough stock options to realize a pretax profit of $270 million from selling shares. To many, it seems counterintuitive to not recognize compensation expense for plans that routinely provide executives with a substantial part of their total compensation.

FINANCIAL Reporting Case

Q3, p. 1001

FAILED ATTEMPT TO REQUIRE EXPENSING. This is where the controversy ensues. In 1993, the FASB issued an Exposure Draft of a new standard that would have required companies to measure options at their *fair values* at the time they are granted and to expense that amount over the appropriate service period. To jump straight to the punch line, the FASB bowed to public pressure and agreed to withdraw the requirement before it became a standard. The FASB consented to encourage, rather than require, that fair value compensation be recognized as expense. Companies were permitted to continue accounting under *APB Opinion 25* (the intrinsic value method referred to in the previous paragraph).[3] Before we discuss the details of accounting for stock options, it's helpful to look back at what led the FASB to first propose fair value accounting and later rescind that proposal.

After lengthy debate, the FASB consented to encourage, rather than require, that the fair value of options be recognized as expense.

As the 1990s began, the public was becoming increasingly aware of the enormity of executive compensation in general and compensation in the form of stock options in particular. The lack of accounting for this compensation was apparent, prompting the SEC to encourage the FASB to move forward on its stock option project. Even Congress got into the fray when, in 1992, a bill was introduced that would require firms to report compensation expense based on the fair value of options. Motivated by this encouragement, the FASB issued its exposure draft in 1993. The real disharmony began then. Opposition to the proposed standard was broad and vehement; and that perhaps is an understatement. Critics based their opposition on one or more of three objections:

1. *Options with no intrinsic value at issue have zero fair value and should not give rise to expense recognition.* The FASB, and even some critics of the proposal, were adamant that options provide valuable compensation at the grant date to recipients.
2. *It is impossible to measure the fair value of the compensation on the grant date.* The FASB argued vigorously that value can be approximated using one of several **option pricing models.** These are statistical models that use computers to incorporate information about a company's stock and the terms of the stock option to estimate the options' fair value. We might say the FASB position is that it's better to be approximately right than precisely wrong.
3. *The proposed standard would have unacceptable economic consequences.* Essentially, this argument asserted that requiring this popular means of compensation to be expensed would cause companies to discontinue the use of options.

There were consistent criticisms of the FASB's requirement to expense option compensation.

The opposition included corporate executives, auditors, members of Congress, and the SEC.[4] Ironically, the very groups that provided the most impetus for the rule change

[3]"Accounting for Stock Issued to Employees," *Opinions of the Accounting Principles Board No. 25* (New York: AICPA, 1972).

[4]All of the "Big Six" CPA firms lobbied against the proposal. Senator Lieberman of Connecticut introduced a bill in Congress that if passed would have forbidden the FASB from passing a requirement to expense option compensation.

initially—the SEC and Congress—were among the most effective detractors in the end. The only group that offered much support at all was the academic community, and that was by-and-large nonvocal support. In reversing its decision, the FASB was not swayed by any of the specific arguments of any opposition group. Dennis Beresford, chair of the FASB at the time, indicated that it was fear of government control of the standard-setting process that prompted the Board to modify its position. The Board remained steadfast that the proposed change was appropriate.

VOLUNTARY EXPENSING. Prior to 2002, only two companies—**Boeing** and **Winn-Dixie**—reported stock option compensation expense at fair value. However, in 2002 public outrage mounted amid high-profile accounting scandals at **Enron, WorldCom, Tyco,** and others. Some degree of consensus emerged that greed on the part of some corporate executives contributed to the fraudulent and misleading financial reporting at the time. In fact, many in the media were pointing to the proliferation of stock options as a primary form of compensation as a culprit in fueling that greed. An episode of the PBS series *Frontline* argued that not expensing the value of stock options contributed to the collapse of Enron. For these reasons, renewed interest surfaced in requiring stock option compensation to be reported in income statements.

FRANK PARTNOY—AUTHOR, INFECTIOUS GREED

. . . the increase in the use of stock options coincided with a massive increase in accounting fraud by corporate executives, who benefited from short-term increases in their stock prices.[5]

CURRENT REQUIREMENT TO EXPENSE. Emerging from the rekindled debate was an FASB Standard that now requires fair value accounting for employee stock options, eliminating altogether the intrinsic value approach.[6] As you might expect, the proposal did not come without opposition. Many of the same groups that successfully blocked the FASB from enacting a similar requirement in 1995 led the opposition. Not surprisingly, at the forefront of the resistance were the high-tech companies that extensively use stock options as a primary form of compensating employees and thus are most susceptible to a reduction in reported earnings when that compensation is included in income statements. For example, consider **Apple Computer**'s earnings for the 12 months ending March 27, 2004. Reported net income of $179 million would have been only $56 million, or 69% less, if the Standard had been in effect then.[7]

An FASB Standard now requires companies to record the value of options in their income statements.

It's important to note that the way we account for stock options has no effect whatsoever on cash flows, only on whether the value of stock options is included among expenses. This is not to say that companies haven't altered their compensation strategies. Already, we have seen a shift in the way some companies compensate their employees. Partly due to the negative connotation that has become associated with executive stock options, we've seen fewer options and more bonuses and restricted stock awards. Let's examine the way stock options are accounted for now.

We've witnessed a discernable shift in the way executives are compensated—fewer options, more stock awards and bonuses.

Recognizing the Fair Value of Options

Accounting for stock options parallels the accounting for restricted stock we discussed in the first part of this chapter. That is, we measure compensation as the fair value of the stock options at the grant date and then record that amount as compensation expense over the service period for which employees receive the options. Estimating the fair value requires the use of one of several option pricing models. These mathematical models assimilate a variety of information about a company's stock and the terms of the stock option to estimate the option's fair value. The model should take into account the:

The fair value of a stock option can be determined by employing a recognized option pricing model.

- Exercise price of the option.
- Expected term of the option.
- Current market price of the stock.

[5]Frank Partnoy, *Infectious Greed: How Deceit and Risk Corrupted the Financial Markets* (New York: Henry Holt/Times Books, Spring 2003), p. 159.

[6]"Share-Based Payment," *Statement of Financial Accounting Standards No. 123 (revised 2004)*, (Norwalk, Conn.: FASB 2004).

[7]Alex Salkever, "What Could Crunch Apple Shares," *BusinessWeek*, July 12, 2004, p. 11.

An option pricing model takes into account several variables.

- Expected dividends.
- Expected risk-free rate of return during the term of the option.
- Expected volatility of the stock.

The techniques for estimating fair value have been among the most controversial issues in the debate.

SFAS No. 123(r) modified the way companies actually measure fair value. It calls for using models that permit greater flexibility in modeling the ways employees are expected to exercise options and their expected employment termination patterns after options vest.[8] Option-pricing theory, on which the pricing models are based, is a topic explored in depth in finance courses and is subject to active empirical investigation and development. A simplified discussion is provided in Appendix 19A.[9]

The total compensation as estimated by the options' fair value is reported as compensation expense over the period of service for which the options are given. Recipients normally are not allowed to exercise their options for a specified number of years. This delay provides added incentive to remain with the company. The time between the date options are granted and the first date they can be exercised is the vesting period and usually is considered to be the service period over which the compensation expense is reported. The process is demonstrated in Illustration 19–2.

ILLUSTRATION 19–2
Stock Options

At January 1, 2009, Universal Communications grants options that permit key executives to acquire 10 million of the company's $1 par common shares within the next eight years, but not before December 31, 2012 (the vesting date). The exercise price is the market price of the shares on the date of grant, $35 per share. The fair value of the options, estimated by an appropriate option pricing model, is $8 per option.

January 1, 2009
No entry

Fair value is estimated at the date of grant.

Calculate total compensation expense:

$ 8	Estimated fair value per option
× 10 million	Options granted
= $80 million	Total compensation

The total compensation is to be allocated to expense over the four-year service (vesting) period: 2009–2010

The value of the award is expensed over the service period for which the compensation is provided.

$80 million ÷ 4 years = $20 million per year

December 31, 2009, 2010, 2011, 2012	($ in millions)	
Compensation expense ($80 million ÷ 4 years)	20	
Paid-in capital—stock options		20

ESTIMATED FORFEITURES. If previous experience indicates that a material number of the options will be forfeited before they vest (due to employee turnover or violation of other terms of the options), we adjust the fair value estimate on the grant date to reflect that expectation. For instance, if a forfeiture rate of 5% is expected, Universal's estimated total compensation would be 95% of $80 million, or $76 million. In that case, the annual compensation expense in Illustration 19–2 would have been $19 million ($76/4) instead of $20 million. We see the effect of that possibility in Illustration 19–2A.

Option compensation expense is based on the number of options expected to vest.

What if that expectation changes later? Universal should adjust the cumulative amount of compensation expense recorded to date in the year the estimate changes.[10] Suppose, for instance, that during 2011, the third year, Universal revises its estimate of forfeitures from 5% to 10%. The new estimate of total compensation would then be $80 million × 90%, or $72 million. For the first three years, the portion of the total compensation that should have been reported would be $72 million × 3/4, or $54 million, and since $38 million ($19 × 2)

When forfeiture estimates change, the cumulative effect on compensation is reflected in current earnings.

[8]"Share-Based Payment," *Statement of Financial Accounting Standards No.123 (revised 2004),* (Norwalk, Conn.: FASB 2004), par. A27-A29.
[9]An expanded discussion is provided in *SFAS No. 123* (revised 2004).
[10]"Share-Based Payment," *Statement of Financial Accounting Standards No.123 (revised 2004),* (Norwalk, Conn.: FASB 2004), par. 43.

	($ in millions)	
2009		
Compensation expense ($80 × 95% ÷ 4)	19	
Paid-in capital—stock options		19
2010		
Compensation expense ($80 × 95% ÷ 4)	19	
Paid-in capital—stock options		19
2011		
Compensation expense [($80 × 90% × 3/4) − ($19 + 19)]	16	
Paid-in capital—stock options		16
2012		
Compensation expense [($80 × 90% × 4/4) − ($19 + 19 + 16)]	18	
Paid-in capital—stock options		18

ILLUSTRATION 19–2A
Estimated Forfeitures

The value of the compensation is estimated to be $76 million, or $19 million per year.

The expense each year is the current estimate of total compensation that should have been recorded to date less the amount already recorded.

of that was recorded in 2009–2010 before the estimate changed, an additional $16 million would now be recorded in 2011. Then if the estimate isn't changed again, the remaining $18 million ($72 − 54) would be recorded in 2012.

ADDITIONAL CONSIDERATION

Notice that the $18 million is the amount that would have been reported in each of the four years if Universal had assumed a 10% forfeiture rate from the beginning. Also be aware that this approach is contrary to the usual way companies account for changes in estimates. For instance, assume a company acquires a four-year depreciable asset having an estimated residual value of 5% of cost. The $76 million depreciable cost would be depreciated straight line at $19 million over the four-year useful life. If the estimated residual value changes after two years to 10%, the new estimated depreciable cost of $72 would be reduced by the $38 million depreciation recorded the first two years, and the remaining $34 million would be depreciated equally, $17 million per year, over the remaining two years.

When Options are Exercised

If half the options in Illustration 19–2 (five million shares) are exercised on July 11, 2015, when the market price is $50 per share, the following journal entry is recorded:

	($ in millions)	
July 11, 2015		
Cash ($35 exercise price × 5 million shares)	175	
Paid-in capital—stock options (½ account balance)	40	
Common stock (5 million shares at $1 par per share)		5
Paid-in capital—excess of par (to balance)		210

Recording the exercise of options is not affected by the market price on the exercise date.

Notice that the market price at exercise is irrelevant. Changes in the market price of underlying shares do not influence the previously measured fair value of options.

When Unexercised Options Expire

If options that have vested expire without being exercised, the following journal entry is made (assuming the remaining 5 million options in our illustration are allowed to expire):

	($ in millions)	
Paid-in capital—stock options (account balance)	40	
Paid-in capital—expiration of stock options		40

***Paid-in capital—stock options* becomes *paid-in capital—expiration of stock options*, when options expire without being exercised.**

In effect, we rename the paid-in capital attributable to the stock option plan. Compensation expense for the four years' service, as of the measurement date, is not affected.

ADDITIONAL CONSIDERATION

Tax Consequences of Stock-Based Compensation Plans

Tax treatment favors the employer in a nonqualified stock option plan.

In Illustration 19–2 we ignored the tax effect. To illustrate the effect of taxes, let's assume Universal Communications' income tax rate is 40%.

For tax purposes, plans can either qualify as "incentive stock option plans" under the Tax Code or be "unqualified plans." Among the requirements of a qualified option plan is that the exercise price be equal to the market price at the grant date. Under a qualified **incentive plan,** the recipient pays no income tax until any shares acquired are subsequently sold. On the other hand, the company gets no tax deduction at all. With a **nonqualified plan** the employee can't delay paying income tax, but the employer is permitted to deduct the difference between the exercise price and the market price at the exercise date. Let's consider both.

Because an incentive plan provides no tax deduction, it has no deferred tax consequences.

Case 1. With an incentive plan, the employer receives no tax deduction at all. If Universal's plan qualifies as an incentive plan, the company will receive no tax deduction upon exercise of the options and thus no tax consequences.

Case 2. On the other hand, if we assume the plan does not qualify as an incentive plan, Universal will deduct from taxable income the difference between the exercise price and the market price at the exercise date. Recall from Chapter 16 that this creates a temporary difference between accounting income (for which compensation expense is recorded currently) and taxable income (for which the tax deduction is taken later upon the exercise of the options). We assume the temporary difference is the cumulative amount expensed for the options. The following entries would be recorded on the dates shown:

A deferred tax asset is recognized now for the future tax savings from the tax deduction when the options are exercised.

December 31, 2009, 2010, 2011, 2012	($ in millions)	
Compensation expense ($80 million ÷ 4 years)	20	
Paid-in capital—stock options		20
Deferred tax asset (40% × $20 million)	8	
Income tax expense		8

The after-tax effect on earnings is thus $12 million each year ($20 – 8).

If all of the options (ten million shares) are exercised on April 4, 2014:

Cash ($35 exercise price × 10 million shares)	350	
Paid-in capital—stock options (account balance)	80	
Common stock (10 million shares at $1 par per share)		10
Paid-in capital—excess of par (to balance)		420

If the eventual tax savings exceed the deferred tax asset, the difference is recognized as equity.

a. Options exercised when the tax benefit *exceeds* the deferred tax asset:
If the market price on April 4, 2014, is $50 per share:

Income taxes payable [($50 – 35) × 10 million shares × 40%]	60	
Deferred tax asset (4 years × $8 million)		32
Paid-in capital—tax effect of stock options (remainder)*		28

b. Options exercised when the tax benefit is *less than* the deferred tax asset:
If the market price on April 4, 2014, is $40 per share:

Income taxes payable [($40 – 35) × 10 million shares × 40%]	20	
Income tax expense or paid-in capital—tax effect of stock options† (remainder)	12	
Deferred tax asset (4 years × $8 million)		32

The tax consequences of all nonqualifying stock options as well as restricted stock plans also are accounted for in the manner demonstrated above.

*This treatment is consistent with a provision of *SFAS 109* (par. 36C) that requires the tax effect of an increase or decrease in equity (paid-in capital—stock options, in this case) be allocated to equity.

†Paid-in capital—tax effect of stock options is debited only if that account has a sufficient credit balance from previous transactions in which the tax benefit exceeded the deferred tax asset.

INTERNATIONAL FINANCIAL REPORTING STANDARDS

Recognition of Deferred Tax Asset for Stock Options. Under U.S. GAAP, a deferred tax asset is created for the cumulative amount of the fair value of the options expensed. Under IFRS, the deferred tax asset isn't created until the award is "in the money"; that is, has intrinsic value.

Plans with Performance or Market Conditions

Stock option (and other share-based) plans often specify a performance condition or a market condition that must be satisfied before employees are allowed the benefits of the award. The objective is to provide employees with additional incentive for managerial achievement. For instance, an option might not be exercisable until a performance target is met. The target could be divisional revenue, earnings per share, sales growth, or rate of return on assets. The possibilities are limitless. On the other hand, the target might be market-related, perhaps a specified stock price or a stock price change exceeding a particular index. The way we account for such plans depends on whether the condition is performance-based or market-based.

The terms of performance options vary with some measure of performance to tie rewards to productivity.

PLANS WITH PERFORMANCE CONDITIONS. Whether we recognize compensation expense for performance-based options depends (a) initially on whether it's probable[11] that the performance target will be met and (b) ultimately on whether the performance target actually is met. Accounting is as described earlier for other stock options. Initial estimates of compensation cost as well as subsequent revisions of that estimate take into account the likelihood of both forfeitures and achieving performance targets. For example, in Illustration 19–2, if the options described also had included a condition that the options would become exercisable only if sales increase by 10% after four years, we would estimate the likelihood of that occurring; specifically, is it probable? Let's say we initially estimate that it is probable that sales will increase by 10% after four years. Then, our initial estimate of the total compensation would have been unchanged at:

If compensation from a stock option depends on meeting a performance target, compensation is recorded only if we feel it's probable the target will be met.

$10 million	×	$8	=	$80 million
Options expected to vest		Fair value		Estimated total compensation

Suppose, though, that after two years, we estimate that it is *not* probable that sales will increase by 10% after four years. Then, our new estimate of the total compensation would change to:

0	×	$8	=	0
Options expected to vest		Fair value		Estimated total compensation

If it later becomes probable that a performance target will *not* be met, we reverse any compensation expense already recorded.

In that case, we would reverse the $40 million expensed in 2009–2010 because no compensation can be recognized for options that don't vest due to performance targets not being met, and that's our expectation.

Conversely, assume that our initial expectation is that it is *not* probable that sales will increase by 10% after four years and so we record no annual compensation expense. But then, in the third year, we estimate that it *is* probable that sales will increase by 10% after four years. At that point, our revised estimate of the total compensation would change to

When we revise our estimate of total compensation because our expectation of probability changes, we record the effect of the change in the current period.

[11]"Probable" means the same as it did in Chapter 13 when we were estimating the likelihood that payment would be made for a loss contingency.

$80 million, and we would reflect the cumulative effect on compensation in 2011 earnings and record compensation thereafter:

2011		
Compensation expense [($80 × ¾) – $0]	60	
Paid-in capital—stock options		60
2012		
Compensation expense [($80 × 4/4) – $60]	20	
Paid-in capital—stock options		20

If we had begun with our new estimate of total compensation, $60 million would have been expensed in the first three years.

PLANS WITH MARKET CONDITIONS. If the award contains a market condition (e.g., a share option with an exercisability requirement based on the stock price reaching a specified level), then no special accounting is required. The fair value estimate of the share option already implicitly reflects market conditions due to the nature of share option pricing models. So, we recognize compensation expense regardless of when, if ever, the market condition is met.

If the target is based on changes in the market rather than on performance, we record compensation as if there were no target.

DECLINE IN POPULARITY OF OPTIONS. Recent years have witnessed a steady shift in the way companies compensate their top executives. In the wake of recent accounting scandals, the image of stock options has been tarnished in the view of many who believe that the potential to garner millions in stock option gains created incentives for executives to boost company stock prices through risky or fraudulent behavior. That image has motivated many firms to move away from stock options in favor of other forms of share-based compensation, particularly restricted stock awards. Also contributing to the rise of restricted stock is the feeling by many that it better aligns pay with performance. As of 2008, the value of restricted stock awards given to top executives had surpassed the value of stock options awarded.

In today's world, stock options are still important, but other equity compensation plans are rapidly assuming greater importance. Companies such as Amazon.com and Microsoft are moving from stock options to restricted stock.[12]

Employee Share Purchase Plans

Share purchase plans permit employees to buy shares directly from the corporation.

● LO3

Employee share purchase plans often permit all employees to buy shares directly from their company at favorable terms. The primary intent of these plans is to encourage employee ownership of the company's shares. Presumably loyalty is enhanced among employee-shareholders. The employee also benefits because, typically, these plans allow employees to buy shares from their employer without brokerage fees and, perhaps, at a slight discount. Some companies even encourage participation by matching or partially matching employee purchases.

As long as (a) substantially all employees can participate, (b) employees have no longer than one month after the price is fixed to decide whether to participate, and (c) the discount is no greater than 5% (or can be justified as reasonable), accounting is straightforward. Simply record the sale of new shares as employees buy shares.

If these criteria for the plan being noncompensatory are not met, say the discount is 15%, accounting is similar to other share-based plans. The 15% discount to employees, then, is considered to be compensation, and that amount is recorded as expense.[13] Compensation expense replaces the cash debit for any employer-paid portion. Say an employee buys shares (no par) under the plan for $850 rather than the current market price of $1,000. The $150 discount is recorded as compensation expense:

Cash (discounted price)	850	
Compensation expense ($1,000 × 15%)	150	
Common stock (market value)		1,000

[12] "Beyond Stock Options," *National Center for Employee Ownership*, 5th ed. (February 2007).

[13] "Share-Based Payment," *Statement of Financial Accounting Standards No.123 (revised 2004)*, (Norwalk, Conn.: FASB 2004), par. 12–13.

DECISION MAKERS' PERSPECTIVE

In several previous chapters, we have revisited the concept of "earnings quality" (as first defined in Chapter 4). We also have noted that one rather common practice that negatively influences earnings quality is earnings management, which refers to companies' use of one or more of several techniques designed to artificially increase (or decrease) earnings. A frequent objective of earnings management is to meet analysts' expectations regarding projections of income. The share-based compensation plans we discuss in this chapter suggest another motive managers sometimes have to manipulate income. If a manager's personal compensation includes company stock, stock options, or other compensation based on the value of the firm's stock, it's not hard to imagine an increased desire to ensure that market expectations are met and that reported earnings have a positive effect on stock prices. In fact, as we discussed earlier, that is precisely the reaction these incentive compensation plans are designed to elicit. Investors and creditors, though, should be alert to indications of attempts to artificially manipulate income and realize that the likelihood of earnings management is probably higher for companies with generous share-based compensation plans.

Analysts should be aware of the possibility of earnings management as a way to increase managers' compensation.

One way managers might manipulate numbers is to low-ball the data that go into the option-pricing models. The models used to estimate fair value are built largely around subjective assumptions. That possibility emphasizes the need for investors to look closely at the assumptions used as reported in the stock option footnote, and particularly at how those assumptions change from year to year.

CONCEPT REVIEW EXERCISE

SHARE-BASED COMPENSATION PLANS

Listed below are transactions dealing with various stock benefit plans of Fortune-Time Corporation during the period 2009–2011. The market price of the stock is $45 at January 1, 2009.

a. On January 1, 2009, the company issued 10 million common shares to divisional managers under its restricted stock award plan. The shares are subject to forfeiture if employment is terminated within three years.
b. On January 1, 2009, the company granted incentive stock options to its senior management exercisable for 1.5 million common shares. The options must be exercised within five years, but not before January 1, 2011. The exercise price of the stock options is equal to the fair value of the common stock on the date the options are granted. An option pricing model estimates the fair value of the options to be $4 per option. All recipients are expected to remain employed through the vesting date.
c. Recorded compensation expense on December 31, 2009.
d. A divisional manager holding 1 million of the restricted shares left the company to become CEO of a competitor on September 15, 2010, before the required service period ended.
e. Recorded compensation expense on December 31, 2010.

Required:
Prepare the journal entries that Fortune-Time recorded for each of these transactions. (Ignore any tax effects.)

SOLUTION

January 1, 2009

Restricted Stock Award Plan
No entry.
Total compensation is measured as 10 million shares × $45 = $450 million

Stock Options
No entry.
Total compensation is measured as 1.5 million shares × $4 = $6 million

December 31, 2009

Restricted Stock	($ in millions)	
Compensation expense ($450 million ÷ 3 years)	150	
Paid-in capital—restricted stock		150

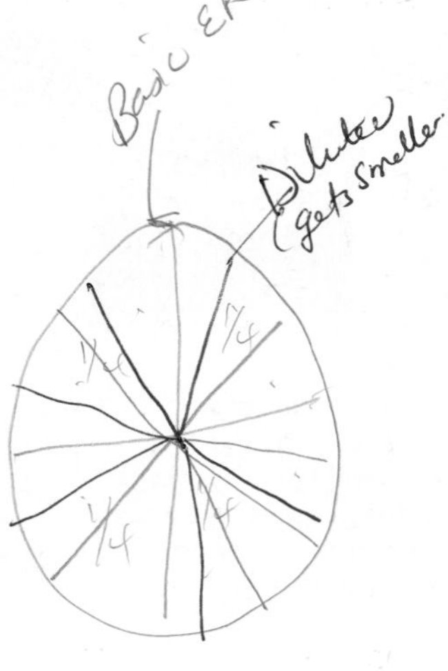

Stock Options		
Compensation expense ($6 million ÷ 2 years)	3	
Paid-in capital—stock options		3
September 15, 2010		
Restricted Stock		
Paid-in capital—restricted stock (10% × $150)	15	
Compensation expense		15
December 31, 2010		
Restricted Stock		
Compensation expense [($450 − .10 × $450 − 150 + 15) ÷ 2 years]	135	
Paid-in capital—restricted stock		135
Stock Options		
Compensation expense ($6 million ÷ 2 years)	3	
Paid-in capital—stock options		3

PART B EARNINGS PER SHARE

Earnings per share is the single accounting number that receives the most media attention.

A typical corporate annual report contains four comparative financial statements, an extensive list of disclosure notes and schedules, and several pages of charts, tables, and textual descriptions. Of these myriad facts and figures, the single accounting number that is reported most frequently in the media and receives by far the most attention by investors and creditors is **earnings per share.** The reasons for the considerable attention paid to earnings per share certainly include the desire to find a way to summarize the performance of business enterprises into a single number.

> Information . . . gains greatly in usefulness if it can be compared with similar information about other enterprises and with similar information about the same enterprise for other time periods.[14]

Summarizing performance in a way that permits comparisons is difficult because the companies that report the numbers are different from one another. And yet, the desire to condense performance to a single number has created a demand for EPS information. The profession has responded with rules designed to maximize the comparability of EPS numbers by minimizing the inconsistencies in their calculation from one company to the next.[15]

Comparability is a qualitative characteristic of relevant accounting information *(Concept Statement 2)*.

Keep in mind as you study the requirements that a primary goal is comparability. As a result, many of the rules devised to achieve consistency are unavoidably arbitrary, meaning that other choices the FASB might have made in many instances would be equally adequate.

INTERNATIONAL FINANCIAL REPORTING STANDARDS

Earnings per Share. The earnings per share requirements used in the United States, *SFAS No. 128*, are a result of the FASB's cooperation with the IASB to narrow the differences between IFRS and U.S. GAAP. A few differences remain. The FASB and the IASB plan to issue an Exposure Draft for public comment in the first quarter of 2008, designed to converge the computations of basic and diluted EPS with IFRS.

IAS No. 33 and *SFAS No. 128* are similar in most respects. The differences that remain are the result of differences in the application of the treasury stock method, the treatment of contracts that may be settled in shares or cash, and contingently issuable shares.

[14] "Qualitative Characteristics of Accounting Information," *FASB Statement of Concepts No. 2*, FASB, 1980, par. 111.

[15] "Earnings per Share," *Statement of Financial Accounting Standards No. 128* (Norwalk, Conn.: FASB, 1977).

Basic Earnings Per Share

A firm is said to have a **simple capital structure** if it has no outstanding securities that could potentially dilute earnings per share. In this context, to dilute means to *reduce* earnings per share. For instance, if a firm has convertible bonds outstanding and those bonds are converted, the resulting increase in common shares could decrease (or dilute) earnings per share. That is, the new shares represented by the bonds might participate in future earnings. So convertible bonds are referred to as **potential common shares.** Other potential common shares are convertible preferred stock, stock options, and contingently issuable shares. We will see how the potentially dilutive effects of these securities are included in the calculation of EPS later in this chapter. Now, though, our focus is on the calculation of EPS for a simple capital structure—when no potential common shares are present. In these cases, the calculation is referred to as **basic EPS,** and is simply earnings available to common shareholders divided by the weighted-average number of common shares outstanding.

A firm has a simple capital structure if it has no *potential* common shares.

● LO4

***Basic EPS* reflects no dilution, only shares now outstanding.**

In the most elemental setting, earnings per share (or net loss per share) is merely a firm's net income (or net loss) divided by the number of shares of common stock outstanding throughout the year. The calculation becomes more demanding (a) when the number of shares has changed during the reporting period, (b) when the earnings available to common shareholders are diminished by dividends to preferred shareholders, or (c) when we attempt to take into account the impending effect of potential common shares (which we do in a later section of the chapter). To illustrate the calculation of EPS in each of its dimensions, we will use only one example in this chapter. We'll start with the most basic situation and then add one new element at a time until we have considered all the principal ways the calculation can be affected. In this way you can see the effect of each component of earnings per share, not just in isolation, but in relation to the effects of other components as well. The basic calculation is shown in Illustration 19–3.

EPS expresses a firm's profitability on a per share basis.

ILLUSTRATION 19–3
Fundamental Calculation

Sovran Financial Corporation reported net income of $154 million in 2009 (tax rate 40%). Its capital structure consisted of:

Common Stock

Jan. 1	60 million common shares outstanding
	(amounts in millions, except per share amount)

Basic EPS:

$$\frac{\text{Net income } \$154}{60 \text{ Shares outstanding}} = \$2.57$$

In the most elemental setting, earnings per share is simply a company's earnings divided by the number of shares outstanding.

Issuance of New Shares

Because the shares discussed in Illustration 19–3 remained unchanged throughout the year, the denominator of the EPS calculation is simply the number of shares outstanding. But if the number of shares has changed, it's necessary to find the weighted average of the shares outstanding during the period the earnings were generated. For instance, if an additional 12 million shares had been issued on March 1 of the year just ended, we calculate the weighted-average number of shares to be 70 million as demonstrated in Illustration 19–4 on the next page.

● LO5

Because the new shares were outstanding only 10 months, or 10/12 of the year, we increase the 60 million shares already outstanding by the additional shares—weighted by the fraction of the year (10/12) they were outstanding. The weighted average is $60 + 12\,(10/12) = 60 + 10 = 70$ million shares. The reason for time-weighting the shares issued is that the resources the stock sale provides the company are available for generating income only after the date the shares are sold. So, weighting is necessary to make the shares in the fraction's denominator consistent with the income in its numerator.

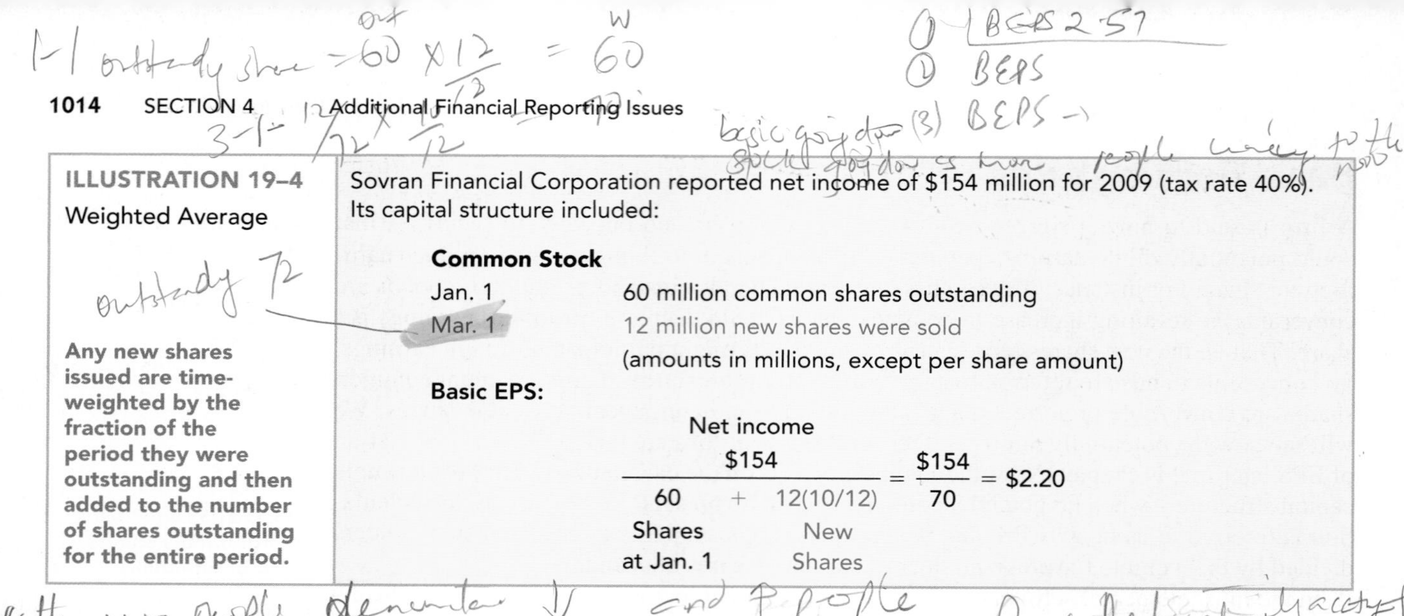

ILLUSTRATION 19–4
Weighted Average

Any new shares issued are time-weighted by the fraction of the period they were outstanding and then added to the number of shares outstanding for the entire period.

Sovran Financial Corporation reported net income of $154 million for 2009 (tax rate 40%). Its capital structure included:

Common Stock

Jan. 1	60 million common shares outstanding
Mar. 1	12 million new shares were sold
	(amounts in millions, except per share amount)

Basic EPS:

$$\frac{\text{Net income } \$154}{\underset{\text{Shares at Jan. 1}}{60} + \underset{\text{New Shares}}{12(10/12)}} = \frac{\$154}{70} = \$2.20$$

Stock Dividends and Stock Splits

● LO6

Recall that a stock dividend or a stock split is a distribution of additional shares to existing shareholders. But there's an important and fundamental difference between the increase in shares caused by a stock dividend and an increase from selling new shares. When new shares are sold, both assets and shareholders' equity are increased by an additional investment in the firm by shareholders. On the other hand, a stock dividend or stock split merely increases the number of shares without affecting the firm's assets. In effect, the same pie is divided into more pieces. The result is a larger number of less valuable shares.[16] This fundamental change in the nature of the shares is reflected in a calculation of EPS by simply increasing the number of shares.

In Illustration 19–5, notice that the additional shares created by the stock dividend are *not* weighted for the time period they were outstanding. Instead, the increase is treated as if it occurred at the beginning of the year.

ILLUSTRATION 19–5
Stock Dividends and Stock Splits

Shares outstanding prior to the stock dividend are retroactively restated to reflect the 10% increase in shares—that is, treated as if the distribution occurred at the beginning of the period.

Sovran Financial Corporation reported net income of $154 million in 2009 (tax rate 40%). Its capital structure included:

Common Stock

Jan. 1	60 million common shares outstanding
Mar. 1	12 million new shares were sold
June 17	A 10% stock dividend was distributed
	(amounts in millions, except per share amount)

Basic EPS:

$$\frac{\text{Net income } \$154}{\underset{\text{Shares at Jan. 1}}{60}\ (1.10) + \underset{\text{New Shares}}{12(10/12)}\ (1.10)} = \frac{\$154}{77} = \$2.00$$

(1.10) — Stock dividend adjustment

The number of shares outstanding after a 10% stock dividend is 1.10 times higher than before. This multiple is applied to both the beginning shares and the new shares sold before the stock distribution. If this had been a 25% stock dividend, the multiple would have been 1.25; a 2-for-1 stock split means a multiple of 2; and so on.

Notice that EPS without the 10% stock dividend ($2.20) is 10% more than it is with the stock distribution ($2). This is caused by the increase in the number of shares. But, unlike

[16]For a more complete discussion of why the market price per share declines in proportion to the increase in the number of shares, see Chapter 18.

a sale of new shares, this should not be interpreted as a "dilution" of earnings per share. Shareholders' interests in their company's earnings have not been diluted. Instead, each shareholder's interest is represented by more—though less valuable—shares.

A simplistic but convenient way to view the effect is to think of the predistribution shares as having been "blue." After the stock dividend, the more valuable "blue" shares are gone, replaced by a larger number of, let's say, "green" shares. From now on, we compute the earnings per "green" share, whereas we previously calculated earnings per "blue" share. We restate the number of shares retroactively to reflect the stock dividend, as if the shares always had been "green." After all, our intent is to let the calculation reflect the fundamental change in the nature of the shares.

ADDITIONAL CONSIDERATION

When last year's EPS is reported again for comparison purposes in the current year's comparative income statements, it too should reflect the increased shares from the stock dividend. For instance, suppose last year's EPS were $2.09: $115 million net income divided by 55 million weighted-average shares. When reported again for comparison purposes in the 2009 comparative income statements, that figure would be restated to reflect the 10% stock dividend [$115 ÷ (55 × 1.10) = $1.90]:

Earnings per Share:	2009	2008
	$2.00	$1.90

The EPS numbers now are comparable—both reflect the stock dividend. Otherwise we would be comparing earnings per "green" share with earnings per "blue" share; this way both are earnings per "green" share.

Reacquired Shares

If shares were reacquired during the period (either retired or as treasury stock), the weighted-average number of shares is reduced. The number of reacquired shares is time-weighted for the *fraction of the year they were **not** outstanding,* prior to being *subtracted* from the number of shares outstanding during the period. Let's modify our continuing illustration to assume 8 million shares were reacquired on October 1 as treasury stock (Illustration 19–6).

ILLUSTRATION 19–6
Reacquired Shares

Sovran Financial Corporation reported net income of $154 million in 2009 (tax rate 40%). Its capital structure included:

Common Stock

Jan. 1	60 million common shares outstanding
Mar. 1	12 million new shares were sold
June 17	A 10% stock dividend was distributed
Oct. 1	8 million shares were reacquired as treasury stock

(amounts in millions, except per share amounts)

Basic EPS:

Net income

$$\frac{\$154}{60\ (1.10) + 12(10/12)\ (1.10) - 8(3/12)} = \frac{\$154}{75} = \$2.05$$

60 = Shares at Jan. 1; 12(10/12) = New Shares; 8(3/12) = Treasury shares; (1.10) = Stock dividend adjustment*

The 8 million shares reacquired as treasury stock are weighted by (3/12) to reflect the fact they were not outstanding the last three months of the year.

*Not necessary for the treasury shares since they were reacquired after the stock dividend and thus already reflect the adjustment (that is, the shares repurchased are 8 million "new green" shares).

The adjustment for reacquired shares is the same as for new shares sold except the shares are deducted rather than added.

Any sales or purchases of shares that occurred before, but not after, a stock dividend or split are affected by the distribution.

Compare the adjustment for treasury shares with the adjustment for new shares sold. Each is time-weighted for the fraction of the year the shares were or were not outstanding. But also notice two differences. The new shares are added, while the reacquired shares are subtracted. The second difference is that the reacquired shares are not multiplied by 1.10 to adjust for the 10% stock dividend. The reason is the shares were repurchased after the June 17 stock dividend; the reacquired shares are 8 million of the new post-distribution shares. (To use our earlier representation, these are 8 million "green" shares.) To generalize, when a stock distribution occurred during the reporting period, any sales or purchases of shares that occurred *before* the distribution are increased by the distribution. But the stock distribution does not increase the number of shares sold or purchased, if any, *after* the distribution.

Earnings Available to Common Shareholders

● LO7

The denominator in an EPS calculation is the weighted-average number of common shares outstanding. Logically, the numerator should similarly represent earnings available to common shareholders. This was automatic in our illustrations to this point because the only shares outstanding were common shares. But when a senior class of shareholders (like preferred shareholders) is entitled to a specified allocation of earnings (like preferred dividends), those amounts are subtracted from earnings before calculating earnings per share.[17] This is demonstrated in Illustration 19–7.

ILLUSTRATION 19–7
Preferred Dividends

Sovran Financial Corporation reported net income of $154 million in 2009 (tax rate 40%). Its capital structure included:

Common Stock

January 1	60 million common shares outstanding
March 1	12 million new shares were sold
June 17	A 10% stock dividend was distributed
October 1	8 million shares were reacquired as treasury stock

Preferred Stock, Nonconvertible

January 1–December 31	5 million 8%, $10 par, shares

(amounts in millions, except per share amount)

Basic EPS:

Net income — Preferred dividends

$$\frac{\$154 \quad -\$4^{*}}{60\,(1.10) + 12(10/12)\,(1.10) - 8(3/12)} = \frac{\$150}{75} = \$2.00$$

60 (1.10): Shares at Jan. 1; 12(10/12) (1.10): New Shares; 8(3/12): Treasury shares. (1.10): Stock dividend adjustment*

Preferred dividends are subtracted from net income so that "earnings available to common shareholders" is divided by the weighted-average number of common shares.

*8% × $10 par × 5 million shares.

Preferred dividends reduce earnings available to common shareholders unless the preferred stock is noncumulative and no dividends were declared that year.

Suppose no dividends were declared for the year. Should we adjust for preferred dividends? Yes, if the preferred stock is cumulative—and most preferred stock is. This means that when dividends are not declared, the unpaid dividends accumulate to be paid in a future year when (if) dividends are subsequently declared. Obviously, the presumption is that, although the year's dividend preference isn't distributed this year, it eventually will be paid.

We have encountered no potential common shares to this point in our continuing illustration. As a result, we have what is referred to as a simple capital structure. (Although, at this point, you may question this label.) For a simple capital structure, a single presentation of basic earnings per common share is appropriate. We turn our attention now to situations described as complex capital structures. In these situations, two separate presentations are required: basic EPS and diluted EPS.

[17]You learned in Chapter 18 that when dividends are declared, preferred shareholders have a preference (over common shareholders) to a specified amount.

Diluted Earnings Per Share

Potential Common Shares

Imagine a situation in which convertible bonds are outstanding that will significantly increase the number of common shares if bondholders exercise their options to exchange their bonds for shares of common stock. Should these be ignored when earnings per share is calculated? After all, they haven't been converted as yet, so to assume an increase in shares for a conversion that may never occur might mislead investors and creditors. On the other hand, if conversion is imminent, not taking into account the dilutive effect of the share increase might mislead investors and creditors. The profession's solution to the dilemma is to calculate earnings per share twice.

Securities like these convertible bonds, while not being common stock, may become common stock through their exercise or conversion. Therefore, they may dilute (reduce) earnings per share and are called **potential common shares.** A firm is said to have a **complex capital structure** if potential common shares are outstanding. Besides convertible bonds, other potential common shares are convertible preferred stock, stock options, rights, or warrants, and contingently issuable securities. (We'll discuss each of these shortly.) A firm with a complex capital structure reports two EPS calculations. **Basic EPS** ignores the dilutive effect of such securities, **diluted EPS** incorporates the dilutive effect of all potential common shares.

In a complex capital structure, a second EPS computation takes into account the assumed effect of *potential common shares*, essentially a "worst case scenario."

Options, Rights, and Warrants

LO8

Stock options, stock rights, and stock warrants are similar. Each gives its holders the right to exercise their option to purchase common stock, usually at a specified exercise price. The dilution that would result from their exercise should be reflected in the calculation of diluted EPS, but not basic EPS.

To include the dilutive effect of a security means to calculate EPS *as if* the potential increase in shares already has occurred (even though it hasn't yet). So, for a stock option (or right, or warrant), we pretend the option has been exercised. In fact, we assume the options were exercised at the beginning of the reporting period, or when the options were issued if that's later. We then assume the cash proceeds from selling the new shares at the exercise price are used to buy back as many shares as possible at the shares' average market price during the year. This is demonstrated in Illustration 19–8 on the next page.

Stock options are assumed to have been exercised when calculating diluted EPS.

When we simulate the exercise of the stock options, we calculate EPS as if 15 million shares were sold at the beginning of the year. This obviously increases the number of shares in the denominator by 15 million shares. But it is insufficient to simply add the additional shares without considering the accompanying consequences. Remember, if this hypothetical scenario had occurred, the company would have had \$300 million cash proceeds from the exercise of the options (15 million shares × \$20 exercise price per share). What would have been the effect on earnings per share? This depends on what the company would have done with the \$300 million cash proceeds. Would the proceeds have been used to buy more equipment? Increase the sales force? Expand facilities? Pay dividends?

FINANCIAL Reporting Case

Q4, p. 1001

Obviously, there are literally hundreds of choices, and it's unlikely that any two firms would spend the \$300 million exactly the same way. But remember, our objective is to create some degree of uniformity in the way firms determine earnings per share so the resulting numbers are comparable. So, standard-setters decided on a single assumption for all firms to provide some degree of comparability.

For diluted EPS, we assume the proceeds from exercise of the options were used to reacquire shares as treasury stock at the average market price of the common stock during the reporting period. Consequently, the weighted-average number of shares is increased by the difference between the shares assumed issued and those assumed reacquired—in our illustration: 15 million shares issued minus 12 million shares reacquired (\$300 million ÷ \$25 per share) equals 3 million net increase in shares.

The way we take into account the dilutive effect of stock options is called the *treasury stock method* because of our assumption that treasury shares are purchased with the cash proceeds of the exercise of the options. Besides providing comparability, this assumption actually is plausible because, if the options were exercised, more shares would be needed to issue to option-holders. And, as discussed in the previous chapter, many firms routinely buy back shares either to issue to option-holders or, equivalently, to offset the issuance of new shares.

ILLUSTRATION 19–8
Stock Options

Sovran Financial Corporation reported net income of $154 million in 2009 (tax rate 40%). Its capital structure included:

Common Stock

Jan. 1	60 million common shares outstanding
Mar. 1	12 million new shares were sold
June 17	A 10% stock dividend was distributed
Oct. 1	8 million shares were reacquired as treasury stock

(The average market price of the common shares during 2009 was $25 per share.)

Preferred Stock, Nonconvertible

January 1–December 31 5 million 8%, $10 par, shares

Incentive Stock Options

Executive stock options granted in 2004, exercisable after 2008 for 15 million common shares* at an exercise price of $20 per share

(amounts in millions, except per share amounts)

Stock options give their holders (company executives in this case) the right to purchase common stock at a specified exercise price ($20 in this case).

The stock options do not affect the calculation of basic EPS.

Basic EPS (unchanged)

$$\frac{\overset{\text{Net income}}{\$154} \qquad \overset{\text{Preferred dividends}}{-\$4}}{60\ (1.10) + 12\ (10/12)\ (1.10) - 8\ (3/12)} = \frac{\$150}{75} = \$2$$

Shares at Jan. 1 — New Shares — Treasury shares — Stock dividend adjustment

The calculation of diluted EPS assumes that the shares specified by stock options were issued at the exercise price and that the proceeds were used to buy back (as treasury stock) as many of those shares as can be purchased at the average market price during the period.

Diluted EPS

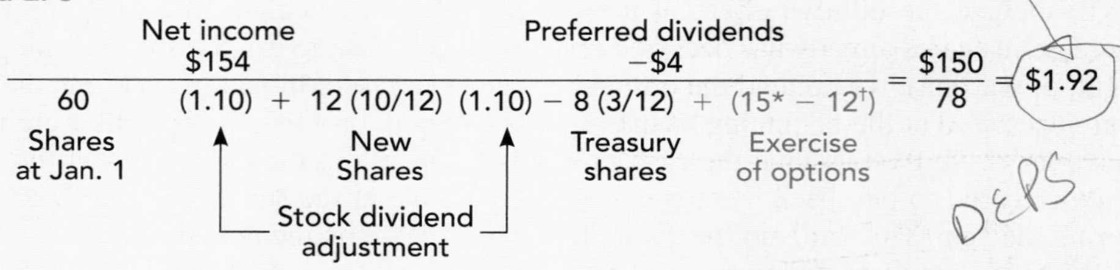

$$\frac{\$154 - \$4}{60\ (1.10) + 12\ (10/12)\ (1.10) - 8\ (3/12) + (15^{*} - 12^{\dagger})} = \frac{\$150}{78} = \$1.92$$

*Adjusted for the stock dividend. Prior to the stock dividend, the options were exercisable for 13 7/11 million of the "old" shares. Upon the stock dividend, the new equivalent of 13 7/11 became 15 million (13 7/11 × 1.10) of the "new" shares.

†Shares Reacquired for Diluted EPS

15 million shares
× $ 20 (exercise price)
$300 million
÷ $ 25 (average market price)
12 million shares reacquired

ADDITIONAL CONSIDERATION

For the treasury stock method, "proceeds" include:

1. **the cash amount, if any, received from the hypothetical exercise of options or vesting of restricted stock,**
2. **the total compensation from the award that's not yet expensed, and**

The proceeds for the calculation should include the amount received from the hypothetical exercise of the options ($300 million in our illustration), the first of three possible components.

The second component of the proceeds is the total compensation from the award that's not yet expensed. If the fair value of an option had been $4 at the grant date, the total compensation would have been 15 million shares times $4, or $60 million. In our illustration, though, we assumed the options were fully vested before 2009, so all $60 million already had been expensed so this second component of the proceeds was zero. If the options had been only half vested, half the compensation would not yet have been expensed and $30 million would have been added to the $300 million cash proceeds.

The third potential component of the proceeds is what's called the "excess tax benefit." We expense the fair value of stock options at the date of grant. If the options were nonqualified options, rather than incentive stock options, the corporation receives a tax deduction at exercise equal to the difference between the stock's market value and its exercise price. That amount usually is higher than the fair value at the grant date, and the difference times the tax rate is the excess tax benefit. In our illustration, though, we assumed the options were incentive stock options, hence no tax benefit. Had they been nonqualified options, the proceeds also would have included a $6 million excess tax benefit:

$25	average market price during 2009 (and price at hypothetical exercise)
(20)	exercise price
$ 5	tax deduction at hypothetical exercise
(4)	fair value at grant date (and amount expensed over the vesting period)
$ 1	excess tax deduction per option
× 15	million options
$15	million excess tax deduction
× 40%	tax rate
$ 6	million excess tax benefit[18]

3. the difference between the eventual tax benefit and the amount recognized in expense.

Why do the proceeds include these three components? We might think of it like this. The "proceeds" include everything the firm will receive from the award: (1) cash, if any, at exercise; (2) services from the recipient (value of award given as compensation); and (3) tax savings. The reason we *exclude the expensed portion* of the compensation is that, when it's expensed, earnings are reduced, and that dilution is reflected in EPS. Excluding that expensed portion from the proceeds avoids the additional dilution that would occur if more proceeds are available in our hypothetical buy back of shares. Hence, we avoid double-counting the dilutive effect of the compensation.

Restricted Stock Awards in EPS Calculations. As we discussed earlier, restricted stock awards are quickly replacing stock options as the share-based compensation plan of choice. Like stock options, they represent potential common shares and their dilutive effect is included in diluted EPS. In fact, they too are included using the treasury stock method. That is, the shares are added to the denominator and then reduced by the number of shares that can be bought back with the "proceeds" at the average market price of the company's stock during the year. Unlike stock options, though, the first component of the proceeds usually is absent; executives don't pay cash to acquire their shares.

Also, only *unvested* shares are included in hypothetical EPS calculations; fully vested shares are actually outstanding. The proceeds for the EPS calculation include the total compensation from the *unvested* stock award that's not yet expensed, the second component. For an example, refer back to the restricted stock in Illustration 19–1 on page xxx. The total compensation for the award is $60 million ($12 market price per share × 5 million shares). Because the stock award vests over four years, it is expensed as $15 million each year for four years. At the end of 2009, the first year, $45 million remains unexpensed, so $45 million would be the assumed proceeds in an EPS calculation.[19] If we assume the market price remains at $12, the $45 million will buy back 3.75 million shares and we would add to the denominator of diluted EPS 1.25 million common shares:

No adjustment to the numerator
5 million − 3.75* million = **1.25 million**

***Assumed purchase of treasury shares**

$45	million
÷ $12	(average market price)
3.75 million shares	

At the end of 2010, the *second* year, $30 million remains unexpensed, so assuming the average market price again is $12, we would add to the denominator of diluted EPS 2.5 million common shares:

No adjustment to the numerator
5 million − 2.5* million = **2.5 million**

***Assumed purchase of treasury shares**

$30	million
÷ $12	(average market price)
2.5 million shares	

[18] Journal entries for the tax benefit are described in the Additional Consideration on p. 1008.

[19] *SFAS No. 123(r)* also requires the proceeds to be increased (or decreased) by any tax benefits that would be added to (or deducted from) paid-in capital when the eventual tax deduction differs from the amount expensed as described for the stock options above and in the Additional Consideration on p. xxx. Since that occurs when the stock price at vesting differs from the stock price at the grant date, our assumption above that the market price remained at $12 avoided that complexity.

LO9

Convertible Securities

Sometimes corporations include a conversion feature as part of a bond offering, a note payable, or an issue of preferred stock. Convertible securities can be converted into (exchanged for) shares of stock at the option of the holder of the security. For that reason, convertible securities are potentially dilutive. EPS will be affected if and when such securities are converted and new shares of common stock are issued. In the previous section you learned that the potentially dilutive effect of stock options is reflected in diluted EPS calculations by assuming the options were exercised. Similarly, the potentially dilutive effect of convertible securities is reflected in diluted EPS calculations by assuming they were converted.

When we assume conversion, the denominator of the EPS fraction is increased by the additional common shares that would have been issued upon conversion.

By the *if converted method* as it's called, we assume the conversion into common stock occurred at the beginning of the period (or at the time the convertible security is issued, if that's later). We increase the denominator of the EPS fraction by the additional common shares that would have been issued upon conversion. We increase the numerator by the interest (after-tax) on bonds or other debt or preferred dividends that would have been avoided if the convertible securities had not been outstanding due to having been converted.

The numerator is increased by the after-tax interest that would have been avoided.

CONVERTIBLE BONDS. Now, let's return to our continuing illustration and modify it to include the existence of convertible bonds (Illustration 19–9). We increase the denominator by the 12 million shares that would have been issued if the bonds had been converted. However, if that hypothetical conversion had occurred, the bonds would not have been outstanding during the year. What effect would the absence of the bonds have had on income? Obviously, the bond interest expense (10% × \$300 million = \$30 million) would have been saved, causing income to be higher. But saving the interest paid would also have meant losing a \$30 million tax deduction on the income tax return. With a 40% tax rate that would mean paying \$12 million more income taxes. So, to reflect in earnings the \$18 million after-tax interest that would have been avoided in the event of conversion, we add back the \$30 million of interest expense, but deduct 40% × \$30 million for the higher tax expense.

ILLUSTRATION 19–9
Convertible Bonds

Sovran Financial Corporation reported net income of \$154 million in 2009 (tax rate 40%). Its capital structure included:

Common Stock

Jan. 1	60 million common shares outstanding
Mar. 1	12 million new shares were sold
June 17	A 10% stock dividend was distributed
Oct. 1	8 million shares were reacquired as treasury stock

(The average market price of the common shares during 2009 was \$25 per share.)

Preferred Stock, Nonconvertible

January 1–December 31 5 million 8%, \$10 par, shares

Incentive Stock Options

Executive stock options granted in 2004, exercisable after 2008 for 15 million common shares* at an exercise price of \$20 per share

Convertible Bonds

10%, \$300 million face amount issued in 2008, convertible into 12 million common shares

(amounts in millions, except per share amounts)

The convertible bonds do not affect the calculation of basic EPS.

Basic EPS (unchanged)

$$\frac{\underset{\text{Net income}}{\$154} \quad \underset{\text{Preferred dividends}}{-\$4}}{\underset{\text{Shares at Jan. 1}}{60}\ (1.10) + \underset{\text{New Shares}}{12\ (10/12)}\ (1.10) - \underset{\text{Treasury shares}}{8\ (3/12)}} = \frac{\$150}{75} = \$2.00$$

(1.10) factors: Stock dividend adjustment

(continued)

Diluted EPS

Net income	Preferred dividends		After-tax interest savings		
$154	−$4		+ $30 − 40% (30)	= $168	= $1.87
60 (1.10) + 12 (10/12) (1.10) − 8 (3/12)		+ (15 − 12)	+12	90	

Shares at Jan. 1 — New Shares — Stock dividend adjustment (applied to shares at Jan. 1 and new shares) — Treasury shares — Exercise of options — Conversion of bonds

ILLUSTRATION 19–9

(concluded)

If the bonds had been converted, 12 million more common shares would have been issued, and net income would have been higher by the interest saved (after tax) from not having the bonds outstanding.

*Adjusted for the stock dividend. For example, prior to the stock dividend, the bonds were exercisable for 10 10/11 million of the "old" shares which became 12 million (10 10/11 × 1.10) of the "new" shares after the stock dividend.

ADDITIONAL CONSIDERATION

The $300 million of convertible bonds in our illustration were issued at face value. Suppose the bonds had been issued for $282 million. In that case, the adjustment to earnings would be modified to include the amortization of the $18 million bond discount. Assuming straight-line amortization and a 10-year maturity, the adjustment to the diluted EPS calculation would have been:

$$\frac{+\,[\$30 + (\$18 \div 10\text{ years})] \times (1 - 40\%)^{*}}{+\,12}$$

to reflect the fact that the interest expense would include the $30 million stated interest plus one-tenth of the bond discount.[†]

*This is an alternative way to represent the after-tax adjustment to interest since subtracting 40% of the interest expense is the same as multiplying interest expense by 60%.

[†]See Chapter 14 if you need to refresh your memory about bond discount amortization.

Our illustration describes the treatment of convertible bonds. The same treatment pertains to other debt that is convertible into common shares such as convertible notes payable. Remember from our discussion of debt in earlier chapters that all debt is similar whether in the form of bonds, notes, or other configurations.

ADDITIONAL CONSIDERATION

Notice that we assumed the bonds were converted at the beginning of the reporting period since they were outstanding all year. However, if the convertible bonds had been issued during the reporting period, we would assume their conversion occurred on the date of issue. It would be illogical to assume they were converted before they were issued. If the convertible bonds in our illustration had been sold on September 1, for instance, the adjustment to the EPS calculation would have been:

$$\frac{+\,[\$30 - 40\%\,(\$30)]\,(4/12)}{+\,12\,(4/12)}$$

to reflect the fact that the after-tax interest savings and the net increase in shares would have been effective for only four months of the year.

This is our approach not just for convertible bonds, but for any potential common shares. For example, we assumed the options in our illustration were exercised at the beginning of the reporting period so the net increase in shares was not weighted for a fraction of the year outstanding. If the options had been granted to company executives on April 1 the adjustment to the weighted-average number of shares would have been:

$$+\,(15 - 12)\,(9/12)$$

to reflect the fact that the net increase in shares would have been effective for only nine months of the year.

We assume convertible securities were converted (or options exercised) at the beginning of the reporting period or at the time the securities are issued, if later.

CONVERTIBLE PREFERRED STOCK. The potentially dilutive effect of convertible preferred stock is reflected in EPS calculations in much the same way as convertible debt. That is, we calculate EPS as if conversion already had occurred. Specifically, we add shares to the denominator of the EPS fraction and add back to earnings available to common shareholders the preferred dividends that would have been avoided if the preferred stock had been converted. In Illustration 19–10 we assume our preferred stock is convertible into 3 million shares of common stock.

ILLUSTRATION 19–10
Convertible Preferred Stock

Sovran Financial Corporation reported net income of $154 million in 2009 (tax rate 40%). Its capital structure included:

Common Stock

Jan. 1	60 million common shares outstanding
Mar. 1	12 million new shares were sold
June 17	A 10% stock dividend was distributed
Oct. 1	8 million shares were reacquired as treasury stock

(The average market price of the common shares during 2009 was $25 per share.)

Preferred Stock, Convertible into 3 million common shares*
January 1–December 31 5 million 8%, $10 par, shares

Incentive Stock Options
Executive stock options granted in 2004, exercisable after 2008 for 15 million common shares* at an exercise price of $20 per share

Convertible Bonds
10%, $300 million face amount issued in 2008, convertible into 12 million common shares

(amounts in millions, except per share amounts)

Basic EPS

Numerator: Net income $154 − Preferred dividends $4

$$\frac{\$154 - \$4}{60\ (1.10) + 12\ (10/12)\ (1.10) - 8\ (3/12)} = \frac{\$150}{75} = \$2.00$$

Denominator: Shares at Jan. 1; New Shares; Treasury shares; (1.10) factors = Stock dividend adjustment

Diluted EPS

Numerator: Net income $154 − Preferred dividends $4 + After-tax interest savings (+$30 − 40% ($30)) + Preferred dividends +$4

$$\frac{\$154 - \$4 + \$30 - 40\%(\$30) + \$4}{60\ (1.10) + 12\ (10/12)(1.10) - 8\ (3/12) + (15 - 12) + 12 + 3^*} = \frac{\$172}{93} = \$1.85$$

Denominator: Shares at Jan. 1; New Shares; Treasury shares; Exercise of options; Conversion of bonds; Conversion of preferred shares; (1.10) factors = Stock dividend adjustment

Since diluted EPS is calculated as if the preferred shares had been converted, there are no dividends. Earnings available to common shareholders is increased by the dividends that otherwise would have been distributed to preferred shareholders.

*Adjusted for the stock dividend. For example, prior to the stock dividend, the preferred shares were convertible into $2\frac{8}{11}$ million of the "old" shares which became 3 million ($2\frac{8}{11} \times 1.10$) of the "new" shares after the stock dividend.

The adjustment for the conversion of the preferred stock is applied only to diluted EPS computations. Basic EPS is unaffected.

However, when diluted EPS is calculated, we hypothetically assume the convertible preferred stock was *not* outstanding. Accordingly, no preferred dividends on these shares would have been paid. So we add back the $4 million preferred dividends in much the same way we added back the interest saved when we assumed convertible bonds were converted. An important difference, though, is that, unlike interest expense, dividends have no tax effect. Dividends are not an expense and no income tax deduction is lost when dividends are not paid. Of course, adding back the preferred dividends that otherwise would have been deducted is equivalent to simply not deducting them in the first place.

Antidilutive Securities

At times, the effect of the conversion or exercise of potential common shares would be to increase, rather than decrease, EPS. These we refer to as **antidilutive securities.** Such securities are ignored when calculating both basic and diluted EPS.

Options, Warrants, Rights

For illustration, recall the way we treated the stock options in our continuing illustration. In applying the treasury stock method, the number of shares assumed repurchased is fewer than the number of shares assumed sold. This is the case any time the buyback (average market) price is higher than the exercise price. Consequently, there will be a net increase in the number of shares, so earnings per share will decline.

On the other hand, when the exercise price is *higher* than the market price, to assume shares are sold at the exercise price and repurchased at the market price would mean buying back *more* shares than were sold. This would produce a net decrease in the number of shares. EPS would increase, not decrease. These would have an antidilutive effect and would not be considered exercised. In fact, a rational investor would not exercise options at an exercise price higher than the current market price anyway. Let's look at the example provided by Illustration 19–11.

Antidilutive securities are ignored when calculating both basic and diluted EPS.

ILLUSTRATION 19–11
Antidilutive Warrants

Sovran Financial Corporation reported net income of $154 million in 2009 (tax rate 40%). Its capital structure included:

Common Stock

Jan. 1	60 million common shares outstanding
Mar. 1	12 million new shares were sold
June 17	A 10% stock dividend was distributed
Oct. 1	8 million shares were reacquired as treasury stock

(The average market price of the common shares during 2009 was $25 per share.)

Preferred Stock, Convertible into 3 million common shares.
January 1–December 31 5 million 8%, $10 par, shares

Incentive Stock Options
Executive stock options granted in 2004, exercisable after 2008 for 15 million common shares* at an exercise price of $20 per share

Convertible Bonds
10%, $300 million face amount issued in 2008, convertible into 12 million common shares

Stock warrants
Warrants granted in 2008, exercisable for 4 million common shares* at an exercise price of $32.50 per share

Calculations:
The calculations of both basic and diluted EPS are unaffected by the warrants because the effect of exercising the warrants would be antidilutive.

The $32.50 exercise price is higher than the market price, $25, so to assume shares are sold at the exercise price and repurchased at the market price would mean reacquiring more shares than were sold.

*Adjusted for the stock dividend. For example, prior to the stock dividend, the warrants were exercisable for $3\frac{7}{11}$ million of the "old" shares which became 4 million ($3\frac{7}{11}$ 1.10) of the "new" shares after the stock dividend.

To assume 4 million shares were sold at the $32.50 exercise price and repurchased at the lower market price ($25) would mean reacquiring 5.2 million shares. That's more shares than were assumed sold. Because the effect would be antidilutive, we would simply ignore the warrants in the calculations.

In our continuing illustration, only the stock warrants were antidilutive. The other potential common shares caused EPS to decline when we considered them exercised or converted. In the case of the executive stock options, it was readily apparent that their effect would be dilutive because the exercise price was less than the market price, indicating that fewer shares could be repurchased (at the average market price) than were assumed issued (at the exercise price).

As a result, the denominator increased. When only the denominator of a fraction increases, the fraction itself decreases. On the other hand, in the case of the warrants, it was apparent that their effect would be antidilutive because the exercise price was higher than the market price, which would have decreased the denominator and therefore increased the fraction.

When a company has a net loss, rather than net income, it reports a loss per share. In that situation, stock options that otherwise are dilutive will be antidilutive. Here's why. Suppose we have a loss per share of $2.00 calculated as ($150 million) ÷ 75 million shares = ($2.00). Now suppose stock options are outstanding that, if exercised, will increase the number of shares by 5 million. If that increase is included in the calculation, the loss per share will be $1.88 calculated as ($150 million) ÷ 80 million shares = ($1.88). The *loss* per share *declines*. This represents an *increase* in performance—not a dilution of performance. The options would be considered antidilutive, then, and not included in the calculation of the net loss per share. Any potential common shares not included in dilutive EPS because they are antidilutive should be revealed in the disclosure notes.

Convertible Securities

For convertible securities, though, it's not immediately obvious whether the effect of their conversion would be dilutive or antidilutive because the assumed conversion would affect both the numerator and the denominator of the EPS fraction. We discovered each was dilutive only after including the effect in the calculation and observing the result—a decline in EPS. But there's an easier way.

To determine whether convertible securities are dilutive and should be included in a diluted EPS calculation, we can compare the "incremental effect" of the conversion (expressed as a fraction) with the EPS fraction before the effect of any convertible security is considered. This, of course is our basic EPS. Recall from Illustration 19–10 that basic EPS is $2.00.

For comparison, we determine the "earnings per incremental share" of the two convertible securities:

The incremental effect (of conversion) of the bonds is the after-tax interest saved divided by the additional common shares from conversion.

Conversion of bonds.

$$\frac{\overset{\text{After-tax interest savings}}{+\$30 - 40\%\ (\$30)}}{\underset{\text{Conversion of bonds}}{+12}} = \frac{\$18}{12} = \$1.50$$

The incremental effect (of conversion) of the preferred stock is the dividends that wouldn't be paid divided by the additional common shares from conversion.

Conversion of preferred stock.

$$\frac{\overset{\text{Preferred dividends}}{+\$4}}{\underset{\text{Conversion of preferred shares}}{+3}} = \$1.33$$

If the incremental effect of a security is *higher* than basic EPS, it is antidilutive. That's not the case in our illustration.

Order of Entry for Multiple Convertible Securities

A convertible security might seem to be dilutive when looked at individually but, in fact, may be antidilutive when included in combination with other convertible securities. This is because the *order of entry* for including their effects in the EPS calculation determines by how much, or even whether, EPS decreases as a result of their assumed conversion. Because our goal is to reveal the maximum potential dilution that might result, theoretically we should calculate diluted EPS using every possible combination of potential common shares to find the combination that yields the lowest EPS. But that's not necessary.

We can use the earnings per incremental share we calculated to determine the sequence of including securities' effects in the calculation. We include the securities in reverse order, beginning with the lowest incremental effect (that is, most dilutive), followed by the next lowest, and so on. This is, in fact, the order in which we included the securities in our continuing illustration.

ADDITIONAL CONSIDERATION

Actually, the order of inclusion made no difference in our example, but would in many instances. For example, suppose the preferred stock had been convertible into 2.1 million shares, rather than 3 million shares. The incremental effect of its conversion would have been:

Conversion of Preferred Stock

$$\frac{\text{Preferred dividends } +\$4}{+2.1 \text{ conversion of preferred shares}} = \$1.90$$

On the surface, the effect would seem to be dilutive because $1.90 is less than $2.00, basic EPS. In fact, if this were the only convertible security, it would be dilutive. But, after the convertible bonds are assumed converted first, then the assumed conversion of the preferred stock would be *antidilutive:*

With Conversion of Bonds

Numerator: Net income $154 − Preferred dividends $4 + After-tax interest savings [$30 − 40% ($30)]

Denominator: 60 (Shares at Jan. 1) (1.10) + 12 (New shares) (10/12) (1.10) [Stock divident adjustment] − 8 (3/12) (Treasury shares) + (15 − 12) (Exercise of options) + 12 (Conversion of bonds)

$$= \frac{\$168}{90} = \$1.867$$

With Conversion of Preferred Stock

Numerator: Net income $154 − Preferred dividends $4 + After-tax interest savings [$30 − 40% ($30)] + Preferred dividends $4

Denominator: 60 (Shares at Jan. 1) (1.10) + 12 (New Shares) (10/12) (1.10) [Stock dividend adjustment] − 8 (3/12) (Treasury shares) + (15 − 12) (Exercise of options) + 12 (Conversion of bonds) + 2.1 (Conversion of preferred shares)

$$= \frac{\$172}{92.1} = \$1.868$$

Although the incremental effect of the convertible preferred stock ($1.90) is lower than basic EPS ($2.00), when included in the calculation after the convertible bonds the effect is antidilutive (EPS increases).

Because the incremental effect of the convertible bonds ($1.50) is lower than the incremental effect of the convertible preferred stock ($1.90), it is included first.

A convertible security might seem to be dilutive when looked at individually but may be antidilutive when included in combination with other convertible securities.

CONCEPT REVIEW EXERCISE

BASIC AND DILUTED EPS

At December 31, 2009, the financial statements of Clevenger Casting Corporation included the following:

Net income for 2009	$500 million
Common stock, $1 par:	
Shares outstanding on January 1	150 million shares
Shares retired for cash on February 1	24 million shares
Shares sold for cash on September 1	18 million shares
2-for-1 split on July 23	
Preferred stock, 10%, $60 par, cumulative, nonconvertible	$ 70 million
Preferred stock, 8%, $50 par, cumulative, convertible into 4 million shares of common stock	$100 million
Incentive stock options outstanding, fully vested, for 4 million shares of common stock; the exercise price is $15	
Bonds payable, 12.5%, convertible into 20 million shares of common stock	$200 million

Additional data:
The market price of the common stock averaged $20 during 2009.
The convertible preferred stock and the bonds payable had been issued at par in 2007. The tax rate for the year was 40%.

Required:
Compute basic and diluted earnings per share for the year ended December 31, 2009.

SOLUTION

(amounts in millions, except per share amounts)

Basic EPS

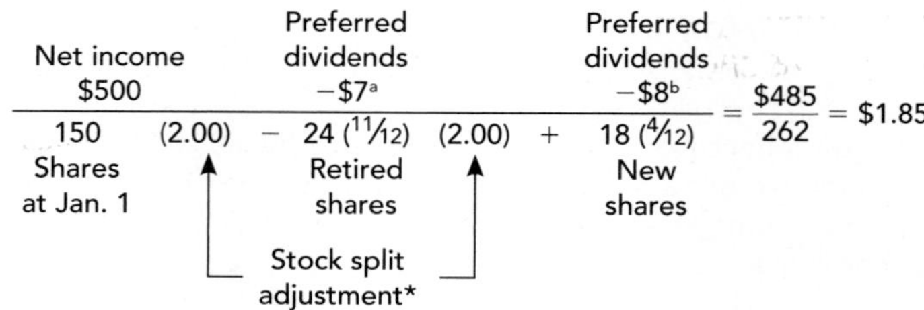

Net income $500
Preferred dividends −$7ᵃ
Preferred dividends −$8ᵇ
150 (2.00) − 24 (11⁄12) (2.00) + 18 (4⁄12)
Shares at Jan. 1
Retired shares
New shares
= $485 / 262 = $1.85
Stock split adjustment*

Diluted EPS

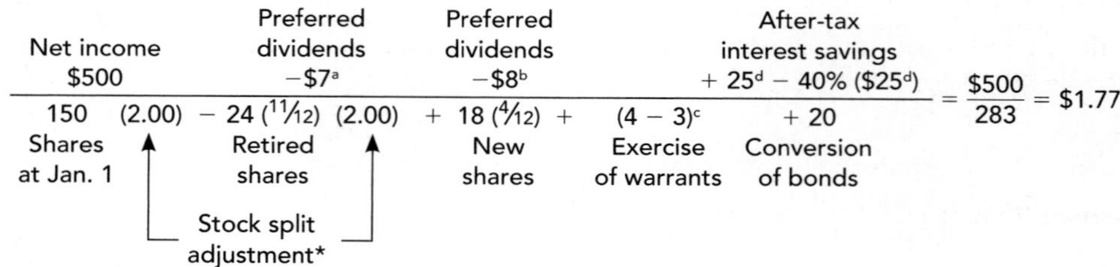

[a]10% × $70 million = $7 million
[b]8% × $100 million = $8 million
[c]**Exercise of warrants:**

4 million shares
× $15 (exercise price)
$60 million
÷ $20 (average market price)
3 million shares

[d]12.5% × $200 million = $25 million

Dilution:

Conversion of Bonds

After-tax interest savings
$$\frac{+\$25 - 40\%(\$25)}{+20} = \$0.75$$
Conversion of bonds

Conversion of 8% Preferred Stock

Preferred dividends
$$\frac{+\$8}{+4} = \$2.00^*$$
Conversion of preferred shares

*Because the incremental effect of conversion of the preferred stock ($2) is higher than EPS without the conversion of the preferred stock, the conversion would be *antidilutive* and is *not* considered in the calculation of diluted EPS.

Additional EPS Issues

Contingently Issuable Shares

LO10

Sometimes an agreement specifies that additional shares of common stock will be issued, contingent on the occurrence of some future circumstance. For instance, in the disclosure note reproduced in Graphic 19–2, **Hunt Manufacturing Co.** reported contingent shares in connection with its acquisition of **Feeny Manufacturing Company.**

At times, contingent shares are issuable to shareholders of an acquired company, certain key executives, or others in the event a certain level of performance is achieved. Contingent performance may be a desired level of income, a target stock price, or some other measurable activity level.

GRAPHIC 19–2

Contingently Issuable Shares—Hunt Manufacturing Company

Real World Financials

Note 12: Acquisitions (in part)

The Company acquired Feeny Manufacturing Company of Muncie, Indiana, for 135,000 shares of restricted common stock with a value of $7.71 per share. Feeny Manufacturing Company is a manufacturer of kitchen storage products. The acquisition was accounted for as a purchase. The purchase agreement calls for the issuance of up to 135,000 additional shares of common stock in the next fiscal year based on the earnings of Feeny Manufacturing Company. . . .

Contingently issuable shares are considered outstanding in the computation of diluted EPS.

When calculating EPS, **contingently issuable shares** are considered to be outstanding in the computation of diluted EPS if the target performance level already is being met (assumed to remain at existing levels until the end of the contingency period). For example, if shares will be issued at a future date if a certain level of income is achieved and that level of income or more was already earned this year, those additional shares are simply added to the denominator of the diluted EPS fraction.[20]

For clarification, refer to our continuing illustration and assume 3 million additional shares will become issuable to certain executives in the following year (2010) if net income that year is $150 million or more. Recall that net income in 2009 was $154 million, so the additional shares would be considered outstanding in the computation of diluted EPS by simply adding 3 million additional shares to the denominator of the EPS fraction. Obviously, the 2010 condition ($150 million net income or more) has not been met yet since it's only year 2009. But because that level of income was achieved in 2009, the presumption is it's likely to be earned in 2010 as well.

Assumed Issuance of Contingently Issuable Shares (diluted EPS):

No adjustment to the numerator
―――――――――――――――――
+3
Additional shares

If a level of income must be attained before the shares will be issued, and income already is that amount or more, the additional shares are simply added to the denominator.

On the other hand, if the target income next year is $160 million, the contingent shares would simply be ignored in our calculation.

Summary of the Effect of Potential Common Shares on Earnings Per Share

You have seen that under certain circumstances, securities that have the potential of reducing earnings per share by becoming common stock are assumed already to have become common stock for the purpose of calculating EPS. The table in Graphic 19–3 summarizes the circumstances under which the dilutive effect of these securities is reflected in the calculation of basic and diluted EPS.

GRAPHIC 19–3

When Potential Common Shares Are Reflected in EPS

	Is the Dilutive Effect Reflected in the Calculation of EPS?*	
Potential Common Shares	**Basic EPS**	**Diluted EPS**
• Stock options (or warrants, rights)	no	yes
• Convertible securities (bonds, notes, preferred stock)	no	yes
• Contingently issuable shares	no	yes†

*The effect is not included for any security if its effect is antidilutive.
†Unless shares are contingent upon some level of performance not yet achieved.

Graphic 19–4 summarizes the specific effects on the diluted EPS fraction when the dilutive effect of a potentially dilutive security is reflected in the calculation.

[20]The shares should be included in both basic and diluted EPS if all conditions have actually been met so that there is no circumstance under which those shares would not be issued. In essence, these are no longer contingent shares.

GRAPHIC 19–4
How Potential Common Shares Are Reflected in a Diluted EPS Calculation

	Modification to the Diluted EPS Fractions:	
Potential Common Shares	**Numerator**	**Denominator**
• Stock options (or warrants, rights)	None	Add the shares that would be created by their exercise,* reduced by shares repurchased at the average share price.
• Convertible bonds (or notes)	Add the interest (after-tax) that would have been avoided if the debt had been converted.	Add shares that would be created by the conversion* of the bonds (or notes).
• Convertible preferred stock	Do not deduct the dividends that would have been avoided if the preferred stock had been converted.	Add shares that would have been created by the conversion* of the preferred stock.
• Contingently issuable shares: Issuable when specified conditions are met, and those conditions currently are being met	None	Add shares that are issuable.
• Contingently issuable shares: Issuable when specified conditions are met, and those conditions are **not** currently being met	None	None

*At the beginning of the year or when potential common shares were issued, whichever is later (time-weight the increase in shares if assumed exercised or converted in midyear).

Actual Conversions

When calculating EPS in our example, we "pretended" the convertible bonds had been converted at the beginning of the year. What if they actually had been converted, let's say on November 1? Interestingly, diluted EPS would be precisely the same. Here's why:

1. The actual conversion would cause an actual increase in shares of 12 million on November 1. These would be time-weighted so the denominator would increase by 12 ($^2/_{12}$) Also, the numerator would be higher because net income actually would be increased by the after-tax interest saved on the bonds for the last two months, [\$30 − 40% (\$30)] × ($^2/_{12}$). Be sure to note that this would not be an adjustment in the EPS calculation. Instead, net income would actually have been higher by [\$30 − 40% (\$30)] × ($^2/_{12}$) = \$3. That is, reported net income would have been \$157 rather than \$154.
2. We would assume conversion for the period before November 1 because they were potentially dilutive during that period. The 12 million shares assumed outstanding from January 1 to November 1 would be time-weighted for that 10-month period: 12 ($^{10}/_{12}$). Also, the numerator would be increased by the after-tax interest assumed saved on the bonds for the first 10 months, [\$30 − 40% (\$30)] × ($^{10}/_{12}$).

Notice that the incremental effect on diluted EPS is the same either way:

EPS would be precisely the same whether convertible securities were actually converted or not.

Not Actually Converted: **Converted on November 1:**

$$\frac{\underset{\text{Assumed after-tax interest savings}}{+\$30 - 40\%(\$30)}}{\underset{\text{Assumed conversion of bonds}}{+12}} = \frac{\underset{\text{Actual after-tax interest savings}}{+[\$30 - 40\%(\$30)] \times (^2/_{12})} - \underset{\text{Assumed after-tax interest savings}}{[\$30 - 40\%(\$30)] \times (^{10}/_{12})}}{\underset{\text{Actual conversion of bonds}}{+12\,(^2/_{12})} \qquad \underset{\text{Assumed conversion of bonds}}{+12\,(^{10}/_{12})}}$$

Graphic 19–5 shows the disclosure note **Clorox Company** reported after the conversion of convertible notes during the year.

GRAPHIC 19–5
Conversion of Notes—The Clorox Company
Real World Financials

Note 1: Significant Accounting Policies—Earnings Per Common Share (in part)
A $9,000,000 note payable to Henkel Corporation was converted into 1,200,000 shares of common stock on August 1. . . . Earnings per common share and weighted-average shares outstanding reflect this conversion as if it were effective during all periods presented.

Financial Statement Presentation of Earnings Per Share Data

● LO11

Recall from Chapter 4 that the income statement sometimes includes items that require separate presentation within the statement as follows:

Income from Continuing Operations
Discontinued operations
Extraordinary items
Net income

When the income statement includes one or more of the separately reported items, EPS data (both basic and diluted) must also be reported separately for income from continuing operations and net income. Per share amounts for discontinued operations and extraordinary items would be disclosed either on the face of the income statement or in the notes to financial statements. Presentation on the face of the income statement is illustrated by the partial income statements of **Newport Corporation** from its 2006 annual report and exhibited in Graphic 19–6.

GRAPHIC 19–6
EPS Disclosure—Newport Corporation
Real World Financials

Consolidated Statements of Operations (partial)

	($ in thousands, except per share data)		
	2006	**2005**	**2004**
Income (loss) from continuing operations	$38,502	$25,714	$(20,413)
Loss from discontinued operations, net of income tax	(1,075)	(16,973)	(61,023)
Extraordinary gain on settlement of litigation	—	2,891	—
Net income (loss)	$37,427	$11,632	$(81,436)
Basic income (loss) per share:			
Income (loss) from continuing operations	$ 0.95	$ 0.62	$ (0.50)
Loss from discontinued operations, net of income tax	(0.03)	(0.41)	(1.49)
Extraordinary gain on settlement of litigation	—	0.07	—
Net income (loss)	$ 0.92	$ 0.28	$ (1.99)
Diluted income (loss) per share:			
Income (loss) from continuing operations	$ 0.91	$ 0.60	$ (0.50)
Loss from discontinued operations, net of income tax	(0.02)	(0.40)	(1.49)
Extraordinary gain on settlement of litigation	—	0.07	—
Net income (loss)	$ 0.89	$ 0.27	$ (1.99)

Basic and diluted EPS data should be reported on the face of the income statement for all reporting periods presented in the comparative statements. Businesses without potential common shares present basic EPS only. Disclosure notes should provide additional disclosures including:

1. A reconciliation of the numerator and denominator used in the basic EPS computations to the numerator and the denominator used in the diluted EPS computations. An example of this is presented in Graphic 19–7 using the situation described in Illustration 19–10.
2. Any adjustments to the numerator for preferred dividends.
3. Any potential common shares that weren't included because they were antidilutive.
4. Any transactions that occurred after the end of the most recent period that would materially affect earnings per share.

GRAPHIC 19–7
Reconciliation of Basic EPS Computations to Diluted EPS Computations

Earnings per Share Reconciliation:

	Income (Numerator)	**Share (Denominator)**	**Per Share Amount**
Net income	$154		
Preferred dividends	(4)		
Basic earnings per share	150	75	$2.00
Stock options	None	3*	
Convertible debt	18	12	
Convertible preferred stock	4	3	
Diluted earnings per share	$172	93	$1.85

Note: Stock warrants to purchase an additional 4 million shares at $32.50 per share were outstanding throughout the year but were not included in diluted EPS because the warrants' exercise price is greater than the average market price of the common shares.
*15 million – [(15 million × $20)/$25] = 3 million net additional shares

ADDITIONAL CONSIDERATION

It is possible that potential common shares would have a dilutive effect on one component of net income but an antidilutive effect on another. When the inclusion of the potential common shares has a dilutive effect on "income from continuing operations," the effect should be included in all calculations of diluted EPS. In other words, the same number of potential common shares used in computing the diluted per-share amount for income from continuing operations is used in computing all other diluted per-share amounts, even when amounts are antidilutive to the individual per-share amounts.

DECISION MAKERS' PERSPECTIVE

We noted at the beginning of the chapter that investors and creditors pay a great deal of attention to earnings per share information. Because of the importance analysts attach to earnings announcements, companies are particularly eager to meet earnings expectations. As we first noted in Chapter 4, this desire has contributed to a relatively recent trend, especially among technology firms, to report **pro forma** earnings per share. What exactly are pro forma earnings? Unfortunately there is no answer to that question. Essentially, pro forma earnings are actual (GAAP) earnings reduced by any expenses the reporting company feels

Make sure you pay lots of attention to the man behind the curtain. If any earnings figure says pro forma, you should immediately look for a footnote or explanation telling you just what is and is not included in the calculation.[21]

[21] Bill Mann, "Qualcomm's Globalstar Headache," *MotleyFool.com*, January 25, 2001.

are unusual and should be excluded. Always, though, the pro forma results of a company look better than the real results. **Broadcom Corporation,** a provider of broadband and network products, reported pro forma *earnings* of $0.49 per share. However on a GAAP basis, it actually had a *loss* of $3.29 per share. This is not an isolated example.

When companies report pro forma results, they argue they are trying to help investors by giving them numbers that more accurately reflect their normal business activities, because they exclude unusual expenses. Analysts should be skeptical, though. Because of the purely discretionary nature of pro forma reporting and several noted instances of abuse, analysts should, at a minimum, find out precisely what expenses are excluded and what the actual GAAP numbers are.

Another way management might enhance the appearance of EPS numbers is by massaging the denominator of the calculation. Reducing the number of shares increases earnings *per share.* Some companies judiciously use share buyback programs to manipulate the number of shares and therefore EPS. There is nothing inherently wrong with share buybacks and, as we noted in Chapter 18, they can benefit shareholders. The motivation for buybacks, though, can sometimes be detected in the year-to-year pattern. A *Fortune* article asserts that, "One way Big Blue has kept the fabulous EPS growth going has been by buying back shares of its own stock. Since 1995, **IBM** has spent a stunning $34.1 billion to shrink shares outstanding. Indeed, $34.1 billion is more than IBM reported in net income ($31.3 billion) over the same period."[22]

One way analysts use EPS data is in connection with the price-earnings ratio. This ratio is simply the market price per share divided by the earnings per share. It measures the market's perception of the quality of a company's earnings by indicating the price multiple the capital market is willing to pay for the company's earnings. Presumably, this ratio reflects the information provided by all financial information in that the market price reflects analysts' perceptions of the company's growth potential, stability, and relative risk. The price-earnings ratio relates these performance measures with the external judgment of the marketplace concerning the value of the firm.

The price-earnings ratio measures the quality of a company's earnings.

The ratio measures the quality of earnings in the sense that it represents the market's expectation of future earnings as indicated by current earnings. Caution is called for in comparing price-earnings ratios. For instance, a ratio might be low, not because earnings expectations are low, but because of abnormally elevated current earnings. On the contrary, the ratio might be high, not because earnings expectations are high, but because the company's current earnings are temporarily depressed. Similarly, an analyst should be alert to differences among accounting methods used to measure earnings from company to company when making comparisons.

Another ratio frequently calculated by shareholders and potential shareholders is the dividend payout ratio. This ratio expresses the percentage of earnings that is distributed to shareholders as dividends. The ratio is calculated by dividing dividends per common share by the earnings per share.

The dividend payout ratio indicates the percentage of earnings that is distributed to shareholders as dividends.

This ratio provides an indication of a firm's reinvestment strategy. A low payout ratio suggests that a company is retaining a large portion of earnings for reinvestment for new facilities and other operating needs. Low payouts often are found in growth industries and high payouts in mature industries. Often, though, the ratio is merely a reflection of managerial strategy concerning the mix of internal versus external financing. The ratio also is considered by investors who, for tax or other reasons, prefer current income over market price appreciation, or vice versa.

CONCEPT REVIEW EXERCISE

ADDITIONAL EPS ISSUES

At December 31, 2009, the financial statements of Bahnson General, Inc., included the following:

Net income for 2009 (including a net-of-tax extraordinary loss of $10 million)	$180 million
Common stock, $1 par:	
Shares outstanding on January 1	44 million

The share price was $25 and $28 at the beginning and end of the year, respectively.

[22]"Bethany McLean, Hocus-Pocus: How IBM Grew 27% a Year," *Fortune,* June 26, 2000.

Additional data:

- At January 1, 2009, \$200 million of 10% convertible notes were outstanding. The notes were converted on April 1 into 16 million shares of common stock.
- An agreement with company executives calls for the issuance of up to 12 million additional shares of common stock in 2010 and 2011 based on the Bahnson's net income in those years. Executives will receive 2 million shares at the end of each of those two years if the company's stock price is at least \$26 and another 4 million shares each year if the stock price is at least \$29.50.

The tax rate is 40%.

Required:

Compute basic and diluted earnings per share for the year ended December 31, 2009.

SOLUTION

(amounts in millions, except per share amounts)

Basic EPS

$$\frac{\underset{\text{Net income}}{\$180}}{\underset{\text{Shares at Jan. 1}}{44} + \underset{\text{Actual conversion of notes}}{16\,(9/12)}} = \frac{\$180}{56} = \$3.21$$

Diluted EPS

$$\frac{\underset{\text{Net income}}{\$180} + \underset{\text{Assumed after-tax interest savings}}{[\$20 - 40\%\,(\$20)] \times (3/12)}}{\underset{\text{Shares at Jan. 1}}{44} + \underset{\text{Actual conversion of notes}}{16\,(9/12)} + \underset{\text{Assumed conversion of notes}}{16\,(3/12)} + \underset{\text{Contingent shares}}{(2 + 2)}} = \frac{\$183}{64} = \$2.86$$

Convertible Notes: Notice that the effect on diluted EPS would be precisely the same whether the convertible notes were actually converted or not.
Converted on April 1:

Converted on April 1:

$$\frac{\underset{\text{Net income including actual after-tax interest savings}}{\$180} + \underset{\text{Assumed after-tax interest savings}}{[\$20 - 40\%\,(\$20)] \times (3/12)}}{\underset{\text{Shares at Jan. 1}}{44} + \underset{\text{Actual conversion of notes}}{16\,(9/12)} + \underset{\text{Assumed conversion of notes}}{16\,(3/12)}} = \frac{\$183}{60}$$

Not Actually Converted:

$$\frac{\underset{\text{Net income without actual after-tax interest savings}}{\$171^*} + \underset{\text{Assumed after-tax interest savings}}{[\$20 - 40\%\,(\$20)]}}{\underset{\text{Shares at Jan. 1}}{44} + \underset{\text{Assumed conversion of notes}}{16}} = \frac{\$183}{60}$$

*$\$180 - \{[\$20 - 40\%\,(\$20)] \times (9/12)\} = \$171$
After-tax interest from Apr. 1 to Dec. 31

Contingently Issuable Shares:

Because the conditions are met for issuing 4 million shares (2 million for each of two years), those shares are simply added to the denominator of diluted EPS. The current share price (\$28) is projected to remain the same throughout the contingency period, so the other 8 million shares (4 million for each of two years) are excluded.

Income Statement Presentation:

To determine the per share amounts for income before extraordinary items, we substitute that amount for net income in the numerator (in this case, that means adding back the $10 million extraordinary loss):

$$\text{Basic: } \frac{\$180 + 10}{56} = \$3.39 \qquad \text{Diluted: } \frac{\$183 + 10}{64} = \$3.02$$

Earnings per Share:	**Basic***	**Diluted**
Income before extraordinary items	$3.39	$3.02
Extraordinary loss	(.18)	(.16)
Net income	$3.21	$2.86

*Only diluted EPS is required on the face of the income statement. Basic EPS is reported in the EPS reconciliation shown in the disclosure note (below).

Disclosure Note:

Earnings per Share Reconciliation:

	Income (Numerator)	**Shares (Denominator)**	**Per Share Amount**
Basic Earnings per Share			
Income before extraordinary items	$190	56	$3.39
Extraordinary loss	(10)	56	(.18)
Net income	$180	56	$3.21
Convertible debt	3	4	
Contingently issuable shares	—	4	
Diluted Earnings per Share			
Income before extraordinary items	$193	64	$3.02
Extraordinary loss	(10)	64	(.16)
Net income	$183	64	$2.86

FINANCIAL REPORTING CASE SOLUTION

1. **How can a compensation package such as this serve as an incentive to Ms. Veres?** *(p. 1002)* Stock-based plans like the restricted stock and stock options that Ms. Veres is receiving are designed to motivate recipients. If the shares awarded are restricted so that Ms. Veres is not free to sell the shares during the restriction period, she has an incentive to remain with the company until rights to the shares vest. Likewise, stock options can be made exercisable only after a specified period of employment. An additional incentive of stock-based plans is that the recipient will be motivated to take actions that will maximize the value of the shares.
2. **Ms. Veres received a "grant of restricted stock." How should NEV account for the grant?** *(p. 1002)* The compensation associated with restricted stock is the market price of unrestricted shares of the same stock. NEV will accrue this amount as compensation expense over the service period from the date of grant to when restrictions are lifted.
3. **Included were stock options to buy more than 800,000 shares. How will the options affect NEV's compensation expense?** *(p. 1004)* Similar to the method used for restricted stock, the value of the options is recorded as compensation over the service period, usually the vesting period.
4. **How will the presence of these and other similar stock options affect NEV's earnings per share?** *(p. 1017)* If outstanding stock options were exercised, the resulting increase in shares would reduce or dilute EPS. If we don't take into account the dilutive effect of the share increase, we might mislead investors and creditors. So, in addition to basic EPS, we also calculate diluted EPS to include the dilutive effect of options and other potential common shares. This means calculating EPS as if the potential increase in shares already has occurred (even though it hasn't yet). ●

THE BOTTOM LINE

- **LO1** We measure the fair value of stock issued in a restricted stock award plan and expense it over the service period, usually from the date of grant to the vesting date. (p. 1002)
- **LO2** Similarly, we estimate the fair value of stock options at the grant date and expense it over the service period, usually from the date of grant to the vesting date. Fair value is estimated at the grant date using an option-pricing model that considers the exercise price and expected term of the option, the current market price of the underlying stock and its expected volatility, expected dividends, and the expected risk-free rate of return. (p. 1003)
- **LO3** Employee share purchase plans allow employees to buy company stock under convenient or favorable terms. Most such plans are considered compensatory and require any discount to be recorded as compensation expense. (p. 1010)
- **LO4** A company has a simple capital structure if it has no outstanding securities that could potentially dilute earnings per share. For such a firm, EPS is simply earnings available to common shareholders divided by the weighted-average number of common shares outstanding. When potential common shares are outstanding, the company is said to have a complex capital structure. In that case, two EPS calculations are reported. Basic EPS assumes no dilution. Diluted EPS assumes maximum potential dilution. (p. 1013)
- **LO5** EPS calculations are based on the weighted-average number of shares outstanding during the period. Any new shares issued during the period are time-weighted by the fraction of the period they were outstanding and then added to the number of shares outstanding for the period. (p. 1013)
- **LO6** For a stock dividend or stock split, shares outstanding prior to the stock distribution are retroactively restated to reflect the increase in shares. When shares are reacquired, as treasury stock or to be retired, they are time-weighted for the fraction of the period they were not outstanding, prior to being subtracted from the number of shares outstanding during the reporting period. (p. 1014)
- **LO7** The numerator in the EPS calculation should reflect earnings available to common shareholders. So, any dividends on preferred stock outstanding should be subtracted from reported net income. This adjustment is made for cumulative preferred stock whether or not dividends are declared that period. (p. 1016)
- **LO8** For diluted EPS, it is assumed that stock options, rights, and warrants are exercised at the beginning of the period (or at the time the options are issued, if later) and the cash proceeds received are used to buy back (as treasury stock) as many of those shares as can be acquired at the average market price during the period. (p. 1017)
- **LO9** To incorporate convertible securities into the calculation of diluted EPS, the conversion is assumed to have occurred at the beginning of the period (or at the time the convertible security is issued, if later). The denominator of the EPS fraction is adjusted for the additional common shares assumed and the numerator is increased by the interest (after-tax) or preferred dividends that would have been avoided in the event of conversion. (p. 1020)
- **LO10** Contingently issuable shares are considered outstanding in the computation of diluted EPS when they will later be issued upon the mere passage of time or because of conditions that currently are met. (p. 1026)
- **LO11** EPS data (both basic and diluted) must be reported for (a) income before any separately reported items, (b) the separately reported items (discontinued operations and extraordinary gains and losses), and (c) net income. Disclosures also should include a reconciliation of the numerator and denominator used in the computations. (p. 1029)

APPENDIX 19A OPTION-PRICING THEORY

Option values have two essential components: (1) intrinsic value and (2) time value.

Intrinsic Value

Intrinsic value is the benefit the holder of an option would realize by exercising the option rather than buying the underlying stock directly. An option that permits an employee to buy $25 stock for $10 has an intrinsic value of $15. An option that has an exercise price equal to or exceeding the market price of the underlying stock has zero intrinsic value.

TIME VALUE

In addition to their intrinsic value, options also have a time value due to the fact that (a) the holder of an option does not have to pay the exercise price until the option is exercised and (b) the market price of the underlying stock may yet rise and create additional intrinsic value. All options have time value so long as time remains before expiration. The longer the time until expiration, other things being equal, the greater the time value. For instance, the option described above with an intrinsic value of $15, might have a fair value of, say, $22 if time still remains until the option expires. The $7 difference represents the time value of the option. Time value can be subdivided into two components: (1) the effects of time value of money and (2) volatility value.

TIME VALUE OF MONEY

The time value of money component arises because the holder of an option does not have to pay the exercise price until the option is exercised. Instead, the holder can invest funds elsewhere while waiting to exercise the option. For measurement purposes, the time value of money component is assumed to be the rate of return available on risk-free U.S. Treasury Securities. The higher the time value of money, the higher the value of being able to delay payment of the exercise price.

An option's value is enhanced by the delay in paying cash for the shares.

When the underlying stock pays no dividends, the time value of money component is the difference between the exercise price (a future amount) and its discounted present value. Let's say the exercise price is $30. If the present value (discounted at the risk-free rate) is $24, the time value of money component is $6. On the other hand, if the stock pays a dividend (or is expected to during the life of the option), the time value of money component is lower. The value of being able to delay payment of the exercise price would be partially off-set by the cost of forgoing the dividend in the meantime. For instance, if the stock underlying the options just described were expected to pay dividends and the discounted present value of the expected dividends were $2, the time value of money component in that example would be reduced from $6 to $4.

The time value of money component is the difference between the exercise price and its discounted present value minus the present value of expected dividends.

VOLATILITY VALUE

The volatility value represents the possibility that the option holder might profit from market price appreciation of the underlying stock while being exposed to the loss of only the value of the option, rather than the full market value of the stock. For example, fair value of an option to buy a share at an exercise price of $30 might be measured as $7. The potential profit from market price appreciation is conceptually unlimited. And yet, the potential loss from the stock's value failing to appreciate is only $7.

A stock's volatility is the amount by which its price has fluctuated previously or is expected to fluctuate in the future. The greater a stock's volatility, the greater the potential profit. It usually is measured as one standard deviation of a statistical distribution. Statistically, if the expected annualized volatility is 25%, the probability is approximately 67% that the stock's year-end price will fall within roughly plus or minus 25% of its beginning-of-year price. Stated differently, the probability is approximately 33% that the year-end stock price will fall outside that range.

Volatility enhances the likelihood of stock price appreciation.

Option-pricing models make assumptions about the likelihood of various future stock prices by making assumptions about the statistical distribution of future stock prices that take into account the expected volatility of the stock price. One popular option pricing model, the Black–Scholes model, for instance, assumes a log-normal distribution. This assumption posits that the stock price is as likely to fall by half as it is to double and that large price movements are less likely than small price movements. The higher a stock's volatility, the higher the probability of large increases or decreases in market price. Because the cost of large decreases is limited to the option's current value, but the profitability from large increases is unlimited, an option on a highly volatile stock has a higher probability of a large profit than does an option on a less volatile stock.

Summary

In summary, the fair value of an option is (a) its intrinsic value plus (b) its time value of money component plus (c) its volatility component. The variables that affect an option's fair value and the effect of each are indicated in Graphic 19A–1.

GRAPHIC 19A–1
Effect of Variables on an Option's Fair Value

All Other Factors Being Equal, If the:	The Option Value Will Be:
Exercise price is higher	Lower
Term of the option is longer	Higher
Market price of the stock is higher	Higher
Dividends are higher	Lower
Risk-free rate of return is higher	Higher
Volatility of the stock is higher	Higher

APPENDIX 19B STOCK APPRECIATION RIGHTS

Stock appreciation rights (SARs) overcome a major disadvantage of stock option plans that require employees to actually buy shares when the options are exercised. Even though the options' exercise price may be significantly lower than the market value of the shares, the employee still must come up with enough cash to take advantage of the bargain. This can be quite a burden if the award is sizable. In a nonqualified stock option plan, income taxes also would have to be paid when the options are exercised.[23]

In an SAR plan, the employer pays compensation equal to the increase in share price from a specified level.

SARs offer a solution. Unlike stock options, these awards enable an employee to benefit by the amount that the market price of the company's stock rises without having to buy shares. Instead, the employee is awarded the share appreciation, which is the amount by which the market price on the exercise date exceeds a prespecified price (usually the market price at the date of grant). For instance, if the share price rises from $35 to $50, the employee receives $15 cash for each SAR held. The share appreciation usually is payable in cash or the recipient has the choice between cash and shares. A plan of this type offered by **IBM** is described in Graphic 19B–1.

GRAPHIC 19B–1
Stock Appreciation Rights—IBM Corporation

Real World Financials

Long-Term Performance Plan (in part)

SARs offer eligible optionees the alternative of electing not to exercise the related stock option, but to receive payment in cash and/or stock, equivalent to the difference between the option price and the average market price of IBM stock on the date of exercising the right.

IS IT DEBT OR IS IT EQUITY?

If an employer can elect to settle in shares of stock rather than cash, the award is considered to be equity.

In some plans, the employer chooses whether to issue shares or cash at exercise. In other plans, the choice belongs to the employee.[24] Who has the choice determines the way it's accounted for. More specifically, the accounting treatment depends on whether the award is considered an equity instrument or a liability. If the employer can elect to settle in shares of stock rather than cash, the award is considered to be equity. On the other hand, if the employee will receive cash or can elect to receive cash, the award is considered to be a liability.

If an employee can elect to receive cash, the award is considered to be a liability.

The distinction between share-based awards that are considered equity and those that are considered liabilities is based on the definition of liabilities in *SFAC No. 6*.[25] That statement classifies an instrument as a liability if it obligates the issuer to transfer its assets to the holder. A stock option is an equity instrument if it requires only the issuance of stock. A cash SAR, on the other hand, requires the transfer of assets, and therefore is a liability. This does not mean that a stock option whose issuer may later choose to settle in cash is not an equity instrument. Instead, cash settlement would be considered equivalent to repurchasing an equity instrument for cash.

[23]The tax treatment of share-based plans is discussed in an earlier Additional Consideration.

[24]Many such plans are called tandem plans and award an employee both a cash SAR and an SAR that calls for settlement in an equivalent amount of shares. The exercise of one cancels the other.

[25]"Elements of Financial Statements," *Statement of Financial Accounting Concepts No. 6* (Stamford, Conn.: FASB 1985).

SARS PAYABLE IN SHARES (EQUITY)

When an SAR is considered to be equity (because the employer can elect to settle in shares of stock rather than cash), we estimate the fair value of the SARs at the grant date and accrue that compensation to expense over the service period. Normally, the fair value of an SAR is the same as the fair value of a stock option with the same terms. The fair value is determined at the grant date and accrued to compensation expense over the service period the same way as for other share-based compensation plans. The total compensation is not revised for subsequent changes in the price of the underlying stock. This is demonstrated in Case 1 of Illustration 19B–1 on the next page.

The cash settlement of an equity award is considered the repurchase of an equity instrument.

SARS PAYABLE IN CASH (LIABILITY)

When an SAR is considered to be a liability (because the employee can elect to receive cash upon settlement), we estimate the fair value of the SARs and recognize that amount as compensation expense over the requisite service period consistent with the way we account for options and other share-based compensation. However, because these plans are considered to be liabilities, it's necessary to periodically re-estimate the fair value in order to continually adjust the liability (and corresponding compensation) until it is paid. Be sure to note that this is consistent with the way we account for other liabilities. Recall from our discussions in Chapter 16, for instance, that when a tax rate change causes a change in the eventual liability for deferred income taxes, we adjust that liability.

Compensation expense reported to date is the estimated total compensation multiplied by the fraction of the service period that has expired.

The periodic expense (and adjustment to the liability) is the fraction of the total compensation earned to date by recipients of the SARs (based on the elapsed fraction of the service period) reduced by any amounts expensed in prior periods. For example, if the fair value of SARs at the end of a period is $8, the total compensation would be $80 million if 10 million SARs are expected to vest. Let's say two years of a four-year service period have elapsed, and $21 million was expensed the first year. Then, compensation expense the second year would be $19 million, calculated as (2/4 of $80 million) minus $21. An example spanning several years is provided in Illustration 19B–1, case 2.

We make up for incorrect previous estimates by adjusting expense in the period the estimate is revised.

Note that the way we treat changes in compensation estimates entails a catch-up adjustment in the period of change, *inconsistent* with the usual treatment of a change in estimate.

Remember that for most changes in estimate, revisions are allocated over remaining periods, rather than all at once in the period of change. The treatment is, however, consistent with the way we treat changes in forfeiture rate estimates as we discussed earlier in the chapter.

The liability continues to be adjusted after the service period if the rights haven't been exercised yet.

December 31, 2013	($ in millions)	
Compensation expense [($5 × 10 million × all) − 21 − 19 − 5 + 2]	7	
Liability—SAR plan		7

Compensation expense and the liability continue to be adjusted until the SARs expire or are exercised.

It's necessary to continue to adjust both compensation expense and the liability until the SARs ultimately either are exercised or lapse.[26] Assume for example that the SARs are exercised on October 11, 2014, when their fair value is $4.50, and executives choose to receive the market price appreciation in cash:

Adjustment continues after the service period if the SARs have not yet been exercised.

October 11, 2014	($ in millions)	
Liability—SAR plan	5	
Compensation expense [($4.50 × 10 million × all) − 50]		5
Liability—SAR plan (balance)	45	
Cash		45

[26]Except that the cumulative compensation expense cannot be negative; that is, the liability cannot be reduced below zero.

ILLUSTRATION 19B–1
Stock Appreciation Rights
Case 1: Equity
Case 2: Liability

At January 1, 2009, Universal Communications issued SARs that, upon exercise, entitle key executives to receive compensation equal in value to the excess of the market price at exercise over the share price at the date of grant. The SARs vest at the end of 2012 (cannot be exercised until then) and expire at the end of 2016. The fair value of the SARs, estimated by an appropriate option pricing model, is $8 per SAR at January 1, 2009. The fair value re-estimated at December 31, 2009, 2010, 2011, 2012, and 2013, is $8.40, $8, $6, $4.30, and $5, respectively.

Case 1: SARs considered to be equity because Universal can elect to settle in shares of Universal stock at exercise

January 1, 2009
No entry
Calculate total compensation expense:

Fair value is estimated at the date of grant.

$ 8	Estimated fair value per SAR
× 10 million	SARs granted
= $80 million	Total compensation

The value of the award is expensed over the service period for which the compensation is provided.

The total compensation is allocated to expense over the four-year service (vesting) period: 2009–2012

$80 million ÷ 4 years = $20 million per year

December 31, 2009, 2010, 2011, 2012	($ in millions)	
Compensation expense ($80 million ÷ 4 years)	20	
Paid-in capital—SAR plan		20

The value of the compensation is estimated each year at the fair value of the SARs.

Case 2: SARs considered to be a liability because employees can elect to receive cash at exercise

January 1, 2009
No entry

The expense each year is the current estimate of total compensation that should have been recorded to date less the amount already recorded.

If the fair value falls below the amount expensed to date, both the liability and expense are reduced.

December 31, 2009	($ in millions)	
Compensation expense ($8.40 × 10 million × 1/4)	21	
Liability—SAR plan		21
December 31, 2010		
Compensation expense [($8 × 10 million × 2/4) – 21]	19	
Liability—SAR plan		19
December 31, 2011		
Compensation expense [($6 × 10 million × 3/4) – 21 – 19]	5	
Liability—SAR plan		5
December 31, 2012		
Liability—SAR plan	2	
Compensation expense [($4.30 × 10 million × 4/4) – 21 – 19 – 5]		2

Let's look at the changes in the liability—SAR plan account during the 2009–2014 period:

The liability is adjusted each period as changes in the fair value estimates cause changes in the liability.

Liability—SAR Plan

			($ in millions)
		21	2009
		19	2010
		5	2011
2012	2		
		7	2013
2014	5		
2014	45		
		0	Balance after exercise

QUESTIONS FOR REVIEW OF KEY TOPICS

Q 19–1 What is restricted stock? Describe how compensation expense is determined and recorded for a restricted stock award plan.

Q 19–2 Stock option plans provide employees the option to purchase: (a) a specified number of shares of the firm's stock, (b) at a specified price, (c) during a specified period of time. One of the most controversial aspects of accounting for stock-based compensation is how the fair value of stock options should be measured. Describe the general approach to measuring fair value.

Q 19–3 The Tax Code differentiates between qualified option plans, including incentive plans, and nonqualified plans. What are the major differences in tax treatment between incentive plans and nonqualified plans?

Q 19–4 The fair value of stock options can be considered to comprise two main components. What are they?

Q 19–5 Stock option (and other share-based) plans often specify a performance condition or a market condition that must be satisfied before employees are allowed the benefits of the award. Describe the general approach we use to account for performance-based options and options with market-related conditions.

Q 19–6 What is a simple capital structure? How is EPS determined for a company with a simple capital structure?

Q 19–7 When calculating the weighted average number of common shares, how are stock dividends and stock splits treated? Compare this treatment with that of additional shares sold for cash in midyear.

Q 19–8 Blake Distributors had 100,000 common shares outstanding at the beginning of the year, January 1. On May 13, Blake distributed a 5% stock dividend. On August 1, 1,200 shares were retired. What is the weighted average number of shares for calculating EPS?

Q 19–9 Why are preferred dividends deducted from net income when calculating EPS? Are there circumstances when this deduction is not made?

Q 19–10 Distinguish between basic and diluted EPS.

Q 19–11 The treasury stock method is used to incorporate the dilutive effect of stock options, stock warrants, and similar securities. Describe this method as it applies to diluted EPS.

Q 19–12 The potentially dilutive effect of convertible securities is reflected in EPS calculations by the if-converted method. Describe this method as it relates to convertible bonds.

Q 19–13 How is the potentially dilutive effect of convertible preferred stock reflected in EPS calculations by the if-converted method? How is this different from the way convertible bonds are considered?

Q 19–14 A convertible security may appear to be dilutive when looked at individually but might be antidilutive when included in combination with other convertible securities. How should the order be determined for inclusion of convertible securities in an EPS calculation to avoid including an antidilutive security?

Q 19–15 Wiseman Electronics has an agreement with certain of its division managers that 50,000 contingently issuable shares will be issued next year in the event operating income exceeds $2.1 million that year. In what way, if any, is the calculation of EPS affected by these contingently issuable shares assuming this year's operating income was $2.2 million? $2.0 million?

Q 19–16 Diluted EPS would be precisely the same whether convertible securities were actually converted or not. Why?

Q 19–17 When the income statement includes one or more of the separately reported items, such as discontinued operations or extraordinary items, which amounts require per share presentation?

Q 19–18 In addition to EPS numbers themselves, what additional disclosures should be provided concerning the EPS information?

Q 19–19 (Based on Appendix B) LTV Corporation grants SARs to key executives. Upon exercise, the SARs entitle executives to receive either cash or stock equal in value to the excess of the market price at exercise over the share price at the date of grant. How should LTV account for the awards?

BRIEF EXERCISES

BE 19–1
Restricted stock award

● LO1

First Link Services granted 8 million of its $1 par common shares to executives, subject to forfeiture if employment is terminated within three years. The common shares have a market price of $6 per share on the grant date. Ignoring taxes, what is the total compensation cost pertaining to the restricted shares? What is the effect on earnings in the year after the shares are granted to executives?

BE 19–2
Stock options

● LO2

Under its executive stock option plan, National Corporation granted options on January 1, 2009, that permit executives to purchase 12 million of the company's $1 par common shares within the next six years, but not before December 31, 2011 (the vesting date). The exercise price is the market price of the shares on the date of grant, $17 per share. The fair value of the options, estimated by an appropriate option pricing model, is $5 per option.

No forfeitures are anticipated. Ignoring taxes, what is the total compensation cost pertaining to the stock options? What is the effect on earnings in the year after the options are granted to executives?

BE 19–3
Stock options; forfeiture
● LO2

Refer to the situation described in BE 19–2. Suppose that unexpected turnover during 2010 caused the forfeiture of 5% of the stock options. Ignoring taxes, what is the effect on earnings in 2010? In 2011?

BE 19–4
Stock options; exercise
● LO2

Refer to the situation described in BE 19–2. Suppose that the options are exercised on April 3, 2012, when the market price is $19 per share. Ignoring taxes, what journal entry will National record?

BE 19–5
Stock options; expiration
● LO2

Refer to the situation described in BE 19–2. Suppose that the options expire without being exercised. Ignoring taxes, what journal entry will National record?

BE 19–6
Performance-based options
● LO2

On October 1, 2009, Farmer Fabrication issued stock options for 100,000 shares to a division manager. The options have an estimated fair value of $6 each. To provide additional incentive for managerial achievement, the options are not exercisable unless divisional revenue increases by 5% in three years. Farmer initially estimates that it is probable the goal will be achieved. How much compensation will be recorded in each of the next three years?

BE 19–7
Performance-based options
● LO2

Refer to the situation described in BE 19–6. Suppose that after one year, Farmer estimates that it is *not* probable that divisional revenue will increase by 5% in three years. What action will be taken to account for the options in 2010?

BE 19–8
Performance-based options
● LO2

Refer to the situation described in BE 19–6. Suppose that Farmer initially estimates that it is *not* probable the goal will be achieved, but then after one year, Farmer estimates that it *is* probable that divisional revenue will increase by 5% by the end of 2011. What action will be taken to account for the options in 2010 and thereafter?

BE 19–9
Options with market-based conditions
● LO2

On October 1, 2009, Farmer Fabrication issued stock options for 100,000 shares to a division manager. The options have an estimated fair value of $6 each. To provide additional incentive for managerial achievement, the options are not exercisable unless Farmer Fabrication's stock price increases by 5% in three years. Farmer initially estimates that it is not probable the goal will be achieved. How much compensation will be recorded in each of the next three years?

BE 19–10
EPS; shares issued, shares retired
● LO5 LO6

McDonnell-Myer Corporation reported net income of $741 million. The company had 544 million common shares outstanding at January 1 and sold 36 million shares on Feb. 28. As part of an annual share repurchase plan, 6 million shares were retired on April 30 for $47 per share. Calculate McDonnell-Myer's earnings per share for the year.

BE 19–11
EPS; nonconvertible preferred shares
● LO7

At December 31, 2008 and 2009, Funk & Noble Corporation had outstanding 820 million shares of common stock and 2 million shares of 8%, $100 par value cumulative preferred stock. No dividends were declared on either the preferred or common stock in 2008 or 2009. Net income for 2009 was $426 million. The income tax rate is 40%. Calculate earnings per share for the year ended December 31, 2009.

BE 19–12
EPS; stock options
● LO8

Fully vested incentive stock options exercisable at $50 per share to obtain 24,000 shares of common stock were outstanding during a period when the average market price of the common stock was $60 and the ending market price was $55. By how many shares will the assumed exercise of these options increase the weighted-average number of shares outstanding when calculating diluted earnings per share?

BE 19–13
EPS; convertible preferred shares
● LO9

Ahnberg Corporation had 800,000 shares of common stock issued and outstanding at January 1. No common shares were issued during the year, but on January 1 Ahnberg issued 100,000 shares of convertible preferred stock. The preferred shares are convertible into 200,000 shares of common stock. During the year Ahnberg paid $60,000 cash dividends on the preferred stock. Net income was $1,500,000. What were Ahnberg's basic and diluted earnings per share for the year?

EXERCISES

available with McGraw-Hill's Homework Manager www.mhhe.com/spiceland5e 

An alternate exercise and problem set is available on the text website: www.mhhe.com/spiceland5e

E 19–1
Restricted stock award plan
● LO1

Allied Paper Products, Inc. offers a restricted stock award plan to its vice presidents. On January 1, 2009, the company granted 16 million of its $1 par common shares, subject to forfeiture if employment is terminated within two years. The common shares have a market price of $5 per share on the grant date.

Required:
1. Determine the total compensation cost pertaining to the restricted shares.
2. Prepare the appropriate journal entries related to the restricted stock through December 31, 2010.

E 19–2
Restricted stock award plan
● LO1

On January 1, 2009, VKI Corporation awarded 12 million of its $1 par common shares to key personnel, subject to forfeiture if employment is terminated within three years. On the grant date, the shares have a market price of $2.50 per share.

Required:
1. Determine the total compensation cost pertaining to the restricted shares.
2. Prepare the appropriate journal entry to record the award of restricted shares on January 1, 2009.
3. Prepare the appropriate journal entry to record compensation expense on December 31, 2009.
4. Prepare the appropriate journal entry to record compensation expense on December 31, 2010.
5. Prepare the appropriate journal entry to record compensation expense on December 31, 2011.
6. Prepare the appropriate journal entry to record the lifting of restrictions on the shares at December 31, 2011.

E 19–3
Restricted stock award; Kmart
● LO1
Real World Financials

Kmart Holding Co. included the following disclosure note in a recent annual report:

RESTRICTED STOCK (in part)

. . . , we issued 111,540 shares of restricted stock at market prices ranging from $23.00 to $29.65. . . . The restricted stock generally vests over three years, during which time we will recognize total compensation expense of approximately $3 million.

Required:
1. Based on the information provided in the disclosure note, determine the weighted average market price of the restricted stock issued.
2. How much compensation expense did Kmart report for the year following the year in which the restricted stock was issued?

E 19–4
Restricted stock award plan; forfeitures anticipated
● LO1

Magnetic-Optical Corporation offers a variety of share-based compensation plans to employees. Under its restricted stock award plan, the company on January 1, 2009, granted 4 million of its $1 par common shares to various division managers. The shares are subject to forfeiture if employment is terminated within three years. The common shares have a market price of $22.50 per share on the grant date.

Required:
1. Determine the total compensation cost pertaining to the restricted shares.
2. Prepare the appropriate journal entry to record the award of restricted shares on January 1, 2009.
3. Prepare the appropriate journal entry to record compensation expense on December 31, 2009.
4. Suppose Magnetic-Optical expected a 10% forfeiture rate on the restricted shares prior to vesting. Determine the total compensation cost, assuming the company chooses to follow the elective fair value approach for fixed compensation plans and chooses to anticipate forfeitures at the grant date.

E 19–5
Stock options
● LO2

American Optical Corporation provides a variety of share-based compensation plans to its employees. Under its executive stock option plan, the company granted options on January 1, 2009, that permit executives to acquire 4 million of the company's $1 par common shares within the next five years, but not before December 31, 2010 (the vesting date). The exercise price is the market price of the shares on the date of grant, $14 per share. The fair value of the 4 million options, estimated by an appropriate option pricing model, is $3 per option. No forfeitures are anticipated. Ignore taxes.

Required:
1. Determine the total compensation cost pertaining to the options.
2. Prepare the appropriate journal entry to record the award of options on January 1, 2009.
3. Prepare the appropriate journal entry to record compensation expense on December 31, 2009.
4. Prepare the appropriate journal entry to record compensation expense on December 31, 2010.

E 19–6
Stock options; forfeiture of options

● LO2

On January 1, 2009, Adams-Meneke Corporation granted 25 million incentive stock options to division managers, each permitting holders to purchase one share of the company's $1 par common shares within the next six years, but not before December 31, 2011 (the vesting date). The exercise price is the market price of the shares on the date of grant, currently $10 per share. The fair value of the options, estimated by an appropriate option pricing model, is $3 per option.

Required:

1. Determine the total compensation cost pertaining to the options on January 1, 2009.
2. Prepare the appropriate journal entry to record compensation expense on December 31, 2009.
3. Unexpected turnover during 2010 caused the forfeiture of 6% of the stock options. Determine the adjusted compensation cost, and prepare the appropriate journal entry(s) on December 31, 2010 and 2011.

E 19–7
Stock options exercise; forfeitures

● LO2

Walters Audio Visual, Inc. offers an incentive stock option plan to its regional managers. On January 1, 2009, options were granted for 40 million $1 par common shares. The exercise price is the market price on the grant date—$8 per share. Options cannot be exercised prior to January 1, 2011, and expire December 31, 2015. The fair value of the 40 million options, estimated by an appropriate option pricing model, is $1 per option.

Required:

1. Determine the total compensation cost pertaining to the incentive stock option plan.
2. Prepare the appropriate journal entry to record compensation expense on December 31, 2009.
3. Prepare the appropriate journal entry to record compensation expense on December 31, 2010.
4. Prepare the appropriate journal entry to record the exercise of 75% of the options on March 12, 2011, when the market price is $9 per share.
5. Prepare the appropriate journal entry on December 31, 2015, when the remaining options that have vested expire without being exercised.

E 19–8
Stock options

● LO2

SSG Cycles manufactures and distributes motorcycle parts and supplies. Employees are offered a variety of share-based compensation plans. Under its nonqualified stock option plan, SSG granted options to key officers on January 1, 2009. The options permit holders to acquire 12 million of the company's $1 par common shares for $11 within the next six years, but not before January 1, 2012 (the vesting date). The market price of the shares on the date of grant is $13 per share. The fair value of the 12 million options, estimated by an appropriate option pricing model, is $3 per option.

Required:

1. Determine the total compensation cost pertaining to the incentive stock option plan.
2. Prepare the appropriate journal entries to record compensation expense on December 31, 2009, 2010, and 2011.
3. Record the exercise of the options if all of the options are exercised on May 11, 2013, when the market price is $14 per share.

E 19–9
Employee share purchase plan

● LO3

In order to encourage employee ownership of the company's $1 par common shares, Washington Distribution permits any of its employees to buy shares directly from the company through payroll deduction. There are no brokerage fees and shares can be purchased at a 15% discount. During March, employees purchased 50,000 shares at a time when the market price of the shares on the New York Stock Exchange was $12 per share.

Required:

Prepare the appropriate journal entry to record the March purchases of shares under the employee share purchase plan.

E 19–10
EPS; shares issued; stock dividend

● LO5 LO6

For the year ended December 31, 2009, Norstar Industries reported net income of $655,000. At January 1, 2009, the company had 900,000 common shares outstanding. The following changes in the number of shares occurred during 2009:

Apr. 30	Sold 60,000 shares in a public offering.
May 24	Declared and distributed a 5% stock dividend.
June 1	Issued 72,000 shares as part of the consideration for the purchase of assets from a subsidiary.

Required:

Compute Norstar's earnings per share for the year ended December 31, 2009.

E 19–11
EPS; stock dividend; nonconvertible preferred stock

● LO5 LO6 LO7

Hardaway Fixtures' balance sheet at December 31, 2008, included the following:

Shares issued and outstanding:	
Common stock, $1 par	$800,000
Nonconvertible preferred stock, $50 par	20,000

On July 21, 2009, Hardaway issued a 25% stock dividend on its common stock. On December 12 it paid $50,000 cash dividends on the preferred stock. Net income for the year ended December 31, 2009, was $2,000,000.

Required:

Compute Hardaway's earnings per share for the year ended December 31, 2009.

E 19–12
EPS; net loss; nonconvertible preferred stock; shares sold
● LO5 LO7

At December 31, 2008, Albrecht Corporation had outstanding 373,000 shares of common stock and 8,000 shares of 9.5%, $100 par value cumulative, nonconvertible preferred stock. On May 31, 2009, Albrecht sold for cash 12,000 shares of its common stock. No cash dividends were declared for 2009. For the year ended December 31, 2009, Albrecht reported a net loss of $114,000.

Required:

Calculate Albrecht's net loss per share for the year ended December 31, 2009.

E 19–13
EPS; treasury stock; new shares; stock dividends; two years
● LO5 LO6

The Alford Group had 202,000 shares of common stock outstanding at January 1, 2009. The following activities affected common shares during the year. There are no potential common shares outstanding.

2009	
Feb. 28	Purchased 6,000 shares of treasury stock.
Oct. 31	Sold the treasury shares purchased on February 28.
Nov. 30	Issued 24,000 new shares.
Dec. 31	Net income for 2009 is $400,000.
2010	
Jan. 15	Declared and issued a 2-for-1 stock split.
Dec. 31	Net income for 2010 is $400,000.

Required:

1. Determine the 2009 EPS.
2. Determine the 2010 EPS.
3. At what amount will the 2009 EPS be presented in the 2010 comparative financial statements?

E 19–14
EPS; stock dividend; nonconvertible preferred stock; treasury shares; shares sold
● LO5 LO6 LO7

On December 31, 2008, Berclair, Inc. had 200 million shares of common stock and 3 million shares of 9%, $100 par value cumulative preferred stock issued and outstanding. On March 1, 2009, Berclair purchased 24 million shares of its common stock as treasury stock. Berclair issued a 5% common stock dividend on July 1, 2009. Four million treasury shares were sold on October 1. Net income for the year ended December 31, 2009, was $150 million.

Required:

Compute Berclair's earnings per share for the year ended December 31, 2009.

E 19–15
EPS; stock dividend; nonconvertible preferred stock; treasury shares; shares sold; stock options
● LO5 through LO8

(Note: This is a variation of the previous exercise, modified to include stock options.) On December 31, 2008, Berclair, Inc. had 200 million shares of common stock and 3 million shares of 9%, $100 par value cumulative preferred stock issued and outstanding. Berclair issued a 5% common stock dividend on July 1, 2009. On March 1, 2009, Berclair purchased 24 million shares of its common stock as treasury stock. Four million treasury shares were sold on October 1. Net income for the year ended December 31, 2009, was $150 million.

Also outstanding at December 31 were incentive stock options granted to key executives on September 13, 2004. The options are exercisable as of September 13, 2008, for 30 million common shares at an exercise price of $56 per share. During 2009, the market price of the common shares averaged $70 per share, peaking at $80 on December 31.

Required:

Compute Berclair's basic and diluted earnings per share for the year ended December 31, 2009.

E 19–16
EPS; stock dividend; nonconvertible preferred stock; treasury shares; shares sold; stock options exercised
● LO5 through LO8

(Note: This is a variation of the previous exercise, modified to include the exercise of stock options.) On December 31, 2008, Berclair, Inc. had 200 million shares of common stock and 3 million shares of 9%, $100 par value cumulative preferred stock issued and outstanding. Berclair issued a 5% common stock dividend on July 1, 2009. On March 1, 2009, Berclair purchased 24 million shares of its common stock as treasury stock. Four million treasury shares were sold on October 1. Net income for the year ended December 31, 2009, was $150 million.

Also outstanding at December 31 were incentive stock options granted to key executives on September 13, 2004. The options are exercisable as of September 13, 2008, for 30 million common shares at an exercise price of $56 per share. During 2009, the market price of the common shares averaged $70 per share, peaking at $80 on December 31.

The options were exercised on September 1, 2009.

Required:

Compute Berclair's basic and diluted earnings per share for the year ended December 31, 2009.

E 19–17
EPS; stock dividend; nonconvertible preferred stock; treasury shares; shares sold; stock options; convertible bonds

● LO5 through LO9

(Note: This is a variation of E 19–15 modified to include convertible bonds).
On December 31, 2008, Berclair, Inc. had 200 million shares of common stock and 3 million shares of 9%, $100 par value cumulative preferred stock issued and outstanding. Berclair issued a 5% common stock dividend on July 1, 2009. On March 1, 2009, Berclair purchased 24 million shares of its common stock as treasury stock. Four million treasury shares were sold on October 1. Net income for the year ended December 31, 2009, was $150 million. The income tax rate is 40%.

Also outstanding at December 31 were incentive stock options granted to key executives on September 13, 2004. The options are exercisable as of September 13, 2008, for 30 million common shares at an exercise price of $56 per share. During 2009, the market price of the common shares averaged $70 per share, peaking at $80 on December 31.

$62.5 million of 8% bonds, convertible into 6 million common shares, were issued at face value in 2005.

Required:
Compute Berclair's basic and diluted earnings per share for the year ended December 31, 2009.

E 19–18
EPS; convertible preferred stock; convertible bonds

● LO7 LO9

Information from the financial statements of the Ames Fabricators, Inc., included the following:

	December 31	
	2009	**2008**
Common shares	100,000	100,000
Convertible preferred shares (convertible into 32,000 shares of common)	12,000	12,000
10% convertible bonds (convertible into 30,000 shares of common)	$1,000,000	$1,000,000

Ames's net income for the year ended December 31, 2009, is $500,000. The income tax rate is 40%. Ames paid dividends of $5 per share on its preferred stock during 2009.

Required:
Compute basic and diluted earnings per share for the year ended December 31, 2009.

E 19–19
EPS; shares issued; stock options

● LO6 through LO9

Stanley Department Stores reported net income of $720,000 for the year ended December 31, 2009.

Additional Information:

Common shares outstanding at Jan. 1, 2009	80,000
Incentive stock options (vested in 2008) outstanding throughout 2009	24,000

(Each option is exercisable for one common share at an exercise price of $37.50)
During the year, the market price of Stanley's common stock averaged $45, ending 2009 at $50 per share.
On Aug. 30 Stanley sold 15,000 common shares.
Stanley's only debt consisted of $50,000 of 10% short term bank notes.
The company's income tax rate is 40%.

Required:
Compute Stanley's basic and diluted earnings per share for the year ended December 31, 2009.

E 19–20
EPS; contingently issuable shares

● LO10

During its first year of operations, McCollum Tool Works entered into the following transactions relating to shareholders' equity. The corporation was authorized to issue 100 million common shares, $1 par per share.

Jan. 2	Issued 35 million common shares for cash.
3	Entered an agreement with the company president to issue up to 2 million additional shares of common stock in 2010 based on the earnings of McCollum in 2010. If net income exceeds $140 million, the president will receive 1 million shares; 2 million shares if net income exceeds $150 million.
Mar. 31	Issued 4 million shares in exchange for plant facilities.

Net income for 2009 was $148 million.

Required:
Compute basic and diluted earnings per share for the year ended December 31, 2009.

E 19–21
EPS; new shares; contingent agreements

● LO10

Anderson Steel Company began 2009 with 600,000 shares of common stock outstanding. On March 31, 2009, 100,000 new shares were sold at a price of $45 per share. The market price has risen steadily since that time to a high of $50 per share at December 31. No other changes in shares occurred during 2009, and no securities are outstanding that can become common stock. However, there are two agreements with officers of the company for future issuance of common stock. Both agreements relate to compensation arrangements reached in 2008. The first agreement grants to the company president a right to 10,000 shares of stock each year the closing market price is at least $48. The agreement begins in 2010 and expires in 2013. The second agreement grants to the controller a right to 15,000 shares of stock if she is still with the firm at the end of 2017. Net income for 2009 was $2,000,000.

Required:

Compute Anderson Steel Company's basic and diluted EPS for the year ended December 31, 2009.

E 19–22
EPS; concepts; terminology

● LO5 through LO11

Listed below are several terms and phrases associated with earnings per share. Pair each item from List A (by letter) with the item from List B that is most appropriately associated with it.

List A	List B
____ 1. Subtract preferred dividends.	a. Options exercised.
____ 2. Time-weighted by 5/12.	b. Simple capital structure.
____ 3. Time-weighted shares assumed issued plus time-weighted actual shares.	c. Basic EPS.
____ 4. Midyear event treated as if it occurred at the beginning of the reporting period.	d. Convertible preferred stock.
____ 5. Preferred dividends do not reduce earnings.	e. Earnings available to common shareholders.
____ 6. Single EPS presentation.	f. Antidilutive.
____ 7. Stock split.	g. Increased marketability.
____ 8. Potential common shares.	h. Extraordinary items.
____ 9. Exercise price exceeds market price.	i. Stock dividend.
____ 10. No dilution assumed.	j. Add after-tax interest to numerator.
____ 11. Convertible bonds.	k. Diluted EPS.
____ 12. Contingently issuable shares.	l. Noncumulative, undeclared preferred dividends.
____ 13. Maximum potential dilution.	m. Common shares retired at the beginning of August.
____ 14. Per share amounts for net income and for income from continuing operations.	n. Include in diluted EPS when conditions for issuance are met.

E 19–23
Stock appreciation rights; settlement in shares

● (Appendix B)

As part of its stock-based compensation package, International Electronics granted 24 million stock appreciation rights (SARs) to top officers on January 1, 2009. At exercise, holders of the SARs are entitled to receive stock equal in value to the excess of the market price at exercise over the share price at the date of grant. The SARs cannot be exercised until the end of 2012 (vesting date) and expire at the end of 2014. The $1 par common shares have a market price of $46 per share on the grant date. The fair value of the SARs, estimated by an appropriate option pricing model, is $3 per SAR at January 1, 2009. The fair value reestimated at December 31, 2009, 2010, 2011, 2012, and 2013, is $4, $3, $4, $2.50, and $3, respectively. All recipients are expected to remain employed through the vesting date.

Required:

1. Prepare the appropriate journal entry to record the award of SARs on January 1, 2009.
2. Prepare the appropriate journal entries pertaining to the SARs on December 31, 2009–December 31, 2012.
3. The SARs remain unexercised on December 31, 2013. Prepare the appropriate journal entry on that date.
4. The SARs are exercised on June 6, 2014, when the share price is $50. Prepare the appropriate journal entry(s) on that date.

E 19–24
Stock appreciation rights; cash settlement

● (Appendix B)

(Note: This is a variation of the previous exercise, modified to allow settlement in cash.) As part of its stock-based compensation package, International Electronics granted 24 million stock appreciation rights (SARs) to top officers on January 1, 2009. At exercise, holders of the SARs are entitled to receive cash or stock equal in value to the excess of the market price at exercise over the share price at the date of grant. The SARs cannot be exercised until the end of 2012 (vesting date) and expire at the end of 2014. The $1 par common shares have a market price of $46 per share on the grant date. The fair value of the SARs, estimated by an appropriate option pricing model, is $3 per SAR at January 1, 2009. The fair value re-estimated at December 31, 2009, 2010, 2011, 2012, and 2013, is $4, $3, $4, $2.50, and $3, respectively. All recipients are expected to remain employed through the vesting date.

Required:

1. Prepare the appropriate journal entry to record the award of SARs on January 1, 2009.
2. Prepare the appropriate journal entries pertaining to the SARs on December 31, 2009–December 31, 2012.
3. The SARs remain unexercised on December 31, 2013. Prepare the appropriate journal entry on that date.
4. The SARs are exercised on June 6, 2014, when the share price is $50, and executives choose to receive the market price appreciation in cash. Prepare the appropriate journal entry(s) on that date.

CPA AND CMA REVIEW QUESTIONS

CPA Exam Questions

The following questions are used in the Kaplan CPA Review Course to study share-based compensation and earnings per share while preparing for the CPA examination. Determine the response that best completes the statements or questions.

● LO2

1. On January 1, 2009, Pall Corp. granted stock options to key employees for the purchase of 40,000 shares of the company's common stock at $25 per share. The options are intended to compensate employees for the next two years. The options are exercisable within a four-year period beginning January 1, 2011, by the grantees still in the employ of the company. No options were terminated during 2009, but the company does have an experience of 4% forfeitures over the life of the stock options. The market price of the common stock was $32 per share at the date of the grant. Pall Corp. used the binomial pricing model and estimated the fair value of each of the options at $10. What amount should Pall charge to compensation expense for the year ended December 31, 2009?
   a. $153,600
   b. $160,000
   c. $192,000
   d. $200,000

● LO2

2. On January 1, 2009, Doro Corp. granted an employee an option to purchase 3,000 shares of Doro's $5 par value common stock at $20 per share. The options became exercisable on December 31, 2010, after the employee completed two years of service. The options were exercised on January 10, 2011. The market prices of Doro's stock were as follows: January 1, 2009, $30; December 31, 2010, $50; and January 10, 2011, $45. The Black-Scholes-Merton option pricing model estimated the value of the options at $8 each on the grant date. For 2009, Doro should recognize compensation expense of
   a. $0
   b. $12,000
   c. $15,000
   d. $45,000

● LO6

3. The following information pertains to Jet Corp.'s outstanding stock for 2009:

Common stock, $5 par value	
Shares outstanding, 1/1/09	20,000
2-for-1 stock split, 4/1/09	20,000
Shares issued, 7/1/09	10,000
Preferred stock, $10 par value, 5% cumulative	
Shares outstanding, 1/1/09	4,000

   What is the number of shares Jet should use to calculate 2009 basic earnings per share?
   a. 40,000
   b. 45,000
   c. 50,000
   d. 54,000

● LO7

4. At December 31, 2009 and 2008, Gow Corp. had 100,000 shares of common stock and 10,000 shares of 5%, $100 par value cumulative preferred stock outstanding. No dividends were declared on either the preferred or common stock in 2009 or 2008. Net income for 2009 was $1,000,000. For 2009, basic earnings per common share amounted to
   a. $ 5.00
   b. $ 9.50
   c. $ 9.00
   d. $10.00

● LO8

5. January 1, 2009, Hage Corporation granted options to purchase 9,000 of its common shares at $7 each. The market price of common stock was $10.50 per share on March 31, 2009, and averaged $9 per share during the quarter then ended. There was no change in the 50,000 shares of outstanding common stock during the

quarter ended March 31, 2009. Net income for the quarter was $8,268. The number of shares to be used in computing diluted earnings per share for the quarter is

a. 50,000
b. 52,000
c. 53,000
d. 59,000

● LO9

6. During 2009, Moore Corp. had the following two classes of stock issued and outstanding for the entire year:
   - 100,000 shares of common stock, $1 par.
   - 1,000 shares of 4% preferred stock, $100 par, convertible share for share into common stock.

   Moore's 2009 net income was $900,000, and its income tax rate for the year was 30%. In the computation of diluted earnings per share for 2009, the amount to be used in the numerator is

   a. $896,000
   b. $898,800
   c. $900,000
   d. $901,200

● LO9

7. On January 2, 2009, Lang Co. issued at par $10,000 of 4% bonds convertible in total into 1,000 shares of Lang's common stock. No bonds were converted during 2009.

   Throughout 2009, Lang had 1,000 shares of common stock outstanding. Lang's 2009 net income was $1,000. Lang's income tax rate is 50%.

   No potential common shares other than the convertible bonds were outstanding during 2009.

   Lang's diluted earnings per share for 2009 would be

   a. $ .50
   b. $ .60
   c. $ .70
   d. $1.00

CMA Exam Questions

The following questions dealing with share-based compensation and earnings per share are adapted from questions that previously appeared on Certified Management Accountant (CMA) examinations. The CMA designation sponsored by the Institute of Management Accountants (www.imanet.org) provides members with an objective measure of knowledge and competence in the field of management accounting. Determine the response that best completes the statements or questions.

● LO2

1. Noncompensatory stock option plans have all of the following characteristics except
   a. participation by substantially all full-time employees who meet limited employment qualifications.
   b. equal offers of stock to all eligible employees.
   c. a limited amount of time permitted to exercise the option.
   d. a provision related to the achievement of certain performance criteria.

● LO2

2. A stock option plan may or may not be intended to compensate employees for their work. The compensation expense for compensatory stock option plans should be recognized in the periods the
   a. employees become eligible to exercise the options.
   b. employees perform services.
   c. stock is issued.
   d. options are granted.

PROBLEMS

available with McGraw-Hill's Homework Manager www.mhhe.com/spiceland5e

An alternate exercise and problem set is available on the text website: www.mhhe.com/spiceland5e

P 19–1
Steve Jobs' restricted stock; tax effects

● LO1

Apple Inc. provides its executives compensation under a variety of share-based compensation plans including restricted stock awards. The following disclosure note from Apple's 2007 annual report describes the plan created for the company's chief executive officer, Steve Jobs:

Real World Financials

CEO Restricted Stock Award

On March 19, 2003, the Company's Board of Directors granted 10 million shares of restricted stock to the Company's CEO that vested on March 19, 2006. The amount of the restricted stock award expensed by the Company was based on the closing market price of the Company's common stock on the date of grant and was amortized ratably on a straight-line basis over the three-year requisite service period. Upon vesting during 2006, the 10 million shares of restricted stock had a fair value of $646.6 million and had grant-date fair value of $7.48 per share. The restricted stock award was net-share settled such that the Company withheld shares with value equivalent to the CEO's minimum statutory obligation for the applicable income and other employment taxes, and remitted the cash to the appropriate taxing authorities. The total shares withheld of 4.6 million were based on the value of the restricted stock award on the vesting date as determined by the Company's closing stock price of $64.66. The remaining shares net of those withheld were delivered to the Company's CEO. Total payments for the CEO's tax obligations to the taxing authorities were $296 million in 2006 and are reflected as a financing activity within the Consolidated Statements of Cash Flows. The net-share settlement had the effect of share repurchases by the Company as it reduced and retired the number of shares outstanding and did not represent an expense to the Company. The Company's CEO has no remaining shares of restricted stock.

Required:

1. How much compensation did Apple record for its CEO related to the restricted stock in its fiscal year ended September 24, 2005?
2. What was the CEO's combined income tax and employment tax rate that Apple used to determine the shares to be withheld at vesting?
3. From the information provided in the disclosure note, recreate the journal entries Apple used to record compensation expense and its related tax effects on September 24, 2005, the end of the 2005 fiscal year.
4. From the information provided in the disclosure note, recreate the journal entries Apple used to record the vesting of the restricted stock and its related tax effects on March 16, 2006, assuming the remaining compensation expense already has been recorded.

P 19–2
Stock options; forfeiture; exercise

● LO2

On October 15, 2008, the board of directors of Ensor Materials Corporation approved a stock option plan for key executives. On January 1, 2009, 20 million stock options were granted, exercisable for 20 million shares of Ensor's $1 par common stock. The options are exercisable between January 1, 2012, and December 31, 2014, at 80% of the quoted market price on January 1, 2009, which was $15. The fair value of the 20 million options, estimated by an appropriate option pricing model, is $6 per option.

Two million options were forfeited when an executive resigned in 2010. All other options were exercised on July 12, 2013, when the stock's price jumped unexpectedly to $19 per share.

Required:

1. When is Ensor's stock option measurement date?
2. Determine the compensation expense for the stock option plan in 2009. (Ignore taxes.)
3. What is the effect of forfeiture of the stock options on Ensor's financial statements for 2010 and 2011?
4. Is this effect consistent with the general approach for accounting for changes in estimates? Explain.
5. How should Ensor account for the exercise of the options in 2013?

P 19–3
Stock option plan; deferred tax effect recognized

● LO2

Walters Audio Visual, Inc., offers a stock option plan to its regional managers. On January 1, 2009, options were granted for 40 million $1 par common shares. The exercise price is the market price on the grant date, $8 per share. Options cannot be exercised prior to January 1, 2011, and expire December 31, 2015. The fair value of the options, estimated by an appropriate option pricing model, is $2 per option. Because the plan does not qualify as an incentive plan, Walters will receive a tax deduction upon exercise of the options equal to the excess of the market price at exercise over the exercise price. The income tax rate is 40%.

Required:

1. Determine the total compensation cost pertaining to the stock option plan.
2. Prepare the appropriate journal entries to record compensation expense and its tax effect on December 31, 2009.
3. Prepare the appropriate journal entries to record compensation expense and its tax effect on December 31, 2010.
4. Record the exercise of the options and their tax effect if *all* of the options are exercised on March 20, 2014, when the market price is $12 per share.
5. Assume the option plan qualifies as an incentive plan. Prepare the appropriate journal entries to record compensation expense and its tax effect on December 31, 2009.
6. Assuming the option plan qualifies as an incentive plan, record the exercise of the options and their tax effect if *all* of the options are exercised on March 20, 2014, when the market price is $11 per share.

P 19–4
Stock option plan; deferred tax effect of a nonqualifying plan

● LO2

JBL Aircraft manufactures and distributes aircraft parts and supplies. Employees are offered a variety of share-based compensation plans. Under its nonqualified stock option plan, JBL granted options to key officers on January 1, 2009. The options permit holders to acquire six million of the company's $1 par common shares for $22 within the next six years, but not before January 1, 2012 (the vesting date). The market price of the shares on the date of grant is $26 per share. The fair value of the 6 million options, estimated by an appropriate option pricing model, is $6 per option. Because the plan does not qualify as an incentive plan, JBL will receive a tax deduction upon exercise of the options equal to the excess of the market price at exercise over the exercise price. The tax rate is 40%.

Required:
1. Determine the total compensation cost pertaining to the incentive stock option plan.
2. Prepare the appropriate journal entries to record compensation expense and its tax effect on December 31, 2009, 2010, and 2011.
3. Record the exercise of the options and their tax effect if *all* of the options are exercised on August 21, 2013, when the market price is $27 per share.

P 19–5
Performance option plan

● LO2

LCI Cable Company grants 1 million performance stock options to key executives at January 1, 2009. The options entitle executives to receive 1 million of LCI $1 par common shares, subject to the achievement of specific financial goals over the next four years. Attainment of these goals is considered probable initially and throughout the service period. The options have a current fair value of $12 per option.

Required:
1. Prepare the appropriate entry when the options are awarded on January 1, 2009.
2. Prepare the appropriate entries on December 31 of each year 2009–2012.
3. Suppose at the beginning of 2011, LCI decided it is not probable that the performance objectives will be met. Prepare the appropriate entries on December 31 of 2011 and 2012.

P 19–6
EPS; net loss; stock dividend; nonconvertible preferred stock; treasury shares; shares sold; extraordinary loss

● LO5 through LO7 LO11

On December 31, 2008, Ainsworth, Inc., had 600 million shares of common stock outstanding. Twenty million shares of 8%, $100 par value cumulative, nonconvertible preferred stock were sold on January 2, 2009. On April 30, 2009, Ainsworth purchased 30 million shares of its common stock as treasury stock. Twelve million treasury shares were sold on August 31. Ainsworth issued a 5% common stock dividend on June 12, 2009. No cash dividends were declared in 2009. For the year ended December 31, 2009, Ainsworth reported a net loss of $140 million, including an after-tax extraordinary loss of $400 million from a litigation settlement.

Required:
1. Determine Ainsworth's net loss per share for the year ended December 31, 2009.
2. Determine the per share amount of income or loss from continuing operations for the year ended December 31, 2009.
3. Prepare an EPS presentation that would be appropriate to appear on Ainsworth's 2009 and 2008 comparative income statements. Assume EPS was reported in 2008 as $.75, based on net income (no extraordinary items) of $450 million and a weighted-average number of common shares of 600 million.

P 19–7
EPS from statement of retained earnings

● LO4 through LO6

(Note: Problem 19–7 is based on the same situation described in Problem 18–4 in Chapter 18, modified to focus on EPS rather than recording the events that affected retained earnings.)

Comparative Statements of Retained Earnings for Renn-Dever Corporation were reported as follows for the fiscal years ending December 31, 2007, 2008, and 2009.

RENN-DEVER CORPORATION
Statements of Retained Earnings

For the Years Ended December 31	2009	2008	2007
Balance at beginning of year	$6,794,292	$5,464,052	$5,624,552
Net income (loss)	3,308,700	2,240,900	(160,500)
Deductions:			
Stock dividend (34,900 shares)	242,000		
Common shares retired, September 30 (110,000 shares)		212,660	
Common stock cash dividends	889,950	698,000	0
Balance at end of year	$8,971,042	$6,794,292	$5,464,052

At December 31, 2006, paid-in capital consisted of the following:

Common stock, 1,855,000 shares at $1 par,	$1,855,000
Paid in capital—excess of par	7,420,000

No preferred stock or potential common shares were outstanding during any of the periods shown.

Required:

Compute Renn-Dever's earnings per share as it would have appeared in income statements for the years ended December 31, 2007, 2008, and 2009.

P 19–8
EPS from statement of shareholders' equity

● LO4 through LO6

eXcel

Comparative Statements of Shareholders' Equity for Locke Intertechnology Corporation were reported as follows for the fiscal years ending December 31, 2007, 2008, and 2009.

LOCKE INTERTECHNOLOGY CORPORATION
Statements of Shareholders' Equity
For the Years Ended Dec. 31, 2007, 2008, and 2009
($ in millions)

	Preferred Stock, $10 par	Common Stock, $1 par	Additional Paid-In Capital	Retained Earnings	Total Shareholder's Equity
Balance at January 1, 2007		55	495	1,878	2,428
Sale of preferred shares	10		470		480
Sale of common shares, 7/1		9	81		90
Cash dividend, preferred				(1)	(1)
Cash dividend, common				(16)	(16)
Net income				290	290
Balance at December 31, 2007	10	64	1,046	2,151	3,271
Retirement of common shares, 4/1		(4)	(36)	(20)	(60)
Cash dividend, preferred				(1)	(1)
Cash dividend, common				(20)	(20)
3-for-2 split effected in the form of a common stock dividend, 8/12		30	(30)		
Net income				380	380
Balance at December 31, 2008	10	90	980	2,490	3,570
10% common stock dividend, 5/1		9	90	(99)	
Sale of common shares, 9/1		3	31		34
Cash dividend, preferred				(2)	(2)
Cash dividend, common				(22)	(22)
Net income				412	412
Balance at December 31, 2009	10	102	1,101	2,779	3,992

Required:

Infer from the statements the events and transactions that affected Locke Intertechnology Corporation's shareholders' equity and compute earnings per share as it would have appeared on the income statements for the years ended December 31, 2007, 2008, and 2009. No potential common shares were outstanding during any of the periods shown.

P 19–9
EPS; nonconvertible preferred stock; treasury shares; shares sold; stock dividend

● LO4 through LO7

On December 31, 2008, Dow Steel Corporation had 600,000 shares of common stock and 300,000 shares of 8%, noncumulative, nonconvertible preferred stock issued and outstanding. Dow issued a 4% common stock dividend on May 15 and paid cash dividends of $400,000 and $75,000 to common and preferred shareholders, respectively, on December 15, 2009.

On February 28, 2009, Dow sold 60,000 common shares. In keeping with its long-term share repurchase plan, 2,000 shares were retired on July 1. Dow's net income for the year ended December 31, 2009, was $2,100,000. The income tax rate is 40%.

Required:

Compute Dow's earnings per share for the year ended December 31, 2009.

P 19–10
EPS; nonconvertible preferred stock; treasury shares; shares sold; stock dividend; options

● LO4 through LO8

(Note: This is a variation of the previous problem, modified to include stock options.)
On December 31, 2008, Dow Steel Corporation had 600,000 shares of common stock and 300,000 shares of 8%, noncumulative, nonconvertible preferred stock issued and outstanding. Dow issued a 4% common stock dividend on May 15 and paid cash dividends of $400,000 and $75,000 to common and preferred shareholders, respectively, on December 15, 2009.

On February 28, 2009, Dow sold 60,000 common shares. In keeping with its long-term share repurchase plan, 2,000 shares were retired on July 1. Dow's net income for the year ended December 31, 2009, was $2,100,000. The income tax rate is 40%.

As part of an incentive compensation plan, Dow granted incentive stock options to division managers at December 31 of the current and each of the previous two years. Each option permits its holder to buy one share of common stock at an exercise price equal to market value at the date of grant and can be exercised one year from that date. Information concerning the number of options granted and common share prices follows:

Date Granted	Options Granted	Share Price
	(adjusted for the stock dividend)	
December 31, 2007	8,000	$24
December 31, 2008	3,000	$33
December 31, 2009	6,500	$31

The market price of the common stock averaged $32 per share during 2009.

Required:

Compute Dow's earnings per share for the year ended December 31, 2009.

P 19–11
EPS; nonconvertible preferred stock; treasury shares; shares sold; stock dividend; options; convertible bonds; contingently issuable shares

● LO4 through LO10

(Note: This is a variation of the previous problem, modified to include convertible bonds and contingently issuable shares.)

On December 31, 2008, Dow Steel Corporation had 600,000 shares of common stock and 300,000 shares of 8%, noncumulative, nonconvertible preferred stock issued and outstanding. Dow issued a 4% common stock dividend on May 15 and paid cash dividends of $400,000 and $75,000 to common and preferred shareholders, respectively, on December 15, 2009.

On February 28, 2009, Dow sold 60,000 common shares. Also, as a part of a 2008 agreement for the acquisition of Merrill Cable Company, another 23,000 shares (already adjusted for the stock dividend) are to be issued to former Merrill shareholders on December 31, 2010, if Merrill's 2010 net income is at least $500,000. In 2009, Merrill's net income was $630,000.

In keeping with its long-term share repurchase plan, 2,000 shares were retired on July 1. Dow's net income for the year ended December 31, 2009, was $2,100,000. The income tax rate is 40%.

As part of an incentive compensation plan, Dow granted incentive stock options to division managers at December 31 of the current and each of the previous two years. Each option permits its holder to buy one share of common stock at an exercise price equal to market value at the date of grant and can be exercised one year from that date. Information concerning the number of options granted and common share prices follows:

Date Granted	Options Granted	Share Price
	(adjusted for the stock dividend)	
December 31, 2007	8,000	$24
December 31, 2008	3,000	$33
December 31, 2009	6,500	$31

The market price of the common stock averaged $32 per share during 2009.

On July 12, 2007, Dow issued $800,000 of convertible 10% bonds at face value. Each $1,000 bond is convertible into 30 common shares (adjusted for the stock dividend).

Required:

Compute Dow's basic and diluted earnings per share for the year ended December 31, 2009.

P 19–12
EPS; antidilution

● LO4 through LO10

Alciatore Company earned a net income of $150,000 in 2009. The weighted-average number of common shares outstanding for 2009 was 40,000. The average stock price for 2009 was $33. Assume an income tax rate of 40%.

Required:

For each of the following independent situations, indicate whether the effect of the security is antidilutive for diluted EPS.

1. 10,000 shares of 7.7% of $100 par convertible, cumulative preferred stock. Each share may be converted into two common shares.
2. 8% convertible 10-year, $500,000 of bonds, issued at face value. The bonds are convertible to 5,000 shares of common stock.
3. Stock options exercisable at $30 per share after January 1, 2011.
4. Warrants for 1,000 common shares with an exercise price of $35 per share.
5. A contingent agreement to issue 5,000 shares of stock to the company president if net income is at least $125,000 in 2010.

P 19–13
EPS; convertible bonds; treasury shares

At December 31, 2009, the financial statements of Hollingsworth Industries included the following:

LO4 through LO6 LO9

Net income for 2009	$560 million
Bonds payable, 10%, convertible into 36 million shares of common stock	$300 million
Common stock:	
Shares outstanding on January 1	400 million
Treasury shares purchased for cash on September 1	30 million

Additional data:

The bonds payable were issued at par in 2007. The tax rate for 2009 was 40%.

Required:
Compute basic and diluted EPS for the year ended December 31, 2009.

P 19–14
EPS; options; convertible preferred; additional shares

LO4 through LO9

On January 1, 2009, Tonge Industries had outstanding 440,000 common shares (par $1) that originally sold for $20 per share, and 4,000 shares of 10% cumulative preferred stock (par $100), convertible into 40,000 common shares.

On October 1, 2009, Tonge sold and issued an additional 16,000 shares of common stock at $33. At December 31, 2009, there were incentive stock options outstanding, issued in 2008, and exercisable after one year for 20,000 shares of common stock at an exercise price of $30. The market price of the common stock at year-end was $48. During the year the price of the common shares had averaged $40.

Net income was $650,000. The tax rate for the year was 40%.

Required:
Compute basic and diluted EPS for the year ended December 31, 2009.

P 19–15
EPS; stock options; nonconvertible preferred; convertible bonds; shares sold

LO4 through LO9

At January 1, 2009, Canaday Corporation had outstanding the following securities:

600 million common shares
20 million 6% cumulative preferred shares, $50 par
8% convertible bonds, $2,000 million face amount, convertible into 80 million common shares

The following additional information is available:

- On September 1, 2009, Canaday sold 72 million additional shares of common stock.
- Incentive stock options to purchase 60 million shares of common stock after July 1, 2008, at $12 per share were outstanding at the beginning and end of 2009. The average market price of Canaday's common stock was $18 per share during 2009.
- Canaday's net income for the year ended December 31, 2009, was $1,476 million. The effective income tax rate was 40%.

Required:
1. Calculate basic earnings per common share for the year ended December 31, 2009.
2. Calculate the diluted earnings per common share for the year ended December 31, 2009.

P 19–16
EPS; options; restricted stock; additional components for "proceeds" in treasury stock method

LO1 LO2 LO4 LO8

Witter House is a calendar-year firm with 300 million common shares outstanding throughout 2009 and 2010. As part of its executive compensation plan, at January 1, 2008, the company had issued 30 million executive stock options permitting executives to buy 30 million shares of stock for $10 within the next eight years, but not prior to January 1, 2011. The fair value of the options was estimated on the grant date to be $3 per option.

In 2009, Witter House began granting employees stock awards rather than stock options as part of its equity compensation plans and granted 15 million restricted common shares to senior executives at January 1, 2009. The shares vest four years later. The fair value of the stock was $12 per share on the grant date. The average price of the common shares was $12 and $15 during 2009 and 2010, respectively.

The stock options qualify for tax purposes as an incentive plan. The restricted stock does not. The company's net income was $150 million and $160 million in 2009 and 2010, respectively. Its income tax rate is 40%.

Required:
1. Determine basic and diluted earnings per share for Witter House in 2009.
2. Determine basic and diluted earnings per share for Witter House in 2010.

BROADEN YOUR PERSPECTIVE

Apply your critical-thinking ability to the knowledge you've gained. These cases will provide you an opportunity to develop your research, analysis, judgment, and communication skills. You also will work with other students, integrate what you've learned, apply it in real world situations, and consider its global and ethical ramifications. This practice will broaden your knowledge and further develop your decision-making abilities.

Real World Case 19–1
Restricted stock plan; Microsoft

● LO1

Real World Financials

Microsoft provides compensation to executives in the form of a variety of incentive compensation plans including restricted stock award grants. The following is an excerpt from a disclosure note from Microsoft's 2007 annual report:

Note 14 Employee Stock and Savings Plans (in part)

In fiscal year 2004, we began granting employees stock awards rather than stock options as part of our equity compensation plans.

Stock awards are grants that entitle the holder to shares of common stock as the award vests. Our stock awards generally vest over a five-year period. During fiscal year 2007, the following activity occurred under our existing plans:

	Shares (in millions)	Weighted Average Grant-Date Fair Value
Stock awards:		
Nonvested balance at June 30, 2006	98	$24.25
Granted	57	25.15
Vested	(24)	24.15
Forfeited	(7)	24.44
Nonvested balance at June 30, 2007	**124**	**$24.67**

Required:

1. What is the "incentive" provided by Microsoft's restricted stock grants?
2. If all awards are granted, vested, and forfeited evenly throughout the year, what is the compensation expense in fiscal 2007 pertaining to the previous and current stock awards? Explain. Assume forfeited shares were granted evenly throughout the four previous years.

Communication Case 19–2
Stock options; basic concepts; prepare a memo

● LO2

You are Assistant Controller of Stamos & Company, a medium-size manufacturer of machine parts. On October 22, 2008, the board of directors approved a stock option plan for key executives. On January 1, 2009, a specific number of stock options were granted. The options were exercisable between January 1, 2011, and December 31, 2013, at 100% of the quoted market price at the grant date. The service period is for 2009 through 2011.

Your boss, the controller, is one of the executives to receive options. Neither he nor you have had occasion to deal with the FASB pronouncement on accounting for stock options. He and you are aware of the traditional approach your company used previously but do not know the newer method. Your boss understands how options might benefit him personally but wants to be aware also of how the options will be reported in the financial statements. He has asked you for a one-page synopsis of accounting for stock options under the fair value approach. He instructed you, "I don't care about the effect on taxes or earnings per share—just the basics, please."

Required:

Prepare such a report that includes the following:

1. At what point should the compensation cost be measured? How should it be measured?
2. How should compensation expense be measured for the stock option plan in 2009 and later?
3. If options are forfeited because an executive resigns before vesting, what is the effect of that forfeiture of the stock options on the financial statements?
4. If options are allowed to lapse after vesting, what is the effect on the financial statements?

Ethics Case 19–3
Stock options

● LO2

You are in your second year as an auditor with Dantly and Regis, a regional CPA firm. One of the firm's long-time clients is Mayberry-Cleaver Industries, a national company involved in the manufacturing, marketing, and sales of hydraulic devices used in specialized manufacturing applications. Early in this year's audit you discover that Mayberry-Cleaver has changed its method of determining inventory from LIFO to FIFO. Your client's explanation is that FIFO is consistent with the method used by some other companies in the industry. Upon further investigation, you discover an executive stock option plan whose terms call for a significant increase in the shares available to executives if net income this year exceeds $44 million. Some quick calculations convince you that without the change in inventory methods, the target will not be reached; with the change, it will.

Required:

Do you perceive an ethical dilemma? What would be the likely impact of following the controller's suggestions? Who would benefit? Who would be injured?

Trueblood Accounting Case 19–4
Modification of share-based awards

The following Trueblood case is recommended for use with this chapter. The case provides an excellent opportunity for class discussion, group projects, and writing assignments. The case, along with Professor's Discussion Material, can be obtained from the Deloitte Foundation at its website: www.deloitte.com/us/truebloodcases.

● LO1 LO2

Case 07-4: *Murray Compensation, Inc.*

This case gives students the opportunity to consider accounting for share-based compensation plans under *SFAS No. 123(R)* when a company modifies the existing award.

Real World Case 19–5
Share-based plans; Cisco Systems

● LO1 LO2 Appendix B

Real World Financials

Cisco Systems offers its employees a variety of share-based compensation plans including stock options, stock appreciation rights, and restricted stock. The following is an excerpt from a disclosure note from Cisco's 2007 financial statements:

Note 10 Employee Benefit Plans (in part)

. . . , the Company adopted *SFAS 123(R)*, which requires the measurement and recognition of compensation expense for all share-based payment awards made to the Company's employees and directors including employee stock options and employee stock purchase rights, based on estimated fair values. Employee share-based compensation expense under *SFAS 123(R)* was as follows (in millions):

	July 28	July 29	July 30
Years Ended	**2007**	2006	2005
Total employee share-based compensation expense	**$931**	$1,050	$—

Required:

1. Cisco's share-based compensation includes stock options, stock appreciation rights, restricted stock awards, and performance-based awards. What is the general financial reporting objective when recording compensation expense for these forms of compensation?
2. Cisco reported share-based expense of $931 million in 2007. Without referring to specific numbers and ignoring other forms of share-based compensation, describe how this amount reflects the value of stock options.

Real World Case 19–6
Employee stock purchase plan; Microsoft

● LO3

Real World Financials

Microsoft Corporation offers compensation to its employees and executives through a variety of compensation plans. One such plan is its employee stock purchase plan, which is described in the following disclosure note from its fiscal 2007 annual report:

Employee Stock Purchase Plan. We have an employee stock purchase plan for all eligible employees. Compensation expense for the employee stock purchase plan is recognized in accordance with *SFAS No. 123(R)*. Shares of our common stock may be purchased by employees at three-month intervals at 90% of the fair market value on the last day of each three-month period. Employees may purchase shares having a value not exceeding 15% of their gross compensation during an offering period. Employees purchased the following shares:

(Shares in millions)	**2007**	**2006**	**2005**
Shares purchased	**17**	17	16
Average price per share	**$25.36**	$23.02	$23.33

At June 30, 2007, 125 million shares were reserved for future issuance.

Required:

Describe the way "Compensation expense for the employee stock purchase plan is recognized in accordance with *SFAS No. 123(R)*" by Microsoft. Include in your explanation the journal entry that summarizes employee share purchases during 2007.

Judgment Case 19–7
Where are the profits?

● LO4 through LO7 LO9

Del Conte Construction Company has experienced generally steady growth since its inception in 1953. Management is proud of its record of having maintained or increased its earnings per share in each year of its existence.

Inflationary pressures in the construction industry have led to disturbing dips in revenues the past two years. Despite concerted cost-cutting efforts, profits have actually declined in each of the two previous years. Net income in 2007, 2008, and 2009 was as follows:

2007	$145 million
2008	$134 million
2009	$ 95 million

A major shareholder has hired you to provide advice on whether to continue her present investment position or to curtail that position. Of particular concern is the declining profitability, despite the fact that earnings per share has continued a pattern of growth:

	Basic	**Diluted**
2007	$2.15	$1.91
2008	$2.44	$2.12
2009	$2.50	$2.50

She specifically asks you to explain this apparent paradox. During the course of your investigation you discover the following events:

- For the decade ending December 31, 2006, Del Conte had 60 million common shares and 20 million shares of 8%, $10 par nonconvertible preferred stock outstanding. Cash dividends have been paid quarterly on both.
- On July 1, 2008, half the preferred shares were retired in the open market. The remaining shares were retired on December 30, 2008.
- $55 million of 8% nonconvertible bonds were issued at the beginning of 2009 and a portion of the proceeds were used to call and retire $50 million of 10% debentures (outstanding since 2004) that were convertible into 9 million common shares.
- In 2007 management announced a share repurchase plan by which up to 24 million common shares would be retired. 12 million shares were retired on March 1 of both 2008 and 2009.
- Del Conte's income tax rate is 40% and has been for the last several years.

Required:
Explain the apparent paradox to which your client refers. Include calculations that demonstrate your explanation.

Communication Case 19–8
Dilution

● LO9

"I thought I understood earnings per share," lamented Brad Dawson, "but you're telling me we need to pretend our convertible bonds have been converted! Or maybe not?"

Dawson, your boss, is the new manager of the Fabricating division of BVT Corporation. His background is engineering and he has only a basic understanding of earnings per share. Knowing you are an accounting graduate, he asks you to explain the questions he has about the calculation of the company's EPS. His reaction is to your explanation that the company's convertible bonds might be included in this year's calculation.

"Put it in a memo!" he grumbled as he left your office.

Required:
Write a memo to Dawson. Explain the effect on earnings per share of each of the following:

1. Convertible securities.
2. Antidilutive securities.

Real World Case 19–9
Reporting EPS; discontinued operations; Alberto-Culver Company

● LO11

Real World Financials

The Alberto-Culver Company develops, manufactures, distributes, and markets branded beauty care products as well as branded food and household products in the United States and more than 100 other countries. The following is an excerpt from the comparative income statements (beginning with earnings from continuing operations) from Alberto-Culver's 2007 annual report ($ in thousands):

	2007	2006	2005
Earnings from continuing operations	$81,227	79,515	69,839
Earnings (loss) from discontinued operations, net of income taxes	(2,963)	125,806	141,062
Net earnings	$78,264	205,321	210,901

An income statement sometimes includes items that require separate presentation (net of income taxes) within the statement. The two possible "separately reported items" are discontinued operations and extraordinary items. Alberto-Culver reports one of these items.

A disclosure note from Alberto-Culver's 2007 annual report is shown below:

Weighted Average Shares Outstanding

The following table provides information about basic and diluted weighted average shares outstanding:

(shares in thousands)	2007	2006	2005
Basic weighted average shares outstanding	95,896	92,426	91,451
Effect of dilutive securities:			
Assumed exercise of stock options	2,443	1,110	1,252
Assumed vesting of restricted stock	237	199	177
Effect of unrecognized stock-based compensation related to future services	(218)	(250)	(42)
Diluted weighted average shares outstanding	98,358	93,485	92,838

The computations of diluted weighted average shares outstanding exclude 1.4 million shares in fiscal year 2007, 2.1 million shares in fiscal year 2006 and 38,000 shares in fiscal year 2005 since the options were antidilutive.

Required:

1. The disclosure note shows adjustments for "assumed exercise of stock options and assumed vesting of restricted stock." What other adjustments might be needed? Explain why and how these adjustments are made to the weighted-average shares outstanding.

2. The disclosure note indicates that the effect of some of the stock options were not included because they would be antidilutive. What does that mean? Why not include antidilutive securities?
3. Based on the information provided, prepare the presentation of basic and diluted earnings per share for 2007, 2006, and 2005 that Alberto-Culver reports in its 2007 annual report.

Analysis Case 19–10

Analyzing financial statements; price–earnings ratio; dividend payout ratio

● LO11

IGF Foods Company is a large, primarily domestic, consumer foods company involved in the manufacture, distribution and sale of a variety of food products. Industry averages are derived from Troy's *The Almanac of Business and Industrial Financial Ratios* and Dun and Bradstreet's *Industry Norms and Key Business Ratios.* Following are the 2009 and 2008 comparative income statements and balance sheets for IGF. The market price of IGF's common stock is $47 during 2009. (The financial data we use are from actual financial statements of a well-known corporation, but the company name used in our illustration is fictitious and the numbers and dates have been modified slightly to disguise the company's identity.)

IGF FOODS COMPANY
Years Ended December 31, 2009 and 2008

($ in millions)	2009	2008
Comparative Income Statements		
Net sales	$6,440	$5,800
Cost of goods sold	(3,667)	(3,389)
Gross profit	2,773	2,411
Operating expenses	(1,916)	(1,629)
Operating income	857	782
Interest expense	(54)	(53)
Income from operations before tax	803	729
Income taxes	(316)	(287)
Net income	$ 487	$ 442
Net income per share	$ 2.69	$2.44
Average shares outstanding	181 million	181 million
Comparative Balance Sheets		
Assets		
Total current assets	$1,879	$1,490
Property, plant, and equipment (net)	2,592	2,291
Intangibles (net)	800	843
Other assets	74	60
Total assets	$5,345	$4,684
Liabilities and Shareholders' Equity		
Total current liabilities	$1,473	$ 941
Long term debt	534	728
Deferred income taxes	407	344
Total liabilities	2,414	2,013
Shareholders' equity:		
Common stock	180	180
Additional paid-in capital	21	63
Retained earnings	2,730	2,428
Total shareholders' equity	2,931	2,671
Total liabilities and shareholders' equity	$5,345	$4,684

Some ratios express income, dividends, and market prices on a per share basis. As such, these ratios appeal primarily to common shareholders, particularly when weighing investment possibilities. These ratios focus less on the fundamental soundness of a company and more on its investment characteristics.

Required:

1. Earnings per share expresses a firm's profitability on a per share basis. Calculate 2009 earnings per share for IGF.
2. Calculate IGF's 2009 price-earnings ratio. The average price-earnings ratio for the stocks listed on the New York Stock Exchange in a comparable time period was 18.5. What does your calculation indicate about IGF's earnings?
3. Calculate IGF's 2009 dividend payout ratio. What information does the calculation provide an investor?

Ethics Case 19–11
International Network Solutions

● LO6

International Network Solutions provides products and services related to remote access networking. The company has grown rapidly during its first 10 years of operations. As its segment of the industry has begun to mature, though, the fast growth of previous years has begun to slow. In fact, this year revenues and profits are roughly the same as last year.

One morning, nine weeks before the close of the fiscal year, Rob Mashburn, CFO, and Jessica Lane, controller, were sharing coffee and ideas in Lane's office.

Lane: About the Board meeting Thursday. You may be right. This may be the time to suggest a share buyback program.

Mashburn: To begin this year, you mean?

Lane: Right! I know Barber will be lobbying to use the funds for our European expansion. She's probably right about the best use of our funds, but we can always issue more notes next year. Right now, we need a quick fix for our EPS numbers.

Mashburn: Our shareholders are accustomed to increases every year.

Required:

1. How will a buyback of shares provide a "quick fix" for EPS?
2. Is the proposal ethical?
3. Who would be affected if the proposal is implemented?

Research Case 19–12
Determining and comparing price-earnings ratios; retrieving stock prices and earnings per share numbers from the Internet

● LO11

Many sites on the Internet allow the retrieval of current stock price information. Among those sites are Marketwatch (cbs.marketwatch.com) and Quicken (www.quicken.com).

Required:

1. Access any site on the Internet that permits you to get a current stock quote. Determine the current price of Microsoft Corporation's common stock (MSFT) and that of Intel Corporation (INTC).
2. Access EDGAR on the Internet at www.sec.gov. Search for Microsoft and access its most recent 10-K filing. Search or scroll to find the income statement and related note(s). Determine the most recent earnings per share. Repeat this step for Intel.
3. Calculate the price-earnings ratio for each company.
4. Compare the PE ratios of Microsoft and Intel. What information might be gleaned from your comparison?

Analysis Case 19–13
Kellogg's EPS; PE ratio; dividend payout

● LO11

Real World Financials

While eating his Kellogg's Frosted Flakes one January morning, Tony noticed the following article in his local paper:

Kellogg Affirms 2008 Guidance, Reports 2007 EPS Growth of 10%
BATTLE CREEK, Mich., Jan. 30, 2008 (PRIME NEWSWIRE)—Kellogg Company (NYSE: News - K) today reported strong 2007 earnings. Fourth quarter earnings were $0.44 per share. Annual earnings were $2.76 per share, representing the sixth consecutive year that the Company has met or exceeded its long-term EPS targets.

As a shareholder, Tony is well aware that Kellogg pays a regular cash dividend of $.31 per share quarterly. A quick click on a price quote service indicated that Kellogg's shares closed at $52.43 on December 31. That web page also reported Kellogg's previous year's EPS as $2.51.

Required:

1. Using the numbers provided, determine the price/earnings ratio for Kellogg Company for 2007. What information does this ratio impart?
2. What is the dividend payout ratio for Kellogg? What does it indicate?

Analysis Case 19–14
EPS concepts

● LO4 through LO8

The shareholders' equity of Proactive Solutions, Inc. included the following at December 31, 2009:

Common stock, $1 par
Paid-in capital—excess of par on common stock
7% cumulative convertible preferred stock, $100 par value
Paid-in capital—excess of par on preferred stock
Retained earnings

Additional information:

- Proactive had 7 million shares of preferred stock authorized of which 2 million were outstanding. All 2 million shares outstanding were issued in 2003 for $112 a share. The preferred stock is convertible into common stock on a two-for-one basis until December 31, 2011, after which the preferred stock no longer is convertible. None of the preferred stock has been converted into common stock at December 31, 2009. There were no dividends in arrears.
- Of the 13 million common shares authorized, there were 8 million shares outstanding at January 1, 2009. Proactive also sold 3 million shares at the beginning of September 2009 at a price of $52 a share.

- The company has an employee stock option plan where certain key employees and officers may purchase shares of common stock at the market price at the date of the option grant. All options are exercisable beginning one year after the date of the grant and expire if not exercised within five years of the grant date. On January 1, 2009, options for 2 million shares were outstanding at prices ranging from $45 to $53 a share. Options for 1 million shares were exercised at $49 a share at the end of June 2009. No options expired during 2009. Additional options for 1.5 million shares were granted at $55 a share during the year. The 2.5 million options outstanding at December 31, 2009, were exercisable at $45 to $55 a share.

The only changes in the shareholders' equity for 2009 were those described above, 2009 net income, and cash dividends paid.

Required:

Explain how each of the following amounts should be determined when computing earnings per share for presentation in the income statements. For each, be specific as to the treatment of each item.

1. Numerator for basic EPS.
2. Denominator for basic EPS.
3. Numerator for diluted EPS.
4. Denominator for diluted EPS.

Real World Case 19–15

Per share data; stock options; antidilutive securities; Sun Microsystems

● LO8

Real World Financials

Sun Microsystems, Inc., headquartered in Santa Clara, California, is a prominent provider of products and services for network computing. Sun's 2007 annual report included the following disclosure note:

Computation of Net Income (Loss) per Common Share (in part)

Basic net income (loss) per common share is computed using the weighted-average number of common shares outstanding (adjusted for treasury stock and common stock subject to repurchase activity) during the period.

Diluted net income (loss) per common share is computed using the weighted-average number of common and dilutive common equivalent shares outstanding during the period. Common equivalent shares are anti-dilutive when their conversion would increase earnings per share. Dilutive common equivalent shares consist primarily of stock options and restricted stock awards (restricted stock and restricted stock units that are settled in stock).

The following table sets forth the computation of basic and diluted income (loss) per share for each of the past three fiscal years (in millions, except per share amounts):

	Fiscal Years Ended June 30,		
	2007	**2006**	**2005**
Basic earnings per share			
Net income (loss)	$ 473	$ (864)	$ (107)
Basic weighted average shares outstanding	3,531	3,437	3,368
Net Income (loss) per common share-basic	$ 0.13	$ (0.25)	$ (0.03)
Diluted earnings per share			
Net income (loss)	$ 473	$ (864)	$ (107)
Diluted weighted average shares outstanding	3,606	3,437	3,368
Net Income (loss) per common share-diluted	$ 0.13	$ (0.25)	$ (0.03)

For fiscal 2007, we added 75 million common equivalent shares to our basic weighted-average shares outstanding to compute the diluted weighted-average shares outstanding. We are required to include these dilutive shares in our calculations of net income per share for fiscal 2007 because we earned a profit. If we had earned a profit during fiscal 2006 and 2005, we would have added 25 million and 23 million common equivalent shares, respectively, to our basic weighted-average shares outstanding to compute the diluted weighted-average shares outstanding for these periods.

Required:

1. The note indicates that "diluted net income (loss) per common share is computed using the weighted-average number of common and dilutive common equivalent shares outstanding during the period." What are dilutive common equivalent shares?
2. The note indicates that "For fiscal 2007, we added 75 million common equivalent shares to our basic weighted-average shares outstanding to compute the diluted weighted-average shares outstanding." Does that mean Sun had a total of 75 million stock options and restricted shares outstanding? Explain.
3. Sun does not include potential common shares from employee stock options and restricted stock when calculating EPS for fiscal 2006 and 2005. Why not? If Sun had included dilutive potential common shares from employee stock options and restricted stock awards, what would have been the amount of diluted loss per share for fiscal 2006?

Analysis Case 19–16
EPS; AAON, Inc.

● LO5 through LO8

Real World Financials

"I guess I'll win that bet!" you announced to no one in particular.

"What bet?" Renee asked. Renee Patey was close enough to overhear you.

"When I bought my AAON stock last year Randy insisted it was a mistake, that they were going downhill. I bet him a Coke he was wrong. This press release says earnings are up 11%," you bragged. Renee was looking over your shoulder now at the article you were pointing at:

> TULSA, OK—(MARKET WIRE)—11/07/07—AAON, Inc. (NASDAQ: AAON) today announced its operating results for the third quarter and nine-month period ended September 30, 2007.
>
> In the quarter, net sales were a record high of $70.9 million, up 11% from $64.2 million during the corresponding period in 2006, and net income equaled the third quarter record level of $5.4 million or $0.28 per share set in the same period a year ago. Per share earnings are on a diluted basis and reflect the three-for-two stock split on August 21, 2007.
>
> It was also announced that the Board of Directors has authorized the Company to repurchase up to 10% (approximately 1.8 million shares) of its outstanding common stock.

Excerpt from: "AAON Reports Third Quarter Results and Announces New Stock Buyback Plan," November 11, 2007.

"Twenty-eight cents a share, huh?" Renee asked. "How many shares do you have? When do you get the check?"

Required:

1. Renee's questions imply that she thinks you will get cash dividends of 28 cents a share. What does earnings per share really tell you?
2. The press release says, "Per share earnings are on a diluted basis and reflect the three-for-two stock split on August 21, 2007." What does that mean?
3. The press release indicates that AAON may repurchase up to $1.8 million of its stock. Would that reduction in shares be taken into account when EPS is calculated? How?
4. You know from statements AAON mailed you that AAON grants stock options to company executives. If those options are exercised, you know the resulting increase in shares might reduce earnings per share. Is that possibility taken into account when EPS is calculated? Explain.

CPA SIMULATION 19–1

Houston County Energy
EPS and Share-Based Compensation

CPA Review

Test your knowledge of the concepts discussed in this chapter, practice critical professional skills necessary for career success, and prepare for the computer-based CPA exam by accessing our CPA simulations at the text website: www.mhhe.com/spiceland5e.

The Houston County Energy simulation tests your knowledge of a variety of earnings per share and share-based compensation reporting issues.

As on the CPA exam itself, you will be asked to use tools including a spreadsheet, a calculator, and profes sional accounting standards, to conduct research, derive solutions, and communicate conclusions related to these issues in a simulated environment headed by the following interactive tabs:

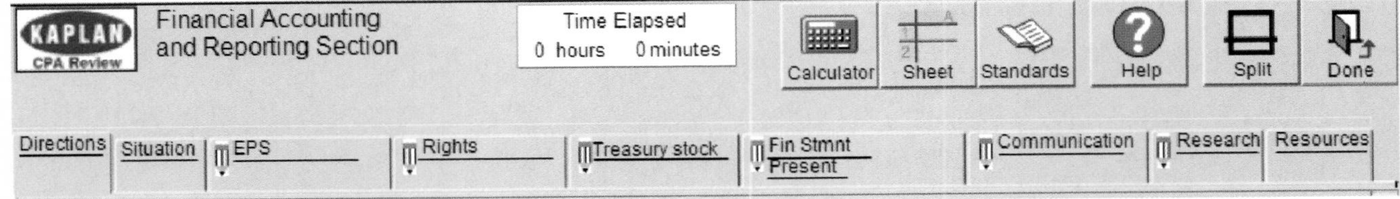

Specific tasks in the simulation include:

- Calculating basic and diluted earnings per share.
- Applying judgment in deciding the financial reporting implications of the issuance, exercise, and expiration of stock rights and the conversion of preferred shares.
- Demonstrating an understanding of appropriate financial statement reporting of earnings per share.
- Analyzing the financial statement effects of treasury stock transactions.
- Communicating the financial reporting implications of stock options.
- Researching the purpose of and procedures for a quasi-reorganization.

CHAPTER 20

Accounting Changes and Error Corrections

/// OVERVIEW

Chapter 4 provided an overview of accounting changes and error correction. Later, we discussed changes encountered in connection with specific assets and liabilities as we dealt with those topics in subsequent chapters.

Here we revisit accounting changes and error correction to synthesize the way these are handled in a variety of situations that might be encountered in practice. We see that most changes in accounting principle are reported retrospectively. Changes in estimates are accounted for prospectively. A change in depreciation methods is considered a change in estimate resulting from a change in principle. Both changes in reporting entities and the correction of errors are reported retrospectively.

LEARNING OBJECTIVES

After studying this chapter, you should be able to:

- **LO1** Differentiate among the three types of accounting changes and distinguish between the retrospective and prospective approaches to accounting for and reporting accounting changes.
- **LO2** Describe how changes in accounting principle typically are reported.
- **LO3** Explain how and why some changes in accounting principle are reported prospectively.
- **LO4** Explain how and why changes in estimates are reported prospectively.
- **LO5** Describe the situations that constitute a change in reporting entity.
- **LO6** Understand and apply the four-step process of correcting and reporting errors, regardless of the type of error or the timing of its discovery.

FINANCIAL REPORTING CASE

In a Jam

"What the heck!" Martin yelped as he handed you the annual report of J.M. Smucker he'd received in the mail today. "It looks like Smucker found a bunch of lost jelly. It says here that their inventory was $54 million last year. I distinctly remember them reporting that number last year as $52 million because my dad was born in '52, and I did a little wordplay in my mind about him 'taking inventory' of his life when he bought the red Mustang." He had circled the number in the comparative balance sheets. "When I bought Smucker shares last year, I promised myself I would monitor things pretty closely, but it's not as easy as I thought it would be."

As an accounting graduate, you can understand Martin's confusion. Flipping to the footnote on accounting changes, you proceed to clear things up for him.

By the time you finish this chapter, you should be able to respond appropriately to the questions posed in this case. Compare your response to the solution provided at the end of the chapter.

QUESTIONS ///

1. How can an accounting change cause a company to increase a previously reported inventory amount? (page 1064)
2. Are all accounting changes reported this way? (page 1071)

You learned early in your study of accounting that two of the qualitative characteristics of accounting information that contribute to its relevance and reliability are *consistency* and *comparability*. Though we strive to achieve and maintain these financial reporting attributes, we cannot ignore the forces of change. Ours is a dynamic business environment. The economy is increasingly a global one. Technological advances constantly transform both day-to-day operations and the flow of information about those operations. The accounting profession's response to the fluid environment often means issuing new standards that require companies to change accounting methods. Often, developments within an industry or the economy will prompt a company to voluntarily switch methods of accounting or to revise estimates or expectations. In short, change is inevitable. The question then becomes a matter of how best to address change when reporting financial information from year to year.

In the first part of this chapter, we differentiate among the various types of accounting changes that businesses face, with a focus on the most meaningful and least disruptive ways to report those changes. Then, in the second part of the chapter, we direct our attention to a closely related circumstance—the correction of errors.

PART A

ACCOUNTING CHANGES

Accounting changes fall into one of three categories listed in Graphic 20–1.[1]

GRAPHIC 20–1
Types of Accounting Changes

● LO1

Type of Change	Description	Examples
Change in accounting principle	Change from one generally accepted accounting principle to another.	• Adopt a new FASB standard. • Change methods of inventory costing. • Change from cost method to equity method, or vice versa. • Change from completed contract to percentage-of-completion, or vice versa.
Change in accounting estimate	Revision of an estimate because of new information or new experience.	• Change depreciation methods. • Change estimate of useful life of depreciable asset. • Change estimate of residual value of depreciable asset. • Change estimate of bad debt percentage. • Change estimate of periods benefited by intangible assets. • Change actuarial estimates pertaining to a pension plan.
Change in reporting entity	Change from reporting as one type of entity to another type of entity.	• Consolidate a subsidiary not previously included in consolidated financial statements. • Report consolidated financial statements in place of individual statements.

A change in depreciation methods is a change in estimate that is achieved by a change in accounting principle.

The correction of an error is another adjustment sometimes made to financial statements that is not actually an accounting change but is accounted for similarly. Errors occur when transactions are either recorded incorrectly or not recorded at all as shown in Graphic 20–2.

GRAPHIC 20–2
Correction of Errors

Type of Change	Description	Examples
Error correction	Correction of an error caused by a transaction being recorded incorrectly or not at all.	• Mathematical mistakes. • Inaccurate physical count of inventory. • Change from the cash basis of accounting to the accrual basis. • Failure to record an adjusting entry. • Recording an asset as an expense, or vice versa. • Fraud or gross negligence.

Two approaches to reporting accounting changes and error corrections are used, depending on the situation.

The *retrospective* approach offers consistency and comparability.

1. Using the **retrospective approach**, financial statements issued in previous years are revised to reflect the impact of the change whenever those statements are presented again for comparative purposes. An advantage of this approach is that it achieves comparability among financial statements. All financial statements presented are prepared on the same basis. However, some argue that public confidence in the

[1]"Accounting Changes," *Accounting Principles Board Opinion No. 20* (New York: AICPA, 1971).

integrity of financial data suffers when numbers previously reported as correct are later superseded. On the other hand, proponents argue the opposite—that it's impossible to maintain public confidence unless the financial statements are comparable.

For each year in the comparative statements reported, the balance of each account affected is revised. In other words, those statements are made to appear as if the newly adopted accounting method had been applied all along or that the error had never occurred. Then, a journal entry is created to adjust all account balances affected to what those amounts would have been. In addition, if retained earnings is one of the accounts whose balance requires adjustment, that adjustment is made to the beginning balance of retained earnings for the earliest period reported in the comparative statements of shareholders' equity.

2. The **prospective approach** requires neither a modification of prior years' financial statements nor a journal entry to adjust account balances. Instead, the change is simply implemented now, and its effects are reflected in the financial statements of the current and future years only.

The effects of a change are reflected in the financial statements of only the current and future years under the *prospective approach*.

Now, let's look at each type of accounting change, one at a time, focusing on the selective application of these approaches.

Change in Accounting Principle

Accounting is not an exact science. Professional judgment is required to apply a set of principles, concepts, and objectives to specific sets of circumstances. This means choices must be made. In your study of accounting to date, you've encountered many areas where choices are necessary. For example, management must choose whether to use accelerated or straight-line depreciation. Is FIFO, LIFO, or average cost most appropriate to measure inventories? Would the completed contract or percentage-of-completion method best reflect the performance of our construction operations? Should we adopt a new FASB standard early or wait until it's mandatory? These are but a few of the accounting choices management makes.

You also probably recall that consistency and comparability are two fundamental qualitative characteristics of accounting information. To achieve these attributes of information, accounting choices, once made, should be consistently followed from year to year. This doesn't mean, though, that methods can never be changed. Changing circumstances might make a new method more appropriate. A change in economic conditions, for instance, might prompt a company to change accounting methods. The most extensive voluntary accounting change ever—a switch by hundreds of companies from FIFO to LIFO in the mid-1970s, for example—was a result of heightened inflation. Changes within a specific industry, too, can lead a company to switch methods, often to adapt to new technology or to be consistent with others in the industry. And, of course, a change might be mandated. This happens when the FASB issues a new accounting standard. In 1993, all firms were required to switch from accounting for income taxes according to *APB 11*[2] to the method prescribed by *SFAS No. 109*. For these reasons, it's not uncommon for a company to switch from one accounting method to another. This is called a **change in accounting principle.**

Although consistency and comparability are desirable, changing to a new method sometimes is appropriate.

DECISION MAKERS' PERSPECTIVE—Motivation for Accounting Choices

It would be nice to think that all accounting choices are made by management in the best interest of fair and consistent financial reporting. Unfortunately, other motives influence the choices among accounting methods and whether to change methods. It has been suggested that the effect of choices on management compensation, on existing debt agreements, and on union negotiations each can affect management's selection of accounting methods.[3] For instance, research has suggested that managers of companies with bonus plans are more likely to choose accounting methods that maximize their bonuses (often those that increase

[2]*SFAS No. 96* for those companies that voluntarily adopted that interim standard.

[3]R. L. Watts and J. L. Zimmerman, "Towards a Positive Theory of the Determination of Accounting Standards," *The Accounting Review*, January 1978, and "Positive Accounting Theory: A Ten Year Perspective," *The Accounting Review*, January 1990.

net income).[4] Other research has indicated that the existence and nature of debt agreements and other aspects of a firm's capital structure can influence accounting choices.[5] Whether a company is forbidden from paying dividends if retained earnings fall below a certain level, for example, can affect the choice of accounting methods.

A financial analyst must be aware that different accounting methods used by different firms and by the same firm in different years complicate comparisons. Financial ratios, for example, will differ when different accounting methods are used, even when there are no differences in attributes being compared.

Investors and creditors also should be alert to instances in which companies change accounting methods. They must consider not only the effect on comparability but also possible hidden motivations for making the changes. Are managers trying to compensate for a downturn in actual performance with a switch to methods that artificially inflate reported earnings? Is the firm in danger of violating debt covenants or other contractual agreements regarding financial position? Are executive compensation plans tied to reported performance measures? Fortunately, the nature and effect of changes are reported in the financial statements. Although a justification for a change is provided by management, analysts should be wary of accepting the reported justification at face value without considering a possible hidden agenda.

Choices are not always those that tend to increase income. As you learned in Chapter 8, many companies use the LIFO inventory method because it reduces income and therefore reduces the amount of income taxes that must be paid currently. Also, some very large and visible companies might be reluctant to report high income that might render them vulnerable to union demands, government regulations, or higher taxes.[6]

Another reason managers sometimes choose accounting methods that don't necessarily increase earnings was mentioned earlier. Most managers tend to prefer to report earnings that follow a regular, smooth trend from year to year. The desire to "smooth" earnings means that any attempt to manipulate earnings by choosing accounting methods is not always in the direction of higher income. Instead, the choice might be to avoid irregular earnings, particularly those with wide variations from year to year, a pattern that might be interpreted by analysts as denoting a risky situation.

Obviously, any time managers make accounting choices for any of the reasons discussed here, when the motivation is an objective other than to provide useful information, earnings quality suffers. As mentioned frequently throughout this text, earnings quality refers to the ability of reported earnings (income) to predict a company's future earnings.

Let's turn our attention now to situations involving changes in methods and how we account for those changes.

The Retrospective Approach: Most Changes in Accounting Principle

● LO2

We report most voluntary changes in accounting principles retrospectively.[7] This means reporting all previous period's financial statements as if the new method had been used in all prior periods. An example is provided in Illustration 20–1.

FINANCIAL Reporting Case

Q1, p. 1061

1. REVISE COMPARATIVE FINANCIAL STATEMENTS. For each year reported in the comparative statements, Air Parts makes those statements appear as if the newly adopted accounting method (FIFO) had been applied all along. As you learned in Chapter 1, consistency is one of the important qualitative characteristics of accounting information.

---

[4]For example, see P. M. Healy, "The Effect of Bonus Schemes on Accounting Decisions," *Journal of Accounting and Economics,* April 1985, and D. Dhaliwal, G. Salamon, and E. Smith, "The Effect of Owner versus Management Control on the Choice of Accounting Methods," *Journal of Accounting and Economics,* July 1992.

[5]R. M. Bowen, E. W. Noreen, and J. M. Lacy, "Determinants of the Corporate Decision to Capitalize Interest," *Journal of Accounting and Economics,* August 1981.

[6]This political cost motive is suggested by R. L. Watts and J. L. Zimmerman, "Positive Accounting Theory: A Ten Year Perspective," *The Accounting Review,* January 1990, and M. Zmijewski and R. Hagerman, "An Income Strategy Approach to the Positive Theory of Accounting Standard Setting/Choice," *Journal of Accounting and Economics,* August 1981.

[7]"Accounting Changes and Error Corrections—A Replacement of APB Opinion No. 20 and FASB Statement No. 3," *Statement of Financial Accounting Standards No. 154,* (Norwalk, Conn: FASB, 2005).

Air Parts Corporation used the LIFO inventory costing method. At the beginning of 2009, Air Parts decided to change to the FIFO method. Income components for 2009 and prior years were as follows ($ in millions):

	2009	2008	2007	Previous Years
Cost of goods sold (LIFO)	$430	$420	$405	$2,000
Cost of goods sold (FIFO)	370	365	360	1,700
Difference	$ 60	$ 55	$ 45	$ 300
Revenues	$950	$900	$875	$4,500
Operating expenses	230	210	205	1,000

Air Parts has paid dividends of $40 million each year beginning in 2002. Its income tax rate is 40%. Retained earnings on January 1, 2007, was $700 million; inventory was $500 million.

ILLUSTRATION 20–1
Change in Accounting Principle

LIFO usually produces higher cost of goods sold than does FIFO because more recently purchased goods (usually higher priced) are assumed sold first.

When accounting changes occur, the usefulness of the comparative financial statements is enhanced with retrospective application of those changes.

Income statements.

($ in millions)	2009	2008	2007
Revenues	$950	$900	$875
Cost of goods sold (FIFO)	(370)	(365)	(360)
Operating expenses	(230)	(210)	(205)
Income before tax	$350	$325	$310
Income tax expense (40%)	(140)	(130)	(124)
Net income	$210	$195	$186

The company recasts the comparative statements to appear as if the accounting method adopted in 2009 (FIFO) had been used in 2008 and 2007 as well.

Earnings per share each year, of course, also will be based on the revised net income numbers.

Balance Sheets.

Inventory. In its comparative balance sheets, Air Parts will report 2009 inventory by its newly adopted method, FIFO, and also will revise the amounts it reported last year for its 2008 and 2007 inventory. Each year, inventory will be higher than it would have been by LIFO. Here's why:

Since the cost of goods *available for sale* each period is the sum of the cost of goods *sold* and the cost of goods *unsold* (inventory), a difference in cost of goods sold resulting from having used LIFO rather than FIFO means there also is an opposite difference in inventory. Because cost of goods sold by the FIFO method is *less* than by LIFO, inventory by FIFO is *greater* than by LIFO. The amounts of the differences and also the cumulative differences over the years are calculated in Illustration 20–1A on the next page.

FIFO usually produces *lower* cost of goods sold and thus *higher* inventory than does LIFO.

Retained earnings. Similarly, Air Parts will report retained earnings by FIFO each year as well. Retained earnings is different because the two inventory methods affect income differently. Because cost of goods sold by FIFO is *less* than by LIFO, income and therefore retained earnings by FIFO are *greater* than by LIFO.

Comparative balance sheets, then, will report retained earnings for 2009, 2008, and 2007 at amounts $276, $240, and $207 million higher than would have been reported if the switch from LIFO had not occurred. These are the cumulative net income differences shown in Illustration 20–1A.

When costs are rising, FIFO produces *lower* cost of goods sold than does LIFO and thus *higher* net income and retained earnings.

Retained earnings is revised each year to reflect FIFO.

Statements of shareholders' equity.

Recall that a statement of shareholders' equity reports changes that occur in each shareholders' equity account starting with the beginning balances in the earliest year reported.

ILLUSTRATION 20–1A
Effects of Switch to FIFO

By FIFO, cost of goods sold is lower.

The cumulative income effect increases each year by the annual after-tax difference in COGS.

Inventory, pretax income, income taxes, net income, and retained earnings all are higher.

	Years Ending Dec. 31:			
($ in millions)	**2009**	**2008**	**2007**	**Previous Years**
Cost of goods sold (LIFO)	$430	$420	$405	$2,000
Cost of goods sold (FIFO)	370	365	360	1,700
Differences	$ 60	$ 55	$ 45	$ 300
Cumulative differences:				
Cost of goods sold	$460	$400	$345	$ 300
Income taxes (40%)	184	160	138	120
Net income and retained earnings	$276	$240	$207	$ 180

Comparative balance sheets, then, will report 2007 inventory $345 million higher than it was reported in last year's statements. Likewise, 2008 inventory will be increased by $400 million. Inventory for 2009, being reported for the first time, is $460 million higher than it would have been if the switch from LIFO had not occurred.

Because it's the earliest year reported, 2007's beginning retained earnings is increased by the $180 million cumulative income effect of the difference in inventory methods that occurred before 2007.

So, if retained earnings is one of the accounts whose balance requires adjustment due to a change in accounting principle (and it usually is), we must adjust the beginning balance of retained earnings for the earliest period reported in the comparative statements of shareholders' equity. The amount of the revision is the cumulative effect of the change on years prior to that date. Air Parts will revise its 2007 beginning retained earnings since that's the earliest year in its comparative statements. That balance had been reported in prior statements as $700 million. If FIFO had been used for inventory rather than LIFO, that amount would have been higher by $180 million as calculated in Illustration 20–1A. The disclosure note pertaining to the inventory change should point out the amount of the adjustment. The January 1, 2007, retained earnings balance reported in the comparative statements of shareholders' equity below has been adjusted from $700 million to $880 million.

ILLUSTRATION 20–1B
Comparative Statements of Shareholders' Equity

A footnote should indicate that the beginning retained earnings balance has been increased by $180 million from $700 million to $880 million.

($ in millions)	**Common Stock**	**Additional Paid-In Capital**	**Retained Earnings**	**Total Shareholders' Equity**
Jan. 1, 2007			$ 880	
Net income (revised to FIFO)			186	
Dividends			(40)	
Dec. 31, 2007			$1,026	
Net income (revised to FIFO)			195	
Dividends			(40)	
Dec. 31, 2008			$1,181	
Net income (using FIFO)			210	
Dividends			(40)	
Dec. 31, 2009			$1,351	

2. ADJUST ACCOUNTS FOR THE CHANGE. Besides reporting revised amounts in the comparative financial statements, Air Parts must also adjust the book balances of affected accounts. It does so by creating a journal entry to change those balances from their current amounts (from using LIFO) to what those balances would have been using the newly adopted method (FIFO). As discussed in the previous section, differences in cost of goods sold and income are reflected in retained earnings, as are the income tax effects of changes in income. So, the journal entry updates inventory, retained earnings, and the income tax liability for revisions resulting from differences in the LIFO and FIFO methods prior to the switch, pre-2009. Repeating a portion of the calculation we made in Illustration 20–1A, we determine the difference in cost of goods sold and therefore in inventory.

($ in millions)

	2008	2007	Cumulative Difference pre-2007	Cumulative Difference pre-2009
Cost of goods sold (LIFO)	$420	$405	$1,000	
Cost of goods sold (FIFO)	365	360	700	
Difference	$ 55	$ 45	$ 300	$400

Cost of goods sold would have been $400 million *less* if FIFO rather than LIFO had been used in years before the change.

The $400 million cumulative difference in cost of goods sold also is the difference between the balance in inventory and what that balance would have been if the FIFO method, rather than LIFO, had been used before 2009. Inventory must be increased by that amount. Retained earnings must be increased also, but by only 60% of that amount because income taxes would have been higher by 40% of the change in pretax income.

Journal entry to record the change in principle.

January 1, 2009		
Inventory (additional inventory if FIFO had been used)	400	
Retained earnings (additional net income if FIFO had been used)		240
Deferred tax liability ($400 × 40%)		160

Inventory would have been $400 million more and cumulative prior earnings $240 more if FIFO rather than LIFO had been used.

Notice that the income tax effect is reflected in the deferred income tax liability. The reason is that an accounting method used for tax purposes cannot be changed retrospectively for prior years. The Internal Revenue Code requires that taxes saved previously ($160 million in this case) from having used another inventory method must now be repaid (over no longer than six years). Recall from Chapter 16 that in the meantime, there is a temporary difference, reflected in the deferred tax liability.

ADDITIONAL CONSIDERATION

What if the tax law did not require a recapture of the tax difference? There still would be a credit to the deferred tax liability. That's because retrospectively increasing accounting income, but not taxable income, creates a temporary difference between the two that will reverse over time as the unsold inventory becomes cost of goods sold. When that happens, taxable income will become higher than accounting income—a future taxable amount, creating a deferred tax liability.

If we were switching *from* FIFO to, say, the average method, we would record a deferred tax asset instead. For financial reporting purposes, but not for tax, we would be retrospectively *decreasing* accounting income, but not taxable income. This creates a temporary difference between the two that will reverse over time as the unsold inventory becomes cost of goods sold. When that happens, taxable income will be less than accounting income. When taxable income will be less than accounting income as a temporary difference reverses, we have a "future deductible amount" and record a deferred tax asset.

3. DISCLOSURE NOTES. To achieve consistency and comparability, accounting choices once made should be consistently followed from year to year. Any change, then, requires that the new method be justified as clearly more appropriate. In the first set of financial statements after the change, a disclosure note is needed to provide that justification. The note also should point out that comparative information has been revised, or that retrospective revision has not been made because it is impracticable, and report any per share amounts affected for the current period and all prior periods presented. Disclosure of a recent change by **Hormel Foods Corporation** in its 2007 annual report provides us the example shown in Graphic 20–3 on the next page.

Footnote disclosure explains why the change was needed as well as its effects on items not reported on the face of the primary statements.

GRAPHIC 20–3
Disclosure of a change in inventory method—Hormel Foods

Real World Financials

Change in Accounting Principle

In the first quarter of fiscal 2006, the company changed its method of accounting for the materials portion of turkey products and substantially all inventoriable expenses, packages, and supplies (in total approximately 23.0 percent of total gross inventory at the end of fiscal 2005) that had previously been accounted for utilizing the Last-In First-Out (LIFO) method to the First-In First-Out (FIFO) method. As a result, all inventories are now stated at the lower of cost, determined on a FIFO basis, or market. The change is preferable because it provides a more meaningful presentation of the company's financial position as it values inventory in a manner which more closely approximates current cost; it provides a consistent and uniform costing method across the company's operations; FIFO inventory values better represent the underlying commercial substance of selling the oldest products first; it is the prevalent method used by other entities within the company's industry; and it enhances the comparability of the financial statements with those of our industry peers. As required by U.S. generally accepted accounting principles, the change has been reflected in the consolidated statements of financial position, consolidated statements of operations, and consolidated statements of cash flows through retrospective application of the FIFO method. Inventories as of the beginning of fiscal 2005 were increased by the LIFO reserve ($36.7 million), the net current deferred tax assets were decreased ($7.9 million), current tax liabilities were increased ($5.8 million), and shareholders' investment was increased by the after-tax effect ($23.0 million). Previously reported net earnings for fiscal years 2005 and 2004 were increased by $1.1 million and $1.9 million, respectively.

The Prospective Approach

Although we usually report voluntary changes in accounting principles retrospectively, it's not always practicable or appropriate to do so.

● LO3

Sometimes a lack of information makes it impracticable to report a change retrospectively so the new method is simply applied prospectively.

THE PROSPECTIVE APPROACH: WHEN RETROSPECTIVE APPLICATION IS IMPRACTICABLE. For some changes in principle, insufficient information is available for retrospective application to be practicable. Revising balances in prior years means knowing what those balances should be. But suppose we're switching from the FIFO method of inventory costing to the LIFO method. Recall from your study of inventory costing methods that LIFO inventory consists of "layers" added in prior years at costs existing in those years. If another method has been used, though, the company likely hasn't kept track of those costs. So, accounting records of prior years usually are inadequate to report the change retrospectively. In that case, a company changing to LIFO usually reports the change prospectively, and the beginning inventory in the year the LIFO method is adopted becomes the base year inventory for all future LIFO calculations. Footnote disclosure should indicate reasons why retrospective application was impracticable.

When **Books A Million, Inc.** adopted the LIFO cost flow assumption for valuing its inventories, the change was reported in a disclosure note as shown in Graphic 20–4.

GRAPHIC 20–4
Disclosure of a Change to LIFO—Books A Million, Inc.

Real World Financials

Inventories (in part)

. . . the Company changed from the first-in, first-out (FIFO) method of accounting for inventories to the last-in, first-out (LIFO) method. Management believes this change was preferable in that it achieves a more appropriate matching of revenues and expenses. The impact of this accounting change was to increase "Costs of Products Sold" in the consolidated statements of operations by $0.7 million for the fiscal year. . . . The cumulative effect of a change in accounting principle from the FIFO method to LIFO method is not determinable. Accordingly, such change has been accounted for prospectively.

When it is impracticable to determine some period-specific effects. A company may have some, but not all, the information it needs to account for a change retrospectively.

For instance, let's say a company changes to the LIFO inventory method effective as of the beginning of 2009. It has information that would allow it to revise all assets and liabilities on the basis of the newly adopted method for 2008 in its comparative statements, but not for 2007. In that case, the company should report 2008 statement amounts (revised) and 2009 statement amounts (reported for the first time) based on LIFO, but not revise 2007 numbers. Then, account balances should be retrospectively adjusted at the beginning of 2008 since that's the earliest date it's practicable to do so.

If it's impracticable to adjust each year reported, the change is applied retrospectively as of the earliest year practicable.

When it is impracticable to determine the cumulative effect of prior years? Another possibility is that the company doesn't have the information necessary to retrospectively adjust retained earnings, but does have information that would allow it to revise all assets and liabilities for one or more specific years. Let's say the records of inventory purchases and sales are not available for some previous years, which would have allowed it to determine the cumulative effect of applying this change to LIFO retrospectively. However, it does have all of the information necessary to apply the LIFO method on a prospective basis beginning in, say, 2007. In that case, the company should report numbers for years beginning in 2007 as if it had carried forward the 2006 ending balance in inventory (measured on the previous inventory costing basis) and then had begun applying LIFO as of January 1, 2007. Of course there would be no adjustment to retained earnings for the cumulative income effect of not using LIFO prior to that.

If full retrospective application isn't possible, the new method is applied prospectively beginning in the earliest year practicable.

THE PROSPECTIVE APPROACH: WHEN MANDATED BY AUTHORITATIVE PRONOUNCEMENTS. Another exception to retrospective application of voluntary changes in accounting principle is when an FASB Statement or another authoritative pronouncement requires prospective application for specific changes in accounting methods. For instance, for a change from the equity method to another method of accounting for long-term investments, *APB Opinion 18* requires the prospective application of the new method.[8] Recall from Chapter 12 that when an investor's level of influence changes, it may be necessary to change from the equity method to another method. This could happen, for instance, if a sale of shares causes the investor's ownership interest to fall from, say, 25% to 15%, resulting in the equity method no longer being appropriate. When this situation happens, no adjustment is made to the remaining carrying amount of the investment. Instead, the equity method is simply discontinued and the new method applied from then on. The balance in the investment account when the equity method is discontinued would serve as the new "cost" basis for writing the investment up or down to fair value on the next set of financial statements.

If an authoritative pronouncement specifically requires prospective accounting, that requirement is followed.

INTERNATIONAL FINANCIAL REPORTING STANDARDS

The FASB and the International Accounting Standards Board have a continuing commitment to converge their accounting standards. As part of their short-term convergence effort, they identified how companies report accounting changes as an area in which the FASB could improve its guidance by converging it with the provisions of *IAS No. 8*, "Accounting Policies, Changes in Accounting Estimates and Errors." The product of this effort is *SFAS No. 154*, "Accounting Changes and Error Corrections," issued in 2005. Few differences remain, so it's unlikely we will see much change in this area.

THE PROSPECTIVE APPROACH: CHANGING DEPRECIATION, AMORTIZATION, AND DEPLETION METHODS. A change in depreciation methods is considered to be a change in accounting estimate that is achieved by a change in accounting principle. As a result, we account for such a change prospectively—precisely the way we account for changes in estimates. We discuss that approach in the next section.

We account for a change in depreciation method as a change in accounting estimate.

[8] "Reporting Accounting Changes in Interim Financial Statements," *Accounting Principles Board Opinion No. 18* (New York: AICPA, 1971).

Change in Accounting Estimate

● LO4

You've encountered many instances during your study of accounting in which it's necessary to make estimates of uncertain future events. Depreciation, for example, entails estimates not only of the useful lives of depreciable assets, but their anticipated residual values as well. Anticipating uncollectible accounts receivable, predicting warranty expenses, amortizing intangible assets, and making actuarial assumptions for pension benefits are but a few of the accounting tasks that require estimates.

Revisions are viewed as a natural consequence of making estimates.

Accordingly, estimates are an inherent aspect of accounting. Unfortunately, though, estimates routinely turn out to be wrong. No matter how carefully known facts are considered and forecasts are prepared, new information and experience frequently force the revision of estimates. Of course, if the original estimate was based on erroneous information or calculations or was not made in good faith, the revision of that estimate constitutes the correction of an error.

A change in estimate is reflected in the financial statements of the current period and future periods.

Changes in accounting estimates are accounted for prospectively. When a company revises a previous estimate, prior financial statements are *not* revised. Instead, the company merely incorporates the new estimate in any related accounting determinations from then on. So, it usually will affect some aspects of both the balance sheet and the income statement in the current period and future periods. A disclosure note should describe the effect of a change in estimate on income before extraordinary items, net income, and related per share amounts for the current period.

When **Owens-Corning Fiberglass** revised estimates of the useful lives of some of its depreciable assets, the change was disclosed in its annual report as shown in Graphic 20–5.

GRAPHIC 20–5
Change in Estimate—Owens-Corning Fiberglass Corporation

Real World Financials

Note 6: Depreciation of Plant and Equipment (in part)

. . . the Company completed a review of its fixed asset lives. The Company determined that as a result of actions taken to increase its preventative maintenance and programs initiated with its equipment suppliers to increase the quality of their products, actual lives for certain asset categories were generally longer than the useful lives for depreciation purposes. Therefore, the Company extended the estimated useful lives of certain categories of plant and equipment, effective . . . The effect of this change in estimate reduced depreciation expense for the year ended . . . , by $14 million and increased income before cumulative effect of accounting change by $8 million ($.19 per share).

An example of another change in estimate is provided in Illustration 20–2.

ILLUSTRATION 20–2
Change in Accounting Estimate

Universal Semiconductors estimates bad debt expense as 2% of credit sales. After a review during 2009, Universal determined that 3% of credit sales is a more realistic estimate of its collection experience. Credit sales in 2009 are $300 million. The effective income tax rate is 40%.

Neither bad debt expense nor the allowance for uncollectible accounts reported in prior years is restated. No account balances are adjusted. The cumulative effect of the estimate change is not reported in current income. Rather, in 2009 and later years, the adjusting entry to record bad debt expense simply will reflect the new percentage. In 2009, the entry would be:

	($ in millions)	
Bad debt expense (3% × $300 million)	9	
Allowance for uncollectible accounts		9

The after-tax effect of the change in estimate is $1.8 million [$300 million × (3% − 2%) = $3 million, less 40% of $3 million]. Assuming 100 million outstanding shares of common stock, the effect is described in a disclosure note to the financial statements as follows:

Note A: Accounts Receivable

In 2009, the company revised the percentage used to estimate bad debts. The change provides a better indication of collection experience. The effect of the change was to decrease 2009 net income by $1.8 million, or $.018 per share.

Changing Depreciation, Amortization, and Depletion Methods

FINANCIAL Reporting Case

Q2, p. 1061

When a company acquires an asset that will provide benefits for several years, it allocates the cost of the asset over the asset's useful life. If the asset is a building, equipment, or other tangible operational asset, the allocation process is called *depreciation.* It's referred to as *amortization* if an intangible asset or *depletion* if a natural resource. In each case, estimates are essential to the allocation process. How long will benefits accrue? What will be the value of the asset when its use is discontinued? Will the benefits be realized evenly over the asset's life or will they be higher in some years than in others?

An exception to retrospective application of a change in accounting principle is a change in the method of depreciation (or amortization or depletion).

The choice of depreciation method and application reflects these estimates. Likewise, when a company changes the way it depreciates an asset in midstream, the change would be made to reflect a change in (a) estimated future benefits from the asset, (b) the pattern of receiving those benefits, or (c) the company's knowledge about those benefits. For instance, suppose Universal Semiconductors originally chose an accelerated depreciation method because it expected greater benefits in the earlier years of an asset's life. Then, two years later, when it became apparent that remaining benefits would be realized approximately evenly over the remaining useful life, Universal Semiconductor switched to straight-line depreciation. Even though the company is changing its depreciation method, it is doing so to reflect changes in its estimates of future benefits. As a result, we report a change in depreciation method as a change in estimate, rather than as a change in accounting principle.

Companies report a change in depreciation prospectively.

For this reason, a company reports a change in depreciation method (say to straight line) prospectively; previous financial statements are not revised. Instead, the company simply employs the straight-line method from then on. The undepreciated cost remaining at the time of the change would be depreciated straight-line over the remaining useful life. Illustration 20–3 on the next page provides an example.

A company must justify any change in principle as preferable to the previous method.

Is a change in depreciation method a change in accounting principle, or is it a change in estimate? As we've seen, it's both. Even though it's considered to reflect a change in estimate and is accounted for as such, a change to a new depreciation method requires the company to justify the new method as being preferable to the previous method, just as for any other change in principle. A disclosure note should justify that the change is preferable and describe the effect of a change on any financial statement line items and per share amounts affected for all periods reported.

In practice, the situation arises infrequently. Most companies changing depreciation methods do not apply the change to existing assets, but instead to assets placed in service after that date. In those cases, of course, the new method is simply applied prospectively (see Graphic 20–6).

Note 12: Land, Buildings, and Equipment, Net (in part)

. . . the company changed its method of depreciation for newly acquired buildings and equipment to the straight-line method. The change had no cumulative effect on prior years' earnings but did increase [current year] net earnings by $9 million, or $.14 per share . . .

GRAPHIC 20–6

Change in depreciation method for newly acquired assets—**Rohm and Haas Company**

Real World Financials

ILLUSTRATION 20–3
Change in depreciation methods

Universal Semiconductors switched from the SYD depreciation method to straight-line depreciation in 2009. The change affects its precision equipment purchased at the beginning of 2007 at a cost of $63 million. The machinery has an expected useful life of five years and an estimated residual value of $3 million.

The depreciation prior to the change is as follows ($ in millions):

Sum-of-the-Years'-Digits Depreciation:	
2007 depreciation	$20 ($60 × 5/15)
2008 depreciation	16 ($60 × 4/15)
Accumulated depreciation	$36

A change in depreciation method is considered a change in accounting estimate resulting from a change in accounting principle. So, Universal Semiconductors reports the change prospectively; previous financial statements are not revised. Instead, the company simply employs the straight-line method from 2009 on. The undepreciated cost remaining at the time of the change is depreciated straight-line over the remaining useful life.

The $24 million depreciable cost not yet depreciated is spread over the asset's remaining three years.

Calculation of Straight-Line Depreciation:	($ in millions)
Asset's cost	$63
Accumulated depreciation to date (calculated above)	(36)
Undepreciated cost, Jan. 1, 2009	$27
Estimated residual value	(3)
To be depreciated over remaining 3 years	$24
	3 years
Annual straight-line depreciation 2009–2011	$ 8

Adjusting entry (2009, 2010, and 2011 depreciation):	($ in millions)	
Depreciation expense (calculated above)	8	
Accumulated depreciation		8

When it's not possible to distinguish between a change in principle and a change in estimate, the change should be treated as a change in estimate.

Sometimes, it's not easy to distinguish between a change in principle and a change in estimate. For example, if a company begins to capitalize rather than expense the cost of tools because their benefits beyond one year become apparent, the change could be construed as either a change in principle or a change in the estimated life of the asset. When the distinction is not possible, the change should be treated as a change in estimate. This treatment also is appropriate when both a change in principle and a change in estimate occur simultaneously.

Change in Reporting Entity

● LO5

The issuance of *SFAS No. 94* resulted in many companies consolidating previously unconsolidated subsidiaries.

A reporting entity can be a single company, or it can be a group of companies that reports a single set of financial statements. For example, the consolidated financial statements of **PepsiCo Inc.** report the financial position and results of operations not only for the parent company but also for its subsidiaries which include **Frito-Lay** and **Gatorade.** A **change in reporting entity** occurs as a result of (1) presenting consolidated financial statements in place of statements of individual companies or (2) changing specific companies that constitute the group for which consolidated or combined statements are prepared.[9]

Some changes in reporting entity are a result of changes in accounting rules. For example, *SFAS No. 94* requires companies like **Ford, General Motors** and **General Electric** to consolidate their manufacturing operations with their financial subsidiaries, creating a new

[9]"Consolidation of All Majority-Owned Subsidiaries," *Statement of Financial Accounting Standards No. 94* (Stamford, Conn.: FASB, 1987).

entity that includes them both.[10] For those changes in entity, *SFAS No. 154* requires that the prior-period financial statements that are presented for comparative purposes be restated to appear as if the new entity existed in those periods.

However, the more frequent change in entity occurs when one company acquires another one. In those circumstances, the financial statements of the acquirer include the acquiree as of the date of acquisition, and the acquirer's prior-period financial statements that are presented for comparative purposes are not restated. This makes it difficult to make year-to-year comparisons for a company that frequently acquires other companies. Acquiring companies are required to provide a footnote that presents key financial statement information as if the acquisition had occurred before the beginning of the previous year. At a minimum, the supplemental pro forma information should display revenue, income before extraordinary items, net income, and earnings per share.

A change in reporting entity requires that financial statements of prior periods be retrospectively revised to report the financial information for the new reporting entity in all periods.

A change in reporting entity is reported by recasting all previous periods' financial statements as if the new reporting entity existed in those periods.[11] In the first set of financial statements after the change, a disclosure note should describe the nature of the change and the reason it occurred. Also, the effect of the change on net income, income before extraordinary items, and related per share amounts should be indicated for all periods presented. These disclosures aren't necessary in subsequent financial statements. **Dalrada Financial Corporation,** a financial services company, changed the composition of its reporting entity following a spin-off of one of its subsidiaries and described it this way:

GRAPHIC 20–7

Change in Reporting Entity—Dalrada Financial Corporation

Real World Financials

Note 3. Change in Reporting Entity (in part)

On March 29, 2007, the Company completed a separation and sale agreement with an effective date of January 1, 2007, with its majority owned subsidiary, The Solvis Group, Inc. The purpose of this transaction between the Company and Solvis was to separate the two companies into unrelated reporting entities.

For accounting purposes, this transaction has been recorded as a change in reporting entity. The Company has reported the effect of this change in reporting entity in the financial statements as a prior-period adjustment by adjusting the assets and liabilities balances of the first reporting period presented. An offsetting adjustment of $160 has been made to the opening balance of accumulated deficit for the first period presented in the accompanying financial statements. The accompanying financial statements have been restated to reflect this change in reporting entity as if it occurred on the beginning of the earliest period presented.

Error Correction

The correction of an error is not actually an accounting change but is accounted for similarly. In fact, it's accounted for retrospectively like a change in reporting entity and like most changes in accounting principle.

Previous years' financial statements are retrospectively restated to reflect the correction of an error.

More specifically, previous years' financial statements that were incorrect as a result of the error are retrospectively restated to reflect the correction. And, of course, any account balances that are incorrect as a result of the error are corrected by a journal entry. If retained earnings is one of the incorrect accounts, the correction is reported as a prior period adjustment to the beginning balance in a statement of shareholders' equity (or statement of retained earnings if that's presented instead).[12] And, as for accounting changes, a disclosure note is needed to describe the nature of the error and the impact of its correction on operations. We discuss the correction of errors in more detail in Part B of this chapter. But first, let's compare the two approaches for reporting accounting changes and error corrections (Graphic 20–8).

[10]The issuance of *SFAS No. 94,* Consolidation of All Majority-Owned Subsidiaries," resulted in hundreds of entities consolidating previously unconsolidated finance subsidiaries.

[11]Any prior periods' statements are recast when those statements are presented again for comparative purposes.

[12]"Prior Period Adjustments," *Statement of Financial Accounting Standards No. 16* (Stamford, CT: FASB, 1977).

GRAPHIC 20–8 Approaches to Reporting Accounting Changes and Error Corrections

Previous Years	Current Year	Later Years

← Retrospective:
Most changes in accounting principle
Change in reporting entity
Corrections of errors

Prospective →
Changes in estimate including changes in depreciation method
Changes in accounting principle when retrospective application is impractical
Changes in accounting principle when prospective application is mandated

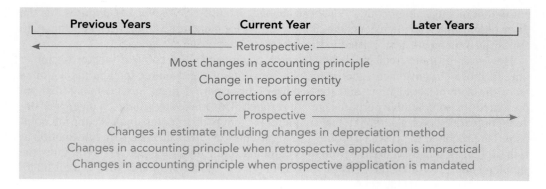

A comparison of accounting treatments is provided by Graphic 20–9.

GRAPHIC 20–9 Accounting Changes and Errors: A Summary

	Change in Accounting Principle		Change in Estimate (including depreciation changes)	Change in Reporting Entity	Error
	Most Changes*	Exceptions†			
Method of accounting	Retrospective	Prospective	Prospective	Retrospective	Retrospective
• Revise prior years' statements?	Yes	No	No	Yes	Yes
• Cumulative effect on prior years' income reported:	As adjustment to retained earnings of earliest year reported.‡	Not reported.	Not reported.	Not reported.	As adjustment to retained earnings of earliest year reported.‡
• Journal entry	To adjust affected balances to new method.	None, but subsequent accounting is affected by the change.	None, but subsequent accounting is affected by the new estimate.	Involves consolidated financial statements discussed in other courses.	To correct any balances that are incorrect as a result of the error.
• Disclosure note?	Yes	Yes	Yes	Yes	Yes

*Changes in depreciation, amortization, and depletion methods are considered changes in estimates.
†When retrospective application is impracticable such as most changes to LIFO and certain mandated changes.
‡On the statement of shareholders' equity or statement of retained earnings.

CONCEPT REVIEW EXERCISE

ACCOUNTING CHANGES

Modern Business Machines recently conducted an extensive review of its accounting and reporting policies. The following accounting changes are an outgrowth of that review:

1. MBM has a patent on a copier design. The patent has been amortized on a straight-line basis since it was acquired at a cost of $400,000 in 2006. During 2009, it was decided that the benefits from the patent would be experienced over a total of 13 years rather than the 20-year legal life now being used to amortize its cost.
2. At the beginning of 2009, MBM changed its method of valuing inventory from the FIFO cost method to the average cost method. At December 31, 2008 and 2007, MBM's inventories were $560 and $540 million, respectively, on a FIFO cost basis but would have totaled $500 and $490 million, respectively, if determined on an average cost basis. MBM's income tax rate is 40%.

Required:

Prepare all journal entries needed in 2009 related to each change. Also, briefly describe any other measures MBM would take in connection with reporting the changes.

SOLUTION

1. Change in estimate

	($ in 000s)	
Patent amortization expense (determined below)	34	
Patent		34

Calculation of Annual Amortization after the Estimate Change

	$400,000	Cost
$20,000		Old annual amortization ($400,000 ÷ 20 years)
× 3 years	(60,000)	Amortization to date (2006, 2007, 2008)
	340,000	Unamortized cost
	÷ 10	Estimated remaining life (13 years − 3 years)
	$ 34,000	New annual amortization

A disclosure note should describe the effect of a change in estimate on income before extraordinary items, net income, and related per-share amounts for the current period.

2. Change in principle

MBM creates a journal entry to bring up to date all account balances affected.

	($ in millions)	
Retained earnings (The difference in net income before 2008)	36	
Deferred tax asset ($60 million × 40%)	24	
Inventory ($560 million − $500 million)		60

For financial reporting purposes, but not for tax, MBM is retrospectively *decreasing* accounting income, but not taxable income. This creates a temporary difference between the two that will reverse over time as the unsold inventory becomes cost of goods sold. When that happens, taxable income will be less than accounting income. When taxable income will be less than accounting income as a temporary difference reverses, we have a "future deductible amount" and record a deferred tax asset.

Prior years' financial statements are revised to reflect the use of the new accounting method.

Also, MBM will revise all previous period's financial statements (in this case 2008) as if the new method (average cost) were used in those periods. In other words, for each year in the comparative statements reported, the balance of each account affected will be revised to appear as if the average method had been applied all along.

Since it's the earliest year reported, 2008's beginning retained earnings is adjusted for the portion of the cumulative income effect of the change attributable to prior years.

Since retained earnings is one of the accounts whose balance requires adjustment (and it usually is), MBM makes an adjustment to the beginning balance of retained earnings for the earliest period (2008) reported in the comparative statements of shareholders' equity. Also, in the first set of financial statements after the change, a *disclosure note* describes the nature of the change, justifies management's decision to make the change, and indicates its effect on each item affected in the financial statements.

PART B

CORRECTION OF ACCOUNTING ERRORS

● LO6

Nobody's perfect. People make mistakes, even accountants. When errors are discovered, they should be corrected.[13] Graphic 20–10 describes the steps to be taken to correct an error, if the effect of the error is material.[14]

[13]Interestingly, it appears that not all accounting errors are unintentional. Research has shown that firms with errors that overstate income are more likely "to have diffuse ownership, lower growth in earnings and fewer income-increasing GAAP alternatives available, and are less likely to have audit committees," suggesting that "overstatement errors are the result of managers responding to economic incentives." M. L. DeFond and J. Jiambaolvo, "Incidence and Circumstances of Accounting Errors," *The Accounting Review,* July, 1991.

[14]In practice, the vast majority of errors are not material with respect to their effect on the financial statements and are, therefore, simply corrected in the year discovered (step 1 only).

GRAPHIC 20–10
Steps to Correct an Error

The retrospective approach is used for the correction of errors.

The correction of an error is treated as a prior period adjustment.

1. A journal entry is made to correct any account balances that are incorrect as a result of the error.
2. Previous years' financial statements that were incorrect as a result of the error are retrospectively restated to reflect the correction (for all years reported for comparative purposes).
3. If retained earnings is one of the accounts incorrect as a result of the error, the correction is reported as a prior period adjustment to the beginning balance in a statement of shareholders' equity (or statement of retained earnings if that's presented instead).
4. A disclosure note should describe the nature of the error and the impact of its correction on net income.

Prior Period Adjustments

Before we see these steps applied to the **correction of an error**, one of the steps requires elaboration. As discussed in Chapter 4, the correction of errors is the more common of only two situations that are considered to be prior period adjustments.[15] **A prior period adjustment** refers to an addition to or reduction in the beginning retained earnings balance in a statement of shareholders' equity (or statement of retained earnings if that's presented instead).

In an earlier chapter we saw that a statement of shareholders' equity is the most commonly used way to report the events that cause components of shareholders' equity to change during a particular reporting period. Some companies, though, choose to report the changes that occur in the balance of retained earnings separately in a statement of retained earnings. When it's discovered that the ending balance of retained earnings in the period prior to the discovery of an error was incorrect as a result of that error, the balance must be corrected when it appears as the beginning balance the following year. However, simply reporting a corrected amount might cause misunderstanding for someone familiar with the previously reported amount. Explicitly reporting a prior period adjustment on the statement itself avoids this confusion. Assume, for example, the following comparative statements of retained earnings:

A statement of retained earnings reports the events that cause changes in retained earnings.

STATEMENTS OF RETAINED EARNINGS
For the Years Ended December 31, 2005 and 2004

	2008	2007
Balance at beginning of year	$600,000	$450,000
Net income	400,000	350,000
Less: Dividends	(200,000)	(200,000)
Balance at end of year	$800,000	$600,000

Now suppose that in 2009 it's discovered that an error in 2007 caused that year's net income to be overstated by $20,000 (it should have been $330,000). This means retained earnings both years were overstated. Comparative statements the following year, when the error is discovered, would include a prior period adjustment as shown below:

The incorrect balance as previously reported is corrected by the prior period adjustment.

STATEMENTS OF RETAINED EARNINGS
For the Years Ended December 31, 2009 and 2008

	2009	2008
Balance at beginning of year	$ 780,000	$600,000
Prior period adjustment		(20,000)
Corrected balance		$580,000
Net Income	500,000	400,000
Less: Dividends	(200,000)	(200,000)
Balance at end of year	$1,080,000	$780,000

[15]The other is an adjustment that results from the realization of income tax benefits of preacquisition operating loss carryforwards of purchased subsidiaries. See "Prior Period Adjustments," *Statement of Financial Accounting Standards No. 16* (Stamford, Conn.: FASB, 1977). This situation arises in connection with consolidation which is covered in many advanced accounting courses.

At least two years' (as in our example) and often three years' statements are reported in comparative financial statements. The prior period adjustment is applied to beginning retained earnings for the year following the error, or for the earliest year being reported in the comparative financial statements when the error occurs prior to the earliest year presented.[16]

Error Correction Illustrated

Now, let's discuss these procedures to correct errors in the context of a variety of the most common types of errors. Since there are literally thousands of possibilities, it's not practical to describe every error in every stage of its discovery. However, by applying the process to the situations described below, you should become sufficiently comfortable with the *process* that you could apply it to whatever situation you might encounter.

As you study these examples, be sure to notice that it's significantly more complicated to deal with an error if (a) it affected net income in the reporting period in which it occurred and (b) it is not discovered until a later period.

You shouldn't try to memorize how specific errors are corrected; you should learn the process needed to analyze whatever errors you might encounter.

Error Discovered in the Same Reporting Period That It Occurred

If an accounting error is made and discovered in the same accounting period, the original erroneous entry should simply be reversed and the appropriate entry recorded. The possibilities are limitless. Let's look at the one in Illustration 20–4.

G. H. Little, Inc. paid $3 million for replacement computers and recorded the expenditure as maintenance expense. The error was discovered a week later.

	($ in millions)	
To Reverse Erroneous Entry		
Cash	3	
Maintenance expense		3
To Record Correct Entry		
Equipment	3	
Cash		3

ILLUSTRATION 20–4
Error Discovered in the Same Reporting Period That It Occurred

Note: These entries can, of course, be combined.

Error Affecting Previous Financial Statements, but Not Net Income

If an error did *not* affect net income in the year it occurred, it's relatively easy to correct. Examples are incorrectly recording salaries payable as accounts payable, recording a loss as an expense, or classifying a cash flow as an investing activity rather than a financing activity on the statement of cash flows. A 2005 restatement by **Kirklands, Inc.,** reproduced in Graphic 20–11 provides an example. Illustration 20–5 provides another.

Note 2 Restatement of Financial Statements (in part)

On December 8, 2004, we determined that our accounting for tenant allowances received from landlords in connection with store construction did not comply with FASB Technical Bulletin No. 88-1, Issues Relating to Accounting for Leases (FTB 88-1). . . . Accordingly, we have restated our balance sheet as of January 31, 2004 and the statement of cash flows for the 39-week period ended November 1, 2003. Additionally, this adjustment results in an increase to depreciation and amortization expense and a corresponding decrease to cost of sales as the liability is amortized over the lease term. This change does not have any impact on net income, net sales or shareholders equity.

GRAPHIC 20–11
Error Correction; Kirkland's, Inc.

Real World Financials

[16]The retained earnings balances in years after the first year also are adjusted to what those balances would be if the error had not occurred, but a company may choose not to explicitly report those adjustments as separate line items.

ILLUSTRATION 20–5

Error Affecting Previous Financial Statements, but Not Net Income

MDS Transportation incorrectly recorded a $2 million note receivable as accounts receivable. The error was discovered a year later.

Step 1

To Correct Incorrect Accounts ($ in millions)

Note receivable	2	
Accounts receivable		2

Step 2

When reported for comparative purposes in the current year's annual report, last year's balance sheet would be restated to report the note as it should have been reported last year.

Step 3

Since last year's net income was not affected by the error, the balance in retained earnings was not incorrect. So no prior period adjustment to that account is necessary.

Step 4

A disclosure note would describe the nature of the error, but there would be no impact on net income, income before extraordinary items, and earnings per share to report.

Error Affecting a Prior Year's Net Income

Most errors affect net income in some way. When they do, they affect the balance sheet as well. Both statements must be retrospectively restated; the statement of cash flows sometimes is affected, too. As with any error, all incorrect account balances must be corrected. Because these errors affect income, one of the balances that will require correcting is retained earnings. Complicating matters, income taxes often are affected by income errors. In those cases, amended tax returns are prepared either to pay additional taxes or to claim a tax refund for taxes overpaid.

In Illustration 20–6 (except as indicated), we ignore the tax effects of the errors and their correction to allow us to focus on the errors themselves rather than their tax aspects.

ILLUSTRATION 20–6

Error Affecting Net Income: Recording an Asset as an Expense

In 2009, internal auditors discovered that Seidman Distribution, Inc. had debited an expense account for the $7 million cost of sorting equipment purchased at the beginning of 2007. The equipment's useful life was expected to be five years with no residual value. Straight-line depreciation is used by Seidman.

Sometimes, the analysis is easier if you re-create the entries actually recorded incorrectly and those that would have been recorded if the error hadn't occurred and then compare them.

Analysis:

($ in millions)

	Correct (Should have been recorded)			**Incorrect** (As recorded)		
2007	Equipment	7.0		Expense	7.0	
	Cash		7.0	Cash		7.0
2007	Expense	1.4		Depreciation entry omitted		
	Accum. deprec.		1.4			
2008	Expense	1.4		Depreciation entry omitted		
	Accum. deprec.		1.4			

During the two-year period, depreciation expense was understated by $2.8 million, but other expenses were overstated by $7 million, so net income during the period was understated by $4.2 million. This means retained earnings is currently understated by that amount.

Accumulated depreciation is understated by $2.8 million.

Step 1

To Correct Incorrect Accounts ($ in millions)

Equipment	7.0	
Accumulated depreciation		2.8
Retained earnings		4.2

Step 2
Restate previous years' financial statements

The 2007 and 2008 financial statements that were incorrect as a result of the error are retrospectively restated to report the equipment acquired and to reflect the correct amount of depreciation expense and accumulated depreciation, assuming both statements are reported again for comparative purposes in the 2009 annual report.

Step 3

Because retained earnings is one of the accounts that is incorrect as a result of the error, a correction to that account of $4.2 million is reported as a prior period adjustment

ILLUSTRATION 20–6
Concluded

to the 2009 beginning retained earnings balance in Seidman's comparative statements of shareholders' equity. A correction would be made also to the 2008 beginning retained earnings balance. That prior period adjustment, though, would be for the pre-2008 difference: $7 million − 1.4 million = $5.6 million. If 2007 statements also are included in the comparative report, no adjustment would be necessary for that period because the error didn't occur until after the beginning of 2007.

Prior period adjustment

Also, a disclosure note accompanying Seidman's 2009 financial statements should describe the nature of the error and the impact of its correction on each year's net income (understated by $5.6 million in 2007 and overstated by $1.4 million in 2008), income before extraordinary items (same as net income), and earnings per share.

Step 4 Disclosure note

The effect of most errors is different, depending on ***when*** the error is discovered. For example, if the error in Illustration 20–6 is not discovered until 2010, rather than 2009, accumulated depreciation would be understated by another $1.4 million, or a total of $4.2 million. If not discovered until 2013 or after, no correcting entry at all would be needed. By then, the sum of the omitted depreciation amounts ($1.4 million × 5 years) would equal the expense incorrectly recorded in 2007 ($7 million), so the retained earnings balance would be the same as if the error never had occurred. Also, the asset would have been disposed of—if the useful life estimate was correct—so neither the equipment nor accumulated depreciation would need to be recorded. Of course, any statements of prior years that were affected and are reported again in comparative statements still would be restated, and a footnote would describe the error.

Most errors, in fact, eventually self-correct. An example of an uncommon instance in which an error never self-corrects would be an expense account debited for the cost of land. Because land doesn't depreciate, the error would continue until the land is sold.

Most self correct.

ADDITIONAL CONSIDERATION

We ignored the tax impact of the error and its correction in Illustration 20–6. To consider taxes, we need to know whether depreciation was also omitted from the tax return and the depreciation methods used for tax reporting. Let's say that depreciation was omitted from the tax return also, and that straight-line depreciation is used by Seidman for both tax and financial reporting. The tax rate is 40%.

Total operating expenses (nontax) still would have been overstated by $4.2 million over the two-year period. But that would have caused taxable income to be understated and the tax liability and income tax expense to be understated by 40% of $4.2 million, or $1.68 million. So net income and retained earnings would have been understated by only $2.52 million:

Operating expenses *overstated*	$4.20 million
Income tax expense *understated*	(1.68) million
Net income (and retained earnings) *understated*	$2.52 million

To Correct Incorrect Accounts:	($ in millions)	
Equipment	7.00	
Accumulated depreciation		2.80
Income tax payable (40% × $4.2 million)		1.68
Retained earnings		2.52

If depreciation had been omitted from the income statement but not from the tax return, or if accelerated depreciation was used for tax reporting but straight-line depreciation for financial reporting, the credit to income tax payable in the correcting entry would be replaced by a credit to deferred tax liability.

Some errors correct themselves the following year. For instance, if a company's ending inventory is incorrectly counted or otherwise misstated, the income statement would be in error for the year of the error and the following year, but the balance sheet would be incorrect only for the year the error occurs. After that, all account balances will be correct. This is demonstrated in Illustration 20–7 on the next page.

Even errors that eventually correct themselves cause financial statements to be misstated in the meantime.

ILLUSTRATION 20–7
Error Affecting Net Income: Inventory Misstated

In early 2009, Overseas Wholesale Supply discovered that $1 million of inventory had been inadvertently excluded from its 2007 ending inventory count.

Analysis:
U = Understated O = Overstated

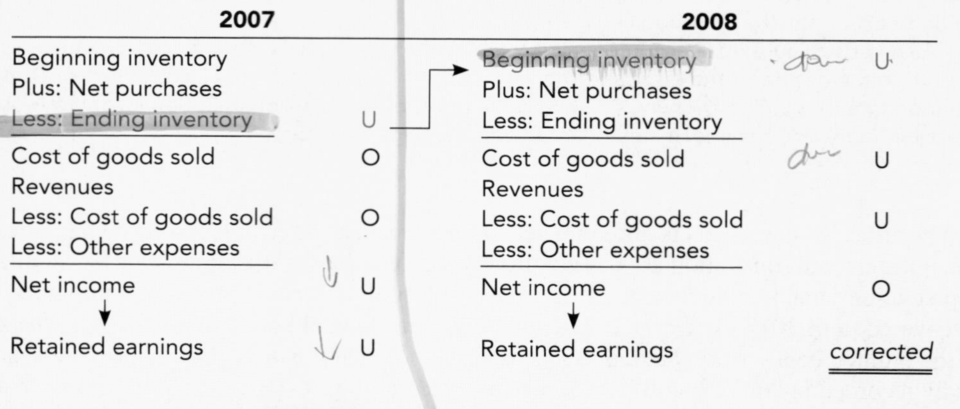

2007		2008	
Beginning inventory		Beginning inventory	U
Plus: Net purchases		Plus: Net purchases	
Less: Ending inventory	U	Less: Ending inventory	
Cost of goods sold	O	Cost of goods sold	U
Revenues		Revenues	
Less: Cost of goods sold	O	Less: Cost of goods sold	U
Less: Other expenses		Less: Other expenses	
Net income	U	Net income	O
Retained earnings	U	Retained earnings	*corrected*

When analyzing inventory errors or other errors that affect cost of goods sold, you may find it helpful to visualize the determination of cost of goods sold, net income, and retained earnings.

Step 1

If Error Is Discovered in 2008 (before closing):

	($ in millions)	
Inventory	1	
Retained earnings		1

If Error Discovered in 2009 or Later:
No correcting entry needed

Step 2

If the error is discovered in 2008, the 2007 financial statements that were incorrect as a result of the error are retrospectively restated to reflect the correct inventory amounts, cost of goods sold, and retained earnings when those statements are reported again for comparative purposes in the 2008 annual report. If the error is discovered in 2009, the 2008 financial statements also are retrospectively restated to reflect the correct inventory amounts and cost of goods sold (retained earnings would not require adjustment), even though no correcting entry would be needed at that point.

Step 3

Because retained earnings is one of the accounts incorrect if the error is discovered in 2008, the correction to that account is reported as a prior period adjustment to the 2008 beginning retained earnings balance in Overseas' statement of shareholders' equity. Of course, no prior period adjustment is needed if the error isn't discovered until 2009 or later.

Step 4

Also, a disclosure note in Overseas' annual report should describe the nature of the error and the impact of its correction on each year's net income (understated by $1 million in 2007, overstated by $1 million in 2008), income before extraordinary items (same as net income), and earnings per share.

Other error corrections that benefit from a similar analysis are the overstatement of ending inventory, the overstatement or understatement of beginning inventory, and errors in recording merchandise purchases (or returns).

An error also would occur if a revenue or an expense is recorded in the wrong accounting period. Illustration 20–8 on the next page offers an example.

ETHICAL DILEMMA

As a second-year accountant for McCormack Chemical Company, you were excited to be named assistant manager of the Agricultural Chemicals Division. After two weeks in your new position, you were supervising the year-end inventory count when the senior manager mentioned that two carloads of herbicides were omitted from the count and should be added. Upon checking, you confirm your understanding that the inventory in question had been deemed to be unsaleable. "Yes," your manager agreed, "but we'll write that off next year when our bottom line won't be so critical to the continued existence of the Agricultural Chemicals Division. Jobs and families depend on our division showing well this year."

IL

Erro
Income
to Recor
Revenue

In 2009, General Paper Company discovered that $3,000 of merchandise (credit) sales the last week of 2008 were not recorded until the first week of 2009. The merchandise sold was appropriately excluded from 2008 ending inventory.

Analysis:

($ in 000s)

	Correct (Should have been recorded)			**Incorrect** (As recorded)		
2008	Accounts receivable	3		No entry		
	Sales revenue		3			
2009	No entry			Accounts receivable	3	
				Sales revenue		3

2008 sales revenue was incorrectly recorded in 2009, so 2008 net income was understated. Retained earnings is currently understated in 2009. 2009 sales revenue is overstated.

To Correct Incorrect Accounts	($ in 000s)	
Sales revenue	3	
Retained earnings		3

Step 1

Note: If the sales revenue had not been recorded at all, the correcting entry would include a debit to accounts receivable rather than sales revenue.

Step 2

The 2008 financial statements that were incorrect as a result of the error are retroactively restated to reflect the correct amount of sales revenue and accounts receivable when those statements are reported again for comparative purposes in the 2009 annual report.

Step 3

Because retained earnings is one of the accounts incorrect as a result of the error, the correction to that account is reported as a prior period adjustment to the 2008 beginning retained earnings balance in General Paper's comparative statements of shareholders' equity.

Step 4

Also, a disclosure note in General Paper's 2009 annual report should describe the nature of the error and the impact of its correction on each year's net income ($3,000 in 2008), income before extraordinary items ($3,000 in 2008), and earnings per share.

Graphic 20–12 illustrates how **Benihana, Inc.,** corrected its financial statements for having incorrectly expensed leasehold improvements and assets on leased properties in past years. Benihana was one of hundreds of firms making similar correction in 2005 following a Securities and Exchange Commission letter on February 7, 2005, urging companies to follow long-standing accounting standards in this area. As the note indicates, Benihana's

GRAPHIC 20–12

Error Correction; Benihana, Inc.

Real World Financials

2. Restatement of Previously Issued Financial Statements (in part)

Following a February 2005 review . . . we have restated our consolidated financial statements for the fiscal years through 2004 and for the third quarter of fiscal 2004 included herein. Previously, when accounting for leases with renewal options, we recorded rent expense on a straight-line basis over the initial noncancelable lease term, with the term commencing when actual rent payments began. We depreciate our buildings, leasehold improvements and other long-lived assets on those properties over a period that includes both the initial noncancelable lease term and all option periods provided for in the lease (or the useful life of the assets if shorter). We previously believed that these long-standing accounting treatments were appropriate under generally accepted accounting principles. We now have restated our financial statements to recognize rent expense on a straight-line basis over the expected lease term, including cancelable option periods where failure to exercise such options would result in an economic penalty and including the period that commences when the underlying property is made available to us for construction.

The cumulative effect of the Restatement through fiscal 2004 is an increase in deferred rent liability of $3.6 million and a decrease in deferred income tax liability of $1.4 million. As a result, retained earnings at the end of fiscal 2004 decreased by $2.2 million. Rent expense for fiscal year ended 2004 and for the three and ten periods ended January 4, 2004 increased by $0.4 million, and $0.1 million and $0.3, respectively. The Restatement decreased reported diluted net earnings per share $0.01 and $0.03 for the three and ten periods ended January 4, 2004, respectively.

ings had been overstated by $2.2 million as a result of the error and the balance rnings was accordingly decreased in the correcting journal entry. At about the Donald's Corp. recorded a similar charge of $139 million.

d at the outset, we've made no attempt to demonstrate the correction process f error in every stage of its discovery. However, after seeing the process v situations described, you should feel comfortable that the process is the the specific situation you might encounter.

d Error Corrections 1081

LUSTRATION 20–8 Affecting Net : Failure d Sales

ERNATIONAL FINANCIAL REPORTING STANDARDS

Error Corrections. When correcting errors in previously issued financial statements, IFRS permits the effect of the error to be reported in the current period if it's not considered practicable to report it retrospectively as is required by U.S. GAAP.

CONCEPT REVIEW EXERCISE

CORRECTION OF ERRORS

In 2009, the following errors were discovered by the internal auditors of Development Technologies, Inc.

1. 2008 accrued wages of $2 million were not recognized until they were paid in 2009.
2. A $3 million purchase of merchandise in 2009 was recorded in 2008 instead. The physical inventory count at the end of 2008 was correct.

Required:
Prepare the journal entries needed in 2009 to correct each error. Also, briefly describe any other measures Development Technologies would take in connection with correcting the errors. (Ignore income taxes.)

SOLUTION

Step 1:

1. To reduce 2009 wages expense and reduce retained earnings to what it would have been if the expense had reduced net income in 2008.

	($ in millions)	
Retained earnings	2	
Wages expense		2

2. To include the $3 million in 2009 purchases and increase retained earnings to what it would have been if 2008 cost of goods sold had not included the $3 million purchases.

Analysis

U = Understated O = Overstated

2008		2009	
Beginning inventory		Beginning inventory	
Purchases	O	Purchases	U
Less: Ending inventory			
Cost of goods sold	O		
Revenues			
Less: Cost of goods sold	O		
Less: Other expenses			
Net income	U		
↓			
Retained earnings	U		

	($ in millions)	
Purchases	3	
Retained earnings		3

Step 2:
The 2008 financial statements that were incorrect as a result of the errors would be *retrospectively restated* to reflect the correct wages expense, cost of goods sold (income tax expense if taxes are considered), net income, and retained earnings when those statements are reported again for comparative purposes in the 2009 annual report.

Step 3:
Because retained earnings is one of the accounts that is incorrect, the correction to that account is reported as a *"prior period adjustment"* to the 2009 beginning retained earnings balance in the comparative Statements of Shareholders' Equity.

Step 4:
Also, a *disclosure note* should describe the nature of the error and the impact of its correction on each year's net income, income before extraordinary items, and earnings per share.

FINANCIAL REPORTING CASE SOLUTION

1. **How can an accounting change cause a company to increase a previously reported inventory amount?** *(page 1064)* Smucker didn't find any lost jelly. The company increased last year's inventory number by $2 million to reflect its change from LIFO to FIFO this year. If it had not revised the number, last year's inventory would be based on LIFO and this year's inventory on FIFO. Analysts would be comparing apples and oranges (or apple jelly and orange jelly). Retrospective application of an accounting change provides better comparability in accounting information.
2. **Are all accounting changes reported this way?** *(page 1071)* Not all accounting changes are reported retrospectively. Besides most changes in accounting principle, changes in reporting entity and the correction of errors are reported that way, but some changes are reported prospectively instead. Changes in depreciation method, changes in accounting estimate, and some changes for which retrospective application is either impracticable or prohibited are reported prospectively in current and future periods only.

THE BOTTOM LINE

- **LO1** Accounting changes are categorized as:
  a. Changes in *principle,*
  b. Changes in *estimates,* or
  c. Changes in *reporting entity.*

  Accounting changes can be accounted for retrospectively (prior years revised) or prospectively (only current and future years affected). (p. 1062)
- **LO2** Most voluntary changes in accounting principles are reported retrospectively. This means revising all previous periods' financial statements to appear as if the newly adopted accounting method had been applied all along. A journal entry is created to adjust all account balances affected as of the date of the change. In the first set of financial statements after the change, a disclosure note describes the change and justifies the new method as preferable. It also describes the effects of the change on all items affected, including the fact that the retained earnings balance was revised in the statement of shareholders' equity. (p. 1064)
- **LO3** Some changes are reported prospectively. These include (a) changes in the method of depreciation, amortization, or depletion, (b) some changes in principle for which retrospective application is impracticable, and (c) a few changes for which an authoritative pronouncement requires prospective application. (p. 1068)

● LO4 Changes in estimates are accounted for prospectively. When a company revises a previous estimate, prior financial statements are not revised. Instead, the company merely incorporates the new estimate in any related accounting determinations from then on. (p. 1070)

● LO5 A change in reporting entity requires that financial statements of prior periods be retrospectively revised to report the financial information for the new reporting entity in all periods. (p. 1071)

● LO6 When errors are discovered, they should be corrected and accounted for retrospectively. Previous years' financial statements that were incorrect as a result of an error are retrospectively restated, and any account balances that are incorrect are corrected by a journal entry. If retained earnings is one of the incorrect accounts, the correction is reported as a prior period adjustment to the beginning balance in a statement of shareholders' equity. And, a disclosure note should describe the nature of the error and the impact of its correction on operations. (p. 1075) ●

QUESTIONS FOR REVIEW OF KEY TOPICS

Q 20–1 For accounting purposes, we classify accounting changes into three categories. What are they? Provide a short description of each.

Q 20–2 There are two basic accounting approaches to reporting accounting changes. What are they?

Q 20–3 We report most changes in accounting principle retrospectively. Describe this general way of recording and reporting changes in accounting principle.

Q 20–4 Lynch Corporation changes from the sum-of-the-years'-digits method of depreciation for existing assets to the straight-line method. How should the change be reported?

Q 20–5 Sugarbaker Designs, Inc. changed from the FIFO inventory costing method to the average cost method during 2009. Which items from the 2008 financial statements should be restated on the basis of the average cost method when reported in the 2009 comparative financial statements?

Q 20–6 Most accounting principles are recorded and reported retrospectively. In a few situations, though, the changes should be reported prospectively. When is prospective application appropriate?

Q 20–7 Southeast Steel, Inc. changed from the FIFO inventory costing method to the LIFO method during 2008. How would this change likely be reported in the 2009 comparative financial statements?

Q 20–8 Direct Assurance Company revised the estimates of the useful life of a trademark it had acquired three years earlier. How should Direct account for the change?

Q 20–9 It's not easy sometimes to distinguish between a change in principle and a change in estimate. In these cases, how should the change be accounted for?

Q 20–10 For financial reporting, a reporting entity can be a single company, or it can be a group of companies that reports a single set of financial statements. When changes occur that cause the financial statements to be those of a different reporting entity, we account for the situation as a change in reporting entity. What are the situations deemed to constitute a change in reporting entity?

Q 20–11 The issuance of *SFAS No. 94,* "Consolidation of All Majority-Owned Subsidiaries," required **Ford Motors** to include a previously unconsolidated finance subsidiary as part of the reporting entity. How did Ford report the change?

Q 20–12 Describe the process of correcting an error when it's discovered in a subsequent reporting period.

Q 20–13 If merchandise inventory is understated at the end of 2008, and the error is not discovered, how will net income be affected in 2009?

Q 20–14 If it is discovered that an extraordinary repair in the previous year was incorrectly debited to repair expense, how will retained earnings be reported in the current year's statement of shareholders' equity?

Q 20–15 What action is required when it is discovered that a five-year insurance premium payment of $50,000 two years ago was debited to insurance expense? (Ignore taxes.)

Q 20–16 Suppose the error described in the previous question is not discovered until six years later. What action will the discovery of this error require?

BRIEF EXERCISES

BE 20–1
Change in inventory methods
● LO2

In 2009, the Carney Company changed its method of valuing inventory from the FIFO method to the average cost method. At December 31, 2008, Carney's inventories were $32 million (FIFO). Carney's records indicated that the inventories would have totaled $23.8 million at December 31, 2008, if determined on an average cost basis. Ignoring income taxes, what journal entry will Carney use to record the adjustment? Briefly describe other steps Carney should take to report the change.

BE 20–2
Change in inventory methods
● LO2

In 2009, DeWash Industries changed its method of valuing inventory from the average cost method to the FIFO method. At December 31, 2008, DeWash's inventories were $47.6 million (average cost). DeWash's records indicated that the inventories would have totaled $64 million at December 31, 2008, if determined on a FIFO basis. Ignoring income taxes, what journal entry will DeWash use to record the adjustment?

BE 20–3
Change in inventory methods
● LO3

In 2009, Dorsey Markets changed its method of valuing inventory from the FIFO method to the LIFO method. At December 31, 2008, Dorsey's inventories were $96 million (FIFO). Dorsey's records were insufficient to determine what inventories would have totaled if determined on a LIFO cost basis. Briefly describe the steps Dorsey should take to report the change.

BE 20–4
Change in depreciation methods
● LO3

Irwin, Inc., constructed a machine at a total cost of $35 million. Construction was completed at the end of 2005 and the machine was placed in service at the beginning of 2006. The machine was being depreciated over a 10-year life using the sum-of-the-years'-digits method. The residual value is expected to be $2 million. At the beginning of 2009, Irwin decided to change to the straight-line method. Ignoring income taxes, what journal entry(s) should Irwin record relating to the machine for 2009?

BE 20–5
Change in depreciation methods
● LO3

Refer to the situation described in BE 20–4. Suppose Irwin has been using the straight-line method and switches to the sum-of-the-years'-digits method. Ignoring income taxes, what journal entry(s) should Irwin record relating to the machine for 2009?

BE 20–6
Change in estimate; useful life of patent
● LO4

Van Frank Telecommunications has a patent on a cellular transmission process. The company has amortized the patent on a straight-line basis since 2005, when it was acquired at a cost of $18 million at the beginning of that year. Due to rapid technological advances in the industry, management decided that the patent would benefit the company over a total of six years rather than the nine-year life being used to amortize its cost. The decision was made at the end of 2009 (before adjusting and closing entries). What is the appropriate adjusting entry for patent amortization in 2009 to reflect the revised estimate?

BE 20–7
Error correction
● LO6

When DeSoto Water Works purchased a machine at the end of 2008 at a cost of $65,000, the company debited Buildings and credited Cash $65,000. The error was discovered in 2009. What journal entry will DeSoto use to correct the error? What other step(s) would be taken in connection with the error?

BE 20–8
Error correction
● LO6

In 2009, internal auditors discovered that PKE Displays, Inc., had debited an expense account for the $350,000 cost of a machine purchased on January 1, 2006. The machine's useful life was expected to be five years with no residual value. Straight-line depreciation is used by PKE. Ignoring income taxes, what journal entry will PKE use to correct the error?

BE 20–9
Error correction
● LO6

Refer to the situation described in BE 20–8. Assume the error was discovered in 2011 after the 2010 financial statements are issued. Ignoring income taxes, what journal entry will PKE use to correct the error?

BE 20–10
Error correction
● LO6

In 2009, the internal auditors of Development Technologies, Inc., discovered that (a) 2008 accrued wages of $2 million were not recognized until they were paid in 2009 and (b) a $3 million purchase of merchandise in 2009 was recorded in 2008 instead. The physical inventory count at the end of 2008 was correct. Ignoring income taxes, what journal entries are needed in 2009 to correct each error? Also, briefly describe any other measures Development Technologies would take in connection with correcting the errors.

EXERCISES

available with McGraw-Hill's Homework Manager www.mhhe.com/spiceland5e

An alternate exercise and problem set is available on the text website: www.mhhe.com/spiceland5e

E 20–1
Change in principle; change in inventory methods
● LO2

During 2007 (its first year of operations) and 2008, Batali Foods used the FIFO inventory costing method for both financial reporting and tax purposes. At the beginning of 2009, Batali decided to change to the average method for both financial reporting and tax purposes.

Income components before income tax for 2009, 2008, and 2007 were as follows ($ in millions):

	2009	2008	2007
Revenues	$420	$390	$380
Cost of goods sold (FIFO)	(46)	(40)	(38)
Cost of goods sold (average)	(62)	(56)	(52)
Operating expenses	(254)	(250)	(242)

Dividends of $20 million were paid each year. Batali's fiscal year ends December 31.

Required:

1. Prepare the journal entry at the beginning of 2009 to record the change in principle. (Ignore income taxes.)
2. Prepare the 2009–2008 comparative income statements.
3. Determine the balance in retained earnings at January 1, 2008, as Batali reported previously using the FIFO method.
4. Determine the adjustment to the January 1, 2008, balance in retained earnings that Batali would include in the 2009–2008 comparative statements of retained earnings or retained earnings column of the statements of shareholders' equity to revise it to the amount it would have been if Batali had used the average method.

E 20–2
Change in principle; change in inventory methods
● LO2

Aquatic Equipment Corporation decided to switch from the LIFO method of costing inventories to the FIFO method at the beginning of 2009. The inventory as reported at the end of 2008 using LIFO would have been $60,000 higher using FIFO. Retained earnings had been reported at the end of 2008 as $780,000 (reflecting the LIFO method). The tax rate is 40%.

Required:

1. Calculate the balance in retained earnings at the time of the change (beginning of 2009) as it would have been reported if FIFO had been used in prior years.
2. Prepare the journal entry at the beginning of 2009 to record the change in principle.

E 20–3
Change in principle; change to the percentage-of completion method
● LO2

The Long Island Construction Company has used the completed contract method of accounting for construction contracts. At the beginning of 2009, the company decides to change to the percentage-of-completion method for financial reporting purposes, but will continue to use the completed contract method for tax reporting. The following table presents information concerning the change. The income tax rate for all years is 40%.

	Income before Income Tax		
	Percentage of Completion Method	Completed Contract Method	Difference
Before 2008	$15 million	$8 million	$7 million
2008	8 million	5 million	3 million
2009	10 million	9 million	1 million

Required:

1. Prepare the journal entry to record the change in principle. (All tax effects should be reflected in the deferred tax liability account.)
2. Determine the net income to be reported in the 2009–2008 comparative income statements.
3. Which other 2008 amounts would be reported differently in the 2009–2008 comparative income statements and 2009–2008 comparative balance sheets than they were reported the previous year?
4. How would the change be reflected in the 2009–2008 comparative statements of shareholders' equity? Cash dividends were $1 million each year.

E 20–4
Classifying accounting changes
● LO1 through LO5

Indicate with the appropriate letter the nature of each situation described below:

Type of Change

PR	Change in principle reported retrospectively
PP	Change in principle reported prospectively
E	Change in estimate
EP	Change in estimate resulting from a change in principle
R	Change in reporting entity
N	Not an accounting change

____ 1. Change from declining balance depreciation to straight-line.
____ 2. Change in the estimated useful life of office equipment.
____ 3. Technological advance that renders worthless a patent with an unamortized cost of $45,000.
____ 4. Change from determining lower of cost or market for the inventories by the individual item approach to the aggregate approach.
____ 5. Change from LIFO inventory costing to the weighted-average inventory costing.
____ 6. Settling a lawsuit for less than the amount accrued previously as a loss contingency.
____ 7. Including in the consolidated financial statements a subsidiary acquired several years earlier that was appropriately not included in previous years.
____ 8. Change by a retail store from reporting bad debt expense on a pay-as-you-go basis to the allowance method.

____ 9. A shift of certain manufacturing overhead costs to inventory that previously were expensed as incurred to more accurately measure cost of goods sold. (Either method is generally acceptable.)

____ 10. Pension plan assets for a defined benefit pension plan achieving a rate of return in excess of the amount anticipated.

E 20–5
Change from the treasury stock method to retired stock

● LO2

In keeping with a modernization of corporate statutes in its home state, UMC Corporation decided in 2009 to discontinue accounting for reacquired shares as treasury stock. Instead, shares repurchased will be viewed as having been retired, reassuming the status of unissued shares. As part of the change, treasury shares held were reclassified as retired stock. At December 31, 2008, UMC's balance sheet reported the following shareholders' equity:

	($ in millions)
Common stock, $1 par	$ 200
Paid-in capital—excess of par	800
Retained earnings	956
Treasury stock (4 million shares at cost)	(25)
Total shareholders' equity	$1,931

Required:
Identify the type of accounting change this decision represents and prepare the journal entry to effect the reclassification of treasury shares as retired shares.

E 20–6
Change in principle; change to the equity method

● LO2

The Trump Companies, Inc., has ownership interests in several public companies. At the beginning of 2009, the company's ownership interest in the common stock of Milken Properties increased to the point that it became appropriate to begin using the equity method of accounting for the investment. The balance in the investment account was $31 million at the time of the change. Accountants working with company records determined that the balance would have been $48 million if the account had been adjusted to reflect the equity method.

Required:
1. Prepare the journal entry to record the change in principle. (Ignore income taxes.)
2. Briefly describe other steps Trump should take to report the change.
3. Suppose Trump is changing *from* the equity method rather than *to* the equity method. How would your answers to requirements 1 and 2 differ?

E 20–7
Change in inventory methods; incomplete information

● LO3

Moulton Foods has always used the FIFO inventory costing method for both financial reporting and tax purposes. At the beginning of 2009, Moulton decided to change to the LIFO method. Net income in 2009 was $80 million. If the company had used LIFO in 2008, its cost of goods sold would have been higher by $6 million that year. Moulton's records of inventory purchases and sales are not available for 2007 and several previous years. Last year, Moulton reported the following net income amounts in its comparative income statements:

($ in millions)	2008	2007	2006
Net income	$84	$82	$80

Required:
1. Prepare the journal entry at the beginning of 2009 to record the change in principle. (Ignore income taxes.)
2. Briefly describe other steps Moulton will take to report the change.
3. What amounts will Moulton report for net income in its 2009–2007 comparative income statements?

E 20–8
Change in inventory methods; incomplete information

● LO3

Wolfgang Kitchens has always used the FIFO inventory costing method for both financial reporting and tax purposes. At the beginning of 2009, Wolfgang decided to change to the LIFO method. Net income in 2009 was $90 million. If the company had used LIFO in 2008, its cost of goods sold would have been higher by $7 million that year. Company accountants are able to determine that the cumulative net income for all years prior to 2008 would have been lower by $23 million if LIFO had been used all along, but have insufficient information to determine specific effects of using LIFO in 2007. Last year, Wolfgang reported the following net income amounts in its comparative income statements:

($ in millions)	2008	2007	2006
Net income	$94	$92	$90

Required:
1. Prepare the journal entry at the beginning of 2009 to record the change in principle. (Ignore income taxes.)
2. Briefly describe other steps Wolfgang will take to report the change.
3. What amounts will Wolfgang report for net income in its 2009–2007 comparative income statements?

E 20–9
Change in depreciation methods

● LO3

For financial reporting, Clinton Poultry Farms has used the declining-balance method of depreciation for conveyor equipment acquired at the beginning of 2006 for $2,560,000. Its useful life was estimated to be six years with a $160,000 residual value. At the beginning of 2009, Clinton decides to change to the straight-line method. The effect of this change on depreciation for each year is as follows ($ in 000s):

Year	Straight-Line	Declining Balance	Difference
2006	$ 400	$ 853	$453
2007	400	569	169
2008	400	379	(21)
	$1,200	$1,801	$601

Required:

1. Briefly describe the way Clinton should report this accounting change in the 2008–2009 comparative financial statements.
2. Prepare any 2009 journal entry related to the change.

E 20–10
Change in depreciation methods

● LO3

The Canliss Milling Company purchased machinery on January 2, 2007, for $800,000. A five-year life was estimated and no residual value was anticipated. Canliss decided to use the straight-line depreciation method and recorded $160,000 in depreciation in 2007 and 2008. Early in 2009, the company changed its depreciation method to the sum-of-the-years'-digits (SYD) method.

Required:

1. Briefly describe the way Canliss should report this accounting change in the 2008–2009 comparative financial statements.
2. Prepare any 2009 journal entry related to the change.

E 20–11
Book royalties

● LO4

Dreighton Engineering Group receives royalties on a technical manual written by two of its engineers and sold to William B. Irving Publishing, Inc. Royalties are 10% of net sales, receivable on October 1 for sales in January through June and on April 1 for sales in July through December of the prior year. Sales of the manual began in July 2008, and Dreighton accrued royalty revenue of $31,000 at December 31, 2008, as follows:

Receivable—royalty revenue	31,000	
Royalty revenue		31,000

Dreighton received royalties of $36,000 on April 1, 2009, and $40,000 on October 1, 2009. Irving indicated to Dreighton on December 31 that book sales subject to royalties for the second half of 2009 are expected to be $500,000.

Required:

1. Prepare any journal entries Dreighton should record during 2009 related to the royalty revenue.
2. What adjustments, if any, should be made to retained earnings or to the 2008 financial statements? Explain.

E 20–12
Loss contingency

● LO4

The Commonwealth of Virginia filed suit in October 2007, against Northern Timber Corporation seeking civil penalties and injunctive relief for violations of environmental laws regulating forest conservation. When the financial statements were issued in 2008, Northern had not reached a settlement with state authorities, but legal counsel advised Northern Timber that it was probable the ultimate settlement would be $1,000,000 in penalties. The following entry was recorded:

Loss—litigation	1,000,000	
Liability—litigation		1,000,000

Late in 2009, a settlement was reached with state authorities to pay a total of $600,000 to cover the cost of violations.

Required:

1. Prepare any journal entries related to the change.
2. Briefly describe other steps Northern should take to report the change.

E 20–13
Warranty expense

● LO4

Woodmier Lawn Products introduced a new line of commercial sprinklers in 2008 that carry a one-year warranty against manufacturer's defects. Because this was the first product for which the company offered a warranty, trade publications were consulted to determine the experience of others in the industry. Based on that experience, warranty costs were expected to approximate 2% of sales. Sales of the sprinklers in 2008 were $2,500,000. Accordingly, the following entries relating to the contingency for warranty costs were recorded during the first year of selling the product:

Accrued liability and expense		
Warranty expense (2% × $2,500,000)	50,000	
Estimated warranty liability		50,000
Actual expenditures (summary entry)		
Estimated warranty liability	23,000	
Cash, wages payable, parts and supplies, etc		23,000

In late 2009, the company's claims experience was evaluated and it was determined that claims were far more than expected—3% of sales rather than 2%.

Required:

1. Assuming sales of the sprinklers in 2009 were $3,600,000 and warranty expenditures in 2009 totaled $88,000, prepare any journal entries related to the warranty.
2. Assuming sales of the sprinklers were discontinued after 2008, prepare any journal entry(s) in 2009 related to the warranty.

E 20–14
Deferred taxes; change in tax rates
● LO4

Bronson Industries reported a deferred tax liability of $8 million for the year ended December 31, 2008, related to a temporary difference of $20 million. The tax rate was 40%. The temporary difference is expected to reverse in 2010 at which time the deferred tax liability will become payable. There are no other temporary differences in 2008–2010. Assume a new tax law is enacted in 2009 that causes the tax rate to change from 40% to 30% beginning in 2010. (The rate remains 40% for 2009 taxes.) Taxable income in 2009 is $30 million.

Required:

Determine the effect of the change and prepare the appropriate journal entry to record Bronson's income tax expense in 2009. What adjustment, if any, is needed to revise retained earnings as a result of the change?

E 20–15
Accounting change
● LO4

The Peridot Company purchased machinery on January 2, 2007, for $800,000. A five-year life was estimated and no residual value was anticipated. Peridot decided to use the straight-line depreciation method and recorded $160,000 in depreciation in 2007 and 2008. Early in 2009, the company revised the total estimated life of the machinery to eight years.

Required:

1. What type of change is this?
2. Briefly describe the accounting treatment for this change.
3. Determine depreciation for 2009.

E 20–16
Change in estimate; useful life and residual value of equipment
● LO4

Wardell Company purchased a mini computer on January 1, 2007, at a cost of $40,000. The computer has been depreciated using the straight-line method over an estimated five-year useful life with an estimated residual value of $4,000. On January 1, 2009, the estimate of useful life was changed to a total of 10 years, and the estimate of residual value was changed to $900.

Required:

1. Prepare the appropriate adjusting entry for depreciation in 2009 to reflect the revised estimate.
2. Repeat requirement 1 assuming that the company uses the sum-of-the-years'-digits method instead of the straight-line method.

E 20–17
Error correction; inventory error
● LO6

During 2007, WMC Corporation discovered that its ending inventories reported on its financial statements were misstated by the following amounts:

2007	understated by	$120,000
2008	overstated by	150,000

WMC uses the periodic inventory system and the FIFO cost method.

Required:

1. Determine the effect of these errors on retained earnings at January 1, 2009, before any adjustments. Explain your answer. (Ignore income taxes.)
2. Prepare a journal entry to correct the error.
3. What other step(s) would be taken in connection with the error?

E 20–18
Error corrections; investment
● LO6

On December 12, 2009, an investment costing $80,000 was sold for $100,000. The total of the sale proceeds was credited to the investment account.

Required:

1. Prepare the journal entry to correct the error assuming it is discovered before the books are adjusted or closed in 2009. (Ignore income taxes.)
2. Prepare the journal entry to correct the error assuming it is not discovered until early 2010. (Ignore income taxes.)

E 20–19
Error in amortization schedule

● LO6

Wilkins Food Products, Inc., acquired a packaging machine from Lawrence Specialists Corporation. Lawrence completed construction of the machine on January 1, 2007. In payment for the machine Wilkins issued a three-year installment note to be paid in three equal payments at the end of each year. The payments include interest at the rate of 10%.

Lawrence made a conceptual error in preparing the amortization schedule which Wilkens failed to discover until 2009. The error had caused Wilkens to understate interest expense by $45,000 in 2007 and $40,000 in 2008.

Required:

1. Determine which accounts are incorrect as a result of these errors at January 1, 2009, before any adjustments. Explain your answer. (Ignore income taxes.)
2. Prepare a journal entry to correct the error.
3. What other step(s) would be taken in connection with the error?

E 20–20
Error correction; accrued interest on bonds

● LO6

At the end of 2008, Majors Furniture Company failed to accrue $61,000 of interest expense that accrued during the last five months of 2008 on bonds payable. The bonds mature in 2022. The discount on the bonds is amortized by the straight-line method. The following entry was recorded on February 1, 2009, when the semiannual interest was paid:

Interest expense	73,200	
Discount on bonds payable		1,200
Cash		72,000

Required:

Prepare any journal entry necessary to correct the error as well as any adjusting entry for 2009 related to the situation described. (Ignore income taxes.)

E 20–21
Error correction; three errors

● LO6

Below are three independent and unrelated errors.

a. On December 31, 2008, Wolfe-Bache Corporation failed to accrue office supplies expense of $1,800. In January 2009, when it received the bill from its supplier, Wolfe-Bache made the following entry:

Office supplies expense	1,800	
Cash		1,800

b. On the last day of 2008, Midwest Importers received a $90,000 prepayment from a tenant for 2009 rent of a building. Midwest recorded the receipt as rent revenue.

c. At the end of 2008, Dinkins-Lowery Corporation failed to accrue interest of $8,000 on a note receivable. At the beginning of 2009, when the company received the cash, it was recorded as interest revenue.

Required:

For each error:

1. What would be the effect of each error on the income statement and the balance sheet in the 2008 financial statements?
2. Prepare any journal entries each company should record in 2009 to correct the errors.

E 20–22
Inventory errors

● LO6

For each of the following inventory errors occurring in 2009, determine the effect of the error on 2009's cost of goods sold, net income, and retained earnings. Assume that the error is not discovered until 2010 and that a periodic inventory system is used. Ignore income taxes.

U = Understated O = Overstated NE = No effect

		Cost of Goods Sold	Net Income	Retained Earnings
(Example) 1.	Overstatement of ending inventory	U	O	O
2.	Overstatement of purchases			
3.	Understatement of beginning inventory			
4.	Freight in charges are understated			
5.	Understatement of ending inventory			
6.	Understatement of purchases			
7.	Overstatement of beginning inventory			
8.	Understatement of purchases and understatement of ending inventory, by the same amount			

E 20–23
Classifying accounting changes and errors

● LO1 through LO6

Indicate with the appropriate letter the nature of each adjustment described below:

Type of Adjustment

A. Change in principle (reported retrospectively)
B. Change in principle (exception reported prospectively)
C. Change in estimate
D. Change in estimate resulting from a change in principle
E. Change in reporting entity
F. Correction of an error

____ 1. Change from expensing extraordinary repairs to capitalizing the expenditures.
____ 2. Change in the residual value of machinery.
____ 3. Change from FIFO inventory costing to LIFO inventory costing.
____ 4. Change in the percentage used to determine bad debts.
____ 5. Change from LIFO inventory costing to FIFO inventory costing.
____ 6. Change from reporting an investment by the equity method due to a reduction in the percentage of shares owned.
____ 7. Change in the composition of a group of firms reporting on a consolidated basis.
____ 8. Change from sum-of-the-years'-digits depreciation to straight-line.
____ 9. Change from the percentage-of-completion method by a company in the long-term construction industry.
____ 10. Change in actuarial assumptions for a defined benefit pension plan.

CPA AND CMA REVIEW QUESTIONS

CPA Exam Questions

KAPLAN SCHWESER

The following questions are used in the Kaplan CPA Review Course to study accounting changes and errors while preparing for the CPA examination. Determine the response that best completes the statements or questions.

● LO3

1. Kap Company switched from the sum-of-the-years-digits depreciation method to straight-line depreciation in 2009. The change affects machinery purchased at the beginning of 2007 at a cost of $36,000. The machinery has an estimated life of five years and an estimated residual value of $1,800. What is Kap's 2009 depreciation expense?
   a. $4,200
   b. $4,560
   c. $4,800
   d. $7,920

● LO4

2. Retrospective restatement usually is appropriate for a change in:

	Accounting Principle	Accounting Estimate
a.	Yes	Yes
b.	Yes	No
c.	No	Yes
d.	No	No

● LO4

3. For 2008, Pac Co. estimated its two-year equipment warranty costs based on $100 per unit sold in 2008. Experience during 2009 indicated that the estimate should have been based on $110 per unit. The effect of this $10 difference from the estimate is reported
   a. In 2009 income from continuing operations.
   b. As an accounting change, net of tax, below 2009 income from continuing operations.
   c. As an accounting change requiring 2008 financial statements to be restated.
   d. As a correction of an error requiring 2008 financial statements to be restated.

LO5

4. A company has included in its consolidated financial statements this year a subsidiary acquired several years ago that was appropriately excluded from consolidation last year. This results in
   a. An accounting change that should be reported prospectively.
   b. An accounting change that should be reported by restating the financial statements of all prior periods presented.
   c. A correction of an error.
   d. Neither an accounting change nor a correction of an error.

LO6

5. Conn Co. reported a retained earnings balance of $400,000 at December 31, 2008. In August 2009, Conn determined that insurance premiums of $60,000 for the three-year period beginning January 1, 2008, had been paid and fully expensed in 2008. Conn has a 30% income tax rate. What amount should Conn report as adjusted beginning retained earnings in its 2009 statement of retained earnings?
   a. $420,000
   b. $428,000
   c. $440,000
   d. $442,000

LO6

6. During 2010, Paul Company discovered that the ending inventories reported on its financial statements were incorrect by the following amounts:

2008	$ 60,000 understated
2009	75,000 overstated

   Paul uses the periodic inventory system to ascertain year-end quantities that are converted to dollar amounts using the FIFO cost method. Prior to any adjustments for these errors and ignoring income taxes, Paul's retained earnings at January 1, 2010, would be
   a. Correct.
   b. $15,000 overstated.
   c. $75,000 overstated.
   d. $135,000 overstated.

CMA Exam Questions

The following questions dealing with accounting changes and errors are adapted from questions that previously appeared on Certified Management Accountant (CMA) examinations. The CMA designation sponsored by the Institute of Management Accountants (**www.imanet.org**) provides members with an objective measure of knowledge and competence in the field of management accounting. Determine the response that best completes the statements or questions.

LO6

1. In a review of the May 31, 2009 financial statements during the normal year-end closing process, it was discovered that the interest income accrual on Simpson Company's notes receivable was omitted. The amounts omitted were calculated as follows:

May 31, 2008	$ 91,800
May 31, 2009	100,200

   The May 31, 2009 entry to correct for these errors, ignoring the effect of income taxes, includes a
   a. credit to retained earnings for $91,800.
   b. credit to interest revenue for $91,800.
   c. debit to interest revenue for $100,200.
   d. credit to interest receivable for $100,200.

LO4

2. A change in the liability for warranty costs requires
   a. presenting prior-period financial statements as previously reported.
   b. presenting the effect of pro forma data on income and earnings per share for all prior periods presented.
   c. reporting an adjustment to the beginning retained earnings balance in the statement of retained earnings.
   d. reporting current and future financial statements on the new basis.

LO6

3. An example of an item that should be reported as a prior-period adjustment in a company's annual financial statements is
   a. a settlement resulting from litigation.
   b. an adjustment of income taxes.
   c. a correction of an error that occurred in a prior period.
   d. an adjustment of utility revenue because of rate revisions ordered by a regulatory commission.

PROBLEMS

available with McGraw-Hill's Homework Manager www.mhhe.com/spiceland5e 

An alternate exercise and problem set is available on the text website: www.mhhe.com/spiceland5e

P 20–1
Change in inventory costing methods; comparative income statements

● LO2

The Cecil-Booker Vending Company changed its method of valuing inventory from the average cost method to the FIFO cost method at the beginning of 2009. At December 31, 2008, inventories were $120,000 (average cost basis) and were $124,000 a year earlier. Cecil-Booker's accountants determined that the inventories would have totaled $155,000 at December 31, 2008, and $160,000 at December 31, 2007, if determined on a FIFO basis. A tax rate of 40% is in effect for all years.

One hundred thousand common shares were outstanding each year. Income from continuing operations was $400,000 in 2008 and $525,000 in 2009. There were no extraordinary items either year.

Required:

1. Prepare the journal entry to record the change in principle. (All tax effects should be reflected in the deferred tax liability account.)
2. Prepare the 2009–2008 comparative income statements beginning with income from continuing operations. Include per share amounts.

P 20–2
Change in principle; change in method of accounting for longterm construction

● LO2

The Pyramid Construction Company has used the completed-contract method of accounting for construction contracts during its first two years of operation, 2007 and 2008. At the beginning of 2009, Pyramid decides to change to the percentage-of-completion method for both tax and financial reporting purposes. The following table presents information concerning the change for 2007–2009. The income tax rate for all years is 40%.

	Income before Income Tax				
	Percentage of Completion Method	Completed Contract Method	Difference	Income Tax Effect	Difference after Tax
2007	$ 90,000	$60,000	$30,000	$12,000	$18,000
2008	45,000	36,000	9,000	3,600	5,400
Total	$135,000	$96,000	$39,000	$15,600	$23,400
2009	$ 51,000	$46,000	$ 5,000	$ 2,000	$ 3,000

Pyramid issued 50,000 $1 par, common shares for $230,000 when the business began, and there have been no changes in paid-in capital since then. Dividends were not paid the first year, but $10,000 cash dividends were paid in both 2008 and 2009.

Required:

1. Prepare the journal entry to record the change in principle. (All tax effects should be reflected in the deferred tax liability account.)
2. Prepare the 2009–2008 comparative income statements beginning with income before income taxes.
3. Prepare the 2009–2008 comparative statements of shareholders' equity. (Hint: The 2007 statements reported retained earnings of $36,000. This is $60,000 − [$60,000 × 40%]).

P 20–3
Change in inventory costing methods; comparative income statements

● LO2 LO3

Shown below are net income amounts as they would be determined by Weihrich Steel Company by each of three different inventory costing methods ($ in 000s).

	FIFO	Average Cost	LIFO
Pre-2008	$2,800	$2,540	$2,280
2008	750	600	540
	$3,550	$3,140	$2,820

Required:

1. Assume that Weihrich used FIFO before 2009, and then in 2009 decided to switch to average cost. Prepare the journal entry to record the change in principle and briefly describe any other steps Weihrich should take to appropriately report the situation. (Ignore income tax effects.)
2. Assume that Weihrich used FIFO before 2009, and then in 2009 decided to switch to LIFO. Assume accounting records are inadequate to determine LIFO information prior to 2009. Therefore, the 2008 ($540) and pre-2008 ($2,280) data are not available. Prepare the journal entry to record the change in principle and briefly describe any other steps Weihrich should take to appropriately report the situation. (Ignore income tax effects.)

3. Assume that Weihrich used FIFO before 2009, and then in 2009 decided to switch to LIFO cost. Weihrich's records of inventory purchases and sales are not available for several previous years. Therefore, the pre-2008 LIFO information ($2,280) is not available. However, Weihrich does have the information needed to apply LIFO on a prospective basis beginning in 2008. Prepare the journal entry to record the change in principle and briefly describe any other steps Weihrich should take to appropriately report the situation. (Ignore income tax effects.)

P 20–4
Change in inventory methods

● LO2

The Rockwell Corporation uses a periodic inventory system and has used the FIFO cost method since inception of the company in 1974. In 2009, the company decided to switch to the average cost method. Data for 2009 are as follows:

Beginning inventory, FIFO (5,000 units @ $30.00)		$150,000
Purchases:		
5,000 units @ $36.00	$180,000	
5,000 units @ $40.00	200,000	380,000
Cost of goods available for sale		$530,000
Sales for 2009 (8,000 units @ $70.00)		$560,000

Additional information:

1. The company's effective income tax rate is 40% for all years.
2. If the company had used the average cost method prior to 2009, ending inventory for 2008 would have been $130,000.
3. 7,000 units remained in inventory at the end of 2009.

Required:

1. Prepare the journal entry at the beginning of 2009 to record the change in principle.
2. In the 2009–2007 comparative financial statements, what will be the amounts of cost of goods sold and inventory reported for 2009?

P 20–5
Change in inventory methods

● LO2

Fantasy Fashions has used the LIFO method of costing inventories, but at the beginning of 2009 decided to change to the FIFO method. The inventory as reported at the end of 2008 using LIFO would have been $20 million higher using FIFO.

Retained earnings had been reported at the end of 2007 and 2008 as $240 million and $260 million, respectively (reflecting the LIFO method). Those amounts reflecting the FIFO method would have been $250 million and $272 million, respectively. 2008 net income had been reported at the end of 2008 as $28 million (LIFO method) but would have been $30 million using FIFO. After changing to FIFO, 2009 net income was $36 million. Dividends of $8 million were paid each year. The tax rate is 40%.

Required:

1. Prepare the journal entry at the beginning of 2009 to record the change in principle.
2. In the 2009–2008 comparative income statements, what will be the amounts of net income reported for 2008 and 2009?
3. Prepare the 2009–2008 retained earnings column of the comparative statements of shareholders' equity.

P 20–6
Change in principle; change in depreciation methods

● LO3

During 2007 and 2008, Faulkner Manufacturing used the sum-of-the-years'-digits (SYD) method of depreciation for its operational assets, for both financial reporting and tax purposes. At the beginning of 2009, Faulkner decided to change to the straight-line method for both financial reporting and tax purposes. A tax rate of 40% is in effect for all years.

For an asset that cost $21,000 with an estimated residual value of $1,000 and an estimated useful life of 10 years, the depreciation under different methods is as follows:

Year	Straight Line	SYD	Difference
2007	$2,000	$3,636	$1,636
2008	2,000	3,273	1,273
	$4,000	$6,909	$2,909

Required:

1. Describe the way Faulkner should account for the change described. Include in your answer any journal entry Faulkner will record in 2009 related to the change and any required footnote disclosures.
2. Suppose instead that Faulkner had previously used straight-line depreciation and changed to sum-of-the-years'-digits in 2009. Describe the way Faulkner should account for the change. Include in your answer any journal entry Faulkner will record in 2009 related to the change and any required footnote disclosures.

P 20–7
Depletion; change in estimate

● LO4

In 2009, the Marion Company purchased land containing a mineral mine for $1,600,000. Additional costs of $600,000 were incurred to develop the mine. Geologists estimated that 400,000 tons of ore would be extracted. After the ore is removed, the land will have a resale value of $100,000.

To aid in the extraction, Marion built various structures and small storage buildings on the site at a cost of $150,000. These structures have a useful life of 10 years. The structures cannot be moved after the ore has been removed and will be left at the site. In addition, new equipment costing $80,000 was purchased and installed at the site. Marion does not plan to move the equipment to another site, but estimates that it can be sold at auction for $4,000 after the mining project is completed.

In 2009, 50,000 tons of ore were extracted and sold. In 2010, the estimate of total tons of ore in the mine was revised from 400,000 to 487,500. During 2010, 80,000 tons were extracted.

Required:

1. Compute depletion and depreciation of the mine and the mining facilities and equipment for 2009 and 2010. Marion uses the units-of-production method to determine depreciation on mining facilities and equipment.
2. Compute the book value of the mineral mine, structures, and equipment as of December 31, 2010.

P 20–8
Accounting changes; six situations

● LO1 LO3 LO4

Described below are six independent and unrelated situations involving accounting changes. Each change occurs during 2009 before any adjusting entries or closing entries were prepared. Assume the tax rate for each company is 40% in all years. Any tax effects should be adjusted through the deferred tax liability account.

a. Fleming Home Products introduced a new line of commercial awnings in 2008 that carry a one-year warranty against manufacturer's defects. Based on industry experience, warranty costs were expected to approximate 3% of sales. Sales of the awnings in 2008 were $3,500,000. Accordingly, warranty expense and a warranty liability of $105,000 were recorded in 2008. In late 2009, the company's claims experience was evaluated and it was determined that claims were far fewer than expected: 2% of sales rather than 3%. Sales of the awnings in 2009 were $4,000,000 and warranty expenditures in 2009 totaled $91,000.
b. On December 30, 2005, Rival Industries acquired its office building at a cost of $1,000,000. It has been depreciated on a straight-line basis assuming a useful life of 40 years and no salvage value. However, plans were finalized in 2009 to relocate the company headquarters at the end of 2013. The vacated office building will have a salvage value at that time of $700,000.
c. Hobbs-Barto Merchandising, Inc. changed inventory cost methods to LIFO from FIFO at the end of 2009 for both financial statement and income tax purposes. Under FIFO, the inventory at January 1, 2010, is $690,000.
d. At the beginning of 2006, the Hoffman Group purchased office equipment at a cost of $330,000. Its useful life was estimated to be 10 years with no salvage value. The equipment has been depreciated by the sum-of-the-years'-digits method. On January 1, 2009, the company changed to the straight-line method.
e. In November 2007, the State of Minnesota filed suit against Huggins Manufacturing Company, seeking penalties for violations of clean air laws. When the financial statements were issued in 2008, Huggins had not reached a settlement with state authorities, but legal counsel advised Huggins that it was probable the company would have to pay $200,000 in penalties. Accordingly, the following entry was recorded:

Loss—litigation	200,000	
Liability—litigation		200,000

Late in 2009, a settlement was reached with state authorities to pay a total of $350,000 in penalties.
f. At the beginning of 2009, Jantzen Specialties, which uses the sum-of-the-years'-digits method changed to the straight-line method for newly acquired buildings and equipment. The change increased current year net earnings by $445,000.

Required:

For each situation:

1. Identify the type of change.
2. Prepare any journal entry necessary as a direct result of the change as well as any adjusting entry for 2009 related to the situation described.
3. Briefly describe any other steps that should be taken to appropriately report the situation.

P 20–9
Accounting changes; identify type and reporting approach

● LO1 through LO4

At the beginning of 2009, Wagner Implements undertook a variety of changes in accounting methods, corrected several errors, and instituted new accounting policies.

Required:

On a sheet of paper numbered from 1 to 10, indicate for each item below the type of change and the reporting approach Wagner would use.

Type of Change (choose one)	Reporting Approach (choose one)
P. Change in accounting principle	R. Retrospective approach
E. Change in accounting estimate	P. Prospective approach
EP. Change in estimate resulting from a change in principle	
X. Correction of an error	
N. Neither an accounting change nor an accounting error.	

Change:

1. By acquiring additional stock, Wagner increased its investment in Wise, Inc. from a 12% interest to 25% and changed its method of accounting for the investment from an available-for-sale investment to the equity method.
2. Wagner instituted a postretirement benefit plan for its employees in 2009 and adopted *SFAS No. 106,* "Accounting for Postretirement Benefit Plans Other than Pensions." Wagner had not previously had such a plan.
3. Wagner changed its method of depreciating computer equipment from the SYD method to the straight-line method.
4. Wagner determined that a liability insurance premium it both paid and expensed in 2008 covered the 2008–2010 period.
5. Wagner custom-manufactures farming equipment on a contract basis. Wagner switched its accounting for these long-term contracts from the completed-contract method to the percentage-of-completion method.
6. Due to an unexpected relocation, Wagner determined that its office building previously to be depreciated over 45 years should be depreciated over 18 years.
7. Wagner offers a three-year warranty on the farming equipment it sells. Manufacturing efficiencies caused Wagner to reduce its expectation of warranty costs from 2% of sales to 1% of sales.
8. Wagner changed from LIFO to FIFO to account for its materials and work in process inventories.
9. Wagner changed from FIFO to average cost to account for its equipment inventory.
10. Wagner sells extended service contracts on some of its equipment sold. Wagner performs services related to these contracts over several years, so in 2009 Wagner changed from recognizing revenue from these service contracts on a cash basis to the accrual basis.

P 20–10
Inventory errors

● LO6

You have been hired as the new controller for the Ralston Company. Shortly after joining the company in 2009, you discover the following errors related to the 2007 and 2008 financial statements:

a. Inventory at 12/31/07 was understated by $6,000.
b. Inventory at 12/31/08 was overstated by $9,000.
c. On 12/31/08, inventory was purchased for $3,000. The company did not record the purchase until the inventory was paid for early in 2009. At that time, the purchase was recorded by debit to purchases and a credit to cash.

The company uses a periodic inventory system.

Required:

1. Assuming that the errors were discovered after the 2008 financial statements were issued, analyze the effect of the errors on 2008 and 2007 cost of goods sold, net income, and retained earnings. (Ignore income taxes.)
2. Prepare a journal entry to correct the errors.
3. What other step(s) would be taken in connection with the error?

P 20–11
Error correction; change in depreciation method

● LO6

The Collins Corporation purchased office equipment at the beginning of 2007 and capitalized a cost of $2,000,000. This cost included the following expenditures:

Purchase price	$1,850,000
Freight charges	30,000
Installation charges	20,000
Annual maintenance charge	100,000
Total	$2,000,000

The company estimated an eight-year useful life for the equipment. No residual value is anticipated. The double-declining-balance method was used to determine depreciation expense for 2007 and 2008.

In 2009, after the 2008 financial statements were issued, the company decided to switch to the straightline depreciation method for this equipment. At that time, the company's controller discovered that the original cost of the equipment incorrectly included one year of annual maintenance charges for the equipment.

Required:

1. Ignoring income taxes, prepare the appropriate correcting entry for the equipment capitalization error discovered in 2009.
2. Ignoring income taxes, prepare any 2009 journal entry(s) related to the change in depreciation methods.

P 20–12
Accounting changes and error correction; eight situations; tax effects ignored

● LO1 through LO4

Williams-Santana, Inc., is a manufacturer of high-tech industrial parts that was started in 1997 by two talented engineers with little business training. In 2009, the company was acquired by one of its major customers. As part of an internal audit, the following facts were discovered. The audit occurred during 2009 before any adjusting entries or closing entries were prepared.

a. A five-year casualty insurance policy was purchased at the beginning of 2007 for $35,000. The full amount was debited to insurance expense at the time.
b. Effective January 1, 2009, the company changed the salvage value used in calculating depreciation for its office building. The building cost $600,000 on December 29, 1998, and has been depreciated on a straight-line basis assuming a useful life of 40 years and a salvage value of $100,000. Declining real estate values in the area indicate that the salvage value will be no more than $25,000.
c. On December 31, 2008, merchandise inventory was overstated by $25,000 due to a mistake in the physical inventory count using the periodic inventory system.
d. The company changed inventory cost methods to FIFO from LIFO at the end of 2009 for both financial statement and income tax purposes. The change will cause a $960,000 increase in the beginning inventory at January 1, 2010.
e. At the end of 2008, the company failed to accrue $15,500 of sales commissions earned by employees during 2008. The expense was recorded when the commissions were paid in early 2009.
f. At the beginning of 2007, the company purchased a machine at a cost of $720,000. Its useful life was estimated to be 10 years with no salvage value. The machine has been depreciated by the double-declining balance method. Its carrying amount on December 31, 2008, was $460,800. On January 1, 2009, the company changed to the straight-line method.
g. Bad debt expense is determined each year as 1% of credit sales. Actual collection experience of recent years indicates that 0.75% is a better indication of uncollectible accounts. Management effects the change in 2009. Credit sales for 2009 are $4,000,000; in 2008 they were $3,700,000.

Required:

For each situation:

1. Identify whether it represents an accounting change or an error. If an accounting change, identify the type of change.
2. Prepare any journal entry necessary as a direct result of the change or error correction as well as any adjusting entry for 2009 related to the situation described. (Ignore tax effects.)
3. Briefly describe any other steps that should be taken to appropriately report the situation.

P 20–13
Accounting changes and error correction; eight situations; tax effects considered

● LO1 through LO4 LO6

(Note: This problem is a variation of the previous problem, modified to consider income tax effects.) Williams-Santana, Inc., is a manufacturer of high-tech industrial parts that was started in 1997 by two talented engineers with little business training. In 2009, the company was acquired by one of its major customers. As part of an internal audit, the following facts were discovered. The audit occurred during 2009 before any adjusting entries or closing entries were prepared. The income tax rate is 40% for all years.

a. A five-year casualty insurance policy was purchased at the beginning of 2007 for $35,000. The full amount was debited to insurance expense at the time.
b. Effective January 1, 2009, the company changed the salvage values used in calculating depreciation for its office building. The building cost $600,000 on December 29, 1998, and has been depreciated on a straight-line basis assuming a useful life of 40 years and a salvage value of $100,000. Declining real estate values in the area indicate that the salvage value will be no more than $25,000.
c. On December 31, 2008, merchandise inventory was overstated by $25,000 due to a mistake in the physical inventory count using the periodic inventory system.
d. The company changed inventory cost methods to FIFO from LIFO at the end of 2009 for both financial statement and income tax purposes. The change will cause a $960,000 increase in the beginning inventory at January 1, 2010.
e. At the end of 2008, the company failed to accrue $15,500 of sales commissions earned by employees during 2008. The expense was recorded when the commissions were paid in early 2009.
f. At the beginning of 2007, the company purchased a machine at a cost of $720,000. Its useful life was estimated to be ten years with no salvage value. The machine has been depreciated by the double-declining balance method. Its carrying amount on December 31, 2008, was $460,800. On January 1, 2009, the company changed to the straight-line method.

g. Bad debt expense is determined each year as 1% of credit sales. Actual collection experience of recent years indicates that 0.75% is a better indication of uncollectible accounts. Management effects the change in 2009. Credit sales for 2009 are $4,000,000; in 2008 they were $3,700,000.

Required:

For each situation:

1. Identify whether it represents an accounting change or an error. If an accounting change, identify the type of change.
2. Prepare any journal entry necessary as a direct result of the change or error correction as well as any adjusting entry for 2009 related to the situation described. Any tax effects should be adjusted for through the deferred tax liability account.
3. Briefly describe any other steps that should be taken to appropriately report the situation.

P 20–14
Errors; change in estimate; change in principle; restatement of previous financial statements

● LO1 LO3 LO4 LO6

Whaley Distributors is a wholesale distributor of electronic components. Financial statements for the year ended December 31, 2008, reported the following amounts and subtotals ($ in millions):

	Assets	Liabilities	Shareholders' Equity	Net Income	Expenses
2007	$740	$330	$410	$210	$150
2008	820	400	420	230	175

In 2009 the following situations occurred or came to light:

a. Internal auditors discovered that ending inventories reported on the financial statements the two previous years were misstated due to faulty internal controls. The errors were in the following amounts:

2007 inventory	Overstated by $12 million
2008 inventory	Understated by $10 million

b. A liability was accrued in 2007 for a probable payment of $7 million in connection with a lawsuit ultimately settled in December 2009 for $4 million.

c. A patent costing $18 million at the beginning of 2007, expected to benefit operations for a total of six years, has not been amortized since acquired.

d. Whaley's conveyer equipment has been depreciated by the sum-of-the-years'-digits (SYD) basis since constructed at the beginning of 2007 at a cost of $30 million. It has an expected useful life of five years and no expected residual value. At the beginning of 2009, Whaley decided to switch to straight-line depreciation.

Required:

For each situation:

1. Prepare any journal entry necessary as a direct result of the change or error correction as well as any adjusting entry for 2009 related to the situation described. (Ignore tax effects.)
2. Determine the amounts to be reported for each of the five items shown above from the 2007 and 2008 financial statements when those amounts are reported again in the 2007–2009 comparative financial statements.

P 20–15
Correction of errors; six errors

● LO6

Conrad Wholesale Supply underwent a restructuring in 2009. The company conducted a thorough internal audit, during which the following facts were discovered. The audit occurred during 2009 before any adjusting entries or closing entries are prepared.

a. Additional computers were acquired at the beginning of 2007 and added to the company's office network. The $45,000 cost of the computers was inadvertently recorded as maintenance expense. Computers have five-year useful lives and no material salvage value. This class of equipment is depreciated by the straight-line method.

b. Two weeks prior to the audit, the company paid $17,000 for assembly tools and recorded the expenditure as office supplies. The error was discovered a week later.

c. On December 31, 2008, merchandise inventory was understated by $78,000 due to a mistake in the physical inventory count. The company uses the periodic inventory system.

d. Two years earlier, the company recorded a 4% stock dividend (2,000 common shares, $1 par) as follows:

Retained earnings	2,000	
Common stock		2,000

The shares had a market price at the time of $12 per share.

e. At the end of 2008, the company failed to accrue $104,000 of interest expense that accrued during the last four months of 2008 on bonds payable. The bonds which were issued at face value mature in 2013. The following entry was recorded on March 1, 2009, when the semiannual interest was paid:

Interest expense	156,000	
Cash		156,000

f. A three-year liability insurance policy was purchased at the beginning of 2008 for $72,000. The full premium was debited to insurance expense at the time.

Required:
For each error, prepare any journal entry necessary to correct the error as well as any year-end adjusting entry for 2009 related to the situation described. (Ignore income taxes.)

P 20–16
Integrating problem; errors; deferred taxes; contingency; change in tax rates

● LO6

You are internal auditor for Shannon Supplies, Inc., and are reviewing the company's preliminary financial statements. The statements, prepared after making the adjusting entries, but before closing entries for the year ended December 31, 2009, are as follows:

SHANNON SUPPLIES, INC.
Balance Sheet
December 31, 2009

Assets	($ in 000s)
Cash	$2,400
Investments	250
Accounts receivable, net	810
Inventory	1,060
Property, plant, and equipment	1,240
Less: Accumulated depreciation	(560)
Total assets	$5,200
Liabilities and Stockholders' Equity	
Accounts payable and accrued expenses	$3,320
Income tax payable	220
Common stock, $1 par	200
Additional paid-in capital	750
Retained earnings	710
Total liabilities and shareholders' equity	$5,200

SHANNON SUPPLIES, INC.
Income Statement
For the Year Ended December 31, 2009

Sales revenue		$3,400
Operating expenses:		
Cost of goods sold	$1,140	
Selling and administrative	896	
Depreciation	84	2,120
Income before income tax		$1,280
Income tax expense		(512)
Net income		$ 768

Shannon's income tax rate was 40% in 2009 and previous years. During the course of the audit, the following additional information (not considered when the above statements were prepared) was obtained:

a. Shannon's investment portfolio consists of blue chip stocks held for long-term appreciation. To raise working capital some of the shares that had cost $180,000 were sold in May 2009. Shannon accountants debited cash and credited investments for the $220,000 proceeds of the sale.

b. At December 31, 2009, the fair value of the remaining securities in the portfolio was $274,000.

c. The state of Alabama filed suit against Shannon in October 2007 seeking civil penalties and injunctive relief for violations of environmental regulations regulating emissions. Shannon's legal counsel previously believed that an unfavorable outcome was not probable, but based on negotiations with state attorneys in 2009, now believe eventual payment to the state of $130,000 is probable, most likely to be paid in 2012.

d. The $1,060,000 inventory total, which was based on a physical count at December 31, 2009, was priced at cost. Based on your conversations with company accountants, you determined that the inventory cost was overstated by $132,000.

e. Electronic counters costing $80,000 were added to the equipment on December 29, 2008. The cost was charged to repairs.

f. Shannon's equipment to which the counters were added had a remaining useful life of four years on December 29, 2008, and is being depreciated by the straight-line method for both financial and tax reporting.

g. A new tax law was enacted in 2009 which will cause Shannon's income tax rate to change from 40% to 35% beginning in 2010.

Required:

Prepare journal entries to record the effects on Shannon's accounting records at December 31, 2009, for each of the items described above. Show all calculations.

P 20–17
Integrating problem; error; depreciation; deferred taxes

● LO6

George Young Industries (GYI) acquired industrial robots at the beginning of 2006 and added them to the company's assembly process. During 2009, management became aware that the $1 million cost of the machinery was inadvertently recorded as repair expense on GYI's books and on its income tax return. The industrial robots have 10-year useful lives and no material salvage value. This class of equipment is depreciated by the straight-line method for financial reporting purposes and for tax purposes it is considered to be MACRS 7-year property (cost deducted over 7 years by the modified accelerated recovery system as follows):

Year	MACRS Deductions
2006	$ 142,900
2007	244,900
2008	174,900
2009	124,900
2010	89,300
2011	89,200
2012	89,300
2013	44,600
Totals	1,000,000

The tax rate is 40% for all years involved.

Required:

1. Prepare any journal entry necessary as a direct result of the error described.
2. Briefly describe any other steps GYI would take to appropriately report the situation.
3. Prepare the adjusting entry for 2009 depreciation.

BROADEN YOUR PERSPECTIVE

Apply your critical-thinking ability to the knowledge you've gained. These cases will provide you an opportunity to develop your research, analysis, judgment, and communication skills. You also will work with other students, integrate what you've learned, apply it in real world situations, and consider its global and ethical ramifications. This practice will broaden your knowledge and further develop your decision-making abilities.

Judgment Case 20–1
Accounting changes; independent situations

● LO1 through LO5

Sometimes a business entity will change its method of accounting for certain items. The change may be classified as a change in accounting principle, a change in accounting estimate, or a change in reporting entity.

Listed below are three independent, unrelated sets of facts relating to accounting changes.

Situation I: A company determined that the depreciable lives of its fixed assets are presently too long to fairly match the cost of the fixed assets with the revenue produced. The company decided at the beginning of the current year to reduce the depreciable lives of all of its existing fixed assets by five years.

Situation II: On December 31, 2008, Gary Company owned 51% of Allen Company, at which time Gary reported its investment on a nonconsolidated basis due to political uncertainties in the country in which Allen was located. On January 2, 2009, the management of Gary Company was satisfied that the political uncertainties were resolved and the assets of the company were in no danger of nationalization. Accordingly, Gary will prepare consolidated financial statements for Gary and Allen for the year ended December 31, 2009.

Situation III: A company decides in January 2009 to adopt the straight-line method of depreciation for plant equipment. The straight-line method will be used for new acquisitions as well as for previously acquired plant equipment for which depreciation had been provided on an accelerated basis.

Required:

For each of the situations described above, provide the information indicated below. Complete your discussion of each situation before going on to the next situation.

1. Type of accounting change.
2. Manner of reporting the change under current generally accepted accounting principles including a discussion, where applicable, of how amounts are computed.
3. Effect of the change on the balance sheet and income statement.
4. Footnote disclosures that would be necessary.

Analysis Case 20–2
Various changes

● LO1 through LO5

DRS Corporation changed the way it depreciates its computers from the sum-of-the-year's-digits method to the straight-line method beginning January 1, 2009, DRS also changed its estimated residual value used in computing depreciation for its office building. At the end of 2009, DRS changed the specific subsidiaries constituting the group of companies for which its consolidated financial statements are prepared.

Required:

1. For each accounting change DRS undertook, indicate the type of change and how DRS should report the change. Be specific.
2. Why should companies disclose changes in accounting principles?

Analysis Case 20–3
Various changes

● LO1 through LO4

Ray Solutions decided to make the following changes in its accounting policies on January 1, 2009:

a. Changed from the cash to the accrual basis of accounting for recognizing revenue on its service contracts.
b. Adopted straight-line depreciation for all future equipment purchases, but continued to use accelerated depreciation for all equipment acquired before 2009.
c. Changed from the LIFO inventory method to the FIFO inventory method.

Required:

For each accounting change Ray undertook, indicate the type of change and how Ray should report the change. Be specific.

Integrating Case 20–4
Change to dollar-value LIFO

● LO3

Webster Products, Inc., adopted the dollar-value LIFO method of determining inventory costs for financial and income tax reporting on January 1, 2009. Webster continues to use the FIFO method for internal decision-making purposes. Webster's FIFO inventories at December 31, 2009, 2010, and 2011, were $300,000, $412,500, and $585,000, respectively. Internally generated cost indexes are used to convert FIFO inventory amounts to dollar-value LIFO amounts. Webster estimated these indexes as follows:

2009	1.00
2010	1.25
2011	1.50

Required:

1. Determine Webster's dollar-value LIFO inventory at December 31, 2010 and 2011.
2. Describe how the change should have been reported in Webster's 2009 financial statements.

Communication Case 20–5
Change in loss contingency; write a memo

● LO4

Late in 2009, you and two other officers of Curbo Fabrications Corporation just returned from a meeting with officials of The City of Jackson. The meeting was unexpectedly favorable even though it culminated in a settlement with city authorities that your company pay a total of $475,000 to cover the cost of violations of city construction codes. Jackson had filed suit in November 2007 against Curbo Fabrications Corporation, seeking civil penalties and injunctive relief for violations of city construction codes regulating earth- quake damage standards. Alleged violations involved several construction projects completed during the previous three years. When the financial statements were issued in 2008, Curbo had not reached a settlement with state authorities, but legal counsel had advised the company that it was probable the ultimate settlement would be $750,000 in penalties. The following entry had been recorded:

Loss—litigation	750,000	
Liability—litigation		750,000

The final settlement, therefore, was a pleasant surprise. While returning from the meeting, conversation turned to reporting the settlement in the 2009 financial statements. You drew the short straw and were selected to write a memo to Janet Zeno, the financial vice president, advising the proper course of action.

Required:

Write the memo. Include descriptions of any journal entries related to the change in amounts. Briefly describe other steps Curbo should take to report the settlement.

Analysis Case 20–6
Two wrongs make a right?

● LO4

Early one Wednesday afternoon, Ken and Larry studied in the dormitory room they shared at Fogelman College. Ken, an accounting major, was advising Larry, a management major, regarding a project for Larry's Business Policy class. One aspect of the project involved analyzing the 2008 annual report of Craft Paper Company. Though not central to his business policy case, a footnote had caught Larry's attention.

Depreciation and Cost of Timber Harvested (in part)
($ in millions)

	2008	2007	2006
Depreciation of buildings, machinery and equipment	$260.9	$329.8	$322.5
Cost of timber harvested and amortization of logging roads	4.9	4.9	4.9
	$265.8	$334.7	$327.4

Beginning in 2008, the Company revised the estimated average useful lives used to compute depreciation for most of its pulp and paper mill equipment from 16 years to 20 years and for most of its finishing and converting equipment from 12 years to 15 years. These revisions were made to more properly reflect the true economic lives of the assets and to better align the Company's depreciable lives with the predominant practice in the industry. The change had the effect of increasing net income by approximately $55 million.

"If I understand this right, Ken, the company is not going back and recalculating a lower depreciation for earlier years. Instead they seem to be leaving depreciation overstated in earlier years and making up for that by understating it in current and future years," Larry mused. "Is that the way it is in accounting? Two wrongs make a right?"

Required:

What are the two wrongs to which Larry refers? Is he right?

Ethics Case 20–7
Softening the blow

● LO1 LO2 LO3

Late one Thursday afternoon, Joy Martin, a veteran audit manager with a regional CPA firm, was reviewing documents for a long-time client of the firm, AMT Transport. The year-end audit was scheduled to begin Monday.

For three months, the economy had been in a down cycle and the transportation industry was particularly hard hit. As a result, Joy expected AMT's financial results would not be pleasant news to shareholders. However, what Joy saw in the preliminary statements made her sigh aloud. Results were much worse than she feared.

"Larry (the company president) already is in the doghouse with shareholders," Joy thought to herself. "When they see these numbers, they'll hang him out to dry."

"I wonder if he's considered some strategic accounting changes," she thought, after reflecting on the situation. "The bad news could be softened quite a bit by changing inventory methods from LIFO to FIFO or reconsidering some of the estimates used in other areas."

Required:

1. How would the actions contemplated contribute toward "softening" the bad news?
2. Do you perceive an ethical dilemma? What would be the likely impact of following up on Joy's thoughts? Who would benefit? Who would be injured?

Research Case 20–8
Researching the way changes in postretirement benefit estimates are reported; retrieving disclosures from the Internet

● LO4

It's financial statements preparation time at Center Industries where you have been assistant controller for two months. Ben Huddler, the controller, seems to be pleasant but unpredictable. Today, although your schedule is filled with meetings with internal and outside auditors and two members of the board of directors, Ben made a request. "As you know, we're decreasing the rate at which we assume health care costs will rise when measuring our postretirement benefit obligation. I'd like to know how others have reported similar changes. Can you find me an example?" he asked. "I'd bet you could get one off the Internet you're always using." As a matter of fact, you often use EDGAR, the Electronic Data Gathering, Analysis, and Retrieval system (www.sec.gov) to access financial statements filed with the U.S. Securities and Exchange Commission (SEC).

Required:

1. Access EDGAR on the Internet. You might want to use one of the EDGAR retrieval sites listed at the course website. Access a recent 10-K filing of a firm you think might have a postretirement health care plan. You may need to look up several companies before you find what you're looking for. Older, established companies are most likely to have such benefit plans.
   (Note: You may be able to focus your search by searching with key words and phrases in one of the several "search engines" available on the Internet.)
2. Copy the portion of the disclosures that reports the effect of a change in health care cost trends.
3. What information is provided about the effect of the change on the company's estimated benefit obligation?

Analysis Case 20–9
Change in inventory methods; concepts
● LO2 LO3

Generally accepted accounting principles should be applied consistently from period to period. However, changes within a company, as well as changes in the external economic environment, may force a company to change an accounting method. The specific reporting requirements when a company changes from one generally accepted inventory method to another depend on the methods involved.

Required:

Explain the accounting treatment for a change in inventory method (a) not involving LIFO, (b) from the LIFO method, and (c) to the LIFO method. Explain the logic underlying those treatments. Also, describe how disclosure requirements are designed to address the departure from consistency and comparability of changes in accounting principle.

Real World Case 20–10
Change in inventory method
● LO2
Real World Financials

On November 8, 2007, AMCON Distributing Company ("AMCON" or "Company") issued a press release announcing its financial results for the fiscal year ended September 30, 2007. Included was the following information regarding a change in inventory method (in part):

In the fourth quarter of fiscal 2007, the Company changed its inventory valuation method from the Last-In First-Out (LIFO) method to the First-In First-Out (FIFO) method. The change is preferable as it provides a more meaningful presentation of the Company's financial position as it values inventory in a manner which more closely approximates current cost; better represents the underlying commercial substance of selling the oldest products first; and more accurately reflects the Company's realized periodic income.

As required by U.S. generally accepted accounting principles, this change in accounting principle has been reflected in the consolidated statements of financial position, consolidated statements of operations, and consolidated statements of cash flows through retroactive application of the FIFO method. Previously reported net income (loss) available to common shareholders' for the fiscal years 2006 and 2005 were increased by $0.1 million and $0.5 million after income taxes, respectively.

Required:

1. Why does GAAP require AMCON to retrospectively adjust prior years' financial statements for this type of accounting change?
2. Assuming that the quantity of inventory remained stable during the previous two years, did the cost of AMCON's inventory move up or down during that year?

Communication Case 20–11
Change in inventory method; disclosure note
● LO2

Mayfair Department Stores, Inc., operates over 30 retail stores in the Pacific Northwest. Prior to 2009, the company used the FIFO method to value its inventory. In 2009, Mayfair decided to switch to the dollar- value LIFO retail inventory method. One of your responsibilities as assistant controller is to prepare the disclosure note describing the change in method that will be included in the company's 2009 financial statements. Kenneth Meier, the controller, provided the following information:

- Internally developed retail price indexes are used to adjust for the effects of changing prices.
- If the change had not been made, cost of goods sold for the year would have been $22 million lower. The company's income tax rate is 40% and there were 100 million shares of common stock outstanding during 2009.
- The cumulative effect of the change on prior years' income is not determinable.
- The reasons for the change were (a) to provide a more consistent matching of merchandise costs with sales revenue, and (b) the new method provides a more comparable basis of accounting with competitors that also use the LIFO method.

Required:

1. Prepare for Kenneth Meier the disclosure note that will be included in the 2009 financial statements.
2. Explain why the "cumulative effect of the change on prior years' income is not determinable."

Judgment Case 20–12
Inventory errors
● LO6

Some inventory errors are said to be "self-correcting" in that the error has the opposite financial statement effect in the period following the error, thereby "correcting" the original account balance errors.

Required:

Despite this self-correcting feature, discuss why these errors should not be ignored and describe the steps required to account for the error correction.

Ethics Case 20–13
Overstatement of ending inventory
● LO6

Danville Bottlers is a wholesale beverage company. Danville uses the FIFO inventory method to determine the cost of its ending inventory. Ending inventory quantities are determined by a physical count. For the fiscal year-end June 30, 2009, ending inventory was originally determined to be $3,265,000. However, on July 17, 2009, John Howard, the company's controller, discovered an error in the ending inventory count. He determined that the correct ending inventory amount should be $2,600,000.

Danville is a privately owned corporation with significant financing provided by a local bank. The bank requires annual audited financial statements as a condition of the loan. By July 17, the auditors had completed their review of the financial statements which are scheduled to be issued on July 25. They did not discover the inventory error.

John's first reaction was to communicate his finding to the auditors and to revise the financial statements before they are issued. However, he knows that his and his fellow workers' profit-sharing plans are based on annual pretax earnings and that if he revises the statements, everyone's profit sharing bonus will be significantly reduced.

Required:

1. Why will bonuses be negatively affected? What is the effect on pretax earnings?
2. If the error is not corrected in the current year and is discovered by the auditors during the following year's audit, how will it be reported in the company's financial statements?
3. Discuss the ethical dilemma Howard faces.

Trueblood Case 20–14
Preferability of accounting changes

● LO2

The following Trueblood case is recommended for use with this chapter. The case provides an excellent opportunity for class discussion, group projects, and writing assignments. The case, along with Professor's Discussion Material, can be obtained from the Deloitte Foundation at its website: **www.deloitte.com/us/truebloodcases**.

Case 07-2: *Western Aluminum*

This case gives students the opportunity to consider the treatment of changes in accounting principle. It requires a judgment as to the preferability of one accounting method over another when making a change. Assuming that the change is preferable, it requires calculating the financial statement impact of the change.

CHAPTER 21

The Statement of Cash Flows Revisited

/// OVERVIEW

The objective of financial reporting is to provide investors and creditors with useful information, primarily in the form of financial statements. The balance sheet and the income statement—the focus of your study in earlier chapters—do not provide all the information needed by these decision makers. Here you will learn how the statement of cash flows fills the information gap left by the other financial statements.

The statement lists all cash inflows and cash outflows, and classifies them as cash flows from (a) operating, (b) investing, or (c) financing activities. Investing and financing activities that do not directly affect cash also are reported.

LEARNING OBJECTIVES

After studying this chapter, you should be able to:

- **LO1** Explain the usefulness of the statement of cash flows.
- **LO2** Define cash equivalents.
- **LO3** Determine cash flows from operating activities by the direct method.
- **LO4** Determine cash flows from operating activities by the indirect method.
- **LO5** Identify transactions that are classified as investing activities.
- **LO6** Identify transactions that are classified as financing activities.
- **LO7** Identify transactions that represent noncash investing and financing activities.
- **LO8** Prepare a statement of cash flows with the aid of a spreadsheet or T-accounts.

FINANCIAL REPORTING CASE

Where's the Cash?

"What do you mean you can't afford a wage increase?" union negotiator Vince Barr insisted. "We've all seen your income statement. You had record earnings this year."

This is the first day of negotiations with the company's union representatives. As company controller, you know it's going to be up to you to explain the company's position on the financial aspects of the negotiations. In fact, you've known for some time that a critical point of contention would be the moderate increase in this year's profits after three years of level or slightly declining earnings. Not helping the situation is that the company has always used accelerated depreciation on its equipment which it began replacing this year at considerably higher prices than it cost several years back.

By the time you finish this chapter, you should be able to respond appropriately to the questions posed in this case. Compare your response to the solution provided at the end of the chapter.

QUESTIONS ///

1. What are the cash flow aspects of the situation that Mr. Barr may be overlooking in making his case for a wage increase? How can a company's operations generate a healthy profit and yet produce meager or even negative cash flows? (page 1112)
2. What information can a statement of cash flows provide about a company's investing activities that can be useful in decisions such as this? (page 1114)
3. What information can a statement of cash flows provide about a company's financing activities that can be useful in decisions such as this? (page 1115)

PART A THE CONTENT AND VALUE OF THE STATEMENT OF CASH FLOWS

DECISION MAKERS' PERSPECTIVE—Usefulness Of Cash Flow Information

● LO1

Investors and creditors require cash flows from the corporation.

A fund manager of a major insurance company, considering investing $8,000,000 in the common stock of **The Coca-Cola Company**, asks herself: "What are the prospects of future dividends and market-price appreciation? Will we get a return commensurate with the cost and risk of our investment?" A bank officer, examining an application for a business loan, asks himself: "If I approve this loan, what is the likelihood of the borrower making interest payments on time and repaying the loan when due?" Investors and creditors continually face these and similar decisions that require projections of the relative ability of a business to generate future cash flows and of the risk associated with those forecasts.

To make these projections, decision makers rely heavily on the information reported in periodic financial statements. In the final analysis, cash flows into and out of a business enterprise are the most fundamental events on which investors and creditors base their decisions. Naturally, these decisions focus on the prospects of the decision makers receiving cash returns from their dealings with the firm. However, it is the ability of the firm to generate cash flows to itself that ultimately determines the potential for cash flows from the firm to investors and creditors.

Cash flows to investors and creditors depend on the corporation generating cash flows to itself.

The financial statements that have been the focus of your study in earlier chapters—the income statement and the balance sheet—offer information helpful in forecasting future cash-generating ability. Some important questions, however, are not easily answered from the information these statements provide. For example, meaningful projections of a company's future profitability and risk depend on answers to such questions as:

- In what types of activities is the company investing?
- Are these activities being financed with debt? with equity? by cash generated from operations?
- Are facilities being acquired to accommodate future expansion?
- How does the amount of cash generated from operations compare with net income over time?
- Why isn't the increase in retained earnings reflected as an increase in dividends?
- What happens to the cash received from the sale of assets?
- By what means is debt being retired?

Many decisions benefit from information about the company's underlying cash flow process.

The information needed to answer these and similar questions is found in the continuous series of cash flows that the income statement and the balance sheet describe only indirectly. This underlying cash flow process is considered next. ●

Cash Inflows and Outflows

Cash continually flows into and out of an active business. Businesses disburse cash to acquire operational assets to maintain or expand productive capacity. When no longer needed, these assets may be sold for cash. Cash is paid to produce or purchase inventory for resale, as well as to pay for the expenses of selling these goods. The ultimate outcome of these selling activities is an inflow of cash. Cash might be invested in securities of other firms. These investments provide cash inflows during the investment period in the form of dividends or interest and at the end of the investment period when the securities are sold. To raise cash to finance their operations, firms sell stock and/or acquire debt. Cash payments are made as dividends to shareholders and interest to creditors. When debt is repaid or stock repurchased, cash flows out of the firm. To help you visualize the continual process of cash receipts and cash payments, that process is diagrammed in Graphic 21–1. The diagram also previews the way we will later classify the cash flows on a statement of cash flows.

GRAPHIC 21–1
Cash Inflows and Cash Outflows

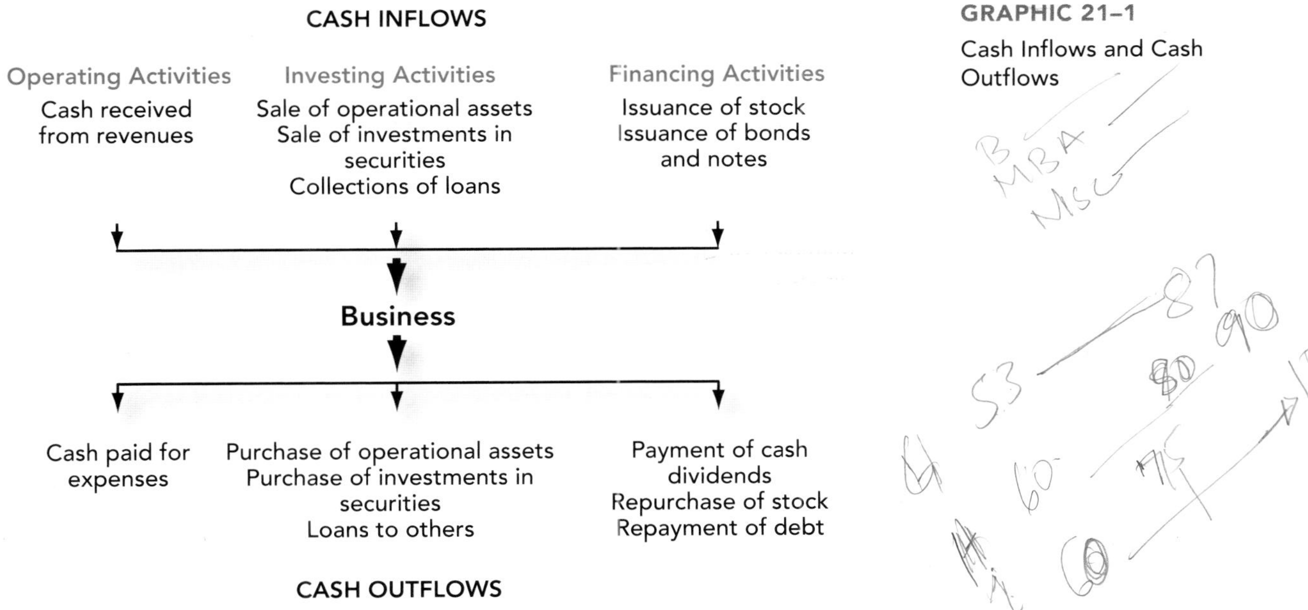

Embodied in this assortment of cash flows is a wealth of information that investors and creditors require to make educated decisions. Much of the value of the underlying information provided by the cash flows is lost when reported only indirectly by the balance sheet and the income statement. Each cash flow eventually impacts decision makers by affecting the balances of various accounts on the balance sheet. Also, many of the cash flows—those related to income-producing activities—are represented on the income statement. However, they are not necessarily reported in the period the cash flows occur because the income statement measures activities on an accrual basis. The statement of cash flows fills the information gap by reporting the cash flows directly.

Role of the Statement of Cash Flows

A statement of cash flows is shown in Graphic 21–2. The statement lists all cash inflows and cash outflows during the reporting period. To enhance the informational value of the presentation, the cash flows are classified according to the nature of the activities that bring about the cash flows. The three primary categories of cash flows are (1) cash flows from operating activities, (2) cash flows from investing activities, and (3) cash flows from financing activities. Classifying each cash flow by source (operating, investing, or financing activities) is more informative than simply listing the various cash flows. Notice, too, that the noncash investing and financing activities—investing and financing activities that do not directly increase or decrease cash—also are reported. *FASB Statement 95,* requiring the statement of cash flows, was issued in direct response to *FASB Concept Statement 1,* which states that the primary objective of financial reporting is to "provide information to help investors and creditors, and others assess the amounts, timing, and uncertainty of prospective net cash inflows to the related enterprise."[1]

The statement of cash flows provides information about cash flows that is lost when reported only indirectly by the balance sheet and the income statement.

Many companies have experienced bankruptcy because they were unable to generate sufficient cash to satisfy their obligations. Doubtless, many investors in the stock of these firms would have been spared substantial losses if the financial statements had been designed to foresee the cash flow problems the companies were experiencing. A noted illustration is the demise of **W. T. Grant** during the 1970s. Grant, a general retailer in the days before malls, was a blue chip stock of its time. Grant's statement of changes in financial position (the predecessor of the statement of cash flows) reported working capital from operations of $46 million in 1972. Yet, if presented, a statement of cash flows would have reported cash

[1] "Objectives of Financial Reporting by Business Enterprises," *FASB Statement of Financial Accounting Concepts* No. 1, par 37.

GRAPHIC 21–2
Statement of Cash Flows

UNITED BRANDS CORPORATION
Statement of Cash Flows
For Year Ended December 31, 2009
($ in millions)

Cash Flows from Operating Activities		
Cash inflows:		
From customers	$98	
From investment revenue	3	
Cash outflows:		
To suppliers of goods	(50)	
To employees	(11)	
For interest	(3)	
For insurance	(4)	
For income taxes	(11)	
Net cash flows from operating activities		$22
Cash Flows from Investing Activities		
Purchase of land	(30)	
Purchase of short-term investment	(12)	
Sale of land	18	
Sale of equipment	5	
Net cash flows from investing activities		(19)
Cash Flows from Financing Activities		
Sale of common shares	26	
Retirement of bonds payable	(15)	
Payment of cash dividends	(5)	
Net cash flows from financing activities		6
Net increase in cash		9
Cash balance, January 1		20
Cash balance, December 31		$29

Note X:	
Noncash Investing and Financing Activities	
Acquired $20 million of equipment by issuing a 12%, 5-year note.	$20
Reconciliation of Net Income to Cash Flows from Operating Activities:	
Net income	$12
Adjustments for noncash effects:	
Gain on sale of land	(8)
Depreciation expense	3
Loss on sale of equipment	2
Changes in operating assets and liabilities:	
Increase in accounts receivable	(2)
Decrease in inventory	4
Increase in accounts payable	6
Increase in salaries payable	2
Discount on bonds payable	2
Decrease in prepaid insurance	3
Decrease in income tax payable	(2)
Net cash flows from operating activities	$22

flows from operating activities of negative $10 million. In fact, the unreported cash flow deficiency grew to $114 million in 1973, while working capital from operations was reported as having increased by $1 million. That year, without the benefit of cash flow information, investors were buying Grant's stock at prices that represented up to 20 times its earnings.[2]

[2]Cheryl A. Zega, "The New Statement of Cash Flows," *Management Accounting,* September 1988.

More recently, even with cash flow information available, cash flow problems can go unnoticed. An example is the rapid growth and subsequent bankruptcy of the **Wicks 'N' Sticks** franchise. The company's drive for rapid growth led to a dependence on the sale of new franchises in order to generate cash flow instead of doing so in a more healthy way through its operations. As we see shortly, a statement of cash flows can indicate not just the amount of cash flows, but also whether those cash flows are coming from operations or from outside sources. Wicks 'N' Sticks was able to emerge from bankruptcy through restructuring and a new perspective on cash flow management.

The statement of cash flows for United Brands Corporation (UBC), shown in Graphic 21–2, is intended at this point in the discussion to illustrate the basic structure and composition of the statement. Later we will see how the statement of cash flows for UBC is prepared from the information typically available for this purpose. We will refer to UBC's statement of cash flows frequently throughout the chapter as the discussion becomes more specific regarding the criteria for classifying cash flows in the three primary categories and as we identify the specific cash flows to be reported on the statement. We will examine the content of the statement in more detail following a look at how this relatively recent financial statement has evolved to its present form over the course of the last several decades.

Cash and Cash Equivalents

● LO2

Skilled cash managers will invest temporarily idle cash in short-term investments to earn interest on those funds, rather than maintain an unnecessarily large balance in a checking account. The FASB views short-term, highly liquid investments that can be readily converted to cash, with little risk of loss, as **cash equivalents.** Amounts held as investments of this type are essentially equivalent to cash because they are quickly available for use as cash. Therefore, on the statement of cash flows there is no differentiation between amounts held as cash (e.g., currency and checking accounts) and amounts held in cash equivalent investments. So, when we refer in this chapter to cash, we are referring to the total of cash and cash equivalents.

There is no differentiation between amounts held as cash and amounts held in cash equivalent investments.

Examples of cash equivalents are money market funds, Treasury bills, and commercial paper. To be classified as cash equivalents, these investments must have a maturity date not longer than three months from the date of purchase. Flexibility is permitted in designating cash equivalents. Each company must establish a policy regarding which short-term, highly liquid investments it classifies as cash equivalents. The policy should be consistent with the company's customary motivation for acquiring various investments and should be disclosed in the notes to the statement.[3] A recent annual report of **ExxonMobil Corporation** provides this description of its cash equivalents (Graphic 21–3):

Each firm's policy regarding which short-term, highly liquid investments it classifies as cash equivalents should be disclosed in the notes to the financial statements.

GRAPHIC 21–3
Disclosure of Cash Equivalents—ExxonMobil Corporation

Note 4: Cash Flow Information (in part)
The consolidated statement of cash flows provides information about changes in cash and cash equivalents. Highly liquid investments with maturities of three months or less when acquired are classified as cash equivalents.

Transactions that involve merely transfers from cash to cash equivalents (such as the purchase of a three-month Treasury bill), or from cash equivalents to cash (such as the sale of a Treasury bill), should not be reported on the statement of cash flows. The total of cash and cash equivalents is not altered by such transactions.[4] The cash balance reported on the balance sheet also represents the total of cash and cash equivalents, which allows us to compare the change in that balance with the net increase or decrease in the cash flows reported on the statement of cash flows.

Primary Elements of the Statement of Cash Flows

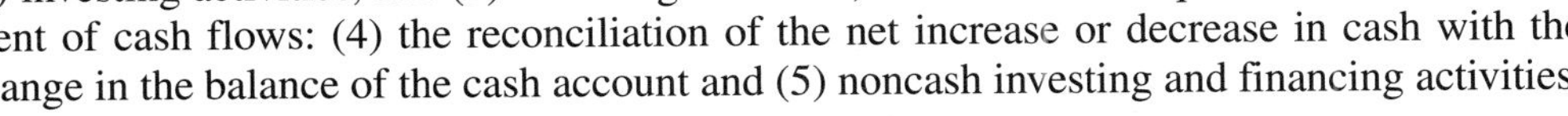

This section describes the three primary activity classifications: (1) operating activities, (2) investing activities, and (3) financing activities; and two other requirements of the statement of cash flows: (4) the reconciliation of the net increase or decrease in cash with the change in the balance of the cash account and (5) noncash investing and financing activities.

[3]A change in that policy is treated as a change in accounting principle.

[4]An exception is the sale of a cash equivalent at a gain or loss. This exception is described in more detail later in the chapter.

FINANCIAL Reporting Case

Q1, p. 1107

● LO3

CASH FLOWS FROM OPERATING ACTIVITIES. The income statement reports the success of a business in generating a profit from its operations. Net income (or loss) is the result of netting together the revenues earned during the reporting period, regardless of when cash is received, and the expenses incurred in generating those revenues, regardless of when cash is paid. This is the accrual concept of accounting that has been emphasized throughout your study of accounting. Information about net income and its components, measured by the accrual concept, generally provides a better indication of current operating performance than does information about current cash receipts and payments.[5] Nevertheless, as indicated earlier, the cash effects of earning activities also provide useful information that is not directly accessible from the income statement. The first cash flow classification in the statement of cash flows reports that information.

The cash effects of the elements of net income are reported as cash flows from operating activities.

Cash flows from operating activities are both inflows and outflows of cash that result from activities reported on the income statement. In other words, this classification of cash flows includes the elements of net income, but reported on a cash basis. The components of this section of the statement of cash flows, and their relationship with the elements of the income statement, are illustrated in Graphic 21–4.

GRAPHIC 21–4
Relationship between the Income Statement and Cash Flows from Operating Activities (Direct Method)

Income Statement	Cash Flows from Operating Activities
Revenues:	Cash inflows:
Sales and service revenue	Cash received from customers
Investment revenue	Cash revenue received (e.g., dividends, interest)
Noncash revenues and gains (e.g., gain on sale of assets)	(Not reported)
Less: Expenses:	Less: Cash outflows:
Cost of goods sold	Cash paid to suppliers of inventory
Salaries expense	Cash paid to employees
Noncash expenses and losses (e.g., depreciation, amortization, bad debts, loss on sale of assets)	(Not reported)
Interest expense	Cash paid to trade creditors
Other operating expenses	Cash paid to insurance companies and others
Income tax expense	Cash paid to the government
Net income	*Net cash flows from operating activities*

To see the concept applied, let's look again at the cash flows from operating activities reported by United Brands Corporation. That section of the statement of cash flows is extracted from Graphic 21–2 and reproduced in Graphic 21–5.

GRAPHIC 21–5
Cash Flows from Operating Activities

Cash Flows from Operating Activities:		
Cash inflows:		
From customers	$98	
From investment revenue	3	
Cash outflows:		
To suppliers of goods	(50)	
To employees	(11)	
For interest	(3)	
For insurance	(4)	
For income taxes	(11)	
Net cash flows from operating activities		$22

Cash flows from operating activities are the elements of net income, but reported on a cash basis.

Cash inflows from operating activities exceeded cash outflows for expenses by $22 million. We'll see later (in Illustration 21–1) that UBC's net income from the same operating activities was only $12 million. Why did operating activities produce net cash inflows greater

[5] *FASB Statement of Financial Accounting Concepts No. 1,* par. 44.

than net income? The reason will become apparent when we determine, in a later section, the specific amounts of these cash flows.

You also should be aware that the generalization stated earlier that cash flows from operating activities include the elements of net income reported on a cash basis is not strictly true for all elements of the income statement. Notice in Graphic 21–5 that no cash effects are reported for depreciation and amortization of operational assets, nor for gains and losses from the sale of those assets. Cash outflows occur when operational assets are acquired, and cash inflows occur when the assets are sold. However, as described later, the acquisition and subsequent resale of operational assets are classified as investing activities, rather than as operating activities.

Quite the opposite, the purchase and the sale of inventory are considered operating activities. The cash effects of these transactions—namely, (1) cash payments to suppliers and (2) cash receipts from customers—are included in the determination of cash flows from operating activities. Why are inventories and operational assets treated differently when classifying their cash effects if both are acquired for the purpose of producing revenues? The essential difference is that inventory typically is purchased for the purpose of being sold as part of the firm's current operations, while an operational asset is purchased as an investment to benefit the business over a relatively long period of time.

DIRECT METHOD OR INDIRECT METHOD OF REPORTING CASH FLOWS FROM OPERATING ACTIVITIES. The presentation by UBC of cash flows from operating activities illustrated in Graphic 21–2 and reproduced in Graphic 21–5 above is referred to as the **direct method**. The method is named for the fact that the cash effect of each operating activity (i.e., income statement item) is reported *directly* on the statement of cash flows. For instance, UBC reports "cash received from customers" as the cash effect of sales activities, "cash paid to suppliers" as the cash effect of cost of goods sold, and so on. Then, UBC simply omits from the presentation any income statement items that do not affect cash at all, such as depreciation expense.

Another way UBC might have reported cash flows from operating activities is by the **indirect method.** By this approach, the net cash increase or decrease from operating activities ($22 million in our example) would be derived *indirectly* by starting with reported net income and working backwards to convert that amount to a cash basis. As we see later in the chapter, UBC's net income is $12 million. Using the indirect method, UBC would replace the previous presentation of net cash flows from operating activities with the one shown in Graphic 21–6.

● LO4

GRAPHIC 21–6
Indirect Method

Cash Flows from Operating Activities:		
Net income	$12	
Adjustments for noncash effects:		
Gain on sale of land	(8)	
Depreciation expense	3	
Loss on sale of equipment	2	
Changes in operating assets and liabilities:		
Increase in accounts receivable	(2)	
Decrease in inventory	4	
Increase in accounts payable	6	
Increase in salaries payable	2	
Discount on bonds payable	2	
Decrease in prepaid insurance	3	
Decrease in income tax payable	(2)	
Net cash flows from operating activities		$22

By the indirect method, UBC derives the net cash increase or decrease from operating activities *indirectly*, by starting with reported net income and working backwards to convert that amount to a cash basis.

Be sure to note that the indirect method generates the same $22 million net cash flows from operating activities as did the direct method. Rather than directly reporting only the components of the income statement that *do* represent increases or decreases in cash, by the indirect method we begin with net income—which includes both cash and noncash components—and back out all amounts that *don't* reflect increases or decreases in cash. Later in the chapter, we explore the specific adjustments made to net income to achieve this result. At this point it is sufficient to realize that two alternative methods are permitted for reporting net cash flows from operating activities. Either way, we convert accrual-based income to cash flows produced by those same operating activities.

Notice also that the indirect method presentation is identical to what UBC reported earlier as the "Reconciliation of Net Income to Cash Flows from Operating Activities" in Note X of Graphic 21–2. Whether cash flows from operating activities are reported by the direct method or by the indirect method, the financial statements must reconcile the difference between net income and cash flows from operating activities. When a company uses the *direct method,* the company presents the reconciliation in a separate schedule as UBC did. That presentation is precisely the same as the presentation of net cash flows from operating activities by the indirect method. On the other hand, a company choosing to use the indirect method is not required to provide a separate reconciliation schedule because the "cash flows from operating activities" section of the statement of cash flows serves that purpose. Most companies use the indirect method.[6]

It's important to understand, too, that regardless of which method a company chooses to report *operating* activities, that choice has no effect on the way it identifies and reports cash flows from *investing* and *financing* activities. We turn our attention now to those two sections of the statement of cash flows. Later in Part C, we'll return for a more thorough discussion of the alternative methods of reporting the operating activities section.

FINANCIAL Reporting Case

Q2, p. 1107

CASH FLOWS FROM INVESTING ACTIVITIES. Companies periodically invest cash to replace or expand productive facilities such as property, plant, and equipment. Investments might also be made in other assets, such as securities of other firms, with the expectation of a return on those investments. Information concerning these investing activities can provide valuable insight to decision makers regarding the nature and magnitude of operational assets being acquired for future use, as well as provide clues concerning the company's ambitions for the future.

● LO5

Cash outflows and cash inflows due to the acquisition and disposition of assets (other than inventory and assets classified as cash equivalents) are reported as cash flows from investing activities.

Cash flows from investing activities are both outflows and inflows of cash caused by the acquisition and disposition of assets. Included in this classification are cash payments to acquire (1) property, plant, and equipment and other productive assets (except inventories), (2) investments in securities (except cash equivalents and trading securities[7]), and (3) nontrade receivables.[8] When these assets later are liquidated, any cash receipts from their disposition also are classified as investing activities. For instance, cash received from the sale of the assets or from the collection of a note receivable (principal amount only) represents cash inflows from investing activities. Be sure to realize that, unlike the label might imply, any investment revenue like interest, dividends, or other cash return from these investments is not an investing activity. The reason, remember, is that investment revenue is an income statement item and therefore is an operating activity.

For illustration, notice the cash flows reported as investing activities by UBC. That section of the statement of cash flows is extracted from Graphic 21–2 and reproduced in Graphic 21–7.

UBC reports as investing activities the cash paid to purchase both land and a short-term investment. The other two investing activities reported are cash receipts for the sale of assets—equipment and land—that were acquired in earlier years. The specific transactions creating these cash flows are described in a later section of this chapter.

The purchase and sale of inventories are not considered investing activities. Inventories are purchased for the purpose of being sold as part of the firm's primary operations, so their purchase and sale are classified as operating activities.

[6]According to the *AICPA, Accounting Trends and Techniques,* 2004, a recent survey of 600 companies showed that 593 companies chose to use the indirect method, only 7 the direct method.

[7]Inflows and outflows of cash from buying and selling trading securities typically are considered operating activities because financial institutions that routinely transact in trading securities consider them an appropriate part of their normal operations.

[8]A nontrade receivable differs from a trade receivable in that it is not one associated with the company's normal trade; that is, it's not received from a customer. A trade receivable, or accounts receivable, is an *operating asset.* A nontrade receivable, on the other hand, might be a loan to an affiliate company or to an officer of the firm. To understand how the creation of a nontrade receivable is an *investing* activity, you might view such a loan as an investment in the receivable.

GRAPHIC 21–7
Cash Flows from Investing Activities

Cash flows from investing activities include investments in assets and their subsequent sale.

Cash Flows from Investing Activities:		
Purchase of land	(30)	
Purchase of short-term investment	(12)	
Sale of land	18	
Sale of equipment	5	
Net cash flows from investing activities		(19)

Also, the purchase and sale of assets classified as cash equivalents are not reported as investing activities. In fact, these activities usually are not reported on the statement of cash flows. For example, when temporarily idle cash is invested in a money market fund considered to be a cash equivalent, the total of cash and cash equivalents does not change. Likewise, when the cash is later withdrawn from the money market fund, the total remains unchanged. The exception is when cash equivalents are sold at a gain or a loss. In that case, the total of cash and cash equivalents actually increases or decreases in the process of transferring from one cash equivalent account to another cash equivalent account. As a result, the change in cash would be reported as a cash flow from operating activities. This is illustrated later in the chapter.

FINANCIAL Reporting Case

Q3, p. 1107

● LO6

CASH FLOWS FROM FINANCING ACTIVITIES. Not only is it important for investors and creditors to be informed about how a company is investing its funds, but also how its investing activities are being financed. Hopefully, the primary operations of the firm provide a source of internal financing. Information revealed in the cash flows from operating activities section of the statement of cash flows lets statement users know the extent of available internal financing. However, a major portion of financing for many companies is provided by external sources, specifically by shareholders and creditors.

Cash inflows and cash outflows due to the external financing of a business are reported as cash flows from financing activities.

Cash flows from financing activities are both inflows and outflows of cash resulting from the external financing of a business. We include in this classification cash inflows from (a) the sale of common and preferred stock and (b) the issuance of bonds and other debt securities. Subsequent transactions related to these financing transactions, such as a buyback of stock (to retire the stock or as treasury stock), the repayment of debt, and the payment of cash dividends to shareholders, also are classified as financing activities.

For illustration, refer to Graphic 21–8 excerpted from Graphic 21–2.

GRAPHIC 21–8
Cash Flows from Financing Activities

Cash flows from financing activities include the sale or repurchase of shares, the issuance or repayment of debt securities, and the payment of cash dividends.

Cash Flows from Financing Activities		
Sale of common shares	26	
Retirement of bonds payable	(15)	
Payment of cash dividends	(5)	
Net cash flows from financing activities		6

The cash received from the sale of common stock is reported as a financing activity. Since the sale of common stock is a financing activity, providing a cash return (dividend) to common shareholders also is a financing activity. Similarly, when the bonds being retired were sold in a prior year, that cash inflow was reported as a financing activity. In the current year, when the bonds are retired, the resulting cash outflow is likewise classified as a financing activity.

Interest, unlike dividends, is a determinant of net income and therefore an operating activity.

At first glance, it may appear inconsistent to classify the payment of cash dividends to shareholders as a financing activity when, as stated earlier, paying interest to creditors is classified as an operating activity. But remember, cash flows from operating activities should reflect the cash effects of items that enter into the determination of net income. Interest expense is a determinant of net income. A dividend, on the other hand, is a distribution of net income and not an expense.[9]

[9]Not all accountants are satisfied with the FASB's distinctions among operating, investing, and financing activities. See, for example, Hugo Nurnberg, "Inconsistencies and Ambiguities in Cash Flow Statements under *FASB Statement No. 95*," *Accounting Horizons*, June 1993.

RECONCILIATION WITH CHANGE IN CASH BALANCE. One of the first items you may have noticed about UBC's statement of cash flows is that there is a net change in cash of $9 million. Is this a significant item of information provided by the statement? The primary objective of the statement of cash flows is not to tell us that cash increased by $9 million. We can readily see the increase or decrease in cash by comparing the beginning and ending balances in the cash account in comparative balance sheets. Instead, the purpose of the statement of cash flows is to explain *why* cash increased by $9 million.

To reinforce the fact that the net amount of cash inflows and outflows explains the change in the cash balance, the statement of cash flows includes a reconciliation of the net increase (or decrease) in cash with the company's beginning and ending cash balances. Notice, for instance, that on UBC's statement of cash flows, the reconciliation appears as:

The net amount of cash inflows and outflows reconciles the change in the company's beginning and ending cash balances.

Net Increase in Cash	**$ 9**
Cash balance, January 1	20
Cash balance, December 31	$29

NONCASH INVESTING AND FINANCING ACTIVITIES. Suppose UBC were to borrow $20 million cash from a bank, issuing a long-term note payable for that amount. This transaction would be reported on a statement of cash flows as a financing activity. Now suppose UBC used that $20 million cash to purchase new equipment. This second transaction would be reported as an investing activity.

● LO7

Instead of two separate transactions, as indicated by Graphic 21–2, UBC acquired $20 million of new equipment by issuing a $20 million long-term note payable in a single transaction. Undertaking a significant investing activity and a significant financing activity as two parts of a single transaction does not diminish the value of reporting these activities. For that reason, transactions that do not increase or decrease cash, but which result in significant investing and financing activities, must be reported in related disclosures.

These **noncash investing and financing activities,** such as UBC's acquiring equipment (an investing activity) by issuing a long-term note payable (a financing activity), are reported in a separate disclosure schedule or note. UBC reported this transaction in the following manner:

Noncash investing and financing activities are reported also.

Noncash Investing and Financing Activities:
Acquired $20 million of equipment by issuing a 12%, 5-year note.

It's convenient to report noncash investing and financing activities on the same page as the statement of cash flows as did UBC only if there are few such transactions. Otherwise, precisely the same information would be reported in disclosure notes to the financial statements.[10]

Examples of noncash transactions that would be reported in this manner are:

1. Acquiring an asset by incurring a debt payable to the seller.
2. Acquiring an asset by entering into a capital lease.
3. Converting debt into common stock or other equity securities.
4. Exchanging noncash assets or liabilities for other noncash assets or liabilities.

Noncash transactions that do not affect a company's assets or liabilities, such as the distribution of stock dividends, are not considered investing or financing activities and are not reported. Recall from Chapter 18 that stock dividends merely increase the number of shares of stock owned by existing shareholders. From an accounting standpoint, the stock dividend causes a dollar amount to be transferred from one part of shareholders' equity (retained earnings) to another part of shareholders' equity (paid-in capital). Neither assets nor liabilities are affected; therefore, no investing or financing activity has occurred.

● LO8

Preparation of the Statement of Cash Flows

The objective in preparing the statement of cash flows is to identify all transactions and events that represent operating, investing, or financing activities and to list and classify those activities in proper statement format. A difficulty in preparing a statement of cash flows is

[10]"Statement of Cash Flows," *Statement of Financial Accounting Standards No. 95* (Stamford, Conn.: FASB, 1987), par. 74.

ADDITIONAL CONSIDERATION

A transaction involving an investing and financing activity may be part cash and part noncash. For example, a company might pay cash for a part of the purchase price of new equipment and issue a long-term note for the remaining amount. In our previous illustration, UBC issued a note payable for the $20 million cost of the equipment it acquired. Suppose the equipment were purchased in the following manner:

Equipment	20	
Cash		6
Note payable		14

In that case, $6 million would be reported under the caption "Cash flows from investing activities," and the noncash portion of the transaction—issuing a $14 million note payable for $14 million of equipment—would be reported as a "noncash investing and financing activity." UBC's statement of cash flows, if modified by the assumption of a part cash/part noncash transaction, would report these two elements of the transaction as follows:

Cash Flows from Investing Activities:		
Purchase of land	$(30)	
Purchase of short-term investments	(12)	
Sale of land	18	
Sale of equipment	5	
Purchase of equipment	(6)	
Net cash flows from investing activities		(25)
Noncash Investing and Financing Activities:		
Acquired $20 million of equipment by paying cash and issuing a 12%, 5-year note as follows:		
Cost of equipment		$20 million
Cash paid		6 million
Note issued		$14 million

that typical accounting systems are not designed to produce the specific information we need for the statement. At the end of a reporting cycle, balances exist in accounts reported on the income statement (sales revenue, cost of goods sold, etc.) and the balance sheet (accounts receivable, common stock, etc.). However, the ledger contains no balances for cash paid to acquire equipment, or cash received from sale of land, or any other cash flow needed for the statement. As a result, it's necessary to find a way of using information that is available to reconstruct the various cash flows that occurred during the reporting period. Typically, the information available to assist the statement preparer includes an income statement for the year and balance sheets for both the current and preceding years (comparative statements). The accounting records also can provide additional information about transactions that caused changes in account balances during the year.

The typical year-end data is provided for UBC in Illustration 21–1 on the next page. We have referred frequently to the statement of cash flows of UBC to illustrate the nature of the activities the statement reports. Now we will see how that statement is developed from the data provided in that illustration.

In situations involving relatively few transactions, it is possible to prepare the statement of cash flows by merely inspecting the available data and logically determining the reportable activities. Few real-life situations are sufficiently simple to be solved this way. Usually, it is more practical to use some systematic method of analyzing the available data to ensure that all operating, investing, and financing activities are detected. A common approach is to use either a manual or electronic spreadsheet to organize and analyze the information used to prepare the statement.[11]

[11]The T-account method is a second systematic approach to the preparation of the statement of cash flows. This method is identical in concept and similar in application to the spreadsheet method. The T-account method is used to prepare the statement of cash flows for UBC in Appendix 21B.

ILLUSTRATION 21–1
Comparative Balance Sheets and Income Statement

UNITED BRANDS CORPORATION
Comparative Balance Sheets
December 31, 2009 and 2008
($ in millions)

	2009		2008
Assets			
Cash	$ 29		$ 20
Accounts receivable	32		30
Short-term investments	12		0
Inventory	46		50
Prepaid insurance	3		6
Land	80		60
Buildings and equipment	81		75
Less: Accumulated depreciation	(16)		(20)
	$267		$221
Liabilities			
Accounts payable	$ 26		$ 20
Salaries payable	3		1
Income tax payable	6		8
Notes payable	20		0
Bonds payable	35		50
Less: Discount on bonds	(1)		(3)
Shareholders' Equity			
Common stock	130		100
Paid-in capital—excess of par	29		20
Retained earnings	19		25
	$267		$221
Revenues			
Sales revenue	$100		
Investment revenue	3		
Gain on sale of land	8	$111	
Expenses			
Cost of goods sold	60		
Salaries expense	13		
Depreciation expense	3		
Bond interest expense	5		
Insurance expense	7		
Loss on sale of equipment	2		
Income tax expense	9	99	
Net income		$ 12	

Additional Information from the Accounting Records

a. A portion of company land, purchased in a previous year for $10 million, was sold for $18 million.
b. Equipment that originally cost $14 million, and which was one-half depreciated, was sold for $5 million cash.
c. The common shares of Mazuma Corporation were purchased for $12 million as a short-term investment.
d. Property was purchased for $30 million cash for use as a parking lot.
e. On December 30, 2009, new equipment was acquired by issuing a 12%, five-year, $20 million note payable to the seller.
f. On January 1, 2009, $15 million of bonds were retired at maturity.
g. The increase in the common stock account is attributable to the issuance of a 10% stock dividend (1 million shares) and the subsequent sale of 2 million shares of common stock. The market price of the $10 par value common stock was $13 per share on the dates of both transactions.
h. Cash dividends of $5 million were paid to shareholders.

Whether the statement of cash flows is prepared by an unaided inspection and analysis or with the aid of a systematic technique such as spreadsheet analysis, the analytical process is the same. To identify the activities to be reported on the statement, we use available data to reconstruct the events and transactions that involved operating, investing, and financing activities during the year. It is helpful to reproduce the journal entries that were recorded at the time of the transaction. Examining reconstructed journal entries makes it easier to visualize whether a reportable activity is involved and how that activity is to be classified.

Reconstructing events and transactions that occurred during the period helps identify the operating, investing, and financing activities to be reported.

Next, in Part B, we see how a spreadsheet simplifies the process of preparing a statement of cash flows. Even if you choose not to use a spreadsheet, the summary entries described can be used to help you find the cash inflows and outflows you need to prepare a statement of cash flows. For this demonstration, we assume the direct method is used to determine and report cash flows from operating activities. Appreciation of the direct method provides the backdrop for a thorough understanding of the indirect method that we explore in Part C.

PREPARING AN SCF: THE DIRECT METHOD OF REPORTING CASH FLOWS FROM OPERATING ACTIVITIES

PART B

Using a Spreadsheet

An important advantage gained by using a spreadsheet is that it ensures that no reportable activities are inadvertently overlooked. Spreadsheet analysis relies on the fact that, in order for cash to increase or decrease, there must be a corresponding change in a noncash account. Therefore, if we can identify the events and transactions that caused the change in each noncash account during the year, we will have identified all the operating, investing, and financing activities that are to be included in the statement of cash flows.

There can be no cash inflow or cash outflow without a corresponding change in a noncash account.

The beginning and ending balances of each account are entered on the spreadsheet. Then, as journal entries are reconstructed in our analysis of the data, those entries are recorded on the spreadsheet so that the debits and credits of the spreadsheet entries explain the changes in the account balances. Only after spreadsheet entries have explained the changes in all account balances, can we feel confident that all operating, investing, and financing activities have been identified. The spreadsheet is designed in such a way that, as we record spreadsheet entries that explain account balance changes, we are simultaneously identifying and classifying the activities to be reported on the statement of cash flows.

Recording spreadsheet entries that explain account balance changes simultaneously identifies and classifies the activities to be reported on the statement of cash flows.

We begin by transferring the comparative balance sheets and income statement to a blank spreadsheet. For illustration, refer to the 2009 and 2008 balances in the completed spreadsheet for UBC, shown in Illustration 21–1A on the next two pages. Notice that the amounts for elements of the income statement are ending balances resulting from accumulations during the year. Beginning balances in each of these accounts are always zero.

Following the balance sheets and income statement, we allocate space on the spreadsheet for the statement of cash flows. Although at this point we have not yet identified the specific cash flow activities shown in the completed spreadsheet, we can include headings for the major categories of activities: cash flows from operating activities, cash flows from investing activities, and cash flows from financing activities. Leaving several lines between headings allows adequate space to include the specific cash flows identified in subsequent analysis.

The spreadsheet entries shown in the two changes columns, which separate the beginning and ending balances, explain the increase or decrease in each account balance. You will see in the next section how these entries were reconstructed. Although spreadsheet entries are in the form of debits and credits like journal entries, they are entered on the spreadsheet only. They are not recorded in the formal accounting records. In effect, these entries duplicate, frequently in summary form, the actual journal entries used to record the transactions as they occurred during the year.

Spreadsheet entries duplicate the actual journal entries used to record the transactions as they occurred during the year.

To reconstruct the journal entries, we analyze each account, one at a time, deciding at each step what transaction or event caused the change in that account. Often, the reason for the change in an account balance is readily apparent from viewing the change in conjunction with

ILLUSTRATION 21–1A

Spreadsheet—Direct method

UNITED BRANDS CORPORATION
Spreadsheet for the Statement of Cash Flows

	Dec. 31 2008	Changes: Debits		Changes: Credits		Dec. 31 2009
Balance Sheet						
Assets:						
Cash	20	(19)	9			29
Accounts receivable	30	(1)	2			32
Short-term investments	0	(12)	12			12
Inventory	50			(4)	4	46
Prepaid insurance	6			(8)	3	3
Land	60	(13)	30	(3)	10	80
Buildings and equipment	75	(14)	20X	(9)	14	81
Less: Accumulated depreciation	(20)	(9)	7	(6)	3	(16)
	221					267
Liabilities:						
Accounts payable	20			(4)	6	26
Salaries payable	1			(5)	2	3
Income tax payable	8	(10)	2			6
Notes payable	0			(14)	20X	20
Bonds payable	50	(15)	15			35
Less: Discount on bonds	(3)			(7)	2	(1)
Shareholders' Equity:						
Common stock	100			(16)	10	
				(17)	20	130
Paid-in capital—excess of par	20			(16)	3	
				(17)	6	29
Retained earnings	25	(16)	13			
		(18)	5	(11)	12	19
	221					267
Income Statement						
Revenues:						
Sales revenue				(1)	100	100
Investment revenue				(2)	3	3
Gain on sale of land				(3)	8	8
Expenses:						
Cost of goods sold		(4)	60			(60)
Salaries expense		(5)	13			(13)
Depreciation expense		(6)	3			(3)
Bond interest expense		(7)	5			(5)
Insurance expense		(8)	7			(7)
Loss on sale of equipment		(9)	2			(2)
Income tax expense		(10)	9			(9)
Net income		(11)	**12**			**12**
Statement of Cash Flows						
Operating Activities:						
Cash inflows:						
From customers		(1)	98			
From investment revenue		(2)	3			
Cash outflows:						
To suppliers of goods				(4)	50	
To employees				(5)	11	
To bondholders				(7)	3	
For insurance expense				(8)	4	
For income taxes				(10)	11	
Net cash flows						22

(continued)

	Dec. 31 2008	Changes Debits		Credits		Dec. 31 2009
Investing Activities:						
Sale of land		(3)	18			
Sale of equipment		(9)	5			
Purchase of S-T investment				(12)	12	
Purchase of land				(13)	30	
Net cash flows						(19)
Financing Activities:						
Retirement of bonds payable				(15)	15	
Sale of common shares		(17)	26			
Payment of cash dividends				(18)	5	
Net cash flows						6
Net increase in cash				(19)	9	9
Totals			376		376	

ILLUSTRATION 21–1A (concluded)

X—As explained later, the X's serve as a reminder to report this noncash transaction.

that of a related account elsewhere in the financial statements. Sometimes it is necessary to consult the accounting records for additional information to help explain the transaction that resulted in the change.

You may find it helpful to diagram in T-account format the relationship between accounts to better visualize certain changes, particularly in your initial study of the chapter. The analysis that follows is occasionally supplemented with such diagrams to emphasize *why,* rather than merely *how,* specific cash flow amounts emerge from the analysis.

Although there is no mandatory order in which to analyze the accounts, it is convenient to begin with the income statement accounts, followed by the balance sheet accounts. We analyze the accounts of UBC in that order below. Although our analysis of each account culminates in a spreadsheet entry, keep in mind that the analysis described also is appropriate to identify reportable activities when a spreadsheet is not used.[12]

Income Statement Accounts

As described in an earlier section, cash flows from operating activities are inflows and outflows of cash that result from activities reported on the income statement. Thus, to identify those cash inflows and outflows, we begin by analyzing the components of the income statement. It is important to keep in mind that the amounts reported in the income statement usually do not represent the cash effects of the items reported. For example, UBC reports sales revenue of $100 million. This does not mean, however, that it collected $100 million cash from customers during the year. In fact, by referring to the beginning and ending balances in accounts receivable, we see that cash received from customers could not have been $100 million. Since accounts receivable increased during the year, some of the sales revenue earned must not yet have been collected. This is explained further in the next section.

Amounts reported in the income statement usually are not the same as the cash effects of the items reported.

The cash effects of other income statement elements can be similarly discerned by referring to changes in the balances of the balance sheet accounts that are directly related to those elements. So, to identify cash flows from operating activities we examine, one at a time, the elements of the income statement in conjunction with any balance sheet accounts affected by each element.

1. SALES REVENUE. Accounts receivable is the balance sheet account that is affected by sales revenue. Specifically, accounts receivable is increased by credit sales and is decreased as cash is received from customers. We can compare sales and the change in accounts

[12]The spreadsheet entries also are used to record the same transactions when the T-account method is used. We refer again to these entries when that method is described in Appendix 21B.

receivable during the year to determine the amount of cash received from customers. This relationship can be viewed in T-account format as follows:

Accounts Receivable

Beginning balance	30		
Credit sales (increases A/R)	100	?	Cash received (decreases A/R)
Ending balance	32		

We see from this analysis that cash received from customers must have been $98 million. Note that even if some of the year's sales were cash sales, say $40 million cash sales and $60 million credit sales, the result is the same:

Accounts Receivable

Beginning balance	30		Cash sales	$40
Credit sales	60	58 →	Received on account	58
Ending balance	32		Cash received	$98

Relating sales and the change in accounts receivable during the period helps determine the amount of cash received from customers.

Thus, cash flows from operating activities should include cash received from customers of $98 million. The net effect of sales revenue activity during the year can be summarized in the following entry.

	($ in millions)	
Entry (1) Cash (received from customers)	98	
Accounts receivable (given)	2	
Sales revenue ($100 – 0)		100

The entry above appears as entry (1) in the completed spreadsheet for UBC, shown in Illustration 21–1A. The entry explains the changes in two account balances—accounts receivable and sales revenue. Since the entry affects cash, it also identifies a cash flow to be reported on the statement of cash flows. The $98 million debit to cash is therefore entered in the statement of cash flows section of the spreadsheet under the heading of cash flows from operating activities.

ADDITIONAL CONSIDERATION

The preceding discussion describes the most common situation—companies earn revenue by selling goods and services, increase accounts receivable, and then collect the cash and decrease accounts receivable later. Some companies, though, often collect the cash in advance of earning it, record unearned revenue, and then later record revenue and decrease unearned revenue. In those cases, we need to analyze any changes in the unearned revenue account for differences between revenue reported and cash collected. For instance, if UBC also had a $1 million increase in unearned revenue, the summary entry would be modified as follows:

	($ in millions)	
Entry (1) Cash (received from customers)	99	
Accounts receivable (given)	2	
Unearned revenue (given)		1
Sales revenue ($100 – 0)		100

Notice that we enter the cash portion of entry (1) as one of several cash flows on the statement of cash flows rather than as a debit to the cash account. Only after all cash inflows and outflows have been identified will the net change in cash be entered as a debit to the cash account. In fact, the entry to reconcile the $9 million increase in the cash account and the $9 million net increase in cash on the statement of cash flows will serve as a final check of the accuracy of our spreadsheet analysis.

ADDITIONAL CONSIDERATION

Notice that bad debt expense does not appear on the income statement and allowance for uncollectible accounts does not appear on the balance sheet. We have assumed that bad debts are immaterial for UBC. When this is not the case, it's necessary to consider the write-off of bad debts as we determine cash received from customers. Here's why.

When using the allowance method to account for bad debts, a company estimates the dollar amount of customer accounts that will ultimately prove uncollectible and records both bad debt expense and allowance for uncollectible accounts for that estimate.

Bad debt expense	xxx	
Allowance for uncollectible accounts		xxx

Then, when accounts actually prove uncollectible, accounts receivable and the allowance are reduced.

Allowance for uncollectible accounts	xxx	
Accounts receivable		xxx

In our illustration, we concluded that UBC received $2 million less cash ($98 million) than sales for the year ($100 million) because accounts receivable increased by that amount. However, if a portion of the change in accounts receivable had been due to write-offs of bad debts, that conclusion would be incorrect. Let's say, for instance, that UBC had bad debt expense of $2 million and its allowance for uncollectible accounts had increased by $1 million. Because the allowance for uncollectible accounts would be credited by $2 million in the adjusting entry for bad debts expense, necessarily there also would have been a $1 million debit to the account in order for there to have been a net increase (credit) in its balance of only $1 million. That debit would occur due to write-offs of bad debts totaling $1 million.

	($ in millions)	
Allowance for uncollectible accounts	1	
Accounts receivable		1

This would indicate that a portion ($1 million credit) of the total change in accounts receivable ($2 million debit) would have been due to write-offs of bad debts, and the remaining change ($3 million debit) would have been due to cash collections being less than sales revenue. Cash received from customers would have been only $97 million in that case. We can view this in the framework of our T-account analysis as follows:

Accounts Receivable

Beginning balance	30		
Credit sales	100	97	Cash received
		1	Bad Debt write-offs
Ending balance	32		

The effect of write-offs of bad debts can be explicitly considered by combining all the accounts related to sales and collection activities into a single summary spreadsheet entry:

	($ in millions)	
Entry (1) Cash (received from customers)	97	
Accounts receivable ($32 – 30)	2	
Bad debt expense (from income statement)	2	
Allowance for uncollectible accounts ($3 – 2)		1
Sales revenue ($100 – 0)		100

This single entry summarizes all transactions related to sales, bad debts expense, write-offs of accounts receivable, and cash collections from sales.

The remaining spreadsheet entries are described in subsections 2 through 19. When including the entries on the spreadsheet, it is helpful to number the entries sequentially to provide a means of retracing the steps taken in the analysis if the need arises. You also may find it helpful to put a check mark (✔) to the right of the ending balance when the change in that balance has been explained. Then, once you have check marks next to every noncash account, you will know you are finished.

2. INVESTMENT REVENUE. The income statement reports investment revenue of \$3 million. Before concluding that this amount was received in cash, we first refer to the balance sheets to see whether a change in an account there indicates otherwise. A change in either of two balance sheet accounts, (a) investment revenue receivable or (b) long-term investments, might indicate that cash received from investment revenue differs from the amount reported on the income statement.

Changes in related accounts might indicate that investment revenue reported on the income statement is a different amount from cash received from the investment.

a. If we observe either an increase or a decrease in an *investment revenue receivable* account (e.g., interest receivable, dividends receivable), we would conclude that the amount of cash received during the year was less than (if an increase) or more than (if a decrease) the amount of revenue reported. The analysis would be identical to that of sales revenue and accounts receivable.

b. Also, an unexplained increase in a *long-term investment* account might indicate that a portion of investment revenue has not yet been received in cash. Recall from Chapter 12 that when using the equity method to account for investments in the stock of another corporation, investment revenue is recognized as the investor's percentage share of the investee's income, whether or not the revenue is received currently as cash dividends. For example, assume the investor owns 25% of the common stock of a corporation that reports net income of \$12 million and pays dividends of \$4 million. This situation would have produced a \$2 million increase in long-term investments, which can be demonstrated by reconstructing the journal entries for the recognition of investment and the receipt of cash dividends:

	($ in millions)	
Long-term investments	3	
Investment revenue ($12 × 25%)		3
Cash ($4 × 25%)	1	
Long-term investments		1

A combined entry would produce the same results:

Long-term investments	2	
Cash ($4 × 25%)	1	
Investment revenue ($12 × 25%)		3

The \$2 million net increase in long-term investments would represent the investment revenue not received in cash. This would also explain why there is a \$3 million increase (credit) in investment revenue. If these events had occurred, we would prepare a spreadsheet entry identical to the combined entry above. The spreadsheet entry would (a) explain the \$2 million increase in long-term investments, (b) explain the \$3 million increase in investment revenue, and (c) identify a \$1 million cash inflow from operating activities.

However, because neither an investment revenue receivable account nor a long-term investment account appears on the comparative balance sheets, we can conclude that \$3 million of investment revenue was collected in cash. Entry (2) on the spreadsheet is:

Because no other transactions are apparent that would have caused a change in investment revenue, we can conclude that \$3 million of investment revenue was collected in cash.

	($ in millions)	
Entry (2) Cash (received from investment revenue)	3	
Investment revenue ($3 – 0)		3

3. GAIN ON SALE OF LAND. The third item reported on the income statement is an \$8 million gain on the sale of land. Recall that our objective in analyzing each element of the statement is to determine the cash effect of that element. To do so, we need additional information about the transaction that caused this gain. The accounting records—item (a) in Illustration 21–1—indicate that land that originally cost $10 million was sold for $18 million. The entry recorded in the journal when the land was sold also serves as our spreadsheet entry:

	($ in millions)	
Entry (3) Cash (received from sale of land)	18	
Land (given)		10
Gain on sale of land ($8 – 0)		8

A gain (or loss) is simply the difference between cash received in the sale of an asset and the book value of the asset—not a cash flow.

The cash effect of this transaction is a cash increase of $18 million. We therefore include the debit as a cash inflow in the statement of cash flows section of the spreadsheet. However, unlike the cash effect of the previous two spreadsheet entries, it is not reported as an operating activity. The sale of land is an *investing* activity, so this cash inflow is listed under that heading of the spreadsheet. The entry also accounts for the $8 million gain on sale of land. The $10 million credit to land does not, by itself, explain the $20 million increase in that account. As we will later discover, another transaction also affected the land account.

It is important to understand that the gain is simply the difference between cash received in the sale of land (reported as an investing activity) and the book value of the land. To report the $8 million gain as a cash flow from operating activities, in addition to reporting $18 million as a cash flow from investing activities, would be to report the $8 million twice.

4. COST OF GOODS SOLD. During the year UBC sold goods that had cost $60 million. This does not necessarily indicate that $60 million cash was paid to suppliers of those goods. To determine the amount of cash paid to suppliers, we look to the two current accounts affected by merchandise purchases—inventory and accounts payable. The analysis can be viewed as a two-step process.

First, we compare cost of goods sold with the change in inventory to determine the cost of goods *purchased* (not necessarily cash paid) during the year. To facilitate our analysis, we can examine the relationship in T-account format:

Inventory

Beginning balance	50		
Cost of goods **purchased** *(increases inventory)*	?	60	Cost of goods **sold** *(decreases inventory)*
Ending balance	46		

From this analysis, we see that $56 million of goods were *purchased* during the year. It is not necessarily true, though, that $56 million cash was paid to suppliers of these goods. By looking in accounts payable, we can determine the cash paid to suppliers:

Determining the amount of cash paid to suppliers means looking at not only the cost of goods sold, but also the changes in both inventory and accounts payable.

Accounts Payable

		20	Beginning balance
Cash paid to suppliers *(decreases A/P)*	?	56	Cost of goods *purchased* *(increases A/P)*
		26	Ending Balance

We now see that cash paid to suppliers was $50 million. The spreadsheet entry that summarizes merchandise acquisitions is:

	($ in millions)	
Entry (4) Cost of goods sold ($60 – 0)	60	
Inventory ($46 – 50)		4
Accounts payable ($26 – 20)		6
Cash (paid to suppliers of goods)		50

Although $60 million of goods were sold during the year, only $50 million cash was paid to suppliers of these goods.

5. SALARIES EXPENSE. The balance sheet account affected by salaries expense is salaries payable. By analyzing salaries expense in relation to the change in salaries payable, we can determine the amount of cash paid to employees:

Salaries Payable

		1	Beginning balance
Cash paid to employees *(decreases salaries payable)*	?	13	Salaries expense *(increases salaries payable)*
		3	Ending Balance

This analysis indicates that only $11 million cash was paid to employees; the remaining $2 million of salaries expense is reflected as an increase in salaries payable.

Viewing the relationship in journal entry format provides the same conclusion and also gives us the entry in our spreadsheet analysis:

Although salaries expense was $13 million, only $11 million cash was paid to employees.

	($ in millions)	
Entry (5) Salaries expense ($13 – 0)	13	
Salaries payable ($3 – 1)		2
Cash (paid to employees)		11

6. DEPRECIATION EXPENSE. The income statement reports depreciation expense of $3 million. The entry used to record depreciation, which also serves as our spreadsheet entry, is:

Depreciation expense does not require a current cash expenditure.

	($ in millions)	
Entry (6) Depreciation expense ($3 – 0)	3	
Accumulated depreciation		3

Depreciation is a noncash expense. It is merely an allocation in the current period of a prior cash expenditure (for the depreciable asset). Therefore, unlike the other entries to this point, the depreciation entry has no effect on the statement of cash flows. However, it does explain the change in the depreciation expense account and a portion of the change in accumulated depreciation.

7. INTEREST EXPENSE. Recall from Chapter 14 that bond interest expense differs from the amount of cash paid to bondholders when bonds are issued at either a premium or a discount. The difference between the two amounts is the reduction of the premium or discount. By referring to the balance sheet, we see that UBC's bonds were issued at a discount. Since we know that bond interest expense is $5 million and that $2 million of the discount was reduced in 2009, we can determine that $3 million cash was paid to bondholders by recreating the entry that summarizes the recording of bond interest expense.

Bond interest expense is not the same as the amount of cash paid to bondholders when bonds are issued at either a premium or a discount.

	($ in millions)	
Entry (7) Interest expense ($5 – 0)	5	
Discount on bonds payable ($1 – 3)		2
Cash (paid to bondholders)		3

Recording this entry on the spreadsheet explains the change in both the bond interest expense and discount on bonds payable accounts. It also provides us with another cash outflow from operating activities. Of course, if a premium were being reduced, rather than a discount, the cash outflow would be *greater* than the expense.

8. INSURANCE EXPENSE. A decrease of $3 million in the prepaid insurance account indicates that cash paid for insurance coverage was $3 million less than the $7 million insurance expense for the year. Viewing prepaid insurance in T-account format clarifies this point.

ADDITIONAL CONSIDERATION

If the balance sheet had revealed an increase or decrease in an accrued bond interest payable account, the entry calculating cash paid to bondholders would require modification. For example, if UBC had a bond interest payable account, and that account had increased (a credit) by $1 million, the entry would have been:

	($ in millions)	
Entry (7) Interest expense	5	
(revised) Discount on bonds payable		2
Interest payable		1
Cash (paid to bondholders)		2

If the amount owed to bondholders increased by $1 million, they obviously were paid $1 million less cash than if there had been no change in the amount owed them. Similarly, if bond interest payable decreased by $1 million, the opposite would be true; that is, cash paid to them would have been $1 million more.

Prepaid Insurance

Beginning balance	6		
Cash paid for insurance *(increases prepaid insurance)*	?	7	Insurance expense *(decreases prepaid insurance)*
Ending balance	3		

From this analysis, we can conclude that $4 million was paid for insurance. We reach the same conclusion by preparing the following spreadsheet entry:

	($ in millions)	
Entry (8) Insurance expense ($7 – 0)	7	
Prepaid insurance ($3 – 6)		3
Cash (paid for insurance)		4

Since $3 million of prepaid insurance was allocated to insurance expense, only $4 million of the expense was paid in cash during the period.

The entry accounts for the change in both the insurance expense and prepaid insurance accounts and also identifies a cash outflow from operating activities.

9. LOSS ON SALE OF EQUIPMENT. A $2 million loss on the sale of equipment is the next item reported on the income statement. To determine the cash effect of the sale of equipment, we need additional information about the transaction. The information we need is provided in item (b) of Illustration 21–1. Recreating the journal entry for the transaction described gives us the following entry:

	($ in millions)	
Entry (9) Cash (from the sale of equipment)	5	
Loss on sale of equipment ($2 – 0)	2	
Accumulated depreciation ($14 × 50%)	7	
Buildings and equipment (given)		14

Recreating the journal entry for the sale of equipment reveals a $5 million cash inflow from investing activities.

The $5 million cash inflow is entered in the statement of cash flows section of the spreadsheet as an investing activity. The $2 million debit to the loss on sale of equipment explains the change in that account balance. Referring to the spreadsheet, we see that a portion of the change in accumulated depreciation was accounted for in entry (6). The debit to accumulated depreciation in the entry above completes the explanation for the change in that account. However, the credit to buildings and equipment only partially justifies the change in that account. We must assume that the analysis of a subsequent transaction will account for the unexplained portion of the change.

Recognize too that the loss, like the gain in entry (3), has no cash effect in the current period. Therefore, it is not reported in the statement of cash flows when using the direct method.

10. INCOME TAX EXPENSE. The final expense reported on the income statement is income tax expense. Since income taxes payable is the balance sheet account affected by this expense, we look to the change in that account to help determine the cash paid for income taxes. A T-account analysis can be used to find the cash effect as follows:

Income Tax Payable

		8	Beginning balance
Cash paid for income tax *(decreases the liability)*	?	9	Income tax expense
		6	Ending Balance

This analysis reveals that $11 million cash was paid for income taxes, $2 million more than the year's expense. The overpayment explains why the liability for income taxes decreased by $2 million.

The same conclusion can be reached from the following spreadsheet entry, which represents the net effect of income taxes on UBC's accounts.

	($ in millions)	
Entry (10) Income tax expense ($9 – 0)	9	
Income tax payable ($6 – 8)	2	
Cash (paid for income taxes)		11

ADDITIONAL CONSIDERATION

Entry (10) would require modification in either of the two independent situations described below.

1. Note that UBC does not have a deferred income tax account. Recall from Chapter 16 that temporary differences between taxable income and pretax accounting income give rise to deferred taxes. If temporary differences had been present, which would be evidenced by a change in a deferred income taxes account, the calculation of cash paid for income taxes would require modification. Assume, for example, that a deferred income tax liability account had experienced a credit change of $1 million for the year. In that case, the previous spreadsheet entry would be revised as follows:

	($ in millions)	
Entry (10) Income tax expense	9	
(revised) Income tax payable	2	
Deferred income tax liability		1
Cash (paid for income taxes)		10

As the revised entry indicates, only $10 million cash would have been paid in this situation, rather than $11 million. The $1 million difference represents the portion of the income tax expense whose payment is deferred to a later year.

2. The spreadsheet entry also would be affected if the income statement includes either an extraordinary gain or an extraordinary loss. Recall from Chapter 3 and Chapter 16 that the income tax effect of an extraordinary item is not reflected in income tax expense, but instead is separately reported as a reduction in the extraordinary item. For example, if UBC's loss on the sale of equipment had been due to an extraordinary event, the tax savings from that loss would be reported as a reduction in the extraordinary loss rather than as a reduction in income tax expense. (Since the loss reduces taxable income by $2 million, assuming a marginal tax rate of 50%, taxes would be reduced by $1 million.) The lower portion of the income statement would have appeared as shown below, in comparison with the presentation in Illustration 21–1:

Ordinary Loss (from Illustration 21–1)		**Extraordinary Loss**		
		Income tax expense		(10)
		Income before extraordinary items		$13
Loss on sale of equipment	(2)	Extraordinary loss—sale of equipment	$2	
Income tax expense	(9)	Less: Tax savings	(1)	(1)
Net income	$12	Net income		$12

Without the tax savings produced by the loss, income tax expense would have been $10 million, rather than $9 million. But the tax savings still reduces the amount of cash paid for income taxes, even though it is reported separately from the income tax expense. Therefore, whether the loss is extraordinary or not, the amount of cash paid for income taxes is the same. If the loss is extraordinary, entry (10) would be modified as follows:

	($ in millions)	
Entry (10) Income tax expense (on ordinary income)	10	
(revised) Income tax payable	2	
Income tax expense (savings from extraordinary loss)		1
Cash (paid for income taxes)		11

Entry (9) would be unaffected. Whether or not the loss is extraordinary, it is not reported in the statement of cash flows, and the cash inflow from the sale is reported as an investing activity.

11. NET INCOME. The balance in the retained earnings account at the end of the year includes an increase due to net income. If we are to account for all changes in each of the accounts, we must include the following spreadsheet entry, which represents the closing of net income to retained earnings.

	($ in millions)	
Entry (11) Net income	12	
Retained earnings		12

This entry partially explains the change in the retained earnings account.

This entry does not affect amounts reported on the statement of cash flows. We include the entry in the spreadsheet analysis only to help explain account balance changes.

Balance Sheet Accounts

To identify all the operating, investing, and financing activities when using a spreadsheet, we must account for the changes in each account on both the income statement and the balance sheet. Thus far, we have explained the change in each income statement account. Since the transactions that gave rise to some of those changes involved balance sheet accounts as well, some changes in balance sheet accounts have already been explained. We now reconstruct the transactions that caused changes in the remaining balances.

With the exception of the cash account, the accounts are analyzed in the order of their presentation in the balance sheet. As noted earlier, we save the entry that reconciles the change in the cash account with the net change in cash from the statement of cash flows as a final check on the accuracy of the spreadsheet.

12. SHORT-TERM INVESTMENTS. Since the change in accounts receivable was explained previously [in entry (1)], we proceed to the next asset on the balance sheet. The balance in short-term investments increased from zero to $12 million. In the absence of evidence to the contrary, we could assume that the increase is due to the purchase of short-term investments during the year. This assumption is confirmed by item (c) of Illustration 21–1.

The entry to record the investment and our spreadsheet entry is:

The $12 million increase in the short-term investments account is due to the purchase of short-term investments during the year.

	($ in millions)	
Entry (12) Short-term investment ($12 − 0)	12	
Cash (purchase of short-term investment)		12

The $12 million cash outflow is entered in the statement of cash flows section of the spreadsheet as an investing activity. An exception is when an investment is classified as a "trading security," in which case the cash outflow is reported as an operating activity.

ADDITIONAL CONSIDERATION

Recall that some highly liquid, short-term investments such as money market funds, Treasury bills, or commercial paper might be classified as cash equivalents. If the short-term investment above were classified as a cash equivalent, its purchase would have no effect on the total of cash and cash equivalents. In other words, since cash would include this investment, its purchase would constitute both a debit and a credit to cash. We would neither prepare a spreadsheet entry nor report the transaction on the statement of cash flows.

Likewise, a sale of a cash equivalent would not affect the total of cash and cash equivalents and would not be reported.

An exception would be if the cash equivalent investment were sold for either more or less than its acquisition cost. For example, assume a Treasury bill classified as a cash equivalent were sold for $1 million more than its $2 million cost. The sale would constitute both a $3 million increase and a $2 million decrease in cash. We see the effect more clearly if we reconstruct the transaction in journal entry format:

	($ in millions)	
Cash	3	
Gain on sale of cash equivalent		1
Cash (cash equivalent investment)		2

The spreadsheet entry to reflect the net increase in cash would be:

Entry (X) Cash (from sale of cash equivalents)	1	
Gain on sale of cash equivalent		1

The $1 million net increase in cash and cash equivalents would be reported as a cash inflow from *operating* activities.

13. LAND. The changes in the balances of both inventory and prepaid insurance were accounted for in previous spreadsheet entries: (4) and (8). Land is the next account whose change has yet to be fully explained. We discovered in a previous transaction that a sale of land caused a $10 million reduction in the account. Yet, the account shows a net *increase* of $20 million. It would be logical to assume that the unexplained increase of $30 million was due to a purchase of land. The transaction described in item (d) of Illustration 21–1 supports that assumption and is portrayed in the following spreadsheet entry:

A $30 million purchase of land accounts for the portion of the $20 million increase in the account that was not previously explained by the sale of land.

	($ in millions)	
Entry (13) Land (given)	30	
Cash (purchase of land)		30

The $30 million payment is reported as a cash outflow from investing activities.

14. BUILDINGS AND EQUIPMENT. When examining a previous transaction [entry (9)], we determined that the buildings and equipment account was reduced by $14 million from the sale of used equipment. And yet the account shows a net *increase* of $6 million for the year. The accounting records [item (e) of Illustration 21–1] reveal the remaining unexplained cause of the net increase. New equipment costing $20 million was purchased by issuing a $20 million note payable. Recall from the discussion in a previous section of this chapter that, although this is a noncash transaction, it represents both a significant investing activity (investing in new equipment) and a significant financing activity (financing the acquisition with long-term debt).

The journal entry used to record the transaction when the equipment was acquired also serves as our spreadsheet entry:

	($ in millions)	
Entry (14) Buildings and equipment (given)	20	
Note payable (given)		20

Investing in new equipment is a significant investing activity and financing the acquisition with long-term debt is a significant financing activity.

Remember that the statement of cash flows section of the spreadsheet will serve as the basis for our preparation of the formal statement. But the noncash entry above will not affect the cash flows section of the spreadsheet. Because we want to report this noncash investing and financing activity when we prepare the statement of cash flows, it is helpful to "mark" the spreadsheet entry as a reminder not to overlook this transaction when the statement is prepared. Crosses (*X*) serve this purpose on the spreadsheet in Illustration 21–1A.

ADDITIONAL CONSIDERATION

Payments on Debt

When a debt, such as the note payable above, is paid, the payment is reported on a statement of cash flows as a financing activity. However, any interest paid on the debt is reported as a cash outflow from operating activities. The reason is that interest expense is a component of net income, and the cash effects of income statement elements are reported as cash flows from operating activities. If the note is an installment note, each installment payment includes both an amount that represents interest and an amount that represents a reduction of principal. In a statement of cash flows, then, the interest portion is reported as a cash outflow from operating activities and the principal portion as a cash outflow from financing activities.

Leases

As we discussed in Chapter 15, lease arrangements vary greatly, in both their purpose and the ways we account for them. Consistent with those differences, we also report leases differently in a statement of cash flows depending on their type. Lease payments for **operating leases,** for instance, represent rent—expense to the lessee, revenue for the lessor. These amounts are included in net income, so both the lessee and lessor report cash payments for operating leases in a statement of cash flows as cash flows from operating activities. **Capital leases,** on the other hand, are agreements that we identify as being formulated outwardly as leases, but which are in reality installment purchases, so we account for them as such. Each rental payment (except the first if paid at inception) includes both an amount that represents interest and an amount that represents a reduction of principal. In a statement of cash flows, then, the lessee reports the interest portion as a cash outflow from operating activities and the principal portion as a cash outflow from financing activities. On the other side of the transaction, the lessor in a **direct financing lease** reports the interest portion as a cash inflow from operating activities and the principal portion as a cash inflow from investing activities. Both the lessee and lessor report the lease at its inception as a noncash investing/financing activity. Remember, though, that a **sales-type lease** differs from a direct financing lease for the lessor in that we assume the lessor is actually selling its product. Consistent with reporting sales of products under installment sales agreements rather than lease agreements, the lessor reports cash receipts from a sales-type lease as cash inflows from operating activities.

15. BONDS PAYABLE. The balance in the bonds payable account decreased during the year by $15 million. Illustration 21–1, item (f), reveals the cause. Cash was paid to retire $15 million face value of bonds. The spreadsheet entry that duplicates the journal entry that was recorded when the bonds were retired is:

	($ in millions)	
Entry (15) Bonds payable ($35 – 50)	15	
Cash (retirement of bonds payable)		15

The cash outflow is reported as a financing activity.

ADDITIONAL CONSIDERATION

The description of the transaction stipulated that $15 million of bonds were retired at their maturity on the first day of the year. Thus, any discount or premium on the bonds would have been completely amortized before the start of the year. If bonds are retired prior to their scheduled maturity, any unamortized discount or premium would be removed from the accounts at that time. For instance, assume that the bonds above were callable at $16 million and that $1 million of unamortized discount remained when they were retired by a call at that price. The spreadsheet entry would be revised as follows:

	($ in millions)	
Entry (15) Bonds payable	15	
(revised) Loss on early extinguishment of bonds	2	
Discount on bonds payable		1
Cash (retirement of bonds payable)		16

The loss, of course, would not be reported in the statement of cash flows. The amortization of the discount, however, would affect a previous spreadsheet entry. In entry (7) we concluded that the decrease in discount on bonds payable was due to the amortization of $2 million of the discount when recording bond interest expense. However, if the early retirement assumed above had occurred, that transaction would have accounted for $1 million of the $2 million decrease in the discount. Entry (7) would be modified as follows:

	($ in millions)	
Entry (7) Interest expense	5	
(revised) Discount on bonds payable		1
Cash (paid to bondholders)		4

16–17. COMMON STOCK. The comparative balance sheets indicate that the common stock account balance increased by $30 million. We look to the accounting records—Illustration 21–1, item (g)—for an explanation. Two transactions, a stock dividend and a sale of new shares of common stock, combined to cause the increase. To create the spreadsheet entries for our analysis, we replicate the journal entries for the two transactions as described below.

Remember from Chapter 18 that to record a small stock dividend, we capitalize retained earnings for the market value of the shares distributed—in this case, 1 million shares times $13 per share, or $13 million. The entry is:

Although this transaction does not identify a cash flow, nor does it represent an investing or financing activity, we include the spreadsheet entry to help explain changes in the three account balances affected.

	($ in millions)	
Entry (16) Retained earnings (1 million shares × $13)	13	
Common stock (1 million shares × $10 par)		10
Paid-in capital—excess of par (difference)		3

Also recall from the discussion of noncash investing and financing activities earlier in the chapter, that stock dividends do not represent a significant investing or financing activity. Therefore, this transaction is not reported in the statement of cash flows. We include the entry in our spreadsheet analysis only to help explain changes in the account balances affected.

The sale of 2 million shares of common stock at $13 per share is represented by the following spreadsheet entry:

	($ in millions)	
Entry (17) Cash (from sale of common stock)	26	
Common stock ([$130 – 100] – 10)		20
Paid-in capital—excess of par ([$29 – 20] – 3)		6

The sale of common shares explains the remaining increase in the common stock account and the remaining increase in paid-in capital—excess of par.

The cash inflow is reported in the statement of cash flows as a financing activity.

ADDITIONAL CONSIDERATION

If cash is paid to retire outstanding shares of stock or to purchase those shares as treasury stock, the cash outflow would be reported in a statement of cash flows as a financing activity.

Together, the two entries above account for both the $30 million increase in the common stock account and the $9 million increase in paid-in capital—excess of par.

18. RETAINED EARNINGS. The stock dividend in entry (16) above includes a $13 million reduction of retained earnings. Previously, we saw in entry (11) that net income increased retained earnings by $12 million. The net reduction of $1 million accounted for by these two entries leaves $5 million of the $6 million net decrease in the account unexplained.

Retained Earnings

		25	Beginning balance
(16) Stock dividend	13	12	Net income (11)
(18) ?	?		
		19	Ending balance

Without additional information about the $5 million decrease in retained earnings, we might assume it was due to a $5 million cash dividend. This assumption is unnecessary, though, because the cash dividend is described in Illustration 21–1, item (h).

Retained Earnings

		25	Beginning balance
(16) Stock dividend	13	12	Net income (11)
(18) Cash dividend	5		
		19	Ending balance

The spreadsheet entry is:

	($ in millions)	
Entry (18) Retained earnings	5	
Cash (payment of cash dividends)		5

The cash dividend accounts for the previously unexplained change in retained earnings.

19. COMPLETING THE SPREADSHEET. In preparing the spreadsheet to this point, we have analyzed each noncash account on both the income statement and the balance sheet. Our purpose was to identify the transactions that, during the year, had affected each account. By recreating each transaction in the form of a spreadsheet entry—in effect, duplicating the journal entry that had been used to record the transaction—we were able to explain the change in the balance of each account. That is, the debits and credits in the changes columns of the spreadsheet account for the increase or decrease in each noncash account. When a transaction being entered on the spreadsheet included an operating, investing, or financing activity, we entered that portion of the entry under the corresponding heading of the statement of cash flows section of the spreadsheet. Since, as noted earlier, there can be no operating, investing, or financing activity without a corresponding change in one or more of the noncash accounts, we should feel confident at this point that we have identified all of the activities that should be reported on the statement of cash flows.

The cash flows section of the spreadsheet provides the information to be reported in the statement of cash flows.

To check the accuracy of the analysis, we compare the change in the balance of the cash account with the net change in cash flows produced by the activities listed in the statement of cash flows section of the spreadsheet. The net increase or decrease in cash flows from each of the statement of cash flows categories is extended to the extreme right column of the spreadsheet. By reference to Illustration 21–1A, we see that net cash flows from operating, investing, and financing activities are: $22 million; ($19 million); and $6 million, respectively. Together these activities provide a net increase in cash of $9 million. This amount corresponds to the increase in the balance of the cash account from $20 million to $29 million. To complete the spreadsheet, we include the final spreadsheet entry:

	($ in millions)	
Entry (19) Cash	9	
Net increase in cash		
(from statement of cash flows activities)		9

As a final check of accuracy, we can confirm that the total of the debits is equal to the total of the credits in the changes columns of the spreadsheet.[13]

[13]The mechanical and computational aspects of the spreadsheet analysis are simplified greatly when performed on an electronic spreadsheet such as Microsoft Excel.

ETHICAL DILEMMA

"We must get it," Courtney Lowell, president of Industrial Fasteners, roared. "Without it we're in big trouble." The "it" Mr. Lowell referred to is the renewal of a $14 million loan with Community First Bank. The big trouble he fears is the lack of funds necessary to repay the existing debt and few, if any, prospects for raising the funds elsewhere.

Mr. Lowell had just hung up the phone after a conversation with a bank vice-president in which it was made clear that this year's statement of cash flows must look better than last year's. Mr. Lowell knows that improvements are not on course to happen. In fact, cash flow projections were dismal.

Later that day, Tim Cratchet, assistant controller, was summoned to Mr. Lowell's office. "Cratchet," Lowell barked, "I've looked at our accounts receivable. I think we can generate quite a bit of cash by selling or factoring most of those receivables. I know it will cost us more than if we collect them ourselves, but it sure will make our cash flow picture look better."

Is there an ethical question facing Cratchet?

INTERNATIONAL FINANCIAL REPORTING STANDARDS

Both U.S. GAAP and IFRS require a statement of cash flows classifying cash flows as operating, investing, or financing. A difference, though, is that *SFAS No. 95* designates cash outflows for interest payments and cash inflows from interest and dividends received as operating cash flows. *IAS No. 7* allows companies to report cash outflows from interest payments as either operating *or* financing cash flows and cash inflows from interest and dividends as either operating *or* investing cash flows. U.S. GAAP classifies dividends paid to shareholders as financing cash flows. The international standard allows companies to report dividends paid as either financing *or* operating cash flows.

The spreadsheet is now complete. The statement of cash flows can now be prepared directly from the spreadsheet simply by presenting the items included in the statement of cash flows section of the spreadsheet in the appropriate format of the statement.

The statements of cash flows from an annual report of **Hooker Furniture Corporation** are shown in Graphic 21–9. Notice that the reconciliation schedule was reported by Hooker Furniture in the statement of cash flows itself shown below. Many companies report the schedule separately in the disclosure notes.

GRAPHIC 21–9 Statement of Cash Flows—Hooker Furniture Corporation

HOOKER FURNITURE CORPORATION AND SUBSIDIARIES
Consolidated Statements of Cash Flows
(In thousands)

For The Years Ended November 30,	2006	2005	2004
Cash flows from operating activities			
Cash received from customers	$ 349,075	$ 339,041	$ 341,296
Cash paid to suppliers and employees	(317,895)	(308,957)	(320,677)
Income taxes paid, net	(8,741)	(9,614)	(11,981)
Interest paid, net	(111)	(846)	(1,189)
Net cash provided by operating activities	22,328	19,624	7,449
Cash flows from investing activities			
Purchase of property, plant and equipment	(4,268)	(3,590)	(3,702)
Proceeds received on notes issued for the sale of property	52	18	900
Proceeds from the sale of property and equipment	3,357	5,208	181
Net cash (used in) provided by investing activities	(859)	1,636	(2,621)
Cash flows from financing activities			
Proceeds from long-term debt			2,000
Payments on long-term debt	(2,283)	(9,871)	(9,671)
Payments to terminate interest rate swap agreements		(38)	
Cash dividends paid	(3,687)	(3,286)	(2,786)
Purchase and retirement of common stock		(930)	
Net cash used in financing activities	(5,970)	(14,125)	(10,457)
Net increase (decrease) in cash and cash equivalents	15,499	7,135	(5,629)
Cash and cash equivalents at beginning of year	16,365	9,230	14,859
Cash and cash equivalents at end of year	$ 31,864	$ 16,365	$ 9,230
Reconciliation of net income to net cash provided by operating activities			
Net income	$ 14,138	$ 12,485	$ 18,204
Depreciation and amortization	4,645	6,296	7,422
Non-cash ESOP cost and restricted stock awards	2,664	3,225	3,784
Restructuring and related asset impairment charges	6,881	5,250	1,604
Gain (loss) on disposal of property	2	(10)	(27)
Provision for doubtful accounts	1,920	569	1,255
Deferred income tax (benefit) provision	(3,273)	(1,479)	41
Changes in assets and liabilities:			
Trade accounts receivable	(3,371)	(3,602)	(4,614)
Inventories	579	992	(27,333)
Prepaid expenses and other assets	(1,224)	(2,550)	(720)
Trade accounts payable	(2,621)	(1,058)	7,985
Accrued salaries, wages and benefits	(1,340)	(2,440)	647
Accrued income taxes	2,489		(308)
Other accrued expenses	313	300	581
Other long-term liabilities	526	1,646	(1,072)
Net cash provided by operating activities	$ 22,328	$ 19,624	$ 7,449

CONCEPT REVIEW EXERCISE

COMPREHENSIVE REVIEW

The comparative balance sheets for 2009 and 2008 and the income statement for 2009 are given below for Beneficial Drill Company. Additional information from Beneficial Drill's accounting records is provided also.

Required:

Prepare the statement of cash flows of Beneficial Drill Company for the year ended December 31, 2009. Present cash flows from operating activities by the direct method and use a spreadsheet to assist in your analysis.

BENEFICIAL DRILL COMPANY
Comparative Balance Sheets
December 31, 2009 and 2008
($ in millions)

Assets	2009	2008
Cash	$ 20	$ 40
Accounts receivable	99	100
Less: Allowance for uncollectible accounts	(5)	(4)
Investment revenue receivable	3	2
Inventory	115	110
Prepaid insurance	2	3
Long-term investments	77	60
Land	110	80
Buildings and equipment	220	240
Less: Accumulated depreciation	(35)	(60)
Patent	15	16
	$621	$587
Liabilities		
Accounts payable	$ 23	$ 30
Salaries payable	2	5
Bond interest payable	4	2
Income tax payable	6	7
Deferred income tax liability	5	4
Notes payable	15	0
Bonds payable	150	130
Less: Discount on bonds	(9)	(10)
Shareholders' Equity		
Common stock	210	200
Paid-in capital—excess of par	44	40
Retained earnings	178	179
Less: Treasury stock (at cost)	(7)	0
	$621	$587

BENEFICIAL DRILL COMPANY
Income Statement
For Year Ended December 31, 2009
($ in millions)

Revenues		
Sales revenue	$200	
Investment revenue	6	
Investment revenue—sale of treasury bills	1	$207

(continued)

(concluded)

Expenses			
Cost of goods sold		110	
Salaries expense		30	
Depreciation expense		5	
Patent amortization expense		1	
Bad debts expense		4	
Insurance expense		3	
Bond interest expense		14	
Extraordinary loss on destruction of equipment	$ 10		
Less: Tax savings	(5)	5	
Income tax expense		12	(184)
Net income			$ 23

Additional information from the accounting records:

a. During 2009, $3 million of customer accounts were written off as uncollectible.
b. Investment revenue includes Beneficial Drill Company's $3 million share of the net income of Hammer Company, an equity method investee.
c. Treasury bills were sold during 2009 at a gain of $1 million. Beneficial Drill Company classifies its investments in Treasury bills as cash equivalents.
d. A machine that originally cost $60 million and was one-half depreciated, was rendered unusable by a freak bolt of lightning. Most major components of the machine were unharmed and were sold for $20 million.
e. Temporary differences between pretax accounting income and taxable income caused the deferred income tax liability to increase by $1 million.
f. The common stock of Wrench Corporation was purchased for $14 million as a long-term investment.
g. Land costing $30 million was acquired by paying $15 million cash and issuing a 13%, seven-year, $15 million note payable to the seller.
h. New equipment was purchased for $40 million cash.
i. $20 million of bonds were sold at face value.
j. On January 19, Drill issued a 5% stock dividend (1 million shares). The market price of the $10 par value common stock was $14 per share at that time.
k. Cash dividends of $10 million were paid to shareholders.
l. In November, 500,000 common shares were repurchased as treasury stock at a cost of $7 million. Drill uses the cost method to account for treasury stock.

SOLUTION

BENEFICIAL DRILL COMPANY
Spreadsheet for the Statement of Cash Flows

	Dec. 31 2008	Changes				Dec. 31 2009
		Debits		Credits		
Balance Sheet						
Assets						
Cash	40			(20)	20	20
Accounts receivable	100			(1)	1	99
Less: Allowance for uncollectible accounts	(4)			(1)	1	(5)
Investment revenue receivable	2	(2)	1			3
Inventory	110	(4)	5			115
Prepaid insurance	3			(8)	1	2
Long-term investments	60	(2)	3			
		(13)	14			77
Land	80	(14)	30			110
Buildings and equipment	240	(15)	40	(10)	60	220
Less: Accumulated depreciation	(60)	(10)	30	(6)	5	(35)
Patent	16			(7)	1	15
	587					621

(continued)

(continued)

Liabilities						
Accounts payable	30	(4)	7			23
Salaries payable	5	(5)	3			2
Bond interest payable	2			(9)	2	4
Income tax payable	7	(11)	1			6
Deferred income tax liability	4			(11)	1	5
Notes payable	0			(14)	15X	15
Bonds payable	130			(16)	20	150
Less: Discount on bonds	(10)			(9)	1	(9)
Shareholders' Equity						
Common stock	200			(17)	10	210
Paid-in capital—excess of par	40			(17)	4	44
Retained earnings	179	(17)	14			
		(18)	10	(12)	23	178
Less: Treasury stock	0	(19)	7			(7)
	587					621
Income Statement						
Revenues:						
Sales revenue				(1)	200	200
Investment revenue				(2)	6	6
Investment revenue—sale of Treasury bills				(3)	1	1
Expenses:						
Cost of goods sold		(4)	110			(110)
Salaries expense		(5)	30			(30)
Depreciation expense		(6)	5			(5)
Patent amortization expense		(7)	1			(1)
Bad debts expense		(1)	4			(4)
Insurance expense		(8)	3			(3)
Bond interest expense		(9)	14			(14)
Extraordinary loss		(10)	10			(10)
Less: Tax savings				(11)	5	5
Income tax expense		(11)	12			(12)
Net income		(12)	23			23
Statement of Cash Flows						
Operating Activities:						
Cash inflows:						
From customers		(1)	198			
From investment revenue		(2)	2			
From sale of Treasury bills		(3)	1			
Cash outflows:						
To suppliers of goods				(4)	122	
To employees				(5)	33	
For insurance expense				(8)	2	
For bond interest expense				(9)	11	
For income taxes				(11)	7	
Net cash flows						26
Investing Activities:						
Sale of equipment		(10)	20			
Purchase of LT investments				(13)	14	
Purchase of land				(14)	15	
Purchase of equipment				(15)	40	
Net cash flows						(49)

(continued)

(concluded)

Financing Activities:					
Sale of bonds payable	(16)	20			
Payment of cash dividends			(18)	10	
Purchase of treasury stock			(19)	7	
Net cash flows					3
Net decrease in cash	(20)	20			(20)
Totals		638		638	

BENEFICIAL DRILL COMPANY
Statement of Cash Flows
For Year Ended December 31, 2009
($ in millions)

Cash Flows from Operating Activities		
Cash inflows:		
From customers	$198	
From investment revenue	2	
From sale of Treasury bills	1	
Cash outflows:		
To suppliers of goods	(122)	
To employees	(33)	
For insurance expense	(2)	
For bond interest expense	(11)	
For income taxes	(7)	
Net cash flows from operating activities		$26
Cash Flows from Investing Activities		
Sale of equipment	$ 20	
Purchase of long-term investments	(14)	
Purchase of land	(15)	
Purchase of equipment	(40)	
Net cash flows from investing activities		(49)
Cash Flows from Financing Activities		
Sale of bonds payable	$ 20	
Payment of cash dividends	(10)	
Purchase of treasury stock	(7)	
Net cash flows from financing activities		3
Net decrease in cash		($20)
Cash balance, January 1		40
Cash balance, December 31		$20
Noncash Investing and Financing Activities		
Acquired $30 million of land by paying cash and issuing a 13%, 7-year note as follows:		
Cost of land	$ 30	
Cash paid	15	
Note issued	$ 15	

PART C

PREPARING AN SCF: THE INDIRECT METHOD OF REPORTING CASH FLOWS FROM OPERATING ACTIVITIES

Getting There through the Back Door

The presentation of cash flows from operating activities illustrated in Part B is referred to as the *direct method.* By this method, the cash effect of each operating activity (i.e., income statement item) is reported directly on the statement of cash flows. For instance, cash received from customers is reported as the cash effect of sales activities, and cash paid to suppliers is reported as the cash effect of cost of goods sold. Income statement items that have *no* cash effect, such as depreciation expense, bad debt expense, gains, and losses, are simply not reported.

As pointed out previously, a permissible alternative is the *indirect method,* by which the net cash increase or decrease from operating activities is derived indirectly by starting with reported net income and working backwards to convert that amount to a cash basis. The derivation by the indirect method of net cash flows from operating activities for UBC is shown in Illustration 21–1B. For the adjustment amounts, you may wish to refer back to UBC's balance sheets and income statement presented in Illustration 21–1.

ILLUSTRATION 21–1B
Indirect Method

The indirect method derives the net cash increase or decrease from operating activities indirectly, by starting with reported net income and "working backwards" to convert that amount to a cash basis.

Cash Flows from Operating Activities—Indirect Method
and
Reconciliation of Net Income to Net Cash Flows from Operating Activities

Net Income	$12
Adjustments for noncash effects:	
Gain on sale of land	(8)
Depreciation expense	3
Loss on sale of equipment	2
Changes in operating assets and liabilities:	
Increase in accounts receivable	(2)
Decrease in inventory	4
Increase in accounts payable	6
Increase in salaries payable	2
Discount on bonds payable	2
Decrease in prepaid insurance	3
Decrease in income tax payable	(2)
Net cash flows from operating activities	$22

Notice that the indirect method yields the same $22 million net cash flows from operating activities as does the direct method. This is understandable when you consider that the indirect method simply reverses the differences between the accrual-based income statement and cash flows from operating activities. We accomplish this as described in the next two sections.

Components of Net Income that Do Not Increase or Decrease Cash

Amounts that were subtracted in determining net income but did not reduce cash are *added back to* net income to reverse the effect of their having been subtracted. For example, depreciation expense and the loss on sale of equipment are added back to net income. Other things being equal, this restores net income to what it would have been had depreciation and the loss not been subtracted at all.

Similarly, amounts that were added in determining net income but did not increase cash are subtracted from net income to reverse the effect of their having been added. For example, UBC's gain on sale of land is deducted from net income. Here's why. UBC sold for $18 million land that originally cost $10 million. Recording the sale produced a gain of $8 million, which UBC appropriately included in its income statement. But did this gain increase UBC's cash? No. Certainly selling the land increased cash—by $18 million. We therefore include the $18 million as a cash inflow in the statement of cash flows. However, the sale of land is an investing activity. The gain itself, though, is simply the difference between cash received in the sale of land (reported as an investing activity) and the original cost of the land. If UBC also reported the $8 million gain as a cash flow from operating activities, in addition to reporting $18 million as a cash flow from investing activities, UBC would report the $8 million twice. So, because UBC added the gain in determining its net income but the gain had no effect on cash, the gain must now be subtracted from net income to reverse the effect of its having been added.

Components of Net Income that Do Increase or Decrease Cash

For components of net income that increase or decrease cash, but by an amount different from that reported on the income statement, net income is adjusted for changes in the balances of related balance sheet accounts to *convert the effects of those items to a cash basis.* For example, sales of $100 million are included on the income statement as a component of net income, and yet, since accounts receivable increased by $2 million, only $98 million cash was collected from customers during the reporting period. Sales are converted to a cash basis by subtracting the $2 million increase in accounts receivable. Here's another example:

The income statement reports salaries expense as $13 million. Just because employees earned $13 million during the reporting period, though, doesn't necessarily mean UBC paid those employees $13 million in cash during the same period. In fact, we see in the comparative balance sheets that salaries payable increased from $1 million to $3 million; UBC owes its employees $2 million more than before the year started. The company must not have paid the entire $13 million expense. By analyzing salaries expense in relation to the change in salaries payable, we can determine the amount of cash paid to employees:

Salaries Payable

		1	Beginning balance
Cash paid to employees (*decreases salaries payable*)	?	13	Salaries expense (*increases salaries payable*)
		3	Ending balance

This inspection indicates that UBC paid only $11 million cash to its employees; the remaining $2 million of salaries expense is reflected as an increase in salaries payable. From a cash perspective, then, by subtracting $13 million for salaries in the income statement, UBC has subtracted $2 million more than the reduction in cash. Adding back the $2 million leaves UBC in the same position as if it had deducted only the $11 million cash paid to employees.

Following a similar analysis of the cash effects of the remaining components of net income, those items are likewise converted to a cash basis by adjusting net income for increases and decreases in related accounts.

For components of net income that increase or decrease cash by an amount exactly the same as that reported on the income statement, no adjustment of net income is required. For example, investment revenue of $3 million is included in UBC's $12 million net income amount. Because $3 million also is the amount of cash received from that activity, this element of net income already represents its cash effect and needs no adjustment.[14]

Comparison with the Direct Method

The indirect method is compared with the direct method in Graphic 21–10, using the data of UBC. To better illustrate the relationship between the two methods, the adjustments to net income using the indirect method are presented parallel to the related cash inflows and cash outflows of the direct method. The income statement is included in the graphic to

[14]We determined in Part B (subsection 2) that there is no evidence that cash received from investments differs from investment revenue.

GRAPHIC 21–10 Comparison of the Indirect Method and the Direct Method of Determining Cash Flows from Operating Activities

		Cash Flows from Operating Activities			
Income Statement		**Indirect Method**		**Direct Method**	
		Net income	$12		
		Adjustments:			
Sales	$100	Increase in accounts receivable	(2)	Cash received from customers	$98
Investment revenue	3	(No adjustment—no investment revenue receivable or long-term investments)		Cash received from investments	3
Gain on sale of land	8	Gain on sale of land	(8)	(Not reported—no cash effect)	
Cost of goods sold	(60)	Decrease in inventory	4		
		Increase in accounts payable	6	Cash paid to suppliers	(50)
Salaries expense	(13)	Increase in salaries payable	2	Cash paid to employees	(11)
Depreciation expense	(3)	Depreciation expense	3	(Not reported—no cash effect)	
Interest expense	(5)	Decrease in bond discount	2	Cash paid for interest	(3)
Insurance expense	(7)	Decrease in prepaid insurance	3	Cash paid for insurance	(4)
Loss on sale of equipment	(2)	Loss on sale of equipment	2	(Not reported—no cash effect)	
Income tax expense	(9)	Decrease in income tax payable	(2)	Cash paid for income taxes	(11)
Net Income	$ 12	**Net cash flows from operating activities**	**$22**	**Net cash flows from operating activities**	**$22**

demonstrate that the indirect method also serves to reconcile differences between the elements of that statement and the cash flows reported by the direct method.

As a practical consideration, you might notice that the adjustments to net income using the indirect method follow a convenient pattern. *Increases* in related assets are deducted from net income (i.e., the increase in accounts receivable) when converting to cash from operating activities. Conversely, *decreases* in assets are added (inventory and prepaid insurance in this case). Changes in related liabilities are handled in just the opposite way. Increases in related liabilities are *added* to net income (i.e., the increases in accounts payable and salaries payable) while decreases in liabilities are subtracted (i.e., decrease in income tax payable).[15]

Of course, these are adjustments to net income that effectively convert components of income from reported accrual amounts to a cash basis. The other adjustments to net income (gain, depreciation, loss) as pointed out earlier are to get rid of the three income statement components that have no effect at all on cash. This pattern is summarized in Graphic 21–11 on the next page.

Although either the direct method or the indirect method is permitted, the FASB strongly encourages companies to report cash flows from operating activities by the direct method. The obvious appeal of this approach is that it reports specific operating cash receipts and operating cash payments, which is consistent with the primary objective of the statement of cash flows. Investors and creditors gain additional insight into the specific sources of cash receipts and payments from operating activities revealed by this reporting method. Also, statement users can more readily interpret and understand the information presented because the direct method avoids the confusion caused by reporting noncash items and other reconciling adjustments under the caption *cash flows from operating activities.* Nonetheless, the vast majority of companies choose to use the indirect method. Reasons for this choice

[15]The adjustment for the decrease in bond discount is logically consistent with this pattern as well. Bond discount is a contra liability. It's logical, then, that an adjustment for a decrease in this account be added—the opposite of the way a decrease in a liability is treated.

GRAPHIC 21–11
Adjustments to Convert Net Income to a Cash Basis—Indirect Method

Type of Adjustment	To Adjust for Noncash Effect
Adjustments for Noncash Effects:	
Income statement components that have *no effect* at all on cash but are *additions* to income	Deduct from net income
Income statement components that have *no effect* at all on cash but are *deductions* from income	Add to net income
Changes in Operating Assets and Liabilities:	
Increases in assets related to an income statement component	Deduct from net income
Decreases in assets related to an income statement component	Add to net income
Increases in liabilities related to an income statement component	Add to net income
Decreases in liabilities related to an income statement component	Deduct from net income

range from longstanding tradition to the desire to withhold as much information as possible from competitors.[16]

Reconciliation of Net Income to Cash Flows from Operating Activities

As we discussed earlier, whether cash flows from operating activities are reported by the direct method or by the indirect method, the financial statements must report a reconciliation of net income to net cash flows from operating activities. When the direct method is used, the reconciliation is presented in a separate schedule and is identical to the presentation of net cash flows from operating activities by the indirect method. In other words, Illustration 21–1B also serves as the reconciliation schedule to accompany a statement of cash flows using the direct method. Obviously, a separate reconciliation schedule is not required when using the indirect method because the cash flows from operating activities section of the statement of cash flows *is* a reconciliation of net income to net cash flows from operating activities.[17]

Remember that the direct and indirect methods are alternative approaches to deriving net cash flows from *operating* activities only. The choice of which method is used for that purpose does not affect the way cash flows from *investing* and *financing* activities are identified and reported.

The statements of cash flows from the annual report of **Hewlett-Packard Company,** which uses the indirect method, are shown in Graphic 21–12 on the next page.

For most companies, expenditures for interest and for taxes are significant. Cash payments for interest and for taxes usually are specifically indicated when the direct method is employed as is the case for **Hooker Furniture Corporation** reported earlier in Graphic 21–9. When the indirect method is used, those amounts aren't readily apparent and are *separately reported* either on the face of the statement or in an accompanying disclosure note as Hewlett-Packard does.

We use a spreadsheet to help prepare a statement of cash flows by the indirect method in Appendix 21A.

[16]Strong arguments are made for the FASB requiring the direct method by Paul R. Bahnson, Paul B. W. Miller, and Bruce P. Budge in "Nonarticulation in Cash Flow Statements and Implications for Education, Research and Practice," *Accounting Horizons,* December 1996, and by G. V. Krishnan and J. A. Largay III in "The Predictive Ability of Direct Method Cash Flow Information," *Journal of Business Finance & Accounting,* January 2000.

[17]It is permissible to present the reconciliation in a separate schedule and to report the net cash flows from operating activities as a single line item on the statement of cash flows.

GRAPHIC 21–12 Statement of Cash Flows—Indirect Method; Hewlett-Packard

HEWLETT PACKARD
Consolidated Statements of Cash Flows

	For the Fiscal Years Ended October 31		
	2007	**2006**	**2005**
		$ in millions	
Cash Flows from Operating Activities:			
Net earnings	$ 7,264	$ 6,198	$ 2,398
Adjustments to reconcile net earnings to net cash provided by operating activities:			
Depreciation and amortization	2,705	2,353	2,344
Stock-based compensation expense	629	536	104
Provision (benefit) for doubtful accounts—accounts and financing receivables	47	4	(22)
Provision for inventory	362	267	398
Restructuring charges	387	158	1,684
Pension curtailments and pension settlements, net	(517)	—	(199)
In-process research and development charges	190	52	2
Deferred taxes on earnings	415	693	(162)
Excess tax benefit from stock-based compensation	(481)	(251)	—
(Gains) losses on investments	(14)	(25)	13
Other, net	(86)	18	(82)
Changes in assets and liabilities:			
Accounts and financing receivables	(2,808)	(882)	666
Inventory	(633)	(1,109)	(208)
Accounts payable	(346)	1,879	846
Taxes on earnings	502	(513)	748
Restructuring	(606)	(810)	(247)
Other assets and liabilities	2,605	2,785	(255)
Net cash provided by operating activities	9,615	11,353	8,028
Cash Flows from Investing Activities:			
Investment in property, plant and equipment	(3,040)	(2,536)	(1,995)
Proceeds from sale of property, plant and equipment	568	556	542
Purchases of available-for-sale securities and other investments	(283)	(46)	(1,729)
Maturities and sales of available-for-sale securities and other investments	425	94	2,066
Payments made in connection with business acquisitions, net	(6,793)	(855)	(641)
Net cash used in investing activities	(9,123)	(2,787)	(1,757)
Cash Flows from Financing Activities:			
Issuance (repayment) of commercial paper and notes payable, net	1,863	(55)	(1)
Issuance of debt	4,106	1,121	84
Payment of debt	(3,419)	(1,259)	(1,827)
Issuance of common stock under employee stock plans	3,103	2,538	1,161
Repurchase of common stock	(10,887)	(6,057)	(3,514)
Prepayment of common stock repurchase	—	(1,722)	—
Excess tax benefit from stock-based compensation	481	251	—
Dividends	(846)	(894)	(926)
Net cash used in financing activities	(5,599)	(6,077)	(5,023)
(Decrease) increase in cash and cash equivalents	(5,107)	2,489	1,248
Cash and cash equivalents at beginning of period	16,400	13,911	12,663
Cash and cash equivalents at end of period	$ 11,293	$ 16,400	$ 13,911

(continued)

GRAPHIC 21–12 concluded

Note 5: Supplemental Cash Flow Information

Supplemental cash flow information was as follows for the following fiscal years ended October 31:

	2007	2006	2005
		$ in millions	
Cash paid for income taxes, net	$ 956	$ 637	$ 884
Cash paid for interest	$ 489	$ 299	$ 447
Non-cash investing and financing activities:			
Issuance of common stock and options assumed in business acquisitions	$ 41	$ 13	$ 12
Purchase of assets under financing arrangement	$ 57	$ —	$ —
Purchase of assets under capital leases	$ —	$ 19	$ —

DECISION MAKERS' PERSPECTIVE—Cash Flow Ratios

We have emphasized the analysis of financial statements from a decision maker's perspective throughout this text. Often that analysis included the development and comparison of financial ratios. Ratios based on income statement and balance sheet amounts enjoy a long tradition of acceptance from which several standard ratios, including those described in earlier chapters, have evolved. To gain another viewpoint, some analysts supplement their investigation with cash flow ratios. Some cash flow ratios are derived by simply substituting cash flow from operations (CFFO) from the statement of cash flows in place of net income in many ratios, not to replace those ratios but to complement them. For example, the times interest earned ratio can be modified to reflect the number of times the cash outflow for interest is provided by cash inflow from operations and any of the profitability ratios can be modified to determine the cash generated from assets, shareholders' equity, sales, etc. Graphic 21–13 summarizes the calculation and usefulness of several representative cash flow ratios.

GRAPHIC 21–13
Cash Flow Ratios

	Calculation	Measures
Performance Ratios		
Cash flow to sales	CFFO / Net sales	Cash generated by each sales dollar
Cash return on assets	CFFO / Average total assets	Cash generated from all resources
Cash return on shareholders' equity	CFFO / Average shareholders' equity	Cash generated from owner-provided resources
Cash to income	CFFO / Income from continuing operations	Cash-generating ability of continuing operations
Cash flow per share	(CFFO − preferred dividends) / Weighted-average shares	Operating cash flow on a per share basis
Sufficiency Ratios		
Debt coverage	Total liabilities / CFFO	Financial risk and financial leverage
Interest coverage	(CFFO + interest + taxes) / Interest	Ability to satisfy fixed obligations
Reinvestment	CFFO / Cash outflow for noncurrent assets	Ability to acquire assets with operating cash flows
Debt payment	CFFO / Cash outflow for LT debt repayment	Ability to pay debts with operating cash flows

(continued)

GRAPHIC 21–13
(concluded)

	Calculation	Measures
Dividend payment	CFFO / Cash outflow for dividends	Ability to pay dividends with operating cash flows
Investing and financing activity	CFFO / Cash outflows for investing and financing activities	Ability to acquire assets, pay debts, and make distributions to owners

Cash flow ratios have received limited acceptance to date due, in large part, to the long tradition of accrual-based ratios coupled with the relatively brief time that all companies have published statements of cash flows. A lack of consensus on cash flow ratios by which to make comparisons also has slowed their acceptance. Nevertheless, cash flow ratios offer insight in the evaluation of a company's profitability and financial strength.[18]

FINANCIAL REPORTING CASE **SOLUTION**

1. **What are the cash flow aspects of the situation that Mr. Barr may be overlooking in making his case for a wage increase? How can a company's operations generate a healthy profit and yet produce meager or even negative cash flows?** *(p. 1112)* Positive net income does not necessarily indicate a healthy cash position. A statement of cash flows provides information about cash flows not seen when looking only at the balance sheet and the income statement. Although cash flows from operating activities result from the same activities that are reported on the income statement, the income statement reports the activities on an accrual basis. That is, revenues reported are those earned during the reporting period, regardless of when cash is received, and the expenses incurred in generating those revenues, regardless of when cash is paid. Thus, the very same operations can generate a healthy profit and yet produce meager or even negative cash flows.
2. **What information can a statement of cash flows provide about a company's investing activities that can be useful in decisions such as this?** *(p. 1114)* Cash flows from investing activities result from the acquisition and disposition of assets. Information about investing activities is useful to decision makers regarding the nature and magnitude of productive assets being acquired for future use. In the union negotiations, for instance, Mr. Barr may not be aware of the substantial investments underway to replace and update equipment and the cash requirements of those investments. Relatedly, the relatively low depreciation charges accelerated depreciation provides in the later years of assets' lives may cause profits to seem artificially high given the necessity to replace those assets at higher prices.
3. **What information can a statement of cash flows provide about a company's financing activities that can be useful in decisions such as this?** *(p. 1115)* Information about financing activities provides insights into sources of a company's external financing. Recent debt issues, for instance, might indicate a need for higher cash flows to maintain higher interest charges. Similarly, recent external financing activity may suggest that a company might be near its practical limits from external sources and, therefore, may need a greater reliance on internal financing through operations.

[18] Proposals for informative sets of cash flow ratios are offered by Charles Carslaw and John Mills, "Developing Ratios for Effective Cash Flow Analysis," *Journal of Accountancy,* November 1991; Don Giacomino and David Mielke, "Cash Flows: Another Approach to Ratio Analysis," *Journal of Accountancy,* March 1993; and John Mills and Jeanne Yamamura, "The Power of Cash Flows Ratios," *Journal of Accountancy,* October 1998.

THE BOTTOM LINE

- **LO1** Decision makers focus on the prospects of receiving a cash return from their dealings with a firm. But it is the ability of the firm to generate cash flows to itself that ultimately determines the potential for cash flows to investors and creditors. The statement of cash flows fills an information gap left by the balance sheet and the income statement by presenting information about cash flows that the other statements either do not provide or provide only indirectly. The stipulation that companies present the statement of cash flows is a relatively recent requirement. *SFAS No. 95* completed a full-cycle movement of accounting thought back to cash flow reporting, which, in different form, was common practice several decades ago. (p. 1108)
- **LO2** Cash includes cash equivalents. These are short-term, highly liquid investments that can readily be converted to cash with little risk of loss. (p. 1111)
- **LO3** Cash flows from operating activities are both inflows and outflows of cash that result from activities reported on the income statement. (p. 1112)
- **LO4** Unlike the direct method, which directly lists cash inflows and outflows, the indirect method derives cash flows indirectly, by starting with reported net income and working backwards to convert that amount to a cash basis. (p. 1113)
- **LO5** Cash flows from investing activities are related to the acquisition and disposition of assets, other than inventory and assets classified as cash equivalents. (p. 1114)
- **LO6** Cash flows from financing activities result from the external financing of a business. (p. 1115)
- **LO7** Noncash investing and financing activities, such as acquiring equipment (an investing activity) by issuing a long-term note payable (a financing activity), are reported in a related disclosure schedule or note. (p. 1116)
- **LO8** A spreadsheet provides a systematic method of preparing a statement of cash flows by analyzing available data to insure that all operating, investing, and financing activities are detected. Recording spreadsheet entries that explain account balance changes simultaneously identifies and classifies the activities to be reported on the statement of cash flows. (p. 1116)

SPREADSHEET FOR THE INDIRECT METHOD

APPENDIX 21A

A spreadsheet is equally useful in preparing a statement of cash flows whether we use the direct or the indirect method of determining cash flows from operating activities. The format of the spreadsheet differs only with respect to operating activities. The analysis of transactions for the purpose of identifying cash flows to be reported is the same. To illustrate, Illustration 21A–1 on the next page provides a spreadsheet analysis of the data for UBC.

Two differences should be noted between the spreadsheet in Illustration 21A–1 and the spreadsheet we used earlier for the direct method. First, in the statement of cash flows section of the spreadsheet, under the heading of "cash flows from operating activities," specific cash inflows and cash outflows are replaced by net income and the required adjustments for noncash effects. Second, we do not include an income statement section. This section is unnecessary because, using the indirect method, we are not interested in identifying specific operating activities that cause increases and decreases in cash. Instead, we need from the income statement only the amount of net income, which is converted to a cash basis by adjusting for any noncash amounts included in net income. The spreadsheet entries in journal entry form for the indirect method are illustrated in Illustration 21A–2 on page 1149.

Remember that there is no mandatory order in which the account changes must be analyzed. However, since we determine net cash flows from operating activities by working backwards from net income when using the indirect method, it is convenient to start with the spreadsheet entry that represents the credit to retained earnings due to net income. This entry corresponds to spreadsheet entry (11) using the direct method. By entering the debit portion of the entry as the first item under the cash flows from operating activities (CFOA), we establish net income as the initial amount of cash flows from operating activities, which is then adjusted to a cash basis by subsequent entries. Entries (2)–(4) duplicate the transactions that involve noncash components of net income. Changes in current assets and current liabilities that represent differences between revenues and expenses and the cash effects of those revenues and expenses are accounted for by entries (5)–(11). Spreadsheet entries

ILLUSTRATION 21A–1
Indirect Method

UNITED BRANDS CORPORATION
Spreadsheet for the Statement of Cash Flows

	Dec. 31 2008	Changes Debits		Changes Credits		Dec. 31 2009
Balance Sheet						
Assets						
Cash	20	(19)	9			29
Accounts receivable	30	(5)	2			32
Short-term investments	0	(12)	12			12
Inventory	50			(6)	4	46
Prepaid insurance	6			(8)	3	3
Land	60	(13)	30	(2)	10	80
Buildings and equipment	75	(14)	20X	(3)	14	81
Less: Accumulated depreciation	(20)	(3)	7	(4)	3	(16)
	221					267
Liabilities						
Accounts payable	20			(7)	6	26
Salaries payable	1			(9)	2	3
Income tax payable	8	(11)	2			6
Notes payable	0			(14)	20X	20
Bonds payable	50	(15)	15			35
Less: Discount on bonds	(3)			(10)	2	(1)
Shareholders' Equity						
Common stock	100			(16)	10	
				(17)	20	130
Paid-in capital—excess of par	20			(16)	3	
				(17)	6	29
Retained earnings	25	(16)	13			
		(18)	5	(1)	12	19
	221					267
Statement of Cash Flows						
Operating activities:						
Net income		(1)	12			
Adjustments for noncash effects:						
Gain on sale of land				(2)	8	
Depreciation expense		(4)	3			
Loss on sale of equipment		(3)	2			
Increase in accounts receivable				(5)	2	
Decrease in inventory		(6)	4			
Decrease in prepaid insurance		(8)	3			
Increase in accounts payable		(7)	6			
Increase in salaries payable		(9)	2			
Decrease in income tax payable				(11)	2	
Amortization of discount		(10)	2			
Net cash flows						22
Investing activities:						
Purchase of land				(13)	30	
Purchase of S-T investment				(12)	12	
Sale of land		(2)	18			
Sale of equipment		(3)	5			
Net cash flows						(19)
Financing activities:						
Sale of common shares		(17)	26			
Retirement of bonds payable				(15)	15	
Payment of cash dividends				(18)	5	
Net cash flows						6
Net increase in cash				(19)	9	9
Totals			198		198	

ILLUSTRATION 21A–2

Spreadsheet Entries for the Indirect Method

Entry	Account	Debit	Credit
Entry (1)	Net income—CFOA	12	
	Retained earnings		12
	Establishes net income as the initial amount of cash flows from operating activities, to be adjusted to a cash basis by subsequent entries.		
Entry (2)	Cash (received from sale of land)	18	
	Land		10
	Gain on sale of land—CFOA		8
	Deducts the noncash gain added in determining net income, explains a portion of the change in land, and identifies a cash inflow from investing activities.		
Entry (3)	Cash (received from sale of equipment)	5	
	Loss on sale of equipment—CFOA	2	
	Accumulated depreciation	7	
	Buildings and equipment		14
	Adds back the noncash loss subtracted in determining net income, explains portions of the changes in accumulated depreciation and buildings and equipment, and identifies a cash inflow from investing activities.		
Entry (4)	Depreciation expense—CFOA	3	
	Accumulated depreciation		3
	Adds back the noncash expense subtracted in determining net income.		
Entry (5)	Accounts receivable	2	
	Increase in accounts receivable—CFOA		2
	Reduces net income to reflect $98 million cash received from customers rather than $100 million sales.		
Entry (6)	Decrease in inventory—CFOA	4	
	Inventory		4
	Increases net income to reflect a deduction of $56 million cost of goods purchased rather than $60 million cost of goods sold.		
Entry (7)	Increase in accounts payable—CFOA	6	
	Accounts payable		6
	Increases net income to reflect a deduction of $50 million cash paid to suppliers rather than $56 million cost of goods purchased.		
Entry (8)	Decrease in prepaid insurance—CFOA	3	
	Prepaid insurance		3
	Increases net income to reflect a deduction of $4 million cash paid for insurance rather than $7 million insurance expense.		
Entry (9)	Increase in salaries payable—CFOA	2	
	Salaries payable		2
	Increases net income to reflect a deduction of $11 million cash paid to employees rather than $13 million salaries expense.		
Entry (10)	Amortization of discount on bonds—CFOA	2	
	Discount on bonds		2
	Increases net income to reflect a deduction of $3 million cash paid for bond interest rather than $5 million bond interest expense.		
Entry (11)	Income taxes payable	2	
	Decrease in income taxes payable—CFOA		2
	Reduces net income to reflect a deduction of $11 million cash paid for income taxes rather than $9 million income tax expense.		
Entry (12)	Short-term investment	12	
	Cash (purchase of short-term investment)		12
	Explains the increase in the short-term investment account and identifies a cash outflow from investing activities.		
Entry (13)	Land	30	
	Cash (purchase of land)		30
	Explains a portion of the change in the land account and identifies a cash outflow from investing activities.		

(continued)

ILLUSTRATION 21A–2
(concluded)

		Debit	Credit
Entry (14)	Buildings and equipment	20	
	Note payable		20
	Partially explains the changes in the buildings and equipment and notes payable accounts and identifies a noncash investing and financing activity.		
Entry (15)	Bonds payable	15	
	Cash (retirement of bonds payable)		15
	Explains the decrease in the bonds payable account and identifies a cash outflow from financing activities.		
Entry (16)	Retained earnings	13	
	Common stock		10
	Paid-in capital—excess of par		3
	Partially explains the changes in the retained earnings, common stock, and paid-in capital—excess of par accounts.		
Entry (17)	Cash (from sale of common stock)	26	
	Common stock		20
	Paid-in capital—excess of par		6
	Partially explains the changes in the common stock and paid-in capital—excess of par accounts and identifies a cash inflow from financing activities.		
Entry (18)	Retained earnings	5	
	Cash (payment of cash dividends)		5
	Partially explains the change in the retained earnings account and identifies a cash outflow from financing activities.		
Entry (19)	Cash	9	
	Net increase in cash (from statement of cash flows activities)		9
	Reconciles the net increase in cash from operating, investing, and financing activities to the increase in the cash balance.		

(12)–(19) explain the changes in the balance sheet not already accounted for by previous entries, and are identical to entries (12)–(19) recorded using the direct method.

The statement of cash flows presenting net cash flows from operating activities by the indirect method is illustrated in Illustration 21A–3.

ILLUSTRATION 21A–3
Statement of Cash Flows—Indirect Method

All parts of the statement of cash flows except operating activities are precisely the same as in the direct method.

UNITED BRANDS CORPORATION
Statement of Cash Flows
For Year Ended December 31, 2009
($ in millions)

Cash Flows from Operating Activities		
Net income	$12	
Adjustments for noncash effects:		
Gain on sale of land	(8)	
Depreciation expense	3	
Loss on sale of equipment	2	
Increase in accounts receivable	(2)	
Decrease in inventory	4	
Decrease in prepaid insurance	3	
Increase in accounts payable	6	
Increase in salaries payable	2	
Decrease in income tax payable	(2)	
Amortization of discount on bonds	2	
Net cash flows from operating activities		$22
Cash Flows from Investing Activities		
Purchase of land	(30)	
Purchase of short-term investment	(12)	
Sale of land	18	
Sale of equipment	5	
Net cash from investing activities		(19)

(continued)

Cash Flows from Financing Activities		
Sale of common shares	26	
Retirement of bonds payable	(15)	
Payment of cash dividends	(5)	
Net cash flows from financing activities		6
Net increase in cash		9
Cash balance, January 1		20
Cash balance, December 31		$29
Noncash Investing and Financing Activities		
Acquired $20 million of equipment by issuing a 12%, 5-year note		$20

ILLUSTRATION 21A–3 (concluded)

APPENDIX 21B

THE T-ACCOUNT METHOD OF PREPARING THE STATEMENT OF CASH FLOWS

The T-account method serves the same purpose as a spreadsheet in assisting in the preparation of a statement of cash flows.

This chapter demonstrates the use of a spreadsheet to prepare the statement of cash flows. A second systematic approach to the preparation of the statement is referred to as the T-account method. The two methods are identical in concept. Both approaches reconstruct the transactions that caused changes in each account balance during the year, simultaneously identifying the operating, investing, and financing activities to be reported on the statement of cash flows. The form of the two methods differs only by whether the entries for those transactions are recorded on a spreadsheet or in T-accounts. In both cases, entries are recorded until the net change in each account balance has been explained.

Some accountants feel that the T-account method is less time-consuming than preparing a spreadsheet but accomplishes precisely the same goal. Since both methods are simply analytical techniques to assist in statement preparation, the choice is a matter of personal preference. The following five steps outline the T-account method:

1. Draw T-accounts for each income statement and balance sheet account.
2. The T-account for cash should be drawn considerably larger than other T-accounts because more space is required to accommodate the numerous debits and credits to cash. Also, the cash T-account will serve the same purpose as the statement of cash flows section of the spreadsheet in that the formal statement of cash flows is developed from the cash flows reported there. Therefore, it is convenient to partition the cash T-account with headings for "Operating Activities," "Investing Activities," and "Financing Activities" before entries are recorded.
3. Enter each account's net change on the appropriate side (debit or credit) of the uppermost portion of each T-account. These changes will serve as individual check figures for determining whether the increase or decrease in each account balance has been explained. These first three steps establish the basic work form for the T-account method.
4. Reconstruct the transactions that caused changes in each account balance during the year and record the entries for those transactions directly in the T-accounts. Again using UBC as an example, the entries we record in the T-accounts are exactly the same as the spreadsheet entries we created in the chapter when using the spreadsheet method. The analysis we used in creating those spreadsheet entries is equally applicable to the T-account method. For that reason, that analysis is not repeated here. The complete T-account work form for UBC is presented below. Account balance changes are provided by Illustration 21–1.

BALANCE SHEET ACCOUNTS

Cash (statement of cash flows)

		Debit	Credit		
		9			
Operating Activities:					
From customers	(1)	98	50	(4)	To suppliers of goods
From investment revenue	(2)	3	11	(5)	To employees
			3	(7)	For interest
			4	(8)	For insurance
			11	(10)	For income taxes
Investing Activities:					
Sale of land	(3)	18	12	(12)	Purchase of short-term investment
Sale of equipment	(9)	5	30	(13)	Purchase of land
Financing Activities:					
Sale of common stock	(17)	26	15	(15)	Retirement of bonds payable
			5	(18)	Payment of cash dividends

Accounts Receivable

	Debit	Credit	
	2		
(1)	2		

Short-Term Investments

	Debit	Credit	
	12		
(12)	12		

Inventory

	Debit	Credit	
		4	
		4	(4)

Prepaid Insurance

	Debit	Credit	
		3	
		3	(8)

Land

	Debit	Credit	
	20		
(13)	30	10	(3)

Buildings and Equipment

	Debit	Credit	
	6		
X(14)	20	14	(9)

Accumulated Depreciation

	Debit	Credit	
	4		
(9)	7	3	(6)

Accounts Payable

	Debit	Credit	
		6	
		6	(4)

Salaries Payable

	Debit	Credit	
		2	
		2	(5)

Income Tax Payable

	Debit	Credit	
	2		
(10)	2		

Notes Payable

	Debit	Credit	
		20	
		20	(14)X

Bonds Payable

	Debit	Credit	
	15		
(15)	15		

Discount on Bonds

	Debit	Credit	
		2	
		2	(7)

Common Stock

	Debit	Credit	
		30	
		10	(16)
		20	(17)

Paid-in Capital—excess of par

	Debit	Credit	
		9	
		3	(16)
		6	(17)

Retained Earnings

	Debit	Credit	
	6		
(16)	13		
(18)	5	12	(11)

X Noncash Investing and Financing Activity

(continued)

(concluded)

INCOME STATEMENT ACCOUNTS

Sales Revenue

	Debit	Credit	
		100	
		100	(1)

Investment Revenue

	Debit	Credit	
		3	
		3	(2)

Gain on Sale of Land

	Debit	Credit	
		8	
		8	(3)

Cost of Goods Sold

	Debit	Credit
	60	
(4)	60	

Salaries Expense

	Debit	Credit
	13	
(5)	13	

Depreciation Expense

	Debit	Credit
	3	
(6)	3	

Interest Expense

	Debit	Credit
	5	
(7)	5	

Insurance Expense

	Debit	Credit
	7	
(8)	7	

Loss on Sale of Equipment

	Debit	Credit
	2	
(9)	2	

Income Tax Expense

	Debit	Credit
	9	
(10)	9	

Net Income (Income Summary)

	Debit	Credit
	12	
(11)	12	

5. After all account balances have been explained by T-account entries, prepare the statement of cash flows from the cash T-account, being careful also to report noncash investing and financing activities. The statement of cash flows for UBC appears in Graphic 21–2 on page 1110. ●

QUESTIONS FOR REVIEW OF KEY TOPICS

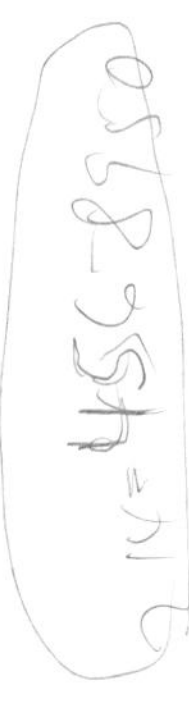

Q 21–1 Effects of all cash flows affect the balances of various accounts reported on the balance sheet. Also, the activities that cause some of these cash flows are reported on the income statement. What, then, is the need for an additional financial statement that reports cash flows?

Q 21–2 The statement of cash flows has been a required financial statement only since 1988. Is cash flow reporting a totally new concept? Explain.

Q 21–3 Is an investment in Treasury bills always classified as a cash equivalent? Explain.

Q 21–4 Transactions that involve merely purchases or sales of cash equivalents generally are not reported on a statement of cash flows. Describe an exception to this generalization. What is the essential characteristic of the transaction that qualifies as an exception?

Q 21–5 What are the differences between cash flows from operating activities and the elements of an income statement?

Q 21–6 Do cash flows from operating activities report all the elements of the income statement on a cash basis? Explain.

Q 21–7 Investing activities include the acquisition and disposition of assets. Provide four specific examples. Identify two exceptions.

Q 21–8 The sale of stock and the sale of bonds are reported as financing activities. Are payments of dividends to shareholders and payments of interest to bondholders also reported as financing activities? Explain.

Q 21–9 Does the statement of cash flows report only transactions that cause an increase or a decrease in cash? Explain.

Q 21–10 How would the acquisition of a building be reported on a statement of cash flows if purchased by issuing a mortgage note payable in addition to a significant cash down payment?

Q 21–11 Perhaps the most noteworthy item reported on an income statement is net income—the amount by which revenues exceed expenses. The most noteworthy item reported on a statement of cash flows is *not* the amount of net cash flows. Explain.

Q 21–12 What is the purpose of the "changes" columns of a spreadsheet to prepare a statement of cash flows?

Q 21–13 Given sales revenue of $200,000, how can it be determined whether or not $200,000 cash was received from customers?

Q 21–14 When an asset is sold at a gain, why is the gain not reported as a cash inflow from operating activities?

Q 21–15 Are ordinary losses and extraordinary losses treated alike in preparing a statement of cash flows? Explain.

Q 21–16 When determining the amount of cash paid for income taxes, what would be indicated by an increase in the deferred income tax liability account?

Q 21–17 When using the indirect method of determining net cash flows from operating activities, how is bad debt expense reported? Why? What other expenses are reported in a like manner?

Q 21–18 When using the indirect method of determining net cash flows from operating activities, how are revenues and expenses reported on the statement of cash flows if their cash effects are identical to the amounts reported on the income statement?

Q 21–19 Why does the FASB recommend the direct method over the indirect method?

Q 21–20 Compare the manner in which investing activities are reported on a statement of cash flows prepared by the direct method and by the indirect method.

BRIEF EXERCISES

BE 21–1
Determine cash received from customers
● LO3

Horton Housewares' accounts receivable decreased during the year by $5 million. What is the amount of cash Horton received from customers during the reporting period if its sales were $33 million? Prepare a summary entry that represents the net effect of the selling and collection activities during the reporting period.

BE 21–2
Determine cash received from customers
● LO3

April Wood Products' accounts receivable increased during the year by $4 million. Its bad debt expense was $2 million, and its allowance for uncollectible accounts increased by $1 million. What is the amount of cash April Wood Products received from customers during the reporting period if its sales were $44 million? Prepare a summary entry that represents the net effect of the selling and collection activities during the reporting period.

BE 21–3
Determine cash paid to suppliers
● LO3

LaRoe Lawns' inventory increased during the year by $6 million. Its accounts payable increased by $5 million during the same period. What is the amount of cash LaRoe paid to suppliers of merchandise during the reporting period if its cost of goods sold was $25 million? Prepare a summary entry that represents the net effect of merchandise purchases during the reporting period.

BE 21–4
Determine cash paid to employees
● LO3

Sherriane Baby Products' salaries expense was $17 million. What is the amount of cash Sherriane paid to employees during the reporting period if its salaries payable increased by $3 million? Prepare a summary entry that represents the net effect of salaries expense incurred and paid during the reporting period.

BE 21–5
Bond interest and discount
● LO3 LO6

Agee Technology, Inc., issued 9% bonds, dated January 1, with a face amount of $400 million on July 1, 2009, at a price of $380 million. For bonds of similar risk and maturity, the market yield is 10%. Interest is paid semiannually on June 30 and December 31. Prepare the journal entry to record interest at December 31. What would be the amount(s) related to the bonds that Agee would report in its statement of cash flows for the year ended December 31, 2009, if it uses the direct method?

BE 21–6
Bond interest and discount
● LO4 LO6

Refer to the situation described in BE 21–5. What would be the amount(s) related to the bonds that Agee would report in its statement of cash flows for the year ended December 31, 2009, if it uses the indirect method**?**

BE 21–7
Installment note
● LO3 LO6

On January 1, 2009, the Merit Group issued to its bank a $41 million, five-year installment note to be paid in five equal payments at the end of each year. Installment payments of $10 million annually include interest at the rate of 7%. What would be the amount(s) related to the note that Merit would report in its statement of cash flows for the year ended December 31, 2009?

BE 21–8
Sale of land
● LO3 LO4 LO5

On July 15, 2009, M.W. Morgan Distribution sold land for $35 million that it had purchased in 2004 for $22 million. What would be the amount(s) related to the sale that Morgan would report in its statement of cash flows for the year ended December 31, 2009, using the direct method? The indirect method?

BE 21–9
Investing activities
● LO5

Carter Containers sold marketable securities, land, and common stock for $30 million, $15 million, and $40 million, respectively. Carter also purchased treasury stock, equipment, and a patent for $21 million, $25 million, and $12 million, respectively. What amount should Carter report as net cash from investing activities?

BE 21–10
Financing activities

● LO6

Refer to the situation described in BE 21–9. What amount should Carter report as net cash from financing activities?

BE 21–11
Indirect method

● LO4

Sheen Awnings reported net income of $90 million. Included in that number were depreciation expense of $3 million and a loss on the sale of equipment of $2 million. Records reveal increases in accounts receivable, accounts payable, and inventory of $1 million, $4 million, and $3 million, respectively. What were Sheen's cash flows from operating activities?

BE 21–12
Indirect method

● LO4

Sunset Acres reported net income of $60 million. Included in that number were trademark amortization expense of $2 million and a gain on the sale of land of $1 million. Records reveal decreases in accounts receivable, accounts payable, and inventory of $2 million, $5 million, and $4 million, respectively. What were Sunset's cash flows from operating activities?

EXERCISES

available with McGraw-Hill's Homework Manager www.mhhe.com/spiceland5e 

An alternate exercise and problem set is available on the text website: www.mhhe.com/spiceland5e

E 21–1
Classification of cash flows

● LO3 through LO6

Listed below are several transactions that typically produce either an increase or a decrease in cash. Indicate by letter whether the cash effect of each transaction is reported on a statement of cash flows as an operating (**O**), investing (**I**), or financing (**F**) activity.

	Transactions
F	1. Sale of common stock
____	2. Sale of land
____	3. Purchase of treasury stock
____	4. Merchandise sales
____	5. Issuance of a long-term note payable
____	6. Purchase of merchandise
____	7. Repayment of note payable
____	8. Employee salaries
____	9. Sale of equipment at a gain
____	10. Issuance of bonds
____	11. Acquisition of bonds of another corporation
____	12. Payment of semiannual interest on bonds payable
____	13. Payment of a cash dividend
____	14. Purchase of a building
____	15. Collection of nontrade note receivable (principal amount)
____	16. Loan to another firm
____	17. Retirement of common stock
____	18. Income taxes
____	19. Issuance of a short-term note payable
____	20. Sale of a copyright

E 21–2
Determine cash paid to suppliers of merchandise

● LO3

Shown below in T-account format are the beginning and ending balances ($ in millions) of both inventory and accounts payable.

Inventory

	Debit	Credit
Beginning balance	90	
Ending balance	93	

Accounts Payable

Debit	Credit	
	14	Beginning balance
	16	Ending balance

Required:
1. Use a T-account analysis to determine the amount of cash paid to suppliers of merchandise during the reporting period if cost of goods sold was $300 million.
2. Prepare a summary entry that represents the net effect of merchandise purchases during the reporting period.

E 21–3
Determine cash received from customers

Determine the amount of cash received from customers for each of the six independent situations below. All dollars are in millions.

● LO3

Situation	Sales Revenue	Accounts Receivable Increase (Decrease)	Bad Debt Expense	Allowance for Uncollectible Accounts Increase (Decrease)	Cash Received from Customers
1	100	–0–	–0–	–0–	?
2	100	5	–0–	–0–	?
3	100	(5)	–0–	–0–	?
4	100	5	2	2	?
5	100	(5)	2	1	?
6	100	5	2	(1)	?

E 21–4
Summary entries for cash received from customers

● LO3

For each of the four independent situations below, prepare journal entries that summarize the selling and collection activities for the reporting period in order to determine the amount of cash received from customers and to explain the change in each account shown. All dollars are in millions.

Situation	Sales Revenue	Accounts Receivable Increase (Decrease)	Bad Debt Expense	Allowance for Uncollectible Accounts Increase (Decrease)	Cash Received from Customers
1	200	–0–	–0–	–0–	?
2	200	10	–0–	–0–	?
3	200	10	4	4	?
4	200	10	4	(2)	?

E 21–5
Determine cash paid to suppliers of merchandise

● LO3

Determine the amount of cash paid to suppliers of merchandise for each of the nine independent situations below. All dollars are in millions.

Situation	Cost of Goods Sold	Inventory Increase (Decrease)	Accounts Payable Increase (Decrease)	Cash Paid to Suppliers
1	100	0	0	?
2	100	3	0	?
3	100	(3)	0	?
4	100	0	7	?
5	100	0	(7)	?
6	100	3	7	?
7	100	3	(7)	?
8	100	(3)	(7)	?
9	100	(3)	7	?

E 21–6
Summary entries for cash paid to suppliers of merchandise

● LO3

For each of the five independent situations below, prepare a journal entry that summarizes the purchases, sales, and payments related to inventories in order to determine the amount of cash paid to suppliers and explain the change in each account shown. All dollars are in millions.

Situation	Cost of Goods Sold	Inventory Increase (Decrease)	Accounts Payable Increase (Decrease)	Cash Paid to Suppliers
1	200	0	0	?
2	200	6	0	?
3	200	0	14	?
4	200	6	14	?
5	200	(6)	(14)	?

E 21–7
Determine cash paid for bond interest

● LO3

Determine the amount of cash paid to bondholders for bond interest for each of the six independent situations below. All dollars are in millions.

Situation	Bond Interest Expense	Bond Interest Payable Increase (Decrease)	Unamortized Discount Increase (Decrease)	Cash Paid for Interest
1	10	0	0	?
2	10	2	0	?
3	10	(2)	0	?
4	10	0	(3)	?
5	10	2	(3)	?
6	10	(2)	(3)	?

E 21–8
Determine cash paid for bond interest

For each of the four independent situations below, prepare a single journal entry that summarizes the recording and payment of interest in order to determine the amount of cash paid for bond interest and explain the change (if any) in each of the accounts shown. All dollars are in millions.

● LO3

Situation	Bond Interest Expense	Bond Interest Payable Increase (Decrease)	Unamortized Discount Increase (Decrease)	Cash Paid for Interest
1	20	0	0	?
2	20	4	0	?
3	20	0	(6)	?
4	20	(4)	(6)	?

E 21–9
Determine cash paid for income taxes

● LO3

Determine the amount of cash paid for income taxes in each of the nine independent situations below. All dollars are in millions.

Situation	Income Tax Expense	Income Tax Payable Increase (Decrease)	Deferred Tax Liability Increase (Decrease)	Cash Paid for Taxes
1	10	0	0	?
2	10	3	0	?
3	10	(3)	0	?
4	10	0	2	?
5	10	0	(2)	?
6	10	3	2	?
7	10	3	(2)	?
8	10	(3)	(2)	?
9	10	(3)	2	?

E 21–10
Summary entries for cash paid for income taxes

● LO3

For each of the five independent situations below, prepare a single journal entry that summarizes the recording and payment of income taxes in order to determine the amount of cash paid for income taxes and explain the change (if any) in each of the accounts shown. All dollars are in millions.

Situation	Income Tax Expense	Income Tax Payable Increase (Decrease)	Deferred Tax Liability Increase (Decrease)	Cash Paid for Taxes
1	10	0	0	?
2	10	3	0	?
3	10	0	(2)	?
4	10	3	2	?
5	10	(3)	(2)	?

E 21–11
Bonds; statement of cash flow effects

● LO3

Most Solutions, Inc., issued 10% bonds, dated January 1, with a face amount of $640 million on January 1, 2009. The bonds mature in 2019 (10 years). For bonds of similar risk and maturity the market yield is 12%. Interest is paid semiannually on June 30 and December 31. Most recorded the sale as follows:

January 1, 2009		
Cash (price)	566,589,440	
Discount on bonds (difference)	73,410,560	
Bonds payable (face amount)		640,000,000

Required:
What would be the amount(s) related to the bonds that Most would report in its statement of cash flows for the year ended December 31, 2009?

E 21–12
Installment note; statement of cash flow effects

● LO3 LO6

National Food Services, Inc., borrowed $4 million from its local bank on January 1, 2009, and issued a 4-year installment note to be paid in four equal payments at the end of each year. The payments include interest at the rate of 10%. Installment payments are $1,261,881 annually.

Required:
What would be the amount(s) related to the note that National would report in its statement of cash flows for the year ended December 31, 2009?

E 21–13
Identifying cash flows from investing activities and financing activities

● LO5 LO6

In preparation for developing its statement of cash flows for the year ended December 31, 2009, RapidPac, Inc., collected the following information:

	($ in millions)
Fair value of shares issued in a stock dividend	$ 65
Payment for the early extinguishment of long-term bonds (carrying amount: $97 million)	102
Proceeds from the sale of treasury stock (cost: $17 million)	22
Gain on sale of land	4

(continued)

(concluded)

Proceeds from sale of land	12
Purchase of Microsoft common stock	160
Declaration of cash dividends	44
Distribution of cash dividends declared in 2008	40

Required:

1. In RapidPac's statement of cash flows, what were net cash inflows (or outflows) from investing activities for 2009?
2. In RapidPac's statement of cash flows, what were net cash inflows (or outflows) from financing activities for 2009?

E 21–14
Identifying cash flows from investing activities and financing activities

● LO5 LO6

In preparation for developing its statement of cash flows for the year ended December 31, 2009, Millennium Solutions, Inc., collected the following information ($ in millions):

Payment for the early extinguishments of long-term notes (book value: $50 million)	$ 54
Sale of common shares	176
Retirement of common shares	122
Loss on sale of equipment	2
Proceeds from sale of equipment	8
Issuance of short-term note payable for cash	10
Acquisition of building for cash	7
Purchase of marketable securities (not a cash equivalent)	5
Purchase of marketable securities (considered a cash equivalent)	1
Cash payment for 3-year insurance policy	3
Collection of note receivable with interest (principal amount, $11)	13
Declaration of cash dividends	33
Distribution of cash dividends declared in 2008	30

Required:

1. In Millennium's statement of cash flows, what were net cash inflows (or outflows) from investing activities for 2009?
2. In Millennium's statement of cash flows, what were net cash inflows (or outflows) from financing activities for 2009?

E 21–15
Capital lease; lessee; statement of cash flows effects

● LO3 LO5 LO6

Wilson Foods Corporation leased a commercial food processor on September 30, 2009. The five-year lease agreement calls for Wilson to make quarterly lease payments of $195,774, payable each September 30, December 31, March 31, June 30, with the first payment at September 30, 2009. Wilson's incremental borrowing rate is 12%. Wilson records depreciation on a straight-line basis at the end of each fiscal year. Wilson recorded the lease as follows:

September 30, 2009		
Leased equipment (calculated below)	3,000,000	
Lease payable (calculated below)		3,000,000
Lease payable	195,774	
Cash (rental payment)		195,774

Calculation of the present value of lease payments

$195,774 × 15.32380* = $3,000,000 (rounded)

*Present value of an annuity due of $1: n = 20, i = 3% (from Table 6)

Required:

What would be the pretax amounts related to the lease that Wilson would report in its statement of cash flows for the year ended December 31, 2009?

E 21–16
Equity method investment; statement of cash flow effects

● LO3 LO5

On January 1, 2009, Beilich Enterprises bought 20% of the outstanding common stock of Wolfe Construction Company for $600 million cash. Wolfe's net income for the year ended December 31, 2009, was $300 million. During 2009, Wolfe declared and paid cash dividends of $60 million. Beilich recorded the investment as follows:

	($ in millions)	
Purchase		
Investment in Wolfe Construction shares	600	
Cash		600
Net income		
Investment in Wolfe Construction shares (20% × $300 million)	60	
Investment revenue		60
Dividends		
Cash (20% × $60 million)	12	
Investment in Wolfe Construction shares		12

Required:
What would be the pretax amounts related to the investment that Beilich would report in its statement of cash flows for the year ended December 31, 2009?

E 21–17
Indirect method; reconciliation of net income to net cash flows from operating activities

● LO4

The accounting records of EZ Company provided the data below. Prepare a reconciliation of net income to net cash flows from operating activities.

Net income	$50,000
Depreciation expense	7,000
Increase in inventory	1,500
Decrease in salaries payable	800
Decrease in accounts receivable	2,000
Amortization of patent	500
Amortization of premium on bonds	1,000
Increase in accounts payable	4,000
Cash dividends	12,000

E 21–18
Spreadsheet entries from statement of retained earnings

● LO3 through LO8

The statement of retained earnings of Gary Larson Publishers is presented below.

GARY LARSON PUBLISHERS
Statement of Retained Earnings
For the Year Ended December 31, 2009
($ in millions)

Retained earnings, January 1		$200
Add:	Net income	75
Deduct:	Cash dividend	(25)
	Stock dividend (1 million shares of $1 par common stock)	(16)
	Property dividend (Garfield Company preferred stock held as a short-term investment)	(12)
	Sale of treasury stock (cost $53 million)	(10)
Retained earnings, December 31		$212

Required:
For the transactions that affected Larson's retained earnings, reconstruct the journal entries for the transactions that affected retained earnings and that can be used to determine cash flows to be reported in a statement of cash flows. Also indicate any investing and financing activities you identify from this analysis that should be reported on the statement of cash flows.

E 21–19
Relationship between the income statement and cash flows from operating activities (direct method and indirect method)

● LO3 LO4

The following schedule relates the income statement with cash flows from operating activities, derived by both the direct and indirect methods, in the format illustrated by Graphic 21–10 in the chapter. The amounts for income statement elements are missing.

Income Statement		Cash Flows from Operating Activities: Indirect Method		Direct Method	
		Net income	$?		
		Adjustments:			
Sales	$?	Decrease in accounts receivable	12	Cash received from customers	$612
Cost of goods sold	?	Increase in inventory	(24)		
		Decrease in accounts payable	(36)	Cash paid to suppliers	(420)
Salaries expense	?	Increase in salaries payable	12	Cash paid to employees	(66)
Depreciation expense	?	Depreciation expense	18	(Not reported—no cash effect)	
Insurance expense	?	Decrease in prepaid insurance	18	Cash paid for insurance	(24)
Loss on sale of land	?	Loss on sale of land	12	(Not reported—no cash effect)	
Income tax expense	?	Increase in income tax payable	12	Cash paid for income taxes	(42)
Net income	$?	**Net cash flows from operating activities**	$60	**Net cash flows from operating activities**	$ 60

Required:
Deduce the missing amounts and prepare the income statement.

E 21–20
Reconciliation of net cash flows from operating activities to net income

● LO3 LO4

The income statement and the cash flows from the operating activities section of the statement of cash flows are provided below for Syntric Company. The merchandise inventory account balance neither increased nor decreased during the reporting period. Syntric had no liability for either insurance, deferred income taxes, or interest at any time during the period.

SYNTRIC COMPANY
Income Statement
For the Year Ended December 31, 2009
($ in 000s)

Sales		$312
Cost of goods sold		(188)
Gross margin		124
Salaries expense	$41	
Insurance expense	22	
Depreciation expense	11	
Depletion expense	5	
Bond interest expense	10	(89)
Gains and losses:		
Gain on sale of equipment		25
Loss on sale of land		(8)
Income before tax		52
Income tax expense		(26)
Net income		$ 26
Cash Flows from Operating Activities:		
Cash received from customers		$258
Cash paid to suppliers		(175)
Cash paid to employees		(37)
Cash paid for interest		(9)
Cash paid for insurance		(16)
Cash paid for income taxes		(14)
Net cash flows from operating activities		$ 7

Required:
Prepare a schedule to reconcile net income to net cash flows from operating activities.

E 21–21
Cash flows from operating activities (direct method) derived from an income statement and cash flows from operating activities (indirect method)

● LO3 LO4

The income statement and a schedule reconciling cash flows from operating activities to net income are provided below ($ in 000s) for Peach Computers.

PEACH COMPUTERS
Income Statement
For the Year Ended December 31, 2009

Sales		$305
Cost of goods sold		(185)
Gross margin		120
Salaries expense	$41	
Insurance expense	19	
Depreciation expense	11	
Loss on sale of land	5	76
Income before tax		44
Income tax expense		(22)
Net income		$ 22

Reconciliation of Net Income
To Net Cash Flows from Operating Activities

Net income	$22
Adjustments for Noncash Effects	
Depreciation expense	11
Loss on sale of land	5
Changes in operating assets and liabilities:	
Decrease in accounts receivable	6
Increase in inventory	(13)
Decrease in accounts payable	(8)
Increase in salaries payable	5
Decrease in prepaid insurance	9
Increase in income tax payable	20
Net cash flows from operating activities	$57

Required:
1. Calculate each of the following amounts for Peach Computers:
   a. Cash received from customers during the reporting period.
   b. Cash paid to suppliers of goods during the reporting period.
   c. Cash paid to employees during the reporting period.

d. Cash paid for insurance during the reporting period.
e. Cash paid for income taxes during the reporting period.

2. Prepare the cash flows from operating activities section of the statement of cash flows (direct method).

E 21–22
Indirect method; reconciliation of net income to net cash flows from operating activities

● LO4

The accounting records of Baddour Company provided the data below. Prepare a reconciliation of net income to net cash flows from operating activities.

Net loss	$5,000
Depreciation expense	6,000
Increase in salaries payable	500
Decrease in accounts receivable	2,000
Increase in inventory	2,300
Amortization of patent	300
Reduction in discount on bonds	200

E 21–23
Cash flows from operating activities (direct method)— includes loss on sale of cash equivalents and extraordinary loss

● LO3

Portions of the financial statements for Myriad Products are provided below.

MYRIAD PRODUCTS COMPANY
Income Statement
For the Year Ended December 31, 2009
($ in millions)

Sales		$660
Cost of goods sold		(250)
Gross margin		410
Salaries expense	$110	
Depreciation expense	90	
Patent amortization expense	5	
Interest expense	20	
Loss on sale of cash equivalents	3	(228)
Income before taxes and extraordinary loss		182
Income tax expense		(91)
Income before extraordinary loss		91
Extraordinary loss (earthquake)	10	
Less: Tax savings	(5)	(5)
Net Income		$86

MYRIAD PRODUCTS COMPANY
Selected Accounts from Comparative Balance Sheets
December 31, 2009 and 2008
($ in millions)

	Year		
	2009	2008	Change
Cash	$102	$100	$ 2
Accounts receivable	220	232	(12)
Inventory	440	450	(10)
Accounts payable	140	134	6
Salaries payable	80	86	(6)
Interest payable	25	20	5
Income taxes payable	15	10	5

Required:
Prepare the cash flows from operating activities section of the statement of cash flows for Myriad Products Company using the *direct method.*

E 21–24
Cash flows from operating activities (indirect method) includes loss on sale of cash equivalents and extraordinary loss

● LO4

Refer to the data provided in the previous exercise for Myriad Products Company.

Required:
Prepare the cash flows from operating activities section of the statement of cash flows for Myriad Products Company using the *indirect method.*

E 21–25
Cash flows from operating activities (direct method)—includes loss on sale of cash equivalents and extraordinary gain

● LO3

Portions of the financial statements for Clear Transmissions Company are provided below.

CLEAR TRANSMISSIONS COMPANY
Income Statement
For the Year Ended December 31, 2009 ($ in 000s)

Sales		$1,320
Cost of goods sold		(500)
Gross margin		820
Salaries expense	$220	
Depreciation expense	180	
Patent amortization expense	10	
Interest expense	40	
Loss on sale of cash equivalents	6	(456)
Income before taxes and extraordinary gain		364
Income tax expense		(182)
Income before extraordinary gain		182
Extraordinary gain (sale of subsidiary)	20	
Less: Tax on gain	(10)	10
Net Income		$ 192

CLEAR TRANSMISSIONS COMPANY
Selected Accounts from Comparative Balance Sheets
December 31, 2009 and 2008 ($ in 000s)

	Year		
	2009	2008	Change
Cash	$102	$100	$ 2
Accounts receivable	220	232	(12)
Inventory	440	450	(10)
Accounts payable	140	134	6
Salaries payable	80	86	(6)
Interest payable	25	20	5
Income taxes payable	15	10	5

Required:
Prepare the cash flows from operating activities section of the statement of cash flows for Clear Transmissions Company using the *direct method.*

E 21–26
Cash flows from operating activities (indirect method)— includes loss on sale of cash equivalents and extraordinary gain

● LO4

Refer to the data provided in the previous exercise for Clear Transmissions Company.

Required:
Prepare the cash flows from operating activities section of the statement of cash flows for Clear Transmissions Company using the *indirect method.*

E 21–27
Statement of cash flows; direct method

● LO3 LO5 LO6 LO8

Comparative balance sheets for 2009 and 2008, a statement of income for 2009, and additional information from the accounting records of Red, Inc., are provided below.

RED, INC.
Comparative Balance Sheets
December 31, 2009 and 2008 ($ in millions)

	2009	2008
Assets		
Cash	$ 24	$110
Accounts receivable	178	132
Prepaid insurance	7	3
Inventory	285	175
Buildings and equipment	400	350
Less: Accumulated depreciation	(119)	(240)
	$775	$530

(continued)

(concluded)

Liabilities		
Accounts payable	$ 87	$100
Accrued expenses payable	6	11
Notes payable	50	0
Bonds payable	160	0
Shareholders' Equity		
Common stock	400	400
Retained earnings	72	19
	$775	$530

RED, INC.
Statement of Income
For Year Ended December 31, 2009 ($ in millions)

Revenues		
Sales revenue		$2,000
Expenses		
Cost of goods sold	$1,400	
Depreciation expense	50	
Operating expenses	447	1,897
Net income		$ 103

Additional information from the accounting records:

a. During 2009, $230 million of equipment was purchased to replace $180 million of equipment (95% depreciated) sold at book value.

b. In order to maintain the usual policy of paying cash dividends of $50 million, it was necessary for Red to borrow $50 million from its bank.

Required:

Prepare the statement of cash flows of Red, Inc., for the year ended December 31, 2009. Present cash flows from operating activities by the direct method. (You may omit the schedule to reconcile net income with cash flows from operating activities.)

E 21–28
Pension plan funding

● LO3

Mayer Corporation has a defined benefit pension plan. Mayer's policy is to fund the plan annually, cash payments being made at the end of each year. Data relating to the pension plan for 2009 are as follows:

	December 31 ($ in millions)	
	2009	**2008**
Plan assets	$1,080	$900
Net Pension Expense for 2009:		
Service cost	$ 112	
Interest cost (6% × $850)	51	
Actual return on the plan assets (11% × $900 = $99)		
Adjusted for: $9 gain on the plan assets*	(90)	
Amortization of prior service cost	8	
Amortization of net loss	1	
	$ 82	

*(11% × $900) – (10% × $900)

Required:

Recreate the journal entries used to record Mayer's 2009 pension expense, gain on plan assets, and funding of plan assets in order to determine the cash paid to the pension trustee as reported in the statement of cash flows.

E 21–29
Statement of cash flows; indirect method

● LO4 LO5 LO6 LO8

Refer to the data provided in Exercise 21–27 for Red, Inc.

Required:

Prepare the statement of cash flows for Red, Inc., using the indirect method to report operating activities.

E 21–30
Statement of cash flows; T-account method

● LO8
Appendix B

Refer to the data provided in Exercise 21–27 for Red, Inc.

Required:

Prepare the statement of cash flows (direct method) for Red, Inc. Use the T-account method to assist in your analysis.

CPA AND CMA REVIEW QUESTIONS

CPA Exam Questions

The following questions are used in the Kaplan CPA Review Course to study the statement of cash flows while preparing for the CPA examination. Determine the response that best completes the statements or questions.

SCHWESER

● LO3

1. In a statement of cash flows in which operating activities are reported by the direct method, which of the following would increase reported cash flows from operating activities?
   a. Gain on sale of land.
   b. Interest revenue.
   c. Gain on early extinguishment of bonds.
   d. Proceeds from sale of equipment.

2. During 2009, TEL Company engaged in the following activities:

Distribution of cash dividends declared in 2008	$ 24
Fair value of shares issued in a stock dividend	110
Payment to retire bonds	226
Proceeds from the sale of treasury stock (cost: $26)	30

   In TEL's statement of cash flows, what were net cash outflows from financing activities for 2009?
   a. $196
   b. $220
   c. $280
   d. $366

● LO4

3. SOL Company reported net income for 2009 in the amount of $200,000. The company's financial statements also included the following:

Increase in accounts receivable	$ 40,000
Decrease in inventory	30,000
Increase in accounts payable	100,000
Depreciation expense	52,000
Gain on sale of land	74,000

   What is net cash provided by operating activities under the indirect method?
   a. $216,000
   b. $268,000
   c. $290,000
   d. $416,000

● LO3

4. Which of the following does *not* represent a cash flow relating to operating activities?
   a. Dividends paid to stockholders.
   b. Cash received from customers.
   c. Interest paid to bondholders.
   d. Cash paid for salaries.

● LO5

5. Which of the following would *not* be a component of cash flows from investing activities?
   a. Sale of land.
   b. Purchase of securities.
   c. Purchase of equipment.
   d. Dividends paid.

● LO4

6. An analyst compiled the following information for Universe, Inc., for the year ended December 31, 2009:
   - Net income was $850,000.
   - Depreciation expense was $200,000.
   - Interest paid was $100,000.
   - Income taxes paid were $50,000.

- Common stock was sold for $100,000.
- Preferred stock (8% annual dividend) was sold at par value of $125,000.
- Common stock dividends of $25,000 were paid.
- Preferred stock dividends of $10,000 were paid.
- Equipment with a book value of $50,000 was sold for $100,000.

Using the indirect method, what was Universe, Inc.'s net cash flow from operating activities for the year ended December 31, 2009?

a. $1,000,000
b. $1,015,000
c. $1,040,000
d. $1,050,000

CMA Exam Questions

The following questions dealing with the statement of cash flows are adapted from questions that previously appeared on Certified Management Accountant (CMA) examinations. The CMA designation sponsored by the Institute of Management Accountants (www.imanet.org) provides members with an objective measure of knowledge and competence in the field of management accounting. Determine the response that best completes the statements or questions.

● LO3

1. When preparing the statement of cash flows, companies are required to report separately as operating cash flows all of the following except
   a. interest received on investments in bonds.
   b. interest paid on the company's bonds.
   c. cash collected from customers.
   d. cash dividends paid on the company's stock.

● LO5 LO6

2. The following information was taken from the accounting records of Oak Corporation for the year ended December 31:

Proceeds from issuance of preferred stock	$4,000,000
Dividends paid on preferred stock	400,000
Bonds payable converted to common stock	2,000,000
Payment for purchase of machinery	500,000
Proceeds from sale of plant building	1,200,000
2% stock dividend on common stock	300,000
Gain on sale of plant building	200,000

   The net cash flows from investing and financing activities that should be presented on Oak's statement of cash flows for the year ended December 31 are, respectively
   a. $700,000 and $3,600,000.
   b. $700,000 and $3,900,000.
   c. $900,000 and $3,900,000.
   d. $900,000 and $3,600,000.

● LO5

3. The net income for Cypress Inc. was $3,000,000 for the year ended December 31. Additional information is as follows:

Depreciation on fixed assets	$1,500,000
Gain from cash sale of land	200,000
Increase in accounts payable	300,000
Dividends paid on preferred stock	400,000

   The net cash provided by operating activities in the statement of cash flows for the year ended December 31 should be
   a. $4,200,000.
   b. $4,500,000.
   c. $4,600,000.
   d. $4,800,000.

PROBLEMS

available with McGraw-Hill's Homework Manager www.mhhe.com/spiceland5e

An alternate exercise and problem set is available on the text website: www.mhhe.com/spiceland5e

P 21–1
Classification of cash flows from investing and financing activities

● LO2 LO5 through LO7

Listed below are transactions that might be reported as investing and/or financing activities on a statement of cash flows. Possible reporting classifications of those transactions are provided also.

Required:

Indicate the reporting classification of each transaction by entering the appropriate classification code.

Classifications	
+I	Investing activity (cash inflow)
−I	Investing activity (cash outflow)
+F	Financing activity (cash inflow)
−F	Financing activity (cash outflow)
N	Noncash investing and financing activity
X	Not reported as an investing and/or a financing activity

Transactions

Example _+I_ 1. Sale of land.

____ 2. Issuance of common stock for cash.
____ 3. Purchase of treasury stock.
____ 4. Conversion of bonds payable to common stock.
____ 5. Lease of equipment by capital lease.
____ 6. Sale of patent.
____ 7. Acquisition of building for cash.
____ 8. Issuance of common stock for land.
____ 9. Collection of note receivable (principal amount).
____ 10. Issuance of bonds.
____ 11. Issuance of stock dividend.
____ 12. Payment of property dividend.
____ 13. Payment of cash dividends.
____ 14. Issuance of short-term note payable for cash.
____ 15. Issuance of long-term note payable for cash.
____ 16. Purchase of marketable securities ("avaible for sale").
____ 17. Payment of note payable.
____ 18. Cash payment for 5-year insurance policy.
____ 19. Sale of equipment.
____ 20. Issuance of note payable for equipment.
____ 21. Acquisition of common stock of another corporation.
____ 22. Repayment of long-term debt by issuing common stock.
____ 23. Appropriation of retained earnings for plant expansion.
____ 24. Payment of semiannual interest on bonds payable.
____ 25. Retirement of preferred stock.
____ 26. Loan to another firm.
____ 27. Sale of inventory to customers.
____ 28. Purchase of marketable securities (cash equivalents).

P 21–2
Statement of cash flows; direct method

● LO3 LO8

The comparative balance sheets for 2009 and 2008 and the statement of income for 2009 are given below for Wright Company. Additional information from Wright's accounting records is provided also.

WRIGHT COMPANY
Comparative Balance Sheets
December 31, 2009 and 2008
($ in 000s)

	2009	2008
Assets		
Cash	$ 42	$ 30
Accounts receivable	73	75
Short-term investment	40	15
Inventory	75	70
Land	50	60
Buildings and equipment	550	400
Less: Accumulated depreciation	(115)	(75)
	$ 715	$575

(continued)

(concluded)

Liabilities		
Accounts payable	$ 28	$ 35
Salaries payable	2	5
Interest payable	5	3
Income tax payable	9	12
Notes payable	0	30
Bonds payable	160	100
Shareholders' Equity		
Common stock	250	200
Paid-in capital—excess of par	126	100
Retained earnings	135	90
	$ 715	$575

WRIGHT COMPANY
Income Statement
For Year Ended December 31, 2009
($ in 000s)

Revenues		
Sales revenue		$380
Expenses		
Cost of goods sold	$130	
Salaries expense	45	
Depreciation expense	40	
Interest expense	12	
Loss on sale of land	3	
Income tax expense	70	300
Net income		$ 80

Additional information from the accounting records:

a. Land that originally cost $10,000 was sold for $7,000.
b. The common stock of Microsoft Corporation was purchased for $25,000 as a short-term investment not classified as a cash equivalent.
c. New equipment was purchased for $150,000 cash.
d. A $30,000 note was paid at maturity on January 1.
e. On January 1, 2009, $60,000 of bonds were sold at face value.
f. Common stock ($50,000 par) was sold for $76,000.
g. Net income was $80,000 and cash dividends of $35,000 were paid to shareholders.

Required:
Prepare the statement of cash flows of Wright Company for the year ended December 31, 2009. Present cash flows from operating activities by the direct method. (You may omit the schedule to reconcile net income with cash flows from operating activities.)

P 21–3
Statement of cash flows; direct method

● LO3 LO8

The comparative balance sheets for 2009 and 2008 and the statement of income for 2009 are given below for National Intercable Company. Additional information from NIC's accounting records is provided also.

NATIONAL INTERCABLE COMPANY
Comparative Balance Sheets
December 31, 2009 and 2008
($ in millions)

	2009	2008
Assets		
Cash	$ 72	$ 55
Accounts receivable	181	170
Less: Allowance for uncollectible accounts	(8)	(6)
Prepaid insurance	7	12
Inventory	170	165
Long-term investment	66	90
Land	150	150
Buildings and equipment	290	270
Less: Accumulated depreciation	(85)	(75)
Trademark	24	25
	$867	$856

(continued)

(concluded)

Liabilities		
Accounts payable	$ 30	$ 45
Salaries payable	3	8
Deferred income tax liability	18	15
Lease liability	80	0
Bonds payable	145	275
Less: Discount on bonds	(22)	(25)
Shareholders' Equity		
Common stock	310	290
Paid-in capital—excess of par	95	85
Preferred stock	50	0
Retained earnings	158	163
	$867	$856

NATIONAL INTERCABLE COMPANY
Income Statement
For Year Ended December 31, 2009
($ in millions)

Revenues		
Sales revenue	$320	
Investment revenue	15	
Gain on sale of investments	5	$ 340
Expenses		
Cost of goods sold	125	
Salaries expense	55	
Depreciation expense	25	
Trademark amortization expense	1	
Bad debt expense	7	
Insurance expense	13	
Bond interest expense	30	(256)
Income before tax and extraordinary items		84
Income tax expense		(38)
Income before extraordinary items		46
Extraordinary loss (tornado)	42	
Less: Tax savings	(21)	(21)
Net income		$ 25

Additional information from the accounting records:

a. During 2009, $5 million of customer accounts were written off as uncollectible.

b. Investment revenue includes National Intercable Company's $6 million share of the net income of Central Fiber Optics Corporation, an equity method investee.

c. A long-term investment in bonds, originally purchased for $30 million, was sold for $35 million.

d. Pretax accounting income exceeded taxable income causing the deferred income tax liability to increase by $3 million.

e. A building that originally cost $60 million, and which was one-fourth depreciated, was destroyed by a tornado. Some undamaged parts were sold for $3 million.

f. A building was acquired by a seven-year capital lease; present value of lease payments, $80 million.

g. $130 million of bonds were retired at maturity.

h. $20 million par value of common stock was sold for $30 million, and $50 million of preferred stock was sold at par.

i. Shareholders were paid cash dividends of $30 million.

Required:

1. Prepare a spreadsheet for preparation of the statement of cash flows (direct method) of National Intercable Company for the year ended December 31, 2009.
2. Prepare the statement of cash flows. (A reconciliation schedule is not required.)

P 21–4
Statement of cash flows; direct method

● LO3 LO8

The comparative balance sheets for 2009 and 2008 and the statement of income for 2009 are given below for Dux Company. Additional information from Dux's accounting records is provided also.

DUX COMPANY
Comparative Balance Sheets
December 31, 2009 and 2008
($ in 000s)

	2009	2008
Assets		
Cash	$ 33	$ 20
Accounts receivable	48	50
Less: Allowance for uncollectible accounts	(4)	(3)
Dividends receivable	3	2
Inventory	55	50
Long-term investment	15	10
Land	70	40
Buildings and equipment	225	250
Less: Accumulated depreciation	(25)	(50)
	$420	$369
Liabilities		
Accounts payable	$ 13	$ 20
Salaries payable	2	5
Interest payable	4	2
Income tax payable	7	8
Notes payable	30	0
Bonds payable	95	70
Less: Discount on bonds	(2)	(3)
Shareholders' Equity		
Common stock	210	200
Paid-in capital—excess of par	24	20
Retained earnings	45	47
Less: Treasury stock	(8)	0
	$420	$369

DUX COMPANY
Income Statement
For the Year Ended December 31, 2009
($ in 000s)

Revenues		
Sales revenue	$200	
Dividend revenue	3	$203
Expenses		
Cost of goods sold	120	
Salaries expense	25	
Depreciation expense	5	
Bad debt expense	1	
Interest expense	8	
Loss on sale of building	3	
Income tax expense	16	178
Net income		$ 25

Additional information from the accounting records:

a. A building that originally cost $40,000, and which was three-fourths depreciated, was sold for $7,000.
b. The common stock of Byrd Corporation was purchased for $5,000 as a long-term investment.
c. Property was acquired by issuing a 13%, seven-year, $30,000 note payable to the seller.
d. New equipment was purchased for $15,000 cash.
e. On January 1, 2009, $25,000 of bonds were sold at face value.
f. On January 19, Dux issued a 5% stock dividend (1,000 shares). The market price of the $10 par value common stock was $14 per share at that time.

g. Cash dividends of $13,000 were paid to shareholders.

h. On November 12, 500 shares of common stock were repurchased as treasury stock at a cost of $8,000. Dux uses the cost method to account for treasury stock.

Required:

Prepare the statement of cash flows of Dux Company for the year ended December 31, 2009. Present cash flows from operating activities by the direct method. (You may omit the schedule to reconcile net income with cash flows from operating activities.)

P 21–5
Statement of cash flows; direct method

● LO3 LO8

Comparative balance sheets for 2009 and 2008 and a statement of income for 2009 are given below for Metagrobolize Industries. Additional information from the accounting records of Metagrobolize also is provided.

METAGROBOLIZE INDUSTRIES
Comparative Balance Sheets
December 31, 2009 and 2008
($ in 000s)

	2009	2008
Assets		
Cash	$ 600	$ 375
Accounts receivable	600	450
Inventory	900	525
Land	675	600
Building	900	900
Less: Accumulated depreciation	(300)	(270)
Equipment	2,850	2,250
Less: Accumulated depreciation	(525)	(480)
Patent	1,200	1,500
	$6,900	$5,850
Liabilities		
Accounts payable	$ 750	$ 450
Accrued expenses payable	300	225
Lease liability—land	150	0
Shareholders' Equity		
Common stock	3,150	3,000
Paid-in capital—excess of par	750	675
Retained earnings	1,800	1,500
	$6,900	$5,850

METAGROBOLIZE INDUSTRIES
Income Statement
For the Year Ended December 31, 2009
($ in 000s)

Revenues		
Sales revenue	$2,645	
Gain on sale of land	90	$2,735
Expenses		
Cost of goods sold	$ 600	
Depreciation expense—building	30	
Depreciation expense—equipment	315	
Loss on sale of equipment	15	
Amortization of patent	300	
Operating expenses	500	1,760
Net income		$ 975

Additional information from the accounting records:

a. During 2009, equipment with a cost of $300,000 (90% depreciated) was sold.

b. The statement of retained earnings reveals reductions of $225,000 and $450,000 for stock dividends and cash dividends, respectively.

Required:

Prepare the statement of cash flows of Metagrobolize for the year ended December 31, 2009. Present cash flows from operating activities by the direct method. (You may omit the schedule to reconcile net income with cash flows from operating activities.)

P 21–6
Cash flows from operating activities (direct method) derived from an income statement and cash flows from operating activities (indirect method)

● LO3 LO4

The income statement and a schedule reconciling cash flows from operating activities to net income are provided below ($ in millions) for Mike Roe Computers.

MIKE ROE COMPUTERS
Income Statement
For the Year Ended December 31, 2009

Sales		$150
Cost of goods sold		(90)
Gross margin		60
Salaries expense	$20	
Insurance expense	10	
Depreciation expense	5	
Bad debt expense	2	
Interest expense	6	(43)
Gains and losses:		
Gain on sale of equipment		12
Loss on sale of land		(3)
Income before tax		26
Income tax expense		(13)
Net income		$ 13

Reconciliation of Net Income to Net Cash Flows from Operating Activities

Net income	$13
Adjustments for noncash effects:	
Decrease in accounts receivable	3
Gain on sale of equipment	(12)
Increase in inventory	(6)
Increase in accounts payable	9
Increase in salaries payable	3
Depreciation expense	5
Increase in allowance for uncoll.	2
Decrease in bond discount	3
Decrease in prepaid insurance	2
Loss on sale of land	3
Increase in income tax payable	6
Net cash flows from operating activities	$31

Required:
1. Calculate each of the following amounts for Mike Roe Computers:
   a. Cash received from customers during the reporting period.
   b. Cash paid to suppliers of goods during the reporting period.
   c. Cash paid to employees during the reporting period.
   d. Cash paid for interest during the reporting period.
   e. Cash paid for insurance during the reporting period.
   f. Cash paid for income taxes during the reporting period.
2. Prepare the cash flows from operating activities section of the statement of cash flows (direct method).

P 21–7
Cash flows from operating activities (direct method) derived from an income statement and cash flows from operating activities (indirect method)

● LO3 LO4

The income statement and a schedule reconciling cash flows from operating activities to net income are provided below for Macrosoft Corporation.

MACROSOFT CORPORATION
Income Statement
For the Year Ended December 31, 2009
($ in millions)

Sales		$310
Cost of goods sold		(120)
Gross margin		$190
Salaries expense	$40	
Insurance expense	20	
Depreciation expense	10	
Patent amortization expense	4	
Interest expense	12	(86)
Loss on sale of land		(6)
Gain on sale of cash equivalents		2
Income before taxes and extraordinary gain		100
Income tax expense		(50)
Income before extraordinary gain		50
Extraordinary gain (sale of subsidiary)	24	
Less: Tax on gain	(12)	12
Net income		$ 62

Reconciliation of Net Income to Net Cash Flows from Operating Activities

Net income	$62
Adjustments for noncash effects:	
Depreciation expense	10
Patent amortization expense	4
Loss on sale of land	6
Extraordinary gain (sale of subsidiary)	(24)
Decrease in accounts receivable	6
Increase in inventory	(12)
Increase in accounts payable	18
Decrease in bond discount	1
Increase in salaries payable	6
Decrease in prepaid insurance	4
Increase in income tax payable	10
Net cash flows from operating activities	$91

Required:
Prepare the cash flows from operating activities section of the statement of cash flows (direct method).

P 21–8
Cash flows from operating activities (direct method and indirect method)—deferred income tax liability and amortization of bond discount

● LO3 LO4

Portions of the financial statements for Parnell Company are provided below.

PARNELL COMPANY
Income Statement
For the Year Ended December 31, 2009
($ in 000s)

Sales		$ 800
Cost of goods sold		(300)
Gross margin		500
Salaries expense	$120	
Insurance expense	40	
Depreciation expense	123	
Interest expense	50	(333)
Gains and losses:		
Gain on sale of buildings		11
Loss on sale of machinery		(12)
Income before tax		166
Income tax expense		(78)
Net income		$ 88

PARNELL COMPANY
Selected Accounts from Comparative Balance Sheets
December 31, 2009 and 2008
($ in 000s)

	Year		
	2009	2008	Change
Cash	$134	$100	$ 34
Accounts receivable	324	216	108
Inventory	321	425	(104)
Prepaid insurance	66	88	(22)
Accounts payable	210	117	93
Salaries payable	102	93	9
Deferred income tax liability	60	52	8
Bond discount	190	200	(10)

Required:

1. Prepare the cash flows from operating activities section of the statement of cash flows for Parnell Company using the direct method.
2. Prepare the cash flows from operating activities section of the statement of cash flows for Parnell Company using the indirect method.

P 21–9
Cash flows from operating activities (direct method and indirect method)—gain on sale of cash equivalents and extraordinary loss

● LO3 LO4

Portions of the financial statements for Hawkeye Company are provided below.

HAWKEYE COMPANY
Income Statement
For the Year Ended December 31, 2009

Sales		$900
Cost of goods sold		(350)
Gross margin		550
Salaries expense	$220	
Depreciation expense	190	
Bad debt expense	12	
Interest expense	40	
Gain on sale of cash equivalents	(4)	(458)
Income before taxes and extraordinary loss		92
Income tax expense		(46)
Income before extraordinary loss		46
Extraordinary loss (flood damage)	12	
Less: Tax savings	(6)	(6)
Net Income		$ 40

(continued)

(concluded)

HAWKEYE COMPANY
Selected Accounts from Comparative Balance Sheets
December 31, 2009 and 2008

	Year		
	2009	2008	Change
Cash	$212	$200	$ 12
Accounts receivable	418	432	(14)
Allowance for uncollectibles	23	11	12
Inventory	860	850	10
Accounts payable	210	234	(24)
Salaries payable	180	188	(8)
Interest payable	55	50	5
Income taxes payable	90	104	(14)

Required:

1. Prepare the cash flows from operating activities section of the statement of cash flows for Hawkeye Company using the direct method.
2. Prepare the cash flows from operating activities section of the statement of cash flows for Hawkeye Company using the indirect method.

P 21–10
Relationship between the income statement and cash flows from operating activities (direct method and indirect method)

● LO3 LO4

The following schedule relates the income statement with cash flows from operating activities, derived by both the direct and indirect methods, in the format illustrated by Graphic 21–10 in the chapter. Some elements necessary to complete the schedule are missing.

Cash Flows from Operating Activities

Income Statement		Indirect Method		Direct Method	
		Net income	$?		
		Adjustments:			
Sales	$300	Decrease in accounts receivable	6	Cash received from customers	$?
Gain on sale of equipment	24	Gain on sale of equipment	(24)	(Not reported—no cash effect)	
		Increase in inventory	(12)		
Cost of goods sold	(?)	Increase in accounts payable	18	Cash paid to suppliers	(174)
Salaries expense	(39)	? in salaries payable	6	Cash paid to employees	(33)
Depreciation expense	(9)	Depreciation expense	9	Cash paid for depreciation	?
Bad debt expense	(3)	Bad debt expense	3	(Not reported—no cash effect)	
Interest expense	(?)	Decrease in bond discount	3	Cash paid for interest	(9)
Insurance expense	(21)	Decrease in prepaid insurance	9	Cash paid for insurance	(?)
Loss on sale of land	(6)	Loss on sale of land	6	(Not reported—no cash effect)	
Income tax expense	(27)	Increase in income tax payable	?	Cash paid for income taxes	(21)
Net Income	$?	**Net cash flows from operating activities**	$ 57	**Net cash flows from operating activities**	**$ 57**

Required:

Complete the schedule by determining each of the following missing elements:

1. Cash received from customers
2. Cost of goods sold
3. ? in salaries payable (Increase? or decrease?)
4. Cash paid for depreciation
5. Interest expense
6. Cash paid for insurance
7. Increase in income tax payable
8. Net income

P 21–11
Prepare a statement of cash flows; direct method

● LO3 LO8

The comparative balance sheets for 2009 and 2008 and the income statement for 2009 are given below for Arduous Company. Additional information from Arduous's accounting records is provided also.

ARDUOUS COMPANY
Comparative Balance Sheets
December 31, 2009 and 2008
($ in millions)

	2009	2008
Assets		
Cash	$ 116	$ 81
Accounts receivable	200	202
Less: Allowance for uncollectible accounts	(10)	(8)
Investment revenue receivable	6	4
Inventory	205	200
Prepaid insurance	4	8
Long-term investment	156	125
Land	196	150
Buildings and equipment	412	400
Less: Accumulated depreciation	(97)	(120)
Patent	30	32
	$1,218	$1,074
Liabilities		
Accounts payable	$ 50	$ 65
Salaries payable	6	11
Bond interest payable	8	4
Income tax payable	12	14
Deferred income tax liability	11	8
Notes payable	23	0
Lease liability	82	0
Bonds payable	215	275
Less: Discount on bonds	(22)	(25)
Shareholders' Equity		
Common stock	430	410
Paid-in capital—excess of par	95	85
Preferred stock	75	0
Retained earnings	242	227
Less: Treasury stock	(9)	0
	$1,218	$1,074

ARDUOUS COMPANY
Income Statement
For Year Ended December 31, 2009
($ in millions)

Revenues			
Sales revenue		$410	
Investment revenue		11	
Gain on sale of treasury bills		2	$423
Expenses			
Cost of goods sold		180	
Salaries expense		65	
Depreciation expense		12	
Patent amortization expense		2	
Bad debt expense		8	
Insurance expense		7	
Bond interest expense		28	
Extraordinary loss (flood)	$18		
Less: Tax savings	(9)	9	
Income tax expense		45	356
Net income			$ 67

Additional information from the accounting records:

a. During 2009, $6 million of customer accounts were written off as uncollectible.

b. Investment revenue includes Arduous Company's $6 million share of the net income of Demur Company, an equity method investee.

c. Treasury bills were sold during 2009 at a gain of $2 million. Arduous Company classifies its investments in Treasury bills as cash equivalents.
d. A machine originally costing $70 million that was one-half depreciated was rendered unusable by a rare flood. Most major components of the machine were unharmed and were sold for $17 million.
e. Temporary differences between pretax accounting income and taxable income caused the deferred income tax liability to increase by $3 million.
f. The preferred stock of Tory Corporation was purchased for $25 million as a long-term investment.
g. Land costing $46 million was acquired by issuing $23 million cash and a 15%, four-year, $23 million note payable to the seller.
h. A building was acquired by a 15-year capital lease; present value of lease payments, $82 million.
i. $60 million of bonds were retired at maturity.
j. In February, Arduous issued a 4% stock dividend (4 million shares). The market price of the $5 par value common stock was $7.50 per share at that time.
k. In April, 1 million shares of common stock were repurchased as treasury stock at a cost of $9 million. Arduous uses the cost method to account for treasury stock.

Required:

Prepare the statement of cash flows of Arduous Company for the year ended December 31, 2009. Present cash flows from operating activities by the direct method. (A reconciliation schedule is not required.)

P 21–12
Transactions affecting retained earnings

● LO5 LO6 LO8

Shown below in T-account format are the changes affecting the retained earnings of Brenner-Jude Corporation during 2009. At January 1, 2009, the corporation had outstanding 105 million common shares, $1 par per share.

Retained Earnings ($ in millions)

		90	Beginning balance
Retirement of 5 million common shares for $22 million	2		
		88	Net income for the year
Declaration and payment of a $.33 per share cash dividend	33		
Declaration and distribution of a 4% stock dividend	20		
		123	Ending balance

Required:

1. From the information provided by the account changes you should be able to re-create the transactions that affected Brenner-Jude's retained earnings during 2009. Reconstruct the journal entries which can be used as spreadsheet entries in the preparation of a statement of cash flows. Also indicate any investing and financing activities you identify from this analysis that should be reported on the statement of cash flows.
2. Prepare a statement of retained earnings for Brenner-Jude for the year ended 2009. (You may wish to compare your solution to this problem with the parallel situation described in Exercise 18–12.)

P 21–13
Various cash flows

● LO3 through LO8

Following are selected balance sheet accounts of Del Conte Corp. at December 31, 2009 and 2008, and the increases or decreases in each account from 2008 to 2009. Also presented is selected income statement information for the year ended December 31, 2009, and additional information.

Selected Balance Sheet Accounts	2009	2008	Increase (Decrease)
Assets			
Accounts receivable	$ 34,000	$ 24,000	$ 10,000
Property, plant, and equipment	277,000	247,000	30,000
Accumulated depreciation	(178,000)	(167,000)	11,000
Liabilities and Stockholders' Equity			
Bonds payable	49,000	46,000	3,000
Dividends payable	8,000	5,000	3,000
Common stock, $1 par	22,000	19,000	3,000
Additional paid-in capital	9,000	3,000	6,000
Retained earnings	104,000	91,000	13,000

Selected Income Statement Information for the Year Ended December 31, 2009

Sales revenue	$ 155,000
Depreciation	33,000
Gain on sale of equipment	13,000
Net income	28,000

Additional information:

a. Accounts receivable relate to sales of merchandise.

b. During 2009, equipment costing $40,000 was sold for cash.

c. During 2009, $20,000 of bonds payable were issued in exchange for property, plant, and equipment. There was no amortization of bond discount or premium.

Required:

Items 1 through 5 represent activities that will be reported in Del Conte's statement of cash flows for the year ended December 31, 2009. The following two responses are required for each item:

- Determine the amount that should be reported in Del Conte's 2009 statement of cash flows.
- Using the list below, determine the category in which the amount should be reported in the statement of cash flows.

O. Operating activity
I. Investing activity
F. Financing activity

	Amount	Category
1. Cash collections from customers (direct method).	____	____
2. Payments for purchase of property, plant, and equipment.	____	____
3. Proceeds from sale of equipment.	____	____
4. Cash dividends paid.	____	____
5. Redemption of bonds payable.	____	____

(AICPA adapted)

P 21–14
Statement of cash flows; indirect method; limited information

● LO4 LO8

The comparative balance sheets for 2009 and 2008 are given below for Surmise Company. Net income for 2009 was $50 million.

SURMISE COMPANY
Comparative Balance Sheets
December 31, 2009 and 2008
($ in millions)

	2009	2008
Assets		
Cash	$ 45	$ 40
Accounts receivable	92	96
Less: Allowance for uncollectible accounts	(12)	(4)
Prepaid expenses	8	5
Inventory	145	130
Long-term investment	80	40
Land	100	100
Buildings and equipment	411	300
Less: Accumulated depreciation	(142)	(120)
Patent	16	17
	$ 743	$ 604
Liabilities		
Accounts payable	$ 17	$ 32
Accrued liabilities	(2)	10
Notes payable	35	0
Lease liability	111	0
Bonds payable	65	125
Shareholders' Equity		
Common stock	60	50
Paid-in capital—excess of par	245	205
Retained earnings	212	182
	$ 743	$ 604

Required:

Prepare the statement of cash flows of Surmise Company for the year ended December 31, 2009. Use the indirect method to present cash flows from operating activities because you do not have sufficient information to use the direct method. You will need to make reasonable assumptions concerning the reasons for changes in some account balances. A spreadsheet or T-account analysis will be helpful.

P 21–15
Integrating problem; bonds; lease transactions; lessee and lessor; statement of cash flow effects

● LO3 LO5 LO6

Digital Telephony issued 10% bonds, dated January 1, with a face amount of $32 million on January 1, 2009. The bonds mature in 2019 (10 years). For bonds of similar risk and maturity the market yield is 12%. Interest is paid semiannually on June 30 and December 31. Digital recorded the issue as follows:

Cash	28,329,472	
Discount on bonds	3,670,528	
Bonds payable		32,000,000

Digital also leased switching equipment to Midsouth Communications, Inc., on September 30, 2009. Digital purchased the equipment from MDS Corp. at a cost of $6 million. The five-year lease agreement calls for Midsouth to make quarterly lease payments of $391,548, payable each September 30, December 31, March 31, and June 30, with the first payment on September 30, 2009. Digital's implicit interest rate is 12%.

Required:

1. What would be the amount(s) related to the bonds that Digital would report in its statement of cash flows for the year ended December 31, 2009, if Digital uses the direct method? The indirect method?
2. What would be the amounts related to the lease that *Midsouth* would report in its statement of cash flows for the year ended December 31, 2009?
3. What would be the amounts related to the lease that *Digital* would report in its statement of cash flows for the year ended December 31, 2009?
4. Assume MDS manufactured the equipment at a cost of $5 million and that Midsouth leased the equipment directly from MDS. What would be the amounts related to the lease that *MDS* would report in its statement of cash flows for the year ended December 31, 2009?

P 21–16
Statement of cash flows; indirect method

● LO4 LO8

Refer to the data provided in the Problem 21–4 for Dux Company.

Required:

Prepare the statement of cash flows for Dux Company using the *indirect method.*

P 21–17
Statement of cash flows; indirect method

● LO4 LO8

Refer to the data provided in the Problem 21–5 for Metagrobolize Industries.

Required:

Prepare the statement of cash flows for Metagrobolize Industries using the *indirect method.*

P 21–18
Statement of cash flows; indirect method

● LO4 LO8

Refer to the data provided in the Problem 21–11 for Arduous Company.

Required:

Prepare the statement of cash flows for Arduous Company using the *indirect method.*

(Note: The following problems use the technique learned in Appendix 21B.)

P 21–19
Statement of cash flows; T-account method

● LO3 LO8

Refer to the data provided in the Problem 21–4 for Dux Company.

Required:

Prepare the statement of cash flows for Dux Company. Use the T-account method to assist in your analysis.

P 21–20
Statement of cash flows; T-account method

● LO3 LO8

Refer to the data provided in the Problem 21–5 for Metagrobolize Industries.

Required:

Prepare the statement of cash flows for Metagrobolize Industries. Use the T-account method to assist in your analysis.

P 21–21
Statement of cash flows; T-account method

● LO3 LO8

Refer to the data provided in the Problem 21–11 for Arduous Company.

Required:

Prepare the statement of cash flows for Arduous Company. Use the T-account method to assist in your analysis.

BROADEN YOUR PERSPECTIVE

Apply your critical-thinking ability to the knowledge you've gained. These cases will provide you an opportunity to develop your research, analysis, judgment, and communication skills. You also will work with other students, integrate what you've learned, apply it in real world situations, and consider its global and ethical ramifications. This practice will broaden your knowledge and further develop your decision-making abilities.

Communication Case 21–1
Distinguish income and cash flows

● LO1 LO3 LO4

"Why can't we pay our shareholders a dividend?" shouted your new boss. "This income statement you prepared for me says we earned $5 million in our first half-year!"

You were hired last month as the chief accountant for Enigma Corporation which was organized on July 1 of the year just ended. You recently prepared the financial statements below:

ENIGMA CORPORATION
Income Statement
For the Six Months Ended December 31, 2009
($ in millions)

Sales revenue	$ 75
Cost of goods sold	(30)
Depreciation expense	(5)
Remaining expenses	(35)
Net income	$ 5

ENIGMA CORPORATION
Balance Sheet
December 31, 2009 ($ in millions)

Cash	$ 1
Accounts receivable (net)	20
Merchandise inventory	15
Machinery (net)	44
Total	$80
Accounts payable	$ 2
Accrued expenses payable	7
Notes payable	36
Common stock	30
Retained earnings	5
Total	$80

You have just explained to your boss, Robert James, that although net income was $5 million, operating activities produced a net decrease in cash. Unable to understand your verbal explanation, he has asked you to prepare a written report.

Required:

Prepare a report explaining the apparent discrepancy between Enigma's profitability and its cash flows. To increase the chances of your boss's understanding the situation, include in your report a determination of net cash flows from operating activities by both the direct and indirect methods. Your report should also include a narrative explanation of how it is possible for operating activities to simultaneously produce a positive net income and negative net cash flows.

Judgment Case 21–2
Distinguish income and cash flows

● LO3 LO8

You are a loan officer for First Benevolent Bank. You have an uneasy feeling as you examine a loan application from Daring Corporation. The application included the following financial statements.

DARING CORPORATION
Income Statement
For the Year Ended December 31, 2009

Sales revenue	$100,000
Cost of goods sold	(50,000)
Depreciation expense	(5,000)
Remaining expenses	(25,000)
Net income	$ 20,000

DARING CORPORATION
Balance Sheet
December 31, 2009

Cash	$ 5,000
Accounts receivable	25,000
Inventory	20,000
Operational assets	55,000
Accumulated depreciation	(5,000)
Total	$100,000
Accounts payable	$ 10,000
Interest payable	5,000
Note payable	45,000
Common stock	20,000
Retained earnings	20,000
Total	$100,000

It is not Daring's profitability that worries you. The income statement submitted with the application shows net income of $20,000 in Daring's first year of operations. By referring to the balance sheet, you see that this net income represents a 20% rate of return on assets of $100,000. Your concern stems from the recollection that the note payable reported on Daring's balance sheet is a two-year loan you approved earlier in the year.

You also recall another promising new company that, just last year, defaulted on another of your bank's loans when it failed due to its inability to generate sufficient cash flows to meet its obligations. Before requesting additional information from Daring, you decide to test your memory of the intermediate accounting class you took in night school by attempting to prepare a statement of cash flows from the information available in the loan application.

Research Case 21–3
Information from cash flow activities; FedEx

● LO3 through LO8

Real World Financials

Locate the most recent financial statements and related disclosure notes of **FedEx Corporation.** You can locate the report online at www.fedex.com or by accessing EDGAR at www.sec.gov.

Required:

1. From the information provided in the statement of cash flows, explain what allows FedEx Corporation to expand its business as evidenced by the investing activities, while at the same time not raising as much cash through financing activities.
2. Describe the activities listed under financing activities for the most recent fiscal year. [*Hint:* FedEx's Statement of Changes in Common Stockholders' Investment (statement of shareholders' equity) will help you determine the nature of the stock activity.] What is the most notable financing activity reported?
3. What are the cash payments FedEx made for interest and for income taxes in the three years reported? (*Hint:* See the disclosure notes.)

Research Case 21–4
Locate and extract relevant information for a financial reporting issue; integrative; Microsoft Corporation

● LO4

A meeting of your accounting department is scheduled for early tomorrow morning. One topic of discussion is certain to be the appropriate adjustments to net income in your company's statement of cash flows using the indirect method of reporting operating activities. Hallway discussions have suggested some degree of uncertainty, particularly regarding unearned revenues, which are substantial for the company. Because your firm went public only seven months ago, this reporting issue is a new one for you and most other members of the department. In preparation for the meeting, you sought out the financial statements of **Microsoft Corporation,** knowing that it too had substantial unearned revenues. The operating activities section of the comparative statements of cash flows for Microsoft is presented below.

Real World Financials

Cash Flows Statements (in millions)

Year Ended June 30	2007	2006	2005
Operations			
Net income	$ 14,065	$ 12,599	$ 12,254
Depreciation, amortization, and other noncash items	1,440	903	855
Stock-based compensation	1,550	1,715	2,448
Net recognized gains on investments	(292)	(270)	(527)
Stock option income tax benefits	—	—	668
Excess tax benefits from stock-based payment arrangements	(77)	(89)	—
Deferred income taxes	421	219	(179)
Unearned revenue	21,032	16,453	13,831
Recognition of unearned revenue	(19,382)	(14,729)	(12,919)
Accounts receivable	(1,764)	(2,071)	(1,243)
Other current assets	232	(1,405)	(245)
Other long-term assets	(435)	(49)	21
Other current liabilities	(552)	(145)	396
Other long-term liabilities	1,558	1,273	1,245
Net cash from operations	17,796	14,404	16,605

Required:

1. Locate the financial statements of Microsoft Corporation on the Internet. Search the disclosure notes for information about how Microsoft accounts for its unearned revenues. What percentage of Microsoft's sales of Windows XP Professional does the company record as unearned revenue initially?
2. Why does the statement of cash flows include "unearned revenue" as an addition to net income in the operations section? Why is "recognition of unearned revenue" included as a deduction from net income? Why do you think Microsoft reported these two items separately rather than just adjusting net income for the change in the unearned revenue account balance?
3. Why is stock-based compensation added to net income?

Analysis Case 21–5

Smudged ink; find missing amounts

● LO3 LO4

"Be careful with that coffee!" Your roommate is staring in disbelief at the papers in front of her. "This was my contribution to our team project," she moaned. "When you spilled your coffee, it splashed on this page. Now I can't recognize some of these numbers, and Craig has my source documents."

Knowing how important this afternoon's presentation is to your roommate, you're eager to see what can be done. "Let me see that," you offer. "I think we can figure this out." The statement of cash flows and income statement are intact. The reconciliation schedule and the comparative balance sheets are coffee casualties.

DISTINCTIVE INDUSTRIES
Statement of Cash Flows
For the Year Ended December 31, 2009
($ in millions)

Cash Flows from Operating Activities:		
Collections from customers	$213	
Payment to suppliers	(90)	
Payment of general & administrative expenses	(54)	
Payment of income taxes	(27)	
Net cash flows from operating activities		$ 42
Cash Flows from Investing Activities:		
Sale of equipment		120
Cash Flows from Financing Activities:		
Issuance of common stock	30	
Payment of dividends	(9)	
Net cash flows from financing activities		21
Net increase in cash		$183

Reconciliation of net income to cash flows from operating activities:		
Net income	$ 84	
Adjustments for noncash items:		
Depreciation expense	☐	
☐	☐	
☐	☐	
☐	☐	
☐	☐	
☐	☐	
Net cash flows from operating activities		☐

(continued)

(concluded)

DISTINCTIVE INDUSTRIES
Income Statement
For the Year Ended December 31, 2009

Sales revenue		$240
Cost of goods sold		96
Gross profit		144
Operating expenses:		
General and administrative	$54	
Depreciation	30	
Total operating expenses		84
Operating income		60
Other income:		
Gain on sale of equipment		45
Income before income taxes		105
Income tax expense		21
Net income		$ 84

DISTINCTIVE INDUSTRIES
Comparative Balance Sheets
At December 31

	2009	2008
Assets:		
Cash	$360	☐
Accounts receivable (net)	☐	252
Inventory	180	☐
Property, plant, & equipment	450	600
Less: Accumulated depreciation	(120)	☐
Total assets	☐	☐
Liabilities and shareholders' equity:		
Accounts payable	$120	$ 90
General and administrative expenses payable	27	27
Income taxes payable	66	☐
Common stock	720	690
Retained earnings	☐	141
Total liabilities and shareholders' equity	☐	☐

Required:

1. Determine the missing amounts.
2. Reconstruct the reconciliation of net income to cash flows from operating activities (operating cash flows using the indirect method).

Real World Case 21–6
Analyze cash flow activities; Procter & Gamble

● LO1 through LO8

Real World Financials

The Procter & Gamble Company is a multinational manufacturer of products including personal care, household cleaning, laundry detergents, prescription drugs, and disposable nappies.

($ in millions)	2007	2006	2005
Cash and Cash Equivalents, Beginning of Year	$ 6,693	$ 6,389	$ 4,232
Operating Activities			
Net earnings	10,340	8,684	6,923
Depreciation and amortization	3,130	2,627	1,884
Share-based compensation expense	668	585	524
Deferred income taxes	253	(112)	564
Change in accounts receivable	(729)	(524)	(86)
Change in inventories	(389)	383	(644)
Change in accounts payable, accrued and other liabilities	(273)	230	(101)
Change in other operating assets and liabilities	(157)	(508)	(498)
Other	592	10	113
Total Operating Activities	13,435	11,375	8,679
Investing Activities			
Capital expenditures	(2,945)	(2,667)	(2,181)
Proceeds from asset sales	281	882	517
Acquisitions, net of cash acquired	(492)	171	(572)
Change in investment securities	673	884	(100)
Total Investing Activities	(2,483)	(730)	(2,336)

(continued)

(concluded)

Financing Activities			
Dividends to shareholders	(4,209)	(3,703)	(2,731)
Change in short-term debt	8,981	(8,627)	2,016
Additions to long-term debt	4,758	22,545	3,108
Reductions of long-term debt	(17,929)	(5,282)	(2,013)
Impact of stock options and other	1,499	1,319	521
Treasury purchases	(5,578)	(16,830)	(5,026)
Total Financing Activities	(12,478)	(10,578)	(4,125)
Effect of Exchange Rate Changes on Cash and Cash Equivalents	187	237	(61)
Change in Cash and Cash Equivalents	(1,339)	304	2,157
Cash and Cash Equivalents, End of Year	$ 5,354	$ 6,693	$ 6,389

Required:

1. In the three years reported, what were P&G's primary investing activities? How were these activities financed? Be specific.
2. During the most recent fiscal year, P&G purchased certificates of deposit. How were these purchases reported in the statement of cash flows? (Note: This is not an investing activity.)
3. How are issuances of debt securities and issuances of equity securities classified in a statement of cash flows?
4. How are payments to investors in debt securities (interest) and payments to investors in equity securities (dividends) classified in a statement of cash flows? Is this a conceptual inconsistency? Explain.
5. P&G's statement of cash flows reports expenditures for acquisition of businesses. It also reports the issuance of debt securities. Suppose the businesses had been acquired, not with cash, but by exchange for debt securities. Would such a transaction be reported? Explain.

Ethics Case 21–7
Where's the cash?

● LO1 LO3

After graduating near the top of his class, Ben Naegle was hired by the local office of a Big 4 CPA firm in his hometown. Two years later, impressed with his technical skills and experience, Park Electronics, a large regional consumer electronics chain, hired Ben as assistant controller. This was last week. Now Ben's initial excitement has turned to distress.

The cause of Ben's distress is the set of financial statements he's stared at for the last four hours. For some time prior to his recruitment, he had been aware of the long trend of moderate profitability of his new employer. The reports on his desk confirm the slight, but steady, improvements in net income in recent years. The trend he was just now becoming aware of, though, was the decline in cash flows from operations.

Ben had sketched out the following comparison ($ in millions):

	2009	2008	2007	2006
Income from operations	$140.0	$132.0	$127.5	$127.0
Net income	38.5	35.0	34.5	29.5
Cash flow from operations	1.6	17.0	12.0	15.5

Profits? Yes. Increasing profits? Yes. The cause of his distress? The ominous trend in cash flow which is consistently lower than net income.

Upon closer review, Ben noticed three events in the last two years that, unfortunately, seemed related:

a. Park's credit policy had been loosened; credit terms were relaxed and payment periods were lengthened.
b. Accounts receivable balances had increased dramatically.
c. Several of the company's compensation arrangements, including that of the controller and the company president, were based on reported net income.

Required:

1. What is so ominous about the combination of events Ben sees?
2. What course of action, if any, should Ben take?

Real World Case 21–8
Cash flow despite losses; Northwest Airlines

● LO3 LO4

"I've been reading that the airline industry is having money problems—big losses and budget cuts," said Bee Del Conte as you walked with her to the library. "How is it, then, that I hear on the radio this morning that Northwest Airlines had over a billion dollar cash flow from its operations last year?" Curious, the two of you stop by a computer terminal on the way to the reference section and do a quick search. A few clicks later you're looking at the operating activities section of Northwest's 2006 cash flow statement:

Real World Financials

($ in millions)	Year Ended December 31 2006	2005	2004
Cash Flows from Operating Activities			
Net income (loss)	$ (2,835)	$ (2,533)	$ (862)
Adjustments to reconcile net income (loss) to net cash provided by operating activities:			
Reorganization items, net	3,165	1,081	—
Depreciation and amortization	519	552	731
Income tax expense (benefit)	(29)	7	1
Net receipts (payments) of income taxes	2	(3)	(3)
Pension and other postretirement benefit contributions less than expense	261	457	190
Net loss (earnings) of affiliates	(1)	14	(8)
Net loss (gain) on disposition of property, equipment and other	16	(80)	(95)
Other, net	(16)	20	78
Changes in certain assets and liabilities:			
Decrease (increase) in accounts receivable	(3)	(102)	46
Decrease (increase) in flight equipment spare parts	23	(3)	7
Decrease (increase) in vendor deposits/holdbacks	(35)	(290)	—
Decrease (increase) in supplies, prepaid expenses and other	67	(34)	(57)
Increase (decrease) in air traffic liability	(33)	144	186
Increase (decrease) in accounts payable	287	206	33
Increase (decrease) in other liabilities	(164)	127	29
Net cash provided by (used in) operating activities	1,224	(437)	276

Required:

1. Without regard to Northwest specifically, explain to Bee the difference between net income or net loss and cash flows from operating activities.
2. What is the major contributor to Northwest having positive cash flows from operating activities despite a net loss in 2006?
3. Why did Northwest add $16 million in the determination of cash flows from operating activities for the loss on disposition of property, equipment, and other?

Research Case 21–9
Researching the way cash flows are reported; retrieving information from the Internet

● LO3 through LO8

EDGAR, the Electronic Data Gathering, Analysis, and Retrieval system, performs automated collection, validation, indexing, acceptance, and forwarding of submissions by companies and others who are required by law to file forms with the U.S. Securities and Exchange Commission (SEC). All publicly traded domestic companies use EDGAR to make the majority of their filings. (Filings by foreign companies are not required to be filed on EDGAR, but some of these companies do so voluntarily.) Form 10-K, which includes the annual report, is required to be filed on EDGAR. The SEC makes this information available on the Internet.

Required:

1. Access EDGAR on the Internet. The web address is www.sec.gov.
2. Search for a public company with which you are familiar. Access its most recent 10-K filing. Search or scroll to find the statement of cash flows and related note(s).
3. Is the direct or indirect method used to report operating activities? What is the largest adjustment to net income in reconciling net income and cash flows from operations in the most recent year?
4. What are the cash payments for interest and for taxes?
5. What has been the most significant investing activity for the company in the most recent three years?
6. What has been the most significant financing activity for the company in requirements 2–6 for another company.

Analysis Case 21–10
Information from cash flow activities; Google

● LO3 through LO8

Google

Refer to the financial statements and related disclosure notes of Google Inc. located in the company's 2007 annual report included with all new copies of the text. You also can locate the 2007 report online at www.google.com.

Notice that Google's net income has steadily increased over the three years reported. To supplement their analysis of profitability, many analysts like to look at "free cash flow." A popular way to measure this metric is "structural free cash flow" (or as Warren Buffett calls it "owner's earnings"), which is calculated as net income from operations plus depreciation and amortization minus capital expenditures. Before *SFAS No. 123 (revised)* began requiring "excess tax benefits from stock options" to be reported as a financing activity rather than an operating activity, that amount, too, often was added back in.

Required:

Determine free cash flows for Google in each of the three years reported. Compare that amount with net income each year. What pattern do you detect?

CPA SIMULATION 21–1

Ark Company
Statement of Cash Flows

CPA Review

Test your knowledge of the concepts discussed in this chapter, practice critical professional skills necessary for career success, and prepare for the computer-based CPA exam by accessing our CPA simulations at the text website: **www.mhhe.com/spiceland5e**.

The Ark Company simulation tests your knowledge of a variety of statement of cash flows reporting issues.

As on the CPA exam itself, you will be asked to use tools including a spreadsheet, a calculator, and professional accounting standards, to conduct research, derive solutions, and communicate conclusions related to these issues in a simulated environment headed by the following interactive tabs:

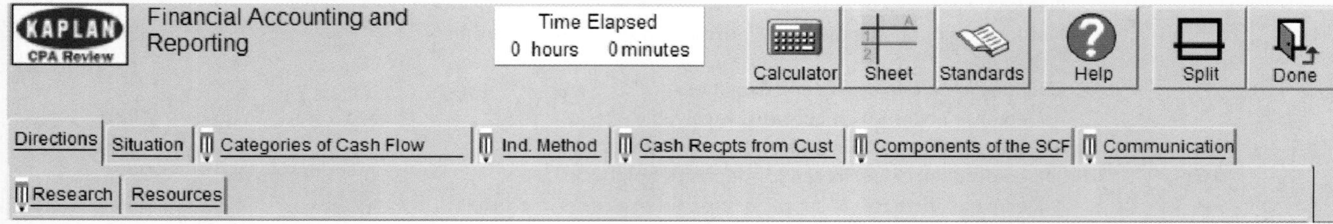

Specific tasks in the simulation include:

- Analyzing accrual transactions to determine their related cash flows.
- Applying judgment in deciding the appropriate financial statement classification of various cash flows.
- Calculating cash flows from operations.
- Determining cash flows from a trial balance.
- Communicating the definition and role of cash equivalents.
- Researching the disclosure requirements for the direct and indirect method of reporting operating activities.

Derivatives

Appendix A

In today's global economy and evolving financial markets, businesses are increasingly exposed to a variety of risks, which, unmanaged, can have major impacts on earnings or even threaten a company's very existence. Risk management, then, has become critical. Derivative financial instruments have become the key tools of risk management.[1]

Derivatives are financial instruments that "derive" their values or contractually required cash flows from some other security or index. For instance, a contract allowing a company to buy a particular asset (say steel, gold, or flour) at a designated future date, at a predetermined price is a financial instrument that derives its value from expected and actual changes in the price of the underlying asset. Financial futures, forward contracts, options, and interest rate swaps are the most frequently used derivatives. Derivatives are valued as tools to manage or hedge companies' increasing exposures to risk, including interest rate risk, price risk, and foreign exchange risk. The variety, complexity, and magnitude of derivatives have grown rapidly in recent years. Tens of trillions of dollars in derivative contracts are used every year. Accounting standard-setters have scrambled to keep pace.

***Derivatives* are financial instruments that "derive" their values from some other security or *index*.**

A persistent stream of headline stories has alerted us to multimillion-dollar losses by **Dell Computer, Procter & Gamble,** and **Orange County** (California), to name a few. Focusing on these headlines, it would be tempting to conclude that derivatives are risky business indeed. Certainly they can be quite risky, if misused, but the fact is, these financial instruments exist to lessen, not increase, risk. Properly used, they serve as a form of "insurance" against risk. In fact, if a company is exposed to a substantial risk and does not hedge that risk, it is taking a gamble. On the other hand, if a derivative is used improperly, it can be a huge gamble itself.

Derivatives serve as a form of "insurance" against risk.

Derivatives Used to Hedge Risk

Hedging means taking an action that is expected to produce exposure to a particular type of risk that is precisely the *opposite* of an actual risk to which the company already is exposed. For instance, the volatility of interest rates creates exposure to interest-rate risk for companies that issue debt—which, of course, includes most companies. So, a company that frequently arranges short-term loans from its bank under a floating (variable) interest rate agreement is exposed to the risk that interest rates might increase and adversely affect borrowing costs. Similarly, a company that regularly reissues commercial paper as it matures faces the possibility that new rates will be higher and cut into forecasted income. When borrowings are large, the potential cost can be substantial. So, the firm might choose to hedge its position by entering into a transaction that would produce a *gain* of roughly the same amount as the potential loss if interest rates do, in fact, increase.

***Hedging* means taking a risk position that is opposite to an actual position that is exposed to risk.**

Hedging is used to deal with three areas of risk exposure: fair value risk, cash flow risk, and foreign currency risk. Let's look at some of the more common derivatives.

Financial Futures

A futures contract is an agreement between a seller and a buyer that requires the seller to deliver a particular commodity (say corn, gold, or pork bellies) at a designated future date, at a *predetermined* price. These contracts are actively traded on regulated futures exchanges. When the "commodity" is a *financial instrument,* such as a Treasury bond, Treasury bill,

A *futures contract* allows a firm to sell (or buy) a financial instrument at a designated future date, at today's price.

[1]Almost all financial institutions and over half of all nonfinancial companies use derivatives.

commercial paper, or a certificate of deposit, the agreement is referred to as a *financial futures contract.*[2]

To appreciate the way these hedges work, you need to remember that when interest rates rise, the market price of interest-bearing securities goes down. For instance, if you have an investment in a 10% bond and market interest rates go up to, say, 12%, your 10% bond is less valuable relative to other bonds paying the higher rate. Conversely, when interest rates decline, the market price of interest-bearing securities goes up. This risk that the investment's value might change is referred to as *fair value risk.* The company that issued the securities is faced with fair value risk also. If interest rates decline, the fair value of that company's debt would rise, a risk the borrower may want to hedge against. Later in this section, we'll look at an illustration of how the borrower would account for and report such a hedge.

The seller in a financial futures contract realizes a gain (loss) when interest rates rise (decline).

Now let's look at the effect on a contract to sell or buy securities (or any asset for that matter) at preset prices. One who is contracted to *sell* securities at a *preset* price after their market price has fallen, benefits from the rise in interest rates. Consequently, the value of the *contract* that gives one the right to sell securities at a preset price goes up as the market price declines. The seller in a futures contract derives a gain (loss) when interest rates rise (decline).[3] Conversely, the one obligated to *buy* securities at a preset price experiences a loss. This risk of having to pay more cash or receive less cash is referred to as *cash flow risk.*

Another example of cash flow risk would be borrowing money by issuing a variable (floating) rate note. If market interest rates rise, the borrower would have to pay more interest. Similarly, the lender (investor) in the variable (floating) rate note transaction would face cash flow risk that interest rates would decline, resulting in lower cash interest receipts.

Let's look closer at how a futures contract can mitigate cash flow risk. Consider a company in April that will replace its $10 million of 8.5% bank notes when they mature in June. The company is exposed to the risk that interest rates in June will have risen, increasing borrowing costs. To counteract that possibility, the firm might enter a contract in April to deliver (sell) bonds in June at their *current* price. Since there are no corporate bond futures contracts, the company buys Treasury bond futures, which will accomplish essentially the same purpose. In essence, the firm agrees to sell Treasury bonds in June at a price established now (April). Let's say it's April 6 and the price of Treasury bond futures on the International Monetary Market of the Chicago Mercantile Exchange is quoted as 95.24.[4] Since the trading unit of Treasury bond futures is a 15-year, $100,000, 8% Treasury bond, the company might sell 105 Treasury bond futures to hedge the June issuance of debt. This would effectively provide a hedge of 105 $\times$ $100,000 $\times$ 95.24% = $10,000,200.[5]

Here's what happens then. If interest rates rise, borrowing costs will go up for our example company because it will have to sell debt securities at a higher interest cost (or lower price). But that loss will be offset (approximately) by the gain produced by being in the opposite position on Treasury bond futures. Take note, though, this works both ways. If interest rates go down causing debt security prices to rise, the potential benefit of being able to issue debt at that lower interest rate (higher price) will be offset by a loss on the futures position.

A very important point about futures contracts is that the seller does not need to have actual possession of the commodity (the Treasury bonds, in this case), nor is the purchaser of the contract required to take possession of the commodity. In fact, virtually all financial futures contracts are "netted out" before the actual transaction is to take place. This is simply a matter of reversing the original position. A seller closes out his transaction with a purchase. Likewise, a purchaser would close out her transaction with a sale. After all, the objective is not to actually buy or sell Treasury bonds (or whatever the commodity might be), but to incur the financial impact of movements in interest rates as reflected in changes in Treasury bond prices. Specifically, it will buy at the lower price (to reverse the original seller position) at the same time it's selling its new bond issue at that same lower price. The

[2]Note that a financial futures contract meets the definition of a financial instrument because it entails the exchange of financial instruments (cash for Treasury bonds, for instance). But, a futures contract for the sale or purchase of a nonfinancial commodity like corn or gold does not meet the definition because one of the items to be exchanged is not a financial instrument.

[3]The seller of a futures contract is obligated to sell the bonds at a future date. The buyer of a futures contract is obligated to buy the bonds at a future date. The company in our example, then, is the seller of the futures contract.

[4]Price quotes are expressed as a percentage of par.

[5]This is a simplification of the more sophisticated way financial managers determine the optimal number of futures.

financial futures market is an "artificial" exchange in that its reason for existing is to provide a mechanism to transfer risk from those exposed to it to those willing to accept the risk, not to actually buy and sell the underlying financial instruments.

If the impending debt issue being hedged is a short-term issue, the company may attain a more effective hedge by selling Treasury *bill* futures since Treasury bills are 90-day securities, or maybe certificate of deposit (CD) futures that also are traded in futures markets. The object is to get the closest association between the financial effects of interest rate movements on the actual transaction and the effects on the financial instrument used as a hedge.

The effectiveness of a hedge is influenced by the closeness of the match between the item being hedged and the financial instrument chosen as a hedge.

Financial Forward Contracts

A **forward contract** is similar to a futures contract but differs in three ways:

1. A forward contract calls for delivery on a specific date, whereas a futures contract permits the seller to decide later which specific day within the specified month will be the delivery date (if it gets as far as actual delivery before it is closed out).
2. Unlike a futures contract, a forward contract usually is not traded on a market exchange.
3. Unlike a futures contract, a forward contract does not call for a daily cash settlement for price changes in the underlying contract. Gains and losses on forward contracts are paid only when they are closed out.

Options

Options frequently are purchased to hedge exposure to the effects of changing interest rates. Options serve the same purpose as futures in that respect but are fundamentally different. An option on a financial instrument—say a Treasury bill—gives its holder the right either to buy or to sell the Treasury bill at a specified price and within a given time period. Importantly, though, the option holder has no obligation to exercise the option. On the other hand, the holder of a futures contract must buy or sell within a specified period unless the contract is closed out before delivery comes due.

Foreign Currency Futures

Foreign loans frequently are denominated in the currency of the lender (Japanese yen, Swiss franc, Euro, and so on). When loans must be repaid in foreign currencies, a new element of risk is introduced. This is because if exchange rates change, the dollar equivalent of the foreign currency that must be repaid differs from the dollar equivalent of the foreign currency borrowed.

To hedge against "foreign exchange risk" exposure, some firms buy or sell **foreign currency futures** contracts. These are similar to financial futures except specific foreign currencies are specified in the futures contracts rather than specific debt instruments. They work the same way to protect against foreign exchange risk as financial futures protect against fair value or cash flow risk.

Foreign exchange risk often is hedged in the same manner as interest rate risk.

Interest Rate Swaps

Over 70% of derivatives are **interest rate swaps.** These contracts exchange fixed interest payments for floating rate payments, or vice versa, without exchanging the underlying principal amounts. For example, suppose you owe $100,000 on a 10% fixed rate home loan. You envy your neighbor who also is paying 10% on her $100,000 mortgage, but hers is a floating rate loan, so if market rates fall, so will her loan rate. To the contrary, she is envious of your fixed rate, fearful that rates will rise, increasing her payments. A solution would be for the two of you to effectively swap interest payments using an interest rate swap agreement. The way a swap works, you both would continue to actually make your own interest payments, but would exchange the net cash difference between payments at specified intervals. So, in this case, if market rates (and thus floating payments) increase, you would pay your neighbor; if rates fall, she pays you. The net effect is to exchange the consequences of rate changes. In other words, you have effectively converted your fixed-rate debt to floating-rate debt; your neighbor has done the opposite.

***Interest rate swaps* exchange fixed interest payments for floating rate payments, or vice versa, without exchanging the underlying notional amounts.**

Of course, this technique is not dependent on happening into such a fortuitous pairing of two borrowers with opposite philosophies on interest rate risk. Instead, banks or other intermediaries offer, for a fee, one-sided swap agreements to companies desiring to be either fixed-rate payers or variable-rate payers. Intermediaries usually strive to maintain a balanced portfolio of matched, offsetting swap agreements.

Theoretically, the two parties to such a transaction exchange principal amounts, say the $100,000 amount above, in addition to the interest on those amounts. It makes no practical sense, though, for the companies to send each other $100,000. So, instead, the principal amount is not actually exchanged, but serves merely as the computational base for interest calculations and is called the *notional amount.* Similarly, the fixed-rate payer doesn't usually send the entire fixed interest amount (say 10% × $100,000 = $10,000) and receive the entire variable interest amount (say 9% × $100,000 = $9,000). Generally, only the net amount ($1,000 in this case) is exchanged. This is illustrated in Graphic A–1.

GRAPHIC A–1
Interest Rate Swap

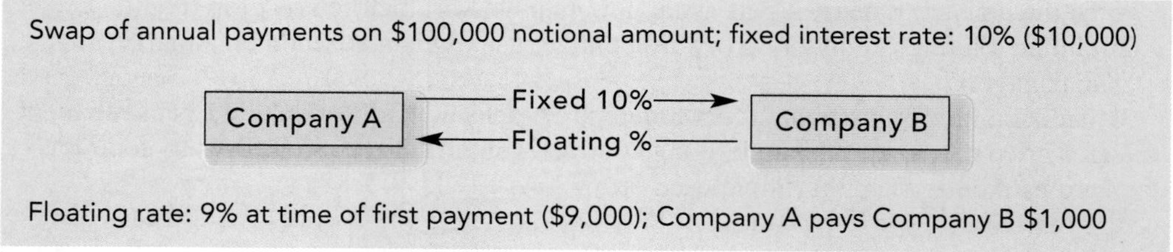

From an accounting standpoint, the central issue is not the operational differences among various hedge instruments, but their similarities in functioning as hedges against risk.

Accounting for Derivatives

A key to accounting for derivatives is knowing the purpose for which a company holds them and whether the company is effective in serving that purpose. Derivatives, for instance, may be held for risk management (hedging activities). The desired effect, and often the real effect, is a reduction in risk. On the other hand, derivatives sometimes are held for speculative position taking, hoping for large profits. The effect of this activity usually is to increase risk. Perhaps more important, derivatives acquired as hedges and intended to reduce risk may, in fact, unintentionally increase risk instead.

Derivatives not serving as hedges are extremely speculative due to the high leverage inherent in such investments.

It's important to understand that, serving as investments rather than as hedges, derivatives are extremely speculative. This is due to the high leverage inherent in derivatives. Here's why. The investment outlay usually is negligible, but, the potential gain or loss on the investment usually is quite high. A small change in interest rates or another underlying event can trigger a large change in the fair value of the derivative. Because the initial investment was minimal, the change in value relative to the investment itself represents a huge percentage gain or loss. Accounting for derivatives is designed to treat differently (a) derivatives designated as hedges and those not designated as hedges as well as (b) the effective portion and the ineffective portion of gains and losses from intended hedges.

All derivatives are reported on the balance sheet at fair value.

The basic approach to accounting for derivatives is fairly straightforward, although implementation can be quite cumbersome. All derivatives, no exceptions, are carried on the balance sheet as either assets or liabilities at fair (or market) value.[6] The reasoning is that (a) derivatives create either rights or obligations that meet the definition of assets or liabilities, and (b) fair value is the most meaningful measurement.

Accounting for the gain or loss on a derivative depends on how it is used. Specifically, if the derivative is not designated as a hedging instrument, or doesn't qualify as one, any gain or loss from fair value changes is recognized immediately in earnings. On the other hand, if a derivative is used to hedge against exposure to risk, any gain or loss from fair value changes is either (a) recognized immediately in earnings along with an offsetting loss or gain on the item being hedged or (b) deferred in comprehensive income until it can be recognized in earnings

[6]"Accounting for Derivative Instruments and Hedging Activities," *Statement of Financial Accounting Standards No. 133* (Norwalk, Conn.: FASB, 1998).

at the same time as earnings are affected by a hedged transaction. Which way depends on whether the derivative is designated as a (a) fair value hedge, (b) cash flow hedge, or (c) foreign currency hedge. Let's look now at each of the three hedge designations.

Fair Value Hedges

A company can be adversely affected when a change in either prices or interest rates causes a change in the fair value of one of its assets, its liabilities, or a commitment to buy or sell assets or liabilities. If a derivative is used to hedge against the exposure to changes in the fair value of an asset or liability or a firm commitment, it can be designated as a **fair value hedge.** In that case, when the derivative is adjusted to reflect changes in fair value, the other side of the entry recognizes a gain or loss to be included *currently* in earnings. At the same time, though, the loss or gain from changes in the fair value (due to the risk being hedged)[7] of the item being hedged also is included currently in earnings. This means that, to the extent the hedge is effective in serving its purpose, the gain or loss on the derivative will be offset by the loss or gain on the item being hedged. In fact, this is precisely the concept behind the procedure.

A gain or loss from a *fair value hedge* is recognized immediately in earnings along with the loss or gain from the item being hedged.

The reasoning is that as interest rates or other underlying events change, a hedge instrument will produce a gain approximately equal to a loss on the item being hedged (or vice versa). These income effects are interrelated and offsetting, so it would be improper to report the income effects in different periods. More critically, the intent and effect of having the hedge instrument is to *lessen* risk. And yet, recognizing gains in one period and counterbalancing losses in another period would tend to cause fluctuations in income that convey an *increase* in risk. However, to the extent that a hedge is ineffective and produces gains or losses different from the losses or gains being hedged, the ineffective portion is recognized in earnings immediately.

The income effects of the hedge instrument and the income effects of the item being hedged should affect earnings at the same time.

Some of the more common fair value hedges use:

- An interest rate swap to synthetically convert fixed-rate debt (for which interest rate changes could change the fair value of the debt) into floating-rate debt.
- A futures contract to hedge changes in the fair value (due to price changes) of aluminum, sugar, or some other type of inventory.
- A futures contract to hedge the fair value (due to price changes) of a firm commitment to sell natural gas or some other asset.

Illustration

Because interest rate swaps comprise over 70% of derivatives in use, we will use swaps to illustrate accounting for derivatives. Let's look at the example in Illustration A–1 on the next page.

When the floating rate declined from 10% to 9%, the fair values of both the derivative (swap) and the note increased. This created an offsetting gain on the derivative and holding loss on the note. Both are recognized in earnings at the same time (at June 30, 2009).

January 1, 2009		
Cash	1,000,000	
Notes payable		1,000,000
To record the issuance of the note.		
June 30, 2009		
Interest expense (10% × ½ × $1 million)	50,000	
Cash		50,000
To record interest.		
Cash ($50,000 – [9% × ½ × $1 million])	5,000	
Interest expense		5,000
To record the net cash settlement.		

The interest rate swap is designated as a fair value hedge on this note at issuance.

The swap settlement is the difference between the fixed interest (5%) and variable interest (4.5%).

(continued)

[7] The fair value of a hedged item might also change for reasons other than from effects of the risk being hedged. For instance, the hedged risk may be that a change in interest rates will cause the fair value of a bond to change. The bond price might also change, though, if the market perceives that the bond's default risk has changed.

ILLUSTRATION A–1
Interest Rate Swap

Wintel Semiconductors issued $1 million of 18-month, 10% bank notes on January 1, 2009. Wintel is exposed to the risk that general interest rates will decline, causing the fair value of its debt to rise. (If the fair value of Wintel's debt increases, its effective borrowing cost is higher relative to the market.) To hedge against this fair value risk, the firm entered into an 18-month interest rate swap agreement on January 1 and designated the swap as a hedge against changes in the fair value of the note. The swap calls for the company to *receive payment* based on a 10% fixed interest rate on a notional amount of $1 million and to *make payment* based on a floating interest rate tied to changes in general rates.[8] As the Illustration will show, this effectively converts Wintel's fixed-rate debt to floating-rate debt. Cash settlement of the net interest amount is made semiannually at June 30 and December 31 of each year with the net interest being the difference between the $50,000 fixed interest [$1 million × (10% × ½)] and the floating interest rate times $1 million at those dates.

Floating (market) settlement rates were 9% at June 30, 2009, 8% at December 31, 2009, and 9% at June 30, 2010. Net interest receipts can be calculated as shown below. Fair values of both the derivative and the note resulting from those market rate changes are assumed to be quotes obtained from securities dealers.

	1/1/09	6/30/09	12/31/09	6/30/10
Fixed rate	10%	10%	10%	10%
Floating rate	10%	9%	8%	9%
Fixed payments ($1 million × [10% × ½])		$ 50,000	$ 50,000	$ 50,000
Floating payments ($1 million × ½ floating rate)		45,000	40,000	45,000
Net interest receipts		$ 5,000	$ 10,000	$ 5,000
Fair value of interest rate swap	0	$ 9,363	$ 9,615	0
Fair value of note payable	$1,000,000	$1,009,363	$1,009,615	$1,000,000

The fair value of derivatives is recognized in the balance sheet.

The hedged liability (or asset) is adjusted to fair value as well.

June 30, 2009 entries continued from previous page:

Interest rate swap[9] ($9,363 – 0)	9,363	
Holding gain—interest rate swap		9,363
To record change in fair value of the derivative.		
Holding loss—hedged note	9,363	
Note payable ($1,009,363 – 1,000,000)		9,363
To record change in fair value of the note due to interest rate changes.		

The net interest settlement on June 30, 2009, is $5,000 because the fixed rate is 5% (half of the 10% annual rate) and the floating rate is 4.5% (half of the 9% annual rate).

As with any debt, interest expense is the effective rate times the outstanding balance.

The settlement is the difference between the fixed interest (5%) and variable interest (4%).

The derivative is increased by the change in fair value.

The note is increased by the change in fair value.

December 31, 2009

Interest expense	50,000	
Cash (10% × ½ × $1,000,000)		50,000
To record interest.		
Cash ($50,000 – [8% × ½ × $1 million])	10,000	
Interest expense		10,000
To record the net cash settlement.		
Interest rate swap ($9,615 – 9,363)	252	
Holding gain—interest rate swap		252
To record the change in fair value of the derivative.		
Holding loss—hedged note	252	
Note payable ($1,009,615 – 1,009,363)		252
To record the change in fair value of the note due to interest rate changes.		

[8]A common measure for benchmarking variable interest rates is LIBOR, the London Interbank Offered Rate, a base rate at which large international banks lend funds to each other.

[9]This would be a liability rather than an investment (asset) if the fair value had declined.

The fair value of the swap increased by $252 (from $9,363 to $9,615). Similarly, we adjust the note's carrying value by the amount necessary to increase it to fair value. This produces a holding loss on the note that exactly offsets the gain on the swap. This result is the hedging effect that motivated Wintel to enter the fair value hedging arrangement in the first place.

At June 30, 2010, Wintel repeats the process of adjusting to fair value both the derivative investment and the note being hedged.

The net interest received is the difference between the fixed interest (5%) and floating interest (4.5%).

The swap's fair value now is zero.

June 30, 2010		
Interest expense	50,000	
Cash (10% × ½ × $1,000,000)		50,000
To record interest.		
Cash [$50,000 − (9% × ½ × $1 million)]	5,000	
Interest expense		5,000
To record the net cash settlement.		
Holding loss—interest rate swap	9,615	
Interest rate swap ($0 − 9,615)		9,615
To record the change in fair value of the derivative.		
Note payable ($1,000,000 − 1,009,615)	9,615	
Holding gain—hedged note		9,615
To record the change in fair value of the note due to interest rate changes.		
Note payable	1,000,000	
Cash		1,000,000
To repay the loan.		

The net interest received is the difference between the fixed rate (5%) and floating rate (4.5%) times $1 million. The fair value of the swap decreased by $9,615 (from $9,615 to zero).[10] That decline represents a holding *loss* that we recognize in earnings. Similarly, we record an offsetting holding *gain* on the note for the change in its fair value.

Now let's see how the carrying values changed for the swap account and the note:

	Swap (debit)	Swap (credit)	Note (debit)	Note (credit)
Jan. 1, 2009				1,000,000
June 30, 2009	9,363			9,363
Dec. 31, 2009	252			252
June 30, 2010		9,615	9,615 1,000,000	
	0			0

The income statement is affected as follows:

	Income Statement + (−)	
June 30, 2009	(50,000)	Interest expense—fixed payment
	5,000	Interest expense—net cash settlement
	9,363	Holding gain—interest rate swap
	(9,363)	Holding loss—hedged note
	(45,000)	Net effect—same as floating interest payment
Dec. 31, 2009	(50,000)	Interest expense—fixed payment
	10,000	Interest expense—net cash settlement
	252	Holding gain—interest rate swap
	(252)	Holding loss—hedged note
	(40,000)	Net effect—same as floating interest payment
June 30, 2010	(50,000)	Interest expense—fixed payment
	5,000	Interest expense—net cash settlement
	9,615	Holding gain—interest rate swap
	(9,615)	Holding loss—hedged note
	(45,000)	Net effect—same as floating interest payment

[10]Because there are no future cash receipts from the swap arrangement at this point, the fair value of the swap is zero.

As this demonstrates, the swap effectively converts fixed-interest debt to floating-interest debt.

ADDITIONAL CONSIDERATION

Fair Value of the Swap

The fair value of a derivative typically is based on a quote obtained from a derivatives dealer. That fair value will approximate the present value of the expected net interest settlement receipts for the remaining term of the swap. In fact, we can actually calculate the fair value of the swap that we accepted as given in our illustration.

Since the June 30, 2009, floating rate of 9% caused the cash settlement on that date to be $5,000, it's reasonable to look at 9% as the best estimate of future floating rates and therefore assume the remaining two cash settlements also will be $5,000 each. We can then calculate at June 30, 2009, the present value of those expected net interest settlement receipts for the remaining term of the swap:

Fixed interest	10% × ½ × $1 million	$ 50,000
Expected floating interest	9% × ½ × $1 million	45,000
Expected cash receipts for both Dec. 31, 2009 and June 30, 2010		$ 5,000
		× 1.87267*
Present value		$ 9,363

*Present value of an ordinary annuity of $1: $n = 2$, $i = 4.5\%$ (½ of 9%) (from Table 4)

Fair Value of the Notes

The fair value of the note payable will be the present value of principal and remaining interest payments discounted at the *market rate*. The market rate will vary with the designated floating rate but might differ due to changes in default (credit) risk and the term structure of interest rates. Assuming it's 9% at June 30, 2009, we can calculate the fair value (present value) of the notes:

Interest	$50,000* × 1.87267† =	$ 93,633
Principal	$1,000,000 × .91573‡ =	915,730
		$1,009,363

*½ of 10% × $1,000,000
†Present value of an ordinary annuity of $1: $n = 2$, $i = 4.5\%$ (from Table 4)
‡Present value of $1: $n = 2$, $i = 4.5\%$ (from Table 2)

Note: Often the cash settlement rate is "reset" as of each cash settlement date (thus the floating rate actually used at the end of each period to determine the payment is the floating market rate as of the *beginning* of the same period). In our illustration, for instance, there would have been no cash settlement at June 30, 2009, since we would use the beginning floating rate of 10% to determine payment. Similarly, we would have used the 9% floating rate at June 30, 2009, to determine the cash settlement six months later at December 31. In effect, each cash settlement would be delayed six months. Had this arrangement been in effect in the current illustration, there would have been one fewer cash settlement payments (two rather than three), but would not have affected the fair value calculations above because, either way, our expectation would be cash receipts of $5,000 for both Dec. 31, 2009, and June 30, 2010.

Cash Flow Hedges

A gain or loss from a *cash flow hedge* is deferred as Other comprehensive income until it can be recognized in earnings along with the earnings effect of the item being hedged.

The risk in some transactions or events is the risk of a change in cash flows, rather than a change in fair values. We noted earlier, for instance, that *fixed-rate* debt subjects a company to the risk that interest rate changes could change the fair value of the debt. On the other hand, if the obligation is *floating-rate* debt, the fair value of the debt will not change when interest rates do, but cash flows will. If a derivative is used to hedge against the exposure to changes in cash inflows or cash outflows of an asset or liability or a forecasted transaction (like a future purchase or sale), it can be designated as a **cash flow hedge.** In that case, when the derivative is adjusted to reflect changes in fair value, the other side of the entry is a gain or loss to be deferred as a **component of Other comprehensive income** and included in earnings later, at the same time as earnings are affected by the hedged transaction. Once again, the effect is matching the earnings effect of the derivative with the earnings effect of the item being hedged, precisely the concept behind hedge accounting.

To understand the deferral of the gain or loss, we need to revisit the concept of comprehensive income. Comprehensive income, as you may recall from Chapters 4, 12, 17, and 18 is a more expansive view of the change in shareholders' equity than traditional net income. In fact, it encompasses all changes in equity other than from transactions with owners.[11] So, in addition to net income itself, comprehensive income includes up to four other changes in equity that don't (yet) belong in net income, namely, net holding gains (losses) on investments (Chapter 12), gains (losses) from and amendments to postretirement benefit plans (Chapter 17), gains (losses) from foreign currency translation, and deferred gains (losses) from derivatives designated as cash flow hedges.[12]

Some of the more commonly used cash flow hedges are:

- An interest rate swap to synthetically convert floating rate debt (for which interest rate changes could change the cash interest payments) into fixed rate debt.
- A futures contract to hedge a forecasted sale (for which price changes could change the cash receipts) of natural gas, crude oil, or some other asset.

Foreign Currency Hedges

Today's economy is increasingly a global one. The majority of large "U.S." companies are, in truth, multinational companies that may receive only a fraction of their revenues from U.S. operations. Many operations of those companies are located abroad. Foreign operations often are denominated in the currency of the foreign country (the Euro, Japanese yen, Russian rubles, and so on). Even companies without foreign operations sometimes hold investments, issue debt, or conduct other transactions denominated in foreign currencies. As exchange rates change, the dollar equivalent of the foreign currency changes. The possibility of currency rate changes exposes these companies to the risk that some transactions require settlement in a currency other than the entities' functional currency or that foreign operations will require translation adjustments to reported amounts.

The possibility that foreign currency exchange rates might change exposes many companies to foreign currency risk.

A **foreign currency hedge** can be a hedge of foreign currency exposure of:

- A firm commitment—treated as a fair value hedge.
- An available-for-sale security—treated as a fair value hedge.
- A forecasted transaction—treated as a cash flow hedge.
- A company's net investment in a foreign operation—the gain or loss is reported in *other comprehensive income* as part of unrealized gains and losses from foreign currency translation.[13]

Hedge Effectiveness

When a company elects to apply hedge accounting, it must establish at the inception of the hedge the method it will use to assess the effectiveness of the hedging derivative as well as the measurement approach it will use to determine the ineffective portion of the hedge.[14] The key criterion for qualifying as a hedge is that the hedging relationship must be highly effective in achieving offsetting changes in fair values or cash flows based on the hedging company's specified risk management objective and strategy.

To qualify as a hedge, the hedging relationship must be highly effective in achieving offsetting changes in fair values or cash flows.

An assessment of this effectiveness must be made at least every three months and whenever financial statements are issued. There are no precise guidelines for assessing effectiveness, but it generally means a high correlation between changes in the fair value or cash flows of the derivative and of the item being hedged, not necessarily a specific reduction in risk. Hedge accounting must be terminated for hedging relationships that no longer are highly effective.

Hedge Ineffectiveness

In Illustration A–1, the loss on the hedged note exactly offset the gain on the swap. This is because the swap in this instance was highly effective in hedging the risk due to interest rate

[11]Transactions with owners primarily include dividends and the sale or purchase of shares of the company's stock.

[12]"Reporting Comprehensive Income," *Statement of Financial Accounting Standards No. 130* (Norwalk, Conn.: FASB, 1997)

[13]This is the same treatment previously prescribed for these translation adjustments by *Statement of Financial Accounting Standards No. 52.*

[14]Remember, if a derivative is not designated as a hedge, any gains or losses from changes in its fair value are recognized immediately in earnings.

changes. However, the loss and gain would not have exactly offset each other if the hedging arrangement had been ineffective. For instance, suppose the swap's term had been different from that of the note (say a three-year swap term compared with the 18-month term of the note) or if the notional amount of the swap differed from that of the note (say $500,000 rather than $1 million). In that case, changes in the fair value of the swap and changes in the fair value of the note would not be the same. The result would be a greater (or lesser) amount recognized in earnings for the swap than for the note. Because there would not be an exact offset, earnings would be affected, an effect resulting from hedge ineffectiveness. That is a desired effect of hedge accounting; to the extent that a hedge is effective, the earnings effect of a derivative cancels out the earnings effect of the item being hedged. However, even if a hedge is highly effective, all ineffectiveness is recognized currently in earnings.

Imperfect hedges result in part of the derivative gain or loss being included in current earnings.

Fair Value Changes Unrelated to the Risk Being Hedged

In Illustration A–1, the fair value of the hedged note and the fair value of the swap changed by the same amounts each year because we assumed the fair values changed only due to interest rate changes. It's also possible, though, that the note's fair value would change by an amount different from that of the swap for reasons unrelated to interest rates. Remember from our earlier discussion that the market's perception of a company's creditworthiness, and thus its ability to pay interest and principal when due, also can affect the value of debt, whether interest rates change or not. In hedge accounting, we ignore those changes. We recognize only the fair value changes in the hedged item that we can attribute to the risk being hedged (interest rate risk in this case). For example, if a changing perception of default risk had caused the note's fair value to increase by an additional, say $5,000, our journal entries in Illustration A–1 would have been unaffected. Notice, then, that although we always mark a *derivative* to fair value, the reported amount of the *item being hedged* may not be its fair value. We mark a hedged item to fair value only to the extent that its fair value changed due to the risk being hedged.

Fair value changes unrelated to the risk being hedged are ignored.

Disclosure of Derivatives and Risk

To be adequately informed about the adequacy of a company's risk management, investors and creditors need information about strategies for holding derivatives and specific hedging activities. Toward that end, extensive disclosure requirements provide information that includes:

- Objectives and strategies for holding and issuing derivatives.
- A description of the items for which risks are being hedged.
- For forecasted transactions: a description, time before the transaction is expected to occur, the gains and losses accumulated in other comprehensive income, and the events that will trigger their recognition in earnings.
- Beginning balance of, changes in, and ending balance of the derivative component of other comprehensive income.
- The net amount of gain or loss reported in earnings (representing aggregate hedge ineffectiveness).
- Qualitative and quantitative information about failed hedges: canceled commitments or previously hedged forecasted transactions no longer expected to occur.

The intent is to provide information about the company's success in reducing risks and consequently about risks not managed successfully. Remember, too, that when derivatives are employed ineffectively, risks can escalate. Ample disclosures about derivatives are essential to maintain awareness of potential opportunities and problems with risk management.

In addition, *SFAS No. 161* requires companies to provide enhanced disclosures indicating (a) how and why the company uses derivative instruments, (b) how the company accounts for derivative instruments and related hedged items, and (c) how derivative instruments and related hedged items affect the company's balance sheet, income statement, and cash flows.[15] The required disclosures includes two tables, one that highlights the location and

[15] "Disclosures about Derivative Instruments and Hedging Activities—an amendment of FASB Statement No. 133)," *Statement of Financial Accounting Standards No. 161* (Stamford, Conn.: FASB, 2008)

fair values of derivative instruments in the balance sheet, and another that indicates the location and amounts of gains and losses on derivative instruments in the income statement. The two tables distinguish between derivative instruments that are designated as hedging instruments under *SFAS No. 133* and those that are not. The tables also categorize derivative instruments by each major type—interest rate contracts, foreign exchange contracts, equity contracts, commodity contracts, credit contracts and other types of contracts.

Even for some traditional liabilities, the amounts reported on the face of the financial statements provide inadequate disclosure about the degree to which a company is exposed to risk of loss. To provide adequate disclosure about a company's exposure to risk, additional information must be provided about (a) concentrations of credit risk and (b) the fair value of all financial instruments.[16]

Extended Method for Interest Rate Swap Accounting

A shortcut method for accounting for an interest rate swap is permitted by *SFAS No. 133* when a hedge meets certain criteria. In general, the criteria are designed to see if the hedge supports the assumption of "no ineffectiveness." Illustration A–1 of a fair value hedge met those criteria, in particular, (a) the swap's notional amount matches the note's principal amount, (b) the swap's expiration date matches the note's maturity date, (c) the fair value of the swap is zero at inception, and (d) the floating payment is at the market rate.[17] Because Wintel can conclude that the swap will be highly effective in offsetting changes in the fair value of the debt, it can use the changes in the fair value of the swap to measure the offsetting changes in the fair value of the debt. That's the essence of the shortcut method used in Illustration A–1. The extended method required when the criteria are *not* met for the shortcut method is described in this section (Illustration A–2). It produces the same effect on earnings and in the balance sheet as does the procedure shown in Illustration A–1.

ILLUSTRATION A–2
Interest Rate Swap—Extended Method

Wintel Semiconductors issued $1 million of 18-month, 10% bank notes on January 1, 2009. Wintel is exposed to the risk that general interest rates will decline, causing the fair value of its debt to rise. (If the fair value of Wintel's debt increases, its effective borrowing cost is higher relative to the market.) To hedge against this fair value risk, the firm entered into an 18-month interest rate swap agreement on January 1 and designated the swap as a hedge against changes in the fair value of the note. The swap calls for the company to *receive payment* based on a 10% fixed interest rate on a notional amount of $1 million and to *make payment* based on a floating interest rate tied to changes in general rates. Cash settlement of the net interest amount is made semiannually at June 30 and December 31 of each year with the net interest being the difference between the $50,000 fixed interest [$1 million × (10% × ½)] and the floating interest rate times $1 million at those dates.

Floating (market) settlement rates were 9% at June 30, 2009, 8% at December 31, 2009, and 8% at June 30, 2010. Net interest receipts can be calculated as shown below. Fair values of both the derivative and the note resulting from those market rate changes are assumed to be quotes obtained from securities dealers.

	1/1/09	6/30/09	12/31/09	6/30/10
Fixed rate	10%	10%	10%	10%
Floating rate	10%	9%	8%	9%
Fixed payments				
[$1 million × (10% × ½)]		$ 50,000	$ 50,000	$ 50,000
Floating payments				
($1 million × ½ floating rate)		45,000	40,000	45,000
Net interest receipts		$ 5,000	$ 10,000	$ 5,000
Fair value of interest rate swap	0	$ 9,363	$ 9,615	0
Fair value of note payable	$1,000,000	$1,009,363	$1,009,615	$1,000,000

[16]"Disclosures About Fair Values of Financial Instruments," *Statement of Financial Accounting Standards No. 107* (Norwalk, Conn.: FASB, 1991) as amended by *Statement of Financial Accounting Standards No. 133*, "Accounting for Derivative Instruments and Hedging Activities" (Norwalk, Conn.: FASB, 1998).

[17]There is no precise minimum interval, though it generally is three to six months or less. Other criteria are specified by *SFAS No. 133* (para. 68) in addition to the key conditions listed here.

When the floating rate declined in Illustration A–2 from 10% to 9%, the fair values of both the derivative (swap) and the note increased. This created an offsetting gain on the derivative and holding loss on the note. Both are recognized in earnings the same period (June 30, 2009).

The interest rate swap is designated as a fair value hedge on this note at issuance.

January 1, 2009		
Cash	1,000,000	
Notes payable		1,000,000
To record the issuance of the note.		

The swap settlement is the difference between the fixed interest (5%) and variable interest (4.5%).

The fair value of derivatives is recognized in the balance sheet.

The hedged liability (or asset) is adjusted to fair value as well.

June 30, 2009		
Interest expense (10% × ½ × $1 million)	50,000	
Cash		50,000
To record interest.		
Cash ($50,000 – [9% × ½ × × $1 million])	5,000	
Interest rate swap ($9,363 – 0)	9,363	
Interest revenue (10% × ½ × $0)		0
Holding gain—interest rate swap (to balance)		14,363
To record the net cash settlement, accrued interest on the swap, and change in the fair value of the derivative.		
Holding loss—hedged note	9,363	
Notes payable ($1,009,363 – 1,000,000)		9,363
To record change in fair value of the note due to interest rate changes.		

The net interest settlement on June 30, 2009, is $5,000 because the fixed rate is 5% (half of the 10% annual rate) and the floating rate is 4.5% (half of the 9% annual rate). A holding gain ($14,363) is produced by holding the derivative security during a time when an interest rate decline caused an increase in the value of that asset. A portion ($5,000) of the gain was received in cash and another portion ($9,363) is reflected as an increase in the value of the asset.

We also have holding loss of the same amount. This is because we also held a liability during the same time period, and the interest rate change caused its fair value to increase as well.

As with any debt, interest expense is the effective rate times the outstanding balance.

The cash settlement is the difference between the fixed interest (5%) and variable interest (4%).

Interest ($421) accrues on the asset.

The note is increased by the change in fair value.

December 31, 2009		
Interest expense (9% × ½ × $1,009,363)	45,421	
Notes payable (difference)*	4,579	
Cash (10% × ½ × $1,000,000)		50,000
To record interest.		
Cash [$50,000 – (8% × ½ × $1 million)]	10,000	
Interest rate swap ($9,615 – 9,363)	252	
Interest revenue (9% × ½ × $9,363)		421
Holding gain—interest rate swap (to balance)		9,831
To record the net cash settlement, accrued interest on the swap, and change in the fair value of the derivative.		
Holding loss—hedged note	4,831	
Notes payable ($1,009,615 – 1,009,363 + 4,579)		4,831
To record the change in fair value of the note due to interest rate changes.		

*We could use a premium on the note to adjust its carrying amount.

We determine interest on the note the same way we do for any liability, as you learned earlier—at the effective rate (9% × ½) times the outstanding balance ($1,009,363). This results in reducing the note's carrying amount for the cash interest paid in excess of the interest expense.

The fair value of the swap increased due to the interest rate decline by $252 (from $9,363 to $9,615). The holding gain we recognize in earnings consists of that increase (a) plus the $10,000 cash settlement also created by the interest rate decline and (b) minus the $421 increase that results not from the interest rate decline, but from interest accruing on the asset.[18] Similarly, we adjust the note's carrying value by the amount necessary to increase it to fair value, allowing for the $4,579 reduction in the note in the earlier entry to record interest.

At June 30, 2010, Wintel repeats the process of adjusting to fair value both the derivative investment and the note being hedged.

June 30, 2010		
Interest expense (8% × ½ × $1,009,615)	40,385	
Notes payable (difference)	9,615	
Cash (10% × ½ × $1,000,000)		50,000
To record interest.		
Cash [$50,000 – (9% × ½ × $1 million)]	5,000	
Holding loss—interest rate swap (to balance)	5,000	
Interest rate swap ($0 – $9,615)		9,615
Interest revenue (8% × ½ × $9,615)		385
To record the net cash settlement, accrued interest on the swap, and change in the fair value of the derivative.		
Notes payable ($1,000,000 – 1,009,615 + 9,615)	0	
Holding gain—hedged note		0
To record the change in fair value of the note due to interest rate changes.		
Note payable	1,000,000	
Cash		1,000,000
To repay the loan		

Interest expense is the effective rate times the outstanding balance.

The net interest received is the difference between the fixed interest (5%) and floating interest (4.5%).

The swap's fair value now is zero.

The net interest received is the difference between the fixed rate (5%) and floating rate (4.5%) times $1 million. The fair value of the swap decreased by $9,615 (from $9,615 to zero).[19] The holding loss we recognize in earnings consists of that decline (a) minus the $5,000 portion of the decline resulting from it being realized in cash settlement and (b) plus the $385 increase that results not from the interest rate change, but from interest accruing on the asset.

Now let's see how the carrying values changed for the swap account and the note:

	Swap		Note	
Jan. 1, 2009				1,000,000
June 30, 2009	9,363			9,363
Dec. 31, 2009	252		4,579	4,831
June 30, 2010		9,615	9,615	
			1,000,000	
	0			0

The income statement is affected as follows:

	Income Statement + (−)	
June 30, 2009	(50,000)	Interest expense
	0	Interest revenue (no time has passed)
	14,363	Holding gain interest rate swap
	(9,363)	Holding loss—hedged note
	(45,000)	Net effect—same as floating interest payment
Dec. 31, 2009	(45,421)	Interest expense
	421	Interest revenue
	9,831	Holding gain—interest rate swap
	(4,831)	Holding loss—hedged note
	(40,000)	Net effect—same as floating interest payment

[18]The investment in the interest rate swap represents the present value of expected future net interest receipts. As with other such assets, interest accrues at the effective rate times the outstanding balance. You also can think of the accrued interest mathematically as the increase in present value of the future cash flows as we get one period nearer to the dates when the cash will be received.

[19]Because there are no future cash receipts or payments from the swap arrangement at this point, the fair value of the swap is zero.

June 30, 2010	(40,385)	Interest expense
	385	Interest revenue
	(5,000)	Holding gain—interest rate swap
	0	Holding loss—hedged note
	(45,000)	Net effect—same as floating interest payment

As this demonstrates, the swap effectively converts Wintel's fixed-interest debt to floating-interest debt.

THE BOTTOM LINE

1. All derivatives are reported in the balance sheet at fair value.
2. *Hedging* means taking a risk position that is opposite to an actual position that is exposed to risk. For a derivative used to hedge against exposure to risk, treatment of any gain or loss from fair value changes depends on whether the derivative is designated as (a) a fair value hedge or (b) a cash flow hedge.
3. We recognize a gain or loss from a *fair value hedge* immediately in earnings along with the loss or gain from the item being hedged. This is so the income effects of the hedge instrument and the income effects of the item being hedged will affect earnings at the same time.
4. We defer a gain or loss from a *cash flow hedge* as part of Other comprehensive income until it can be recognized in earnings along with the earnings effect of the item being hedged.
5. Imperfect hedges result in part of the derivative gain or loss being included in current earnings. We ignore market value changes unrelated to the risk being hedged.
6. Extensive disclosure requirements about derivatives are designed to provide investors and creditors information about the adequacy of a company's risk management and the company's success in reducing risks, including risks not managed successfully. ●

QUESTIONS FOR REVIEW OF KEY TOPICS

Q A–1 Some financial instruments are called derivatives. Why?

Q A–2 Should gains and losses on a fair value hedge be recorded as they occur, or should they be recorded to coincide with losses and gains on the item being hedged?

Q A–3 Hines Moving Company held a fixed-rate debt of $2 million. The company wanted to hedge its fair value exposure with an interest rate swap. However, the only notional available at the time on the type of swap it desired was $2.5 million. What will be the effect of any gain or loss on the $500,000 notional difference?

Q A–4 What is a futures contract?

Q A–5 What is the effect on interest of an interest rate swap?

Q A–6 How are derivatives reported on the balance sheet? Why?

Q A–7 When is a gain or a loss from a cash flow hedge reported in earnings?

EXERCISES

available with McGraw-Hill's Homework Manager www.mhhe.com/spiceland5e 

E A–1
Derivatives—hedge classification

Indicate (by abbreviation) the type of hedge each activity described below would represent.

Hedge Type

FV	Fair value hedge
CF	Cash flow hedge
FC	Foreign currency hedge
N	Would not qualify as a hedge

Activity

____ 1. An options contract to hedge possible future price changes of inventory.

____ 2. A futures contract to hedge exposure to interest rate changes prior to replacing bank notes when they mature.

____ 3. An interest rate swap to synthetically convert floating rate debt into fixed rate debt.

____ 4. An interest rate swap to synthetically convert fixed rate debt into floating rate debt.

____ 5. A futures contract to hedge possible future price changes of timber covered by a firm commitment to sell.

____ 6. A futures contract to hedge possible future price changes of a forecasted sale of tin.
____ 7. ExxonMobil's net investment in a Kuwait oil field.
____ 8. An interest rate swap to synthetically convert floating rate interest on a stock investment into fixed rate interest.
____ 9. An interest rate swap to synthetically convert fixed rate interest on a held-to-maturity debt investment into floating rate interest.
____ 10. An interest rate swap to synthetically convert floating rate interest on a held-to-maturity debt investment into fixed rate interest.
____ 11. An interest rate swap to synthetically convert fixed rate interest on a stock investment into floating rate interest.

E A–2
Derivatives; interest rate swap; fixed rate debt

On January 1, 2009, LLB Industries borrowed $200,000 from Trust Bank by issuing a two-year, 10% note, with interest payable quarterly. LLB entered into a two-year interest rate swap agreement on January 1, 2009, and designated the swap as a fair value hedge. Its intent was to hedge the risk that general interest rates will decline, causing the fair value of its debt to increase. The agreement called for the company to receive payment based on a 10% fixed interest rate on a notional amount of $200,000 and to pay interest based on a floating interest rate. The contract called for cash settlement of the net interest amount quarterly.

Floating (LIBOR) settlement rates were 10% at January 1, 8% at March 31, and 6% June 30, 2009. The fair values of the swap are quotes obtained from a derivatives dealer. Those quotes and the fair values of the note are as indicated below.

	January 1	March 31	June 30
Fair value of interest rate swap	0	$ 6,472	$ 11,394
Fair value of note payable	$200,000	$206,472	$211,394

Required:
1. Calculate the net cash settlement at March 31 and June 30, 2009.
2. Prepare the journal entries through June 30, 2009, to record the issuance of the note, interest, and necessary adjustments for changes in fair value.

E A–3
Derivatives; interest rate swap; fixed rate investment

(This is a variation of Exercise A–2, modified to consider an investment in debt securities.)

On January 1, 2009, S&S Corporation invested in LLB Industries' negotiable two-year, 10% notes, with interest receivable quarterly. The company classified the investment as available-for-sale. S&S entered into a two-year interest rate swap agreement on January 1, 2009, and designated the swap as a fair value hedge. Its intent was to hedge the risk that general interest rates will decline, causing the fair value of its investment to increase. The agreement called for the company to make payment based on a 10% fixed interest rate on a notional amount of $200,000 and to receive interest based on a floating interest rate. The contract called for cash settlement of the net interest amount quarterly.

Floating (LIBOR) settlement rates were 10% at January 1, 8% at March 31, and 6% June 30, 2009. The fair values of the swap are quotes obtained from a derivatives dealer. Those quotes and the fair values of the investment in notes are as follows:

	January 1	March 31	June 30
Fair value of interest rate swap	0	$ 6,472	$ 11,394
Fair value of the investment in notes	$200,000	$206,472	$211,394

Required:
1. Calculate the net cash settlement at March 31 and June 30, 2009
2. Prepare the journal entries through June 30, 2009, to record the investment in notes, interest, and necessary adjustments for changes in fair value.

E A–4
Derivatives; interest rate swap; fixed rate debt; fair value change unrelated to hedged risk

(This is a variation of Exercise A–2, modified to consider fair value change unrelated to hedged risk.)

LLB Industries borrowed $200,000 from Trust Bank by issuing a two-year, 10% note, with interest payable quarterly. LLB entered into a two-year interest rate swap agreement on January 1, 2009 and designated the swap as a fair value hedge. Its intent was to hedge the risk that general interest rates will decline, causing the fair value of its debt to increase. The agreement called for the company to receive payment based on a 10% fixed interest rate on a notional amount of $200,000 and to pay interest based on a floating interest rate.

Floating (LIBOR) settlement rates were 10% at January 1, 8% at March 31, and 6% at June 30, 2009. The fair values of the swap are quotes obtained from a derivatives dealer. Those quotes and the fair values of the note are as indicated below. The additional rise in the fair value of the note (higher than that of the swap) on June 30 was due to investors' perceptions that the creditworthiness of LLB was improving.

	January 1	March 31	June 30
Fair value of interest rate swap	0	$ 6,472	$ 11,394
Fair value of note payable	$200,000	$206,472	$220,000

Required:
1. Calculate the net cash settlement at June 30, 2009
2. Prepare the journal entries on June 30, 2009, to record the interest and necessary adjustments for changes in fair value.

E A–5
Derivatives; interest rate swap; fixed rate debt; extended method

This is a variation of Exercise A–2, modified to consider the extended method.

On January 1, 2009, LLB Industries borrowed $200,000 from Trust Bank by issuing a two-year, 10% note, with interest payable quarterly. LLB entered into a two-year interest rate swap agreement on January 1, 2009, and designated the swap as a fair value hedge. Its intent was to hedge the risk that general interest rates will decline, causing the fair value of its debt to increase. The agreement called for the company to receive payment based on a 10% fixed interest rate on a notional amount of $200,000 and to pay interest based on a floating interest rate. The contract called for cash settlement of the net interest amount quarterly.

Floating (LIBOR) settlement rates were 10% at January 1, 8% at March 31, and 6% at June 30, 2009. The fair values of the swap are quotes obtained from a derivatives dealer. Those quotes and the fair values of the note are as follows:

	January 1	March 31	June 30
Fair value of interest rate swap	0	$ 6,472	$ 11,394
Fair value of note payable	$200,000	$206,472	$211,394

Required:
Prepare the journal entries through June 30, 2009, to record the issuance of the note, interest, and necessary adjustments for changes in fair value. Use the extended method demonstrated in Illustration A–2.

E A–6
Derivatives; interest rate swap; fixed-rate debt; fair value change unrelated to hedged risk; extended method

(Note: This is a variation of Exercise A–5, modified to consider fair value change unrelated to hedged risk.)

On January 1, 2009, LLB Industries borrowed $200,000 from trust Bank by issuing a two-year, 10% note, with interest payable quarterly. LLB entered into a two-year interest rate swap agreement on January 1, 2009, and designated the swap as a fair value hedge. Its intent was to hedge the risk that general interest rates will decline, causing the fair value of its debt to increase. The agreement called for the company to receive payment based on a 10% fixed interest rate on a notional amount of $200,000 and to pay interest based on a floating interest rate. The contract called for cash settlement of the net interest amount quarterly.

Floating (LIBOR) settlement rates were 10% at January 1, 8% at March 31, and 6% June 30, 2009. The fair values of the swap are quotes obtained from a derivatives dealer. Those quotes and the fair values of the note are as indicated below. The additional rise in the fair value of the note (higher than that of the swap) on June 30 was due to investors' perceptions that the creditworthiness of LLB was improving.

	January 1	March 31	June 30
Fair value of interest rate swap	0	$ 6,472	$ 11,394
Fair value of note payable	$200,000	206,472	220,000

Required:
1. Calculate the net cash settlement at June 30, 2009.
2. Prepare the journal entries on June 30, 2009, to record the interest and necessary adjustments for changes in fair value. Use the extended method demonstrated in Illustration A–2.

PROBLEMS

available with McGraw-Hill's Homework Manager www.mhhe.com/spiceland5e 

P A–1
Derivatives—interest rate swap

On January 1, 2009, Labtech Circuits borrowed $100,000 from First Bank by issuing a three-year, 8% note, payable on December 31, 2011. Labtech wanted to hedge the risk that general interest rates will decline, causing the fair value of its debt to increase. Therefore, Labtech entered into a three-year interest rate swap agreement on January 1, 2009, and designated the swap as a fair value hedge. The agreement called for the company to receive payment based on an 8% fixed interest rate on a notional amount of $100,000 and to pay interest based on a floating interest rate tied to LIBOR. The contract called for cash settlement of the net interest amount on December 31 of each year.

Floating (LIBOR) settlement rates were 8% at inception and 9%, 7%, and 7% at the end of 2009, 2010, and 2011, respectively. The fair values of the swap are quotes obtained from a derivatives dealer. These quotes and the fair values of the note are as follows:

	January 1	December 31		
	2009	2009	2010	2011
Fair value of interest rate swap	0	$ (1,759)	$ 935	0
Fair value of note payable	$100,000	$98,241	$100,935	$100,000

Required:

1. Calculate the net cash settlement at the end of 2009, 2010, and 2011.
2. Prepare the journal entries during 2009 to record the issuance of the note, interest, and necessary adjustments for changes in fair value.
3. Prepare the journal entries during 2010 to record interest, net cash interest settlement for the interest rate swap, and necessary adjustments for changes in fair value.
4. Prepare the journal entries during 2011 to record interest, net cash interest settlement for the interest rate swap, necessary adjustments for changes in fair value, and repayment of the debt.
5. Calculate the carrying values of both the swap account and the note in each of the three years.
6. Calculate the net effect on earnings of the hedging arrangement in each of the three years. (Ignore income taxes.)
7. Suppose the fair value of the note at December 31, 2009, had been $97,000 rather than $98,217 with the additional decline in fair value due to investors' perceptions that the creditworthiness of Labtech was worsening. How would that affect your entries to record changes in the fair values?

P A–2
Derivatives; interest rate swap; comprehensive

CMOS Chips is hedging a 20-year, $10 million, 7% bond payable with a 20-year interest rate swap and has designated the swap as a fair value hedge. The agreement called for CMOS to receive payment based on a 7% fixed interest rate on a notional amount of $10 million and to pay interest based on a floating interest rate tied to LIBOR. The contract calls for cash settlement of the net interest amount on December 31 of each year.

At December 31, 2009, the fair value of the derivative and of the hedged bonds has increased by $100,000 because interest rates declined during the reporting period.

Required:

1. Does CMOS have an unrealized gain or loss on the derivative for the period? On the bonds? Will earnings increase or decrease due to the hedging arrangement? Why?
2. Suppose interest rates increased, rather than decreased, causing the fair value of both the derivative and of the hedged bonds to decrease by $100,000. Would CMOS have an unrealized gain or loss on the derivative for the period? On the bonds? Would earnings increase or decrease due to the hedging arrangement? Why?
3. Suppose the fair value of the bonds at December 31, 2009, had increased by $110,000 rather than $100,000, with the additional increase in fair value due to investors' perceptions that the creditworthiness of CMOS was improving. Would CMOS have an unrealized gain or loss on the derivative for the period? On the bonds? Would earnings increase or decrease due to the hedging arrangement? Why?
4. Suppose the notional amount of the swap had been $12 million, rather than the $10 million principal amount of the bonds. As a result, at December 31, 2009, the swap's fair value had increased by $120,000 rather than $100,000. Would CMOS have an unrealized gain or loss on the derivative for the period? On the bonds? Would earnings increase or decrease due to the hedging arrangement? Why?
5. Suppose BIOS Corporation is an investor having purchased all $10 million of the bonds issued by CMOS as described in the original situation above. BIOS is hedging its investment, classified as available-for-sale, with a 20-year interest rate swap and has designated the swap as a fair value hedge. The agreement called for BIOS to make *payment* based on a 7% fixed interest rate on a notional amount of $10 million and to *receive* interest based on a floating interest rate tied to LIBOR. Would BIOS have an unrealized gain or loss on the derivative for the period due to interest rates having declined? On the bonds? Would earnings increase or decrease due to the hedging arrangement? Why?

P A–3
Derivatives; interest rate swap; fixed rate debt; extended method

(Note: This is a variation of Problem A–1, modified to consider the extended method demonstrated in Illustration A–2.)

On January 1, 2009, Labtech Circuits borrowed $100,000 from First Bank by issuing a three-year, 8% note, payable on December 31, 2011. Labtech wanted to hedge the risk that general interest rates will decline, causing the fair value of its debt to increase. Therefore, Labtech entered into a three-year interest rate swap agreement on January 1, 2009, and designated the swap as a fair value hedge. The agreement called for the company to receive payment based on an 8% fixed interest rate on a notional amount of $100,000 and to pay interest based on a floating interest rate tied to LIBOR. The contract called for cash settlement of the net interest amount on December 31 of each year.

Floating (LIBOR) settlement rates were 8% at inception and 9%, 7%, and 7% at the end of 2009, 2010, and 2011, respectively. The fair values of the swap are quotes obtained from a derivatives dealer. Those quotes and the fair values of the note are as follows:

	January 1	December 31		
	2009	2009	2010	2011
Fair value of interest rate swap	0	$ (1,759)	$ 935	0
Fair value of note payable	$100,000	$ 98,241	100,935	$100,000

Required:

Use the extended method demonstrated in Illustration A–2.

1. Calculate the net cash settlement at the end of 2009, 2010, and 2011.
2. Prepare the journal entries during 2009 to record the issuance of the note, interest, and necessary adjustments for changes in fair value.
3. Prepare the journal entries during 2010 to record interest, net cash interest settlement for the interest rate swap, and necessary adjustments for changes in fair value.
4. Prepare the journal entries during 2011 to record interest, net cash interest settlement for the interest rate swap, necessary adjustments for changes in fair value, and repayment of the debt.
5. Calculate the carrying values of both the swap account and the note in each of the three years.
6. Calculate the net effect on earnings of the hedging arrangement in each of the three years. (Ignore income taxes.)
7. Suppose the fair value of the note at December 31, 2009, had been $97,000 rather than $98,217 with the additional decline in fair value due to investors' perceptions that the creditworthiness of Labtech was worsening. How would that affect your entries to record changes in the fair values?

BROADEN YOUR PERSPECTIVE

Apply your critical-thinking ability to the knowledge you've gained. These cases will provide you an opportunity to develop your research, analysis, judgment, and communication skills. You also will work with other students, integrate what you've learned, apply it in real world situations, and consider its global and ethical ramifications. This practice will broaden your knowledge and further develop your decision-making abilities.

Real World Case A–1
Derivative losses; recognition in earnings

The following is an excerpt from a disclosure note of **Johnson & Johnson**:

15. Financial Instruments (in part)

As of December 31, 2006, the balance of deferred net losses on derivatives included in accumulated other comprehensive income was $9 million after-tax. The Company expects that substantially all of this amount will be reclassified into earnings over the next 12 months as a result of transactions that are expected to occur over that period.

Required:

1. Johnson & Johnson indicates that it expects that substantially all of the balance of deferred net losses on derivatives will be reclassified into earnings over the next 12 months as a result of transactions that are expected to occur over that period. What is meant by "reclassified into earnings"?
2. What type(s) of hedging transaction might be accounted for in this way?

Communication Case A–2
Derivatives; hedge accounting

A conceptual question in accounting for derivatives is: Should gains and losses on a hedge instrument be recorded as they occur, or should they be recorded to coincide (match) with income effects of the item being hedged?

ABI Wholesalers plans to issue long-term notes in May that will replace its $20 million of 9.5% bonds when they mature in July. ABI is exposed to the risk that interest rates in July will have risen, increasing borrowing costs (reducing the selling price of its notes). To hedge that possibility, ABI entered a (Treasury bond) futures contract in May to deliver (sell) bonds in July at their *current* price.

As a result, if interest rates rise, borrowing costs will go up for ABI because it will sell notes at a higher interest cost (or lower price). But that loss will be offset (approximately) by the gain produced by being in the opposite position on Treasury bond futures.

Two opposing viewpoints are:

View 1: Gains and losses on instruments designed to hedge anticipated transactions should be recorded as they occur.

View 2: Gains and losses on instruments designed to hedge anticipated transactions should be recorded to coincide (match) with income effects of the item being hedged.

In considering this question, focus on conceptual issues regarding the practicable and theoretically appropriate treatment, unconstrained by GAAP. Your instructor will divide the class into two to six groups depending on the size of the class. The mission of your group is to reach consensus on the appropriate accounting for the gains and losses on instruments designed to hedge anticipated transactions.

Required:

1. Each group member should deliberate the situation independently and draft a tentative argument prior to the class session for which the case is assigned.

2. In class, each group will meet for 10 to 15 minutes in different areas of the classroom. During that meeting, group members will take turns sharing their suggestions for the purpose of arriving at a single group treatment.
3. After the allotted time, a spokesperson for each group (selected during the group meetings) will share the group's solution with the class. The goal of the class is to incorporate the views of each group into a consensus approach to the situation.

Real World Case A–3
Researching the way interest rate futures prices are quoted on the Chicago Mercantile Exchange; retrieving information from the Internet

The **Chicago Mercantile Exchange,** or Merc, at 30 S. Wacker Drive in Chicago, is the world's largest financial exchange, an international marketplace enabling institutions and businesses to trade futures and options contracts including currencies, interest rates, stock indices, and agricultural commodities.

Required:

1. Access the Merc on the Internet. The web address is **www.cme.com.**
2. Access the daily settlement prices within the site. Scroll to find the 13-week Treasury bill futures.
3. What are the settlement prices for September and December futures contracts?
4. In terms of dollars, how can we interpret the settlement price?

Research Case A–4
Issue related to the derivatives standard; research an article

In an effort to keep up with the rapidly changing global financial markets, the FASB issued a standard—*SFAS No. 133*—on accounting for derivative financial instruments. A *Journal of Accountancy* article that discusses this standard is "The Decision on Derivatives," by Arlette C. Wilson, Gary Waters and Barry J. Bryan, November 1998.

Required:

On the Internet, go to the AICPA site at **www.aicpa.org** and find the article mentioned.

1. What are the primary problems or issues the FASB is attempting to address with the new standard?
2. In considering the issues, the FASB made four fundamental decisions that became the cornerstones of the proposed statement. What are those fundamental decisions? Which do you think is most critical to fair financial reporting?

Glossary

Accounting equation the process used to capture the effect of economic events; Assets = Liabilities + Owner's Equity.

Accounting Principles Board (APB) the second private sector body delegated the task of setting accounting standards.

Accounts storage areas to keep track of the increases and decreases in financial position elements.

Accounts payable obligations to suppliers of merchandise or of services purchased on open account.

Accounts receivable receivables resulting from the sale of goods or services on account.

Accounts receivable aging schedule applying different percentages to accounts receivable balances depending on the length of time outstanding.

Accrual accounting measurement of the entity's accomplishments and resource sacrifices during the period, regardless of when cash is received or paid.

Accruals when the cash flow comes after either expense or revenue recognition.

Accrued interest interest that has accrued since the last interest date.

Accrued liabilities expenses already incurred but not yet paid (accrued expenses).

Accrued receivables the recognition of revenue earned before cash is received.

Accumulated benefit obligation (ABO) the discounted present value of estimated retirement benefits earned so far by employees, applying the plan's pension formula using existing compensation levels.

Accumulated other comprehensive income amount of other comprehensive income (nonowner changes in equity other than net income) accumulated over the current and prior periods.

Accumulated postretirement benefit obligation (APBO) portion of the EPBO attributed to employee service up to a particular date.

Acid-test ratio current assets, excluding inventories and prepaid items, divided by current liabilities.

Acquisition costs the amounts paid to acquire the rights to explore for undiscovered natural resources or to extract proven natural resources.

Activity-based method allocation of an asset's cost base using a measure of the asset's input or output.

Actuary a professional trained in a particular branch of statistics and mathematics to assess the various uncertainties and to estimate the company's obligation to employees in connection with its pension plan.

Additions the adding of a new major component to an existing asset.

Adjusted trial balance trial balance after adjusting entries have been recorded.

Adjusting entries internal transactions recorded at the end of any period when financial statements are prepared.

Allocation base the value of the usefulness that is expected to be consumed.

Allocation method the pattern in which the usefulness is expected to be consumed.

Allowance method recording bad debt expense and reducing accounts receivable indirectly by crediting a contra account (allowance for uncollectible accounts) to accounts receivable for an estimate of the amount that eventually will prove uncollectible.

American Institute of Accountants (AIA)/American Institute of Certified Public Accountants (AICPA) national organization of professional public accountants.

Amortization cost allocation for intangibles.

Amortization schedule schedule that reflects the changes in the debt over its term to maturity.

Annuity cash flows received or paid in the same amount each period.

Annuity due cash flows occurring at the beginning of each period.

Antidilutive securities the effect of the conversion or exercise of potential common shares would be to increase rather than decrease, EPS.

Articles of incorporation statement of the nature of the firm's business activities, the shares to be issued, and the composition of the initial board of directors.

Asset retirement obligations (AROs) obligations associated with the disposition of an operational asset.

Assets probable future economic benefits obtained or controlled by a particular entity as a result of past transactions or events.

Asset turnover ratio measure of a company's efficiency in using assets to generate revenue.

Assigning using receivables as collateral for loans; nonpayment of a debt will require the proceeds from collecting the assigned receivables to go directly toward repayment of the debt.

Attribution process of assigning the cost of benefits to the years during which those benefits are assumed to be earned by employees.

Auditors independent intermediaries who help ensure that management has appropriately applied GAAP in preparing the company's financial statements.

Auditor's report report issued by CPAs who audit the financial statements that informs users of the audit findings.

Average collection period indication of the average age of accounts receivable.

Average cost method assumes cost of goods sold and ending inventory consist of a mixture of all the goods available for sale.

Average days in inventory indicates the average number of days it normally takes to sell inventory.

Bad debt expense an operating expense incurred to boost sales; inherent cost of granting credit.

Balance sheet a position statement that presents an organized list of assets, liabilities, and equity at a particular point in time.

Balance sheet approach determination of bad debt expense by estimating the net realizable value of accounts receivable to be reported in the balance sheet.

Bank reconciliation comparison of the bank balance with the balance in the company's own records.

Bargain purchase option (BPO) provision in the lease contract that gives the lessee the option of purchasing the leased property at a bargain price.

Bargain renewal option gives the lessee the option to renew the lease at a bargain rate.

Basic EPS computed by dividing income available to common stockholders (net income less any preferred stock dividends) by the weighted-average number of common shares outstanding for the period.

Billings of construction contract contra account to the asset construction in progress; subtracted from construction in progress to determine balance sheet presentation.

Board of directors establishes corporate policies and appoints officers who manage the corporation.

Bond indenture document that describes specific promises made to bondholders.

Bonds A form of debt consisting of separable units (bonds) that obligates the issuing corporation to repay a stated amount at a specified maturity date and to pay interest to bondholders between the issue date and maturity.

Book value assets minus liabilities as shown in the balance sheet.

Callable allows the issuing company to buy back, or call, outstanding bonds from the bondholders before their scheduled maturity date.

Capital budgeting The process of evaluating the purchase of operational assets.

Capital leases installment purchases/sales that are formulated outwardly as leases.

Capital markets mechanisms that foster the allocation of resources efficiently.

Cash currency and coins, balances in checking accounts, and items acceptable for deposit in these accounts, such as checks and money orders received from customers.

Cash basis accounting/net operating cash flow difference between cash receipts and cash disbursements during a reporting period from transactions related to providing goods and services to customers.

Cash disbursements journal record of cash disbursements.

Cash discounts sales discounts; represent reductions not in the selling price of a good or service but in the amount to be paid by a credit customer if paid within a specific period of time.

Cash equivalents certain negotiable items such as commercial paper, money market funds, and U.S. Treasury bills that are highly liquid investments quickly convertible to cash.

Cash equivalents short-term, highly liquid investments that can be readily converted to cash with little risk of loss.

Cash flow hedge a derivative used to hedge against the exposure to changes in cash inflows or cash outflows of an asset or liability or a forecasted transaction (like a future purchase or sale).

Cash flows from financing activities both inflows and outflows of cash resulting from the external financing of a business.

Cash flows from investing activities both outflows and inflows of cash caused by the acquisition and disposition of assets.

Cash flows from operating activities both inflows and outflows of cash that result from activities reported on the income statement.

Cash receipts journal record of cash receipts.

Certified Public Accountants (CPAs) licensed individuals who can represent that the financial statements have been audited in accordance with generally accepted auditing standards.

Change in accounting estimate a change in an estimate when new information comes to light.

Change in accounting principle switch by a company from one accounting method to another.

Change in reporting entity presentation of consolidated financial statements in place of statements of individual companies, or a change in the specific companies that constitute the group for which consolidated or combined statements are prepared.

Closing process the temporary accounts are reduced to zero balances, and these temporary account balances are closed (transferred) to retained earnings to reflect the changes that have occurred in that account during the period.

Commercial paper unsecured notes sold in minimum denominations of $25,000 with maturities ranging from 30 to 270 days.

Committee on Accounting Procedure (CAP) the first private sector body that was delegated the task of setting accounting standards.

Comparability the ability to help users see similarities and differences among events and conditions.

Comparative financial statements corresponding financial statements from the previous years accompanying the issued financial statements.

Compensating balance a specified balance (usually some percentage of the committee amount) a borrower of a loan is asked to maintain in a low-interest or noninterest-bearing account at the bank.

Completed contract method recognition of revenue for a long-term contract when the project is complete.

Complex capital structure potential common shares are outstanding.

Composite depreciation method physically dissimilar assets are aggregated to gain the convenience of group depreciation.

Compound interest interest computed not only on the initial investment but also on the accumulated interest in previous periods.

Comprehensive income traditional net income plus other nonowner changes in equity.

Conceptual framework deals with theoretical and conceptual issues and provides an underlying structure for current and future accounting and reporting standards.

Conservatism practice followed in an attempt to ensure that uncertainties and risks inherent in business situations are adequately considered.

Consignment the consignor physically transfers the goods to the other company (the consignee), but the consignor retains legal title.

Consistency permits valid comparisons between different periods.

Consolidated financial statements combination of the separate financial statements of the parent and subsidiary each period into a single aggregate set of financial statements as if there were only one company.

Construction in progress asset account equivalent to the asset work-in-progress inventory in a manufacturing company.

Contingently issuable shares additional shares of common stock to be issued, contingent on the occurrence of some future circumstance.

Conventional retail method applying the retail inventory method in such a way that LCM is approximated.

Convertible bonds bonds for which bondholders have the option to convert the bonds into shares of stock.

Copyright exclusive right of protection given to a creator of a published work, such as a song, painting, photograph, or book.

Corporation the dominant form of business organization that acquires capital from investors in exchange for ownership interest and from creditors by borrowing.

Correction of an error an adjustment a company makes due to an error made.

Cost effectiveness the perceived benefit of increased decision usefulness exceeds the anticipated cost of providing that information.

Cost of goods sold cost of the inventory sold during the period.

Cost recovery method deferral of all gross profit recognition until the cost of the item sold has been recovered.

Cost-to-retail percentage ratio found by dividing goods available for sale at cost by goods available for sale at retail.

Coupons bonds name of the owner was not registered; the holder actually clipped an attached coupon and redeemed it in accordance with instructions on the indenture.

Credits represent the right side of the account.

Cumulative if the specified dividend is not paid in a given year, the unpaid dividends accumulate and must be made up in a later dividend year before any dividends are paid on common shares.

Current assets includes assets that are cash, will be converted into cash, or will be used up within one year or the operating cycle, whichever is longer.

Current liabilities expected to require current assets and usually are payable within one year.

Current maturities of long-term debt the current installment due on long-term debt, reported as a current liability.

Current ratio current assets divided by current liabilities.

Date of record specific date stated as to when the determination will be made of the recipient of the dividend.

Debenture bond secured only by the "full faith and credit" of the issuing corporation.

Debits represent the left side of the account.

Debt issue cost with either publicly or privately sold debt, the issuing company will incur costs in connection with issuing bonds or notes, such as legal and accounting fees and printing costs, in addition to registration and underwriting fees.

Debt to equity ratio compares resources provided by creditors with resources provided by owners.

Decision usefulness the quality of being useful to decision making.

Default risk a company's ability to pay its obligations when they come due.

Deferred annuity the first cash flow occurs more than the one period after the date the agreement begins.

Deferred tax asset taxes to be saved in the future when future deductible amounts reduce taxable income (when the temporary differences reverse).

Deferred tax liability taxes to be paid in the future when future taxable amounts become taxable (when the temporary differences reverse).

Deficit debit balance in retained earnings.

Defined benefit pension plans fixed retirement benefits defined by a designated formula, based on employees' years of service and annual compensation.

Defined contribution pension plans fixed annual contributions to a pension fund; employees choose where funds are invested—usually stocks or fixed-income securities.

Depletion allocation of the cost of natural resources.

Depreciation cost allocation for plant and equipment.

Derivatives financial instruments usually created to hedge against risks created by other financial instruments or by transactions that have yet to occur but are anticipated and that "derive" their values or contractually required cash flows from some other security or index.

Detachable stock purchase warrants the investor has the option to purchase a stated number of shares of common stock at a specified option price, within a given period of time.

Development costs for natural resources, costs incurred after the resource has been discovered but before production begins.

Diluted EPS incorporates the dilutive effect of all potential common shares.

Direct financing lease lease in which the lessor finances the asset for the lessee and earns interest revenue over the lease term.

Direct method the cash effect of each operating activity (i.e., income statement item) is reported directly on the statement of cash flows.

Direct write-off method an allowance for uncollectible accounts is not used; instead bad debts that do arise are written off as bad debt expense.

Disclosure notes additional insights about company operations, accounting principles, contractual agreements, and pending litigation.

Discontinued operations The discontinuance of a component of an entity whose operations and cash flows can be clearly distinguished from the rest of the entity.

Discount Arises when bonds are sold for less than face amount.

Discounting the transfer of a note receivable to a financial institution.

Distributions to owners decreases in equity resulting from transfers to owners.

Dividend distribution to shareholders of a portion of assets earned.

Dollar-value LIFO (DVL) Inventory is viewed as a quantity of value instead of a physical quantity of goods. Instead of layers of units from different purchases, the DVL inventory pool is viewed as comprising layers of dollar value from different years.

Dollar-value LIFO retail method LIFO retail method combined with dollar-value LIFO.

Double-declining-balance (DDB) method 200% of the straight-line rate is multiplied by book value.

Double-entry system dual effect that each transaction has on the accounting equation when recorded.

DuPont framework depict return on equity as determined by profit margin (representing profitability), asset turnover (representing efficiency), and the equity multiplier (representing leverage).

Early extinguishment of debt debt is retired prior to its scheduled maturity date.

Earnings per share (EPS) the amount of income earned by a company expressed on a per share basis.

Earnings quality refers to the ability of reported earnings (income) to predict a company's future earnings.

Economic events any event that directly affects the financial position of the company.

Effective interest method recording interest each period as the effective rate of interest multiplied by the outstanding balance of the debt.

Effective rate the actual rate at which money grows per year.

Emerging Issues Task Force (EITF) responsible for providing more timely responses to emerging financial reporting issues.

Employee share purchase plans permit all employees to buy shares directly from their company, often at favorable terms.

Equity method used when an investor can't control, but can significantly influence, the investee.

Equity multiplier depicts leverage as total assets divided by total equity.

Equity/net assets called shareholders' equity or stockholders' equity for a corporation; the residual interest in the assets of an entity that remains after deducting liabilities.

Estimates prediction of future events.

Ethics a code or moral system that provides criteria for evaluating right and wrong.

Ex-dividend date date usually two business days before the date of the record and is the first day the stock trades without the right to receive the declared dividend.

Executory costs maintenance, insurance, taxes, and any other costs usually associated with ownership.

Expected cash flow approach adjusts the cash flows, not the discount rate, for the uncertainty or risk of those cash flows.

Expected economic life useful life of an asset.

Expected postretirement benefit obligation (EPBO) discounted present value of the total net cost to the employer of postretirement benefits.

Expected return on plan assets estimated long-term return on invested assets.

Expenses outflows or other using up of assets or incurrences of liabilities during a period from delivering or producing good, rendering services, or other activities that constitute the entity's ongoing major, or central, operations.

Exploration costs for natural resources, expenditures such as drilling a well, or excavating a mine, or any other costs of searching for natural resources.

External events exchange between the company and a separate economic entity.

Extraordinary items material events and transactions that are both unusual in nature and infrequent in occurrence.

F.O.B. (free on board) shipping point legal title to the goods changes hands at the point of shipment when the seller delivers the goods to the common carrier, and the purchaser is responsible for shipping costs and transit insurance.

F.O.B. destination the seller is responsible for shipping and the legal title does not pass until the goods arrive at their destination.

Factor financial institution that buys receivables for cash, handles the billing and collection of the receivables, and charges a fee for this service.

Fair value hedge a derivative is used to hedge against the exposure to changes in the fair value of an asset or liability or a firm commitment.

Fair value hierarchy prioritizes the inputs companies should use when determinig fair value.

Fair value option allows companies to report their financial assets and liabilities at fair value.

Financial accounting provides relevant financial information to various external users.

Financial Accounting Foundation (FAF) responsible for selecting the members of the FASB and its Advisory Council, ensuring adequate funding of FASB activities, and exercising general oversight of the FASB's activities.

Financial Accounting Standards Board (FASB) the current private sector body that has been delegated the task of setting accounting standards.

Financial activities cash inflows and outflows from transactions with creditors and owners.

Financial instrument cash; evidence of an ownership interest in an entity; a contract that imposes on one entity an obligation to deliver cash or another financial instrument, and conveys to the second entity a right to receive cash or another financial instrument; and a contract that imposes on one entity an obligation to exchange financial instruments on potentially unfavorable terms and conveys to a second entity a right to exchange other financial instruments on potentially favorable terms.

Financial leverage by earning a return on borrowed funds that exceeds the cost of borrowing the funds, a company can provide its shareholders with a total return higher than it could achieve by employing equity funds alone.

Financial reporting process of providing financial statement information to external users.

Financial statements primary means of communicating financial information to external parties.

Finished goods costs that have accumulated in work in process are transferred to finished goods once the manufacturing process is completed.

Fiscal year the annual time period used to report to external users.

Fixed-asset turnover ratio used to measure how effectively managers used PP&E.

$$\text{Fixed-asset turnover ratio} = \frac{\text{Net sales}}{\text{Average-fixed assets}}$$

Foreign currency futures contract agreement that requires the seller to deliver a specific foreign currency at a designated future date at a specific price.

Foreign currency hedge if a derivative is used to hedge the risk that some transactions require settlement in a currency other than the entities' functional currency or that foreign operations will require translation adjustments to reported amounts.

Forward contract calls for delivery on a specific date; is not traded on a market exchange; does not call for a daily cash settlement for price changes in the underlying contract.

Fractional shares a stock dividend or stock split results in some shareholders being entitled to fractions of whole shares.

Franchise contractual arrangement under which the franchisor grants the franchisee the exclusive right to use the franchisor's trademark or tradename within a geographical area, usually for specified period of time.

Franchisee individual or corporation given the right to sell the franchisor's products and use its name for a specified period of time.

Franchisor grants to the franchisee the right to sell the franchisor's products and use its name for a specific period of time.

Freight-in transportation-in; in a periodic system, freight costs generally are added to this temporary account, which is added to purchases in determining net purchases.

Full-cost method allows costs incurred in searching for oil and gas within a large geographical area to be capitalized as assets and expensed in the future as oil and gas from the successful wells are removed from that area.

Full-disclosure principle the financial reports should include any information that could affect the decisions made by external users.

Funded status difference between the employer's obligation (PBO) and the resources available to satisfy that obligation (plan assets).

Future deductible amounts the future tax consequence of a temporary difference will be to decrease taxable income relative to accounting income.

Futures contract agreement that requires the seller to deliver a particular commodity at a designated future date at a specified price.

Future taxable amounts the future tax consequence of temporary difference will be to increase taxable income relative to accounting income.

Future value amount of money that a dollar will grow to at some point in the future.

Gain or loss on the PBO the decrease or increase in the PBO when one or more estimates used in determining the PBO require revision.

Gains increases in equity from peripheral, or incidental, transactions of an entity.

General journal used to record any type of transaction.

General ledger collection of accounts.

Generally Accepted Accounting Principles (GAAP) set of both broad and specific guidelines that companies should follow when measuring and reporting the information in their financial statements and related notes.

Going concern assumption in the absence of information to the contrary, it is anticipated that a business entity will continue to operate indefinitely.

Goodwill unique intangible asset in that its cost can't be directly associated with any specifically identifiable right and it is not separable from the company itself.

Government Accounting Standards Board (GASB) responsible for developing accounting standards for governmental units such as states and cities.

Gross investment in the lease total of periodic rental payments and residual value.

Gross method For the buyer, views a discount not taken as part of the cost of inventory. For the seller, views a discount not taken by the customer as part of sales of revenue.

Gross profit method (gross margin method) estimates cost of goods sold which is then subtracted from cost of goods available for sale to estimate ending inventory.

Gross profit/ratio highlights the important relationship between net sales revenue and cost of goods sold.

$$\text{Gross profit ratio} = \frac{\text{Gross profit}}{\text{Net sales}}$$

Group depreciation method collection of assets defined as depreciable assets that share similar service lives and other attributes.

Half-year convention record one-half of a full year's depreciation in the year of acquisition and another half year in the year of disposal.

Hedging taking an action that is expected to produce exposure to a particular type of risk that is precisely the opposite of an actual risk to which the company already is exposed.

Historical costs original transaction value.

Horizontal analysis comparison by expressing each item as a percentage of that same item in the financial statements of another year (base amount) in order to more easily see year-to-year changes.

Illegal acts violations of the law, such as bribes, kickbacks, and illegal contributions to political candidates.

Impairment of value operational assets should be written down if there has been a significant impairment (fair value less than book value) of value.

Implicit rate of interest rate implicit in the agreement.

Improvements replacement of a major component of an operational asset.

Income from continuing operations revenues, expenses (including income taxes), gain, and losses, excluding those related to discontinued operations and extraordinary items.

Income statement statement of operations or statement of earnings is used to summarize the profit-generating activities that occurred during a particular reporting period.

Income statement approach estimating bad debt expense as a percentage of each period's net credit sales; usually determined by reviewing the company's recent history of the relationship between credit sales and actual bad debts.

Income summary account that is a bookkeeping convenience used in the closing process that provides a check that all temporary accounts have been properly closed.

Income tax expense provision for income taxes; reported as a separate expense in corporate income statements.

Indirect method the net cash increase or decrease from operating activities is derived indirectly by starting with reported net income and working backwards to convert that amount to a cash basis.

Initial direct costs costs incurred by the lessor that are associated directly with originating a lease and are essential to acquire the lease.

In-process research and development the amount of the purchase price in a business acquisition that is allocated to projects that have not yet reached technological feasibility.

Installment notes Notes payable for which equal installment payments include both an amount that represents interest and an amount that represents a reduction of the outstanding balance so that at maturity the note is completely paid.

Installment sales method recognizes revenue and costs only when cash payments are received.

Institute of Internal Auditors national organization of accountants providing internal auditing services for their own organizations.

Institute of Management Accountants (IMA) primary national organization of accountants working in industry and government.

Intangible assets operational assets that lack physical substance; examples include patents, copyrights, franchises, and goodwill.

Interest "rent" paid for the use of money for some period of time.

Interest cost interest accrued on the projected benefit obligation calculated as the discount rate multiplied by the projected benefit obligation at the beginning of the year.

Interest rate swap agreement to exchange fixed interest payments for floating rate payments, or vice versa, without exchanging the underlying principal amounts.

Internal control a company's plan to encourage adherence to company policies and procedures, promote operational efficiency, minimize errors and theft, and enhance the reliability and accuracy of accounting data.

Internal events events that directly affect the financial position of the company but don't involve an exchange transaction with another entity.

International Accounting Standards Board (IASB) objectives are to develop a single set of high-quality, understandable global accounting standards, to promote the use of those standards, and to bring about the convergence of national accounting standards and International Accounting Standards.

International Accounting Standards Committee (IASC) umbrella organization formed to develop global accounting standards.

International Financial Reporting Standards developed by the ISAB and used by more than 100 countries.

Intraperiod tax allocation associates (allocates) income tax expense (or income tax Gross profit Net sales benefit if there is a loss) with each major component of income that causes it.

Intrinsic value the difference between the market price of the shares and the option price at which they can be acquired.

Inventories goods awaiting sale (finished goods), goods in the course of production (work in process), and goods to be consumed directly or indirectly in production (raw materials).

Inventory goods acquired, manufactured, or in the process of being manufactured for sale.

Inventory turnover ratio measures a company's efficiency in managing its investment in inventory.

Investing activities involve the acquisition and sale of long-term assets used in the business and non-operating investment assets.

Investments by owners increases in equity resulting from transfers of resources (usually cash) to a company in exchange for ownership interest.

Irregularities intentional distortions of financial statements.

Journal a chronological record of all economic events affecting financial position.

Journal entry captures the effect of a transaction on financial position in debit/credit form.

Just-in-time (JIT) system a system used by a manufacturer to coordinate production with suppliers so that raw materials or components arrive just as they are needed in the production process.

Land improvements the cost of parking lots, driveways, and private roads and the costs of fences and lawn and garden sprinkler systems.

Last-in, first-out (LIFO) method assumes units sold are the most recent units purchased.

Leasehold improvements account title when a lessee makes improvements to leased property that reverts back to the lessor at the end of the lease.

Lessee user of a leased asset.

Lessor owner of a leased asset.

Leveraged lease a third-party, long-term creditor provides nonrecourse financing for a lease agreement between a lessor and a lessee.

Liabilities probable future sacrifices of economic benefits arising from present obligations of a particular entity to transfer assets or provide services to other entities in the future as a result of past transactions or events.

LIFO conformity rule if a company uses LIFO to measure taxable income, the company also must use LIFO for external financial reporting.

LIFO inventory pools simplifies recordkeeping and reduces the risk of LIFO liquidation by grouping inventory units into pools based on physical similarities of the individual units.

LIFO liquidation the decline in inventory quantity during the period.

Limited liability company owners are not liable for the debts of the business, except to the extent of their investment; all members can be involved with managing the business without losing liability protection; no limitations on the number of owners.

Limited liability partnership similar to a limited liability company, except it doesn't offer all the liability protection available in the limited liability company structure.

Line of credit allows a company to borrow cash without having to follow formal loan procedures and paperwork.

Liquidating dividend when a dividend exceeds the balance in retained earnings.

Liquidity period of time before an asset is converted to cash or until a liability is paid.

Long-term solvency the riskiness of a company with regard to the amount of liabilities in its capital structure.

Loss contingency existing, uncertain situation involving potential loss depending on whether some future event occurs.

Losses decreases in equity arising from peripheral, or incidental, transactions of the entity.

Lower-of-cost-or-market (LCM) recognizes losses in the period that the value of inventory declines below its cost.

Management discussion and analysis (MDA) provides a biased but informed perspective of a company's operations, liquidity, and capital resources.

Managerial accounting deals with the concepts and methods used to provide information to an organization's internal users (i.e., its managers).

Matching principle expenses are recognized in the same period as the related revenues.

Materiality if a more costly way of providing information is not expected to have a material effect on decisions made by those using the information, the less costly method may be acceptable.

Measurement process of associating numerical amounts to the elements.

Minimum lease payments payments the lessee is required to make in connection with the lease.

Minimum pension liability an employer must report a pension liability at least equal to the amount by which its ABO exceeds its plan assets.

Model Business Corporation Act designed to serve as a guide to states in the development of their corporation statutes.

Modified accelerated cost recovery system (MACRS) The federal income tax code allows taxpayers to compute depreciation for their tax returns using this method.

Monetary assets money and claims to receive money, the amount of which is fixed or determinable.

Monetary liabilities obligations to pay amounts of cash, the amount of which is fixed or determinable.

Mortgage bond backed by a lien on specified real estate owned by the issuer.

Multiple-deliverable arrangements require allocation of revenue to multiple elements that qualify for separate revenue recognition.

Multiple-step income statement format that includes a number of intermediate subtotals before arriving at income from continuing operations.

Natural resources oil and gas deposits, timber tracts, and mineral deposits.

Net income/net loss revenue + gains − (expenses and losses for a period) income statement bottom line.

Net markdown net effect of the change in selling price (increase, decrease, increase).

Net markup net effect of the change in selling price (increase, increase, decrease).

Net method For the buyer, considers the cost of inventory to include the net, after-discount amount, and any discounts not taken are reported as interest expense. For the seller, considers sales revenue to be the net amount, after discount, and any discounts not taken by the customer as interest revenue.

Net operating loss negative taxable income because tax-deductible expenses exceed taxable revenues.

Net realizable less a normal profit margin (NRV − NP) lower limit of market.

Net realizable value: the amount of cash the company expects to actually collect from customers.

Net realizable value (NRV) upper limit of market.

Neutrality neutral with respect to parties potentially affected.

Noncash investing and financing activities transactions that do not increase or decrease cash but that result in significant investing and financing activities.

Noninterest-bearing note notes that bear interest, but the interest is deducted (or discounted) from the face amount to determine the cash proceeds made available to the borrower at the outset.

Nonoperating income includes gains and losses and revenues and expenses related to peripheral or incidental activities of the company.

Nontemporary difference difference between pretax accounting income and taxable income and, consequently, between the reported amount of an asset or liability in the financial statements and its tax basis that will not "reverse" resulting from transactions and events that under existing tax law will never affect taxable income or taxes payable.

Note payable A promissory note (essentially an IOU) that obligates the issuing corporation to repay a stated amount at or by a specified maturity date and to pay interest to the lender between the issue date and maturity.

Notes receivable receivables supported by a formal agreement or note that specifies payment terms.

Objectives-oriented/principles-based accounting standards approach to standard setting stresses professional judgment, as opposed to following a list of rules.

Operating activities inflows and outflows of cash related to transactions entering into the determination of net income.

Operating cycle period of time necessary to convert cash to raw materials, raw materials to finished product, the finished product to receivables, and then finally receivables back to cash.

Operating income includes revenues and expenses directly related to the principal revenue-generating activities of the company.

Operating leases fundamental rights and responsibilities of ownership are retained by the lessor and that the lessee merely is using the asset temporarily.

Operating loss carryback reduction of prior (up to two) years' taxable income by a current net operating loss.

Operating loss forward reduction of future (up to 20) years' taxable income by a current net operating loss.

Operating segment a component of an enterprise that engages in business activities from which it may earn revenues and incur expenses (including revenues and expenses relating to transactions with other companies of the same enterprise); whose operating results are regularly reviewed by the enterprise's chief operating decision maker to make decisions about resources to be allocated to the segment and assess its performance; for which discrete financial information is available.

Operational assets property, plant, and equipment, along with intangible assets.

Operational risk how adept a company is at withstanding various events and circumstances that might impair its ability to earn profits.

Option gives the holder the right either to buy or sell a financial instrument at a specified price.

Option pricing models statistical models that incorporate information about a company's stock and the terms of the stock option to estimate the option's fair value.

Ordinary annuity cash flows occur at the end of each period.

Other comprehensive income certain gains and losses that are excluded from the calculation of net income, but included in the calculation of comprehensive income.

Paid-in capital invested capital consisting primarily of amounts invested by shareholders when they purchase shares of stock from the corporation.

Parenthetical comments/modifying comments supplemental information disclosed on the face of financial statements.

Participating preferred shareholders are allowed to receive additional dividends beyond the stated amount.

Patent exclusive right to manufacture a product or to use a process.

Pension plan assets employer contributions and accumulated earnings on the investment of those contributions to be used to pay retirement benefits to retired employees.

Percentage-of-completion method allocation of a share of a project's revenues and expenses to each reporting period during the contract period.

Periodic inventory system the merchandise inventory account balance is not adjusted as purchases and sales are made but only periodically at the end of a reporting period when a physical count of the period's ending inventory is made and costs are assigned to the quantities determined.

Periodicity assumption allows the life of a company to be divided into artificial time periods to provide timely information.

Permanent accounts represent assets, liabilities, and shareholders' equity at a point in time.

Perpetual inventory system account inventory is continually adjusted for each change in inventory, whether it's caused by a purchase, a sale, or a return of merchandise by the company to its supplier.

Pledging trade receivables in general rather than specific receivables are pledged as collateral; the responsibility for collection of the receivables remains solely with the company.

Point-of-sale the goods or services sold to the buyer are delivered (the title is transferred).

Post-closing trial balance verifies that the closing entries were prepared and posted correctly and that the accounts are now ready for next year's transactions.

Posting transferring debits and credits recorded in individual journal entries to the specific accounts affected.

Postretirement benefits all types of retiree benefits; may include medical coverage, dental coverage, life insurance, group legal services, and other benefits.

Potential common shares Securities that, while not being common stock may become common stock through their exercise, conversion, or issuance and therefore dilute (reduce) earnings per share.

Predictive value/feedback value confirmation of investor expectations about future cash-generating ability.

Preferred stock typically has a preference (a) to specified amount of dividends (stated dollar amount per share or percentage of par value per share) and (b) to distribution of assets in the event the corporation is dissolved.

Premium arises when bonds are sold for more than face amount.

Prepaid expense represents an asset recorded when an expense is paid in advance, creating benefits beyond the current period.

Prepayments/deferrals the cash flow precedes either expense or revenue recognition.

Present value today's equivalent to a particular amount in the future.

Prior period adjustment addition to or reduction in the beginning retained earnings balance in a statement of shareholders' equity due to a correction of an error.

Prior service cost the cost of credit given for an amendment to a pension plan to employee service rendered in prior years.

Product costs costs associated with products and expensed as cost of goods sold only when the related products are sold.

Profit margin on sales net income divided by net sales; measures the amount of net income achieved per sales dollar.

Pro forma earnings actual (GAAP) earnings reduced by any expenses the reporting company feels are unusual and should be excluded.

Projected benefit obligation (PBO) the discounted present value of estimated retirement benefits earned so far by employees, applying the plan's pension formula using projected future compensation levels.

Property dividend when a noncash asset is distributed.

Property, plant, and equipment land, buildings, equipment, machinery, autos, and trucks.

Prospective approach the accounting change is implemented in the present, and its effects are reflected in the financial statements of the current and future years only.

Proxy statement contains disclosures on compensation to directors and executives; sent to all shareholders each year.

Purchase commitments contracts that obligate a company to purchase a specified amount of merchandise or raw materials at specified prices on or before specified dates.

Purchase discounts reductions in the amount to be paid if remittance is made within a designated period of time.

Purchase return a reduction in both inventory and accounts payable (if the account has not yet been paid) at the time of the return.

Purchases journal records the purchase of merchandise on account.

Quasi reorganization a firm undergoing financial difficulties, but with favorable future prospects, may use a quasi reorganization to write down inflated asset values and eliminate an accumulated deficit.

Rate of return on stock investment

$$\frac{\text{Dividends} + \text{Share price appreciation}}{\text{Initial investment}}$$

Ratio analysis comparison of accounting numbers to evaluate the performance and risk of a firm.

Raw materials cost of components purchased from other manufacturers that will become part of the finished product.

Real estate lease involves land—exclusively or in part.

Realization principle requires that the earnings process is judged to be complete or virtually complete, and there is reasonable certainty as to the collectibility of the asset to be received (usually cash) before revenue can be recognized.

Rearrangements expenditures made to restructure an asset without addition, replacement, or improvement.

Receivables a company's claims to the future collection of cash, other assets, or services.

Receivables turnover ratio indicates how quickly a company is able to collect its accounts receivable.

Recognition process of admitting information into the basic financial statements.

Redemption privilege might allow preferred shareholders the option, under specified conditions, to return their shares for a predetermined redemption price.

Related-party transactions transactions with owners, management, families of owners or management, affiliated companies, and other parties that can significantly influence or be influenced by the company.

Relevance one of the primary decision-specific qualities that make accounting information useful; made up of predictive value and/or feedback value, and timeliness.

Reliability the extent to which information is verifiable, representationally faithful, and neutral.

Rent abatement lease agreements may call for uneven rent payments during the term of the lease, e.g., when the initial payment (or maybe several payments) is waived.

Replacement cost (RC) the cost to replace the item by purchase or manufacture.

Replacement depreciation method depreciation is recorded when assets are replaced.

Representational faithfulness agreement between a measure or description and the phenomenon it purports to represent.

Residual value or salvage value, the amount the company expects to receive for the asset at the end of its service life less any anticipated disposal costs.

Restoration costs costs to restore land or other property to its original condition after extraction of the natural resource ends.

Restricted stock shares subject to forfeiture by the employee if employment is terminated within some specified number of years from the date of grant.

Retail inventory method relies on the relationship between cost and selling price to estimate ending inventory and cost of goods sold; provides a more accurate estimate than the gross profit method.

Retained earnings amounts earned by the corporation on behalf of its shareholders and not (yet) distributed to them as dividends.

Retired stock shares repurchased and not designated as treasury stock.

Retirement depreciation method Records depreciation when assets are disposed of and measures depreciation as the difference between the proceeds received and cost.

Retrospective approach financial statements issued in previous years are revised to reflect the impact of an accounting change whenever those statements are presented again for comparative purpose.

Return on assets (ROA) indicates a company's overall profitability.

Return on shareholders' equity: Amount of profit management can generate from the assets that owners provide.

Revenues inflows or other enhancements of assets or settlements of liabilities from delivering or producing goods, rendering services, or other activities that constitute the entity's ongoing major, or central, operations.

Reverse stock split when a company decreases, rather than increases, its outstanding shares.

Reversing entries optional entries that remove the effects of some of the adjusting entries made at the end of the previous reporting period for the sole purpose of simplifying journal entries made during the new period.

Right of conversion shareholders' right to exchange shares of preferred stock for common stock at specified conversion ratio.

Right of return customers' right to return merchandise to retailers if they are not satisfied.

Rules-based accounting standards a list of rules for choosing the appropriate accounting treatment for a transaction.

S corporation characteristics of both regular corporations and partnerships.

SAB No. 101 *Staff Accounting Bulletin 101* summarizes the SEC's views on revenue recognition.

Sale-leaseback transaction the owner of an asset sells it and immediately leases it back from the new owner.

Sales journal records credit sales.

Sales return the return of merchandise for a refund or for credit to be applied to other purchases.

Sales-type lease in addition to interest revenue earned over the lease term, the lessor receives a manufacturer's or dealer's profit on the sale of the asset.

Sarbanes-Oxley Act law provides for the regulation of the key players in the financial reporting process.

Secondary market transactions provide for the transfer of stocks and bonds among individuals and institutions.

Securities and Exchange Commission (SEC) responsible for setting accounting and reporting standards for companies whose securities are publicly traded.

Securities available-for-sale equity or debt securities the investor acquires, not for an active trading account or to be held to maturity.

Securities to be held-to-maturity debt securities for which the investor has the "positive intent and ability" to hold the securities to maturity.

Securitization the company creates a special purpose entity (SPE), usually a trust or a subsidiary; the SPE buys a pool of trade receivables, credit card receivables, or loans from the company and then sells related securities.

Serial bonds more structured (and less popular) way to retire bonds on a piecemeal basis.

Service cost increase in the projected benefit obligation attributable to employee service performed during the period.

Service life (useful life) the estimated use that the company expects to receive from the asset.

Service method allocation approach that reflects the declining service pattern of the prior service cost.

Share purchase contract shares ordinarily are sold in exchange for a promissory note from the subscriber—in essence, shares are sold on credit.

Short-term investments investments not classified as cash equivalents that will be liquidated in the coming year or operating cycle, whichever is longer.

Significant influence effective control is absent but the investor is able to exercise significant influence over the operating and financial policies of the investee (usually between 20% and 50% of the investee's voting shares are held).

Simple capital structure a firm that has no potential common shares (outstanding securities that could potentially dilute earnings per share).

Simple interest computed by multiplying an initial investment times both the applicable interest rate and the period of time for which the money is used.

Single-step income statement format that groups all revenues and gains together and all expenses and losses together.

Sinking fund debentures bonds that must be redeemed on a prespecified year-by-year basis; administered by a trustee who repurchases bonds in the open market.

Source documents relay essential information about each transaction to the accountant, e.g., sales invoices, bills from suppliers, cash register tapes.

Special journal record of a repetitive type of transaction, e.g., a sales journal.

Specific identification method each unit sold during the period or each unit on hand at the end of the period to be matched with its actual cost.

Specific interest method for interest capitalization, rates from specific construction loans to the extent of specific borrowings are used before using the average rate of other debt.

Start-up costs whenever a company introduces a new product or service, or commences business in a new territory or with a new customer, it incurs one-time costs that are expensed in the period incurred.

Statement of cash flows change statement summarizing the transactions that caused cash to change during the period.

Statement of shareholders' equity statement disclosing the source of changes in the shareholders' equity accounts.

Stock appreciation rights (SARs) awards that enable an employee to benefit by the amount that the market price of the company's stock rises above a specified amount without having to buy shares.

Stock dividend distribution of additional shares of stock to current shareholders of the corporation.

Stock options employees aren't actually awarded shares, but rather are given the option to buy shares at a specified exercise price within some specified number of years from the date of grant.

Stock split stock distribution of 25% or higher, sometimes call a *large* stock dividend.

Straight line an equal amount of depreciable base is allocated to each year of the asset's service life.

Straight-line method recording interest each period at the same dollar amount.

Subordinated debenture the holder is not entitled to receive any liquidation payments until the claims of other specified debt issues are satisfied.

Subsequent event a significant development that takes place after the company's fiscal year-end but before the financial statements are issued.

Subsidiary ledger record of a group of subsidiary accounts associated with a particular general ledger control account.

Successful efforts method requires that exploration costs that are known not to have resulted in the discovery of oil or gas be included as expense in the period the expenditures are made.

Sum-of-the-years'-digits (SYD) method systematic acceleration of depreciation by multiplying the depreciable base by a fraction that declines each year.

Supplemental financial statements reports containing more detailed information than is shown in the primary financial statements.

T-account account with space at the top for the account title and two sides for recording increases and decreases.

Taxable income comprises revenues, expenses, gains, and losses as measured according to the regulations of the appropriate taxing authority.

Technological feasibility established when the enterprise has completed all planning, designing, coding, and testing activities that are necessary to establish that the product can be produced to meet its design specifications including functions, features, and technical performance requirements.

Temporary accounts represent changes in the retained earnings component of shareholders' equity for a corporation caused by revenue, expense, gain, and loss transactions.

Temporary difference difference between pretax accounting income and taxable income and, consequently, between the reported amount of an asset or liability in the financial statements and its tax basis which will "reverse" in later years.

Time-based methods allocates the cost base according to the passage of time.

Timeliness information that is available to users early enough to allow its use in the decision process.

Times interest earned ratio a way to gauge the ability of a company to satisfy its fixed debt obligations by comparing interest charges with the income available to pay those charges.

Time value of money money can be invested today to earn interest and grow to a larger dollar amount in the future.

Trade discounts percentage reduction from the list price.

Trademark (tradename) exclusive right to display a word, a slogan, a symbol, or an emblem that distinctively identifies a company, a product, or a service.

Trade notes payable formally recognized by a written promissory note.

Trading securities equity or debt securities the investor (usually a financial institution) acquires principally for the purpose of selling in the near term.

Transaction analysis process of reviewing the source documents to determine the dual effect on the accounting equation and the specific elements involved.

Transaction obligation the unfunded accumulated postretirement benefit obligation existing when *SFAS 106* was adopted.

Transactions economic events.

Treasury stock shares repurchased and not retired.

Troubled debt restructuring the original terms of a debt agreement are changed as a result of financial difficulties experienced by the debtor (borrower).

Trustee person who accepts employer contributions, invests the contributions, accumulates the earnings on the investments, and pays benefits from the plan assets to retired employees or their beneficiaries.

Unadjusted trial balance a list of the general ledger accounts and their balances at a particular date.

Understandability users must understand the information within the context of the decision being made.

Unearned revenues cash received from a customer in one period for goods or services that are to be provided in a future period.

Units-of-production method computes a depreciation rate per measure of activity and then multiplies this rate by actual activity to determine periodic depreciation.

Unqualified opinion auditors are satisfied that the financial statements present fairly the company's financial position, results of operations, and cash flows and are in conformity with generally accepted accounting principles.

Valuation allowance indirect reduction (contra account) in a deferred tax asset when it is more likely than not that some portion or all of the deferred tax asset will not be realized.

Verifiability implies a consensus among different measurers.

Vertical analysis expression of each item in the financial statements as a percentage of an appropriate corresponding total, or base amount, but within the same year.

Vested benefits benefits that employees have the right to receive even if their employment were to cease today.

Weighted-average interest method for interest capitalization, weighted-average rate on all interest-bearing debt, including all construction loans, is used.

Without recourse the buyer assumes the risk of uncollectibility.

With recourse the seller retains the risk of uncollectibility.

Working capital differences between current assets and current liabilities.

Work-in-process inventory products that are not yet complete.

Worksheet used to organize the accounting information needed to prepare adjusting and closing entries and the financial statements.

Photo Credits

3 Banana Stock/Jupiter Images
51 Jon Riley/Getty Images
111 Zuma Press/Newscom
165 Getty Images
227 Ken Reid/Photographers Choice/Getty Images
289 Michael Newman/Photoedit
327 Jim Arbogast/Getty Images
375 Tim Boyle/Getty Images
425 Jeff Zelevansky/Bloomberg News/Landov
477 Steve Vidler/eStock Photo
533 Michel Touraine/pixland/Corbis
587 Nasha Lee/Bloomberg News/Landov
651 © LWA-Stephen Welstead/Corbis
703 David De Lossy/Photodisc/Getty Images
759 John F. Rizzo/Photodisc/Getty Images
821 Ryan McVay/Getty Images
881 Photodisc/Getty Images
945 Courtesy of Cessna Corp./Newsmakers/Getty Images
1001 Will Woods/Digital Vision/Getty Images
1061 Lisa Poole/AP Images
1107 © Corbis

Subject Index

Note: page numbers followed by *n* indicate material in footnotes.

J

K

L

M

S

Accounting Standards Index

Note: page numbers followed by *n* indicate material in footnotes.

Present and Future Value Tables

This table shows the future value of $1 at various interest rates (i) and time periods (n). It is used to calculate the future value of any single amount.

TABLE 1 Future Value of $1

$FV = \$1\,(1 + i)^n$

n/i	1.0%	1.5%	2.0%	2.5%	3.0%	3.5%	4.0%	4.5%	5.0%	5.5%	6.0%	7.0%	8.0%	9.0%	10.0%	11.0%	12.0%	20.0%
1	1.01000	1.01500	1.02000	1.02500	1.03000	1.03500	1.04000	1.04500	1.05000	1.05500	1.06000	1.07000	1.08000	1.09000	1.10000	1.11000	1.12000	1.20000
2	1.02010	1.03022	1.04040	1.05063	1.06090	1.07123	1.08160	1.09203	1.10250	1.11303	1.12360	1.14490	1.16640	1.18810	1.21000	1.23210	1.25440	1.44000
3	1.03030	1.04568	1.06121	1.07689	1.09273	1.10872	1.12486	1.14117	1.15763	1.17424	1.19102	1.22504	1.25971	1.29503	1.33100	1.36763	1.40493	1.72800
4	1.04060	1.06136	1.08243	1.10381	1.12551	1.14752	1.16986	1.19252	1.21551	1.23882	1.26248	1.31080	1.36049	1.41158	1.46410	1.51807	1.57352	2.07360
5	1.05101	1.07728	1.10408	1.13141	1.15927	1.18769	1.21665	1.24618	1.27628	1.30696	1.33823	1.40255	1.46933	1.53862	1.61051	1.68506	1.76234	2.48832
6	1.06152	1.09344	1.12616	1.15969	1.19405	1.22926	1.26532	1.30226	1.34010	1.37884	1.41852	1.50073	1.58687	1.67710	1.77156	1.87041	1.97382	2.98598
7	1.07214	1.10984	1.14869	1.18869	1.22987	1.27228	1.31593	1.36086	1.40710	1.45468	1.50363	1.60578	1.71382	1.82804	1.94872	2.07616	2.21068	3.58318
8	1.08286	1.12649	1.17166	1.21840	1.26677	1.31681	1.36857	1.42210	1.47746	1.53469	1.59385	1.71819	1.85093	1.99256	2.14359	2.30454	2.47596	4.29982
9	1.09369	1.14339	1.19509	1.24886	1.30477	1.36290	1.42331	1.48610	1.55133	1.61909	1.68948	1.83846	1.99900	2.17189	2.35795	2.55804	2.77308	5.15978
10	1.10462	1.16054	1.21899	1.28008	1.34392	1.41060	1.48024	1.55297	1.62889	1.70814	1.79085	1.96715	2.15892	2.36736	2.59374	2.83942	3.10585	6.19174
11	1.11567	1.17795	1.24337	1.31209	1.38423	1.45997	1.53945	1.62285	1.71034	1.80209	1.89830	2.10485	2.33164	2.58043	2.85312	3.15176	3.47855	7.43008
12	1.12683	1.19562	1.26824	1.34489	1.42576	1.51107	1.60103	1.69588	1.79586	1.90121	2.01220	2.25219	2.51817	2.81266	3.13843	3.49845	3.89598	8.91610
13	1.13809	1.21355	1.29361	1.37851	1.46853	1.56396	1.66507	1.77220	1.88565	2.00577	2.13293	2.40985	2.71962	3.06580	3.45227	3.88328	4.36349	10.69932
14	1.14947	1.23176	1.31948	1.41297	1.51259	1.61869	1.73168	1.85194	1.97993	2.11609	2.26090	2.57853	2.93719	3.34173	3.79750	4.31044	4.88711	12.83918
15	1.16097	1.25023	1.34587	1.44830	1.55797	1.67535	1.80094	1.93528	2.07893	2.23248	2.39656	2.75903	3.17217	3.64248	4.17725	4.78459	5.47357	15.40702
16	1.17258	1.26899	1.37279	1.48451	1.60471	1.73399	1.87298	2.02237	2.18287	2.35526	2.54035	2.95216	3.42594	3.97031	4.59497	5.31089	6.13039	18.48843
17	1.18430	1.28802	1.40024	1.52162	1.65285	1.79468	1.94790	2.11338	2.29202	2.48480	2.69277	3.15882	3.70002	4.32763	5.05447	5.89509	6.86604	22.18611
18	1.19615	1.30734	1.42825	1.55966	1.70243	1.85749	2.02582	2.20848	2.40662	2.62147	2.85434	3.37993	3.99602	4.71712	5.55992	6.54355	7.68997	26.62333
19	1.20811	1.32695	1.45681	1.59865	1.75351	1.92250	2.10685	2.30786	2.52695	2.76565	3.02560	3.61653	4.31570	5.14166	6.11591	7.26334	8.61276	31.94800
20	1.22019	1.34686	1.48595	1.63862	1.80611	1.98979	2.19112	2.41171	2.65330	2.91776	3.20714	3.86968	4.66096	5.60441	6.72750	8.06231	9.64629	38.33760
21	1.23239	1.36706	1.51567	1.67958	1.86029	2.05943	2.27877	2.52024	2.78596	3.07823	3.39956	4.14056	5.03383	6.10881	7.40025	8.94917	10.80385	46.00512
25	1.28243	1.45095	1.64061	1.85394	2.09378	2.36324	2.66584	3.00543	3.38635	3.81339	4.29187	5.42743	6.84848	8.62308	10.83471	13.58546	17.00006	95.39622
30	1.34785	1.56308	1.81136	2.09757	2.42726	2.80679	3.24340	3.74532	4.32194	4.98395	5.74349	7.61226	10.06266	13.26768	17.44940	22.89230	29.95992	237.37631
40	1.48886	1.81402	2.20804	2.68506	3.26204	3.95926	4.80102	5.81636	7.03999	8.51331	10.28572	14.97446	21.72452	31.40942	45.25926	65.00087	93.05097	1469.77160

This table shows the present value of $1 at various interest rates (i) and time periods (n). It is used to calculate the present value of any single amount.

TABLE 2 Present Value of $1

$$PV = \frac{\$1}{(1 + i)^n}$$

n/i	1.0%	1.5%	2.0%	2.5%	3.0%	3.5%	4.0%	4.5%	5.0%	5.5%	6.0%	7.0%	8.0%	9.0%	10.0%	11.0%	12.0%	20.0%
1	0.99010	0.98522	0.98039	0.97561	0.97087	0.96618	0.96154	0.95694	0.95238	0.94787	0.94340	0.93458	0.92593	0.91743	0.90909	0.90090	0.89286	0.83333
2	0.98030	0.97066	0.96117	0.95181	0.94260	0.93351	0.92456	0.91573	0.90703	0.89845	0.89000	0.87344	0.85734	0.84168	0.82645	0.81162	0.79719	0.69444
3	0.97059	0.95632	0.94232	0.92860	0.91514	0.90194	0.88900	0.87630	0.86384	0.85161	0.83962	0.81630	0.79383	0.77218	0.75131	0.73119	0.71178	0.57870
4	0.96098	0.94218	0.92385	0.90595	0.88849	0.87144	0.85480	0.83856	0.82270	0.80722	0.79209	0.76290	0.73503	0.70843	0.68301	0.65873	0.63552	0.48225
5	0.95147	0.92826	0.90573	0.88385	0.86261	0.84197	0.82193	0.80245	0.78353	0.76513	0.74726	0.71299	0.68058	0.64993	0.62092	0.59345	0.56743	0.40188
6	0.94205	0.91454	0.88797	0.86230	0.83748	0.81350	0.79031	0.76790	0.74622	0.72525	0.70496	0.66634	0.63017	0.59627	0.56447	0.53464	0.50663	0.33490
7	0.93272	0.90103	0.87056	0.84127	0.81309	0.78599	0.75992	0.73483	0.71068	0.68744	0.66506	0.62275	0.58349	0.54703	0.51316	0.48166	0.45235	0.27908
8	0.92348	0.88771	0.85349	0.82075	0.78941	0.75941	0.73069	0.70319	0.67684	0.65160	0.62741	0.58201	0.54027	0.50187	0.46651	0.43393	0.40388	0.23257
9	0.91434	0.87459	0.83676	0.80073	0.76642	0.73373	0.70259	0.67290	0.64461	0.61763	0.59190	0.54393	0.50025	0.46043	0.42410	0.39092	0.36061	0.19381
10	0.90529	0.86167	0.82035	0.78120	0.74409	0.70892	0.67556	0.64393	0.61391	0.58543	0.55839	0.50835	0.46319	0.42241	0.38554	0.35218	0.32197	0.16151
11	0.89632	0.84893	0.80426	0.76214	0.72242	0.68495	0.64958	0.61620	0.58468	0.55491	0.52679	0.47509	0.42888	0.38753	0.35049	0.31728	0.28748	0.13459
12	0.88745	0.83639	0.78849	0.74356	0.70138	0.66178	0.62460	0.58966	0.55684	0.52598	0.49697	0.44401	0.39711	0.35553	0.31863	0.28584	0.25668	0.11216
13	0.87866	0.82403	0.77303	0.72542	0.68095	0.63940	0.60057	0.56427	0.53032	0.49856	0.46884	0.41496	0.36770	0.32618	0.28966	0.25751	0.22917	0.09346
14	0.86996	0.81185	0.75788	0.70773	0.66112	0.61778	0.57748	0.53997	0.50507	0.47257	0.44230	0.38782	0.34046	0.29925	0.26333	0.23199	0.20462	0.07789
15	0.86135	0.79985	0.74301	0.69047	0.64186	0.59689	0.55526	0.51672	0.48102	0.44793	0.41727	0.36245	0.31524	0.27454	0.23939	0.20900	0.18270	0.06491
16	0.85282	0.78803	0.72845	0.67362	0.62317	0.57671	0.53391	0.49447	0.45811	0.42458	0.39365	0.33873	0.29189	0.25187	0.21763	0.18829	0.16312	0.05409
17	0.84438	0.77639	0.71416	0.65720	0.60502	0.55720	0.51337	0.47318	0.43630	0.40245	0.37136	0.31657	0.27027	0.23107	0.19784	0.16963	0.14564	0.04507
18	0.83602	0.76491	0.70016	0.64117	0.58739	0.53836	0.49363	0.45280	0.41552	0.38147	0.35034	0.29586	0.25025	0.21199	0.17986	0.15282	0.13004	0.03756
19	0.82774	0.75361	0.68643	0.62553	0.57029	0.52016	0.47464	0.43330	0.39573	0.36158	0.33051	0.27651	0.23171	0.19449	0.16351	0.13768	0.11611	0.03130
20	0.81954	0.74247	0.67297	0.61027	0.55368	0.50257	0.45639	0.41464	0.37689	0.34273	0.31180	0.25842	0.21455	0.17843	0.14864	0.12403	0.10367	0.02608
21	0.81143	0.73150	0.65978	0.59539	0.53755	0.48557	0.43883	0.39679	0.35894	0.32486	0.29416	0.24151	0.19866	0.16370	0.13513	0.11174	0.09256	0.02174
24	0.78757	0.69954	0.62172	0.55288	0.49193	0.43796	0.39012	0.34770	0.31007	0.27666	0.24698	0.19715	0.15770	0.12640	0.10153	0.08170	0.06588	0.01258
25	0.77977	0.68921	0.60953	0.53939	0.47761	0.42315	0.37512	0.33273	0.29530	0.26223	0.23300	0.18425	0.14602	0.11597	0.09230	0.07361	0.05882	0.01048
28	0.75684	0.65910	0.57437	0.50088	0.43708	0.38165	0.33348	0.29157	0.25509	0.22332	0.19563	0.15040	0.11591	0.08955	0.06934	0.05382	0.04187	0.00607
29	0.74934	0.64936	0.56311	0.48866	0.42435	0.36875	0.32065	0.27902	0.24295	0.21168	0.18456	0.14056	0.10733	0.08215	0.06304	0.04849	0.03738	0.00506
30	0.74192	0.63976	0.55207	0.47674	0.41199	0.35628	0.30832	0.26700	0.23138	0.20064	0.17411	0.13137	0.09938	0.07537	0.05731	0.04368	0.03338	0.00421
31	0.73458	0.63031	0.54125	0.46511	0.39999	0.34423	0.29646	0.25550	0.22036	0.19018	0.16425	0.12277	0.09202	0.06915	0.05210	0.03935	0.02980	0.00351
40	0.67165	0.55126	0.45289	0.37243	0.30656	0.25257	0.20829	0.17193	0.14205	0.11746	0.09722	0.06678	0.04603	0.03184	0.02209	0.01538	0.01075	0.00068

This table shows the future value of an ordinary annuity of $1 at various interest rates (i) and time periods (n). It is used to calculate the future value of any series of equal payments made at the *end* of each compounding period.

TABLE 3 Future Value of an Ordinary Annuity of $1

$$FVA = \frac{(1+i)^n - 1}{i}$$

n/i	1.0%	1.5%	2.0%	2.5%	3.0%	3.5%	4.0%	4.5%	5.0%	5.5%	6.0%	7.0%	8.0%	9.0%	10.0%	11.0%	12.0%	20.0%
1	1.0000	1.0000	1.0000	1.0000	1.0000	1.0000	1.0000	1.0000	1.0000	1.0000	1.0000	1.0000	1.0000	1.0000	1.0000	1.0000	1.0000	1.0000
2	2.0100	2.0150	2.0200	2.0250	2.0300	2.0350	2.0400	2.0450	2.0500	2.0550	2.0600	2.0700	2.0800	2.0900	2.1000	2.1100	2.1200	2.2000
3	3.0301	3.0452	3.0604	3.0756	3.0909	3.1062	3.1216	3.1370	3.1525	3.1680	3.1836	3.2149	3.2464	3.2781	3.3100	3.3421	3.3744	3.6400
4	4.0604	4.0909	4.1216	4.1525	4.1836	4.2149	4.2465	4.2782	4.3101	4.3423	4.3746	4.4399	4.5061	4.5731	4.6410	4.7097	4.7793	5.3680
5	5.1010	5.1523	5.2040	5.2563	5.3091	5.3625	5.4163	5.4707	5.5256	5.5811	5.6371	5.7507	5.8666	5.9847	6.1051	6.2278	6.3528	7.4416
6	6.1520	6.2296	6.3081	6.3877	6.4684	6.5502	6.6330	6.7169	6.8019	6.8881	6.9753	7.1533	7.3359	7.5233	7.7156	7.9129	8.1152	9.9299
7	7.2135	7.3230	7.4343	7.5474	7.6625	7.7794	7.8983	8.0192	8.1420	8.2669	8.3938	8.6540	8.9228	9.2004	9.4872	9.7833	10.0890	12.9159
8	8.2857	8.4328	8.5830	8.7361	8.8923	9.0517	9.2142	9.3800	9.5491	9.7216	9.8975	10.2598	10.6366	11.0285	11.4359	11.8594	12.2997	16.4991
9	9.3685	9.5593	9.7546	9.9545	10.1591	10.3685	10.5828	10.8021	11.0266	11.2563	11.4913	11.9780	12.4876	13.0210	13.5795	14.1640	14.7757	20.7989
10	10.4622	10.7027	10.9497	11.2034	11.4639	11.7314	12.0061	12.2882	12.5779	12.8754	13.1808	13.8164	14.4866	15.1929	15.9374	16.7220	17.5487	25.9587
11	11.5668	11.8633	12.1687	12.4835	12.8078	13.1420	13.4864	13.8412	14.2068	14.5835	14.9716	15.7836	16.6455	17.5603	18.5312	19.5614	20.6546	32.1504
12	12.6825	13.0412	13.4121	13.7956	14.1920	14.6020	15.0258	15.4640	15.9171	16.3856	16.8699	17.8885	18.9771	20.1407	21.3843	22.7132	24.1331	39.5805
13	13.8093	14.2368	14.6803	15.1404	15.6178	16.1130	16.6268	17.1599	17.7130	18.2868	18.8821	20.1406	21.4953	22.9534	24.5227	26.2116	28.0291	48.4966
14	14.9474	15.4504	15.9739	16.5190	17.0863	17.6770	18.2919	18.9321	19.5986	20.2926	21.0151	22.5505	24.2149	26.0192	27.9750	30.0949	32.3926	59.1959
15	16.0969	16.6821	17.2934	17.9319	18.5989	19.2957	20.0236	20.7841	21.5786	22.4087	23.2760	25.1290	27.1521	29.3609	31.7725	34.4054	37.2797	72.0351
16	17.2579	17.9324	18.6393	19.3802	20.1569	20.9710	21.8245	22.7193	23.6575	24.6411	25.6725	27.8881	30.3243	33.0034	35.9497	39.1899	42.7533	87.4421
17	18.4304	19.2014	20.0121	20.8647	21.7616	22.7050	23.6975	24.7417	25.8404	26.9964	28.2129	30.8402	33.7502	36.9737	40.5447	44.5008	48.8837	105.9306
18	19.6147	20.4894	21.4123	22.3863	23.4144	24.4997	25.6454	26.8551	28.1324	29.4812	30.9057	33.9990	37.4502	41.3013	45.5992	50.3959	55.7497	128.1167
19	20.8109	21.7967	22.8406	23.9460	25.1169	26.3572	27.6712	29.0636	30.5390	32.1027	33.7600	37.3790	41.4463	46.0185	51.1591	56.9395	63.4397	154.7400
20	22.0190	23.1237	24.2974	25.5447	26.8704	28.2797	29.7781	31.3714	33.0660	34.8683	36.7856	40.9955	45.7620	51.1601	57.2750	64.2028	72.0524	186.6880
21	23.2392	24.4705	25.7833	27.1833	28.6765	30.2695	31.9692	33.7831	35.7193	37.7861	39.9927	44.8652	50.4229	56.7645	64.0025	72.2651	81.6987	225.0256
30	34.7849	37.5387	40.5681	43.9027	47.5754	51.6227	56.0849	61.0071	66.4388	72.4355	79.0582	94.4608	113.2832	136.3075	164.4940	199.0209	241.3327	1181.8816
40	48.8864	54.2679	60.4020	67.4026	75.4013	84.5503	95.0255	107.0303	120.7998	136.6056	154.7620	199.6351	259.0565	337.8824	442.5926	581.8261	767.0914	7343.8578

This table shows the present value of an ordinary annuity of $1 at various interest rates (i) and time periods (n). It is used to calculate the present value of any series of equal payments made at the *end* of each compounding period.

TABLE 4 Present Value of an Ordinary Annuity of $1

$$PVA = \frac{1 - \frac{1}{(1+i)^n}}{i}$$

n/i	1.0%	1.5%	2.0%	2.5%	3.0%	3.5%	4.0%	4.5%	5.0%	5.5%	6.0%	7.0%	8.0%	9.0%	10.0%	11.0%	12.0%	20.0%
1	0.99010	0.98522	0.98039	0.97561	0.97087	0.96618	0.96154	0.95694	0.95238	0.94787	0.94340	0.93458	0.92593	0.91743	0.90909	0.90090	0.89286	0.83333
2	1.97040	1.95588	1.94156	1.92742	1.91347	1.89969	1.88609	1.87267	1.85941	1.84632	1.83339	1.80802	1.78326	1.75911	1.73554	1.71252	1.69005	1.52778
3	2.94099	2.91220	2.88388	2.85602	2.82861	2.80164	2.77509	2.74896	2.72325	2.69793	2.67301	2.62432	2.57710	2.53129	2.48685	2.44371	2.40183	2.10648
4	3.90197	3.85438	3.80773	3.76197	3.71710	3.67308	3.62990	3.58753	3.54595	3.50515	3.46511	3.38721	3.31213	3.23972	3.16987	3.10245	3.03735	2.58873
5	4.85343	4.78264	4.71346	4.64583	4.57971	4.51505	4.45182	4.38998	4.32948	4.27028	4.21236	4.10020	3.99271	3.88965	3.79079	3.69590	3.60478	2.99061
6	5.79548	5.69719	5.60143	5.50813	5.41719	5.32855	5.24214	5.15787	5.07569	4.99553	4.91732	4.76654	4.62288	4.48592	4.35526	4.23054	4.11141	3.32551
7	6.72819	6.59821	6.47199	6.34939	6.23028	6.11454	6.00205	5.89270	5.78637	5.68297	5.58238	5.38929	5.20637	5.03295	4.86842	4.71220	4.56376	3.60459
8	7.65168	7.48593	7.32548	7.17014	7.01969	6.87396	6.73274	6.59589	6.46321	6.33457	6.20979	5.97130	5.74664	5.53482	5.33493	5.14612	4.96764	3.83716
9	8.56602	8.36052	8.16224	7.97087	7.78611	7.60769	7.43533	7.26879	7.10782	6.95220	6.80169	6.51523	6.24689	5.99525	5.75902	5.53705	5.32825	4.03097
10	9.47130	9.22218	8.98259	8.75206	8.53020	8.31661	8.11090	7.91272	7.72173	7.53763	7.36009	7.02358	6.71008	6.41766	6.14457	5.88923	5.65022	4.19247
11	10.36763	10.07112	9.78685	9.51421	9.25262	9.00155	8.76048	8.52892	8.30641	8.09254	7.88687	7.49867	7.13896	6.80519	6.49506	6.20652	5.93770	4.32706
12	11.25508	10.90751	10.57534	10.25776	9.95400	9.66333	9.38507	9.11858	8.86325	8.61852	8.38384	7.94269	7.53608	7.16073	6.81369	6.49236	6.19437	4.43922
13	12.13374	11.73153	11.34837	10.98319	10.63496	10.30274	9.98565	9.68285	9.39357	9.11708	8.85268	8.35765	7.90378	7.48690	7.10336	6.74987	6.42355	4.53268
14	13.00370	12.54338	12.10625	11.69091	11.29607	10.92052	10.56312	10.22283	9.89864	9.58965	9.29498	8.74547	8.24424	7.78615	7.36669	6.98187	6.62817	4.61057
15	13.86505	13.34323	12.84926	12.38138	11.93794	11.51741	11.11839	10.73955	10.37966	10.03758	9.71225	9.10791	8.55948	8.06069	7.60608	7.19087	6.81086	4.67547
16	14.71787	14.13126	13.57771	13.05500	12.56110	12.09412	11.65230	11.23402	10.83777	10.46216	10.10590	9.44665	8.85137	8.31256	7.82371	7.37916	6.97399	4.72956
17	15.56225	14.90765	14.29187	13.71220	13.16612	12.65132	12.16567	11.70719	11.27407	10.86461	10.47726	9.76322	9.12164	8.54363	8.02155	7.54879	7.11963	4.77463
18	16.39827	15.67256	14.99203	14.35336	13.75351	13.18968	12.65930	12.15999	11.68959	11.24607	10.82760	10.05909	9.37189	8.75563	8.20141	7.70162	7.24967	4.81219
19	17.22601	16.42617	15.67846	14.97889	14.32380	13.70984	13.13394	12.59329	12.08532	11.60765	11.15812	10.33560	9.60360	8.95011	8.36492	7.83929	7.36578	4.84350
20	18.04555	17.16864	16.35143	15.58916	14.87747	14.21240	13.59033	13.00794	12.46221	11.95038	11.46992	10.59401	9.81815	9.12855	8.51356	7.96333	7.46944	4.86958
21	18.85698	17.90014	17.01121	16.18455	15.41502	14.69797	14.02916	13.40472	12.82115	12.27524	11.76408	10.83553	10.01680	9.29224	8.64869	8.07507	7.56200	4.89132
25	22.02316	20.71961	19.52346	18.42438	17.41315	16.48151	15.62208	14.82821	14.09394	13.41393	12.78336	11.65358	10.67478	9.82258	9.07704	8.42174	7.84314	4.94759
30	25.80771	24.01584	22.39646	20.93029	19.60044	18.39205	17.29203	16.28889	15.37245	14.53375	13.76483	12.40904	11.25778	10.27365	9.42691	8.69379	8.05518	4.97894
40	32.83469	29.91585	27.35548	25.10278	23.11477	21.35507	19.79277	18.40158	17.15909	16.04612	15.04630	13.33171	11.92461	10.75736	9.77905	8.95105	8.24378	4.99660

This table shows the future value of an annuity due of $1 at various interest rates (i) and time periods (n). It is used to calculate the future value of any series of equal payments made at the *beginning* of each compounding period.

TABLE 5 Future Value of an Annuity Due of $1

$$FVAD = \left[\frac{(1+i)^n - 1}{i}\right] \times (1+i)$$

n/i	1.0%	1.5%	2.0%	2.5%	3.0%	3.5%	4.0%	4.5%	5.0%	5.5%	6.0%	7.0%	8.0%	9.0%	10.0%	11.0%	12.0%	20.0%
1	1.0100	1.0150	1.0200	1.0250	1.0300	1.0350	1.0400	1.0450	1.0500	1.0550	1.0600	1.0700	1.0800	1.0900	1.1000	1.1100	1.1200	1.2000
2	2.0301	2.0452	2.0604	2.0756	2.0909	2.1062	2.1216	2.1370	2.1525	2.1680	2.1836	2.2149	2.2464	2.2781	2.3100	2.3421	2.3744	2.6400
3	3.0604	3.0909	3.1216	3.1525	3.1836	3.2149	3.2465	3.2782	3.3101	3.3423	3.3746	3.4399	3.5061	3.5731	3.6410	3.7097	3.7793	4.3680
4	4.1010	4.1523	4.2040	4.2563	4.3091	4.3625	4.4163	4.4707	4.5256	4.5811	4.6371	4.7507	4.8666	4.9847	5.1051	5.2278	5.3528	6.4416
5	5.1520	5.2296	5.3081	5.3877	5.4684	5.5502	5.6330	5.7169	5.8019	5.8881	5.9753	6.1533	6.3359	6.5233	6.7156	6.9129	7.1152	8.9299
6	6.2135	6.3230	6.4343	6.5474	6.6625	6.7794	6.8983	7.0192	7.1420	7.2669	7.3938	7.6540	7.9228	8.2004	8.4872	8.7833	9.0890	11.9159
7	7.2857	7.4328	7.5830	7.7361	7.8923	8.0517	8.2142	8.3800	8.5491	8.7216	8.8975	9.2598	9.6366	10.0285	10.4359	10.8594	11.2997	15.4991
8	8.3685	8.5593	8.7546	8.9545	9.1591	9.3685	9.5828	9.8021	10.0266	10.2563	10.4913	10.9780	11.4876	12.0210	12.5795	13.1640	13.7757	19.7989
9	9.4622	9.7027	9.9497	10.2034	10.4639	10.7314	11.0061	11.2882	11.5779	11.8754	12.1808	12.8164	13.4866	14.1929	14.9374	15.7220	16.5487	24.9587
10	10.5668	10.8633	11.1687	11.4835	11.8078	12.1420	12.4864	12.8412	13.2068	13.5835	13.9716	14.7836	15.6455	16.5603	17.5312	18.5614	19.6546	31.1504
11	11.6825	12.0412	12.4121	12.7956	13.1920	13.6020	14.0258	14.4640	14.9171	15.3856	15.8699	16.8885	17.9771	19.1407	20.3843	21.7132	23.1331	38.5805
12	12.8093	13.2368	13.6803	14.1404	14.6178	15.1130	15.6268	16.1599	16.7130	17.2868	17.8821	19.1406	20.4953	21.9534	23.5227	25.2116	27.0291	47.4966
13	13.9474	14.4504	14.9739	15.5190	16.0863	16.6770	17.2919	17.9321	18.5986	19.2926	20.0151	21.5505	23.2149	25.0192	26.9750	29.0949	31.3926	58.1959
14	15.0969	15.6821	16.2934	16.9319	17.5989	18.2957	19.0236	19.7841	20.5786	21.4087	22.2760	24.1290	26.1521	28.3609	30.7725	33.4054	36.2797	71.0351
15	16.2579	16.9324	17.6393	18.3802	19.1569	19.9710	20.8245	21.7193	22.6575	23.6411	24.6725	26.8881	29.3243	32.0034	34.9497	38.1899	41.7533	86.4421
16	17.4304	18.2014	19.0121	19.8647	20.7616	21.7050	22.6975	23.7417	24.8404	25.9964	27.2129	29.8402	32.7502	35.9737	39.5447	43.5008	47.8837	104.9306
17	18.6147	19.4894	20.4123	21.3863	22.4144	23.4997	24.6454	25.8551	27.1324	28.4812	29.9057	32.9990	36.4502	40.3013	44.5992	49.3959	54.7497	127.1167
18	19.8109	20.7967	21.8406	22.9460	24.1169	25.3572	26.6712	28.0636	29.5390	31.1027	32.7600	36.3790	40.4463	45.0185	50.1591	55.9395	62.4397	153.7400
19	21.0190	22.1237	23.2974	24.5447	25.8704	27.2797	28.7781	30.3714	32.0660	33.8683	35.7856	39.9955	44.7620	50.1601	56.2750	63.2028	71.0524	185.6880
20	22.2392	23.4705	24.7833	26.1833	27.6765	29.2695	30.9692	32.7831	34.7193	36.7861	38.9927	43.8652	49.4229	55.7645	63.0025	71.2651	80.6987	224.0256
21	23.4716	24.8376	26.2990	27.8629	29.5368	31.3289	33.2480	35.3034	37.5052	39.8643	42.3923	48.0057	54.4568	61.8733	70.4027	80.2143	91.5026	270.0307
25	28.5256	30.5140	32.6709	35.0117	37.5530	40.3131	43.3117	46.5706	50.1135	53.9660	58.1564	67.6765	78.9544	92.3240	108.1818	126.9988	149.3339	566.3773
30	35.1327	38.1018	41.3794	45.0003	49.0027	53.4295	58.3283	63.7524	69.7608	76.4194	83.8017	101.0730	122.3459	148.5752	180.9434	220.9132	270.2926	1418.2579
40	49.3752	55.0819	61.6100	69.0876	77.6633	87.5095	98.8265	111.8467	126.8398	144.1189	164.0477	213.6096	279.7810	368.2919	486.8518	645.8269	859.1424	8812.6294